Artificial Intelligence

Structures and Strategies for Complex Problem Solving

Visit the *Artificial Intelligence* Companion Website at **www.booksites.net/luger** to find valuable **student** learning material including:

- Program code

Artificial intelligence

Structures and Strategies for
Complex Problem Solving

Fifth Edition

George F Luger

ADDISON-WESLEY

Harlow, England • London • New York • Boston • San Francisco • Toronto • Sydney • Singapore • Hong Kong
Tokyo • Seoul • Taipei • New Delhi • Cape Town • Madrid • Mexico City • Amsterdam • Munich • Paris • Milan

Pearson Education Limited
Edinburgh Gate
Harlow
Essex CM20 2JE
England

and Associated Companies throughout the world

Visit us on the World Wide Web at:
www.pearsoned.co.uk

First edition 1988
Fourth edition 2002

Fifth edition published 2005

ISBN 0 321 26318 9

British Library Cataloguing-in-Publication Data
A catalogue record for this book is available from the British Library

Library of Congress Cataloging-in-Publication Data
A catalog record for this book is available from the Library of Congress

10   9   8   7   6   5   4   3   2
08   07   06   05   04

Typeset in 10/12pt Times by 35
Printed and bound in the United States of America

The publisher's policy is to use paper manufactured from sustainable forests.

For my wife, Kathleen, and our children Sarah, David, and Peter.

Si quid est in me ingenii, judices . . .
Cicero, Pro Archia Poeta

GFL

PREFACE

What we have to learn to do
we learn by doing . . .

—ARISTOTLE, *Ethics*

Welcome to the Fifth Edition!

I was very pleased to be asked to produce a fifth edition of our artificial intelligence book. It is a compliment to the earlier editions, started almost twenty years ago, that our approach to AI has been so highly valued. It is also exciting that, as new development in the field emerges, we are able to present much of it in each new edition. We thank our readers, colleagues, and students for keeping our topics relevant and presentation up to date.

Many sections of the earlier editions have endured remarkably well, including the presentation of logic, search algorithms, knowledge representation, production systems, machine learning, and the programming techniques developed in LISP and PROLOG. These remain central to the practice of artificial intelligence, and required a relatively small effort to bring them up to date. We created a new introductory chapter on stochastic methods for the fifth edition. We feel that the stochastic technology is having an increasingly larger impact on AI, especially in areas such as diagnostic reasoning, natural language analysis, and learning. To support these technologies we expand the presentation of Bayes' theorem, Bayesian networks and related graphical models, probabilistic finite state machines, dynamic programming with the Viterbi algorithm, and Markov modeling. Other topics, such as emergent computation, case-based reasoning, and model-based problem solving, that were treated cursorily in the first editions, have grown sufficiently in importance to merit a more complete discussion. The changes in the fifth edition reflect the evolving research questions and are evidence of the continued vitality of the field of artificial intelligence.

As the scope of our AI project grew, we have been sustained by the support of our publisher, editors, friends, colleagues, and, most of all, by our readers, who have given our work such a long and productive life. We remain excited at the writing opportunity we are afforded: scientists are rarely encouraged to look up from their own, narrow research interests and chart the larger trajectories of their chosen field. Our readers have asked us to do just that. We are grateful to them for this opportunity. We are also encouraged that our earlier editions have been used in AI communities worldwide and translated into a number of languages including German, Polish, Portuguese, Russian, and two dialects of Chinese!

Although artificial intelligence, like most engineering disciplines, must justify itself to the world of commerce by providing solutions to practical problems, we entered the field of AI for the same reasons as many of our colleagues and students: we want to understand and explore the mechanisms of mind that enable intelligent thought and action. We reject the rather provincial notion that intelligence is an exclusive ability of humans, and believe that we can effectively investigate the space of possible intelligences by designing and evaluating intelligent artifacts. Although the course of our careers has given us no cause to change these commitments, we have arrived at a greater appreciation for the scope, complexity, and audacity of this undertaking. In the preface to our earlier editions, we outlined three assertions that we believed distinguished our approach to teaching artificial intelligence. It is reasonable, in writing a preface to this fifth edition, to return to these themes and see how they have endured as our field has grown.

The first of these goals was to "unify the diverse branches of AI through a detailed discussion of its theoretical foundations". At the time we adopted that goal, it seemed that the main problem was reconciling researchers who emphasized the careful statement and analysis of formal theories of intelligence (the *neats*) with those who believed that intelligence itself was some sort of grand hack that could be best approached in an application-driven, *ad hoc* manner (the *scruffies*). That dichotomy has proven far too simple. In contemporary AI, debates between neats and scruffies have given way to dozens of other debates between proponents of physical symbol systems and students of neural networks, between logicians and designers of artificial life forms that evolve in a most illogical manner, between architects of expert systems and case-based reasoners and, finally, between those who believe artificial intelligence has already been achieved and those who believe it will never happen. Our original image of AI as frontier science where outlaws, prospectors, wild-eyed prairie prophets and other dreamers were being slowly tamed by the disciplines of formalism and empiricism has given way to a different metaphor: that of a large, chaotic but mostly peaceful city, where orderly bourgeois neighborhoods draw their vitality from diverse, chaotic, bohemian districts. Over the years that we have devoted to the different editions of this book, a compelling picture of the architecture of intelligence has started to emerge from this city's structure, art, and industry.

Intelligence is too complex to be described by any single theory; instead, researchers are constructing a hierarchy of theories that characterize it at multiple levels of abstraction. At the lowest levels of this hierarchy, neural networks, genetic algorithms and other forms of emergent computation have enabled us to address the processes of adaptation, perception, embodiment, and interaction with the physical world that must underlie any form of intelligent activity. Through some still partially understood resolution, this chaotic population of blind and primitive actors gives rise to the cooler patterns of logical inference. Working at this higher level, logicians have built on Aristotle's gift, tracing the outlines of deduction, abduction, induction, truth-maintenance, and countless other modes and manners of reason. At even higher levels of abstraction, designers of expert systems, intelligent agents, and natural language understanding programs have come to recognize the role of social processes in creating, transmitting, and sustaining knowledge. Finally, as philosophers we are charged to critique the epistemological validity of the AI enterprise. For this task we discuss the rationalist project, the empiricists dilemma, and propose a constructivist rapprochement. In this fifth edition, we have touched on all these levels of the developing AI endeavour.

The second commitment we made in the earlier editions was to the central position of "advanced representational formalisms and search techniques" in AI methodology. This is, perhaps, the most controversial aspect of our previous editions and of much early work in AI, with many researchers in emergent computation questioning whether symbolic reasoning and referential semantics have any role at all in thought. Although the idea of representation as giving names to things has been challenged by the implicit representation provided by the emerging patterns of a neural network or an artificial life, we believe that an understanding of representation and search remains essential to any serious practitioner of artificial intelligence. We also feel that an overview of the historical traditions and the skills acquired through the study of representation and search are critical components for AI education. Furthermore, these are invaluable tools for analyzing such aspects of non-symbolic AI as the expressive power of a neural network or the progression of candidate problem solutions through the fitness landscape of a genetic algorithm. Comparisons, contrasts, and a critique of the various approaches of modern AI are offered in Chapter 17.

The third commitment we made at the beginning of this book's life cycle, to "place artificial intelligence within the context of empirical science," has remained unchanged. To quote from the preface to the third edition, we continue to believe that AI is not

. . . some strange aberration from the scientific tradition, but . . . part of a general quest for knowledge about, and the understanding of intelligence itself. Furthermore, our AI programming tools, along with the exploratory programming methodology . . . are ideal for exploring an environment. Our tools give us a medium for both understanding and questions. We come to appreciate and know phenomena constructively, that is, by progressive approximation.

Thus we see each design and program as an experiment with nature: we propose a representation, we generate a search algorithm, and then we question the adequacy of our characterization to account for part of the phenomenon of intelligence. And the natural world gives a response to our query. Our experiment can be deconstructed, revised, extended, and run again. Our model can be refined, our understanding extended.

New with The Fifth Edition

The most general change for the fifth edition was the extension of the material related to the stochastic approaches to AI. To accomplish we added a completely new Chapter 5 that introduces the stochastic methodology. From the basic foundations of set theory and counting we develop the notions of probabilities, random variables, and independence. We present and use Bayes' theorem first with one symptom and one disease and then in its full general form. We examine the hypotheses that underlie the use of Bayes and then present the *argmax* and *naive Bayes* approaches. We present examples of stochastic reasoning, including several from work in the analysis of language phenomena. We also introduce the idea of conditional independence that leads to our presentation of Bayesian belief networks (BBNs) and d-separation in Chapter 9.

We supplemented the presentation of materials throughout the book with more on these stochastic methods. This included introducing *probabilistic finite state machines* and *probabilistic acceptors*, and the presentation of algorithms for *dynamic programming*, especially using stochastic measures (sometimes referred to as the *Viterbi algorithm*). We extended the material in Chapter 9 (reasoning under conditions of uncertainty) to include Bayesian belief nets, hidden Markov, and other graphical models. We added a stochastic English language parser (based on the work of Mark Steedman at the University of Edinburgh) to Chapter 15, the PROLOG material in the book.

We also extended material in several sections of the book to recognize the continuing importance of agent-based problem solving and embodiment in AI technology. In discussions of the foundations of AI we recognize intelligence as physically embodied and situated in a natural and social world context. Apropos of this, we present in Chapter 7 the evolution of AI representational schemes from associative and early logic-based, through weak and strong method approaches, including connectionist and evolutionary/emergent models, to the situated and social aspects of created intelligence. Chapter 17 contains a critique of each of these representational approaches.

Chapter 14 presents issues in natural language understanding, including a section on stochastic models for language comprehension. The presentation includes Markov models, CART trees, mutual information clustering, and statistic-based parsing. The chapter closes with several examples, including the applications of text mining and text summarization techniques for the WWW.

Finally, in a revised Chapter 17, we return to the deeper questions of the nature of intelligence and the possibility of intelligent machines. We comment on the AI endeavour from the perspectives of philosophy, psychology, and neuro-physiology.

The Contents

Chapter 1 (Part I) introduces artificial intelligence. We begin with a brief history of attempts to understand mind and intelligence in philosophy, psychology, and other related areas. In an important sense, AI is an old science, tracing its roots back at least to Aristotle. An appreciation of this background is essential for an understanding of the issues addressed in modern research. We also present an overview of some of the important applications of AI. Our goal in Chapter 1 is to provide both background and a motivation for the theory and applications that follow.

Chapters 2, 3, 4, 5, and 6 (Part II) introduce the research tools for AI problem solving. These include, in Chapter 2, the predicate calculus presented both as a mathematical system as well as a representation language to describe the essential features of a problem. Search, and the algorithms and data structures used to implement search, are introduced in Chapter 3, to organize the exploration of problem situations. In Chapter 4, we discuss the essential role of heuristics in focusing and constraining search-based problem solving. In Chapter 5, we introduce the stochastic methodology, important technology for reasoning in situations of uncertainty. In Chapter 6, we present a number of software architectures, including the blackboard and production system, for implementing these search algorithms.

Chapters 7, 8, and 9 make up Part III: representations for AI, knowledge-intensive problem solving, and reasoning in changing and ambiguous situations. In Chapter 7 we present the evolving story of AI representational schemes. We begin with a discussion of association-based networks and extend this model to include conceptual dependency theory, frames, and scripts. We then present an in-depth examination of a particular formalism, conceptual graphs, emphasizing the epistemological issues involved in representing knowledge and showing how these issues are addressed in a modern representation language. Expanding on this formalism in Chapter 14, we show how conceptual graphs can be used to implement a natural language database front end. We conclude Chapter 7 with more modern approaches to representation, including Copycat and agent-oriented architectures.

Chapter 8 presents the rule-based expert system along with case-based and model-based reasoning, including examples from the NASA space program. These approaches to problem solving are presented as a natural evolution of the material in Part II: using a production system of predicate calculus expressions to orchestrate a graph search. We end with an analysis of the strengths and weaknesses of each of these approaches to knowledge-intensive problem solving.

Chapter 9 presents models for reasoning with uncertainty as well as the use of unreliable information. We introduce Bayesian models, belief networks, Dempster–Shafer, causal models, and the Stanford certainty algebra for reasoning in uncertain situations. Chapter 9 also contains algorithms for truth maintenance, reasoning with minimum models, logic-based abduction, and the clique-tree algorithm for Bayesian belief networks.

Part IV, Chapters 10 through 12, is an extensive presentation of issues in machine learning. In Chapter 10 we offer a detailed look at algorithms for symbol-based learning, a fruitful area of research spawning a number of different problems and solution approaches. These learning algorithms vary in their goals, the training data considered, their learning strategies, and the knowledge representations they employ. Symbol-based learning includes induction, concept learning, version-space search, and ID3. The role of inductive bias is considered, generalizations from patterns of data, as well as the effective use of knowledge to learn from a single example in explanation-based learning. Category learning, or conceptual clustering, is presented with unsupervised learning. Reinforcement learning, or the ability to integrate feedback from the environment into a policy for making new decisions concludes the chapter.

In Chapter 11 we present neural networks, often referred to as sub-symbolic or connectionist models of learning. In a neural net, information is implicit in the organization and weights on a set of connected processors, and learning involves a re-arrangement and modification of the overall weighting of nodes and structure of the system. We present a number of connectionist architectures, including perceptron learning, backpropagation, and counterpropagation. We demonstrate Kohonen, Grossberg, and Hebbian models. We present associative learning and attractor models, including Hopfield networks.

Genetic algorithms and evolutionary approaches to learning are introduced in Chapter 12. On this viewpoint, learning is cast as an emerging and adaptive process. After several examples of problem solutions based on genetic algorithms, we introduce the application of genetic techniques to more general problem solvers. These include classifier systems and genetic programming. We then describe society-based learning with examples from artificial life, called *a-life*, research. We conclude the chapter with an example of emergent computation from research at the Santa Fe Institute. We compare, contrast, and critique the three approaches we present to machine learning (symbol-based, connectionist, social and emergent) in Chapter 17.

Part V, Chapters 13 and 14, presents automated reasoning and natural language understanding. Theorem proving, often referred to as automated reasoning, is one of the oldest areas of AI research. In Chapter 13, we discuss the first programs in this area, including the Logic Theorist and the General Problem Solver. The primary focus of the chapter is binary resolution proof procedures, especially resolution refutations. More advanced inferencing with hyper-resolution and paramodulation is also presented. Finally, we describe the PROLOG interpreter as a Horn clause and resolution-based inferencing system, and see PROLOG computing as an instance of the logic programming paradigm.

Chapter 14 presents natural language understanding. Our traditional approach to language understanding, exemplified by many of the semantic structures presented in Chapter 7, is complemented with the stochastic approach. These include Markov models, CART trees, mutual information clustering, and statistics-based parsing. The chapter concludes with examples applying these natural language techniques to database query systems and also to a text summarization system for use on the WWW.

Part VI develops in LISP and PROLOG many of the algorithms presented in the earlier chapters. Chapter 15 covers PROLOG and Chapter 16 LISP. We demonstrate these languages as tools for AI problem solving by building the search and representation techniques of the earlier chapters, including breadth-, depth-, and best-first search algorithms. We implement these search techniques in a problem-independent fashion so that they may be extended to create shells for search in rule-based expert systems, to build semantic networks, natural language understanding systems, and learning applications.

Finally, Chapter 17 serves as an epilogue for the book. It addresses the issue of the possibility of a science of intelligent systems, and considers contemporary challenges to AI; it discusses AI's current limitations, and projects its exciting future.

Using This Book

Artificial intelligence is a big field, and consequently, this is a large book. Although it would require more than a single semester to cover all of the material offered, we have designed our book so that a number of paths may be taken through the material. By selecting subsets of the material, we have used this text for single semester and full year (two semester) courses.

We assume that most students will have had introductory courses in discrete mathematics, including predicate calculus, set theory, counting, and graph theory. If this is not true, the instructor should spend more time on these concepts in the optional sections at the beginning of the introductory chapters (2.1, 3.1, and 5.1). We also assume that students have had courses in data structures including trees, graphs, and recursion-based search, using stacks, queues, and priority queues. If they have not, then spend more time on the beginning sections of Chapters 3, 4, and 6.

In a one quarter or one semester course, we go quickly through the first two parts of the book. With this preparation, students are able to appreciate the material in Part III. We then consider the PROLOG and LISP in Part VI and require students to build many of the representation and search techniques of the first sections. Alternatively, one of the languages, PROLOG, for example, can be introduced early in the course and be used to test out the data structures and search techniques as they are encountered. We feel the meta-interpreters presented in the language chapters are very helpful for building rule-based and other knowledge-intensive problem solvers. PROLOG and LISP are both excellent tools for building natural language understanding and learning systems.

In a two-semester or three-quarter course, we are able to cover the application areas of Parts IV and V, especially the machine learning chapters, in appropriate detail. We also expect a much more detailed programming project from students. We think that it is very important in the second semester for students to revisit many of the primary sources in the AI literature. It is crucial for students to see both where we are, as well as how we got here, and to have an appreciation of the future promises of artificial intelligence. We use a collected set of readings for this purpose, such as *Computation and Intelligence* (Luger 1995).

The algorithms of our book are described using a Pascal-like pseudo-code. This notation uses the control structures of Pascal along with English descriptions of the tests and operations. We have added two useful constructs to the Pascal control structures. The first is a modified case statement that, rather than comparing the value of a variable with constant case labels, as in standard Pascal, lets each item be labeled with an arbitrary boolean test. The case evaluates these tests in order until one of them is true and then performs the associated action; all other actions are ignored. Those familiar with LISP will note that this has the same semantics as the LISP cond statement.

The other addition to our pseudo-code language is a return statement which takes one argument and can appear anywhere within a procedure or function. When the return is encountered, it causes the program to immediately exit the function, returning its argument as a result. Other than these modifications we used Pascal structure, with a reliance on the English descriptions, to make the algorithms clear.

Supplemental Material Available via the Internet

The fifth edition has an important attached web site maintained by Addison-Wesley Pearson. This site, built by two UNM graduate students, Alejandro CdeBaca and Cheng Liu, includes supplementary ideas for most chapters, some sample problems with their solutions, and many ideas for student projects. Besides the LISP and PROLOG materials in Chapters 15 and 16, we have included many AI algorithms in Java and C++ on the web site. Students are welcome to use these materials and supplement them with their own comments, code, and critiques. The web url for this book is www.booksites.net/luger.

The PROLOG and LISP code presented in the book is available to readers on the book web page just described as well as via the internet at www.cs.unm.edu/~luger/. Follow the pointers to the fifth edition.

Addison-Wesley and Pearson Education: www.aw-bc.com/cs/ and www.booksites.net/luger support this book with an Instructor's Guide, which has many of the book's exercises worked out, several practice tests with solutions, and ideas for teaching the material. They also have a full set of PowerPoint presentation materials for use by instructors. See your local A-W Pearson representative for access to these materials.

My e-mail address is luger@cs.unm.edu, and I very much enjoy hearing from my readers.

Acknowledgements

Although I am the sole author of the fifth edition, this book has always been the product of my efforts as Professor of Computer Science, Psychology, and Linguistics at the University of New Mexico together with the contributions of my fellow faculty, my professional colleagues, graduate students, and friends, especially the members of the UNM artificial intelligence community. The fifth edition is also the product of the many readers that have e-mailed me comments, corrections, and suggestions. The book will continue this way, reflecting this "community" effort; consequently, I will continue using the prepositions *we, our,* and *us* when presenting material.

I thank Bill Stubblefield, the co-author for the first three editions, for more than fifteen years of contributions, but even more importantly, for his friendship over the past twenty-five years. I also thank the many reviewers that have helped develop these five editions. These include Dennis Bahler, Leonardo Bottaci, Skona Brittain, Philip Chan, Peter Collingwood, Mehdi Dastani, John Donald, Sarah Douglas, Christophe Giraud-Carrier, Andrew Kosoresow, Terran Lane, Chris Malcolm, Ray Mooney, Marek Perkowski, Barak Pearlmutter, Dan Pless, Bruce Porter, Julian Richardson, Jude Shavlik, John Sheppard, Carl Stern, Leon van der Torre, Marco Valtorta, and Bob Veroff. We also appreciate the numerous suggestions and comments sent directly by e-mail from people using the book. Finally, Chris Malcolm, Brendan McGonnigle, and Akasha Tang, critiqued Chapter 17.

From our UNM colleagues, we thank Dan Pless for his major role in developing material in Chapters 5 and 9, Joseph Lewis for his efforts on Chapters 9 and 17, Carl Stern for his help in developing Chapter 10 on connectionist learning, Bob Veroff for his critique of the automated reasoning material in Chapter 13, and Jared Saia and Monique Morin for helping with the stochastic approaches to natural language understanding of Chapter 14. Alejandro CdeBaca and Cheng Liu checked the bibliographic references and did the indexing.

We thank Academic Press for permission to reprint much of the material of Chapter 11; this appeared in the book *Cognitive Science: The Science of Intelligent Systems* (Luger

1994). Finally, we thank more than a decade of students who have used this text and software at UNM for their help in expanding our horizons, as well as in removing typos and bugs from the book.

We thank our many friends at Benjamin-Cummings, Addison-Wesley-Longman, and Pearson Education for their support and encouragement in completing the writing task of our five editions, especially Alan Apt in helping us with the first edition, Lisa Moller and Mary Tudor for their help on the second, Victoria Henderson, Louise Wilson, and Karen Mosman for their assistance on the third, Keith Mansfield, Karen Sutherland, and Anita Atkinson for support on the fourth, and Keith Mansfield, Owen Knight, Mary Lince, and Bridget Allen for their help on this fifth edition. Katherine Haratunian of Addison Wesley USA has had a huge role in seeing that Professors received their Instructor Guides and PowerPoint presentation materials. These are maintained by Addison-Wesley Pearson and available only through your local sales representative. We appreciate Linda Cicarella's work at the University of New Mexico helping prepare figures for publication.

Individual debts for permissions to include copyright materials in all five editions are listed in the *Publisher's Acknowledgments* section which follows this preface.

We thank Thomas Barrow, internationally recognized artist and University of New Mexico Professor of Art (emeritus), who created the seven photograms for this book.

Artificial intelligence is an exciting and rewarding discipline; may you enjoy your study as you come to appreciate its power and challenges.

George Luger
1 July 2004
Albuquerque

PUBLISHER'S ACKNOWLEDGEMENTS

We are grateful to the following for permission to reproduce copyright material:

Figures 4.8, 4.9, 9.21 and 9.22, Tables 5.2 and 5.3 adapted from Figure 5.6, p. 157, Figure 5.18, p.178, Figure 5.20, p.180 and data on p.167, from *Speech and Language Processing: an introduction to natural language processing, computational linguistics, and speech recognition*, Prentice Hall, (Pearson Education, Inc.), (Jurafsky, D., and Martin, J.H., 2000); Figure 5.3 adapted from Figure 5.12, p. 170, from *Speech and Language Processing: an introduction to natural language processing, computational linguistics, and speech recognition*, Prentice Hall, (Pearson Education, Inc.), (Jurafsky, D., and Martin, J.H., 2000), which was itself adapted from a figure from *Artificial Intelligence: A Modern Approach*, 1st Edition, Prentice Hall, (Pearson Education, Inc.), (Russell, S.J., and Norvig, P., 1995); Figure 7.1 from figure from *Expert Systems: Artificial Intelligence in Business*, by Harmon, P. and King, D., John Wiley & Sons, Inc., Copyright © 1985 Paul Harmon and David King. This material is used by permission of John Wiley & Sons, Inc.; Figures 7.6, 7.9, and 7.10 from figures from 'Inference and the computer understanding of natural language', in *Artificial Intelligence*, Vol. 5, No. 4, 1974, pp. 373–412, Copyright © 1974, reprinted with permission from Elsevier Science, (Schank, R.C., and Reiger, C.J., 1974); Figures 7.27 and 7.28 from figures from *Analogy-Making as Perception: A Computer Model*, The MIT Press, (Mitchell, M., 1993); Figure 9.2 from 'An improved algorithm for non-monotonic dependency net update', in *Technical Report LITH-MAT-R-82-23*, reprinted by permission of the author, (Goodwin, J., 1982); Figure 10.21 adapted from figure from 'Models of incremental concept formation', in *Artificial Intelligence*, Vol. 40, Nos. 1–3, 1989, pp. 11–62, Copyright © 1989, reprinted with permission from Elsevier Science, (Gennari, J.H., Langley, P., and Fisher, D., 1989); Figure 11.18 from part of Figure 6.2, p. 102, from *Introduction to Support Vector Machines: and other kernel-based learning methods*, Cambridge University Press, (Cristianini, N., and Shawe-Taylor, J., 2000).

Academic Press for Chapter 11, adapted from *Cognitive Science: The Science of Intelligent Systems*, (Luger, G.F., 1994). American Society for Public Administration for an abridged extract from 'Decision-making and administrative organization', in *Public Administration Review*, Vol. 4, Winter 1944, (Simon, H.A., 1944).

In some instances we have been unable to trace the owners of copyright material, and we would appreciate any information that would enable us to do so.

BRIEF CONTENTS

Companion Website resources

Visit the Companion Website at **www.booksites.net/luger**

For students
- Program code

For lecturers
- Complete, downloadable Instructor's Manual
- PowerPoint slides that can be downloaded and used as OHTs

Also: This website has a Syllabus and Profile Manager, online help, search functions, and email results functions.

CONTENTS

PART I

ARTIFICIAL INTELLIGENCE: ITS ROOTS AND SCOPE

Everything must have a beginning, to speak in Sanchean phrase; and that beginning must be linked to something that went before. Hindus give the world an elephant to support it, but they make the elephant stand upon a tortoise. Invention, it must be humbly admitted, does not consist in creating out of void, but out of chaos; the materials must, in the first place, be afforded. . . .

—MARY SHELLEY, Frankenstein

Artificial Intelligence: An Attempted Definition

Artificial intelligence (AI) may be defined as the branch of computer science that is concerned with the automation of intelligent behavior. This definition is particularly appropriate to this book in that it emphasizes our conviction that AI is a part of computer science and, as such, must be based on sound theoretical and applied principles of that field. These principles include the data structures used in knowledge representation, the algorithms needed to apply that knowledge, and the languages and programming techniques used in their implementation.

However, this definition suffers from the fact that intelligence itself is not very well defined or understood. Although most of us are certain that we know intelligent behavior when we see it, it is doubtful that anyone could come close to defining intelligence in a way that would be specific enough to help in the evaluation of a supposedly intelligent computer program, while still capturing the vitality and complexity of the human mind.

Thus the problem of defining artificial intelligence becomes one of defining intelligence itself: is intelligence a single faculty, or is it just a name for a collection of distinct and unrelated abilities? To what extent is intelligence learned as opposed to having an a priori existence? Exactly what does happen when learning occurs? What is creativity? What is intuition? Can intelligence be inferred from observable behavior, or does it require evidence of a particular internal mechanism? How is knowledge represented in the nerve tissue of a living being, and what lessons does this have for the design of intelligent machines? What is self-awareness; what role does it play in intelligence? Furthermore, is it necessary to pattern an intelligent computer program after what is known about human intelligence, or is a strict "engineering" approach to the problem sufficient? Is it even possible to achieve intelligence on a computer, or does an intelligent entity require the richness of sensation and experience that might be found only in a biological existence?

These are unanswered questions, and all of them have helped to shape the problems and solution methodologies that constitute the core of modern AI. In fact, part of the appeal of artificial intelligence is that it offers a unique and powerful tool for exploring exactly these questions. AI offers a medium and a test-bed for theories of intelligence: such theories may be stated in the language of computer programs and consequently tested and verified through the execution of these programs on an actual computer.

For these reasons, our initial definition of artificial intelligence seems to fall short of unambiguously defining the field. If anything, it has only led to further questions and the paradoxical notion of a field of study whose major goals include its own definition. But this difficulty in arriving at a precise definition of AI is entirely appropriate. Artificial intelligence is still a young discipline, and its structure, concerns, and methods are less clearly defined than those of a more mature science such as physics.

Artificial intelligence has always been more concerned with expanding the capabilities of computer science than with defining its limits. Keeping this exploration grounded in sound theoretical principles is one of the challenges facing AI researchers in general and this book in particular.

Because of its scope and ambition, artificial intelligence defies simple definition. For the time being, we will simply define it as *the collection of problems and methodologies studied by artificial intelligence researchers*. This definition may seem silly and meaningless, but it makes an important point: artificial intelligence, like every science, is a human endeavor, and perhaps, is best understood in that context.

There are reasons that any science, AI included, concerns itself with a certain set of problems and develops a particular body of techniques for approaching these problems. In Chapter 1, a short history of artificial intelligence and the people and assumptions that have shaped it will explain why certain sets of questions have come to dominate the field and why the methods discussed in this book have been taken for their solution.

AI: EARLY HISTORY AND APPLICATIONS

All men by nature desire to know . . .

—ARISTOTLE, Opening sentence of the Metaphysics

Hear the rest, and you will marvel even more at the crafts and resources I have contrived. Greatest was this: in the former times if a man fell sick he had no defense against the sickness, neither healing food nor drink, nor unguent; but through the lack of drugs men wasted away, until I showed them the blending of mild simples wherewith they drive out all manner of diseases. . . .

It was I who made visible to men's eyes the flaming signs of the sky that were before dim. So much for these. Beneath the earth, man's hidden blessing, copper, iron, silver, and gold—will anyone claim to have discovered these before I did? No one, I am very sure, who wants to speak truly and to the purpose. One brief word will tell the whole story: all arts that mortals have come from Prometheus.

—AESCHYLUS, Prometheus Bound

1.1   From Eden to ENIAC: Attitudes toward Intelligence, Knowledge, and Human Artifice

Prometheus speaks of the fruits of his transgression against the gods of Olympus: his purpose was not merely to steal fire for the human race but also to enlighten humanity through the gift of intelligence or *nous*: the *rational mind*. This intelligence forms the foundation for all of human technology and ultimately all human civilization. The work of Aeschylus, the classical Greek dramatist, illustrates a deep and ancient awareness of the extraordinary power of knowledge. Artificial intelligence, in its very direct concern for Prometheus's gift, has been applied to all the areas of his legacy—medicine, psychology, biology, astronomy, geology—and many areas of scientific endeavor that Aeschylus could not have imagined.

Though Prometheus's action freed humanity from the sickness of ignorance, it also earned him the wrath of Zeus. Outraged over this theft of knowledge that previously belonged only to the gods of Olympus, Zeus commanded that Prometheus be chained to a barren rock to suffer the ravages of the elements for eternity. The notion that human efforts to gain knowledge constitute a transgression against the laws of God or nature is deeply ingrained in Western thought. It is the basis of the story of Eden and appears in the work of Dante and Milton. Both Shakespeare and the ancient Greek tragedians portrayed intellectual ambition as the cause of disaster. The belief that the desire for knowledge must ultimately lead to disaster has persisted throughout history, enduring the Renaissance, the Age of Enlightenment, and even the scientific and philosophical advances of the nineteenth and twentieth centuries. Thus, we should not be surprised that artificial intelligence inspires so much controversy in both academic and popular circles.

Indeed, rather than dispelling this ancient fear of the consequences of intellectual ambition, modern technology has only made those consequences seem likely, even imminent. The legends of Prometheus, Eve, and Faustus have been retold in the language of technological society. In her introduction to *Frankenstein*, subtitled, interestingly enough, *The Modern Prometheus*, Mary Shelley writes:

> Many and long were the conversations between Lord Byron and Shelley to which I was a devout and silent listener. During one of these, various philosophical doctrines were discussed, and among others the nature of the principle of life, and whether there was any probability of its ever being discovered and communicated. They talked of the experiments of Dr. Darwin (I speak not of what the doctor really did or said that he did, but, as more to my purpose, of what was then spoken of as having been done by him), who preserved a piece of vermicelli in a glass case till by some extraordinary means it began to move with a voluntary motion. Not thus, after all, would life be given. Perhaps a corpse would be reanimated; galvanism had given token of such things: perhaps the component parts of a creature might be manufactured, brought together, and endued with vital warmth (Butler 1998).

Mary Shelley shows us the extent to which scientific advances such as the work of Darwin and the discovery of electricity had convinced even nonscientists that the workings of nature were not divine secrets, but could be broken down and understood systematically. Frankenstein's monster is not the product of shamanistic incantations or unspeakable transactions with the underworld: it is assembled from separately "manufactured" components and infused with the vital force of electricity. Although nineteenth-century science was inadequate to realize the goal of understanding and creating a fully intelligent agent, it affirmed the notion that the mysteries of life and intellect might be brought into the light of scientific analysis.

1.1.1 A Brief History of the Foundations for AI

By the time Mary Shelley finally and perhaps irrevocably joined modern science with the Promethean myth, the philosophical foundations of modern work in artificial intelligence had been developing for several thousand years. Although the moral and cultural issues raised by artificial intelligence are both interesting and important, our introduction is more properly concerned with AI's intellectual heritage. The logical starting point for such a history is the genius of Aristotle, or as Dante in the *Divine Comedy* refers to him, "the master of them that know". Aristotle wove together the insights, wonders, and fears of the early Greek tradition with the careful analysis and disciplined thought that were to become the standard for more modern science.

For Aristotle, the most fascinating aspect of nature was change. In his *Physics*, he defined his "philosophy of nature" as the "study of things that change". He distinguished between the *matter* and *form* of things: a sculpture is fashioned from the *material* bronze and has the *form* of a human. Change occurs when the bronze is molded to a new form. The matter/form distinction provides a philosophical basis for modern notions such as symbolic computing and data abstraction. In computing (even with numbers) we are manipulating patterns that are the forms of electromagnetic material, with the changes of form of this material representing aspects of the solution process. Abstracting the form from the medium of its representation not only allows these forms to be manipulated computationally but also provides the promise of a theory of data structures, the heart of modern computer science.

In his *Metaphysics*, beginning with the words "All men by nature desire to know", Aristotle developed a science of things that never change, including his cosmology and theology. More relevant to artificial intelligence, however, was Aristotle's epistemology or analysis of how humans "know" their world, discussed in his *Logic*. Aristotle referred to logic as the "instrument" (*organon*), because he felt that the study of thought itself was at the basis of all knowledge. In his *Logic*, he investigated whether certain propositions can be said to be "true" because they are related to other things that are known to be "true". Thus if we know that "all men are mortal" and that "Socrates is a man", then we can conclude that "Socrates is mortal". This argument is an example of what Aristotle referred to as a syllogism using the deductive form *modus ponens*. Although the formal axiomatization of reasoning needed another two thousand years for its full flowering in the works of Gottlob Frege, Bertrand Russell, Kurt Gödel, Alan Turing, Alfred Tarski, and others, its roots may be traced to Aristotle.

Renaissance thought, building on the Greek tradition, initiated the evolution of a different and powerful way of thinking about humanity and its relation to the natural world. Science began to replace mysticism as a means of understanding nature. Clocks and, eventually, factory schedules superseded the rhythms of nature for thousands of city dwellers. Most of the modern social and physical sciences found their origin in the notion that processes, whether natural or artificial, could be mathematically analyzed and understood. In particular, scientists and philosophers realized that thought itself, the way that knowledge was represented and manipulated in the human mind, was a difficult but essential subject for scientific study.

Perhaps the major event in the development of the modern world view was the Copernican revolution, the replacement of the ancient Earth-centered model of the universe with the idea that the Earth and other planets are actually in orbits around the sun. After centuries of an "obvious" order, in which the scientific explanation of the nature of the cosmos was consistent with the teachings of religion and common sense, a drastically different and not at all obvious model was proposed to explain the motions of heavenly bodies. For perhaps the first time, *our ideas about the world were seen as fundamentally distinct from that world's appearance.* This split between the human mind and its surrounding reality, between ideas about things and things themselves, is essential to the modern study of the mind and its organization. This breach was widened by the writings of Galileo, whose scientific observations further contradicted the "obvious" truths about the natural world and whose development of mathematics as a tool for describing that world emphasized the distinction between the world and our ideas about it. It is out of this breach that the modern notion of the mind evolved: introspection became a common motif in literature, philosophers began to study epistemology and mathematics, and the systematic application of the scientific method rivaled the senses as tools for understanding the world.

In 1620, Francis Bacon's *Novum Organun* offered a set of search techniques for this emerging scientific methodology. Based on the Aristotelian and Platonic idea that the "form" of an entity was equivalent to the sum of its necessary and sufficient "features", Bacon articulated an algorithm for determining the essence of an entity. First, he made an organized collection of all instances of the entity, enumerating the features of each in a table. Then he collected a similar list of negative instances of the entity, focusing especially on near instances of the entity, that is, those that deviated from the "form" of the entity by single features. Then Bacon attempts—this step is not totally clear—to make a systematic list of all the features essential to the entity, that is, those that are common to all positive instances of the entity and missing from the negative instances.

It is interesting to see a form of Francis Bacon's approach to concept learning reflected in modern AI algorithms for Version Space Search, Chapter 10.2. An extension of Bacon's algorithms was also part of an AI program for discovery learning, suitably called *Bacon* (Langley et al. 1981). This program was able to induce many physical laws from collections of data related to the phenomena. It is also interesting to note that the question of whether a general purpose algorithm was possible for producing scientific proofs awaited the challenges of the early twentieth century mathematician Hilbert (his *Entscheidungsproblem*) and the response of the modern genius of Alan Turing (his *Turing Machine* and proofs of *computability* and the *haltying problem*); see Davis et al. (1976).

Although the first calculating machine, the abacus, was created by the Chinese in the twenty-sixth century BC, further mechanization of algebraic processes awaited the skills of the seventeenth century Europeans. In 1614, the Scots mathematician, John Napier, created logarithms, the mathematical transformations that allowed multiplication and the use of exponents to be reduced to addition and multiplication. Napier also created his *bones* that were used to represent overflow values for arithmetic operations. These bones were later used by Wilhelm Schickard (1592–1635), a German mathematician and clergyman of Tübingen, who in 1623 invented a *Calculating Clock* for performing addition and subtraction. This machine recorded the overflow from its calculations by the chiming of a clock.

Another famous calculating machine was the *Pascaline* that Blaise Pascal, the French philosopher and mathematician, created in 1642. Although the mechanisms of Schickard and Pascal were limited to addition and subtraction—including carries and borrows—they showed that processes that previously were thought to require human thought and skill could be fully automated. As Pascal later stated in his *Pensees* (1670), "The arithmetical machine produces effects which approach nearer to thought than all the actions of animals".

Pascal's successes with calculating machines inspired Gottfried Wilhelm von Leibniz in 1694 to complete a working machine that become known as the *Leibniz Wheel*. It integrated a moveable carriage and hand crank to drive wheels and cylinders that performed the more complex operations of multiplication and division. Leibniz was also fascinated by the possibility of an automated logic for proofs of propositions. Returning to Bacon's entity specification algorithm, where concepts were characterized as the collection of their necessary and sufficient features, Leibniz conjectured a machine that could calculate with these features to produce logically correct conclusions. Leibniz (1887) also envisioned a machine, reflecting modern ideas of deductive inference and proof, by which the production of scientific knowledge could become automated, a calculus for reasoning.

The seventeenth and eighteenth centuries also saw a great deal of discussion of epistemological issues; perhaps the most influential was the work of René Descartes, a central figure in the development of the modern concepts of thought and theories of mind. In his *Meditations*, Descartes (1680) attempted to find a basis for reality purely through introspection. Systematically rejecting the input of his senses as untrustworthy, Descartes was forced to doubt even the existence of the physical world and was left with only the reality of thought; even his own existence had to be justified in terms of thought: "Cogito ergo sum" (I think, therefore I am). After he established his own existence purely as a thinking entity, Descartes inferred the existence of God as an essential creator and ultimately reasserted the reality of the physical universe as the necessary creation of a benign God.

We can make two observations here: first, the schism between the mind and the physical world had become so complete that the process of thinking could be discussed in isolation from any specific sensory input or worldly subject matter; second, the connection between mind and the physical world was so tenuous that it required the intervention of a benign God to support reliable knowledge of the physical world! This view of the duality between the mind and the physical world underlies all of Descartes's thought, including his development of analytic geometry. How else could he have unified such a seemingly worldly branch of mathematics as geometry with such an abstract mathematical framework as algebra?

Why have we included this mind/body discussion in a book on artificial intelligence? There are two consequences of this analysis essential to the AI enterprise:

1. By attempting to separate the mind from the physical world, Descartes and related thinkers established that the structure of ideas about the world was not necessarily the same as the structure of their subject matter. This underlies the methodology of AI, along with the fields of epistemology, psychology, much of higher mathematics, and most of modern literature: mental processes have an existence of their own, obey their own laws, and can be studied in and of themselves.

2. Once the mind and the body are separated, philosophers found it necessary to find a way to reconnect the two, because interaction between Descartes mental, *res cogitans*, and physical, *res extensa*, is essential for human existence.

Although millions of words have been written on this *mind–body problem*, and numerous solutions proposed, no one has successfully explained the obvious interactions between mental states and physical actions while affirming a fundamental difference between them. The most widely accepted response to this problem, and the one that provides an essential foundation for the study of AI, holds that the mind and the body are not fundamentally different entities at all. On this view, mental processes are indeed achieved by physical systems such as brains (or computers). Mental processes, like physical processes, can ultimately be characterized through formal mathematics. Or, as acknowledged in his *Leviathan* by the 17th century English philosopher Thomas Hobbes (1651), "By ratiocination, I mean computation".

1.1.2   AI and the Rationalist and Empiricist Traditions

Modern research issues in artificial intelligence, as in other scientific disciplines, are formed and evolve through a combination of historical, social, and cultural pressures. Two of the most prominent pressures for the evolution of AI are the empiricist and rationalist traditions in philosophy.

The rationalist tradition, as seen in the previous section, had an early proponent in Plato, and was continued on through the writings of Pascal, Descartes, and Leibniz. For the rationalist, the external world is reconstructed through the clear and distinct ideas of a mathematics. A criticism of this dualistic approach is the forced disengagement of representational systems from their field of reference. The issue is whether the meaning attributed to a representation can be defined independent of its application conditions. If the world is different from our beliefs about the world, can our created concepts and symbols still have meaning?

Many AI programs have very much of this rationalist flavor. Early robot planners, for example, would describe their application domain or "world" as sets of predicate calculus statements and then a "plan" for action would be created through proving theorems about this "world" (Fikes et al. 1972, see also Section 8.4). Newell and Simon's *Physical Symbol System Hypothesis* (Introduction to Part II and Chapter 17) is seen by many as the archetype of this approach in modern AI. Several critics have commented on this rationalist bias as part of the failure of AI at solving complex tasks such as understanding human languages (Searle 1980, Winograd and Flores 1986, Brooks 1991a).

Rather than affirming as "real" the world of clear and distinct ideas, empiricists continue to remind us that "nothing enters the mind except through the senses". This constraint leads to further questions of how the human can possibly perceive general concepts or the pure forms of Plato's cave (Plato 1961). Aristotle was an early empiricist, emphasizing in his *De Anima* the limitations of the human perceptual system. More modern empiricists, especially Hobbes, Locke, and Hume, emphasize that knowledge must be explained through an introspective but empirical psychology. They distinguish two types of mental phenomena, perceptions on one hand, and thought, memory, and imagination on the other. The Scots philosopher, David Hume, for example, distinguishes between *impressions* and *ideas*. Impressions are lively and vivid, reflecting the presence and existence of an external object and not subject to voluntary control. Ideas, on the other hand, are less vivid and detailed and more subject to the subject's voluntary control.

Given this distinction between impressions and ideas, how can knowledge arise? For Hobbes, Locke, and Hume the fundamental explanatory mechanism is *association*.

Particular perceptual properties are associated through repeated experience. This repeated association creates a disposition in the mind to associate the corresponding ideas. A fundamental property of this account is presented with Hume's skepticism. Hume's purely descriptive account of the origins of ideas cannot, he claims, support belief in causality. Even the use of logic and induction cannot be rationally supported in this radical empiricist epistemology.

In *An Inquiry Concerning Human Understanding* (1748), Hume's skepticism extended to the analysis of miracles. Although Hume didn't address the nature of miracles directly, he did question the testimony-based belief in the miraculous. This skepticism, of course, was seen as a direct threat by believers in the bible as well as many other purveyors of religious traditions. The Reverend Thomas Bayes was both a mathematician and a minister. One of his papers, called *Essay towards Solving a Problem in the Doctrine of Chances* (1763) addressed Hume's questions mathematically. Bayes' theorem demonstrates formally how, through learning the correlations of the effects of actions, we can determine the probability of their causes.

The associational account of knowledge plays a significant role in the development of AI representational structures and programs, for example, in memory organization with *semantic networks* and *MOPS* and work in natural language understanding (see Sections 7.0, 7.1, and Chapter 14). Associational accounts have important influences of machine learning, especially with connectionist networks (see Sections 10.6, 10.7, and Chapter 11). Associationism also plays an important role in cognitive psychology including the *schemas* of Bartlett and Piaget as well as the entire thrust of the behaviorist tradition (Luger 1994). Finally, with AI tools for stochastic analysis, including the *Bayesian belief network* (BBN) and its current extensions to first-order Turing-complete systems for stochastic modeling, associational theories have found a sound mathematical basis and mature expressive power. Bayesian tools are important for research including diagnostics, machine learning, and natural language understanding (see Chapter 5 and Section 9.3).

Immanuel Kant, a German philosopher trained in the rationalist tradition, was strongly influenced by the writing of Hume. As a result, he began the modern synthesis of these two traditions. Knowledge for Kant contains two collaborating energies, an a priori component coming from the subject's reason along with an a posteriori component coming from active experience. Experience is meaningful only through the contribution of the subject. Without an active organizing form proposed by the subject, the world would be nothing more than passing transitory sensations. Finally, at the level of judgement, Kant claims, passing images or representations are bound together by the active subject and taken as the diverse appearances of an identity, of an "object". Kant's realism began the modern enterprise of psychologists such as Bartlett, Brunner, and Piaget. Kant's work influences the modern AI enterprise of machine learning (Part IV) as well as the continuing development of a constructivist epistemology (see Chapter 17).

1.1.3 The Development of Formal Logic

Once thinking had come to be regarded as a form of computation, its formalization and eventual mechanization were obvious next steps. As noted in Section 1.1.1, Gottfried

Wilhelm von Leibniz, with his *Calculus Philosophicus*, introduced the first system of formal logic as well as proposing a machine for automating its tasks (Leibniz 1887). Furthermore, the steps and stages of this mechanical solution can be represented as movement through the states of a tree or graph. Leonhard Euler, in the eighteenth century, with his analysis of the "connectedness" of the bridges joining the riverbanks and islands of the city of Königsberg (see the introduction to Chapter 3), introduced the study of representations that can abstractly capture the structure of relationships in the world as well as the discrete steps within a computation (Euler 1735).

The formalization of graph theory also afforded the possibility of *state space search*, a major conceptual tool of artificial intelligence. We can use graphs to model the deeper structure of a problem. The nodes of a *state space graph* represent possible stages of a problem solution; the arcs of the graph represent inferences, moves in a game, or other steps in a problem solution. Solving the problem is a process of searching the state space graph for a path to a solution (Introduction to Part II and Chapter 3). By describing the entire space of problem solutions, state space graphs provide a powerful tool for measuring the structure and complexity of problems and analyzing the efficiency, correctness, and generality of solution strategies.

As one of the originators of the science of operations research, as well as the designer of the first programmable mechanical computing machines, Charles Babbage, a nineteenth century mathematician, may also be considered an early practitioner of artificial intelligence (Morrison and Morrison 1961). Babbage's *difference engine* was a special-purpose machine for computing the values of certain polynomial functions and was the forerunner of his *analytical engine*. The analytical engine, designed but not successfully constructed during his lifetime, was a general-purpose programmable computing machine that presaged many of the architectural assumptions underlying the modern computer.

In describing the analytical engine, Ada Lovelace (1961), Babbage's friend, supporter, and collaborator, said:

> We may say most aptly that the Analytical Engine weaves algebraical patterns just as the Jacquard loom weaves flowers and leaves. Here, it seems to us, resides much more of originality than the difference engine can be fairly entitled to claim.

Babbage's inspiration was his desire to apply the technology of his day to liberate humans from the drudgery of making arithmetic calculations. In this sentiment, as well as with his conception of computers as mechanical devices, Babbage was thinking in purely nineteenth century terms. His analytical engine, however, also included many modern notions, such as the separation of memory and processor, the *store* and the *mill* in Babbage's terms, the concept of a digital rather than analog machine, and programmability based on the execution of a series of operations encoded on punched pasteboard cards. The most striking feature of Ada Lovelace's description, and of Babbage's work in general, is its treatment of the "patterns" of algebraic relationships as entities that may be studied, characterized, and finally implemented and manipulated mechanically without concern for the particular values that are finally passed through the mill of the calculating machine. This is an example implementation of the "abstraction and manipulation of form" first described by Aristotle and Leibniz.

The goal of creating a formal language for thought also appears in the work of George Boole, another nineteenth-century mathematician whose work must be included in any discussion of the roots of artificial intelligence (Boole 1847, 1854). Although he made contributions to a number of areas of mathematics, his best known work was in the mathematical formalization of the laws of logic, an accomplishment that forms the very heart of modern computer science. Though the role of Boolean algebra in the design of logic circuitry is well known, Boole's own goals in developing his system seem closer to those of contemporary AI researchers. In the first chapter of *An Investigation of the Laws of Thought, on which are founded the Mathematical Theories of Logic and Probabilities*, Boole (1854) described his goals as

> to investigate the fundamental laws of those operations of the mind by which reasoning is performed: to give expression to them in the symbolical language of a Calculus, and upon this foundation to establish the science of logic and instruct its method; ...and finally to collect from the various elements of truth brought to view in the course of these inquiries some probable intimations concerning the nature and constitution of the human mind.

The greatness of Boole's accomplishment is in the extraordinary power and simplicity of the system he devised: three operations, "AND" (denoted by $*$ or $\wedge$), "OR" (denoted by $+$ or $\vee$), and "NOT" (denoted by $\neg$), formed the heart of his logical calculus. These operations have remained the basis for all subsequent developments in formal logic, including the design of modern computers. While keeping the meaning of these symbols nearly identical to the corresponding algebraic operations, Boole noted that "the Symbols of logic are further subject to a special law, to which the symbols of quantity, as such, are not subject". This law states that for any X, an element in the algebra, $X*X=X$ (or that once something is known to be true, repetition cannot augment that knowledge). This led to the characteristic restriction of Boolean values to the only two numbers that may satisfy this equation: 1 and 0. The standard definitions of Boolean multiplication (AND) and addition (OR) follow from this insight.

Boole's system not only provided the basis of binary arithmetic but also demonstrated that an extremely simple formal system was adequate to capture the full power of logic. This assumption and the system Boole developed to demonstrate it form the basis of all modern efforts to formalize logic, from Russell and Whitehead's *Principia Mathematica* (Whitehead and Russell 1950), through the work of Turing and Gödel, up to modern automated reasoning systems.

Gottlob Frege, in his *Foundations of Arithmetic* (Frege 1879, 1884), created a mathematical specification language for describing the basis of arithmetic in a clear and precise fashion. With this language Frege formalized many of the issues first addressed by Aristotle's *Logic*. Frege's language, now called the *first-order predicate calculus*, offers a tool for describing the propositions and truth value assignments that make up the elements of mathematical reasoning and describes the axiomatic basis of "meaning" for these expressions. The formal system of the predicate calculus, which includes predicate symbols, a theory of functions, and quantified variables, was intended to be a language for describing mathematics and its philosophical foundations. It also plays a fundamental role in creating a theory of representation for artificial intelligence (Chapter 2). The first-order predicate calculus offers the tools necessary for automating reasoning: a language for expressions, a theory for assumptions related to the meaning of expressions, and a logically sound calculus for inferring new true expressions.

Whitehead and Russell's (1950) work is particularly important to the foundations of AI, in that their stated goal was to derive the whole of mathematics through formal operations on a collection of axioms. Although many mathematical systems have been constructed from basic axioms, what is interesting is Russell and Whitehead's commitment to mathematics as a purely formal system. This meant that axioms and theorems would be treated solely as strings of characters: proofs would proceed solely through the application of well-defined rules for manipulating these strings. There would be no reliance on intuition or the meaning of theorems as a basis for proofs. Every step of a proof followed from the strict application of formal (syntactic) rules to either axioms or previously proven theorems, even where traditional proofs might regard such a step as "obvious". What "meaning" the theorems and axioms of the system might have in relation to the world would be independent of their logical derivations. This treatment of mathematical reasoning in purely formal (and hence mechanical) terms provided an essential basis for its automation on physical computers. The logical syntax and formal rules of inference developed by Russell and Whitehead are still a basis for automatic theorem-proving systems, presented in Chapter 13, as well as for the theoretical foundations of artificial intelligence.

Alfred Tarski is another mathematician whose work is essential to the foundations of AI. Tarski created a *theory of reference* wherein the *well-formed formulae* of Frege or Russell and Whitehead can be said to refer, in a precise fashion, to the physical world (Tarski 1944, 1956; see Chapter 2). This insight underlies most theories of formal semantics. In his paper *The Semantic Conception of Truth and the Foundation of Semantics*, Tarski describes his theory of reference and truth value relationships. Modern computer scientists, especially Scott, Strachey, Burstall (Burstall and Darlington 1977), and Plotkin have related this theory to programming languages and other specifications for computing.

Although in the eighteenth, nineteenth, and early twentieth centuries the formalization of science and mathematics created the intellectual prerequisite for the study of artificial intelligence, it was not until the twentieth century and the introduction of the digital computer that AI became a viable scientific discipline. By the end of the 1940s electronic digital computers had demonstrated their potential to provide the memory and processing power required by intelligent programs. It was now possible to implement formal reasoning systems on a computer and empirically test their sufficiency for exhibiting intelligence. An essential component of the science of artificial intelligence is this commitment to digital computers as the vehicle of choice for creating and testing theories of intelligence.

Digital computers are not merely a vehicle for testing theories of intelligence. Their architecture also suggests a specific paradigm for such theories: intelligence is a form of information processing. The notion of search as a problem-solving methodology, for example, owes more to the sequential nature of computer operation than it does to any biological model of intelligence. Most AI programs represent knowledge in some formal language that is then manipulated by algorithms, honoring the separation of data and program fundamental to the von Neumann style of computing. Formal logic has emerged as an important representational tool for AI research, just as graph theory plays an indispensable role in the analysis of problem spaces as well as providing a basis for semantic networks and similar models of semantic meaning. These techniques and formalisms are discussed in detail throughout the body of this text; we mention them here to emphasize the symbiotic relationship between the digital computer and the theoretical underpinnings of artificial intelligence.

We often forget that the tools we create for our own purposes tend to shape our conception of the world through their structure and limitations. Although seemingly restrictive, this interaction is an essential aspect of the evolution of human knowledge: a tool (and scientific theories are ultimately only tools) is developed to solve a particular problem. As it is used and refined, the tool itself seems to suggest other applications, leading to new questions and, ultimately, the development of new tools.

1.1.4   The Turing Test

One of the earliest papers to address the question of machine intelligence specifically in relation to the modern digital computer was written in 1950 by the British mathematician Alan Turing. *Computing Machinery and Intelligence* (Turing 1950) remains timely in both its assessment of the arguments against the possibility of creating an intelligent computing machine and its answers to those arguments. Turing, known mainly for his contributions to the theory of computability, considered the question of whether or not a machine could actually be made to think. Noting that the fundamental ambiguities in the question itself (what is thinking? what is a machine?) precluded any rational answer, he proposed that the question of intelligence be replaced by a more clearly defined empirical test.

The *Turing test* measures the performance of an allegedly intelligent machine against that of a human being, arguably the best and only standard for intelligent behavior. The test, which Turing called the *imitation game*, places the machine and a human counterpart in rooms apart from a second human being, referred to as the *interrogator* (Figure 1.1). The interrogator is not able to see or speak directly to either of them, does not know which entity is actually the machine, and may communicate with them solely by use of a textual device such as a terminal. The interrogator is asked to distinguish the computer from the human being solely on the basis of their answers to questions asked over this device. If the interrogator cannot distinguish the machine from the human, then, Turing argues, the machine may be assumed to be intelligent.

By isolating the interrogator from both the machine and the other human participant, the test ensures that the interrogator will not be biased by the appearance of the machine or any mechanical property of its voice. The interrogator is free, however, to ask any questions, no matter how devious or indirect, in an effort to uncover the computer's identity. For example, the interrogator may ask both subjects to perform a rather involved arithmetic calculation, assuming that the computer will be more likely to get it correct than the human; to counter this strategy, the computer will need to know when it should fail to get a correct answer to such problems in order to seem like a human. To discover the human's identity on the basis of emotional nature, the interrogator may ask both subjects to respond to a poem or work of art; this strategy will require that the computer have knowledge concerning the emotional makeup of human beings.

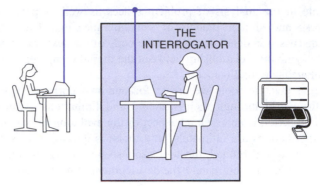

Figure 1.1 The Turing test.

The important features of Turing's test are:

1. It attempts to give an objective notion of intelligence, i.e., the behavior of a known intelligent being in response to a particular set of questions. This provides a standard for determining intelligence that avoids the inevitable debates over its "true" nature.

2. It prevents us from being sidetracked by such confusing and currently unanswerable questions as whether or not the computer uses the appropriate internal processes or whether or not the machine is actually conscious of its actions.

3. It eliminates any bias in favor of living organisms by forcing the interrogator to focus solely on the content of the answers to questions.

Because of these advantages, the Turing test provides a basis for many of the schemes actually used to evaluate modern AI programs. A program that has potentially achieved intelligence in some area of expertise may be evaluated by comparing its performance on a given set of problems to that of a human expert. This evaluation technique is just a variation of the Turing test: a group of humans are asked to blindly compare the performance of a computer and a human being on a particular set of problems. As we will see, this methodology has become an essential tool in both the development and verification of modern expert systems.

The Turing test, in spite of its intuitive appeal, is vulnerable to a number of justifiable criticisms. One of the most important of these is aimed at its bias toward purely symbolic problem-solving tasks. It does not test abilities requiring perceptual skill or manual dexterity, even though these are important components of human intelligence. Conversely, it is sometimes suggested that the Turing test needlessly constrains machine intelligence to fit a human mold. Perhaps machine intelligence is simply different from human intelligence and trying to evaluate it in human terms is a fundamental mistake. Do we really wish a machine would do mathematics as slowly and inaccurately as a human? Shouldn't an intelligent machine capitalize on its own assets, such as a large, fast, reliable memory, rather than trying to emulate human cognition? In fact, a number of modern AI practitioners (e.g., Ford and Hayes 1995) see responding to the full challenge of Turing's test as a mistake and a major distraction to the more important work at hand: developing general theories to explain the mechanisms of intelligence in humans and machines and applying those theories to the development of tools to solve specific, practical problems. Although we agree with the Ford and Hayes concerns in the large, we still see Turing's test as an important component in the verification and validation of modern AI software.

Turing also addressed the very feasibility of constructing an intelligent program on a digital computer. By thinking in terms of a specific model of computation (an electronic discrete state computing machine), he made some well-founded conjectures concerning the storage capacity, program complexity, and basic design philosophy required for such a system. Finally, he addressed a number of moral, philosophical, and scientific objections to the possibility of constructing such a program in terms of an actual technology. The reader is referred to Turing's article for a perceptive and still relevant summary of the debate over the possibility of intelligent machines.

Two of the objections cited by Turing are worth considering further. *Lady Lovelace's Objection*, first stated by Ada Lovelace, argues that computers can only do as they are told and consequently cannot perform original (hence, intelligent) actions. This objection has become a reassuring if somewhat dubious part of contemporary technological folklore. Expert systems (Section 1.2.3 and Chapter 8), especially in the area of diagnostic reasoning, have reached conclusions unanticipated by their designers. Indeed, a number of researchers feel that human creativity can be expressed in a computer program.

The other related objection, the *Argument from Informality of Behavior*, asserts the impossibility of creating a set of rules that will tell an individual exactly what to do under every possible set of circumstances. Certainly, the flexibility that enables a biological intelligence to respond to an almost infinite range of situations in a reasonable if not necessarily optimal fashion is a hallmark of intelligent behavior. While it is true that the control structure used in most traditional computer programs does not demonstrate great flexibility or originality, it is not true that all programs must be written in this fashion. Indeed, much of the work in AI over the past 25 years has been to develop programming languages and models such as production systems, object-based systems, network representations, and others discussed in this book that attempt to overcome this deficiency.

Many modern AI programs consist of a collection of modular components, or rules of behavior, that do not execute in a rigid order but rather are invoked as needed in response to the structure of a particular problem instance. Pattern matchers allow general rules to apply over a range of instances. These systems have an extreme flexibility that enables relatively small programs to exhibit a vast range of possible behaviors in response to differing problems and situations.

Whether these systems can ultimately be made to exhibit the flexibility shown by a living organism is still the subject of much debate. Nobel laureate Herbert Simon has argued that much of the originality and variability of behavior shown by living creatures is due to the richness of their environment rather than the complexity of their own internal programs. In *The Sciences of the Artificial*, Simon (1981) describes an ant progressing circuitously along an uneven and cluttered stretch of ground. Although the ant's path seems quite complex, Simon argues that the ant's goal is very simple: to return to its colony as quickly as possible. The twists and turns in its path are caused by the obstacles it encounters on its way. Simon concludes that

> An ant, viewed as a behaving system, is quite simple. The apparent complexity of its behavior over time is largely a reflection of the complexity of the environment in which it finds itself.

This idea, if ultimately proved to apply to organisms of higher intelligence as well as to such simple creatures as insects, constitutes a powerful argument that such systems are relatively simple and, consequently, comprehensible. It is interesting to note that if one applies this idea to humans, it becomes a strong argument for the importance of culture in the forming of intelligence. Rather than growing in the dark like mushrooms, intelligence seems to depend on an interaction with a suitably rich environment. Culture is just as important in creating humans as human beings are in creating culture. Rather than denigrating our intellects, this idea emphasizes the miraculous richness and coherence of the cultures that have formed out of the lives of separate human beings. In fact, the idea that intelligence emerges from the interactions of individual elements of a society is one of the insights supporting the approach to AI technology presented in the next section.

1.1.5   Biological and Social Models of Intelligence: Agents Theories

So far, we have approached the problem of building intelligent machines from the viewpoint of mathematics, with the implicit belief of logical reasoning as paradigmatic of intelligence itself, as well as with a commitment to "objective" foundations for logical reasoning. This way of looking at knowledge, language, and thought reflects the rationalist tradition of western philosophy, as it evolved through Plato, Galileo, Descartes, Leibniz, and many of the other philosophers discussed earlier in this chapter. It also reflects the underlying assumptions of the Turing test, particularly its emphasis on symbolic reasoning as a test of intelligence, and the belief that a straightforward comparison with human behavior was adequate to confirming machine intelligence.

The reliance on logic as a way of representing knowledge and on logical inference as the primary mechanism for intelligent reasoning are so dominant in Western philosophy that their "truth" often seems obvious and unassailable. It is no surprise, then, that approaches based on these assumptions have dominated the science of artificial intelligence from its inception through to the present day.

The latter half of the twentieth century has, however, seen numerous challenges to rationalist philosophy. Various forms of philosophical relativism question the objective basis of language, science, society, and thought itself. Ludwig Wittgenstein's later philosophy (Wittgenstein 1953), has forced us to reconsider the basis on meaning in both natural and formal languages. The work of Godel, Nagel and Newman (1958), and Turing has cast doubt on the very foundations of mathematics itself. Post-modern thought has changed our understanding of meaning and value in the arts and society. Artificial intelligence has not been immune to these criticisms; indeed, the difficulties that AI has encountered in achieving its goals are often taken as evidence of the failure of the rationalist viewpoint (Winograd and Flores 1986, Lakoff and Johnson 1999).

Two philosophical traditions, that of Wittgenstein (1953) as well as that of Husserl (1970, 1972) and Heidegger (1962), are central to this reappraisal of the Western philosophical tradition. In his later work, Wittgenstein questioned many of the assumptions of the rationalist tradition, including the foundations of language, science, and knowledge. Natural language was a major focus of Wittgenstein's analysis: he challenged the notion that human language derived its meaning from any sort of objective foundation.

For Wittgenstein, as well as the speech act theory developed by Austin (1962) and his followers (Grice 1975, Searle 1969), the meaning of any utterance depends on its being situated in a human, cultural context. Our understanding of the meaning of the word "chair", for example, is dependent on having a physical body that conforms to a sitting posture and the cultural conventions for using chairs. When, for example, is a large, flat rock a chair? Why is it odd to refer to the throne of England as a chair? What is the difference between a human being's understanding of a chair and that of a dog or cat, incapable of sitting in the human sense? Based on his attacks on the foundations of meaning, Wittgenstein argued that we should view the use of language in terms of choices made and actions taken in a shifting cultural context. Wittgenstein even extended his criticisms to science and mathematics, arguing that they are just as much social constructs as is language use.

Husserl (1970, 1972), the father of phenomenology, was committed to abstractions as rooted in the concrete *Lebenswelt* or *life-world*: a rationalist model was very much secondary to the concrete world that supported it. For Husserl, as well as for his student Heidegger (1962), and their proponent Merleau-Ponty (1962), intelligence was not knowing what was true, but rather knowing how to cope in a world that was constantly changing and evolving. Gadamer (1976) also contributed to this tradition. For the existentialist/phenomenologist, intelligence is seen as survival in the world, rather than as a set of logical propositions about the world (combined with some inferencing scheme).

Many authors, for example Dreyfus and Dreyfus (1985) and Winograd and Flores (1986), have drawn on Wittgenstein's and the Husserl/Heidegger work in their criticisms of AI. Although many AI practitioners continue developing the rational/logical agenda, also known as *GOFAI*, or *Good Old Fashioned AI*, a growing number of researchers in the field have incorporated these criticisms into new and exciting models of intelligence. In keeping with Wittgenstein's emphasis on the anthropological and cultural roots of knowledge, they have turned to social, sometimes referred to as *situated*, models of intelligent behavior for their inspiration.

As an example of an alternative to a logic-based approach, research in connectionist learning (Section 1.2.9 and Chapter 11) de-emphasizes logic and the functioning of the rational mind in an effort to achieve intelligence by modeling the architecture of the physical brain. Neural models of intelligence emphasize the brain's ability to adapt to the world in which it is situated by modifying the relationships between individual neurons. Rather than representing knowledge in explicit logical sentences, they capture it implicitly, as a property of patterns of relationships.

Another biologically based model of intelligence takes its inspiration from the processes by which entire species adapt to their surroundings. Work in artificial life and genetic algorithms (Chapter 12) applies the principles of biological evolution to the problems of finding solutions to difficult problems. These programs do not solve problems by reasoning logically about them; rather, they spawn populations of competing candidate solutions and drive them to evolve ever better solutions through a process patterned after biological evolution: poor candidate solutions tend to die out, while those that show the promise for solving a problem survive and reproduce by constructing new solutions out of components of their successful parents.

Social systems provide another metaphor for intelligence in that they exhibit global behaviors that enable them to solve problems that would confound any of their individual members. For example, although no individual could accurately predict the number of loaves of bread to be consumed in New York City on a given day, the entire system of New York bakeries does an excellent job of keeping the city stocked with bread, and doing so with minimal waste. The stock market does an excellent job of setting the relative values of hundreds of companies, even though each individual investor has only limited knowledge of a few companies. A final example comes from modern science. Individuals located in universities, industry, or government environments focus on common problems. With conferences and journals as the main communication media, problems important to society at large are attacked and solved by individual agents working semi-independently, although progress in many instances is also driven by funding agencies.

These examples share two themes: first, the view of intelligence as rooted in culture and society and, as a consequence, emergent. The second theme is that intelligence is reflected by the collective behaviors of large numbers of very simple interacting, semi-autonomous individuals, or agents. Whether these agents are neural cells, individual members of a species, or a single person in a society, their interactions produce intelligence.

What are the main themes supporting an agent-oriented and emergent view of intelligence? They include:

1. Agents are autonomous or semi-autonomous. That is, each agent has certain responsibilities in problem solving with little or no knowledge of either what other agents do or how they do it. Each agent does its own independent piece of the problem solving and either produces a result itself (does something) or reports results back to others in the community (communicating agent).

2. Agents are "situated." Each agent is sensitive to its own surrounding environment and (usually) has no knowledge of the full domain of all agents. Thus, an agent's knowledge is limited to the tasks to hand: "the-file-I'm-processing" or "the-wall-next-to-me" with no knowledge of the total range of files or physical constraints in the problem solving task.

3. Agents are interactional. That is, they form a collection of individuals that cooperate on a particular task. In this sense they may be seen as a "society" and, as with human society, knowledge, skills, and responsibilities, even when seen as collective, are distributed across the population of individuals.

4. The society of agents is structured. In most views of agent-oriented problem solving, each individual, although having its own unique environment and skill set, will coordinate with other agents in the overall problem solving. Thus, a final solution will not only be seen as collective, but also as cooperative.

5. Finally, the phenomenon of intelligence in this environment is "emergent." Although individual agents are seen as possessing sets of skills and responsibilities, the overall cooperative result can be viewed as greater than the sum of its individual contributors. Intelligence is seen as a phenomenon resident in and emerging from a society and not just a property of an individual agent.

Based on these observations, we define an agent as an element of a society that can perceive (often limited) aspects of its environment and affect that environment either directly or through cooperation with other agents. Most intelligent solutions require a variety of agents. These include rote agents, that simply capture and communicate pieces of information, coordination agents that can support the interactions between other agents, search agents that can examine multiple pieces of information and return some chosen bit of it, learning agents that can examine collections of information and form concepts or generalizations, and decision agents that can both dispatch tasks and come to conclusions in the light of limited information and processing. Going back to an older definition of intelligence, agents can be seen as the mechanisms supporting decision making in the context of limited processing resources.

The main requisites for designing and building such a society are:

1. structures for the representation of information,

2. strategies for the search through alternative solutions, and

3. the creation of architectures that can support the interaction of agents.

The remaining chapters of our book, especially Section 7.4, include prescriptions for the construction of support tools for this society of agents, as well as many examples of agent-based problem solving.

Our preliminary discussion of the possibility of a theory of automated intelligence is in no way intended to overstate the progress made to date or minimize the work that lies ahead. As we emphasize throughout this text, it is important to be aware of our limitations and to be honest about our successes. For example, there have been only limited results with programs that in any interesting sense can be said to "learn." Our accomplishments in modeling the semantic complexities of a natural language such as English have also been very modest. Even fundamental issues such as organizing knowledge or fully managing the complexity and correctness of very large computer programs (such as large knowledge bases) require considerable further research. Knowledge-based systems, though they have achieved marketable engineering successes, still have many limitations in the quality and generality of their reasoning. These include their inability to perform *commonsense reasoning* or to exhibit knowledge of rudimentary physical reality, such as how things change over time.

But we must maintain a reasonable perspective. It is easy to overlook the accomplishments of artificial intelligence when honestly facing the work that remains. In the next section, we establish this perspective through an overview of several areas of artificial intelligence research and development.

1.2   Overview of AI Application Areas

The Analytical Engine has no pretensions whatever to originate anything. It can do whatever we know how to order it to perform.

—ADA BYRON, *Countess of Lovelace*

I'm sorry Dave; I can't let you do that.

—HAL 9000 in *2001: A Space Odyssey* by Arthur C. Clarke

We now return to our goal of defining artificial intelligence through an examination of the ambitions and accomplishments of workers in the field. The two most fundamental concerns of AI researchers are *knowledge representation* and *search*. The first of these addresses the problem of capturing in a language, i.e., one suitable for computer manipulation, the full range of knowledge required for intelligent behavior. Chapter 2 introduces predicate calculus as a language for describing the properties and relationships among objects in problem domains that require qualitative reasoning rather than arithmetic calculations for their solutions. Later, Part III discusses the tools that artificial intelligence has developed for representing the ambiguities and complexities of areas such as commonsense reasoning and natural language understanding. Chapters 15 and 16 demonstrate the use of LISP and PROLOG to implement these representations.

Search is a problem-solving technique that systematically explores a space of *problem states*, i.e., successive and alternative stages in the problem-solving process. Examples of problem states might include the different board configurations in a game or intermediate steps in a reasoning process. This space of alternative solutions is then searched to find an answer. Newell and Simon (1976) have argued that this is the essential basis of human problem solving. Indeed, when a chess player examines the effects of different moves or a doctor considers a number of alternative diagnoses, they are searching among alternatives. The implications of this model and techniques for its implementation are discussed in Chapters 3, 4, 6, and 17.

Like most sciences, AI is decomposed into a number of subdisciplines that, while sharing an essential approach to problem solving, have concerned themselves with different applications. In this section we outline several of these major application areas and their contributions to artificial intelligence as a whole.

1.2.1   Game Playing

Much of the early research in state space search was done using common board games such as checkers, chess, and the 15-puzzle. In addition to their inherent intellectual appeal, board games have certain properties that made them ideal subjects for this early work. Most games are played using a well-defined set of rules: this makes it easy to generate the search space and frees the researcher from many of the ambiguities and complexities inherent in less structured problems. The board configurations used in playing these games are easily represented on a computer, requiring none of the complex formalisms needed to capture the semantic subtleties of more complex problem domains. As games can be easily played, testing a game-playing program presents no financial or ethical burden. State space search, the paradigm underlying most game-playing research, is presented in Chapters 3 and 4.

Games can generate extremely large search spaces. These are large and complex enough to require powerful techniques for determining what alternatives to explore in the problem space. These techniques are called *heuristics* and constitute a major area of AI research. A heuristic is a useful but potentially fallible problem-solving strategy, such as checking to make sure that an unresponsive appliance is plugged in before assuming that it is broken or to castle in order to try and protect your king from capture in a chess game. Much of what we commonly call intelligence seems to reside in the heuristics used by humans to solve problems.

Because most of us have some experience with these simple games, it is possible to devise and test the effectiveness of our own heuristics. We do not need to find and consult an expert in some esoteric problem area such as medicine or mathematics (chess is an obvious exception to this rule). For these reasons, games provide a rich domain for the study of heuristic search. Chapter 4 introduces heuristics using these simple games; Chapter 8 extends their application to expert systems. Game-playing programs, in spite of their simplicity, offer their own challenges, including an opponent whose moves may not be deterministically anticipated, Chapters 5 and 8. This presence of the opponent further complicates program design by adding an element of unpredictability and the need to consider psychological as well as tactical factors in game strategy.

1.2.2　Automated Reasoning and Theorem Proving

We could argue that automatic theorem proving is the oldest branch of artificial intelligence, tracing its roots back through Newell and Simon's Logic Theorist (Newell and Simon 1963*a*) and General Problem Solver (Newell and Simon 1963*b*), through Russell and Whitehead's efforts to treat all of mathematics as the purely formal derivation of theorems from basic axioms, to its origins in the writings of Babbage and Leibniz. In any case, it has certainly been one of the most fruitful branches of the field. Theorem-proving research was responsible for much of the early work in formalizing search algorithms and developing formal representation languages such as the predicate calculus (Chapter 2) and the logic programming language PROLOG (Chapter 15).

Most of the appeal of automated theorem proving lies in the rigor and generality of logic. Because it is a formal system, logic lends itself to automation. A wide variety of problems can be attacked by representing the problem description and relevant background information as logical axioms and treating problem instances as theorems to be proved. This insight is the basis of work in automatic theorem proving and mathematical reasoning systems (Chapter 13).

Unfortunately, early efforts at writing theorem provers failed to develop a system that could consistently solve complicated problems. This was due to the ability of any reasonably complex logical system to generate an infinite number of provable theorems: without powerful techniques (heuristics) to guide their search, automated theorem provers proved large numbers of irrelevant theorems before stumbling onto the correct one. In response to this inefficiency, many argue that purely formal, syntactic methods of guiding search are inherently incapable of handling such a huge space and that the only alternative is to rely on the informal, *ad hoc* strategies that humans seem to use in solving problems. This is the approach underlying the development of expert systems (Chapter 8), and it has proved to be a fruitful one.

Still, the appeal of reasoning based in formal mathematical logic is too strong to ignore. Many important problems such as the design and verification of logic circuits, verification of the correctness of computer programs, and control of complex systems seem to respond to such an approach. In addition, the theorem-proving community has enjoyed success in devising powerful solution heuristics that rely solely on an evaluation of the syntactic form of a logical expression, and as a result, reducing the complexity of the search space without resorting to the *ad hoc* techniques used by most human problem solvers.

Another reason for the continued interest in automatic theorem provers is the realization that such a system does not have to be capable of independently solving extremely complex problems without human assistance. Many modern theorem provers function as intelligent assistants, letting humans perform the more demanding tasks of decomposing a large problem into subproblems and devising heuristics for searching the space of possible proofs. The theorem prover then performs the simpler but still demanding task of proving lemmas, verifying smaller conjectures, and completing the formal aspects of a proof outlined by its human associate (Boyer and Moore 1979, Bundy 1988, Veroff 1997).

1.2.3 Expert Systems

One major insight gained from early work in problem solving was the importance of domain-specific knowledge. A doctor, for example, is not effective at diagnosing illness solely because she possesses some innate general problem-solving skill; she is effective because she knows a lot about medicine. Similarly, a geologist is effective at discovering mineral deposits because he is able to apply a good deal of theoretical and empirical knowledge about geology to the problem at hand. Expert knowledge is a combination of a theoretical understanding of the problem and a collection of heuristic problem-solving rules that experience has shown to be effective in the domain. Expert systems are constructed by obtaining this knowledge from a human expert and coding it into a form that a computer may apply to similar problems.

This reliance on the knowledge of a human domain expert for the system's problem solving strategies is a major feature of expert systems. Although some programs are written in which the designer is also the source of the domain knowledge, it is far more typical to see such programs growing out of a collaboration between a domain expert such as a doctor, chemist, geologist, or engineer and a separate artificial intelligence specialist. The domain expert provides the necessary knowledge of the problem domain through a general discussion of her problem-solving methods and by demonstrating those skills on a carefully chosen set of sample problems. The AI specialist, or *knowledge engineer,* as expert systems designers are often known, is responsible for implementing this knowledge in a program that is both effective and seemingly intelligent in its behavior. Once such a program has been written, it is necessary to refine its expertise through a process of giving it example problems to solve, letting the domain expert criticize its behavior, and making any required changes or modifications to the program's knowledge. This process is repeated until the program has achieved the desired level of performance.

One of the earliest systems to exploit domain-specific knowledge in problem solving was DENDRAL, developed at Stanford in the late 1960s (Lindsay et al. 1980). DENDRAL was designed to infer the structure of organic molecules from their chemical formulas and mass spectrographic information about the chemical bonds present in the molecules. Because organic molecules tend to be very large, the number of possible structures for these molecules tends to be huge. DENDRAL addresses the problem of this large search space by applying the heuristic knowledge of expert chemists to the structure elucidation problem. DENDRAL's methods proved remarkably effective, routinely finding the correct structure out of millions of possibilities after only a few trials. The approach has proved so successful that descendants of the system are used in chemical and pharmaceutical laboratories throughout the world.

Whereas DENDRAL was one of the first programs to effectively use domain-specific knowledge to achieve expert level problem-solving performance, MYCIN established the methodology of contemporary expert systems (Buchanan and Shortliffe 1984). MYCIN uses expert medical knowledge to diagnose and prescribe treatment for spinal meningitis and bacterial infections of the blood.

MYCIN, developed at Stanford in the mid-1970s, was one of the first programs to address the problems of reasoning with uncertain or incomplete information. MYCIN provided clear and logical explanations of its reasoning, used a control structure appropriate to the specific problem domain, and identified criteria to reliably evaluate its performance. Many of the expert system development techniques currently in use were first developed in the MYCIN project (Chapter 8).

Other classic expert systems include the PROSPECTOR program for determining the probable location and type of ore deposits based on geological information about a site (Duda et al. 1979a, 1979b), the INTERNIST program for performing diagnosis in the area of internal medicine, the Dipmeter Advisor for interpreting the results of oil well drilling logs (Smith and Baker 1983), and XCON for configuring VAX computers. XCON was developed in 1981, and at one time every VAX sold by Digital Equipment Corporation was configured by that software. Numerous other expert systems are currently solving problems in areas such as medicine, education, business, design, and science (Waterman 1986, Durkin 1994).

It is interesting to note that most expert systems have been written for relatively specialized, expert level domains. These domains are generally well studied and have clearly defined problem-solving strategies. Problems that depend on a more loosely defined notion of "common sense" are much more difficult to solve by these means. In spite of the promise of expert systems, it would be a mistake to overestimate the ability of this technology. Current deficiencies include:

1. Difficulty in capturing "deep" knowledge of the problem domain. MYCIN, for example, lacks any real knowledge of human physiology. It does not know what blood does or the function of the spinal cord. Folklore has it that once, when selecting a drug for treatment of meningitis, MYCIN asked whether the patient was pregnant, even though it had been told that the patient was male. Whether this actually occurred or not, it does illustrate the potential narrowness of knowledge in expert systems.

2. Lack of robustness and flexibility. If humans are presented with a problem instance that they cannot solve immediately, they can generally return to an examination of first principles and come up with some strategy for attacking the problem. Expert systems generally lack this ability.

3. Inability to provide deep explanations. Because expert systems lack deep knowledge of their problem domains, their explanations are generally restricted to a description of the steps they took in finding a solution. For example, they often cannot tell "why" a certain approach was taken.

4. Difficulties in verification. Though the correctness of any large computer system is difficult to prove, expert systems are particularly difficult to verify. This is a serious problem, as expert systems technology is being applied to critical applications such as air traffic control, nuclear reactor operations, and weapons systems.

5. Little learning from experience. Current expert systems are handcrafted; once the system is completed, its performance will not improve without further attention from its programmers, leading to doubts about the intelligence of such systems.

In spite of these limitations, expert systems have proved their value in a number of important applications. It is hoped that these limitations will only encourage the student to pursue this important branch of computer science. Expert systems are a major topic in this text and are discussed in Chapters 7 and 8.

1.2.4   Natural Language Understanding and Semantics

One of the long-standing goals of artificial intelligence is the creation of programs that are capable of understanding and generating human language. Not only does the ability to use and understand natural language seem to be a fundamental aspect of human intelligence, but also its successful automation would have an incredible impact on the usability and effectiveness of computers themselves. Much effort has been put into writing programs that understand natural language. Although these programs have achieved success within restricted contexts, systems that can use natural language with the flexibility and generality that characterize human speech are beyond current methodologies.

Understanding natural language involves much more than parsing sentences into their individual parts of speech and looking those words up in a dictionary. Real understanding depends on extensive background knowledge about the domain of discourse and the idioms used in that domain as well as an ability to apply general contextual knowledge to resolve the omissions and ambiguities that are a normal part of human speech.

Consider, for example, the difficulties in carrying on a conversation about baseball with an individual who understands English but knows nothing about the rules, players, or history of the game. Could this person possibly understand the meaning of the sentence: "With none down in the top of the ninth and the go-ahead run at second, the manager called his relief from the bull pen"? Even though all of the words in the sentence may be individually understood, this sentence would be gibberish to even the most intelligent non-baseball fan.

The task of collecting and organizing this background knowledge in such a way that it may be applied to language comprehension forms the major problem in automating natural language understanding. Responding to this need, researchers have developed many of the techniques for structuring semantic meaning used throughout artificial intelligence (Chapters 7 and 14).

Because of the tremendous amounts of knowledge required for understanding natural language, most work is done in well-understood, specialized problem areas. One of the earliest programs to exploit this "micro world" methodology was Winograd's SHRDLU, a natural language system that could "converse" about a simple configuration of blocks of different shapes and colors (Winograd 1973). SHRDLU could answer queries such as "what color block is on the blue cube?" as well as plan actions such as "move the red pyramid onto the green brick". Problems of this sort, involving the description and manipulation of simple arrangements of blocks, have appeared with surprising frequency in AI research and are known as "blocks world" problems.

In spite of SHRDLU's success in conversing about arrangements of blocks, its methods did not generalize from that domain. The representational techniques used in the program were too simple to capture the semantic organization of richer and more complex domains in a useful way. Much of the current work in natural language understanding is devoted to finding representational formalisms that are general enough to be used in a wide range of applications yet adapt themselves well to the specific structure of a given domain. A number of different techniques (many of which are extensions or modifications of *semantic networks*) are explored for this purpose and used in the development of programs that can understand natural language in constrained but interesting knowledge domains. Finally, in current research (Marcus 1980, Manning and Schutze 1999, Jurafsky and Martin 2000) stochastic models, describing how words and language structures "occur" in use, are employed to characterize both syntax and semantics. Full computational understanding of language, however, remains beyond the current state of the art.

1.2.5 Modeling Human Performance

Although much of the above discussion uses human intelligence as a reference point in considering artificial intelligence, it does not follow that programs should pattern themselves after the organization of the human mind. Indeed, many AI programs are engineered to solve some useful problem without regard for their similarities to human mental architecture. Even expert systems, while deriving much of their knowledge from human experts, do not really attempt to simulate human internal mental problem solving processes. If performance is the only criterion by which a system will be judged, there may be little reason to attempt to simulate human problem-solving methods; in fact, programs that take nonhuman approaches to solving problems are often more successful than their human counterparts. Still, the design of systems that explicitly model aspects of human performance is a fertile area of research in both artificial intelligence and psychology.

Human performance modeling, in addition to providing AI with much of its basic methodology, has proved to be a powerful tool for formulating and testing theories of human cognition. The problem-solving methodologies developed by computer scientists have given psychologists a new metaphor for exploring the human mind. Rather than casting theories of cognition in the vague language used in early research or abandoning the problem of describing the inner workings of the human mind entirely (as suggested by the behaviorists), many psychologists have adopted the language and theory of computer science to formulate models of human intelligence. Not only do these techniques provide a new vocabulary for describing human intelligence, but also computer implementations of these theories offer psychologists an opportunity to empirically test, critique, and refine their ideas (Luger 1994). Further discussion of the relationship between artificial and human intelligence is found throughout this book and is summarized in Chapter 17.

1.2.6   Planning and Robotics

Research in planning began as an effort to design robots that could perform their tasks with some degree of flexibility and responsiveness to the outside world. Briefly, planning assumes a robot that is capable of performing certain atomic actions. It attempts to find a sequence of those actions that will accomplish some higher-level task, such as moving across an obstacle-filled room.

Planning is a difficult problem for a number of reasons, not the least of which is the size of the space of possible sequences of moves. Even an extremely simple robot is capable of generating a vast number of potential move sequences. Imagine, for example, a robot that can move forward, backward, right, or left, and consider how many different ways that robot can possibly move around a room. Assume also that there are obstacles in the room and that the robot must select a path that moves around them in some efficient fashion. Writing a program that can intelligently discover the best path under these circumstances, without being overwhelmed by the huge number of possibilities, requires sophisticated techniques for representing spatial knowledge and controlling search through possible environments.

One method that human beings use in planning is *hierarchical problem decomposition*. If you are planning a trip from Albuquerque to London, you will generally treat the problems of arranging a flight, getting to the airport, making airline connections, and finding ground transportation in London separately, even though they are all part of a bigger overall plan. Each of these may be further decomposed into smaller subproblems such as finding a map of the city, negotiating the subway system, and finding a decent pub. Not only does this approach effectively restrict the size of the space that must be searched, but also allows saving of frequently used subplans for future use.

While humans plan effortlessly, creating a computer program that can do the same is a difficult challenge. A seemingly simple task such as breaking a problem into independent subproblems actually requires sophisticated heuristics and extensive knowledge about the planning domain. Determining what subplans should be saved and how they may be generalized for future use is an equally difficult problem.

A robot that blindly performs a sequence of actions without responding to changes in its environment or being able to detect and correct errors in its own plan could hardly be considered intelligent. Often, a robot will have to formulate a plan based on incomplete information and correct its behavior as it executes the plan. A robot may not have adequate sensors to locate all obstacles in the way of a projected path. Such a robot must begin moving through the room based on what it has "perceived" and correct its path as other obstacles are detected. Organizing plans in a fashion that allows response to changing environmental conditions is a major problem for planning (Lewis and Luger 2000).

Finally, robotics was one of the research areas in AI that produced many of the insights supporting agent-oriented problem solving (Section 1.1.5). Frustrated by both the complexities of maintaining the large representational space as well as the design of adequate search algorithms for traditional planning, researchers, including Agre and Chapman (1987) and Brooks (1991a), restated the larger problem in terms of the interaction of multiple semi-autonomous agents. Each agent was responsible for its own portion of the problem task and through their coordination the larger solution would emerge.

Planning research now extends well beyond the domains of robotics, to include the coordination of any complex set of tasks and goals. Modern planners are applied to agents (Nilsson 1994) as well as to control of particle beam accelerators (Klein et al. 1999, 2000).

1.2.7 Languages and Environments for AI

Some of the most important by-products of artificial intelligence research have been advances in programming languages and software development environments. For a number of reasons, including the size of many AI application programs, the importance of a prototyping methodology, the tendency of search algorithms to generate huge spaces, and the difficulty of predicting the behavior of heuristically driven programs, AI programmers have been forced to develop a powerful set of programming methodologies.

Programming environments include knowledge-structuring techniques such as object-oriented programming. High-level languages, such as LISP and PROLOG (Part VI), which support modular development, help manage program size and complexity. Trace packages allow a programmer to reconstruct the execution of a complex algorithm and make it possible to unravel the complexities of heuristic search. Without such tools and techniques, it is doubtful that many significant AI systems could have been built.

Many of these techniques are now standard tools for software engineering and have little relationship to the core of AI theory. Others, such as object-oriented programming, are of significant theoretical and practical interest. Finally, many AI algorithms are also now built in more traditional computing languages, such as C++ and Java.

The languages developed for artificial intelligence programming are intimately bound to the theoretical structure of the field. We cover both LISP and PROLOG in this book and prefer to remain apart from religious debates over their relative merits. Rather, we adhere to the adage "a good worker knows all her tools." The language chapters (15 and 16) discuss the advantages of each language for specific programming tasks.

1.2.8   Machine Learning

Learning has remained a challenging area for AI. The importance of learning, however, is beyond question, particularly as this ability is one of the most important components of intelligent behavior. An expert system may perform extensive and costly computations to solve a problem. Unlike a human being, however, if it is given the same or a similar problem a second time, it usually does not remember the solution. It performs the same sequence of computations again. This is true the second, third, fourth, and every time it solves that problem—hardly the behavior of an intelligent problem solver. The obvious solution to this problem is for programs to learn on their own, either from experience, analogy, examples, or by being "told" what to do.

Although learning is a difficult area, there are several programs that suggest that it is not impossible. One striking program is AM, the *Automated Mathematician*, designed to discover mathematical laws (Lenat 1977, 1982). Initially given the concepts and axioms of set theory, AM was able to induce such important mathematical concepts as cardinality, integer arithmetic, and many of the results of number theory. AM conjectured new theorems by modifying its current knowledge base and used heuristics to pursue the "best" of a number of possible alternative theorems. More recently, Cotton et al. (2000) designed a program that automatically invents "interesting" integer sequences.

Early influential work includes Winston's research on the induction of structural concepts such as "arch" from a set of examples in the blocks world (Winston 1975a). The ID3 algorithm has proved successful in learning general patterns from examples (Quinlan 1986a). *Meta-DENDRAL* learns rules for interpreting mass spectrographic data in organic chemistry from examples of data on compounds of known structure. *Teiresias*, an intelligent "front end" for expert systems, converts high-level advice into new rules for its knowledge base (Davis 1982). *Hacker* devises plans for performing blocks world manipulations through an iterative process of devising a plan, testing it, and correcting any flaws discovered in the candidate plan (Sussman 1975). Work in explanation-based learning has shown the effectiveness of prior knowledge in learning (Mitchell et al. 1986, DeJong and Mooney 1986). There are also now many important biological and sociological models of learning; we review these in the connectionist and emergent learning chapters (11 and 12).

The success of machine learning programs suggests the existence of a set of general learning principles that will allow the construction of programs with the ability to learn in realistic domains. We present several approaches to learning in Part IV.

1.2.9   Alternative Representations: Neural Nets and Genetic Algorithms

Most of the techniques presented in this AI book use explicitly represented knowledge and carefully designed search algorithms to implement intelligence. A very different approach seeks to build intelligent programs using models that parallel the structure of neurons in the human brain or the evolving patterns found in genetic algorithms and artificial life.

A simple schematic of a neuron (Figure 1.2) consists of a cell body that has a number of branched protrusions, called *dendrites*, and a single branch called the *axon*. Dendrites receive signals from other neurons. When these combined impulses exceed a certain threshold, the neuron fires and an impulse, or *spike*, passes down the axon. Branches at the end of the axon form *synapses* with the dendrites of other neurons. The synapse is the point of contact between neurons; synapses may be either *excitatory* or *inhibitory*, either adding to the total of signals reaching the neuron or subtracting from that total.

This description of a neuron is excessively simple, but it captures those features that are relevant to neural models of computation. In particular, each computational unit computes some function of its inputs and passes the result along to connected units in the network: the final results are produced by the parallel and distributed processing of this network of neural connections and threshold weights.

Neural architectures are appealing mechanisms for implementing intelligence for a number of reasons. Traditional AI programs can be brittle and overly sensitive to noise. Human intelligence is much more flexible and good at interpreting noisy input, such as a face in a darkened room or a conversation at a noisy party. Neural architectures, because they capture knowledge in a large number of fine-grained units distributed about a network, seem to have more potential for partially matching noisy and incomplete data.

With genetic algorithms and artificial life we evolve new problem solutions from components of previous solutions. The genetic operators, such as crossover and mutation, much like their genetic equivalents in the natural world, work to produce, for each new generation, ever better potential problem solutions. Artificial life produces its new generation as a function of the "quality" of its neighbors in previous generations.

Both neural architectures and genetic algorithms provide a natural model for parallelism, because each neuron or segment of a solution is an independent unit. Hillis (1985) has commented on the fact that humans get faster at a task as they acquire more knowledge, while computers tend to slow down. This slowdown is due to the cost of sequentially searching a knowledge base; a massively parallel architecture like the human brain would not suffer from this problem. Finally, something is intrinsically appealing about approaching the problems of intelligence from a neural or genetic point of view. After all, the evolved brain achieves intelligence and it does so using a neural architecture. We present neural networks, genetic algorithms, and artificial life, in Chapters 11 and 12.

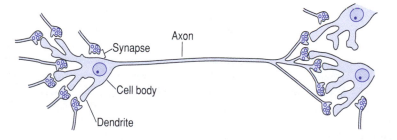

Axon

Synapse

Cell body

Dendrite

Figure 1.2 A simplified diagram of a neuron, from Crick and Asanuma (1986).

1.2.10 AI and Philosophy

In Section 1.1 we presented the philosophical, mathematical, and sociological roots of artificial intelligence. It is important to realize that modern AI is not just a product of this rich intellectual tradition but also contributes to it.

For example, the questions that Turing posed about intelligent programs reflect back on our understanding of intelligence itself. What is intelligence, and how is it described? What is the nature of knowledge? Can knowledge be represented? How does knowledge in an application area relate to problem-solving skill in that domain? How does *knowing what* is true, Aristotle's *theoria*, relate to *knowing how* to perform, his *praxis*?

Answers proposed to these questions make up an important part of what AI researchers and designers do. In the scientific sense, AI programs can be viewed as experiments. A design is made concrete in a program and the program is run as an experiment. The program designers observe the results and then redesign and rerun the experiment. In this manner we can determine whether our representations and algorithms are sufficient models of intelligent behavior. Newell and Simon (1976) proposed this approach to scientific understanding in their 1976 Turing Award lecture (Part VII). Newell and Simon (1976) also propose a stronger model for intelligence with their physical symbol system hypothesis: *the necessary and sufficient condition for a physical system to exhibit intelligence is that it be a physical symbol system.* We take up in Part VII what this hypothesis means in practice as well as how it has been criticized by many modern thinkers.

A number of AI application areas also open up deep philosophical issues. In what sense can we say that a computer can understand natural language expressions? To produce or understand a language requires interpretation of symbols. It is not sufficient to be able to say that a string of symbols is well formed. A mechanism for understanding must be able to impute meaning or interpret symbols in context. What is meaning? What is interpretation? In what sense does interpretation require responsibility?

Similar philosophical issues emerge from many AI application areas, whether they be building expert systems to cooperate with human problem solvers, designing computer vision systems, or designing algorithms for machine learning. We look at many of these issues as they come up in the chapters of this book and address the general issue of relevance to philosophy again in Part VII.

1.3 Artificial Intelligence—A Summary

We have attempted to define artificial intelligence through discussion of its major areas of research and application. This survey reveals a young and promising field of study whose primary concern is finding an effective way to understand and apply intelligent problem solving, planning, and communication skills to a wide range of practical problems. In spite of the variety of problems addressed in artificial intelligence research, a number of important features emerge that seem common to all divisions of the field; these include:

1. The use of computers to do reasoning, pattern recognition, learning, or some other form of inference.

2. A focus on problems that do not respond to algorithmic solutions. This underlies the reliance on heuristic search as an AI problem-solving technique.

3. A concern with problem solving using inexact, missing, or poorly defined information and the use of representational formalisms that enable the programmer to compensate for these problems.

4. Reasoning about the significant qualitative features of a situation.

5. An attempt to deal with issues of semantic meaning as well as syntactic form.

6. Answers that are neither exact nor optimal, but are in some sense "sufficient". This is a result of the essential reliance on heuristic problem-solving methods in situations where optimal or exact results are either too expensive or not possible.

7. The use of large amounts of domain-specific knowledge in solving problems. This is the basis of expert systems.

8. The use of meta-level knowledge to effect more sophisticated control of problem solving strategies. Although this is a very difficult problem, addressed in relatively few current systems, it is emerging as an essential area of research.

We hope that this introduction provides some feel for the overall structure and significance of the field of artificial intelligence. We also hope that the brief discussions of such technical issues as search and representation were not excessively cryptic and obscure; they are developed in proper detail throughout the remainder of the book, but included here to demonstrate their significance in the general organization of the field.

As we mentioned in the discussion of agent-oriented problem solving, objects take on meaning through their relationships with other objects. This is equally true of the facts, theories, and techniques that constitute a field of scientific study. We have intended to give a sense of those interrelationships, so that when the separate technical themes of artificial intelligence are presented, they will find their place in a developing understanding of the overall substance and directions of the field. We are guided in this process by an observation made by Gregory Bateson (1979), the psychologist and systems theorist:

> Break the pattern which connects the items of learning and you necessarily destroy all quality.

1.4   Epilogue and References

The field of AI reflects some of the oldest concerns of Western civilization in the light of the modern computational model. The notions of rationality, representation, and reason are now under scrutiny as perhaps never before, because we computer scientists demand to understand them algorithmically! At the same time, the political, economic, and ethical situation of our species forces us to confront our responsibility for the effects of our artifices.

Many excellent sources are available on the topics raised in this chapter: *Mind Design* (Haugeland 1997), *Artificial Intelligence: The Very Idea* (Haugeland 1985), *Brainstorms*

(Dennett 1978), *Mental Models* (Johnson-Laird 1983), *Elbow Room* (Dennett 1984), *The Body in the Mind* (Johnson 1987), *Consciousness Explained* (Dennett 1991), and *Darwin's Dangerous Idea* (Dennett 1995), and *Prehistory of Android Epistemology* (Glymour, Ford, and Hayes 1995*a*).

Several of the primary sources are also readily available, including Aristotle's *Physics*, *Metaphysics*, and *Logic*; papers by Frege; and the writings of Babbage, Boole, and Russell and Whitehead. Turing's papers are also very interesting, especially his discussions of the nature of intelligence and the possibility of designing intelligent programs (Turing 1950). Turing's famous 1937 paper *On Computable Numbers, with an Application to the Entscheidungsproblem* worked out the theory of Turing machines and the definition of computability. Turing's biography, *Alan Turing: The Enigma* (Hodges 1983), makes excellent reading. Selfridge's *Pandemonium* (1959) is an early example of learning. An important collection of early papers in AI may be found in Webber and Nilsson (1981).

Computer Power and Human Reason (Weizenbaum 1976) and *Understanding Computers and Cognition* (Winograd and Flores 1986) offer sobering comments on the limitations of and ethical issues in AI. *The Sciences of the Artificial* (Simon 1981) is a positive statement on the possibility of artificial intelligence and its role in society.

The AI applications mentioned in Section 1.2 are intended to introduce the reader to the broad interests of AI researchers and outline many of the important questions under investigation. Each of these subsections referenced the primary areas in this book where these topics are presented. *The Handbook of Artificial Intelligence* (Barr and Feigenbaum 1989) also offers an introduction to many of these areas. The *Encyclopedia of Artificial Intelligence* (Shapiro 1992) offers a clear and comprehensive treatment of the field of artificial intelligence.

Natural language understanding is a dynamic field of study; some important points of view are expressed in *Natural Language Understanding* (Allen 1995), *Language as a Cognitive Process* (Winograd 1983), *Computer Models of Thought and Language* (Schank and Colby 1973), *Grammar, Meaning and the Machine Analysis of Language* (Wilks 1972), *The Language Instinct* (Pinker 1994), *Philosophy in the Flesh* (Lakoff and Johnson 1999), and *Speech and Language Processing* (Jurafsky and Martin 2000); an introduction to the field is presented in our Chapters 7 and 14.

Using computers to model human performance, which we address briefly in Chapter 17, is discussed in some depth in *Human Problem Solving* (Newell and Simon 1972), *Computation and Cognition* (Pylyshyn 1984), *Arguments Concerning Representations for Mental Imagery* (Anderson 1978), *Cognitive Science: the Science of Intelligent Systems* (Luger 1994), and *Problem Solving as Model Refinement: Towards a Constructivist Epistemology* (Luger et al. 2002).

The subject of AI-oriented languages and environments is explored in Chapters 15 and 16 of this text. Machine learning is discussed in Part IV; the multi-volume set, *Machine Learning* (Michalski et al. 1983, 1986; Kodratoff and Michalski 1990), the *Journal of Artificial Intelligence* and the *Journal of Machine Learning* are important sources.

Chapter 12 presents a view of intelligence that emphasizes its modular structure and adaptation within a social and natural context. Minsky's *Society of Mind* (1985) is one of the earliest and most thought provoking articulations of this point of view. Also see *Android Epistemology* (Ford et al. 1995) and *Artificial Life* (Langton 1995).

1.5 Exercises

1. Create and justify your own definition of artificial intelligence.

2. Give several other examples of Aristotle's distinction between *matter* and *form*. Can you show how your examples might fit into a theory of abstraction?

3. Much traditional Western thought has dwelt on the mind–body relationship. Are the mind and body:

   a.   distinct entities somehow interacting, or
   b.   is mind an expression of "physical processes", or
   c.   is body just an illusion of the rational mind?

   Discuss your thoughts on the mind–body problem and its importance for a theory of artificial intelligence.

4. Criticize Turing's criteria for computer software being "intelligent".

5. Describe your own criteria for computer software to be considered "intelligent".

6. Although computing is a relatively new discipline, philosophers and mathematicians have been thinking about the issues involved in automating problem solving for thousands of years. What is your opinion of the relevance of these philosophical issues to the design of a device for intelligent problem solving? Justify your answer.

7. Given the differences between the architectures of modern computers and that of the human brain, what relevance does research into the physiological structure and function of biological systems have for the engineering of AI programs? Justify your answer.

8. Pick one problem area that you feel would justify the energy required to design an expert system solution. Spell the problem out in some detail. Based on your own intuition, which aspects of this solution would be most difficult to automate?

9. Add two more benefits for expert systems to those already listed in the text. Discuss these in terms of intellectual, social, or financial results.

10. Discuss why you think the problem of machines "learning" is so difficult.

11. Discuss whether or not you think it is possible for a computer to understand and use a natural (human) language.

12. List and discuss two potentially negative effects on society of the development of artificial intelligence techniques.

PART II

ARTIFICIAL INTELLIGENCE AS REPRESENTATION AND SEARCH

A PROPOSAL FOR THE DARTMOUTH SUMMER RESEARCH PROJECT ON ARTIFICIAL INTELLIGENCE (url IIa)

We propose that a 2 month, 10 man (sic) study of artificial intelligence be carried out during the summer of 1956 at Dartmouth College in Hanover, New Hampshire. The study is to proceed on the basis of the conjecture that every aspect of learning or any other feature of intelligence can in principle be so precisely described that a machine can be made to simulate it. An attempt will be made to find how to make machines use language, form abstractions and concepts, solve kinds of problems now reserved for humans, and improve themselves. We think that a significant advance can be made in one or more of these problems if a carefully selected group of scientists work on it together for a summer.

J. MCCARTHY, *Dartmouth College*
M. L. MINSKY, *Harvard University*
N. ROCHESTER, *I.B.M. Corporation*
C.E. SHANNON, *Bell Telephone Laboratories*

August 31, 1955

Introduction to Representation and Search

From an engineering perspective, the description of artificial intelligence presented in Section 1.3 may be summarized as *the study of representation and search through which intelligent activity can be enacted on a mechanical device*. This perspective has dominated the origins and growth of AI.

The first modern workshop/conference for AI practitioners was held at Dartmouth College in the summer of 1956. The proposal for this workshop is presented as the introductory quotation for Part II. This workshop, where the name *artificial intelligence* itself was chosen, brought together many of the then current researchers focused on the integration of computation and intelligence. There were also a few computer programs written by that time reflecting these early ideas. The main topics for discussion at this conference, abridged here from the original workshop proposal (url IIa), were:

1. Automatic Computers

If a machine can do a job, then an automatic calculator can be programmed to simulate the machine.

2. How Can a Computer be Programmed to Use a Language

It may be speculated that a large part of human thought consists of manipulating words according to rules of reasoning and rules of conjecture.

3. Neuron Nets

How can a set of (hypothetical) neurons be arranged so as to form concepts?

4. Theory of the Size of a Calculation

If we are given a well-defined problem (one for which it is possible to test mechanically whether or not a proposed answer is a valid answer) one way of solving it is to try all possible answers in order. This method is inefficient, and to exclude it one must have some criterion for efficiency of calculation.

5. Self-improvement (Machine Learning)

Probably a truly intelligent machine will carry out activities which may best be described as self-improvement.

6. Abstractions

A number of types of "abstraction" can be distinctly defined and several others less distinctly. A direct attempt to classify these and to describe machine methods of forming abstractions from sensory and other data would seem worthwhile.

7. Randomness and Creativity

A fairly attractive and yet clearly incomplete conjecture is that the difference between creative thinking and unimaginative competent thinking lies in the injection of some randomness.

It is interesting to note that the topics proposed for this first conference on artificial intelligence capture many of the issues, such as complexity theory, methodologies for abstraction, language design, and machine learning, that make up the focus of modern computer science. In fact, many of the defining characteristics of computer science as we know it today have their roots in AI. AI has also had its own historical and political struggles, with several of these early topics proposed for research, such as "neuron nets" and "randomness and creativity", put into background mode for decades.

A powerful new computational tool, the LISP language, emerged at about this time, built under the direction of John McCarthy, one of the original proposers of the Dartmouth Workshop. LISP, as we see in great detail in Chapter 16, addressed several of the topics of the Workshop, supporting the ability to create relationships that could themselves be manipulated by other structures of the language. LISP gave artificial intelligence a highly expressive language, rich in abstraction, as well as a medium for interpretation of these expressions.

The availability of the LISP programming language did shape much of the early development of AI, in particular, the use of the predicate calculus as a representational medium as well as search to explore the efficacy of different logical alternatives, what we now call *graph search*. PROLOG, created in the late 1970s, would offer AI a similar powerful computational tool; see Chapter 15.

An introduction to the fundamental representation and search techniques supporting work in artificial intelligence make up the five chapters of Part II. The predicate calculus, graph search, heuristic and stochastic methods, and architectures (control systems) for intelligent problem solving make up the material of Part II. These technologies reflect the dominant techniques explored by the AI community during its first two decades.

Representational Systems

The function of any representation scheme is to capture the essential features of a problem domain and make that information accessible to a problem-solving procedure. *Abstraction*, the representation of exactly that information needed for a given purpose, is an essential tool for managing complexity. It is also important that the resulting programs be computationally efficient. *Expressiveness* and *efficiency* are major dimensions for evaluating knowledge representation languages. Sometimes, expressiveness must be sacrificed to improve efficiency. This must be done without limiting the representation's ability to capture essential problem-solving knowledge. Optimizing the trade-off between efficiency and expressiveness is a major task for designers of intelligent programs.

Knowledge representation languages are also tools for helping humans solve problems. As such, a representation should provide a *natural* framework for expressing problem-solving knowledge; it should make that knowledge available to the computer and assist the programmer in its organization.

The computer representation of floating-point numbers illustrates these trade-offs (see Figure II.1). In general, real numbers require an infinite string of digits to be fully described; this cannot be accomplished on a finite device such as a computer. One answer to this dilemma is to represent the number in two pieces: its *significant* digits and the location within those digits of the decimal point. Although it is not possible to actually store a real number in a computer, it is possible to create a representation that functions adequately in most practical applications.

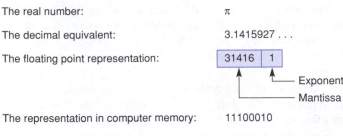

The real number:	π
The decimal equivalent:	3.1415927 . . .
The floating point representation:	31416 1

The real number: π

The decimal equivalent: 3.1415927 . . .

The floating point representation: 31416 | 1

Exponent
Mantissa

The representation in computer memory: 11100010

Figure II.1 Different representations of the real number π.

Floating-point representation thus sacrifices full expressive power to make the representation efficient, in this case to make it possible. The representation allows algorithms for multiple-precision arithmetic, giving effectively infinite precision by limiting round-off error to any pre-specified tolerance. It also guarantees well-behaved round-off errors. Like all representations, it is only an abstraction, a symbol pattern that designates a desired entity and not the entity itself.

The array is another representation common in computer science. For many problems, it is more natural and efficient than the memory architecture implemented in computer hardware. This gain in naturalness and efficiency involves compromises in expressiveness, as illustrated by the following example from image processing. Figure II.2 is a digitized image of human chromosomes in a stage called *metaphase*. The image is processed to determine the number and structure of the chromosomes, looking for breaks, missing pieces, and other abnormalities.

The visual scene is made up of a number of picture points. Each picture point, or *pixel*, has both a location and a number value representing its intensity or *gray level*. It is natural, then, to collect the entire scene into a two-dimensional array where the row and column address gives the location of a pixel (X and Y coordinates) and the content of the array element is the gray level at that point. Algorithms are designed to perform operations like looking for isolated points to remove noise from the image, finding threshold levels for discerning objects and edges, summing contiguous elements to determine size or density, and in various other ways transforming the picture point data. Implementing these algorithms is straightforward, given the array representation and the FORTRAN language, for example. This task would be quite cumbersome using other representations such as the predicate calculus, records, or assembly code, because these do not have a natural fit with the material being represented.

When we represent the picture as an array of pixel points, we sacrifice fineness of resolution (compare a photo in a newspaper to the original print of the same picture). In addition, pixel arrays cannot express the deeper semantic organization of the image. For example, a pixel array cannot represent the organization of chromosomes in a single cell nucleus, their genetic function, or the role of metaphase in cell division. This knowledge is more easily captured using a representation such as predicate calculus (Chapter 2) or semantic networks (Chapter 7). In summary, a representational scheme should be adequate to express all of the necessary information, support efficient execution of the resulting code, and provide a natural scheme for expressing the required knowledge.

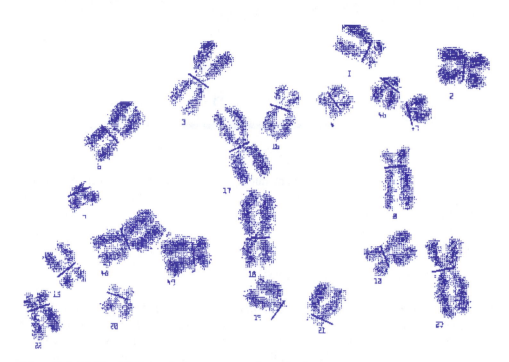

Figure II.2 Digitized image of chromosomes in metaphase.

In general, the problems AI attempts to solve do not lend themselves to the representations offered by more traditional formalisms such as arrays. Artificial intelligence is concerned with qualitative rather than quantitative problem solving, with reasoning rather than numeric calculation, and with organizing large and varied amounts of knowledge rather than implementing a single, well-defined algorithm.

For example, consider Figure II.3, the arrangement of blocks on a table. Suppose we wish to capture the properties and relations required to control a robot arm. We must determine which blocks are stacked on other blocks and which blocks have clear tops so that they can be picked up. The *predicate calculus* offers a medium to capture this descriptive information. The first word of each expression (on, ontable, etc.) is a *predicate* denoting some property or relationship among its *arguments* (appearing in the parentheses). The arguments are symbols denoting objects (blocks) in the domain. The collection of logical clauses describes the important properties and relationships of this *blocks world*:

```
clear(c)
clear(a)
ontable(a)
ontable(b)
on(c, b)
cube(b)
cube(a)
pyramid(c)
```

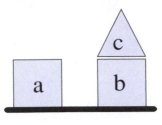

Figure II.3 A blocks world.

Predicate calculus provides artificial intelligence programmers with a well-defined language for describing and reasoning about qualitative aspects of a system. Suppose, in the blocks world example, we want to define a test to determine whether a block is clear, that is, has nothing stacked on top of it. This is important if the robot hand is to pick it up or stack another block on top of it. We can define a general rule:

$$\forall X \neg \exists Y \; on(Y,X) \Rightarrow clear(X)$$

This is read "for all X, X is clear if there does not exist a Y such that Y is on X." This general rule can be applied to a variety of situations by substituting different block names, a, b, c, etc., for X and Y. By supporting general inference rules, predicate calculus allows economy of representation, as well as the possibility of designing systems that are flexible and general enough to respond intelligently to a range of situations.

The predicate calculus may also be used to represent the properties of individuals and groups. It is often not sufficient, for example, to describe a car by simply listing its component parts; we may want to describe the ways in which those parts are combined and the interactions between them. This view of structure is essential to a range of situations including taxonomic information, such as the classification of plants by genus and species, or a description of complex objects such as a diesel engine or a human body in terms of their component parts. For example, a simple description of a bluebird might be "a bluebird is a small blue-colored bird and a bird is a feathered flying vertebrate", which may be represented as the set of logical predicates:

hassize(bluebird,small)
hascovering(bird,feathers)
hascolor(bluebird,blue)
hasproperty(bird,flies)
isa(bluebird,bird)
isa(bird,vertebrate)

This predicate description can be represented graphically by using the *arcs*, or *links*, in a graph instead of predicates to indicate relationships (Figure II.4). This *semantic network*, is a technique for representing semantic meaning. Because relationships are explicitly denoted in the graph, an algorithm for reasoning about the domain could make relevant associations by following the links. In the bluebird illustration, for example, the program need only follow two links in order to determine that a bluebird is a vertebrate.

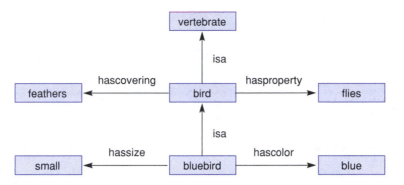

Figure II.4 Semantic network description of a bluebird.

Perhaps the most important application for semantic networks is to represent meanings for language understanding programs. When it is necessary to understand a child's story, the details of a journal article, or the contents of a web page, semantic networks may be used to encode the information and relationships that reflect the knowledge in that application. Semantic networks are discussed in Chapter 7, and their application to language understanding in Chapter 14.

Search

Given a representation, the second component of intelligent problem solving is *search*. Humans generally consider a number of alternative strategies on their way to solving a problem. A chess player typically reviews alternative moves, selecting the "best" according to criteria such as the opponent's possible responses or the degree to which various moves support some global game strategy. A player also considers short-term gain (such as taking the opponent's queen), opportunities to sacrifice a piece for positional advantage, or conjectures concerning the opponent's psychological makeup and level of skill. This aspect of intelligent behavior underlies the problem-solving technique of *state space search*.

Consider, for example, the game of tic-tac-toe. Given any board situation, there is only a finite number of moves that a player can make. Starting with an empty board, the first player may place an X in any one of nine places. Each of these moves yields a different board that will allow the opponent eight possible responses, and so on. We can represent this collection of possible moves and responses by regarding each board configuration as a *node* or *state* in a graph. The *links* of the graph represent legal moves from one board configuration to another. The resulting structure is a *state space graph*.

The state space representation thus enables us to treat all possible games of tic-tac-toe as different paths through the state space graph. Given this representation, an effective game strategy will search through the graph for the paths that lead to the most wins and fewest losses and play in a way that always tries to force the game along one of these optimal paths, as in Figure II.5.

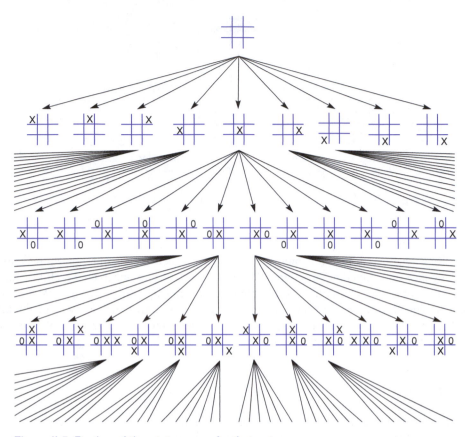

Figure II.5 Portion of the state space for tic-tac-toe.

As an example of how search is used to solve a more complicated problem, consider the task of diagnosing a mechanical fault in an automobile. Although this problem does not initially seem to lend itself to state space search as easily as tic-tac-toe or chess, it actually fits this strategy quite well. Instead of letting each node of the graph represent a "board state," we let it represent a state of partial knowledge about the automobile's mechanical problems. The process of examining the symptoms of the fault and inducing its cause may be thought of as searching through states of increasing knowledge. The starting node of the graph is empty, indicating that nothing is known about the cause of the problem. The first thing a mechanic might do is ask the customer which major system (engine, transmission, steering, brakes, etc.) seems to be causing the trouble. This is represented by a collection of arcs from the start state to states that indicate a focus on a single subsystem of the automobile, as in Figure II.6.

Each of the states in the graph has arcs (corresponding to basic diagnostic checks) that lead to states representing further accumulation of knowledge in the diagnostic process. For example, the engine trouble node has arcs to nodes labeled engine starts and engine won't start. From the won't start node we may move to nodes labeled turns over

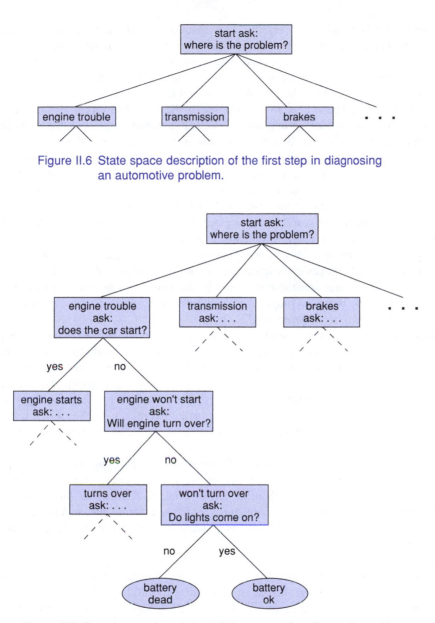

Figure II.6 State space description of the first step in diagnosing
an automotive problem.

Figure II.7 State space description of the automotive diagnosis problem.

and won't turn over. The won't turn over node has arcs to nodes labeled **battery dead** and **battery ok**, see Figure II.7. A problem solver can diagnose car trouble by searching for a path through this graph that is consistent with the symptoms of a particular defective car. Although this problem is very different from that of finding an optimal way to play tic-tac-toe or chess, it is equally amenable to solution by state space search.

In spite of this apparent universality, state space search is not, by itself, sufficient for automating intelligent problem-solving behavior; rather it is an important tool for the design of intelligent programs. If state space search were sufficient, it would be fairly simple to write a program that plays chess by searching through the entire space for the sequence of moves that brought a victory, a method known as *exhaustive search*. Though exhaustive search can be applied to any state space, the overwhelming size of the space for interesting problems makes this approach a practical impossibility. Chess, for example, has approximately 10^{120} different board states. This is a number larger than the number of molecules in the universe or the number of nanoseconds that have passed since the *big bang*. Search of this space is beyond the capabilities of any computing device, whose dimensions must be confined to the known universe and whose execution must be completed before the universe succumbs to the ravages of entropy.

Humans use intelligent search: a chess player considers a number of possible moves, a doctor examines several possible diagnoses, a computer scientist entertains different designs before beginning to write code. Humans do not use exhaustive search: the chess player examines only moves that experience has shown to be effective, the doctor does not require tests that are not somehow indicated by the symptoms at hand. Human problem solving seems to be based on judgmental rules that guide search to those portions of the state space that seem most "promising".

These rules are known as *heuristics*, and they constitute one of the central topics of AI research. A heuristic (the name is taken from the Greek word "to discover") is a strategy for selectively searching a problem space. It guides search along lines that have a high probability of success while avoiding wasted or apparently stupid efforts. Human beings use a large number of heuristics in problem solving. If you ask a mechanic why your car is overheating, she may say something like, "Usually that means the thermostat is bad." If you ask a doctor what could cause nausea and stomach pains, he might say it is "probably either stomach flu or food poisoning."

State space search gives us a means of formalizing the problem-solving process, and heuristics allow us to infuse that formalism with intelligence. These techniques are discussed in detail in the early chapters of this book and remain at the heart of most modern work in AI. In summary, state space search is a formalism, independent of any particular search strategies, and used as a launch point for many problem solving approaches.

Throughout the text we continue to explore the theoretical aspects of knowledge representation and search and the use of this theory in building effective programs. The treatment of knowledge representation begins with Chapter 2 and the predicate calculus. Chapter 3 introduces search in the context of game graphs and other applications. In Chapter 4, heuristics are introduced and applied to graph search, including games. In Chapter 5 we present stochastic techniques for building and organizing search spaces; these will be used later in machine learning and natural language processing. Finally, Chapter 6 introduces the production system, blackboards and other software architectures for building intelligent problem solvers.

THE PREDICATE CALCULUS

We come to the full possession of our power of drawing inferences, the last of our faculties;
for it is not so much a natural gift as a long and difficult art.

—C. S. PIERCE

The essential quality of a proof is to compel belief.

—FERMAT

2.0 Introduction

In this chapter we introduce the predicate calculus as a representation language for
artificial intelligence. The importance of the predicate calculus was discussed in the
introduction to Part II; these advantages include a well-defined *formal semantics* and
sound and *complete* inference rules. This chapter begins with a brief review of the
propositional calculus (Section 2.1). Section 2.2 defines the syntax and semantics of the
predicate calculus. In Section 2.3 we discuss predicate calculus inference rules and their
use in problem solving. Finally, the chapter demonstrates the use of the predicate calculus
to implement a knowledge base of financial investment advice.

2.1 The Propositional Calculus

2.1.1 Symbols and Sentences

The propositional calculus and, in the next subsection, the predicate calculus are first of all
languages. Using their words, phrases, and sentences, we can represent and reason about
properties and relationships in the world. The first step in describing a language is to
introduce the pieces that make it up: its set of symbols.

PROPOSITIONAL CALCULUS SYMBOLS

The *symbols* of propositional calculus are the propositional symbols:

P, Q, R, S, …

truth symbols:

true, false

and connectives:

$\land, \lor, \lnot, \rightarrow, \equiv$

Propositional symbols denote *propositions*, or statements about the world that may be either true or false, such as "the car is red" or "water is wet." Propositions are denoted by uppercase letters near the end of the English alphabet. Sentences in the propositional calculus are formed from these atomic symbols according to the following rules:

PROPOSITIONAL CALCULUS SENTENCES

Every propositional symbol and truth symbol is a sentence.

For example: true, P, Q, and R are sentences.

The *negation* of a sentence is a sentence.

For example: $\lnot$ P and $\lnot$ false are sentences.

The *conjunction*, or *and*, of two sentences is a sentence.

For example: P $\land$ $\lnot$ P is a sentence.

The *disjunction*, or *or*, of two sentences is a sentence.

For example: P $\lor$ $\lnot$ P is a sentence.

The *implication* of one sentence from another is a sentence.

For example: P $\rightarrow$ Q is a sentence.

The *equivalence* of two sentences is a sentence.

For example: P $\lor$ Q $\equiv$ R is a sentence.

Legal sentences are also called *well-formed formulas* or *WFFs*.

In expressions of the form P $\land$ Q, P and Q are called the *conjuncts*. In P $\lor$ Q, P and Q are referred to as *disjuncts*. In an implication, P $\rightarrow$ Q, P is the *premise* or *antecedent* and Q, the *conclusion* or *consequent*.

In propositional calculus sentences, the symbols ( ) and [ ] are used to group symbols into subexpressions and so to control their order of evaluation and meaning. For example, $(P \lor Q) \equiv R$ is quite different from $P \lor (Q \equiv R)$, as can be demonstrated using truth tables, see Section 2.1.2.

An expression is a sentence, or well-formed formula, of the propositional calculus if and only if it can be formed of legal symbols through some sequence of these rules. For example,

$$((P \land Q) \rightarrow R) \equiv \neg P \lor \neg Q \lor R$$

is a well-formed sentence in the propositional calculus because:

P, Q, and R are propositions and thus sentences.

$P \land Q$, the conjunction of two sentences, is a sentence.

$(P \land Q) \rightarrow R$, the implication of a sentence for another, is a sentence.

$\neg P$ and $\neg Q$, the negations of sentences, are sentences.

$\neg P \lor \neg Q$, the disjunction of two sentences, is a sentence.

$\neg P \lor \neg Q \lor R$, the disjunction of two sentences, is a sentence.

$((P \land Q) \rightarrow R) \equiv \neg P \lor \neg Q \lor R$, the equivalence of two sentences, is a sentence.

This is our original sentence, which has been constructed through a series of applications of legal rules and is therefore "well formed".

2.1.2 The Semantics of the Propositional Calculus

Section 2.1.1 presented the syntax of the propositional calculus by defining a set of rules for producing legal sentences. In this section we formally define the *semantics* or "meaning" of these sentences. Because AI programs must reason with their representational structures, it is important to demonstrate that the truth of their conclusions depends only on the truth of their initial knowledge, i.e., that logical errors are not introduced by the inference procedures. A precise treatment of semantics is essential to this goal.

A proposition symbol corresponds to a statement about the world. For example, P may denote the statement "it is raining" or Q, the statement "I live in a brown house." A proposition may be either true or false, given some state of the world. The truth value assignment to propositional sentences is called an *interpretation*, an assertion about their truth in some *possible world*.

Formally, an interpretation is a mapping from the propositional symbols into the set {T, F}. As mentioned in the previous section, the symbols true and false are part of the set of well-formed sentences of the propositional calculus; i.e., they are distinct from the truth value assigned to a sentence. To enforce this distinction, the symbols T and F are used for truth value assignment.

Each possible mapping of truth value onto propositions corresponds to a possible world of interpretation. For example, if P denotes the proposition "it is raining" and Q denotes "I am at work," then the set of propositions {P, Q} has four different functional mappings into the truth values {T, F}. These mappings correspond to four different interpretations. The semantics of propositional calculus, like its syntax, is defined inductively:

DEFINITION

PROPOSITIONAL CALCULUS SEMANTICS

An *interpretation* of a set of propositions is the assignment of a truth value, either T or F, to each propositional symbol.

The symbol true is always assigned T, and the symbol false is assigned F.

The interpretation or truth value for sentences is determined by:

The truth assignment of *negation*, ¬ P, where P is any propositional symbol, is F if the assignment to P is T, and T if the assignment to P is F.

The truth assignment of *conjunction*, ∧, is T only when both conjuncts have truth value T; otherwise it is F.

The truth assignment of *disjunction*, ∨, is F only when both disjuncts have truth value F; otherwise it is T.

The truth assignment of *implication*, →, is F only when the premise or symbol before the implication is T and the truth value of the consequent or symbol after the implication is F; otherwise it is T.

The truth assignment of *equivalence*, ≡, is T only when both expressions have the same truth assignment for all possible interpretations; otherwise it is F.

The truth assignments of compound propositions are often described by *truth tables*. A truth table lists all possible truth value assignments to the atomic propositions of an expression and gives the truth value of the expression for each assignment. Thus, a truth table enumerates all possible worlds of interpretation that may be given to an expression. For example, the truth table for P ∧ Q, Figure 2.1, lists truth values for each possible truth assignment of the operands. P ∧ Q is true only when both P and Q are both T. Or (∨), not (¬), implies (→), and equivalence (≡) are defined in a similar fashion. The construction of these truth tables is left as an exercise.

Two expressions in the propositional calculus are equivalent if they have the same value under all truth value assignments. This equivalence may be demonstrated using truth tables. For example, a proof of the equivalence of P → Q and ¬ P ∨ Q is given by the truth table of Figure 2.2.

By demonstrating that two different sentences in the propositional calculus have identical truth tables, we can prove the following equivalences. For propositional expressions P, Q, and R:

$\neg\,(\neg\,P) \equiv P$

$(P \lor Q) \equiv (\neg\,P \rightarrow Q)$

the contrapositive law: $(P \rightarrow Q) \equiv (\neg\,Q \rightarrow \neg\,P)$

de Morgan's law: $\neg\,(P \lor Q) \equiv (\neg\,P \land \neg\,Q)$ and $\neg\,(P \land Q) \equiv (\neg\,P \lor \neg\,Q)$

the commutative laws: $(P \land Q) \equiv (Q \land P)$ and $(P \lor Q) \equiv (Q \lor P)$

the associative law: $((P \land Q) \land R) \equiv (P \land (Q \land R))$

the associative law: $((P \lor Q) \lor R) \equiv (P \lor (Q \lor R))$

the distributive law: $P \lor (Q \land R) \equiv (P \lor Q) \land (P \lor R)$

the distributive law: $P \land (Q \lor R) \equiv (P \land Q) \lor (P \land R)$

Identities such as these can be used to change propositional calculus expressions into a syntactically different but logically equivalent form. These identities may be used instead of truth tables to prove that two expressions are equivalent: find a series of identities that transform one expression into the other. An early AI program, the *Logic Theorist* (Newell and Simon 1956), designed by Newell, Simon, and Shaw, used transformations between equivalent forms of expressions to prove many of the theorems in Whitehead and Russell's *Principia Mathematica* (1950). The ability to change a logical expression into a different form with equivalent truth values is also important when using inference rules (modus ponens, Section 2.3, and resolution, Chapter 13) that require expressions to be in a specific form.

P	Q	P∧Q
T	T	T
T	F	F
F	T	F
F	F	F

Figure 2.1 Truth table for the operator ∧.

P	Q	¬P	¬P∨Q	P⇒Q	(¬P∨Q)=(P⇒Q)
T	F	F	F	F	T
F	T	T	T	T	T
F	F	T	T	T	T

Figure 2.2 Truth table demonstrating the equivalence of
$P \rightarrow Q$ and $\neg\,P \lor Q$.

2.2   The Predicate Calculus

In propositional calculus, each atomic symbol (P, Q, etc.) denotes a proposition of some complexity. There is no way to access the components of an individual assertion. Predicate calculus provides this ability. For example, instead of letting a single propositional symbol, P, denote the entire sentence "it rained on Tuesday," we can create a predicate weather that describes a relationship between a date and the weather: weather(tuesday, rain). Through inference rules we can manipulate predicate calculus expressions, accessing their individual components and inferring new sentences.

Predicate calculus also allows expressions to contain variables. Variables let us create general assertions about classes of entities. For example, we could state that for all values of X, where X is a day of the week, the statement weather(X, rain) is true; i.e., it rains every day. As with propositional calculus, we will first define the syntax of the language and then discuss its semantics.

2.2.1   The Syntax of Predicates and Sentences

Before defining the syntax of correct expressions in the predicate calculus, we define an alphabet and grammar for creating the *symbols* of the language. This corresponds to the lexical aspect of a programming language definition. Predicate calculus symbols, like the *tokens* in a programming language, are irreducible syntactic elements: they cannot be broken into their component parts by the operations of the language.

In this text we represent predicate calculus symbols as strings of letters and digits beginning with a letter. Blanks and nonalphanumeric characters cannot appear within the string, although the underscore, _, may be used to improve readability.

DEFINITION

PREDICATE CALCULUS SYMBOLS

The alphabet that makes up the symbols of the predicate calculus consists of:

1.   The set of letters, both upper- and lowercase, of the English alphabet.
2.   The set of digits, 0, 1, …, 9.
3.   The underscore, _.

Symbols in the predicate calculus begin with a letter and are followed by any sequence of these legal characters.

Legitimate characters in the alphabet of predicate calculus symbols include

    a R 6 9 p _ z

Examples of characters not in the alphabet include

    # % @ / & " "

Legitimate predicate calculus symbols include

    George fire3 tom_and_jerry bill XXXX friends_of

Examples of strings that are not legal symbols are

    3jack "no blanks allowed" ab%cd ***71 duck!!!

Symbols, as we see in Section 2.2.2, are used to denote objects, properties, or relations in a world of discourse. As with most programming languages, the use of "words" that suggest the symbol's intended meaning assists us in understanding program code. Thus, even though l(g,k) and likes(george, kate) are formally equivalent (i.e., they have the same structure), the second can be of great help (for human readers) in indicating what relationship the expression represents. It must be stressed that these descriptive names are intended solely to improve the readability of expressions. The only meaning that predicate calculus expressions may be said to have is through their formal semantics.

Parentheses "( )", commas ",", and periods "." are used solely to construct well-formed expressions and do not denote objects or relations in the world. These are called *improper symbols*.

Predicate calculus symbols may represent either *variables, constants, functions,* or *predicates*. Constants name specific objects or properties in the world. Constant symbols must begin with a lowercase letter. Thus george, tree, tall, and blue are examples of well-formed constant symbols. The constants true and false are reserved as *truth symbols*.

Variable symbols are used to designate general classes of objects or properties in the world. Variables are represented by symbols beginning with an uppercase letter. Thus George, BILL, and KAte are legal variables, whereas geORGE and bill are not.

Predicate calculus also allows functions on objects in the world of discourse. Function symbols (like constants) begin with a lowercase letter. Functions denote a mapping of one or more elements in a set (called the *domain* of the function) into a unique element of another set (the *range* of the function). Elements of the domain and range are objects in the world of discourse. In addition to common arithmetic functions such as addition and multiplication, functions may define mappings between nonnumeric domains.

Note that our definition of predicate calculus symbols does not include numbers or arithmetic operators. The number system is not included in the predicate calculus primitives; instead it is defined axiomatically using "pure" predicate calculus as a basis (Manna and Waldinger 1985). While the particulars of this derivation are of theoretical interest, they are less important to the use of predicate calculus as an AI representation language. For convenience, we assume this derivation and include arithmetic in the language.

Every function symbol has an associated *arity*, indicating the number of elements in the domain mapped onto each element of the range. Thus father could denote a function of arity 1 that maps people onto their (unique) male parent. plus could be a function of arity 2 that maps two numbers onto their arithmetic sum.

A *function expression* is a function symbol followed by its arguments. The arguments are elements from the domain of the function; the number of arguments is equal to the arity of the function. The arguments are enclosed in parentheses and separated by commas. For example,

    f(X,Y)
    father(david)
    price(bananas)

are all well-formed function expressions.

Each function expression denotes the mapping of the arguments onto a single object in the range, called the *value* of the function. For example, if father is a unary function, then

    father(david)

is a function expression whose value (in the author's world of discourse) is george. If plus is a function of arity 2, with domain the integers, then

    plus(2,3)

is a function expression whose value is the integer 5. The act of replacing a function with its value is called *evaluation*.

The concept of a predicate calculus symbol or term is formalized in the following definition:

DEFINITION

SYMBOLS and TERMS

Predicate calculus symbols include:

1. *Truth symbols* true and false (these are reserved symbols).

2. *Constant symbols* are symbol expressions having the first character lowercase.

3. *Variable symbols* are symbol expressions beginning with an uppercase character.

4. *Function symbols* are symbol expressions having the first character lowercase. Functions have an attached arity indicating the number of elements of the domain mapped onto each element of the range.

A *function expression* consists of a function constant of arity n, followed by n terms, $t_1, t_2, ..., t_n$, enclosed in parentheses and separated by commas.

A predicate calculus *term* is either a constant, variable, or function expression.

Thus, a predicate calculus *term* may be used to denote objects and properties in a problem domain. Examples of terms are:

cat
times(2,3)
X
blue
mother(jane)
kate

Symbols in predicate calculus may also represent predicates. Predicate symbols, like constants and function names, begin with a lowercase letter. A predicate names a relationship between zero or more objects in the world. The number of objects so related is the arity of the predicate. Examples of predicates are

likes   equals   on   near   part_of

An *atomic sentence*, the most primitive unit of the predicate calculus language, is a predicate of arity n followed by n terms enclosed in parentheses and separated by commas. Examples of atomic sentences are

likes(george,kate)	likes(X,george)
likes(george,susie)	likes(X,X)
likes(george,sarah,tuesday)	friends(bill,richard)
friends(bill,george)	friends(father_of(david),father_of(andrew))
helps(bill,george)	helps(richard,bill)

The predicate symbols in these expressions are likes, friends, and helps. A predicate symbol may be used with different numbers of arguments. In this example there are two different likes, one with two and the other with three arguments. When a predicate symbol is used in sentences with different arities, it is considered to represent two different relations. Thus, a predicate relation is defined by its name and its arity. There is no reason that the two different likes cannot make up part of the same description of the world; however, this is avoided because it can often cause confusion.

In the predicates above, bill, george, kate, etc., are constant symbols and represent objects in the problem domain. The arguments to a predicate are terms and may also include variables or function expressions. For example,

friends(father_of(david),father_of(andrew))

is a predicate describing a relationship between two objects in a domain of discourse. These arguments are represented as function expressions whose mappings (given that the father_of david is george and the father_of andrew is allen) form the parameters of the predicate. If the function expressions are evaluated, the expression becomes

friends(george,allen)

These ideas are formalized in the following definition.

Atomic sentences are also called *atomic expressions*, *atoms*, or *propositions*.

We may combine atomic sentences using logical operators to form *sentences* in the predicate calculus. These are the same logical connectives used in propositional calculus: $\land, \lor, \neg, \rightarrow$, and $\equiv$.

When a variable appears as an argument in a sentence, it refers to unspecified objects in the domain. First order (Section 2.2.2) predicate calculus includes two symbols, the *variable quantifiers* $\forall$ and $\exists$, that constrain the meaning of a sentence containing a variable. A quantifier is followed by a variable and a sentence, such as

$\exists$ Y friends(Y, peter)
$\forall$ X likes(X, ice_cream)

The *universal quantifier*, $\forall$, indicates that the sentence is true for all values of the variable. In the example, $\forall$ X likes(X, ice_cream) is true for all values in the domain of the definition of X. The *existential quantifier*, $\exists$, indicates that the sentence is true for at least one value in the domain. $\exists$ Y friends(Y, peter) is true if there is at least one object, indicated by Y that is a friend of peter. Quantifiers are discussed in more detail in Section 2.2.2.

Sentences in the predicate calculus are defined inductively.

5. If s_1 and s_2 are sentences, then so is their equivalence, $s_1 \equiv s_2$.

6. If X is a variable and s a sentence, then $\forall$ X s is a sentence.

7. If X is a variable and s a sentence, then $\exists$ X s is a sentence.

Examples of well-formed sentences follow. Let times and plus be function symbols of arity 2 and let equal and foo be predicate symbols with arity 2 and 3, respectively.

plus(two,three) is a function and thus not an atomic sentence.

equal(plus(two,three), five) is an atomic sentence.

equal(plus(2, 3), seven) is an atomic sentence. Note that this sentence, given the standard interpretation of plus and equal, is false. Well-formedness and truth value are independent issues.

$\exists$ X foo(X,two,plus(two,three)) $\land$ equal(plus(two,three),five) is a sentence because both conjuncts are sentences.

(foo(two,two,plus(two,three))) $\rightarrow$ (equal(plus(three,two),five) $\equiv$ true) is a sentence because all its components are sentences, appropriately connected by logical operators.

The definition of predicate calculus sentences and the examples just presented suggest a method for verifying that an expression is a sentence. This is written as a recursive algorithm, verify_sentence. verify_sentence takes as argument a candidate expression and returns success if the expression is a sentence.

```
function verify_sentence(expression);
begin
  case
    expression is an atomic sentence: return SUCCESS;
    expression is of the form Q X s, where Q is either " or $, X is a variable,
      if verify_sentence(s) returns SUCCESS
      then return SUCCESS
      else return FAIL;
    expression is of the form ¬ s:
      if verify_sentence(s) returns SUCCESS
      then return SUCCESS
      else return FAIL;
    expression is of the form s₁ op s₂, where op is a binary logical operator:
      if verify_sentence(s₁) returns SUCCESS and
         verify_sentence(s₂) returns SUCCESS
      then return SUCCESS
      else return FAIL;
    otherwise: return FAIL
  end
end.
```

We conclude this section with an example of the use of predicate calculus to describe a simple world. The domain of discourse is a set of family relationships in a biblical genealogy:

```
mother(eve,abel)
mother(eve,cain)
father(adam,abel)
father(adam,cain)
```

$$\forall X \forall Y \; father(X, Y) \lor mother(X, Y) \rightarrow parent(X, Y)$$
$$\forall X \forall Y \forall Z \; parent(X, Y) \land parent(X, Z) \rightarrow sibling(Y, Z)$$

In this example we use the predicates mother and father to define a set of parent–child relationships. The implications give general definitions of other relationships, such as parent and sibling, in terms of these predicates. Intuitively, it is clear that these implications can be used to infer facts such as sibling(cain,abel). To formalize this process so that it can be performed on a computer, care must be taken to define inference algorithms and to ensure that such algorithms indeed draw correct conclusions from a set of predicate calculus assertions. In order to do so, we define the semantics of the predicate calculus (Section 2.2.2) and then address the issue of inference rules (Section 2.3).

2.2.2 A Semantics for the Predicate Calculus

Having defined well-formed expressions in the predicate calculus, it is important to determine their meaning in terms of objects, properties, and relations in the world. Predicate calculus semantics provide a formal basis for determining the truth value of well-formed expressions. The truth of expressions depends on the mapping of constants, variables, predicates, and functions into objects and relations in the domain of discourse. The truth of relationships in the domain determines the truth of the corresponding expressions.

For example, information about a person, George, and his friends Kate and Susie may be expressed by

```
friends(george,susie)
friends(george,kate)
```

If it is indeed true that George is a friend of Susie and George is a friend of Kate then these expressions would each have the truth value (assignment) T. If George is a friend of Susie but not of Kate, then the first expression would have truth value T and the second would have truth value F.

To use the predicate calculus as a representation for problem solving, we describe objects and relations in the domain of interpretation with a set of well-formed expressions. The terms and predicates of these expressions denote objects and relations in the domain. This database of predicate calculus expressions, each having truth value T, describes the "state of the world." The description of George and his friends is a simple example of such a database. Another example is the *blocks world* in the introduction to Part II.

Based on these intuitions, we formally define the semantics of predicate calculus. First, we define an *interpretation* over a domain D. Then we use this interpretation to determine the *truth value assignment* of sentences in the language.

DEFINITION

INTERPRETATION

Let the domain D be a nonempty set.

An *interpretation* over D is an assignment of the entities of D to each of the constant, variable, predicate, and function symbols of a predicate calculus expression, such that:

1. Each constant is assigned an element of D.

2. Each variable is assigned to a nonempty subset of D; these are the allowable substitutions for that variable.

3. Each function f of arity m is defined on m arguments of D and defines a mapping from D^m into D.

4. Each predicate p of arity n is defined on n arguments from D and defines a mapping from D^n into {T, F}.

Given an interpretation, the meaning of an expression is a truth value assignment over the interpretation.

DEFINITION

TRUTH VALUE OF PREDICATE CALCULUS EXPRESSIONS

Assume an expression E and an interpretation I for E over a nonempty domain D. The truth value for E is determined by:

1. The value of a constant is the element of D it is assigned to by I.

2. The value of a variable is the set of elements of D it is assigned to by I.

3. The value of a function expression is that element of D obtained by evaluating the function for the parameter values assigned by the interpretation.

4. The value of truth symbol "true" is T and "false" is F.

5. The value of an atomic sentence is either T or F, as determined by the interpretation I.

Quantification of variables is an important part of predicate calculus semantics. When a variable appears in a sentence, such as X in likes(george,X), the variable functions as a placeholder. Any constant allowed under the interpretation can be substituted for it in the expression. Substituting kate or susie for X in likes(george,X) forms the statements likes(george,kate) and likes(george,susie).

The variable X stands for all constants that might appear as the second parameter of the sentence. This variable name might be replaced by any other variable name, such as Y or PEOPLE, without changing the meaning of the expression. Thus the variable is said to be a *dummy*. In the predicate calculus, variables must be *quantified* in either of two ways: *universally* or *existentially*. A variable is considered *free* if it is not within the scope of either the universal or existential quantifiers. An expression is *closed* if all of its variables are quantified. A *ground expression* has no variables at all. In the predicate calculus all variables must be quantified.

The symbol indicating universal quantification is ∀. Parentheses are often used to indicate the *scope* of quantification, that is, the instances of a variable name over which a quantification holds. Thus

$$\forall\ X\ (p(X) \lor q(Y) \to r(X))$$

indicates that X is universally quantified in both p(X) and r(X).

Universal quantification introduces problems in computing the truth value of a sentence, because all the possible values of a variable symbol must be tested to see whether the expression remains true. For example, to test the truth value of ∀ X likes(george,X), where X ranges over the set of all humans, all possible values for X must be tested. If the domain of an interpretation is infinite, exhaustive testing of all substitutions to a universally quantified variable is computationally impossible: the algorithm may never halt. Because of this problem, the predicate calculus is said to be *undecidable*. Because the propositional calculus does not support variables, sentences can only have a finite number of truth assignments, and we can exhaustively test all these possible assignments. This is done with the truth table, Section 2.1.

Variables may also be quantified *existentially*. In this case the expression containing the variable is said to be true for at least one substitution from the domain of definition. The existential quantifier is indicated by ∃. The scope of an existentially quantified variable is also indicated by enclosing the quantified occurrences of the variable in parentheses.

Evaluating the truth of an expression containing an existentially quantified variable may be no easier than evaluating the truth of expressions containing universally quantified variables. Suppose we attempt to determine the truth of the expression by trying substitutions until one is found that makes the expression true. If the domain of the variable is infinite and the expression is false under all substitutions, the algorithm will never halt.

Several relationships between negation and the universal and existential quantifiers are given below. These relationships are used in resolution refutation systems described in Chapter 12. The notion of a variable name as a dummy symbol that stands for a set of constants is also noted. For predicates p and q and variables X and Y:

$$\neg \exists\, X\, p(X) \equiv \forall\, X\, \neg\, p(X)$$

$$\neg \forall\, X\, p(X) \equiv \exists\, X\, \neg\, p(X)$$

$$\exists\, X\, p(X) \equiv \exists\, Y\, p(Y)$$

$$\forall\, X\, q(X) \equiv \forall\, Y\, q(Y)$$

$$\forall\, X\, (p(X) \wedge q(X)) \equiv \forall\, X\, p(X) \wedge \forall\, Y\, q(Y)$$

$$\exists\, X\, (p(X) \vee q(X)) \equiv \exists\, X\, p(X) \vee \exists\, Y\, q(Y)$$

In the language we have defined, universally and existentially quantified variables may refer only to objects (constants) in the domain of discourse. Predicate and function names may not be replaced by quantified variables. This language is called the *first-order predicate calculus*.

DEFINITION

FIRST-ORDER PREDICATE CALCULUS

First-order predicate calculus allows quantified variables to refer to objects in the domain of discourse and not to predicates or functions.

For example,

∀ (Likes) Likes(george,kate)

is not a well-formed expression in the first-order predicate calculus. There are *higher-order* predicate calculi where such expressions are meaningful. Some researchers (McCarthy

1968, Appelt 1985) have used higher-order languages to represent knowledge in natural language understanding programs.

Many grammatically correct English sentences can be represented in the first-order predicate calculus using the symbols, connectives, and variable symbols defined in this section. It is important to note that there is no unique mapping of sentences into predicate calculus expressions; in fact, an English sentence may have any number of different predicate calculus representations. A major challenge for AI programmers is to find a scheme for using these predicates that optimizes the expressiveness and efficiency of the resulting representation. Examples of English sentences represented in predicate calculus are:

If it doesn't rain on Monday, Tom will go to the mountains.
¬ weather(rain, monday) → go(tom, mountains)

Emma is a Doberman pinscher and a good dog.
gooddog(emma) ∧ isa(emma, doberman)

All basketball players are tall.
∀ X (basketball_player(X) → tall(X))

Some people like anchovies.
∃ X (person(X) ∧ likes(X, anchovies))

If wishes were horses, beggars would ride.
equal(wishes, horses) → ride(beggars)

Nobody likes taxes.
¬ ∃ X likes(X, taxes)

2.2.3   A "Blocks World" Example of Semantic Meaning

We conclude this section by giving an extended example of a truth value assignment to a set of predicate calculus expressions. Suppose we want to model the blocks world of Figure 2.3 to design, for example, a control algorithm for a robot arm. We can use predicate calculus sentences to represent the qualitative relationships in the world: does a given block have a clear top surface? can we pick up block a? etc. Assume that the computer has knowledge of the location of each block and the arm and is able to keep track of these locations (using three-dimensional coordinates) as the hand moves blocks about the table.

We must be very precise about what we are proposing with this "blocks world" example. First, we are creating a set of predicate calculus expressions that is to represent a static snapshot of the blocks world problem domain. As we will see in Section 2.3, this set of blocks offers an *interpretation* and a possible *model* for the set of predicate calculus expressions.

Second, the predicate calculus is *declarative*, that is, there is no assumed timing or order for considering each expression. Nonetheless, in the planning section of this book, Section 8.4, we will add a "procedural semantics", or a clearly specified methodology for evaluating these expressions over time. A concrete example of a procedural semantics for

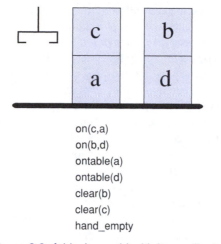

on(c,a)
on(b,d)
ontable(a)
ontable(d)
clear(b)
clear(c)
hand_empty

Figure 2.3 A blocks world with its predicate
calculus description.

predicate calculus expressions is PROLOG, Chapter 15. This situation calculus we are creating will introduce a number of issues, including the *frame problem* and the issue of *non-monotonicity* of logic interpretations, that will be addressed later in this book. For this example, however, it is sufficient to say that our predicate calculus expressions will be evaluated in a left-to-right fashion.

To pick up a block and stack it on another block, both blocks must be clear. In Figure 2.3, block a is not clear. Because the arm can move blocks, it can change the state of the world and clear a block. Suppose it removes block c from block a and updates the knowledge base to reflect this by deleting the assertion on(c,a). The program needs to be able to infer that block a has become clear.

The following rule describes when a block is clear:

$$\forall\, X\, (\neg\, \exists\, Y\ on(Y,X) \rightarrow clear(X))$$

That is, for all X, X is clear if there does not exist a Y such that Y is on X.

This rule not only defines what it means for a block to be clear but also provides a basis for determining how to clear blocks that are not. For example, block d is not clear, because if variable X is given value d, substituting b for Y will make the statement false. Therefore, to make this definition true, block b must be removed from block d. This is easily done because the computer has a record of all the blocks and their locations.

Besides using implications to define when a block is clear, other rules may be added that describe operations such as stacking one block on top of another. For example: to stack X on Y, first empty the hand, then clear X, then clear Y, and then pick_up X and put_down X on Y.

$$\forall\, X\, \forall\, Y\, ((hand\_empty \wedge clear(X) \wedge clear(Y) \wedge pick\_up(X) \wedge put\_down(X,Y))$$
$$\rightarrow stack(X,Y))$$

Note that in implementing the above description it is necessary to "attach" an action of the robot arm to each predicate such as pick_up(X). As noted previously, for such an implementation it was necessary to augment the semantics of predicate calculus by requiring that the actions be performed in the order in which they appear in a rule premise. However, much is gained by separating these issues from the use of predicate calculus to define the relationships and operations in the domain.

Figure 2.3 gives a semantic interpretation of these predicate calculus expressions. This interpretation maps the constants and predicates in the set of expressions into a domain D, here the blocks and relations between them. The interpretation gives truth value T to each expression in the description. Another interpretation could be offered by a different set of blocks in another location, or perhaps by a team of four acrobats. The important question is not the uniqueness of interpretations, but whether the interpretation provides a truth value for all expressions in the set and whether the expressions describe the world in sufficient detail that all necessary inferences may be carried out by manipulating the symbolic expressions. The next section uses these ideas to provide a formal basis for predicate calculus inference rules.

2.3   Using Inference Rules to Produce Predicate Calculus Expressions

2.3.1   Inference Rules

The semantics of the predicate calculus provides a basis for a formal theory of *logical inference*. The ability to infer new correct expressions from a set of true assertions is an important feature of the predicate calculus. These new expressions are correct in that they are *consistent* with all previous interpretations of the original set of expressions. First we discuss these ideas informally and then we create a set of definitions to make them precise.

An interpretation that makes a sentence true is said to *satisfy* that sentence. An interpretation that satisfies every member of a set of expressions is said to satisfy the set. An expression X *logically follows* from a set of predicate calculus expressions S if every interpretation that satisfies S also satisfies X. This notion gives us a basis for verifying the correctness of rules of inference: the function of logical inference is to produce new sentences that logically follow a given set of predicate calculus sentences.

It is important that the precise meaning of *logically follows* be understood: for expression X to *logically follow* S, it must be true for every interpretation that satisfies the original set of expressions S. This would mean, for example, that any new predicate calculus expression added to the blocks world of Figure 2.3 must be true in that world as well as in any other interpretation that that set of expressions may have.

The term itself, "logically follows," may be a bit confusing. It does not mean that X is deduced from or even that it is deducible from S. It simply means that X is true for every (potentially infinite) interpretation that satisfies S. However, because systems of predicates can have a potentially infinite number of possible interpretations, it is seldom practical to try all interpretations. Instead, *inference rules* provide a computationally feasible way to determine when an expression, a component of an interpretation, logically follows for that interpretation. The concept "logically follows" provides a formal basis for proofs of the soundness and correctness of inference rules.

An inference rule is essentially a mechanical means of producing new predicate calculus sentences from other sentences. That is, inference rules produce new sentences based on the syntactic form of given logical assertions. When every sentence X produced by an inference rule operating on a set S of logical expressions logically follows from S, the inference rule is said to be *sound*.

If the inference rule is able to produce every expression that logically follows from S, then it is said to be *complete*. *Modus ponens*, to be introduced below, and *resolution*, introduced in Chapter 12, are examples of inference rules that are sound and, when used with certain appropriate strategies, complete. Logical inference systems generally use sound rules of inference, although later chapters (6, 10, 11, and 15) examine heuristic reasoning and commonsense reasoning, both of which relax this requirement.

We formalize these ideas through the following definitions.

DEFINITION

SATISFY, MODEL, VALID, INCONSISTENT

For a predicate calculus expression X and an interpretation I:

If X has a value of T under I and a particular variable assignment, then I is said to *satisfy* X.

If I satisfies X for all variable assignments, then I is a *model* of X.

X is *satisfiable* if and only if there exist an interpretation and variable assignment that satisfy it; otherwise, it is *unsatisfiable*.

A set of expressions is *satisfiable* if and only if there exist an interpretation and variable assignment that satisfy every element.

If a set of expressions is not satisfiable, it is said to be *inconsistent*.

If X has a value T for all possible interpretations, X is said to be *valid*.

In the blocks world example of Figure 2.3, the blocks world was a model for its logical description. All of the sentences in the example were true under this interpretation. When a knowledge base is implemented as a set of true assertions about a problem domain, that domain is a model for the knowledge base.

The expression $\exists X (p(X) \wedge \neg p(X))$ is inconsistent, because it cannot be satisfied under any interpretation or variable assignment. On the other hand, the expression $\forall X (p(X) \vee \neg p(X))$ is valid.

The truth table method can be used to test validity for any expression not containing variables. Because it is not always possible to decide the validity of expressions containing variables (as mentioned above, the process may not terminate), the full predicate calculus is "undecidable." There are *proof procedures*, however, that can produce any expression that logically follows from a set of expressions. These are called *complete* proof procedures.

DEFINITION

PROOF PROCEDURE

A *proof procedure* is a combination of an inference rule and an algorithm for applying that rule to a set of logical expressions to generate new sentences.

We present proof procedures for the *resolution* inference rule in Chapter 12.

Using these definitions, we may formally define "logically follows."

DEFINITION

LOGICALLY FOLLOWS, SOUND, and COMPLETE

A predicate calculus expression X *logically follows* from a set S of predicate calculus expressions if every interpretation and variable assignment that satisfies S also satisfies X.

An inference rule is *sound* if every predicate calculus expression produced by the rule from a set S of predicate calculus expressions also logically follows from S.

An inference rule is *complete* if, given a set S of predicate calculus expressions, the rule can infer every expression that logically follows from S.

Modus ponens is a sound inference rule. If we are given an expression of the form P → Q and another expression of the form P such that both are true under an interpretation I, then modus ponens allows us to infer that Q is also true for that interpretation. Indeed, because modus ponens is sound, Q is true for *all* interpretations for which P and P → Q are true.

Modus ponens and a number of other useful inference rules are defined below.

DEFINITION

MODUS PONENS, MODUS TOLLENS, AND ELIMINATION, AND INTRODUCTION, and UNIVERSAL INSTANTIATION

If the sentences P and P → Q are known to be true, then *modus ponens* lets us infer Q.

> Under the inference rule *modus tollens*, if P → Q is known to be true and Q is known to be false, we can infer ¬ P.
>
> *And elimination* allows us to infer the truth of either of the conjuncts from the truth of a conjunctive sentence. For instance, P ∧ Q lets us conclude P and Q are true.
>
> *And introduction* lets us infer the truth of a conjunction from the truth of its conjuncts. For instance, if P and Q are true, then P ∧ Q is true.
>
> *Universal instantiation* states that if any universally quantified variable in a true sentence is replaced by any appropriate term from the domain, the result is a true sentence. Thus, if a is from the domain of X, ∀ X p(X) lets us infer p(a).

As a simple example of the use of modus ponens in the propositional calculus, assume the following observations: "if it is raining then the ground will be wet" and "it is raining." If P denotes "it is raining" and Q is "the ground is wet" then the first expression becomes P → Q. Because it is indeed now raining (P is true), our set of axioms becomes

    P → Q
    P

Through an application of modus ponens, the fact that the ground is wet (Q) may be added to the set of true expressions.

Modus ponens can also be applied to expressions containing variables. Consider as an example the common syllogism "all men are mortal and Socrates is a man; therefore Socrates is mortal." "All men are mortal" may be represented in predicate calculus by

    ∀ X (man(X) → mortal(X)).

"Socrates is a man" is

    man(socrates).

Because the X in the implication is universally quantified, we may substitute any value in the domain for X and still have a true statement under the inference rule of universal instantiation. By substituting socrates for X in the implication, we infer the expression

    man(socrates) → mortal(socrates).

We can now apply modus ponens and infer the conclusion mortal(socrates). This is added to the set of expressions that logically follow from the original assertions. An algorithm called *unification* can be used by an automated problem solver to determine that socrates may be substituted for X in order to apply modus ponens. Unification is discussed in Section 2.3.2.

Chapter 13 discusses a more powerful rule of inference called *resolution*, which is the basis of many automated reasoning systems.

2.3.2 Unification

To apply inference rules such as modus ponens, an inference system must be able to determine when two expressions are the same or *match*. In propositional calculus, this is trivial: two expressions match if and only if they are syntactically identical. In predicate calculus, the process of matching two sentences is complicated by the existence of variables in the expressions. Universal instantiation allows universally quantified variables to be replaced by terms from the domain. This requires a decision process for determining the variable substitutions under which two or more expressions can be made identical (usually for the purpose of applying inference rules).

Unification is an algorithm for determining the substitutions needed to make two predicate calculus expressions match. We have already seen this done in the previous subsection, where socrates in man(socrates) was substituted for X in ∀ X(man(X) ⇒ mortal(X)). This allowed the application of modus ponens and the conclusion mortal(socrates). Another example of unification was seen previously when dummy variables were discussed. Because p(X) and p(Y) are equivalent, Y may be substituted for X to make the sentences match.

Unification and inference rules such as modus ponens allow us to make inferences on a set of logical assertions. To do this, the logical database must be expressed in an appropriate form.

An essential aspect of this form is the requirement that all variables be universally quantified. This allows full freedom in computing substitutions. Existentially quantified variables may be eliminated from sentences in the database by replacing them with the constants that make the sentence true. For example, ∃ X parent(X,tom) could be replaced by the expression parent(bob,tom) or parent(mary,tom), assuming that bob and mary are tom's parents under the interpretation.

The process of eliminating existentially quantified variables is complicated by the fact that the value of these substitutions may depend on the value of other variables in the expression. For example, in the expression ∀ X ∃ Y mother(X,Y), the value of the existentially quantified variable Y depends on the value of X. *Skolemization* replaces each existentially quantified variable with a function that returns the appropriate constant as a function of some or all of the other variables in the sentence. In the above example, because the value of Y depends on X, Y could be replaced by a *skolem function*, f, of X. This yields the predicate ∀ X mother(X,f(X)). Skolemization, a process that can also bind universally quantified variables to constants, is discussed in more detail in Chapter 13.

Once the existentially quantified variables have been removed from a logical database, unification may be used to match sentences in order to apply inference rules such as modus ponens.

Unification is complicated by the fact that a variable may be replaced by any term, including other variables and function expressions of arbitrary complexity. These expressions may themselves contain variables. For example, father(jack) may be substituted for X in man(X) to infer that jack's father is mortal.

Some instances of the expression

foo(X,a,goo(Y)).

generated by legal substitutions are given below:

1) foo(fred,a,goo(Z))
2) foo(W,a,goo(jack))
3) foo(Z,a,goo(moo(Z)))

In this example, the substitution instances or *unifications* that would make the initial expression identical to each of the other three are written as

1) {fred/X, Z/Y}
2) {W/X, jack/Y}
3) {Z/X, moo(Z)/Y}

The notation X/Y, … indicates that X is substituted for the variable Y in the original expression. Substitutions are also referred to as *bindings*. A variable is said to be *bound* to the value substituted for it.

In defining the unification algorithm that computes the substitutions required to match two expressions, a number of issues must be taken into account.

Although a constant may be systematically substituted for a variable, any constant is considered a "ground instance" and may not be replaced. Neither can two different ground instances be substituted for one variable.

A variable cannot be unified with a term containing that variable. X cannot be replaced by p(X) as this creates an infinite expression: p(p(p(p(...X)...). The test for this situation is called the *occurs check*.

Generally, a problem-solving process will require multiple inferences and, consequently, multiple successive unifications. Logic problem solvers must maintain consistency of variable substitutions. It is important that any unifying substitution be made consistently across all occurrences of the variable in both expressions being matched. This was seen before when socrates was substituted not only for the variable X in man(X) but also for the variable X in mortal(X).

Once a variable has been bound, future unifications and inferences must take the value of this binding into account. If a variable is bound to a constant, that variable may not be given a new binding in a future unification. If a variable X_1 is substituted for another variable X_2 and at a later time X_1 is replaced by a constant, then X_2 must also reflect this binding. The set of substitutions used in a sequence of inferences is important, because it may contain the answer to the original query (Section 13.2.5). For example, if p(a,X) unifies with the premise of p(Y,Z) $\Rightarrow$ q(Y,Z) with substitution {a/Y, X/Z}, modus ponens lets us infer q(a,X) under the same substitution. If we match this result with the premise of q(W,b) $\Rightarrow$ r(W,b), we infer r(a,b) under the substitution set {a/W, b/X}.

Another important concept is the *composition* of unification substitutions. If S and S′ are two substitution sets, then the composition of S and S′ (written SS′) is obtained by applying S′ to the elements of S and adding the result to S. Consider the example of composing the following three sets of substitutions:

{X/Y, W/Z}, {V/X}, {a/V, f(b)/W}.

Composing the third set, {a/V, f(b)/W}, with the second, {V/X}, produces:

{a/X, a/V, f(b)/W}.

Composing this result with the first set, {X/Y, W/Z}, produces the set of substitutions:

{a/Y, a/X, a/V, f(b)/Z, f(b)/W}.

Composition is the method by which unification substitutions are combined and returned in the recursive function unify, presented next. Composition is associative but not commutative. The exercises present these issues in more detail.

A further requirement of the unification algorithm is that the unifier be as general as possible: that the *most general unifier* be found. This is important, as will be seen in the next example, because, if generality is lost in the solution process, it may lessen the scope of the eventual solution or even eliminate the possibility of a solution entirely.

For example, in unifying p(X) and p(Y) any constant expression such as {fred/X, fred/Y} will work. However, fred is not the most general unifier; any variable would produce a more general expression: {Z/X, Z/Y}. The solutions obtained from the first substitution instance would always be restricted by having the constant fred limit the resulting inferences; i.e., fred would be a unifier, but it would lessen the generality of the result.

DEFINITION

MOST GENERAL UNIFIER (mgu)

If s is any unifier of expressions E, and g is the most general unifier of that set of expressions, then for s applied to E there exists another unifier s' such that Es = Egs', where Es and Egs' are the composition of unifiers applied to the expression E.

The most general unifier for a set of expressions is unique except for alphabetic variations; i.e., whether a variable is eventually called X or Y really does not make any difference to the generality of the resulting unifications.

Unification is important for any artificial intelligence problem solver that uses the predicate calculus for representation. Unification specifies conditions under which two (or more) predicate calculus expressions may be said to be equivalent. This allows use of inference rules, such as *resolution*, with logic representations, a process that often requires backtracking to find all possible interpretations. For example, see PROLOG, Chapter 15.

We next present pseudo-code for a function, unify, that computes the unifying substitutions (when this is possible) between two predicate calculus expressions. Unify takes as arguments two expressions in the predicate calculus and returns either the most general unifying substitutions or the constant FAIL if no unification is possible. It is defined as a recursive function: first, it recursively attempts to unify the initial components of the expressions. If this succeeds, any substitutions returned by this unification are applied to the remainder of both expressions. These are then passed in a second recursive call to unify, which attempts to complete the unification. The recursion stops when either argument is a symbol (a predicate, function name, constant, or variable) or the elements of the expression have all been matched.

To simplify the manipulation of expressions, the algorithm assumes a slightly modified syntax. Because unify simply performs syntactic pattern matching, it can effectively ignore the predicate calculus distinction between predicates, functions, and arguments. By representing an expression as a *list* (an ordered sequence of elements) with the predicate or function name as the first element followed by its arguments, we simplify the manipulation of expressions. Expressions in which an argument is itself a predicate or function expression are represented as lists within the list, thus preserving the structure of the expression. Lists are delimited by parentheses, ( ), and list elements are separated by spaces. Examples of expressions in both predicate calculus (PC) and list syntax are:

PC SYNTAX	LIST SYNTAX
p(a,b)	(p a b)
p(f(a),g(X,Y))	(p (f a) (g X Y))
equal(eve,mother(cain))	(equal eve (mother cain))

We next present the function unify:

```
function unify(E1, E2);
  begin
    case
      both E1 and E2 are constants or the empty list:          %recursion stops
        if E1 = E2 then return {}
          else return FAIL;
      E1 is a variable:
        if E1 occurs in E2 then return FAIL
          else return {E2/E1};
      E2 is a variable:
        if E2 occurs in E1 then return FAIL
          else return {E1/E2}
      either E1 or E2 are empty then return FAIL        %the lists are of different sizes
      otherwise:                                        %both E1 and E2 are lists
        begin
            HE1 := first element of E1;
            HE2 := first element of E2;
            SUBS1 := unify(HE1,HE2);
            if SUBS1 : = FAIL then return FAIL;
            TE1 := apply(SUBS1, rest of E1);
            TE2 : = apply (SUBS1, rest of E2);
            SUBS2 : = unify(TE1, TE2);
            if SUBS2 = FAIL then return FAIL;
                else return composition(SUBS1,SUBS2)
        end
    end                                                 %end case
  end
```

2.3.3 A Unification Example

The behavior of the preceding algorithm may be clarified by tracing the call

unify((parents X (father X) (mother bill)), (parents bill (father bill) Y)).

When unify is first called, because neither argument is an atomic symbol, the function will attempt to recursively unify the first elements of each expression, calling

unify(parents, parents).

This unification succeeds, returning the empty substitution, { }. Applying this to the remainder of the expressions creates no change; the algorithm then calls

unify((X (father X) (mother bill)), (bill (father bill) Y)).

A tree depiction of the execution at this stage appears in Figure 2.4.

In the second call to unify, neither expression is atomic, so the algorithm separates each expression into its first component and the remainder of the expression. This leads to the call

unify(X, bill).

This call succeeds, because both expressions are atomic and one of them is a variable. The call returns the substitution {bill/X}. This substitution is applied to the remainder of each expression and unify is called on the results, as in Figure 2.5:

unify(((father bill) (mother bill)), ((father bill)Y)).

The result of this call is to unify (father bill) with (father bill). This leads to the calls

unify(father, father)
unify(bill, bill)
unify(( ), ( ))

All of these succeed, returning the empty set of substitutions as seen in Figure 2.6.
Unify is then called on the remainder of the expressions:

unify(((mother bill)), (Y)).

This, in turn, leads to calls

unify((mother bill), Y)

unify(( ),( )).

In the first of these, (mother bill) unifies with Y. Notice that unification substitutes the whole *structure* (mother bill) for the variable Y. Thus, unification succeeds and returns the substitution {(mother bill)/Y}. The call

   unify(( ),( ))

returns { }. These are composed, along with the earlier substitution {bill/X}, to return the answer {bill/X (mother bill)/Y}. A trace of the entire execution appears in Figure 2.6. Each call is numbered to indicate the order in which it was made; the substitutions returned by each call are noted on the arcs of the tree.

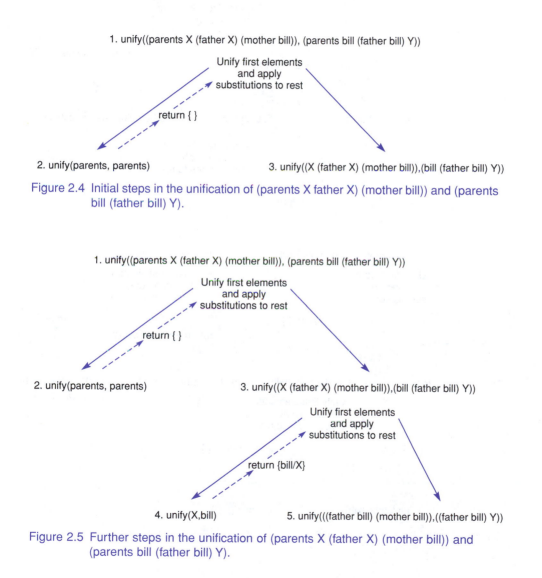

Figure 2.4 Initial steps in the unification of (parents X father X) (mother bill)) and (parents bill (father bill) Y).

Figure 2.5 Further steps in the unification of (parents X (father X) (mother bill)) and (parents bill (father bill) Y).

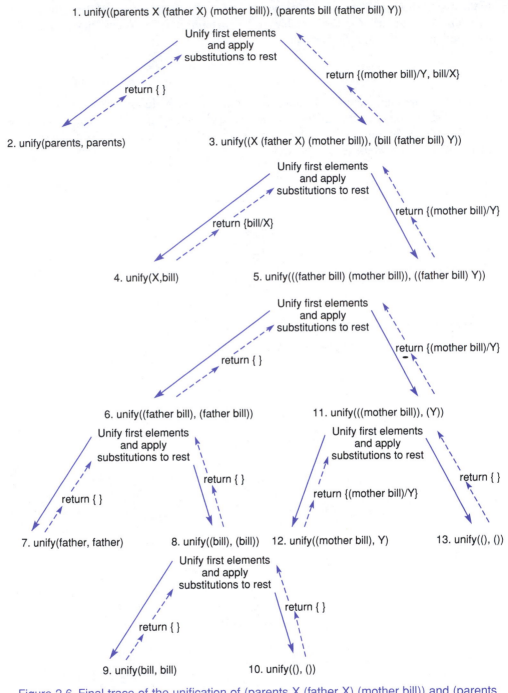

Figure 2.6 Final trace of the unification of (parents X (father X) (mother bill)) and (parents bill (father bill) Y).

2.4   Application: A Logic-Based Financial Advisor

As a final example of the use of predicate calculus to represent and reason about problem domains, we design a simple financial advisor using predicate calculus. Although a simple example, it illustrates many of the issues involved in realistic applications.

The function of the advisor is to help a user decide whether to invest in a savings account or the stock market. Some investors may want to split their money between the two. The investment that will be recommended for individual investors depends on their income and the current amount they have saved according to the following criteria:

1. Individuals with an inadequate savings account should always make increasing the amount saved their first priority, regardless of their income.

2. Individuals with an adequate savings account and an adequate income should consider a riskier but potentially more profitable investment in the stock market.

3. Individuals with a lower income who already have an adequate savings account may want to consider splitting their surplus income between savings and stocks, to increase the cushion in savings while attempting to increase their income through stocks.

The adequacy of both savings and income is determined by the number of dependents an individual must support. Our rule is to have at least $5,000 in the bank for each dependent. An adequate income must be a steady income and supply at least $15,000 per year plus an additional $4,000 for each dependent.

To automate this advice, we translate these guidelines into sentences in the predicate calculus. The first task is to determine the major features that must be considered. Here, they are the adequacy of the savings and the income. These are represented by the predicates savings_account and income, respectively. Both of these are unary pre- dicates, and their argument could be either adequate or inadequate. Thus,

    savings_account(adequate).
    savings_account(inadequate).
    income(adequate).
    income(inadequate).

are their possible values.

Conclusions are represented by the unary predicate investment, with possible values of its argument being stocks, savings, or combination (implying that the investment should be split).

Using these predicates, the different investment strategies are represented by implications. The first rule, that individuals with inadequate savings should make increased savings their main priority, is represented by

    savings_account(inadequate) → investment(savings).

Similarly, the remaining two possible investment alternatives are represented by

savings_account(adequate) ∧ income(adequate) → investment(stocks).
savings_account(adequate) ∧ income(inadequate)
        → investment(combination).

Next, the advisor must determine when savings and income are adequate or inadequate. This will also be done using implication. The need to do arithmetic calculations requires the use of functions. To determine the minimum adequate savings, the function minsavings is defined. minsavings takes one argument, the number of dependents, and returns 5000 times that argument.

Using minsavings, the adequacy of savings is determined by the rules

∀ X amount_saved(X) ∧ ∃ Y (dependents(Y) ∧ greater(X, minsavings(Y)))
        → savings_account(adequate).
∀ X amount_saved(X) ∧ ∃ Y (dependents(Y) ∧ ¬ greater(X, minsavings(Y)))
        → savings_account(inadequate).

where minsavings(X) ≡ 5000 ∗ X.

In these definitions, amount_saved(X) and dependents(Y) assert the current amount in savings and the number of dependents of an investor; greater(X,Y) is the standard arithmetic test for one number being greater than another and is not formally defined in this example.

Similarly, a function minincome is defined as

minincome(X) ≡ 15000 + (4000 ∗ X).

minincome is used to compute the minimum adequate income when given the number of dependents. The investor's current income is represented by a predicate, earnings. Because an adequate income must be both steady and above the minimum, earnings takes two arguments: the first is the amount earned, and the second must be equal to either steady or unsteady. The remaining rules needed for the advisor are

∀ X earnings(X, steady) ∧ ∃ Y (dependents(Y) ∧ greater(X, minincome(Y)))
        → income(adequate).

∀ X earnings(X, steady) ∧ ∃ Y (dependents(Y) ∧ ¬ greater(X, minincome(Y)))
        → income(inadequate).

∀ X earnings(X, unsteady) → income(inadequate).

In order to perform a consultation, a description of a particular investor is added to this set of predicate calculus sentences using the predicates amount_saved, earnings, and dependents. Thus, an individual with three dependents, $22,000 in savings, and a steady income of $25,000 would be described by

amount_saved(22000).

earnings(25000, steady).
dependents(3).

This yields a logical system consisting of the following sentences:

1. savings_account(inadequate) → investment(savings).

2. savings_account(adequate) ∧ income(adequate) → investment(stocks).

3. savings_account(adequate) ∧ income(inadequate)
    → investment(combination).

4. ∀ X amount_saved(X) ∧ ∃ Y (dependents(Y) ∧
    greater(X, minsavings(Y))) → savings_account(adequate).

5. ∀ X amount_saved(X) ∧ ∃ Y (dependents(Y) ∧
    ¬ greater(X, minsavings(Y))) → savings_account(inadequate).

6. ∀ X earnings(X, steady) ∧ ∃ Y (dependents (Y) ∧
    greater(X, minincome(Y))) → income(adequate).

7. ∀ X earnings(X, steady) ∧ ∃ Y (dependents(Y) ∧
    ¬ greater(X, minincome(Y))) → income(inadequate).

8. ∀ X earnings(X, unsteady) → income(inadequate).

9. amount_saved(22000).

10. earnings(25000, steady).

11. dependents(3).

where minsavings(X) ≡ 5000 * X and minincome(X) ≡ 15000 + (4000 * X).

This set of logical sentences describes the problem domain. The assertions are numbered so that they may be referenced in the following trace.

Using unification and modus ponens, a correct investment strategy for this individual may be inferred as a logical consequence of these descriptions. A first step would be to unify the conjunction of 10 and 11 with the first two components of the premise of 7; i.e.,

earnings(25000,steady) ∧ dependents(3)

unifies with

earnings(X,steady) ∧ dependents(Y)

under the substitution {25000/X, 3/Y}. This substitution yields the new implication:

earnings(25000, steady) ∧ dependents(3) ∧ ¬ greater(25000, minincome(3))
    → income(inadequate).

Evaluating the function minincome yields the expression

earnings(25000, steady) ∧ dependents(3) ∧ ¬ greater(25000, 27000)
    → income(inadequate).

Because all three components of the premise are individually true, by 10, 3, and the mathematical definition of greater, their conjunction is true and the entire premise is true. Modus ponens may therefore be applied, yielding the conclusion income(inadequate). This is added as assertion 12.

12. income(inadequate).

Similarly,

amount_saved(22000) ∧ dependents(3)

unifies with the first two elements of the premise of assertion 4 under the substitution {22000/X, 3/Y}, yielding the implication

amount_saved(22000) ∧ dependents(3) ∧ greater(22000, minsavings(3))
    → savings_account(adequate).

Here, evaluating the function minsavings(3) yields the expression

amount_saved(22000) ∧ dependents(3) ∧ greater(22000, 15000)
    → savings_account(adequate).

Again, because all of the components of the premise of this implication are true, the entire premise evaluates to true and modus ponens may again be applied, yielding the conclusion savings_account(adequate), which is added as expression 13.

13. savings_account(adequate).

As an examination of expressions 3, 12, and 13 indicates, the premise of implication 3 is also true. When we apply modus ponens a third time, the conclusion is investment(combination). This is the suggested investment for this individual.

This example illustrates how predicate calculus may be used to reason about a realistic problem, drawing correct conclusions by applying inference rules to the initial problem description. We have not discussed exactly how an algorithm can determine the correct inferences to make to solve a given problem or the way in which this can be implemented on a computer. These topics are presented in Chapters 3, 4, and 6.

2.5 Epilogue and References

In this chapter we introduced predicate calculus as a representation language for AI problem solving. The symbols, terms, expressions, and semantics of the language were described and defined. Based on the semantics of predicate calculus, we defined inference rules that allow us to derive sentences that logically follow from a given set of expressions. We defined a unification algorithm that determines the variable substitutions that make two expressions match, which is essential for the application of inference rules. We concluded the chapter with the example of a financial advisor that represents financial knowledge in predicate calculus and demonstrates logical inference as a problem-solving technique.

Predicate calculus is discussed in detail in a number of computer science books, including: *The Logical Basis for Computer Programming* by Zohar Manna and Richard Waldinger (1985), *Logic for Computer Science* by Jean H. Gallier (1986), *Symbolic Logic and Mechanical Theorem Proving* by Chin-liang Chang and Richard Char-tung Lee (1973), and *An Introduction to Mathematical Logic and Type Theory* by Peter B. Andrews (1986). We present more modern proof techniques in Chapter 13, Automated Reasoning.

Books that describe the use of predicate calculus as an artificial intelligence representation language include: *Logical Foundations of Artificial Intelligence* by Michael Genesereth and Nils Nilsson (1987), *Artificial Intelligence* by Nils Nilsson (1998), *The Field of Automated Reasoning* by Larry Wos (1995), *Computer Modelling of Mathematical Reasoning* by Alan Bundy (1983, 1988), and *Readings in Knowledge Representation* by Ronald Brachman and Hector Levesque (1985). See *Automated Reasoning* by Bob Veroff (1997) for interesting modern applications of automated inference.

2.6 Exercises

1. Using truth tables, prove the identities of Section 2.1.2.

2. A new operator, $\oplus$, or *exclusive-or*, may be defined by the following truth table:

P	Q	P $\oplus$ Q
T	T	F
T	F	T
F	T	T
F	F	F

Create a propositional calculus expression using only $\wedge$, $\vee$, and $\neg$ that is equivalent to P $\oplus$ Q.
Prove their equivalence using truth tables.

3. The logical operator "↔" is read "if and only if." $P \leftrightarrow Q$ is defined as being equivalent to $(P \rightarrow Q) \land (Q \rightarrow P)$. Based on this definition, show that $P \leftrightarrow Q$ is logically equivalent to $(P \lor Q) \rightarrow (P \land Q)$:

   a. By using truth tables.
   b. By a series of substitutions using the identities on page 51.

4. Prove that implication is transitive in the propositional calculus, that is, that $((P \rightarrow Q) \land (Q \rightarrow R)) \rightarrow (P \rightarrow R)$.

5.   a. Prove that modus ponens is sound for propositional calculus. Hint: use truth tables to enumerate all possible interpretations.
   b. *Abduction* is an inference rule that infers P from $P \rightarrow Q$ and Q. Show that abduction is not sound (see Chapter 8).
   c. Show modus tollens $((P \rightarrow Q) \land \neg Q) \rightarrow \neg P$ is sound.

6. Attempt to unify the following pairs of expressions. Either show their most general unifiers or explain why they will not unify.

   a. p(X,Y) and p(a,Z)
   b. p(X,X) and p(a,b)
   c. ancestor(X,Y) and ancestor(bill,father(bill))
   d. ancestor(X,father(X)) and ancestor(david,george)
   e. q(X) and $\neg$ q(a)

7.   a. Compose the substitution sets {a/X, Y/Z} and {X/W, b/Y}.
   b. Prove that composition of substitution sets is associative.
   c. Construct an example to show that composition is not commutative.

8. Implement the unify algorithm of Section 2.3.2 in the computer language of your choice.

9. Give two alternative interpretations for the blocks world description of Figure 2.3.

10. Jane Doe has four dependents, a steady income of $30,000, and $15,000 in her savings account. Add the appropriate predicates describing her situation to the general investment advisor of the example in Section 2.4 and perform the unifications and inferences needed to determine her suggested investment.

11. Write a set of logical predicates that will perform simple automobile diagnostics (e.g., if the engine won't turn over and the lights won't come on, then the battery is bad). Don't try to be too elaborate, but cover the cases of bad battery, out of gas, bad spark plugs, and bad starter motor.

12. The following story is from N. Wirth's (1976) *Algorithms + data structures = programs.*
I married a widow (let's call her W) who has a grown-up daughter (call her D). My father (F), who visited us quite often, fell in love with my step-daughter and married her. Hence my father became my son-in-law and my step-daughter became my mother. Some months later, my wife gave birth to a son (S_1), who became the brother-in-law of my father, as well as my uncle. The wife of my father, that is, my step-daughter, also had a son (S_2).
Using predicate calculus, create a set of expressions that represent the situation in the above story. Add expressions defining basic family relationships such as the definition of father-in-law and use modus ponens on this system to prove the conclusion that "I am my own grandfather."

STRUCTURES AND STRATEGIES FOR STATE SPACE SEARCH

3

In order to cope, an organism must either armor itself (like a tree or a clam) and "hope for the best," or else develop methods for getting out of harm's way and into the better neighborhoods of the vicinity. If you follow this latter course, you are confronted with the primordial problem that every agent must continually solve: Now what do I do?

—DANIEL C. DENNETT, *"Consciousness Explained"*

Two roads diverged in a yellow wood,
And sorry I could not travel both
And be one traveler, long I stood
And looked down one as far as I could
To where it bent in the undergrowth;
Then took the other . . .

—ROBERT FROST, *"The Road Not Taken"*

3.0 Introduction

Chapter 2 introduced predicate calculus as an example of an artificial intelligence representation language. Well-formed predicate calculus expressions provide a means of describing objects and relations in a problem domain, and inference rules such as modus ponens allow us to infer new knowledge from these descriptions. These inferences define a space that is searched to find a problem solution. Chapter 3 introduces the theory of state space search.

To successfully design and implement search algorithms, a programmer must be able to analyze and predict their behavior. Questions that need to be answered include:

Is the problem solver guaranteed to find a solution?

Will the problem solver always terminate, or can it become caught in an infinite loop?

When a solution is found, is it guaranteed to be optimal?

What is the complexity of the search process in terms of time usage? Memory usage?

How can the interpreter most effectively reduce search complexity?

How can an interpreter be designed to most effectively utilize a representation language?

The theory of *state space search* is our primary tool for answering these questions. By representing a problem as a *state space graph*, we can use *graph theory* to analyze the structure and complexity of both the problem and the search procedures that we employ to solve it.

A graph consists of a set of *nodes* and a set of *arcs* or *links* connecting pairs of nodes. In the state space model of problem solving, the nodes of a graph are taken to represent discrete *states* in a problem-solving process, such as the results of logical inferences or the different configurations of a game board. The arcs of the graph represent transitions between states. These transitions correspond to logical inferences or legal moves of a game. In expert systems, for example, states describe our knowledge of a problem instance at some stage of a reasoning process. Expert knowledge, in the form of *if . . . then* rules, allows us to generate new information; the act of applying a rule is represented as an arc between states.

Graph theory is our best tool for reasoning about the structure of objects and relations; indeed, this is precisely the need that led to its creation in the early eighteenth century. The Swiss mathematician Leonhard Euler invented graph theory to solve the "bridges of Königsberg problem" (Newman 1956). The city of Königsberg occupied both banks and two islands of a river. The islands and the riverbanks were connected by seven bridges, as indicated in Figure 3.1.

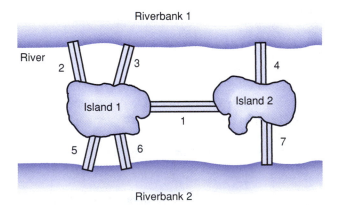

Figure 3.1 The city of Königsberg.

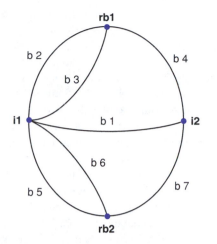

Figure 3.2 Graph of the Königsberg bridge system.

The bridges of Königsberg problem asks if there is a walk around the city that crosses each bridge exactly once. Although the residents had failed to find such a walk and doubted that it was possible, no one had proved its impossibility. Devising a form of graph theory, Euler created an alternative representation for the map, presented in Figure 3.2. The riverbanks (rb1 and rb2) and islands (i1 and i2) are described by the nodes of a graph; the bridges are represented by labeled arcs between nodes (b1, b2, ..., b7). The graph representation preserves the essential structure of the bridge system, while ignoring extraneous features such as distance and direction.

Alternatively, we may represent the Königsberg bridge system using predicate calculus. The connect predicate corresponds to an arc of the graph, asserting that two land masses are connected by a particular bridge. Each bridge requires two connect predicates, one for each direction in which the bridge may be crossed. A predicate expression, connect(X, Y, Z) = connect (Y, X, Z), indicating that any bridge can be crossed in either direction, would allow removal of half the following connect facts:

connect(i1, i2, b1)	connect(i2, i1, b1)
connect(rb1, i1, b2)	connect(i1, rb1, b2)
connect(rb1, i1, b3)	connect(i1, rb1, b3)
connect(rb1, i2, b4)	connect(i2, rb1, b4)
connect(rb2, i1, b5)	connect(i1, rb2, b5)
connect(rb2, i1, b6)	connect(i1, rb2, b6)
connect(rb2, i2, b7)	connect(i2, rb2, b7)

The predicate calculus representation is equivalent to the graph representation in that the connectedness is preserved. Indeed, an algorithm could translate between the two representations with no loss of information. However, the structure of the problem can be visualized more directly in the graph representation, whereas it is left implicit in the predicate calculus version. Euler's proof illustrates this distinction.

In proving that the walk was impossible, Euler focused on the *degree* of the nodes of the graph, observing that a node could be of either *even* or *odd* degree. An *even* degree node has an even number of arcs joining it to neighboring nodes. An *odd* degree node has an odd number of arcs. With the exception of its beginning and ending nodes, the desired walk would have to leave each node exactly as often as it entered it. Nodes of odd degree could be used only as the beginning or ending of the walk, because such nodes could be crossed only a certain number of times before they proved to be a dead end. The traveler could not exit the node without using a previously traveled arc.

Euler noted that unless a graph contained either exactly zero or two nodes of odd degree, the walk was impossible. If there were two odd-degree nodes, the walk could start at the first and end at the second; if there were no nodes of odd degree, the walk could begin and end at the same node. The walk is not possible for graphs containing any other number of nodes of odd degree, as is the case with the city of Königsberg. This problem is now called finding an *Euler path* through a graph.

Note that the predicate calculus representation, though it captures the relationships between bridges and land in the city, does not suggest the concept of the degree of a node. In the graph representation there is a single instance of each node with arcs between the nodes, rather than multiple occurrences of constants as arguments in a set of predicates. For this reason, the graph representation suggests the concept of node degree and the focus of Euler's proof. This illustrates graph theory's power for analyzing the structure of objects, properties, and relationships.

In Section 3.1 we review basic graph theory and then present finite state machines and the state space description of problems. In section 3.2 we introduce graph search as a problem-solving methodology. Depth-first and breadth-first search are two strategies for searching a state space. We compare these and make the added distinction between goal-driven and data-driven search. Section 3.3 demonstrates how state space search is used to characterize logical reasoning. Throughout the chapter, we use graph theory to analyze the structure and complexity of a variety of problems.

3.1 Graph Theory (optional)

3.1.1 Structures for State Space Search

A *graph* is a set of *nodes* or *states* and a set of *arcs* that connect the nodes. A *labeled* graph has one or more descriptors (labels) attached to each node that distinguish that node from any other node in the graph. In a *state space graph*, these descriptors identify states in a problem-solving process. If there are no descriptive differences between two nodes, they are considered the same. The arc between two nodes is indicated by the labels of the connected nodes.

The arcs of a graph may also be labeled. Arc labels are used to indicate that an arc represents a named relationship (as in a semantic network) or to attach weights to arcs (as in the traveling salesperson problem). If there are different arcs between the same two nodes (as in Figure 3.2), these can also be distinguished through labeling.

A graph is *directed* if arcs have an associated directionality. The arcs in a directed graph are usually drawn as arrows or have an arrow attached to indicate direction. Arcs that can be crossed in either direction may have two arrows attached but more often have no direction indicators at all. Figure 3.3 is a labeled, directed graph: arc (a, b) may only be crossed from node a to node b, but arc (b, c) is crossable in either direction.

A *path* through a graph connects a sequence of nodes through successive arcs. The path is represented by an ordered list that records the nodes in the order they occur in the path. In Figure 3.3, [a, b, c, d] represents the path through nodes a, b, c, and d, in that order.

A *rooted* graph has a unique node, called the *root*, such that there is a path from the root to all nodes within the graph. In drawing a rooted graph, the root is usually drawn at the top of the page, above the other nodes. The state space graphs for games are usually rooted graphs with the start of the game as the root. The initial moves of the tic-tac-toe game graph are represented by the rooted graph of Figure II.5. This is a directed graph with all arcs having a single direction. Note that this graph contains no cycles; players cannot (as much as they might sometimes wish!) undo a move.

A *tree* is a graph in which two nodes have at most one path between them. Trees often have roots, in which case they are usually drawn with the root at the top, like a rooted graph. Because each node in a tree has only one path of access from any other node, it is impossible for a path to *loop* or *cycle* continuously through a sequence of nodes.

For rooted trees or graphs, relationships between nodes include *parent*, *child*, and *sibling*. These are used in the usual familial fashion with the parent preceding its child along a directed arc. The children of a node are called *siblings*. Similarly, an *ancestor* comes before a *descendant* in some path of a directed graph. In Figure 3.4, b is a *parent* of nodes e and f (which are, therefore, *children* of b and *siblings* of each other). Nodes a and c are *ancestors* of states g, h, and i, and g, h, and i are *descendants* of a and c.

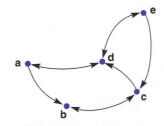

Nodes = {a,b,c,d,e}
Arcs = {(a,b),(a,d),(b,c),(c,b),(c,d),(d,a),(d,e),(e,c),(e,d)}

Figure 3.3 A labeled directed graph.

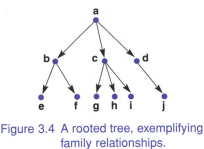

Figure 3.4 A rooted tree, exemplifying
family relationships.

Before introducing the state space representation of problems we formally define these concepts.

DEFINITION

GRAPH

A graph consists of:

A set of *nodes* N_1, N_2, N_3, ..., N_n, ..., which need not be finite.

A set of *arcs* that connect pairs of nodes.

Arcs are ordered pairs of nodes; i.e., the arc (N_3, N_4) connects node N_3 to node N_4. This indicates a direct connection from node N_3 to N_4 but not from N_4 to N_3, unless (N_4, N_3) is also an arc, and then the arc joining N_3 and N_4 is undirected.

If a directed arc connects N_j and N_k, then N_j is called the *parent* of N_k and N_k, the *child* of N_j. If the graph also contains an arc (N_j, N_l), then N_k and N_l are called *siblings*.

A *rooted* graph has a unique node N_S from which all paths in the graph originate. That is, the root has no parent in the graph.

A *tip* or *leaf* node is a node that has no children.

An ordered sequence of nodes [N_1, N_2, N_3, ..., N_n], where each pair N_i , N_{i+1} in the sequence represents an arc, i.e., (N_i, N_{i+1}), is called a *path* of length $n - 1$.

On a path in a rooted graph, a node is said to be an *ancestor* of all nodes positioned after it (to its right) as well as a *descendant* of all nodes before it.

A path that contains any node more than once (some N_j in the definition of path above is repeated) is said to contain a *cycle* or *loop*.

A *tree* is a graph in which there is a unique path between every pair of nodes. (The paths in a tree, therefore, contain no cycles.)

> The edges in a rooted tree are directed away from the root. Each node in a rooted tree has a unique parent.
>
> Two nodes are said to be *connected* if a path exists that includes them both.

Next we introduce the finite state machine, an abstract representation for computational devices, that may be viewed as an automaton for traversing paths in a graph.

3.1.2　The Finite State Machine (FSM)

We think of a machine as a system that can accept input values, possibly produce output values, and can have some sort of internal mechanism (states) to keep track of information about previous input values. A *finite state machine* (FSM) is a finite, directed, connected graph, having a set of states, a set of input values, and a state transition function that describes the effect that the elements of the input stream have on the states of the graph. The stream of input values produces a path within the graph of the states of this finite machine. Thus the FSM can be seen as an abstract model of computation.

The primary use for such a machine is to recognize components of a formal language. These components are often strings of characters ("words" made from characters of an "alphabet"). In Section 5.3 we extend this definition to a probabilistic finite state machine. These state machines have an important role in analyzing expressions in languages, whether computational or human, as we see in Sections 5.3, 9.3, and Chapter 14.

> **DEFINITION**
>
> **FINITE STATE MACHINE (FSM)**
>
> A *finite state machine* is an ordered triple (S, I, F), where:
>
> S is a finite set of *states* in a connected graph $s_1, s_2, s_3, ..., s_n$.
>
> I is a finite set of *input* values $i_1, i_2, i_3, ..., i_m$.
>
> F is a state transition function that for any $i \in I$, describes its effect on the states S of the machine, thus $\forall i \in I, F_i : (S \rightarrow S)$. If the machine is in state s_i and input i occurs, the next state of the machine will be $F_i(s_j)$.

For a simple example of a finite state machine, let $S = \{s_0, s_1\}$, $I = \{0,1\}$, $f_0(s_0) = s_0$, $f_0(s_1) = (s_1)$, $f_1(s_0) = s_1$, and $f_1(s_1) = s_0$. With this device, sometimes called a *flip-flop*, an input value of zero leaves the state unchanged, while input 1 changes the state of the machine. We may visualize this machine from two equivalent perspectives, as a finite graph with labelled, directed arcs, as in Figure 3.5a, or as a transition matrix, Figure 3.5b. In the transition matrix, input values are listed along the top row, the states are in the left-most column, and the output for an input applied to a state is at the intersection point.

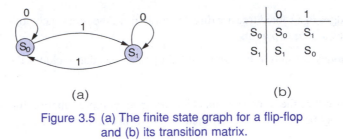

(a)   (b)

Figure 3.5 (a) The finite state graph for a flip-flop
and (b) its transition matrix.

A second example of a finite state machine is represented by the directed graph of Figure 3.6a and the (equivalent) transition matrix of Figure 3.6b. One might ask what the finite state machine of Figure 3.6 could represent. With two assumptions, this machine could be seen as a recognizer of all strings of characters from the alphabet {a, b, c, d} that contain the exact sequence "abc". The two assumptions are, first, that state s_0 has a special role as the *starting state*, and second, that s_3 is the *accepting state*. Thus, the input stream will present its first element to state s_0. If the stream later terminates with the machine in state s_3, it will have recognized that there is the sequence "abc" within that input stream.

What we have just described is a *finite state accepting machine*, sometimes called a *Moore machine*. We use the convention of placing an arrow from no state that terminates in the starting state of the Moore machine, and represent the accepting state (or states) as special, often using a doubled circle, as in Figure 3.6. We now present a formal definition of the Moore machine:

DEFINITION

FINITE STATE ACCEPTOR (MOORE MACHINE)

A *finite state acceptor* is a finite state machine (S, I, F), where:

$\exists s_0 \in S$ such that the input stream starts at s_0, and

$\exists s_n \in S$, an *accept* state. The input stream is accepted if it terminates in that state. In fact, there may be a set of accept states.

The finite state acceptor is represented as (S, s_0, {s_n}, I, F)

We have presented two fairly simple examples of a powerful concept. As we will see in natural language understanding (Chapter 14), finite state recognizers are an important tool for determining whether or not patterns of characters, words, or sentences have desired properties. We will see that a finite state acceptor implicitly defines a formal language on the basis of the sets of letters (characters) and words (strings) that it accepts.

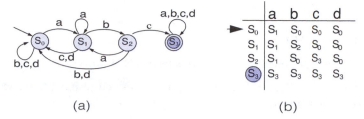

Figure 3.6 (a) The finite state graph and (b) the transition matrix for string recognition example.

We have also shown only *deterministic* finite state machines, where the transition function for any input value to a state gives a unique next state. *Probabilistic finite state machines*, where the transition function defines a distribution of output states for each input to a state, are also an important modeling technique. We consider these in Section 5.3 and again in Chapter 14. We next consider a more general graphical representation for the analysis of problem solving: the state space.

3.1.3 The State Space Representation of Problems

In the *state space representation* of a problem, the nodes of a graph correspond to partial problem solution *states* and the arcs correspond to steps in a problem-solving process. One or more *initial states*, corresponding to the given information in a problem instance, form the root of the graph. The graph also defines one or more *goal* conditions, which are solutions to a problem instance. *State space search* characterizes problem solving as the process of finding a *solution path* from the start state to a goal.

A goal may describe a state, such as a winning board in tic-tac-toe (Figure II.5) or a goal configuration in the 8-puzzle (Figure 3.7). Alternatively, a goal can describe some property of the solution path itself. In the traveling salesperson problem (Figures 3.9 and 3.10), search terminates when the "shortest" path is found through all nodes of the graph. In the parsing problem (Section 3.3), the path of successful analysis of a sentence indicates termination.

Arcs of the state space correspond to steps in a solution process and paths through the space represent solutions in various stages of completion. Paths are searched, beginning at the start state and continuing through the graph, until either the goal description is satisfied or they are abandoned. The actual generation of new states along the path is done by applying operators, such as "legal moves" in a game or inference rules in a logic problem or expert system, to existing states on a path. The task of a search algorithm is to find a solution path through such a problem space. Search algorithms must keep track of the paths from a start to a goal node, because these paths contain the series of operations that lead to the problem solution.

We now formally define the state space representation of problems:

DEFINITION

STATE SPACE SEARCH

A *state space* is represented by a four-tuple [N,A,S,GD], where:

N is the set of nodes or states of the graph. These correspond to the states in a problem-solving process.

A is the set of arcs (or links) between nodes. These correspond to the steps in a problem-solving process.

S, a nonempty subset of N, contains the start state(s) of the problem.

GD, a nonempty subset of N, contains the goal state(s) of the problem. The states in GD are described using either:

1. A measurable property of the states encountered in the search.
2. A property of the path developed in the search, for example, the transition costs for the arcs of the path.

A *solution path* is a path through this graph from a node in S to a node in GD.

One of the general features of a graph, and one of the problems that arise in the design of a graph search algorithm, is that states can sometimes be reached through different paths. For example, in Figure 3.3 a path can be made from state a to state d either through b and c or directly from a to d. This makes it important to choose the *best* path according to the needs of a problem. In addition, multiple paths to a state can lead to loops or cycles in a solution path that prevent the algorithm from reaching a goal. A blind search for goal state e in the graph of Figure 3.3 might search the sequence of states abcdabcdabcd . . . forever!

If the space to be searched is a tree, as in Figure 3.4, the problem of cycles does not occur. It is, therefore, important to distinguish between problems whose state space is a tree and those that may contain loops. General graph search algorithms must detect and eliminate loops from potential solution paths, whereas tree searches may gain efficiency by eliminating this test and its overhead.

Tic-tac-toe and the 8-puzzle exemplify the state spaces of simple games. Both of these examples demonstrate termination conditions of type 1 in our definition of state space search. Example 3.1.3, the traveling salesperson problem, has a goal description of type 2, the total cost of the path itself.

EXAMPLE 3.1.1: TIC-TAC-TOE

The state space representation of tic-tac-toe appears in Figure II.5. The start state is an empty board, and the termination or goal description is a board state having three Xs in a row, column, or diagonal (assuming that the goal is a win for X). The path from the start state to a goal state gives the series of moves in a winning game.

The states in the space are all the different configurations of Xs and Os that the game can have. Of course, although there are 3^9 ways to arrange {blank, X, O} in nine spaces, most of them could never occur in an actual game. Arcs are generated by legal moves of the game, alternating between placing an X and an O in an unused location. The state space is a graph rather than a tree, as some states on the third and deeper levels can be reached by different paths. However, there are no cycles in the state space, because the directed arcs of the graph do not allow a move to be undone. It is impossible to "go back up" the structure once a state has been reached. No checking for cycles in path generation is necessary. A graph structure with this property is called a *directed acyclic graph*, or *DAG*, and is common in state space search.

The state space representation provides a means of determining the complexity of the problem. In tic-tac-toe, there are nine first moves with eight possible responses to each of them, followed by seven possible responses to each of these, and so on. It follows that $9 \times 8 \times 7 \times \ldots$ or 9! different paths can be generated. Although it is not impossible for a computer to search this number of paths (362,880) exhaustively, many important problems also exhibit factorial or exponential complexity, although on a much larger scale. Chess has 10^{120} possible game paths; checkers has 10^{40}, some of which may never occur in an actual game. These spaces are difficult or impossible to search exhaustively. Strategies for searching such large spaces rely on heuristics to reduce the complexity of the search (Chapter 4).

EXAMPLE 3.1.2: THE 8-PUZZLE

In the *15-puzzle* of Figure 3.7, 15 differently numbered tiles are fitted into 16 spaces on a grid. One space is left blank so that tiles can be moved around to form different patterns. The goal is to find a series of moves of tiles into the blank space that places the board in a goal configuration. This is a common game that most of us played as children. (The version I remember was about 3 inches square and had red and white tiles in a black frame.)

A number of interesting aspects of this game have made it useful to researchers in problem solving. The state space is large enough to be interesting but is not completely intractable (16! if symmetric states are treated as distinct). Game states are easy to represent. The game is rich enough to provide a number of interesting heuristics (see Chapter 4).

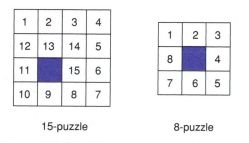

15-puzzle   8-puzzle

Figure 3.7 The 15-puzzle and the 8-puzzle.

The *8-puzzle* is a 3 × 3 version of the 15-puzzle in which eight tiles can be moved around in nine spaces. Because it generates a smaller state space than the full 15-puzzle, it is used for many of the examples in this text.

Although in the physical puzzle moves are made by moving tiles ("move the 7 tile right, provided the blank is to the right of the tile" or "move the 3 tile down"), it is much simpler to think in terms of "moving the blank space" instead. This simplifies the definition of move rules because there are eight tiles but only a single blank. In order to apply a move, we must make sure that it does not move the blank off the board. Therefore, all four moves are not applicable at all times; for example, when the blank is in one of the corners only two moves are possible.

The legal moves are:

move the blank up	↑
move the blank right	→
move the blank down	↓
move the blank left	←

If we specify a beginning state and a goal state for the 8-puzzle, it is possible to give a state space accounting of the problem-solving process (Figure 3.8). States could be

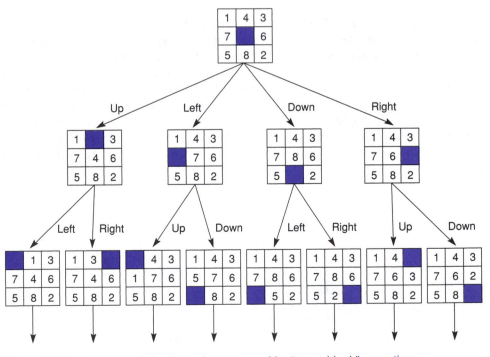

Figure 3.8 State space of the 8-puzzle generated by "move blank" operations.

represented using a simple 3 × 3 array. A predicate calculus representation could use a "state" predicate with nine parameters (for the locations of numbers in the grid). Four procedures, describing each of the possible moves of the blank, define the arcs in the state space.

As with tic-tac-toe, the state space for the 8-puzzle is a graph (with most states having multiple parents), but unlike tic-tac-toe, cycles are possible. The GD or goal description of the state space is a particular state or board configuration. When this state is found on a path, the search terminates. The path from start to goal is the desired series of moves.

It is interesting to note that the complete state space of the 8- and 15-puzzles consists of two disconnected (and in this case equal-sized) subgraphs. This makes half the possible states in the search space impossible to reach from any given start state. If we exchange (by prying loose!) two immediately adjacent tiles, states in the other component of the space become reachable.

EXAMPLE 3.1.3: THE TRAVELING SALESPERSON

Suppose a salesperson has five cities to visit and then must return home. The goal of the problem is to find the shortest path for the salesperson to travel, visiting each city, and then returning to the starting city. Figure 3.9 gives an instance of this problem. The nodes of the graph represent cities, and each arc is labeled with a weight indicating the cost of traveling that arc. This cost might be a representation of the miles necessary in car travel or cost of an air flight between the two cities. For convenience, we assume the salesperson lives in city A and will return there, although this assumption simply reduces the problem of N cities to a problem of (N − 1) cities.

The path [A,D,C,B,E,A], with associated cost of 450 miles, is an example of a possible circuit. The goal description requires a complete circuit with minimum cost. Note that the

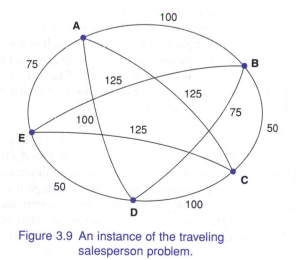

Figure 3.9 An instance of the traveling salesperson problem.

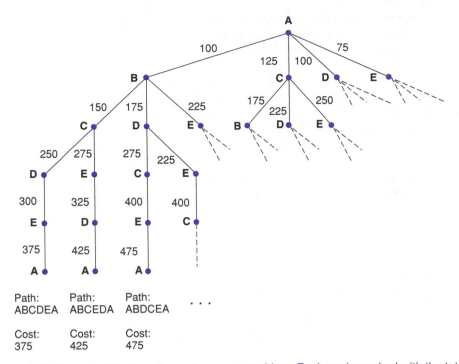

Figure 3.10 Search of the traveling salesperson problem. Each arc is marked with the total weight of all paths from the start node (A) to its endpoint.

goal description is a property of the entire path, rather than of a single state. This is a goal description of type 2 from the definition of state space search.

Figure 3.10 shows one way in which possible solution paths may be generated and compared. Beginning with node A, possible next states are added until all cities are included and the path returns home. The goal is the lowest-cost path.

As Figure 3.10 suggests, the complexity of exhaustive search in the traveling salesperson problem is (N − 1)!, where N is the number of cities in the graph. For 9 cities we may exhaustively try all paths, but for any problem instance of interesting size, for example with 50 cities, simple exhaustive search cannot be performed within a practical length of time. In fact complexity for an N! search grows so fast that very soon the search combinations become intractable.

Several techniques can reduce the search complexity. One is called *branch and bound* (Horowitz and Sahni 1978). Branch and bound generates paths one at a time, keeping track of the best circuit found so far. This value is used as a *bound* on future candidates. As paths are constructed one city at a time, the algorithm examines each partially completed path. If the algorithm determines that the best possible extension to a path, the branch, will have greater cost than the bound, it eliminates that partial path and *all* of its possible extensions. This reduces search considerably but still leaves an exponential number of paths (1.26^N rather than N!).

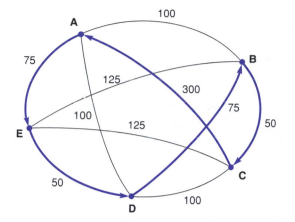

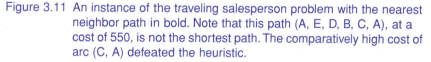

Figure 3.11 An instance of the traveling salesperson problem with the nearest
neighbor path in bold. Note that this path (A, E, D, B, C, A), at a
cost of 550, is not the shortest path. The comparatively high cost of
arc (C, A) defeated the heuristic.

Another strategy for controlling search constructs the path according to the rule "go to
the closest unvisited city." The *nearest neighbor* path through the graph of Figure 3.11 is
[A,E,D,B,C,A], at a cost of 375 miles. This method is highly efficient, as there is only one
path to be tried! The nearest neighbor heuristic is fallible, as graphs exist for which it does
not find the shortest path, see Figure 3.11, but it is a possible compromise when the time
required makes exhaustive search impractical.

Section 3.2 examines strategies for state space search.

3.2 Strategies for State Space Search

3.2.1 Data-Driven and Goal-Driven Search

A state space may be searched in two directions: from the given data of a problem instance
toward a goal or from a goal back to the data.

In *data-driven search*, sometimes called *forward chaining*, the problem solver begins
with the given facts of the problem and a set of legal moves or rules for changing state.
Search proceeds by applying rules to facts to produce new facts, which are in turn used by
the rules to generate more new facts. This process continues until (we hope!) it generates
a path that satisfies the goal condition.

An alternative approach is possible: take the goal that we want to solve. See what rules
or legal moves could be used to generate this goal and determine what conditions must be
true to use them. These conditions become the new goals, or *subgoals*, for the search.
Search continues, working backward through successive subgoals until (we hope!) it works
back to the facts of the problem. This finds the chain of moves or rules leading from data

to a goal, although it does so in backward order. This approach is called *goal-driven* reasoning, or *backward chaining*, and it recalls the simple childhood trick of trying to solve a maze by working back from the finish to the start.

To summarize: data-driven reasoning takes the facts of the problem and applies the rules and legal moves to produce new facts that lead to a goal; goal-driven reasoning focuses on the goal, finds the rules that could produce the goal, and chains backward through successive rules and subgoals to the given facts of the problem.

In the final analysis, both data-driven and goal-driven problem solvers search the same state space graph; however, the order and actual number of states searched can differ. The preferred strategy is determined by the properties of the problem itself. These include the complexity of the rules, the "shape" of the state space, and the nature and availability of the problem data. All of these vary for different problems.

As an example of the effect a search strategy can have on the complexity of search, consider the problem of confirming or denying the statement "I am a descendant of Thomas Jefferson." A solution is a path of direct lineage between the "I" and Thomas Jefferson. This space may be searched in two directions, starting with the "I" and working along ancestor lines to Thomas Jefferson or starting with Thomas Jefferson and working through his descendants.

Some simple assumptions let us estimate the size of the space searched in each direction. Thomas Jefferson was born about 250 years ago; if we assume 25 years per generation, the required path will be about length 10. As each person has exactly two parents, a search back from the "I" would examine on the order of 2^{10} ancestors. A search that worked forward from Thomas Jefferson would examine more states, as people tend to have more than two children (particularly in the eighteenth and nineteenth centuries). If we assume an average of only three children per family, the search would examine on the order of 3^{10} nodes of the family tree. Thus, a search back from the "I" would examine fewer nodes. Note, however, that both directions yield exponential complexity.

The decision to choose between data- and goal-driven search is based on the structure of the problem to be solved. Goal-driven search is suggested if:

1. A goal or hypothesis is given in the problem statement or can easily be formulated. In a mathematics theorem prover, for example, the goal is the theorem to be proved. Many diagnostic systems consider potential diagnoses in a systematic fashion, confirming or eliminating them using goal-driven reasoning.

2. There are a large number of rules that match the facts of the problem and thus produce an increasing number of conclusions or goals. Early selection of a goal can eliminate most of these branches, making goal-driven search more effective in pruning the space (Figure 3.12). In a mathematics theorem prover, for example, the total number of rules used to produce a given theorem is usually much smaller than the number of rules that may be applied to the entire set of axioms.

3. Problem data are not given but must be acquired by the problem solver. In this case, goal-driven search can help guide data acquisition. In a medical diagnosis program, for example, a wide range of diagnostic tests can be applied. Doctors order only those that are necessary to confirm or deny a particular hypothesis.

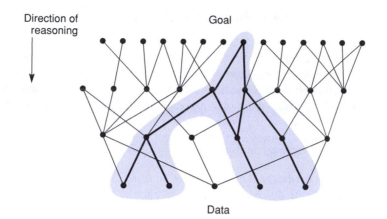

Figure 3.12 State space in which goal-directed search
effectively prunes extraneous search paths.

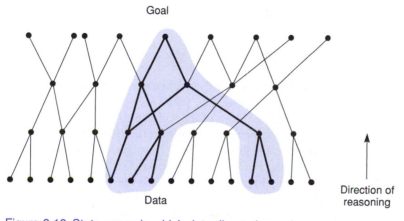

Figure 3.13 State space in which data-directed search prunes
irrelevant data and their consequents and determines
one of a number of possible goals.

Goal-driven search thus uses knowledge of the desired goal to guide the search through relevant rules and eliminate branches of the space.

Data-driven search (Figure 3.13) is appropriate to problems in which:

1. All or most of the data are given in the initial problem statement. Interpretation problems often fit this mold by presenting a collection of data and asking the system to provide a high-level interpretation. Systems that analyze particular data (e.g., the PROSPECTOR or Dipmeter programs, which interpret geological data or

attempt to find what minerals are likely to be found at a site) fit the data-driven approach.

2. There are a large number of potential goals, but there are only a few ways to use the facts and given information of a particular problem instance. The DENDRAL program, an expert system that finds the molecular structure of organic compounds based on their formula, mass spectrographic data, and knowledge of chemistry, is an example of this. For any organic compound, there are an enormous number of possible structures. However, the mass spectrographic data on a compound allow DENDRAL to eliminate all but a few of these.

3. It is difficult to form a goal or hypothesis. In using DENDRAL, for example, little may be known initially about the possible structure of a compound.

Data-driven search uses the knowledge and constraints found in the given data of a problem to guide search along lines known to be true.

To summarize, there is no substitute for careful analysis of the particular problem, considering such issues as the *branching factor* of rule applications (see Chapter 4; on average, how many new states are generated by rule applications in both directions?), availability of data, and ease of determining potential goals.

3.2.2   Implementing Graph Search

In solving a problem using either goal- or data-driven search, a problem solver must find a path from a start state to a goal through the state space graph. The sequence of arcs in this path corresponds to the ordered steps of the solution. If a problem solver were given an oracle or other infallible mechanism for choosing a solution path, search would not be required. The problem solver would move unerringly through the space to the desired goal, constructing the path as it went. Because oracles do not exist for interesting problems, a problem solver must consider different paths through the space until it finds a goal. *Backtracking* is a technique for systematically trying all paths through a state space.

We begin with backtrack because it is one of the first search algorithms computer scientists study, and it has a natural implementation in a stack oriented recursive environment. We will see a simpler version of backtrack in *depth-first search* (Section 3.2.3) which we will build in LISP and PROLOG in Part VI.

Backtracking search begins at the start state and pursues a path until it reaches either a goal or a "dead end." If it finds a goal, it quits and returns the solution path. If it reaches a dead end, it "backtracks" to the most recent node on the path having unexamined siblings and continues down one of these branches, as described in the following recursive rule:

If the present state S does not meet the requirements of the goal description, then generate its first descendant S_{child1}, and apply the backtrack procedure recursively to this node. If backtrack does not find a goal node in the subgraph rooted at S_{child1}, repeat the procedure for its sibling, S_{child2}. This continues until either some descendant of a child is a goal node or all the children have been searched. If none of the children of S leads to a goal, then backtrack "fails back" to the parent of S, where it is applied to the siblings of S, and so on.

The algorithm continues until it finds a goal or exhausts the state space. Figure 3.14 shows the backtrack algorithm applied to a hypothetical state space. The direction of the dashed arrows on the tree indicates the progress of search up and down the space. The number beside each node indicates the order in which it is visited. We now define an algorithm that performs a backtrack, using three lists to keep track of nodes in the state space:

SL, for state list, lists the states in the current path being tried. If a goal is found, SL contains the ordered list of states on the solution path.

NSL, for new state list, contains nodes awaiting evaluation, i.e., nodes whose descendants have not yet been generated and searched.

DE, for dead ends, lists states whose descendants have failed to contain a goal node. If these states are encountered again, they will be detected as elements of DE and eliminated from consideration immediately.

In defining the backtrack algorithm for the general case (a graph rather than a tree), it is necessary to detect multiple occurrences of any state so that it will not be reentered and cause (infinite) loops in the path. This is accomplished by testing each newly generated state for membership in any of these three lists. If a new state belongs to any of these lists, then it has already been visited and may be ignored.

```
function backtrack;
begin
    SL := [Start];  NSL := [Start];  DE := [ ];  CS := Start;            % initialize:
    while NSL π [ ] do                              % while there are states to be tried
        begin
            if CS = goal (or meets goal description)
                then return SL;                     % on success, return list of states in path.
            if CS has no children (excluding nodes already on DE, SL, and NSL)
                then begin
                    while SL is not empty and CS = the first element of SL do
                        begin
                            add CS to DE;                       % record state as dead end
                            remove first element from SL;                       %backtrack
                            remove first element from NSL;
                            CS := first element of NSL;
                        end
                    add CS to SL;
                end
            else begin
                place children of CS (except nodes already on DE, SL, or NSL) on NSL;
                CS := first element of NSL;
                add CS to SL
            end
        end;
        return FAIL;
end.
```

In backtrack, the state currently under consideration is called CS for current state. CS is always equal to the state most recently added to SL and represents the "frontier" of the solution path currently being explored. Inference rules, moves in the game, or other appropriate problem-solving operators are ordered and applied to CS. The result is an ordered set of new states, the children of CS. The first of these children is made the new current state and the rest are placed in order on NSL for future examination. The new current state is added to SL and search continues. If CS has no children, it is removed from SL (this is where the algorithm "backtracks") and any remaining children of its predecessor on SL are examined.

A trace of backtrack on the graph of Figure 3.14 is given by:

Initialize: SL = [A]; NSL = [A]; DE = [ ]; CS = A;

AFTER ITERATION	CS	SL	NSL	DE
0	A	[A]	[A]	[ ]
1	B	[B A]	[B C D A]	[ ]
2	E	[E B A]	[E F B C D A]	[ ]
3	H	[H E B A]	[H I E F B C D A]	[ ]
4	I	[I E B A]	[I E F B C D A]	[H]
5	F	[F B A]	[F B C D A]	[E I H]
6	J	[J F B A]	[J F B C D A]	[E I H]
7	C	[C A]	[C D A]	[B F J E I H]
8	G	[G C A]	[G C D A]	[B F J E I H]

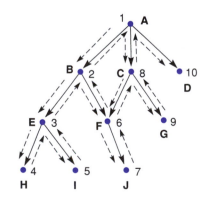

Figure 3.14 Backtracking search of a hypothetical state space space.

As presented here, backtrack implements data-driven search, taking the root as a start state and evaluating its children to search for the goal. The algorithm can be viewed as a goal-driven search by letting the goal be the root of the graph and evaluating descendants back in an attempt to find a start state. If the goal description is of type 2 (see Section 3.1.3), the algorithm must determine a goal state by examining the path on SL.

backtrack is an algorithm for searching state space graphs. The graph search algorithms in the remainder of the text, including depth-first, breadth-first, and best-first search, exploit the ideas used in backtrack, including:

1. The use of a list of unprocessed states (NSL) to allow the algorithm to return (backtrack) to any of these states.

2. A list of "bad" states (DE) to prevent the algorithm from retrying useless paths.

3. A list of nodes (SL) on the current solution path that is returned if a goal is found.

4. Explicit checks for membership of new states in these lists to prevent looping.

The next section introduces search algorithms that, like backtrack, use lists to keep track of states in a search space. These algorithms, including *depth-first*, *breadth-first*, and *best-first* (Chapter 4) search, differ from backtrack in providing a more flexible basis for implementing alternative graph search strategies.

3.2.3   Depth-First and Breadth-First Search

In addition to specifying a search direction (data-driven or goal-driven), a search algorithm must determine the order in which states are examined in the tree or the graph. This section considers two possibilities for the order in which the nodes of the graph are considered: *depth-first* and *breadth-first* search.

Consider the graph represented in Figure 3.15. States are labeled (A, B, C, . . .) so that they can be referred to in the discussion that follows. In depth-first search, when a state is examined, all of its children and their descendants are examined before any of its siblings. Depth-first search goes deeper into the search space whenever this is possible. Only when no further descendants of a state can be found are its siblings considered. Depth-first search examines the states in the graph of Figure 3.15 in the order A, B, E, K, S, L, T, F, M, C, G, N, H, O, P, U, D, I, Q, J, R. The backtrack algorithm of Section 3.2.2 implemented depth-first search.

Breadth-first search, in contrast, explores the space in a level-by-level fashion. Only when there are no more states to be explored at a given level does the algorithm move on to the next level. A breadth-first search of the graph of Figure 3.15 considers the states in the order A, B, C, D, E, F, G, H, I, J, K, L, M, N, O, P, Q, R, S, T, U.

We implement breadth-first search using lists, open and closed, to keep track of progress through the state space. open, like NSL in backtrack, lists states that have been generated but whose children have not been examined. The order in which states are removed from open determines the order of the search. closed records states already examined. closed is the union of the DE and SL lists of the backtrack algorithm.

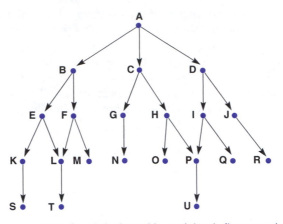

Figure 3.15 Graph for breadth- and depth-first search examples.

```
function breadth_first_search;

begin
    open := [Start];                                          % initialize
    closed := [ ];
    while open π [ ] do                                       % states remain
        begin
            remove leftmost state from open, call it X;
                if X is a goal then return SUCCESS            % goal found
                    else begin
                        generate children of X;
                        put X on closed;
                        discard children of X if already on open or closed;   % loop check
                        put remaining children on right end of open          % queue
                    end
        end
    return FAIL                                               % no states left
end.
```

Child states are generated by inference rules, legal moves of a game, or other state transition operators. Each iteration produces all children of the state X and adds them to open. Note that open is maintained as a *queue*, or first-in-first-out (FIFO) data structure. States are added to the right of the list and removed from the left. This biases search toward the states that have been on open the longest, causing the search to be breadth-first. Child states that have already been discovered (already appear on either open or closed) are discarded. If the algorithm terminates because the condition of the "while" loop is no longer satisfied (open = [ ]) then it has searched the entire graph without finding the desired goal: the search has failed.

A trace of breadth_first_search on the graph of Figure 3.15 follows. Each successive number, 2,3,4, . . . , represents an iteration of the "while" loop. U is the goal state.

1. open = [A]; closed = [ ]
2. open = [B,C,D]; closed = [A]
3. open = [C,D,E,F]; closed = [B,A]
4. open = [D,E,F,G,H]; closed = [C,B,A]
5. open = [E,F,G,H,I,J]; closed = [D,C,B,A]
6. open = [F,G,H,I,J,K,L]; closed = [E,D,C,B,A]
7. open = [G,H,I,J,K,L,M] (as L is already on open); closed = [F,E,D,C,B,A]
8. open = [H,I,J,K,L,M,N]; closed = [G,F,E,D,C,B,A]
9. and so on until either U is found or open = [ ].

Figure 3.16 illustrates the graph of Figure 3.15 after six iterations of breadth_first_search. The states on open and closed are highlighted. States not shaded have not been discovered by the algorithm. Note that open records the states on the "frontier" of the search at any stage and that closed records states already visited.

Because breadth-first search considers every node at each level of the graph before going deeper into the space, all states are first reached along the shortest path from the start state. Breadth-first search is therefore guaranteed to find the shortest path from the start state to the goal. Furthermore, because all states are first found along the shortest path, any states encountered a second time are found along a path of equal or greater length. Because there is no chance that duplicate states were found along a better path, the algorithm simply discards any duplicate states.

It is often useful to keep other information on open and closed besides the names of the states. For example, note that breadth_first_search does not maintain a list of states on the current path to a goal as backtrack did on the list SL; all visited states are kept on closed. If the path is required for a solution, it can be returned by the algorithm. This can be done by storing ancestor information along with each state. A state may be saved along with a record of its parent state, i.e., as a (state, parent) pair. If this is done in the search of Figure 3.15, the contents of open and closed at the fourth iteration would be:

open = [(D,A), (E,B), (F,B), (G,C), (H,C)]; closed = [(C,A), (B,A), (A,nil)]

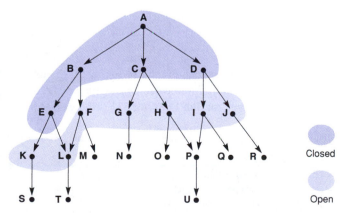

Figure 3.16 Graph of Figure 3.15 at iteration 6 of breadth-first search. States on open and closed are highlighted.

The path (A, B, F) that led from A to F could easily be constructed from this information. When a goal is found, the algorithm may construct the solution path by tracing back along parents from the goal to the start state. Note that state A has a parent of nil, indicating that it is a start state; this stops reconstruction of the path. Because breadth-first search finds each state along the shortest path and retains the first version of each state, this is the shortest path from a start to a goal.

Figure 3.17 shows the states removed from open and examined in a breadth-first search of the graph of the 8-puzzle. As before, arcs correspond to moves of the blank up, to the right, down, and to the left. The number next to each state indicates the order in which it was removed from open. States left on open when the algorithm halted are not shown.

Next, we create a depth-first search algorithm, a simplification of the backtrack algorithm already presented in Section 3.2.3. In this algorithm, the descendant states are added and removed from the *left* end of open: open is maintained as a *stack*, or last-in-first-out (LIFO), structure. The organization of open as a stack directs search toward the most recently generated states, producing a depth-first search order:

```
function depth_first_search;

begin
    open := [Start];                                    % initialize
    closed := [ ];
    while open π [ ] do                                 % states remain
        begin
            remove leftmost state from open, call it X;
            if X is a goal then return SUCCESS          % goal found
                else begin
                    generate children of X;
                    put X on closed;
                    discard children of X if already on open or closed;   % loop check
                    put remaining children on left end of open           % stack
                end
        end;
    return FAIL                                         % no states left
end.
```

A trace of depth_first_search on the graph of Figure 3.15 appears below. Each successive iteration of the "while" loop is indicated by a single line (2, 3, 4, . . .). The initial states of open and closed are given on line 1. Assume U is the goal state.

1. open = [A]; closed = [ ]
2. open = [B,C,D]; closed = [A]
3. open = [E,F,C,D]; closed = [B,A]
4. open = [K,L,F,C,D]; closed = [E,B,A]
5. open = [S,L,F,C,D]; closed = [K,E,B,A]
6. open = [L,F,C,D]; closed = [S,K,E,B,A]
7. open = [T,F,C,D]; closed = [L,S,K,E,B,A]

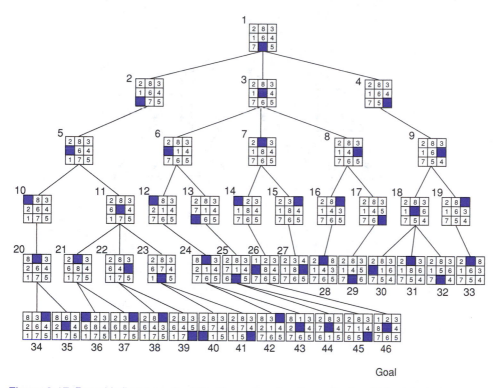

Figure 3.17 Breadth-first search of the 8-puzzle, showing order in which states were removed from open.

8. open = [F,C,D]; closed = [T,L,S,K,E,B,A]
9. open = [M,C,D], (as L is already on closed); closed = [F,T,L,S,K,E,B,A]
10. open = [C,D]; closed = [M,F,T,L,S,K,E,B,A]
11. open = [G,H,D]; closed = [C,M,F,T,L,S,K,E,B,A]

and so on until either U is discovered or open = [ ].

As with breadth_first_search, open lists all states discovered but not yet evaluated (the current "frontier" of the search), and closed records states already considered. Figure 3.18 shows the graph of Figure 3.15 at the sixth iteration of the depth_first_search. The contents of open and closed are highlighted. As with breadth_first_search, the algorithm could store a record of the parent along with each state, allowing the algorithm to reconstruct the path that led from the start state to a goal.

Unlike breadth-first search, a depth-first search is not guaranteed to find the shortest path to a state the first time that state is encountered. Later in the search, a different path may be found to any state. If path length matters in a problem solver, when the algorithm encounters a duplicate state, the algorithm should save the version reached along the shortest path. This could be done by storing each state as a triple: (state, parent,

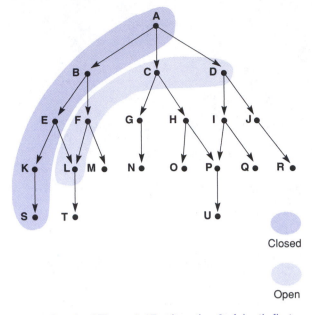

Closed

Open

Figure 3.18 Graph of Figure 3.15 at iteration 6 of depth-first search.
States on open and closed are highlighted.

length_of_path). When children are generated, the value of the path length is simply incremented by one and saved with the child. If a child is reached along multiple paths, this information can be used to retain the best version. This is treated in more detail in the discussion of *algorithm A* in Chapter 4. Note that retaining the best version of a state in a simple depth-first search does not guarantee that a goal will be reached along the shortest path.

Figure 3.19 gives a depth-first search of the 8-puzzle. As noted previously, the space is generated by the four "move blank" rules (up, down, left, and right). The numbers next to the states indicate the order in which they were considered, i.e., removed from open. States left on open when the goal is found are not shown. A depth bound of 5 was imposed on this search to keep it from getting lost deep in the space.

As with choosing between data- and goal-driven search for evaluating a graph, the choice of depth-first or breadth-first search depends on the specific problem being solved. Significant features include the importance of finding the shortest path to a goal, the branching factor of the space, the available compute time and space resources, the average length of paths to a goal node, and whether we want all solutions or only the first solution. In making these decisions, there are advantages and disadvantages for each approach.

Breadth-First Because it always examines all the nodes at level n before proceeding to level n + 1, breadth-first search always finds the shortest path to a goal node. In a problem where it is known that a simple solution exists, this solution will be found. Unfortunately, if there is a bad branching factor, i.e., states have a high average number of descendants,

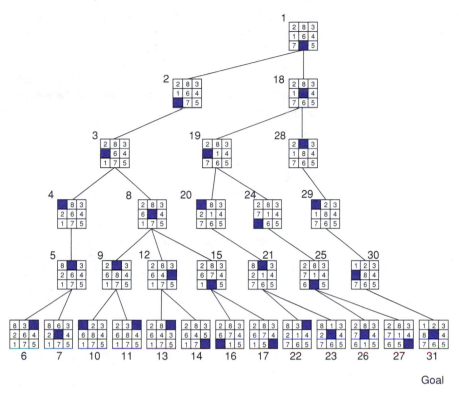

Figure 3.19 Depth-first search of the 8-puzzle with a depth bound of 5.

the combinatorial explosion may prevent the algorithm from finding a solution using the available space. This is due to the fact that all unexpanded nodes for each level of the search must be kept on open. For deep searches, or state spaces with a high branching factor, this can become quite cumbersome.

The space utilization of breadth-first search, measured in terms of the number of states on open, is an exponential function of the length of the path at any time. If each state has an average of B children, the number of states on a given level is B times the number of states on the previous level. This gives B^n states on level n. Breadth-first search would place all of these on open when it begins examining level n. This can be prohibitive if solution paths are long.

Depth-First   Depth-first search gets quickly into a deep search space. If it is known that the solution path will be long, depth-first search will not waste time searching a large number of "shallow" states in the graph. On the other hand, depth-first search can get "lost" deep in a graph, missing shorter paths to a goal or even becoming stuck in an infinitely long path that does not lead to a goal.

Depth-first search is much more efficient for search spaces with many branches because it does not have to keep all the nodes at a given level on the open list. The space usage of depth-first search is a linear function of the length of the path. At each level, open retains only the children of a single state. If a graph has an average of B children per state, this requires a total space usage of B × n states to go n levels deep into the space.

The best answer to the "depth-first versus breadth-first" issue is to examine the problem space carefully and consult experts in the area. In chess, for example, breadth-first search simply is not possible. In simpler games, breadth-first search not only may be possible but also may be the only way to avoid losing.

3.2.4   Depth-First Search with Iterative Deepening

A nice compromise on these trade-offs is to use a depth bound on depth-first search. The depth bound forces a failure on a search path once it gets below a certain level. This causes a breadth-like sweep of the search space at that depth level. When it is known that a solution lies within a certain depth or when time constraints, such as those that occur in an extremely large space like chess, limit the number of states that can be considered; then a depth-first search with a depth bound may be most appropriate. Figure 3.19 showed a depth-first search of the 8-puzzle in which a depth bound of 5 caused the sweep across the space at that depth.

This insight leads to a search algorithm that remedies many of the drawbacks of both depth-first and breadth-first search. *Depth-first iterative deepening* (Korf 1987) performs a depth-first search of the space with a depth bound of 1. If it fails to find a goal, it performs another depth-first search with a depth bound of 2. This continues, increasing the depth bound by one at each iteration. At each iteration, the algorithm performs a complete depth-first search to the current depth bound. No information about the state space is retained between iterations.

Because the algorithm searches the space in a level-by-level fashion, it is guaranteed to find a shortest path to a goal. Because it does only depth-first search at each iteration, the space usage at any level n is B × n, where B is the average number of children of a node.

Interestingly, although it seems as if depth-first iterative deepening would be much less time efficient than either depth-first or breadth-first search, its time complexity is actually of the same order of magnitude as either of these: $O(B^n)$. An intuitive explanation for this seeming paradox is given by Korf (1987):

> Since the number of nodes in a given level of the tree grows exponentially with depth, almost all the time is spent in the deepest level, even though shallower levels are generated an arithmetically increasing number of times.

Unfortunately, all the search strategies discussed in this chapter—depth-first, breadth-first, and depth-first iterative deepening—may be shown to have worst-case exponential time complexity. This is true for all *uninformed* search algorithms. The only approaches to search that reduce this complexity employ heuristics to guide search. *Best-first search* is a search algorithm that is similar to the algorithms for depth- and breadth-first search just presented. However, best-first search orders the states on the open list, the current fringe of the search, according to some measure of their heuristic merit. At each iteration, it considers neither the deepest nor the shallowest but the "best" state. Best-first search is the main topic of Chapter 4.

3.3 Using the State Space to Represent Reasoning with the Predicate Calculus

3.3.1 State Space Description of a Logical System

When we defined state space graphs in Section 3.1, we noted that nodes must be distinguishable from one another, with each node representing some state of the solution process. Predicate calculus can be used as the formal specification language for making these distinctions as well as for mapping the nodes of a graph onto the state space. Furthermore, inference rules can be used to create and describe the arcs between states. In this fashion, problems in the predicate calculus, such as determining whether a particular expression is a logical consequence of a given set of assertions, may be solved using search.

The soundness and completeness of predicate calculus inference rules guarantee the correctness of conclusions derived through this form of graph-based reasoning. This ability to produce a formal proof of the integrity of a solution through the same algorithm that produces the solution is a unique attribute of much artificial intelligence and theorem proving based problem solving.

Although many problems' states, e.g., tic-tac-toe, can be more naturally described by other data structures, such as arrays, the power and generality of logic allow much of AI problem solving to use the predicate calculus descriptions and inference rules. Other AI representations such as rules (Chapter 8), semantic networks, or frames (Chapter 7) employ search strategies similar to those just presented.

EXAMPLE 3.3.1: THE PROPOSITIONAL CALCULUS

The first example of how a set of logical relationships may be viewed as defining a graph is from the propositional calculus. If p, q, r, . . . are propositions, assume the assertions:

$q \rightarrow p$
$r \rightarrow p$
$v \rightarrow q$
$s \rightarrow r$
$t \rightarrow r$
$s \rightarrow u$
s
t

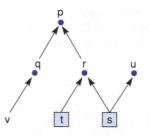

Figure 3.20 State space graph of a set of implications
in the propositional calculus.

From this set of assertions and the inference rule modus ponens, certain propositions (p, r, and u) may be inferred; others (such as v and q) may not be so inferred and indeed do not logically follow from these assertions. The relationship between the initial assertions and these inferences is expressed in the directed graph in Figure 3.20.

In Figure 3.20 the arcs correspond to logical implications ($\rightarrow$). Propositions that are given as true (s and t) correspond to the given data of the problem. Propositions that are logical consequences of this set of assertions correspond to the nodes that may be reached along a directed path from a state representing a true proposition; such a path corresponds to a sequence of applications of modus ponens. For example, the path [s, r, p] corresponds to the sequence of inferences:

s and s $\rightarrow$ r yields r.
r and r $\rightarrow$ p yields p.

Given this representation, determining whether a given proposition is a logical consequence of a set of propositions becomes a problem of finding a path from a boxed node (the start node) to the proposition (the goal node). Thus, the task can be cast as a graph search problem. The search strategy used here is data-driven, because it proceeds from what is known (the true propositions) toward the goal. Alternatively, a goal-directed strategy could be applied to the same state space by starting with the proposition to be proved (the goal) and searching back along arcs to find support for the goal among the true propositions. We can also search this space of inferences in either a depth-first or breadth-first fashion.

3.3.2 And/Or Graphs

In the propositional calculus example of Section 3.3.1, all of the assertions were implications of the form p $\rightarrow$ q. We did not discuss the way in which the logical operators and and or could be represented in such a graph. Expressing the logical relationships defined by these operators requires an extension to the basic graph model known as an *and/or graph*. And/or graphs are an important tool for describing the search spaces generated by many AI problems, including those solved by logical theorem provers and expert systems.

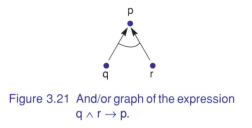

Figure 3.21 And/or graph of the expression
$q \wedge r \rightarrow p$.

In expressions of the form $q \wedge r \rightarrow p$, both q and r must be true for p to be true. In expressions of the form $q \vee r \rightarrow p$, the truth of either q or r is sufficient to prove p is true. Because implications containing disjunctive premises may be written as separate implications, this expression is often written as $q \rightarrow p, r \rightarrow p$. To represent these different relationships graphically, and/or graphs distinguish between and nodes and or nodes. If the premises of an implication are connected by an $\wedge$ operator, they are called and nodes in the graph and the arcs from this node are joined by a curved link. The expression $q \wedge r \rightarrow p$ is represented by the and/or graph of Figure 3.21.

The link connecting the arcs in Figure 3.21 captures the idea that both q and r must be true to prove p. If the premises are connected by an or operator, they are regarded as or nodes in the graph. Arcs from or nodes to their parent node are not so connected (Figure 3.22). This captures the notion that the truth of any one of the premises is independently sufficient to determine the truth of the conclusion.

An and/or graph is actually a specialization of a type of graph known as a *hypergraph*, which connects nodes by sets of arcs rather than by single arcs. A hypergraph is defined as follows:

DEFINITION

HYPERGRAPH

A hypergraph consists of:

N, a set of nodes.

H, a set of hyperarcs defined by ordered pairs in which the first element of the pair is a single node from N and the second element is a subset of N.

An ordinary graph is a special case of hypergraph in which all the sets of descendant nodes have a cardinality of 1.

Hyperarcs are also known as *k-connectors*, where k is the cardinality of the set of descendant nodes. If k = 1, the descendant may be thought of as an or node. If k > 1, the elements of the set of descendants may be thought of as and nodes. In this case, the connector is drawn with individual edges from the parent to each of the descendant nodes; these individual edges are then joined with a curved link as in Figure 3.21.

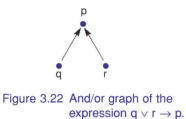

Figure 3.22 And/or graph of the
expression q ∨ r → p.

EXAMPLE 3.3.2: AND/OR GRAPH SEARCH

The second example is also from the propositional calculus but generates a graph that contains both and and or descendants. Assume a situation in the world where the following propositions are true:

a
b
c
a ∧ b → d
a ∧ c → e
b ∧ d → f
f → g
a ∧ e → h

This set of assertions generates the and/or graph in Figure 3.23.

Questions that might be asked (answers deduced by the search of this graph) are:

1.   Is h true?

2.   Is h true if b is no longer true?

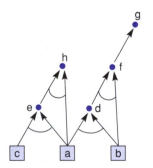

Figure 3.23 And/or graph of a set of propositional
calculus expressions.

3. What is the shortest path (i.e., the shortest sequence of inferences) to show that X (some proposition) is true?

4. Show that the proposition p (note that p is not supported) is false. What does this mean? What would be necessary to achieve this conclusion?

And/or graph search requires only slightly more record keeping than search in regular graphs, an example of which was the backtrack algorithm, previously discussed. The or descendants are checked as they were in backtrack: once a path is found connecting a goal to a start node along or nodes, the problem will be solved. If a path leads to a failure, the algorithm may backtrack and try another branch. In searching and nodes, however, all of the and descendants of a node must be solved (or proved true) to solve the parent node.

In the example of Figure 3.23, a goal-directed strategy for determining the truth of h first attempts to prove both a and e. The truth of a is immediate, but the truth of e requires the truth of both c and a; these are given as true. Once the problem solver has traced all these arcs down to true propositions, the true values are recombined at the and nodes to verify the truth of h.

A data-directed strategy for determining the truth of h, on the other hand, begins with the known facts (c, a, and b) and begins adding new propositions to this set of known facts according to the constraints of the and/or graph. e or d might be the first proposition added to the set of facts. These additions make it possible to infer new facts. This process continues until the desired goal, h, has been proved.

One way of looking at and/or graph search is that the $\land$ operator (hence the and nodes of the graph) indicates a problem decomposition in which the problem is broken into subproblems such that all of the subproblems must be solved to solve the original problem. An $\lor$ operator in the predicate calculus representation of the problem indicates a selection, a point in the problem solution at which a choice may be made between alternative problem-solving paths or strategies, any one of which, if successful, is sufficient to solve the problem.

3.3.3 Further Examples and Applications

EXAMPLE 3.3.3: MACSYMA

One natural example of an and/or graph is a program for symbolically integrating mathematical functions. MACSYMA is a well-known program that is used extensively by mathematicians. The reasoning of MACSYMA can be represented as an and/or graph. In performing integrations, one important class of strategies involves breaking an expression into sub-expressions that may be integrated independently of one another, with the result being combined algebraically into a solution expression. Examples of this strategy include the rule for integration by parts and for decomposing the integral of a sum into the sum of the integrals of the individual terms. These strategies, representing the decomposition of a problem into independent subproblems, can be represented by and nodes in the graph.

Another class of strategies involves the simplification of an expression through various algebraic substitutions. Because any given expression may allow a number of different

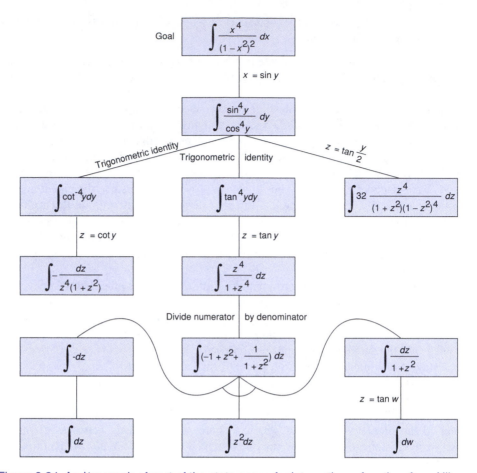

Figure 3.24 And/or graph of part of the state space for integrating a function, from Nilsson (1971).

substitutions, each representing an independent solution strategy, these strategies are represented by or nodes of the graph. Figure 3.24 illustrates the space searched by such a problem solver. The search of this graph is goal-directed, in that it begins with the query "find the integral of a particular function" and searches back to the algebraic expressions that define that integral. Note that this is an example in which goal-directed search is the obvious strategy. It would be practically impossible for a problem solver to determine the algebraic expressions that formed the desired integral without working back from the query.

EXAMPLE 3.3.4: GOAL-DRIVEN AND/OR SEARCH

This example is taken from the predicate calculus and represents a goal-driven graph search where the goal to be proved true in this situation is a predicate calculus expression containing variables. The axioms are the logical descriptions of a relationship between a dog, Fred, and his master, Sam. We assume that a cold day is not a warm day, bypassing issues such as the complexity added by equivalent expressions for predicates, an issue discussed further in Chapters 7 and 13. The facts and rules of this example are given as English sentences followed by their predicate calculus equivalents:

1. Fred is a collie.
    collie(fred).

2. Sam is Fred's master.
    master(fred,sam).

3. The day is Saturday.
    day(saturday).

4. It is cold on Saturday.
    ¬ (warm(saturday)).

5. Fred is trained.
    trained(fred).

6. Spaniels are good dogs and so are trained collies.
    ∀ X[spaniel(X) ∨ (collie(X) ∧ trained(X)) → gooddog(X)].

7. If a dog is a good dog and has a master then he will be with his master.
    ∀ (X,Y,Z) [gooddog(X) ∧ master(X,Y) ∧ location(Y,Z) → location(X,Z)].

8. If it is Saturday and warm, then Sam is at the park.
    (day(saturday) ∧ warm(saturday)) → location(sam,park).

9. If it is Saturday and not warm, then Sam is at the museum.
    (day(saturday) ∧ ¬ (warm(saturday))) → location(sam,museum).

The goal is the expression ∃ X location(fred,X), meaning "where is Fred?" A backward search algorithm examines alternative means of establishing this goal: "if Fred is a good dog and Fred has a master and Fred's master is at a location then Fred is at that location also." The premises of this rule are then examined: what does it mean to be a "good dog," etc.? This process continues, constructing the and/or graph of Figure 3.25.

Let us examine this search in more detail, particularly because it is an example of goal-driven search using the predicate calculus and it illustrates the role of unification in the generation of the search space. The problem to be solved is "where is Fred?" More formally, it may be seen as determining a substitution for the variable X, if such a substitution exists, under which location(fred,X) is a logical consequence of the initial assertions.

When it is desired to determine Fred's location, clauses are examined that have location as their conclusion, the first being clause 7. This conclusion, location(X,Z), is then unified with location(fred, X) by the substitutions {fred/X, X/Z}. The premises of this rule, under the same substitution set, form the and descendants of the top goal:

gooddog(fred) ∧ master(fred,Y) ∧ location(Y,X).

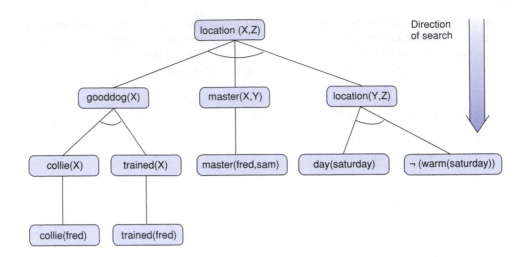

Substitutions = {fred/X, sam/Y, museum/Z}

Figure 3.25 The solution subgraph showing that fred is at the museum.

This expression may be interpreted as meaning that one way to find Fred is to see if Fred is a good dog, find out who Fred's master is, and find out where the master is. The initial goal has thus been replaced by three subgoals. These are and nodes and all of them must be solved.

To solve these subgoals, the problem solver first determines whether Fred is a good dog. This matches the conclusion of clause 6 using the substitution {fred/X}. The premise of clause 6 is the or of two expressions:

spaniel(fred) ∨ (collie(fred) ∧ trained(fred)).

The first of these or nodes is spaniel(fred). The database does not contain this assertion, so the problem solver must assume it is false. The other or node is (collie(fred) ∧ trained(fred)), i.e., is Fred a collie and is Fred trained. Both of these need to be true, which they are by clauses 1 and 5.

This proves that gooddog(fred) is true. The problem solver then examines the second of the premises of clause 7: master(X,Y). Under the substitution {fred/X}, master(X,Y) becomes master(fred,Y), which unifies with the fact (clause 2) of master(fred,sam). This produces the unifying substitution of {sam/Y}, which also gives the value of sam to the third subgoal of clause 7, creating the new goal location(sam,X).

In solving this, assuming the problem solver tries rules in order, the goal location(sam,X) will first unify with the conclusion of clause 7. Note that the same rule is being tried with different bindings for X. Recall (Chapter 2) that X is a "dummy" variable and could have any name (any string beginning with an uppercase letter). Because the extent of the meaning of any variable name is contained within the clause in which it appears, the predicate calculus has no global variables. Another way of saying this is that values of variables are passed to other clauses as parameters and have no fixed (memory) locations. Thus, the multiple occurrences of X in different rules in this example indicate *different* formal parameters (Section 13.3).

In attempting to solve the premises of rule 7 with these new bindings, the problem solver will fail because sam is not a gooddog. Here, the search will backtrack to the goal location(sam,X) and try the next match, the conclusion of rule 8. This will also fail, which will cause another backtrack and a unification with the conclusion of clause 9, at(sam,museum).

Because the premises of clause 9 are supported in the set of assertions (clauses 3 and 4), it follows that the conclusion of 9 is true. This final unification goes all the way back up the tree to finally answer ∃ X location(fred,X) with location(fred, museum).

It is important to examine carefully the nature of the goal-driven search of a graph and compare it with the data-driven search of Example 3.3.2. Further discussion of this issue, including a more rigorous comparison of these two methods of searching a graph, continues in the next example, but is seen in full detail only in the discussion of production systems in Chapter 6 and in the application to expert systems in Part IV. Another point implicit in this example is that the order of clauses affects the order of search. In the example above, the multiple location clauses were tried in order, with backtracking search eliminating those that failed to be proved true.

EXAMPLE 3.3.5: THE FINANCIAL ADVISOR REVISITED

In the last example of Chapter 2 we used predicate calculus to represent a set of rules for giving investment advice. In that example, modus ponens was used to infer a proper investment for a particular individual. We did not discuss the way in which a program might determine the appropriate inferences. This is, of course, a search problem; the present example illustrates one approach to implementing the logic-based financial advisor, using goal-directed, depth-first search with backtracking. The discussion uses the predicates found in Section 2.4; these predicates are not duplicated here.

Assume that the individual has two dependents, $20,000 in savings, and a steady income of $30,000. As discussed in Chapter 2, we can add predicate calculus expressions describing these facts to the set of predicate calculus expressions. Alternatively, the program may begin the search without this information and ask the user to add it as needed. This has the advantage of not requiring data that may not prove necessary for a solution. This approach, often taken in expert systems, is illustrated in this example.

In performing a consultation, the goal is to find an investment; this is represented with the predicate calculus expression ∃ X investment(X), where X in the goal variable we seek to bind. There are three rules (1, 2, and 3) that conclude about investments, because the query will unify with the conclusion of these rules. If we select rule 1 for initial exploration, its premise savings_account(inadequate) becomes the subgoal, i.e., the child node that will be expanded next.

In generating the children of savings_account(inadequate), the only rule that may be applied is rule 5. This produces the and node:

amount_saved(X) ∧ dependents(Y) ∧ ¬ greater(X,minsavings(Y)).

If we attempt to satisfy these in left-to-right order, amount_saved(X) is taken as the first subgoal. Because the system contains no rules that conclude this subgoal, it will query the user. When amount_saved(20000) is added the first subgoal will succeed, with unification substituting 20000 for X. Note that because an and node is being searched, a failure here would eliminate the need to examine the remainder of the expression.

Similarly, the subgoal dependents(Y) leads to a user query, and the response, dependents(2), is added to the logical description. The subgoal matches this expression with the substitution {2/Y}. The search will then evaluate the truth of

¬ greater(X, minsavings(Y)).

This evaluates to false, causing failure of the entire and node. The search then backtracks to the parent node, savings_account(inadequate), and attempts to find an alternative way to prove that node true. This corresponds to the generation of the next child in the search. Because no other rules conclude this subgoal, search fails back to the top-level goal, investment(X). The next rule whose conclusions unify with this goal is rule 2, producing the new subgoals

savings_account(adequate) ∧ income(adequate).

Continuing the search, savings_account(adequate) is proved true as the conclusion of rule 4, and income(adequate) follows as the conclusion of rule 6. Although the details of the remainder of the search will be left to the reader, the and/or graph that is ultimately explored appears in Figure 3.26.

EXAMPLE 3.3.6: AN ENGLISH LANGUAGE PARSER AND SENTENCE GENERATOR

The final example is not from the predicate calculus but consists of a set of rewrite rules for parsing sentences in a subset of English grammar. Rewrite rules take an expression and transform it into another by replacing the pattern on one side of the arrow (↔) with the pattern on the other side. For example, a set of rewrite rules could be defined to change an expression in one language, such as English, into another language (perhaps French or a predicate calculus clause). The rewrite rules given here transform a subset of English sentences into higher level grammatical constructs such as noun phrase, verb phrase, and sentence. These rules are used to *parse* sequences of words, i.e., to determine whether they are well-formed sentences (are grammatically correct or not) and to model the linguistic structure of the sentences.

Five rules for a simple subset of English grammar are:

1. sentence ↔ np vp
   (A sentence is a noun phrase followed by a verb phrase.)

2. np ↔ n
   (A noun phrase is a noun.)

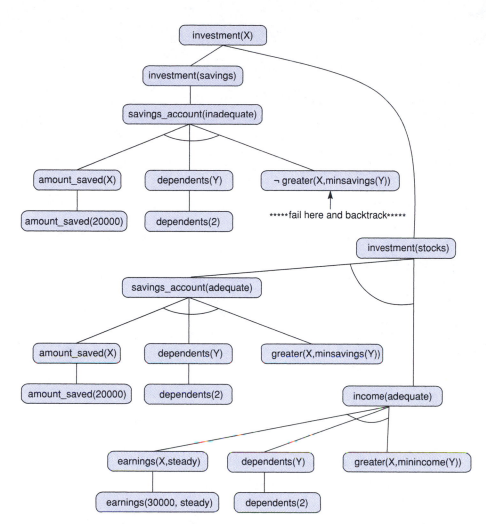

Figure 3.26 And/or graph searched by the financial advisor.

3. np ↔ art n
    (A noun phrase is an article followed by a noun.)

4. vp ↔ v
    (A verb phrase is a verb.)

5. vp ↔ v np
    (A verb phrase is a verb followed by a noun phrase.)

In addition to these grammar rules, a parser needs a dictionary of words in the language. These words are called the *terminals* of the grammar. They are defined by their parts of speech using rewrite rules. In the following "dictionary," "a," "the," "man," "dog," "likes," and "bites" are the terminals of our simple grammar:

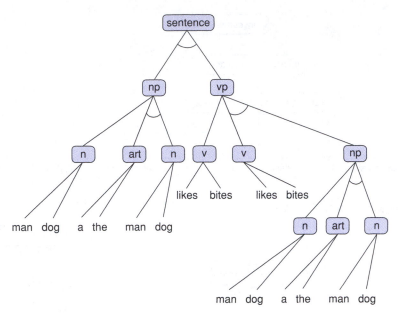

Figure 3.27 And/or graph for the grammar of Example 3.3.6. Some of the nodes (np, art, etc.) have been written more than once to simplify drawing the graph.

6. art $\leftrightarrow$ a

7. art $\leftrightarrow$ the
    ("a" and "the" are articles)

8. n $\leftrightarrow$ man

9. n $\leftrightarrow$ dog
    ("man" and "dog" are nouns)

10. v $\leftrightarrow$ likes

11. v $\leftrightarrow$ bites
    ("likes" and "bites" are verbs)

These rewrite rules define the and/or graph of Figure 3.27. sentence is the root. The elements on the left of a rewrite rule correspond to and nodes in the graph. Multiple rules with the same conclusion form the or nodes. Notice that the leaf or terminal nodes of this graph are the English words in the grammar (hence, they are called *terminals*).

An expression is *well formed* in a grammar if it consists entirely of terminal symbols and there is a series of substitutions in the expression using rewrite rules that reduce it to the sentence symbol. Alternatively, this may be seen as constructing a *parse tree* that has the words of the expression as its leaves and the sentence symbol as its root.

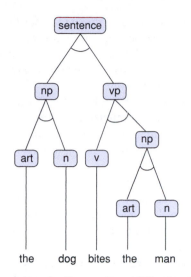

Figure 3.28 Parse tree for the sentence "The dog bites the man."
Note that this is a subtree of the graph of Figure 3.27.

For example, we may parse the sentence the dog bites the man, constructing the parse tree of Figure 3.28. This tree is a subtree of the and/or graph of Figure 3.27 and is constructed by searching this graph. A *data-driven parsing* algorithm would implement this by matching right-hand sides of rewrite rules with patterns in the sentence, trying these matches in the order in which the rules are written. Once a match is found, the part of the expression matching the right-hand side of the rule is replaced by the pattern on the left-hand side. This continues until the sentence is reduced to the symbol sentence (indicating a successful parse) or no more rules can be applied (indicating failure). A trace of the parse of the dog bites the man is:

1. The first rule that will match is 7, rewriting the as art. This yields: art dog bites the man.

2. The next iteration would find a match for 7, yielding art dog bites art man.

3. Rule 8 will fire, producing art dog bites art n.

4. Rule 3 will fire to yield art dog bites np.

5. Rule 9 produces art n bites np.

6. Rule 3 may be applied, giving np bites np.

7. Rule 11 yields np v np.

8. Rule 5 yields np vp.

9. Rule 1 reduces this to sentence, accepting the expression as correct.

The above example implements a data-directed depth-first parse, as it always applies the highest-level rule to the expression; e.g., art n reduces to np before bites reduces to v. Parsing could also be done in a goal-directed fashion, taking sentence as the starting string and finding a series of replacements of patterns that match left-hand sides of rules leading to a series of terminals that match the target sentence.

Parsing is important, not only for natural language (Chapter 14) but also for constructing compilers and interpreters for computer languages (Aho and Ullman 1977). The literature is full of parsing algorithms for all classes of languages. For example, many goal-directed parsing algorithms look ahead in the input stream to determine which rule to apply next.

In this example we have taken a very simple approach of searching the and/or graph in an uninformed fashion. One thing that is interesting in this example is the implementation of the search. This approach of keeping a record of the current expression and trying to match the rules in order is an example of using the *production system* to implement search. This is a major topic of Chapter 6.

Rewrite rules are also used to generate legal sentences according to the specifications of the grammar. Sentences may be generated by a goal-driven search, beginning with sentence as the top-level goal and ending when no more rules can be applied. This produces a string of terminal symbols that is a legal sentence in the grammar. For example:

A sentence is a np followed by a vp (rule 1).

np is replaced by n (rule 2), giving n vp.

man is the first n available (rule 8), giving man vp.

Now np is satisfied and vp is attempted. Rule 3 replaces vp with v, man v.

Rule 10 replaces v with likes.

man likes is found as the first acceptable sentence.

If it is desired to create all acceptable sentences, this search may be systematically repeated until all possibilities are tried and the entire state space has been searched exhaustively. This generates sentences including a man likes, the man likes, and so on. There are 84 correct sentences that are produced by an exhaustive search. These include such semantic anomalies as the man bites the dog.

Parsing and generation can be used together in a variety of ways to handle different problems. For instance, if it is desired to find all sentences to complete the string "the man," then the problem solver may be given an incomplete string the man... . It can work upward in a data-driven fashion to produce the goal of completing the sentence rule (rule 1), where np is replaced by the man, and then work in a goal-driven fashion to determine all possible vps that will complete the sentence. This would create sentences such as the man likes, the man bites the man, and so on. Again, this example deals only with syntactic correctness. The issue of semantics (whether the string has a mapping into some "world" with "truth") is entirely different. Chapter 2 examined the issue of constructing a semantics for expressions in formal logic; for expressions in natural language, the issue is much more difficult and is discussed in Chapter 14.

This last example illustrates the extreme flexibility with which state spaces may be searched. In the next chapter we discuss the use of heuristics to focus search on the smallest possible portion of the state space. Chapter 6 discusses the production system and other formalisms for controlling the application of problem-solving rules as well as other techniques for implementing search in a variety of problems and representation languages.

3.4 Epilogue and References

Chapter 3 introduced the theoretical foundations of state space search, using graph theory to analyze the structure and complexity of problem-solving strategies. In reviewing the basics of graph theory, we showed how it may be used to model problem solving as a search through a graph of problem states. The chapter compared data-driven and goal-driven reasoning and depth-first and breadth-first search.

And/or graphs allow us to apply state space search to the implementation of logical reasoning. The search strategies of Chapter 3 were demonstrated on a number of examples, including the financial advisor introduced in Chapter 2.

Basic graph search is discussed in a number of textbooks on computer algorithms. These include *Introduction to Algorithms* by Thomas Cormen, Charles Leiserson, and Ronald Rivest (1990), *Walls and Mirrors* by Paul Helman and Robert Veroff (1986), *Algorithms* by Robert Sedgewick (1983), and *Fundamentals of Computer Algorithms* by Ellis Horowitz and Sartaj Sahni (1978). Finite automata are presented in Lindenmayer and Rosenberg (1976). More algorithms for and/or search are presented in Chapter 13, Automated Reasoning, and are built in the PROLOG and LISP chapters (15 and 16).

The use of graph search to model intelligent problem solving is presented in *Human Problem Solving* by Alan Newell and Herbert Simon (1972). Artificial intelligence texts that discuss search strategies include Nils Nilsson's *Artificial Intelligence* (1998), Patrick Winston's *Artificial Intelligence* (1992), and *Artificial Intelligence* by Eugene Charniak and Drew McDermott (1985). *Heuristics* by Judea Pearl (1984) presents search algorithms and lays a groundwork for the material we present in Chapter 4. Developing new techniques for graph search are often topics at the annual AI conferences.

3.5 Exercises

1. A Hamiltonian path is a path that uses every node of the graph exactly once. What conditions are necessary for such a path to exist? Is there such a path in the Königsberg map?

2. Give the graph representation for the farmer, wolf, goat, and cabbage problem of Section 15.3 (see Figures 15.1 and 15.2). Let the nodes represent states of the world; e.g., the farmer and the goat are on the west bank and the wolf and cabbage on the east. Discuss the advantages of breadth-first and depth-first for searching this space.

3. Build a finite state acceptor that recognizes all strings of binary digits a) that contain "111", b) that end in "111", c) that contain "111" but not more that three consecutive "1"s.

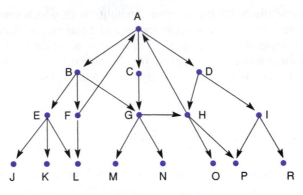

Figure 3.29 A graph to be searched.

4. Give an instance of the traveling salesperson problem for which the nearest-neighbor strategy fails to find an optimal path. Suggest another heuristic for this problem.

5. "Hand run" the **backtrack** algorithm on the graph in Figure 3.29. Begin from state A. Keep track of the successive values of NSL, SL, CS, etc.

6. Implement a backtrack algorithm in a programming language of your choice.

7. Determine whether goal-driven or data-driven search would be preferable for solving each of the following problems. Justify your answer.

   a. Diagnosing mechanical problems in an automobile.
   b. You have met a person who claims to be your distant cousin, with a common ancestor named John Doe. You would like to verify her claim.
   c. Another person claims to be your distant cousin. He does not know the common ancestor's name but knows that it was no more than eight generations back. You would like to either find this ancestor or determine that she did not exist.
   d. A theorem prover for plane geometry.
   e. A program for examining sonar readings and interpreting them, such as telling a large submarine from a small submarine from a whale from a school of fish.
   f. An expert system that will help a human classify plants by species, genus, etc.

8. Choose and justify a choice of breadth- or depth-first search for examples of Exercise 6.

9. Write a backtrack algorithm for and/or graphs.

10. Trace the goal-driven *good-dog* problem of Example 3.3.4 in a data-driven fashion.

11. Give another example of an and/or graph problem and develop part of the search space.

12. Trace a data-driven execution of the *financial advisor* of Example 3.3.5 for the case of an individual with four dependents, $18,000 in the bank, and a steady income of $25,000 per year. Based on a comparison of this problem and the example in the text, suggest a generally "best" strategy for solving the problem.

13. Add rules for adjectives and adverbs to the *English grammar* of Example 3.3.6.

14. Add rules for (multiple) prepositional phrases to the *English grammar* of Example 3.3.6.

15. Add grammar rules to the *English grammar* of Example 3.3.6 that allow complex sentences such as, sentence ↔ sentence AND sentence.

HEURISTIC SEARCH

The task that a symbol system is faced with, then, when it is presented with a problem and a problem space, is to use its limited processing resources to generate possible solutions, one after another, until it finds one that satisfies the problem defining test. If the symbol system had some control over the order in which potential solutions were generated, then it would be desirable to arrange this order of generation so that actual solutions would have a high likelihood of appearing early. A symbol system would exhibit intelligence to the extent that it succeeded in doing this. Intelligence for a system with limited processing resources consists in making wise choices of what to do next. . . .

—NEWELL AND SIMON, 1976, Turing Award Lecture

I been searchin' . . .
Searchin' . . . Oh yeah,
Searchin' every which-a-way . . .

—LIEBER AND STOLLER

4.0 Introduction

George Polya defines *heuristic* as "the study of the methods and rules of discovery and invention" (Polya 1945). This meaning can be traced to the term's Greek root, the verb *eurisco*, which means "I discover." When Archimedes emerged from his famous bath clutching the golden crown, he shouted "Eureka!" meaning "I have found it!". In state space search, *heuristics* are formalized as rules for choosing those branches in a state space that are most likely to lead to an acceptable problem solution.

AI problem solvers employ heuristics in two basic situations:

1. A problem may not have an exact solution because of inherent ambiguities in the problem statement or available data. Medical diagnosis is an example of this. A given set of symptoms may have several possible causes; doctors use heuristics to

choose the most likely diagnosis and formulate a plan of treatment. Vision is another example of an inexact problem. Visual scenes are often ambiguous, allowing multiple interpretations of the connectedness, extent, and orientation of objects. Optical illusions exemplify these ambiguities. Vision systems often use heuristics to select the most likely of several possible interpretations of a scene.

2. A problem may have an exact solution, but the computational cost of finding it may be prohibitive. In many problems (such as chess), state space growth is combinatorially explosive, with the number of possible states increasing exponentially or factorially with the depth of the search. In these cases, exhaustive, *brute-force* search techniques such as depth-first or breadth-first search may fail to find a solution within any practical length of time. Heuristics attack this complexity by guiding the search along the most "promising" path through the space. By eliminating unpromising states and their descendants from consideration, a heuristic algorithm can (its designer hopes) defeat this *combinatorial explosion* and find an acceptable solution.

Unfortunately, like all rules of discovery and invention, heuristics are fallible. A heuristic is only an informed guess of the next step to be taken in solving a problem. It is often based on experience or intuition. Because heuristics use limited information, such as knowledge of the present situation or descriptions of states currently on the open list, they are seldom able to predict the exact behavior of the state space farther along in the search. A heuristic can lead a search algorithm to a suboptimal solution or fail to find any solution at all. This is an inherent limitation of heuristic search. It cannot be eliminated by "better" heuristics or more efficient search algorithms (Garey and Johnson 1979).

Heuristics and the design of algorithms to implement heuristic search have long been a core concern of artificial intelligence. Game playing and theorem proving are two of the oldest applications in artificial intelligence; both of these require heuristics to prune spaces of possible solutions. It is not feasible to examine every inference that can be made in a mathematics domain or every possible move that can be made on a chessboard. Heuristic search is often the only practical answer.

Expert systems research has affirmed the importance of heuristics as an essential component of problem solving. When a human expert solves a problem, he or she examines the available information and makes a decision. The "rules of thumb" that a human expert uses to solve problems efficiently are largely heuristic in nature. These heuristics are extracted and formalized by expert systems designers.

It is useful to think of heuristic search from two perspectives: the heuristic measure and an algorithm that uses heuristics to search the state space. In Section 4.1, we implement heuristics with *hill-climbing* and *dynamic programming* algorithms. In Section 4.2 we present an algorithm for *best-first* search. The design and evaluation of the effectiveness of heuristics is presented in Section 4.3, and game playing heuristics in Section 4.4.

Consider heuristics in the game of tic-tac-toe, Figure II.5. The combinatorics for exhaustive search are high but not insurmountable. Each of the nine first moves has eight possible responses, which in turn have seven continuing moves, and so on. A simple analysis puts the total number of states for exhaustive search at $9 \times 8 \times 7 \times \cdots$ or $9!$.

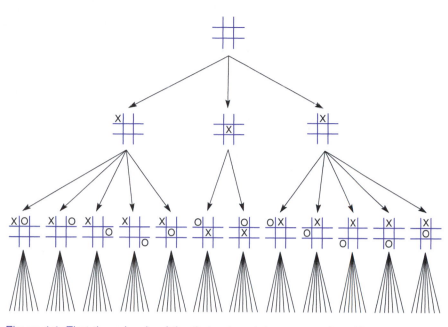

Figure 4.1 First three levels of the tic-tac-toe state space reduced by symmetry.

Symmetry reduction decreases the search space. Many problem configurations are actually equivalent under symmetric operations of the game board. Thus, there are not nine but really three initial moves: to a corner, to the center of a side, and to the center of the grid. Use of symmetry on the second level further reduces the number of paths through the space to $12 \times 7!$, as seen in Figure 4.1. Symmetries in a game space such as this may be described as mathematical invariants, that, when they exist, can often be used to tremendous advantage in reducing search.

A simple heuristic, however, can almost eliminate search entirely: we may move to the state in which X has the most winning opportunities. (The first three states in the tic-tac-toe game are so measured in Figure 4.2.) In case of states with equal numbers of potential wins, take the first such state found. The algorithm then selects and moves to the state with the highest number of opportunities. In this case X takes the center of the grid. Note that not only are the other two alternatives eliminated, but so are all their descendants. Two-thirds of the full space is pruned away with the first move, Figure 4.3.

After the first move, the opponent can choose either of two alternative moves (as seen in Figure 4.3). Whichever is chosen, the heuristic can be applied to the resulting state of the game, again using "most winning opportunities" to select among the possible moves. As search continues, each move evaluates the children of a single node; exhaustive search is not required. Figure 4.3 shows the reduced search after three steps in the game. States are marked with their heuristic values. Although not an exact calculation of search size for

| Three wins through a corner square | Four wins through the center square | Two wins through a side square |

Figure 4.2 The "most wins" heuristic applied to the first children in tic-tac-toe.

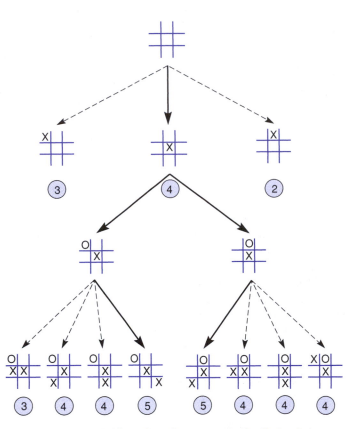

Figure 4.3 Heuristically reduced state space for tic-tac-toe.

this "most wins" strategy for tic-tac-toe, a crude upper bound can be computed by assuming a maximum of five moves in a game with five options per move. In reality, the number of states is smaller, as the board fills and reduces options. This crude bound of 25 states is an improvement of four orders of magnitude over 9!.

The next section presents two algorithms for implementing heuristic search: *hill-climbing* and *dynamic programming*. Section 4.2 uses the priority queue for *best-first* search. In Section 4.3 we discuss theoretical issues related to heuristic search, such as *admissibility* and *monotonicity*. Section 4.4 examines the use of *minimax* and *alpha-beta pruning* to apply heuristics to two-person games. The final section examines the complexity of heuristic search and reemphasizes its essential role in intelligent problem solving.

4.1 Hill-Climbing and Dynamic Programming

4.1.1 Hill-Climbing

The simplest way to implement heuristic search is through a procedure called *hill-climbing* (Pearl 1984). Hill-climbing strategies expand the current state of the search and evaluate its children. The best child is selected for further expansion; neither its siblings nor its parent are retained. Hill-climbing is named for the strategy that might be used by an eager, but blind mountain climber: go uphill along the steepest possible path until you can go no farther up. Because it keeps no history, the algorithm cannot recover from failures of its strategy. An example of hill-climbing in tic-tac-toe was the "take the state with the most possible wins" that we demonstrated in Section 4.0.

A major problem of hill-climbing strategies is their tendency to become stuck at *local maxima*. If they reach a state that has a better evaluation than any of its children, the algorithm halts. If this state is not a goal, but just a local maximum, the algorithm may fail to find the best solution. That is, performance might well improve in a limited setting, but because of the shape of the entire space, it may never reach the overall best. An example of local maxima in games occurs in the 8-puzzle. Often, in order to move a particular tile to its destination, other tiles already in goal position need be moved out. This is necessary to solve the puzzle but temporarily worsens the board state. Because "better" need not be "best" in an absolute sense, search methods without backtracking or some other recovery mechanism are unable to distinguish between local and global maxima.

Figure 4.4 is an example of the local maximum dilemma. Suppose, exploring this search space, we arrive at state X, wanting to maximize state values. The evaluations of X's children, grandchildren, and great grandchildren demonstrate that hill-climbing can get confused even with multiple level look ahead. There are methods for getting around this problem, such as randomly perturbing the evaluation function, but in general there is no way of guaranteeing optimal performance with hill-climbing techniques. Samuel's (1959) checker program offers an interesting variant of the hill-climbing algorithm.

Samuel's program was exceptional for its time, 1959, particularly given the limitations of the 1950s computers. Not only did Samuel's program apply heuristic search to checker playing, but it also implemented algorithms for optimal use of limited memory, as well as a simple form of learning. Indeed, it pioneered many of the techniques still used in game-playing and machine learning programs.

Samuel's program evaluated board states with a weighted sum of several different heuristic measures:

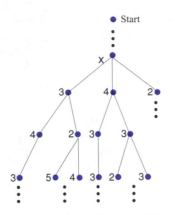

Figure 4.4 The local maximum problem for hill-climbing with 3-level look ahead.

$$\sum_i a_i x_i$$

The x_i in this sum represented features of the game board such as piece advantage, piece location, control of center board, opportunities to sacrifice pieces for advantage, and even a calculation of moments of inertia of one player's pieces about an axis of the board. The a_i coefficients of these x_i were specially tuned weights that tried to model the importance of that factor in the overall board evaluation. Thus, if piece advantage was more important than control of the center, the piece advantage coefficient would reflect this.

Samuel's program would look ahead in the search space the desired number of levels or *plies* (usually imposed by space and/or time limitations of the computer) and evaluate all the states at that level with the evaluation polynomial. Using a variation on *minimax* (Section 4.3), it propagated these values back up the graph. The checker player would then move to the best state; after the opponent's move, the process would be repeated for the new board state.

If the evaluation polynomial led to a losing series of moves, the program adjusted its coefficients in an attempt to improve performance. Evaluations with large coefficients were given most of the blame for losses and had their weights decreased, while smaller weights were increased to give these evaluations more influence. If the program won, the opposite was done. The program trained by playing either against a human partner or against another version of itself.

Samuel's program thus took a hill-climbing approach to learning, attempting to improve performance through local improvements on the evaluation polynomial. Samuel's checker player was able to improve its performance until it played a very good game of checkers. Samual addressed some of the limitations of hill-climbing by checking the effectiveness of the individual weighted heuristic measures, and replacing the less effective. The program also retained certain interesting limitations. For example, because of a limited global strategy, it was vulnerable to evaluation functions leading to traps. The learning component of the program was also vulnerable to inconsistencies in opponent's play; for example, if the opponent used widely varying strategies, or simply played foolishly, the weights on the evaluation polynomial might begin to take on "random" values, leading to an overall degradation of performance.

4.1.2   Dynamic Programming

Dynamic programming (DP) is sometimes called the *forward-backward*, or, when using probabilities, the *Viterbi* algorithm. Created by Richard Bellman (1956), dynamic programming addresses the issue of restricted memory search in problems composed of multiple interacting and interrelated subproblems. DP keeps track of and reuses subproblems already searched and solved within the solution of the larger problem. An example of this would be the reuse the subseries solutions within the solution of the Fibonacci series. The technique of subproblem caching for reuse is sometimes called *memoizing* partial subgoal solutions. The result is an important algorithm often used for string matching, spell checking, and related areas in natural language processing (see Sections 9.4 and 14.4).

We demonstrate dynamic programming using two examples, both from text processing; first, finding an optimum global alignment of two strings of characters and, second, finding the minimum edit difference between two strings of characters. Suppose we wanted to find the best possible alignment for the characters in the strings BAADDCABDDA and BBADCBA. One optimal alignment, among several possible, would be:

BAADDCABDDA
BBADC B A

Dynamic programming requires a data structure to keep track of the subproblems related to the state currently being processed. We use an array. The size of the dimensions of this array, because of initialization requirements, is one more than the length of each string, in our example 12 by 8, as in Figure 4.5. The value of each row-column element of

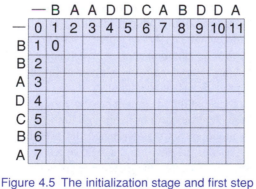

Figure 4.5 The initialization stage and first step
in completing the array for character
alignment using dynamic programming.

	—	B	A	A	D	D	C	A	B	D	D	A
—	0	1	2	3	4	5	6	7	8	9	10	11
B	1	0	1	2	3	4	5	6	7	8	9	10
B	2	1	2	3	4	5	6	7	6	7	8	9
A	3	2	1	2	3	4	5	6	7	8	9	8
D	4	3	2	3	2	3	4	5	6	7	8	9
C	5	4	3	4	3	4	3	4	5	6	7	8
B	6	5	6	5	4	5	4	5	4	5	6	7
A	7	6	5	4	5	6	5	4	5	6	7	6

Figure 4.6 The completed array reflecting the maximum alignment information for the strings.

the array reflects the global alignment success to that point in the matching process. There are three possible costs for the current state: if a character is shifted along in the shorter string for better possible alignment, the cost is 1 and is recorded by the array's *column* score. If a new character is inserted, the cost is 1 and reflected in the array's *row* score. If the characters to be aligned are different, shift and insert, the cost is 2; or if they are identical the cost is 0; this is reflected in the array's *diagonal*. Figure 4.5 shows initialization, the increasing +1s in the first row and column reflect the continued shifting or insertion of characters to the "_" or empty string.

In the *forward* stage of the dynamic programming algorithm, we fill the array from the upper left corner by considering the partial matching successes to the current point of the solution. That is, the value of the intersection of row x and column y, (x, y), is a function (for the minimum alignment problem, the minimum cost) of one of the three values in row x − 1 column y, row x − 1 column y − 1, or row x column y − 1. These three array locations hold the alignment information *up to* the present point of the solution. If there is a match of characters at location (x, y) add 0 to the value at location (x − 1, y − 1); if there is no match add 2 (for shift and insert). We add 1 by either shifting the shorter character string (add to the previous value of column y) or inserting a character (add to the previous value of row x). Continuing this approach produces the filled array of Figure 4.6. It can be observed that the minimum match usually takes place close to the "diagonal" of the array; only when strings have few or no common characters is it necessary to complete the array.

Once the array is filled, we begin the *backward* stage of the algorithm. That is, from the best alignment count, we produce a specific alignment of the characters (often one of several possible). We begin this process at the maximum row by column value, in our example the 6 in row 7 column 12. From there we move back through the array, at each step selecting one of the immediate state's predecessors that produced the present state from the *forward* stage of the solution, whether it is the previous diagonal or row or column that produced the state. Whenever there is a forced decreasing difference, as in the 6 and 5 at the beginning of the trace back, we select the previous diagonal, as that is where the match came from; otherwise we use the value of the preceding row or column. The trace back of Figure 4.7, one of several possible, produces the optimal string alignment of the previous page.

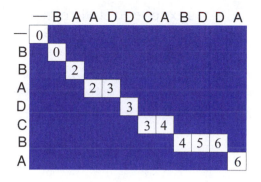

Figure 4.7 A completed backward component of the dynamic programming example giving one (of several possible) string alignments.

In the second example of dynamic programming we consider the idea of the *minimum edit difference* between two strings. If we were building an intelligent spelling checker, for example, we might want to determine what words from our set of correctly spelled words best approximate a certain unrecognized string of characters. A similar approach could be used to determine what known spoken words most closely matched a particular string of phonemes. The next example of establishing a systematic "distance" between two strings of characters is adapted from Jurafsky and Martin (2000).

Suppose you produce an unrecognized string of characters. The task of the spell checker is to produce an ordered list of the most likely words from the dictionary that you meant to type. The question is then, how can a difference be measured between pairs of strings of characters, the string you typed and the character strings in the dictionary. For your string, we want to produce an ordered list of possibly correct words in the dictionary. For each of these words, the source, we want a numerical measure of how "different" each word is from your string.

A *minimum edit difference* between two strings can be (arbitrarily) specified as the number of character insertions, deletions, and replacements necessary to turn the first string, the source, into the second string, the target. This is sometimes called the *Levenshtein distance* (Jurafsky and Martin 2000). We now implement a dynamic programming search for determining the minimum edit difference between two strings of characters. We let intention be the source string and execution be the target. The edit cost for transforming the first string to the second is 1 for a character insertion or deletion and 2 for a replacement (a deletion plus an insertion). We want to determine a minimum cost difference between these two strings.

Our array for subgoals will again be one character longer than each of the strings, in this case 10 by 10. The initialization is as in Figure 4.8 (a sequence of insertions is necessary, starting at the null string, to make either string resemble the other. The array location (2, 2) is 2, because a replacement (or delete plus insert) is required to turn an i into an e.

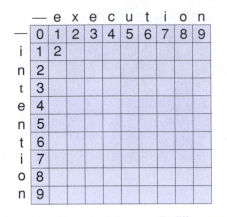

Figure 4.8 Initialization of minimum edit difference matrix between *intention* and *execution* (adapted from Jurafsky and Martin 2000).

Figure 4.9 gives the full result of applying the dynamic programming algorithm to transform intention into execution. The value at each location (x, y) in the array is the cost of the minimum editing to that point plus the (minimum) cost of either an insertion, deletion, or replacement. Thus the cost of (x, y) is the minimum of the cost of (x − 1, y) plus cost of insertion, or cost (x − 1, y − 1) plus cost of replacement, or cost of (x, y − 1) plus the deletion cost. Pseudocode for this algorithm is a function taking the two strings (a source and a target) and their lengths and returning the minimum edit difference cost:

```
function dynamic (source, sl, target, tl) return cost (i, j);
```

```
create array cost(sl + 1, tl + 1)
cost (0,0) := 0                                                          % initialize
for i := 1 to sl + 1 do
     for j := 1 to tl + 1 do
          cost (i, j) := min [ cost (i − 1, j) + insertion cost target_{i−1}      % add 1
                              cost (i − 1, j − 1) + replace cost source_{j−1} target_{i−1}  % add 2
                              cost(i, j − 1) + delete cost source_{j−1}]          % add 1
```

Using the results (bold) in Figure 4.9, the following edits will translate intention into execution with total edit cost of 8:

intention
ntention   delete i, cost 1
etention   replace n with e, cost 2
exention   replace t with x, cost 2
exenution   insert u, cost 1
execution   replace n with c, cost 2

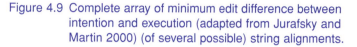

	—	e	x	e	c	u	t	i	o	n
—	0	1	2	3	4	5	6	7	8	9
i	1	2	3	4	5	6	7	8	9	10
n	2	3	4	5	6	7	8	9	10	11
t	3	4	5	6	7	8	9	10	11	12
e	4	5	6	5	6	7	8	9	10	11
n	5	6	7	6	7	8	9	10	11	12
t	6	7	8	7	8	9	8	9	10	11
i	7	8	9	8	9	10	9	8	9	10
o	8	9	10	9	10	11	10	9	8	9
n	9	10	11	10	11	12	11	10	9	8

Figure 4.9 Complete array of minimum edit difference between intention and execution (adapted from Jurafsky and Martin 2000) (of several possible) string alignments.

In the spell check situation of proposing a cost-based ordered list of words for replacing an unrecognized string, the backward segment of the dynamic programming algorithm is not needed. Once the minimum edit measure is calculated for the set of related strings a prioritized order of alternatives is proposed from which the user chooses an appropriate string.

The justification for dynamic programming is the cost of time/space in computation. Dynamic programming, as seen in our two examples, has cost of n^2, where n is the length of the largest string; the cost in the worse case is n^3, if other related subproblems need to be considered (other row/column values) to determine the current state. Exhaustive search for comparing two strings is exponential, costing between 2^n and 3^n.

There are a number of obvious heuristics that can be used to prune the search in dynamic programming. First, useful solutions will usually lie around the upper left to lower right diagonal of the array; this leads to ignoring development of array extremes. Second, it can be useful to prune the search as it evolves, e.g., for edit distances passing a certain threshold, cut that solution path or even abandon the whole problem, i.e., the source string will be so distant from the target string of characters as to be useless. There is also a stochastic approach to the pattern comparison problem we will see in Section 5.3.

4.2 The Best-First Search Algorithm

4.2.1 Implementing Best-First Search

In spite of their limitations, algorithms such as backtrack, hill climbing, and dynamic programming can be used effectively if their evaluation functions are sufficiently informative to avoid local maxima, dead ends, and related anomalies in a search space. In general, however, use of heuristic search requires a more flexible algorithm: this is provided by *best-first search*, where, with a priority queue, recovery from these situations is possible.

Like the depth-first and breadth-first search algorithms of Chapter 3, best-first search uses lists to maintain states: open to keep track of the current fringe of the search and closed to record states already visited. An added step in the algorithm orders the states on open according to some heuristic estimate of their "closeness" to a goal. Thus, each iteration of the loop considers the most "promising" state on the open list. The pseudo-code for the function best-first search appears below.

```
function best_first_search;

begin
    open := [Start];                                      % initialize
    closed := [ ];
    while open ≠ [ ] do                                   % states remain
        begin
            remove the leftmost state from open, call it X;
            if X = goal then return the path from Start to X
            else begin
                    generate children of X;
                    for each child of X do
                    case
                        the child is not on open or closed:
                            begin
                                assign the child a heuristic value;
                                add the child to open
                            end;
                        the child is already on open:
                            if the child was reached by a shorter path
                            then give the state on open the shorter path
                        the child is already on closed:
                            if the child was reached by a shorter path then
                                begin
                                    remove the state from closed;
                                    add the child to open
                                end;
                    end;                                   % case
                    put X on closed;
                    re-order states on open by heuristic merit (best leftmost)
                end;
    return FAIL                                            % open is empty
    end.
```

At each iteration, best_first_search removes the first element from the open list. If it meets the goal conditions, the algorithm returns the solution path that led to the goal. Note that each state retains ancestor information to determine if it had previously been reached by a shorter path and to allow the algorithm to return the final solution path. (See Section 3.2.3.)

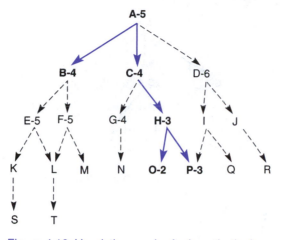

Figure 4.10 Heuristic search of a hypothetical state space.

If the first element on open is not a goal, the algorithm applies all matching production rules or operators to generate its descendants. If a child state is already on open or closed, the algorithm checks to make sure that the state records the shorter of the two partial solution paths. Duplicate states are not retained. By updating the ancestor history of nodes on open and closed when they are rediscovered, the algorithm is more likely to find a shorter path to a goal.

best_first_search then applies a heuristic evaluation to the states on open, and the list is sorted according to the heuristic values of those states. This brings the "best" states to the front of open. Note that because these estimates are heuristic in nature, the next state to be examined may be from any level of the state space. When open is maintained as a sorted list, it is often referred to as a *priority queue*.

Figure 4.9 shows a hypothetical state space with heuristic evaluations attached to some of its states. The states with attached evaluations are those actually generated in best_first_search. The states expanded by the heuristic search algorithm are indicated in bold; note that it does not search all of the space. The goal of best-first search is to find the goal state by looking at as few states as possible; the more *informed* (Section 4.2.3) the heuristic, the fewer states are processed in finding the goal.

A trace of the execution of best_first_search on this graph appears below. Suppose P is the goal state in the graph of Figure 4.10. Because P is the goal, states along the path to P tend to have low heuristic values. The heuristic is fallible: the state O has a lower value than the goal itself and is examined first. Unlike hill climbing, which does not maintain a priority queue for the selection of "next" states, the algorithm recovers from this error and finds the correct goal.

1.   open = [A5]; closed = [ ]

2.   evaluate A5; open = [B4,C4,D6]; closed = [A5]

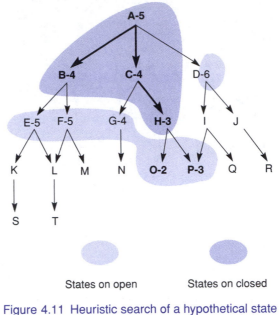

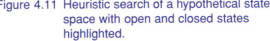

States on open   States on closed

Figure 4.11 Heuristic search of a hypothetical state
space with open and closed states
highlighted.

3.   evaluate B4; open = [C4,E5,F5,D6]; closed = [B4,A5]

4.   evaluate C4; open = [H3,G4,E5,F5,D6]; closed = [C4,B4,A5]

5.   evaluate H3; open = [O2,P3,G4,E5,F5,D6]; closed = [H3,C4,B4,A5]

6.   evaluate O2; open = [P3,G4,E5,F5,D6]; closed = [O2,H3,C4,B4,A5]

7.   evaluate P3; the solution is found!

Figure 4.11 shows the space as it appears after the fifth iteration of the while loop. The states contained in open and closed are indicated. open records the current frontier of the search and closed records states already considered. Note that the frontier of the search is highly uneven, reflecting the opportunistic nature of best-first search.

The best-first search algorithm always selects the most promising state on open for further expansion. However, as it is using a heuristic that may prove erroneous, it does not abandon all the other states but maintains them on open. In the event a heuristic leads the search down a path that proves incorrect, the algorithm will eventually retrieve some previously generated, "next best" state from open and shift its focus to another part of the space. In the example of Figure 4.10, after the children of state B were found to have poor heuristic evaluations, the search shifted its focus to state C. The children of B were kept on open in case the algorithm needed to return to them later. In best_first_search, as in the algorithms of Chapter 3, the open list allows backtracking from paths that fail to produce a goal.

4.2.2   Implementing Heuristic Evaluation Functions

We now evaluate the performance of several different heuristics for solving the 8-puzzle. Figure 4.12 shows a start and goal state for the 8-puzzle, along with the first three states generated in the search.

The simplest heuristic counts the tiles out of place in each state when it is compared with the goal. This is intuitively appealing, because it would seem that, all else being equal, the state that had fewest tiles out of place is probably closer to the desired goal and would be the best to examine next.

However, this heuristic does not use all of the information available in a board configuration, because it does not take into account the distance the tiles must be moved. A "better" heuristic would sum all the distances by which the tiles are out of place, one for each square a tile must be moved to reach its position in the goal state.

Both of these heuristics can be criticized for failing to acknowledge the difficulty of tile reversals. That is, if two tiles are next to each other and the goal requires their being in opposite locations, it takes (many) more than two moves to put them back in place, as the tiles must "go around" each other (Figure 4.13).

A heuristic that takes this into account multiplies a small number (2, for example) times each direct tile reversal (where two adjacent tiles must be exchanged to be in the order of the goal). Figure 4.14 shows the result of applying each of these three heuristics to the three child states of Figure 4.12.

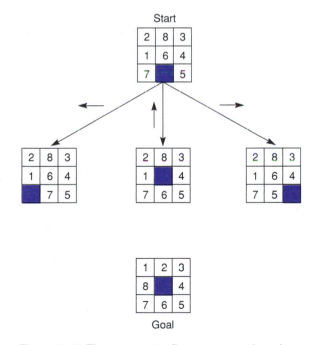

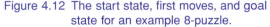

Figure 4.12 The start state, first moves, and goal
state for an example 8-puzzle.

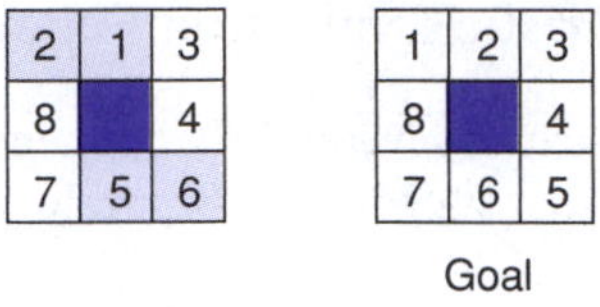

Figure 4.13 An 8-puzzle state with a goal and two
reversals: 1 and 2, 5 and 6.

In Figure 4.14's summary of evaluation functions, the sum of distances heuristic does indeed seem to provide a more accurate estimate of the work to be done than the simple count of the number of tiles out of place. Also, the tile reversal heuristic fails to distinguish between these states, giving each an evaluation of 0. Although it is an intuitively appealing heuristic, it breaks down since none of these states have any direct reversals. A fourth heuristic, which may overcome the limitations of the tile reversal heuristic, adds the sum of the distances the tiles are out of place and 2 times the number of direct reversals.

This example illustrates the difficulty of devising good heuristics. Our goal is to use the limited information available in a single state descriptor to make intelligent choices. Each of the heuristics proposed above ignores some critical bit of information and is subject to improvement. The design of good heuristics is an empirical problem; judgment and intuition help, but the final measure of a heuristic must be its actual performance on problem instances.

If two states have the same or nearly the same heuristic evaluations, it is generally preferable to examine the state that is nearest to the root state of the graph. This state will have a greater probability of being on the *shortest* path to the goal. The distance from the

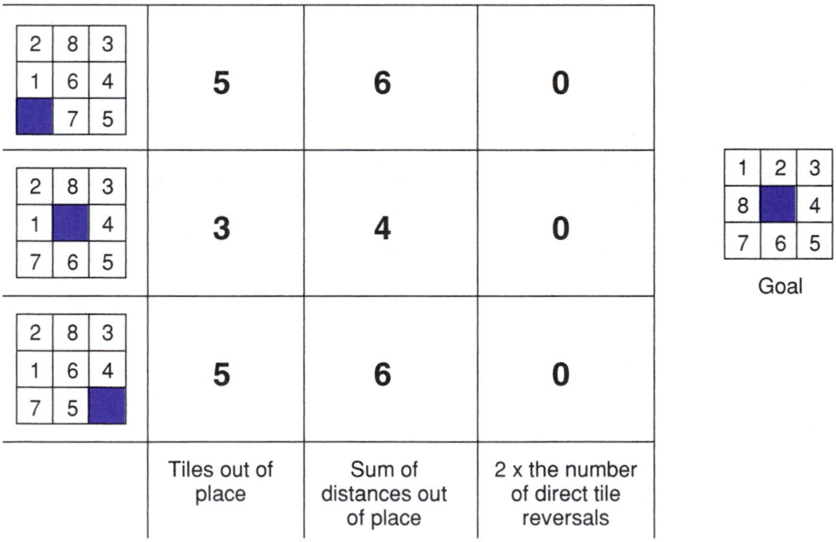

State	Tiles out of place	Sum of distances out of place	2 x the number of direct tile reversals
2 8 3 / 1 6 4 / _ 7 5	5	6	0
2 8 3 / 1 _ 4 / 7 6 5	3	4	0
2 8 3 / 1 6 4 / 7 5 _	5	6	0

Goal: 1 2 3 / 8 _ 4 / 7 6 5

Figure 4.14 Three heuristics applied to states in the 8-puzzle.

starting state to its descendants can be measured by maintaining a depth count for each state. This count is 0 for the beginning state and is incremented by 1 for each level of the search. This depth measure can be added to the heuristic evaluation of each state to bias search in favor of states found shallower in the graph.

This makes our evaluation function, f, the sum of two components:

$$f(n) = g(n) + h(n)$$

where g(n) measures the actual length of the path from any state n to the start state and h(n) is a heuristic estimate of the distance from state n to a goal.

In the 8-puzzle, for example, we can let h(n) be the number of tiles out of place. When this evaluation is applied to each of the child states in Figure 4.12, their f values are 6, 4, and 6, respectively, see Figure 4.15.

The full best-first search of the 8-puzzle graph, using f as defined above, appears in Figure 4.16. Each state is labeled with a letter and its heuristic weight, f(n) = g(n) + h(n). The number at the top of each state indicates the order in which it was taken off the open list. Some states (h, g, b, d, n, k, and i) are not so numbered, because they were still on open when the algorithm terminated.

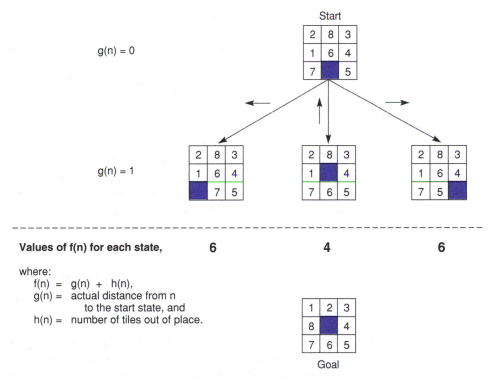

Figure 4.15 The heuristic f applied to states in the 8-puzzle.

The successive stages of open and closed that generate this graph are:

1. open = [a4];
   closed = [ ]

2. open = [c4, b6, d6];
   closed = [a4]

3. open = [e5, f5, b6, d6, g6];
   closed = [a4, c4]

4. open = [f5, h6, b6, d6, g6, I7];
   closed = [a4, c4, e5]

5. open = [j5, h6, b6, d6, g6, k7, I7];
   closed = [a4, c4, e5, f5]

6. open = [l5, h6, b6, d6, g6, k7, I7];
   closed = [a4, c4, e5, f5, j5]

7. open = [m5, h6, b6, d6, g6, n7, k7, I7];
   closed = [a4, c4, e5, f5, j5, l5]

8. success, m = goal!

In step 3, both e and f have a heuristic of 5. State e is examined first, producing children, h and i. Although h, the child of e, has the same number of tiles out of place as f, it is one level deeper in the space. The depth measure, g(n), causes the algorithm to select f for evaluation in step 4. The algorithm goes back to the shallower state and continues to the goal. The state space graph at this stage of the search, with open and closed highlighted, appears in Figure 4.17. Notice the opportunistic nature of best-first search.

In effect, the g(n) component of the evaluation function gives the search more of a breadth-first flavor. This prevents it from being misled by an erroneous evaluation: if a heuristic continuously returns "good" evaluations for states along a path that fails to reach a goal, the g value will grow to dominate h and force search back to a shorter solution path. This guarantees that the algorithm will not become permanently lost, descending an infinite branch. Section 4.3 examines the conditions under which best-first search using this evaluation function can actually be guaranteed to produce the shortest path to a goal.

To summarize:

1. Operations on states generate children of the state currently under examination.

2. Each new state is checked to see whether it has occurred before (is on either open or closed), thereby preventing loops.

3. Each state n is given an f value equal to the sum of its depth in the search space g(n) and a heuristic estimate of its distance to a goal h(n). The h value guides search toward heuristically promising states while the g value prevents search from persisting indefinitely on a fruitless path.

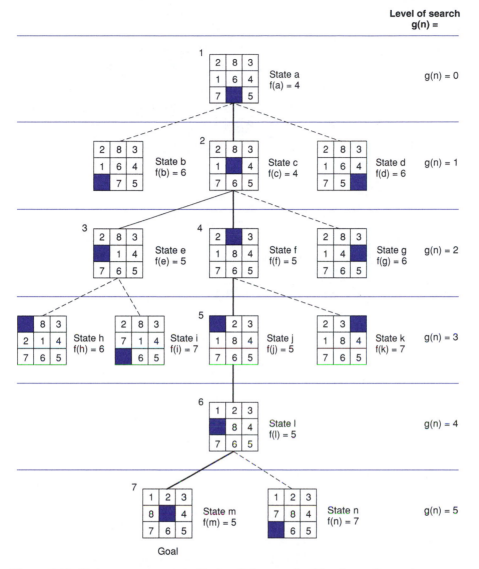

Figure 4.16 State space generated in heuristic search of the 8-puzzle graph.

4. States on open are sorted by their f values. By keeping all states on open until they are examined or a goal is found, the algorithm recovers from dead ends.

5. As an implementation point, the algorithm's efficiency can be improved through maintenance of the open and closed lists, perhaps as *heaps* or *leftist trees*.

Best-first search is a general algorithm for heuristically searching any state space graph (as were the breadth- and depth-first algorithms presented earlier). It is equally applicable

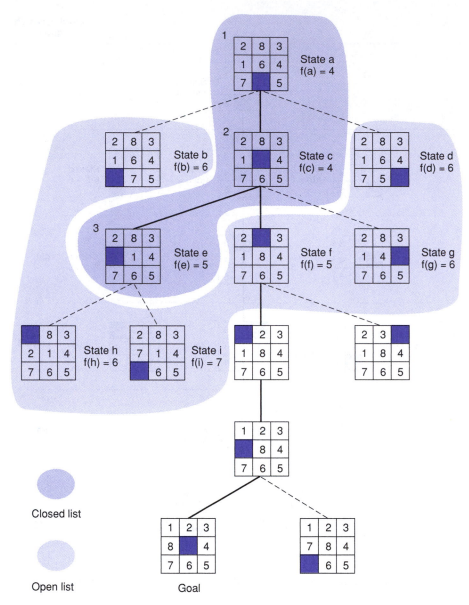

Figure 4.17 open and closed as they appear after the third iteration of heuristic search.

to data- and goal-driven searches and supports a variety of heuristic evaluation functions. It will continue (Section 4.3) to provide a basis for examining the behavior of heuristic search. Because of its generality, best-first search can be used with a variety of heuristics, ranging from subjective estimates of state's "goodness" to sophisticated measures based on the probability of a state leading to a goal. Bayesian statistical measures (Chapters 5 and 8) offer an important example of this approach.

Another interesting approach to implementing heuristics is the use of confidence measures by expert systems to weigh the results of a rule. When human experts employ a heuristic, they are usually able to give some estimate of their confidence in its conclusions. Expert systems employ *confidence measures* to select the conclusions with the highest likelihood of success. States with extremely low confidences can be eliminated entirely. This approach to heuristic search is examined in the next section.

4.2.3   Heuristic Search and Expert Systems

Simple games such as the 8-puzzle are ideal vehicles for exploring the design and behavior of heuristic search algorithms for a number of reasons:

1. The search spaces are large enough to require heuristic pruning.

2. Most games are complex enough to suggest a rich variety of heuristic evaluations for comparison and analysis.

3. Games generally do not involve complex representational issues. A single node of the state space is just a board description and usually can be captured in a straightforward fashion. This allows researchers to focus on the behavior of the heuristic, rather than the problems of knowledge representation.

4. Because each node of the state space has a common representation (e.g., a board description), a single heuristic may be applied throughout the search space. This contrasts with systems such as the financial advisor, where each node represents a different subgoal with its own distinct description.

More realistic problems greatly complicate the implementation and analysis of heuristic search by requiring multiple heuristics to deal with different situations in the problem space. However, the insights gained from simple games generalize to problems such as those found in expert systems applications, planning, intelligent control, and machine learning. Unlike the 8-puzzle, a single heuristic may not apply to each state in these domains. Instead, situation specific problem-solving heuristics are encoded in the syntax and content of individual problem solving operators. Each solution step incorporates its own heuristic that determines when it should be applied; the pattern matcher matches the appropriate operation (heuristic) with the relevant state in the space.

EXAMPLE 4.2.1: THE FINANCIAL ADVISOR, REVISITED

The use of heuristic measures to guide search is a general approach in AI. Consider again the financial advisor problem of Chapters 2 and 3, where the knowledge base was treated as a set of logical implications, whose conclusions are either true or false. In actuality, these rules are highly heuristic in nature. For example, one rule states that an individual with adequate savings and income should invest in stocks:

savings_account(adequate) ∧ income(adequate) ⇒ investment(stocks).

In reality, it is possible that such an individual may prefer the added security of a combination strategy or even that of placing all investment money in savings. Thus, the rule is a heuristic, and the problem solver should try to account for this uncertainty. We could take additional factors, such as the age of the investor and the long-term prospects for security and advancement in the investor's profession, into account to make the rules more informed and capable of finer distinctions. However, this does not change the fundamentally heuristic nature of financial advice.

One way in which expert systems have addressed this issue is to attach a numeric weight (called a *confidence measure* or *certainty factor*) to the conclusion of each rule. This measures the confidence that may be placed in their conclusions.

Each rule conclusion is given a confidence measure, a real number between −1 and 1, with 1 corresponding to certainty (true) and −1 to a definite value of false. Values in between reflect varying confidence in the conclusion. For example, the preceding rule may be given a confidence of, say, 0.8, reflecting a small possibility that it may not be correct. Other conclusions may be drawn with different confidence weights:

savings_account(adequate) ∧ income(adequate) ⇒ investment(stocks)
   with confidence = 0.8.

savings_account(adequate) ∧ income(adequate) ⇒ investment(combination)
   with confidence = 0.5.

savings_account(adequate) ∧ income(adequate) ⇒ investment(savings)
   with confidence = 0.1.

These rules reflect the common investment advice that, although an individual with adequate savings and income would be most strongly advised to invest in stocks, there is some possibility that a combination strategy should be pursued and a slight chance that they may want to continue investing in savings. Heuristic search algorithms can use these certainty factors in a number of ways. For example, the results of all applicable rules could be produced along with their associated confidences. This exhaustive search of all possibilities may be appropriate in domains such as medicine. Alternatively, the program might return only the result with the strongest confidence value, if alternative solutions are not of interest. This can allow the program to ignore other rules, radically pruning the search space. A more conservative pruning strategy could ignore rules that draw a conclusion with a confidence less than a certain value, 0.2 for example.

A number of important issues must be addressed in using confidence measures to weight rule conclusions. What does it really mean to have a "numeric confidence measure"? For example, how are the confidences handled if the conclusion of one rule is used as the premise of others? How are confidences combined in the event that more than one rule draws the same conclusion? How are the proper confidence measures assigned to rules in the first place? These issues are discussed in more detail in Chapter 8.

4.3 Admissibility, Monotonicity, and Informedness

We may evaluate the behavior of heuristics along a number of dimensions. For instance, we may not only desire a solution but also may require the algorithm to find the shortest path to the goal. This could be important when an application might have an excessive cost for extra solution steps, such as planning a path for an autonomous robot through a dangerous environment. Heuristics that find the shortest path to a goal whenever it exists are said to be *admissible*. In other applications a minimal solution path might not be as important as overall problem-solving efficiency.

We may want to ask whether any better heuristics are available. In what sense is one heuristic "better" than another? This is the *informedness* of a heuristic.

When a state is discovered by using heuristic search, is there any guarantee that the same state won't be found later in the search at a cheaper cost (with a shorter path from the start state)? This is the property of *monotonicity*. The answers to these and other questions related to the effectiveness of heuristics make up the content of this section.

4.3.1 Admissibility Measures

A search algorithm is *admissible* if it is guaranteed to find a minimal path to a solution whenever such a path exists. Breadth-first search is an admissible search strategy. Because it looks at every state at level n of the graph before considering any state at the level n + 1, any goal nodes are found along the shortest possible path. Unfortunately, breadth-first search is often too inefficient for practical use.

Using the evaluation function f(n) = g(n) + h(n) that was introduced in the last section, we may characterize a class of admissible heuristic search strategies. If n is a node in the state space graph, g(n) measures the depth at which that state has been found in the graph, and h(n) is the heuristic estimate of the distance from n to a goal. In this sense f(n) estimates the total cost of the path from the start state through n to the goal state. In determining the properties of admissible heuristics, we define an evaluation function f*:

$$f^*(n) = g^*(n) + h^*(n)$$

where g*(n) is the cost of the *shortest* path from the start node to node n and h* returns the *actual* cost of the shortest path from n to the goal. It follows that f*(n) is the actual cost of the optimal path from a start node to a goal node that passes through node n.

As we will see, when we employ best_first_search with the evaluation function f*, the resulting search strategy is admissible. Although *oracles* such as f* do not exist for most real problems, we would like the evaluation function f to be a close estimate of f*. In algorithm A, g(n), the cost of the current path to state n, is a reasonable estimate of g*, but they may not be equal: g(n) ≥ g*(n). These are equal only if the graph search has discovered the optimal path to state n.

Similarly, we replace h*(n) with h(n), a heuristic estimate of the minimal cost to a goal state. Although we usually may not compute h*, it is often possible to determine whether or not the heuristic estimate, h(n), is bounded from above, i.e., is always less than or equal to the actual cost of a minimal path, h*(n). If algorithm A uses an evaluation function f in which h(n) ≤ h*(n), it is called *algorithm A**.

DEFINITION

ALGORITHM A, ADMISSIBILITY, ALGORITHM A*

Consider the evaluation function $f(n) = g(n) + h(n)$, where

> n is any state encountered in the search.
>
> g(n) is the cost of n from the start state.
>
> h(n) is the heuristic estimate of the cost of going from n to a goal.

If this evaluation function is used with the best_first_search algorithm of Section 4.1, the result is called *algorithm A*.

A search algorithm is *admissible* if, for any graph, it always terminates in the optimal solution path whenever a path from the start to a goal state exists.

If algorithm A is used with an evaluation function in which h(n) is less than or equal to the cost of the minimal path from n to the goal, the resulting search algorithm is called *algorithm* A* (pronounced "A STAR").

It is now possible to state a property of A* algorithms:

> All A* algorithms are admissible.

The admissibility of A* algorithms is a theorem. An exercise at the end of the chapter gives directions for developing its proof (see also Nilsson 1980, p 76–78). The theorem says that any A* algorithm, i.e., one that uses a heuristic h(n) such that h(n) ≤ h*(n) for all n, is guaranteed to find the minimal path from n to the goal, if such a path exists.

Note that breadth-first search may be characterized as an A* algorithm in which f(n) = g(n) + 0. The decision for considering a state is based solely on its distance from the start state. We will show (Section 4.3.3) that the set of nodes considered by an A* algorithm is a subset of the states examined in breadth-first search.

Several heuristics from the 8-puzzle provide examples of A* algorithms. Although we may not be able to compute the value of h*(n) for the 8-puzzle, we may determine when a heuristic is bounded from above by the actual cost of the shortest path to a goal.

For instance, the heuristic of counting the number of tiles not in the goal position is certainly less than or equal to the number of moves required to move them to their goal position. Thus, this heuristic is admissible and guarantees an optimal (or shortest) solution path. The sum of the direct distances of tiles out of place is also less than or equal to the minimum actual path. Using small multipliers for direct tile reversals gives an admissible heuristic.

This approach to proving admissibility of 8-puzzle heuristics may be applied to any heuristic search problem. Even though the actual cost of the shortest path to a goal may not always be computed, we can often prove that a heuristic is bounded from above by this value. When this can be done, the resulting search will terminate in the discovery of the shortest path to the goal, when such a path exists.

4.3.2 Monotonicity

Recall that the definition of A* algorithms did not require that $g(n) = g^*(n)$. This means that admissible heuristics may initially reach non-goal states along a suboptimal path, as long as the algorithm eventually finds an optimal path to all states on the path to a goal. It is natural to ask if there are heuristics that are "locally admissible," i.e., that consistently find the minimal path to each state they encounter in the search. This property is called *monotonicity*.

DEFINITION

MONOTONICITY

A heuristic function h is monotone if

1. For all states n_i and n_j, where n_j is a descendant of n_i,

    $$h(n_i) - h(n_j) \leq cost(n_i, n_j),$$

    where $cost(n_i, n_j)$ is the actual cost (in number of moves) of going from state n_i to n_j.

2. The heuristic evaluation of the goal state is zero, or $h(Goal) = 0$.

One way of describing the monotone property is that the search space is everywhere locally consistent with the heuristic employed. The difference between the heuristic measure for a state and any one of its successors is bound by the actual cost of going between that state and its successor. This is to say that the heuristic is everywhere admissible, reaching each state along the shortest path from its ancestors.

If the graph search algorithm for best-first search is used with a monotonic heuristic, an important step may be omitted. Because the heuristic finds the shortest path to any state the first time that state is discovered, when a state is encountered a second time, it is not necessary to check whether the new path is shorter. It won't be! This allows any state that is rediscovered in the space to be dropped immediately without updating the path information retained on open or closed.

When using a monotonic heuristic, as the search moves through the space, the heuristic measure for each state n is replaced by the actual cost for generating that piece of the path to n. Because the actual cost is equal to or larger than the heuristic in each instance, f will not decrease; i.e., f is monotonically nondecreasing (hence the name).

A simple argument can show that any monotonic heuristic is admissible. This argument considers any path in the space as a sequence of states $s_1, s_2, ..., s_g$, where s_1 is the start state and s_g is the goal. For the sequence of moves in this arbitrarily selected path:

s_1 to s_2	$h(s_1) - h(s_2) \leq cost(s_1, s_2)$	by monotone property
s_2 to s_3	$h(s_2) - h(s_3) \leq cost(s_2, s_3)$	by monotone property
s_3 to s_4	$h(s_3) - h(s_4) \leq cost(s_3, s_4)$	by monotone property
.	. . .	by monotone property
.	. . .	by monotone property
s_{g-1} to s_g	$h(s_{g-1}) - h(s_g) \leq cost(s_{g-1}, s_g)$	by monotone property

Summing each column and using the monotone property of $h(s_g) = 0$:

path s_1 to s_g $h(s_1) \leq cost(s_1, s_g)$

This means that monotone heuristic h is A* and admissible. It is left as an exercise whether the admissibility property of a heuristic implies monotonicity.

4.3.3   When One Heuristic Is Better: More Informed Heuristics

The final issue of this subsection compares two heuristics' ability to find the minimal path. An interesting case occurs when the heuristics are A*.

> **DEFINITION**
>
> **INFORMEDNESS**
>
> For two A* heuristics h_1 and h_2, if $h_1(n) \leq h_2(n)$, for all states n in the search space, heuristic h_2 is said to be *more informed* than h_1.

We can use this definition to compare the heuristics proposed for solving the 8-puzzle. As pointed out previously, breadth-first search is equivalent to the A* algorithm with heuristic h_1 such that $h_1(x) = 0$ for all states x. This is, trivially, less than h*. We have also shown that h_2, the number of tiles out of place with respect to the goal state, is a lower bound for h*. In this case $h_1 \leq h_2 \leq h^*$. It follows that the "number of tiles out of place" heuristic is more informed than breadth-first search. Figure 4.18 compares the spaces searched by these two heuristics. Both h_1 and h_2 find the optimal path, but h_2 evaluates many fewer states in the process.

Similarly, we can argue that the heuristic that calculates the sum of the direct distances by which all the tiles are out of place is again more informed than the calculation of the number of tiles that are out of place with respect to the goal state, and indeed this is the case. One can visualize a sequence of search spaces, each smaller than the previous one, converging on the direct optimal path solution.

If a heuristic h_2 is more informed than h_1, then the set of states examined by h_2 is a subset of those expanded by h_1. This can be verified by assuming the opposite (that there is at least one state expanded by h_2 and not by h_1). But since h_2 is more informed than h_1, for all n, $h_2(n) \leq h_1(n)$, and both are bounded above by h*, our assumption is contradictory.

In general, then, the more informed an A* algorithm, the less of the space it needs to expand to get the optimal solution. We must be careful, however, that the computations

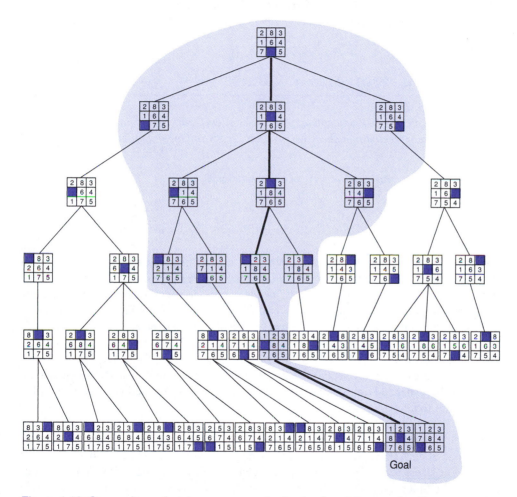

Figure 4.18 Comparison of state space searched using heuristic search with space searched by breadth-first search. The portion of the graph searched heuristically is shaded. The optimal solution path is in bold. Heuristic used is f(n) = g(n) + h(n) where h(n) is tiles out of place.

necessary to employ the more informed heuristic are not so inefficient as to offset the gains from reducing the number of states searched.

Computer chess programs provide an interesting example of this trade-off. One school of thought uses simple heuristics and relies on computer speed to search deeply into the search space. These programs often use specialized hardware for state evaluation to increase the depth of the search. Another school relies on more sophisticated heuristics to reduce the number of board states searched. These heuristics include calculations of piece advantages, control of board geography, possible attack strategies, passed pawns, and so on. Calculation of heuristics itself may involve exponential complexity (an issue discussed in Section 4.5). Since the total time for the first 40 moves of the game is limited, it is important to optimize this trade-off between search and heuristic evaluation. The optimal blend of search and heuristics remains an open empirical question in computer chess.

4.4 Using Heuristics in Games

At that time two opposing concepts of the game called forth commentary and discussion. The foremost players distinguished two principal types of Game, the formal and the psychological . . .

—HERMANN HESSE, "*Magister Ludi*" (The Glass Bead Game)

4.4.1 The Minimax Procedure on Exhaustively Searchable Graphs

Games have always been an important application area for heuristic algorithms. Two-person games are more complicated than simple puzzles because of the existence of a "hostile" and essentially unpredictable opponent. Thus, they provide some interesting opportunities for developing heuristics, as well as greater difficulties in developing search algorithms.

First we consider games whose state space is small enough to be exhaustively searched; here the problem is systematically searching the space of possible moves and counter-moves by the opponent. Then we look at games in which it is either impossible or undesirable to exhaustively search the game graph. Because only a portion of the state space can be generated and searched, the game player must use heuristics to guide play along a path to a winning state.

We first consider a variant of the game *nim*, whose state space may be exhaustively searched. To play this game, a number of tokens are placed on a table between the two opponents; at each move, the player must divide a pile of tokens into two nonempty piles of different sizes. Thus, 6 tokens may be divided into piles of 5 and 1 or 4 and 2, but not 3 and 3. The first player who can no longer make a move loses the game. For a reasonable number of tokens, the state space can be exhaustively searched. Figure 4.19 illustrates the space for a game with 7 tokens.

In playing games whose state space may be exhaustively delineated, the primary difficulty is in accounting for the actions of the opponent. A simple way to handle this

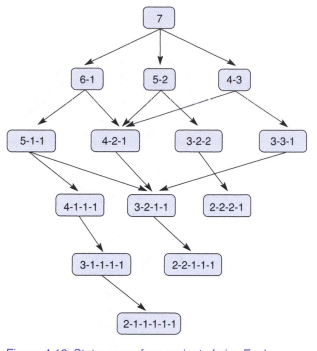

Figure 4.19 State space for a variant of nim. Each
state partitions the seven matches
into one or more piles.

assumes that your opponent uses the same knowledge of the state space as you use and
applies that knowledge in a consistent effort to win the game. Although this assumption
has its limitations (which are discussed in Section 4.4.2), it provides a reasonable basis
for predicting an opponent's behavior. *Minimax* searches the game space under this
assumption.

The opponents in a game are referred to as MIN and MAX. Although this is partly for
historical reasons, the significance of these names is straightforward: MAX represents the
player trying to win, or to MAXimize her advantage. MIN is the opponent who attempts
to MINimize MAX's score. We assume that MIN uses the same information and always
attempts to move to a state that is worst for MAX.

In implementing minimax, we label each level in the search space according to whose
move it is at that point in the game, MIN or MAX. In the example of Figure 4.20, MIN is
allowed to move first. Each leaf node is given a value of 1 or 0, depending on whether it is
a win for MAX or for MIN. Minimax propagates these values up the graph through
successive parent nodes according to the rule:

If the parent state is a MAX node, give it the maximum value among its children.

If the parent is a MIN node, give it the minimum value of its children.

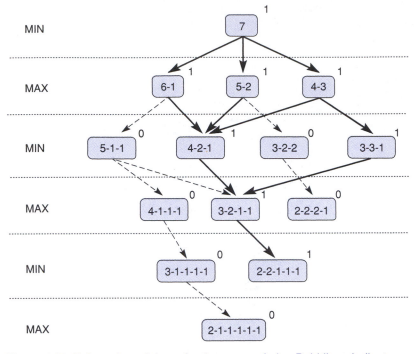

Figure 4.20 Exhaustive minimax for the game of nim. Bold lines indicate forced win for MAX. Each node is marked with its derived value (0 or 1) under minimax.

The value that is thus assigned to each state indicates the value of the best state that this player can hope to achieve (assuming the opponent plays as predicted by the minimax algorithm). These derived values are used to choose among possible moves. The result of applying minimax to the state space graph for nim appears in Figure 4.20.

The values of the leaf nodes are propagated up the graph using minimax. Because all of MIN's possible first moves lead to nodes with a derived value of 1, the second player, MAX, always can force the game to a win, regardless of MIN's first move. MIN could win only if MAX played foolishly. In Figure 4.20, MIN may choose any of the first move alternatives, with the resulting win paths for MAX in bold arrows.

Although there are games where it is possible to search the state space exhaustively, most interesting games do not. We examine fixed depth search next.

4.4.2 Minimaxing to Fixed Ply Depth

In applying minimax to more complicated games, it is seldom possible to expand the state space graph out to the leaf nodes. Instead, the state space is searched to a predefined number of levels, as determined by available resources of time and memory. This strategy is called an n-*ply look-ahead*, where n is the number of levels explored. As the leaves of this subgraph are not final states of the game, it is not possible to give them values that reflect a win or a loss. Instead, each node is given a value according to some heuristic evaluation function. The value that is propagated back to the root node is not an indication of whether or not a win can be achieved (as in the previous example) but is simply the heuristic value of the best state that can be reached in n moves from the root. Look-ahead increases the power of a heuristic by allowing it to be applied over a greater area of the state space. Minimax consolidates these separate evaluations for the ancestor state.

In a game of conflict, each player attempts to overcome the other, so many game heuristics directly measure the advantage of one player over another. In checkers or chess, piece advantage is important, so a simple heuristic might take the difference in the number of pieces belonging to MAX and MIN and try to maximize the difference between these piece measures. A more sophisticated strategy might assign different values to the pieces, depending on their value (e.g., queen vs. pawn or king vs. ordinary checker) or location on the board. Most games provide limitless opportunities for designing heuristics.

Game graphs are searched by level, or *ply*. As we saw in Figure 4.20, MAX and MIN alternately select moves. Each move by a player defines a new ply of the graph. Game playing programs typically look ahead a fixed ply depth, often determined by the space/time limitations of the computer. The states on that ply are measured heuristically and the values are propagated back up the graph using minimax. The search algorithm then uses these *derived values* to select among possible next moves.

After assigning an evaluation to each state on the selected ply, the program propagates a value up to each parent state. If the parent is on a MIN level, the minimum value of the children is backed up. If the parent is a MAX node, minimax assigns it the maximum value of its children.

Maximizing for MAX parents and minimizing for MIN, the values go back up the graph to the children of the current state. These values are then used by the current state to select among its children. Figure 4.21 shows minimax on a hypothetical state space with a four-ply look-ahead.

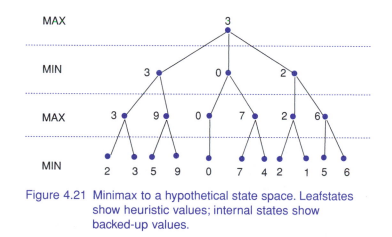

Figure 4.21 Minimax to a hypothetical state space. Leafstates show heuristic values; internal states show backed-up values.

We can make several final points about the minimax procedure. First, and most important, evaluations to any (previously decided) fixed ply depth may be seriously misleading. When a heuristic is applied with limited look-ahead, it is possible the depth of the look-ahead may not detect that a heuristically promising path leads to a bad situation later in the game. If your opponent in chess offers a rook as a lure to take your queen, and the evaluation only looks ahead to the ply where the rook is offered, the evaluation is going to be biased toward this state. Unfortunately, selection of the state may cause the entire game to be lost! This is referred to as the *horizon effect*. It is usually countered by searching several plies deeper from states that look exceptionally good. This selective deepening of search in important areas will not make the horizon effect go away, however. The search must stop somewhere and will be blind to states beyond that point.

There is another effect that occurs in minimaxing on the basis of heuristic evaluations. The evaluations that take place very deep in the space can be biased by their very depth (Pearl 1984). In the same way that the average of products differs from the product of averages, the estimate of minimax (which is what we desire) is different from the minimax of estimates (which is what we are doing). In this sense, deeper search with evaluation and minimax normally does, but need not always, mean better search. Further discussion of these issues and possible remedies may be found in Pearl (1984).

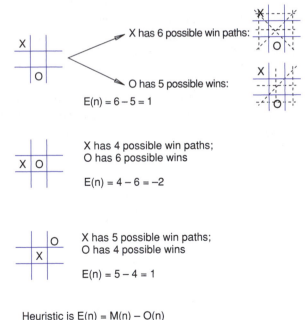

Heuristic is $E(n) = M(n) - O(n)$
where $M(n)$ is the total of My possible winning lines
$O(n)$ is total of Opponent's possible winning lines
$E(n)$ is the total Evaluation for state n

Figure 4.22 Heuristic measuring conflict applied to states of tic-tac-toe.

In concluding the discussion of minimax, we present an application to tic-tac-toe (Section 4.0), adapted from Nilsson (1980). A slightly more complex heuristic is used, one that attempts to measure the conflict in the game. The heuristic takes a state that is to be measured, counts all winning lines open to MAX, and then subtracts the total number of winning lines open to MIN. The search attempts to maximize this difference. If a state is a forced win for MAX, it is evaluated as $+\infty$; a forced win for MIN, as $-\infty$. Figure 4.22 shows this heuristic applied to several sample states.

Figures 4.23, 4.24, and 4.25 demonstrate the heuristic of Figure 4.22 in a two-ply minimax. These figures show the heuristic evaluation, minimax backup, and MAX's move, with some type of tiebreaker applied to moves of equal value, from Nilsson (1971).

4.4.3   The Alpha-Beta Procedure

Straight minimax requires a two-pass analysis of the search space, the first to descend to the ply depth and there apply the heuristic and the second to propagate values back up the tree. Minimax pursues all branches in the space, including many that could be ignored or pruned by a more intelligent algorithm. Researchers in game playing developed a class of search techniques called *alpha-beta* pruning, first proposed in the late 1950s (Newell and Simon 1976), to improve search efficiency in two-person games (Pearl 1984).

The idea for alpha-beta search is simple: rather than searching the entire space to the ply depth, alpha-beta search proceeds in a depth-first fashion. Two values, called *alpha* and *beta*, are created during the search. The alpha value, associated with MAX nodes, can never decrease, and the beta value, associated with MIN nodes, can never increase. Suppose a MAX node's alpha value is 6. Then MAX need not consider any backed-up value less than

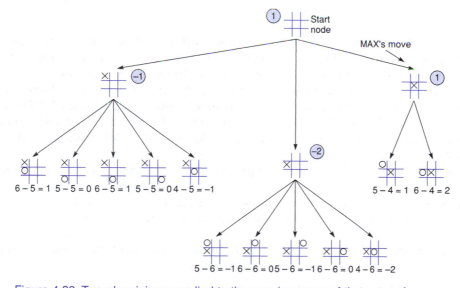

Figure 4.23 Two-ply minimax applied to the opening move of tic-tac-toe, from Nilsson (1971).

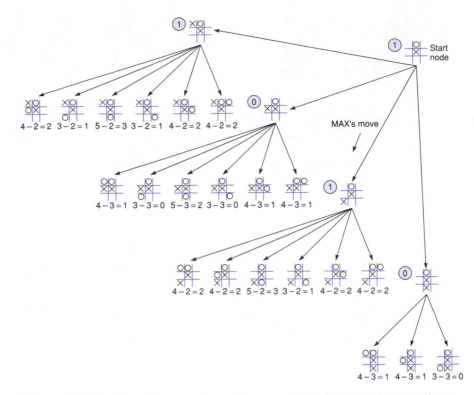

Figure 4.24 Two-ply minimax and one of two possible MAX second moves, from Nilsson (1971).

or equal to 6 that is associated with any MIN node below it. Alpha is the worst that MAX can "score" given that MIN will also do its "best." Similarly, if MIN has beta value 6, it does not need to consider any MAX node below that has a value of 6 or more.

To begin alpha-beta search, we descend to full ply depth in a depth-first fashion and apply our heuristic evaluation to a state and all its siblings. Assume these are MIN nodes. The maximum of these MIN values is then backed up to the parent (a MAX node, just as in minimax). This value is then offered to the grandparent of these MINs as a potential beta cutoff.

Next, the algorithm descends to other grandchildren and terminates exploration of their parent if any of their values is equal to or larger than this beta value. Similar procedures can be described for alpha pruning over the grandchildren of a MAX node.

Two rules for terminating search, based on alpha and beta values, are:

1. Search can be stopped below any MIN node having a beta value less than or equal to the alpha value of any of its MAX ancestors.

2. Search can be stopped below any MAX node having an alpha value greater than or equal to the beta value of any of its MIN node ancestors.

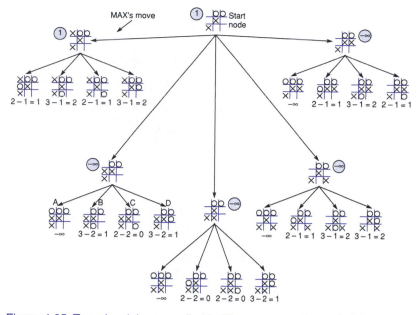

Figure 4.25 Two-ply minimax applied to X's move near the end of the game, from Nilsson (1971).

Alpha-beta pruning thus expresses a relation between nodes at ply n and nodes at ply n + 2 under which entire subtrees rooted at level n + 1 can be eliminated from consideration. As an example, Figure 4.26 takes the space of Figure 4.21 and applies alpha-beta pruning. Note that the resulting backed-up value is identical to the minimax result and the search saving over minimax is considerable.

With a fortuitous ordering of states in the search space, alpha-beta can effectively double the depth of the search space considered with a fixed space/time computer commitment (Nilsson 1980). If there is a particular unfortunate ordering, alpha-beta searches no more of the space than normal minimax; however, the search is done in only one pass.

4.5 Complexity Issues

The most difficult aspect of combinatorial problems is that the "explosion" often takes place without program designers realizing that it is happening. Because most human activity, computational and otherwise, takes place in a linear-time world, we have difficulty appreciating exponential growth. We hear the complaint: "If only I had a larger (or faster or highly parallel) computer my problem would be solved." Such claims, often made in the aftermath of the explosion, are usually rubbish. The problem wasn't understood properly and/or appropriate steps were not taken to address the combinatorics of the situation.

The full extent of combinatorial growth staggers the imagination. It has been estimated that the number of states produced by a full search of the space of possible chess moves is

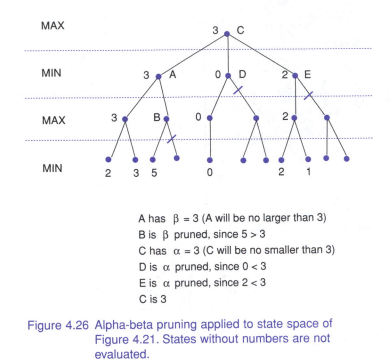

A has $\beta = 3$ (A will be no larger than 3)
B is β pruned, since $5 > 3$
C has $\alpha = 3$ (C will be no smaller than 3)
D is α pruned, since $0 < 3$
E is α pruned, since $2 < 3$
C is 3

Figure 4.26 Alpha-beta pruning applied to state space of Figure 4.21. States without numbers are not evaluated.

about 10^{120}. This is not "just another large number;" it is comparable to the number of molecules in the universe or the number of nanoseconds since the "big bang."

Several measures have been developed to help calculate complexity. One of these is the *branching factor* of a space. We define branching factor as the average number of branches (children) that are expanded from any state in the space. The number of states at depth n of the search is equal to the branching factor raised to the nth power. Once the branching factor is computed for a space it is possible to estimate the search cost to generate a path of any particular length. Figure 4.27 gives the relationship between B (branching), L (path length), and T (total states in the search) for small values. The figure is logarithmic in T, so L is not the straight line it looks in the graph.

Several examples using this figure show how bad things can get. If the branching factor is 2, it takes a search of about 100 states to examine all paths that extend six levels deep into the search space. It takes a search of about 10,000 states to consider paths 12 moves deep. If the branching can be cut down to 1.5 (by some heuristic), then a path twice as long can be examined for the same number of states searched.

The mathematical formula that produced the relationships of Figure 4.27 is:

$$T = B + B^2 + B^3 + \cdots + B^L$$

with T total states, L path length, and B branching factor. This equation reduces to:

$$T = B(B^L - 1)/(B - 1)$$

Measuring a search space is usually an empirical process done by considerable playing with a problem and testing its variants. Suppose, for example, we wish to establish the branching factor of the 8-puzzle. We calculate the total number of possible moves: 2 from each corner for a total of 8 corner moves, 3 from the center of each side for a total of 12, and 4 from the center of the grid for a grand total of 24. This divided by 9, the different number of possible locations of the blank, gives an average branching factor of 2.67. As can be seen in Figure 4.27, this is not very good for a deep search. If we eliminate moves directly back to a parent state (already built into the search algorithms of this chapter) there is one move fewer from each state. This gives a branching factor of 1.67, a considerable improvement, which might (in some state spaces) make exhaustive search possible.

As we considered in Chapter 3, the complexity cost of an algorithm can also be measured by the sizes of the open and closed lists. One method of keeping the size of open reasonable is to save on open only a few of the (heuristically) best states. This can produce a better focused search but has the danger of possibly eliminating the best, or even the only, solution path. This technique of maintaining a size bound, often a function of the number of steps taken in the search, is called *beam search*.

In the attempt to bring down the branching of a search or otherwise constrain the search space, we presented the notion of *more informed* heuristics. The more informed the search, the less the space must be searched to get the minimal path solution. As we pointed out in Section 4.4, the computational costs of the additional information needed to further cut down the search space may not always be acceptable. In solving problems on a computer, it is not enough to find a minimum path. We must also minimize total cpu costs.

Figure 4.28, taken from an analysis by Nilsson (1980), is an informal attempt to get at these issues. The "informedness" coordinate marks the amount of information costs that are included in the evaluation heuristic that are intended to improve performance. The cpu coordinate marks the cpu costs for implementing state evaluation and other aspects of the search. As the information included in the heuristic increases, the cpu cost of the heuristic increases. Similarly, as the heuristic gets more informed, the cpu cost of evaluating states gets smaller, because fewer states are considered. The critical cost, however, is the total cost of computing the heuristic PLUS evaluating states, and it is usually desirable that this cost be minimized.

Finally, heuristic search of and/or graphs is an important area of concern, as the state spaces for expert systems are often of this form. The fully general search of these structures is made up of many of the components already discussed in this and the preceding chapter. Because all and children must be searched to find a goal, the heuristic estimate of the cost of searching an and node is the sum of the estimates of searching the children.

There are many further heuristic issues, however, besides the numerical evaluation of individual and states, in the study of and/or graphs, such as are used in knowledge based systems. For instance, if the satisfaction of a set of and children is required for solving a parent state, which child should be considered first? The state most costly to evaluate? The state most likely to fail? The state the human expert considers first? The decision is important both for computational efficiency as well as overall cost, e.g., in medical or other diagnostic tests, of the knowledge system. These, as well as other related heuristic issues, are visited again in Chapter 8.

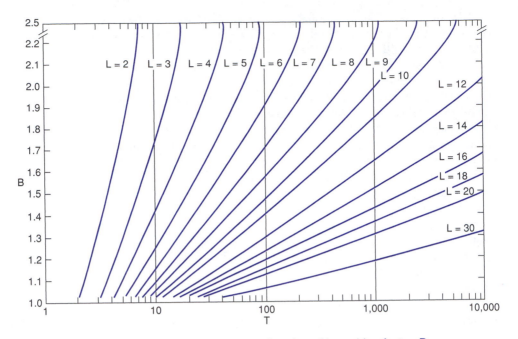

Figure 4.27 Number of nodes generated as a function of branching factor, B, for various lengths, L, of solution paths. The relating equation is: $T = B(B^L - 1)/(B - 1)$, adapted from Nilsson (1980).

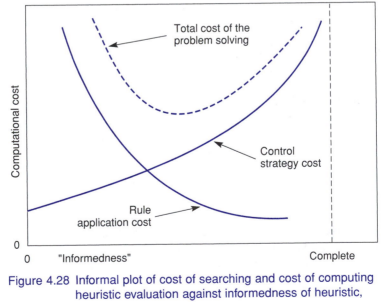

Figure 4.28 Informal plot of cost of searching and cost of computing heuristic evaluation against informedness of heuristic, adapted from Nilsson (1980).

4.6   Epilogue and References

The search spaces for interesting problems tend to grow exponentially; heuristic search is a primary tool for managing this combinatorial complexity. Various control strategies for implementing heuristic search were presented in this chapter.

We began the chapter with two traditional algorithms, both of them inherited from the discipline of operations research, hill-climbing and dynamic programming. We recommend reading the paper by Arthur Samuel (1959) discussing his checker playing program and its sophisticated use of hill-climbing and minimax search. Samuel also presents early interesting examples of a sophisticated memory management system and a program that is able to learn. Bellman's (1956) design of algorithms for dynamic programming remains important in areas such as natural language processing where it is necessary to compare strings of characters, words, or phonemes. Dynamic programming is often called the forward/backward or Viterbi algorithm. For impotant examples of use of dynamic programming for language analysis see Jurafsky and Martin (2000) and Chapter 14.

We next presented heuristics in the context of traditional state space search. We presented the A and A* algorithms for implementing best-first search. Heuristic search was demonstrated using simple games such as the 8-puzzle and extended to the more complex problem spaces generated by rule-based expert systems (Chapter 8). The chapter also applied heuristic search to two-person games, using look-ahead with minimax and alpha-beta pruning to try to predict the behavior of the opponent. After discussing A* algorithms, we analyzed their behavior, considering properties including admissibility, monotonicity, and informedness.

The discipline of complexity theory has essential ramifications for virtually every branch of computer science, especially the analysis of state space growth and heuristic pruning. Complexity theory examines the inherent complexity of problems (as opposed to algorithms). The key conjecture in complexity theory is that there exists a class of inherently intractable problems. This class, referred to as NP-hard (Nondeterministically Polynomial), consists of problems that may not be solved in less than exponential time without resorting to the use of heuristics. Almost all interesting search problems belong to this class. We especially recommend *Computers and Intractability* by Michael R. Garey and David S. Johnson (1979) and *Algorithms from P to NP, Vol. I: Design and Efficiency* by Bernard Moret and Henry Shapiro (1991) for discussing these issues.

The book *Heuristics* by Judea Pearl (1984) provides a comprehensive treatment of the design and analysis of heuristic algorithms. R. E. Korf (1987, 1998, 1999) continues research on search algorithms, including an analysis of iterative deepening and the development of the IDA* algorithm. IDA* integrates iterative deepening with A* to obtain linear bounds on open for heuristic search. Chess and other game playing programs have held an abiding interest across the history of AI, with results often presented and discussed at the annual conferences.

We are indebted to Nils Nilsson (1980) for the approach and many of the examples of this chapter.

4.7 Exercises

1. Extend the the "most wins" heuristic for tic-tac-toe two plys deeper in the search space of Figure 4.3. What is the total number of states examined using this heuristic? Would the traditional hill-climbing algorithm work in this situation? Why?

2. Use the backward component of the dynamic programing algorithm to find another optimal alignment of the characters of Figure 4.6. How many optimal alignments are there?

3. With the Levenshtein metric of Section 4.1.2, use dynamic programming to determine the minimum edit distance from source strings sensation and excitation to target string execution.

4. Give a heuristic that a block-stacking program might use to solve problems of the form "stack block X on block Y." Is it admissible? Monotonic?

5. The sliding-tile puzzle consists of three black tiles, three white tiles, and an empty space in the configuration shown in Figure 4.29.
   The puzzle has two legal moves with associated costs:

   > A tile may move into an adjacent empty location. This has a cost of 1. A tile can hop over one or two other tiles into the empty position. This has a cost equal to the number of tiles jumped over.

   The goal is to have all the white tiles to the left of all the black tiles. The position of the blank is not important.

   a. Analyze the state space with respect to complexity and looping.
   b. Propose a heuristic for solving this problem and analyze it with respect to admissibility, monotonicity, and informedness.

6. Compare the three 8-puzzle heuristics of Figure 4.14 with the heuristic of adding the sum of distances out of place to 2 times the number of direct reversals. Compare them in terms of:

   a. Accuracy in estimating distance to a goal. This requires that you first derive the shortest path solution and use it as a standard.
   b. Informedness. Which heuristic most effectively prunes the state space?
   c. Are any of these three 8-puzzle heuristics monotonic?
   d. Admissibility. Which of these heuristics are bounded from above by the actual cost of a path to the goal? Either prove your conclusions for the general case or give a counterexample.

7. a. As presented in the text, best-first search uses the **closed** list to implement loop detection. What would be the effect of eliminating this test and relying on the depth test, $g(n)$, to detect loops? Compare the efficiencies of the two approaches.

Figure 4.29 The sliding block puzzle.

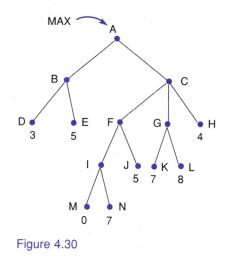

Figure 4.30

b. **best_first_search** does not test a state to see whether it is a goal until it is removed from the **open** list. This test could be performed when new states are generated. What effect would doing so have on the efficiency of the algorithm? Admissibility?

8. Prove **A*** is admissible. Hint: the proof should show that:

   a. A* search will terminate.
   b. During its execution there is always a node on **open** that lies on an optimal path to the goal.
   c. If there is a path to a goal, **A*** will terminate by finding the optimal path.

9. Does admissibility imply monotonicity of a heuristic? If not, can you describe when admissibility would imply monotonicity?

10. Prove that the set of states expanded by algorithm A* is a subset of those examined by breadth-first search.

11. Prove that more informed heuristics develop the same or less of the search space. Hint: formalize the argument presented in Section 4.3.3.

12. A Caesar cipher is an encryption scheme based on cyclic permutations of the alphabet, with the i-th letter of the alphabet replaced by the (i + n)-th letter of the alphabet. For example, in a Caesar cipher with a shift of 4, "Caesar" would be encrypted as "Geiwev."

   a. Give three heuristics that might be used for solving Caesar ciphers.
   b. In a simple substitution cipher, each letter is replaced by another letter under some arbitrary one-to-one mapping. Which of the heuristics proposed for the Caesar cipher may be used to solve substitution ciphers? Explain. (Thanks to Don Morrison for this problem.)

13. Perform minimax on the tree shown in Figure 4.30.

14. Perform a left-to-right alpha-beta prune on the tree of Exercise 13. Perform a right-to-left prune on the same tree. Discuss why a different pruning occurs.

15. Consider three-dimensional tic-tac-toe. Discuss representational issues; analyze the complexity of the state space. Propose a heuristic for playing this game.

16. Perform alpha-beta pruning on the tic-tac-toe search of Figures 4.23, 4.24, and 4.25. How many leaf nodes can be eliminated in each case?

17. a.   Create an algorithm for heuristically searching and/or graphs. Note that all descendants of an **and** node must be solved to solve the parent. Thus, in computing heuristic estimates of costs to a goal, the estimate of the cost to solve an **and** node must be at least the sum of the estimates to solve the different branches.

    b.   Use this algorithm to search the graph in Figure 4.31.

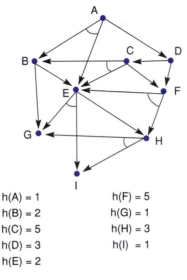

h(A) = 1   h(F) = 5
h(B) = 2   h(G) = 1
h(C) = 5   h(H) = 3
h(D) = 3   h(I) = 1
h(E) = 2

Figure 4.31

STOCHASTIC METHODS

Probable impossibilities are to be preferred to improbable possibilities. . .

—ARISTOTLE As quoted by Bobby Wolfe in *"Aces on Bridge"*, 2003

God does not play dice. . .

—ALBERT EINSTEIN   (His answer to the credibility of Quantum Theory)

God not only plays dice, but he sometimes throws them where they can't be seen. . .

—STEPHEN HAWKING

5.0   Introduction

Chapter 4 introduced heuristic search as an approach to problem solving in domains where either a problem does not have an exact solution or where the full state space may be too costly to calculate. In this chapter we propose the stochastic methodology as also appropriate for these situations. Probabilistic reasoning is also suitable for situations where state information is found from sampling an information base and causal models are learned from data.

One important application domain for the use of the stochastic methodology is diagnostic reasoning where cause/effect relationships are not always captured in a purely deterministic fashion, as is often possible in the knowledge-based approaches to problem solving that we saw in Chapters 2, 3, 4, and will see again in Chapter 8. A diagnostic situation usually presents evidence, such as fever or headache, without further causative justification. In fact, the evidence can often be indicative of several different causes, e.g., fever can be caused by either flu or an infection. In these situations probabilistic information can often indicate and prioritize possible explanations for the evidence.

Another interesting application for the stochastic methodology is gambling, where supposedly random events such as the roll of dice, the dealing of shuffled cards, or the spin of a roulette wheel produce possible player payoff. In fact, in the 18th century, the attempt to provide a mathematical foundation for gambling was an important motivation for Pascal (and later Laplace) to develop a probabilistic calculus.

Finally, as observed in Section 1.1.4, a "situated" accounting of intelligence suggests that human decisions often emerge from complex, time-critical, and embodied environments where a fully mechanistic calculus may simply not be definable, or, if defined, may not compute answers in a usable time frame. In these situations intelligent actions may best be seen as stochastic responses to anticipated costs and benefits.

We next describe several problem areas, among many, where the stochastic methodology is often used in the computational implementation of intelligence; these areas will be major topics in later chapters.

1. **Diagnostic reasoning.** In medical diagnosis, for example, there is not always an obvious cause/effect relationship between the set of symptoms presented by the patient and the causes of these symptoms. In fact, the same sets of symptoms often suggest multiple possible causes. Probabilistic models are also important in complex mechanical situations, such as monitoring aircraft or helicopter flight systems. Rule-based (Chapter 8) and probabilistic (Chapter 9) systems have both been applied in these and other diagnostic domains.

2. **Natural language understanding.** If a computer is to understand and use a human language, that computer must be able to characterize how humans themselves use that language. Words, expressions, and metaphors are learned, but also change and evolve as they are used over time. The stochastic methodology supports the understanding of language; for example, when a computational system is trained on a database of specific language use (called a *corpus linguistics*). We consider these language issues further in this chapter as well as in Chapter 14.

3. **Planning and scheduling.** When an agent forms a plan, for example, a vacation trip by automobile, it is often the case that no deterministic sequence of operations is guaranteed to succeed. What happens if the car breaks down, if the car ferry is cancelled on a specific day, if a hotel is fully booked, even though a reservation was made? Specific plans, whether for humans or robots, are often expressed in probabilistic language. Planning is considered in Section 8.4.

4. **Learning.** The three previous areas mentioned for stochastic technology can also be seen as domains for automated learning. An important component of many stochastic systems is that they have the ability to sample situations and learn over time. Some sophisticated systems are able to both sample data and predict outcomes as well as learn new probabilistic relationships based on the data and outcomes. We consider learning in Part IV.

The stochastic methodology has its foundation in the properties of counting. The probability of an event in a situation is described as the ratio of the number of ways the event can occur to the total number of possible outcomes of that event. Thus, the probability that an even number results from the roll of a fair die is the total number of even outcomes (here 2, 4, or 6) over the total number of outcomes (1, 2, 3, 4, 5, or 6), or

1/2. Again, the probability of drawing a marble of a certain color from a bag of marbles is the ratio of the number of marbles of that color to the total number of marbles in the bag. In Section 5.1 we introduce basic counting techniques, including the sum and product rules. Because of their importance in counting, we also present the *permutations* and *combinations* of discrete events. This is an optional section that can be skipped by readers with a sufficient background in discrete mathematics.

In Section 5.2, we introduce a formal language for reasoning with the stochastic methodology. This includes the definitions of independence and types of random variables that may be applied to situations. For example, for probabilistic propositions, random variables may be *boolean*—true or false, *discrete*, as in the example of rolling the fair die, or *continuous*, a function defined on the real numbers. In Section 5.3 we present several applications of stochastic methods, including probabilistic finite state automata and a methodology for predicting word patterns based on sampled data.

In Section 5.4, we present Bayes' theorem which supports most current systems for probabilistic inference. Bayes' rule is important for interpreting new evidence in the context of the prior knowledge or experience of situations.

In Chapter 9 we continue our presentation of stochastic models and inference. The topics of Chapter 9 include *Bayesian belief networks (BBNs)*, *hidden Markov models (HMMs)*, and first-order representation systems that support stochastic modeling. These methodologies based on graphs, in our examples the directed acyclic graph (or DAG) formalism, are often referred to as *graphical models*.

5.1　The Elements of Counting (optional)

The foundation for the stochastic methodology is the ability to count the elements of an application domain. The basis for collecting and counting elements is, of course, set theory, in which we must be able to unequivocally determine whether an element is or is not a member of a set of elements. Once this is determined, there are methodologies for counting elements of sets, of the complement of a set, and the union and intersection of multiple sets. We review these techniques in this section.

5.1.1　The Addition and Multiplication Rules

If we have a set A, the *number of the elements* in set A is denoted by $|A|$, called the *cardinality* of A. Of course, A may be empty (the number of elements is zero), finite, countably infinite, or uncountably infinite. Each set is defined in terms of a domain of interest or *universe*, U, of elements that might be in that set. For example, the set of male people in a classroom may be defined in the context, or universe, of all the people in that room. Similarly, the roll of a 3 on a fair die may be seen as one of a set of six possible outcomes.

The domain or universe of a set A is thus also a set and is used to determine the *complement* of that set, $\overline{A}$. For example, the complement of the set of all males in the classroom just mentioned is the set of all females, and the complement of the {3} roll of the fair die is {1, 2, 4, 5, 6}. One set A is a *subset* of another set B, A ⊆ B, if every element of the set A is also an element of the set B. Thus, trivially, every set is a subset of itself, any set A is a subset of its universe, and the empty set, denoted { } or φ, is a subset of every set.

The *union* of two sets A and B, A ∪ B, may now be described as the set of all elements in either set. The number of elements in the union of two sets is the total of all the elements in each of the sets minus the number of elements that are in both sets. The justification for this, of course, is the fact that each distinct element in a set may only be counted once. Trivially, if the two sets have no elements in common, the number of the elements in their union is the sum of the number of elements in each set.

The *intersection* of two sets A and B, A ∩ B, is the set of all elements common to both sets. We now give examples of a number of the concepts just defined.

Suppose the universe, U, is the set {0, 1, 2, 3, 4, 5, 6, 7, 8, 9}
Let A be the set {1, 3, 5, 7, 9}
Let B be the set {0, 2, 4, 6, 8}
Let C be the set {4, 5, 6}
Then |A| is 5, |B| is 5, |C| is 3, and |U| is 10.
Also, A ⊆ U, B ⊆ U and A ∪ B = U, |B| = |A|, A = $\overline{B}$
Further, |A ∪ B| = |A| + |B| = 10, since A ∩ B = { }, but
|A ∪ C| = |A| + |C| − |A ∩ C| = 7, since A ∩ C = {5}

We have just presented the major components for the *addition rule* for combining two sets. For any two sets A and C, the number of elements in the union of these sets is:

$$|A \cup C| = |A| + |C| - |A \cap C|$$

Note that this addition rule holds whether the two sets are disjoint or have elements in common. A similar addition rule holds for three sets A, B, and C, again whether or not they have elements in common:

$$|A \cup B \cup C| = |A| + |B| + |C| - |A \cap B| - |A \cap C| - |B \cap C| + |A \cap B \cap C|$$

An argument similar to that made earlier can be used to justify this equation. Similar inclusion/exclusion equations are available, and easily demonstrated, for the addition of sets of elements of more than three sets.

The *multiplication principle for counting* states that if we have two sets of elements A and B of size a and b respectively, then there are a x b unique ways of combining the elements of the sets together. The justification for this, of course, is that for each of the a elements of A there are b pairings for that element. The multiplication principle supports many of the techniques used in counting, including the Cartesian product of sets, as well as permutations and combinations of sets.

The *Cartesian product* of two sets A and B, denoted A X B, is the set of all ordered pairs (a, b) where a is an element of set A and b is an element of set B; or more formally:

$$A \times B = \{(a, b) \mid (a \in A) \wedge (b \in B)\}$$

and by the multiplication principle of counting:

$$|A \times B| = |A| \times |B|$$

The Cartesian product can, of course, be defined across any number of sets. The product for n sets will be the set of n-tuples where the first component of the n-tuple is any element of the first set, the second component of the n-tuple is any element of the second set, and so on. Again, the number of unique n-tuples that result is the product of the number of elements in each set.

5.1.2 Permutations and Combinations

A *permutation* of a set of elements is an arranged sequence of the elements of that set. In this arrangement of elements, each may be used only once. An example permutation is an arrangement or ordering of a set of ten books on a shelf that can hold all ten. Another example is the assignment of specific jobs to four of a group of six children.

We often wish to know how many (unique) permutations there are of a set of n elements. We use multiplication to determine this. If there are n elements in set A, then the set of permutations of these elements is a sequence of length n, where the first element of the sequence is any of the n elements of A, the second element of the sequence is any of the (n − 1) remaining elements of A, the third element of the sequence is any of the (n − 2) remaining elements, and so on.

The order in which the elements are placed in the permutation sequence is unimportant, i.e., any of the n elements of the set may be placed first in any location in the sequence, any of the n − 1 remaining elements may be placed second in any of the n − 1 remaining locations of the permutation sequence, and so on. Finally, by the multiplication principle, there are n! permutation sequences for this set of n elements.

We can restrict the number of elements in a permutation of a set A to be any number greater than or equal to zero, and less than or equal to the number of elements n in the original set A. For example, we might want to know how many distinct orderings there are of ten possible books on a shelf that can only hold six of them at a time. If we wanted to determine the number of permutations of the n elements of A taken r at a time, where $0 \leq r \leq n$, we use multiplication as before, except that now we only have r places in each permutation sequence:

$$n \times (n-1) \times (n-2) \times (n-3) \times ... \times (n-(r-1))$$

Alternatively, we can represent this equation as:

$$\frac{n \times (n-1) \times (n-2) \times (n-3) \times ... \times (n-(r-1)) \times (n-r) \times (n-r-1) \times ... \times 2 \times 1}{(n-r) \times (n-r-1) \times ... \times 2 \times 1}$$

or equivalently, the number of permutations of n elements taken r at a time, which is symbolized as $_nP_r$, is:

$$_nP_r = \frac{n!}{(n-r)!}$$

The *combination* of a set of n elements is any *subset* of these elements that can be formed. As with permutations, we often want to count the number of combinations of items that can be formed, given a set of items. Thus, there is only one combination of the n elements of a set of n items. The key idea here is that the number of combinations represents the number of *subsets of the full set of elements* that can be created. In the bookshelf example, combinations represent the different subsets of six books, the books on the shelf, that can be formed from the full set of ten books. Another example of combinations is the task of forming four-member committees from a group of fifteen people. Each person is either on the committee or not, and it doesn't make any difference whether they are the first or last member chosen. A further example is a five-card hand in a poker game. The order in which the cards are dealt makes no difference to the ultimate value of the hand. (It can make a huge difference to the value of the betting, if the last four cards are dealt face-up as in stud poker, but the ultimate value of the hand is independent of the dealt order).

The number of combinations of n elements taken r at a time, where $0 \le r \le n$, is symbolized by $_nC_r$. A straightforward method for determining the number of these combinations is to take the number of permutations, $_nP_r$, as we did already, and then divide out the number of duplicate sets. Since any r element subset of n elements has r! permutations, to get the number of combinations of n elements taken r at a time we divide the number of permutations of n elements taken r at a time by r!. Thus we have:

$$_nC_r = \frac{_nP_r}{r!} = \frac{n!}{(n-r)!\,r!}$$

There are many other variations of the counting principles just presented, some of which will be found in the Chapter 5 exercises. We recommend any discrete mathematics textbook for further development of these counting techniques.

5.2 Elements of Probability Theory

With the foundation in the counting rules presented in Section 5.1, we can now introduce probability theory. First, in Section 5.2.1, we consider some fundamental definitions, such as the notion of whether two or more events are independent of each other. In Section 5.2.2 we demonstrate how to infer explanations for particular data sets. This will set us up to consider several examples of probabilistic inference in Section 5.3 and Bayes' theorem in Section 5.4.

5.2.1 The Sample Space, Probabilities, and Independence

The following definitions, the foundation for a theory for probability, were first formalized by the French mathematician Laplace (1816) in the early nineteenth century. As mentioned in the introduction to Chapter 5, Laplace was in the process of creating a calculus for gambling!

For example, what is the probability that a 7 or an 11 is the result of the roll of two fair dice? We first determine the sample space for this situation. Using the multiplication principle of counting, each die has 6 outcomes, so the total set of outcomes of the two dice is 36. The number of combinations of the two dice that can give a 7 is 1,6; 2,5; 3,4; 4,3; 5,2; and 6,1—6 altogether. The probability of rolling a 7 is thus $6/36 = 1/6$. The number of combinations of the two dice that can give an 11 is 5,6; 6,5—or 2, and the probability of rolling an 11 is $2/36 = 1/18$. Using the additive property of distinct outcomes, there is $1/6 + 1/18$ or $2/9$ probability of rolling either a 7 or 11 with two fair dice.

In this 7/11 example, the two events are getting a 7 and getting an 11. The elementary events are the distinct results of rolling the two dice. Thus the event of a 7 is made up of the six atomic events (1,6), (2,5), (3,4), (4,3), (5,2), and (6,1). The full sample space is the union of all 36 possible atomic events, the set of all pairs that result from rolling the dice. As we see soon, because the events of getting a 7 and getting an 11 have no atomic events in common, they are *independent*, and the probability of their sum (union) is just the sum of their individual probabilities.

In a second example, how many four-of-a-kind hands can be dealt in all possible five-card poker hands? First, the set of atomic events that make up the full space of all five-card poker hands is the combination of 52 cards taken 5 at a time. To get the total number of four-of-a-kind hands we use the multiplication principle. We multiply the number of combinations of 13 cards taken 1 at a time (the number of different kinds of cards: ace, 2, 3..., king) times the number of ways to pick all four cards of the same kind (the combination of 4 cards taken 4 at a time) times the number of possible other cards that fill out the 5 card hand (48 cards remain). Thus, the probability of a four-of-a-kind poker hand is:

$$(_{13}C_1 \times {}_4C_4 \times {}_{48}C_1) \ / \ {}_{52}C_5 \ = 13 \times 1 \times 48 \ / \ 2{,}598{,}960 \approx 0.00024$$

Several results follow immediately from the definitions just made. First, the probability of any event E from the sample space S is:

$$0 \le p(E) \le 1, \text{ where } E \subseteq S$$

A second result is that the sum of the probabilities of all possible outcomes in S is 1. To see this, note that the definition for sample space S indicates that it is made up of the union of all individual events E in the problem.

As a third result of the definitions, note that the *probability of the complement* of an event is:

$$p(\overline{E}) = (|S| - |E|) \ / \ |S| \ = \ (|S| \ / \ |S|) - (|E| \ / \ |S|) = 1 - p(E).$$

The complement of an event is an important relationship. Many times it is easier to determine the probability of an event happening as a function of it not happening, for example, determining the probability that at least one element of a randomly generated bit string of length n is a 1. The complement is that all the bits in the string are 0, with probability 2^{-n}, with n the length of the string. Thus, the probability of the original event is $1 - 2^{-n}$.

Finally, from the probability of the complement of an event set we work out the probability when no event occurs, sometimes referred to as a *contradictory* or *false* outcome:

$$p(\{ \ \}) = 1 - \ p(\overline{\{\ \}}) = 1 - p(S) = 1 - 1 = 0, \text{ or alternatively,}$$
$$= |\{ \ \}| \ / \ |S| = 0 \ / \ |S| = 0$$

A final important relationship, the probability of the union of two sets of events, may be determined from the principle of counting presented in Section 5.1, namely that for any two sets A and B: $|A \cup B| = |A| + |B| - |A \cap B|$. From this relationship we can determine the probability of the union of any two sets taken from the sample space S:

$$p(A \cup B) = |A \ \cup \ B| \ / \ |S| \ = \ (|A| \ + \ |B| \ - \ |A \ \cap \ B|) \ / \ |S|$$
$$= |A| \ / \ |S| \ + \ |B| \ / \ |S| \ - \ |A \cap B| \ / \ |S| \ = \ p(A) \ + \ p(B) \ - \ p(A \ \cap \ B)$$

Of course, this result may be extended to the union of any number of sets, along the line of the principle of inclusion/exclusion presented in Section 5.1.

We already presented an example of determining the probability of the union of two sets: the probability of rolling a 7 or an 11 with two fair dice. In this example, the formula just presented was used with the probability of the pairs of dice that gave a 7 disjoint from the pairs of dice that gave an 11. We may also use this formula in the more general case when the sets are not disjoint. Suppose we wanted to determine, rolling two fair dice, the probability of rolling an 8 or of rolling pairs of the same number. We would simply calculate the probability of this union where there is one elementary event—(4,4)—that is in the intersection of both desired outcome events.

We next consider the probability of two independent events. Suppose that you are a player in a four-person card game where all the cards are dealt out equally. If you do not have the queen of spades, you can conclude that each of the other players has it with probability 1/3. Similarly, you can conclude that each player has the ace of hearts with probability 1/3 and that any one player has both cards with probability $1/3 \times 1/3$, or 1/9. In this situation we assumed that the events of getting these two cards are independent, even though this is only approximately true. We formulize this intuition with a definition.

Because the description of independence of events as just presented is an *if and only if* relationship, we can determine whether two events are independent by working out their probabilistic relationships. Consider the situation where bit strings of length four are randomly generated. We want to know whether the event of the bit string containing an even number of 1s is independent of the event where the bit string ends with a 0. Using the multiplication principle, with each bit having 2 values, there are a total of $2^4 = 16$ bit strings of length 4.

There are 8 bit strings of length 4 that end with a 0: {1110, 1100, 1010, 1000, 0010, 0100, 0110, 0000}. There are also 8 bit strings that have an even number of 1s: {1111, 1100, 1010, 1001, 0110, 0101, 0011, 0000}. The number of bit strings that have both an even number of 1s and end with a 0 is 4: {1100, 1010, 0110, 0000}. Now these two events are independent since

$p(\{\text{even number of 1s}\} \cap \{\text{end with 0}\}) = p(\{\text{even number of 1s}\}) \times p(\{\text{end with 0}\})$
$4/16 = 8/16 \times 8/16 = 1/4$

Consider this same example of randomly generated bit strings of length 4. Are the two following events independent: *the bit strings have an even number of 1s*, and *the bit strings end in a 1*? When two or more events are not independent, that is the probability of any one event affects the probability of the others, it requires the notion of *conditional probability* to work out their relationships. We see this in Section 5.2.4.

Before closing this section, we note that other axiom systems supporting the foundations of probability theory are possible, for instance, as an extension to the propositional calculus (Section 2.1). As an example of our set-based approach, the Russian mathematician Kolmogorov (1950) proposed a variant of the following axioms, equivalent to our definitions. From these three axioms Kolmogorov systematically constructed all of probability theory.

1. The probability of event E in sample space S is between 0 and 1, i.e., $0 \le p(E) \le 1$.

2. When the union of all $E = S$, $p(S) = 1$, and $p(\overline{S}) = 0$.

3. The probability of the union of two sets of events A and B is:

$$p(A \cup B) = p(A) + p(B) - p(A \cap B)$$

In the next section we present a simple example of probabilistic inference.

5.2.2   Probabilistic Inference: An Example

We now demonstrate examples of reasoning with the ideas just presented. Suppose you are driving the interstate highway system and realize you are gradually slowing down because of increased traffic congestion. You begin to search for possible explanations of the slowdown. Could it be road construction? Has there been an accident? All you are aware of is that you are slowing down. But wait! You have access to the state highway statistics, and with your new automobile based GUI and inferencing system you can download to your car's computer the relevant statistical information. Okay, so you have the data; what can you do with them?

For this example we assume we have three true or false parameters (we will define this type parameter as a *boolean random variable* in Section 5.2.4). First, there is whether or not the traffic—and you—are slowing down. This situation will be labeled S, with assignment of t or f. Second, there is the probability of whether or not there is an accident, A, with assignments t or f. Finally, the probability of whether or not there is road construction at the time, C; again either t or f. We can express these relationships for the interstate highway traffic, thanks to our car-based data download system, in Table 5.1.

The entries of Table 5.1 are interpreted, of course, just like the truth tables of Section 2.1, except that the right hand column gives the probability of the situation on the left hand side happening. Thus, the third row of the table gives the probability of the traffic slowing down and there being an accident but with no construction as 0.16:

$$S \cap \overline{C} \cap A = 0.16$$

It should be noted that we have been developing our probabilistic calculus in the context of *sets* of events. Figure 5.1 demonstrates how the probabilities of Table 5.1 may be represented with the traditional Venn diagram. We could equally well have presented this situation as the probabilistic truth assignments of *propositions*, in which case the $\cap$ would be replaced by a $\wedge$ and Table 5.1 would be interpreted as the truth values of the conjunction of propositions.

Next, we note that the sum of all possible outcomes of the joint distribution of Table 5.1 is 1.0; this is as one would expect with the axioms of probability presented in Section

S	C	A	p
t	t	t	0.01
t	t	f	0.03
t	f	t	0.16
t	f	f	0.12
f	t	t	0.01
f	t	f	0.05
f	f	t	0.01
f	f	f	0.61

Table 5.1 The joint probability distribution for the traffic slowdown, S, accident, A, and construction, C, variables of the example of Section 5.3.2.

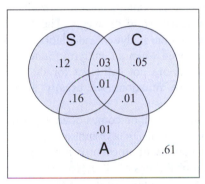

Figure 5.1 A Venn diagram representation of the probability distributions of Table 5.1; S is traffic slowdown, A is accident, C is construction.

5.2.1. We can also work out the probability of any simple or complex set of events. For example, we can calculate the probability that there is traffic slowdown S. The value for slow traffic is 0.32, the sum of the first four lines of Table 5.1; that is, all the situations where S = t. This is sometimes called the *unconditional* or *marginal probability* of slow traffic, S. This process is called *marginalization* because all the probabilities other than slow traffic are summed out. That is, the distribution of a variable can be obtained by summing out all the other variables from the joint distribution containing that variable.

In a like manner, we can calculate the probability of construction C with no slowdown $\overline{S}$—a phenomenon not uncommon in the State of New Mexico! This situation is captured by $p(C \cap \overline{S}) = t$, as the sum of the 5th and the 6th lines of Table 5.1, or 0.06. If we consider the negation of the situation $C \cap \overline{S}$, we would get (using deMorgan's laws), $p(\overline{C} \cup S)$. Calculating the probability of the union of two sets, as presented in Section 5.2.1, we obtain:

$$0.16 + 0.12 + 0.01 + 0.61 + 0.01 + 0.03 + 0.16 + 0.12 - (0.16 + 0.12) = .94$$

And again the total probability of $C \cap \overline{S}$ and its complement (negation) is 1.0.

5.2.3 Random Variables

In the theory of probability, individual probabilities are either computed analytically, through combinatorial methods, or empirically, by sampling a population of events. To this point most of our probabilities have been determined analytically. For example, there are six sides to a die, and two sides to a coin. When the die or coin is "fair" we say that each outcome, from rolling or flipping, is equally likely. As a result, it is straightforward to determine the event space for these problem situations we later call *parametric*.

More interesting probabilistic reasoning, however, results from the sampling based analysis of situations in the actual world of events. These situations often lack a well defined specification that supports the analytical calculation of probabilities. It can also be the case that some situations, even when an analytic foundation exists, are so complex that time and computation costs are not sufficient for the deterministic calculation of probabilistic outcomes. In these situations we usually adopt an empirical sampling methodology.

Most importantly, we assume that all outcomes of an experiment are not equally likely. We retain, however, the basic axioms or assumptions we have made in the previous sections; namely, that the probability of an event is a number between (and including) 0 and 1, and that the summed probabilities of all outcomes is 1. We also retain our rule for the probability of unioned sets of events. We define the idea of a *random variable* as a method for making this calculus precise.

DEFINITION

RANDOM VARIABLE
A *random variable* is a function whose domain is a sample space and range a set of outcomes, most often real numbers. Rather than using a problem-specific event space, a random variable allows us to talk about probabilities as numerical values that are related to an event space.

BOOLEAN, DISCRETE, and CONTINUOUS RANDOM VARIABLES
A *boolean random variable* is a function from an event space to {true, false} or to the subset of real numbers {0.0, 1.0}. A boolean random variable is sometimes called a *Bernoulli trial*.

A *discrete random variable*, which includes boolean random variables as a subset, is a function from the sample space to (a countable subset of) real numbers in [0.0, 1.0].

A *continuous random variable* has as its range the set of real numbers.

An example using a discrete random variable on the domain of Season, where the atomic events of Season are {spring, summer, fall, winter}, assigns .75, say, to the domain element Season = spring. In this situation we say p(Season = spring) = .75. An example of a boolean random variable in the same domain would be the mapping p(Season = spring) = true. Most of the probabilistic examples that we consider will be of discrete random variables.

Another example of the use of a boolean random variable would be to calculate the probability of obtaining 5 heads in 7 flips of a fair coin. This would be the combination of 5 of 7 flips being heads times the 1/2 probability of heads to the 5th power times the 1/2 probability of not getting heads to the 2nd power, or:

$$_7C_5 \times (1/2)^5 \times (1/2)^2$$

This coin flip situation is an example of what is called the *binomial distribution*. In fact, the outcome of any situation where we want to measure r successes in n trials, where p is the known probability of success, may be represented as:

$$_nC_r \times p^r \times (1 - p)^{(n-r)}$$

An important natural extension to associating probabilistic measures to events is the notion of the expected cost or payoff for that outcome. For example, we can calculate the prospective payback from betting specific money values of the draw of a card or the spin of a roulette wheel. We define the *expectation of a random variable or event*, ex(E):

DEFINITION

EXPECTATION OF AN EVENT

If the reward for the occurrence of an event E, with probability $p(E)$, is r, and the cost of the event not occurring, $1 - p(E)$, is c, then the *expectation* for an event occurring, $ex(E)$, is:

$$ex(E) = r \times p(E) + c \times (1 - p(E))$$

For example, suppose that a fair roulette wheel has integers 0 through 36 equally spaced on the slots of the wheel. In the game each player places $1 on any number she chooses: if the wheel stops on the number chosen, she wins $35; otherwise she loses the dollar. The reward of a win is $35; the cost of a loss, $1. Since the probability of winning is 1/37, of losing, 36/37, the expected value for this event, $ex(E)$, is:

$$\text{ex}(E) = 35 \ (1/37) \ + \ (-1) \ (36/37) \ \approx \ -0.027$$

Thus the player loses, on average, about $0.03 per play!

We conclude this subsection with a brief discussion and summary of the origins of the values of probabilities used in stochastic reasoning. As noted above, in most of our examples so far, we considered probabilistic values that can be determined by reasoning about known situations such as the flip of a fair coin or the spin of a fair roulette wheel. When we have these situations, we can draw many conclusions about aspects of the probability space, such as its *mean*, the statistically-based probability measure, and how far from this mean the sampled values usually vary, the *standard deviation* of the outcomes in this domain.

We refer to this well understood situation as the *parametric* approach to the generation of a sample outcome space. The parametric approach is justified in stochastic situations where there exist a priori expectations for the structure of the results of experimental trials. Our task is to "fill in" the parameters of this well understood situation. An example is flipping a fair coin with the outcome as the binomial distribution. We then can build our expectations of the situation with the binomial model for possible outcomes.

There are a number of advantages of parametric approaches. The first is that fewer data points are needed to calibrate the expected outcomes, since the shape of the outcome curve is known in advance. A further advantage is that it is often possible to determine a priori the number of outcomes or the amount of training data sufficient to make quality probability estimates. In fact, in the parametric situation, besides calculating the mean and standard deviation of the expectations, we can make an accurate determination of when certain data points are outside normal expectations.

Of course, many, if not most, interesting situations do not have clear expected outcomes. One example is diagnostic reasoning, in medicine, say. A second example is the use and interpretation of a natural language expression. With language it is quite common to take a *non parametric* approach to expectations by sampling a large number of situations, as one might have, for example, in a language *corpus*. By analyzing collected examples of language use in newspapers, say, or in conversations from a help-desk for computer support, it is possible to infer meaning for ambiguous expressions in these domains. We demonstrate this methodology analyzing possible phoneme relationships (for ni) in Section 5.3.

With sufficient data points, the resulting discrete distribution in non parametric environments can often be smoothed by interpolation to be continuous. Then new situations can be inferred in the context of this created distribution. A major disadvantage of non parametric methods is that, with the absence of the constraints from prior expectations, a large amount of training data is often required to compensate. We present examples of this type of reasoning in Section 5.3.

5.2.4 Conditional Probability

The probability measures discussed to this point in Chapter 5 are often called *prior probabilities*, because they are worked out prior to having any new information about the expected outcomes of events in a particular situation. In this present section we consider the *conditional probability* of an occurrence of an event, that is, the probability of the event, given some new information or constraint on that event.

As seen earlier in this chapter, the *prior probability* of getting a 2 or a 3 on the roll of a fair die is the sum of these two individual results divided by the total number of possible outcomes of the roll of a fair die, or 2/6. The prior probability of a person having a disease is the number of people with the disease divided by the number of people in the domain of concern.

An example of a *conditional* or *posterior probability* is the situation of a patient entering the doctor's office with a set of symptoms, headaches and nausea, say. The experienced doctor will know a set of prior expectations for different diseases based on symptoms, but will want to determine a specific diagnosis for this patient currently suffering from the headaches and nausea. To make these ideas more precise we make two important definitions.

DEFINITION

PRIOR PROBABILITY

The *prior probability*, generally an *unconditioned probability*, of an event is the probability assigned based on all knowledge supporting its occurrence or absence, that is, the probability of the event prior to any new evidence. The prior probability of an event is symbolized: p(event).

POSTERIOR PROBABILITY

The *posterior* (after the fact) *probability*, generally a *conditional probability*, of an event is the probability of an event given some new evidence. The posterior probability of an event given some evidence is symbolized: p(event | evidence).

We next begin the presentation of Bayes' theorem, whose general form is seen in Section 5.4. The idea supporting Bayes is that the probability of a new (posterior) situation of an hypothesis given evidence can be seen as a function of known probabilities for the evidence given that hypothesis. We can say that we wish to determine the function f, such that $p(h|e) = f(p(e|h))$. We usually want to determine the value on the left side of this equation while it is often much easier to compute the values on the right hand side.

We now prove Bayes' theorem for one symptom and one disease. Based on the previous definitions, the posterior probability of a person having disease d, from a set of diseases D, with symptom or evidence, s, from a set of symptoms S, is:

$$p(d|s) = |d \cap s| / |s|$$

As in Section 5.1, the "|"'s surrounding a set is the cardinality or number of elements in that set. The right side of this equation is the number of people having both (the intersection) the disease d and the symptom s divided by the total number of people having the symptom s. Figure 5.2 presents a Venn diagram of this situation. We expand the right

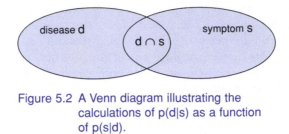

Figure 5.2 A Venn diagram illustrating the
calculations of p(d|s) as a function
of p(s|d).

hand side of this equation. Since the sample space for determining the probabilities of the numerator and denominator are the same, we get:

p(d|s) = p(d ∩ s) / p(s).

There is an equivalent relationship for p(s|d); again, see Figure 5.2:

p(s|d) = p(s ∩ d) / p(d).

We next solve the p(s|d) equation to determine the value for p(s ∩ d):

p(s ∩ d) = p(s|d) p(d).

Substituting this result in the previous equation for p(d|s) produces Bayes' rule for one disease and one symptom:

$$p(d|s) = \frac{p(s|d)p(d)}{p(s)}$$

Thus, the posterior probability of the disease given the symptom is the product of the likelihood of the symptom given the disease and the likelihood of the disease, normalized by the probability of that symptom. We generalize this rule in Section 5.4.

We next present the *chain rule*, an important technique used across most domains of stochastic reasoning, especially in natural language processing. We have just developed the equations for any two sets, A_1 and A_2:

p(A_1 ∩ A_2) = p(A_1 | A_2) p(A_2) = p(A_2 | A_1) p(A_1).

and now, the generalization to multiple sets A_i, called the chain rule:

$$p(A_1 \cap A_2 \cap ... \cap A_n) = p(A_1)\, p(A_2 | A_1)\, p(A_3 | A_1 \cap A_2) ... p(A_n | \bigcap_{i=1}^{n-1} A_i)$$

We make an inductive argument to prove the chain rule, consider the nth case:

$$p(A_1 \cap A_2 \cap ... \cap A_{n-1} \cap A_n) = p((A_1 \cap A_2 \cap ... \cap A_{n-1}) \cap A_n),$$

We apply the intersection of two sets rule to get:

$$p((A_1 \cap A_2 \cap ... \cap A_{n-1}) \cap A_n) = p(A_1 \cap A_2 \cap ... \cap A_{n-1}) \, p(A_n \mid A_1 \cap A_2 \cap ... \cap A_{n-1})$$

and then reduce again, considering that:

$$p(A_1 \cap A_2 \cap ... A_{n-1}) = p((A_1 \cap A_2 \cap ... \cap A_{n-2}) \cap A_{n-1})$$

until $p(A_1 \cap A_2)$ is reached, the base case, which we have already demonstrated.

We close this section with several definitions based on the use of the chain rule relationship just developed. First, we redefine independent events (see Section 5.2.1) in the context of conditional probabilities, and then we define conditionally independent events, or the notion of how events can be independent of each other, given some third event.

DEFINITION

INDEPENDENT EVENTS
Two events A and B are *independent* of each other if and only if $p(A \cap B) = p(A) \, p(B)$. When $p(B) \neq 0$ this is the same as saying that $p(A) = p(A|B)$. That is, knowing that B is true does not affect the probability of A being true.

CONDITIONALLY INDEPENDENT EVENTS
Two events A and B are said to be *conditionally independent* of each other, given event C if and only if $p((A \cap B) \mid C) = p(A \mid C) \, p(B \mid C)$.

As a result of the simplification of general chain rule offered by conditionally independent events, larger stochastic systems can be built with smaller computational cost; that is, conditionally independent events simplify joint distributions. An example from our slow traffic situation: suppose that as we slow down we notice orange control barrels along the side of the traffic lane. Besides suggesting that the cause of our slowdown is now more likely to be from road construction than a traffic accident, the presence of orange barrels will have its own probabilistic measure. In fact, the variables representing traffic slowdown and the presence of orange barrels are conditionally independent since they are both caused by road construction. Thus, we say that the variable road construction *separates* traffic slowdown from orange barrels.

Because of the statistical efficiencies gained by conditional independence, a major task in the construction of large stochastic computational systems is to break out a complex problem into more weakly connected subproblems. The subproblem interaction relationships are then controlled by the various conditional separation relationships. We see this idea further formalized with the definition of *d-separation* in Section 9.3.

Next, Section 5.3, we present examples of reasoning based on probability measures. Finally, Section 5.4, we present the general form of Bayes' theorem and demonstrate how, in complex situations, the computation necessary to support full Bayesian inference can become intractable.

5.3   Applications of the Stochastic Methodology

You say [t ow m ey t ow] and I say [t ow m aa t ow]. . .

—IRA GERSHWIN, *"Let's Call the Whole Thing Off"*

In this section we present several examples that use probability measures to reason about the interpretation of ambiguous information. First, we define an important modeling tool based on the finite state machine of Section 3.1, *the probabilistic finite state machine.*

D E F I N I T I O N

PROBABILISTIC FINITE STATE MACHINE

A *probabilistic finite state machine* is a finite state machine where the next state function is a probability distribution over the full set of states of the machine.

PROBABILISTIC FINITE STATE ACCEPTOR

A *probabilistic finite state machine* is an *acceptor*, when one or more states are indicated as the *start* states and one or more as the *accept* states.

It can be seen that these two definitions are simple extensions to the finite state and the Moore machines presented in Section 3.1. The addition for non-determinism is that the next state function is no longer a function in the strict sense. That is, there is no longer a unique range state for each state of the domain. Rather, for any state, the next state function is a probability distribution over all possible next states.

Figure 5.3 presents a probabilistic finite state acceptor that represents different pronunciations of the word "tomato". A particular acceptable pronunciation for the word

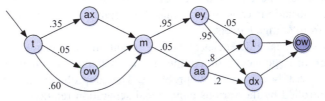

Figure 5.3 A probabilistic finite state acceptor for the pronunciation of "tomato", adapted from Jurafsky and Martin (2000).

tomato is characterized by a path from the start state to the accept state. The decimal values that label the arcs of the graph represent the probability that the speaker will make that particular transition in the state machine. For example, 60% of all speakers in this data set go directly from the t phone to the m without producing any vowel phone between.

Besides characterizing the various ways people in the pronunciation database speak the word "tomato", this model can be used to help interpret ambiguous collections of phonemes. This is done by seeing how well the phonemes match the paths through the state machine of this and related words. Furthermore, given a partially formed word, the state machine can be used to determine possible paths to complete that word.

In a second example, also adapted from Jurafsky and Martin (2000), we consider the *phoneme recognition* problem, often called *decoding*. Suppose a phoneme recognition algorithm has identified the phone ni (as in "knee") that occurs just after the recognized word (phone) l, and we want to associate ni with either a word or the first part of a word. In this case we have linguistic *corpora*, the *Brown and Switchboard corpora*, to assist us.

The *Brown corpus* is a one million word collection of sentences from 500 written texts, including newspapers, novels, academic writings, and others, collected at Brown University in the 1960s (Kucera and Francis 1967, Francis 1979). The *Switchboard corpus* is a 1.4 million word collection of telephone conversations. These corpora together contain about 2,500,000 words that let us sample both written and spoken information bases.

There are a number of ways to proceed in identifying the most likely word to associate with the ni phone. First we can determine which word, with this phone first, is the most likely to be used. Table 5.2 presents the raw frequencies of these words along with the probability of their occurrence, that is, the frequency of the word divided by the total number of words in these combined corpora. This table is adapted from Jurafsky and Martin (2000); see Section 5.8 of their book for a justification that "the" belongs to this collection. From this data, the word "the" would seem to be the first choice for matching ni.

We next apply a form of Bayes' theorem. We developed, in the previous section, the formula for using Bayes with one outcome and one piece of evidence. Our second attempt at analyzing the phone ni following l, uses a simplification (justified in Section 5.4) of that formula:

p(word | [ni]) ∝ p([ni] | word) x p(word)

word	frequency	probability
knee	61	.000024
the	114834	.046
neat	338	.00013
need	1417	.00056
new	2625	.001

Table 5.2. The *ni* words with their frequencies and probabilities from the Brown and Switchboard corpora of 2.5M words, adapted from Jurafsky and Martin (2000).

word	p([ni] | word)	p(word)	p([ni] | word) x p(word)
new	0.36	0.001	0.00036
neat	0.52	0.00013	0.000068
need	0.11	0.00056	0.000062
knee	1.0	0.000024	0.000024
the	0.0	0.046	0.0

Table 5.3. The *ni* phone/word probabilities from the Brown and Switchboard corpora (Jurafsky and Martin 2000).

The results of this calculation, ordered from most recommended to least, are found in Table 5.3. (Jurafsky and Martin 2000, p 167) and explain why p(ni | the) is impossible. The results of Table 5.3 also suggest that new is the most likely word for decoding ni. But the two-word combination I new doesn't seem to make much sense, whereas other combinations, such as I need does. Part of the problem in this situation is that we are still reasoning on the phone level, that is, determining the probability p(ni | new). There is, in fact, a straightforward way of addressing this issue, and that is to look for explicit two word combinations in the corpora. Following this line of reasoning, it turns out that I need is a much more likely pair of consecutive words than is I new, or of any of the other I-word combinations, for that matter.

The methodology for deriving probabilities from pairs, or triples, of word combinations in corpora is called *n-gram analysis*. With two words, we were using *bigrams*, with three, *trigrams*. The probabilities derived from word combinations using n-grams are important, as we see again in Chapter 14. We conclude this chapter with the presentation of Bayes' theorem.

5.4 Bayes' Theorem

The Reverend Thomas Bayes was a mathematician and a minister. His famous theorem was published in 1763, four years after his death. His paper, entitled *Essay towards Solving a Problem in the Doctrine of Chances* was published in the *Philosophical Transactions of the Royal Society of London*. Bayes' theorem relates cause and effect in such a way that by understanding the effect we can learn the probability of its causes. As a result Bayes' theorem is important both for determining the causes of diseases, such as cancer, as well as useful for determining the effects of some particular medication on that disease.

5.4.1 Introduction

One of the most important results of probability theory is the general form of Bayes' theorem. First, we revisit one of the results of Section 5.2.4, Bayes' equation for one disease and one symptom. To help keep our diagnostic relationships in context, we rename the variables used previously to indicate individual hypotheses, h_i, from a set of hypotheses, H, and a set of evidence, E. Furthermore, we will now consider the set of individual hypotheses h_i as disjoint, and having the union of all h_i to be equal to H.

$$p(h_i|E) = (p(E|h_i) \times p(h_i)) / p(E)$$

This equation may be read, "The probability of an hypothesis h_i given a set of evidence E is . . ." First, note that the denominator $p(E)$ on the right hand side of the equation is very much a normalizing factor for any of the hypotheses h_i from the set H. It is often the case that Bayes' theorem is used to determine which hypothesis out of a set of possible hypotheses is strongest, given a particular evidence set E. In this case we often drop the $p(E)$ denominator which is identical for all the h_i, with the saving of a possibly large computational cost. Without the denominator, we have created the *maximum a posteriori* value for an hypothesis:

$$\arg \max(h_i)\, p(E|h_i)\, p(h_i)$$

We read this expression as "The maximum value over all h_i of $p(E|h_i)\, p(h_i)$". The simplification just described is highly important for diagnostic reasoning as well as in natural language processing. Of course, the *arg max*, or maximum likelihood hypothesis, is no longer a random variable as defined previously.

Next consider the calculation of the denominator $p(E)$ in the situation where the entire sample space *is partitioned by* the set of hypotheses h_i. The partition of a set is defined as the split of that set into disjoint non overlapping subsets, the union of which make up the entire set. Assuming that the set of hypotheses h_i partition the entire sample space, we get:

$$p(E) = \Sigma_i\, p(E|h_i)\, p(h_i)$$

This relationship is demonstrated by considering the fact that the set of hypotheses h_i forms a partition of the full set of evidence E along with the rule for the probability of the intersection of two sets. So:

$$E = (E \cap h_1) \cup (E \cap h_2) \cup ... \cup (E \cap h_n)$$

But by the generalized union of sets rule developed in Section 5.2.1:

$$p(E) = p((E \cap h_1) \cup (E \cap h_2) \cup ... \cup (E \cap h_n))$$
$$= p(E \cap h_1) + p(E \cap h_2) + ... + p(E \cap h_n) - p(E \cap h_1 \cap E \cap h_2 \cap ... \cap h_n)$$
$$= p(E \cap h_1) + p(E \cap h_2) + ... + p(E \cap h_n)$$

since the set of hypotheses h_i partition E and their intersection is empty.

This calculation of $p(E)$ produces the general form of Bayes' theorem, where we assume that the set of hypotheses, h_i partition the evidence set E:

$$p(H_i|E) = \frac{p(E|H_i) \times p(H_i)}{\sum\limits_{k=1}^{n} p(E|H_k) \times p(H_k)}$$

$p(h_i|E)$ is the probability that h_i is true given evidence E.

$p(h_i)$ is the probability that h_i is true overall.

$p(E|h_i)$ is the probability of observing evidence E when h_i is true.

n is the number of possible hypotheses.

Bayes' theorem provides a way of computing the probability of a hypothesis h_i, given a particular piece of evidence, given only the probabilities with which the evidence follows from actual causes (the hypotheses).

As an example, suppose we want to examine the geological evidence at some location to see whether or not it is suited to finding copper. We must know in advance the probability of finding each of a set of minerals and the probability of certain evidence being present when each particular mineral is found. Then we can use Bayes' theorem, with evidence found at the particular location, to determine the likelihood of copper. This approach is used by PROSPECTOR, built at Stanford University and SRI International and employed in mineral exploration (copper, molybdenum, and others). PROSPECTOR has found commercially significant mineral deposits at several sites (Duda et al. 1979*a*).

We next present a simple numerical example demonstrating Bayes' theorem. Suppose that you go out to purchase an automobile. The probability that you will go to dealer 1, d_1, is 0.2. The probability of going to dealer 2, d_2, is 0.4. There are only three dealers you are considering and the probability that you go to the third, d_3, is 0.4. At d_1 the probability of purchasing a particular automobile, a_1, is 0.2; at dealer d_2 the probability of purchasing automobile a_1 is 0.4. Finally, at dealer d_3, the probability of purchasing a_1 is 0.3. Suppose you purchase automobile a_1. What is the probability that you purchased it at dealer d_2?

First, we want to know, given that you purchased automobile a_1, that you bought it from dealer d_2, i.e., to determine $p(d_2|a_1)$. We present Bayes' theorem in variable form for determining $p(d_2|a_1)$ and then with variables bound to the situation in the example.

$p(d_2|a_1) = (p(a_1|d_2) \, p(d_2)) \, / \, ((d_1 \times a_1) + (d_2 \times a_1) + (d_3 \times a_1))$
$\qquad = (0.4) \, (0.4) \, / \, ((0.2) \, (0.2) + (0.4) \, (0.4) + (0.4) \, (0.3))$
$\qquad = 0.16 \, / \, 0.32$
$\qquad = 0.5$

There are two major commitments in using Bayes' theorem: first all the probabilities on the relationships of the evidence with the various hypotheses must be known, as well as the probabilistic relationships among the pieces of evidence. Second, and sometimes more difficult to determine, all the relationships between evidence and hypotheses, or $p(E|h_k)$, must be estimated or empirically sampled. Recall that calculation of $p(E)$ for the general form of Bayes' theorem also required that the hypothesis set h_i partitioned the set of evidence E. In general, and especially in areas such as medicine and natural language processing, an assumption of this partition cannot be justified a priori.

It is interesting to note, however, that many situations that violate this assumption (that the individual pieces of evidence partition the evidence set) behave quite well! Using this partition assumption, even in situations where it is not justified, is called using *naive Bayes* or a *Bayes classifier.* With naive Bayes, the assumption is, for an hypothesis h_j:

$$p(E|h_j) \approx \prod_{i=1}^{n} p(e_i|h_j)$$

i.e., we assume the pieces of evidence are independent, given a particular hypothesis.

Using Bayes' theorem to determine the probability of some hypothesis h_i given a set of evidence E, $p(h_i|E)$, the numbers on the right-hand side of the equation are often easily obtainable. This is especially true when compared to obtaining the values for the left-hand side of the equation, or determining $p(h_i|E)$ directly. For example, because the population is smaller, it is much easier to determine the number of meningitis patients who have headaches than it is to determine the percentage of headache sufferers with meningitis. Even more importantly, for the simple case of a single disease and a single symptom, not very many numbers are needed. Troubles begin, however, when we consider multiple diseases h_i from the domain of diseases H and multiple symptoms e_n from a set E of possible symptoms. When we consider each disease from H and each symptom from E singly, we have m × n measures to collect and integrate. (Actually m × n posterior probabilities plus m + n prior probabilities.)

Unfortunately, our analysis is about to get much more complex. To this point, we considered each symptom e_i individually. In actual situations, single symptoms are rarely the case. When a doctor is considering a patient, for instance, there are often many combinations of symptoms she must consider. We require a form of Bayes' theorem to consider any single hypothesis h_i in the context of the union of multiple symptoms e_i.

$$p(h_i|e_1 \cup e_2 \cup ... \cup e_n) = (p(h_i)\, p(e_1 \cup e_2 \cup ... \cup e_n|h_i)) / p(e_1 \cup e_2 \cup ... \cup e_n)$$

With one disease and a single symptom we needed only m × n measurements. Now, for every pair of symptoms e_i and e_j and a particular disease hypothesis h_i, we need to know both $p(e_i \cup e_j \mid h_i)$ and $p(e_i \cup e_j)$. The number of such pairs is n × (n − 1), or approximately n^2, when there are n symptoms in E. Now, if we want to use Bayes, there will be about (m x n^2 conditional probabilities) + (n^2 symptom probabilities) + (m disease probabilities) or about m x $n^2 + n^2 + m$ pieces of information to collect. In a realistic medical system with 200 diseases and 2000 symptoms, this value is over 800,000,000!

There is some hope, however. As was discussed when we presented conditional independence, many of these symptom pairs will be independent, that is $p(e_i|e_j) = p(e_i)$. Independence means, of course, that the probability of e_i is not affected by the presence of e_j. In medicine, for example, most symptoms are not related, e.g., hair loss and sore elbow. But even if only ten percent of our example symptoms are not independent, there are still about 80,000,000 relationships remaining to consider.

In many diagnostic situations, we must also deal with negative information, e.g., when a patient does not have a symptom such as bad blood pressure. We require both:

$$p(\overline{e_i}) = 1 - p(e_i) \text{ and } p(\overline{h_i}|e_i) = 1 - p(h_i|e_i).$$

We also note that $p(e_i|h_i)$ and $p(h_i|e_i)$ are not the same and will almost always have different values. These relationships, and the avoidance of circular reasoning, are important for the design of *Bayesian belief networks* considered in Section 9.3.1.

A final problem, which again makes keeping the statistics of complex Bayesian systems virtually intractable, is the need to rebuild probability tables when new relationships between hypotheses and evidence sets are discovered. In many active research areas such as medicine, new discoveries happen continuously. Bayesian reasoning requires complete and up-to-date probabilities, including joint probabilities, if its conclusions are to be correct. In many domains, such extensive data collection and verification are not possible, or if possible, quite expensive.

Where these assumptions are met, however, Bayesian approaches offer the benefit of a mathematically well-founded handling of uncertainty. Most expert system domains do not meet these requirements and must rely on heuristic approaches, as presented in Chapter 8. Furthermore, due to complexity issues, we know that even fairly powerful computers cannot use full Bayesian techniques for successful real-time problem solving. We end this section with an example to show how a Bayesian approach might work to organize hypothesis/evidence relationships.

5.4.2 Extending the Road/Traffic Example

We present again and extend the example of Section 5.2.2. Suppose you are driving the interstate highway system and realize you are gradually slowing down because of increased traffic congestion. You begin to search for possible explanations of the slowdown. Could it be road construction? Has there been an accident? Perhaps there are other possible explanations. After a few minutes you come across orange barrels at the side of the road that begin to cut off the outside lane of traffic. At this point you determine that the best explanation is most likely road construction. At the same time the alternative hypothesis of an accident is *explained away*. Similarly if you would have seen flashing lights in the distance ahead, such as those from a police vehicle or an ambulance, the best explanation given this new evidence would be a traffic accident and road construction would have been *explained away*. When an hypothesis is explained away that does not mean that it is no longer possible. Rather, in the context of new evidence, it is simply less likely.

Figure 5.4 presents a Bayesian account of what we have just seen. road construction is correlated with orange barrels and bad traffic. Similarly, accident correlates with flashing lights and bad traffic. We examine Figure 5.4 and build a joint probability distribution for the road construction and bad traffic relationship. We simplify both of these variables to be either true (t) or false (f) and represent the probability distribution in Table 5.4. Note that if construction is f there is not likely to be bad traffic and if it is t

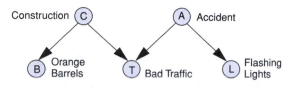

Figure 5.4 The Bayesian representation of the traffic
problem with potential explanations.

$$
\begin{array}{c|c|c}
\text{C} & \text{T} & \text{p} \\
\hline
t & t & .3 \\
t & f & .2 \\
f & t & .1 \\
f & f & .4
\end{array}
$$

C is true = .5   T is true = .4

Table 5.4 The joint probability distribution for the traffic and
construction variables of Figure 5.3.

then bad traffic is likely. Note also that the probability of road construction on the interstate, C = true, is .5 and the probability of having bad traffic, T = true, is .4 (this is New Mexico!).

We next consider the change in the probability of road construction given the fact that we have bad traffic, or p(C|T) or p(C = t | T = t).

p(C|T) = p(C = t , T = t) / (p(C = t , T = t) + p(C = f , T = t)) = .3 / (.3 + .1) = .75

So now, with the probability of road construction being .5, given that there actually is bad traffic, the probability for road construction goes up to .75. This probability will increase even further with the presence of orange barrels, explaining away the hypothesis of accident.

Besides the requirement that we may have knowledge or measurements for any of our parameters being in a particular state, we also must address, as noted in Section 5.4.1, complexity issues. Consider the calculation of the joint probability of all the parameters of Figure 5.4 (using the chain rule and a topologically sorted order of variables):

p(C,A,B,T,L) = p(C) × p(A|C) × p(B|C,A) × p(T|C,A,B) × p(L|C,A,B,T)

This result is a general decomposition of the probability measures that is always true. The cost of producing this joint probability table is exponential in the number of parameters involved, and in this case requires a table of size 2^5 or 32. We are considering a toy problem, of course, with only five parameters. A situation of interesting size, with thirty or more parameters say, requires a joint distribution table of roughly a billion elements! As we will see in Section 9.3, Bayesian belief networks and d-separation give us further tools for addressing this representational and computational complexity.

5.5   Epilogue and References

Games of chance date back, at least, to the Greek and Roman civilizations. It wasn't until the European Renaissance, however, that the mathematical analysis of probability theory began. As noted in the chapter, probabilistic reasoning begins with determining principles of counting and combinatorics. Actually, one of the first combinatorial "machines" is attributed to Ramon Llull (Ford et al. 1995), a Spanish philosopher and Franciscan monk, who created his device, said to automatically enumerate the attributes of God, with the intention of converting heathens. The first publication on probabilities, *De Ratiociniis Ludo Aleae*, was authored by Christian Huygens (1657). Huygens describes earlier results by Blaise Pascal, including a methodology for calculating probabilities, as well as conditional probabilities. Pascal targeted both the "objective" analysis of the world of games as well as the more "subjective" analysis of belief systems, including the existence of God.

The definitions of probabilities presented in Section 5.2.1 are based on the formalism proposed by the French mathematician Pierre Simon Laplace. Laplace's book *Theorie Analytique des Probabilitees* (1816) documents this approach. Laplace's work was based on earlier results published by Gotlob Leibnitz and James Bernoulli.

Thomas Bayes was a mathematician and a minister. His famous theorem was published in 1764, after his death. His paper, entitled *Essay towards Solving a Problem in the Doctrine of Chances* was published in the *Philosophical Transactions of the Royal Society of London*. Ironically, Bayes' theorem is never explicitly stated in this paper, although it is there! Bayes also has extensive discussion of the "reality" of statistical measures.

Bayes' research was partly motivated to answer the philosophical skepticism of the Scots philosopher David Hume. Hume's dismissal of causality destroyed any foundation for arguments for the existence of God. In fact, in a 1763 paper presented to the British Royal Society, the minister Richard Price used Bayes' theorem to show there was good evidence in favor of the miracles described in the New Testament.

The mathematicians of the early twentieth century, including Fisher (1922), Popper (1959), and Carnap (1948) completed the foundation of modern probability theory continuing the "subjective/objective" debates on the nature of probabilities. Kolmogorov (1950, 1965) axiomatized the foundations of probabilistic reasoning (see Section 5.2.1).

It is possible to present the topic of probabilistic reasoning from several vantage points. The two most popular approaches are based on the propositional calculus and set theory. For the propositional calculus, Section 2.1, propositions are assigned a confidence or probabilistic truth value in the range [0.0, 1.0]. This approach offers a natural extension to the semantics of propositional calculus. We have chosen the second approach to probabilistic reasoning, the semantics of set theory. We feel this orientation is a bit more intuitive, bringing to bear all the counting and other techniques of set theory, as seen in Section 5.1. Equivalent axiom systems give both approaches a sound mathematical foundation. In Chapter 9, when we extend our presentation of stochastic systems, we will present a first-order (variable based) representation scheme for stochastic states and inference schemes.

Bayes' theorem has offered a foundation for several expert systems of the 1970s and 1980s, including an extensive analysis of acute abdominal pain at the University of

Glasgow Hospital (de Dombal et al. 1974), and PROSPECTOR, the expert system from Stanford University supporting mineral exploration (Duda et al. 1979a). The naive Bayes approach has been used on a number of classification problems, including pattern recognition (Duda and Hart 1973), natural language processing (Mooney 1996), and elsewhere. Domingos and Pazzani (1997) offer justification for the successes of naive Bayes classifiers in situations which do not meet Bayesian independence assumptions.

There is a large amount of current research in probabilistic reasoning in artificial intelligence, some presented in Chapters 9, 10, 13, and 16. Uncertain reasoning makes up a component of AI conferences, including AAAI, IJCAI, NIPS, and UAI. There are several excellent introductory texts in probabilistic reasoning (Ross 1988, DeGroot 1989), as well as several introductions to use of stochastic methods in artificial intelligence applications (Russell and Norvig 2003, Jurafsky and Martin 2000, Manning and Schutze 1999).

I am indebted to Dan Pless of Sandia National Laboratories for the general approach taken in this chapter, for several of the examples, and also for editorial suggestions.

5.6   Exercises

1. A fair six-sided die is tossed five times and the numbers up are recorded in a sequence. How many different sequences are there?

2. Find the number of distinguishable permutations of the letters in the word MISSISSIPPI, of the letters of the word ASSOCIATIVE.

3. Suppose that an urn contains 15 balls, of which eight are red and seven are black. In how many ways can five balls be chosen so that:

    a.   all five are red? all five are black?
    b.   two are red and three are black?
    c.   at least two are black?

4. How many ways can a committee of three faculty members and two students be selected from a group of five faculty and seven students?

5. In a survey of 250 television viewers, 88 like to watch news, 98 like to watch sports, and 94 like to watch comedy. 33 people like to watch news and sports, 31 like to watch sports and comedy, and 35 like to watch news and comedy. 10 people like to watch all three. Suppose a person from this group is picked at random:

    a.   What is the probability that they watch news but not sports?
    b.   What is the probability that they watch news or sports but not comedy?
    c.   What is the probability that they watch neither sports nor news?

6. What is the probability that a four digit integer with no beginning zeros:

    a.   has 3, 5, or 7 as a digit?
    b.   begins with 3, ends with 5, or has 7 as a digit?

7. Two dice are tossed. Find the probability that their sum is:

    a.   4
    b.   7 or an even number
    c.   10 or greater

8. A card is drawn from the usual fifty-two card deck. What is the probability of:

   a. drawing a face card (jack, queen, king or ace)?
   b. drawing a queen or a spade?
   c drawing a face card or a club?

9. What is the probability of being dealt the following hands in a five card poker game (from the normal deck of fifty-two cards)?

   a. A "flush" or all cards from the same suit.
   b. A "full house" or two cards of the same value and three cards of another value.
   c. A "royal flush" or the ten, jack, queen, king, and ace all of the same suit.

10. The *expectation* is the *mean* or average of the value of a random variable. In throwing a die, for example, it can be calculated by totaling up the resulting values from a large number of throws and then dividing by the number of throws. What is:

   a. the expectation from throwing a fair die?
   b. the value of a roulette wheel with 37 equally likely results?
   c. the value of a draw from a set of cards (ace is valued at 1, all other face cards as 10)?

11. Suppose that we are playing a game where we toss a die and then receive the amount of dollars equal to the value of the die. For example, if a 3 comes up we receive $3. If it costs us $4 to play this game, is this reasonable?

12. Consider the situation where bit strings of length four are randomly generated. Demonstrate whether or not the event of production of bit strings containing an even number of 1s is independent of the event of producing bit strings that end in a 1.

13. Show that the statement $p(A,B|C) = p(A|C)\, p(B|C)$ is equivalent to both $p(A|B,C) = p(A|C)$ and $p(B|A,C) = p(B|C)$.

14. In manufacturing a product, 85% of the products that are produced are not defective. Of the products inspected, 10% of the good ones are seen as defective and not shipped whereas only 5% of the defective products are approved and shipped. If a product is shipped, what is the probability that it is defective?

15. A blood test is 90% effective in detecting a disease. It also falsely diagnoses that a healthy person has the disease 3% of the time. If 10% of those tested have the disease, what is the probability that a person who tests positive will actually have the disease?

16. Suppose an automobile insurance company classifies a driver as good, average, or bad. Of all their insured drivers, 25% are classified good, 50% are average, and 25% are bad. Suppose for the coming year, a good driver has a 5% chance of having an accident, and an average driver has 15% chance of having an accident, and a bad driver has a 25% chance. If you had an accident in the past year what is the probability that you are a good driver?

17. Three prisoners, A, B, C, are in their cells. They are told that one of them will be executed the next day and the others will be pardoned. Only the governor knows who will be executed. Prisoner A asks the guard a favor. "Please ask the governor who will be executed, and then tell either prisoner B or C that they will be pardoned." The guard does as was asked and then comes back and tells prisoner A that he has told prisoner B that he (B) will be pardoned. What are prisoner A's chances of being executed, given this message? Is there more information than before his request to the guard? This problem is adapted from Pearl (1988).

BUILDING CONTROL ALGORITHMS FOR STATE SPACE SEARCH

If we carefully factor out the influences of the task environments from the influences of the underlying hardware components and organization, we reveal the true simplicity of the adaptive system. For, as we have seen, we need postulate only a very simple information processing system in order to account for human problem solving in such tasks as chess, logic, and cryptarithmetic. The apparently complex behavior of the information processing system in a given environment is produced by the interaction of the demands of the environment with a few basic parameters of the system, particularly characteristics of its memories.

—A. Newell and H. A. Simon, "Human Problem Solving" (1972)

What we call the beginning is often the end
And to make an end is to make a beginning.
The end is where we start from . . .

T. S. Eliot, "Four Quartets"

6.0   Introduction

To this point, Part II has represented problem solving as search through a set of problem situations or states. Chapter 2 presented the predicate calculus as a medium for describing states of a problem and sound inference as a method for producing new states. Chapter 3 introduced graphs to represent and link problem situations. The backtrack algorithm, as well as algorithms for depth-first and breadth-first search, can explore these graphs. Chapter 4 presented algorithms for heuristic search. In Chapter 5, given probabilistic states of the world, stochastic inference was used to produce new states. To summarize, Part II has:

1.   Represented a problem solution as a path in a graph from a start state to a goal.

2. Used search to test systematically alternative paths to goals.

3. Employed backtracking, or some other mechanism, to allow algorithms to recover from paths that failed to find a goal.

4. Used lists to keep explicit records of states under consideration.

    a. The *open* list allows the algorithm to explore untried states if necessary.
    b. The *closed* list of visited states allows the algorithm to implement loop detection and avoid repeating fruitless paths.

5. Implemented the *open* list as a *stack* for depth-first search, a *queue* for breadth-first search, and a *priority queue* for best-first search.

Chapter 6 introduces further techniques for building search algorithms. In Section 6.1, *recursive search* implements depth-, breadth-, and best-first search in a more concise and natural fashion than was done in Chapter 3. Further, recursion is augmented with *unification* to search the state space generated by predicate calculus assertions. This *pattern-directed* search algorithm is the basis of PROLOG, see Chapter 15, and several of the expert systems discussed in Chapter 8. In Section 6.2 we introduce *production systems*, a general architecture for pattern-directed problem solving that has been used extensively to model human problem solving, Chapter 17, as well as other AI applications. Finally, in Section 6.3, we present another AI problem-solving control architecture, the *blackboard*.

6.1   Recursion-Based Search (optional)

6.1.1   Recursive Search

In mathematics, a recursive definition uses the term being defined as part of its own definition. In computer science, recursion is used to define and analyze both data structures and procedures. A recursive procedure consists of:

1. A recursive step: the procedure calls itself to repeat a sequence of actions.

2. A terminating condition that stops the procedure from recurring endlessly (the recursive version of an endless loop).

Both these components are essential and appear in all recursive definitions and algorithms. Recursion is a natural control construct for data structures that have a regular structure and no definite size, such as lists, trees, and graphs, and is particularly appropriate for state space search.

A direct translation of the depth-first search algorithm of Chapter 3 into recursive form illustrates the equivalence of recursion and iteration. This algorithm uses global variables closed and open to maintain lists of states. Breadth-first and best-first search can be designed with virtually the same algorithm, that is, by retaining closed as a global data structure and by implementing open as a queue or a priority queue rather than as a stack (build stack becomes build queue or build priority queue):

```
function depthsearch;                                    % open & closed global

   begin
      if open is empty
         then return FAIL;
      current_state := the first element of open;
      if current_state is a goal state
         then return SUCCESS
         else
            begin
               open := the tail of open;
               closed := closed with current_state added;
               for each child of current_state
                  if not on closed or open                % build stack
                     then add the child to the front of open
            end;
      depthsearch                                         % recur
   end.
```

Depth-first search as just presented does not utilize the full power of recursion. It is possible to simplify the procedure further by using recursion itself (rather than an explicit open list) to organize states and paths through the state space. In this version of the algorithm, a global closed list is used to detect duplicate states and prevent loops, and the open list is implicit in the activation records of the recursive environment. Since the open list can no longer be explicitly manipulated, breadth-first and best-first search are no longer natural extensions of the following algorithm:

```
function depthsearch (current_state);                    % closed is global

begin
   if current_state is a goal
      then return SUCCESS;
   add current_state to closed;
   while current_state has unexamined children
      begin
         child := next unexamined child;
         if child not member of closed
            then if depthsearch(child) = SUCCESS
               then return SUCCESS
      end;
   return FAIL                                            % search exhausted
end
```

Rather than generating all children of a state and placing them on an open list, this algorithm produces the child states one at a time and recursively searches the descendants of each child before generating its sibling. Note that the algorithm assumes an order to the state generation operators. In recursively searching a child state, if some descendant of that state is a goal, the recursive call returns success and the algorithm ignores the siblings. If the recursive call on the child state fails to find a goal, the next sibling is generated and all of its descendants are searched. In this fashion, the algorithm searches the entire graph in a depth-first order. The reader should verify that it actually searches the graph in the same order as the depth-first search algorithm of Section 3.2.3.

The omission of an explicit open list is made possible through recursion. The mechanisms by which a programming language implements recursion include a separate *activation record* (Aho and Ullman 1977) of each recursive call. Each activation record captures the local variables and state of execution of each procedure call. When the procedure is called recursively with a new state, a new activation record stores its parameters (the state), any local variables, and the current state of execution. In a recursive search algorithm, the series of states on the current path are recorded in the sequence of activation records of the recursive calls. The record of each call also indicates the last operation used to generate a child state; this allows the next sibling to be generated when needed.

Backtracking is effected when all descendants of a state fail to include a goal, causing the recursive call to fail. This returns fail to the procedure expanding the parent state, which then generates and recurs on the next sibling. In this situation, the internal mechanisms of recursion do the work of the open list used in the iterative version of the algorithm. The recursive implementation allows the programmer to restrict his or her point of view to a single state and its children rather than having to explicitly maintain an open list of states. The ability of recursion to express global concepts in a closed form is a major source of its power.

As these two algorithms demonstrate, state space search is an inherently recursive process. To find a path from a current state to a goal, move to a child state and recur. If that child state does not lead to a goal, try its siblings in order. Recursion breaks a large and difficult problem (searching the whole space) into smaller, simpler pieces (generate the children of a single state) and applies this strategy (recursively) to each of them. This process continues until a goal state is discovered or the space is exhausted.

In the next section, this recursive approach to problem solving is extended into a controller for a logic-based problem solver that uses unification and inference to generate and search a space of logical relations. The algorithm supports the and of multiple goals as well as back chaining from a goal to premises.

6.1.2   A Recursive Search Example: Pattern-Driven Reasoning

In Section 6.1.2 we apply recursive search to a space of logical inferences; the result is a general search procedure for predicate calculus based problem specifications.

Suppose we want to write an algorithm that determines whether a predicate calculus expression is a logical consequence of some set of assertions. This suggests a goal-directed search with the initial query forming the goal, and modus ponens defining the transitions between states. Given a goal (such as p(a)), the algorithm uses unification to select the implications whose conclusions match the goal (e.g., q(X) → p(X)). Because the algorithm treats implications as potential rules for solving the query, they are often simply called *rules*. After unifying the goal with the conclusion of the implication (or rule) and applying the resulting substitutions throughout the rule, the rule premise becomes a new goal (q(a)).

This is called a *subgoal*. The algorithm then recurs on the subgoal. If a subgoal matches a fact in the knowledge base, search terminates. The series of inferences that led from the initial goal to the given facts prove the truth of the original goal.

```
function pattern_search (current_goal);

begin
    if current_goal is a member of closed                          % test for loops
        then return FAIL
        else add current_goal to closed;
    while there remain in data base unifying facts or rules do
        begin
            case
                current_goal unifies with a fact:
                    return SUCCESS;
                current_goal is a conjunction (p ∧ ...):
                    begin
                        for each conjunct do
                            call pattern_search on conjunct;
                        if pattern_search succeeds for all conjuncts
                            then return SUCCESS
                            else return FAIL
                    end;
                current_goal unifies with rule conclusion (p in q → p):
                    begin
                        apply goal unifying substitutions to premise (q);
                        call pattern_search on premise;
                        if pattern_search succeeds
                            then return SUCCESS
                            else return FAIL
                    end;
            end;                                                    % end case
        end;
    return FAIL
end.
```

In the function pattern_search, search is performed by a modified version of the recursive search algorithm that uses unification, Section 2.3.2, to determine when two expressions match and modus ponens to generate the children of states. The current focus of the search is represented by the variable current_goal. If current_goal matches with a fact, the algorithm returns success. Otherwise the algorithm attempts to match current_goal with the conclusion of some rule, recursively attempting to solve the premise. If current_goal does not match any of the given assertions, the algorithm returns fail. This algorithm also handles conjunctive goals.

For simplicity, the algorithm does not address the problem of maintaining consistency among the variable substitutions produced by unification. This is important when solving conjunctive queries with shared variables (as in $p(X) \land q(X)$). Not only must both conjuncts succeed, but they must succeed with unifiable bindings for X, Section 2.3.2.

The major advantage of using general methods such as unification and modus ponens to generate states is that the resulting algorithm may search *any* space of logical inferences. The specifics of a problem are described using predicate calculus assertions. Thus, we have a means of separating problem-solving knowledge from its control and implementation on the computer. pattern_search provides our first implementation of the separation of knowledge and control.

Although the initial version of pattern_search defined the behavior of a search algorithm for predicate calculus expressions, several subtleties must still be addressed. These include the order with which the algorithm tries alternative matches and proper handling of the full set of logical operators ($\wedge$, $\vee$, and $\neg$). Logic is declarative, and without a prescribed search strategy: it defines a space of possible inferences but does not tell a problem solver how to make the useful ones.

To reason with predicate calculus, we need a control regime that systematically searches the space, avoiding meaningless paths and loops. A control algorithm such as pattern_search must try alternative matches in some sequential order. Knowing this order allows the program designer to control search by properly ordering rules in the knowledge base. A simple way to define such an order is to require that the algorithm try rules and facts in the order that they appear in the knowledge base.

A second issue is the existence of logical connectives in the rule premises: e.g., implications of the form "p $\leftarrow$ q $\wedge$ r" or "p $\leftarrow$ q $\vee$ (r $\wedge$ s)." As will be recalled from the discussion of and/or graphs, an $\wedge$ operator indicates that both expressions must be shown to be true for the entire premise to be true. In addition, the conjuncts of the expression must be solved with consistent variable bindings. Thus, to solve p(X) $\wedge$ q(X), it is not sufficient to solve p(X) with the substitution {a/X} and q(X) with the substitution {b/X}. Both must be solved with the same or unifiable bindings for X. An or operator, on the other hand, indicates that either expression must be found to be true. The search algorithm must take this into account.

The last addition to the algorithm is the ability to solve goals involving logical negation ($\neg$). pattern_search handles negated goals by first solving the operand of the $\neg$. If this subgoal succeeds, then pattern_search returns fail. If the operand fails, then pattern_search returns an empty substitution set, indicating success. Note that even though a subgoal may contain variables, the result of solving its negation may not contain any substitutions. This is because $\neg$ can succeed only if its operand *fails*; hence, it cannot return any bindings for the operand.

Finally, the algorithm should not return success but should return the bindings involved in the solution. The complete version of pattern_search, which returns the set of unifications that satisfies each subgoal, is:

```
function pattern_search(current_goal);

begin
    if current_goal is a member of closed              % test for loops
        then return FAIL
        else add current_goal to closed;
    while there remain unifying facts or rules do
```

```
begin
   case

      current_goal unifies with a fact:
         return unifying substitutions;
      current_goal is negated (¬ p):
         begin
            call pattern_search on p;
            if pattern_search returns FAIL
               then return {};                                        % negation is true
               else return FAIL;
         end;

      current_goal is a conjunction (p ∧ ...):
         begin
            for each conjunct do
               begin
                  call pattern_search on conjunct;
                  if pattern_search returns FAIL
                     then return FAIL;
                     else apply substitutions to other conjuncts;
               end;
            if pattern_search returns SUCCESS for all conjuncts
               then return composition of unifications;
               else return FAIL;
         end;

      current_goal is a disjunction (p ∨ ...):
         begin
            repeat for each disjunct
               call pattern_search on disjunct
            until no more disjuncts or SUCCESS;
            if pattern_search returns SUCCESS
               then return substitutions
               else return FAIL;
         end;

      current_goal unifies with rule conclusion (p in p ← q):
         begin
            apply goal unifying substitutions to premise (q);
            call pattern_search on premise;
            if pattern_search returns SUCCESS
               then return composition of p and q substitutions
               else return FAIL;
         end;
      end;                                                            %end case
   end                                                                %end while
   return FAIL
end.
```

This algorithm for searching a space of predicate calculus rules and facts is the basis of PROLOG (where the Horn clause form of predicates is used, Section 13.3) and in many goal-directed expert system shells (Chapter 8). An alternative control structure for pattern-directed search is provided by the *production system*, discussed in the next section.

6.2 Production Systems

6.2.1 Definition and History

The *production system* is a model of computation that has proved particularly important in AI, both for implementing search algorithms and for modeling human problem solving. A production system provides pattern-directed control of a problem-solving process and consists of a set of *production rules*, a *working memory*, and a *recognize–act* control cycle.

DEFINITION

PRODUCTION SYSTEM

A *production system* is defined by:

1. *The set of production rules*. These are often simply called *productions*. A production is a *condition–action* pair and defines a single chunk of problem-solving knowledge. The *condition part* of the rule is a pattern that determines when that rule may be applied to a problem instance. The *action part* defines the associated problem-solving step.

2. *Working memory* contains a description of the *current state of the world* in a reasoning process. This description is a pattern that is matched against the condition part of a production to select appropriate problem-solving actions. When the condition element of a rule is matched by the contents of working memory, the action associated with that condition may then be performed. The actions of production rules are specifically designed to alter the contents of working memory.

3. *The recognize–act cycle*. The control structure for a production system is simple: *working memory* is initialized with the beginning problem description. The current state of the problem-solving is maintained as a set of patterns in working memory. These patterns are matched against the conditions of the production rules; this produces a subset of the production rules, called the *conflict set*, whose conditions match the patterns in working memory. The productions in the conflict set are said to be *enabled*. One of the productions in the conflict set is then selected (*conflict resolution*) and the production is

fired. To fire a rule, its *action* is performed, changing the contents of working memory. After the selected production rule is fired, the control cycle repeats with the modified working memory. The process terminates when the contents of working memory do not match any rule conditions.

Conflict resolution chooses a rule from the conflict set for firing. Conflict resolution strategies may be simple, such as selecting the first rule whose condition matches the state of the world, or may involve complex rule selection heuristics. This is an important way in which a production system allows the addition of heuristic control to a search algorithm.

The *pure* production system model has no mechanism for recovering from dead ends in the search; it simply continues until no more productions are enabled and halts. Many practical implementations of production systems allow backtracking to a previous state of working memory in such situations.

A schematic drawing of a production system is presented in Figure 6.1.

A very simple example of production system execution appears in Figure 6.2. This is a production system program for sorting a string composed of the letters a, b, and c. In this example, a production is enabled if its condition matches a portion of the string in working memory. When a rule is fired, the substring that matched the rule condition is replaced by the string on the right-hand side of the rule. Production systems are a general model of computation that can be programmed to do anything that can be done on a computer. Their real strength, however, is as an architecture for knowledge-based systems.

The idea for the *production*-based design for computing came originally from writings of Post (1943), who proposed a production rule model as a formal theory of computation. The main construct of this theory was a set of rewrite rules for strings in many ways similar to the parsing rules in Example 3.3.6. It is also closely related to the approach taken by Markov algorithms (Markov 1954) and, like them, is equivalent in power to a Turing machine.

An interesting application of production rules to modeling human cognition is found in the work of Newell and Simon at the Carnegie Institute of Technology (now Carnegie Mellon University) in the 1960s and 1970s. The programs they developed, including the *General Problem Solver*, are largely responsible for the importance of production systems in AI. In this research, human subjects were monitored in various problem-solving activities such as solving problems in predicate logic and playing games like chess. The *protocol* (behavior patterns, including verbal descriptions of the problem-solving process, eye movements, etc.) of problem-solving subjects was recorded and broken down to its elementary components. These components were regarded as the basic bits of problem-solving knowledge in the human subjects and were composed as a search through a graph (called the *problem behavior graph*). A production system was then used to implement search of this graph.

The production rules represented the set of problem-solving skills of the human subject. The present focus of attention was represented as the current state of the world. In executing the production system, the "attention" or "current focus" of the problem solver would match a production rule, which would change the state of "attention" to match another production-encoded skill, and so on.

It is important to note that in this work Newell and Simon used the production system not only as a vehicle for implementing graph search but also as an actual model of human problem-solving behavior. The productions corresponded to the problem-solving skills in the human's *long-term memory*. Like the skills in long-term memory, these productions are not changed by the execution of the system; they are invoked by the "pattern" of a

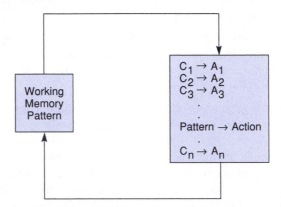

Figure 6.1 A production system. Control loops until working memory pattern no longer matches the conditions of any productions.

Production set:

1. ba $\rightarrow$ ab
2. ca $\rightarrow$ ac
3. cb $\rightarrow$ bc

Iteration #	Working memory	Conflict set	Rule fired
0	cbaca	1, 2, 3	1
1	cabca	2	2
2	acbca	2, 3	2
3	acbac	1, 3	1
4	acabc	2	2
5	aacbc	3	3
6	aabcc	Ø	Halt

Figure 6.2 Trace of a simple production system.

particular problem instance, and new skills may be added without requiring "recoding" of the previously existing knowledge. The production system's working memory corresponds to *short-term memory* or current focus of attention in the human and describes the current stage of solving a problem instance. The contents of working memory are generally not retained after a problem has been solved.

These origins of the production system technology are further described in *Human Problem Solving* by Newell and Simon (1972) and in Luger (1978, 1994). Newell, Simon, and others have continued to use production rules to model the difference between novices and experts (Larkin et al. 1980; Simon and Simon 1978) in areas such as solving algebra word problems and physics problems. Production systems also form a basis for studying learning in both humans and computers (Klahr et al. 1987); ACT* (Anderson 1983*b*) and SOAR (Newell 1990) build on this tradition.

Production systems provide a model for encoding human expertise in the form of rules and designing pattern-driven search algorithms, tasks that are central to the design of the rule-based expert system. In expert systems, the production system is not necessarily assumed to actually model human problem-solving behavior; however, the aspects of production systems that make them useful as a potential model of human problem solving (modularity of rules, separation of knowledge and control, separation of working memory and problem-solving knowledge) make them an ideal tool for designing and building expert systems.

An important family of AI languages comes directly out of the production system language research at Carnegie Mellon. These are the OPS languages; OPS stands for *Official Production System*. Although their origins are in modeling human problem solving, these languages have proved highly effective for programming expert systems and for other AI applications. OPS5 was the implementation language for the VAX configurer XCON and other early expert systems developed at Digital Equipment Corporation (McDermott 1981, 1982; Soloway et al. 1987; Barker and O'Connor 1989). OPS interpreters are widely available for PCs and workstations. CLIPS, implemented in the C programming language, is a widely used, object-oriented version of a production system built by NASA. JESS, a production system implemented in Java, was created by Sandia National Laboratories.

In the next section we give examples of how the production system may be used to solve a variety of search problems.

6.2.2   Examples of Production Systems

EXAMPLE 6.2.1: THE 8-PUZZLE, REVISITED

The search space generated by the 8-puzzle, introduced in Chapter 3, is both complex enough to be interesting and small enough to be tractable, so it is frequently used to explore different search strategies, such as depth-first and breadth-first search, as well as the heuristic strategies of Chapter 4. We now present a production system solution.

Recall that we gain generality by thinking of "moving the blank space" rather than moving a numbered tile. Legal moves are defined by the productions in Figure 6.3. Of course, all four of these moves are applicable only when the blank is in the center; when it

Production set:

Condition		Action
goal state in working memory	→	halt
blank is not on the left edge	→	move the blank left
blank is not on the top edge	→	move the blank up
blank is not on the right edge	→	move the blank right
blank is not on the bottomedge	→	move the blank down

Working memory is the present board state and goal state.

Control regime:

1. Try each production in order.
2. Do not allow loops.
3. Stop when goal is found.

Figure 6.3 The 8-puzzle as a production system.

is in one of the corners only two moves are possible. If a beginning state and a goal state for the 8-puzzle are now specified, it is possible to make a production system accounting of the problem's search space.

An actual implementation of this problem might represent each board configuration with a "state" predicate with nine parameters (for nine possible locations of the eight tiles and the blank); rules could be written as implications whose premise performs the required condition check. Alternatively, arrays or list structures could be used for board states.

An example, taken from Nilsson (1980), of the space searched in finding a solution for the problem given in Figure 6.3 follows in Figure 6.4. Because this solution path can go very deep if unconstrained, a depth bound has been added to the search. (A simple means for adding a depth bound is to keep track of the length/depth of the current path and to force backtracking if this bound is exceeded.) A depth bound of 5 is used in the solution of Figure 6.4. Note that the number of possible states of working memory grows exponentially with the depth of the search.

EXAMPLE 6.2.2: THE KNIGHT'S TOUR PROBLEM

In the game of chess, a knight can move two squares either horizontally or vertically followed by one square in an orthogonal direction as long as it does not move off the board. There are thus at most eight possible moves that the knight may make (Figure 6.5).

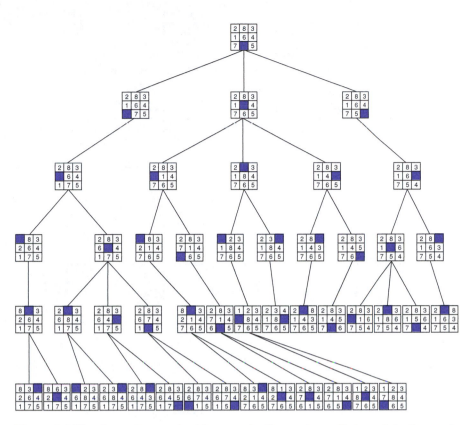

Figure 6.4 The 8-puzzle searched by a production system with loop detection and depth bound 5, from Nilsson (1971).

As traditionally defined, the knight's tour problem attempts to find a series of legal moves in which the knight lands on each square of the chessboard exactly once. This problem has been a mainstay in the development and presentation of search algorithms. The example we use in this chapter is a simplified version of the knight's tour problem. It asks whether there is a series of legal moves that will take the knight from one square to another on a reduced-size (3 × 3) chessboard.

Figure 6.6 shows a 3 × 3 chessboard with each square labeled with integers 1 to 9. This labeling scheme is used instead of the more general approach of giving each space a row and column number in order to further simplify the example. Because of the reduced size of the problem, we simply enumerate the alternative moves rather than develop a general move operator. The legal moves on the board are then described in predicate calculus using a predicate called move, whose parameters are the starting and ending squares of a legal move. For example, move(1,8) takes the knight from the upper left-hand corner to the middle of the bottom row. The predicates of Figure 6.6 enumerate all possible moves for the 3 × 3 chessboard.

The 3 × 3 knight's tour problem may be solved with a production system. Each move can be represented as a rule whose condition is the location of the knight on a particular

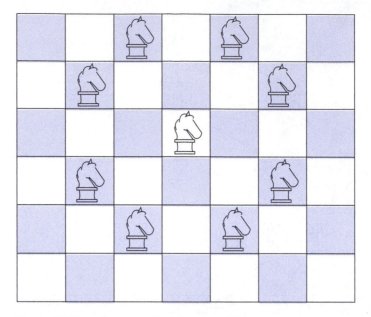

Figure 6.5 Legal moves of a chess knight.

move(1,8)	move(6,1)
move(1,6)	move(6,7)
move(2,9)	move(7,2)
move(2,7)	move(7,6)
move(3,4)	move(8,3)
move(3,8)	move(8,1)
move(4,9)	move(9,2)
move(4,3)	move(9,4)

1	2	3
4	5	6
7	8	9

Figure 6.6 A 3 × 3 chessboard with move rules for the
simplified knight tour problem.

square and whose action moves the knight to another square. Sixteen productions, presented in Table 6.1, represent all possible moves of the knight.

We next specify a recursive procedure to implement a control algorithm for the production system. Because path(X,X) will unify only with predicates such as path(3,3) or path(5,5), it defines the desired terminating condition. If path(X,X) does not succeed we look at the production rules for a possible next state and then recur. The general recursive path definition is then given by two predicate calculus formulas:

$\forall$ X path(X,X)
$\forall$ X,Y [path(X,Y) ← $\exists$ Z [move(X,Z) ∧ path(Z,Y)]]

RULE #	CONDITION		ACTION
1	knight on square 1	→	move knight to square 8
2	knight on square 1	→	move knight to square 6
3	knight on square 2	→	move knight to square 9
4	knight on square 2	→	move knight to square 7
5	knight on square 3	→	move knight to square 4
6	knight on square 3	→	move knight to square 8
7	knight on square 4	→	move knight to square 9
8	knight on square 4	→	move knight to square 3
9	knight on square 6	→	move knight to square 1
10	knight on square 6	→	move knight to square 7
11	knight on square 7	→	move knight to square 2
12	knight on square 7	→	move knight to square 6
13	knight on square 8	→	move knight to square 3
14	knight on square 8	→	move knight to square 1
15	knight on square 9	→	move knight to square 2
16	knight on square 9	→	move knight to square 4

Table 6.1 Production rules for the 3×3 knight problem.

Working memory, the parameters of the recursive path predicate, contains both the current board state and the goal state. The control regime applies rules until the current state equals the goal state and then halts. A simple conflict resolution scheme would fire the first rule that did not cause the search to loop. Because the search may lead to dead ends (from which every possible move leads to a previously visited state and thus a loop), the control regime must also allow backtracking; an execution of this production system that determines whether a path exists from square 1 to square 2 is charted in Figure 6.7. This characterization of the path definition as a production system is given in Figure 6.8.

Production systems are capable of generating infinite loops when searching a state space graph. These loops are particularly difficult to spot in a production system because the rules can fire in any order. That is, looping may appear in the execution of the system, but it cannot easily be found from a syntactic inspection of the rule set. For example, with the "move" rules of the knight's tour problem ordered as in Table 6.1 and a conflict resolution strategy of selecting the first match, the pattern move(2,X) would match with move(2,9), indicating a move to square 9. On the next iteration, the pattern move(9,X) would match with move(9,2), taking the search back to square 2, causing a loop.

To prevent looping, pattern_search checked a global list (closed) of visited states. The actual conflict resolution strategy was therefore: select the first matching move *that leads*

Iteration #	Working memory		Conflict set (rule #'s)	Fire rule
	Current square	Goal square		
0	1	2	1, 2	1
1	8	2	13, 14	13
2	3	2	5, 6	5
3	4	2	7, 8	7
4	9	2	15, 16	15
5	2	2		Halt

Figure 6.7 A production system solution to the 3 × 3
knight's tour problem.

to an unvisited state. In a production system, the proper place for recording such case-specific data as a list of previously visited states is not a global closed list but the working memory itself. We can alter the path predicate to use working memory for loop detection. Assume that our predicate calculus language is augmented by the addition of a special construct, assert(X), which causes its argument X to be entered into the working memory. assert is not an ordinary predicate but an action that is performed; hence, it always succeeds.

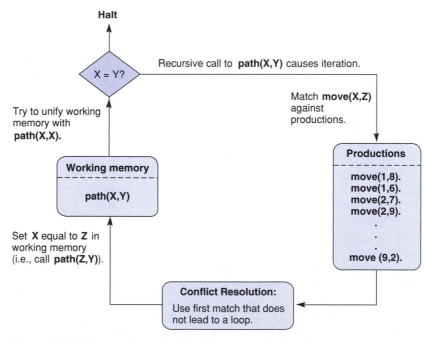

Figure 6.8 The recursive path algorithm as production system.

assert is used to place a "marker" in working memory to indicate when a state has been visited. This marker is represented as a unary predicate, been(X), which takes as its argument a square on the board. been(X) is added to working memory when a new state X is visited. Conflict resolution may then require that been(Z) must not be in working memory before move(X,Z) can fire. For a specific value of Z this can be tested by matching a pattern against working memory.

The modified recursive path controller for the production system is:

$\forall$ X path(X,X)
$\forall$ X,Y [path(X,Y) $\leftarrow$ $\exists$ Z [move(X,Z) $\land \neg$ (been(Z)) $\land$ assert(been(Z)) $\land$ path(Z,Y)]]

In this definition, move(X,Z) succeeds on the first match with a move predicate. This binds a value to Z. If been(Z) matches with an entry in working memory, ¬(been (Z)) will cause a failure (i.e., it will be false). pattern_search will then backtrack and try another match for move(X,Z). If square Z is a new state, the search will continue, with been(Z) asserted to the working memory to prevent future loops. The actual firing of the production takes place when the path algorithm recurs. Thus, the presence of been predicates in working memory implements loop detection in this production system.

EXAMPLE 6.2.3: THE FULL KNIGHT'S TOUR

We may generalize the knight's tour solution to the full 8×8 chessboard. Because it makes little sense to enumerate moves for such a complex problem, we replace the 16 move facts with a set of 8 rules to generate legal knight moves. These moves (productions) correspond to the 8 possible ways a knight can move (Figure 6.5).

If we index the chessboard by row and column numbers, we can define a production rule for moving the knight down two squares and right one square:

CONDITION: current row $\leq$ 6 $\land$ current column $\leq$ 7
ACTION: new row = current row + 2 $\land$ new column = current column + 1

If we use predicate calculus to represent productions, then a board square could be defined by the predicate square(R,C), representing the Rth row and Cth column of the board. The above rule could be rewritten in predicate calculus as:

move(square(Row, Column), square(Newrow, Newcolumn)) $\leftarrow$
    less_than_or_equals(Row, 6) $\land$
    equals(Newrow, plus(Row, 2)) $\land$
    less_than_or_equals(Column, 7) $\land$
    equals(Newcolumn, plus(Column, 1))

plus is a function for addition; less_than_or_equals and equals have the obvious arithmetic interpretations. Seven additional rules can be designed that compute the remaining possible moves. These rules replace the move facts in the 3×3 version of the problem.

The path definition from the 3×3 example defines the control loop for this problem. As we have seen, when predicate calculus descriptions are interpreted procedurally, such as through the pattern_search algorithm, subtle changes are made to the semantics of predicate calculus. One such change is the sequential fashion in which goals are solved. This imposes an ordering, or *procedural semantics*, on predicate calculus expressions. Another change is the introduction of *meta-logical* predicates such as assert, which indicate actions beyond the truth value interpretation of predicate calculus expressions. These issues are discussed in more detail in the PROLOG, Chapter 15, and in the LISP implementation of a logic programming engine, Chapter 16.

EXAMPLE 6.2.4: THE FINANCIAL ADVISOR AS A PRODUCTION SYSTEM

In Chapters 2 and 3, we developed a small financial advisor, using predicate calculus to represent the financial knowledge and graph search to make the appropriate inferences in a consultation. The production system provides a natural vehicle for its implementation. The implications of the logical description form the productions. The case-specific information (an individual's salary, dependents, etc.) is loaded into working memory. Rules are enabled when their premises are satisfied. A rule is chosen from this conflict set and fired, adding its conclusion to working memory. This continues until all possible top-level conclusions have been added to the working memory. Indeed, many expert system "shells" are production systems with added features for supporting the user interface, handling uncertainty in the reasoning, editing the knowledge base, and tracing execution.

6.2.3   Control of Search in Production Systems

The production system model offers a range of opportunities for adding heuristic control to a search algorithm. These include the choice of data-driven or goal-driven strategies, the structure of the rules themselves, and the choice of strategies for conflict resolution.

Control through Choice of Data-Driven or Goal-Driven Search Strategy

Data-driven search begins with a problem description (such as a set of logical axioms, symptoms of an illness, or a body of data that needs interpretation) and infers new knowledge from the data. This is done by applying rules of inference, legal moves in a game, or other state-generating operations to the current description of the world and adding the results to that problem description. This process continues until a goal state is reached.

This description of data-driven reasoning emphasizes its close fit with the production system model of computation. The "current state of the world" (data that have been either assumed to be true or deduced as true with previous use of production rules) is placed in working memory. The recognize–act cycle then matches the current state against the (ordered) set of productions. When these data match (are unified with) the condition(s) of one of the production rules, the action of the production adds (by modifying working memory) a new piece of information to the current state of the world.

All productions have the form CONDITION $\rightarrow$ ACTION. When the CONDITION matches some elements of working memory, its ACTION is performed. If the production rules are formulated as logical implications and the ACTION adds assertions to working

Production set:

1. $p \wedge q \rightarrow goal$
2. $r \wedge s \rightarrow p$
3. $w \wedge r \rightarrow q$
4. $t \wedge u \rightarrow q$
5. $v \rightarrow s$
6. $start \rightarrow v \wedge r \wedge q$

Trace of execution:

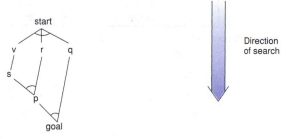

Iteration #	Working memory	Conflict set	Rule fired
0	start	6	6
1	start, v, r, q	6, 5	5
2	start, v, r, q, s	6, 5, 2	2
3	start, v, r, q, s, p	6, 5, 2, 1	1
4	start, v, r, q, s, p, goal	6, 5, 2, 1	halt

Space searched by execution:

Direction of search

Figure 6.9 Data-driven search in a production system.

memory, then the act of firing a rule can correspond to an application of the inference rule modus ponens. This creates a new state of the graph.

Figure 6.9 presents a simple data-driven search on a set of productions expressed as propositional calculus implications. The conflict resolution strategy is a simple one of choosing the enabled rule that has fired least recently (or not at all); in the event of ties, the first rule is chosen. Execution halts when a goal is reached. The figure also presents the sequence of rule firings and the stages of working memory in the execution, along with a graph of the space searched.

To this point we have treated production systems in a data-driven fashion; however they may also be used to produce a goal-driven search. As defined in Chapter 3, goal-driven search begins with a goal and works backward to the facts of the problem to satisfy that goal. To implement this in a production system, the goal is placed in working memory and matched against the ACTIONs of the production rules. These ACTIONs are matched (by unification, for example) just as the CONDITIONs of the productions were matched in the data-driven reasoning. All production rules whose conclusions (ACTIONs) match the goal form the conflict set.

When the ACTION of a rule is matched, the CONDITIONs are added to working memory and become the new subgoals (states) of the search. The new states are then matched to the ACTIONs of other production rules. The process continues until facts are found, usually in the problem's initial description or, as is often the case in expert systems, by directly asking the user for specific information. The search stops when the CONDITIONs of all the productions fired in this backward fashion are found to be true. These CONDITIONs and the chain of rule firings leading to the original goal form a proof

Production set:

1. $p \wedge q \rightarrow$ goal
2. $r \wedge s \rightarrow p$
3. $w \wedge r \rightarrow p$
4. $t \wedge u \rightarrow q$
5. $v \quad \rightarrow s$
6. start $\rightarrow v \wedge r \wedge q$

Trace of execution:

Iteration #	Working memory	Conflict set	Rule fired
0	goal	1	1
1	goal, p, q	1, 2, 3, 4	2
2	goal, p, q, r, s	1, 2, 3, 4, 5	3
3	goal, p, q, r, s, w	1, 2, 3, 4, 5	4
4	goal, p, q, r, s, w, t, u	1, 2, 3, 4, 5	5
5	goal, p, q, r, s, w, t, u, v	1, 2, 3, 4, 5, 6	6
6	goal, p, q, r, s, w, t, u, v, start	1, 2, 3, 4, 5, 6	halt

Space searched by execution:

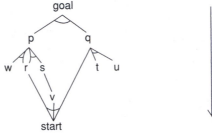

Direction
of search

Figure 6.10 Goal-driven search in a production system.

of its truth through successive inferences such as modus ponens. See Figure 6.10 for an instance of goal-driven reasoning on the same set of productions used in Figure 6.9. Note that the goal-driven search fires a different series of productions and searches a different space than the data-driven version.

As this discussion illustrates, the production system offers a natural characterization of both goal-driven and data-driven search. The production rules are the encoded set of inferences (the "knowledge" in a rule-based expert system) for changing state within the graph. When the current state of the world (the set of true statements describing the world) matches the CONDITIONs of the production rules and this match causes the ACTION part of the rule to create another (true) descriptor for the world, it is referred to as data-driven search.

Alternatively, when the goal is matched against the ACTION part of the rules in the production rule set and their CONDITIONs are then set up as subgoals to be shown to be "true" (by matching the ACTIONs of the rules on the next cycle of the production system), the result is goal-driven problem solving.

Because a set of rules may be executed in either a data-driven or goal-driven fashion, we can compare and contrast the efficiency of each approach in controlling search. The complexity of search for either strategy is measured by such notions as *branching factor* or *penetrance* (Section 4.5). These measures of search complexity can provide a cost estimate for both the data-driven and goal-driven versions of a problem solver and therefore help in selecting the most effective strategy.

Start

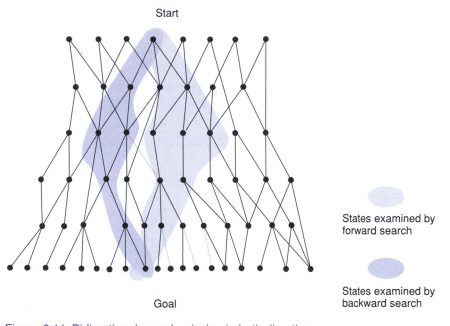

States examined by
forward search

States examined by
backward search

Goal

Figure 6.11 Bidirectional search missing in both directions,
resulting in excessive search.

We can also employ combinations of strategies. For example, we can search in a
forward direction until the number of states becomes large and then switch to a goal
directed search to use possible subgoals to select among alternative states. The danger in
this situation is that, when heuristic or best-first search (Chapter 4) is used, the parts of the
graphs actually searched may "miss" each other and ultimately require more search than a
simpler approach, as in Figure 6.11. However, when the branching of a space is constant
and exhaustive search is used, a combined search strategy can cut back drastically the
amount of space searched, as is seen in Figure 6.12.

Control of Search through Rule Structure

The structure of rules in a production system, including the distinction between the
condition and the action and the order in which conditions are tried, determines the fashion
in which the space is searched. In introducing predicate calculus as a representation
language, we emphasized the *declarative* nature of its semantics. That is, predicate
calculus expressions simply define true relationships in a problem domain and make no
assertion about their order of interpretation. Thus, an individual rule might be $\forall\, X\, (foo(X)$
$\wedge\, goo(X) \rightarrow moo(X))$. Under the rules of predicate calculus, an alternative form of the same
rule is $\forall\, X\, (foo(X) \rightarrow moo(X) \vee \neg\, goo(X))$. The equivalence relationship between these two
clauses is left as an exercise (Chapter 2).

Although these formulations are logically equivalent, they do not lead to the same
results when interpreted as productions because the production system imposes an order

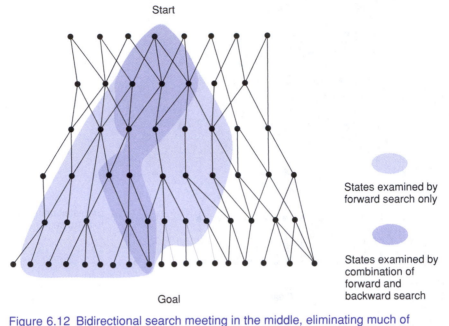

Start

States examined by
forward search only

States examined by
combination of
forward and
backward search

Goal

Figure 6.12 Bidirectional search meeting in the middle, eliminating much of
the space examined by unidirectional search.

on the matching and firing of rules. Thus, the specific form of the rules determines the ease
(or possibility) of matching a rule against a problem instance. This is a result of differences
in the way in which the production system *interprets* the rules. The production system
imposes a *procedural semantics* on the declarative language used to form the rules.

Because the production system tries each of its rules in a specific order, the programmer
may control search through the structure and order of rules in the production set. Although
logically equivalent, $\forall$ X (foo(X) $\wedge$ goo(X) $\rightarrow$ moo(X)) and $\forall$ X (foo(X) $\rightarrow$ moo(X) $\vee$ $\neg$
goo(X)) do not have the same behavior in a search implementation.

Human experts encode crucial heuristics within their rules of expertise. The order of
premises encodes important procedural information for solving the problem. It is
important that this form be preserved in building a program that "solves problems like the
expert". When a mechanic says, "If the engine won't turn over and the lights don't come
on, then check the battery", she is suggesting a specific sequence of actions. This
information is not captured by the logically equivalent statement "the engine turns over or
the lights come on or check the battery." This form of the rules is critical in controlling
search, making the system behave logically and making order of rule firings more
understandable.

Control of Search through Conflict Resolution

Though production systems (like all architectures for knowledge-based systems) allow
heuristics to be encoded in the knowledge content of rules themselves, they offer other

opportunities for heuristic control through conflict resolution. Although the simplest such strategy is to choose the first rule that matches the contents of working memory, any strategy may potentially be applied to conflict resolution. For example, conflict resolution strategies supported by OPS5 (Brownston et al. 1985) include:

1. *Refraction.* Refraction specifies that once a rule has fired, it may not fire again until the working memory elements that match its conditions have been modified. This discourages looping.

2. *Recency.* The recency strategy prefers rules whose conditions match with the patterns most recently added to working memory. This focuses the search on a single line of reasoning.

3. *Specificity.* This strategy assumes that it is appropriate to use a more specific problem-solving rule rather than to use a more general one. One rule is more specific than another if it has more conditions, which implies that it will match fewer working memory patterns.

6.2.4 Advantages of Production Systems for AI

As illustrated by the preceding examples, the production system offers a general framework for implementing search. Because of its simplicity, modifiability, and flexibility in applying problem-solving knowledge, the production system has proved to be an important tool for the construction of expert systems and other AI applications. The major advantages of production systems for artificial intelligence include:

Separation of Knowledge and Control. The production system is an elegant model of separation of knowledge and control in a computer program. Control is provided by the recognize–act cycle of the production system loop, and the problem-solving knowledge is encoded in the rules themselves. The advantages of this separation include ease of modifying the knowledge base without requiring a change in the code for program control and, conversely, the ability to alter the code for program control without changing the set of production rules.

A Natural Mapping onto State Space Search. The components of a production system map naturally into the constructs of state space search. The successive states of working memory form the nodes of a state space graph. The production rules are the set of possible transitions between states, with conflict resolution implementing the selection of a branch in the state space. These rules simplify the implementation, debugging, and documentation of search algorithms.

Modularity of Production Rules. An important aspect of the production system model is the lack of any syntactic interactions between production rules. Rules may only effect the firing of other rules by changing the pattern in working memory; they may not "call" another rule directly as if it were a subroutine, nor may they set the value of variables in other production rules. The scope of the variables of these rules is confined to the individual rule. This syntactic independence supports the incremental development of expert systems by successively adding, deleting, or changing the knowledge (rules) of the system.

Pattern-Directed Control. The problems addressed by AI programs require particular flexibility in program execution. This goal is served by the fact that the rules in a production system may fire in any sequence. The descriptions of a problem that make up the current state of the world determine the conflict set and, consequently, the particular search path and solution.

Opportunities for Heuristic Control of Search. (Several techniques for heuristic control were described in the preceding section.)

Tracing and Explanation. The modularity of rules and the iterative nature of their execution make it easier to trace execution of a production system. At each stage of the recognize–act cycle, the selected rule can be displayed. Because each rule corresponds to a single "chunk" of problem-solving knowledge, the rule content can provide a meaningful explanation of the system's current state and action. Furthermore, the chain of rules used within a solution process reflects both a path in the graph as well as a human expert's "line of reasoning", as we see in detail in Chapter 8. In contrast, a single line of code or procedure in a traditional language such as Pascal or FORTRAN is virtually meaningless.

Language Independence. The production system control model is independent of the representation chosen for rules and working memory, as long as that representation supports pattern matching. We described production rules as predicate calculus implications of the form $A \Rightarrow B$, where the truth of A and the inference rule modus ponens allow us to conclude B. Although there are many advantages to using logic as both the basis for representation of knowledge and the source of sound inference rules, the production system model may be used with other representations.

Although predicate calculus offers the advantage of logically sound inference, many problems require reasoning that is not sound in the logical sense. Instead, they involve probabilistic reasoning, use of uncertain evidence, and default assumptions. Later chapters (7, 8, and 9) discuss alternative inference rules that provide these capabilities. Regardless of the type of inference rules employed, however, the production system provides a vehicle for searching the state space.

A Plausible Model of Human Problem Solving. Modeling human problem solving was among the first uses of production systems, see Newell and Simon (1972). They continue to be used as a model for human performance in many areas of cognitive science research (Chapter 17).

Pattern-directed search gives us the ability to explore the space of logical inferences in the predicate calculus. Many problems build on this technique by using predicate calculus to model specific aspects of the world such as time and change. In the next section *blackboard systems* are presented as a variation of the production system methodology, where task specific groups of production rules are combined into *knowledge sources* and cooperate in problem solving by communication through a global working memory or *blackboard*.

6.3   The Blackboard Architecture for Problem Solving

The *blackboard* is the final control mechanism presented in this chapter. When we want to examine the states in a space of logical inferences in a very deterministic fashion, production systems provide great flexibility by allowing us to represent multiple partial solutions simultaneously in working memory and to select the next state through conflict resolution. Blackboards extend production systems by allowing us to organize production memory into separate modules, each of which corresponds to a different subset of the production rules. Blackboards integrate these separate sets of production rules and coordinate the actions of these multiple problem solving agents, sometimes called *knowledge sources*, within a single global structure, the *blackboard*.

Many problems require the coordination of a number of different types of agents. For example, a speech understanding program may have to first manipulate an utterance represented as a digitized waveform. As the understanding process continues, it must find words in this utterance, form these into sentences, and finally produce a semantic representation of the utterance's meaning.

A related problem occurs when multiple processes must cooperate to solve a single problem. An example of this is the sensor fusion problem (Lesser and Corkill 1983). Assume that we have a network of sensors, each of which is monitored by a separate process. Assume also that the processes can communicate and that proper interpretation of each sensor's data depends on the data received by other sensors in the network. This problem arises in situations as diverse as tracking airplanes across multiple radar sites to combining the readings of multiple sensors in a manufacturing process.

The *blackboard architecture* is a model of control that has been applied to these and other problems requiring the coordination of multiple processes or knowledge sources. A *blackboard* is a central global data base for the communication of independent asynchronous knowledge sources focusing on related aspects of a particular problem. Figure 6.13 gives a schematic of the blackboard design.

In Figure 6.13 each *knowledge source* KS_i gets its data from the blackboard, processes the data, and returns its results to the blackboard to be used by the other knowledge sources. Each KS_i is independent in that it is a separate process operating according to its own specifications and, when a multiprocessing or multiprocessor system is used, it is independent of the other processing in the problem. It is an asynchronous system in that each KS_i begins its operation whenever it finds appropriate input data posted on the blackboard. When it finishes its processing it posts its results to the blackboard and awaits new input data.

The blackboard approach to organizing a large program was first presented in the HEARSAY-II research (Erman et al. 1980, Reddy 1976). HEARSAY-II was a speech understanding program; it was initially designed as the front end for a library database of

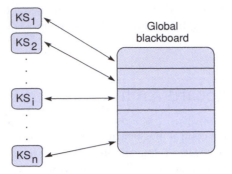

Figure 6.13 Blackboard architecture.

computer science articles. The user of the library would address the computer in spoken English with queries such as, "Are any by Feigenbaum and Feldman?" and the computer would answer the question with information from the library database. Speech understanding requires that we integrate a number of different processes, all of which require very different knowledge and algorithms, all of which can be exponentially complex. Signal processing; recognition of phonemes, syllables, and words; syntactic parsing; and semantic analysis mutually constrain each other in interpreting speech.

The blackboard architecture allowed HEARSAY-II to coordinate the several different knowledge sources required for this complex task. The blackboard is usually organized along two dimensions. With HEARSAY-II these dimensions were *time* as the speech act was produced and the *analysis level* of the utterance. Each level of analysis was processed by a different class of knowledge sources. These analysis levels were:

KS$_1$ The waveform of the acoustic signal.
KS$_2$ The phonemes or possible sound segments of the acoustic signal.
KS$_3$ The syllables that the phonemes could produce.
KS$_4$ The possible words as analyzed by one KS.
KS$_5$ The possible words as analyzed by a second KS (usually considering words from different parts of the data).
KS$_6$ A KS to try to generate possible word sequences.
KS$_7$ A KS that puts word sequences into possible phrases.

We can visualize these processes as components of Figure 6.13. In processing spoken speech, the waveform of the spoken signal is entered at the lowest level. Knowledge sources for processing this entry are enabled and post their interpretations to the blackboard, to be picked up by the appropriate process. Because of the ambiguities of spoken language, multiple competing hypotheses may be present at each level of the blackboard. The knowledge sources at the higher levels attempt to disambiguate these competing hypotheses.

The analysis of HEARSAY-II should not be seen as simply one lower level producing data that the higher levels can then analyze. It is much more complex than that. If a KS at one level cannot process (make sense of) the data sent to it, that KS can request the KS that sent it the data to go back for another try or to make another hypothesis about the data. Furthermore, different KSs can be working on different parts of the utterance at the same time. All the processes, as mentioned previously, are asynchronous and data-driven; they act when they have input data, continue acting until they have finished their task, and then post their results and wait for their next task.

One of the KSs, called the *scheduler*, handles the "consume-data post-result" communication between the KSs. This scheduler has ratings on the results of each KS's activity and is able to supply, by means of a priority queue, some direction in the problem solving. If no KS is active, the scheduler determines that the task is finished and shuts down.

When the HEARSAY program had a database of about 1,000 words it worked quite well, although a bit slowly. When the database was further extended, the data for the knowledge sources got more complex than they could handle. HEARSAY-III (Balzer et al. 1980, Erman et al. 1981) is a generalization of the approach taken by HEARSAY-II. The time dimension of HEARSAY-II is no longer needed, but the multiple KSs for levels of analysis are retained. The blackboard for HEARSAY-III is intended to interact with a general-purpose relational database system. Indeed, HEARSAY-III is a shell for the design of expert systems; see Section 8.1.1.

An important change in HEARSAY-III has been to split off the scheduler KS (as described above for HEARSAY-II) and to make it a separate blackboard controller for the first (or domain) blackboard. This second blackboard allows the scheduling process to be broken down, just as the domain of the problem is broken down, into separate KSs concerned with different aspects of the solution procedure (for example, when and how to apply the domain knowledge). The second blackboard can thus compare and balance different solutions for each problem (Nii and Aiello 1979, Nii 1986a, 1986b). An alternative model of the blackboard retains important parts of the knowledge base in the blackboard, rather than distributing them across knowledge sources (Skinner and Luger 1991, 1992).

6.4 Epilogue and References

Chapter 6 discussed the implementation of search strategies of Chapters 3 and 4. Thus, the references listed in the epilogue to those chapters are also appropriate to this chapter. Chapter 6 presented recursion as an important tool for programming graph search, implementing the depth-first and backtrack algorithms of Chapter 3 in recursive form. Pattern-directed search with unification and inference rules, as in Chapter 2, simplifies the implementation of search through a space of logical inferences.

The production system was shown as a natural architecture for modeling problem solving and implementing search algorithms. The chapter concluded with examples of production system implementations of data-driven and goal-driven search. In fact, the production system has always been an important paradigm for AI programming, beginning with work by Newell and Simon and their colleagues at Carnegie Mellon University (Newell and Simon 1976, Klahr et al. 1987, Neches et al. 1987, Newell et al. 1989). The production system has also been an important architecture supporting research in cognitive science (Newell and Simon 1972, Luger 1994; see also Chapter 17).

References on implementations of production systems are *Programming Expert Systems in OPS5* by Lee Brownston et al. (1985), and *Pattern Directed Inference Systems* by Donald Waterman and Frederick Hayes-Roth (1978).

Early work in blackboard models is described in HEARSAY-II research (Reddy 1976, Erman et al. 1980). Later developments in blackboards is described in the HEARSAY-III work (Lesser and Corkill 1983, Nii 1986*a*, Nii 1986*b*), and *Blackboard Systems*, edited by Robert Engelmore and Tony Morgan (1988). For modern versions of production systems in C and Java, go to the web sites for CLIPS and JESS.

Research in production systems, planning, and blackboard architectures remains an active part of artificial intelligence. We recommend that the interested reader consult recent proceedings of the American Association for Artificial Intelligence Conference and the International Joint Conference on Artificial Intelligence. Morgan Kaufmann has published other conference proceedings, as well as collections of readings on AI topics.

6.5 Exercises

1. a. Write a member-check algorithm to recursively determine whether a given element is a member of a list.
   b. Write an algorithm to count the number of elements in a list.
   c. Write an algorithm to count the number of atoms in a list.
   (The distinction between atoms and elements is that an element may itself be a list. See Section 16.1, if you need help.)

2. Write a recursive algorithm (using **open** and **closed** lists) to implement breadth-first search. Does recursion allow the omission of the **open** list when implementing breadth-first search? Explain.

3. Trace the execution of the recursive depth-first search algorithm (the version that does not use an **open** list) on the state space of Figure 3.14.

4. In an ancient Hindu tea ceremony, there are three participants: an elder, a servant, and a child. The four tasks they perform are feeding the fire, serving cakes, pouring tea, and reading poetry; this order reflects the decreasing importance of the tasks. At the beginning of the ceremony, the child performs all four tasks. They are passed one at a time to the servant and the elder until, at the end of the ceremony, the elder is performing all four tasks. No one can take on a less important task than those they already perform. Generate a sequence of moves to transfer all the tasks from the child to the elder. Write a recursive algorithm to perform the move sequence.

5. Using the **move** and **path** definitions for the knight's tour of Section 6.1.2, trace the execution of **pattern_search** on the goals:
   a. path(1,9).
   b. path(1,5).
   c. path(7,6).

   When the **move** predicates are attempted in order, there is often looping in the search. Discuss loop detection and backtracking in this situation.

6. Write the pseudo-code definition for a breadth-first version of **pattern_search** (Section 6.1.2). Discuss the time and space efficiency of this algorithm.

7. Using the rule in Example 6.2.3 as a model, write the eight move rules needed for the full 8 × 8 version of the knight's tour.

8. Using the goal and start states of Figure 6.5, hand run the production system solution to the 8-puzzle:

   a.   In goal-driven fashion.
   b.   In data-driven fashion.

9. Consider the financial advisor problem discussed in Chapters 2, 3, and 4. Using predicate calculus as a representation language:

   a.   Write the problem explicitly as a production system.
   b.   Generate the state space and stages of working memory for the data-driven solution to the example in Chapter 3.
   c.   Repeat b for a goal-driven solution.

10. Section 6.2.3 presented the general conflict resolution strategies of refraction, recency, and specificity. Propose and justify two more such strategies.

11. Suggest two applications appropriate for solution using the blackboard architecture. Briefly characterize the organization of the blackboard and knowledge sources for each implementation.

PART III

REPRESENTATION AND INTELLIGENCE: THE AI CHALLENGE

Our age of anxiety is, in great part, the result
of trying to do today's jobs with yesterday's tools . . .

—Marshall McLuhan

Might it not be more fruitful to think of brains as controllers for embodied activity? That
small shift in perspective has large implications for how we construct a science of the
mind. It demands, in fact, a sweeping reform in our whole way of thinking about intelligent
behavior. It requires us to abandon the ideas (common since Descartes) of the mental as a
realm distinct from the realm of the body; to abandon the idea of neat dividing lines
between perception, cognition and action; to abandon the idea of an executive center
where the brain carries out high-level reasoning; and most of all to abandon research
methods that artificially divorce thought from embodied action-taking . . .

—Andy Clark, *Being There (1997).*

Representation and Intelligence

The question of *representation*, or how to best capture critical aspects of intelligent activity
for use on a computer, or indeed, for communication with humans, has been a constant
theme across the almost sixty-year history of AI. We begin Part III with a review of the
three predominant approaches to representation taken by the AI research community over
this time period. The first theme, articulated in the 1950s and 1960s by Newell and Simon
in their work with the *Logic Theorist* (Newell and Simon 1956, 1963*a*), is known as the
use of *weak problem-solving methods*. The second theme, common throughout the 1970s
and 1980s, and espoused by the early expert system designers, is *strong method problem
solving* (see Feigenbaum's quote at the beginning of Chapter 8). In more recent research,
especially in the domains of robotics and agent-based methods (Brooks 1987, 1989; Clark
1997), the emphasis is on *distributed and embodied* representations of intelligence. We
next introduce each of these methodologies for representing intelligence. The three
chapters that comprise Part III offer more detailed descriptions of each approach.

In the late 1950s and early 1960s, Alan Newell and Herbert Simon wrote several computer programs to test the hypothesis that intelligent behavior resulted from heuristic search. The *Logic Theorist*, developed with J. C. Shaw (Newell and Simon 1963*a*), proved theorems in elementary logic using the notation and axioms of Whitehead and Russell's (1950) *Principia Mathematica*. The authors describe their research as aimed at understanding

> the complex processes (heuristics) that are effective in problem solving. Hence, we are not interested in methods that guarantee solutions, but which require vast amounts of computation. Rather we wish to understand how a mathematician, for example, is able to prove a theorem even though he does not know when he starts how, or if, he is going to succeed.

In a later program, the *General Problem Solver* or *GPS*, Newell and Simon (1963*b*, 1972) continued this effort to find general principles of intelligent problem solving. The GPS solved problems formulated as state space search; legal problem-solving steps were a set of operations for modifying state representations. GPS searched for a sequence of operations that would transform the start state into the goal state, searching in the same fashion as the algorithms discussed in earlier chapters of this book.

GPS used *means–ends analysis*, a general heuristic for selecting among alternative state transformation operations, to guide search through the problem space. Means–ends analysis examines the *syntactic* differences between the current state and the goal state and selects an operator that can reduce these differences. Suppose, for example, that GPS is attempting to prove the equivalence of two logical expressions. If the current state contains an ∧ operator and the goal does not contain an ∧, then means–ends analysis would select a transformation such as de Morgan's law to remove ∧ from expressions. (For a more detailed description and examples of this research see Section 13.1.)

By using a heuristic that examines only the syntactic form of states, it was hoped that GPS would be a *general* architecture for intelligent problem solving, no matter what the domain. Programs like GPS, which are restricted to syntax-based strategies and intended for a wide variety of applications, are known as *weak method problem solvers*.

Unfortunately, there does not seem to be a single heuristic that can successfully be applied to all problem domains. In general, the methods we use to solve problems employ a great deal of knowledge about a situation. Doctors are able to diagnose illness because they have extensive knowledge of medicine, in addition to their general problem-solving abilities. Architects design houses because they know about architecture. Indeed, the heuristics used in medical diagnosis would be useless in designing an office building.

Weak methods stand in sharp contrast to *strong methods*, which use explicit knowledge of a particular problem domain. Consider a rule for diagnostic analysis of automotive problems:

> if
> the engine does not turn over, and
> the lights do not come on
> then
> the problem is battery or cables (.8)

This heuristic, phrased as an *if... then...* rule, focuses search on the battery/cable subsystem of the automobile, eliminating other components and pruning the search space. Notice that this particular heuristic, unlike means–ends analysis, uses empirical knowledge of how automobiles function, such as knowledge of the relationships between the battery, lights, and starter. It is useless in any problem domain except vehicle repair.

Not only do strong method problem solvers use domain-specific knowledge, but they generally require large amounts of such knowledge to be effective. The bad-battery heuristic, for example, would not be of much use in diagnosing a bad carburetor, and would be totally useless in any domain outside of auto diagnosis. Thus, a major challenge in designing a knowledge-based program is the acquisition and organization of large amounts of specific domain-based knowledge. Domain rules can also contain a measure, .8 in the rule above, to reflect the diagnostician's confidence in this piece of domain knowledge.

In using the strong method approach, program designers are making certain assumptions about the nature of intelligent systems. These assumptions are formalized by Brian Smith (1985) as the *knowledge representation hypothesis*. This hypothesis states that

> any mechanically embodied intelligent process will be comprised of structural ingredients that (a) we as external observers naturally take to represent a propositional account of the knowledge that the overall process exhibits, and (b) independent of such external semantic attribution, play a formal role in engendering the behavior that manifests that knowledge.

The important aspects of this hypothesis include the assumption that knowledge will be represented *propositionally*, that is, in a form that explicitly represents the knowledge in question and that may be seen by an outside observer as a "natural" description of that knowledge. The second major assumption is that the behavior of the system can be seen as formally caused by the propositions in the knowledge base and that this behavior should be consistent with our perceived meaning of those propositions.

The final theme for AI representation is often described as *agent-based*, *embodied*, or *emergent* problem solving. Several researchers working in applied domains such as robotics, game design, and the internet, including Brooks (1987, 1989), Agre and Chapman (1987), Jennings (1995), and Wooldridge (2000), have challenged the requirement of having any centralized knowledge base or general-purpose inferencing scheme. Problem solvers are designed as *distributed* agents: *situated*, *autonomous*, and *flexible*.

On this viewpoint, problem solving is viewed as distributed, with agents performing tasks in different subcontexts of their domains, for example, the activity of an internet browser or security agent. The problem-solving task is laid out into its several components with little or no general coordination of tasks. The situated agent is able to receive sensory input from its particular environment, as well as react in that context without waiting for instructions from some general controller. In interactive game playing, for example, the agent would be addressing a particular local issue, e.g., defending against a particular attack or raising a specific alarm, without any general view of the entire problem situation.

Agents are autonomous, in that they are often required to act without direct intervention of humans or some general control process. Autonomous agents thus have control over their own actions and internal state. Some agent systems are even capable of learning from their own experiences. Finally, agents are flexible in that they are responsive to situations in their local environment. They are also proactive, in that they can anticipate situations. Finally, they must be able to respond flexibly with other agents in the problem domain, communicating about tasks, goals, and appropriate processes.

Several researchers in the domain of robotics have built agent-based systems. Rodney Brooks (1987, 1989) in the MIT Robotics Laboratory has designed what he terms a *subsumption architecture*, a layered sequence of finite state machines, each one acting in its own context but also supporting functionality at higher levels. Manuela Veloso et al. (2000) working in the Robotics Lab at Carnegie Mellon, have designed a team of robotic soccer (football) agents that collaborate in the adversarial environment of soccer games.

Finally, this situated and embodied approach to representation is described by several philosophers of science, including Dan Dennett (1991, 1995) and Andy Clark (1997) as appropriate characterizations of human intelligence. Later in this book we present further representational schemes, including connectionist (Chapter 11) and genetic (Chapter 12) approaches. General representational issues are discussed again in Chapter 17.

In Chapter 7 we examine in detail many of the major approaches the AI community has taken to representation. We begin with the early use of representations, including *semantic networks*, *scripts, frames*, and *objects*. We present these schemes from an evolutionary viewpoint, showing how modern tools grew from these early years of AI research. We next present John Sowa's *conceptual graphs,* a representation for use in natural language understanding. Finally, we present agent-based and situated approaches to representation, including Rodney Brooks' *subsumption architecture*, which calls into question the need for a central base of explicit knowledge used with a general purpose controller.

In Chapter 8 we discuss knowledge-intensive systems and examine the problems involved in the acquisition, formalization, and debugging of a knowledge base. We present different inference schemes for rule systems, including goal-driven and data-driven reasoning. Besides rule-based systems, we present model-based and case-based reasoning. The first of these tries to represent explicitly the theoretical foundations and functionality of a domain, e.g., an electronic circuit, while the second approach builds an explicit database of past successes and failures in a problem domain to assist with future problem solving. We conclude Chapter 8 with a review of *planning*, where explicit knowledge is organized to control problem solving in complex domains such as robotics.

In Chapter 9 we present a number of techniques that address the representation problem for reasoning in situations of vagueness and/or uncertainty. At these times, we try to reach the best explanation for often ambiguous information. This type of reasoning is often termed *abductive*. We first present nonmonotonic and truth-maintenance logics, where traditional predicate logic is extended to capture situations with uncertainty. However, much interesting and important problem solving does not fit comfortably under the umbrella of deductive logic. For reasoning in these situations we introduce a number of other potent tools, including Bayesian techniques, the Dempster–Shafer approach, and the Stanford Certainty Factor algebra. We also have a section on fuzzy reasoning. We conclude Part III with the stochastic methodology for uncertainty, presenting Bayesian belief networks, Markov models, hidden Markov models, and related approaches.

In Part VI we implement many of these representations in LISP and PROLOG.

KNOWLEDGE REPRESENTATION

This grand book, the universe, ... is written in the language of mathematics, and its characters are triangles, circles, and other geometric figures without which it is humanly impossible to understand a word of it; without these one wanders about in a dark labyrinth. . .

—GALILEO GALILEI, *Discorsi E Dimonstrazioni Matematiche Introno a Due Nuove Scienze (1638)*

Since no organism can cope with infinite diversity, one of the basic functions of all organisms is the cutting up of the environment into classifications by which non-identical stimuli can be treated as equivalent. . .

—ELEANOR ROSCH, *Principles of Categorization (1978)*

We have always two universes of discourse—call them "physical" and "phenomenal," or what you will—one dealing with questions of quantitative and formal structure, the other with those qualities that constitute a "world." All of us have our own distinctive mental worlds, our own inner journeyings and landscapes, and these, for most of us, require no clear neurological "correlate."

—OLIVER SACKS, *The Man Who Mistook His Wife for a Hat (1987)*

7.0   Issues in Knowledge Representation

The representation of information for use in intelligent problem solving offers important and difficult challenges that lie at the core of AI. In Section 7.1, we present a brief historical retrospective of early research in representation; topics include *semantic networks*, *conceptual dependencies*, *scripts*, and *frames*. Section 7.2 offers a more modern representation used in natural language programs, John Sowa's *conceptual graphs*. In Section 7.3, we critique the requirement of creating centralized and explicit representational schemes. Brooks' alternative is the *subsumption architecture* for robots. Section 7.4 presents *agents*, another alternative to centralized control. In later chapters we extend our discussion of representations to include the stochastic (Section 9.3), the connectionist (Chapter 11), and the genetic/emergent (Chapter 12).

We begin our discussion of representation from an historical perspective, where a knowledge base is described as a mapping between the objects and relations in a problem domain and the computational objects and relations of a program (Bobrow 1975). The results of inferences in the knowledge base are assumed to correspond to the results of actions or observations in the world. The computational objects, relations, and inferences available to programmers are mediated by the knowledge representation language.

There are general principles of knowledge organization that apply across a variety of domains and can be directly supported by a representation language. For example, class hierarchies are found in both scientific and commonsense classification systems. How may we provide a general mechanism for representing them? How may we represent definitions? Exceptions? When should an intelligent system make default assumptions about missing information and how can it adjust its reasoning should these assumptions prove wrong? How may we best represent time? Causality? Uncertainty? Progress in building intelligent systems depends on discovering the principles of knowledge organization and supporting them in higher-level representational tools.

It is useful to distinguish between a representational *scheme* and the *medium* of its implementation. This is similar to the distinction between data structures and programming languages. Programming languages are the *medium* of implementation; the data structure is the *scheme*. Generally, knowledge representation languages are more constrained than the predicate calculus or programming languages. These constraints take the form of explicit structures for representing categories of knowledge. Their medium of implementation might be PROLOG, LISP, or more common languages such as C++ or Java.

Our discussion to this point illustrates the traditional view of AI representational schemes presented in Sections 7.1 and 7.2. This view often includes a global knowledge base of language structures reflecting a static and "preinterpreted bias" of a "real world." More recent research in robotics (Brooks 1991a, Lewis and Luger 2000), situated cognition (Agre and Chapman 1987, Lakoff and Johnson 1999), agent-based problem solving (Jennings et al. 1998, Wooldridge 2000), and philosophy (Clark 1997) has challenged this traditional approach. These problem domains require distributed knowledge, a world that can itself be used as a partial knowledge structure, the ability to reason with partial information, and even representations that evolve as they come to experience the invariants of a problem domain. These approaches are introduced in Sections 7.3 and 7.4.

7.1 A Brief History of AI Representational Schemes

7.1.1 Associationist Theories of Meaning

Logical representations grew out of the efforts of philosophers and mathematicians to characterize the principles of correct reasoning. The major concern of logic is the development of formal representation languages with sound and complete inference rules.

As a result, the semantics of predicate calculus emphasizes *truth-preserving* operations on well-formed expressions. An alternative line of research has grown out of the efforts of psychologists and linguists to characterize the nature of human understanding. This work is less concerned with establishing a science of correct reasoning than with describing the way in which humans actually acquire, associate, and use knowledge of their world. This approach has proved particularly useful to the AI application areas of natural language understanding and commonsense reasoning.

There are many problems that arise in mapping commonsense reasoning into formal logic. For example, it is common to think of the operators $\lor$ and $\rightarrow$ as corresponding to the English "or" and "if ... then ...". However, these operators in logic are concerned solely with truth values and ignore the fact that the English "if ... then ..." suggests specific relationship (often more coorelational than causal) between its premises and its conclusion. For example, the sentence "If a bird is a cardinal then it is red" (associating the bird cardinal with the color red) can be written in predicate calculus:

$$\forall \; X \; (cardinal(X) \rightarrow red(X)).$$

This may be changed, through a series of truth-preserving operations, Chapter 2, into the logically equivalent expression

$$\forall \; X \; (\neg \, red(X) \rightarrow \neg \, cardinal(X)).$$

These two expressions have the same truth value; that is, the second is true if and only if the first is true. However, truth value equivalence is inappropriate in this situation. If we were to look for physical evidence of the truth of these statements, the fact that this sheet of paper is not red and also not a cardinal is evidence for the truth of the second expression. Because the two expressions are logically equivalent, it follows that it is also evidence for the truth of the first statement. This leads to the conclusion that the whiteness of the sheet of paper is evidence that cardinals are red.

This line of reasoning strikes us as meaningless and rather silly. The reason for this incongruity is that logical implication only expresses a relationship between the truth values of its operands, while the English sentence implied a positive coorelation between membership in a class and the possession of properties of that class. In fact, the genetic makeup of a bird causes it to have a certain color. This relationship is lost in the second version of the expression. Although the fact that the paper is not red is consistent with the truth of both sentences, it is irrelevant to the causal nature of the color of birds.

Associationist theories define the meaning of an object in terms of a network of associations with other objects. For the associationist, when humans perceive and reason about an object, that perception is first mapped into a concept. This concept is part of our entire knowledge of the world and is connected through appropriate relationships to other concepts. These relationships form an understanding of the properties and behavior of objects such as snow. For example, through experience, we associate the concept snow with other concepts such as cold, white, snowman, slippery, and ice. Our understanding of snow and the truth of statements such as "snow is white" and "the snowman is white" manifests itself out of this network of associations.

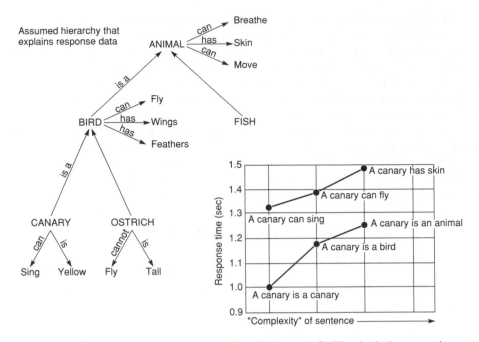

Figure 7.1 Semantic network developed by Collins and Quillian in their research on human information storage and response times (Harmon and King 1985).

There is psychological evidence that, in addition to their ability to associate concepts, humans also organize their knowledge hierarchically, with information kept at the highest appropriate levels of the taxonomy. Collins and Quillian (1969) modeled human information storage and management using a semantic network (Figure 7.1). The structure of this hierarchy was derived from laboratory testing of human subjects. The subjects were asked questions about different properties of birds, such as, "Is a canary a bird?" or "Can a canary sing?" or "Can a canary fly?".

As obvious as the answers to these questions may seem, reaction-time studies indicated that it took longer for subjects to answer "Can a canary fly?" than it did to answer "Can a canary sing?". Collins and Quillian explain this difference in response time by arguing that people store information at its most abstract level. Instead of trying to recall that canaries fly, and robins fly, and swallows fly, all stored with the individual bird, humans remember that canaries are birds and that birds have (usually) the property of flying. Even more general properties such as eating, breathing, and moving are stored at the "animal" level, and so trying to recall whether a canary can breathe should take longer than recalling whether a canary can fly. This is, of course, because the human must travel further up the hierarchy of memory structures to get the answer.

The fastest recall was for the traits specific to the bird, say, that it can sing or is yellow. Exception handling also seemed to be done at the most specific level. When subjects were asked whether an ostrich could fly, the answer was produced faster than when they were asked whether an ostrich could breathe. Thus the hierarchy ostrich → bird → animal seems not to be traversed to get the exception information: it is stored directly with ostrich. This knowledge organization has been formalized in inheritance systems.

Inheritance systems allow us to store information at the highest level of abstraction, which reduces the size of knowledge bases and helps prevent update inconsistencies. For example, if we are building a knowledge base about birds, we can define the traits common to all birds, such as flying or having feathers, for the general class bird and allow a particular species of bird to inherit these properties. This reduces the size of the knowledge base by requiring us to define these essential traits only once, rather than requiring their assertion for every individual. Inheritance also helps us to maintain the consistency of the knowledge base when adding new classes and individuals. Assume that we are adding the species robin to an existing knowledge base. When we assert that robin is a subclass of songbird; robin inherits all of the common properties of both songbirds and birds. It is not up to the programmer to remember (or forget!) to add this information.

Graphs, by providing a means of explicitly representing relations using arcs and nodes, have proved to be an ideal vehicle for formalizing associationist theories of knowledge. A *semantic network* represents knowledge as a graph, with the nodes corresponding to facts or concepts and the arcs to relations or associations between concepts. Both nodes and links are generally labeled. For example, a semantic network that defines the properties of snow and ice appears in Figure 7.2. This network could be used (with appropriate inference rules) to answer a range of questions about snow, ice, and snowmen. These inferences are made by following the links to related concepts. Semantic networks also implement inheritance; for example, frosty inherits all the properties of snowman.

The term "semantic network" encompasses a family of graph-based representations. These differ chiefly in the names that are allowed for nodes and links and the inferences that may be performed. However, a common set of assumptions and concerns is shared by all network representation languages; these are illustrated by a discussion of the history of network representations. In Section 7.2 we examine *conceptual graphs* (Sowa 1984), a more modern network representation language that integrates many of these ideas.

7.1.2   Early Work in Semantic Nets

Network representations have almost as long a history as logic. The Greek philosopher Porphyry created tree-based type hierarchies—with their roots at the top—to describe Aristotle's categories (Porphyry 1887). Frege developed a tree notation for logic expressions. Perhaps the earliest work to have a direct influence on contemporary semantic nets was Charles S. Peirce's system of existential graphs, developed in the nineteenth century (Roberts 1973). Peirce's theory had all the expressive power of first-order predicate calculus, with an axiomatic basis and formal rules of inference.

Graphs have long been used in psychology to represent structures of concepts and associations. Selz (1913, 1922) pioneered this work, using graphs to represent concept hierarchies and the inheritance of properties. He also developed a theory of schematic anticipation that influenced AI work in frames and schemata. Anderson, Norman, Rumelhart, and others have used networks to model human memory and intellectual performance (Anderson and Bower 1973, Norman et al. 1975).

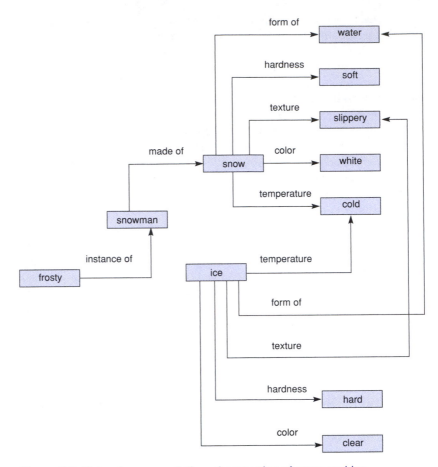

Figure 7.2 Network representation of properties of snow and ice.

Much of the research in network representations has been done in the arena of natural language understanding. In the general case, language understanding requires an understanding of common sense, the ways in which physical objects behave, the interactions that occur between humans, and the ways in which human institutions are organized. A natural language program must understand intentions, beliefs, hypothetical reasoning, plans, and goals. Because of these requirements language understanding has always been a driving force for research in knowledge representation.

The first computer implementations of semantic networks were developed in the early 1960s for use in machine translation. Masterman (1961) defined a set of 100 primitive concept types and used them to define a dictionary of 15,000 concepts. Wilks (1972) continued to build on Masterman's work in semantic network-based natural language systems. Shapiro's (1971) MIND program was the first implementation of a propositional calculus based semantic network. Other early AI workers exploring network representations include Ceccato (1961), Raphael (1968), Reitman (1965), and Simmons (1966).

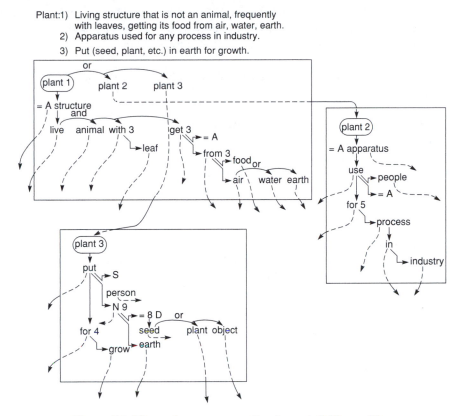

Figure 7.3 Three planes representing three definitions of the word "plant" (Quillian 1967).

An influential program that illustrates many of the features of early semantic networks was written by Quillian in the late 1960s (Quillian 1967). This program defined English words in much the same way that a dictionary does: a word is defined in terms of other words, and the components of the definition are defined in the same fashion. Rather than formally defining words in terms of basic axioms, each definition simply leads to other definitions in an unstructured and sometimes circular fashion. In looking up a word, we traverse this "network" until we are satisfied that we understand the original word.

Each node in Quillian's network corresponded to a *word concept*, with associative links to other word concepts that formed its definition. The knowledge base was organized into *planes*, where each plane was a graph that defined a single word. Figure 7.3, taken from a paper by Quillian (1967), illustrates three planes that capture three different definitions of the word "plant:" a living organism (plant 1), a place where people work (plant 2), and the act of putting a seed in the ground (plant 3).

The program used this knowledge base to find relationships between pairs of English words. Given two words, it would search the graphs outward from each word in a breadth-first fashion, searching for a common concept or *intersection node*. The paths to this node represented a relationship between the word concepts. For example, Figure 7.4 from the same paper, shows the *intersection paths* between cry and comfort.

Using this intersection path, the program was able to conclude:

cry 2 is among other things to make a sad sound. To comfort 3 can be to make 2 something less sad (Quillian 1967).

The numbers in the response indicate that the program has selected from among different meanings of the words.

Quillian (1967) suggested that this approach to semantics might provide a natural language understanding system with the ability to:

1. Determine the meaning of a body of English text by building up collections of these intersection nodes.

2. Choose between multiple meanings of words by finding the meanings with the shortest intersection path to other words in the sentence. For example, it could select a meaning for "plant" in "Tom went home to water his new plant" based on the intersection of the word concepts "water" and "plant."

3. Answer a flexible range of queries based on associations between word concepts in the queries and concepts in the system.

Although this and other early work established the power of graphs to model associative meaning, it was limited by the extreme generality of the formalism. Knowledge was

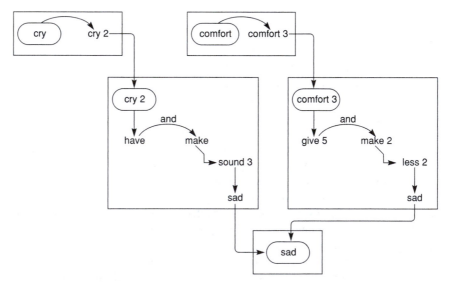

Figure 7.4 Intersection path between "cry" and "comfort" (Quillian 1967).

generally structured in terms of specific relationships such as object/property, class/subclass, and agent/verb/object.

7.1.3 Standardization of Network Relationships

In itself, a graph notation of relationships has little computational advantage over logic; it is just another notation for relationships between objects. In fact, Shapiro's (1979) SNePS (Semantic Net Processing System) worked as a theorem prover with the power of the first-order predicate calculus. The power of his network representations comes from the definition of links and associated inference rules such as inheritance.

Though Quillian's early work established most of the significant features of the semantic network formalism, such as labeled arcs and links, hierarchical inheritance, and inferences along associational links, it proved limited in its ability to deal with the complexities of many domains. One of the main reasons for this failure was the poverty of relationships (links) that captured the deeper semantic aspects of knowledge. Most of the links represented extremely general associations between nodes and provided no real basis for the structuring of semantic relationships. The same problem is encountered in efforts to use predicate calculus to capture semantic meaning. Although the formalism is highly expressive and can represent almost any kind of knowledge, it is too unconstrained and places the burden of constructing appropriate sets of facts and rules on the programmer.

Much of the work in network representations that followed Quillian's focused on defining a richer set of link labels (relationships) that would more fully model the semantics of natural language. By implementing the fundamental semantic relationships of natural language as part of the *formalism*, rather than as part of the *domain knowledge* added by the system builder, knowledge bases require less handcrafting and achieve greater generality and consistency.

Brachman (1979) has stated:

> The key issue here is the isolation of the *primitives* for semantic network languages. The primitives of a network language are those things that the interpreter is programmed in advance to understand, and that are not usually represented in the network language itself.

Simmons (1973) addressed this need for standard relationships by focusing on the *case structure* of English verbs. In this verb-oriented approach, based on work by Fillmore (1968), links define the roles played by nouns and noun phrases in the action of the sentence. Case relationships include *agent*, *object*, *instrument*, *location*, and *time*. A sentence is represented as a verb node, with various case links to nodes representing other participants in the action. This structure is called a *case frame*. In parsing a sentence, the program finds the verb and retrieves the case frame for that verb from its knowledge base. It then binds the values of the agent, object, etc., to the appropriate nodes in the case frame. Using this approach, the sentence "Sarah fixed the chair with glue" might be represented by the network in Figure 7.5.

Thus, the representation language itself captures much of the deep structure of natural language, such as the relationship between a verb and its subject (the agent relation) or that

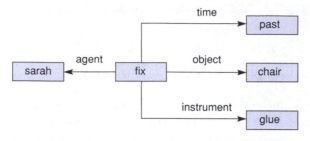

Figure 7.5 Case frame representation of the sentence "Sarah fixed the chair with glue."

between a verb and its object. Knowledge of the case structure of the English language is part of the network formalism itself. When the individual sentence is parsed, these built-in relationships indicate that Sarah is the person doing the fixing and that glue is used to put the chair together. Note that *these linguistic relationships are stored in a fashion that is independent of the actual sentence or even the language in which the sentence was expressed.* A similar approach was also taken in network languages proposed by Norman (1972) and Rumelhart et al. (1972, 1973).

A number of major research endeavors attempted to standardize link names even further (Masterman 1961, Wilks 1972, Schank and Colby 1973, Schank and Nash-Webber 1975). Each effort worked to establish a complete set of primitives that could be used to represent the semantic structure of natural language expressions in a uniform fashion. These were intended to assist in reasoning with language constructs and to be independent of the idiosyncrasies of individual languages or phrasing.

Perhaps the most ambitious attempt to model formally the deep semantic structure of natural language is Roger Schank's *conceptual dependency* theory (Schank and Rieger 1974). Conceptual dependency theory offers a set of four primitive conceptualizations from which the world of meaning is built. These are equal and independent. They are:

ACTs	actions
PPs	objects (picture producers)
AAs	modifiers of actions (action aiders)
PAs	modifiers of objects (picture aiders)

For example, all actions are assumed to reduce to one or more of the primitive ACTs. The primitives listed below are taken as the basic components of action, with more specific verbs being formed through their modification and combination.

ATRANS	transfer a relationship (give)
PTRANS	transfer physical location of an object (go)
PROPEL	apply physical force to an object (push)
MOVE	move body part by owner (kick)
GRASP	grab an object by an actor (grasp)

INGEST	ingest an object by an animal (eat)
EXPEL	expel from an animal's body (cry)
MTRANS	transfer mental information (tell)
MBUILD	mentally make new information (decide)
CONC	conceptualize or think about an idea (think)
SPEAK	produce sound (say)
ATTEND	focus sense organ (listen)

These primitives are used to define *conceptual dependency relationships* that describe meaning structures such as case relations or the association of objects and values. Conceptual dependency relationships are *conceptual syntax rules* and constitute a grammar of meaningful semantic relationships. These relationships can be used to construct an internal representation of an English sentence. A list of basic conceptual dependencies (Schank and Rieger 1974) appears in Figure 7.6. These capture the fundamental semantic structures of natural language. For example, the first conceptual dependency in Figure 7.6 describes the relationship between a subject and its verb, and the third describes the verb–object relation. These can be combined to represent a simple transitive sentence such as "John throws the ball" (see Figure 7.7).

PP $\Leftrightarrow$ ACT	indicates that an actor acts.
PP $\Leftrightarrow$ PA	indicates that an object has a certain attribute.
ACT $\overset{O}{\leftarrow}$ PP	indicates the object of an action.
ACT $\leftarrow$ $\begin{matrix} R \rightarrow PP \\ \leftarrow PP \end{matrix}$	indicates the recipient and the donor of an object within an action.
ACT $\leftarrow$ $\begin{matrix} D \rightarrow PP \\ \leftarrow PP \end{matrix}$	indicates the direction of an object within an action.
ACT $\overset{1}{\leftarrow}$ $\updownarrow$	indicates the instrumental conceptualization for an action.
$\begin{matrix} X \\ \Uparrow \\ Y \end{matrix}$	indicates that conceptualization X caused conceptualization Y. When written with a C this form denotes that X COULD cause Y.
PP $\Leftarrow$ $\begin{matrix} \rightarrow PA2 \\ \leftarrow PA1 \end{matrix}$	indicates a state change of an object.
PP1 $\leftarrow$ PP2	indicates that PP2 is either PART OF or the POSSESSOR OF PP1.

Figure 7.6 Conceptual dependencies (Schank and Rieger 1974).

Figure 7.7 Conceptual dependency representation of the sentence "John throws the ball."

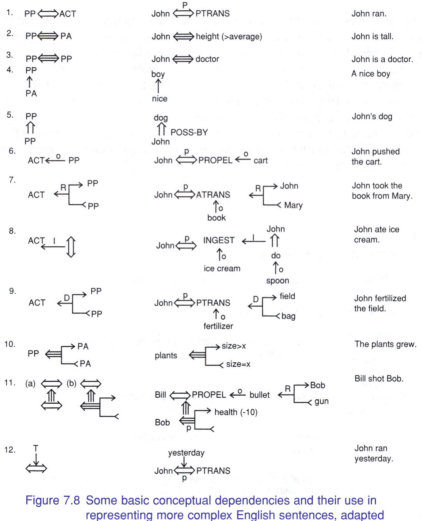

Figure 7.8 Some basic conceptual dependencies and their use in representing more complex English sentences, adapted from Schank and Colby (1973).

Finally, tense and mode information may be added to the set of conceptualizations. Schank supplies a list of attachments or modifiers to the relationships. A partial list of these includes:

p	past
f	future
t	transition
k	continuing
t_s	start transition
?	interrogative
t_f	finish transition
c	conditional
/	negative
nil	present
delta?	timeless

These relations are the first-level constructs of the theory, the simplest semantic relationships out of which more complex structures can be built. Further examples of how these basic conceptual dependencies can be composed to represent the meaning of simple English sentences appear in Figure 7.8.

Based on these primitives, the English sentence "John ate the egg" is represented as shown in Figure 7.9, where the symbols have the following meanings:

←	indicates the direction of dependency
⇔	indicates the agent–verb relationship
p	indicates past tense
INGEST	is a primitive act of the theory
O	object relation
D	indicates the direction of the object in the action

Another example of the structures that can be built using conceptual dependencies is the representation graph for "John prevented Mary from giving a book to Bill" (Figure 7.10). This particular example is interesting because it demonstrates how causality can be represented.

Conceptual dependency theory offers a number of important benefits. By providing a formal theory of natural language semantics, it reduces problems of ambiguity. Second, the representation itself directly captures much of natural language semantics, by attempting to provide a *canonical form* for the meaning of sentences. That is, all sentences that have the same meaning will be represented internally by *syntactically identical*, not just semantically equivalent, graphs. This canonical representation is an effort to simplify the inferences required for understanding. For example, we can demonstrate that two sentences mean the same thing with a simple match of conceptual dependency graphs; a representation that did not provide a canonical form might require extensive operations on differently structured graphs.

Unfortunately, it is questionable whether a program may be written to reliably reduce sentences to canonical form. As Woods (1985) and others have pointed out, reduction to a canonical form is provably uncomputable for monoids, a type of algebraic group that is far simpler than natural language. There is also no evidence that humans store their knowledge in any such sort of canonical form.

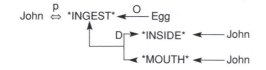

Figure 7.9 Conceptual dependency representing "John ate the egg" (Schank and Rieger 1974).

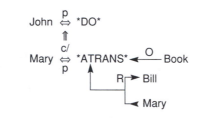
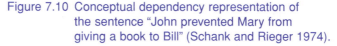

Figure 7.10 Conceptual dependency representation of the sentence "John prevented Mary from giving a book to Bill" (Schank and Rieger 1974).

Other criticisms of this point of view, besides objecting to the computational price paid in reducing everything to such low-level primitives, suggest that the primitives themselves are not adequate to capture many of the more subtle concepts that are important in natural language use. For example, the representation of "tall" in the second sentence of Figure 7.8 does not address the ambiguity of this term as carefully as is done in systems such as fuzzy logic (Zadeh 1983 and Section 9.2.2).

However, no one can say that the conceptual dependency model has not been extensively studied and well understood. More than a decade of research guided by Schank has focused on refining and extending the model. Important extensions of conceptual dependencies include research in *scripts* and *memory organization packets*, or MOPs. The research in scripts examines the organization of knowledge in memory and the role this organization plays in reasoning, see Section 7.1.4. MOPs provided one of the supporting research areas for the design of case-based reasoners, Section 8.3. Conceptual dependency theory is a fully developed model of natural language semantics with consistency of purpose and wide applicability.

7.1.4 Scripts

A natural language understanding program must use a large amount of background knowledge to understand even the simplest conversation (Section 14.0). There is evidence that humans organize this knowledge into structures corresponding to typical situations (Bartlett 1932). If we are reading a story about restaurants, baseball, or politics, we resolve any ambiguities in the text in a way consistent with restaurants, baseball, or politics. If the subject of a story changes abruptly, there is evidence that people pause briefly in their reading, presumably to change knowledge structures. It is hard to understand a poorly organized or structured story, possibly because we cannot easily fit it into any of our existing knowledge structures. There can also be errors in understanding when the subject of a conversation changes abruptly, presumably because we are confused over which context to use in resolving pronoun references and other ambiguities in the conversation.

A *script* is a structured representation describing a stereotyped sequence of events in a particular context. The script was originally designed by Schank and his research group (Schank and Abelson 1977) as a means of organizing *conceptual dependency* structures into descriptions of typical situations. Scripts are used in natural language understanding systems to organize a knowledge base in terms of the situations that the system is to understand.

Most adults are quite comfortable (i.e., they, as customers, know what to expect and how to act) in a restaurant. They are either met at the restaurant entrance or see some sign indicating that they should continue in and find a table. If a menu is not available at the table or if it is not presented by the waiter, then the customer will ask for one. Similarly, customers understand the routines for ordering food, eating, paying, and leaving.

In fact, the restaurant script is quite different from other eating scripts such as the "fast-food" model or the "formal family meal". In the fast-food model the customer enters, gets in line to order, pays for the meal (before eating), waits about for a tray with the food, takes the tray and tries to find a clean table, and so on. These are two different stereotyped sequences of events, and each has a potential script.

The components of a script are:

Entry conditions or descriptors of the world that must be true for the script to be called. In this script, these include an open restaurant and a hungry customer that has some money.

Results or facts that are true once the script has terminated; for example, the customer is full and poorer, the restaurant owner has more money.

Props or the "things" that support the content of the script. These might include tables, waiters, and menus. The set of props supports reasonable default assumptions about the situation: a restaurant is assumed to have tables and chairs unless stated otherwise.

Roles are the actions that the individual participants perform. The waiter takes orders, delivers food, and presents the bill. The customer orders, eats, and pays.

Scenes. Schank breaks the script into a sequence of scenes each of which presents a temporal aspect of the script. In the restaurant there is entering, ordering, eating, etc.

The elements of the script, the basic "pieces" of semantic meaning, are represented using conceptual dependency relationships. Placed together in a framelike structure, they represent a sequence of meanings, or an event sequence. The restaurant script taken from this research is presented in Figure 7.11.

The program reads a small story about restaurants and parses it into an internal conceptual dependency representation. Because the key concepts in this internal description

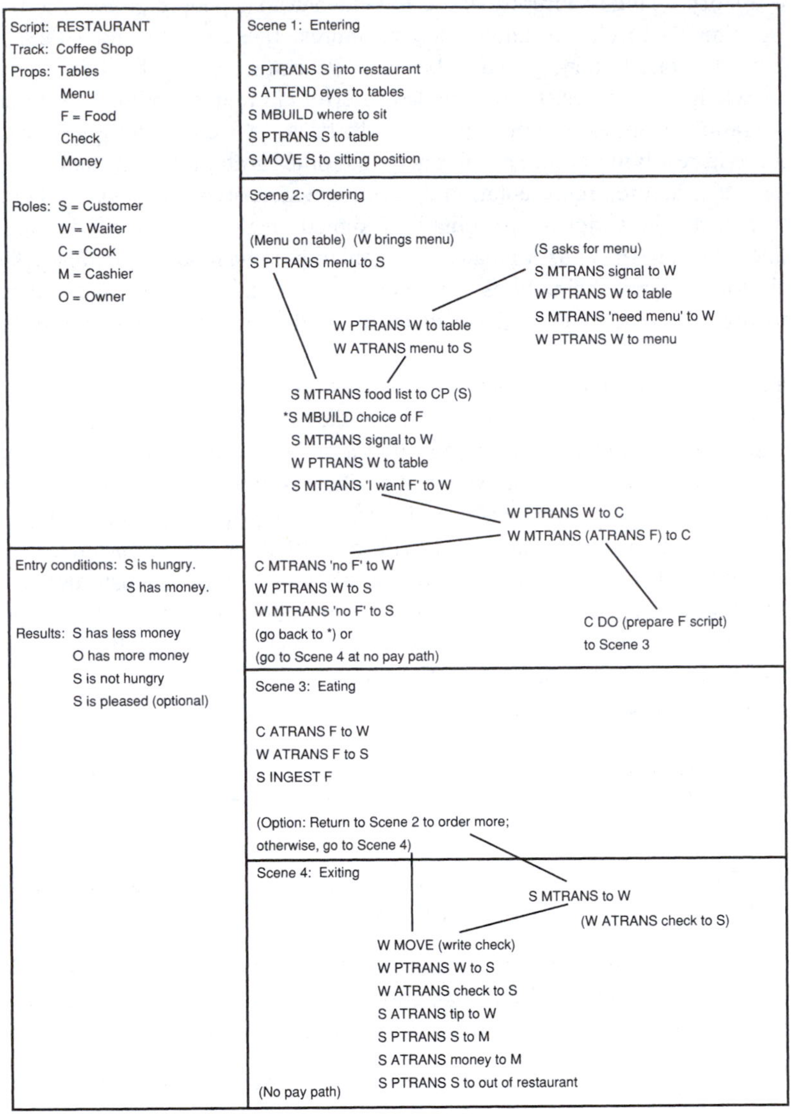

Script: RESTAURANT
Track: Coffee Shop
Props: Tables
Menu
F = Food
Check
Money
Roles: S = Customer
W = Waiter
C = Cook
M = Cashier
O = Owner
Entry conditions: S is hungry.
S has money.
Results: S has less money
O has more money
S is not hungry
S is pleased (optional)
Scene 1: Entering
S PTRANS S into restaurant
S ATTEND eyes to tables
S MBUILD where to sit
S PTRANS S to table
S MOVE S to sitting position
Scene 2: Ordering
(Menu on table) (W brings menu)
S PTRANS menu to S
(S asks for menu)
S MTRANS signal to W
W PTRANS W to table
S MTRANS 'need menu' to W
W PTRANS W to menu
W PTRANS W to table
W ATRANS menu to S
S MTRANS food list to CP (S)
*S MBUILD choice of F
S MTRANS signal to W
W PTRANS W to table
S MTRANS 'I want F' to W
W PTRANS W to C
W MTRANS (ATRANS F) to C
C MTRANS 'no F' to W
W PTRANS W to S
W MTRANS 'no F' to S
(go back to *) or
(go to Scene 4 at no pay path)
C DO (prepare F script)
to Scene 3
Scene 3: Eating
C ATRANS F to W
W ATRANS F to S
S INGEST F
(Option: Return to Scene 2 to order more;
otherwise, go to Scene 4)
Scene 4: Exiting
S MTRANS to W
(W ATRANS check to S)
W MOVE (write check)
W PTRANS W to S
W ATRANS check to S
S ATRANS tip to W
S PTRANS S to M
S ATRANS money to M
S PTRANS S to out of restaurant
(No pay path)

Figure 7.11 A restaurant script (Schank and Abelson 1977).

match with the entry conditions of the script, the program binds the people and things mentioned in the story to the roles and props mentioned in the script. The result is an expanded representation of the story contents, using the script to fill in any missing information and default assumptions. The program then answers questions about the story by referring to the script. The script allows the reasonable default assumptions that are essential to natural language understanding. For example:

EXAMPLE 7.1.1

John went to a restaurant last night. He ordered steak. When he paid he noticed he was running out of money. He hurried home since it had started to rain.

Using the script, the system can correctly answer questions such as: Did John eat dinner last night (the story only implied this)? Did John use cash or a credit card? How could John get a menu? What did John buy?

EXAMPLE 7.1.2

Sue went out to lunch. She sat at a table and called a waitress, who brought her a menu. She ordered a sandwich.

Questions that might reasonably be asked of this story include: Why did the waitress bring Sue a menu? Was Sue in a restaurant? Who paid? Who was the "she" who ordered the sandwich? This last question is difficult. The most recently named female is the waitress, an incorrect conclusion. Script *roles* help to resolve pronoun references and other ambiguities.

Scripts can also be used to interpret unexpected results or breaks in the scripted activity. Thus, in scene 2 of Figure 7.11 there is the choice point of "food" or "no food" delivered to the customer. This allows the following example to be understood.

EXAMPLE 7.1.3

Kate went to a restaurant. She was shown to a table and ordered sushi from the waitress. She sat there and waited for a long time. Finally, she got mad and left.

Questions that can be answered from this story using the restaurant script include: Who is the "she" who sat and waited? Why did she wait? Who was the "she" who got mad and left? Why did she get mad? Note that there are other questions that the script cannot answer, such as why people get upset/mad when the waiter does not come promptly? Like any knowledge-based system, scripts require the knowledge engineer to correctly anticipate the knowledge required.

Scripts, like frames and other structured representations, are subject to certain problems, including the script *match* problem and the *between-the-lines* problem. Consider Example 7.1.4, which could call either the *restaurant* or *concert* scripts. The choice is critical because "bill" can refer to either the restaurant check or the playbill of the concert.

EXAMPLE 7.1.4

John visited his favorite restaurant on the way to the concert. He was pleased by the bill because he liked Mozart.

Since script selection is usually based on matching "key" words, it is often difficult to determine which of two or more potential scripts should be used. The script match problem is "deep" in the sense that no algorithm exists for guaranteeing correct choices. It requires heuristic knowledge about the organization of the world, and scripts assist only in the organization of that knowledge.

The between-the-lines problem is equally difficult: it is not possible to know ahead of time the possible occurrences that can break a script. For instance:

EXAMPLE 7.1.5

Melissa was eating dinner at her favorite restaurant when a large piece of plaster fell from the ceiling and landed on her date.

Questions: Was Melissa eating a date salad? Was Melissa's date plastered? What did she do next? As this example illustrates, structured representations can be inflexible. Reasoning can be locked into a single script, even though this may not be appropriate.

Memory organization packets (MOPs) address the problem of script inflexibility by representing knowledge as smaller components (MOPs) along with rules for dynamically combining them to form a schema that is appropriate to the current situation (Schank 1982). The organization of knowledge in memory is particularly important to implementations of case-based reasoning, in which the problem solver must efficiently retrieve a relevant prior problem solution from memory (Kolodner 1988*a*, Section 8.3).

The problems of organizing and retrieving knowledge are difficult and inherent to the modeling of semantic meaning. Eugene Charniak (1972) illustrated the amount of knowledge required to understand even simple children's stories. Consider a statement about a birthday party: "Mary was given two kites for her birthday so she took one back to the store." We must know about the tradition of giving gifts at a party; we must know what a kite is and why Mary might not want two of them; we must know about stores and their exchange policies. In spite of these problems, programs using scripts and other semantic representations can understand natural language in limited domains. An example of this work is a program that interprets messages coming over the news wire services. Using scripts for natural disasters, coups, or other stereotypic stories, programs have shown remarkable success in this limited but realistic domain (Schank and Riesbeck 1981).

7.1.5 Frames

Another representational scheme, in many ways similar to scripts, that was intended to capture in explicitly organized data structures the implicit connections of information in a problem domain, was called *frames*. This representation supports the organization of knowledge into more complex units that reflect the organization of objects in the domain.

In a 1975 paper, Minsky describes a frame:

Here is the essence of the frame theory: When one encounters a new situation (or makes a substantial change in one's view of a problem) one selects from memory a structure called a "frame". This is a remembered framework to be adapted to fit reality by changing details as necessary (Minsky 1975).

According to Minsky, a frame may be viewed as a static data structure used to represent well-understood stereotyped situations. Framelike structures seem to organize our own knowledge of the world. We adjust to every new situation by calling up information structured by past experiences. We then specially fashion or revise the details of these past experiences to represent the individual differences for the new situation.

Anyone who has stayed in one or two hotel rooms has no trouble with entirely new hotels and their rooms. One expects to see a bed, a bathroom, a place to open a suitcase, a telephone, price and emergency evacuation information on the back of the door, and so on. The details of each room can be supplied when needed: color of the curtains, location and use of light switches, etc. There is also default information supplied with the hotel room frame: no sheets; call housekeeping; need ice: look down the hall; and so on. We do not need to build up our understanding for each new hotel room we enter. All of the pieces of a generic hotel room are organized into a conceptual structure that we access when checking into a hotel; the particulars of an individual room are supplied as needed.

We could represent these higher-level structures directly in a semantic network by organizing it as a collection of separate networks, each of which represents some stereotypic situation. Frames, as well as *object-oriented systems*, provide us with a vehicle for this organization, representing entities as structured objects with named slots and attached values. Thus a frame or schema is seen as a single complex entity.

For example, the hotel room and its components can be described by a number of individual frames. In addition to the bed, a frame could represent a chair: expected height is 20 to 40 cm, number of legs is 4, a default value, is designed for sitting. A further frame represents the hotel telephone: this is a specialization of a regular phone except that billing is through the room, there is a special hotel operator (default), and a person is able to use the hotel phone to get meals served in the room, make outside calls, and to receive other services. Figure 7.12 gives a frame representing the hotel room.

Each individual frame may be seen as a data structure, similar in many respects to the traditional "record", that contains information relevant to stereotyped entities. The slots in the frame contain information such as:

1. *Frame identification information.*

2. *Relationship of this frame to other frames*. The "hotel phone" might be a special instance of "phone," which might be an instance of a "communication device."

3. *Descriptors of requirements for a frame*. A chair, for instance, has its seat between 20 and 40 cm from the floor, its back higher than 60 cm, etc. These requirements may be used to determine when new objects fit the stereotype defined by the frame.

4. *Procedural information on use of the structure described*. An important feature of frames is the ability to attach procedural code to a slot.

5. *Frame default information*. These are slot values that are taken to be true when no evidence to the contrary has been found. For instance, chairs have four legs, telephones are pushbutton, or hotel beds are made by the staff.

6. *New instance information*. Many frame slots may be left unspecified until given a value for a particular instance or when they are needed for some aspect of problem solving. For example, the color of the bedspread may be left unspecified.

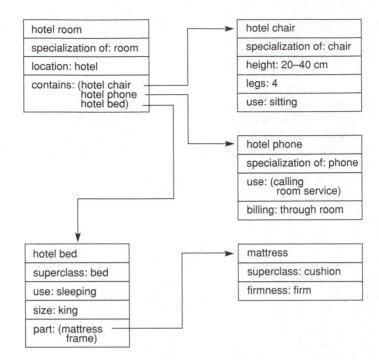

Figure 7.12 Part of a frame description of a hotel room. "Specialization" indicates a pointer to a superclass.

Frames extend semantic networks in a number of important ways. Although the frame description of hotel beds, Figure 7.12, might be equivalent to a network description, the frame version makes it much clearer that we are describing a bed with its various attributes. In the network version, there is simply a collection of nodes and we depend more on our interpretation of the structure to see the hotel bed as the primary object being described. This ability to organize our knowledge into such structures is an important attribute of a knowledge base.

Frames make it easier to organize our knowledge hierarchically. In a network, every concept is represented by nodes and links at the same level of specification. Very often, however, we may like to think of an object as a single entity for some purposes and only consider details of its internal structure for other purposes. For example, we usually are not aware of the mechanical organization of a car until something breaks down; only then do we pull up our "car engine schema" and try to find the problem.

Procedural attachment is an important feature of frames because it supports the linking of specific pieces of code to appropriate entities in the frame representation. For example, we might want to include the ability to generate graphic images in a knowledge base. A graphics language is more appropriate for this than a network language. We use procedural attachment to create *demons*. A demon is a procedure that is invoked as a side effect of some other action in the knowledge base. For example, we may wish the system to perform type checks or to run consistency tests whenever a certain slot value is changed.

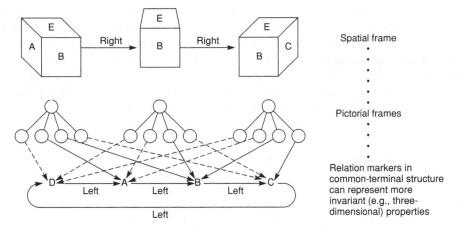

Figure 7.13 Spatial frame for viewing a cube (Minsky 1975).

Frame systems support class inheritance. The slots and default values of a class frame are inherited across the class/subclass and class/member hierarchy. For instance, a hotel phone could be a subclass of a regular phone except that (1) all out-of-building dialing goes through the hotel switchboard (for billing) and (2) hotel services may be dialed directly. Default values are assigned to selected slots to be used only if other information is not available: assume that hotel rooms have beds and are, therefore, appropriate places to go if you want to sleep; if you don't know how to dial the hotel front desk try "zero;" the phone may be assumed (no evidence to the contrary) to be pushbutton.

When an instance of the class frame is created, the system will attempt to fill its slots, either by querying the user, accepting the default value from the class frame, or executing some procedure or demon to obtain the instance value. As with semantic nets, slots and default values are inherited across a class/subclass hierarchy. Of course, default information can cause the data description of the problem to be nonmonotonic, letting us make assumptions about default values that may not always prove correct (see Section 9.1).

Minsky's own work on vision provides an example of frames and their use in default reasoning: the problem of recognizing that different views of an object actually represent the same object. For example, the three perspectives of the one cube of Figure 7.13 actually look quite different. Minsky (1975) proposed a frame system that recognizes these as views of a single object by inferring the hidden sides as default assumptions.

The frame system of Figure 7.13 represents four of the faces of a cube. The broken lines indicate that a particular face is out of view from that perspective. The links between the frames indicate the relations between the views represented by the frames. The nodes, of course, could be more complex if there were colors or patterns that the faces contained. Indeed, each slot in one frame could be a pointer to another entire frame. Also, because given information can fill a number of different slots (face E in Figure 7.13), there need be no redundancy in the information that is stored.

Frames add to the power of semantic nets by allowing complex objects to be represented as a single frame, rather than as a large network structure. This also provides a very natural way to represent stereotypic entities, classes, inheritance, and default values. Although frames, like logical and network representations, are a powerful tool, many of the problems of acquiring and organizing a complicated knowledge base must still be solved by the programmer's skill and intuition. Finally, this MIT research of the 1970s, as well as similar work at Xerox Palo Alto Research Center, led to the "object-oriented" programming design philosophy as well as building important implementation languages, including Smalltalk, Java, C++, and ultimately CLOS (Section 16.12).

7.2 Conceptual Graphs: a Network Language

Following on the early work in AI developing representational schemes (Section 7.1) a number of network languages were developed to model the semantics of natural language and other domains. In this section, we examine a particular formalism in detail, to show how, in this situation, the problems of representing meaning were addressed. John Sowa's *conceptual graphs* (Sowa 1984) is an example of a network representation language. We define the rules for forming and manipulating conceptual graphs and the conventions for representing classes, individuals, and relationships. In Section 14.3.2 we show how this formalism may be used to represent meaning in natural language understanding.

7.2.1 Introduction to Conceptual Graphs

A *conceptual graph* is a finite, connected, bipartite graph. The nodes of the graph are either *concepts* or *conceptual relations*. Conceptual graphs do not use labeled arcs; instead the conceptual relation nodes represent relations between concepts. Because conceptual graphs are bipartite, concepts only have arcs to relations, and vice versa. In Figure 7.14 dog and brown are concept nodes and color a conceptual relation. To distinguish these types of nodes, we represent concepts as boxes and conceptual relations as ellipses.

In conceptual graphs, concept nodes represent either concrete or abstract objects in the world of discourse. Concrete concepts, such as a cat, telephone, or restaurant, are characterized by our ability to form an image of them in our minds. Note that concrete concepts include generic concepts such as cat or restaurant along with concepts of specific cats and restaurants. We can still form an image of a generic cat. Abstract concepts include things such as love, beauty, and loyalty that do not correspond to images in our minds.

Conceptual relation nodes indicate a relation involving one or more concepts. One advantage of formulating conceptual graphs as bipartite graphs rather than using labeled arcs is that it simplifies the representation of relations of any arity. A relation of arity n is represented by a conceptual relation node having n arcs, as shown in Figure 7.14.

Each conceptual graph represents a single proposition. A typical knowledge base will contain a number of such graphs. Graphs may be arbitrarily complex but must be finite. For example, one graph in Figure 7.14 represents the proposition "A dog has a color of brown." Figure 7.15 is a graph of somewhat greater complexity that represents the sentence "Mary gave John the book". This graph uses conceptual relations to represent the cases of

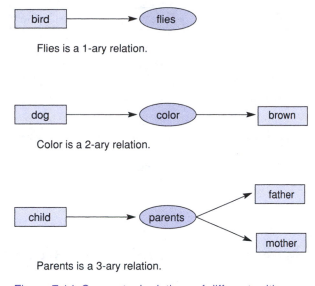

Flies is a 1-ary relation.

Color is a 2-ary relation.

Parents is a 3-ary relation.

Figure 7.14 Conceptual relations of different arities.

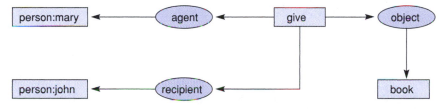

Figure 7.15 Graph of "Mary gave John the book."

the verb "to give" and indicates the way in which conceptual graphs are used to model the semantics of natural language.

7.2.2 Types, Individuals, and Names

Many early designers of semantic networks were careless in defining class/member and class/subclass relationships, with resulting semantic confusion. For example, the relation between an individual and its class is different from the relation between a class (such as dog) and its superclass (carnivore). Similarly, certain properties belong to individuals, and others belong to the class itself; the representation should provide a vehicle for making this distinction. The properties of having fur and liking bones belong to individual dogs; the class "dog" does not have fur or eat anything. Properties that are appropriate to the class include its name and membership in a zoological taxonomy.

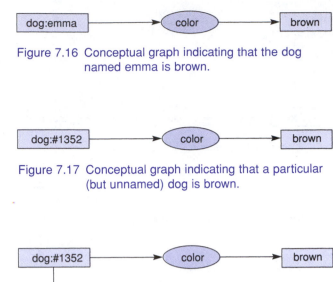

Figure 7.16 Conceptual graph indicating that the dog
named emma is brown.

Figure 7.17 Conceptual graph indicating that a particular
(but unnamed) dog is brown.

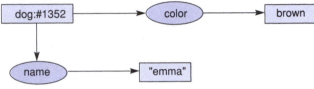

Figure 7.18 Conceptual graph indicating that a dog
named emma is brown.

In conceptual graphs, every concept is a unique individual of a particular type. Each concept box is labeled with a *type* label, which indicates the class or type of individual represented by that node. Thus, a node labeled **dog** represents some individual of that type. Types are organized into a hierarchy. The type **dog** is a subtype of **carnivore**, which is a subtype of **mammal**, etc. Boxes with the same type label represent concepts of the same type; however, these boxes may or may not represent the same individual concept.

Each concept box is labeled with the names of the type and the individual. The type and individual labels are separated by a colon, ":". The graph of Figure 7.16 indicates that the dog "Emma" is brown. The graph of Figure 7.17 asserts that some unspecified entity of type **dog** has a color of **brown**. If the individual is not indicated, the concept represents an unspecified individual of that type.

Conceptual graphs also let us indicate specific but unnamed individuals. A unique token called a *marker* indicates each individual in the world of discourse. This marker is written as a number preceded by a #. Markers are different from names in that they are unique: individuals may have one name, many names, or no name at all, but they have exactly one marker. Similarly, different individuals may have the same name but may not have the same marker. This distinction gives us a basis for dealing with the semantic ambiguities that arise when we give objects names. The graph of Figure 7.17 asserts that a particular dog, #1352, is brown.

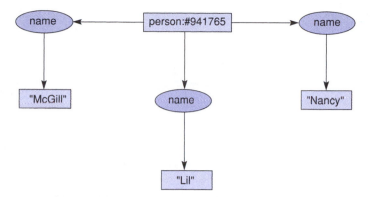

Figure 7.19 Conceptual graph of a person with three names.

Markers allow us to separate an individual from its name. If dog #1352 is named "Emma," we can use a conceptual relation called name to add this to the graph. The result is the graph of Figure 7.18. The name is enclosed in double quotes to indicate that it is a string. Where there is no danger of ambiguity, we may simplify the graph and refer to the individual directly by name. Under this convention, the graph of Figure 7.18 is equivalent to the graph of Figure 7.16.

Although we frequently ignore it both in casual conversation and in formal representations, this distinction between an individual and its name is an important one that should be supported by a representation language. For example, if we say that "John" is a common name among males, we are asserting a property of the name itself rather than of any individual named "John". This allows us to represent such English sentences as "'Chimpanzee' is the name of a species of primates." Similarly, we may want to represent the fact that an individual has several different names. The graph of Figure 7.19 represents the situation described in the song lyric: "Her name was McGill, and she called herself Lil, but everyone knew her as Nancy" (Lennon and McCartney 1968).

As an alternative to indicating an individual by its marker or name, we can also use the generic marker * to indicate an unspecified individual. By convention, this is often omitted from concept labels; a node given just a type label, dog, is equivalent to a node labeled dog:*. In addition to the generic marker, conceptual graphs allow the use of named variables. These are represented by an asterisk followed by the variable name (e.g., *X or *foo). This is useful if two separate nodes are to indicate the same, but unspecified, individual. The graph of Figure 7.20 represents the assertion "The dog scratches its ear with its paw." Although we do not know which dog is scratching its ear, the variable *X indicates that the paw and the ear belong to the same dog that is doing the scratching.

To summarize, each concept node can indicate an individual of a specified type. This individual is the *referent* of the concept. This reference is indicated either individually or generically. If the referent uses an individual marker, the concept is an *individual* concept; if the referent uses the generic marker, then the concept is *generic*.

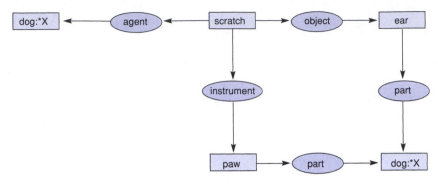

Figure 7.20 Conceptual graph of the sentence "The dog scratches its ear with its paw."

7.2.3   The Type Hierarchy

The type hierarchy, as illustrated by Figure 7.21, is a partial ordering on the set of types, indicated by the symbol $\leq$. If s and t are types and $t \leq s$, then t is said to be a *subtype* of s and s is said to be a *supertype* of t. Because it is a partial ordering, a type may have one or more supertypes as well as one or more subtypes. If s, t, and u are types, with $t \leq s$ and $t \leq u$, then t is said to be a *common subtype* of s and u. Similarly, if $s \leq v$ and $u \leq v$ then v is a *common supertype* of s and u.

The type hierarchy of conceptual graphs forms a lattice, a common form of multiple inheritance system. In a lattice, types may have multiple parents and children. However, every pair of types must have a *minimal common supertype* and a *maximal common subtype*. For types s and u, v is a minimal common supertype if $s \leq v$, $u \leq v$, and for any w, a common supertype of s and u, $v \leq w$. Maximal common subtype has a corresponding definition. The minimal common supertype of a collection of types is the appropriate place to define properties common only to those types. Because many types, such as emotion and rock, have no obvious common supertypes or subtypes, it is necessary to add types that fill these roles. To make the type hierarchy a true lattice, conceptual graphs include two special types. The *universal type*, indicated by $\top$, is a supertype of all types. The *absurd type*, indicated by $\bot$, is a subtype of all types.

7.2.4   Generalization and Specialization

The theory of conceptual graphs includes a number of operations that create new graphs from existing graphs. These allow for the generation of a new graph by either specializing or generalizing an existing graph, operations that are important for representing the semantics of natural language. The four operations are *copy*, *restrict*, *join*, and *simplify*, as seen in Figure 7.22. Assume that g_1 and g_2 are conceptual graphs. Then:

The *copy* rule allows us to form a new graph, g, that is the exact copy of g_1.

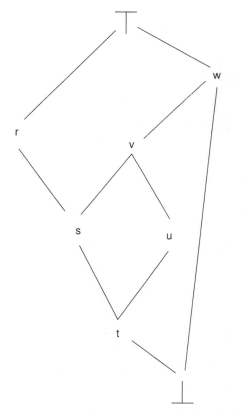

Figure 7.21 A type lattice illustrating subtypes, supertypes, the universal type, and the absurd type. Arcs represent the relationship.

Restrict allows concept nodes in a graph to be replaced by a node representing their specialization. There are two cases:

1. If a concept is labeled with a generic marker, the generic marker may be replaced by an individual marker.

2. A type label may be replaced by one of its subtypes, if this is consistent with the referent of the concept. In Figure 7.22 we can replace animal with dog.

The *join* rule lets us combine two graphs into a single graph. If there is a concept node c_1 in the graph s_1 that is identical to a concept node c_2 in s_2, then we can form a new graph by deleting c_2 and linking all of the relations incident on c_2 to c_1. *Join* is a specialization rule, because the resulting graph is less general than either of its components.

If a graph contains two duplicate relations, then one of them may be deleted, along with all its arcs. This is the *simplify* rule. Duplicate relations often occur as the result of a *join* operation, as in graph g_4 of Figure 7.22.

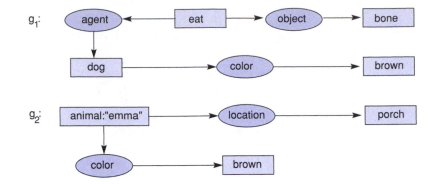

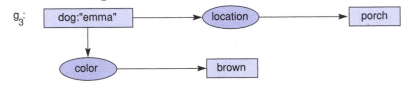

The restriction of g_2:

The join of g_1 and g_3:

The simplify of g_4:

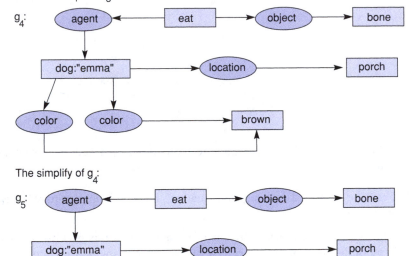

Figure 7.22 Examples of restrict, join, and simplify operations.

One use of the *restrict* rule is to make two concepts match so that a *join* can be performed. Together, *join* and *restrict* allow the implementation of inheritance. For example, the replacement of a generic marker by an individual implements the inheritance of the properties of a type by an individual. The replacement of a type label by a subtype label defines inheritance between a class and a superclass. By joining one graph to another and restricting certain concept nodes, we can implement inheritance of a variety of properties. Figure 7.23 shows how chimpanzees inherit the property of having a hand from the class primates by replacing a type label with its subtype. It also shows how the individual, Bonzo, inherits this property by instantiating a generic concept.

Similarly, we can use joins and restrictions to implement the plausible assumptions that play a role in common language understanding. If we are told that "Mary and Tom went out for pizza together," we automatically make a number of assumptions: they ate a round Italian bread covered with cheese and tomato sauce. They ate it in a restaurant and must have had some way of paying for it. This reasoning can be done using joins and restrictions. We form a conceptual graph of the sentence and then *join* it with the conceptual graphs (from our knowledge base) for pizzas and restaurants. The resulting graph lets us assume that they ate tomato sauce and paid their bill.

Join and *restrict* are specialization rules. They define a partial ordering on the set of derivable graphs. If a graph g_1 is a specialization of g_2, then we may say that g_2 is a generalization of g_1. Generalization hierarchies are important in knowledge representation. Besides providing the basis for inheritance and other commonsense reasoning schemes, generalization hierarchies are used in many learning methods, allowing us, for instance, to construct a generalized assertion from a particular training instance.

These rules are not rules of inference. They do not guarantee that true graphs will be derived from true graphs. For example, in the restriction of the graph of Figure 7.22, the result may not be true; Emma may be a cat. Similarly, the joining example of Figure 7.22 is not truth-preserving either: the dog on the porch and the dog that eats bones may be different animals. These operations are *canonical formation rules*, and although they do not preserve truth, they have the subtle but important property of preserving "meaningfulness". This is an important guarantee when we use conceptual graphs to implement natural language understanding. Consider the three sentences:

Albert Einstein formulated the theory of relativity.

Albert Einstein plays center for the Los Angeles Lakers.

Conceptual graphs are yellow flying popsicles.

The first of these sentences is true and the second is false. The third sentence, however, is meaningless; though grammatically correct, it makes no sense. The second sentence, although false, is meaningful. I can imagine Albert Einstein on a basketball court. The canonical formation rules enforce constraints on semantic meaning; that is, they do not allow us to form nonsensical graphs from meaningful ones. Although they are not sound inference rules, canonical formation rules form a basis for much of the plausible reasoning done in natural language understanding and common sense reasoning.

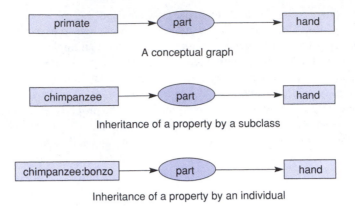

A conceptual graph

Inheritance of a property by a subclass

Inheritance of a property by an individual

Figure 7.23 Inheritance in conceptual graphs.

7.2.5 Propositional Nodes

In addition to using graphs to define relations between objects in the world, we may also want to define relations between propositions. Consider, for example, the statement "Tom believes that Jane likes pizza". "Believes" is a relation that takes a proposition as its argument.

Conceptual graphs include a concept type, *proposition*, that takes a set of conceptual graphs as its referent and allows us to define relations involving propositions. Propositional concepts are indicated as a box that contains another conceptual graph. These proposition concepts may be used with appropriate relations to represent knowledge about propositions. Figure 7.24 shows the conceptual graph for the above assertion about Jane, Tom, and pizza. The experiencer relation is loosely analogous to the agent relation in that it links a subject and a verb. The experiencer link is used with belief states based on the notion that they are something one experiences rather than does.

Figure 7.24 shows how conceptual graphs with propositional nodes may be used to express the *modal* concepts of knowledge and belief. *Modal logics* are concerned with the various ways propositions are entertained: believed, asserted as possible, probably or necessarily true, intended as a result of an action, or counterfactual (Turner 1984).

7.2.6 Conceptual Graphs and Logic

Using conceptual graphs, we can easily represent conjunctive concepts such as "The dog is big and hungry", but we have not established any way of representing negation or disjunction. Nor have we addressed the issue of variable quantification.

We may implement negation using propositional concepts and a unary operation called neg. neg takes as argument a proposition concept and asserts that concept as false. The conceptual graph of Figure 7.25 uses neg to represent the statement "There are no pink dogs".

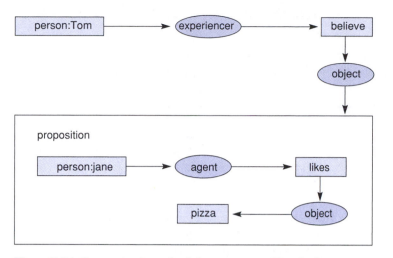

Figure 7.24 Conceptual graph of the statement "Tom believes that Jane likes pizza," showing the use of a propositional concept.

Using negation and conjunction, we may form graphs that represent disjunctive assertions according to the rules of logic. To simplify this, we may also define a relation or, which takes two propositions and represents their disjunction.

In conceptual graphs, generic concepts are assumed to be existentially quantified. For example, the generic concept dog in the graph of Figure 7.14 actually represents an existentially quantified variable. This graph corresponds to the logical expression:

$$\exists X \exists Y (dog(X) \wedge color(X,Y) \wedge brown(Y)).$$

Using negation and existential quantification, Section 2.2.2, we can also represent universal quantification. For example, the graph of Figure 7.25 could be thought of as representing the logical assertion:

$$\forall X \forall Y (\neg (dog(X) \wedge color(X,Y) \wedge pink(Y))).$$

Conceptual graphs are equivalent to predicate calculus in their expressive power. As these examples suggest, there is a straightforward mapping from conceptual graphs into predicate calculus notation. The algorithm, taken from Sowa (1984), for changing a conceptual graph, g, into a predicate calculus expression is:

1. Assign a unique variable, $x_1, x_2, \ldots, x_n$, to each of the n generic concepts in g.

2. Assign a unique constant to each individual concept in g. This constant may simply be the name or marker used to indicate the referent of the concept.

3. Represent each concept node by a unary predicate with the same name as the type of that node and whose argument is the variable or constant given that node.

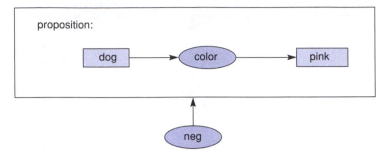

Figure 7.25 Conceptual graph of the proposition "There are no pink dogs."

4. Represent each n-ary conceptual relation in g as an n-ary predicate whose name is the same as the relation. Let each argument of the predicate be the variable or constant assigned to the corresponding concept node linked to that relation.

5. Take the conjunction of all atomic sentences formed under 3 and 4. This is the body of the predicate calculus expressions. All the variables in the expression are existentially quantified.

For example, the graph of Figure 7.16 is given by the predicate calculus expression

$$\exists X_1 \ (dog(emma) \wedge color(emma, X_1) \wedge brown(X_1))$$

Although we can reformulate conceptual graphs into predicate calculus syntax, conceptual graphs support a number of special-purpose inferencing mechanisms, such as *join* and *restrict*, not normally part of the predicate calculus.

We have presented the syntax of conceptual graphs and defined the *restriction* operation as a means of implementing inheritance. We have not yet examined the full range of operations and inferences that may be performed on these graphs, nor have we addressed the problem of defining the concepts and relations needed for domains such as natural language. We address these issues again in Section 14.3.2 where we use conceptual graphs to implement a knowledge base for a simple natural language understanding program.

7.3   Alternatives to Explicit Representation

In recent years, AI researchers have continued to question the role of representation in intelligence. Besides the connectionist and emergent approaches of Chapters 11 and 12, a more direct challenge to the role of explicit representation comes from Rodney Brooks' work at MIT and the problem domain of robotics (Brooks 1991a). Brooks questions the need for *any* centralized representational scheme, and with his *subsumption architecture*, he attempts to show how intelligent beings might evolve from lower and supporting forms of intelligence.

A second challenge to the problem of explicit and static representations comes from the work of Melanie Mitchell and Douglas Hofstadter at Indiana University. The *Copycat* architecture is an evolving network which adjusts itself to the meaning relationships that it encounters through experiment with an external world.

An important aspect of Brooks' and Mitchell's research within applied domains is that their ideas were designed into artifacts and then tested within the constraints of an actual problem situation. As we point out in the Introduction to Chapter 17, this puts both Brooks' and Mitchell's work within the empirical dimensions of science: their experiments are designed and run, and from their results conjectures about intelligence confirmed or falsified, and as a result, the next generation of experiments can be crafted.

7.3.1   Brooks' Hypothesis and the Subsumption Architecture

Brooks conjectures, and offers examples through his robotic creations, that intelligent, rational behavior does not come from disembodied systems like theorem provers, or even from traditional expert systems (Section 8.2). Intelligence, Brooks claims, is the product of the interaction between an appropriately layered system and its environment. Further-more, Brooks espouses the view that intelligent behavior *emerges* from the interactions of architectures of organized simpler behaviors: his *subsumption architecture*.

The subsumption architecture supports Brooks' design of a control system for a robot. This architecture is a collection of task-handling behaviors. Each behavior is accomplished by a finite state machine that continually maps a perception-based input into an action oriented output. This is accomplished through simple sets of *condition* → *action* production rules (Section 6.2). These rules determine, in a fairly blind fashion, that is, with no global state knowledge, what actions are appropriate to the current state of that subsystem. Brooks does allow some feedback to lower level systems.

Before presenting an example of Brooks' architecture in Figure 7.26, we present its supporting philosophy. Brooks feels that "representation is the wrong unit of abstraction in building up the bulkiest of intelligent systems". That in "simple level(s) of intelligence... explicit representations and models of the world simply get in the way. It turns out to be better to use the world as its own model" (Brooks 1991*a*). Thus Brooks wishes to incrementally build the capabilities of intelligent systems. He wants complete systems at each level of his architecture and to ensure that the pieces and their interfaces are valid. At each step of the design he builds complete intelligent systems that are tested in a world requiring actual sensing and acting (Brooks 1991*a*).

Figure 7.26, adapted from Brooks (1991*a*), shows a three-layered subsumption architec-ture. Each layer is composed of a fixed topology network of simple finite state machines, each having a few states, one or two internal registers, one or two internal timers, and access to simple computational devices, for example, to compute vector sums. These finite state machines run asynchronously, sending and receiving fixed length messages over wires. There is no central locus of control. Rather, each finite state machine is data-driven by the messages it receives. The arrival of a message or the expiration of a time period causes the machines to change state. There is no access to global data or to any

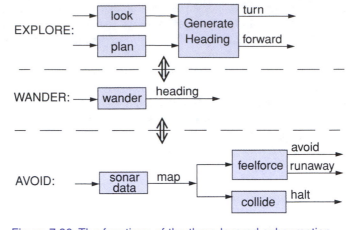

Figure 7.26 The functions of the three-layered subsumption architecture from Brooks (1991a). The layers are described by the AVOID, WANDER, and EXPLORE behaviors.

dynamically created communication links. Thus there is no possibility of global control. All finite state machines are equal and prisoners of their own connectivity.

Figure 7.26 presents a subset of the functions of the three-layered architecture that supported an early robot (Brooks 1991a). The robot had a ring of twelve sonar sensors around it. At every second these sensors gave twelve radial depth measurements. The lowest level layer of the subsumption architecture, AVOID, implements a behavior that keeps the robot from hitting objects, whether these are static or moving. The machine labeled sonar data emits an instantaneous map that is passed on to collide and feelforce, which in turn, are able to generate halt messages for the finite state machine in charge of running the robot forward. When feelforce is activated, it is able to generate either runaway or avoid instructions for object and threat avoidance.

This lowest level network of finite state machines in the architecture generates all halt and avoid instructions for the entire system. The next layer, WANDER, makes the system move about by generating a random heading for the robot about every ten seconds. The AVOID (lower level) machine takes the heading from WANDER and couples it with the forces computed by the AVOID architecture. WANDER uses the result to suppress lower level behavior, forcing the robot to move in a direction close to what wander decided, but at the same time to avoid all obstacles. Finally, if the turn and forward machines (in the top level architecture) are activated, they will suppress any new impulses sent from WANDER.

The top level, EXPLORE, makes the robot try to explore its environment, looking for distant places and trying to reach them by planning a path. This layer is able to suppress the wander instructions and observes how the bottom layer diverts the robot due to obstacles. It corrects for these divergences and keeps the robot focused on its goal, inhibiting the wandering behavior but allowing the lowest level object avoidance to continue its function. When deviations generated at the lower level occur, the EXPLORE level calls plan to keep the system goal oriented. The main point of Brook's subsumption architecture is that the system requires no centralized symbolic reasoning and takes all its actions without searching through possible next states. Although the behavior-based finite state machine is generating suggestions for actions based on its own current state, the global system acts based on the interactions of the systems layered below it.

The three-layer architecture just presented comes from Brooks' early design of a wandering, goal-seeking robot. More recently, his research group has built complex systems with further layers (Brooks 1991a, Brooks and Stein 1994). One system is able to wander around the MIT Robotics Lab looking for empty aluminum drink cans on people's desks. This requires layers for discovering offices, looking for desks, and recognizing drink cans. Further layers are able to guide the robot arm to collect these cans for recycling.

Brooks insists that top level behavior emerges as a result of the design and testing of the individual lower level layers of the architecture. The design for coherent final behaviors, requiring both inter-layer and between-layer communications, is discovered through experiment. Despite this simplicity of design, however, the subsumption architecture has performed successfully in several applications (Brooks 1989, 1991a, 1997).

There remains, however, a number of important questions concerning the subsumption architecture and other related approaches to the design of control systems (see also Section 17.2):

1. There is a problem of the sufficiency of local information at each level of the system. Since at each level, purely reactive state machines make decisions on local information, that is, on local data, it is difficult to see how such decision making could take account of any information not at that local level. By definition, it will be myopic.

2. If there exists absolutely no "knowledge" or "model" of the complete environment, how can the limited input on the local situation be sufficient for determination of globally acceptable actions? How can top level coherence possibly result?

3. How can a purely reactive component with very limited state learn from its environment? At some level in the system, there must be sufficient state for the creation of learning mechanisms if the overall agent is to be called intelligent.

4. There is a problem of scale. Although Brooks and his associates claim to have built subsumption architectures of six and even ten layers, what design principles will allow it to scale to further interesting behavior? Can this approach generalize to very large and complex systems?

Finally, we must ask the question what is "emergence"? Is it magic? At this time in the evolution of science, "emergence" seems to be a word to cover any phenomenon for which we can as yet make no other accounting. We are told to build systems and test them in the world and they will show intelligence. Unfortunately, without further design instruction, emergence just becomes a word to describe what we can't yet understand. As a result, it is very difficult to determine how we can *use* this technology to build ever more complex systems. In the next section we describe *copycat*, a hybrid architecture that is able by exploration to discover invariances in a problem domain and, at the same time, possesses sufficient state to utilize these discovered invariances in the problem-solving process.

7.3.2 The Copycat Architecture

An often-heard criticism of traditional AI representation schemes is that they are static and cannot possibly reflect the dynamic nature of thought processes and intelligence. When a human perceives a new situation, for example, he or she is often struck by relationships with already known or analogous situations. In fact, it is often noted that human perception is both bottom up, that is, stimulated by new patterns in the environment, and top down, mediated by what the agent expects to perceive.

Copycat is a problem-solving architecture built by Melanie Mitchell (1993) as a PhD dissertation under Douglas Hofstadter (1995) at Indiana University. Copycat builds on many of the representational techniques that preceded it, including blackboards, Section 6.3, semantic networks, Section 7.2, connectionist networks, Chapter 11, and classifier systems (Holland 1986). It also follows Brooks' approach to problem solving as active intervention in a problem domain. In contrast with Brooks and connectionist networks, however, copycat requires a global "state" to be part of the problem solver. Secondly, representation is an evolving feature of that state. Copycat supports a semantic network-like mechanism that grows and changes with continuing experience within its environment. Thus, representation is less brittle and more fluid, it is more about what the agent itself has discovered as important, rather than what the program's designer thought would be important. Finally, the components of copycat capture and combine the top down and bottom up synergy of perception and analogy making.

The original problem domain for copycat was the perception and building of simple analogies. In that sense it is building on earlier work by Evans (1968) and Reitman (1965). Examples of this domain are completing the patterns: hot is to cold as tall is to {wall, short, wet, hold} or, based on an hierarchical organization of the world, bear is to pig as chair is to {foot, table, coffee, strawberry}. Copycat worked to discover appropriate completions for alphabetic string patterns such as: abc is to abd as ijk is to ? or again, abc is to abd as iijjkk is to ?.

Copycat is made up of three major components, the *workspace*, the *slipnet*, and the *coderack*. These three components are mediated in their interactions by a *temperature* measure. The temperature mechanism captures the degree of perceptual organization in the system, and based on this measure, controls the degree of randomness used in making decisions. Higher temperatures reflect the fact that there is little information on which to base decisions, lower temperatures reflect the opposite. Thus, decisions are more random at higher temperatures and a temperature drop indicates the system is building consensus.

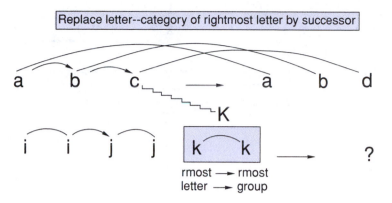

Figure 7.27 A possible state of the copycat workspace. Several examples of bonds and links between the letters are shown; adopted from Mitchell (1993).

Finally, a low temperature indicates that an answer is emerging, as well as reflecting the program's "confidence" in the solution it is producing.

The *workspace* is a global structure, similar to the blackboard of Section 6.3, for creating structures that the other components of the system can inspect. In this sense it is also much like the message area in Holland's (1986) classifier system. The workspace is where perceptual structures are built hierarchically on top of the input (the three strings of alphabetic symbols). Figure 7.27 gives a possible state for the workspace, with bonds (the arrows) built between related components of the strings. Note the link between the c and the pair kk, an early start for analogy building.

The *slipnet* reflects the network of concepts or potential associations for the components of the analogy, a small example of which can be seen in Figure 7.28. One view of the slipnet is as a dynamically deformable semantic network, each of whose nodes has an activation level. Links in the network can be labeled by other nodes. Based on the activation level of the labelling nodes the linked nodes grow or shrink. In this way the system changes the degree of association between the nodes as a function of context, that is the events of significance in building the current solution. The spreading of activation among nodes is encouraged more between nodes that in the current context are more closely related.

The *coderack* is a priority biased probabilistic queue containing *codelets*. Codelets are small pieces of executable code designed to interact with the objects in the workspace and to attempt to further some small part of the evolving solution, or, more simply, to explore different facets of the problem space. Again, the codelets are very much like the individual classifiers of Holland's (1986) system.

Nodes in the slipnet generate codelets and post them to the coderack where they have a probabilistic chance of execution. Thus, the system maintains pieces of code in parallel

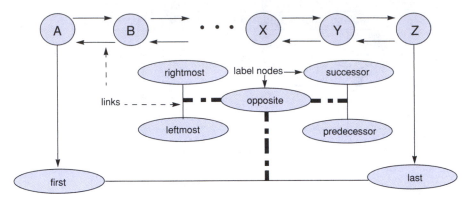

Figure 7.28 A small part of copycat's slipnet with nodes, links, and label nodes shown; adapted from Mitchell (1993).

that compete for the chance to find and build structures in the workspace. These codes correspond to the nodes from which they came. This is a top-down activity, seeking more examples of the things that have already generated interest. Codelets can also work bottom up, trying to identify and build on whatever relationships already exist among the objects in the workspace.

As structures are built in the workspace, an *activation* measure is added to the nodes that generated the codelets that built the structures. This allows the system's behavior in a context of the current state of the problem/solution to impact its future behavior. An important element of the copycat architecture is the use of randomness. Most choices are made randomly, where the probability of selecting an action or structure is biased by the relevance of that item to the current state of the problem solution. The randomness factor also prevents the program from getting stuck. Furthermore, the random chance of doing something "wrong" (not obviously part of the current path) keeps the system open to other potential solution paths. This helps deal with potential "horizon effects" (Section 4.4), where the failure of the current path is hidden. Randomness, thus, adds diversity to the search space, one of the important strengths of genetic algorithms (Chapter 12).

Finally, the *temperature* serves as a feedback mechanism calculating the "cohesion" among the structures built in the workspace. With little cohesion, that is, few structures that offer promise of a solution, the biases of the probabilistic choices made by the system are less important: one choice is just about as useful as another. When the cohesion is high with an internally consistent solution evolving, biases become very important in the probabilistic choices: the choices made are more closely linked to the evolving solution.

Copycat offers a flexible architecture whose structures evolve in both a data-driven and expectation-driven fashion to reflect the invariants in its environment. It is open, however, to several criticisms. First, even though analogical reasoning is a general and important feature of intelligence, the alphabetic domain of copycat is so semantically weak that little appreciation of analogical reasoning results. In this sense, it is, indeed, a toy system.

Secondly, copycat has no learning. It starts anew with each example to try to complete the string patterns. Analogical intelligence requires a system to incorporate each new insight into the sum total of all its insights, the evolving power for analogy-making that it brings to each new encounter with its world.

There are several new projects in the copycat world to test the architecture in richer settings. Hofstadter and his students (Marshall 1999) continue to model analogical relationships. The Madcat Group (Lewis and Luger 2000) has expanded the copycat architecture for use as a control system for a mobile robot. In robotics, the copycat domain is enriched significantly by giving it a concrete environment with which it can have ongoing and learning-oriented interactions. Evolving from this dialogue is a map of the space explored by the robot. Built in a use-oriented fashion, objects are discovered and mapped as well as paths among the objects planned and replanned.

In the next section, with agent-based problem solving, we take a more distributed and component-based view of representation and problem solving.

7.4 Agent-Based and Distributed Problem Solving

There were two insights in the AI research community in the 1980s that had important consequences for future research in the analysis of the role of representation in intelligent problem solving. The first was the research tradition of the "Distributed Artificial Intelligence" or the "DAI" community. The first DAI workshop was held at MIT in 1980 for discussion of issues related to intelligent problem solving with systems consisting of multiple problem solvers. It was decided at that time by the DAI community that they were *not* interested in low level parallelism issues, such as how to distribute processing over different machines or how to parallelize complex algorithms. Rather, their goal was to understand how distributed problem solvers could be effectively coordinated for the intelligent solution of problems. In fact, there had been an even earlier history of distributed processing in artificial intelligence, with the use and coordination of *actors* and *demons* and the design of blackboard systems, as seen in Section 6.3.

The second AI research insight of the 1980s, already presented in Section 7.3, was that of Rodney Brooks and his group at MIT. Brooks' challenge to the AI community's traditional view of representation and reasoning had many important consequences (Section 7.3.1). First, the conjecture that intelligent problem solving does not require a centralized store of knowledge manipulated by some general-purpose inferencing scheme led to the notion of distributed and cooperative models of intelligence, where each element of the distributed representation was responsible for its own component of the problem-solving process. Second, the fact that intelligence is situated and active in the context of particular tasks, allows the problem solver to offload aspects of the solution process into the environment itself. This allows, for example, an individual solver to address a task at hand and at the same time have no knowledge whatsoever of the progress towards solution within the general problem domain. Thus one web agent, say, can check inventory information, while another agent checks credit worthiness of a customer, both agents unaware of the higher-level decision making, for example, whether or not to allow a purchase. Both of these research emphases of the 1980s brought on the current interest in *the design and use of intelligent agents*.

7.4.1   Agent-Oriented Problem Solving: A Definition

Before proceeding further in the discussion of agent research, we define what we mean by "agent", "agent-based system", and "multi-agent system". There are problems here, however, as many different groups in the agent research community have differing opinions as to exactly what agent-based problem solving is all about. Our definition and discussion is based on an extension of the work by Jennings, Sycara, and Wooldridge (1998), Jennings and Wooldridge (1998), Wooldridge (2000), and Lewis and Luger (2000).

For us, a multi-agent system is a computer program with problem solvers situated in interactive environments, which are each capable of flexible, autonomous, yet socially organized actions that can be, but need not be, directed towards predetermined objectives or goals. Thus, the four criteria for an intelligent agent system include software problem solvers that are *situated*, *autonomous*, *flexible*, and *social*.

The *situatedness* of an intelligent agent means that the agent receives input from the environment in which it is active and can also effect changes within that environment. Examples of environments for situated agents include the internet, game playing, or a robotics situation. A concrete example might be a soccer player in a ROBOCUP competition (Veloso et al. 2000) where an agent must interact appropriately with the ball and an opponent without full knowledge of the locations, challenges, and successes of other players in the contest. This situatedness can be contrasted with more traditional AI problem solvers, such as the STRIPS planner, Section 8.4, or the MYCIN expert system, Section 8.3, that maintain centrally located and exhaustive knowledge of application domains.

An *autonomous* system is one that can interact with its environment without the direct intervention of other agents. To do this it must have control over its own actions and internal state. Some autonomous agents can also learn from their experience to improve their performance over time (see Part IV). For example, on the internet, an autonomous agent could do a credit card authentication check independent of other issues in the purchasing transaction. In the ROBOCUP example, an agent could pass the ball to a teammate or kick it on goal depending on its individual situation.

A *flexible* agent is both intelligently *responsive* as well as *proactive* depending on its current situation. A responsive agent receives stimuli from its environment and responds to them in an appropriate and timely fashion. A proactive agent does not simply respond to situations in its environment but is also able to be opportunistic, goal directed, and have appropriate alternatives for various situations. A credit agent, for example, would be able to go back to the user with ambiguous results or find another credit agency if one alternative is not sufficient. The soccer agent could change its dribble depending on the challenge pattern of an opponent.

Finally, an agent is *social* that can interact, as appropriate, with other software or human agents. After all, an agent is only part of a complex problem-solving process. The interactions of the social agent are oriented towards the goals of the larger multi-agent system. This social dimension of the agent system must address many difficult situations. These include: How can different agents bid for a subtask in problem solving? How can agents communicate with each other to facilitate the accomplishment of higher system-level tasks—in the ROBOCUP example, this might be to score a goal. How can one agent support another agent's goals, for example, to handle the security issues of an internet task? All these questions on the social dimension are the subject of ongoing research.

We have described the basis for creating multi-agent systems. Multi-agent systems are ideal for representing problems that include many problem-solving methods, multiple viewpoints, and multiple entities. In these domains, multi-agent systems offer the advantages of distributed and concurrent problem solving along with the advantages of sophisticated schemes for interaction. Examples of interactions include cooperation in working towards a common goal, coordination in organizing problem-solving activity so that harmful interactions are avoided and beneficial possibilities exploited, and negotiation of subproblem constraints so that acceptable performance ensues. It is the flexibility of these social interactions that distinguishes multi-agent systems from more traditional software and which provides the power and excitement to the agent paradigm.

In recent years, the term *multi-agent system* refers to all types of software systems composed of multiple semi-autonomous components. The distributed agent system considers how a particular problem can be solved by a number of modules (agents) which cooperate by dividing and sharing the knowledge about the problem and its evolving solution. Research in multi-agent systems is focused on the behaviors of collections of, sometimes already existing, autonomous agents aimed at solving a given problem. A multi-agent system can also be seen as a loosely coupled network of problem solvers that work together on problems that may be beyond the scope of any of the agents individually (Durfee and Lesser 1989).

The problem solvers of a multi-agent system, besides being autonomous, may also be of heterogeneous design. Based on analysis by Jennings, Sycara, and Wooldridge (1998), there are four important characteristics of multi-agent problem solving. First, each agent has incomplete information and insufficient capabilities for solving the entire problem, and thus can suffer from a limited viewpoint. Second, there is no global system controller for the entire problem solving. Third, the knowledge and input data for the problem is also decentralized, and fourth, the reasoning processes are often asynchronous.

Interestingly, traditional object-oriented programmers often fail to see anything new in an agent-based system. On consideration of the relative properties of agents and objects, this can be understandable. Objects are defined as computational systems with encapsulated state, they have methods associated with this state that support interactions in an environment, and they communicate by message passing.

Differences between objects and agents include the fact that objects rarely exhibit control over their own behavior. We do not see agents as invoking methods on one another, but rather as requesting that actions be performed. Further, agents are designed to have flexible, i.e., reactive, proactive, and social behavior. Finally, interacting agents are often seen to have their own individual threads of control. All these differences are not to indicate that an object-oriented programming language, such as CLOS in Section 16.12, does not offer a suitable medium for building agent systems; quite to the contrary, the power and flexibility of CLOS make it ideal for this task.

7.4.2   Examples of and Challenges to an Agent-Oriented Paradigm

To make the ideas of the previous section more concrete we next describe a number of application domains where agent-based problem solving is appropriate. We also include references to research within these problem areas.

Manufacturing. The manufacturing domain can be modeled as a hierarchy of work areas. There may be work areas for milling, lathing, painting, assembling, and so on. These work areas may then be grouped into manufacturing subsystems, each subsystem a function within the larger manufacturing process. These manufacturing subsystems may then be grouped into a single factory. A larger entity, the company, may then control aspects of each of these factories, for instance, to manage orders, inventory, levels of duplication, profits, and so on. References for agent-based manufacturing include work in production sequencing (Chung and Wu 1997), manufacturing operations (Oliveira et al. 1997), and the collaborative design of products (Cutosky et al. 1993, Darr and Birmingham 1996).

Automated Control. Since process controllers are autonomous, reactive, and often distributed systems, it is not surprising that agent models can be important. There is research in controlling transportation systems (Corera et al. 1996), spacecraft control (Schwuttke and Quan 1993), particle beam accelerators (Perriolat et al. 1996, Klein et al. 2000), air traffic control (Ljunberg and Lucas 1992) and others.

Telecommunications. Telecommunication systems are large distributed networks of interacting components that require real-time monitoring and management. Agent-based systems have been used for network control and management (Schoonderwoerd et al. 1997, Adler et al. 1989), transmission and switching (Nishibe et al. 1993), and service (Busuoic and Griffiths 1994). See Veloso et al. (2000) for a comprehensive overview.

Transportation Systems. Traffic systems are almost by definition distributed, situated, and autonomous. Applications include coordinating commuters and cars for carpooling (Burmeister et al. 1997) and cooperative transportation scheduling (Fischer et al. 1996).

Information Management. The richness, diversity, and complexity of information available to current society is almost overwhelming. Agent systems allow the possibility of intelligent information management, especially on the internet. Both human factors as well as information organization seem to conspire against comfortable access to information. Two critical agent tasks are information filtering, only a tiny portion of the information that we have access to do we actually want, and information gathering, the task of collecting and prioritizing the pieces of information that we actually do want. Applications include WEBMATE (Chen and Sycara 1998), electronic mail filtering (Maes 1994), a web browsing assistant (Lieberman 1995), and an expert locator agent (Kautz et al. 1997).

E-Commerce. Commerce currently seems to be driven by human activity: we decide when to buy or sell, the appropriate quantities and price, even what information might be appropriate at the time. Certainly commerce is a domain appropriate for agent models. Although full development of e-commerce agents may be in the future, several systems are already available. For example, programs can now make many buy and sell decisions in the stock market, based on many diverse pieces of distributed information. Several agent systems are being developed for portfolio management (Sycara et al. 1996), shopping assistance (Doorenbos et al. 1997, Krulwich 1996), and interactive catalogues (Schrooten and van de Velde 1997, Takahashi et al. 1997).

Interactive Games and Theater. Game and theater characters provide a rich interactive simulated environment. These agents can challenge us in war games, finance management scenarios, or even sports. Theater agents play roles analogous to their human counterparts and can offer the illusion of life for working with emotional situations, simulating medical emergencies, or training for diverse tasks. Research in this area includes computer games (Wavish and Graham 1996), and interactive personalities (Hayes-Roth 1995, Trappl and Petta 1997).

There are many other domains, of course, where agent-based approaches are appropriate.

Even though the agent technology offers many potential advantages for intelligent problem solving it still has a number of challenges to overcome. The following research questions are based on ideas from Jennings et al. (1998) and Bond and Gasser (1988).

How can we systematically formalize, decompose, and allocate problems to agents? Furthermore, how do we appropriately synthesize their results?

How can we enable agents to communicate and interact? What communication languages and protocols are available? What and when is communication appropriate?

How can we ensure that agents act coherently in taking actions or making decisions? How can they address nonlocal effects and avoid harmful agent interactions?

How can individual agents represent and reason about the actions, plans, and knowledge of other agents in order to coordinate with them? How can agents reason about the state of their coordinated processes?

How can disparate viewpoints and conflicting intentions between agents be recognized and coordinated?

How can harmful overall system behavior, such as chaotic or oscillatory action, be recognized and avoided?

How can limited resources, both of the individual agent as well as for the full system, be allocated and managed?

Finally, what are the best hardware platforms and software technologies for the support and development of agent systems?

The intelligent software design skills necessary to support agent problem-solving technology are found throughout this book. First, the representational requirements for intelligent problem solving make up a constant theme of our presentation. Second, issues of search, especially heuristic search, may be found in Part II. Third, the area of *planning*, presented in Section 8.4, provides a methodology of ordering and coordinating subgoals in the process of organizing a problem solution. Fourth, we present the idea of stochastic agents reasoning under conditions of uncertainty in Section 9.3. Finally, issues in learning, automated reasoning, and natural language understanding are addressed in Parts V and IV. These subareas of traditional AI have their roles within the creation of agent architectures.

There are a number of other design issues for the agent model that go beyond the scope of this book, for example agent communication languages, bidding schemes, and techniques for distributed control. These are addressed in the agent literature (Jennings, 1995, Jennings, Sycara, and Wooldridge 1998, Wooldridge 1998), and in particular in the appropriate conference proceedings (AAAI, IJCAI, and DAI).

7.5 Epilogue and References

In this chapter, we have examined many of the major alternatives for knowledge representation, including the use of logic, rules, semantic networks, and frames. We also considered systems with no centralized knowledge base or general-purpose reasoning scheme. Finally, we considered distributed problem-solving with agents. The results of careful study include an increased understanding of the advantages and limitations of each of these approaches to representation. Nonetheless, debate continues over the relative naturalness, efficiency, and appropriateness of each approach. We close this chapter with a brief discussion of several important issues in the area of knowledge representation.

The first of these is the *selection and granularity of atomic symbols* for representing knowledge. Objects in the world constitute the domain of the mapping; computational objects in the knowledge base are the range. The nature of the atomic elements in the language largely determines what can be described about the world. For example, if a "car" is the smallest atom of the representation, then the system cannot reason about engines, wheels, or any of the component parts of a car. However, if the atoms correspond to these parts, then a larger structure may be required to represent "car" as a single concept, introducing a cost in efficiency in manipulating this larger structure.

Another example of the trade-off in the choice of symbols comes from work in natural language understanding. Programs that use single words as elements of meaning may have difficulty in representing complex concepts that do not have a one-word denotation. There is also difficulty in distinguishing between different meanings of the same word or different words with the same meaning. One approach to this problem is to use semantic primitives, language-independent conceptual units, as the basis for representing the meaning of natural language. Although this viewpoint avoids the problem of using single words as units of meaning, it involves other trade-offs: many words require complex structures for their definitions; also, by relying on a small set of primitives, many subtle distinctions, such as push vs. shove or yell vs. scream, are difficult to express.

Exhaustiveness is a property of a knowledge base that is assisted by an appropriate representation. A mapping is *exhaustive* with respect to a property or class of objects if all occurrences correspond to an explicit element of the representation. Geographic maps are assumed to be exhaustive to some level of detail; a map with a missing city or river would not be well regarded as a navigational tool. Although most knowledge bases are not exhaustive, exhaustiveness with respect to certain properties or objects is a desirable goal. For example, the ability to assume that a representation is exhaustive may allow a planner to ignore possible effects of the *frame problem*.

When we describe problems as a state of the world that is changed by a series of actions or events, these actions or events generally change only a few components of the description; the program must be able to infer side effects and implicit changes in the world description. The problem of representing the side effects of actions is called the *frame problem*. For example, a robot stacking heavy boxes on a truck must compensate for the lowering of the truck bed due to the weight of each new box. If a representation is exhaustive, there will be no unspecified side effects, and the frame problem effectively disappears. The difficulty of the frame problem results from the fact that it is impossible to build a completely exhaustive knowledge base for most domains. A representation language should assist the programmer in deciding what knowledge may safely be omitted and help deal with the consequences of this omission. (Section 8.4 discusses the frame problem in planning.)

Related to exhaustiveness is the *plasticity* or modifiability of the representation: the addition of knowledge in response to deficiencies is the primary solution to a lack of exhaustiveness. Because most knowledge bases are not exhaustive, it should be easy to modify or update them. In addition to the syntactic ease of adding knowledge, a representation should help to guarantee the consistency of a knowledge base as information is added or deleted. Inheritance, by allowing properties of a class to be inherited by new instances, is an example of how a representational scheme may help ensure consistency.

Several systems, including Copycat (Mitchell 1993, Section 7.3.2), have addressed the plasticity issue by designing network structures that change and evolve as they meet the constraints of the natural world. In these systems, the representation is the result of bottom-up acquisition of new data, constrained by the expectation of the perceiving system. An application of this type of system is analogical reasoning.

Another useful property of representations concerns the extent to which the mapping between the world and the knowledge base is *homomorphic*. Here, homomorphic implies a one-to-one correspondence between objects and actions in the world and the computational objects and operations of the language. In a homomorphic mapping the knowledge base reflects the perceived organization of the domain and can be organized in a more natural and intuitive fashion.

In addition to naturalness, directness, and ease of use, representational schemes may also be evaluated by their *computational efficiency*. Levesque and Brachman (1985) discuss the trade-off between expressiveness and efficiency. Logic, when used as a representational scheme, is highly expressive as a result of its completeness; however, systems based on unconstrained logic pay a considerable price in efficiency, see Chapter 13.

Most of the representation issues just presented relate to any information that is to be captured and used by a computer. There are further issues that the designers of distributed and agent systems must address. Many of these issues relate to making decisions with partial (local) information, distributing the responsibility for accomplishing tasks, agent communication languages, and developing algorithms for the cooperation and information sharing of agents. Many of these issues are presented in Section 7.4.

Finally, if the philosophical approaches of a distributed environment-based intelligence proposed by Clark (1997), Haugeland (1997), and Dennett (1991, 1995) are to be realized, where the so-called "leaky" system utilizes both the environment and other agents as critical media for knowledge storage and use, it may be that entirely new representation languages await invention. Where are the representational tools and support to, as Brooks (1991a) proposes, "use the world as its own model"?

We conclude with further references for the material presented in Chapter 7. Associationist theories have been studied as models of both computer and human memory and reasoning (Selz 1913, 1922; Anderson and Bower 1973; Sowa 1984; Collins and Quillian 1969).

Important work in structured knowledge representation languages includes Bobrow and Winograd's representation language KRL (Bobrow and Winograd 1977) and Brachman's (1979) representation language KL-ONE, which pays particular attention to the semantic foundations of structured representations.

Our overview of conceptual graphs owes a considerable debt to John Sowa's book *Conceptual Structures* (1984). The reader is referred to this book for details that we have omitted. In its full treatment, conceptual graphs combine the expressive power of predicate calculus, as well as that of modal and higher-order logics, with a rich set of built-in concepts and relations derived from epistemology, psychology, and linguistics.

There are a number of other approaches of interest to the representation problem. For example, Brachman, Fikes, and Levesque have proposed a representation that emphasizes *functional* specifications; that is, what information can be asked of or told to a knowledge base (Brachman 1985, Brachman et al. 1985, Levesque 1984).

A number of books can help with an advanced study of these issues. *Readings in Knowledge Representation* by Brachman and Levesque (1985) is a compilation of important articles in this area. Many of the articles referred to in this chapter may be found there, although they were referenced in their original source. *Representation and Understanding* by Bobrow and Collins (1975), *Representations of Commonsense Knowledge* by Davis (1990), *Readings in Qualitative Reasoning about Physical Systems* by Weld and deKleer (1990) are all important. *Principles of Knowledge Representation and Reasoning* (Brachman et al. 1990), *An Overview of Knowledge Representation* (Mylopoulos and Levesque 1984), and the proceedings of the annual conferences on AI are helpful resources.

There is now a considerable number of papers following the directions proposed by Brooks with his subsumption architecture; see especially Brooks (1991a), Brooks and Stein (1994), Maes (1994), and Veloso et al. (2000). There are also contrasting positions, see McGonigle (1990, 1998) and Lewis and Luger (2000). For a philosophical view of distributed and embodied knowledge and intelligence see Clark's *Being There* (1997).

Agent-based research is widespread in modern AI. See Jennings et al. (1998) for an introduction to the area. There are now entire sections of the annual AI conferences (IAAI and IJCAI) devoted to agent research. We recommend reading the recent proceedings of these conferences for more up-to-date discussions of current research issues. We also recommend the conference proceedings and readings in the area of distributed artificial intelligence, or DAI. A summary and references of important application areas for agent-based research was presented in Section 7.4.

Issues in knowledge representation also lie in the middle ground between AI and Cognitive Science; see *Cognitive Science: The Science of Intelligent Systems* (Luger 1994) and *Being There* (Clark 1997). *Computation and Intelligence* edited by George Luger (1995) is a collection of classic papers that emphasizes the development of many different knowledge representation schemes.

7.6   Exercises

1. Common sense reasoning employs such notions as causality, analogy, and equivalence but uses them in a different way than do formal languages. For example, if we say "Inflation caused Jane to ask for a raise," we are suggesting a more complicated causal relationship than that found in simple physical laws. If we say "Use a knife or chisel to trim the wood," we are suggesting an important notion of equivalence. Discuss the problems of translating these and other such concepts into a formal language.

2. In Section 7.2.1 we presented some of the arguments against the use of logic for representing common sense knowledge. Make an argument for the use of logic in representing this knowledge.

3. Translate each of the following sentences into predicate calculus, conceptual dependencies, and conceptual graphs:

    "Jane gave Tom an ice cream cone."
    "Basketball players are tall."
    "Paul cut down the tree with an axe."
    "Place all the ingredients in a bowl and mix thoroughly."

4. Read "What's in a Link" by Woods (1985). Section IV of this article lists a number of problems in knowledge representation. Suggest a solution to each of these problems using logic, conceptual graphs, and frame notations.

5. Translate the conceptual graphs of Figure 7.29 into English sentences.

6. The operations *join* and *restrict* define a generalization ordering on conceptual graphs. Show that the generalization relation is transitive.

7. Specialization of conceptual graphs using *join* and *restrict* is not a truth-preserving operation. Give an example that demonstrates that the restriction of a true graph is not necessarily true. However, the generalization of a true graph is always true; prove this.

8. Define a specialized representation language to describe the activities of a public library. This language will be a set of concepts and relations using conceptual graphs. Do the same thing for a retail business. What concepts and relations would these two languages have in common? Which would exist in both languages but have a different meaning?

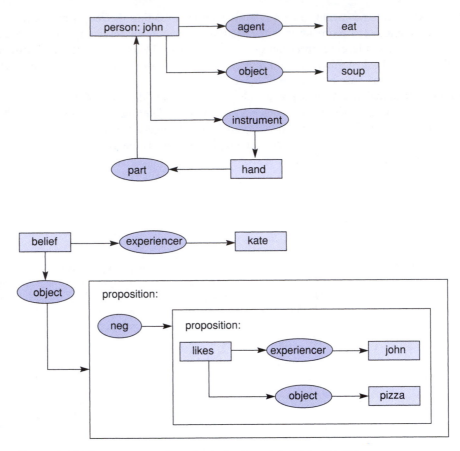

Figure 7.29 Two conceptual graphs to be translated into English.

9. Translate the conceptual graphs of Figure 7.29 into predicate calculus.

10. Translate the financial advisor knowledge base, Section 2.4, into conceptual graph form.

11. Give evidence from your own experience that suggests a script-like or frame-like organization of human memory.

12. Using conceptual dependencies, define a script for:

    a. A fast-food restaurant.
    b. Interacting with a used-car salesperson.
    c. Going to the opera.

13. Construct a hierarchy of subtypes for the concept vehicle; for example, subtypes of vehicle might be land_vehicle or ocean_vehicle. These would have further subtypes. Is this best represented as a tree, lattice, or general graph? Do the same for the concept move; for the concept angry.

14. Construct a type hierarchy in which some types do not have a common supertype. Add types to make this a lattice. Could this hierarchy be expressed using tree inheritance? What problems would arise in doing so?

15. Each of the following sequences of characters is generated according to some general rule. Describe a representation that could be used to represent the rules or relationships required to continue each sequence:

    a. 2,4,6,8, . . .
    b. 1,2,4,8,16, . . .
    c. 1,1,2,3,5,8, . . .
    d. 1,a,2,c,3,f,4, . . .
    e. o,t,t,f,f,s,s, . . .

16. Two examples of analogical reasoning were presented in Section 7.3. Describe an appropriate representation and search strategy that would allow for identification of the best answer in each situation. Create two more example analogies that would work with your proposed representation.

    a. hot is to cold as tall is to {wall, short, wet, hold}
    b. bear is to pig as chair is to {foot, table, coffee, strawberry}

17. Describe a representation that could be used in a program to solve analogy problems like that in Figure 7.30. This class of problems was addressed by T. G. Evans (1968). The representation must be capable of representing the essential features of size, shape, and relative position.

18. Brooks' paper (1991a) offers an important discussion on the role of representation in traditional AI. Read this paper, and comment on the limitations of explicit, general-purpose representational schemes.

19. At the end of Section 7.3.1, there are five potential issues that Brooks' subsumption architecture (1991a) must address to offer a successful general-purpose approach to problem-solving. Pick one or more of these and comment on it (them).

20. Identify five properties that an agent language should have to provide an agent-oriented internet service. Comment on the role of Java as a general-purpose agent language for

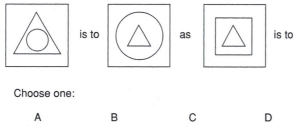

Choose one:

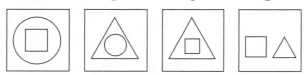

Figure 7.30 Example of an analogy test problem.

building internet services. Do you see a similar role for CLOS? Why or why not? There is plenty of information on this topic on the internet itself.

21. There were a number of important issues presented near the end of Section 7.4 related to the creation of agent-oriented solutions to problems. Pick one of these and discuss the issue further.

22. Suppose you were designing an agent system to represent an American football or alternatively a soccer team. For agents to cooperate in a defensive or in a scoring maneuver, they must have some idea of each other's plans and possible responses to situations. How might you build a model of another cooperating agent's goals and plans?

23 Pick one of the application areas for agent architectures summarized in Section 7.4. Choose a research or application paper in that area. Design an organization of agents that could address the problem. Break the problem down to specify issues of responsibility for each agent. List appropriate cooperation procedures.

STRONG METHOD
PROBLEM SOLVING

8

The first principle of knowledge engineering is that the problem-solving power exhibited by an intelligent agent's performance is primarily the consequence of its knowledge base, and only secondarily a consequence of the inference method employed. Expert systems must be knowledge-rich even if they are methods-poor. This is an important result and one that has only recently become well understood in AI. For a long time AI has focused its attentions almost exclusively on the development of clever inference methods; almost any inference method will do. The power resides in the knowledge.

—EDWARD FEIGENBAUM, Stanford University

Nam et ipsa scientia potestas est (knowledge is power).

—FRANCIS BACON (1620)

8.0   Introduction

We continue studying issues of representation and intelligence by considering an important component of AI: *knowledge-intensive* or *strong method* problem solving.

Human experts are able to perform at a successful level because they know a lot about their areas of expertise. This simple observation is the underlying rationale for the design of strong method or knowledge-based problem solvers (Introduction, Part III). An *expert system*, for example, uses knowledge specific to a problem domain to provide "expert quality" performance in that application area. Generally, expert system designers acquire this knowledge with the help of human domain experts, and the system emulates the human expert's methodology and performance. As with skilled humans, expert systems tend to be specialists, focusing on a narrow set of problems. Also, like humans, their knowledge is both theoretical and practical: the human experts that provide the system's knowledge have generally augmented their own theoretical understanding of the problem domain with tricks, shortcuts, and heuristics for *using* the knowledge they have gained through problem-solving experience.

Because of their heuristic, knowledge-intensive nature, expert systems generally:

1. Support inspection of their reasoning processes, both in presenting intermediate steps and in answering questions about the solution process.

2. Allow easy modification in adding and deleting skills from the knowledge base.

3. Reason heuristically, using (often imperfect) knowledge to get useful solutions.

The reasoning of an expert system should be open to inspection, providing information about the state of its problem solving and explanations of the choices and decisions that the program is making. Explanations are important for a human expert, such as a doctor or an engineer, if he or she is to accept the recommendations from a computer. Indeed, few human experts will accept advice from another human, let alone a machine, without understanding the justifications for it.

The exploratory nature of AI and expert system programming requires that programs be easily prototyped, tested, and changed. AI programming languages and environments are designed to support this iterative development methodology. In a pure production system, for example, the modification of a single rule has no global syntactic side effects. Rules may be added or removed without requiring further changes to the larger program. Expert system designers often comment that easy modification of the knowledge base is a major factor in producing a successful program.

A further feature of expert systems is their use of heuristic problem-solving methods. As expert system designers have discovered, informal "tricks of the trade" and "rules of thumb" are an essential complement to the standard theory presented in textbooks and classes. Sometimes these rules augment theoretical knowledge in understandable ways; often they are simply shortcuts that have, empirically, been shown to work.

Expert systems are built to solve a wide range of problems in domains such as medicine, mathematics, engineering, chemistry, geology, computer science, business, law, defense, and education. These programs address a variety of problems; the following list, from Waterman (1986), is a useful summary of general expert system problem categories.

Interpretation—forming high-level conclusions from collections of raw data.

Prediction—projecting probable consequences of given situations.

Diagnosis—determining the cause of malfunctions in complex situations based on observable symptoms.

Design—finding a configuration of system components that meets performance goals while satisfying a set of design constraints.

Planning—devising a sequence of actions that will achieve a set of goals given certain starting conditions and run-time constraints.

Monitoring—comparing a system's observed behavior to its expected behavior.

Instruction—assisting in the education process in technical domains.

Control—governing the behavior of a complex environment.

In this chapter we first examine the technology that makes knowledge-based problem solving possible. Successful *knowledge engineering* must address a range of problems, from the choice of an appropriate application domain to the acquisition and formalization of problem-solving knowledge. In Section 8.2 we introduce rule-based systems and present the production system as a software architecture for solution and explanation processes. Section 8.3 examines techniques for model-based and case-based reasoning. Section 8.4 presents *planning*, a process of organizing pieces of knowledge into a consistent sequence of actions that will accomplish a goal. Chapter 9 presents techniques for reasoning in uncertain situations, an important component of strong method problem solvers.

8.1 Overview of Expert System Technology

8.1.1 The Design of Rule-Based Expert Systems

Figure 8.1 shows the modules that make up a typical expert system. The user interacts with the system through a *user interface* that simplifies communication and hides much of the complexity, such as the internal structure of the rule base. Expert system interfaces employ a variety of user styles, including question-and-answer, menu-driven, or graphical interfaces. The final decision on the interface type is a compromise between user needs and the requirements of the knowledge base and inferencing system.

The heart of the expert system is the *knowledge base*, which contains the knowledge of a particular application domain. In a rule-based expert system this knowledge is most often represented in the form of *if... then...* rules, as in our examples of Section 8.2. The knowledge base contains both *general knowledge* as well as *case-specific* information.

The *inference engine* applies the knowledge to the solution of actual problems. It is essentially an interpreter for the knowledge base. In the production system, the inference engine performs the recognize-act control cycle. The procedures that implement the

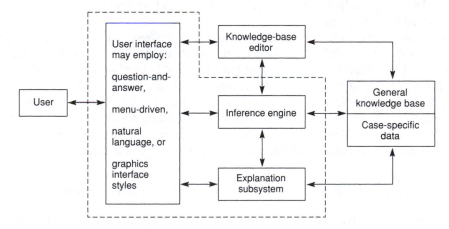

Figure 8.1 Architecture of a typical expert system for a particular problem domain.

control cycle are separate from the production rules themselves. It is important to maintain this separation of the knowledge base and inference engine for several reasons:

1. This separation makes it possible to represent knowledge in a more natural fashion. *If ... then...* rules, for example, are closer to the way in which humans describe their problem-solving skills than is lower-level computer code.

2. Because the knowledge base is separated from the program's lower-level control structures, expert system builders can focus on capturing and organizing problem-solving knowledge rather than on the details of its computer implementation.

3. Ideally, the separation of knowledge and control allows changes to be made in one part of the knowledge base without creating side effects in others.

4. The separation of the knowledge and control elements of the program allows the same control and interface software to be used in a variety of systems. The *expert system shell* has all the components of Figure 8.1 except that the knowledge base and case-specific data are empty and can be added for a new application. The broken lines of Figure 8.1 indicate the shell modules.

The expert system must keep track of *case-specific data*: the facts, conclusions, and other information relevant to the case under consideration. This includes the data given in a problem instance, partial conclusions, confidence measures of conclusions, and dead ends in the search process. This information is separate from the general knowledge base.

The *explanation subsystem* allows the program to explain its reasoning to the user. These explanations include justifications for the system's conclusions, in response to *how queries* (Section 8.2), explanations of why the system needs a particular piece of data, *why queries* (Section 8.2), and, where useful, tutorial explanations or deeper theoretical justifications of the program's actions.

Many systems also include a *knowledge-base editor*. Knowledge-base editors help the programmer locate and correct bugs in the program's performance, often accessing the information provided by the explanation subsystem. They also may assist in the addition of new knowledge, help maintain correct rule syntax, and perform consistency checks on the updated knowledge base.

An important reason for the decrease in design and deployment times for current expert systems is the ready availability of expert system shells. NASA has created and makes available CLIPS, JESS is available from Sandia National Laboratories, and we offer shells in LISP and PROLOG in Part VI. Unfortunately, shell programs do not solve all of the problems involved in building expert systems. Although the separation of knowledge and control, the modularity of the production system architecture, and the use of an appropriate knowledge representation language all help with the building of an expert system, the acquisition and formalization of domain knowledge still remain difficult tasks.

8.1.2   Selecting a Problem and the Knowledge Engineering Process

Expert systems involve a considerable investment of money and human effort. Attempts to solve a problem that is too complex, too poorly understood, or otherwise unsuited to the available technology can lead to costly and embarrassing failures. Researchers have developed guidelines to determine whether a problem is appropriate for expert system solution:

1. **The need for the solution justifies the cost and effort of building an expert system.** Many expert systems have been built in domains such as mineral exploration, business, defense, and medicine where a large potential exists for savings in terms of money, time, and human life.

2. **Human expertise is not available in all situations where it is needed.** In geology, for example, there is a need for expertise at remote mining and drilling sites. Often, geologists and other engineers find themselves traveling large distances to visit sites, with resulting expense and wasted time. By placing expert systems at remote sites, many problems may be solved without needing a visit.

3. **The problem may be solved using symbolic reasoning.** Problem solutions should not require physical dexterity or perceptual skill. Robots and vision systems currently lack the sophistication and flexibility of humans.

4. **The problem domain is well structured and does not require common sense reasoning.** Highly technical fields have the advantage of being well studied and formalized: terms are well defined and domains have clear and specific conceptual models. In contrast, common sense reasoning is difficult to automate.

5. **The problem may not be solved using traditional computing methods.** Expert system technology should not be used where unnecessary. If a problem can be solved satisfactorily using more traditional techniques, then it is not a candidate.

6. **Cooperative and articulate experts exist.** The knowledge used by expert systems comes from the experience and judgment of humans working in the domain. It is important that these experts be both willing and able to share knowledge.

7. **The problem is of proper size and scope.** For example, a program that attempted to capture all of the expertise of a medical doctor would not be feasible; a program that advised MDs on the use of a particular piece of diagnostic equipment or a particular set of diagnoses would be more appropriate.

The primary people involved in building an expert system are the *knowledge engineer*, the *domain expert*, and the *end user*. The knowledge engineer is the AI language and representation expert. His or her main task is to select the software and hardware tools for the project, help the domain expert articulate the necessary knowledge, and implement that knowledge in a correct and efficient knowledge base. Often, the knowledge engineer is initially ignorant of the application domain.

The domain expert provides the knowledge of the problem area. The domain expert is generally someone who has worked in the domain area and understands its problem-solving techniques, such as shortcuts, handling imprecise data, evaluating partial solutions, and all the other skills that mark a person as an expert problem solver. The domain expert is primarily responsible for spelling out these skills to the knowledge engineer.

As in most applications, the end user determines the major design constraints. Unless the user is happy, the development effort is by and large wasted. The skills and needs of the user must be considered throughout the design cycle: Will the program make the user's work easier, quicker, more comfortable? What level of explanation does the user need? Can the user provide correct information to the system? Is the interface appropriate? Does the user's work environment place restrictions on the program's use? An interface that required typing, for example, would not be appropriate for use in the cockpit of a fighter.

Like most AI programming, building expert systems requires a nontraditional development cycle based on early prototyping and incremental revision of the code. Generally, work on the system begins with the knowledge engineer attempting to gain some familiarity with the problem domain. This helps in communicating with the domain expert. This is done in initial interviews with the expert and by observing experts during the performance of their job. Next, the knowledge engineer and expert begin the process of extracting the expert's problem-solving knowledge. This is often done by giving the domain expert a series of sample problems and having him or her explain the techniques used in their solution. Video and/or audio tapes are often essential in this process.

It is often useful for the knowledge engineer to be a novice in the problem domain. Human experts are notoriously unreliable in explaining exactly what goes on in solving a complex problem. Often they forget to mention steps that have become obvious or even automatic to them after years of work in their field. Knowledge engineers, by virtue of their relative naiveté in the domain, can spot these conceptual jumps and ask for help.

Once the knowledge engineer has obtained a general overview of the problem domain and gone through several problem-solving sessions with the expert, he or she is ready to begin actual design of the system: selecting a way to represent the knowledge, such as rules or frames, determining the search strategy, forward, backward, depth-first, best-first etc., and designing the user interface. After making these design commitments, the knowledge engineer builds a prototype.

This prototype should be able to solve problems in a small area of the domain and provide a test bed for preliminary design assumptions. Once the prototype has been implemented, the knowledge engineer and domain expert test and refine its knowledge by giving it problems to solve and correcting its shortcomings. Should the assumptions made in designing the prototype prove correct, the prototype can be incrementally extended until it becomes a final system.

Expert systems are built by progressive approximations, with the program's mistakes leading to corrections or additions to the knowledge base. In a sense, the knowledge base is "grown" rather than constructed. Figure 8.2 presents a flow chart describing the exploratory programming development cycle. This approach to programming was investigated by Seymour Papert with his LOGO language (Papert 1980) as well as Alan Kay's work at Xerox PARC. The LOGO philosophy argues that watching the computer respond to the improperly formulated ideas represented by the code leads to their correction (being *debugged*) and clarification with more precise code. This process of trying and correcting candidate designs is common to expert systems development, and contrasts with such neatly hierarchical processes as top-down design.

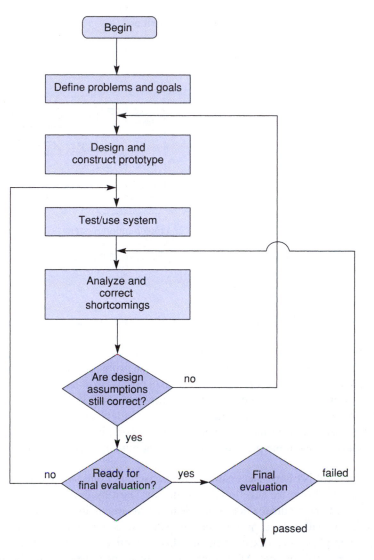

Figure 8.2 Exploratory development cycle.

It is also understood that the prototype may be thrown away if it becomes too cumbersome or if the designers decide to change their basic approach to the problem. The prototype lets program builders explore the problem and its important relationships by actually constructing a program to solve it. After this progressive clarification is complete, they can then often write a cleaner version, usually with fewer rules.

The second major feature of expert system programming is that the program need never be considered "finished." A large heuristic knowledge base will always have limitations. The modularity of the production system model makes it natural to add new rules or makes up for the shortcomings of the present rule base at any time.

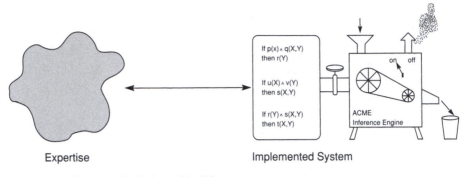

Expertise   Implemented System

Figure 8.3 The standard view of building an expert system.

8.1.3   Conceptual Models and Their Role in Knowledge Acquisition

Figure 8.3 presents a simplified model of the knowledge acquisition process that will serve as a useful "first approximation" for understanding the problems involved in acquiring and formalizing human expert performance. The human expert, working in an application area, operates in a domain of knowledge, skill, and practice. This knowledge is often vague, imprecise, and only partially verbalized. The knowledge engineer must translate this informal expertise into a formal language suited to a computational system. A number of important issues arises in the process of formalizing human skilled performance:

1. Human skill is often inaccessible to the conscious mind. As Aristotle points out in his *Ethics*, "what we have to learn to do, we learn by doing." Skills such as those possessed by medical doctors are learned as much in years of internship and residency, with their constant focus on patients, as they are in physiology lectures, where emphasis is on experiment and theory. Delivery of medical care is to a great extent practice-driven. After years of performance these skills become highly integrated and function at a largely unconscious level. It may be difficult for experts to describe exactly what they are doing in problem solving.

2. Human expertise often takes the form of knowing *how* to cope in a situation rather than knowing *what* a rational characterization of the situation might be, of developing skilled performance mechanisms rather than a fundamental understanding of what these mechanisms are. An obvious example of this is riding a unicycle: the successful rider is not, in real time, consciously solving multiple sets of simultaneous differential equations to keep in balance; rather she is using an intuitive combination of feelings of "gravity," "momentum," and "inertia" to form a usable control procedure.

3. We often think of knowledge acquisition as gaining factual knowledge of an objective reality, the so-called "real world." As both theory and practice have shown, human expertise represents an individual's or a community's *model* of the world. Such models are as influenced by convention, social processes, and hidden agendas as they are by empirical methodologies.

4. Expertise changes. Not only do human experts gain new knowledge, but also existing knowledge may be subject to radical reformulation, as evidenced by ongoing controversies in both scientific and social fields.

Consequently, knowledge engineering is difficult and should be viewed as spanning the life cycle of any expert system. To simplify this task, it is useful to consider, as in Figure 8.4, a *conceptual model* that lies between human expertise and the implemented program. By a conceptual model, we mean the knowledge engineer's evolving conception of the domain knowledge. Although this is undoubtedly different from the domain expert's, it is this model that actually determines the construction of the formal knowledge base.

Because of the complexity of most interesting problems, we should not take this intermediate stage for granted. Knowledge engineers should document and make public their assumptions about the domain through common software engineering methodologies. An expert system should include a requirements document; however, because of the constraints of exploratory programming, expert system requirements should be treated as co-evolving with the prototype. Data dictionaries, graphic representations of state spaces,

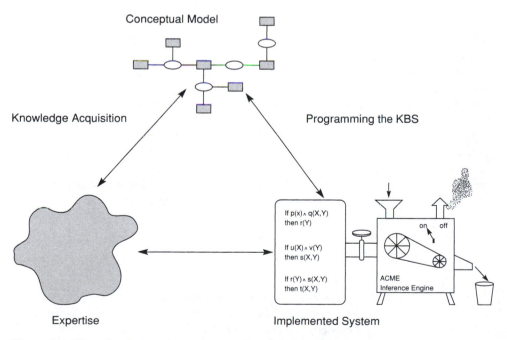

Figure 8.4 The role of mental or conceptual models in problem solving.

and comments in the code itself are all part of this model. By publicizing these design decisions, we reduce errors in both the implementation and maintenance of the program.

Knowledge engineers should save recordings of interviews with domain experts. Often, as knowledge engineers' understanding of the domain grows, they form new interpretations or discover new information about the domain. The recordings, along with documentation of the interpretation given them, play a valuable role in reviewing design decisions and testing prototypes. Finally, this model serves an intermediate role in the formalization of knowledge. The choice of a representation language exerts a strong influence on a knowledge engineer's model of the domain.

The conceptual model is not formal or directly executable on a computer. It is an intermediate design construct, a template to begin to constrain and codify human skill. It can, if the knowledge engineer uses a predicate calculus model, begin as a number of simple networks representing states of reasoning through typical problem-solving situations. Only after further refinement does this network become explicit *if... then...* rules.

Questions often asked in the context of a conceptual model include: Is the problem solution deterministic or search-based? Is the reasoning data-driven, perhaps with a generate and test flavor, or goal-driven, based on a small set of likely hypotheses about situations? Are there stages of reasoning? Is the domain well understood and capable of providing deep predictive models, or is all problem-solving knowledge essentially heuristic? Can we use examples of past problems and their solutions to solve future problems directly, or must we first convert these examples into general rules? Is the knowledge exact or is it "fuzzy" and approximate, lending itself to numeric ratings of certainty (Chapter 9)? Will our reasoning strategies allow us to infer stable facts about the domain, or do change and uncertainty within the system require nonmonotonic reasoning, the ability to make assertions about the domain that may later be modified or retracted (Section 9.1)? Finally, does the structure of the domain knowledge require us to abandon rule-based inference for alternative schemes such as neural networks or genetic algorithms (Part IV)?

The eventual users' needs should also be addressed in the context of the conceptual model: What are their expectations of the eventual program? Where is their level of expertise: novice, intermediate, or expert? What levels of explanation are appropriate? What interface best serves their needs?

Based on the answers to these and other questions, the knowledge obtained from domain experts, and the resulting conceptual model, we can begin development of the expert system. Because the production system, first presented in Chapter 6, offers a number of inherent strengths for organizing and applying knowledge, it is often used as the basis for knowledge representation in rule-based expert systems.

8.2 Rule-Based Expert Systems

Rule-based expert systems represent problem-solving knowledge as *if... then...* rules. This approach lends itself to the architecture of Figure 8.1, and is one of the oldest techniques for representing domain knowledge in an expert system. It is also one of the most natural, and remains widely used in practical and experimental expert systems.

8.2.1　The Production System and Goal-Driven Problem Solving

The architecture of rule-based expert systems may be best understood in terms of the production system model for problem solving presented in Part II. The parallel between the two is more than an analogy: the production system was the intellectual precursor of modern expert system architectures, where application of production rules leads to refinements of understanding of a particular problem situation. When Newell and Simon developed the production system, their goal was to model human performance in problem solving.

If we regard the expert system architecture in Figure 8.1 as a production system, the domain-specific knowledge base is the set of production rules. In a rule-based system, these condition action pairs are represented as *if... then...* rules, with the premises of the rules, the *if* portion, corresponding to the condition, and the conclusion, the *then* portion, corresponding to the action: when the condition is satisfied, the expert system takes the action of asserting the conclusion as true. Case-specific data can be kept in the working memory. The inference engine implements the recognize-act cycle of the production system; this control may be either data-driven or goal-driven.

Many problem domains seem to lend themselves more naturally to forward search. In an interpretation problem, for example, most of the data for the problem are initially given and it is often difficult to formulate an hypotheses or goal. This suggests a forward reasoning process in which the facts are placed in working memory and the system searches for an interpretation, as first presented in Section 3.2.

In a goal-driven expert system, the goal expression is initially placed in working memory. The system matches rule *conclusions* with the goal, selecting one rule and placing its *premises* in the working memory. This corresponds to a decomposition of the problem's goal into simpler subgoals. The process continues in the next iteration of the production system, with these premises becoming the new goals to match against rule conclusions. The system thus works back from the original goal until all the subgoals in working memory are known to be true, indicating that the hypothesis has been verified. Thus, backward search in an expert system corresponds roughly to the process of hypothesis testing in human problem solving, as also first presented in Section 3.2.

In an expert system, subgoals can be solved by asking the user for information. Some expert systems allow the system designer to specify which subgoals may be solved by asking the user. Others simply ask the user about any subgoals that fail to match rules in the knowledge base; i.e., if the program cannot infer the truth of a subgoal, it asks the user.

As an example of goal-driven problem solving with user queries, we next offer a small expert system for analysis of automotive problems. This is not a full diagnostic system, as it contains only four very simple rules. It is intended as an example to demonstrate goal-driven rule chaining, the integration of new data, and the use of explanation facilities:

Rule 1:　if

     the engine is getting gas, and
     the engine will turn over,
     then
     the problem is spark plugs.

Rule 2: if

the engine does not turn over, and
the lights do not come on
then
the problem is battery or cables.

Rule 3: if

the engine does not turn over, and
the lights do come on
then
the problem is the starter motor.

Rule 4: if

there is gas in the fuel tank, and
there is gas in the carburetor
then
the engine is getting gas.

To run this knowledge base under a goal-directed control regime, place the top-level goal, the problem is X, in working memory as shown in Figure 8.5. X is a variable that can match with any phrase, for example the problem is battery or cables; it will become bound to the solution when the problem is solved.

Three rules match with this expression in working memory: rule 1, rule 2, and rule 3. If we resolve conflicts in favor of the lowest-numbered rule, then rule 1 will fire. This causes X to be bound to the value spark plugs and the premises of rule 1 to be placed in the working memory as in Figure 8.6. The system has thus chosen to explore the possible hypothesis that the spark plugs are bad. Another way to look at this is that the system has selected an or branch in an and/or graph (Chapter 3).

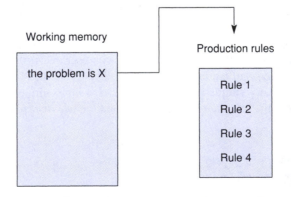

Figure 8.5 The production system at the start of a
consultation in the car diagnostic example.

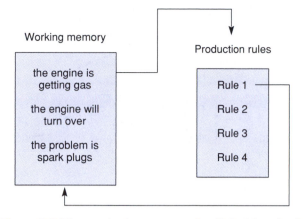

Figure 8.6 The production system after Rule 1 has fired.

Note that there are two premises to rule 1, both of which must be satisfied to prove the conclusion true. These are and branches of the search graph representing a decomposition of the problem (finding whether the problem is spark plugs) into two subproblems (finding whether the engine is getting gas and whether the engine will turn over). We may then fire rule 4, whose conclusion matches with the engine is getting gas, causing its premises to be placed in working memory as in Figure 8.7.

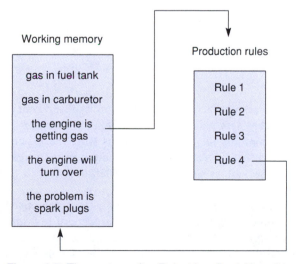

Figure 8.7 The system after Rule 4 has fired. Note the stack-based approach to goal reduction.

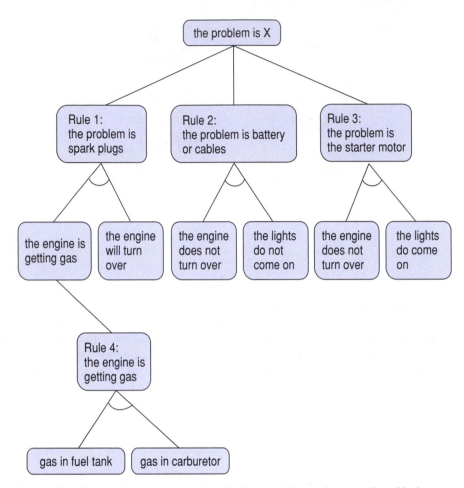

Figure 8.8 The and/or graph searched in the car diagnosis example, with the
conclusion of Rule 4 matching the first premise of Rule 1.

At this point, there are three entries in working memory that do not match with any rule
conclusions. Our expert system will, in this situation, query the user directly about these
subgoals. If the user confirms all three of these as true, the expert system will have
successfully determined that the car will not start because the spark plugs are bad. In
finding this solution, the system has searched the leftmost branch of the and/or graph
presented in Figure 8.8.

This is, of course, a very simple example. Not only is its automotive knowledge limited
at best, but it also ignores a number of important aspects of real implementations. The
rules are phrased in English, rather than a formal language. On finding a solution, a real
expert system will tell the user its diagnosis (our model simply stops). Also, we should
maintain enough of a trace of the reasoning to allow backtracking if necessary. In our
example, had we failed to determine that the spark plugs were bad, we would have needed

to back up to the top level and try rule 2 instead. Notice that this information is implicit in the ordering of subgoals in working memory of Figure 8.7 and in the graph of Figure 8.8. In spite of its simplicity, however, this example underscores the importance of production system based search and its representation by the and/or graph as the foundation for rule-based expert systems.

Earlier we emphasized that an expert system needed to be open to inspection, easily modified, and heuristic in nature. The production system architecture is an important factor in each of these requirements. Ease of modification, for example, is supported by the syntactic independence of production rules: each rule is a chunk of knowledge that can be independently modified. There are semantic constraints, however, in that the meanings of the individual rules are related. These must be reconciled in any editing/modification process. We next discuss the generation of explanations and the monitoring of inference.

8.2.2 Explanation and Transparency in Goal-Driven Reasoning

The production system implements a graph search. The explanation routines of Figure 8.1 keep track of the graph search and use a trace of the search to answer user queries. The production rules themselves document each step of the reasoning process.

In general, the two questions answered by rule-based expert systems are why? and how? A why query occurs when the program asks the user for information and the user responds with why, meaning "why did you ask for that information?" The answer is the current rule that the production system is attempting to fire. The answer to "how did you get that result?" is the sequence of rules that were used to conclude a goal.

Suppose our automotive expert system has an explanation facility, and assume that the consultation has reached the stage represented by the working memory configuration in Figure 8.7. The following dialogue begins with the computer asking the user about the goals present in working memory. User responses are in bold type.

gas in fuel tank?
yes
gas in carburetor?
yes
engine will turn over?
why

Here the user enters a why query, i.e., why do you want to know whether the engine will turn over? The system responds with a literal presentation of the rule under question:

It has been established that:
1.   the engine is getting gas,
therefore if
2.   the engine will turn over,
then the problem is spark plugs.

Because the user answered yes to the first two questions, rule 4 was able to fire, verifying the first premise of rule 1. When the why query was made, the system was trying to solve the second premise of rule 1. Note that the explanation for the system's behavior is just a restatement of the current rule under consideration. However, this provides an adequate explanation for why the program wants to know whether the engine will turn over. In the response to the why query, the system states that it has concluded that the engine is getting gas. Suppose the user then asks:

how the engine is getting gas

The system will respond to how it concluded that the engine is getting gas. The response is a trace of the reasoning that led to this conclusion, working back from the goal along the rules that support it to the user responses:

This follows from rule 4:
if
gas in fuel tank, and
gas in carburetor
then
engine is getting gas.
gas in fuel tank was given by the user
gas in carburetor was given by the user

Once again, the production system architecture provides an essential basis for these explanations. Each cycle of the control loop selects and fires another rule. The program may be stopped after each cycle and inspected. Because each rule represents a complete chunk of problem-solving knowledge, the current rule provides a context for the explanation. Contrast this production system approach with more traditional program architectures: if we stop a C, C++, or Java program in mid execution, it is doubtful that the current statement will have much meaning.

In summary, the knowledge-based system answers why queries by showing the current rule that it is attempting to fire; it answers how queries by giving a trace of the reasoning that led to a goal. Although the mechanisms are conceptually simple, they can exhibit remarkable explanatory power if the knowledge base is organized in a logical fashion. The chapters on LISP and PROLOG, Part VI, demonstrate the use of rule stacks and proof trees to implement these explanations.

If explanations are to behave logically, it is important not only that the knowledge base gets the correct answer but also that each rule corresponds to a single logical step in the problem solving process. If a knowledge base combines several steps into a single rule, or if it breaks up the rules in an arbitrary fashion, it may get correct answers but seem vague, arbitrary, or illogical in responding to how and why queries. This can not only undermine the user's faith in the system but can also make the program much more difficult for its builders to understand and modify.

8.2.3   Using the Production System for Data-Driven Reasoning

The automobile diagnosis demonstration of Section 8.2.1 illustrated the use of a production system to implement goal-driven search. Search was also depth-first in that it searched each subgoal found in the rule base exhaustively before moving onto any sibling goals. As we saw in Section 6.3, however, the production system is also an ideal architecture for data-driven reasoning. Example 6.3.1 demonstrated this process with the 8-puzzle and Examples 6.3.2 and 6.3.3 with the Knight's Tour. In each of these problems we did conflict resolution by taking the first rule found in the knowledge base and then followed the results of that rule. This gave the search a depth-first flavor, although there was no mechanism, such as backtracking, to handle the problem of "dead ends" in the search space.

Breadth-first search is even more common in data-driven reasoning. The algorithm for this is simple: compare the contents of working memory with the conditions of each rule in the rule base according to the order of the rules in the rule base. If the data in working memory supports a rule's firing the result is placed in working memory and then control moves on to the next rule. Once all rules have been considered, search starts again at the beginning of the rule set.

Consider, for example, the automobile diagnosis problem and the rules of Section 8.2.1. If a piece of information that makes up (part of) the premise of a rule is not the conclusion of some other rule then that fact will be deemed "askable" when control comes to the situation (rule) where that information is needed. For example, the engine is getting gas is not askable in the premise of rule 1, because that fact is a conclusion of another rule, namely rule 4.

The breadth-first, data-driven example begins as in Figure 8.5, with no information in working memory, as in Figure 8.9. We first examine premises of the four rules in order to see what information is "askable." The premise, the engine is getting gas, is not askable, so rule 1 fails and control moves to rule 2. The engine does not turn over is askable. Suppose the answer to this query is false, so the engine will turn over is placed in working memory, as in Figure 8.10.

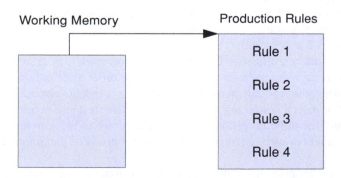

Figure 8.9 The production system at the start of a consultation
for data-driven reasoning.

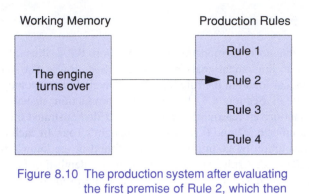

Figure 8.10 The production system after evaluating the first premise of Rule 2, which then fails.

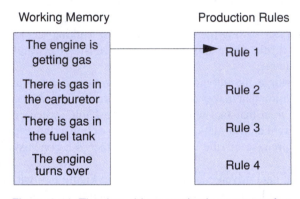

Figure 8.11 The data-driven production system after considering Rule 4, beginning its second pass through the rules.

But rule 2 fails, since the first of two and premises is false, and consideration moves to rule 3, where again, the first premise fails. At rule 4, both premises are askable. Suppose the answer to both questions is true. Then there is gas in the fuel tank and there is gas in the carburetor are placed in working memory, as is the conclusion of the rule, the engine is getting gas.

At this point all the rules have been considered so search now returns, with the new contents of working memory, to consider the rules in order a second time. As is seen in Figure 8.11, when the working memory is matched to rule 1, its conclusion, the problem is spark plugs, is placed in working memory. In this example no more rules will match and fire, and the problem-solving session is completed. A graph of the search process, with the information content of working memory (WM) as the nodes of the graph, is presented as Figure 8.12.

An important refinement on the breadth-first search strategy used in the previous example is what is called *opportunistic search*. This search strategy is simple: whenever a rule fires to conclude new information, control moves to consider those rules which have that new information as a premise. This makes any new *concluded* information (search does not change as the result of "askable" premises) the controlling force for finding the next rules to fire. This is termed *opportunistic* because each conclusion of new information drives the search. By the accident of rule ordering, the very simple example just presented was also opportunistic.

We conclude this section on data-driven reasoning with several comments on explanation and transparency in forward chaining systems. First, in comparison with goal-driven systems, Sections 8.2.1–2, data-driven reasoning is much less "focused" in its search. The reason for this is obvious: in a goal-driven system, reasoning is in pursuit of a particular goal; that goal is broken into subgoals that support the top-level goal and these subgoals may be even further broken down. As a result, search is always directed through this goal and subgoal hierarchy. In data-driven systems this goal orientation does not exist. Rather, the search moves about the tree depending only on rule order and the discovery of new information. As a result, the progress of search can often seem to be very diffuse and unfocused.

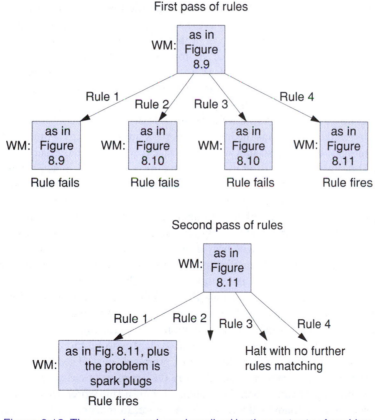

Figure 8.12 The search graph as described by the contents of working memory (WM) for the data-driven breadth-first search of the rule set of Section 8.2.1.

Second, and as a direct result of the first point, the explanation available to the user at any time in the search is quite limited. There is a rule-level accountability in that, when the user asks why some information is required, the why query in Section 8.2.2, the rule under consideration is presented. The explanation cannot go much further, however, unless explicit rule tracking is added into the system, say with opportunistic search. The diffuse nature of the data-driven search makes this difficult to do. Finally, when a goal is achieved, getting a full how explanation for that goal is also difficult. About the only thing that can be used as a partial and very limited explanation is a presentation of the contents of the working memory or a list of rules fired. But again, these will not offer the consistent focused accountability we saw with goal-driven reasoning.

8.2.4 Heuristics and Control in Expert Systems

Because of the separation of the knowledge base and the inference engine, and the fixed control regimes provided by the inference engine, an important method for the programmer to control search is through the structuring and ordering of the rules in the knowledge base. This micro-managing of the rule set offers an important opportunity, especially as the control strategies required for expert-level problem-solving tend to be domain specific and knowledge intensive. Although a rule of the form if p, q, and r then s resembles a logical expression, it may also be interpreted as a series of procedures or steps for solving a problem: to do s, first do p, then do q, then do r. The role of rule and premise ordering was implicit in the examples of Section 8.2 just presented.

This procedural method of rule interpretation is an essential component of practical knowledge use and often reflects the human expert's solution strategy. For example, we can order the premises of a rule so that what is most likely to fail or is easiest to confirm is tried first. This gives the opportunity of eliminating a rule (and hence a portion of the search space) as early as possible. Rule 1 in the automotive example tries to determine whether the engine is getting gas before it asks if the engine turns over. This is inefficient, in that trying to determine whether the engine is getting gas invokes another rule and eventually asks the user two questions. By reversing the order of the premises, a negative response to the query "engine will turn over?" eliminates this rule from consideration before the more involved condition is examined, thus making the system more efficient.

It also makes more sense to determine whether the engine is turning over before checking to see whether it is getting gas; if the engine won't turn over it doesn't matter whether or not it is getting gas! In Rule 4, the user is asked to check the fuel tank before checking the carburetor for gas. In this situation, it is performing the easier check first. There is an important point here, if the overall system is to be more efficient all aspects must be considered: rule order, organization of premises, cost of tests, amount of search eliminated through the answers to tests, the way the majority of cases occur, and so on.

Thus the planning of rule order, the organization of a rule's premises, and the costs of different tests are all fundamentally heuristic in nature. In most rule-based expert systems these heuristic choices reflect the approaches taken by the human expert, and indeed can have erroneous results. In our example, if the engine is getting gas and turning over, the problem may be a bad distributor rather than bad spark plugs.

Data-driven reasoning provides additional problems and opportunities for control of reasoning. Some of these include the high-level heuristics, such as refraction, recency (opportunistic search), and specificity presented in Section 6.3.3. A more domain-specific approach groups sets of rules according to stages of the solution process. For example, in diagnosing car problems we might create the four distinct stages of 1) organize situation, 2) collect the data, 3) do the analysis (there may be more than one problem with the car), and finally, 4) report the conclusions and recommended fixes.

This staged problem solving can be accomplished by creating descriptors for each stage of the solution and placing that description as the first premise in all rules that belong to that stage. For example, we might begin by placing the assertion organize situation in working memory. If no other stage descriptions occur in working memory, then only rules that have organize situation in their set of premises will fire. Of course, this should be the first premise for each of these rules. We would move to the next stage by having the last rule to fire in the organizational stage remove (retract) the fact that that stage is organize solution and assert the new fact that the stage is data collection. All the rules in the data collection stage would then have their first premise IF stage is data collection and . ... When the data collection stage is finished, the last rule would retract this fact, and assert the data analysis fact into working memory to match only those rules whose premises begin with the fact IF stage is data analysis . . ..

In our discussion so far, we have described the behavior of the production system in terms of exhaustive considerations of the rule base. Although this is expensive, it captures the intended semantics of the production system. There are, however, a number of algorithms such as RETE (Forgy 1982) that can be used to optimize search for all potentially usable rules. Essentially, the RETE algorithm compiles rules into a network structure that allow the system to match rules with data by directly following a pointer to the rule. This algorithm greatly speeds execution, especially for larger rule sets, while retaining the semantic behavior we have described in this section.

To summarize, rules are the oldest approach to knowledge representation in expert systems, and remain an important technique for building knowledge-intensive problem solvers. An expert system's rules capture human expert knowledge as it is used in practice; consequently, they are often a blend of theoretical knowledge, heuristics derived from experience, and special-purpose rules for handling odd cases and other exceptions to normal practice. In many situations, this approach has proven effective. Nonetheless, strongly heuristic systems may fail, either on encountering a problem that does not fit any available rules, or by misapplying a heuristic rule to an inappropriate situation. Human experts do not suffer from these problems, because they have a deeper, theoretical understanding of the problem domain that allows them to apply the heuristic rules intelligently, or resort to reasoning from "first principles" in novel situations. *Model-based* approaches, described next in Section 8.3.1, attempt to give an expert system this power and flexibility.

The ability to learn from examples is another human capability that knowledge-intensive problem solvers emulate. *Case-based* reasoners, Section 8.3.3, maintain a knowledge base of example problem solutions, or *cases*. When confronted with a new problem, the reasoner selects from this stored set a case that resembles the present problem, and then attempts to apply a form of its solution strategy to this problem. In legal reasoning, the argument through precedent is a common example of case-based reasoning.

8.3   Model-Based, Case-Based, and Hybrid Systems

8.3.1   Introduction to Model-Based Reasoning

Human expertise is an extremely complex amalgamation of theoretical knowledge, experience-based problem-solving heuristics, examples of past problems and their solutions, perceptual and interpretive skills and other abilities that are so poorly understood that we can only describe them as intuitive. Through years of experience, human experts develop very powerful rules for dealing with commonly encountered situations. These rules are often highly "compiled", taking the form of direct associations between observable symptoms and final diagnoses, and hiding their more deeply explanatory foundations.

For example, the MYCIN expert system would propose a diagnosis based on such observable symptoms as "headaches", "nausea", or "high fever". Although these parameters can be indicative of an illness, rules that link them directly to a diagnosis do not reflect any deeper, causal understanding of human physiology. MYCIN's rules indicate the results of an infection, but do not explain its causes. A more deeply explanatory approach would detect the presence of infecting agents, note the resulting inflammation of cell linings, the presence of inter-cranial pressures, and infer the causal connection to the observed symptoms of headache, elevated temperatures, and nausea.

In a rule-based expert system example for semiconductor failure analysis, a descriptive approach might base a diagnosis of circuit failure on such symptoms as the discoloration of components (possibly indicating a burned-out component), the history of faults in similar devices, or even observations of component interiors using an electron microscope. However, approaches that use rules to link observations and diagnoses do not offer the benefits of a deeper analysis of the device's structure and function. A more robust, deeply explanatory approach would begin with a detailed model of the physical structure of the circuit and equations describing the expected behavior of each component and their interactions. It would base its diagnosis on signal readings from various locations in the device, using this data and its model of the circuit to determine the exact points of failure.

Because first-generation expert systems relied upon heuristic rules gained from the human expert's description of problem-solving techniques, they exhibited a number of fundamental limitations (Clancy 1985). If a problem instance did not match their heuristics, they simply failed, even though a more theoretical analysis would have found a solution. Often, expert systems applied heuristics in inappropriate situations, such as where a deeper understanding of the problem would have indicated a different course. These are the limitations that *model-based* approaches attempt to address. A knowledge-based reasoner whose analysis is founded directly on the specification and functionality of a physical system is called a *model-based system*. In its design and use, a model-based reasoner creates a software simulation, often referred to as "qualitative", of the function of that which is to be understood or fixed. (There are other types of model-based systems, of course, in particular, the logic-based and stochastic, which we present in Chapter 9.)

The earliest model-based reasoners appeared in the mid-1970s and continued to mature through the 1980s (Davis and Hamscher 1992). It is interesting to note that some of the earliest work was intended to create software models of various physical devices, such as electronic circuits, for instructional purposes (deKleer 1976, Brown et al. 1982). In these early intelligent tutoring situations, the specifications for a device or circuit were reflected in sets of rules, e.g., Kirchoff's and Ohm's laws. The tutoring system both tested the student's knowledge of the device or circuit as well as conveyed to the student knowledge he or she might be missing. Rules were both the representation of the functionality of the hardware as well as the medium for conveying this knowledge to the student.

From these early tutoring systems, where the task was to both model and teach the functionality of a system, qualitative model-based reasoners moved to trouble-shooting systems. In trouble-shooting faults in a physical system the model leads to sets of predicted behaviors. A fault is reflected in the discrepancy between predicted and observed behavior. The model-based system tells its user what to expect, and when observations differ from these expectations, how these discrepancies lead to identification of faults.

Qualitative model-based reasoning includes:

1. A description of each component in the device. These descriptions can simulate the behavior of the component.

2. A description of the device's internal structure. This is typically a representation of its components and their interconnections, along with the ability to simulate component interactions. The extent of knowledge of internal structure required depends on the levels of abstraction applied and diagnosis desired.

3. Diagnosis of a particular problem requires observations of the device's actual performance, typically measurements of its inputs and outputs. I/O measurements are easiest to obtain, but in fact, any measure could be used.

The task is then to determine which of the components could have failed in a way that accounts for the observed behaviors. This requires additional rules that describe known failure modes for the different components and their interconnections. The reasoner must find the most probable failures that can explain the observed system behavior.

A number of data structures can be used for representing the causal and structural information in models. Many model-based program designers use rules to reflect the causality and functionality of a device. Rules can also be used to capture the relationships between components. An object-oriented system, see Section 16.12, also offers an excellent representational tool for reflecting device and component structure within a model, with the slots of an object representing a device or component's state, and its methods defining its functionality.

To be more concrete in the design and evaluation of a model, we now consider several examples of device and circuit analysis from Davis and Hamscher (1992). Device behavior is represented by a set of expressions that capture the relationships between values on the terminals of the device. For the adder of Figure 8.13, there will be three expressions:

If we know the values at A and B, the value of C is A + B (the solid line).

If we know C and A the value at B is C − A (the dashed line).

If we know C and B, the value at A is C − B (the dotted line).

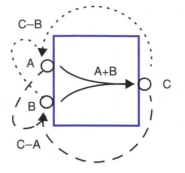

Figure 8.13 The behavior description of an adder,
after Davis and Hamscher (1992).

We need not have used an algebraic form to represent these relationships. We could equally well have used relational tuples or represented the constraints with LISP functions. The goal in model-based reasoning is to represent the knowledge that captures the functionality of the adder.

In a second example, consider the circuit of three multipliers and two adders linked as in Figure 8.14. In this example the input values are given A to E and the output values at F and G. The expected output values are given in ( ) and the actual outputs in [ ]. The task is to determine where the fault lies that will explain this discrepancy. At F we have a conflict, expecting a 12 and getting a 10. We check the dependencies at this point and determine that the value at F is a function of ADD-1 which in turn depends on the outputs of MULT-1 and MULT-2. One of these three devices must have a fault, and so we have three hypotheses to consider: either the adder behavior is bad or one of its two inputs was incorrect, and the problem lies further back in the circuit.

Reasoning from the result (10) at F and assuming correct behavior of ADD-1 and one of its inputs X (6), input Y to ADD-1 must be a 4. But that conflicts with the expectation of 6, which is the correct behavior of MULT-2 and inputs B and D. We have observed these inputs and know they are correct, so MULT-2 must be faulty. In a parallel argument, our second hypothesis is that ADD-1 is correct and MULT-1 is faulty.

Continuing this reasoning, if the first input X to ADD-1 is correct and ADD-1 itself is correct, then the second input Y must be a 4. If it were a 4, G would be 10 rather than 12, so the output of MULT-2 must be a 6 and correct. We are left with the hypotheses that the fault lies in either MULT-1 or ADD-1 and we can continue to constrain these devices with further testing.

In our reasoning about the situation of Figure 8.14 we had three tasks:

1. Hypothesis generation, in which, given a discrepancy, we hypothesized which components of the device could have caused it.

2. Hypothesis testing, in which, given a collection of potential faulty components, we determined which of them could have explained the observed behavior.

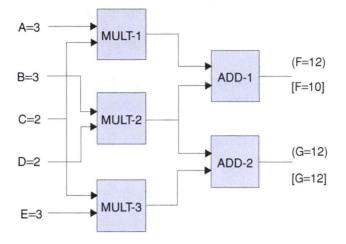

Figure 8.14 Taking advantage of direction of information flow, after Davis and Hamscher (1992).

3. Hypothesis discrimination, in which, when more than one hypothesis survives the testing phase, as happened in the case of Figure 8.14, we must determine what additional information can be gathered to continue the search for the fault.

Finally, we should note that in the example of Figure 8.14 there was assumed to be a single faulty device. The world is not always this simple, although a single fault assumption is a useful, and often correct, heuristic.

Because they are based on a theoretical understanding of the devices in question, qualitative model-based techniques remedy many of the limitations of more heuristic approaches. Rather than reasoning directly from observed phenomena to causal explanations, model-based approaches attempt to represent devices and configurations of devices on a causal or functional level. The program code reflects both the function of devices and the dependencies within a system of devices. Such models are often more robust than heuristic approaches. However, the down side of this explicit modeling of function is that the knowledge acquisition stage can be quite demanding and the resulting program large, cumbersome, and slow. Because heuristic approaches "compile" typical cases into a single rule, they are often more efficient, so long as other system constraints are appropriate.

There are deeper problems, however, with this approach. As with rule-based reasoning, the model of a system is just that, a model. It will of necessity be an abstraction of the system, and at some level of detail, be incorrect. For example, consider the input wires of Figure 8.14. In our discussion we considered these values as given and correct. We did not examine the state of the wire itself, and in particular, the other end where it joined the multipliers. What if the wire were broken, or had a faulty connection to the multiplier? If the user failed to detect this faulty connection, the model would not match the actual device.

Any model attempts to describe the ideal situation, what the system is supposed to do, and not necessarily what the system does do. A "bridging" fault is a contact point in the system where two wires or devices are inadvertently linked, as when a bad solder joint bridges between two wires that should not be in contact. Most model-based reasoning has difficulty hypothesizing a bridging fault because of the a priori assumptions underlying the model and the search methods for determining anomalies. Bridging faults are simply "new" wires that aren't part of the original design. There is an implicit "closed world assumption" (Section 9.1) that the structure description of the model is assumed to be complete and anything not in the model simply doesn't exist.

But, in spite of these shortcomings, model-based reasoning is an important addition to the knowledge engineer's tool kit. Researchers continue to expand our understanding of diagnosis, both how human experts do it so efficiently, as well as how better algorithms can be implemented on machines (Stern and Luger 1997).

8.3.2 Model-Based Reasoning: a NASA Example (Williams and Nayak)

NASA has supported its presence in space by developing a fleet of intelligent space probes that autonomously explore the solar system (Williams and Nayak 1996a, Bernard et al. 1998). This effort was begun with software for the first probe in 1997 and the launch of Deep Space 1 in 1998. To achieve success through years in the harsh conditions of space travel, a craft needs to be able to radically reconfigure its control regime in response to failures and then plan around these failures during its remaining flight. To achieve acceptable cost and fast reconfiguration, one-of-a-kind modules will have to be put together quickly to automatically generate flight software. Finally, NASA expects that the set of potential failure scenarios and possible responses will be much too large to use software that supports preflight enumeration of all contingencies. Instead, the spacecraft will have to reactively think through all the consequences of its reconfiguration options.

Livingstone (Williams and Nayak 1996b) is an implemented kernel for a model-based reactive self-configuring autonomous system. The model-based reasoning representation language for Livingstone is propositional calculus, a shift from the first-order predicate calculus (Chapter 2), the traditional representation language for model-based diagnosis. Williams and Nayak felt, based on their past research on building fast propositional logic conflict-based algorithms for diagnosis (de Kleer and Williams 1989), that a fast reactive system, performing significant deduction in the sense/response loop, was possible.

A long-held vision of model-based reasoning has been to use a single centralized model to support a variety of engineering tasks. For model-based autonomous systems this means using a single model to support a diversity of execution tasks. These include keeping track of developing plans (Section 8.4), confirming hardware modes, reconfiguring hardware, detecting anomalies, diagnosis, and fault recovery. Livingstone automates all these tasks using a single model and a single core algorithm, thus making significant progress towards achieving the vision for model-based problem solvers.

Figure 8.15 shows an idealized schematic of the main engine subassembly of Cassini, the most complex spacecraft built to that time. It consists of a helium tank, a fuel tank, an oxidizer tank, a pair of main engines, regulators, latch valves, pyro valves, and pipes. The helium tank pressurizes the two propellant tanks, with the regulators acting to reduce the high helium pressure to a lower working pressure. When propellant paths to a main engine

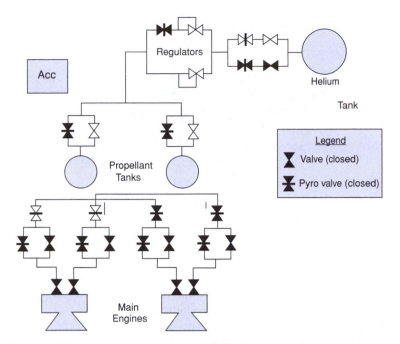

Figure 8.15 A schematic of the simplified Livingstone propulsion system, from Williams and Nayak (1996b).

are open (the valve icon is unfilled), the pressurized tank forces fuel and oxidizer into the main engine, where they combine, spontaneously ignite, and produce thrust. The pyro valves can be fired exactly once, that is, they can change state only once, either going from open to closed or vice versa. Their function is to isolate parts of the main engine subsystem until they are needed, or to permanently isolate failed components. The latch valves are controlled using valve drivers (not shown in Figure 8.15) and the Acc (accelerometer) senses the thrust generated by the main engines.

Starting from the configuration shown in Figure 8.15, the high-level goal of producing thrust can be achieved using a variety of different configurations: thrust can be provided by either of the main engines and there are a number of ways of opening propellant paths to either main engine. For example, thrust can be provided by opening the latch valves leading to the engine on the left, or by firing a pair of pyros and opening a set of latch valves leading to the engine on the right. Other configurations correspond to various combinations of pyro firings. The different configurations have different characteristics since pyro firings are irreversible actions and since firing pyro valves requires significantly more power than opening or closing latch valves.

Suppose the main engine subsystem has been configured to provide thrust from the left main engine by opening the latch valves leading to it. Suppose that this engine fails, for example, by overheating, so that it fails to provide the required thrust. To ensure that the desired thrust is provided even in this situation, the spacecraft must be transitioned to a new configuration in which thrust is now provided by the main engine on the right side.

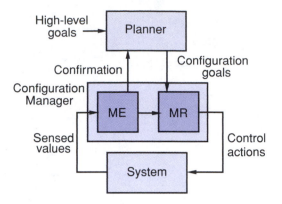

Figure 8.16 A model-based configuration management system, from Williams and Nayak (1996b).

Ideally, this is achieved by firing the two pyro valves leading to the right side and opening the remaining latch valves, rather than firing additional pyro valves.

A *configuration manager* constantly attempts to move the spacecraft into lowest cost configurations that achieve a set of high-level dynamically changing goals. When the spacecraft strays from the chosen configuration due to failures, the manager analyzes sensor data to identify the current configuration of the spacecraft, and then moves the space craft to a new configuration which, once again, achieves the desired configuration goals. A configuration manager is a discrete control system that ensures that the spacecraft's configuration always achieves the set point defined by the configuration goals. The planning algorithms that support the configuration manager are presented in Section 8.4.4.

Reasoning about the configurations (and autonomous reconfigurations) of a system requires the concepts of operating and failure modes, reparable failures, and configuration changes. NASA expresses these concepts in a state space diagram: reparable failures are transitions from a failure state to a nominal state; configuration changes are between nominal states; and failures are transitions from a nominal to a failure state.

Williams and Nayak (1997) view an autonomous system as a combination of a reactive configuration manager and a high-level planner. The planner, for details see Section 8.4, generates a sequence of hardware configuration goals. The configuration manager evolves the transition system of the application domain, here the propulsion system of the spacecraft, along the desired trajectory. Thus configuration management is achieved by sensing and controlling the state of a transition system.

A model-based configuration manager is a configuration manager that uses a specification of the transition system to compute the desired sequence of control values. In the example of Figure 8.15, each hardware component is modeled by a component transition system. Component communication, denoted by wires (links) in the figure is modeled by shared variables between the corresponding component transition systems.

The configuration manager makes extensive use of the model to infer the system's current state and to select optimal control actions to meet configuration goals. This is essential in situations where mistakes can lead to disaster, ruling out simple trial and error methods. The *model-based* configuration manager uses a model to determine the desired control sequence in two stages: mode estimation and mode reconfiguration (ME and MR in Figure 8.16). ME incrementally generates the set of all system trajectories consistent with the plant transition model and the sequence of system control and sensed values. MR uses a plant transition model and the partial trajectories generated by ME up to the current state to determine a set of control values such that all predicted trajectories achieve the configuration goal of the next state. Both ME and MR are reactive. ME infers the current state from knowledge of the previous state and observations within the current state. MR only considers actions that achieve the configuration goal within the next state.

In the next section we consider case-based reasoning, a knowledge-intensive technique that supports the reuse of past experience in a problem domain to address new situations. In Section 8.4 we present planning, and return to the NASA control example.

8.3.3   Introduction to Case-Based Reasoning

Heuristic rules and theoretical models are two types of information human experts use to solve problems. Another powerful strategy experts use is reasoning from cases, examples of past problems and their solutions. *Case-based reasoning* (CBR) uses an explicit database of problem solutions to address new problem-solving situations. These solutions may be collected from human experts through the knowledge engineering process or may reflect the results of previous search-based successes or failures. For example, medical education does not rely solely on theoretical models of anatomy, physiology, and disease; it also depends heavily on case histories and the intern's experience with other patients and their treatment. CASEY (Koton 1988*a, b*) and PROTOS (Bareiss et al. 1988) are examples of case-based reasoning applied to medicine.

Lawyers select past law cases that are similar to their client's and that suggest a favorable decision, and try to convince the court that these similarities merit similar findings. Although general laws are made by democratic processes, their interpretation is usually based on legal precedents. How a law was interpreted in some earlier situation is critical for its current interpretation. Thus, an important component of legal reasoning is identifying from case law precedents for decisions in a particular case. Rissland (1983) and Rissland and Ashley (1987) have designed case-based reasoners to support legal arguments.

Computer programmers often reuse their code, adapting an old program to fit a new situation with similar structure. Architects draw on their knowledge of esthetically pleasing and useful buildings of the past to design new buildings that people find pleasing and comfortable. Historians use stories from the past to help statesmen, bureaucrats, and citizens understand past events and plan for the future. The ability to reason from cases is fundamental to human intelligence.

Other obvious areas for reasoning from cases include design, where aspects of a successfully executed artifact may be appropriate for a new situation, and diagnosis, where the failures of the past often recur. Hardware diagnosis is a good example of this. An expert in this area, besides using extensive theoretical knowledge of electronic and mechanical systems, brings past successful and failed experiences in diagnosis to bear on the current problem. CBR has been an important component of many hardware diagnostic systems, including work on the maintenance of signal sources and batteries in earth orbiting satellites (Skinner and Luger 1992) and the failure analysis of discrete component semiconductors (Stern and Luger 1997).

CBR offers a number of advantages for the construction of expert systems. Knowledge acquisition can be simplified if we record a human expert's solutions to a number of problems and let a case-based reasoner select and reason from the appropriate case. This would save the knowledge engineer the trouble of building general rules from the expert's examples; instead, the reasoner would generalize the rules automatically, through the process of applying them to new situations.

Case-based approaches can also enable an expert system to learn from its experience. After reaching a search-based solution to a problem, a system can save that solution, so that next time a similar situation occurs, search would not be necessary. It can also be important to retain in the case base information about the success or failure of previous solution attempts; thus, CBR offers a powerful model of learning. An early example of this is Samuel's (1959, Section 4.1.1) checker-playing program, where board positions that were found through search or experience to be important are retained in the chance that this position might occur again in a later game.

Case-based reasoners share a common structure. For each new problem they:

1. **Retrieve appropriate cases from memory.** A case is appropriate if its solution may be successfully applied to the new situation. Since reasoners cannot know this in advance, they typically use the heuristic of choosing cases that are similar to the problem instance. Both humans and artificial reasoners determine similarity on the basis of common features: for example, if two patients share a number of common features in their symptoms and medical histories, there is a good probability that they have the same disease and will respond to the same treatment. Retrieving cases efficiently also requires that the case memory be organized to aid such retrieval. Typically, cases are indexed by their significant features, enabling efficient retrieval of cases that have the most features in common with the current problem. The identification of salient features is highly situation dependent.

2. **Modify a retrieved case so that it will apply to the current situation.** Typically a case recommends a sequence of operations that transform a starting state into a goal state. The reasoner must transform the stored solution into operations suitable for the current problem. Analytic methods, such as curve fitting the parameters common to stored cases and new situations can be useful; for example, to determine appropriate temperatures or materials for welding. When analytic relations between cases are not available more heuristic methods may be appropriate; for example, in help desks for hardware diagnosis.

3. **Apply the transformed case.** Step 2 modifies a stored case, which, when applied, may not guarantee a satisfactory problem solution. This may require modifications in the solution case, with further iterations of these first three steps.

4. **Save the solution, with a record of success or failure, for future use.** Storage of the new case requires updating of the index structure. There are methods that can be used to maintain indices, including clustering algorithms (Fisher 1987) and other techniques from machine learning (Stubblefield and Luger 1996).

The data structures for case-based reasoning can be quite varied. In the simplest situation, cases are recorded as relational tuples where a subset of the arguments record the features to be matched and other arguments point to solution steps. Cases can also be represented as more complex structures, such as proof trees. A fairly common mechanism for storing cases is to represent the cases as a set of large situation–action rules. The facts that describe the situation of the rule are the salient features of the recorded case and the operators that make up the action of the rule are the transformations to be used in the new situation. When this type of rule representation is used algorithms such as RETE (Forgy 1982) can be used to organize and optimize the search for appropriate cases.

The most difficult issue in case-based problem solving, regardless of the data structure selected for case representation, is the selection of salient features for the indexing and retrieval of cases. Kolodner (1993) and others actively involved in case-based problem solving set as a cardinal rule that cases be organized by the goals and needs of the problem solver. That is, that a careful analysis be made of case descriptors in the context of how these cases will be used in the solution process.

For example, suppose a *weak communication signal* problem occurs in a satellite at 10:24:35 GMT. Analysis is made, and it is also determined that the power system is low. The low power can occur because the solar panels are not properly oriented towards the sun. The ground controllers make adjustments in the satellite's orientation, the power improves, and the communication signal is again strong. There are a number of salient features that might be used to record this case, the most obvious being that there is a weak communication signal or that the power supply is low. Another feature to describe this case is that the time of the problem was 10:24:35 GMT. The goals and needs of the problem solver in this case suggest that the salient features are weak communication signal and/or low power supply; the time this all happens may well be irrelevant, unless, of course, the fault occurs just after the sun disappears over the horizon (Skinner and Luger 1995).

Another essential problem to be addressed in CBR is the representation of such notions as weak signal or low power. Since the precise situation will probably never again be matched, e.g., some exact real number describing signal strength, the reasoner will probably represent the values as a range of real numbers, i.e., good, borderline-good, weak, and danger-alert levels.

Kolodner (1993) offers a set of possible preference heuristics to help organize the storage and retrieval of cases. These include:

1. *Goal-directed preference.* Organize cases, at least in part, by goal descriptions. Retrieve cases that have the same goal as the current situation.

2. *Salient-feature preference.* Prefer cases that match the most important features or those matching the largest number of important features.

3. *Specify preference.* Look for as exact as possible matches of features before considering more general matches.

4. *Frequency preference.* Check first the most frequently matched cases.

5. *Recency preference.* Prefer cases used most recently.

6. *Ease of adaptation preference.* Use first cases most easily adapted to the current situation.

Case-based reasoning has a number of advantages for the design of expert systems. Once knowledge engineers have arrived at the proper case representation, continued knowledge acquisition is straightforward: simply gather and store more cases. Often, case acquisition can be done from historical records or by monitoring current operations, minimizing demands on the human expert's time.

In addition, CBR raises a number of important theoretical questions relating to human learning and reasoning. One of the most subtle and critical issues raised by CBR is the question of defining *similarity*. Although the notion that similarity is a function of the number of features that two cases have in common is quite reasonable, it masks a number of profound subtleties. For example, most objects and situations have an infinite number of potential descriptive properties; case-based reasoners typically select cases on the basis of a tiny retrieval vocabulary. Typically, case-based reasoners require that the knowledge engineer define an appropriate vocabulary of highly relevant features. Although there has been work on enabling a reasoner to determine relevant features from its own experience (Stubblefield 1995), determining relevance remains a difficult problem.

Another important problem in case-based reasoning deals with store/compute trade-offs. As a case-based reasoner acquires more cases, it becomes more intelligent and better able to solve a variety of target problems. Indeed, as we add cases to a reasoner, its performance will improve – up to a point. The problem is that, as the case base continues to grow, the time needed to retrieve and process an appropriate case also grows. A decline in efficiency for large case bases can also be due to overlapping concepts, noise, and the distribution of problem types. One solution to this problem is to only save the "best" or "prototype" cases, deleting those that are redundant or used infrequently; i.e., forgetting those cases that fail to prove useful. See Samuel's (1959) retention algorithm for saving checker board positions for an important early example of this. In general, however, it is not clear how we can automate such decisions; this remains an active research area (Kolodner 1993).

An automated explanation for why a solution is recommended is also difficult for a case-based reasoner. When asked why a solution was selected to remedy a current situation, the only explanation the system can provide is to say that this particular fix worked at a previous time period. There may also be weak explanations based on similarities of top-level goal descriptions between the current situation and a set of stored cases. In the example of the satellite communication problem, the relevant case was chosen on the basis of a weak communication signal. This mode of reasoning has no deeper explanation than that it worked before in a similar situation. But, as noted previously, this may be sufficient explanation for many situations.

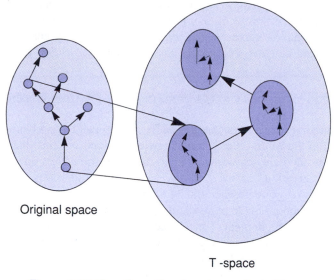

Original space

T -space

Figure 8.17 Transformational analogy, adapted from
Carbonell (1983).

Many researchers, however, feel that the simple repetition of top-level goals and the
case to be applied offers insufficient explanation (Leake 1992, Stern and Luger 1992),
especially when we need an explanation of why some fix doesn't work. Take the satellite
situation again. Suppose the solar panel reorientation works but three hours later the signal
again becomes weak. Using both the frequency and recency heuristics, we again reorient
the solar panel. In three hours the weak signal recurs. And again three hours later; we
always apply the same fix. This example is based on an actual satellite situation in which
it was found that a more complex problem existed, namely a gyroscope was overheating
and giving a distorted reading that disoriented the satellite. The system that finally solved
the problem used a model-based reasoner to simulate the behavior of the satellite to
determine the root causes of the weak communication signal (Skinner and Luger 1995).

Case-based reasoning is related to the problem of learning through analogy. To reuse
past experiences we must both recognize the salient features of the past as well as build a
mapping of how that experience may be used in the present situation. *Transformational
analogy* (Carbonell 1983) is an example of a case-based approach to problem solving. It
solves new problems by modifying existing solutions until they may be applied to the new
instance. Operators that modify complete problem solutions define a higher-level of
abstraction or T-space in which states are problem solutions and operators transform these
solutions, as in Figure 8.17. The goal is to transform a source solution into a possible
solution for the target problem. Operators modify solutions in ways such as inserting or
deleting steps in a solution path, reordering steps in a solution, splicing new solutions into
a portion of an old solution, or changing the bindings of parameters in the current solution.

Transformational analogy typifies the approach used by case-based problem solving.
Later work has refined the approach, considering such issues as the representation of cases,

strategies for organizing a memory of prior cases, retrieval of relevant prior cases, and the use of cases in solving new problems. For further information on case-based reasoning, see Hammond (1989) and Kolodner (1988*a*, *b*). Reasoning through analogies is discussed further in the context of symbol-based machine learning (see Section 10.5.4).

8.3.4　Hybrid Design: Strengths/Weaknesses of Strong Method Systems

Successes in building expert systems that solve hard, practical problems have demonstrated the truth of the central idea behind knowledge-based systems: that the power of a reasoner is in its domain knowledge rather than the sophistication of its reasoning methods. This observation, however, raises one of the central issues in artificial intelligence: that of knowledge representation. At a practical level, every knowledge engineer must make choices about how to represent domain knowledge in a way that will be most appropriate to the given domain. Knowledge representation also raises a number of theoretically important, intellectually difficult issues, such as the handling of missing and uncertain information, the measurement of a representation's expressiveness, the relationship between a representation language and such issues as learning, knowledge acquisition, and the efficiency of a reasoner.

In this chapter, we considered a number of basic approaches to knowledge representation: rule-based expert systems, model-based reasoners, and case-based reasoners. As an aid to practical knowledge engineering, we summarize the strengths and weaknesses of each knowledge-intensive approach to problem solving.

Rule-based Reasoning

The advantages of a rule-based approach include:

1. The ability to use, in a very direct fashion, experiential knowledge acquired from human experts. This is particularly important in domains that rely heavily on heuristics to manage complexity and/or missing information.

2. Rules map into state space search. Explanation facilities support debugging.

3. The separation of knowledge from control simplifies development of expert systems by enabling an iterative development process where the knowledge engineer acquires, implements, and tests individual rules.

4. Good performance is possible in limited domains. Because of the large amounts of knowledge required for intelligent problem solving, expert systems are limited to narrow domains. However, there are many domains where design of an appropriate system has proven extremely useful.

5. Good explanation facilities. Although the basic rule-based framework supports flexible, problem-specific explanations, it must be mentioned that the ultimate quality of these explanations depends upon the structure and content of the rules. Explanation facilities differ widely between data- and goal-driven systems.

Disadvantages of rule-based reasoning include:

1. Often the rules obtained from human experts are highly heuristic in nature, and do not capture functional or model-based knowledge of the domain.

2. Heuristic rules tend to be "brittle" and can have difficulty handling missing information or unexpected data values.

3. Another aspect of the brittleness of rules is a tendency to degrade rapidly near the "edges" of the domain knowledge. Unlike humans, rule-based systems are usually unable to fall back on first principles of reasoning when confronted with novel problems.

4. Explanations function at the descriptive level only, omitting theoretical explanations. This follows from the fact that heuristic rules gain much of their power by directly associating problem symptoms with solutions, without requiring (or enabling) deeper reasoning.

5. The knowledge tends to be very task dependent. Formalized domain knowledge tends to be very specific in its applicability. Currently, knowledge representation languages do not approach the flexibility of human reasoning.

Case-based Reasoning

The advantages of case-based reasoning include:

1. The ability to encode historical knowledge directly. In many domains, cases can be obtained from existing case histories, repair logs, or other sources, eliminating the need for intensive knowledge acquisition with a human expert.

2. Allows shortcuts in reasoning. If an appropriate case can be found, new problems can often be solved in much less time than it would take to generate a solution from rules and search or models.

3. It allows a system to avoid past errors and exploit past successes. CBR provides a model of learning that is both theoretically interesting and practical enough to apply to complex problems.

4. Extensive analysis of domain knowledge is not required. Unlike a rule-based system, where the knowledge engineer must anticipate rule interactions, CBR allows a simple additive model for knowledge acquisition. This requires an appropriate representation for cases, a useful retrieval index, and a case adaptation strategy.

5. Appropriate indexing strategies add insight and problem-solving power. The ability to distinguish differences in target problems and select an appropriate case is an important source of a case-based reasoner's power; often, indexing algorithms can provide this functionality automatically.

The disadvantages of case-based reasoning include:

1. Cases do not often include deeper knowledge of the domain. This handicaps explanation facilities, and in many situations it allows the possibility that cases may be misapplied, leading to wrong or poor quality advice.

2. A large case base can suffer problems from store/compute trade-offs.

3. It is difficult to determine good criteria for indexing and matching cases. Currently, retrieval vocabularies and similarity matching algorithms must be carefully hand crafted; this can offset many of the advantages CBR offers for knowledge acquisition.

Model-based Reasoning

The advantages of model-based reasoning include:

1. The ability to use functional/structural knowledge of the domain in problem-solving. This increases the reasoner's ability to handle a variety of problems, including those that may not have been anticipated by the system's designers.

2. Model-based reasoners tend to be very robust. For the same reasons that humans often retreat to first principles when confronted with a novel problem, model-based reasoners tend to be thorough and flexible problem solvers.

3. Some knowledge is transferable between tasks. Model-based reasoners are often built using scientific, theoretical knowledge. Because science strives for generally applicable theories, this generality often extends to model-based reasoners.

4. Often, model-based reasoners can provide causal explanations. These can convey a deeper understanding of the fault to human users, and can also play an important tutorial role.

The disadvantages of model-based reasoning include:

1. A lack of experiential (descriptive) knowledge of the domain. The heuristic methods used by rule-based approaches reflect a valuable class of expertise.

2. It requires an explicit domain model. Many domains, such as the diagnosis of failures in electronic circuits, have a strong scientific basis that supports model-based approaches. However, many domains, such as some medical specialties, most design problems, or many financial applications, lack a well-defined scientific theory. Model-based approaches cannot be used in such cases.

3. High complexity. Model-based reasoning generally operates at a level of detail that leads to significant complexity; this is, after all, one of the main reasons human experts have developed heuristics in the first place.

4. Exceptional situations. Unusual circumstances, for example, bridging faults or the interaction of multiple failures in electronic components, can alter the functionality of a system in ways difficult to predict a priori.

Hybrid Design

An important area of research and application is the combination of different reasoning models. With a hybrid architecture two or more paradigms are integrated to get a cooperative effect where the strengths of one system can compensate for the weakness of another. In combination, we can address the disadvantages noted in the previous discussion.

For example, the combination of rule-based and case-based systems can:

1. Offer a natural first check against known cases before undertaking rule-based reasoning and the associated search costs.

2. Provide a record of examples and exceptions to solutions through retention in the case base.

3. Record search-based results as cases for future use. By saving appropriate cases, a reasoner can avoid duplicating costly search.

The combination of rule-based and model-based systems can:

1. Enhance explanations with functional knowledge. This can be particularly useful in tutorial applications.

2. Improve robustness when rules fail. If there are no heuristic rules that apply to a given problem instance, the reasoner can resort to reasoning from first principles.

3. Add heuristic search to model-based search. This can help manage the complexity of model-based reasoning and allow the reasoner to choose intelligently between possible alternatives.

The combination of model-based and case-based systems can:

1. Give more mature explanations to the situations recorded in cases.

2. Offer a natural first check against stored cases before beginning the more extensive search required by model-based reasoning.

3. Provide a record of examples and exceptions in a case base that can be used to guide model-based inference.

4. Record results of model-based inference for future use.

Hybrid methods deserve the attention of researchers and application developers alike. However, building such systems is not a simple matter, requiring the resolution of such problems as determining which reasoning method to apply in a given situation, deciding when to change reasoning methods, resolving differences between reasoning methods, and designing representations that allow knowledge to be shared.

We next consider planning, or the organization of procedures into potential solutions.

8.4 Planning

8.4.1 Introduction

The task of a planner is to find a sequence of actions that allow a problem solver, such as a control system, to accomplish some specific task. Traditional planning is very much knowledge-intensive, since plan creation requires the organization of pieces of knowledge and partial plans into a solution procedure. Besides robotics applications, planning plays a role in expert systems in reasoning about events occurring over time. Planning has many applications in manufacturing, such as process control. It is also important in natural language understanding, where humans frequently discuss plans, goals, and intentions.

To begin, we consider examples from traditional robotics. (Much of modern robotics uses reactive control rather than deliberative planning, Sections 6.3.1 and 8.4.3.) The steps of a traditional robot plan are composed of the robot's *atomic actions*. For planning purposes, we do not describe these capabilities in hardware or micro-level terms such as "turn the sixth stepper motor one revolution." Instead, planners specify actions at a higher level, such as by their effects on a world. For example, a blocks world robot might include such actions as "pick up object a" or "go to location x." The micro-control of steps to actually make a robot perform a plan are built into these higher-level actions.

Thus, a sequence of actions to "go get block a from room b" might be:

1. put down whatever is now held

2. go to room b

3. go over to block a

4. pick up block a

5. leave room b

6. return to original location

Plans are created by searching through a space of possible actions until the sequence necessary to accomplish the task is discovered. This space represents states of the world that are changed by applying each of the actions. The search terminates when the goal state (the description of the world) is produced. Thus, many of the issues of heuristic search, including finding A* algorithms, are also appropriate in planning.

The act of planning does not depend on the existence of an actual robot to carry out the plans, however. In the early years of computer planning (1960s), entire plans were formulated before the robot performed its first act. Thus plans were devised without the

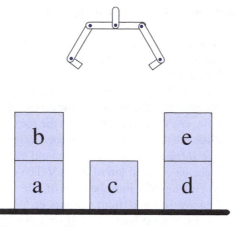

Figure 8.18 The blocks world.

presence of a robot at all! More recently, with the implementation of sophisticated sensing and reactive devices, research has focused on more integrated plan/action sequencing.

Traditional planning relies on search techniques, and raises a number of interesting issues. For one, the description of the states of the world may be considerably more complex than in previous examples of search. Consider the number of predicates necessary to describe rooms and corridors and objects in the robot's environment. Not only must we represent the robot's world; we must also represent the effect of atomic actions on that world. The full description of each state of the problem space can be quite extensive.

Another difference in planning is the need to characterize what is *not* changed by a particular action. Picking up an object does change (a) the location of the object and (b) the fact that the robot hand is now grasping the object. It does not change (a) the locations of the doors and the rooms or (b) the locations of other objects. The specification of what is true in one state of the world and *exactly* what is changed by performing some action in the world has become known as the *frame problem* (McCarthy 1980, McCarthy and Hayes 1969). As the complexity of the problem space increases, the issue of keeping track of the changes that occur with each action and the features of a state description that remain unchanged becomes more important. We present two solutions for coping with the frame problem, but, as will be seen, neither of these is totally satisfactory.

Other important issues include generating plans, saving and generalizing good plans, recovering from unexpected plan failures (part of the world might not be as expected, perhaps by being accidentally moved from its anticipated location), and maintaining consistency between the world and a program's internal model of the world.

In the examples of this section, we limit our robot's world to a set of blocks on a tabletop and the robot's actions to an arm that can stack, unstack, and otherwise move the blocks about the table. In Figure 8.18 we have five blocks, labeled a, b, c, d, e, sitting on the top of a table. The blocks are all cubes of the same size, and stacks of blocks, as in the figure, have blocks directly on top of each other. The robot arm has a gripper that can grasp any clear block (one with no block on top of it) and move it to any location on the tabletop or place it on top of any other clear block.

The robot arm can perform the following tasks (U, V, W, X, Y, and Z are variables):

goto(X,Y,Z)	Goto location described by coordinates X, Y, and Z. This location might be implicit in the command pickup (W) where block W has location X, Y, Z.
pickup(W)	Pick up block W from its current location and hold it. It is assumed that the block is clear on top, the gripper is empty at the time, and the computer knows the location of block W.
putdown(W)	Place block W down at some location on the table and record the new location for W. W must be held by the gripper at the time.
stack(U,V)	Place block U on top of block V. The gripper must be holding U and the top of V must be clear of other blocks.
unstack(U,V)	Remove block U from the top of V. U must be clear of other blocks, V must have block U on top of it, and the hand must be empty before this command can be executed.

The state of the world is described by a set of predicates and predicate relationships:

location(W,X,Y,Z)	Block W is at coordinates X, Y, Z.
on(X,Y)	Block X is immediately on top of block Y.
clear(X)	Block X has nothing on top of it.
gripping(X)	The robot arm is holding block X.
gripping( )	The robot gripper is empty.
ontable(W)	Block W is on the table.

ontable(W) is a short form for the predicate location(W,X,Y,Z), where Z is the table level. Similarly, on(X,Y) indicates that block X is located with its bottom coincident with the top of block Y. We can greatly simplify the world descriptions by having the computer record the present location(X,Y,Z) of each block and keep track of its movements to new locations. With this location assumption, the goto command becomes unnecessary; a command such as pickup(X) or stack(X) implicitly contains the location of X.

The blocks world of Figure 8.18 may now be represented by the following set of predicates. We call this collection of predicates STATE 1 for our continuing example. Because the predicates describing the state of the world for Figure 8.18 are all true at the same time, the full state description is the conjunction (∧) of all these predicates.

STATE 1

ontable(a).	on(b, a).	clear(b).
ontable(c).	on(e, d).	clear(c).
ontable(d).	gripping( ).	clear(e).

Next, a number of truth relations (in the declarative sense) or rules for performance (in the procedural sense) are created for clear(X), ontable(X), and gripping( ):

1. $(\forall\ X)\ (clear(X) \leftarrow \neg\ (\exists\ Y)\ (on(Y,X)))$

2. $(\forall\ Y)\ (\forall\ X)\ \neg\ (on(Y,X) \leftarrow ontable(Y))$

3. $(\forall\ Y)\ gripping(\ ) \leftrightarrow \neg\ (gripping(Y))$

The first statement says that if block X is clear, there does not exist any block Y such that Y is on top of X. Interpreted procedurally, this says "to clear block X go and remove any block Y that might be on top of X."

We now design rules to operate on states and produce new states. In doing so, we again impute a procedural semantics to a predicate logic-like representation. The operators (pickup, putdown, stack, unstack) are:

4. $(\forall\ X)\ (pickup(X) \rightarrow (gripping(X) \leftarrow (gripping(\ ) \wedge clear(X) \wedge ontable(X))))$.

5. $(\forall\ X)\ (putdown(X) \rightarrow ((gripping(\ ) \wedge ontable(X) \wedge clear(X)) \leftarrow gripping(X)))$.

6. $(\forall\ X)\ (\forall\ Y)\ (stack(X,Y) \rightarrow ((on(X,Y) \wedge gripping(\ ) \wedge clear(X)) \leftarrow (clear(Y) \wedge gripping(X))))$.

7. $(\forall\ X)(\forall\ Y)\ (unstack(X,Y) \rightarrow ((clear(Y) \wedge gripping(X)) \leftarrow (on(X,Y) \wedge clear(X) \wedge gripping(\ ))))$.

Consider the fourth rule: for all blocks X, pickup(X) means gripping(X) if the hand is empty and X is clear. Note the form of these rules: $A \rightarrow (B \leftarrow C)$. This says that operator A produces new predicate(s) B when condition(s) C is true. We use these rules to generate new states in a space. That is, if predicates C are true in a state, then B is true in its child state. In other words, operator A can be used to create a new state described by predicates B when predicates C are true. Alternative approaches to creating these operators include STRIPS (Nilsson 1980 and Section 8.4.2) and Rich and Knight's (1991) do function.

We must first address the *frame problem* before we can use these rule relationships to generate new states of the blocks world. *Frame axioms* are rules to tell what predicates describing a state are *not* changed by rule applications and are thus carried over intact to help describe the new state of the world. For example, if we apply the operator pickup block b in Figure 8.18, then all predicates related to the rest of the blocks remain true in the child state. For our world of blocks we can specify several such frame rules:

8. $(\forall\ X)\ (\forall\ Y)\ (\forall\ Z)\ (unstack(Y,Z) \rightarrow (ontable(X) \leftarrow ontable(X)))$.

9. $(\forall\ X)\ (\forall\ Y)\ (\forall\ Z)\ (stack(Y,Z) \rightarrow (ontable(X) \leftarrow ontable(X)))$.

These two rules say that ontable is not affected by the stack and unstack operators. This is true even when X and Z are identical; if Y = Z either 6 or 7 above won't be true.

Other frame axioms say that on and clear are affected by stack and unstack operators only when that particular on relation is unstacked or when a clear relation is stacked. Thus, in our example, on(b,a) is not affected by unstack(c,d).

Similarly, frame axioms say that clear(X) relations are unaffected by gripping(Y) even when X = Y or gripping( ) is true. More axioms say that gripping does not affect on(X,Y) relations but affects only the ontable(X) relation where X is gripped. Thus, a number of other frame axioms need to be specified for our example.

Together, these operators and frame axioms define a state space, as illustrated by the operator unstack. unstack(X,Y) requires three conditions to be true simultaneously, namely on(X,Y), gripping( ), and clear(X). When these conditions are met the new predicates gripping(X) and clear(Y) are produced by applying the unstack operator. A number of other predicates also true for STATE 1 will remain true in STATE 2. These states are preserved for STATE 2 by the frame axioms. We now produce the nine predicates describing STATE 2 by applying the unstack operator and the frame axioms to the nine predicates of STATE 1, where the net result is to unstack block e:

STATE 2

ontable(a).	on(b,a).	clear(b).
ontable(c).	clear(c).	clear(d).
ontable(d).	gripping(e).	clear(e).

To summarize:

1. Planning may be seen as a state space search.

2. New states are produced by general operators such as stack and unstack plus frame rules.

3. The techniques of graph search may be applied to find a path from the start state to the goal state. The operations on this path constitute a plan.

Figure 8.19 shows an example of a state space searched by applying the operators as described above. If a goal description is added to this problem-solving process, then a plan may be seen as a set of operators that produces a path that leads from the present state of this graph to the goal. (See Section 3.1.3.)

This characterization of the planning problem defines its theoretical roots in state space search and predicate calculus representation and inferencing. However, it is important to note how complex this manner of solution can be. In particular, using the frame rules to calculate what remains unchanged between states can add exponentially to the search, as can be seen from the complexity of the very simple blocks problem. In fact, when any new predicate descriptor is introduced, for color, shape, or size, new frame rules must be defined to relate it to all appropriate actions!

This discussion also assumes that the subproblems that make up a task are independent and may thus be solved in an arbitrary order. This is very seldom the case in interesting and/or complex problem domains, where the preconditions and actions required to achieve

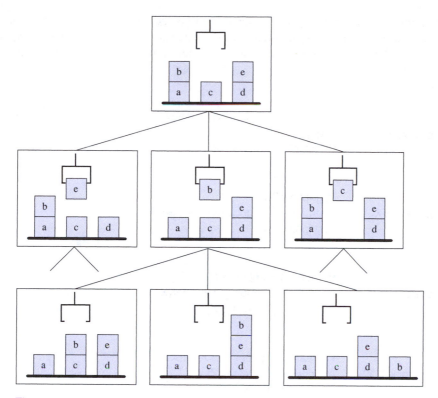

Figure 8.19 Portion of the state space for a portion of the blocks world.

one subgoal can often conflict with the preconditions and actions required to achieve another. Next we illustrate these problems and discuss an approach to planning that greatly assists in handling this complexity.

8.4.2 Using Planning Macros: STRIPS

STRIPS, developed at what is now SRI International, stands for STanford Research Institute Planning System (Fikes and Nilsson 1971, Fikes et al. 1972). This controller was used to drive the *SHAKEY* robot of the early 1970s. STRIPS addressed the problem of efficiently representing and implementing the operations of a planner. It addressed the problem of conflicting subgoals and provided an early model of learning; successful plans were saved and generalized as *macro operators*, which could be used in similar future situations. In the remainder of this section, we present a version of STRIPS-style planning and *triangle tables*, the data structure used to organize and store macro operations.

Using the blocks example, the four operators pickup, putdown, stack, and unstack are represented as triples of descriptions. The first element of the triple is the set of *preconditions* (P), or conditions the world must meet for an operator to be applied. The second element of the triple is the *add* list (A), or the additions to the state description that are a result of applying the operator. Finally, there is the *delete* list (D), or the items that are removed from a state description to create the new state when the operator is applied. These lists eliminate the need for separate frame axioms. We can represent the four operators in this fashion:

pickup(X)
P: gripping( ) ∧ clear(X) ∧ ontable(X)
A: gripping(X)
D: ontable(X) ∧ gripping( )

putdown(X)
P: gripping(X)
A: ontable(X) ∧ gripping( ) ∧ clear(X)
D: gripping(X)

stack(X,Y)
P: clear(Y) ∧ gripping(X)
A: on(X,Y) ∧ gripping( ) ∧ clear(X)
D: clear(Y) ∧ gripping(X)

unstack(X,Y)
P: clear(X) ∧ gripping( ) ∧ on(X,Y)
A: gripping(X) ∧ clear(Y)
D: gripping( ) ∧ on(X,Y)

The important thing about the *add* and *delete* lists is that they specify *everything* that is necessary to satisfy the frame axioms! Some redundancy exists in the add and delete list approach. For example, in unstack the *add* of gripping(X) could imply the *delete* of gripping( ). But the gain of this redundancy is that every descriptor of a state that is not mentioned by the *add* or *delete* remains the same in the new state description.

A related weakness of the precondition-add-delete list approach is that we are no longer using a theorem-proving process to produce (by inference) the new states. This is not a serious problem, however, as proofs of the equivalence of the two approaches can guarantee the correctness of the precondition-add-delete method.

The precondition-add-delete list approach may be used to produce the same results we produced with the inference rules and frame axioms in our earlier example. The state space search, as in Figure 8.19, would be identical for both approaches.

A number of other problems inherent in planning are not solved by either of the two approaches presented so far. In solving a goal we often divide it into subproblems, for instance, unstack(e,d) and unstack(b,a). Attempting to solve these subgoals independently can cause problems if the actions needed to achieve one goal actually undo the other. Incompatible subgoals may result from a false assumption of *linearity* (independence) of subgoals. The non-linearity of a plan/action space can make solution searches unnecessarily difficult or even impossible.

We now show a very simple example of an incompatible subgoal using the start state STATE 1 of Figure 8.18. Suppose the goal of the plan is STATE G as in Figure 8.20, with on(b,a) ∧ on(a,c) and blocks d and e remaining as in STATE 1. It may be noted that one of the parts of the conjunctive goal on(b,a) ∧ on(a,c) is true in STATE 1, namely on(b,a). This already satisfied part of the goal must be undone before the second subgoal, on(a,c), can be accomplished.

The *triangle table* representation (Fikes and Nilsson 1971, Nilsson 1980) is aimed at alleviating some of these anomalies. A triangle table is a data structure for organizing sequences of actions, including potentially incompatible subgoals, within a plan. It addresses the problem of conflicting subgoals within macro actions by representing the global interaction of sequences of operations. A triangle table relates the preconditions of one action to the postconditions, the combined *add* and *delete* lists, of actions preceding it.

Triangle tables are used to determine when that macro operator could be used in building a plan. By saving these macro operators and reusing them, STRIPS increases the efficiency of its planning search. Indeed, we can generalize a macro operator, using variable names to replace the block names in a particular example. Then we can call the new generalized macro to prune search. In Chapter 10, with our presentation of learning in symbol-based environments, we discuss techniques for generalizing macro operations.

The reuse of macro operators also helps to solve the problem of conflicting subgoals. As the following example illustrates, once the planner has developed a plan for goals of the form stack(X,Y) ∧ stack(Y,Z), it may store and reuse that plan. This eliminates the need to break the goal into subgoals and avoids the complications that may follow.

Figure 8.21 presents a triangle table for the macro action stack(X,Y) ∧ stack(Y,Z). This macro action can be applied to states where on(X,Y) ∧ clear(X) ∧ clear(Z) is true. This triangle table is appropriate for starting STATE 1 with X = b, Y = a, and Z = c.

The atomic actions of the plan are recorded along the diagonal. These are the four actions, pickup, putdown, stack, and unstack, discussed earlier in this section. The set of preconditions of each of these actions are in the row preceding that action, and the

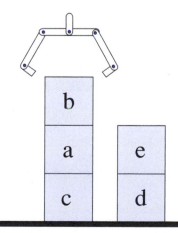

Figure 8.20 Goal state for the blocks world.

postconditions of each action are in the column below it. For example, row 5 lists the preconditions for pickup(X), and column 6 lists the postconditions (the *add* and *delete* lists) of pickup(X). These postconditions are placed in the row of the action that uses them as preconditions, organizing them in a manner relevant to further actions. The triangle table's purpose is to properly interleave the preconditions and postconditions of each of the smaller actions that make up the larger goal. Thus, triangle tables address non-linearity issues in planning on the macro operator level; Partial-Order Planners (Russell and Norvig 1995) and other approaches further address these issues.

One advantage of triangle tables is the assistance they can offer in attempting to recover from unexpected happenings, such as a block being slightly out of place, or accidents, such as dropping a block. Often an accident can require backing up several steps before the plan can be resumed. When something goes wrong with a solution the planner can go back into the rows and columns of the triangle table to check what is still true. Once the planner has figured out what is still true within the rows and columns, it then knows what the next step must be if the larger solution is to be restarted. This is formalized with the notion of a *kernel*.

The *nth kernel* is the intersection of all rows below and including the nth row and all columns to the left of and including the nth column. In Figure 8.21 we have outlined the third kernel in bold. In carrying out a plan represented in a triangle table, the ith operation (that is, the operation in row i) may be performed only if all predicates contained in the ith kernel are true. This offers a straightforward way of verifying that a step can be taken and also allows us to recover systematically from any disruption of a plan. Given a triangle table, we find and execute the highest-numbered action whose kernel is enabled. This not

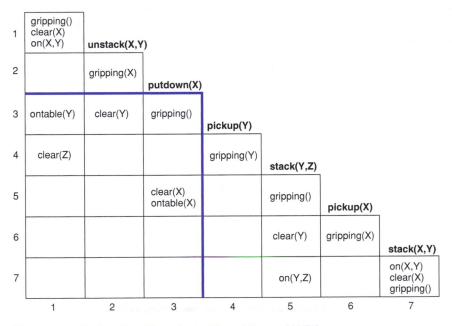

Figure 8.21 A triangle table, adapted from Nilsson (1971).

only lets us back up in a plan but also allows for the possibility that an unexpected event might let us jump forward in a plan.

The conditions in the leftmost column are the preconditions for the macro action as a whole. The conditions in the bottom row are the conditions added to the world by the macro operator. A triangle table may be saved as a *macro operator* with its own set of preconditions and *add* and *delete* lists.

Of course, the triangle table approach does lose some of the semantics of the previous planning models. Notice, for example, that only those postconditions of an act are retained that are also preconditions of later acts. Thus, if guaranteed correctness is a desired result, further verification of the triangle tables, perhaps with additional information that might allow sequences of triangle tables to be composed, might be desirable.

Other problems arise with the use of macro operators in planning. As the number of macro operators increases, the planner has more powerful operations to use, decreasing the size of the state space that must be searched. Unfortunately, at each step of the search, all of these operators must be examined. The pattern matching needed to determine whether an operator may be applied can add considerable overhead to the search process, counteracting the gains made by saving macro operations. The problems of determining when a macro operation should be saved and the best way to determine the next operator to use remain the subject of much research. In the next section we describe an algorithm under which many subgoals may be simultaneously satisfied, teleo-reactive planning.

8.4.3 Teleo-Reactive Planning (Nilsson 1994, Benson 1995)

Since the early work in planning described in the previous section (Fikes and Nilsson 1971), there have been a number of significant advances. Much of this work has been done on domain independent planning, but more recently more domain specific planning, where distributed sense/react mechanisms are employed, has become important. In the next sections we describe a domain independent system, teleo-reactive planning, as well as a more domain dependent planner, Burton, from NASA. For a summary of the first two decades of planning research we recommend Allen et al. (1990).

Teleo-reactive (TR) planning was first proposed by Nilsson (1994) and Benson (1995) at Stanford University. TR planning offers a general purpose architecture, with application to many domains where control of complex subsystems must be coordinated to accomplish a higher level goal. Thus it combines the top-down approach of hierarchical control architectures with an "agent-based" (Section 7.4) or bottom-up assist. The result is a system that can accomplish complex problem solving through the coordination of simple task-specific agents. The justification for this approach is that simple agents have the advantage of working in smaller and more constrained problem spaces. The higher-level controller, on the other hand, can make more global decisions about the entire system, for example, how the current result of a purely local decision can affect the result of the general problem-solving task.

Teleo-reactive control combines aspects of feedback-based control and discrete action planning. Teleo-reactive programs sequence the execution of actions that have been assembled into a goal-oriented plan. Unlike more traditional AI planning environments

(Weld 1994), no assumptions are made that actions are discrete and uninterruptible and that every action's effects are completely predictable. To the contrary, teleo-actions can be sustained over extended periods of time, that is, teleo-actions are executed as long as the actions' preconditions are met and the associated goal has not yet been achieved. Nilsson (1994) refers to this type of action as *durative*. Durative actions can be interrupted when some other action closer to the top-level goal is activated. A short sense-react cycle ensures that when the environment changes the control actions also quickly change to reflect the new state of the problem solution.

Teleo-reactive action sequences are represented by a data structure called a TR tree as in Figure 8.22. A TR tree is described by a set of condition → action pairs (or production rules, Section 6.3). For example:

$$C_0 \rightarrow A_0$$
$$C_1 \rightarrow A_1$$
$$C_2 \rightarrow A_2$$
$$...$$
$$C_n \rightarrow A_n$$

where the C are the conditions and the A_i are the associated actions. We refer to C_0 as the top-level goal of the tree and A_0 as the null action, indicating that nothing further needs to be done once the top-level goal is achieved. At each execution cycle of the teleo-reactive system, each C_i is evaluated from the top of the rules to the bottom (C_0, C_1, ..., C_n) until the first true condition is found. The action associated with this true condition is then performed. The evaluation cycle is then repeated at a frequency that approximates the reactivity of circuit-based control.

The $C_i \rightarrow A_i$ productions are organized in such a way that each action A_i, if continually executed under normal conditions, will eventually make some condition higher in the TR rule tree, Figure 8.22, true. TR tree execution may be seen as adaptive in that if some unanticipated event in the control environment reverses the effect of previous actions, TR execution will fall back to the lower-level rule condition that reflects that condition. From that point it will restart its work towards satisfying all higher-level goals. Similarly, if something good inadvertently happens, TR execution is opportunistic in that control will automatically shift to the action of that true condition.

TR trees can be constructed with a planning algorithm that employs common AI goal reduction methods. Starting from the top-level goal, the planner searches over actions whose effects include achievement of that goal. The preconditions of those actions generate a new set of subgoals, and this procedure recurses. Termination is achieved when the preconditions of the leaf nodes are satisfied by the current state of the environment. Thus the planning algorithm regresses from the top-level goal through goal reduction to the current state. Actions, of course, often have side effects and the planner must be careful to verify that an action at any level does not alter conditions that are required as preconditions of actions at a higher level in the TR tree. Goal reduction is thus coupled with constraint satisfaction, where a variety of action reordering strategies are used to eliminate possible constraint violations.

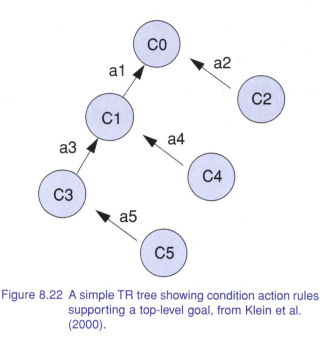

Figure 8.22 A simple TR tree showing condition action rules
supporting a top-level goal, from Klein et al.
(2000).

Thus, TR planning algorithms are used to build plans whose leaf nodes are satisfied by the current state of the problem environment. They usually do not build complete plans, that is plans that can start from any world state, because such plans are generally too large to store or to execute efficiently. This final point is important because sometimes an unexpected environmental event can shift the world to a state in which no action's preconditions in the TR tree are satisfied and some form of replanning is necessary. This is usually done by reactivating the TR planner.

Benson (1995) and Nilsson (1994) have used teleo-reactive planning in a number of application domains including the control of distributed robot agents and building a flight simulator. Klein et al. (1999, 2000) have used a teleo-reactive planner to build and test a portable control architecture for the acceleration of a charged particle beam. These latter researchers gave a number of reasons for the use of a teleo-reactive controller in the domain of particle beam controllers:

1. Accelerator beams and their associated diagnostics are typically dynamic and noisy.

2. The achievement of accelerator tuning goals is often affected by stochastic processes, RF breakdown, or oscillations in the beam source.

3. Many of the actions required for tuning are durative. This is especially true of tweaking and optimization operations that need to be continued until specific criteria are met.

4. TR trees offer an intuitive framework for encoding tuning plans acquired from accelerator physicists. In fact, with very little help, the physicists themselves are able to develop their own TR trees.

Further details of these applications can be found by consulting the references. We next revisit the NASA model-based reasoning example of Section 8.3, to describe control/planning algorithms for the propulsion system of space vehicles.

8.4.4   Planning: a NASA Example (Williams and Nayak)

In this section we describe how a planner can be implemented in the context of a model-based reasoner. We continue the NASA example of Williams and Nayak (1996*b*) introduced in Section 8.3.2. Livingstone is a reactive configuration manager that uses a compositional, component-based model of the space craft propulsion system to determine configurations actions, as is seen in Figure 8.23.

Each propulsion component is modeled as a transition system that specifies the behaviors of the operating and failure modes of the component, the nominal and failure transitions between modes, and the costs and likelihoods of transitions, as in Figure 8.24. In Figure 8.24, open and closed are normal operation modes, but stuck open and stuck closed are failure modes. The open command has unit cost and causes a mode transition from closed to open, similarly for the close command. Failure transitions move the valve from normal operating modes to one of the failure modes with probability 0.01.

Mode behaviors are specified using formulae in propositional logic, but transitions between modes are specified using formulae in a restricted temporal, propositional logic. The restricted temporal, propositional logic is adequate for modeling digital hardware,

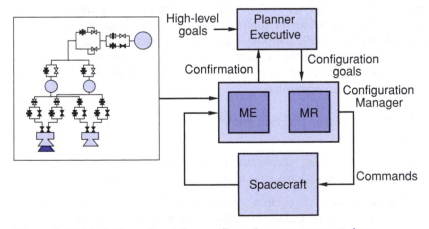

Figure 8.23 Model-based reactive configuration management, from Williams and Nayak (1996b).

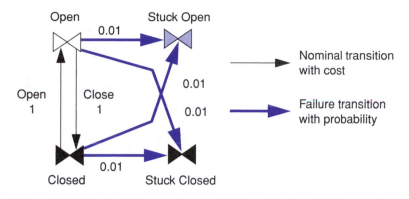

Figure 8.24 The transition system model of a valve, from Williams and Nayak (1996a).

analog hardware using qualitative abstractions (deKleer and Williams 1989, Weld and de Kleer 1990), and real time software using the models of concurrent reactive systems (Manna and Pnueli 1992). The spacecraft transition system model is a composition of its component transition systems in which the set of configurations of the spacecraft is the cross product of the sets of component modes. We assume that the component transition systems operate synchronously; that is, for each spacecraft transition every component performs a transition.

A model-based configuration manager uses its transition-system model to both identify the current configuration of the spacecraft, called *mode estimation* ME, and move the spacecraft into a new configuration that achieves the desired configuration goals, called *mode reconfiguration*, MR. ME incrementally generates all spacecraft transitions from the previous configuration such that the models of the resulting configurations are consistent with the current observations. Thus, in Figure 8.25, a situation is shown where the left engine is firing normally in the previous state, but no thrust is observed in the current state. MEs must identify the configurations into which the spacecraft has transitioned that account for this observation. The figure shows two possible transitions, corresponding to one of the main engine valves failing. The failed or stuck closed valves are circled. Many other transitions, including unlikely double faults, can also account for the observations.

MR determines the commands to be sent to the spacecraft such that the resulting transitions put the spacecraft into a configuration that achieves the configuration goal in the next state, as in Figure 8.26. This figure shows a situation in which mode identification has identified a failed main engine valve leading to the left engine. MR reasons that normal thrust can be restored in the next state if an appropriate set of valves leading to the right engine is opened. The figure shows two of the many configurations that can achieve the desired goal, when the circled valves are commanded to change state. Transitioning to the configuration at the top has lower cost because only necessary pyro valves (see the discussion in Section 8.3.2) are fired. The valves leading to the left engine are turned off

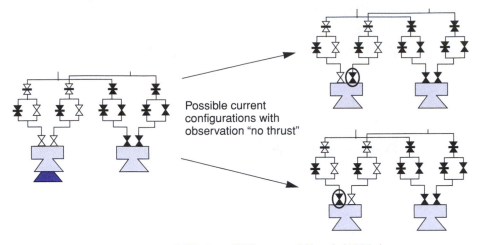

Figure 8.25 Mode estimation (ME), from Williams and Nayak (1996a).

to satisfy a constraint that, at most, one engine can fire at a time. The use of a spacecraft model in both ME and MR ensures that configuration goals are achieved correctly.

Both ME and MR are reactive (see Section 7.4). ME infers the current configuration from knowledge of the previous configuration and current observations. MR only considers commands that achieve the configuration goal in the next state. Given these commitments, the decision to model component transitions as synchronous is key. An alternative is to model multiple component transitions through interleaving. However, interleaving can place an arbitrary distance between the current configuration and a goal configuration, defeating the desire to limit inference to a small fixed number of states. Hence we model component transitions as being synchronous. If component transitions in the underlying hardware-software are not synchronous, Livingstone's modeling assumption is that all interleavings of transitions are correct and support achieving the desired configuration. This assumption is removed in *Burton*, a follow-on of Livingstone, whose planner determines a sequence of control actions that produce all desired transitions (Williams and Nayak 1997). NASA is using the Burton architecture on a mission called Tech Sat 21.

For Livingstone, ME and MR need not generate all transitions and control commands, respectively. Rather all that is required is just the most likely transitions and an optimal control command. These are efficiently regenerated by recasting ME and MR as combinatorial optimization problems. In this reformulation, ME incrementally tracks the likely spacecraft trajectories by always extending the trajectories leading to the current configurations by the most likely transitions. MR then identifies the command with the lowest expected cost that transitions from the likely current configurations to a configuration that achieves the desired goal. These combinatorial optimization problems are efficiently solved using a conflict-directed best-first search algorithm. See Williams and Nayak (1996a, 1996b, 1997) for a more formal characterization of ME and MR as well as a more detailed description of the search and planning algorithms.

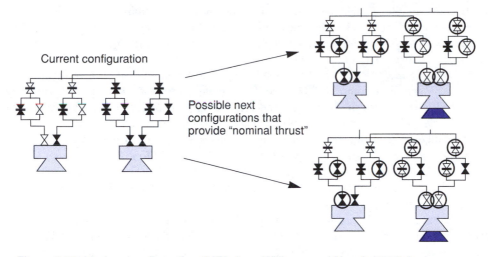

Figure 8.26 Mode reconfiguration (MR), from Williams and Nayak (1996a).

8.5 Epilogue and References

The architecture for the rule-based expert system is the production system. Whether the final product is data-driven or goal-driven, the model for the software is production system-generated graph search, as presented in Chapter 6. We implement production system-based expert system shells in PROLOG and LISP in Chapters 15 and 16, respectively. These shells are able to create a goal-driven search much like MYCIN's. The rules can include certainty measures in a limited form for design of a heuristic-based search.

A number of references complement the material presented in this chapter; especially recommended is a collection of the original MYCIN publications from Stanford entitled *Rule-Based Expert Systems* by Buchanan and Shortliffe (1984). Other early expert systems work is described in Waterman (1968), Michie (1979), Patil et al. (1981), Clancy (1983), and Clancy and Shortliffe (1984*a*, 1984*b*). For a robust implementation of data-driven rule-based search we recommend the CLIPS software, distributed by NASA. An excellent reference for CLIPS is Giarratano and Riley (1989).

Other important books on general knowledge engineering include *Building Expert Systems* by Hayes-Roth et al. (1984), *A Guide to Expert Systems* by Waterman (1986), *Expert Systems: Concepts and Examples* by Alty and Coombs (1984), *Expert Systems Technology: A Guide* by Johnson and Keravnou (1985), and *Expert Systems and Fuzzy Systems* by Negoita (1985), *Introduction to Expert Systems* by Jackson (1986), and *Expert Systems: Tools and Applications* by Harmon et al. (1988). See also *Introduction to Expert Systems* by Ignizio (1991), *An Introduction to Expert Systems* by Mockler and Dologite (1992), and *Expert Systems: Design and Development* by John Durkin (1994).

Because of the domain specificity of expert system solutions, case studies are an important source of knowledge in the area. Books in this category include *Expert Systems: Techniques, Tools and Applications* by Klahr and Waterman (1986), *Competent Expert Systems: A Case Study in Fault Diagnosis* by Keravnou and Johnson (1986), *The CRI Directory of Expert Systems* by Smart and Langeland-Knudsen (1986), *Developments in Expert Systems* by Coombs (1984), and *Developing and Managing Expert Systems* by Prerau (1990). We especially recommend *Expert Systems: Design and Development* by Durkin (1994) for its vast number of practical suggestions on building systems.

A number of techniques for knowledge acquisition have been developed. For more information on specific methodologies see *Knowledge Acquisition: Principles and Guidelines* by McGraw and Harbison-Briggs (1989) and *Knowledge Engineering* by Chorafas (1990), as well as *An Introduction to Expert Systems* by Mockler and Dologite (1992) and other books on expert systems.

Case-based reasoning is an offshoot of earlier research by Schank's group at Yale and their work on scripts (see Sections 7.1.3 and 7.1.4). *Case-Based Reasoning* by Kolodner (1993) is an excellent introduction to the CBR technology. Other CBR-related work from Kolodner and her research group includes Kolodner (1987, 1991). Leake (1992, 1996) offers important comment on explanations in case-based systems. CBR software is now available in commercial software products that support the case-based technology.

Model-based reasoning had its origins in the explicit representation of medicine, logic circuits, and other mathematical domains, often used for teaching purposes (deKleer 1975, Weiss et al. 1977, Brown and Burton 1978, Brown and VanLehn 1980, Genesereth 1982, Brown et al. 1982). More modern research issues in MBR are presented in *Readings in Model-Based Diagnosis* (edited by Hamscher et al. 1992), *Diagnosis Based on Description of Structure and Function* (Davis et al. 1982), and diagnosis in the context of multiple faults (deKleer and Williams 1987, 1989). Skinner and Luger (1995) and other writers on agent architectures (Russell and Norvig 1995, 2003) describe hybrid expert systems, where the interactions of multiple approaches to problem solving can create a synergistic effect with the strengths of one system compensating for the weaknesses of others.

The planning section demonstrates some of the data structures and search techniques used for general-purpose planners. Further references include ABSTRIPS or ABstract specification for STRIPS generator relationships (Sacerdotti 1974), Warren's work (1976), and NOAH for nonlinear or hierarchical planning (Sacerdotti 1975, 1977). For more information on *teleo-reactive planning*, see Section 12.3.2 and Benson and Nilsson (1995).

Meta-planning is a technique for reasoning not just about the plan but also about the process of planning. This can be important in expert systems solutions. References include Meta-DENDRAL for DENDRAL solutions (Lindsay et al. 1980) and Teiresias for MYCIN solutions (Davis 1982). For plans that interact continuously with the world, that is, model a changing environment, see McDermott (1978).

Further research includes *opportunistic planning* using blackboards and planning based on an object-oriented specification (Smoliar 1985). There are several surveys of planning research in the *Handbook of Artificial Intelligence* (Barr and Feigenbaum 1989, Cohen and Feigenbaum 1982) and the *Encyclopedia of Artificial Intelligence* (Shapiro 1992). Nonlinearity issues and partial-order planning are presented in Russell and Norvig (1995). *Readings in Planning* (Allen et al. 1990) is relevant to this chapter.

Our description and analysis of the NASA model-based reasoning and planning algorithms was taken from Williams and Nayak (1996*a*, 1996*b*, 1997). We thank Williams and Nayak, as well as AAAI Press, for allowing us to cite their research.

8.6   Exercises

1. In Section 8.2 we introduced a set of rules for diagnosing automobile problems. Identify possible knowledge engineers, domain experts, and potential end users for such an application. Discuss the expectations, abilities, and needs of each of these groups.

2. Take Exercise 1 above. Create in English or pseudocode 15 *if... then...* rules (other than those prescribed in Section 8.2) to describe relations within this domain. Create a graph to represent the relationships among these 15 rules.

3. Consider the graph of Exercise 2 above. Do you recommend data-driven or goal-driven search? breadth-first or depth-first search? In what ways could heuristics assist the search? Justify your answers to these questions.

4. Pick another area of interest for designing an expert system. Answer Exercises 1–3 for this application.

5. Implement an expert system using a commercial shell program. These are widely available for personal computers as well as larger machines. We especially recommend CLIPS from NASA (Giarratano and Riley 1989) or JESS from Sandia National Laboratories.

6. Critique the shell you used for Exercise 5. What are its strengths and weaknesses? What would you do to improve it? Was it appropriate to your problem? What problems are best suited to that tool?

7. Create a model-based reasoning system for a simple electronic device. Combine several small devices to make a larger system. You can use *if... then...* rules to characterize the system functionality.

8. Read and comment on the paper *Diagnosis based on description of structure and function* (Davis et al., 1982).

9. Read one of the early papers using model-based reasoning to teach children arithmetic (Brown and Burton 1978) or electronic skills (Brown and VanLehn 1980). Comment on this approach.

10. Build a case-based reasoner for an application of your choice. One area might be for selecting computer science and engineering courses to complete an undergraduate major or a MS degree.

11. Use commercial software (check the WWW) for building the case-based reasoning system of Exercise 10. If no software is available, consider building such a system in PROLOG, LISP, or Java.

12. Read and comment on the survey paper *Improving Human Decision Making through Case-Based Decision Aiding* by Janet Kolodner (1991).

13. Create the remaining *frame axioms* necessary for the four operators pickup, putdown, stack, and unstack described in rules 4 through 7 of Section 8.4.

14. Use the operators and frame axioms of the previous question to generate the search space of Figure 8.19.

15. Show how the *add* and *delete* lists can be used to replace the frame axioms in the generation of STATE 2 from STATE 1 in Section 8.4.

16. Use *add* and *delete* lists to generate the search space of Figure 8.19.

17. Design an automated controller that could use *add* and *delete* lists to generate a graph search similar to that of Figure 8.19.

18. Show two more incompatible (precondition) subgoals in the blocks world operators of Figure 8.19.

19. Read the ABSTRIPS research (Sacerdotti 1974) and show how it handles the linearity (or incompatible subgoal) problem in planning.

20. In Section 8.4.3 we presented a planner created by Nilsson and his students at Stanford (Benson and Nilsson 1995). *Teleo-reactive* planning allows actions described as *durative*, i.e., that must continue to be true across time periods. Why might teleo-reactive planning be preferred over a STRIPS-like planner? Build a teleo-reactive planner in PROLOG, LISP, or Java.

21. Read Williams and Nayak (1996, 1996a) for a more complete discussion of their model-based planning system.

22. Expand the propositional calculus representation scheme introduced by Williams and Nayak (1996a, p. 973) for describing state transitions for their propulsion system.

REASONING IN UNCERTAIN SITUATIONS

All traditional logic habitually assumes that precise symbols are being employed. It is therefore not applicable to this terrestrial life but only to an imagined celestial existence.

—BERTRAND RUSSELL

It is the mark of an instructed mind to rest satisfied with that degree of precision which the nature of the subject admits, and not to seek exactness where only an approximation of the truth is possible.

—ARISTOTLE

So far as the laws of mathematics refer to reality they are not certain. And so far as they are certain they do not refer to reality.

—ALBERT EINSTEIN

9.0   Introduction

Through most of Parts I, II, and III, our inference procedures followed the model of reasoning used in the predicate calculus: from correct premises, sound inference rules produce new, guaranteed correct conclusions. As we saw in Chapters 5 and 8 however, there are many situations that will not fit this approach; that is, we must draw useful conclusions from poorly formed and uncertain evidence using unsound inference rules.

Drawing useful conclusions from incomplete and imprecise data with unsound reasoning is not an impossible task; we do it very successfully in almost every aspect of our daily life. We deliver correct medical diagnoses and recommend treatment from ambiguous symptoms; we analyze problems with our cars or stereos; we comprehend language statements that are often ambiguous or incomplete; we recognize friends from their voices or their gestures; and so on.

To demonstrate the problem of reasoning in ambiguous situations, consider Rule 2 from the automobile expert system presented in Section 8.2:

> if
> the engine does not turn over, and
> the lights do not come on
> then
> the problem is battery or cables.

On the surface, this rule looks like a normal predicate relation to be used in sound inferencing (modus ponens). It is not, however; it is heuristic in nature. It could be possible, though very unlikely, that the battery and cables are fine but that the car simply has a bad starter motor and burned-out headlights. Failure of the engine to turn over and the lights to come on does not necessarily imply that the battery and cables are bad. It is interesting that the *converse* of the rule is true:

> if
> the problem is battery or cables
> then
> the engine does not turn over, and
> the lights do not come on.

Barring the supernatural, with a dead battery, neither the lights nor the starter will work!

Our expert system offers an example of *abductive* reasoning. Formally, abduction states that from $P \rightarrow Q$ and Q it is possible to infer P. Abduction is an *unsound* rule of inference, meaning that the conclusion is not necessarily true for every interpretation in which the premises are true (Section 2.3).

Although abduction is unsound, it is often essential to solving problems. The "logically correct" version of the battery rule is not very useful in diagnosing car troubles since its premise, the bad battery, is our goal and its conclusions are the observable symptoms with which we must work. The rule can be used in an abductive fashion, however, as are rules in many diagnostic expert systems. Faults or diseases cause (imply) symptoms, not the other way around; but diagnosis must work from symptoms back to their causes.

In knowledge-based systems, we often attach a certainty factor to the rule to measure confidence in its conclusion. For example, the rule, $P \rightarrow Q$ (.9), expresses the belief "If you believe P to be true, then you believe Q will happen 90% of the time". Thus, heuristic rules can express an explicit policy for belief.

Another issue for expert system reasoning is how to draw useful results from data with missing, incomplete, or incorrect information. We may use certainty measures to reflect our belief in the quality of data, for example, asserting that the lights have full power (.2) can indicate that the headlights do come on, but are weak and barely visible. Beliefs and imperfect data can be propagated through rules to constrain conclusions.

In this chapter, we discuss several ways of managing abductive inference and uncertainty, especially as it is required for knowledge-intensive problem solving. In Section 9.1, we show how logic-based formalisms can be extended to address the abductive task, including the use of nonmonotonic systems supported by truth-maintenance algorithms. In Section 9.2, we consider several alternatives to logic, including the Stanford certainty factor algebra, "fuzzy" reasoning, and the Dempster–Shafer theory of evidence. These simple calculi are often utilized to address some of the complexity issues of using the full Bayesian approach for building expert systems.

In Section 9.3, we introduce stochastic approaches to uncertain reasoning. These techniques are founded on Bayes' theorem for reasoning about the frequency of events, based on prior information about these events. We conclude 9.3 with presentation of graphical models, including Bayesian belief networks and observable and hidden Markov models.

9.1 Logic-Based Abductive Inference

We first present logic-based approaches to abduction. With logic, pieces of knowledge are explicitly used in reasoning, and, as we saw in Chapter 8, can be part of the explanations of derived conclusions. But traditional logic also has its limitations, especially in areas where information is missing, changing, or uncertain; in these situations traditional inference procedures may not be usable. In Section 9.1 we present several extensions to traditional logic that allow it to support abductive inference.

In Section 9.1.1, we extend logic to let it describe a world of changing information and beliefs. Traditional mathematical logic is *monotonic*: it begins with a set of axioms, assumed to be true, and infers their consequences. If we add new information to this system, it may cause the set of true statements to increase. Adding knowledge will never make the set of true statements decrease. This monotonic property leads to problems when we attempt to model reasoning based on beliefs and assumptions. In reasoning with uncertainty, humans draw conclusions based on their current set of beliefs; however, unlike mathematical axioms, these beliefs, along with their consequences, may change over time as more information becomes available.

Nonmonotonic reasoning addresses the problem of changing beliefs. A nonmonotonic reasoning system handles uncertainty by making the most reasonable assumptions in light of uncertain information. It then proceeds with its reasoning as if these assumptions were true. At a later time a belief may change, necessitating a re-examination of any conclusions derived from that belief. Truth maintenance algorithms, Section 9.1.2, may then be employed to keep the knowledge base consistent. Other abductive extensions to logic include "minimum models", Section 9.1.3, and the "set cover" approach, Section 9.1.4.

9.1.1 Logics for Nonmonotonic Reasoning

Nonmonotonicity is an important feature of human problem solving and common sense reasoning. In most planning, for example when we drive to work, we make numerous assumptions about the roads and traffic. If we find that one of these assumptions is violated, perhaps by construction or an accident on our usual route, we change our plans and find an alternative route.

Conventional reasoning using predicate logic is based on three important assumptions. First, the predicate descriptions must be sufficient with respect to our application domain. That is, all the information necessary to solve the problem must be represented. Second, the information base must be consistent; that is, pieces of knowledge cannot contradict each other. Finally, through the use of inference rules, the known information grows monotonically. If any of these three assumptions is not satisfied, the conventional logic-based approach will not work.

Nonmonotonic systems address each of these three issues. First, reasoning systems are often faced with a lack of knowledge about a domain. There is an important issue here: suppose we have no knowledge about the predicate p; does lack of knowledge mean that *we are not sure whether p is true* or *we are sure that not p is true*? This question can be answered in a number of ways. PROLOG, see Chapter 15, uses *the closed world assumption* to determine as false anything that its reasoning system cannot prove to be true. As humans, we often take the alternative approach of assuming something to be true unless it can be explicitly shown to be false.

Another approach to the lack of knowledge problem is to make explicit assumptions of truth. In human reasoning, we assume the innocence of people not directly connected to a crime. We would probably even go further and assume the innocence of those that could not benefit from the crime. The result of these assumptions is to effectively fill in missing details of knowledge and extend our reasoning to reach new conclusions based on these assumptions. We discuss the closed world assumption and its alternatives in Section 9.1.3.

Humans reason based on *how the world usually works*. Most birds fly. Parents usually love and support their children. We make inferences based on the consistency of reasoning with our assumptions about the world. In this section we discuss the addition of modal operators, such as *is consistent with* and *unless*, to perform assumption-based reasoning.

The second assumption required of traditional logic-based systems is that the knowledge supporting reasoning must be consistent. For human reasoners this would be a very limiting assumption. In diagnosing a problem we often entertain multiple possible explanations for a situation, assuming something is true until an alternative assumption proves to be more fruitful. In analysis of an airline accident, for example, a crash expert will consider a number of alternative causes, only eliminating (explaining away) some as new information is discovered. We humans use knowledge of the world *as it usually is* to try to direct reasoning through alternative scenarios. We would like logic systems able to entertain alternative hypotheses.

Finally, if we wish to use logic we must address the problem of how a knowledge base is updated. There are two issues here: first, how can we possibly add knowledge that is based on assumption only, and secondly, what can we do when one of our assumptions is later shown to be incorrect. To address the first issue, we can allow the addition of new knowledge based on assumptions. This new knowledge is assumed to be correct and so it may, in turn, be used to infer more new knowledge. The cost of this practice is that we must keep track of all reasoning and proofs that are based on assumptions: we must be prepared to reconsider any knowledge based on these assumptions.

Nonmonotonic reasoning, because conclusions must sometimes be reconsidered, is called *defeasible*; that is, new information may sometimes invalidate previous results. Representations and search procedures that keep track of the reasoning steps of a logic system are called *truth maintenance systems* or TMS. In defeasible reasoning, the TMS preserves the consistency of the knowledge base, keeping track of conclusions that might later need to be questioned. We consider several approaches to truth maintenance in Section 9.1.2. We first consider operators that can make traditional logic-based reasoning systems defeasible.

In implementing nonmonotonic reasoning, we may extend our logic with the operator unless. unless supports inferences based on the belief that its argument is not true. Suppose we have the following set of predicate logic sentences:

p(X) unless q(X) → r(X)
p(Z)
r(W) → s(W)

The first rule means that we may infer r(X) if p(X) is true and we do not believe q(X) to be true. When these conditions are met, we infer r(X) and, using r(X), can then infer s(X). Subsequently, if we change our belief, or find that q(X) is true, r(X) and also s(X) must be retracted. Note that unless deals with matters of belief rather than truth. Consequently, changing the value of its argument from "either unknown or believed false" to "believed or known to be true" can cause us to retract all inferences that depend upon these beliefs. By extending our logic to reason with beliefs that may later be retracted, we introduce nonmonotonicity into the system.

The reasoning scheme just described can also be used to encode default rules (Reiter 1980). If we replace p(X) unless q(X) → r(X) with p(X) unless ab p(X) → r(X), where ab p(X) represents abnormal p(X), we state that unless we have an abnormal instance of p, such as a bird with a broken wing, we can make the inference that if X is a bird then X can fly.

A second modal operator for extending logic systems is suggested by McDermott and Doyle (1980). They augment first-order predicate logic with the modal operator M, which placed before a predicate is read as *is consistent with*. For example:

∀ X good_student(X) ∧ M study_hard(X) → graduates(X)

This clause can be read: For all X where X is a good student, and if the fact that X studies hard is consistent with everything else we know, then X will graduate. Of course, the difficult part here is defining precisely what *is consistent with everything else we know* might in fact mean.

We first note that *is consistent with everything else we know* may not be decidable. The reason is that a modal operator forms a superset of an already undecidable system, see Section 2.2.2, and will thus be undecidable. There are two ways to address undecidability. First, we can use a *negation as failure* proof to demonstrate *is consistent with*. In our example, we would attempt the proof of not(study_hard(X)) and if we couldn't prove that X doesn't study, then we assume that X does study. We often use this approach in a

PROLOG-like approximation of predicate logic. Unfortunately, negation as failure may unduly restrict our domain of interpretation.

A second approach to the *is consistent with* problem is to make a heuristic-based and limited (time or memory limited) search for the truth of the predicate, in our example study_hard(X), and then, if there is no contrary evidence, assume it to be true with the understanding that we may have to later retract the graduates conclusion and all further conclusions based on it.

We can also produce potentially contradictory results using the *is consistent with* operator. Suppose a person, Peter, is a good student but also seriously enjoys parties. We might then have the following set of predicates that describe the situation:

$\forall$ X good_student(X) $\land$ M study_hard(X) $\rightarrow$ graduates(X)
$\forall$ Y party_person(Y) $\land$ M not(study_hard(Y)) $\rightarrow$ not(graduates(Y))
good_student(peter)
party_person(peter)

With this set of clauses, where we have no further information about Peter's study habits, whether he studies hard or not, we can infer both that Peter will and will not graduate!

One reasoning method that guards against such contradictory results is to keep track of the variable bindings used with the modal operator *is consistent with*. Thus, once Peter was bound to either the study_hard or the not(study_hard) predicate, the system would prevent the binding of Peter to the other predicate. Other nonmonotonic logic systems (McDermott and Doyle 1980) are even more conservative and prevent any conclusions from such potentially contradictory clause sets. We can create another anomaly:

$\forall$ Y very_smart(Y) $\land$ M not(study_hard(Y)) $\rightarrow$ not(study_hard(Y))
$\forall$ X not(very_smart(X)) $\land$ M not(study_hard(X)) $\rightarrow$ not(study_hard(X))

From these clauses we can infer a new clause:

$\forall$ Z M not(study_hard(Z)) $\rightarrow$ not(study_hard(Z))

Further developments of the semantics of the *is consistent with* operator address such anomalous reasoning. One further extension is *autoepistemic logic* (Moore 1985).

Another nonmonotonic logic system is *default logic*, created by Reiter (1980). Default logic employs a new set of inference rules of the form:

A(Z) $\land$: B(Z) $\rightarrow$ C(Z)

which is read: If A(Z) is provable *and it is consistent with what we know to assume* B(Z) then we can conclude C(Z).

To this point default logic sounds much like McDermott and Doyle's nonmonotonic logic just described. An important difference between the two is the method in which reasoning is performed. In default logic, these special inference rules are used to infer sets of plausible extensions of the original axiom/theorem set. Each extension is created by using one of the default logic inferencing rules on the knowledge represented by the original axiom/theorem set. Thus, it would be natural to have a number of plausible extensions to an original knowledge base. This can be seen with the graduates clauses:

$\forall$ X good_student(X) $\wedge$: study_hard(X) $\rightarrow$ graduates(X)
$\forall$ Y party(Y) $\wedge$: not(study_hard(Y)) $\rightarrow$ not(graduates(Y))

Each clause could be used to create a unique plausible extension based on the original set of knowledge.

Default logic then allows any theorem inferred in a plausible extension to be admitted as an axiom for further reasoning. There must be some decision-making guide to finally determine which extension is to be used for further problem solving. Default logic says nothing about how to choose among possible plausible extensions of knowledge base. Reiter (1978), Reiter and Criscuolo (1981), and Touretzky (1986) develop these issues.

Finally, there is also a nonmonotonic reasoning situation created by inheritance search over representations where objects can inherit from more than one parent. Peter, the party-loving good student mentioned earlier, could inherit one set of properties from being a good student, i.e., that he would most likely graduate. Peter could inherit other, and in this case partially conflicting, properties from being a party person, that is, that he would not graduate.

An important problem facing nonmonotonic reasoning systems is the task of efficiently revising a set of conclusions in the light of changing beliefs. If, for example, we use the predicate r to infer s, then removing r removes also the support for s, as well as every other conclusion that used s. Unless there is an independent set of inferences supporting s, it must be retracted. Implementing this retraction process requires, in the worst case, that we recompute all conclusions each time a belief changes. *Truth maintenance systems*, presented next, offer mechanisms for maintaining the consistency of knowledge bases.

9.1.2 Truth Maintenance Systems

A *truth maintenance system* (TMS) can be employed to protect the logical integrity of the conclusions of an inferencing system. As pointed out in the previous section, it is necessary to recompute support for items in a knowledge base whenever beliefs expressed by the clauses of the knowledge base are revised. Reason maintenance systems address this issue by storing justifications for each inference and then reconsidering support for conclusions in the light of new beliefs.

One way of viewing this problem is to review the backtrack algorithm first presented in Section 3.2.2. Backtracking is a systematic method for exploring all the alternatives for decision points in search-based problem solving. An important shortcoming of the backtrack algorithm, however, is the way it systematically (and blindly) backs out of dead end states of the space and looks for alternatives from its most recent choices. This approach is sometimes called *chronological backtracking*. We grant that chronological backtracking will systematically check all alternatives in the space; however, the way it proceeds is time-consuming, inefficient, and in a very large space, useless.

What we really want in logic-based search is the ability to backtrack directly to the point in the space where the problem occurs, and to make adjustments to the solution at that state. This approach is called *dependency-directed backtracking*. Consider an example from nonmonotonic reasoning. We need to find out about p, which we cannot directly infer. There is, however, a plausible assumption q, which, if true, will support p. So we assume q and derive p. Our reasoning continues and based on p we conclude r and s. We continue on in our reasoning and conclude without the support of p, r, or s the results t and u. Finally, we prove that our earlier assumption of q is false. What are we to do?

Chronological backtracking would revisit our reasoning steps in the reverse order in which they were made. Dependency-directed backtracking would go immediately back to the source of the contradictory information, namely the first assumption of q. Then it would go forward retracting p, r, and s. We may, at this time, check to see if r and s can be derived independently of p and q. Just because they were originally produced with an incorrect assumption does not mean that they are not otherwise supported. Finally, because t and u were derived without p, r, or s, we would not need to reconsider them.

In order to use dependency-directed backtracking in a reasoning system, we must:

1. Associate with the production of each conclusion its justification. This justification indicates the derivation process for that conclusion. The justification must contain all the facts, rules, and assumptions used to produce the conclusion.

2. Provide a mechanism that, when given a contradiction along with its justification, finds the set of false assumptions within that justification that led to the contradiction.

3. Retract the false assumption(s).

4. Create a mechanism that follows up the retracted assumption(s) and retracts any conclusion that uses within its justifications the retracted false assumption.

Of course, all retracted conclusions are not necessarily false, so they must be rechecked to see if they can be justified independent of the retracted clauses. We next present two methods for building dependency directed backtracking systems.

Jon Doyle (1979) created one of the earliest truth maintenance systems, called a *justification-based truth maintenance system* or JTMS. Doyle was the first researcher to explicitly separate the truth maintenance system, a network of propositions and their justifications, from the reasoning system operating in a domain. The result of this split is that the JTMS communicates with the problem solver, perhaps an automated theorem prover, receiving information about new propositions and justifications and in turn supplying the problem solver with information about which propositions should be believed based on the current existing justifications.

There are three main operations that are performed by the JTMS. First, the JTMS inspects the network of justifications. This inspection can be triggered by queries from the problem solver such as: Should I believe in proposition p? Why should I believe proposition p? What assumptions underlie proposition p?

The second operation of JTMS is to modify the dependency network, where modifications are driven by information supplied by the problem solver. Modifications include

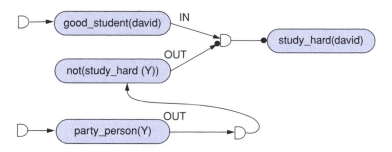

Figure 9.1 A justification network to believe that David studies hard.

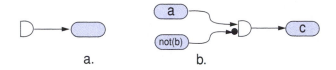

Figure 9.2 9.2(a) is a premise justification, and 9.2(b)
the ANDing of two beliefs, a and not b, to
support c (Goodwin 1982).

adding new propositions, adding or removing premises, adding contradictions, and justifying the belief in a proposition. The final operation of the JTMS is to update the network. This operation is executed whenever a change is made in the dependency network. The update operation recomputes the labels of all propositions in a manner that is consistent with existing justifications.

To demonstrate the JTMS we construct a simple dependency network. Consider the modal operator M presented in Section 9.1.1, which placed before a predicate is read as *is consistent with*. For example:

$\forall$ X good_student(X) $\wedge$ M study_hard(X) $\rightarrow$ study_hard(X)
$\forall$ Y party_person(Y) $\rightarrow$ not (study_hard(Y))
good_student(david)

We now make this set of propositions into a justification network.

In a JTMS, each predicate representing a belief is associated with two other sets of beliefs. The first set, labeled IN in Figure 9.1, is the set of propositions that should be believed for the proposition to hold. The second, labeled OUT, are propositions that should not be believed for the proposition to hold. Figure 9.1 represents the justification that supports study_hard(david) derived from the predicates just listed. The notations of Figure 9.1 are adapted from Goodwin (1982) and explained in Figure 9.2. The premises of justifications are labeled as in Figure 9.2(a) and the combinations of propositions that support a conclusion are labeled as in Figure 9.2(b).

With the information of the network of Figure 9.1, the problem solver can reason that study_hard(david) is supported, because the premise good_student(david) is considered true and it is consistent with the fact that good students study hard. There is also no evidence or other indication in this example that David does not study hard.

Suppose we add the premise party_person(david). This addition enables the derivation not(study_hard(david)), and the belief study_hard(david) is no longer supported. The justifications for this situation are as in Figure 9.3. Note the relabeling of IN and OUT.

As Figures 9.1 and 9.3 demonstrate, the JTMS does not directly represent the predicate relationships as expressed in the original set of propositions. Rather the JTMS is a simple network that only considers the relations between atomic propositions and their negation and organizes these into support relationships for beliefs. The full set of predicate connectives and inferencing schemes ($\forall X$, $\land$, $\lor$, $\rightarrow$, etc.) are used within the problem solver itself. The systems of McAllester (1978) and Martins and Shapiro (1988) merged the TMS and the problem solver into a single representation.

A JTMS is only concerned with the dependencies among beliefs and has no concern with the contents of these beliefs. Therefore, we can replace the beliefs by identifiers, often of the form n_1, n_2, ..., which are associated with objects in the network called nodes. Then the algebra of INs and OUTs that we saw implemented in the study_hard example allows the JTMS to reason about the support for beliefs.

To summarize, a JTMS works with sets of nodes and justifications. Nodes stand for beliefs, and justifications support belief in nodes. Associated with nodes are the labels IN and OUT, which indicate the belief status of the associated node. We can reason about the support for any node by relating it to the INs and OUTs of the other nodes that make up its justification(s). The primary operation of the JTMS algebra is to accomplish the inspection, modification, and updating operators noted above. Finally, since justification checking is enforced by backing over the links of the justification network itself, we have an example of dependency-based backtracking. For further information on this approach to JTMS see Doyle (1983) or Reinfrank (1989).

A second type of truth maintenance system is the *assumption-based truth maintenance system* (ATMS). The term *assumption-based* was first introduced by deKleer (1984), although similar ideas may be found in Martins and Shapiro (1983). In these systems, the labels for nodes in the network are no longer IN and OUT but rather the sets of premises (assumptions) underlying their derivation. deKleer also makes a distinction between premise nodes that hold universally and nodes that can be assumptions made by the problem solver and that may later be retracted.

An advantage of ATMS over JTMS stems from the additional flexibility the ATMS provides in dealing with multiple possible states of belief. By labeling beliefs with the sets of premises under which they hold, there is no longer a single state of belief (in JTMS all the nodes labeled IN), but rather a number of possible states, the set of all subsets of the supporting premises. The creation of different belief sets, or possible worlds, allows a comparison of results from different choices of premises, the existence of different solutions for the problem, and the detection of and recovery from contradictions. The disadvantages of ATMS include the inability to represent premise sets that are themselves nonmonotonic and the control over the problem solver. However, see Dressler (1988) and Forbus and deKleer (1988) for alternatives.

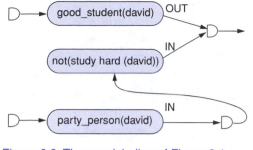

Figure 9.3 The new labeling of Figure 9.1 associated with the new premise party_person(david).

The communication between the ATMS and the problem solver is similar to that between JTMS and its problem solver with operators for *inspection, modification,* and *updating*. The only difference is that with the ATMS there is no longer a single state of belief but rather subsets of potential supporting premises. The goal of computation within the ATMS is to find minimal sets of premises sufficient for the support of each node. This computation is done by propagating and combining labels, beginning with the labels for the premises.

We next present a detailed example adapted from Martins (1991). Suppose we have the ATMS network of Figure 9.4. In this network, n_1, n_2, n_4, and n_5 are premises and assumed true. The dependency network also reflects the relations that from premise n_1 and n_2 we support n_3, with n_3 we support n_7, with n_4 we support n_7, with n_4 and n_5 we support n_6, and finally, with n_6 we support n_7.

Figure 9.5 presents the subset/superset lattice for the premise dependencies found in Figure 9.4. This lattice of subsets of premises offers a useful way to visualize the space of combinations of premises. Thus, if some premise is found to be suspect, the ATMS will be able to determine how that premise relates to other premise support subsets. For example, node n_3 in Figure 9.4 will be supported by all sets of premises that are above $\{n_1, n_2\}$ in the lattice of Figure 9.5.

The ATMS reasoner removes contradictions by removing from the nodes those sets of premises that are discovered to be inconsistent. Suppose, for example, we revise the support for the reasoning reflected by Figure 9.4 to make n_3 a contradiction node. Since the label for n_3 is $\{n_1, n_2\}$, this set of premises is determined to be inconsistent. When this inconsistency is discovered, all the sets of premises that are in the superset relation to $\{n_1, n_2\}$ in Figure 9.5 are marked as inconsistent and removed from the dependency network. In this situation, one of the possible labellings supporting n_7 will have to be removed. A full description of the contradiction-removal algorithm may be obtained from deKleer (1986).

There are several other important contributions to TMS reasoning. *Logic-based TMS* is based on the work of McAllester (1978). In LTMS, relationships between propositions are

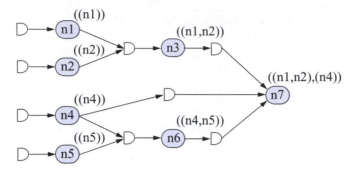

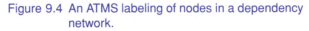

Figure 9.4 An ATMS labeling of nodes in a dependency network.

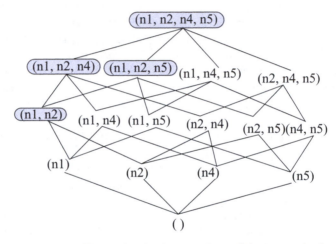

Figure 9.5 The lattice for the premises of the network of Figure 9.4. Circled sets indicate the hierarchy of inconsistencies, after Martins (1991).

represented by clauses which can be used to deduce the truth values of any of the propositions they describe. Another approach, the *multiple belief reasoner* (MBR) is similar to the ATMS reasoner except that the problem solver and the truth maintenance system are merged into a single system. MBR is based on a logic language called SWM* which describes knowledge states. Each knowledge state is composed of a pair of descriptors, the first reflecting a knowledge base and the second a set of sets of known inconsistent premises within the knowledge base. Algorithms for checking inconsistencies during reasoning may be found in Martins (1991). Further discussion on truth maintenance systems may be found in *The Encyclopedia of Artificial Intelligence* (Shapiro 1992).

9.1.3　Logics Based on Minimum Models

In the previous sections, we extended logic by several different modal operators that were specifically designed to reason about the world *as it usually is*, relaxing the requirement that our knowledge of the world be somehow complete. These operators were born of the necessity of creating a more flexible and revisable view of the world. In this section we present logics designed specifically for two situations: first, to reason where a set of assertions specifies only those things that are true and second, to reason where, because of the nature of a problem-solving task, sets of conjectures are usually true. In the first situation we use the *closed world assumption* and in the second *circumscription*. Both of these approaches to logic are often referred to as *reasoning over minimal models*.

We saw in Section 2.3 that a *model* is an interpretation that satisfies S, a set of predicate expressions, for all variable assignments. There are a number of ways of defining what is meant by a *minimum model*. We define a minimum model as *a model such that there are no smaller models that can satisfy the set of expressions S for all variable assignments*.

The idea that makes minimum models important for reasoning is this: there are a (potentially) infinite number of predicates that can be used to describe situations in the world. Consider, for example, the limitless predicates that can be used to describe the situation for the missionaries and cannibals problem (Section 15.10, Exercise 7): the boat is not slowly sinking, the river banks are close enough that rowing will get the boat across, the wind and current are not relevant factors, and so on. When we describe a problem we are usually quite parsimonious in our descriptions. We create only those predicates that are both relevant and needed to solve the problem.

The *closed world assumption* is based on this minimum model of the world. Exactly those predicates that are necessary for a solution are created. The closed world assumption effects the semantics of negation in reasoning. For example, if we wanted to determine whether a student is an enrolled member of a class, we could go to the enrolment database, and if the student is not explicitly listed in that database (the minimal model), he or she would not be enrolled. Similarly, if we wanted to know if two cities were directly connected by a plane flight, we would go to the listing of all airline connections. We would infer, if the direct flight is not listed there (the minimal model), that it does not exist.

The closed world assumption is a statement that if our computational system cannot conclude that p(X) is true, then not(p(X)) must be true. As we will see in Section 13.4, the closed world assumption supports PROLOG inferencing. In Section 13.4 we see the three assumptions (axioms) implicit in the use of minimal models. These axioms are the *unique name*, i.e., that all atoms with distinct names are distinct; *the closed world*, i.e., the only instances of a relation are those implied by the clauses present; and *domain closure*. i.e., the atoms of the domain are exactly those of the model. When these three are satisfied, a minimum model becomes a full logic-based specification. If the axioms are not satisfied, some form of a truth maintenance algorithm is required.

If the closed world requires that all the predicates that make up a model be stated, *circumscription* (McCarthy 1980, Lifschitz 1984, McCarthy 1986) requires that *only* those predicates relevant to the problem solving are stated. In circumscription, axioms are added to a system that forces a minimal interpretation on the predicates of the knowledge base. These *meta-predicates* (predicates about the problem statement's predicates) describe the manner in which particular predicates are to be interpreted. That is, they delimit, or circumscribe, the possible interpretations of predicates.

McCarthy (1980) introduced the idea of circumscription with a thought experiment on the missionaries and cannibals problem. The problem statement asks the solver to devise a series of moves in which six characters, under a set of constraints, can use a boat to cross a river. McCarthy brings up a large number of absurd situations that, quite legitimately, can be asked about the problem statement. A number of these, such as a slowly sinking boat or a wind factor, were presented earlier in this section. Although humans regard these situations as absurd, the reasoning we use to do so is not obvious. The circumscription axioms that McCarthy would add to the problem specification, would precisely delimit the predicates that describe the problem.

As another example of circumscription, consider a predicate expression from an object-oriented common sense reasoning specification, Section 9.5:

$$\forall \, X \; bird(X) \wedge not \, (abnormal(X)) \rightarrow flies(X)$$

This expression might occur in reasoning where one of the properties of *bird* is *flies*. But what could possibly limit the definition of the predicate *abnormal*? That the bird is not a penguin, that it does not have a broken wing, that it is not dead? The specification of the predicate *abnormal* is potentially undecidable.

Circumscription uses an axiom schema, or set of meta rules, within first-order predicate calculus to generate predicates for the problem domain. The schema rules cause certain formulae to have the smallest possible extensions. For example, if B is a belief system including world knowledge K and domain knowledge $A(p)$ about a predicate p, then we may consider p to be minimized, in that as few atoms a_i as possible satisfy $p(a_i)$ as is consistent with $A(p)$ and K. The world knowledge K together with $A(p)$ and the circumscription schema are used to derive conclusions in standard first-order predicate calculus. These conclusions are then added to B, the belief system.

Suppose in the blocks world, Section 8.4, we have the expression:

$$isblock(A) \wedge isblock(B) \wedge isblock(C)$$

asserting that A, B, and C are blocks. Circumscribing the predicate isblock gives:

$$\forall X \, (isblock(X) \leftarrow ((X = A) \vee (X = B) \vee (X = C)))$$

This expression asserts that the only blocks are A, B, and C, i.e., just those objects that the isblock predicate requires to be blocks. In a similar fashion the predicate:

$$isblock(A) \vee isblock(B)$$

can be circumscribed to:

$$\forall X \, (isblock(X) \leftarrow ((X = A) \vee (X = B)))$$

For full details, including the schema axioms used to derive these results, see McCarthy (1980, Section 4).

Circumscription, when used with operators such as abnormal, is much like the closed world assumption in that it produces exactly those variable bindings that abnormal can support. The circumscription algebra, however, allows us to extend this reasoning across predicate representations in that, as we just noted, if we have the predicate p(X) ∨ q(X), we may circumscribe either predicate p or q or both. Thus, unlike the closed world assumption, circumscription allows us to describe the instantiations possible across sets of predicate descriptions.

Further research in circumscriptive logics may be found in Genesereth and Nilsson (1987). Lifschitz (1986) has made an important contribution by proposing a point-wise circumscription in which the minimum model can be carried out for particular predicates and their possible instantiations, rather than for the full domain. Another important contribution is that of Perlis (1988) where reasoning can be about a particular agent's lack of knowledge. For further discussion see also Shapiro (1992).

9.1.4   Set Cover and Logic-Based Abduction (Stern 1996)

As noted in the introduction of this chapter, in abductive reasoning, we have rules of the form p → q, along with a reasonable belief in q. We wish then to make a case for the truth of predicate p. Abductive reasoning is not sound, but what is often called *reasoning to the best explanation* for the presence of the data q. In this section, we look more closely at the generation of explanations in domains of abductive inference.

In addition to the accounts of abductive reasoning already presented, AI researchers have also used set cover and logic supported analyses. The *set cover* approach to abduction attempts to explain the act of adopting a revocable belief in some explanatory hypo-thesis on the grounds that it explains an otherwise unexplainable set of facts. The *logic-based* approach to abduction describes inference rules for abduction along with a definition of their legitimate form(s) for use.

The *set cover* approach, defines an abductive explanation as a covering of predicates describing observations by predicates describing hypotheses. Reggia et al. (1983) describes a cover based on a binary causal relation R where R is a subset of {Hypotheses X Observations}. Thus, an abductive explanation of a set of observations S2 is another set of hypotheses S1 sufficient to cause S2. An optimal explanation according to the set cover approach, is the minimal set cover of S2. The weakness of this approach is that it reduces explanation to a simple list of causal hypotheses (from S1). In situations where there are interrelated or interacting causes or where an understanding of the structure or sequencing of causal interactions is required, the set cover model is inadequate.

Logic-based approaches to abduction, on the other hand, rest on a more sophisticated notion of explanation. Levesque (1989) defines an abductive explanation of some previously unexplained set of observations O as a minimal set of hypotheses H consistent with an agent's background knowledge K. The hypotheses H together with the background knowledge K must entail O. More formally:

abduce(K, O) = H, if and only if

1. K does not entail O
2. H ∪ K entails O
3. H ∪ K is consistent, and
4. No subset of H has properties 1, 2, and 3.

Note that in general many sets of hypotheses may exist; that is, there may be many potential abductive sets of explanations for a given set of observations O.

The logic-based definition of abductive explanation suggests a corresponding mechanism for explanation discovery in the context of a knowledge-based system. If the explanatory hypotheses must entail the observations O, then the way to construct a complete explanation is to reason backwards from O. As we saw in Sections 3.3 and 8.2, we may start from the conjunctive components of O and reason back from consequents to their antecedents.

This backchaining approach also seems natural because the conditionals which support the backchaining can readily be thought of as causal laws, thus capturing the pivotal role which causal knowledge plays in the construction of explanations. The model is also convenient because it fits nicely with something of which the AI community already has experience: backchaining and computational models for deduction.

There are also clever ways of finding the complete set of abductive explanations. Assumption-based truth-maintenance systems, ATMS (deKleer 1986, Section 9.2.3), contain an algorithm for computing minimal support sets, the set of (non-axiom) propositions that logically entail a given proposition in a theory. To find all possible abductive explanations for a set of observations, we merely take the Cartesian product over the support sets.

As simple, precise, and convenient as the logic-based account of abduction is, there are two related shortcomings: high computational complexity and semantic weakness. Selman and Levesque (1990) found the complexity of abduction tasks similar to that involved in computing support sets for an ATMS. The standard proof that the ATMS problem is NP-hard depends on the existence of problem instances with an exponential number of solutions. Selman and Levesque avoid the number of potential solutions complexity issue by asking whether finding a smaller set of solutions is also NP-hard. Given a Horn clause knowledge base, see Section 13.2, Selman and Levesque produce an algorithm that finds a single explanation in order $O(k*n)$ where k indicates the number of propositional variables and n the number of occurrences of literals. However, when restrictions are placed on the kinds of explanations sought, the problem again becomes NP-hard, even for Horn clauses.

One interesting result from the Selman and Levesque (1990) analysis is the fact that adding certain kinds of goals or restrictions to the abduction task actually makes computation significantly harder. From the naive viewpoint of the human problem solver, this added complexity is surprising: the human assumes that the addition of further constraints to the search for relevant explanations makes the task easier. The reason the abduction task is harder in the logic-based model is that it only contributes additional clauses to the problem, not additional structure useful for deriving a solution.

Explanation discovery in the logic-based model is characterized as the task of finding a set of hypotheses with certain logical properties. These properties, including consistency with the background knowledge and entailment of what is to be explained, are meant to capture the *necessary* conditions of explanations: the minimal conditions which a set of explanatory hypotheses must satisfy in order to count as an abductive explanation. Proponents of this approach believe that by adding additional constraints, the approach can be extended to provide a characterization of good or reasonable explanations.

One simple strategy for producing quality explanations is to define a set of fact clauses that are abducible, that is, from which candidate hypotheses must be chosen. This clause set allows search to be restricted in advance to those factors that can potentially play a causal role in the chosen domain. Another strategy is to add selection criteria for evaluating and choosing between explanations. Various selection criteria have been proposed, including *set minimality*, which prefers one hypothesis set over another, where both are consistent and entail what is to be explained, if the first is contained in the second. A *simplicity* criterion gives preference to parsimonious hypothesis sets, those containing fewer unverified assumptions (Levesque 1989).

Both minimality and simplicity can be seen as applications of Occam's razor. Unfortunately, set minimality is of limited power as a search pruning tool; it only eliminates final explanations which are supersets of existing explanations. Simplicity alone is also of questionable validity as a search selection criterion. It is not difficult to construct examples in which an explanation requiring a larger hypothesis set is preferable to some simpler but shallower set of hypotheses. Indeed, complex causal mechanisms will usually require larger hypothesis sets; however, the abduction of such causal mechanisms may well be justified, particularly when the presence of certain key elements of that mechanism has already been verified by observation.

Two other mechanisms for explanation selection are also interesting because they take into account both properties of the hypothesis set as well as properties of the proof procedure. First, *cost-based abduction* places a cost on potential hypotheses as well as a cost on rules. The total cost of the explanation is computed on the basis of the total cost of the hypotheses plus the cost of the rules used to abduce the hypotheses. Competing hypothesis sets are then compared according to cost. One natural semantic that can be attached to this scheme is the probabilistic one (Charniak and Shimony 1990, Section 14.4). Higher costs for hypotheses represent less likely events; higher costs for rules represent less probable causal mechanisms. Cost-based metrics can be combined with least-cost search algorithms, such as best-first search, see Chapter 4, considerably reducing the computational complexity of the task.

A second mechanism, *coherence-based selection*, is particularly appealing when what is to be explained is not a simple proposition but rather a set of propositions. Ng and Mooney (1990) have argued that a coherence metric is superior to a simplicity metric for choosing explanations in the analysis of natural language text. They define coherence as a property of a proof graph where explanations with more connections between any pair of observations and fewer disjoint partitions are more coherent. The coherence criterion is based on the heuristic assumption that what we are asked to explain is a single event or action with multiple aspects. The justification for a coherence metric in natural language understanding is based on Gricean felicity conditions, that is the speaker's obligation to be coherent and pertinent (Grice 1975). It is not difficult to extend their argument to a variety of other situations. For example in diagnosis, the observations which comprise the initial set of things to be explained are brought together because they are believed to be related to the same underlying fault or failure mechanism.

In Section 9.1 we considered extensions to traditional logic that supported reasoning with uncertain or missing data. We next describe non-logic alternatives for reasoning in situations of uncertainty, including the Stanford certainty factor algebra, reasoning with fuzzy sets, and the Dempster-Shafer theory of evidence.

9.2 Abduction: Alternatives to Logic

The logic-based approaches of Section 9.1 are cumbersome and computationally intractable for many applications, especially expert systems. Alternatively, several early expert system projects, e.g., PROSPECTOR, attempted to adapt Bayesian techniques, Section 9.3, for abductive inference. The independence assumptions, continuous updates of statistical data, and the calculations required to support stochastic inference limits this approach. An alternative to these two approaches was used at Stanford for the development of early expert systems, including MYCIN (Buchanan and Shortliffe 1984).

When reasoning with heuristic knowledge, human experts are able to give adequate and useful estimates of the confidences in conclusions. Humans weight conclusions with terms like *highly probable*, *unlikely*, *almost certainly*, or *possible*. These weights are clearly not based in careful analysis of probabilities. Instead, they are themselves heuristics derived from experience in reasoning about the problem domain. In Section 9.2 we introduce three methodologies for abductive inference: Stanford certainty theory, fuzzy reasoning, and the Dempster–Shafer theory of evidence. In Section 9.3 we present stochastic approaches to uncertainty.

9.2.1 The Stanford Certainty Factor Algebra

Stanford certainty theory is based on a number of observations. The first is that in traditional probability theory, the sum of confidence for a relationship and confidence against the same relationship must add to one. However, it is often the case that a human expert might have confidence 0.7 (say) that some relationship is true and have no feeling at all of it being not true. A further assumption that underpins certainty theory is that the knowledge content of the rules is much more important than the algebra for computing the confidences. Confidence measures correspond to the informal evaluations that human experts attach to their conclusions, such as "it is probably true", "it is almost certainly true", or "it is highly unlikely".

The Stanford certainty theory makes some simple assumptions for creating confidence measures and has some equally simple rules for combining these confidences as the program moves toward its conclusion. The first assumption is to split "confidence for" from "confidence against" a relationship:

Call MB(H | E) the measure of belief of a hypothesis H given evidence E.

Call MD(H | E) the measure of disbelief of a hypothesis H given evidence E.

Now either:

$1 > MB(H | E) > 0$ while $MD(H | E) = 0$, or

$1 > MD(H | E) > 0$ while $MB(H | E) = 0$.

These two measures constrain each other in that a given piece of evidence is either for or against a particular hypothesis, an important difference between certainty theory and probability theory. Once the link between measures of belief and disbelief has been established, they may be tied together again, by:

$CF(H | E) = MB(H | E) - MD(H | E)$.

As the certainty factor (CF) approaches 1, the evidence is stronger for a hypothesis; as CF approaches -1, the confidence against the hypothesis gets stronger; and a CF around 0 indicates that either little evidence exists for or against the hypothesis or that the evidence for and against the hypothesis is balanced.

When experts put together a rule base, they must agree on a CF to go with each rule. This CF reflects their confidence in the rule's reliability. Certainty measures may be adjusted to tune the system's performance, although slight variations in the confidence measure tend to have little effect on the overall running of the system. This second role of certainty measures confirms the belief that "the knowledge gives the power," that is, the integrity of the knowledge itself best supports the production of correct diagnoses.

The premises for each rule are formed of ands and ors of a number of facts. When a production rule is used, the certainty factors associated with each condition of the premise are combined to produce a certainty measure for the overall premise as follows. For P1 and P2, premises of the rule:

$CF(P1 \text{ and } P2) = MIN(CF(P1), CF(P2))$, and

$CF(P1 \text{ or } P2) = MAX(CF(P1), CF(P2))$.

The combined CF of the premises, using the above rules, is then multiplied by the CF of the rule itself to get the CF for the conclusions of the rule. For example, consider the rule in a knowledge base:

$(P1 \text{ and } P2) \text{ or } P3 \rightarrow R1 (.7) \text{ and } R2 (.3)$

where P1, P2, and P3 are premises and R1 and R2 are the conclusions of the rule, having CFs 0.7 and 0.3, respectively. These numbers are added to the rule when it is designed and represent the expert's confidence in the conclusion if all the premises are known with complete certainty. If the running program has produced P1, P2, and P3 with CFs of 0.6, 0.4, and 0.2, respectively, then R1 and R2 may be added to the collected case-specific results with CFs 0.28 and 0.12, respectively. Here are the calculations for this example:

CF(P1(0.6) and P2(0.4)) = MIN(0.6,0.4) = 0.4.
CF((0.4) or P3(0.2)) = MAX(0.4,0.2) = 0.4.

The CF for R1 is 0.7 in the rule, so R1 is added to the set of case-specific knowledge with the associated CF of $(0.7) \times (0.4) = 0.28$.

The CF for R2 is 0.3 in the rule, so R2 is added to the set of case-specific knowledge with the associated CF of $(0.3) \times (0.4) = 0.12$.

One further measure is required: how to combine multiple CFs when two or more rules support the same result R. This rule reflects the certainty theory analog of the probability theory procedure of multiplying probability measures to combine independent evidence. By using this rule repeatedly one can combine the results of any number of rules that are used for determining a result R. Suppose CF(R1) is the present certainty factor associated with result R and a previously unused rule produces result R (again) with CF(R2); then the new CF of R is calculated by:

CF(R1) + CF(R2) − (CF(R1) × CF(R2)) when CF(R1) and CF(R2) are positive,

CF(R1) + CF(R2) + (CF(R1) × CF(R2)) when CF(R1) and CF(R2) are negative,

and

$$\frac{CF(R1) + CF(R2)}{1 - MIN(\,|\,CF(R1)\,|\,,\,|\,CF(R2)\,|\,)}$$

otherwise, where $|\,X\,|$ is the absolute value of X.

Besides being easy to compute, these combination equations have other desirable properties. First, the CFs that result from applying this rule are always between 1 and −1. Second, the result of combining contradictory CFs is that they cancel each other, as is desired. Finally, the combined CF measure is a monotonically increasing (decreasing) function in the manner one would expect for combining evidence.

Finally, the confidence measures of the Stanford certainty factor tradition are a human (subjective) estimate of symptom/cause probability measures. As noted in Section 5.4, in the Bayesian tradition if A, B, and C all influence D, we need to isolate and appropriately combine all the prior and posterior probabilities, including P(D), P(D|A), P(D|B), P(D|C), P(A|D), when we want to reason about D. The Stanford Certainty Factor tradition allows the knowledge engineer to wrap all these relationships together into one confidence factor, CF, attached to the rule; that is, if A and B and C then D (CF). It is felt that this simple algebra better reflects how human experts combine and propagate multiple sets of beliefs.

Certainty theory may be criticized as being excessively *ad hoc*. Although it is defined in a formal algebra, the meaning of the certainty measures is not as rigorously founded as is formal probability theory. However, certainty theory does not attempt to produce an algebra for "correct" reasoning. Rather it is the "lubrication" that lets the expert system combine confidences as it moves along through the problem at hand. Its measures are *ad hoc* in the same sense that a human expert's confidence in his or her results is approximate, heuristic, and informal. When MYCIN is run, the CFs are used in the heuristic search to give a priority for goals to be attempted and a cutoff point when a goal need not be considered further. But even though the CF is used to keep the program running and collecting information, the power of the program remains invested in the quality of the rules.

9.2.2   Reasoning with Fuzzy Sets

There are two assumptions that are essential for the use of formal set theory. The first is with respect to set membership: for any element and a set belonging to some universe, the element is either a member of the set or else it is a member of the complement of that set. The second assumption, referred to as *the law of excluded middle*, states that an element cannot belong to both a set and also to its complement. Both these assumptions are violated in Lotfi Zadeh's *fuzzy set theory*. In fact, the sets and reasoning laws of traditional set theory are referred to as *crisp*, from the fuzzy set viewpoint.

Zadeh's main contention (Zadeh 1983) is that, although probability theory is appropriate for measuring randomness of information, it is inappropriate for measuring the *meaning* of information. Indeed, much of the confusion surrounding the use of English words and phrases is related to lack of clarity (vagueness) rather than randomness. This is a crucial point for analyzing language structures and can also be important in creating a measure of confidence in production rules. Zadeh proposes *possibility theory* as a measure of vagueness, just as probability theory measures randomness.

Zadeh's theory expresses lack of precision in a quantitative fashion by introducing a set membership function that can take on real values between 0 and 1. This notion of a *fuzzy set* can be described as follows: let S be a set and s a member of that set. A fuzzy subset F of S is defined by a membership function mF(s) that measures the "degree" to which s belongs to F.

A standard example of a fuzzy set, as presented in Figure 9.6, is for S to be the set of positive integers and F to be the fuzzy subset of S called *small* integers. Now various integer values can have a "possibility" distribution defining their "fuzzy membership" in the set of small integers: mF(1) = 1.0, mF(2) = 1.0, mF(3) = 0.9, mF(4) = 0.8, ..., mF(50) = 0.001, etc. For the statement that positive integer X is a *small integer*, mF creates a possibility distribution across all the positive integers (S).

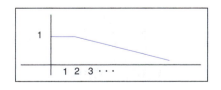

Figure 9.6 The fuzzy set representation for
"small integers."

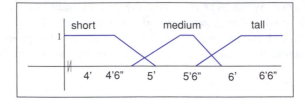

Figure 9.7 A fuzzy set representation for the sets
short, medium, and tall males.

Fuzzy set theory is not concerned with how these possibility distributions are created, but rather with the rules for computing the combined possibilities over expressions that contain fuzzy variables. Thus, it includes rules for combining possibility measures for expressions containing fuzzy variables. The laws for the or, and, and not of these expressions are similar to those just presented for the Stanford certainty factor algebra; see Section 9.2.1.

For the fuzzy set representation of the set of small integers, Figure 9.6, each integer belongs to this set with an associated confidence measure. In the traditional logic of "crisp" sets, the confidence of an element being in a set must be either 1 or 0. Figure 9.7 offers a set membership function for the concept of *short*, *medium*, and *tall* male humans. Note that any one person can belong to more than one set, for example, a 5' 9" male belongs to both the set of *medium* as well as to the set of *tall* males.

We next demonstrate rules for combining and propagating fuzzy measures by presenting part of a problem, now classic in the fuzzy set literature, a control regime for an inverted pendulum. Figure 9.8 presents a pendulum, inverted, which we desire to keep in balance and pointing upward. We keep the pendulum in balance by moving the base of the system to offset the force of gravity acting on the pendulum. There are sets of differential equations that can deterministically keep the pendulum in equilibrium (Ross 1995). The

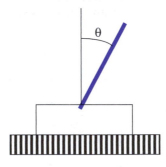

Figure 9.8 The inverted pendulum and the
angle θ and dθ/dt input values.

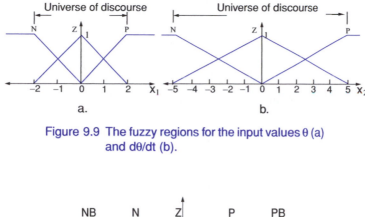

Figure 9.9 The fuzzy regions for the input values θ (a)
and dθ/dt (b).

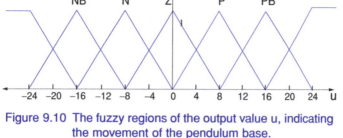

Figure 9.10 The fuzzy regions of the output value u, indicating
the movement of the pendulum base.

advantage of the fuzzy approach to controlling this pendulum system is that an algorithm may be established to control the system efficiently and in real time. We next show this control regime.

We simplify the pendulum problem by presenting it in two dimensions. There are two measurements we use as input values to the controller, as may be seen in Figure 9.8: First the angle θ, deviation of the pendulum from the vertical, and second the speed dθ/dt at which the pendulum is moving. Both these measures are positive in the quadrant to the right of vertical and negative to the left. These two values are given to the fuzzy controller at each iteration of the system. The output of the controller is a movement and a direction for the base of the system. The movement and direction instructions are intended to keep the pendulum in balance.

To clarify the actions of the fuzzy controller we describe the fuzzy set solution process. Data describing the state of the pendulum, θ and dθ/dt, are interpreted as fuzzy measures, see Figure 9.9, and presented to a fuzzy rule set. This step is often made very efficient by use of a structure called a *fuzzy associative matrix* or FAM, Figure 9.12, where input/ output relations are directly encoded. Rules are not chained together as in traditional rule-based problem solving. Rather, all matched rules fire and then their results are combined. This result, usually represented by an area of the fuzzy output parameter space, Figure 9.10, is then defuzzified to return the control response. Note that both the original input and eventual output of the controller are crisp values. These are exact readings of some monitor, the inputs, and a precise instruction for control, the output.

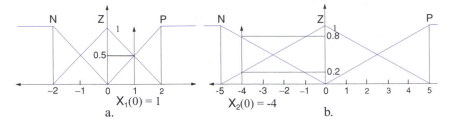

a.

b.

Figure 9.11 The fuzzification of the input
measures $X_1 = 1$, $X_2 = -4$.

X_2 X_1	P	Z	N
P	PB	P	Z
Z	P	Z	N
N	Z	N	NB

Figure 9.12 The Fuzzy Associative Matrix (FAM) for the
pendulum problem. The input values are on
the left and top.

We next describe the fuzzy regions for the input values, θ and $d\theta/dt$. This example
simplifies the situation, for example, in the number of fuzzy regions of input values, but
shows the full cycle of rule application and the response of the controller. The input value
θ is partitioned into three regions, Negative, Zero, and Positive, where θ ranges between
−2 and +2 radians, as may be seen in Figure 9.9a. Figure 9.9b represents the three
regions into which the second input value, $d\theta/dt$, is partitioned, again Negative, Zero, and
Positive, ranging between −5 and +5 degrees per second.

Figure 9.10 represents the partitioning of the output space, where we use the middle five
regions, Negative Big, Negative, Zero, Positive, and Positive Big. The measure, between
−24 and +24 represents the movement and direction of each response.

Suppose the simulation begins and the first values given to the controller are $\theta = 1$ and
$d\theta/dt = -4$. Figure 9.11 reflects the fuzzification of these input measures. In each situation,
the input value impacts two regions of the fuzzy input space. For θ, the values are Zero,
with 0.5, and Positive, with 0.5 possibility measures. For $d\theta/dt$, they are Negative with 0.8,
and Zero with 0.2 possibility measures.

Figure 9.12 presents a simplified form of the fuzzy associative matrix for this problem.
The input values to the table for θ, or x_1, are down the left side, and for $d\theta/dt$, or x_2, are

across the top of the matrix. The 3×3 table of the lower right corner of the FAM then gives the output values. For example, if the θ is Positive, and $d\theta/dt$ is Negative, the FAM returns the value of Zero movement of the pendulum system. Note that the response still must be defuzzified from the Zero output region of Figure 9.10.

In this case, because each input value touched on two regions of the input space, four rules must be applied. As noted above, the combination rules for fuzzy systems are similar to those of the Stanford certainty factor algebra. In fact, Zadeh (Buchanan and Shortliffe 1984) was the first (historically) to propose these combination rules for the algebra of fuzzy reasoning. If the measures of two premises are ANDed together, the minimum of their measures is taken as the measure of the rule. If two premises are ORed, the maximum of their measures is taken.

In our example, all the premise pairs are ANDed together, so the minimum of their measures is taken as the measure of the rule result:

IF x_1 = P AND x_2 = Z THEN u = P
min(0.5, 0.2) = 0.2 P

IF x_1 = P AND x_2 = N THEN u = Z
min(0.5, 0.8) = 0.5 Z

IF x_1 = Z AND x_2 = Z THEN u = Z
min(0.5, 0.2) = 0.2 Z

IF x_1 = Z AND x_2 = N THEN u = N
min(0.5, 0.8) = 0.5 N

Next the output results are combined. In this example, we union together the two areas of Figure 9.10, indicated by the results of this set of two rules firing. There are a number of possible defuzzification techniques (Ross 1995). We have chosen one of the commonest, the *centroid method*. To use this method, the centroid of the union of the areas of the output values becomes the final value the controller applies to the pendulum. The union, as well as the centroid for the union, are presented in Figure 9.13. After this output or result is applied to the system, q and dq/dt are sampled again and the control cycle is repeated.

There are a number of issues we have not addressed in describing fuzzy reasoning systems, including patterns of oscillations within the convergence process and optimum sampling rates. Fuzzy systems, especially in the area of control, offer engineers a powerful and efficient tool for dealing with imprecision in measurement.

9.2.3   The Dempster–Shafer Theory of Evidence

To this point in our discussion of reasoning under uncertainty, we described techniques which consider individual propositions and assign to each a causal influence or a numeric estimate of the degree of belief that we might have, given sets of evidence. One of the limitations of probabilistic approaches to uncertainty is their use of a single quantity to measure what may be a very complex situation. Often, uncertainty results from a

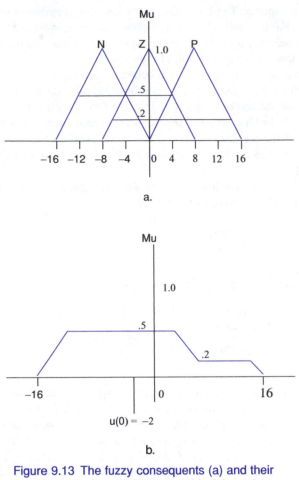

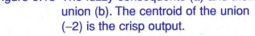

Figure 9.13 The fuzzy consequents (a) and their
union (b). The centroid of the union
(−2) is the crisp output.

combination of missing evidence, the inherent limitations of heuristic rules, and the limitations of our own knowledge.

An alternative approach, called the *Dempster–Shafer theory of evidence,* considers sets of propositions and assigns to each of them an interval [belief, plausibility] within which the degree of belief for each proposition must lie. This *belief measure,* denoted bel, ranges from zero, indicating no evidence of support for a set of propositions, to one, denoting certainty. The *plausibility* of a proposition p, pl(p), is defined:

pl(p) = 1 − bel(not(p))

Thus, plausibility also ranges between zero and one and reflects how evidence of not(p) relates to the possibility for belief in p. If we have certain evidence of not(p) then bel(not(p)) will be one and pl(p) will be zero. The only possible value for bel(p) is also zero.

Suppose we have two competing hypotheses h_1 and h_2. When we have no information supporting either hypothesis, they each have the belief/plausibility range [0,1]. As evidence is gathered, we expect these intervals to shrink, representing the increased confidence for the hypotheses. In a Bayesian domain, we would probably begin (with no evidence) by distributing the prior probabilities equally among the two hypotheses, giving each $p(h_i) = 0.5$. Dempster–Shafer makes it clear that we have no evidence when we start; the Bayesian approach, on the other hand, can result in the same probability measure no matter how much data we have. Thus, Dempster–Shafer can be very useful when it is important to make a decision based on the amount of evidence that has been collected.

To summarize, Dempster and Shafer address the problem of measuring certainty by making a fundamental distinction between lack of certainty and ignorance. In probability theory we are forced to express the extent of our knowledge about an hypothesis h in a single number, p(h). The problem with this approach, say Dempster and Shafer, is that we simply cannot always know the values of its supporting probabilities, and therefore, any particular choice of p(h) may not be justified.

The Dempster–Shafer belief functions satisfy axioms that are weaker than those of probability theory, that is, it reduces to probability theory when all probabilities are obtainable. Belief functions allow us to use our knowledge to bound the assignment of probabilities to events in the absence of exact probabilities.

The Dempster–Shafer theory is based on two ideas: first, the idea of obtaining degrees of belief for one question from subjective probabilities for related questions and second, the use of a rule for combining these degrees of belief when they are based on independent items of evidence. This combination rule was originally proposed by Dempster (1968). Next, we present an informal example of Dempster–Shafer reasoning, then present Dempster's rule, and finally, apply that rule to a more realistic situation.

Suppose I have subjective probabilities for the reliability of my friend Melissa. The probability that she is reliable is 0.9, and that she is unreliable, 0.1. Suppose Melissa tells me that my computer was broken into. This statement is true if Melissa is reliable, but it is not necessarily false if she is unreliable. So Melissa's testimony alone justifies a degree of belief of 0.9 that my computer was broken into and a 0.0 belief that it was not. Belief of 0.0 does not mean that I am sure that my computer was not broken into, as a probability of 0.0 would. It merely means that Melissa's testimony gives me no reason to believe that my computer was not broken into. The plausibility measure, pl, in this situation is:

pl(computer_broken_into) = 1 − bel(not (computer_broken_into)) = 1 − 0.0

or 1.0, and my belief measure for Melissa is [0.9 1.0]. Note that there is still no evidence that my computer was not broken into.

We next consider Dempster's rule for combining evidence. Suppose my friend Bill also tells me that my computer was broken into. Suppose the probability that Bill is reliable is 0.8 and that he is unreliable is 0.2. I also must suppose that Bill's and Melissa's testimonies about my computer are independent of each other; that is, they have separate reasons for telling me that they think my computer was broken into. The event that Bill is reliable must also be independent of Melissa's reliability. The probability that both Bill and Melissa are reliable is the product of their reliabilities, or 0.72; the probability that they both are unreliable is the product 0.02. The probability that at least one of the two is reliable is 1 − 0.02, or 0.98. Since they both said that my computer was broken into and there is a probability of 0.98 that at least one of them is reliable, I will assign to the event of my computer being broken into a [0.98 1.0] degree of belief.

Suppose that Bill and Melissa disagree on whether my computer was broken into: Melissa says that it was, and Bill says that it was not. In this case, they cannot both be correct and they cannot both be reliable. Either both are unreliable or only one is reliable. The prior probability that only Melissa is reliable is $0.9 \times (1 − 0.8) = 0.18$, that only Bill is reliable is $0.8 \times (1 − 0.9) = 0.08$, and that neither is reliable is $0.2 \times 0.1 = 0.02$. Given that at least one is not reliable, $(0.18 + 0.08 + 0.02) = 0.28$, we can also compute the posterior probability that only Melissa is reliable as $0.18 / 0.28 = 0.643$ and my computer was broken into, or the posterior probability that only Bill was right, $0.08 / 0.28 = 0.286$, and my computer was not broken into.

We have just used the Dempster rule to combine beliefs. When Melissa and Bill both reported the computer break-in, we summed the three hypothetical situations that supported the break-in: Bill and Melissa are both reliable; Bill is reliable and Melissa not; and Melissa is reliable and Bill not. The belief, 0.98, was the sum of these possible supporting hypothetical scenarios. In the second use of the Dempster rule, the witnesses disagreed. Again we summed all possible scenarios. The only impossible situation was that they were both reliable; thus either Melissa was reliable and Bill not, Bill was reliable and Melissa not, or neither was reliable. The sum of these three gives a belief of break-in of 0.64. The belief that my computer was not broken into (Bill's opinion) was 0.286; since the plausibility of break-in is 1 − bel(not(break in)) or 0.714, the belief measure is [0.28 0.714].

To use the Dempster rule, we obtain degrees of belief for one question (Was my computer broken into?) from probabilities for another question (Are the witnesses reliable?). The rule begins with the assumption that the questions for which we have probabilities are independent, but that this independence is only a priori. It disappears when we have conflict between the different items of evidence.

Using the Dempster–Shafer approach in a specific situation involves solving two related problems. First, we sort the uncertainties of the situation into a priori independent pieces of evidence. Second, we carry out Dempster's rule. These two tasks are related: Suppose, again, that Bill and Melissa told me, independently, that they believed my computer was broken into. Suppose also that I had called a repair person to check my computer, and that both Bill and Melissa had witnessed this. Because of this common event, I can no longer compare degrees of belief. However, if I consider explicitly the possibility of the repair person's working on my computer, then I have three independent items of evidence: Melissa's reliability, Bill's reliability, and evidence for the presence of the repair person, which I can then combine with Dempster's rule.

Suppose we have an exhaustive set of mutually exclusive hypotheses we call Q. Our goal is to attach some measure of belief, m, to the various subsets Z of Q; m is sometimes called the *probability density function* for a subset of Q. Realistically, not all evidence is directly supportive of individual elements of Q. In fact, evidence most often supports different subsets Z of Q. In addition, since the elements of Q are assumed to be mutually exclusive, evidence in favor of some may have an effect on our belief in others. In a purely Bayesian system, Section 9.3, we address both of these situations by listing all the combinations of conditional probabilities. In the Dempster–Shafer system we handle these interactions by directly manipulating the sets of hypotheses. The quantity $m_n(Z)$ measures the amount of belief that is assigned to the subset Z of hypotheses, and n represents the number of sources of evidence.

Dempster's rule states:

$$m_n(Z) = \frac{\Sigma_{X \cap Y = Z} m_{n-2}(X) m_{n-1}(Y)}{1 - \Sigma_{X \cap Y = \phi} m_{n-2}(X) m_{n-1}(Y)}$$

For example, the belief in an hypothesis Z, with $n = 3$ sources of evidence, $m_3(Z)$, is the sum of the products of the hypothetical situations, $m_1(X)$ and $m_2(Y)$, whose co-occurrence supports Z, that is, $X \cap Y = Z$. The denominator of Dempster's rule acknowledges, as we see in the following example, that X and Y can have an empty intersection, and the sum of the confidences must be normalized by one minus the sum of these values.

We next apply Dempster's rule to a situation of medical diagnosis. Suppose Q represents the domain of our focus, containing four hypotheses: that a patient has a cold (C), flu (F), migraine headaches (H), or meningitis (M). Our task is to associate measures of belief with hypothesis sets within Q. As just noted, these are *hypothesis sets* since evidence need not support individual hypotheses exclusively. For example, having a fever could support {C,F,M}. Since the elements of Q are treated as mutually exclusive hypotheses, evidence in favor of some may affect belief in others. As already noted, the Dempster–Shafer approach addresses interactions by handling the sets of hypotheses directly.

For the probability density function, m, and all subsets Z of the set Q, the quantity $m(q_i)$ represents the belief that is currently assigned to each q_i of Q with the sum of all the $m(q_i)$ equal to one. If Q contains n elements, then there are 2^n subsets of Q. Even though addressing 2^n values may appear daunting, it usually turns out that many of the subsets will never occur. Thus, there is some simplification of the solution process since these values can be ignored, because they have no utility in the problem domain. Finally, the plausibility of Q is $pl(Q) = 1 - \Sigma\ m(q_i)$, where the q_i are the sets of hypotheses that have some supporting belief. If we have no information about any hypotheses, as is often the case when we start a diagnosis, then $pl(Q) = 1.0$.

Suppose the first piece of evidence is that our patient has a fever, and that this supports {C,F,M} at 0.6. We call this first belief m_1. If this is our only hypothesis, then $m_1\{C,F,M\} = 0.6$, where $m_1(Q) = 0.4$, to account for the remaining distribution of belief. It is crucial to note that $m_1(Q) = 0.4$ represents the remainder of our belief distribution, that is, all other possible beliefs across Q and not our belief in the complement of {C,F,M}.

Suppose that we now acquire some new data for our diagnosis, say that the patient has extreme nausea, which suggests {C,F,H} with support level 0.7. For this belief, call it m_2, we have $m_2\{C,F,H\} = 0.7$ and $m_2(Q) = 0.3$. We use Dempster's rule to combine these two beliefs, m_1 and m_2. Let X be the set of subsets of Q to which m_1 assigns a nonzero value and Y be the set of subsets of Q to which m_2 assigns a nonzero value. We then create a combination belief, m_3, defined on subsets Z of Q by using Dempster's rule.

In applying Dempster's rule to the diagnoses, first note that there are no sets $X \cap Y$ that are empty, so the denominator is 1. The belief distribution for m_3 is seen in Table 9.1.

m_1	m_2	m_3
$m_1\{C,F,M\} = 0.6$	$m_2\{C,F,H\} = 0.7$	$m_3\{C,F\} = 0.42$
$m_1(Q) = 0.4$	$m_2\{C,F,H\} = 0.7$	$m_3\{C,F,H\} = 0.28$
$m_1\{C,F,M\} = 0.6$	$m_2(Q) = 0.3$	$m_3\{C,F,M\} = 0.18$
$m_1(Q) = 0.4$	$m_2(Q) = 0.3$	$m_3(Q) = 0.12$

Table 9.1 Using Dempster's rule to obtain a belief distribution for m_3.

Using Dempster's rule, the four sets Z, all possible ways of intersecting X and Y, make up the rightmost column of Table 9.1. Their belief level is computed by multiplying the beliefs for the corresponding elements of X and Y under m_1 and m_2 respectively. Note also that, in this example, each set in Z is unique, which is often not the case.

We extend our example one final time to show how empty belief sets are factored into the analysis. Suppose we have a new fact, the results of a lab culture that are associated with meningitis. We now have $m_4\{M\} = 0.8$ and $m_4(Q) = 0.2$. We may use Dempster's formula to combine m_3, the results of our previous analysis, with m_4 to get m_5, as can be seen in Table 9.2.

m_3	m_4	m_5 (without denominator)
$m_3\{C,F\} = 0.42$	$m_4\{M\} = 0.8$	$m_5\{ \} = 0.336$
$m_3(Q) = 0.12$	$m_4\{M\} = 0.8$	$m_5\{M\} = 0.096$
$m_3\{C,F\} = 0.42$	$m_4(Q) = 0.2$	$m_5\{C,F\} = 0.084$
$m_3(Q) = 0.12$	$m_4(Q) = 0.2$	$m_5(Q) = 0.024$
$m_3\{C,F,H\} = 0.28$	$m_4\{M\} = 0.8$	$m_5\{ \} = 0.224$
$m_3(C,F,M) = 0.18$	$m_4\{M\} = 0.8$	$m_5\{M\} = 0.144$
$m_3\{C,F,H\} = 0.28$	$m_4(Q) = 0.2$	$m_5\{C,F,H\} = 0.056$
$m_3(C.F,M) = 0.18$	$m_4(Q) = 0.2$	$m_5\{C,F,M\} = 0.036$

Table 9.2 Using Dempster's rule to combine m_3 and m_4 to get m_5.

First, note that $m_5\{M\}$ is produced by the intersections of two different pairs of sets, so the total $m_5\{M\} = 0.240$. We also have the case where several set intersections produce the empty set, $\{\}$. Thus the denominator for Dempster's equation is $1 - (0.336 + 0.224) = 1 - 0.56 = 0.44$. The final combined belief function for m_5 is:

$m_5\{M\} = 0.545$ $m_5\{C,F\} = 0.191$ $m_5\{ \} = 0.56$
$m_5\{C,F,H\} = 0.127$ $m_5\{C,F,M\} = 0.082$ $m_5(Q) = 0.055$

Three final comments. First, a large belief assigned to the empty set, as in this final $m_5\{ \} = 0.56$, indicates that there is conflicting evidence within the belief sets m_i. In fact, we designed our example to show several features of Dempster–Shafer reasoning, and, as a consequence, sacrificed medical integrity. Second, when there are large hypothesis sets as well as complex sets of evidence, the calculations for belief sets can get cumbersome, even though, as pointed out earlier, the amount of computation is still considerably less than that for Bayesian reasoning. Finally, the Dempster–Shafer approach is a very useful tool when the stronger Bayesian assumptions may not be justified.

Dempster–Shafer is an example of an algebra supporting the use of subjective probabilities in reasoning. It is sometimes felt that these subjective probabilities better reflect human expert reasoning. In the final section of Chapter 9 we consider further reasoning techniques based on extensions of Bayes' rule, first introduced in Section 5.3.

9.3   The Stochastic Approach to Uncertainty

Using probability theory, we can determine, often from a priori argument, the chances of events occurring. We can also describe how combinations of events are able to influence each other. Although the final touches on probability theory awaited the mathematicians of the early twentieth century, including Fisher, Neyman, and Pearson, the attempt to create a combinatorial algebra goes back through the middle ages to the Greeks, including Llull, Porphyry, and Plato (Glymour et al. 1995a). The insight supporting probability theory is that we can understand the frequency with which events occur and use this information to reason about the frequencies of future combinations of events.

In Chapter 5, we noted that there are a number of situations when probabilistic analysis is appropriate. For example, when the world is genuinely random, as in playing a game with well-shuffled cards, or spinning a fair roulette wheel. Further, although many events in the world are not truly random, it is often impossible to know and measure all causes and their interactions well enough to predict events; statistical correlations are a useful support for this attempted causal analysis. Another important role for statistics is as a basis for automated induction and machine learning (for example, the ID3 algorithm of Section 10.3). Finally, recent work has attempted to directly link the notions of probability and causality (Glymour and Cooper 1999, Pearl 2000).

Our primary inference mechanism in stochastic domains is some form of Bayes' rule. As we noted in Section 5.3, however, the full use of Bayesian inference in complex domains quickly becomes intractable. In the following section we present several inference techniques specifically designed to address this complexity; these include Bayesian belief networks (BBNs), Markov models, and hidden Markov models (HMMs).

9.3.1   A Directed Graphical Model: The Bayesian Belief Network

Although Bayesian probability theory, as presented in Chapter 5, offers a mathematical foundation for reasoning under uncertain conditions, the complexity encountered in

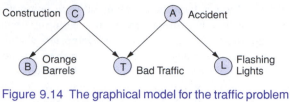

Figure 9.14 The graphical model for the traffic problem
first introduced in Section 5.3.

applying it to realistic problem domains can be prohibitive. Fortunately, we can often prune this complexity by focusing search on a smaller set of more highly relevant events and evidence. One approach, *Bayesian belief networks (BBNs)* (Pearl 1988), offers a computational model for reasoning to the best explanation of a set of data in the context of the expected causal relationships of a problem domain.

Bayesian belief networks can dramatically reduce the number of parameters of the full Bayesian model and show how the data of a domain (or even the absence of data) can partition and focus reasoning. Furthermore, the modularity of a problem domain often allows the program designer to make many independence assumptions not allowed in a full Bayesian treatment. In most reasoning situations, it is not necessary to build a large joint probability table in which the probabilities for all possible combinations of events and evidence are listed. Rather, human experts seem to select the local phenomena that they know will interact and obtain probability or influence measures that reflect only these clusters of events. Experts assume all other events are either conditionally independent or that their correlations are so small that they may be ignored.

As an example Bayesian belief network, consider again the traffic problem of Section 5.4, represented by Figure 9.14. Recall that road construction was C, an accident, A, the presence of orange barrels, B, bad traffic, T, and flashing lights was L. To calculate the joint probability of all the parameters of the example required knowledge or measurements for all parameters being in particular states. Thus, the joint probability, using a topologically sorted order for variables, is:

$$p(C,A,B,T,L) = p(C) * p(A|C) * p(B|C,A) * p(T|C,A,B) * p(L|C,A,B,T)$$

The number of parameters in this joint probability is 2^5 or 32. This table is exponential in the number of parameters involved. For a problem of any complexity, say with thirty or more parameters, the joint distribution table would have more than a billion elements!

Note, however, that if we can support the assumption that the parameters of this problem are only dependent on the probabilities of their parents, that is, we can assume that nodes are independent of all non-descendents, given knowledge of their parents, the calculation of p(C,A,B,T,L) becomes:

$$p(C,A,B,T,L) = p(C) * p(A) * p(B|C) * p(T|C,A) * p(L|A)$$

To better see the simplifications we have made, consider p(B|C,A) from the previous equation. We have reduced this to p(B|C) in our most recent equation. This is based on the assumption that road construction is not a causal effect of there being an accident. Similarly, the presence of orange barrels is not a cause of bad traffic, but construction and accident are, giving as a result p(T|C,A) rather than p(T|C,A,B). Finally, p(L|C,A,B,T) is reduced to p(L|A)! The probability distribution for p(C,A,B,T,L) now has only 20 (rather than 32) parameters. And if we move to a more realistic problem, with 30 variables say, and if each state has at most two parents, there will be at most 240 elements in the distribution. If each state has three parents, the maximum is 490 elements in the distribution: considerably less than the billion required for the full Bayesian approach!

We need to justify this dependence of a node in a belief network on its parents alone. Links between the nodes of a belief network represent the conditioned probabilities for causal influence. Implicit in expert reasoning using causal inference is the assumption that these influences are directed, that is, the presence of some event somehow *causes* other events in the network. Further, causal influence reasoning is not circular in that some effect cannot circle back to cause itself. For these reasons, *Bayesian belief networks* will have a natural representation as a *directed acyclic graph* or DAG (Section 3.1.1), where coherent patterns of reasoning are reflected as paths through cause/effect relationships. Bayesian belief networks are one instance of what are often called *graphical models*.

In the case of our traffic example we have an even stronger situation, with no undirected cycles. This allows us to calculate very simply the probability distribution at every node. The distribution of nodes with no parents are directly looked up. The values of child nodes are computed using only the probability distributions of each child's parents by doing the appropriate computations on the child's conditional probability table and the parent's distributions. This is possible because we don't have to worry about correlations between the parents of any node (since the network is given as a directed and acyclic graph). This produces a natural abductive separation where accident has no correlation at all with the presence of orange barrels, as is seen in Figure 9.14. We summarize our discussion of BBNs and the traffic example with the following definition.

DEFINITION

BAYESIAN BELIEF NETWORK

A graphical model is called a *Bayesian belief network (BBN)* if its graph, annotated with conditional probabilities, is directed and acyclic. Furthermore, BBNs assume nodes are independent of all their non-descendents, given knowledge of their parents.

A *dynamic Bayesian network (DBN)* is a sequence of identical Bayesian networks whose nodes are linked in the (directed) dimension of time. We do not consider the general DBM further; see Friedman (1998) or Ghahramani and Jordan (1997).

In the next section we consider an assumption implicit in much of expert human reasoning: that the presence or absence of data in a domain can partition and focus the search for explanations within that domain. This fact also has important complexity implications for exploring a search space.

9.3.2 Directed Graphical Models: d-separation

An important advantage of representing application domains as graphical models is that the presence or absence of information can lead to partitioning the model and as a result controlling the complexity of the search. We next present several examples of this, and then offer the definition of *d-separation* that supports these intuitions.

Let us consider the diagnosis of oil problems in a car engine: suppose that worn piston rings cause excessive oil consumption which in turn causes a low oil level reading for the car. This situation is reflected by Figure 9.15a, where A is worn piston rings, V is excessive oil consumption, and B is low oil level. Now, if we do not know anything about excessive oil consumption, then we have a causal relationship between worn piston rings and low oil level. However, if some test gives the state of excessive oil consumption, then worn piston rings and low oil level are independent of each other.

In a second example: suppose that worn piston rings can cause both blue exhaust as well as low oil level. This situation is shown in Figure 9.15b, with V as worn piston rings, A as blue exhaust, and B as low oil level. If we know that worn piston rings is either true or false then we don't know whether blue exhaust and low oil level are correlated; if we have no information on worn piston rings then blue exhaust and low oil level are correlated.

Finally, if low oil level can be caused by either excessive oil consumption or by an oil leak then, given knowledge of whether there is low oil level, its two possible causes are correlated. If the state of low oil level is unknown, then its two possible causes are

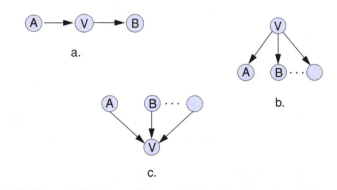

Figure 9.15 Figure 9.15a is a serial connection of nodes where influence runs between A and B unless V is instantiated. Figure 9.15b is a diverging connection, where influence runs between V's children, unless V is instantiated. In Figure 9.15c, a converging connection, if nothing is known about V then its parents are independent, otherwise correlations exist between its parents.

independent. Furthermore, if low oil level is true then establishing oil leak as true will explain away excessive oil consumption. In either case, information on low oil level is a key element in the reasoning process. We see this situation in Figure 9.15c, with A as excessive oil consumption, B as oil leak, and V as low oil level.

We make these intuitions precise by defining the d-separation of nodes in a belief network or other graphical model (after Pearl 1988):

D E F I N I T I O N

d-SEPARATION

Two nodes A and B in a directed acyclic graph are *d-separated* if every path between them is blocked. A path is any continuous series of connections in the graph (linking nodes in any direction, e.g., there is a path from A to B in Figure 9.15b). A path is blocked if there is an intermediate node V in the path with either of the properties:

the connection is *serial* or *diverging* and the state of V is known, or

the connection is *converging* and neither V nor any of V's children have evidence.

We give further instances of serial, diverging, and converging node relationships, as well as how d-separation influences argument paths in the example of Figure 9.16.

Before leaving the graphs of Figure 9.15, we demonstrate how the assumptions of a Bayesian belief network can simplify the computation of conditional probabilities. Using Bayes law, any joint probability distribution can be decomposed into a product of conditional probabilities. Thus, in Figure 9.15a, the joint probability of the three variables A, V, B is:

$$p(A,V,B) = p(A)*p(V|A)*p(B|A,V).$$

We use the assumption of a Bayesian belief network, that the conditional probability of a variable given knowledge of all its predecessors is equal to its conditional probability given knowledge of only its parents. As a result, in the equation above $p(B|A,V)$ becomes $p(B|V)$ because V is a direct parent of B and A is not. The joint probability distributions for the three networks of Figure 9.15 are:

a) $p(A,V,B) = p(A)*p(V|A)*p(B|V)$,
b) $p(V,A,B) = p(V)*p(A|V)*p(B|V)$, and
c) $p(A,B,V) = p(A)*p(B)*p(V|A,B)$.

As the traffic example showed (Figure 9.14), for larger Bayesian belief networks, many more variables in the conditional probabilities can be eliminated. It is this simplification that makes Bayesian belief networks and other graphical models far more statistically tractable than a full Bayesian analysis. We next present a more complex graphical model, one containing an undirected cycle, and propose an efficient inference algorithm, *clique tree propagation*.

9.3.3 Directed Graphical Models: An Inference Algorithm

The next example, adapted from Pearl (1988), shows a more complex Bayesian network. In Figure 9.16, the season of the year determines the probability of rain as well as the probability of water from a sprinkler system. The wet sidewalk will be correlated with rain or water from the sprinkler. Finally, the sidewalk will be slick depending on whether or not it is a wet sidewalk. In the figure we have expressed the probability relationship that each of these parameters has with its parents. Note also that, as compared with the traffic example, the slippery sidewalk example has an undirected cycle.

We now ask the question, how can the probability of wet sidewalk, p(WS), be described? It can't be done as previously, where p(W) = p(W|S) * p(S) or p(R) = p(R|S) * p(S). The two causes of WS are not mutually independent; for example, if S = summer, then p(W) and p(R) could both go up. Thus the complete correlations of the two variables, along with their further correlation with S, must be calculated. In this situation we can do it, but as we will see, this calculation is exponential in the number of possible causes of WS. The calculation is represented in Table 9.4. We now calculate one entry in that table, x where R and W are both true; to make life simpler we assume the season S is either hot or cold.

x = p(R = t, S = t) for all conditions of S, season
  = p(S = hot) * p(R = t | S = hot) * p(W = t | S = hot) +
    p(S = cold) * p(R = t | S = cold) * p(W = t | S = cold)

In a similar fashion the remainder of Table 9.4 can be completed. This makes up the joint probability for rain and water from the sprinkler. This larger "macro element" represents p(WS) = p(WS | R,W) * p(R,W). We have gotten away with a rather reasonable

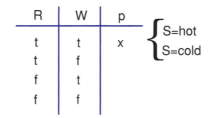

R	W	p	
t	t	x	S=hot
t	f		S=cold
f	t		
f	f		

Table 9.4 The probability distribution for p(WS), a function of p(W) and p(R), given the effect of S. We calculate the effect for x, where R = t and W = t.

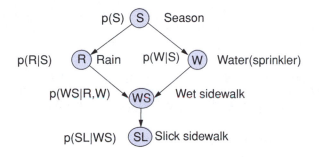

Figure 9.16 An example of a Bayesian probabilistic network, where the probability dependencies are located next to each node. This example is from Pearl (1988).

calculation here; the problem is that this calculation is exponential in the number of parents of the state.

We call this macro element the *combined variable*, or *clique*, for the calculation of p(WS). We employ this concept of a clique in order to replace the constraint propagation of the DAG of Figure 9.16 with an acyclic *clique tree*, as seen in Figure 9.17. The rectangular boxes of Figure 9.17a reflect the variables that the cliques above and below it share. The table that passes the relevant parameters through to the next clique is exponential in the number of these parameters. It should also be noted that a linking variable along with all its parents must be present in the clique. Thus, in setting up a belief network or other graphical model (the knowledge engineering process), we ought to be careful how many variables are parents of any state. The cliques will also overlap, as seen in Figure 9.17b, to pass information through the full tree of cliques, called the *junction tree*. We next present an algorithm developed by Lauritzen and Spiegelhalter (1988) that creates a junction tree from any Bayesian belief network.

1. For all nodes in the belief network make all directed links undirected.

2. For any node draw links between all its parents (the dashed line between R and W in Figure 9.17b).

3. Look for any cycle in the resulting graph of length more than three and add further links that reduce that cycle to three. This process is called *triangulation* and is not necessary in the example of Figure 9.17b.

4. Form the junction tree with the resulting triangulated structure. This is done by finding the *maximal cliques* (cliques that are complete subgraphs and not subgraphs of a larger clique).The variables in these cliques are put into *junctions* and the resulting *junction tree* is created by connecting any two junctions that share at least one variable, as in Figure 9.17a.

The triangulation process described in step 3 above is critical, as we want the resulting junction tree to have minimal computational cost when propagating information.

Unfortunately, this decision of designing optimal cost junction trees is NP hard. Often, fortunately, a simple greedy algorithm can be sufficient for producing useful results. Note that the sizes of the tables required to convey information across the junction tree of Figure 9.17 are 2*2*2, 2*2*2, and 2*2.

Finally, we take the example network of Figure 9.16 and return to the issue of d-separation. Remember, the point of d-separation is that with some information, parts of the belief network can be ignored in calculating probability distributions.

1. SL is d-separated from R, S, and W, given that WS is known.

2. d-separation is symmetric, that is, S is also d-separated from (and not a possible explanation of) SL, given knowledge of WS.

3. R and W are dependent because of S, but knowing S, R and W are d-separated.

4. If we know WS, then R and W are not d-separated; if we don't know S, then R and W are.

5. Given the chain R → WS → SL, if we know WS, then R and SL are d-separated.

We must be careful when we know information about the descendents of a particular state. For example, if we know SL, then R and W are NOT d-separated, since SL is correlated with WS, and knowing WS, R and W are not d-separated.

A final comment: Bayesian belief networks seem to reflect how humans reason in complex domains where some factors are known and related a priori to others. As reasoning proceeds by progressive instantiation of information, search is further restricted, and as a result, more efficient. This search efficiency stands in strong contrast to the approach supported by using a full joint distribution, more information requires an exponentially larger need for statistical relations and a resulting broader search.

There are a number of algorithms available for building belief networks and propagating arguments as new evidence is acquired. We recommend especially Pearl's (1988)

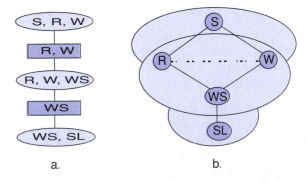

Figure 9.17 A junction tree (a) for the Bayesian probabilistic network of (b). Note that we started to construct the transition table for the rectangle R,W.

message passing approach and the *clique tree triangulation* method proposed by Lauritzen and Spiegelhalter (1988). Druzdel and Henrion (1993) have also proposed algorithms for propagating influence in a network. Dechter (1996) presents the bucket elimination algorithm as a unifying framework for probabilistic inference.

9.3.4 Markov Models: The Discrete Markov Process

In Section 3.1.2 we presented *finite state machines* as graphical representations where states were transitioned depending on the content of an input stream. The states and their transitions reflected properties of a formal language. We then presented a *finite state acceptor* (the Moore machine), a state machine that was able to "recognize" strings having various properties. In Section 5.3 we presented the *probabilistic finite state machine*, a state machine where the next state function was represented by a probability distribution on the current state. The *discrete Markov process* is a specialization of this approach, where the system ignores its input values.

Figure 9.18 is a *Markov state machine* (sometimes called a *Markov chain*) with four distinct states. This general class of system may be described at any time as being in one of a set of S distinct states, $s_1, s_2, s_3, ..., s_n$. The system undergoes changes of state, with the possibility of it remaining in the same state, at regular discrete time intervals. We describe the ordered set of times T that are associated with the discrete intervals as $t_1, t_2, t_3, ..., t_t$. The system changes state according to the distribution of probabilities associated with each state. We denote the actual state of the machine at time t as σ_t.

A full probabilistic description of this system requires, in the general case, the specification of the present state σ_t, in terms of all its predecessor states. Thus the probability of the system being in any particular state σ_t is:

$$p(\sigma_t) = p(\sigma_t \mid \sigma_{t-1}, \sigma_{t-2}, \sigma_{t-3}, ...)$$

where the σ_{t-i} are the predecessor states of σ_t. In a *first-order Markov chain*, the probability of the present state is a function *only* of its direct predecessor state:

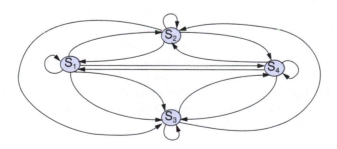

Figure 9.18 A Markov state machine or Markov chain with four states, $s_1, ..., s_4$.

$$p(\sigma_t) = p(\sigma_t \mid \sigma_{t-1})$$

where σ_{t-1} is the predecessor of σ_t. We next assume that the right side of this equation is time invariant, that is, we hypothesize that across all time periods of the system, the transitions between specific states retain the same probabilistic relationships.

Based on these assumptions, we now can create a set of state transition probabilities a_{ij} between any two states s_i and s_j:

$$a_{ij} = p(\sigma_t = s_i \mid \sigma_{t-1} = s_j), \quad 1 \le i, j \le N$$

Recall that i can equal j, in which case the system remains in the same state. The traditional constraints remain on these probability distributions; for each state s_i:

$$a_{ij} \ge 0, \text{ and } \sum_{i=1}^{N} a_{ij} = 1$$

The system we have just described is called a *first-order observable Markov model* since the output of the system is the set of states at each discrete time interval, and each state of the system corresponds to a physical (observable) event. We make the observable Markov model more formal with a definition and then give an example.

DEFINITION

(OBSERVABLE) MARKOV MODEL

A graphical model is called an *(observable) Markov model* if its graph is directed and the probability of arriving at any state s_t from the set of states S at a discrete time t is a function of the probability distributions of its being in previous states of S at previous times. Each state s_t of S corresponds to a physically observable situation.

An observable Markov model is *first-order* if the probability of it being in the present state s_t at any time t is a function only of its being in the previous state s_{t-1} at the time $t - 1$, where s_t and s_{t-1} belong to the set of observable states S.

Note that any probability distribution has the property of being a Markov model. The power of this approach comes from the first-order assumptions. As an example of an observable first-order Markov model, consider the weather at noon, say, for a particular location. We assume this location has four different discrete states for the variable weather: $s_1 = \text{sun}$, $s_2 = \text{cloudy}$, $s_3 = \text{fog}$, $s_4 = \text{precipitation}$. The time intervals for the Markov model will be noon each consecutive day. We also assume the transitions between the states of weather remain constant across time (not true for most locations!), and that the observable, weather, can remain in the same state over multiple days. This situation is represented by Figure 9.18, and is supported by the matrix of state transitions a_{ij}:

$$
a_{ij} = \begin{array}{c|cccc}
 & s_1 & s_2 & s_3 & s_4 \\
\hline
s_1 & 0.4 & 0.3 & 0.2 & 0.1 \\
s_2 & 0.2 & 0.3 & 0.2 & 0.3 \\
s_3 & 0.1 & 0.3 & 0.3 & 0.3 \\
s_4 & 0.2 & 0.3 & 0.3 & 0.2
\end{array}
$$

In this a_{ij} transition matrix the first row represents the transitions from s_1 to each of the states, including staying in the same state; the second row is the transitions from s_2 to each of the states, and so on. This representation is the same as that seen for the transition matrix for finite state machines in Section 3.1.2. Note that the properties required for the transitions to be probability distributions from each state are met (they sum to 1.0).

We now can ask questions of our model. Suppose that today, s_1, is sunny; what is the probability of the next five days remaining sunny? Or again, what is the probability of the next five days being sunny, sunny, cloudy, cloudy, precipitation? We solve this second problem. We wish to determine the probability of observing, given our model, the set of states, where the first day, s_1, is today's observed sunshine:

$$O = s_1, s_1, s_1, s_2, s_2, s_4$$

The probability of this sequence of observed states, given the first-order Markov model, M, is:

$$
\begin{aligned}
p(O \mid M) &= p(s_1, s_1, s_1, s_2, s_2, s_4 \mid M) \\
&= p(s_1) \times p(s_1 \mid s_1) \times p(s_1 \mid s_1) \times p(s_2 \mid s_1) \times p(s_2 \mid s_2) \times p(s_4 \mid s_2) \\
&= 1 \times a_{11} \times a_{11} \times a_{12} \times a_{22} \times a_{24} \\
&= 1 \times (.4) \times (.4) \times (.3) \times (.3) \times (.3) \\
&= .00432
\end{aligned}
$$

This equation follows from the assumptions of the first-order Markov model. Thus the state of weather for each day is a function (only) of the weather the day before and we observe the fact that today is sunshine.

We can extend this example to determine, given that we know today's weather, the probability that the weather will be the same for exactly the next t days, i.e., that the weather remains the same until the t + 1 day at which time it is different. For any weather state s_i, and Markov model M, we have the observation O:

$$O = \{s_i, s_i, s_i, \ldots, s_i, s_j\}, \text{ where there are exactly (t + 1) } s_i, \text{ and where } s_i \neq s_j, \text{ then:}$$
$$p(O \mid M) = 1 \times a_{ii}^t \times (1 - a_{ii})$$

where a_{ii} is the transition probability of taking state s_i to itself. This value is called the *discrete probability density function for the duration of t time periods in state s_i* of model M. This duration density function is indicative of the state duration in a Markov model. Based on this value we can calculate, within model M, the expected number of observations of, or duration d_i within any state s_i, given that the first observation is in that state:

$$d_i = \sum_{d=1}^{n} d(a_{ii})^{(d-1)}(1 - a_{ii}) \quad \text{where } n \text{ approaches } \infty, \text{ or:}$$

$$= \frac{1}{1 - a_{ii}}$$

For example, the expected number of consecutive precipitation days, given this model, is $1/(1 - .3)$ or 1.43. Similarly, the number of consecutive sunny days one might expect is 1.67. In the next section we consider Markov models whose states are not observable events, that is, they are themselves probabilistic functions of the state.

9.3.5   Hidden Markov Models

In the Markov models we have seen to this point, each state corresponded to a discrete physical—or observable—event, such as the value of weather at a certain time of day. This class of model is really fairly limited and we now generalize it to a wider class of problems. In this section we extend Markov models to the situations where the observations are themselves probabilistic functions of a current hidden state. This resulting model, called a *hidden Markov model (HMM)*, is a doubly embedded stochastic process.

The HMM is an observable stochastic process supported by a further nonobservable, or hidden, stochastic process. An example use for an HMM would be to support word recognition through the interpretation of noisy acoustic signals. The phone patterns themselves, that is, which phonemes are more likely to follow others in the particular words of a language, make up the hidden level of the Markov model. An example would be the various pronunciations of the word "tomato" in Figure 5.3. The observations, i.e., the noisy acoustic signals, are a stochastic function of these phonemes. The phoneme level of the model can not be seen except though the top-level stream of acoustic signals. We present an example of this unsupervised learning in Section 9.3.6.

DEFINITION

HIDDEN MARKOV MODEL

A graphical model is called a *hidden Markov model (HMM)* if it is a Markov model whose states are not directly observable but are "hidden" by a further stochastic system interpreting their output. More formally, given a set of states $S = s_1, s_2, ..., s_n$, and given a set of state transition probabilities $A = a_{11}, a_{12}, ..., a_{1n}, a_{21}, a_{22}, ..., ..., a_{nn}$, there is a set of observation likelihoods, $O = p_i(o_t)$, each expressing the probability of an observation o_t (at time t) being from a state i.

We now give two examples of HMMs, suggested by and adapted from Rabiner (1989). First, consider the situation of coin flipping. Suppose there is a person in a room flipping coins, one at a time. We have no idea what is going on in the room, there may in fact be four coins, randomly selected for flipping and each of the coins may have its own biased outcomes, i.e., they may not be "fair" coins. All we observe outside the room is a series of outcomes from the flipping task, such as H, H, T, T, H, T, H, ... Our task is to design a model to capture what is going on in the room.

Given this situation, we attempt to design a model that explains this set of observations from the room. To begin, we select a particular model. We might begin with a simple model assuming there is but one coin being flipped. In this case we would only have to determine the bias of the coin as it is used over time to produce the set of head/tail observations. This simple approach would result in a directly observable zero-order Markov model, which is just a set of Bernoulli trials, but this model may, in fact, be too simple to capture reliably what is going on in the multiple coin flipping problem.

We next consider a two coin model, with two hidden states s_1 and s_2, as seen in Figure 9.19. The probabilistic transition matrix controls which state the system is in at any time. The bias for the states will be different, b_1 and b_2. Suppose we observed the string of coin flips: H, H, T, T, H, T, H, H, H, T, T, H. This set of observations can be accounted for by the following path through the state diagram of Figure 9.19: 2, 1, 1, 2, 2, 2, 1, 2, 2, 1, 2.

A third model for the coin flips is presented in Figure 9.20, where three states are used to describe the system. This model would correspond to the supposition of using three coins to approximate the flipping outcome. Each coin would have its own bias, and the system would decide what state it is in at any time by some probabilistic event based on the values in its transition matrix. The three state machine could account for the same head/tail sequence of the previous paragraph with the following path through the state diagram of Figure 9.20: 3, 1, 2, 3, 3, 1, 1, 2, 3, 1, 3.

The difficult issue in characterizing the coin flipping problem is the choice of a "best" model. The simple one coin model has only one parameter, the bias of a single coin. The two state model has four parameters, the state transitions and the bias of the coins. The three state model of Figure 9.20 has nine parameters. With more degrees of freedom, it would seem that the larger model would be more powerful for capturing the (possibly)

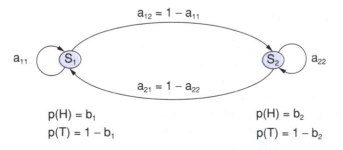

$$p(H) = b_1 \qquad\qquad\qquad p(H) = b_2$$
$$p(T) = 1 - b_1 \qquad\qquad\qquad p(T) = 1 - b_2$$

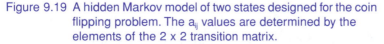

Figure 9.19 A hidden Markov model of two states designed for the coin flipping problem. The a_{ij} values are determined by the elements of the 2 x 2 transition matrix.

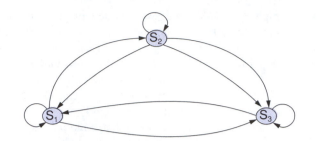

Figure 9.20 A hidden Markov model for the coin flipping problem. Each coin will have its individual bias.

complex situation of the problem than would be the equivalent smaller models. As we saw with full Bayesian reasoning earlier, however, these complexity issues can doom the exercise. Besides, the actual outcomes might be produced by a simpler situation, in which case the larger model would be both an incorrect model of the situation, as well as be under specified.

As a second simple example, consider the problem of N urns, each urn containing a collection of M differently colored balls. The physical process of obtaining observations is, according to some random process, to pick one of the N urns. Once an urn is selected a ball is removed and its color is recorded in the output stream. The ball is then replaced and the random process associated with the current urn selects the next (which might be the same) urn to continue the process. This process generates an observation sequence consisting of a number of colors (of the balls).

It is obvious that the simplest HMM corresponding to this ball selection process is the model in which each state corresponds to a specific urn, the values of the transition matrix for that state produce the next state choice, and in which the ball color probability is defined for each state.

In the next section, we apply the HMM technology to understanding English words, and use the Viterbi algorithm to implement the HMM search.

9.3.6 Using HMMs and Viterbi to Decode Strings of Phonemes

Our final section on graphical models demonstrates an important use of the HMM technology: identifying patterns in spoken natural language. We will also revisit the probabilistic finite state machine (PFSM) introduced in Section 5.3 as a representation technique for capturing pronunciation differences among related sets of words. Finally, we use dynamic programming algorithms, introduced in Section 4.1, for implementing HMM inference. When dynamic programming is used to find the maximum a posteriori string, it is often called the *Viterbi algorithm*.

The following example of computational analysis of human speech patterns and the use of the Viterbi algorithm to interpret strings of phonemes is adapted from Jurafsky and Martin (2000). This example has been simplified in several respects, for example, we

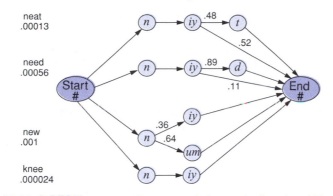

Figure 9.21 A PFSM representing a set of phonemically related English words. The probability of each word occurring is below that word. Adapted from Jurasky and Martin (2000).

assume the acoustic signal has been correctly broken down into an unambiguous string of phonemes, which is certainly not the case in most applications of this technology.

Figure 9.21 presents a segment of a database of words, related by the closeness of the sets of phonemes that make up their acoustic components. Although this set of words, neat, new, need, and knee, is but a small piece of the full English vocabulary, it can be imagined that a large number of these related clusters could support a speech understanding system. Figure 9.21 is an example of a probabilistic finite state machine, as first introduced in Section 5.3.

The input into this probabilistic machine is a string of phones, or basic speech sounds. These could be derived from decomposition of the acoustic signal produced by spoken language. It is unusual in automated speech understanding that acoustic signals would be unambiguously captured as a string of phonemes. Rather speech signals would be interpreted as specific phones probabilistically. We assume unambiguous interpretation of signals to simplify our presentation of the Viterbi algorithm processing the HMM.

The goal of the analysis is to determine which English word from our database of words best represents the input of acoustic signals. This requires use of the HMM technology, because the representation of possible words is itself stochastic, as seen in the non-deterministic finite state machine of Figure 9.21. The string of phones gives us the set of observations that we interpret. Suppose the string of observations is made up of the phones #, n, iy, #; where # indicates a pause or break between sounds. We use the Viterbi algorithm to see which path through the probabilistic finite state machine best captures these observations. In the forward mode of Viterbi we iteratively find the next best state and its value, and then set a pointer to it. In the backward mode we retrace these pointers to obtain the best path. Thus, the output of Viterbi is (one of the) "best" paths of states through the graph associated with the probability of that path.

Using Viterbi, each state of the search is associated with a value. The value for being in state s_i at time t is viterbi$[s_i, t]$. The value associated with the next state s_j in the state machine at time t + 1 is viterbi[s$_j$, t + 1]. The value for the next state is computed as the product of the score of the present state, viterbi[s$_i$, t], times the transition probability of going from the present state to the next state, path[s$_i$, s$_j$], times the probability of observation s$_j$ given s$_i$, p(s$_j$ | s$_i$). The transition probability, path[s$_i$, s$_j$], is taken from the non-deterministic finite state machine and p(s$_j$ | s$_i$) is taken from known observation likelihoods of pairs of phones occurring in the English language.

We next present pseudocode for the Viterbi algorithm (note similarity with dynamic programming, Section 4.1). The array for storing and coordinating values must support iteration over R rows—equal to the number of phones in the probabilistic finite state machine (PFSM) plus two, to handle each state plus the start and end states. It must also iterate over C columns—equal to the number of observations plus two, to handle use of the empty phone #. The columns also indicate the time sequence for observations and each state must be linked with the appropriate observed phone, as seen in Figure 9.22.

```
function Viterbi(Observations, Probabilistic FSM)


begin
    create probability matrix viterbi[R, C];
    viterbi[0, 0] := 1.0;
    for each time step (observation) t from 0 to C do
        for each state s_i from i = 0 to R do
            for each transition s_i to s_j in the Probabilistic FSM do
                begin
                    new-score := viterbi[s_i, t] x path[s_i, s_j] x p(s_j | s_i);
                    if ((new-score = 0) or (new-score < viterbi[s_i, t]))
                        then viterbi[s_j, t + 1] := viterbi[s_i, t]
                        else viterbi[s_j, t + 1] := new-score;
                    add back-pointer s_j ← s_i to back-pointer list
                end;
    return viterbi[R, C];
    return back-pointer list
end.
```

Figure 9.22, adapted from Jurafsky and Martin (2000), presents a trace of the Viterbi algorithm processing the probabilistic finite state machine of Figure 9.21 and the observed phone sequence #, n, iy, #. The back trace links indicate the "best" path through the probabilistic finite state machine. This path indicates that the most likely interpretation of the string of observed phones is the word new.

There remain many limitations in using proposition based graphical models, such as we have presented in Section 9.3. These limitations come both from the knowledge engineering as well as from the computational complexity viewpoints (Xiang et al. 1993, Laskey and Mahoney 1997). Recent research has created a variety of important extensions to graphical models, including hierarchical and decomposable Bayesian models. These new modeling formalisms support model decomposition similar in many respects to object-

Start = 1.0	#	n	iy	#	end
neat .00013 2 paths	1.0	1.0 x .00013 = .00013	.00013 x 1.0 = .00013	.00013 x .52 = .000067 (2 paths)	
need .00056 2 paths	1.0	1.0 x .00056 = .00056	.00056 x 1.0 = .00056	.00056 x .11 = .000062 (2 paths)	
new .001 2 paths	1.0	1.0 x .001 = .001	.001 x .36 = .00036 (2 paths)	.00036 x 1.0 = .00036	
knee .000024 1 path	1.0	1.0 x .000024 = .000024	.000024 x 1.0 = .000024	.000024 x 1.0 = .000024	
Total best					.00036

Figure 9.22 A trace of the Viterbi algorithm on the paths of Figure 9.21. Rows report the maximum value for Viterbi on each word for each input value (top row). Adapted from Jurafsky and Martin (2000).

oriented software design (Koller and Pfeffer 1997, 1998, Pfeffer et al 1999, Xiang et al. 2000, Pless et al. 2000).

Further important extensions to proposition based graphical models include Turing complete first-order languages for stochastic reasoning. First-order systems, of course, have the representational expressiveness equivalent to the first-order predicate calculus. Examples of this first-order stochastic modeling software may be found in the *IBAL* language of Pfeffer (2001), the *Stochastic Lambda Calculus* of Pless and Luger (2001), and the *Loopy Logic* language of Pless and Luger (2003).

Stochastic methods are important across the field of AI, for example, problem solving with probabilistic agents (Kosoresow 1993). We see stochastic methods again in learning, especially reinforcement learning, Section 10.7, and in natural language processing, Chapter 14. Finally, Judea Pearl (2000) uses stochastic methods to discuss the philosophical issues related to "causality".

9.4 Epilogue and References

From the beginning of the AI research enterprise, there has been an important subset of the community that feels logic and its extensions offer a sufficient representation for characterizing intelligence. Important alternatives to first-order predicate calculus have been proposed for describing reasoning under conditions of uncertainty:

1. **Multiple-valued logics.** These extend logic by adding new truth values such as unknown to the standard values of true and false. This can, for example, provide a vehicle for distinguishing between assertions that are known to be false and those that are simply not known to be true.

2. **Modal logics.** Modal logic adds operators that enable it to deal with problems of knowledge and belief, necessity and possibility. We discussed modal operators for *unless* and *is consistent with* in the present chapter.

3. **Temporal logics.** Temporal logics enable us to quantify expressions with regard to time, indicating, for example, that an expression is *always* true or *will be true at some time in the future*.

4. **Higher-order logics.** Many categories of knowledge involve higher-order concepts, where predicates, and not just variables, may be quantified. Do we really need higher-order logics to deal with this knowledge, or can it all be done in first-order logic? If higher-order logics are needed, how may they best be formulated?

5. **Logical formulations of definitions, prototypes, and exceptions.** Exceptions are often seen as a necessary feature of a definitional system. However, careless use of exceptions undermines the semantics of a representation. Another issue is the difference between a definition and a prototype, or representation of a *typical* individual. What is the exact difference between the properties of a class and the properties of a typical member? How should prototypical individuals be represented? When is a prototype more appropriate than a definition?

Logic-based representations continue to be an important area for research (McCarthy 1968, Hayes 1979, Weyhrauch 1980, Moore 1982, Turner 1984).

There are several other important contributions to truth maintenance system (TMS) reasoning. *Logic-based TMS* is based on the work of McAllester (1978). In LTMS relationships between propositions are represented by clauses which can be used to deduce the truth values of any of the propositions they describe. Another approach, the *multiple belief reasoner* MBR, is like the ATMS reasoner (deKleer 1984); similar ideas may be found in Martins and Shapiro (1983). MBR is based on a logic language called SWM* which describes knowledge states. Algorithms for inconsistency checking across reasoning in the knowledge base may be found in Ginsburg (1987) and Martins (1990, 1991). For further information on the node algebra support for JTMS see Doyle (1983) or Reinfrank (1989). Default logic allows any theorem inferred in an extension of a system to be admitted as an axiom for further reasoning. Reiter and Criscuolo (1981) and Touretzky (1986) develop these issues.

There is a rich literature on nonmonotonic reasoning, belief logics, and truth maintenance, besides the original papers in the area (Doyle 1979; Reiter 1985; deKleer 1986; McCarthy 1977, 1980). For stochastic models see *Probabilistic Reasoning in Intelligent Systems* by Pearl (1988), *Readings in Uncertain Reasoning* by Shafer and Pearl (1990), *Representations of Commonsense Knowledge* by Davis (1990), and numerous articles in recent AAAI, UAI, and IJCAI proceedings. We recommend *The Encyclopedia of Artificial Intelligence*, by Stuart Shapiro (2nd edition, 1992), for coverage of many of the reasoning models of this chapter. Josephson and Josephson (1994) have edited a collection of papers in *Abductive Inference: Computation, Philosophy, and Technology*. Also see *Formal Theories of the Commonsense World* (Hobbs and Moore 1985). In *Causality*, Pearl (2000) makes a contribution to understanding the notion of cause-effect relations in the world.

Further research in circumscriptive and minimum model logics may be found in Genesereth and Nilsson (1987) Lifschitz (1986), and McCarthy (1986). Another contribution to circumscriptive inference is Perlis' (1988) reasoning about a particular agent's lack of knowledge. Ginsburg (1987) has edited an important collection of papers on nonmonotonic systems, *Readings in Nonmonotonic Reasoning*.

For further reading on fuzzy systems we recommend the original paper by Lotfi Zadeh (1983) and the more modern integrations of this technology found in *Fuzzy Sets, Neural Networks and Soft Computing* by Yager and Zadeh (1994) and *Fuzzy Logic with Engineering Applications* by Timothy Ross (1995). The solution to the inverted pendulum problem presented in Section 9.2.2 was adapted from Ross.

Algorithms for Bayesian belief network inference include Pearl's (1988) *message passing* and *clique tree triangulation* (Lauritzen and Spiegelhalter 1988, see Section 9.3). For further discussion of these algorithms see the *Encyclopedia of AI* (Shapiro 1992) and (Huang and Darwiche 1996). The spring 1996 issue of the *AISB Quarterly* contains an introduction to *Bayesian belief networks* (van der Gaag 1996); we also recommend the discussions of *qualitative probabilistic networks* by Wellman (1990) and Druzdel (1996).

Stochastic representations and algorithms continue to be a very active research area (Xiang et al. 1993, Laskey and Mahoney 1997). Limitations of Bayesian representations have motivated research in hierarchical and composable Bayesian models (Koller and Pfeffer 1997, 1998, Pfeffer et al. 1999, Xiang et al. 2000). Further extensions of the propositional based graphic models we have presented can be found in the literature. We recommend reading Koller and Pfeffer (1998) and Pless et al. (2000) for ideas on object-oriented stochastic representations. The *IBAL* language of Pfeffer (2001) and the *Stochastic Lambda Calculus* of Pless and Luger (2002) are examples of first-order stochastic functional languages. Cussens (2001), and Pless and Luger (2003) have created first-order logic-based languages for stochastic inference.

9.5 Exercises

1. Identify three application domains where reasoning under conditions of uncertainty is necessary. Pick one of these areas and design six inference rules reflecting reasoning in that domain.

2. Given the following rules in a "back-chaining" expert system application:

   $A \land not(B) \Rightarrow C$ (.9)
   $C \lor D \Rightarrow E$ (.75)
   $F \Rightarrow A$ (.6)
   $G \Rightarrow D$ (.8)

The system can conclude the following facts (with confidences):

F(.9)

B(−.8)

G(.7)

Use the Stanford certainty factor algebra to determine E and its confidence.

3. Consider the simple MYCIN-like rule: if A ∧ (B ∨ C) ⇒ D (.9) ∧ E (.75). Discuss the issues that arise in capturing these uncertainties in a Bayesian context. How might this rule be handled in Dempster–Shafer reasoning?

4. Create a new example of diagnostic reasoning and use the Dempster–Shafer equations of Section 9.2.3 to obtain belief distributions as in Tables 9.1 and 9.2.

5. Use the schema axioms presented in McCarthy (1980, Section 4) to create the circumscription results presented in Section 9.1.3.

6. Create another reasoning network similar to that of Figure 9.4 and show the dependency lattice for its premises, as was done in Figure 9.5.

7. Reasoning by assumption of a minimum model is important in human everyday life. Work out two more examples that assume minimum models.

8. Continue the inverted pendulum example of Section 9.2.2 with two more iterations of the controller where the output of one iteration is the input values for the next iteration.

9. Write a program that implements the fuzzy controller of Section 9.2.2.

10. Go to the literature, for example Ross (1995), and describe two other areas where fuzzy control might be appropriate. Construct a set of fuzzy rules for those domains.

11. Put another link in Figure 9.16, say connecting season directly to slick sidewalk and then create a clique tree to represent this situation. Compare the complexity issues with those of the clique tree of Figure 9.17.

12. Complete the symbolic evaluations that are required to finish Table 9.4.

13. Create an algorithm for Bayesian belief propagation and apply it to the slippery sidewalk domain of Section 9.3.2. You might use Pearl's (1988) message passing approach or the clique triangulation method proposed by Lauritzen and Spiegelhalter (1988).

14. Create a Bayesian belief diagram for another application, for example medical diagnosis, geological discovery, or automobile fault analysis. Point out examples of d-separation and create a clique tree for this network.

15. Create cliques and a junction tree for the following situation (seen in Figure 9.23). Robbery, vandalism and an earthquake can all set off (cause) a house alarm. There is also a measure of the potential dangers in the neighborhood of the house.

16. Take the diagnostic reasoning situation developed in Tables 9.1 and 9.2 of the Dempster–Shafer model of Section 9.2.3 and recast it as a Bayesian belief network. Compare and contrast these two approaches to diagnosis.

17. Given that you wanted to design a second-order Markov model, i.e., where each observable state would be dependent on the previous two observable states. How would you do this? What would the transition probability matrix look like?

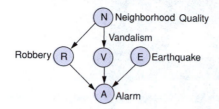

Figure 9.23 A belief network representing the possibility of a house alarm in a dangerous neighborhood.

18. Given the observable Markov model of weather of Section 9.3.4:

    a. Determine the probability that the next five days will be sun.
    b. What is the probability of exactly three days of sun, then one day of precipitation, and then exactly one day of sun?

19. Given the example of the Viterbi algorithm processing the probabilistic finite state machine of Figure 9.21.

    a. Why is new seen as a better interpretation than knee for the observed phones?
    b. How are alternative states in the probabilistic finite state machine handled by the Viterbi algorithm, for example the choice of the phones uw and iy in the word new.

20. Given the hidden Markov model and Viterbi algorithm of Section 9.3.6, perform a full trace, including setting up the appropriate back pointers, that shows how the observation #, n, iy, t, # would be processed.

PART IV

MACHINE LEARNING

Logic is not the end of wisdom, it is the beginning . . .

—SPOCK, "Star Trek VI"

"I know what you're thinking about", said Tweedledum, but it ain't so, nohow".
"Contrariwise", continued Tweedledee, "if it was so, it might be; and if it were so,
it would be; but as it isn't, it ain't. That's logic".

—LEWIS CAROLL, "Through the Looking Glass" (1871)

Let us teach guessing . . .

—GEORGE POLYA

Symbol-Based, Connectionist, and Emergent Learning

When asked what intellectual skills are most essentially human and most difficult to computerize, besides artistic creativity, ethical decision making, and social responsibility, people usually mention language and learning. Over the years, these two areas have functioned as goals, challenges, and as touchstones for the progress of AI. One of the reasons language and learning are difficult yet important research areas is that they encompass many other human intelligent capabilities. If we are ever to make claims of creating an artificial intelligence, we must address issues in natural language, automated reasoning, and machine learning. In Part IV we consider several approaches to machine learning; Part V presents topics in automated reasoning and natural language understanding

In Chapter 10, we consider symbol-based learning methods, beginning with a set of symbols that represent the entities and relationships of a problem domain. Symbolic learning algorithms attempt to infer novel, valid, and useful generalizations that can be expressed using these symbols.

The connectionist approaches discussed in Chapter 11 represent knowledge as patterns of activity in networks of small, individual processing units. Inspired by the architecture of animal brains, connectionist networks learn by modifying their structure and weights in response to training data. Rather than searching through the possible generalizations afforded by a symbolic representation language, connectionist models recognize invariant patterns in data and represent these patterns within their own structure.

Just as connectionist networks are inspired by the biological neural system, the emergent models of Chapter 12 are inspired by genetic and evolutionary analogs. Genetic algorithms begin with a population of candidate problem solutions. Candidate solutions are evaluated according to their ability to solve problem instances: only the fittest survive and combine with each other to produce the next generation of possible solutions. Thus, increasingly powerful solutions emerge as in a Darwinian universe. It is oddly fitting that these approaches should seek the origins of intelligence in the same processes that, it may be argued, gave rise to life itself.

There are a number of important philosophical/epistemological issues that underlie research in machine learning. These include the problem of *generalization* or how a machine can identify invariant patterns in data in a manner sufficient to use these invariants for further intelligent problem solving, for example, as a fit to new previously unseen data. A second problem for machine learning is the nature of an *inductive bias* in learning. This bias refers to how program designers use their own intuitions and heuristics in the design of representations, models, and algorithms that support the learning process. Examples of this include the identification of "important" concepts within the problem domain, the use of "a particular search or reward algorithm", or the selection of a particular neural net architecture for learning. The issue here is that these inductive biases both enable the learning process as well as limit what can be learned by that system. A final philosophical issue, called the *empiricist's dilemma*, looks at the opposite side of things: if there are no predetermined biases in the learning system, how can anything useful be learned, or even worse, how can we even know when something IS learned? This issue often arises in unsupervised and emergent models of machine learning. These three issues are discussed again in Section 17.2.

MACHINE LEARNING: SYMBOL-BASED

10

The mind being, as I have declared, furnished with a great number of the simple ideas conveyed in by the senses, as they are found in exterior things, or by reflection on its own operations, takes notice, also, that a certain number of these simple ideas go constantly together . . . which, by inadvertency, we are apt afterward to talk of and consider as one simple idea.

—JOHN LOCKE, *Essay Concerning Human Understanding*

The mere observing of a thing is no use whatever. Observing turns into beholding, beholding into thinking, thinking into establishing connections, so that one may say that every attentive glance we cast on the world is an act of theorizing. However, this ought to be done consciously, with self criticism, with freedom, and to use a daring word, with irony.

—GOETHE

10.0 Introduction

The ability to learn must be part of any system that would claim to possess general intelligence. Indeed, in our world of symbols and interpretation, the very notion of an unchanging intellect seems a contradiction in terms. Intelligent agents must be able to change through the course of their interactions with the world, as well as through the experience of their own internal states and processes. We present three chapters on machine learning, reflecting three approaches to the problem, first from the symbol-based, second, from the connectionist, and finally, from the genetic or evolutionary perspectives.

Learning is important for practical applications of artificial intelligence. Feigenbaum and McCorduck (1983) have called the "knowledge engineering bottleneck" the major obstacle to the widespread use of intelligent systems. This "bottleneck" is the cost and difficulty of building expert systems using the traditional knowledge acquisition techniques of Section 8.1. One solution to this problem would be for programs to begin with a minimal amount of knowledge and learn from examples, high-level advice, or their own explorations of the domain.

Herbert Simon defines learning as:

> any change in a system that allows it to perform better the second time on repetition of the same task or on another task drawn from the same population (Simon, 1983).

This definition, although brief, suggests many of the issues involved in developing programs that learn. Learning involves generalization from experience: performance should improve not only on the "repetition of the same task," but also on similar tasks in the domain. Because interesting domains tend to be large, a learner usually only examines a fraction of all possible examples; from this limited experience, the learner must generalize correctly to unseen instances of the domain. This is the problem of *induction*, and it is central to learning. In most learning problems, the available data are not sufficient to guarantee optimal generalization, no matter what algorithm is used. Learners must generalize heuristically, that is, they must select those aspects of their experience that are most likely to prove effective in the future. Such selection criteria are known as *inductive biases*.

Simon's definition describes learning as allowing the system to "perform better the second time." As the previous paragraph indicates, selecting the possible changes to a system that will allow it to improve is a difficult task. Learning research must address the possibility that changes may actually degrade performance. Preventing and detecting such problems is another issue for a learning algorithm.

Learning involves changes in the learner; this is clear. However, the exact nature of those changes and the best way to represent them are far from obvious. One approach models learning as the acquisition of explicitly represented domain knowledge. Based on its experience, the learner constructs or modifies expressions in a formal language, such as logic, and retains this knowledge for future use. Symbolic approaches, characterized by the algorithms of Sections 10.2 through 10.6, are built on the assumption that the primary influence on the program's behavior is its base of explicitly represented domain knowledge.

Neural or *connectionist networks*, in contrast, do not learn by acquiring sentences in a symbolic language. Like an animal brain, which consists of a large number of interconnected nerve cells, neural networks are systems of interconnected, artificial neurons. The program's knowledge is implicit in the organization and interaction of these neurons. Rather than constructing an explicit model of the world, they are shaped by it. Neural nets do not learn by adding representations to their knowledge base; instead, they learn by modifying their overall structure in order to adapt to the contingencies of the world they inhabit. In Chapter 10, we examine the neural or connectionist approach.

In Chapter 12, we consider *genetic* and *evolutionary learning*. Certainly one of the strongest models of learning we have may be seen in the human and animal systems that have evolved towards equilibration with the world. This approach to learning through adaptation is reflected in genetic algorithms, genetic programming, and artificial life research.

Machine learning has proven to be a fruitful area of research, spawning a number of different problems and algorithms for their solution. These algorithms vary in their goals, in the available training data, and in the learning strategies and knowledge representation languages they employ. However, all of these algorithms learn by searching through a space of possible concepts to find an acceptable generalization. In Section 10.1, we outline a framework for symbol-based machine learning that emphasizes the common assumptions behind all of this work.

Although Section 10.1 outlines a variety of learning tasks, this chapter focuses primarily on *inductive learning*. Induction, which is learning a generalization from a set of examples, is one of the most fundamental learning tasks. *Concept learning* is a typical inductive learning problem: given examples of some concept, such as "cat," "soybean disease," or "good stock investment," we attempt to infer a definition that will allow the learner to correctly recognize future instances of that concept. Sections 10.2 and 10.3 examine two algorithms used for concept induction, *version space search* and *ID3*.

Section 10.4 considers the role of *inductive bias* in learning. The search spaces encountered in learning tend to be extremely large, even by the standards of search-based problem solving. These complexity problems are exacerbated by the problem of choosing among the different generalizations supported by the training data. Inductive bias refers to any method that a learning program uses to constrain the space of possible generalizations.

The algorithms of Sections 10.2 and 10.3 are data-driven. They use no prior knowledge of the learning domain but rely on large numbers of examples to define the essential properties of a general concept. Algorithms that generalize on the basis of patterns in training data are referred to as *similarity-based*. In contrast to similarity-based methods, a learner may use prior knowledge of the domain to guide generalization. For example, humans do not require large numbers of examples to learn effectively. Often, a single example, analogy, or high-level bit of advice is sufficient to communicate a general concept. The effective use of such knowledge can help an agent to learn more efficiently, and with less likelihood of error. Section 10.5 examines *explanation-based learning*, learning by analogy and other techniques using prior knowledge to learn from limited training data.

The algorithms presented in Sections 10.2 through 10.5, though they differ in search strategies, representation languages, and the amount of prior knowledge used, all assume that the training data are classified by a teacher or some other means. The learner is told whether an instance is a positive or negative example of a target concept. This reliance on training instances of known classification defines the task of *supervised learning*.

Section 10.6 continues the study of induction by examining *unsupervised learning*, which addresses how an intelligent agent can acquire useful knowledge in the absence of correctly classified training data. *Category formation*, or *conceptual clustering*, is a fundamental problem in unsupervised learning. Given a set of objects exhibiting various properties, how may an agent divide the objects into useful categories? How do we even know whether a category will be useful? In this section, we examine CLUSTER/2 and COBWEB, two category formation algorithms.

Finally, in Section 10.7, we present reinforcement learning. Here, an agent is situated in an environment and receives feedback from that context. Learning requires the agent to act and then to interpret feedback from those actions. Reinforcement learning differs from supervised learning in that there is no "teacher" directly responding to each action; rather the agent itself must create a policy for interpreting all feedback. Reinforcement learning fits comfortably with a constructivist epistemology, as described in Section 17.2.

All learning presented in this chapter has one thing in common: it is seen as a variety of state space search. Even reinforcement learning derives a value function over a state space. We next outline a general search-based framework for work in machine learning.

10.1 A Framework for Symbol-Based Learning

Learning algorithms may be characterized along several dimensions, as in Figure 10.1:

1. **The data and goals of the learning task.** One of the primary ways in which we characterize learning problems is according to the goals of the learner and the data it is given. The concept learning algorithms of Sections 10.2 and 10.3, for example, begin with a collection of positive (and usually negative) examples of a target class; the goal is to infer a general definition that will allow the learner to recognize future instances of the class. In contrast to the data-intensive approach taken by these algorithms, *explanation-based learning* (Section 10.5), attempts to infer a general concept from a single training example and a prior base of domain-specific knowledge. The conceptual clustering algorithms discussed in Section 10.6 illustrate another variation on the induction problem: instead of a set of training instances of known categorization, these algorithms begin with a set of unclassified instances. Their task is to discover categorizations that may have some utility to the learner.

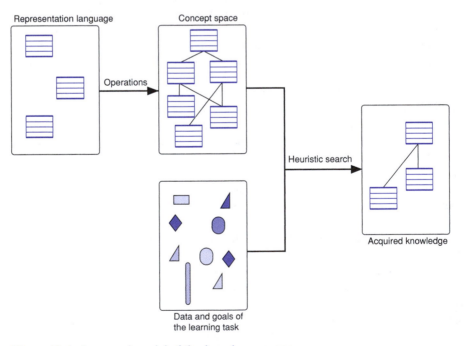

Figure 10.1 A general model of the learning process.

Examples are not the only source of training data. Humans, for instance, often learn from high-level advice. In teaching programming, professors generally tell their students that all loops must achieve a terminating condition. This advice, though correct, is not directly useful: it must be translated into specific rules for manipulating loop counters or logical conditions in a programming language. Analogies (Section 10.5.4) are another type of training data that must be correctly interpreted before they can be of use. If a teacher tells a student that electricity is like water, the student must infer the correct intent of the analogy: as water flows through a pipe, electricity flows through a wire. As with flowing water, we may measure the amount of electricity (amperage) and the pressure behind the flow (voltage). Unlike water, however, electricity does not make things wet or help us wash our hands. The interpretation of analogies involves finding the meaningful similarities and avoiding false or meaningless inferences.

We may also characterize a learning algorithm by the goal, or *target*, of the learner. The goal of many learning algorithms is a *concept*, or a general description of a class of objects. Learning algorithms may also acquire plans, problem-solving heuristics, or other forms of procedural knowledge.

The properties and quality of the training data itself are another dimension along which we classify learning tasks. The data may come from a teacher from the outside environment, or it may be generated by the program itself. Data may be reliable or may contain noise. It can be presented in a well-structured fashion or consist of unorganized data. It may include both positive and negative examples or only positive examples. Data may be readily available, the program may have to construct experiments, or perform some other form of data acquisition.

2. **The representation of learned knowledge.** Machine learning programs have made use of all the representation languages discussed in this text. For example, programs that learn to classify objects may represent these concepts as expressions in predicate calculus or they may use a structured representation such as frames or objects. Plans may be described as a sequence of operations or a triangle table. Heuristics may be represented as problem-solving rules.

A simple formulation of the concept learning problem represents instances of a concept as conjunctive sentences containing variables. For example, two instances of "ball" (not sufficient to learn the concept) may be represented by:

size(obj1, small) $\land$ color(obj1, red) $\land$ shape(obj1, round)
size(obj2, large) $\land$ color(obj2, red) $\land$ shape(obj2, round)

The general concept of "ball" could be defined by:

size(X, Y) $\land$ color(X, Z) $\land$ shape(X, round)

where any sentence that unifies with this general definition represents a ball.

3. **A set of operations.** Given a set of training instances, the learner must construct a generalization, heuristic rule, or plan that satisfies its goals. This requires the ability to manipulate representations. Typical operations include generalizing or

specializing symbolic expressions, adjusting the weights in a neural network, or otherwise modifying the program's representations.

In the concept learning example just introduced, a learner may generalize a definition by replacing constants with variables. If we begin with the concept:

size(obj1, small) $\land$ color(obj1, red) $\land$ shape(obj1, round)

replacing a single constant with a variable produces the generalizations:

size(obj1, X) $\land$ color(obj1, red) $\land$ shape(obj1, round)
size(obj1, small) $\land$ color(obj1, X) $\land$ shape(obj1, round)
size(obj1, small) $\land$ color(obj1, red) $\land$ shape(obj1, X)
size(X, small) $\land$ color(X, red) $\land$ shape(X, round)

4. **The concept space.** The representation language, together with the operations described above, defines a space of potential concept definitions. The learner must search this space to find the desired concept. The complexity of this concept space is a primary measure of the difficulty of a learning problem.

5. **Heuristic search.** Learning programs must commit to a direction and order of search, as well as to the use of available training data and heuristics to search efficiently. In our example of learning the concept "ball," a plausible algorithm may take the first example as a *candidate concept* and generalize it to include subsequent examples. For instance, on being given the single training example

size(obj1, small) $\land$ color(obj1, red) $\land$ shape(obj1, round)

the learner will make that example a candidate concept; this concept correctly classifies the only positive instance seen.

If the algorithm is given a second positive instance

size(obj2, large) $\land$ color(obj2, red) $\land$ shape(obj2, round)

the learner may generalize the candidate concept by replacing constants with variables as needed to form a concept that matches both instances. The result is a more general candidate concept that is closer to our target concept of "ball."

size(X, Y) $\land$ color(X, red) $\land$ shape(X, round)

Patrick Winston's work (1975*a*) on learning concepts from positive and negative examples illustrates these components. His program learns general definitions of structural concepts, such as "arch," in a blocks world. The training data is a series of positive and negative examples of the concept: examples of blocks world structures that fit in the category, along with *near misses*. The latter are instances that almost belong to the category but fail on one property or relation. The near misses enable the program to single out features that can be used to exclude negative instances from the target concept. Figure 10.2 shows positive examples and near misses for the concept "arch."

The program represents concepts as semantic networks, as in Figure 10.3. It learns by refining a candidate description of the target concept as training instances are presented. Winston's program refines candidate descriptions through generalization and specialization. Generalization changes the graph to let it accommodate new examples of the concept. Figure 10.3a shows an arch built of three bricks and a graph that describes it. The next training example, Figure 10.3b, is an arch with a pyramid rather than a brick on top. This example does not match the candidate description. The program matches these graphs, attempting to find a partial isomorphism between them. The graph matcher uses the node names to guide the matching process. Once the program matches the graphs, it may detect differences between them. In Figure 10.3, the graphs match on all components except that the top element in the first graph is brick and the corresponding node of the second example is pyramid. Part of the program's background knowledge is a generalization hierarchy of these concepts, Figure 10.3c. The program generalizes the graph by replacing this node with the least common supertype of brick and pyramid; in this example, it is polygon. The result is the concept of Figure 10.3d.

When presented with a near miss, an example that differs from the target concept in a single property, the program specializes the candidate description to exclude the example. Figure 10.4a is a candidate description. It differs from the near miss of Figure 10.4b in the

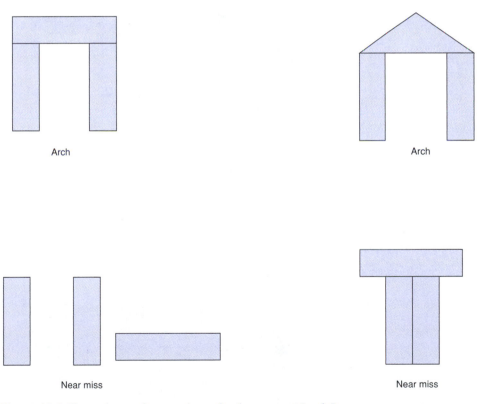

Arch

Arch

Near miss

Near miss

Figure 10.2 Examples and near misses for the concept "arch."

touch relations of the near-miss example. The program specializes the graph by adding must-not-touch links to exclude the near miss, Figure 10.4c. Note that the algorithm depends heavily upon the closeness of the negative examples to the target concept. By differing from the goal in only a single property, a near miss helps the algorithm to determine exactly how to specialize the candidate concept.

a. An example of an arch and its network description

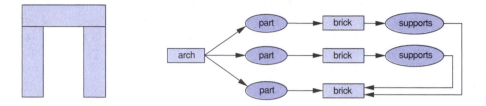

b. An example of another arch and its network description

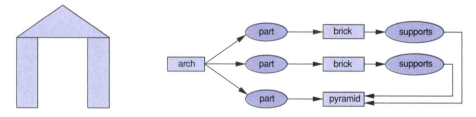

c. Given background knowledge that bricks and pyramids are both types of polygons

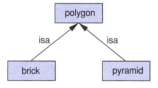

d. Generalization that includes both examples

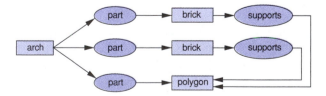

Figure 10.3 Generalization of descriptions to include multiple examples.

These operations—specializing a network by adding links and generalizing it by replacing node or link names with a more general concept—define a space of possible concept definitions. Winston's program performs a hill climbing search on the concept space guided by the training data. Because the program does not backtrack, its performance is highly sensitive to the order of the training examples; a bad ordering can lead the program to dead ends in the search space. Training instances must be presented to the program in an order that assists learning of the desired concept, much as a teacher organizes lessons to help a student learn. The quality and order of the training examples are also important to the program's graph matching algorithm; efficient matching requires that the graphs not be too dissimilar.

a. Candidate description of an arch

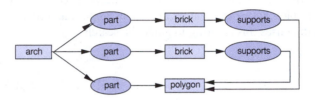

b. A near miss and its description

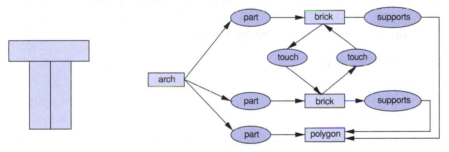

c. Arch description specialized to exclude the near miss

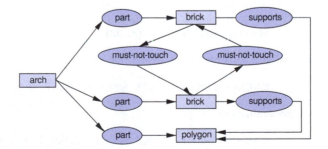

Figure 10.4 Specialization of a description to exclude a near miss. In 10.4c we add constraints to 10.4a so that it can't match with 10.4b.

Although an early example of inductive learning, Winston's program illustrates the features and problems shared by the majority of machine learning techniques: the use of generalization and specialization operations to define a concept space, the use of data to guide search through that space, and the sensitivity of the learning algorithm to the quality of the training data. The next sections examine these problems and the techniques that machine learning has developed for their solution.

10.2 Version Space Search

Version space search (Mitchell 1978, 1979, 1982) illustrates the implementation of inductive learning as search through a concept space. Version space search takes advantage of the fact that generalization operations impose an ordering on the concepts in a space, and then uses this ordering to guide the search.

10.2.1 Generalization Operators and the Concept Space

Generalization and specialization are the most common types of operations for defining a concept space. The primary generalization operations used in machine learning are:

1. Replacing constants with variables. For example,

    color(ball, red)

    generalizes to

    color(X, red)

2. Dropping conditions from a conjunctive expression.

    shape(X, round) ∧ size(X, small) ∧ color(X, red)

    generalizes to

    shape(X, round) ∧ color(X, red)

3. Adding a disjunct to an expression.

    shape(X, round) ∧ size(X, small) ∧ color(X, red)

    generalizes to

    shape(X, round) ∧ size(X, small) ∧ (color(X, red) ∨ color(X, blue))

4. Replacing a property with its parent in a class hierarchy. If we know that primary_color is a superclass of red, then

color(X, red)

generalizes to

color(X, primary_color)

We may think of generalization in set theoretic terms: let P and Q be the sets of sentences matching the predicate calculus expressions p and q, respectively. Expression p is more general than q iff P ⊇ Q. In the above examples, the set of sentences that match color(X, red) contains the set of elements that match color(ball, red). Similarly, in example 2, we may think of the set of round, red things as a superset of the set of small, red, round things. Note that the "more general than" relationship defines a partial ordering on the space of logical sentences. We express this using the "≥" symbol, where p ≥ q means that p is more general than q. This ordering is a powerful source of constraints on the search performed by a learning algorithm.

We formalize this relationship through the notion of *covering*. If concept p is more general than concept q, we say that p *covers* q. We define the covers relation: let p(x) and q(x) be descriptions that classify objects as being positive examples of a concept. In other words, for an object x, p(x) → positive(x) and q(x) → positive(x). p covers q iff q(x) → positive(x) is a logical consequence of p(x) → positive(x).

For example, color(X, Y) covers color(ball, Z), which in turn covers color(ball, red). As a simple example, consider a domain of objects that have properties and values:

Sizes = {large, small}
Colors = {red, white, blue}
Shapes = {ball, brick, cube}

These objects can be represented using the predicate obj(Sizes, Color, Shapes). The generalization operation of replacing constants with variables defines the space of Figure 10.5. We may view inductive learning as searching this space for a concept that is consistent with all the training examples.

10.2.2   The Candidate Elimination Algorithm

This section presents three algorithms (Mitchell 1982) for searching the concept space. These algorithms rely upon the notion of a *version space*, which is the set of all concept descriptions consistent with the training examples. These algorithms work by reducing the size of the version space as more examples become available. The first two algorithms reduce the version space in a specific to general direction and a general to specific direction, respectively. The third algorithm, called *candidate elimination*, combines these approaches into a bi-directional search. We next describe and evaluate these algorithms.

These algorithms are data driven; they generalize based on regularities found in the training data. Also, in using training data of known classification, these algorithms perform a variety of *supervised learning*.

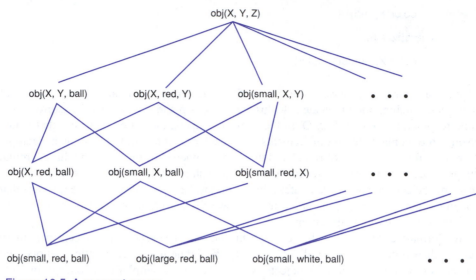

obj(X, Y, Z)

obj(X, Y, ball)   obj(X, red, Y)   obj(small, X, Y)   • • •

obj(X, red, ball)   obj(small, X, ball)   obj(small, red, X)   • • •

obj(small, red, ball)   obj(large, red, ball)   obj(small, white, ball)   • • •

Figure 10.5 A concept space.

As with Winston's program for learning structural descriptions, version space search uses both positive and negative examples of the target concept. Although it is possible to generalize from positive examples only, negative examples are important in preventing the algorithm from overgeneralizing. Not only must the learned concept be general enough to cover all positive examples; it also must be specific enough to exclude all negative examples. In the space of Figure 10.5, one concept that would cover all sets of exclusively positive instances would simply be obj(X, Y, Z). However, this concept is probably too general, because it implies that all instances belong to the target concept. One way to avoid overgeneralization is to generalize as little as possible to cover positive examples; another is to use negative instances to eliminate overly general concepts. As Figure 10.6 illustrates, negative instances prevent overgeneralization by forcing the learner to specialize concepts in order to exclude negative instances. The algorithms of this section use both of these techniques. We define *specific to general* search, for hypothesis set S, as:

```
Begin
Initialize S to the first positive training instance;
N is the set of all negative instances seen so far;

For each positive instance p
    Begin
    For every s ∈ S, if s does not match p, replace s with its most specific
        generalization that matchs p;
    Delete from S all hypotheses more general than some other hypothesis in S;
    Delete from S all hypotheses that match a previously observed negative
        instance in N;
    End;
```

For every negative instance n
    Begin
    Delete all members of S that match n;
    Add n to N to check future hypotheses for overgeneralization;
    End;
End

Specific to general search maintains a set, S, of *hypotheses*, or candidate concept definitions. To avoid overgeneralization, these candidate definitions are the *maximally specific generalizations* from the training data. A concept, c, is maximally specific if it covers all positive examples, none of the negative examples, and for any other concept, c′, that covers the positive examples, $c \leq c'$. Figure 10.7 shows an example of applying this algorithm to the version space of Figure 10.5. The specific to general version space search algorithm is built in PROLOG in Section 15.8.1.

We may also search in a general to specific direction. This algorithm maintains a set, G, of *maximally general concepts* that cover all of the positive and none of the negative instances. A concept, c, is maximally general if it covers none of the negative training instances, and for any other concept, c′, that covers no negative training instance, $c \geq c'$. In this algorithm, negative instances lead to the specialization of candidate concepts; the algorithm uses positive instances to eliminate overly specialized concepts.

Begin
Initialize G to contain the most general concept in the space;
P contains all positive examples seen so far;

For each negative instance n
    Begin
    For each g ∈ G that matches n, replace g with its most general specializations
        that do not match n;
    Delete from G all hypotheses more specific than some other hypothesis in G;
    Delete from G all hypotheses that fail to match some positive example in P;
    End;

For each positive instance p
    Begin
    Delete from G all hypotheses that fail to match p;
    Add p to P;
    End;
End

Figure 10.8 shows an example of applying this algorithm to the version space of Figure 10.5. In this example, the algorithm uses background knowledge that size may have values {large, small}, color may have values {red, white, blue}, and shape may have values {ball, brick, cube}. This knowledge is essential if the algorithm is to specialize concepts by substituting constants for variables.

The *candidate elimination algorithm* combines these approaches into a bi-directional search. This bi-directional approach has a number of benefits for learning. The algorithm

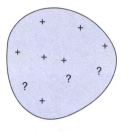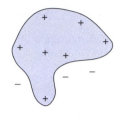

Concept induced from positive examples only

Concept induced from positive and negative examples

Figure 10.6 The role of negative examples in preventing overgeneralization.

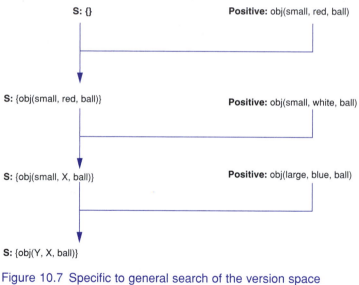

Figure 10.7 Specific to general search of the version space learning the concept "ball."

maintains two sets of candidate concepts: G, the set of maximally general candidate concepts, and S, the set of maximally specific candidates. The algorithm specializes G and generalizes S until they converge on the target concept. The algorithm is defined:

Begin
Initialize G to be the most general concept in the space;
Initialize S to the first positive training instance;

For each new positive instance p
    Begin
    Delete all members of G that fail to match p;
    For every s ∈ S, if s does not match p, replace s with its most specific
        generalizations that match p;
    Delete from S any hypothesis more general than some other hypothesis in S;
    Delete from S any hypothesis more general than some hypothesis in G;
    End;

For each new negative instance n
    Begin
    Delete all members of S that match n;
    For each g ∈ G that matches n, replace g with its most general specializations
        that do not match n;
    Delete from G any hypothesis more specific than some other hypothesis in G;
    Delete from G any hypothesis more specific than some hypothesis in S;
    End;

If G = S and both are singletons, then the algorithm has found a single concept that
    is consistent with all the data and the algorithm halts;

If G and S become empty, then there is no concept that covers all positive instances
    and none of the negative instances;

End

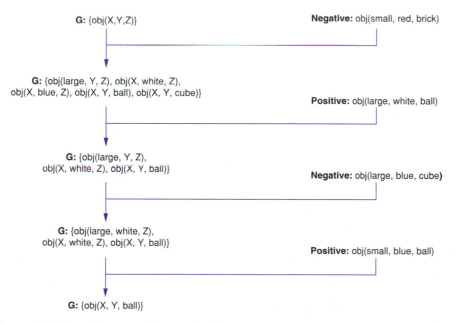

Figure 10.8 General to specific search of the version space learning the concept "ball."

Figure 10.9 illustrates the behavior of the candidate elimination algorithm in searching the version space of Figure 10.5. Note that the figure does not show those concepts that were produced through generalization or specialization but eliminated as overly general or specific. We leave the elaboration of this part of the algorithm as an exercise and show a partial implementation in PROLOG in Section 15.8.2.

Combining the two directions of search into a single algorithm has several benefits. The G and S sets summarize the information in the negative and positive training instances respectively, eliminating the need to save these instances. For example, after generalizing S to cover a positive instance, the algorithm uses G to eliminate concepts in S that do not cover any negative instances. Because G is the set of *maximally general* concepts that do not match any negative training instances, any member of S that is more general than any member of G must match some negative instance. Similarly, because S is the set of *maximally specific* generalizations that cover all positive instances, any new member of G that is more specific than a member of S must fail to cover some positive instance and may also be eliminated.

Figure 10.10 gives an abstract description of the candidate elimination algorithm. The "+" signs represent positive training instances; "−" signs indicate negative instances. The

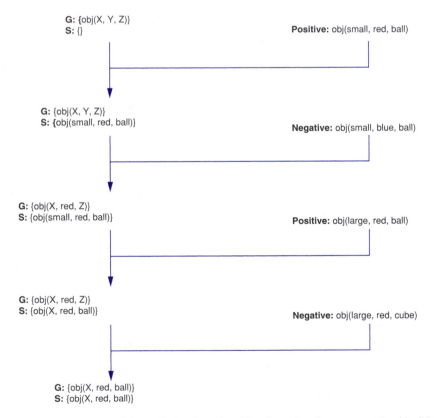

Figure 10.9 The candidate elimination algorithm learning the concept "red ball."

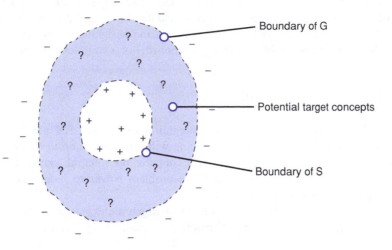

Figure 10.10 Converging boundaries of the G and S sets in the candidate elimination algorithm.

innermost circle encloses the set of known positive instances covered by the concepts in S. The outermost circle encloses the instances covered by G; any instance outside this circle is negative. The shaded portion of the graphic contains the target concept, along with concepts that may be overly general or specific (the ?s). The search "shrinks" the outermost concept as necessary to exclude negative instances; it "expands" the innermost concept to include new positive instances. Eventually, the two sets converge on the target concept. In this fashion, candidate elimination can detect when it has found a single, consistent target concept. When both G and S converge to the same concept the algorithm may halt. If G and S become empty, then there is no concept that will cover all positive instances and none of the negative instances. This may occur if the training data is inconsistent or if the goal concept may not be expressed in the representation language (Section 10.2.4).

An interesting aspect of candidate elimination is its incremental nature. An incremental learning algorithm accepts training instances one at a time, forming a usable, although possibly incomplete, generalization after each example. This contrasts with batch algorithms, (see for example ID3, Section 10.3), which require all training examples to be present before they may begin learning. Even before the candidate elimination algorithm converges on a single concept, the G and S sets provide usable constraints on that concept: if c is the goal concept, then for all $g \in G$ and $s \in S$, $s \le c \le g$. Any concept that is more general than some concept in G will cover negative instances; any concept that is more specific than some concept in S will fail to cover some positive instances. This suggests that instances that have a "good fit" with the concepts bounded by G and S are at least plausible instances of the concept.

In the next section, we clarify this intuition with an example of a program that uses candidate elimination to learn search heuristics. LEX (Mitchell et al. 1983) learns heuristics for solving symbolic integration problems. Not only does this work demonstrate the use of G and S to define partial concepts; it also illustrates such additional issues as the complexities of learning multistep tasks, credit/blame assignment, and the relationship between the learning and problem-solving components of a complex system.

10.2.3 LEX: Inducing Search Heuristics

LEX learns heuristics for solving symbolic integration problems. LEX integrates algebraic expressions through heuristic search, beginning with the expression to be integrated and searching for its goal: an expression that contains no integral signs. The learning component of the system uses data from the problem solver to induce heuristics that improve the problem solver's performance.

LEX searches a space defined by operations on algebraic expressions. Its operators are the typical transformations used in performing integration. They include:

OP1: $\int r\, f(x)\, dx \rightarrow r \int f(x)\, dx$
OP2: $\int u\, dv \rightarrow uv - \int v\, du$
OP3: $1*f(x) \rightarrow f(x)$
OP4: $\int (f_1(x) + f_2(x))\, dx \rightarrow \int f_1(x)\, dx + \int f_2(x)\, dx$

Operators are rules, whose left-hand side defines when they may be applied. Although the left-hand side defines the circumstances under which the operator may be used, it does not include heuristics for when the operator *should* be used. LEX must learn usable heuristics through its own experience. Heuristics are expressions of the form:

If the current problem state matches P then apply operator O with bindings B.

For example, a typical heuristic that LEX might learn is:

If a problem state matches $\int x$ transcendental(x) dx,
    then apply OP2 with bindings
        u = x
        dv = transcendental(x) dx

Here, the heuristic suggests applying integration by parts to solve the integral of x times some transcendental function (e.g., a trigonometric function) in x.

LEX's language for representing concepts consists of the symbols described in Figure 10.11. Note that the symbols exist in a generalization hierarchy, with any symbol matching any of its descendants in the hierarchy. LEX generalizes expressions by replacing a symbol with its ancestor in this hierarchy.

For example, given the expression:

$\int 3x \cos(x)\, dx$

LEX may replace cos with trig. This yields the expression:

∫ 3x trig(x) dx

Alternatively, it may replace 3 with the symbol k, which represents any integer:

∫ kx cos(x) dx

Figure 10.12 shows a version space for OP2 as defined by these generalizations. The overall architecture of LEX consists of four components:

1. a *generalizer* that uses candidate elimination to find heuristics

2. a *problem solver* that produces traces of problem solutions

3. a *critic* that produces positive and negative instances from a problem trace

4. a *problem generator* that produces new candidate problems

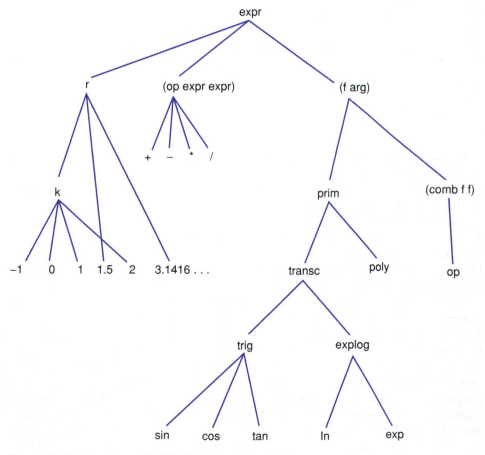

Figure 10.11 A portion of LEX's hierarchy of symbols.

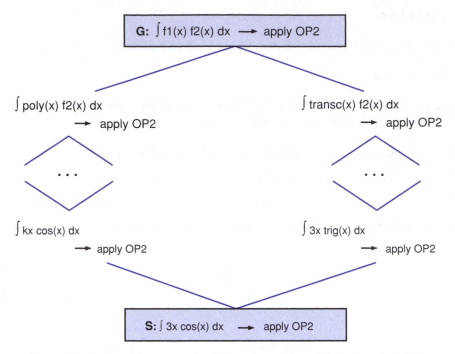

Figure 10.12 A version space for OP2, adapted from Mitchell et al. (1983).

LEX maintains a set of version spaces. Each version space is associated with an operator and represents a partially learned heuristic for that operator. The generalizer updates these version spaces using positive and negative examples of the operator's application, as generated by the critic. On receiving a positive instance, LEX determines whether a version space associated with that operator includes the instance. A version space includes a positive instance if the instance is covered by some of the concepts in G. LEX then uses the positive instance to update that heuristic. If no existing heuristic matches the instance, LEX creates a new version space, using that instance as the first positive example. This can lead to creating multiple version spaces, for different heuristics, and one operator.

LEX's problem solver builds a tree of the space searched in solving an integration problem. It limits the CPU time the problem solver may use to solve a problem. LEX performs best-first search, using its own developing heuristics. An interesting aspect of LEX's performance is its use of G and S as partial definitions of a heuristic. If more than one operator may apply to a given state, LEX chooses the one that exhibits the highest degree of partial match to the problem state. Degree of partial match is defined as the percentage of all the concepts included between G and S that match the current state. Because the computational expense of testing the state against all such candidate concepts would be prohibitive, LEX estimates the degree of match as the percentage of entries actually in G and S that match the state. Note that performance should improve steadily as LEX improves its heuristics. Empirical results have confirmed this conjecture.

LEX obtains positive and negative examples of operator applications from the solution trace generated by the problem solver. In the absence of a teacher, LEX must classify operator applications as positive or negative; this is an example of the *credit assignment* problem. When learning is undertaken in the context of multistep problem solving, it is often unclear which action in a sequence should be given responsibility for the result. If a problem solver arrives at a wrong answer, how do we know which of several steps actually caused the error? LEX's critic approaches this problem by assuming that the solution trace returned by the problem solver represents a shortest path to a goal. LEX classifies applications of operators along this (assumed) shortest path as positive instances; operator applications that diverge from this path are treated as negative instances.

However, in treating the problem solver's trace as a shortest path solution, the critic must address the fact that LEX's evolving heuristics are not guaranteed to be admissible (Chapter 4). The solution path found by the problem solver may not actually be a shortest path solution. To ensure that it has not erroneously classified an operator application as negative, LEX first extends the paths begun by such operators to make sure they do not lead to a better solution. Usually, a problem solution produces 2 to 20 training instances. LEX passes these positive and negative instances on to the generalizer, which uses them to update the version spaces for the associated operators.

The problem generator is the least developed part of the program. Although various strategies were used to automate problem selection, most examples involved hand-chosen instances. However, a problem generator was constructed that explored a variety of strategies. One approach generates instances that were covered by the partial heuristics for two different operators, in order to make LEX learn to discriminate between them.

Empirical tests show that LEX is effective in learning useful heuristics. In one test, LEX was given 5 test problems and 12 training problems. Before training, it solved the 5 test problems in an average of 200 steps; these solutions used no heuristics to guide the search. After developing heuristics from the 12 training problems, it solved these same test problems in an average of 20 steps.

LEX addresses a number of issues in learning, including such problems as credit assignment, the selection of training instances, and the relationship between the problem solving and generalization components of a learning algorithm. LEX also underscores the importance of an appropriate representation for concepts. Much of LEX's effectiveness stems from the hierarchical organization of concepts. This hierarchy is small enough to constrain the space of potential heuristics and to allow efficient search, while being rich enough to represent effective heuristics.

10.2.4 Evaluating Candidate Elimination

The candidate elimination algorithm demonstrates the way in which knowledge representation and state space search can be applied to the problem of machine learning. However, as with most important research, the algorithm should not be evaluated in terms of its successes alone. It raises problems that continue to form a sizeable portion of machine learning's research agenda.

Search-based learning, like all search problems, must deal with the combinatorics of problem spaces. Because the candidate elimination algorithm performs breadth-first search, it can be inefficient. If an application is such that G and S grow excessively, it may be useful to develop heuristics for pruning states from G and S, implementing a *beam search* (see Chapter 4) of the space.

Another approach to this problem, discussed in Section 10.4, involves using an *inductive bias* to further reduce the size of the concept space. Such biases constrain the language used to represent concepts. LEX imposed a bias through the choice of concepts in its generalization hierarchy. Though not complete, LEX's concept language was strong enough to capture many effective heuristics; of equal importance, it reduced the size of the concept space to manageable proportions. Biased languages are essential in reducing the complexity of the concept space, but they may leave the learner incapable of representing the concept it is trying to learn. In this case, candidate elimination would fail to converge on the target concept, leaving G and S empty. This trade-off between expressiveness and efficiency is an essential issue in learning.

Failure of the algorithm to converge may also be due to some noise or inconsistency in the training data. The problem of learning from noisy data is particularly important in realistic applications, where data cannot be guaranteed to be complete or consistent. Candidate elimination is not at all noise resistant. Even a single misclassified training instance can prevent the algorithm from converging on a consistent concept. One solution to this problem maintains multiple G and S sets. In addition to the version space derived from all training instances, it maintains additional spaces based on all but one of the training instances, all but two of the training instances, etc. If G and S fail to converge, the algorithm can examine these alternatives to find those that remain consistent. Unfortunately, this approach leads to a proliferation of candidate sets and is too inefficient to be practical in most cases.

Another issue raised by this research is the role of prior knowledge in learning. LEX's concept hierarchy summarized a great deal of knowledge about algebra; this knowledge was essential to the algorithm's performance. Can greater amounts of domain knowledge make learning even more effective? Section 10.5 examines this problem.

An important contribution of this work is its explication of the relationship between knowledge representation, generalization, and search in inductive learning. Although candidate elimination is only one of many learning algorithms, it raises general questions concerning complexity, expressiveness, and the use of knowledge and data to guide generalization. These problems are central to all machine learning algorithms; we continue to address them throughout this chapter.

10.3 The ID3 Decision Tree Induction Algorithm

ID3 (Quinlan 1986*a*), like candidate elimination, induces concepts from examples. It is particularly interesting for its representation of learned knowledge, its approach to the management of complexity, its heuristic for selecting candidate concepts, and its potential for handling noisy data. ID3 represents concepts as *decision trees*, a representation that allows us to determine the classification of an object by testing its values for certain properties.

For example, consider the problem of estimating an individual's credit risk on the basis of such properties as credit history, current debt, collateral, and income. Table 10.1 lists a sample of individuals with known credit risks. The decision tree of Figure 10.13 represents the classifications in Table 10.1, in that this tree can correctly classify all the objects in the table. In a decision tree, each internal node represents a test on some property, such as credit history or debt; each possible value of that property corresponds to a branch of the tree. Leaf nodes represent classifications, such as low or moderate risk. An individual of unknown type may be classified by traversing this tree: at each internal node, test the individual's value for that property and take the appropriate branch. This continues until reaching a leaf node and the object's classification.

Note that in classifying any given instance, this tree does not use all the properties present in Table 10.1. For instance, if a person has a good credit history and low debt, we may, according to the tree, ignore her collateral and income and classify her as a low risk. In spite of omitting certain tests, this tree correctly classifies all the examples.

NO.	RISK	CREDIT HISTORY	DEBT	COLLATERAL	INCOME
1.	high	bad	high	none	$0 to $15k
2.	high	unknown	high	none	$15 to $35k
3.	moderate	unknown	low	none	$15 to $35k
4.	high	unknown	low	none	$0 to $15k
5.	low	unknown	low	none	over $35k
6.	low	unknown	low	adequate	over $35k
7.	high	bad	low	none	$0 to $15k
8.	moderate	bad	low	adequate	over $35k
9.	low	good	low	none	over $35k
10.	low	good	high	adequate	over $35k
11.	high	good	high	none	$0 to $15k
12.	moderate	good	high	none	$15 to $35k
13.	low	good	high	none	over $35k
14.	high	bad	high	none	$15 to $35k

Table 10.1 Data from credit history of loan applications

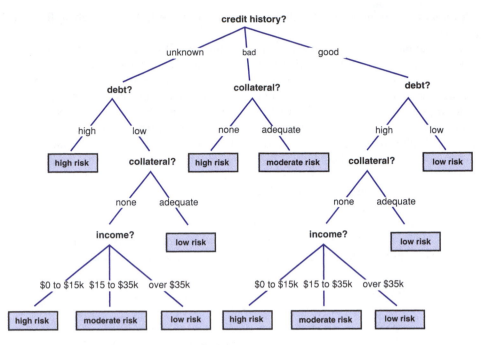

Figure 10.13 A decision tree for credit risk assessment.

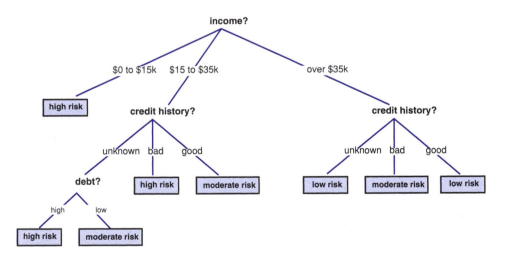

Figure 10.14 A simplified decision tree for credit risk assessment.

In general, the size of the tree necessary to classify a given set of examples varies according to the order with which properties are tested. Figure 10.14 shows a tree that is considerably simpler than that of Figure 10.13 but that also classifies correctly the examples in Table 10.1.

Given a set of training instances and a number of different decision trees that correctly classify them, we may ask which tree has the greatest likelihood of correctly classifying unseen instances of the population. The ID3 algorithm assumes that this is the simplest decision tree that covers all the training examples. The rationale for this assumption is the time-honored heuristic of preferring simplicity and avoiding unnecessary assumptions. This principle, known as *Occam's Razor*, was first articulated by the medieval logician William of Occam in 1324:

> It is vain to do with more what can be done with less. . . . Entities should not be multiplied beyond necessity.

A more contemporary version of Occam's Razor argues that we should always accept the simplest answer that correctly fits our data. In this case, it is the smallest decision tree that correctly classifies all given examples.

Although Occam's Razor has proven itself as a general heuristic for all manner of intellectual activity, its use here has a more specific justification. If we assume that the given examples are sufficient to construct a valid generalization, then our problem becomes one of distinguishing the necessary properties from the extraneous ones. The simplest decision tree that covers all the examples should be the least likely to include unnecessary constraints. Although this idea is intuitively appealing, it is an assumption that must be empirically tested; Section 10.3.3 presents some of these empirical results. Before examining these results, however, we present the ID3 algorithm for inducing decision trees from examples.

10.3.1 Top-Down Decision Tree Induction

ID3 constructs decision trees in a top-down fashion. Note that for any property, we may partition the set of training examples into disjoint subsets, where all the examples in a partition have a common value for that property. ID3 selects a property to test at the current node of the tree and uses this test to partition the set of examples; the algorithm then recursively constructs a subtree for each partition. This continues until all members of the partition are in the same class; that class becomes a leaf node of the tree. Because the order of tests is critical to constructing a simple decision tree, ID3 relies heavily on its criteria for selecting the test at the root of each subtree. To simplify our discussion, this section describes the algorithm for constructing decision trees, assuming an appropriate test selection function. In Section 10.3.2, we present the selection heuristic of the ID3 algorithm.

For example, consider the way in which ID3 constructs the tree of Figure 10.14 from Table 10.1. Beginning with the full table of examples, ID3 selects income as the root property using the selection function described in Section 10.3.2. This partitions the example set as shown in Figure 10.15, with the elements of each partition being listed by their number in the table.

The induction algorithm begins with a sample of correctly classified members of the target categories. ID3 constructs a decision tree according to the algorithm:

```
function induce_tree (example_set, Properties)

    begin
    if all entries in example_set are in the same class
        then return a leaf node labeled with that class
        else if Properties is empty
            then return leaf node labeled with disjunction of all classes in example_set
            else begin
                select a property, P, and make it the root of the current tree;
                delete P from Properties;
                    for each value, V, of P,
                        begin
                            create a branch of the tree labeled with V;
                            let partition_v be elements of example_set with values V for property P;
                            call induce_tree(partition_v, Properties), attach result to branch V
                        end
            end
    end
```

ID3 applies the induce_tree function recursively to each partition. For example, the partition {1, 4, 7, 11} consists entirely of high-risk individuals; ID3 creates a leaf node accordingly. ID3 selects the credit history property as the root of the subtree for the partition {2, 3, 12, 14}. In Figure 10.16, credit history further divides this four element partition into {2, 3}, {14}, and {12}. Continuing to select tests and construct subtrees in this fashion, ID3 eventually produces the tree of Figure 10.14. The reader can work through the rest of this construction; we present a LISP implementation in Section 16.13.

Before presenting ID3's test selection heuristic, it is worth examining the relationship between the tree construction algorithm and our view of learning as search through a concept space. We may think of the set of all possible decision trees as defining a version space. Our operations for moving through this space consist of adding tests to a tree. ID3 implements a form of greedy search in the space of all possible trees: it adds a subtree to the current tree and continues its search; it does not backtrack. This makes the algorithm highly efficient; it also makes it dependent upon the criteria for selecting properties to test.

10.3.2 Information Theoretic Test Selection

We may think of each property of an instance as contributing a certain amount of information to its classification. For example, if our goal is to determine the species of an animal, the discovery that it lays eggs contributes a certain amount of information to that goal. ID3 measures the information gained by making each property the root of the current subtree. It then picks the property that provides the greatest information gain.

Information theory (Shannon 1948) provides a mathematical basis for measuring the information content of a message. We may think of a message as an instance in a universe of possible messages; the act of transmitting a message is the same as selecting one of these possible messages. From this point of view, it is reasonable to define the information

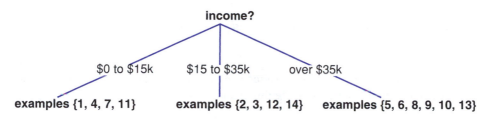

Figure 10.15 A partially constructed decision tree.

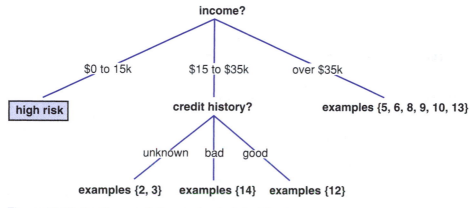

Figure 10.16 Another partially constructed decision tree.

content of a message as depending upon both the size of this universe and the frequency with which each possible message occurs.

The importance of the number of possible messages is evident in an example from gambling: compare a message correctly predicting the outcome of a spin of the roulette wheel with one predicting the outcome of a toss of an honest coin. Because roulette can have more outcomes than a coin toss, a message concerning its outcome is of more value to us: winning at roulette also pays better than winning at a coin toss. Consequently, we should regard this message as conveying more information.

The influence of the probability of each message on the amount of information is evident in another gambling example. Assume that I have rigged a coin so that it will come up heads $^3/_4$ of the time. Because I already know enough about the coin to wager correctly $^3/_4$ of the time, a message telling me the outcome of a given toss is worth less to me than it would be for an honest coin.

Shannon formalized this by defining the amount of information in a message as a function of the probability of occurrence p of each possible message, namely, $-\log_2 p$. Given a universe of messages, $M = \{m_1, m_2, ..., m_n\}$ and a probability, $p(m_i)$, for the occurrence of each message, the expected information content of a message M is given by:

$$I[M] = \left(\sum_{i=1}^{n} - p(m_i) \log_2(p(m_i)) \right) = E[-\log_2 p(m_i)]$$

The information in a message is measured in bits. For example, the information content of a message telling the outcome of the flip of an honest coin is:

$$I[\text{Coin toss}] = -p(\text{heads})\log_2(p(\text{heads})) - p(\text{tails})\log_2(p(\text{tails}))$$

$$= -\frac{1}{2} \log_2 \left(\frac{1}{2}\right) - \frac{1}{2} \log_2 \left(\frac{1}{2}\right)$$

$$= 1 \text{ bit}$$

However, if the coin has been rigged to come up heads 75 per cent of the time, then the information content of a message is:

$$I[\text{Coin toss}] = -\frac{3}{4} \log_2 \left(\frac{3}{4}\right) - \frac{1}{4} \log_2 \left(\frac{1}{4}\right)$$

$$= -\frac{3}{4}*(-0.415) - \frac{1}{4}*(-2)$$

$$= 0.811 \text{ bits}$$

This definition formalizes many of our intuitions about the information content of messages. Information theory is widely used in computer science and telecommunications, including such applications as determining the information-carrying capacity of communications channels, developing data compression algorithms, and developing noise resistant communication strategies. ID3 uses information theory to select the test that gives the greatest information gain in classifying the training examples.

We may think of a decision tree as conveying information about the classification of examples in the decision table; the information content of the tree is computed from the probabilities of the different classifications. For example, if we assume that all the examples in Table 10.1 occur with equal probability, then:

$$p(\text{risk is high}) = {}^6/14, \quad p(\text{risk is moderate}) = {}^3/14, \quad p(\text{risk is low}) = {}^5/14$$

It follows that the distribution described in Table 10.1, $D_{9.1}$, and, consequently, any tree that covers those examples, is:

$$I[D_{9.1}] = -\frac{6}{14} \log_2 \left(\frac{6}{14}\right) - \frac{3}{14} \log_2 \left(\frac{3}{14}\right) - \frac{5}{14} \log_2 \left(\frac{5}{14}\right)$$

$$= -\frac{6}{14}*(-1.222) - \frac{3}{14}*(-2.222) - \frac{5}{14}*(-1.485)$$

$$= 1.531 \text{ bits}$$

The information gain provided by making a test at the root of the current tree is equal to the total information in the tree minus the amount of information needed to complete the classification after performing the test. The amount of information needed to complete the tree is defined as the weighted average of the information in all its subtrees. We compute the weighted average by multiplying the information content of each subtree by the percentage of the examples present in that subtree and summing these products.

Assume a set of training instances, C. If we make property P, with n values, the root of the current tree, this will partition C into subsets, $\{C_1, C_2, ..., C_n\}$. The expected information needed to complete the tree after making P the root is:

$$E[P] = \sum_{i=1}^{n} \frac{|C_i|}{|C|} I[C_i]$$

The gain from property P is computed by subtracting the expected information to complete the tree from the total information content of the tree:

gain(P) = I[C] − E[P]

In the example of Table 10.1, if we make income the property tested at the root of the tree, this partitions the table of examples into the partitions $C_1 = \{1,4,7,11\}$, $C_2 = \{2,3,12,14\}$, and $C_3 = \{5,6,8,9,10,13\}$. The expected information needed to complete the tree is:

$$E[income] = \frac{4}{14} * I[C_1] + \frac{4}{14} * I[C_2] + \frac{6}{14} * I[C_3]$$

$$= \frac{4}{14} * 0.0 + \frac{4}{14} * 1.0 + \frac{6}{14} * 0.650$$

$$= 0.564 \text{ bits}$$

The information gain for the distribution of Table 10.1 is:

$$
\begin{aligned}
\text{gain(income)} \quad &= I[D_{9.1}] - E[income] \\
&= 1.531 - 0.564 \\
&= 0.967 \text{ bits}
\end{aligned}
$$

Similarly, we may show that

$$
\begin{aligned}
\text{gain(credit history)} &= 0.266 \\
\text{gain(debt)} &= 0.633 \\
\text{gain (collateral)} &= 0.206
\end{aligned}
$$

Because income provides the greatest information gain, ID3 will select it as the root of the tree. The algorithm continues to apply this analysis recursively to each subtree until it has completed the tree.

10.3.3 Evaluating ID3

Although the ID3 algorithm produces simple decision trees, it is not obvious that such trees will be effective in predicting the classification of unknown examples. ID3 has been evaluated in both controlled tests and applications and has proven to work well in practice.

Quinlan, for example, has evaluated ID3's performance on the problem of learning to classify boards in a chess endgame (Quinlan 1983). The endgame involved white, playing with a king and a rook, against black, playing with a king and a knight. ID3's goal was to learn to recognize boards that led to a loss for black within three moves. The attributes were different high-level properties of boards, such as "an inability to move the king safely." The test used 23 such attributes.

Once board symmetries were taken into account, the entire problem domain consisted of 1.4 million different boards, of which 474,000 were a loss for black in three moves. ID3 was tested by giving it a randomly selected training set and then testing it on 10,000 different boards, also randomly selected. Quinlan's tests gave the results found in Table 10.2. The predicted maximum errors were derived from a statistical model of ID3's behavior in the domain. For further analysis and details see Quinlan (1983).

These results are supported by further empirical studies and by anecdotal results from further applications. Variations of ID3 have been developed to deal with such problems as noise and excessively large training sets. For more details, see Quinlan (1986a, b).

Size of Training Set	Percentage of Whole Universe	Errors in 10,000 Trials	Predicted Maximum Errors
200	0.01	199	728
1,000	0.07	33	146
5,000	0.36	8	29
25,000	1.79	6	7
125,000	8.93	2	1

Table 10.2 The evaluation of ID3

10.3.4 Decision Tree Data Issues: Bagging, Boosting

Quinlan (1983) was the first to suggest the use of information theory to produce subtrees in decision tree learning and his work was the basis for our presentation. Our examples were clean, however, and their use straightforward. There are a number of issues that we did not address, each of which often occurs in a large data set:

1. The data is bad. This can happen when two (or more) identical attribute sets give different results. What can we do if we have no a priori reason to get rid of data?

2. Data from some attribute sets is missing, perhaps because it is too expensive to obtain. Do we extrapolate? Can we create a new value "unknown?" How can we smooth over this irregularity?

3. Some of the attribute sets are continuous. We handled this by breaking the continuous value "income" into convenient subsets of values, and then used these groupings. Are there better approaches?

4. The data set may be too large for the learning algorithm. How do you handle this?

Addressing these issues produced new generations of decision tree learning algorithms after ID3. The most notable of these is C4.5 (Quinlan 1996). These issues also led to techniques such as bagging and boosting. Since the data for classifier learning systems are attribute-value vectors or instances, it is tempting to manipulate the data to see if different classifiers are produced.

Bagging produces replicate training sets by sampling with replacement from the training instances. *Boosting* uses all instances at each replication, but maintains a weight for each instance in the training set. This weight is intended to reflect that vector's importance. When the weights are adjusted, different classifiers are produced, since the weights cause the learner to focus on different instances. In either case, the multiple classifiers produced are combined by voting to form a composite classifier. In bagging, each component classifier has the same vote, while boosting assigns different voting strengths to component classifiers on the basis of their accuracy.

In working with very large sets of data, it is common to divide the data into subsets, build the decision tree on one subset, and then test its accuracy on other subsets. The literature on decision tree learning is now quite extensive, with a number of data sets on-line, and a number of empirical results published showing the results of using various versions of decision tree algorithms on this data.

Finally, it is straightforward to convert a decision tree into a comparable rule set. What we do is make each possible path through the decision tree into a single rule. The pattern for the rule, its left-hand side (Chapter 6), consists of the decisions leading to the leaf node. The action or right-hand side is the leaf node or outcome of the tree. This rule set may be further customized to capture subtrees within the decision tree. This rule set may then be run to classify new data.

10.4 Inductive Bias and Learnability

So far, our discussion has emphasized the use of empirical data to guide generalization. However, successful induction also depends upon prior knowledge and assumptions about the nature of the concepts being learned. *Inductive bias* refers to any criteria a learner uses to constrain the concept space or to select concepts within that space. In the next section, we examine the need for bias and the types of biases that learning programs typically employ. Section 10.4.2 introduces theoretical results in quantifying the effectiveness of inductive biases.

10.4.1 Inductive Bias

Learning spaces tend to be large; without some way of pruning them, search-based learning would be a practical impossibility. For example, consider the problem of learning a classification of bit strings (strings of 0s and 1s) from positive and negative examples. Because a classification is simply a subset of the set of all possible strings, the total number of possible classifications is equal to the power set, or set of all subsets, of the entire population. If there are m instances, there are 2^m possible classifications. But for strings of n bits, there are 2^n different strings. Thus, there are 2 to the power 2^n different classifications of bit strings of length n. For n = 50, this number is larger than the number of molecules in the known universe! Without some heuristic constraints, it would be impossible for a learner to effectively search such spaces in all but the most trivial domains.

Another reason for the necessity of bias is the nature of inductive generalization itself. Generalization is not truth preserving. For example, if we encounter an honest politician, are we justified in assuming that all politicians are honest? How many honest politicians must we encounter before we are justified in making this assumption? Hume discussed this problem, known as the problem of induction, several hundred years ago:

> You say that the one proposition is an inference from the other; but you must confess that the inference is not intuitive, neither is it demonstrative. Of what nature is it then? To say it is experimental is begging the question. For all inferences from experience suppose, as their foundation, that the future will resemble the past and that similar powers will be conjoined with similar sensible qualities (Hume 1748).

Incidentally, in the eighteenth century Hume's work was seen as an intellectual threat, especially to the religious community's attempts to mathematically prove the existence and attributes of the deity. Among the counter theories proposed to rescue "certainty" was that of Rev. Bayes, an English cleric, as presented in Section 9.3. But back to induction.

In inductive learning, the training data are only a subset of all instances in the domain; consequently, any training set may support many different generalizations. In our example of a bit string classifier, assume that the learner has been given the strings {1100, 1010} as positive examples of some class of strings. Many generalizations are consistent with these examples: the set of all strings beginning with "1" and ending with "0," the set of all strings beginning with "1," the set of all strings of even parity, or any other subset of the entire population that includes {1100, 1010}. What can the learner use to choose from these generalizations? The data alone are not sufficient; all of these choices are consistent with the data. The learner must make additional assumptions about "likely" concepts.

In learning, these assumptions often take the form of heuristics for choosing a branch of the search space. The information theoretic test selection function used by ID3 (Section 10.3.2) is an example of such a heuristic. ID3 performs a hill-climbing search through the space of possible decision trees. At each stage of the search, it examines all the tests that could be used to extend the tree and chooses the test that gains the most information. This is a "greedy" heuristic: it favors branches of the search space that seem to move the greatest distance toward a goal state.

This heuristic allows ID3 to search efficiently the space of decision trees, and it also addresses the problem of choosing plausible generalizations from limited data. ID3 assumes that the smallest tree that correctly classifies all the given examples will be the most likely to classify future training instances correctly. The rationale for this assumption is that small trees are less likely to make assumptions not supported by the data. If the training set is large enough and truly representative of the population, such trees should include all and only the essential tests for determining class membership. As discussed in Section 10.3.3, empirical evaluations have shown this assumption to be quite justified. This preference for simple concept definitions is used in a number of learning algorithms, such as the CLUSTER/2 algorithm of Section 10.6.2.

Another form of inductive bias consists of syntactic constraints on the representation of learned concepts. Such biases are not heuristics for selecting a branch of the concept space. Instead, they limit the size of the space itself by requiring that learned concepts be expressed in a constrained representation language. Decision trees, for example, are a much more constrained language than full predicate calculus. The corresponding reduction in the size of the concept space is essential to ID3's efficiency.

An example of a syntactic bias that might prove effective in classifying bit strings would limit concept descriptions to patterns of symbols from the set $\{0, 1, \#\}$. A pattern defines the class of all matching strings, where matching is determined according to the following rules:

> If the pattern has a "0" in a certain position, then the target string must have a "0" in the corresponding position.

> If the pattern has a "1" in a certain position, then the target string must have a "1" in the corresponding position.

> A "#" in a given position can match either a "1" or a "0".

For example, the pattern, "1##0" defines the set of strings $\{1110, 1100, 1010, 1000\}$.

Considering only those classes that could be represented as a single such pattern reduces the size of the concept space considerably. For strings of length n, we may define 3^n different patterns. This is considerably smaller than the 2 to the power 2^n possible concepts in the unconstrained space. This bias also allows straightforward implementation of version space search, where generalization involves replacing a 1 or a 0 in a candidate pattern with a #. However, the cost we incur for this bias is the inability to represent (and consequently learn) certain concepts. For example, a single pattern of this type cannot represent the class of all strings of even parity.

This trade-off between expressiveness and efficiency is typical. LEX, for example, does not distinguish between odd or even integers in its taxonomy of symbols. Consequently, it cannot learn any heuristic that depends upon this distinction. Although work has been done in programs that can change their bias in response to data (Utgoff 1986), most learning programs assume a fixed inductive bias.

Machine learning has explored a number of representational biases:

Conjunctive biases restrict learned knowledge to conjunctions of literals. This is particularly common because the use of disjunction in concept descriptions creates problems for generalization. For example, assume that we allow arbitrary use of disjuncts in the representation of concepts in the candidate elimination algorithm. Because the maximally specific generalization of a set of positive instances is simply the disjunction of all the instances, the learner will not generalize at all. It will add disjuncts *ad infinitum*, implementing a form of rote learning (Mitchell 1980).

Limitations on the number of disjuncts. Purely conjunctive biases are too limited for many applications. One approach that increases the expressiveness of a representation while addressing the problems of disjunction is to allow a small, bounded number of disjuncts.

Feature vectors are a representation that describes objects as a set of features whose values differ from object to object. The objects presented in Table 10.1 are represented as sets of features.

Decision trees are a concept representation that has proven effective in the ID3 algorithm.

Horn clauses require a restriction on the form of implications that has been used in automated reasoning as well as by a number of programs for learning rules from examples. We present Horn clauses in detail in Section 13.2.

In addition to the syntactic biases discussed in this section, a number of programs use domain-specific knowledge to consider the known or assumed semantics of the domain. Such knowledge can provide an extremely effective bias. Section 10.5 examines these knowledge-based approaches. However, before considering the role of knowledge in learning, we briefly examine theoretical results quantifying inductive bias. We also present a summary discussion of inductive bias in learning systems in Section 17.2.

10.4.2   The Theory of Learnability

The goal of inductive bias is to restrict the set of target concepts in such a way that we may both search the set efficiently and find high-quality concept definitions. An interesting body of theoretical work addresses the problem of quantifying the effectiveness of an inductive bias.

We define the quality of concepts in terms of their ability to correctly classify objects that were not included in the set of training instances. It is not hard to write a learning algorithm that produces concepts that will correctly classify all the examples that it has seen; rote learning would suffice for this. However, due to the large number of instances in most domains, or the fact that some instances are not available, algorithms can only afford to examine a portion of the possible examples. Thus, the performance of a learned concept on new instances is critically important. In testing learning algorithms, we generally divide the set of all instances into nonintersecting sets of training instances and test instances. After training a program on the training set, we test it on the test set.

It is useful to think of efficiency and correctness as properties of the language for expressing concepts, i.e., the inductive bias, rather than of a particular learning algorithm. Learning algorithms search a space of concepts; if this space is manageable and contains concepts that perform well, then any reasonable learning algorithm should find these definitions; if the space is highly complex, an algorithm's success will be limited. An extreme example will clarify this point.

The concept of ball is learnable, given a suitable language for describing the properties of objects. After seeing a relatively small number of balls, a person will be able to define them concisely: balls are round. Contrast this with a concept that is not learnable: suppose a team of people runs around the planet and selects a set of several million objects entirely at random, calling the resulting class bunch_of_stuff. Not only would a concept induced from any sample of bunch_of_stuff require an extremely complex representation, but it also is unlikely that this concept would correctly classify unseen members of the set.

These observations make no assumption about the learning algorithms used, just that they can find a concept in the space consistent with the data. ball is learnable because we can define it in terms of a few features: the concept can be expressed in a biased language. Attempting to describe the concept bunch_of_stuff would require a concept definition as long as the list of all the properties of all the objects in the class.

Thus, rather than defining learnability in terms of specific algorithms, we define it in terms of the language used to represent concepts. Also, to achieve generality, we do not define learnability over specific problem domains, such as learning bunch_of_stuff. Instead we define it in terms of the syntactic properties of the concept definition language.

In defining learnability, we must not only take efficiency into account; we must also deal with the fact that we have limited data. In general we cannot hope to find the exactly correct concept from a random sample of instances. Rather, just as in estimating the mean of a set in statistics, we try to find a concept which is very likely to be nearly correct. Consequently, the correctness of a concept is the probability, over the entire population of instances, that it will correctly classify an instance.

In addition to the correctness of learned concepts, we must also consider the likelihood that an algorithm will find such concepts. That is, there is a small chance that the samples we see are so atypical that learning is impossible. Thus, a particular distribution of positive instances, or a particular training set selected from these instances, may or may not be sufficient to select a high-quality concept. We are therefore concerned with two probabilities: the probability that our samples are not atypical and the probability that the algorithm will find a quality concept, the normal estimation error. These two probabilities are bounded by δ and ε, respectively, in the definition of PAC learability we give below.

To summarize, learnability is a property of concept spaces and is determined by the language required to represent concepts. In evaluating these spaces, we must take into account both the probability that the data is by coincidence quite impoverished and the probability with which the resulting concept will correctly classify the unseen instances.

Valiant (1984) has formalized these intuitions in the theory of probably approximately correct (PAC) learning.

A class of concepts is *PAC learnable* if an algorithm exists that executes efficiently and has a high probability of finding an *approximately correct* concept. By approximately correct, we mean that the concept correctly classifies a high percentage of new instances. Thus, we require both that the algorithm find, with a high probability, a concept that is nearly correct and that the algorithm itself be efficient. An interesting aspect of this definition is that it does not necessarily depend upon the distribution of positive examples in the instance space. It depends upon the nature of the concept language, that is, the bias, and the desired degree of correctness. Finally, by making assumptions about the example distributions, it is often possible to get better performance, that is, to make do with fewer samples than the theory requires.

Formally, Valiant defines PAC learnability as follows. Let C be a set of concepts c and X a set of instances. The concepts may be algorithms, patterns, or some other means of dividing X into positive and negative instances. C is PAC learnable if there exists an algorithm with the following properties:

1. If for concept error ε and failure probability δ, there exists an algorithm which, given a random sample of instances of size $n = |X|$ polynomial in $1/\varepsilon$, and $1/\delta$, the algorithm produces a concept c, an element of C, such that the probability that c has a generalization error greater than ε is less than δ. That is, for y drawn from the same distribution that the samples in X were drawn from:

   $P[P[y$ is misclassified by $c] \geq \varepsilon] \leq \delta$.

2. The execution time for the algorithm is polynomial in n, $1/\varepsilon$, and $1/\delta$.

Using this definition of PAC learnability, researchers have shown the tractability of several inductive biases. For example, Valiant (1984) proves that the class of k-CNF expressions is learnable. k-CNF expressions are sentences in conjunctive normal form with a bound on the number of disjuncts; expressions are formed of the conjunction of clauses, $c_1 \wedge c_2 \wedge \ldots c_n$, where each c_i is the disjunction of no more than k literals. This theoretical result supports the common restriction of concepts to conjunctive form used in many learning algorithms. We do not duplicate the proof here but refer the reader to Valiant's paper, where he proves this result, along with the learnability of other biases. For additional results in learnability and inductive bias see Haussler (1988) and Martin (1997).

10.5 Knowledge and Learning

ID3 and the candidate elimination algorithm generalize on the basis of regularities in training data. Such algorithms are often referred to as *similarity based*, in that generalization is primarily a function of similarities across training examples. The biases employed by these algorithms are limited to syntactic constraints on the form of learned knowledge;

they make no strong assumptions about the semantics of the domains. In this section, we examine algorithms, such as *explanation-based learning*, that use prior domain knowledge to guide generalization.

Initially, the idea that prior knowledge is necessary for learning seems contradictory. However, both machine learning and cognitive scientist researchers have made a case for exactly that notion, arguing that the most effective learning occurs when the learner already has considerable knowledge of the domain. One argument for the importance of knowledge in learning is the reliance of similarity-based learning techniques on relatively large amounts of training data. Humans, in contrast, can form reliable generalizations from as few as a single training instance, and many practical applications require that a learning program do the same.

Another argument for the importance of prior knowledge recognizes that any set of training examples can support an unlimited number of generalizations, most of which are either irrelevant or nonsensical. Inductive bias is one means of making this distinction. In this section, we examine algorithms that go beyond purely syntactic biases to consider the role of strong domain knowledge in learning.

10.5.1   Meta-DENDRAL

Meta-DENDRAL (Buchanan and Mitchell 1978) is one of the earliest and still one of the best examples of the use of knowledge in inductive learning. Meta-DENDRAL acquires rules to be used by the DENDRAL program for analyzing mass spectrographic data. DENDRAL infers the structure of organic molecules from their chemical formula and mass spectrographic data.

A mass spectrograph bombards molecules with electrons, causing some of the chemical bonds to break. Chemists measure the weight of the resulting pieces and interpret these results to gain insight into the structure of the compound. DENDRAL employs knowledge in the form of rules for interpreting mass spectrographic data. The premise of a DENDRAL rule is a graph of some portion of a molecular structure. The conclusion of the rule is that graph with the location of the cleavage indicated.

Meta-DENDRAL infers these rules from spectrographic results on molecules of known structure. Meta-DENDRAL is given the structure of a known compound, along with the mass and relative abundance of the fragments produced by spectrography. It interprets these, constructing an account of where the breaks occurred. These explanations of breaks in specific molecules are used as examples for constructing general rules.

In determining the site of a cleavage in a training run, DENDRAL uses a "half-order theory" of organic chemistry. This theory, though not powerful enough to support the direct construction of DENDRAL rules, does support the interpretation of cleavages within known molecules. The half-order theory consists of rules, constraints, and heuristics such as:

Double and triple bonds do not break.

Only fragments larger than two carbon atoms show up in the data.

Using the half-order theory, meta-DENDRAL constructs explanations of the cleavage. These explanations indicate the likely sites of cleavages along with possible migrations of atoms across the break.

These explanations become the set of positive instances for a rule induction program. This component induces the constraints in the premises of DENDRAL rules through a general to specific search. It begins with a totally general description of a cleavage: X_1*X_2. This pattern means that a cleavage, indicated by the asterisk, can occur between any two atoms. It specializes the pattern by:

adding atoms: $X_1*X_2 \rightarrow X_3 - X_1*X_2$

where the "$-$" operator indicates a chemical bond, or

instantiating atoms or attributes of atoms: $X_1*X_2 \rightarrow C*X_2$

Meta-DENDRAL learns from positive examples only and performs a hill-climbing search of the concept space. It prevents overgeneralization by limiting candidate rules to cover only about half of the training instances. Subsequent components of the program evaluate and refine these rules, looking for redundant rules or modifying rules that may be overly general or specific.

The strength of meta-DENDRAL is in its use of domain knowledge to change raw data into a more usable form. This gives the program noise resistance, through the use of its theory to eliminate extraneous or potentially erroneous data, and the ability to learn from relatively few training instances. The insight that training data must be so interpreted to be fully useful is the basis of explanation-based learning.

10.5.2   Explanation-Based Learning

Explanation-based learning uses an explicitly represented domain theory to construct an explanation of a training example, usually a proof that the example logically follows from the theory. By generalizing from the explanation of the instance, rather than from the instance itself, explanation-based learning filters noise, selects relevant aspects of experience, and organizes training data into a systematic and coherent structure.

There are several alternative formulations of this idea. For example, the STRIPS program for representing general operators for planning (see Sections 6.4 and 15.5) has exerted a powerful influence on this research (Fikes et al. 1972). Meta-DENDRAL, as we have just discussed, established the power of theory-based interpretation of training instances. More recently, a number of authors (DeJong and Mooney 1986, Minton 1988) have proposed alternative formulations of this idea. The *Explanation-Based Generalization* algorithm of Mitchell et al. (1986) is also typical of the genre. In this section, we examine a variation of the explanation-based learning (EBL) algorithm developed by DeJong and Mooney (1986).

EBL begins with:

1. *A target concept*. The learner's task is to determine an effective definition of this concept. Depending upon the specific application, the target concept may be a classification, a theorem to be proven, a plan for achieving a goal, or a heuristic for a problem solver.

2. *A training example*, an instance of the target.

3. *A domain theory*, a set of rules and facts that are used to explain how the training example is an instance of the goal concept.

4. *Operationality criteria*, some means of describing the form that concept definitions may take.

To illustrate EBL, we present an example of learning about when an object is a cup. This is a variation of a problem explored by Winston et al. (1983) and adapted to explanation-based learning by Mitchell et al. (1986). The target concept is a rule that may be used to infer whether an object is a cup:

premise(X) $\rightarrow$ cup(X)

where premise is a conjunctive expression containing the variable X.

Assume a domain theory that includes the following rules about cups:

liftable(X) $\wedge$ holds_liquid(X) $\rightarrow$ cup(X)
part(Z, W) $\wedge$ concave(W) $\wedge$ points_up(W) $\rightarrow$ holds_liquid(Z)
light(Y) $\wedge$ part(Y, handle) $\rightarrow$ liftable(Y)
small(A) $\rightarrow$ light(A)
made_of(A, feathers) $\rightarrow$ light(A)

The training example is an instance of the goal concept. That is, we are given:

cup(obj1)
small(obj1)
part(obj1, handle)
owns(bob, obj1)
part(obj1, bottom)
part(obj1, bowl)
points_up(bowl)
concave(bowl)
color(obj1, red)

Finally, assume the operationality criteria require that target concepts be defined in terms of observable, structural properties of objects, such as part and points_up. We may provide domain rules that enable the learner to infer whether a description is operational, or we may simply list operational predicates.

Using this theory, a theorem prover may construct an explanation of why the example is indeed an instance of the training concept: a proof that the target concept logically follows from the example, as in the first tree in Figure 10.17. Note that this explanation eliminates such irrelevant concepts as color(obj1, red) from the training data and captures those aspects of the example known to be relevant to the goal.

The next stage of explanation-based learning generalizes the explanation to produce a concept definition that may be used to recognize other cups. EBL accomplishes this by substituting variables for those constants in the proof tree that depend solely on the particular training instance, as in Figure 10.17. Based on the generalized tree, EBL defines a new rule whose conclusion is the root of the tree and whose premise is the conjunction of the leaves:

$$small(X) \wedge part(X, handle) \wedge part(X, W) \wedge concave(W) \wedge points\_up(W) \rightarrow cup(X).$$

In constructing a generalized proof tree, our goal is to substitute variables for those constants that are part of the training instance while retaining those constants and constraints that are part of the domain theory. In this example, the constant handle

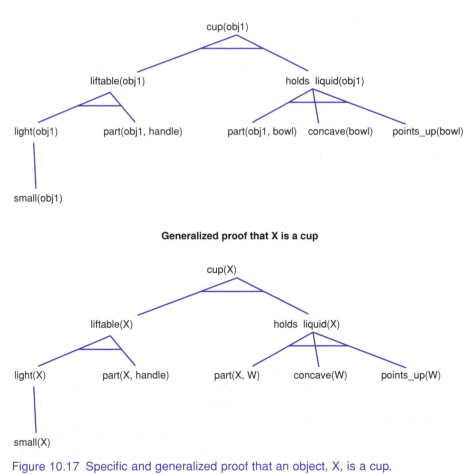

Figure 10.17 Specific and generalized proof that an object, X, is a cup.

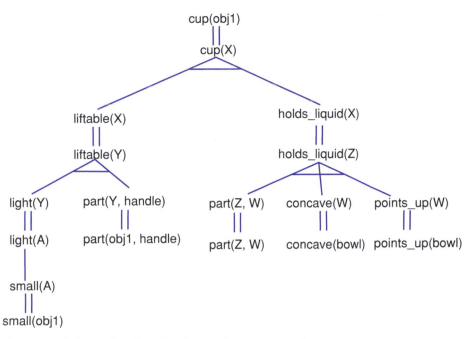

Figure 10.18 An explanation structure of the cup example.

originated in the domain theory rather than the training instance. We have retained it as an essential constraint in the acquired rule.

We may construct a generalized proof tree in a number of ways using a training instance as a guide. Mitchell et al. (1986) accomplish this by first constructing a proof tree that is specific to the training example and subsequently generalizing the proof through a process called *goal regression*. Goal regression matches the generalized goal (in our example, cup(X)) with the root of the proof tree, replacing constants with variables as required for the match. The algorithm applies these substitutions recursively through the tree until all appropriate constants have been generalized. See Mitchell et al. (1986) for a detailed description of this process.

DeJong and Mooney (1986) propose an alternative approach that essentially builds the generalized and the specific trees in parallel. This is accomplished by maintaining a variation of the proof tree consisting of the rules used in proving the goal distinct from the variable substitutions used in the actual proof. This is called an *explanation structure*, as in Figure 10.18, and represents the abstract structure of the proof. The learner maintains two distinct substitution lists for the explanation structure: a list of the specific substitutions required to explain the training example and a list of general substitutions required to explain the generalized goal. It constructs these substitution lists as it builds the explanation structure.

We construct the lists of general and specific substitutions as follows: let s_s and s_g be the lists of specific and general substitutions, respectively. For every match between expressions e_1 and e_2 in the explanation structure, update s_s and s_g according to the following rule:

if e_1 is in the premise of a domain rule and e_2 is the conclusion of a domain rule
then begin

T_s $\ =$ the most general unifier of e_1s_s and e_2s_s % unify e_1 and e_2 under s_s

s_s $\ = s_sT_s$ % update s_s by composing it with T_s

T_g $\ =$ the most general unifier of e_1s_g and e_2s_g % unify e_1 and e_2 under s_g

s_g $\ = s_gT_g$ % update s_g by composing it with T_g

end

if e_1 is in the premise of a domain rule and e_2 is a fact in the training instance
then begin   % only update s_s

T_s $\ =$ the most general unifier of e_1s_s and e_2s_s % unify e_1 and e_2 under s_s

s_s $\ = s_s\,T_s$ % update s_s by composing it with T_s

end

In the example of Figure 10.18:

$s_s = \{obj1/X, obj1/Y, obj1/A, obj1/Z, bowl/W\}$

$s_g = \{X/Y, X/A, X/Z\}$

Applying these substitutions to the explanation structure of Figure 10.18 gives the specific and general proof trees of Figure 10.17.

Explanation-based learning offers a number of benefits:

1. Training examples often contain irrelevant information, such as the color of the cup in the preceding example. The domain theory allows the learner to select the relevant aspects of the training instance.

2. A given example may allow numerous possible generalizations, most of which are either useless, meaningless, or wrong. EBL forms generalizations that are known to be relevant to specific goals and that are guaranteed to be logically consistent with the domain theory.

3. By using domain knowledge EBL allows learning from a single training instance.

4. Construction of an explanation allows the learner to hypothesize unstated relationships between its goals and its experience, such as deducing a definition of a cup based on its structural properties.

EBL has been applied to a number of learning problems. For instance, Mitchell et al. (1983) discuss the addition of EBL to the LEX algorithm. Suppose that the first positive example of the use of OP1 is in solving the instance $\int 7\,x^2\,dx$. LEX will make this instance a member of S, the set of maximally specific generalizations. However, a human would immediately recognize that the techniques used in solving this instance do not depend upon the specific values of the coefficient and exponent but will work for any real values, so long as the exponent is not equal to -1. The learner is justified in inferring that OP1 should be applied to any instance of the form $\int r_1 \, x^{(r_2 \neq -1)} \, dx$, where r_1 and r_2 are any real numbers. LEX has been extended to use its knowledge of algebra with explanation-based learning to make this type of generalization. Finally, we implement an explanation base learning algorithm in Prolog in Section 15.8.3.

10.5.3 EBL and Knowledge-Level Learning

Although it is an elegant formulation of the role of knowledge in learning, EBL raises a number of important questions. One of the more obvious ones concerns the issue of what an explanation-based learner actually learns. Pure EBL can only learn rules that are within the *deductive closure* of its existing theory. This means the learned rules could have been inferred from the knowledge base without using the training instance at all. The sole function of the training instance is to focus the theorem prover on relevant aspects of the problem domain. Consequently, EBL is often viewed as a form of *speed up learning* or knowledge base reformulation; EBL can make a learner work faster, because it does not have to reconstruct the proof tree underlying the new rule. However, because it could always have reconstructed the proof, EBL cannot make the learner do anything new. This distinction has been formalized by Dietterich in his discussion of *knowledge-level learning* (1986).

EBL takes information implicit in a set of rules and makes it explicit. For example, consider the game of chess: a minimal knowledge of the rules of chess, when coupled with an ability to perform unlimited look-ahead on board states, would allow a computer to play extremely well. Unfortunately, chess is too complex for this approach. An explanation-based learner that could master chess strategies would indeed learn something that was, for all practical purposes, new.

EBL also allows us to abandon the requirement that the learner have a complete and correct theory of the domain and focus on techniques for refining incomplete theories within the context of EBL. Here, the learner constructs a partial solution tree. Those branches of the proof that cannot be completed indicate deficiencies in the theory. A number of interesting questions remain to be examined in this area. These include the development of heuristics for reasoning with imperfect theories, credit assignment methodologies, and choosing which of several failed proofs should be repaired.

A further use for explanation-based learning is to integrate it with similarity-based approaches to learning. Again, a number of basic schemes suggest themselves, such as using EBL to refine training data where the theory applies and then passing this partially generalized data on to a similarity-based learner for further generalization. Alternatively, we could use failed explanations as a means of targeting deficiencies in a theory, thereby guiding data collection for a similarity-based learner.

Other issues in EBL research include techniques for reasoning with unsound theories, alternatives to theorem proving as a means of constructing explanations, methods of dealing with noisy or missing training data, and methods of determining which generated rules to save.

10.5.4 Analogical Reasoning

Whereas "pure" EBL is limited to deductive learning, analogies offer a more flexible method of using existing knowledge. Analogical reasoning assumes that if two situations are known to be similar in some respects, it is likely that they will be similar in others. For example, if two houses have similar locations, construction, and condition, then they probably have the same sales value. Unlike the proofs used in EBL, analogy is not logically sound. In this sense it is like induction. As Russell (1989) and others have observed, analogy is a species of single instance induction: in our house example, we are inducing properties of one house from what is known about another.

As we discussed in our presentation of case-based reasoning (Section 8.3), analogy is very useful for applying existing knowledge to new situations. For example, assume that a student is trying to learn about the behavior of electricity, and assume that the teacher tells her that electricity is analogous to water, with voltage corresponding to pressure, amperage to the amount of flow, and resistance to the capacity of a pipe. Using analogical reasoning, the student may more easily grasp such concepts as Ohm's law.

The standard computational model of analogy defines the *source* of an analogy to be a problem solution, example, or theory that is relatively well understood. The *target* is not completely understood. Analogy constructs a *mapping* between corresponding elements of the target and source. Analogical inferences extend this mapping to new elements of the target domain. Continuing with the "electricity is like water" analogy, if we know that this analogy maps switches onto valves, amperage onto quantity of flow, and voltage onto water pressure, we may reasonably infer that there should be some analogy to the capacity (i.e., the cross-sectional area) of a water pipe; this could lead to an understanding of electrical resistance.

A number of authors have proposed a unifying framework for computational models of analogical reasoning (Hall 1989, Kedar-Cabelli 1988, Wolstencroft 1989). A typical framework consists of the following stages:

1. *Retrieval.* Given a target problem, it is necessary to select a potential source analog. Problems in analogical retrieval include selecting those features of the target and source that increase the likelihood of retrieving a useful source analog and indexing knowledge according to those features. Generally, retrieval establishes the initial elements of an analogical mapping.

2. *Elaboration.* Once the source has been retrieved, it is often necessary to derive additional features and relations of the source. For example, it may be necessary to develop a specific problem-solving trace (or explanation) in the source domain as a basis for analogy with the target.

3. *Mapping and inference.* This stage involves developing the mapping of source attributes into the target domain. This involves both known similarities and analogical inferences.

4. *Justification.* Here we determine that the mapping is indeed valid. This stage may require modification of the mapping.

5. *Learning*. In this stage the acquired knowledge is stored in a form that will be useful in the future.

These stages have been developed in a number of computational models of analogical reasoning. For example, *structure mapping theory* (Falkenhainer 1990, Falkenhainer et al. 1989, Gentner 1983) not only addresses the problem of constructing useful analogies but also provides a plausible model of how humans understand analogies. A central question in the use of analogy is how we may distinguish expressive, deep analogies from more superficial comparisons. Gentner argues that true analogies should emphasize systematic, structural features of a domain over more superficial similarities. For example, the analogy, "the atom is like the solar system" is deeper than "the sunflower is like the sun," because the former captures a whole system of causal relations between orbiting bodies whereas the latter describes superficial similarities such as the fact that both sunflowers and the sun are round and yellow. This property of analogical mapping is called *systematicity*.

Structure mapping formalizes this intuition. Consider the example of the atom/solar system analogy, as in Figure 10.19 as explicated by Gentner (1983). The source domain includes the predicates:

```
yellow(sun)
blue(earth)
hotter-than(sun, earth)
causes(more-massive(sun, earth), attract(sun, earth))
causes(attract(sun, earth), revolves-around(earth, sun))
```

The target domain that the analogy is intended to explain includes

```
more-massive(nucleus, electron)
revolves-around(electron, nucleus)
```

Structure mapping attempts to transfer the causal structure of the source to the target. The mapping is constrained by the following rules:

1. Properties are dropped from the source. Because analogy favors systems of relations, the first stage is to eliminate those predicates that describe superficial properties of the source. Structure mapping formalizes this by eliminating predicates of a single argument (unary predicates) from the source. The rationale for this is that predicates of higher arity, by virtue of describing a relationship between two or more entities, are more likely to capture the systematic relations intended by the analogy. In our example, this eliminates such assertions as yellow(sun) and blue(earth). Note that the source may still contain assertions, such as hotter-than(sun, earth), that are not relevant to the analogy.

2. Relations map unchanged from the source to the target; the arguments to the relations may differ. In our example, such relations as revolves-around and more-massive are the same in both the source and the target. This constraint is

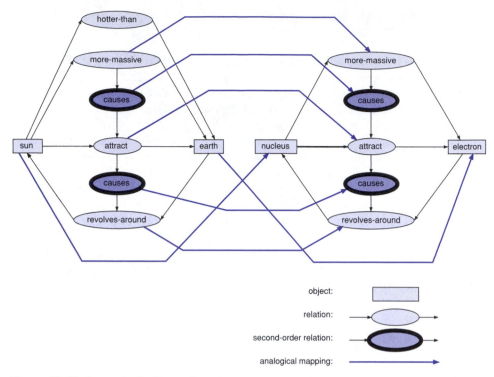

Figure 10.19 An analogical mapping.

used by many theories of analogy and greatly reduces the number of possible mappings. It is also consistent with the heuristic of giving relations preference in the mapping.

3. In constructing the mapping, higher-order relations are preferred as a focus of the mapping. In our example, causes is a higher-order relation, because it takes other relations as its arguments. This is called the *systematicity principle*.

These constraints lead to the mapping:

sun → nucleus
earth → electron

Extending the mapping leads to the inference:

causes(more-massive(nucleus, electron), attract(nucleus, electron))
causes(attract(nucleus, electron), revolves-around(electron, nucleus))

Structure mapping theory has been implemented and tested in a number of domains. Though it remains far from a complete theory of analogy, failing to address such problems as source analog retrieval, it has proven both computationally practical and able to explain many aspects of human analogical reasoning. Finally, as we noted in our presentation of *case-based reasoning*, Section 8.3, there is an essential role for analogy in creating and applying a useful case base.

10.6 Unsupervised Learning

The learning algorithms discussed so far implement forms of *supervised learning*. They assume the existence of a teacher, some fitness measure, or other external method of classifying training instances. *Unsupervised learning* eliminates the teacher and requires that the learners form and evaluate concepts on their own. Science is perhaps the best example of unsupervised learning in humans. Scientists do not have the benefit of a teacher. Instead, they propose hypotheses to explain observations; evaluate their hypotheses using such criteria as simplicity, generality, and elegance; and test hypotheses through experiments of their own design.

10.6.1 Discovery and Unsupervised Learning

AM (Davis and Lenat 1982, Lenat and Brown 1984) is one of the earliest and most successful discovery programs, deriving a number of interesting, even if not original, concepts in mathematics. AM began with the concepts of set theory, operations for creating new knowledge by modifying and combining existing concepts, and a set of heuristics for detecting "interesting" concepts. By searching this space of mathematical concepts, AM discovered the natural numbers along with several important concepts of number theory, such as the existence of prime numbers.

For example, AM discovered the natural numbers by modifying its notion of "bags." A bag is a generalization of a set that allows multiple occurrences of the same element. For example, {a, a, b, c, c} is a bag. By specializing the definition of bag to allow only a single type of element, AM discovered an analogy of the natural numbers. For example, the bag {1, 1, 1, 1} corresponds to the number 4. Union of bags led to the notion of addition: {1,1} ∪ {1,1} = {1,1,1,1}, or 2 + 2 = 4. Exploring further modifications of these concepts, AM discovered multiplication as a series of additions. Using a heuristic that defines new operators by inverting existing operators, AM discovered integer division. It found the concept of prime numbers by noting that certain numbers had exactly two divisors (themselves and 1).

On creating a new concept, AM evaluates it according to a number of heuristics, keeping those concepts that prove "interesting." AM determined that prime numbers were interesting based on the frequency with which they occur. In evaluating concepts using this heuristic, AM generates instances of the concept, testing each to see whether the concept holds. If a concept is true of all instances it is a tautology, and AM gives it a low evaluation. Similarly, AM rejects concepts that are true of no instances. If a concept is true of a significant portion of the examples (as is the case with prime numbers), AM evaluates it as interesting and selects it for further modification.

Although AM discovered prime numbers and several other interesting concepts, it failed to progress much beyond elementary number theory. In a later analysis of this work, Lenat and Brown (1984) examine the reasons for the program's success and its limitations. Although Lenat originally believed that AM's heuristics were the prime source of its power, this later evaluation attributed much of the program's success to the language used to represent mathematical concepts. AM represented concepts as recursive structures in a variation of the LISP programming language. Because of its basis in a well-designed programming language, this representation defined a space that contained a high density of interesting concepts. This was particularly true in the early stages of the search. As exploration continued, the space grew combinatorially, and the percentage of interesting concepts "thinned out." This observation further underscores the relationship between representation and search.

Another reason AM failed to continue the impressive pace of its early discoveries is its inability to "learn to learn." It did not acquire new heuristics as it gained mathematical knowledge; consequently, the quality of its search degraded as its mathematics grew more complex. In this sense, AM never developed a deep understanding of mathematics. Lenat has addressed this problem in later work on a program called EURISKO, which attempts to learn new heuristics (Lenat 1983).

A number of programs have continued to explore the problems of automatic discovery. IL (Sims 1987) applies a variety of learning techniques to mathematical discovery, including methods such as theorem proving and explanation-based learning (Section 10.5). See also the automated invention of integer sequences in Cotton et al. (2000).

BACON (Langley et al. 1986, 1987) has developed computational models of the formation of quantitative scientific laws. For example, using data that related the distances of the planets from the sun and the period of the planets' orbits, BACON "re-discovered" Kepler's laws of planetary motion. By providing a plausible computational model of how humans may have achieved discovery in a variety of domains, BACON has provided a useful tool and methodology for examining the process of human scientific discovery. SCAVENGER (Stubblefield 1995, Stubblefield and Luger 1996) used a variation of the ID3 algorithm to improve its ability to form useful analogies. Shrager and Langley (1990) describe a number of other discovery systems.

Although scientific discovery is an important research area, progress to date has been slight. A more basic, and perhaps more fruitful problem in unsupervised learning, concerns the discovery of categories. Lakoff (1987) suggests that categorization is fundamental to human cognition: higher-level theoretical knowledge depends upon the ability to organize the particulars of our experience into coherent taxonomies. Most of our useful knowledge is about categories of objects, such as cows, rather than about specific individual cows, such as Blossom or Ferdinand. Nordhausen and Langley have emphasized the formation of categories as the basis for a unified theory of scientific discovery (Nordhausen and Langley 1990). In developing explanations of why chemicals react in the ways they do, chemistry built on prior work in classifying compounds into categories such as "acid" and "alkaline."

In the next section, we examine *conceptual clustering*, which is the problem of discovering useful categories in unclassified data.

10.6.2 Conceptual Clustering

The *clustering problem* begins with a collection of unclassified objects and a means for measuring the similarity of objects. The goal is to organize the objects into classes that meet some standard of quality, such as maximizing the similarity of objects in the same class.

Numeric taxonomy is one of the oldest approaches to the clustering problem. Numeric methods rely upon the representation of objects as a collection of features, each of which may have some numeric value. A reasonable similarity metric treats each object (a vector of n feature values) as a point in n-dimensional space. The similarity of two objects is the euclidean distance between them in this space.

Using this similarity metric, a common clustering algorithm builds clusters in a bottom-up fashion. This approach, often called an *agglomerative clustering* strategy, forms categories by:

1. Examining all pairs of objects, selecting the pair with the highest degree of similarity, and making that pair a cluster.

2. Defining the features of the cluster as some function, such as average, of the features of the component members and then replacing the component objects with this cluster definition.

3. Repeating this process on the collection of objects until all objects have been reduced to a single cluster.

4. Many unsupervised learning algorithms can be viewed as performing *maximum likelihood density estimations*, which means finding a distribution from which the data is most likely to have been drawn. An example is the interpretation of a set of phonemes in a natural language application, see Chapter 14.

The result of this algorithm is a binary tree whose leaf nodes are instances and whose internal nodes are clusters of increasing size.

We may extend this algorithm to objects represented as sets of symbolic, rather than numeric, features. The only problem is in measuring the similarity of objects defined using symbolic rather than numeric values. A reasonable approach defines the similarity of two objects as the proportion of features that they have in common. Given the objects

```
object1 = {small, red, rubber, ball}
object2 = {small, blue, rubber, ball}
object3 = {large, black, wooden, ball}
```

this metric would compute the similarity values:

$$\text{similarity(object1, object2)} = {}^3/_4$$
$$\text{similarity(object1, object3)} = \text{similarity(object2, object3)} = {}^1/_4$$

However, similarity-based clustering algorithms do not adequately capture the underlying role of semantic knowledge in cluster formation. For example, constellations of stars are described both on the basis of their closeness in the sky as well as by way of existing human concepts, such as "the big dipper."

In defining categories, we cannot give all features equal weight. In any given context, certain of an object's features are more important than others; simple similarity metrics treat all features equally. Human categories depend upon the goals of the categorization and prior knowledge of the domain much more than on surface similarity. Consider, for example, the classification of whales as mammals instead of fish. Surface similarities cannot account for this classification, which depends upon the wider goals of biological classification and extensive physiological and evolutionary evidence.

Traditional clustering algorithms not only fail to take goals and background knowledge into account, but they also fail to produce meaningful semantic explanations of the resulting categories. These algorithms represent clusters *extensionally*, which means by enumerating all of their members. The algorithms produce no *intensional* definition, or no general rule that defines the semantics of the category and that may be used to classify both known and future members of the category. For example, an extensional definition of the set of people who have served as secretary-general of the United Nations would simply list those individuals. An intensional definition, such as:

{X | X has been elected secretary-general of the United Nations}

would have the added benefits of defining the class semantically and allowing us to recognize future members of the category.

Conceptual clustering addresses these problems by using machine learning techniques to produce general concept definitions and applying background knowledge to the formation of categories. CLUSTER/2 (Michalski and Stepp 1983) is a good example of this approach. It uses background knowledge in the form of biases on the language used to represent categories.

CLUSTER/2 forms k categories by constructing individuals around k *seed* objects. k is a parameter that may be adjusted by the user. CLUSTER/2 evaluates the resulting clusters, selecting new seeds and repeating the process until its quality criteria are met. The algorithm is defined:

1. Select k seeds from the set of observed objects. This may be done randomly or according to some selection function.

2. For each seed, using that seed as a positive instance and all other seeds as negative instances, produce a maximally general definition that covers all of the positive and none of the negative instances. Note that this may lead to multiple classifications of other, nonseed, objects.

3. Classify all objects in the sample according to these descriptions. Replace each maximally general description with a maximally specific description that covers all objects in the category. This decreases likelihood that classes overlap on unseen objects.

4. Classes may still overlap on given objects. CLUSTER/2 includes an algorithm for adjusting overlapping definitions.

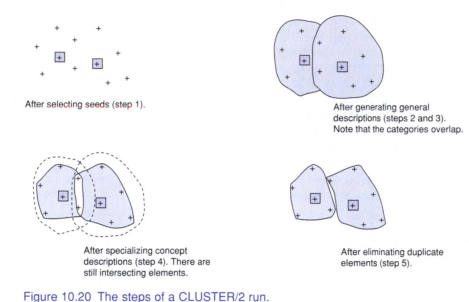

After selecting seeds (step 1).

After generating general
descriptions (steps 2 and 3).
Note that the categories overlap.

After specializing concept
descriptions (step 4). There are
still intersecting elements.

After eliminating duplicate
elements (step 5).

Figure 10.20 The steps of a CLUSTER/2 run.

5. Using a distance metric, select an element closest to the center of each class. The distance metric could be similar to the similarity metric discussed above.

6. Using these central elements as new seeds, repeat steps 1–5. Stop when clusters are satisfactory. A typical quality metric is the complexity of the general descriptions of classes. For instance, a variation of Occam's Razor might prefer clusters that yield syntactically simple definitions, such as those with a small number of conjuncts.

7. If clusters are unsatisfactory and no improvement occurs over several iterations, select the new seeds closest to the edge of the cluster, rather than those at the center.

Figure 10.20 shows the stages of a CLUSTER/2 execution.

10.6.3   COBWEB and the Structure of Taxonomic Knowledge

Many clustering algorithms, as well as many supervised learning algorithms such as ID3, define categories in terms of necessary and sufficient conditions for membership. These conditions are a set of properties possessed by all members of a category and only by members of the category. Though many categories, such as the set of all United Nations delegates, may be so defined, human categories do not always fit this model. Indeed, human categorization is characterized by greater flexibility and a much richer structure than we have so far examined.

For example, if human categories were indeed defined by necessary and sufficient conditions for membership, we could not distinguish degrees of category membership.

However, psychologists have noted a strong sense of prototypicality in human categorization (Rosch 1978, Rosch and Lloyd 1978). For instance, we generally think of a robin as a better example of a bird than a chicken; an oak is a more typical example of a tree than a palm (at least in northern latitudes).

Family resemblance theory (Wittgenstein 1953) supports these notions of prototypicality by arguing that categories are defined by complex systems of similarities between members, rather than by necessary and sufficient conditions for membership. Such categories may not have any properties shared by all of their members. Wittgenstein cites the example of games: not all games require two or more players, such as solitaire; not all games are fun for the players, such as rochambeau; not all games have well-articulated rules, such as children's games of make believe; and not all games involve competition, such as jumping rope. Nonetheless, we consider the category to be well-defined and unambiguous.

Human categories also differ from most formal inheritance hierarchies (Chapter 9) in that not all levels of human taxonomies are equally important. Psychologists (Rosch 1978) have demonstrated the existence of *base-level* categories. The base-level category is the classification most commonly used in describing objects, the terminology first learned by children, and the level that in some sense captures the most fundamental classification of an object. For example, the category "chair" is more basic than either its generalizations, such as "furniture," or its specializations, such as "office chair." "Car" is more basic than either "sedan" or "vehicle."

Common methods of representing class membership and hierarchies, such as logic, inheritance systems, feature vectors, or decision trees, do not account for these effects. Yet doing so is not only important to cognitive scientists, whose goal is the understanding of human intelligence; it is also valuable to the engineering of useful AI applications. Users evaluate a program in terms of its flexibility, its robustness, and its ability to behave in ways that seem reasonable by human standards. Although we do not require that AI algorithms parallel the architecture of the human mind, any algorithm that proposes to discover categories must meet user expectations as to the structure and behavior of those categories.

COBWEB (Fisher 1987) addresses these issues. Although it is not intended as a model of human cognition, it does account for base-level categorization and degrees of category membership. In addition, COBWEB learns incrementally: it does not require that all instances be present before it begins learning. In many applications, the learner acquires data over time. In these situations, it must construct usable concept descriptions from an initial collection of data and update those descriptions as more data become available. COBWEB also addresses the problem of determining the correct number of clusters. CLUSTER/2 produced a prespecified number of categories. Although the user could vary this number or the algorithm could try different values in an effort to improve categorization, such approaches are not particularly flexible. COBWEB uses global quality metrics to determine the number of clusters, the depth of the hierarchy, and the category membership of new instances.

Unlike the algorithms we have seen so far, COBWEB represents categories probabilistically. Instead of defining category membership as a set of values that must be present for each feature of an object, COBWEB represents the probability with which each feature

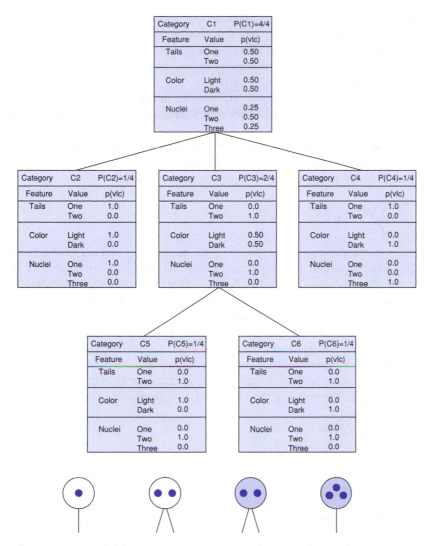

Figure 10.21 A COBWEB clustering for four one-celled organisms, adapted from Gennari et al.(1989).

value is present. $p(f_i = v_{ij} \mid c_k)$ is the conditional probability with which feature f_i will have value v_{ij}, given that an object is in category c_k.

Figure 10.21 illustrates a COBWEB taxonomy taken from Gennari et al. (1989). In this example, the algorithm has formed a categorization of the four single-cell animals at the bottom of the figure. Each animal is defined by its value for the features: color, and numbers of tails and nuclei. Category C3, for example, has a 1.0 probability of having 2 tails, a 0.5 probability of having light color, and a 1.0 probability of having 2 nuclei.

As the figure illustrates, each category in the hierarchy includes probabilities of occurrence for all values of all features. This is essential to both categorizing new instances and modifying the category structure to better fit new instances. Indeed, as an incremental algorithm, COBWEB does not separate these actions. When given a new instance, COBWEB considers the overall quality of either placing the instance in an existing category or modifying the hierarchy to accommodate the instance. The criterion COBWEB uses for evaluating the quality of a classification is called *category utility* (Gluck and Corter 1985). Category utility was developed in research on human categorization. It accounts for base-level effects and other aspects of human category structure.

Category utility attempts to maximize both the probability that two objects in the same category have values in common and the probability that objects in different categories will have different property values. Category utility is defined:

$$\sum_k \sum_i \sum_j p(f_i=v_{ij})p(f_i=v_{ij}|c_k)p(c_k|f_i=v_{ij})$$

This sum is taken across all categories, c_k, all features, f_i, and all feature values, v_{ij}. $p(f_i = v_{ij} | c_k)$, called *predictability*, is the probability that an object has value v_{ij} for feature f_i given that the object belongs to category c_k. The higher this probability, the more likely two objects in a category share the same feature values. $p(c_k | f_i = v_{ij})$, called *predictiveness*, is the probability with which an object belongs to category c_k given that it has value v_{ij} for feature f_i. The greater this probability, the less likely objects not in the category will have those feature values. $p(f_i = v_{ij})$ serves as a weight, assuring that frequently occurring feature values will exert a stronger influence on the evaluation. By combining these values, high category utility measures indicate a high likelihood that objects in the same category will share properties, while decreasing the likelihood of objects in different categories having properties in common.

The COBWEB algorithm is defined:

```
cobweb(Node, Instance)
begin
  if Node is a leaf
    then begin
      create two children of Node, L₁ and L₂;
      set the probabilities of L₁ to those of Node;
      initialize the probabilities for L₂ to those of Instance;
      add Instance to Node, updating Node's probabilities;
    end
  else begin
    add Instance to Node, updating Node's probabilities;
    for each child, C, of Node, compute the category utility of the clustering
      achieved by placing Instance in C;
    let S₁ be the score for the best categorization, C₁;
    let S₂ be the score for the second best categorization, C₂;
    let S₃ be the score for placing instance in a new category;
    let S₄ be the score for merging C₁ and C₂ into one category;
    let S₅ be the score for splitting C₁ (replacing it with its child categories)
  end
```

```
    If S₁ is the best score
        then cobweb(C₁, Instance                          % place the instance in C₁
        else if S₃ is the best score
            then initialize the new category's probabilities to those of Instance
            else if S₄ is the best score
                then begin
                    let Cₘ be the result of merging C₁ and C₂;
                    cobweb(Cₘ, Instance)
                end
                else if S₅ is the best score
                    then begin
                        split C₁;
                        cobweb(Node, Instance)
                    end;
    end
```

COBWEB performs a hill-climbing search of the space of possible taxonomies using category utility to evaluate and select possible categorizations. It initializes the taxonomy to a single category whose features are those of the first instance. For each subsequent instance, the algorithm begins with the root category and moves through the tree. At each level it uses category utility to evaluate the taxonomies resulting from:

1. Placing the instance in the best existing category.

2. Adding a new category containing only the instance.

3. Merging of two existing categories into one new one and adding the instance to that category.

4. Splitting of an existing category into two and placing the instance in the best new resulting category.

Figure 10.22 illustrates the processes of merging and splitting nodes. To merge two nodes, the algorithm creates a new node and makes the existing nodes children of that node. It computes the probabilities for the new node by combining the probabilities for the children. Splitting replaces a node with its children.

This algorithm is efficient and produces taxonomies with a reasonable number of classes. Because it allows probabilistic membership, its categories are flexible and robust. In addition, it has demonstrated base-level category effects and, through its notion of partial category matching, supports notions of prototypicality and degree of membership. Instead of relying on two-valued logic, COBWEB, like fuzzy logic, views the "vagueness" of category membership as a necessary component for learning and reasoning in a flexible and intelligent fashion.

We next present reinforcement learning which, like the classifier systems of Section 12.2, interprets feedback from an environment to learn optimal sets of condition/response relationships for problem solving within that environment.

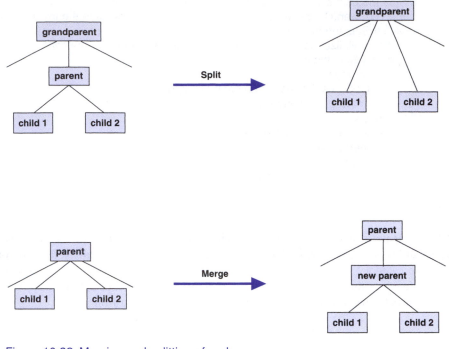

Figure 10.22 Merging and splitting of nodes.

10.7 Reinforcement Learning

We humans (usually!) learn from interacting with our environment. A moment of thought, however, reminds us that feedback from our actions in the world is not always immediate and straightforward. In human relationships, for example, it often takes quite some time to appreciate fully the results of our actions. Interaction with the world demonstrates for us cause and effect (Pearl 2000), the consequences of our actions, and even how to achieve complex goals. As intelligent agents, we make policies for working in and through our world. "The world" *is* a teacher, but her lessons are often subtle and sometimes hard won!

10.7.1   The Components of Reinforcement Learning

In reinforcement learning, we design computational algorithms for transforming world situations into actions in a manner that maximizes a reward measure. Our agent is not told directly what to do or which action to take; rather, the agent discovers through exploration which actions offer the most reward. Agents' actions affect not just immediate reward, but also impact subsequent actions and eventual rewards. These two features, trial-and-error search and delayed reinforcement, are the two most important characteristics of reinforcement learning. Consequently, reinforcement learning is a more general methodology than the learning seen earlier in this chapter.

Reinforcement learning is not defined by particular learning methods, but by actions within and responses from an environment. Any learning method that can address this interaction is an acceptable reinforcement learning method. Reinforcement learning is also not supervised learning, as seen throughout our chapters on machine learning. In supervised learning, a "teacher" uses examples to directly instruct or train the learner. In reinforcement learning, the learning agent itself, through trial, error, and feedback, learns an optimal policy for accomplishing goals within its environment. (In this sense it resembles the classifier learning of Section 12.2.)

Another trade-off that the reinforcement learner must consider is between using only what it presently knows and further exploring its world. To optimize its reward possibilities, the agent must not just do what it already knows, but also explore those parts of its world that are still unknown. Exploration allows the agent to (possibly) make better selections in the future; thus obviously, the agent that either always or never explores will usually fail. The agent must explore a variety of options and at the same time favor those that appear to be best. On tasks with stochastic parameters, exploratory actions must be made many times to gain reliable estimates of rewards.

Many of the problem-solving algorithms presented earlier in this book, including planners, decision makers, and search algorithms, can be viewed in the context of reinforcement learning. For example, we can create a plan with a teleo-reactive controller (Section 8.4) and then evaluate its success with a reinforcement learning algorithm. In fact, the DYNA-Q reinforcement algorithm (Sutton 1990, 1991) integrates model learning with planning and acting. Thus reinforcement learning offers a method for evaluating both plans and models and their utility for accomplishing tasks in complex environments.

We now introduce some terminology for reinforcement learning:

t is a discrete time step in the problem solving process
s_t is the problem state at t, dependent on s_{t-1} and s_{t-1}
a_t is the action at t, dependent on s_t
r_t is the reward at t, dependent on s_{t-1} and a_{t-1}
π is a policy for taking an action in a state. Thus π is a mapping from states to actions
π^* is the optimal policy
V maps a state to its value. Thus, $V^{\pi}(s)$ is the value of state s under policy π

In Section 10.7.2, *temporal difference learning* learns a V for each s with static π.

There are four components of reinforcement learning, a *policy* π, a *reward function* r, a *value mapping* V, and quite often, a *model* of the environment. The *policy* defines the learning agent's choices and method of action at any given time. Thus the policy could be represented by a set of production rules or a simple lookup table. The policy for a particular situation, as just noted, could also be the result of extensive search, consulting a model, or of a planning process. It could also be stochastic. The policy is the critical component of the learning agent in that it alone is sufficient to produce behavior at any time.

The *reward function* r_t defines the state/goal relationships of the problem at time t. It maps each action, or more precisely each state-response pair, into a reward measure, indicating the desirability of that action for achieving the goal. The agent in reinforcement learning has the task of maximizing the total reward it receives in accomplishing its task.

The *value function* V is a property of each state of the environment indicating the reward the system can expect for actions continuing on from that state. While the reward function measures the immediate desirability of state-response pairs, the value function indicates the long-term desirability of a state of the environment. A state gets its value from both its own intrinsic quality as well as from the quality of states likely to follow from it, i.e., the reward of being in those states. For example, a state/action might have a low immediate reward, but have a high value because it is usually followed by other states that do yield a high reward. A low value could also indicate states that are not associated with successful solution paths.

Without a reward function there are no values and the only purpose of estimating values is to gain more rewards. In making decisions, however, it is values that most interest us, as values indicate states and combinations of states that bring highest rewards. It is much harder to determine values for states, however, than to determine rewards. Rewards are given directly by the environment, while values are estimated and then re-estimated from the successes and failures over time. In fact, the most critical as well as most difficult aspect of reinforcement learning is creating a method for efficiently determining values. We demonstrate one method, a temporal difference learning rule, in Section 10.7.2.

A final—and optional—element for reinforcement learning is the *model* of the environment. A model is a mechanism for capturing aspects of the behavior of the environment. As we saw in Section 8.3, models can be used not only for determining faults as in diagnostic reasoning but also as part of determining a plan of action. Models let us evaluate possible future actions without actually experiencing them. Model-based planning is a recent addition to the reinforcement learning paradigm, as early systems tended to create reward and value parameters based on the pure trial and error actions of an agent.

10.7.2　An Example: Tic-Tac-Toe Revisited

We next demonstrate a reinforcement learning algorithm for tic-tac-toe, a problem we have already considered (Chapter 4), and one dealt with in the reinforcement learning literature by Sutton and Barto (1998). It is important to compare and contrast the reinforcement learning approach with other solution methods, for example, mini-max.

As a reminder, tic-tac-toe is a two-person game played on a 3x3 grid, as in Figure II.5. The players, X and O, alternate putting their marks on the grid, with the first player that gets three marks in a row, either horizontal, vertical or diagonal, the winner. As the reader is aware, when this game is played using perfect information and backed up values, Section 4.4, it is always a draw. With reinforcement learning we will be able to do something much more interesting, however. We will show how we can capture the performance of an imperfect opponent, and create a policy that allows us to maximize our advantage over this opponent. Our policy can also evolve as our opponent improves her game, and with the use of a model we will be able to generate forks and other attacking moves!

First, we must set up a table of numbers, one for each possible state of the game. These numbers, that state's *value*, will reflect the current estimate of the probability of winning

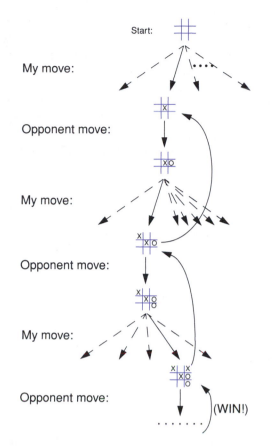

Figure 10.23 A sequence of tic-tac-toe for moves. Dashed arrows indicate possible move choices, down solid arrows indicate selected moves, up solid arrows indicate reward, when reward function changes state's value.

from that state. This will support a policy for a strictly winning strategy, i.e., either a win by our opponent or a drawn game will be considered a loss for us. This draw-as-loss approach allows us to set up a policy focused on winning, and is different from our perfect information win-lose-draw model of Section 4.4. This is an important difference, actually; we are going to capture the skill of an actual opponent and not the perfect information of some idealized opponent. Thus, we will initialize our value table with a 1 for each win position for us, a 0 for each loss or drawn board, and a 0.5 everywhere else, reflecting the initial guess that we have a 50 per cent chance of winning from those states.

We now play many games against this opponent. For simplicity, let us assume that we are the X and our opponent 0. Figure 10.23 reflects a sequence of possible moves, both those considered and those chosen, within a game situation. To generate a move, we first consider each state that is a legal move from our present state, that is, any open state that we can possibly claim with our X. We look up the current value measure for that state kept in our table. Most of the time we can make a greedy move, that is, taking the state that has the best value function. Occasionally, we will want to make an exploratory move and select randomly from the other states. These exploratory moves are to consider alternatives we might not see within the game situation, expanding possible value optimizations.

While we are playing, we change the *value functions* of each of the states we have selected. We attempt to make their latest values better reflect the probability of their being on a winning path. We earlier called this the *reward function* for a state. To do this we back up the value of a state we have selected as a function of the value of the next state we choose. As can be seen with the "up arrows" of Figure 10.23, this back-up action skips the choice of our opponent, and yet it does reflect the set of values that she has directed us towards for our next choice of a state. Thus, the current value of an earlier state we choose is adjusted, rewarded, to better reflect the value of the later state (and ultimately, of course, of the winning or losing value). We usually do this by moving the previous state some fraction of the value difference between itself and the newer state we have selected. This fractional measure, called the *step-size parameter*, is reflected by the multiplier c in the equation:

$$V(s_n) = V(s_n) + c(V(s_{n+1}) - V(s_n))$$

In this equation, s_n represents the state chosen at time n and s_{n+1} the state chosen at time n + 1. This update equation is an example of a *temporal difference learning rule*, since its changes are a function of the difference, $V(s_{n+1}) - V(s_n)$, between value estimates at two different times, n and n + 1. We discuss these learning rules further in the next section.

The temporal difference rule performs quite well for tic-tac-toe. We will want to reduce the step size parameter c over time, so that as the system learns, successively smaller adjustments are made to the state values. This will guarantee convergence of the value functions for each state to the probability of winning, given our opponent. Also, except for periodic exploratory moves, the choices made will in fact be the optimal moves, that is, the optimal policy, against this opponent. What is even more interesting, however, is the fact that if the step size never really gets to zero this policy will continually change to reflect any changes/improvements in the opponent's play!

Our tic-tac-toe example illustrates many of the important features of reinforcement learning. First, there is learning while interacting with the environment, here our opponent. Second, there is an explicit goal (reflected in a number of goal states) and optimal behavior requires planning and look ahead that makes allowance for delayed effects of particular moves. For example, the reinforcement learning algorithm in effect sets up multi move traps for the naive opponent. It is an important feature of reinforcement learning that the effects of look ahead and planning can be in fact achieved, without either an explicit model of the opponent or through extended search.

In our tic-tac-toe example, learning began with no prior knowledge beyond the game's rules. (We simply initialized all non-terminal states to 0.5.) Reinforcement learning certainly does not require this "blank slate" view. Any prior information available can be built into the initial state values. It is also possible to deal with states where there is no information available. Finally, if a model of a situation is available, the resulting model-based information can be used for the state values. But it is important to remember that reinforcement learning can be applied in either situation: no model is required, but models can be used if they are available or if they can be learned.

In the tic-tac-toe example, the reward was amortized over each state-action decision. Our agent was myopic, concerned with maximizing only immediate rewards. Indeed, if we use deeper lookahead with reinforcement learning, we will need to measure the *discounted return* of an eventual reward. We let the discount rate γ represent the present value of a future reward: a reward received k time steps in the future is worth only γ^{k-1} times what it would be worth if it were received immediately. This discounting of the reward measure is important in using the dynamic programming approach to reinforcement learning presented in the next section.

Tic-tac-toe was an example of a two-person game. Reinforcement learning can also be used for situations where there are no opponents, just feedback from an environment. The tic-tac-toe example also had a finite (and actually fairly small) state space. Reinforcement learning can also be employed when the state space is very large, or even infinite. In the latter case, state values are generated only when that state is encountered and used in a solution. Tesauro (1995) for example, used the temporal difference rule we just described, built into a neural network, to learn to play backgammon. Even though the estimated size of the backgammon state space is 10^{20} states, Tesauro's program plays at the level of the best human players.

10.7.3 Inference Algorithms and Applications for Reinforcement Learning

According to Sutton and Barto (1998) there are three different families of reinforcement learning inference algorithms: *temporal difference* learning, *dynamic programming*, and *Monte Carlo* methods. These three form a basis for virtually all current approaches to reinforcement learning. Temporal difference methods learn from sampled trajectories and backup values from state to state. We saw an example of temporal difference learning with tic-tac-toe in the previous section.

Dynamic programming methods compute value functions by backing up values from successor states to predecessor states. Dynamic programming methods systematically update one state after another, based on a model of the next state distribution. The dynamic programming approach to reinforcement is built on the fact that for any policy π and any state s the following recursive consistency equation holds:

$$V^\pi(s) = \sum_a \pi(a \mid s) * \sum_{s'} \pi(s \to s' \mid a) * (R^a(s \to s') + \gamma(V^\pi(s')))$$

$\pi(a \mid s)$ is the probability of action a given state s under stochastic policy π. $\pi(s \to s' \mid a)$ is the probability of s going to s' under action a. This is the Bellman (1957) equation for V^π. It expresses a relationship between the value of a state and the recursively calculated values of its successor states. In Figure 10.24a we present the first step calculation, where from state s we look forward to three possible successor states. With policy π, action a has probability $\pi(a \mid s)$ of occurring. From each of these three states the environment could

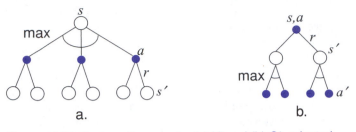

Figure 10.24 Backup diagrams for (a) V* and (b) Q*, adapted from Sutton and Barto (1998).

respond with one of several states, say s' with reward r. The Bellman equation averages over all these possibilities, weighting each by its probability of happening. It states that the value of the start state s must equal the discounted, γ, value of the expected next states plus the reward generated along the path.

Classical dynamic programming models are of limited utility because of their assumption of a perfect model. If n and m denote the number of states and actions, a dynamic programming method is guaranteed to find an optimal policy in polynomial time, even though the total number of deterministic policies is n^m. In this sense dynamic programming is exponentially faster than any direct search in policy space could be, because direct search would have to evaluate each policy exhaustively to give the same guarantee.

Monte Carlo methods do not require a complete model. Instead they sample the entire trajectories of states to update the value function based on the episodes' final outcomes. Monte Carlo methods do require experience, that is, sample sequences of states, actions, and rewards from on-line or simulated interactions with the environment. On-line experience is interesting because it requires no prior knowledge of the environment, yet can still be optimal. Learning from simulated experience is also powerful. A model is required, but it can be generative rather than analytical, that is, a model able to generate trajectories but not able to calculate explicit probabilities. Thus, it need not produce the complete probability distributions of all possible transitions that are required in dynamic programming.

Thus, Monte Carlo methods solve the reinforcement learning problem by averaging sample returns. To ensure well defined returns, Monte Carlo methods are defined only for full episodes, that is, all episodes must eventually terminate. Furthermore, it is only on completion of an episode that the value estimates and policies are changed. Thus, Monte Carlo methods are incremental in an episode by episode sense and not step by step. The term "Monte Carlo" is often used more broadly for any estimation method whose operation involves a significant random component. Here it is used specifically for methods based on averaging complete returns.

There are other methods used for reinforcement learning, the most important being Q-learning (Watkins 1989), a variant of the temporal difference approach. In Q-learning, Q is a function of state-action pairs to learned values. For all states and actions:

Q: (state x action) $\rightarrow$ value

For one step Q-learning:

$$Q(s_t, a_t) \leftarrow (1 - c) * Q(s_t, a_t) + c * [r_{t+1} + \gamma * \max_a Q(s_{t+1}, a) - Q(s_t, a_t)]$$

where both c and γ are ≤ 1 and r_{t+1} is the reward at s_{t+1}. We can visualize the Q approach in Figure 10.24b, and contrast it with Figure 10.24a, where the start node is a state-action situation. This backup rule updates state-action pairs, so that the top state of Figure 10.24b, the root of the backup, is an action node coupled with the state that produced it.

In Q-learning, the backup is from action nodes, maximizing over all the actions possible from the next states, along with their rewards. In full recursively defined Q-learning, the bottom nodes of the backup tree are all terminal nodes reachable by a sequence of actions starting from the root node, together with the rewards of these successor actions. On-line Q-learning, expanding forward from possible actions, does not require building a full world model. Q-learning can also be performed off-line. As one can see, Q-learning is a kind of temporal difference approach. Further details may be found in Watkins (1989) and Sutton and Barto (1998).

There are now a number of significant problems solved with reinforcement learning, including Backgammon (Tesauro 1994, 1995). Sutton and Barto (1998) analyze Samuel's checker program, Section 4.1, from the reinforcement learning viewpoint. They also present the reinforcement learning approach to the acrobat, elevator dispatching, dynamic channel allocation, job shop scheduling, and other problems (Sutton and Barto 1998).

10.8 Epilogue and References

Machine learning is one of the most exciting subfields in artificial intelligence, addressing a problem that is central to intelligent behavior and raising a number of questions about knowledge representation, search, and even the basic assumptions of AI itself. Surveys of machine learning include Pat Langley's (1995) *Elements of Machine Learning*, Tom Mitchell's (1997) book *Machine Learning*, and Anthony Martin's (1997) *Computational Learning Theory: An Introduction* (see also Section 17.2).

Early surveys of learning include *Machine Learning: An Artificial Intelligence Approach* (Kodratoff and Michalski 1990, Michalski et al. 1983, 1986). *Readings in Machine Learning* (Shavlik and Dietterich 1990) collects papers in the field, back as far as 1958. By placing all this research in a single volume, the editors have provided a valuable service to both researchers and those seeking an introduction to the field. Inductive learning is presented by Vere (1975, 1978) and Dietterich and Michalski (1981, 1986). *Production System Models of Learning and Development* (Klahr et al. 1987) collects a number of papers in machine learning, including work (SOAR) reflecting a more cognitive approach.

Computer Systems That Learn (Weiss and Kulikowski 1991) is an introductory survey of the whole field, including treatments of neural networks, statistical methods, and machine learning techniques. Readers interested in a deeper discussion of analogical reasoning should examine Carbonell (1983, 1986), Carbonell et al. (1983), Holyoak (1985), Kedar-Cabelli (1988), and Thagard (1988). For those interested in discovery and theory formation, see *Scientific Discovery: Computational Explorations of the Creative Processes* (Langley et al. 1987) and *Computational Models of Scientific Discovery and Theory Formation* (Shrager and Langley 1990). *Concept Formation: Knowledge and Experience in Unsupervised Learning* (Fisher et al. 1991) presents a number of papers on clustering, concept formation, and other forms of unsupervised learning.

ID3 has a long history within the machine learning community. *EPAM*, the *Elementary Perceiver And Memorizer* in Feigenbaum and Feldman (1963), used a type of decision tree, called a *discrimination net*, to organize sequences of nonsense syllables. Quinlan was the first to use information theory to generate children in the decision tree. Quinlan (1993) and others extended ID3 to C4.5, and address issues such as noise and continuous attributes in data (Quinlan 1996, Auer et al. 1995). Stubblefield and Luger have applied ID3 to the problem of improving the retrieval of sources in an analogical reasoner (1996).

Michie (1961) and Samuel (1959) offer early examples of reinforcement learning. Sutton and Barto's (1998) *Reinforcement Learning* was the source of much of our presentation on this topic. We recommend Watkins (1989) thesis for a more detailed presentation of Q-learning, Sutton's (1988) original paper for analysis of temporal difference learning, and Bertsekas and Tsitsiklis (1996), *Neuro-Dynamic Programming*, for a more formal presentation of all reinforcement learning algorithms.

Machine Learning is the primary journal of the field. Other sources of current research include the yearly proceedings of the International Conference on Machine Learning and the European Conference on Machine Learning as well as the proceedings of the American Association of Artificial Intelligence Conference and the International Joint Conference on Artificial Intelligence.

We present connectionist learning in Chapter 11, and social and emergent learning in Chapter 12. We discuss inductive bias and generalization in learning in Section 17.2.

10.9 Exercises

1. Consider the behavior of Winston's concept learning program when learning the concept "step," where a step consists of a short box and a tall box placed in contact with each other, as in Figure 10.25. Create semantic net representations of three or four examples and near misses and show the development of the concept.

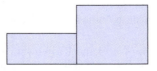

Figure 10.25 A step.

2. The run of the candidate elimination algorithm shown in Figure 10.9 does not show candidate concepts that were produced but eliminated because they were either overly general, overly specific, or subsumed by some other concept. Re-do the execution trace, showing these concepts and the reasons each was eliminated.

3. Build the version space search algorithms in PROLOG, or the language of your choice. If you use PROLOG, see hints in Section 15.14.1.

4. Using the information theoretic selection function of Section 10.4.3, show in detail how ID3 constructs the tree of Figure 10.14 from examples in Table 10.1. Be sure to show the calculations used in computing the information gain for each test and the resulting test selections.

5. Using Shannon's formula, show whether or not a message about the outcome of a spin of a roulette wheel has more information than one about the outcome of a coin toss. What if the roulette wheel message is "not 00"?

6. Develop a simple table of examples in some domain, such as classifying animals by species, and trace the construction of a decision tree by the ID3 algorithm.

7. Implement ID3 in a language of your choice and run it on the credit history example from the text. If you use LISP, consider the algorithms and data structures developed in Section 16.13 for suggestions.

8. Discuss problems that can arise from using continuous attributes in data, such as a monetary cost, dollars and cents, or the height, a real number, of an entity. Suggest some method for addressing this problem of continuous data.

9. Other problems of ID3 are bad or missing data. Data is bad if one set of attributes has two different outcomes. Data is missing if part of the attribute is not present, perhaps because it was too expensive to obtain. How might these issues be dealt with in development of ID3 algorithms?

10. From Quinlan (1993) obtain the C4.5 decision tree algorithm and test it on a data set. There are complete programs and data sets for C4.5 available from this reference.

11. Develop a domain theory for explanation-based learning in some problem area of your choice. Trace the behavior of an explanation-based learner in applying this theory to several training instances.

12. Develop an explanation-based learning algorithm in the language of your choice. If you use PROLOG, consider the algorithms developed in Section 15.8.3.

13. Consider the tic-tac-toe example of Section 10.7.2. Implement the temporal difference learning algorithm in the language of your choice. If you designed the algorithm to take into account problem symmetries, what do you expect to happen? How might this limit your solution?

14. What happens if the temporal difference algorithm of Problem 13 plays tic-tac-toe against itself?

15. Analyze Samuel's checker playing program from a reinforcement learning perspective. Sutton and Barto (1998, Section 11.2) offer suggestions in this analysis.

16. Can you analyze the inverted pendulum problem, Figure 9.8, presented in Section 9.2.2 from a reinforcement learning perspective? Build some simple reward measures and use the temporal difference algorithm in your analysis.

17. Another problem type excellent for reinforcement learning is the so-called gridworld. We present a simple 4×4 gridworld in Figure 10.26. The two greyed corners are the desired terminal states for the agent. From all other states, agent movement is either up, down, left, or right. The agent cannot move off the grid: attempting to leaves the state unchanged. The reward for all transitions, except to the terminal states, is -1. Work through a sequence of grids that produce a solution based on the temporal difference algorithm presented in Section 10.7.2.

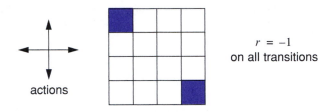

$r = -1$
on all transitions

actions

Figure 10.26 An example of a 4×4 grid world, adapted
from Sutton and Barto (1998).

MACHINE LEARNING: CONNECTIONIST

11

A cat that once sat on a hot stove will never again sit on a hot stove or on a cold one either . . .

—Mark Twain

Everything is vague to a degree you do not realize till you have tried to make it precise . . .

—Bertrand Russell

. . . as if a magic lantern threw the nerves in patterns on a screen . . .

—T. S. Eliot, *The Love Song of J. Alfred Prufrock*

11.0 Introduction

In Chapter 10 we emphasized a symbol-based approach to learning. A central aspect of this hypothesis is the use of symbols to refer to objects and relations in a domain. In the present chapter, we introduce *neurally* or *biology* inspired approaches to learning.

Neurally inspired models, also known as *parallel distributed processing (PDP)* or *connectionist* systems, de-emphasize the explicit use of symbols in problem solving. Instead, they hold that intelligence arises in systems of simple, interacting components (biological or artificial neurons) through a process of learning or adaptation by which the connections between components are adjusted. Processing in these systems is distributed across collections or layers of neurons. Problem solving is parallel in the sense that all the neurons within the collection or layer process their inputs simultaneously and independently. These systems also tend to degrade gracefully because information and processing are distributed across the network's nodes and layers.

In connectionist models there is, however, a strong representational character both in the creation of input parameters as well as in the interpretation of output values. To build a neural network, for example, the designer must create a scheme for encoding patterns in the world into numerical quantities in the net. The choice of an encoding scheme can play a crucial role in the eventual success or failure of the network to learn.

In connectionist systems, processing is parallel and distributed with no manipulation of symbols as symbols. Patterns in a domain are encoded as numerical vectors. The connections *between* components, or neurons, are also represented by numerical values. Finally, the transformation of patterns is the result of numerical operations, usually, matrix multiplications. These "designer's choices" for a connectionist architecture constitute the *inductive bias* of the system.

The algorithms and architectures that implement these techniques are usually trained or conditioned rather than explicitly programmed. Indeed, this is a major strength of the approach: an appropriately designed network architecture and learning algorithm can often capture invariances in the world, even in the form of strange attractors, without being explicitly programmed to recognize them. How this happens makes up the material of Chapter 11.

The tasks for which the connectionist approach is well suited include:

classification, deciding the category or grouping to which an input value belongs;
pattern recognition, identifying structure or pattern in data;
memory recall, including the problem of content addressable memory;
prediction, such as identifying disease from symptoms, causes from effects;
optimization, finding the "best" organization of constraints; and
noise filtering, or separating signal from background, factoring out the irrelevant components of a signal.

The methods of this chapter work best on those tasks that can be difficult to formulate for symbolic models. This typically includes tasks in which the problem domain requires perception-based skills, or lacks a clearly defined syntax.

In Section 11.1 we introduce neurally inspired learning models from an historical viewpoint. We present the basic components of neural network learning, including the "mechanical" neuron, and describe some historically important early work, including the McCulloch–Pitts (1943) neuron. The evolution of the network training paradigms over the past 40 years offers important insights into the present state of the discipline.

In Section 11.2, we continue the historical presentation with the introduction of *perceptron* learning, and the *delta* rule. We present an example of the perceptron used as a classifier. In Section 11.3 we introduce nets with hidden layers, and the *backpropagation* learning rule. These innovations were introduced in the evolution of artificial neural networks to overcome problems the early systems had in generalizing across data points that were not linearly separable. Backpropagation is an algorithm for apportioning "blame" for incorrect responses to the nodes of a multilayered system with continuous thresholding.

In Section 11.4 we present models for *competitive learning* developed by Kohonen (1984) and Hecht-Nielsen (1987). In these models, network weight vectors are used to represent patterns rather than connection strengths. The *winner-take-all* learning algorithm selects the node whose pattern of weights is most like the input vector and adjusts it to make it more like the input vector. It is unsupervised in that *winning* is simply identifying the node whose current weight vector most closely resembles the input vector. The combination of Kohonen with Grossberg (1982) layers in a single network offers an interesting model for stimulus–response learning called *counter propagation* learning.

In Section 11.5 we present Hebb's (1949) model of reinforcement learning. Hebb conjectured that each time one neuron contributes to the firing of another neuron, the strength of the pathway between the neurons is increased. Hebbian learning is modeled by a simple algorithm for adjusting connection weights. We present both unsupervised and supervised versions of Hebbian learning. We also introduce the linear associator, a Hebbian based model for pattern retrieval from memory.

Section 11.6 introduces a very important family of networks called *attractor networks*. These networks employ feedback connections to repeatedly cycle a signal within the network. The network output is considered to be the network state upon reaching equilibrium. Network weights are constructed so that a set of *attractors* is created. Input patterns within an attractor *basin* reach equilibrium at that attractor. The attractors can therefore be used to store patterns in a memory. Given an input pattern, we retrieve either the closest stored pattern in the network or a pattern associated with the closest stored pattern. The first type of memory is called *autoassociative*, the second type *heteroassociative*. John Hopfield (1982), a theoretical physicist, defined a class of attractor networks whose convergence can be represented by energy minimization. Hopfield networks can be used to solve constraint satisfaction problems, such as the traveling salesperson problem, by mapping the optimization function into an energy function (Section 11.6.4).

In Chapter 12, the final chapter of Part IV, we present evolutionary models of learning, such as genetic algorithms and artificial life. We discuss representational issues and bias in learning as well as the strengths of each learning paradigm in Section 17.3.

11.1 Foundations for Connectionist Networks

11.1.1 Early History

Connectionist architectures are often thought of as a recent development, however we can trace their origins to early work in computer science, psychology, and philosophy. John von Neumann, for example, was fascinated by both cellular automata and neurally inspired approaches to computation. Early work in neural learning was influenced by psychological theories of animal learning, especially that of Hebb (1949). In this section, we outline the basic components of neural network learning, and present historically important early work in the field.

The basis of neural networks is the artificial neuron, as in Figure 11.1. An artificial neuron consists of:

Input signals, x_i. These data may come from the environment, or the activation of other neurons. Different models vary in the allowable range of the input values; typically inputs are discrete, from the set $\{0, 1\}$ or $\{-1, 1\}$, or real numbers.

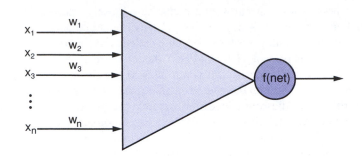

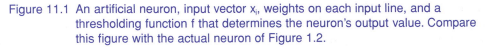

Figure 11.1 An artificial neuron, input vector x_i, weights on each input line, and a thresholding function f that determines the neuron's output value. Compare this figure with the actual neuron of Figure 1.2.

A set of real valued weights, w_i. The weights describe connection strengths.

An activation level, $\Sigma w_i x_i$. The neuron's activation level is determined by the cumulative strength of its input signals where each input signal is scaled by the connection weight w_i along that input line. The activation level is thus computed by taking the sum of the weighted inputs, that is, $\Sigma w_i x_i$.

A threshold function, f. This function computes the neuron's final or output state by determining how far the neuron's activation level is below or above some threshold value. The threshold function is intended to produce the on/off state of actual neurons.

In addition to these properties of individual neurons, a neural network is also characterized by global properties such as:

The network topology. The topology of the network is the pattern of connections between the individual neurons. This topology is a primary source of the net's inductive bias.

The learning algorithm used. A number of algorithms for learning are presented in this chapter.

The encoding scheme. This includes the interpretation placed on the data to the network and the results of its processing.

The earliest example of neural computing is the McCulloch–Pitts neuron (McCulloch and Pitts 1943). The inputs to a McCulloch–Pitts neuron are either excitatory (+1) or inhibitory (−1). The activation function multiplies each input by its corresponding weight and sums the results; if the sum is greater than or equal to zero, the neuron returns 1, otherwise, −1. McCulloch and Pitts showed how these neurons could be constructed to compute any logical function, demonstrating that systems of these neurons provide a complete computational model.

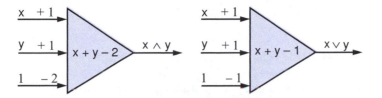

Figure 11.2 McCulloch–Pitts neurons to calculate the logic functions and and or.

Figure 11.2 shows the McCulloch-Pitts neurons for computing logical functions. The *and* neuron has three inputs: x and y are the values to be conjoined; the third, sometimes called a *bias*, has a constant value of +1. The input data and bias have weights of +1, +1, and −2, respectively. Thus, for any values of x and y, the neuron computes the value of x + y − 2: if this value is less than 0, it returns −1, otherwise a 1. Table 11.1 illustrates the neuron computing x ∧ y. In a similar fashion, the weighted sum of input data for the *or* neuron, see Figure 11.2, is greater than or equal to 0 unless both x and y equal −1.

x	y	x + y − 2	Output
1	1	0	1
1	0	−1	−1
0	1	−1	−1
0	0	−2	−1

Table 11.1 The McCulloch-Pitts model for logical and.

Although McCulloch and Pitts demonstrated the power of neural computation, interest in the approach only began to flourish with the development of practical learning algorithms. Early learning models drew heavily on the work of the psychologist D. O. Hebb (1949), who speculated that learning occurred in brains through the modification of synapses. Hebb theorized that repeated firings across a synapse increased its sensitivity and the future likelihood of its firing. If a particular stimulus repeatedly caused activity in a group of cells, those cells come to be strongly associated. In the future, similar stimuli would tend to excite the same neural pathways, resulting in the recognition of the stimuli. (See Hebb's actual description, Section 11.5.1.) Hebb's model of learning worked purely on reinforcement of used paths and ignored inhibition, punishment for error, or attrition. Modern psychologists attempted to implement Hebb's model but failed to produce general results without addition of an inhibitory mechanism (Rochester et al. 1988, Quinlan 1991). We consider the Hebbian model of learning in Section 11.5.

In the next section we extend the McCulloch–Pitts neural model by adding layers of connected neural mechanisms and algorithms for their interactions. The first version of this was called the *perceptron*.

11.2 Perceptron Learning

11.2.1 The Perceptron Training Algorithm

Frank Rosenblatt (1958, 1962) devised a learning algorithm for a type of single layer network called a *perceptron*. In its signal propagation, the perceptron was similar to the McCulloch–Pitts neuron, which we will see in Section 11.2.2. The input values and activation levels of the perceptron are either -1 or 1; weights are real valued. The activation level of the perceptron is given by summing the weighted input values, $\Sigma x_i w_i$. Perceptrons use a simple hard-limiting threshold function, where an activation above a threshold results in an output value of 1, and -1 otherwise. Given input values x_i, weights w_i, and a threshold, t, the perceptron computes its output value as:

$$1 \quad \text{if } \Sigma x_i w_i \geq t$$
$$-1 \quad \text{if } \Sigma x_i w_i < t$$

The perceptron uses a simple form of supervised learning. After attempting to solve a problem instance, a teacher gives it the correct result. The perceptron then changes its weights in order to reduce the error. The following rule is used. Let c be a constant whose size determines the learning rate and d be the desired output value. The adjustment for the weight on the ith component of the input vector, Δw_i, is given by:

$$\Delta w_i = c(d - sign(\Sigma x_i w_i))\, x_i$$

The $sign(\Sigma x_i w_i)$ is the perceptron output value. It is $+1$ or -1. The difference between the desired output and the actual output values will thus be 0, 2, or -2. Therefore for each component of the input vector:

If the desired output and actual output values are equal, do nothing.

If the actual output value is -1 and should be 1, increment the weights on the ith line by $2cx_i$.

If the actual output value is 1 and should be -1, decrement the weights on the ith line by $2cx_i$.

This procedure has the effect of producing a set of weights which are intended to minimize the average error over the entire training set. If there exists a set of weights which give the correct output for every member of the training set, the perceptron learning procedure will learn it (Minsky and Papert 1969).

Perceptrons were initially greeted with enthusiasm. However, Nils Nilsson (1965) and others analyzed the limitations of the perceptron model. They demonstrated that perceptrons could not solve a certain difficult class of problems, namely problems in which the data points are not linearly separable. Although various enhancements of the perceptron model, including multilayered perceptrons, were envisioned at the time, Marvin Minsky and Seymour Papert, in their book *Perceptrons* (1969), argued that the linear separability problem could not be overcome by any form of the perceptron network.

An example of a nonlinearably separable classification is *exclusive-or*. Table 11.2 is the truth table representing exclusive-or.

x_1	x_2	Output
1	1	0
1	0	1
0	1	1
0	0	0

Table 11.2 The truth table for exclusive-or.

Consider a perceptron with two inputs, x_1, x_2, two weights, w_1, w_2, and threshold t. In order to learn this function, a network must find a weight assignment that satisfies the following inequalities, seen graphically in Figure 11.3:

w_1*1 + w_2*1 < t, from line 1 of the truth table.
w_1*1 + 0 > t, from line 2 of the truth table.
0 + w_2*1 > t, from line 3 of the truth table.
0 + 0 < t, or t must be positive, from the last line of the table.

This series of equations on w_1, w_2, and t has no solution, proving that a perceptron that solves *exclusive-or* is impossible. Although multilayer networks would eventually be built that could solve the exclusive-or problem, see Section 11.3.3, the perceptron learning algorithm only worked for single layer networks.

What makes exclusive-or impossible for the perceptron is that the two classes to be distinguished are not *linearly separable*. This can be seen in Figure 11.3. It is impossible to draw a straight line in two dimensions that separates the data points {(0,0), (1,1)} from {(0,1), (1,0)}.

We may think of the set of data values for a network as defining a space. Each parameter of the input data corresponds to one dimension, with each input value defining a point in the space. In the exclusive-or example, the four input values, indexed by the x_1, x_2 coordinates, make up the data points of Figure 11.3. The problem of learning a binary classification of the training instances reduces to that of separating these points into two groups. For a space of n dimensions, a classification is linearly separable if its classes can be separated by an n − 1 dimensional hyperplane. (In two dimensions an n-dimensional hyperplane is a line; in three dimension it is a plane, etc.).

As a result of the linear separability limitation, research shifted toward work in symbol-based architectures, slowing progress in the connectionist methodology. Subsequent work in the 1980s and 1990s has shown these problems to be solvable, however (Ackley et al. 1985, Hinton and Sejnowski 1986, 1987).

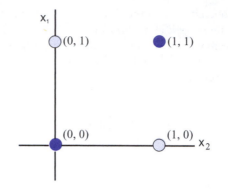

Figure 11.3 The exclusive-or problem. No straight line in two-dimensions can separate the (0, 1) and (1, 0) data points from (0, 0) and (1, 1).

In Section 11.3 we discuss *backpropagation*, an extension of perceptron learning that works for multilayered networks. Before examining backpropagation, we offer an example of a perceptron network that performs classifications. We end Section 11.2 by defining the *generalized delta rule*, a generalization of the perceptron learning algorithm that is used in many neural network architectures, including backpropagation.

11.2.2 An Example: Using a Perceptron Network to Classify

Figure 11.4 offers an overview of the classification problem. Raw data from a space of possible points are selected and transduced to a new data/pattern space. In this new pattern space features are identified, and finally, the entity these features represent is classified. An example would be sound waves recorded on a digital recording device. From there the acoustic signals are translated to a set of amplitude and frequency parameters. Finally, a classifier system might recognize these feature patterns as the voiced speech of a particular person. Another example is the capture of information by medical test equipment, such as heart defibrilators. The features found in this pattern space would then be used to classify symptom sets into different disease categories.

In our classification example, the transducer and feature extractor of Figure 11.4 translates the problem information into parameters of a two-dimensional Cartesian space. Figure 11.5 presents the two-feature perceptron analysis of the information in Table 11.3. The first two columns of the table present the data points on which the network was trained. The third column represents the classification, +1 or −1, used as feedback in network training. Figure 11.5 is a graph of the training data of the problem, showing the linear separation of data classes created when the trained network was run on each data point.

We discuss first the general theory of classification. Each data grouping that a classifier identifies is represented by a region in multidimensional space. Each class R_i has a discriminant function g_i measuring membership in that region. Within the region R_i, the ith discriminant function has the largest value:

$g_i(x) > g_j(x)$ for all j, $1 < j < n$.

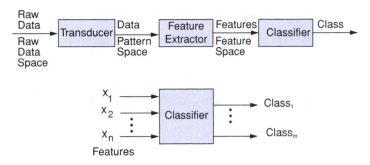

Figure 11.4 A full classification system.

In the simple example of Table 11.3, the two input parameters produce two obvious regions or classes in the space, one represented by 1, the other by −1.

X_1	X_2	Output
1.0	1.0	1
9.4	6.4	−1
2.5	2.1	1
8.0	7.7	−1
0.5	2.2	1
7.9	8.4	−1
7.0	7.0	−1
2.8	0.8	1
1.2	3.0	1
7.8	6.1	−1

Table 11.3 A data set for perceptron classification.

An important special case of discriminant functions is one which evaluates class membership based on the distance from some central point in the region. Classification based on this discriminant function is called *minimum distance classification*. A simple argument shows that if the classes are linearly separable there is a minimum distance classification.

If the regions of R_i and R_j are adjacent, as are the two regions in Figure 11.5, there is a boundary region where the discriminant functions are equal:

$$g_i(x) = g_j(x) \text{ or } g_i(x) - g_j(x) = 0.$$

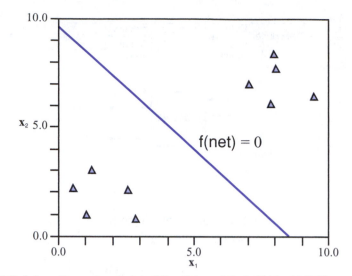

Figure 11.5 A two-dimensional plot of the data points in Table 11.3. The perceptron of Section 11.2.1 provides a linear separation of the data sets.

If the classes are linearly separable, as in Figure 11.5, the discriminant function separating the regions is a straight line, or $g_i(x)$ $g_j(x)$ is linear. Since a line is the locus of points equally distant from two fixed points, the discriminant functions, $g_i(x)$ and $g_j(x)$, are minimum distance functions, measured from the Cartesian center of each of the regions.

The perceptron of Figure 11.6 will compute this linear function. We need two input parameters and will have a bias with a constant value of 1. The perceptron computes:

$f(net) = f(w_1{}^*x_1 + w_2{}^*x_2 + w_3{}^*1)$, where $f(x)$ is the sign of x.

When $f(x)$ is +1, x is interpreted as being in one class, when it is −1, x is in the other class. This thresholding to +1 or −1 is called linear bipolar thresholding (see Figure 11.7a). The bias serves to shift the thresholding function on the horizontal axis. The extent of this shift is learned by adjusting the weight w_3 during training.

We now use the data points of Table 11.3 to train the perceptron of Figure 11.6. We assume random initialization of the weights to [.75, .5, −.6] and use the perceptron training algorithm of Section 11.2.1. The superscripts, e.g. the 1 in $f(net)^1$, represent the current iteration number of the algorithm. We start by taking the first data point in the table:

$f(net)^1 = f(.75^* 1 + .5^*1 − .6^*1) = f(.65) = 1$

Since $f(net)^1 = 1$, the correct output value, we do not adjust the weights. Thus $W^2 = W^1$. For our second data point:

$f(net)^2 = f(.75^* 9.4 + .5^*6.4 − .6^*1) = f(9.65) = 1$

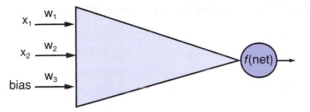

Figure 11.6 The perceptron net for the example data of Table 11.3. The thresholding function is linear and bipolar (see Figure 11.7a).

This time our result should have been −1 so we have to apply the learning rule, described in Section 11.1.1:

$$W^t = W^{t-1} + c(d^{t-1} - \text{sign} (W^{t-1*} X^{t-1})) X^{t-1}$$

where c is the learning constant, X and W are the input and weight vectors, and t the iteration of the net. d^{t-1} is the desired result at time t − 1, or in our situation, at t = 2. The net output at t = 2 is 1. Thus the difference between the desired and actual net output, $d^2 - \text{sign} (W^{2*}X^2)$, is −2. In fact, in a hard limited bipolar perceptron, the learning increment will always be either +2c or else −2c times the training vector. We let the learning constant be a small positive real number, 0.2. We update the weight vector:

$$W^3 = W^2 + 0.2(-1-1)X^2 = \begin{bmatrix} 0.75 \\ 0.50 \\ -0.60 \end{bmatrix} - 0.4 \begin{bmatrix} 9.4 \\ 6.4 \\ 1.0 \end{bmatrix} = \begin{bmatrix} -3.01 \\ -2.06 \\ -1.00 \end{bmatrix}$$

We now consider the third data point with the newly adjusted weights:

$$f(net)^3 = f(-3.01^* 2.5 - 2.06^*2.1 - 1.0^*1) = f(-12.84) = -1$$

Again, the net result is not the desired output. We show the W^4 adjustment:

$$W^4 = W^3 + 0.2(1 - (-1))X^3 = \begin{bmatrix} -3.01 \\ -2.06 \\ -1.00 \end{bmatrix} + 0.4 \begin{bmatrix} 2.5 \\ 2.1 \\ 1.0 \end{bmatrix} = \begin{bmatrix} -2.01 \\ -1.22 \\ -0.60 \end{bmatrix}$$

After 10 iterations of the perceptron net, the linear separation of Figure 11.5 is produced. After repeated training on the data set, about 500 iterations in total, the weight vector converges to [−1.3, −1.1, 10.9]. We are interested in the line separating the two classes. In terms of the discriminant functions g_i and g_j, the line is defined as the locus of points at which $g_i (x) = g_j (x)$ or $g_i (x) - g_j (x) = 0$, that is, where the net output is 0. The equation for the net output is given in terms of the weights. It is:

$$output = w_1x_1 + w_2x_2 + w_3.$$

Consequently, the line separating the two classes is defined by the linear equation:

$$-1.3^*x_1 + -1.1^*x_2 + 10.9 = 0.$$

11.2.3 The Generalized Delta Rule

A straightforward way to generalize the perceptron network is to replace its hard limiting thresholding function with other types of activation functions. For example, continuous activation functions offer the possibility of more sophisticated learning algorithms by allowing for a finer granularity in error measurement.

Figure 11.7 shows the graph of some thresholding functions: a linear bipolar threshold function, Figure 11.7a, similar to that used by the perceptron, and a number of *sigmoidal* functions. Sigmoidal functions are so called because their graph is an "S"-shaped curve, as in Figure 11.7b. A common sigmoidal activation function, called the *logistic* function, is given by the equation:

$$f(net) = 1/(1 + e^{-\lambda^*net}), \text{ where net } = \Sigma x_i w_i$$

As with previously defined functions, x_i is the input on line i, w_i is the weight on line i, and λ a "squashing parameter" used to fine-tune the sigmoidal curve. As λ gets large, the sigmoid approaches a linear threshold function over $\{0,1\}$; as it gets closer to 1 it approaches a straight line.

These threshold graphs plot the input values, the activation level of the neuron, against the scaled activation or output of the neuron. The sigmoidal activation function is continuous, which allows a more precise measure of error. Like the hard limiting thresholding function, the sigmoidal activation function maps most values in its domain into regions close to 0 or 1. However, there is a region of rapid but continuous transition between 0 and 1. In a sense, it approximates a thresholding behavior while providing a continuous output function. The use of λ in the exponent adjusts the slope of the sigmoid shape in the transition region. A weighted *bias* shifts the threshold along the x-axis.

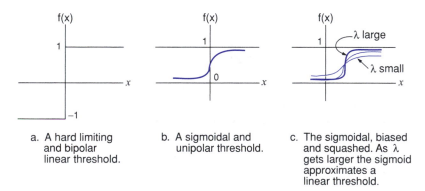

a. A hard limiting and bipolar linear threshold.

b. A sigmoidal and unipolar threshold.

c. The sigmoidal, biased and squashed. As λ gets larger the sigmoid approximates a linear threshold.

Figure 11.7 Thresholding functions.

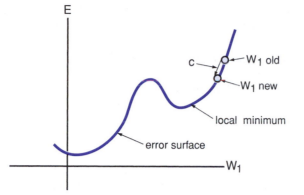

Figure 11.8 An error surface in two dimensions. Constant c dictates the size of the learning step.

The historical emergence of networks with continuous activation functions suggested new approaches to error reduction learning. The Widrow–Hoff (1960) learning rule is independent of the activation function, minimizing the squared error between the desired output value and the network activation, $net_i = WX_i$. Perhaps the most important learning rule for continuous activation functions is the *delta rule* (Rumelhart et al. 1986*a*).

Intuitively, the delta rule is based on the idea of an error surface, as illustrated in Figure 11.8. This error surface represents cumulative error over a data set as a function of network weights. Each possible network weight configuration is represented by a point on this error surface. Given a weight configuration, we want our learning algorithm to find the direction on this surface which most rapidly reduces the error. This approach is called *gradient descent learning* because the gradient is a measure of slope, as a function of direction, from a point on a surface.

To use the delta rule, the network must use an activation function which is continuous and therefore differentiable. The logistic formula just presented has this property. The delta rule learning formula for weight adjustment on the jth input to the ith node is:

$$c\,(d_i - O_i)\,f'(net_i)\,x_j$$

where c is the constant controlling the learning rate, d_i and O_i are the desired and actual output values of the ith node. The derivative of the activation function for the ith node is f', and x_j is the jth input to node i. We now show the derivation of this formula.

The mean squared network error is found by summing the squared error for each node:

$$Error = (1/2)\sum_i (d_i - O_i)^2$$

where d_i is the desired value for each output node and O_i is the actual output of the node. We square each error so that the individual errors, some possibly with negative and others with positive values, will not, in summation, cancel each other out.

We consider here the case where the node is in the output layer; we describe the general case when we present networks with hidden layers in Section 11.3. We want first to measure the rate of change of network error with respect to output of each node. To do this we use the notion of a *partial derivative*, which gives us the rate of change of a multivariable function with respect to a particular variable. The partial derivative of the total error with respect to each output unit i is:

$$\frac{\partial \text{Error}}{\partial O_i} = \frac{\partial(1/2)^*\Sigma(d_i - O_i)^2}{\partial O_i} = \frac{\partial(1/2)^*(d_i - O_i)^2}{\partial O_i}$$

The second simplification is possible because we are considering a node on the output layer, where its error will not affect any other node. Taking the derivative of this quantity, we get:

$$\frac{\partial(1/2)^*(d_i - O_i)^2}{\partial O_i} = -(d_i - O_i)$$

What we want is the rate of change of network error as a function of change in the weights at node i. To get the change in a particular weight, w_k, we rely on the use of the partial derivative, this time taking the partial derivative of the error at each node with respect to the weight, w_k, at that node. The expansion on the right side of the equal sign is given us by the chain rule for partial derivatives:

$$\frac{\partial \text{Error}}{\partial w_k} = \frac{\partial \text{Error}}{\partial O_i} * \frac{\partial O_i}{\partial w_k}$$

This gives us the pieces we need to solve the equation. Using our earlier result, we obtain:

$$\frac{\partial \text{Error}}{\partial w_k} = -(d_i - O_i) * \frac{\partial O_i}{\partial w_k}$$

We continue by considering the right most factor, the partial derivative of the actual output at the ith node taken with respect to each weight at that node. The formula for the output of node i as a function of its weights is:

$$O_i = f(W_i X_i), \text{ where } W_i X_i = \text{net}_i.$$

Since f is a continuous function, taking the derivative we get:

$$\frac{\partial O_i}{\partial w_k} = x_k * f'(W_i X_i) = f'(\text{net}_i)^* x_k$$

Substituting in the previous equation:

$$\frac{\partial \text{Error}}{\partial w_k} = -(d_i - O_i) f'(\text{net}_i)^* x_k$$

The minimization of the error requires that the weight changes be in the direction of the negative gradient component. Therefore:

$$\Delta w_k = -c\frac{\partial Error}{\partial w_k} = -c[-(d_i - O_i)*f'(net_i)*x_k] = c(d_i - O_i)f'(net_i)*x_k$$

We observe that the delta rule is like *hill-climbing*, Section 4.1, in that at every step, it attempts to minimize the local error measure by using the derivative to find the slope of the error space in the region local to a particular point. This makes delta learning vulnerable to the problem of distinguishing local from global minima in the error space.

The learning constant, c, exerts an important influence on the performance of the delta rule, as further analysis of Figure 11.8 illustrates. The value of c determines how much the weight values move in a single learning episode. The larger the value of c, the more quickly the weights move toward an optimal value. However, if c is too large, the algorithm may overshoot the minimum or oscillate around the optimal weights. Smaller values of c are less prone to this problem, but do not allow the system to learn as quickly. The optimal value of the learning rate, sometimes enhanced with a momentum factor (Zurada 1992), is a parameter adjusted for a particular application through experiment.

Although the delta rule does not by itself overcome the limitations of single layer networks, its generalized form is central to the functioning of backpropagation, an algorithm for learning in a multilayer network. This algorithm is presented in the next section.

11.3 Backpropagation Learning

11.3.1 Deriving the Backpropagation Algorithm

As we have seen, single layer perceptron networks are limited as to the classifications that they can perform. We show in Sections 11.3 and 11.4 that the addition of multiple layers

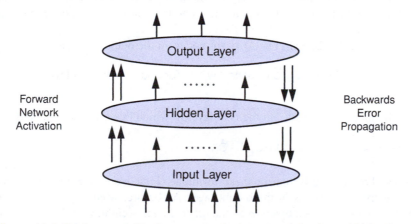

Figure 11.9 Backpropagation in a connectionist network having a hidden layer.

can overcome many of these limitations. In Section 17.3 we observe that multilayered networks are computationally complete, that is, equivalent to the class of Turing machines. Early researchers, however, were not able to design a learning algorithm for their use. We present in this section the generalized delta rule, which offers one solution to this problem.

The neurons in a multilayer network (see Figure 11.9) are connected in layers, with units in layer n passing their activations only to neurons in layer n + 1. Multilayer signal processing means that errors deep in the network can spread and evolve in complex, unanticipated ways through successive layers. Thus, the analysis of the source of error at the output layer is complex. Backpropagation provides an algorithm for apportioning blame and adjusting weights accordingly.

The approach taken by the backpropagation algorithm is to start at the output layer and *propagate* error backwards through the hidden layers. When we analyzed learning with the delta rule, we saw that all the information needed to update the weights on a neuron was local to that neuron, except for the amount of error. For output nodes, this is easily computed as the difference between the desired and actual output values. For nodes in hidden layers, it is considerably more difficult to determine the error for which a node is responsible. The activation function for backpropagation is usually the logistic function:

$$f(net) = 1/(1 + e^{-\lambda*net}), \text{ where } net = \Sigma x_i w_i.$$

This function is used for three reasons. First, it has the sigmoid shape. Second, as a continuous function, it has a derivative everywhere. Third, since the value of the derivative is greatest where the sigmoidal function is changing most rapidly, the assignment of the most error is attributed to those nodes whose activation was least certain. Finally, the derivative is easily computed by a subtraction and multiplication:

$$f'(net) = (1/(1 + e^{-\lambda*net}))' = \lambda(f(net) * (1 - f(net))).$$

Backpropagation training uses the generalized delta rule. This uses the same gradient descent approach presented in Section 11.2. For nodes in the hidden layer we look at their contribution to the error at the output layer. The formulas for computing the adjustment of the weight w_{ki} on the path from the kth to the ith node in backpropagation training are:

1) $\Delta w_{ki} = -c(d_i - O_i) * O_i (1 - O_i) x_k$, for nodes on the output layer, and

2) $\Delta w_{ki} = -c * O_i(1 - O_i) \sum_j (- delta_j * w_{ij}) x_k$, for nodes on hidden layers.

In 2), j is the index of the nodes in the next layer to which i's signals fan out and:

$$delta_j = -\frac{\partial Error}{\partial net_j} = (d_i - O_i) * O_i(1 - O_i).$$

We now show the derivation of these formulae. First we derive 1), the formula for weight adjustment on nodes in the output layer. As before, what we want is the rate of change of network error as a function of change in the kth weight, w_k, of node i. We treated this situation in the derivation of the delta rule, Section 11.2.3, and showed that:

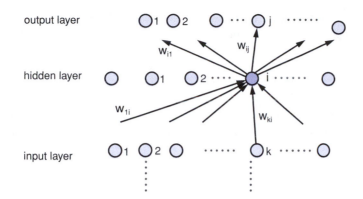

output layer

hidden layer

input layer

Figure 11.10 $\sum\limits_{j} -\text{delta}_j{}^*\text{w}_{ij}$ is the total contribution of node i to the error at the output. Our derivation gives the adjustment for w_{ki}.

$$\frac{\partial \text{Error}}{\partial \text{w}_k} = -((\text{d}_i - \text{O}_i)^*\text{f}'(\text{net}_i)^*\text{x}_k)$$

Since f, which could be any function, is now the logistic activation function, we have:

$$\text{f}'(\text{net}) = \text{f}'(1/(1 + \text{e}^{-\lambda^*\text{net}})) = \text{f}(\text{net}) * (1 - \text{f}(\text{net})).$$

Recall that f (net$_i$) is simply O$_i$. Substituting in the previous equation, we get:

$$\frac{\partial \text{Error}}{\partial \text{w}_k} = -(\text{d}_i - \text{O}_i)^*\text{O}_i{}^*(1 - \text{O}_i)^*\text{x}_k$$

Since the minimization of the error requires that the weight changes be in the direction of the negative gradient component, we multiply by $-c$ to get the weight adjustment for the ith node of the output layer:

$$\Delta \text{w}_k = \text{c}(\text{d}_i - \text{O}_i) * \text{O}_i * (1 - \text{O}_i) * \text{x}_k.$$

We next derive the weight adjustment for hidden nodes. For the sake of clarity we initially assume a single hidden layer. We take a single node i on the hidden layer and analyze its contribution to the total network error. We do this by initially considering node i's contribution to the error at a node j on the output layer. We then sum these contributions across all nodes on the output layer. Finally, we describe the contribution of the kth input weight on node i to the network error. Figure 11.10 illustrates this situation.

We first look at the partial derivative of the network error with respect to the output of node i on the hidden layer. We get this by applying the chain rule:

$$\frac{\partial \text{Error}}{\partial \text{O}_i} = \frac{\partial \text{Error}}{\partial \text{net}_j} * \frac{\partial \text{net}_j}{\partial \text{O}_i}$$

The negative of the first term on the right-hand side, $(\delta Error) / (\delta net_j)$, is called *delta$_j$*. Therefore, we can rewrite the equation as:

$$\frac{\partial Error}{\partial O_i} = -delta_j \cdot \frac{\partial net_j}{\partial O_i}$$

Recall that the activation of node j, net_j, on the output layer is given by the sum of the product of its weights and the output values of the nodes on the hidden layer:

$$net_j = \sum_i w_{ij} O_i$$

Since we are taking the partial derivative with respect to only one component of the sum, namely the connection between node i and node j, we get:

$$\frac{\partial net_j}{\partial O_i} = w_{ij}$$

where w_{ij} is the weight on the connection from node i in the hidden layer to node j in the output layer. Substituting this result:

$$\frac{\partial Error}{\partial O_i} = -delta_j \cdot w_{ij}$$

Now we sum over all the connections of node i to the output layer:

$$\frac{\partial Error}{\partial O_i} = \sum_j -delta_j \cdot w_{ij}$$

This gives us the sensitivity of network error to the output of node i on the hidden layer. We next determine the value of *delta$_i$*, the sensitivity of network error to the net activation at hidden node i. This gives the sensitivity of network error to the incoming weights of node i. Using the chain rule again:

$$-delta_i = \frac{\partial Error}{\partial net_i} = \frac{\partial Error}{\partial O_i} \cdot \frac{\partial O_i}{\partial net_i}$$

Since we are using the logistic activation function,

$$\frac{\partial O_i}{\partial net_i} = O_i \cdot (1 - O_i)$$

We now substitute this value in the equation for delta$_i$ to get:

$$-delta_i = O_i \cdot (1 - O_i) \cdot \sum_j -delta_j \cdot w_{ij}$$

Finally, we can evaluate the sensitivity of the network error on the output layer to the incoming weights on hidden node i. We examine the kth weight on node i, w_k. By the chain rule:

$$\frac{\partial \text{Error}}{\partial w_{ki}} = \frac{\partial \text{Error}}{\partial \text{net}_i} * \frac{\partial \text{net}_i}{\partial w_{ki}} = -\text{delta}_i * \frac{\partial \text{net}_i}{\partial w_{ki}} = -\text{delta}_i * x_k$$

where x_k is the kth input to node i.

We substitute into the equation the value of $-\text{delta}_i$:

$$\frac{\partial \text{Error}}{\partial w_{ki}} = O_i(1 - O_i) \sum_j (-\text{delta}_j * w_{ij}) x_k$$

Since the minimization of the error requires that the weight changes be in the direction of the negative gradient component, we get the weight adjustment for the kth weight of i by multiplying by the negative of the learning constant:

$$\Delta w_{ki} = -c \frac{\partial \text{Error}}{\partial w_{ki}} = c * O_i(1 - O_i) \sum_j (\text{delta}_j * w_{ij}) x_k$$

For networks with more than one hidden layer, the same procedure is applied recursively to propagate the error from hidden layer n to hidden layer n − 1.

Although it provides a solution to the problem of learning in multilayer networks, backpropagation is not without its own difficulties. As with hillclimbing, it may converge to local minima, as in Figure 11.8. Finally, backpropagation can be expensive to compute, especially when the network converges slowly.

11.3.2 Backpropagation Example 1: NETtalk

NETtalk is an interesting example of a neural net solution to a difficult learning problem (Sejnowski and Rosenberg 1987). NETtalk learned to pronounce English text. This can be a difficult task for an explicit symbol approach, for example a rule-based system, since English pronunciation is highly irregular.

NETtalk learned to read a string of text and return a phoneme and an associated stress for each letter in the string. A phoneme is the basic unit of sound in a language; the stress is the relative loudness of that sound. Because the pronunciation of a single letter depends upon its context and the letters around it, NETtalk was given a seven character window. As the text moves through this window, NETtalk returns a phoneme/stress pair for each letter.

Figure 11.11 shows the architecture of NETtalk. The network consists of three layers of units. The input units correspond to the seven character window on the text. Each position in the window is represented by 29 input units, one for each letter of the alphabet, and 3 for punctuation and spaces. The letter in each position activates the corresponding unit. The output units encode phonemes using 21 different features of human articulation. The remaining five units encoded stress and syllable boundaries. NETtalk has 80 hidden units, 26 output values, and 18,629 connections.

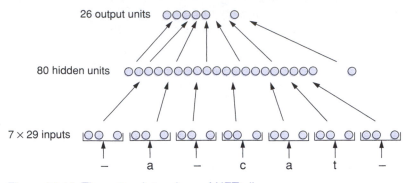

Figure 11.11 The network topology of NETtalk.

NETtalk is trained by giving it a seven character window and letting it attempt to pronounce the middle character. Comparing its attempted pronunciation to the correct pronunciation, it adjusts its weights using backpropagation.

This example illustrates a number of interesting properties of neural networks, many of which reflect the nature of human learning. For example, learning, when measured as a percentage of correct responses, proceeds rapidly at first, and slows as the percentage correct increases. As with humans, the more words the network learns to pronounce, the better it is at correctly pronouncing new words. Experiments in which some of the weights in a fully trained network were randomly altered showed the network to be damage resistant, degrading gracefully as weights were altered. Researchers also found that relearning in a damaged network was highly efficient.

Another interesting aspect of multilayered networks is the role of the hidden layers. Any learning algorithm must learn generalizations that apply to unseen instances in the problem domain. The hidden layers play an important role in allowing a neural network to generalize. NETtalk, like many backpropagation networks, has fewer neurons in the hidden layer than in the input layer. This means that since fewer nodes on the hidden layer are used to encode the information in the training patterns, some form of abstraction is taking place. The shorter encoding implies that different patterns on the input layer can be mapped into identical patterns at the hidden layer. This reduction is a generalization.

NETtalk learns effectively, although it requires a large number of training instances, as well as repeated passes through the training data. In a series of empirical tests comparing backpropagation and ID3 on this problem, Shavlik et al. (1991) found that the algorithms had equivalent results, although their training and use of data was quite different. This research evaluated the algorithms by dividing the total set of examples into separate training and test sets. Both ID3 (Section 10.3) and NETtalk were able to correctly pronounce about 60 per cent of the test data after training on 500 examples. But, where ID3 required only a single pass through the training data, NETtalk required many repetitions of the training set. In this research, NETtalk had 100 passes through the training data.

As our example demonstrates, the relationship between connectionist and symbolic learning is more complicated than it might seem at first. In our next example we work through the details of a backpropagation solution to the exclusive-or problem.

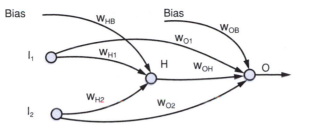

Figure 11.12 A backpropagation net to solve the exclusive-or problem.
The W_{ij} are the weights and H is the hidden node.

11.3.3 Backpropagation Example 2: Exclusive-or

We end this section by presenting a simple hidden layer solution to the *exclusive-or* problem. Figure 11.12 shows a network with two input nodes, one hidden node and one output node. The network also has two bias nodes, the first to the hidden node and the second to the output node. The net values for the hidden and output nodes are calculated in the usual manner, as the vector product of the input values times their trained weights. The bias is added to this sum. The weights are trained by backpropagation and the activation function is sigmoidal.

It should be noted that the input nodes are also directly linked, with trained weights, to the output node. This additional linking can often let the designer get a network with fewer nodes on the hidden layer and quicker convergence. In fact there is nothing unique about the network of Figure 11.12; any number of different networks could be used to compute exclusive-or.

We trained our randomly initialized network with multiple instances of the four patterns that represent the truth values of exclusive-or:

$$(0, 0) \rightarrow 0; (1, 0) \rightarrow 1; (0, 1) \rightarrow 1; (1, 1) \rightarrow 0$$

A total of 1400 training cycles using these four instances produced the following values, rounded to the nearest tenth, for the weight parameters of Figure 11.12:

$$W_{H1} = -7.0 \quad W_{HB} = 2.6 \quad W_{O1} = -5.0 \quad W_{OH} = -11.0$$
$$W_{H2} = -7.0 \quad W_{OB} = 7.0 \quad W_{O2} = -4.0$$

With input values (0, 0), the output of the hidden node is:

$$f(0*(-7.0) + 0*(-7.0) + 1*2.6) = f(2.6) \rightarrow 1$$

The output of the output node for (0,0) is:

$$f(0*(-5.0) + 0*(-4.0) + 1*(-11.0) + 1*(7.0)) = f(-4.0) \rightarrow 0$$

With input values (1, 0), the output of the hidden node is:

f(1*(−7.0) + 0*(−7.0) + 1*2.6) = f(−4.4) → 0

The output of the output node for (1,0) is:

f(1*(−5.0) + 0*(−4.0) + 0*(−11.0) + 1*(7.0)) = f(2.0) →1

The input value of (0, 1) is similar. Finally, let us check our exclusive-or network with input values of (1, 1). The output of the hidden node is:

f(1*(−7.0) + 1*(−7.0) + 1*2.6) = f(−11.4) → 0

The output of the output node for (1,1) is:

f(1*(−5.0) + 1*(−4.0) + 0*(−11.0) + 1*(7.0)) = f(−2.0) →0

The reader can see that this feedforward network with backpropagation learning made a nonlinear separation of these data points. The threshold function f is the sigmoidal of Figure 11.7b, the learned biases have translated it slightly in the positive direction.

We next consider models of competitive learning.

11.4 Competitive Learning

11.4.1 Winner-Take-All Learning for Classification

The winner-take-all algorithm (Kohonen 1984, Hecht-Nielsen 1987) works with the single node in a layer of nodes that responds most strongly to the input pattern. Winner-take-all may be viewed as a competition among a set of network nodes, as in Figure 11.13. In this figure we have a vector of input values, $X=(x_1, x_2, ..., x_m)$, passed into a layer of network nodes, A, B, ..., N. The diagram shows node B the winner of the competition, with an output signal of 1.

Learning for winner-take-all is unsupervised in that the winner is determined by a "maximum activation" test. The weight vector of the winner is then rewarded by bringing its components closer to those of the input vector. For the weights, W, of the winning node and components X of the input vector, the increment is:

$\Delta W^t = c(X^{t-1} − W^{t-1}),$

where c is a small positive learning constant that usually decreases as the learning proceeds. The winning weight vector is then adjusted by adding ΔW^t.

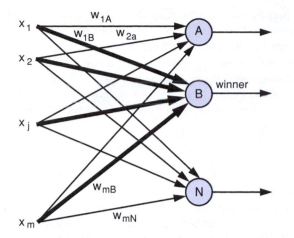

Figure 11.13 A layer of nodes for application of a winner-take-all algorithm. The old input vectors support the winning node.

This reward increments or decrements each component of the winner's weight vector by a fraction of the $x_i - w_i$ difference. The effect is, of course, to make the winning node match more closely the input vector. The winner-take-all algorithm does not need to directly compute activation levels to find the node with the strongest response. The activation level of a node is directly related to the closeness of its weight vector to the input vector. For a node i with a normalized weight vector W_i, the activation level, W_iX, is a function of the Euclidean distance between W_i and the input pattern X. This can be seen by calculating the Euclidean distance, with normalized W_i:

$$\|X - W_i\| = \sqrt{(X - W_i)^2} = \sqrt{X^2 - 2XW_i + W_i^2}$$

From this equation it can be seen that for a set of normalized weight vectors, the weight vector with the smallest Euclidean distance, $\| X - W \|$, will be the weight vector with the maximum activation value, WX. In many cases it is more efficient to determine the winner by calculating Euclidean distances rather than comparing activation levels on normalized weight vectors.

We consider the "winner-take-all" Kohonen learning rule for several reasons. First, we consider it as a classification method and compare it to perceptron classification. Second, it may be combined with other network architectures to offer more sophisticated models of learning. We look at the combination of Kohonen prototype learning with an outstar, supervised learning network. This hybrid, first proposed by Robert Hecht-Nielsen (1987, 1990), is called a *counterpropagation* network. We see, in Section 11.4.3, how we can describe conditioned learning using counterpropagation.

Before we leave this introduction, there are a number of issues important for "winner-take-all" algorithms. Sometimes a "conscience" parameter is set and updated at each iteration to keep individual nodes from winning too often. This ensures that all network nodes eventually participate in representing the pattern space. In some algorithms, rather than identifying a winner that takes all, a *set* of closest nodes are selected and the weights of each are differentially incremented. Another approach is to differentially reward the neighboring nodes of the winner. Weights are typically initialized at random values and then normalized during this learning method (Zurada 1992). Hecht-Nielsen (1990) shows how "winner-take-all" algorithms may be seen as equivalent to the k-means analysis of a set of data. In the next section we present Kohonen's winner-take-all unsupervised method for the learning of clusters.

11.4.2　A Kohonen Network for Learning Prototypes

Classification of data and the role of prototypes in learning are constant concerns of psychologists, linguists, computer scientists, and cognitive scientists (Wittgenstein 1953, Rosch 1978, Lakoff 1987). The role of prototypes and classification in intelligence is also a constant theme of this book. We demonstrated symbol based-classification and probabilistic clustering algorithms with COBWEB and CLUSTER/2 in Section 10.6. In connectionist models, we demonstrated perceptron-based classification in Section 11.2 and now show a Kohonen (1984) winner-take-all clustering algorithm.

Figure 11.14 presents again the data points of Table 11.3. Superimposed on these points are a series of prototypes created during network training. The perceptron training algorithm converged after a number of iterations, resulting in a network weight configuration defining a linear separation between the two classes. As we saw, the line defined by these weights was obtained by implicitly computing the Euclidean "center" of each cluster. This center of a cluster serves in perceptron classification as a prototype of the class.

Kohonen learning, on the other hand, is unsupervised, with a set of prototypes randomly created and then refined until they come to explicitly represent the clusters of data. As the algorithm continues, the learning constant is progressively reduced so that each new input vector will cause less perturbation in the prototypes.

Kohonen learning, like CLUSTER/2, has a strong inductive bias in that the number of desired prototypes is explicitly identified at the beginning of the algorithm and then continuously refined. This allows the net algorithm designer to identify a specific number of prototypes to represent the clusters of data. Counterpropagation (Section 11.4.3) allows further manipulation of this selected number of prototypes.

Figure 11.15 is a Kohonen learning network for classification of the data of Table 11.3. The data are represented in Cartesian two dimensional space, so prototypes to represent the data clusters will also be ordered pairs. We select two prototypes, one to represent each data cluster. We have randomly initialized node A to (7, 2) and node B to (2, 9). Random initialization only works in simple problems such as ours; an alternative is to set the weight vectors equal to representatives of each of the clusters.

The winning node will have a weight vector closest to that of the input vector. This weight vector for the winning node will be rewarded by being moved even closer to the input data, while the weights on the losing nodes are left unchanged. Since we are explicitly calculating the Euclidean distance of the input vector from each of the prototypes we will not need to normalize the vectors, as described in Section 11.4.1.

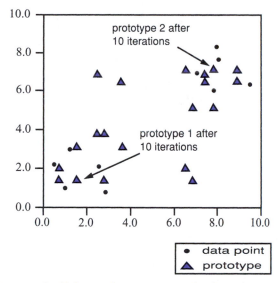

Figure 11.14 The use of a Kohonen layer, unsupervised, to generate a sequence of prototypes to represent the classes of Table 11.3.

Kohonen learning is unsupervised, in that a simple measure of the distance between each prototype and the data point allows selection of the winner. Classification will be "discovered" in the context of this *self-organizing* network. Although Kohonen learning selects data points for analysis in random order, we take the points of Table 11.3 in top to bottom order. For point (1, 1), we measure the distance from each prototype:

$$\|(1, 1) - (7, 2)\| = (1 - 7)^2 + (1 - 2)^2 = 37, \text{ and}$$
$$\|(1, 1) - (2, 9)\| = (1 - 2)^2 + (1 - 9)^2 = 65.$$

Node A (7, 2) is the winner since it is closest to (1, 1). $\|(1, 1) - (7, 2)\|$ represents the distance between these two points; we do not need to apply the square root function in the Euclidean distance measure because the relation of magnitudes is invariant. We now reward the winning node, using the learning constant c set to 0.5. For the second iteration:

$$W^2 = W^1 + c(X^1 - W^1)$$
$$= (7, 2) + .5((1, 1) - (7, 2)) = (7, 2) + .5((1 - 7), (1 - 2))$$
$$= (7, 2) + (-3, -.5) = (4, 1.5)$$

At the second iteration of the learning algorithm we have, for data point (9.4, 6.4):

$$\|(9.4, 6.4) - (4, 1.5)\| = (9.4 - 4)^2 + (6.4 - 1.5)^2 = 53.17 \text{ and}$$
$$\|(9.4, 6.4) - (2, 9)\| = (9.4 - 2)^2 + (6.4 - 9)^2 = 60.15$$

Again, node A is the winner. The weight for the third iteration is:

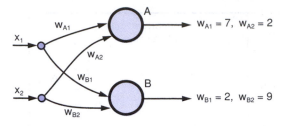

Figure 11.15 The architecture of the Kohonen based learning network for the data of Table 11.3 and classification of Figure 11.14.

$$W^3 = W^2 + c(X^2 - W^2)$$
$$= (4, 1.5) + .5((9.4, 6.4) - (4, 1.5))$$
$$= (4, 1.5) + (2.7, 2.5) = (6.7, 4)$$

At the third iteration we have, for data point (2.5, 2.1):

$$\|(2.5, 2.1) - (6.7, 4)\| = (2.5 - 6.7)^2 + (2.1 - 4)^2 = 21.25, \text{ and}$$
$$\|(2.5, 2.1) - (2, 9)\| = (2.5 - 2)^2 + (2.1 - 9)^2 = 47.86.$$

Node **A** wins again and we go on to calculate its new weight vector. Figure 11.14 shows the evolution of the prototype after 10 iterations. The algorithm used to generate the data of Figure 11.14 selected data randomly from Table 11.3, so the prototypes shown will differ from those just created. The progressive improvement of the prototypes can be seen moving toward the centers of the data clusters. Again, this is an unsupervised, winner-take-all reinforcement algorithm. It builds a set of evolving and explicit prototypes to represent the data clusters. A number of researchers, including Zurada (1992) and Hecht-Nielsen (1990), point out that Kohonen unsupervised classification of data is basically the same as k-means analysis.

We next consider, with a Grossberg, or outstar, extension of Kohonen winner-take-all analysis, an algorithm that will let us extend the power of prototype selection.

11.4.3 Outstar Networks and Counterpropagation

To this point we considered the unsupervised clustering of input data. Learning here requires little *a priori* knowledge of a problem domain. Gradually detected characteristics of the data, as well as the training history, lead to the identification of classes and the discovery of boundaries between them. Once data points are clustered according to similarities in their vector representations, a teacher can assist in calibrating or giving names to data classes. This is done by a form of supervised training, where we take the output nodes of a "winner-take-all" network layer and use them as input to a second network layer. We will then explicitly reinforce decisions at this output layer.

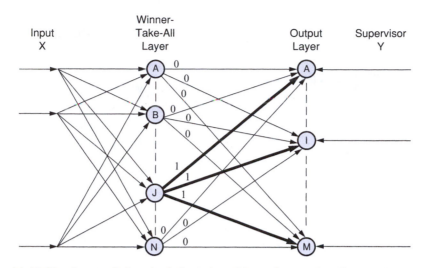

Figure 11.16 The "outstar" of node J, the "winner" in a winner-take-all network. The Y vector supervises the response on the output layer in Grossberg training. The "outstar" is bold with all weights 1; all other weights are 0.

This supervised training and then reinforced output allows us, for example, to map the results of a Kohonen net into an output pattern or class. A Grossberg (1982, 1988) layer, implementing an algorithm called *outstar*, allows us to do this. The combined network, a Kohonen layer joined to a Grossberg layer, is called *counterpropagation* and was first proposed by Robert Hecht-Nielsen (1987, 1990).

In Section 11.4.2 we considered in some detail the Kohonen layer; here we consider the Grossberg layer. Figure 11.16 shows a layer of nodes, A, B, ..., N, where one node, J, is selected as the winner. Grossberg learning is supervised in that we wish, with feedback from a teacher, represented by vector Y, to reinforce the weight connecting J to the node I in the output layer which is supposed to fire. With outstar learning, we identify and increase the weight w_{JI} on the outbound link of J to I.

To train the counterpropagation net we first train the Kohonen layer. When a winner is found, the values on all the links going out from it will be 1, while all the output values of its competitors remain 0. That node, together with all the nodes on the output layer to which it is connected, form what is called an *outstar* (see Figure 11.16). Training for the Grossberg layer is based on outstar components.

If each cluster of input vectors represents a single class and we want all members of a class to map onto the same value at the output layer, we do not need an iterative training. We need only determine which node in the winner-take-all layer is linked to which class and then assign weights from those nodes to output nodes based on the association between classes and desired output values. For example, if the Jth winner-take-all unit wins for all elements of the cluster for which I = 1 is the desired output of the network, we set $w_{JI} = 1$ and $w_{JK} = 0$ for all other weights on the outstar of J.

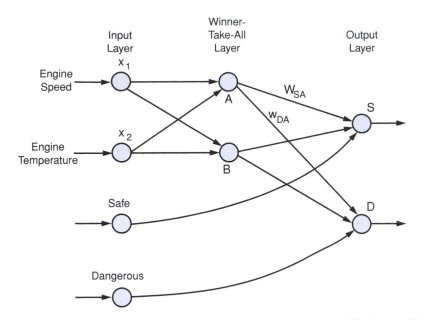

Figure 11.17 A counterpropagation network to recognize the classes in Table 11.3. We train the outstar weights of node A, w_{SA} and w_{DA}.

If the desired output for elements of a cluster vary, then there is an iterative procedure, using the supervision vector Y, for adjusting outstar weights. The result of this training procedure is to *average* the desired output values for elements of a particular cluster. We train the weights on the outstar connections from the winning node to the output nodes according to the equation:

$$W^{t+1} = W^t + c(Y - W^t)$$

where c is a small positive learning constant, W^t is the weight vector of the outstar component, and Y is the desired output vector. Note that this learning algorithm has the effect of increasing the connection between node J on the Kohonen layer and node I on the output layer precisely when I is a winning node with an output of 1 and the desired output of J is also 1. This makes it an instance of Hebbian learning, a form of learning in which a neural pathway is strengthened every time one node contributes to the firing of another. We discuss Hebbian learning in more detail in Section 11.5.

We next apply the rule for training a counterpropagation network to recognize the data clusters of Table 11.3. We also show with this example how counterpropagation nets implement conditioned learning. Suppose the x_1 parameter in Table 11.3 represents engine speed in a propulsion system. x_2 represents engine temperature. Both the speed and the temperature of the system are calibrated to produce data points in the range [0, 10]. Our monitoring system samples data points at regular intervals. Whenever speed and temperature are excessively high, we want to broadcast a warning. Let us rename the output values of Table 11.3 from +1 to "safe" and from −1 to "dangerous." Our counterpropagation network will look like Figure 11.17.

Since we know exactly what values we want each winning node of the Kohonen net to map to on the output layer of the Grossberg net, we could directly set those values. To demonstrate outstar learning, however, we will train the net using the formula just given. If we make the (arbitrary) decision that node S on the output layer should signal safe situations and node D dangerous, then the outstar weights for node A on the output layer of the Kohonen net should be [1, 0] and the outstar weights for B should be [0, 1]. Because of the symmetry of the situation, we show the training of the outstar for node A only.

The Kohonen net must have stabilized before the Grossberg net can be trained. We demonstrated the Kohonen convergence of this same net in Section 11.4.2. The input vectors for training the A outstar node are of the form $[x_1, x_2, 1, 0]$. x_1 and x_2 are values from Table 11.3 that are clustered at Kohonen output node A, and the last two components indicate that when A is the Kohonen winner, safe is "true" and dangerous is "false," as in Figure 11.15. We initialize the outstar weights of A to [0, 0] and use .2 as the learning constant:

$$W^1 = [0, 0] + .2[[1, 0] − [0, 0]] = [0, 0] + [.2, 0] = [.2, 0]$$
$$W^2 = [.2, 0] + .2[[1, 0] − [.2, 0]] = [.2, 0] + [.16, 0] = [.36, 0]$$
$$W^3 = [.36, 0] + .2[[1, 0] − [.36, 0]] = [.36, 0] + [.13, 0] = [.49, 0]$$
$$W^4 = [.49, 0] + .2[[1, 0] − [.49, 0]] = [.49, 0] + [.10, 0] = [.59, 0]$$
$$W^5 = [.59, 0] + .2[[1, 0] − [.59, 0]] = [.59, 0] + [.08, 0] = [.67, 0].$$

As we can see, with training these weights are moving toward [1, 0]. Of course, since in this case elements of the cluster associated with A always map into [1,0], we could have used the simple assignment algorithm rather than the averaging algorithm for training.

We now show that this assignment gives the appropriate response from the counter-propagation net. When the first input vector from Table 11.3 is applied to the network in Figure 11.17, we get activation of [1, 1] for the outstar weights of node A and [0, 0] for the outstar of B. The dot product of activation and weights for node S of the output layer is [1, 0] * [1, 0]; this gives activation 1 to the S output node. With outstar weights of B trained to [0, 1], the activation for node D is [1, 0] * [0, 1]; these are the values that we expect. Testing the second row of data points on Table 11.3, we get activation [0, 0] from the A node and [1,1] from the B at the winner-take-all level. The dot product of these values and the trained weights gives 0 to the S node and 1 to D, again what is expected. The reader may continue to test other data from Table 11.3.

From a cognitive perspective, we can give an associationist interpretation to the counterpropagation net. Consider again Figure 11.17. The learning on the Kohonen layer can be seen as acquiring a conditioned stimulus, since the network is learning patterns in events. The learning on the Grossberg level, on the other hand, is an association of nodes (unconditioned stimuli) to some response. In our situation the system learns to broadcast a danger warning when data fit into a certain pattern. Once the appropriate response is learned, then even without the continued coaching of a teacher, the system responds appropriately to new data.

A second cognitive interpretation of counterpropagation is as the reinforcement of memory links for pattern of phenomena. This is similar to building a lookup table for responses to data patterns.

Counterpropagation has, in certain cases, a considerable advantage over backpropagation. Like backpropagation it is capable of learning nonlinearly separable classifications. It does this, however, by virtue of the preprocessing which goes on in the Kohonen layer, where the data set is partitioned into clusters of homogenous data. This partitioning can result in a significant advantage over backpropagation in learning rate since the explicit partitioning of data into separate clusters replaces the often extensive search required on the hidden layers in backpropagation networks.

11.4.4 Support Vector Machines (Harrison and Luger 2002)

Support vector machines (SVM), offer another example of competitive learning. In the support vector approach, statistical measures are used to determine a minimum set of data points (the support vectors) that maximally separate the positive and negative instances of a learned concept. These support vectors, representing selected data points from both the positive and negative instances of the concept, implicitly define a hyperplane separating these two data sets. For example, running the SVM algorithm identifies points (2.5, 2.1) and (1.2, 3.0) as support vectors for the positive instances and (7.0, 7.0) and (7.8. 6.1) as support vectors for the negative instances of the data of Table 11.3 and Figure 11.5. Once the support vectors are learned other data points need no longer be retained, the support vectors alone are sufficient to determine the separating hyperplane.

The support vector machine is a linear classifier where the learning of the support vectors is supervised. The data for SVM learning is assumed to be produced independently and identically from a fixed, although unknown, distribution of data. The hyperplane, implicitly defined by the support vectors themselves, divides the positive from the negative data instances. Data points nearest the hyperplane are in the *decision margin* (Burges 1998). Any addition or removal of a support vector changes the hyperplane boundary. As previously noted, after training is complete, it is possible to reconstruct the hyperplane and classify new data sets from the support vectors alone.

The SVM algorithm classifies data elements by computing the distance of a data point from the separating hyperplane as an optimization problem. Successfully controlling the increased flexibility of feature spaces, the (often transformed) parameters of the instances to be learned require a sophisticated theory of generalization. This theory must be able to precisely describe the features that have to be controlled to form a good generalization. Within statistics, this issue is known as the *study of the rates of uniform convergence*. We have already seen an example of this in Section 10.4.2, where the probably approximately correct, or PAC, model of learning is presented. The results of PAC learning can be seen as establishing bounds on the number of examples required to guarantee a specific error bound. For this generalization task Bayesian or other data compression techniques are employed. In SVM learning the theory of Vapnik and Chervonenkis is often used.

The Vapnik Chervonenkis (VC) dimension is defined as the maximum number of training points that can be divided into two categories by a set of functions (Burges 1998).

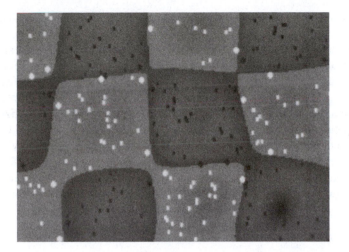

Figure 11.18 A SVM learning the boundaries of a chess board from points generated according to the uniform distribution using Gaussian kernels. The dots are the data points with the larger dots comprising the set of support vectors, the darker areas indicate the confidence in the classification. Adapted from Cristianini and Shawe-Taylor (2000).

Thus VC theory provides a distribution free bound on the generalization of the consistent hypothesis (Cristianini and Shawe-Taylor 2000). The SVM algorithm uses this VC theory to compute the hyperplane and controls the margin of error for the generalizations accuracy, sometimes called the *capacity* of the function.

SVMs use a dot product similarity measure to map data from a feature space. Dot product results representing mapped vectors are linearly combined by weights found by solving a quadratic program (Scholkopf et al. 1998). A kernel function, such as a polynomial, spline, or Gaussian, is used to create the feature vector mapping, where kernel choice is determined by the problem distribution. SVMs compute distances to determine data element classification. These decision rules created by the SVM represent statistical regularities in the data. Once the SVM is trained, classification of new data points is simply a matter of comparison with the support vectors. In the support vectors, critical features characterizing the learned concept are clustered on one side of the hyperplane, those describing its negation on the other, and features that don't discriminate aren't used.

For the perceptron algorithm of Section 11.2, the linear separability of data is important: if the data is not separable the algorithm will not converge. The SVM, alternatively, attempts to maximize the decision margin and is more robust in its ability to handle poor separation caused by overlapping data points. It is able to use *slack* variables to relax the linear constraints to find a soft margin, with values that denote the confidence level of the classification boundary (Cristianini and Shawe-Taylor 2000). As a result some support vectors that are outliers may be misclassified to produce the hyperplane and consequently the decision margin will be narrowed when the data is noisy.

SVMs may be generalized from two category classification problems to the discrimination of multiple classes by repeatedly running the SVM on each category of interest against all the other categories. SVMs are best suited to problems with numerical data rather than categorical; as a result, their applicability for many classic categorization problems with qualitative boundaries is limited. Their strength lies in their mathematical foundations: minimization of a convex quadratic function under linear inequality constraints.

SVMs are applied to many learning situations, including the classification of web pages. In text categorization, the presence of search and/or other related words are weighted. Each document then becomes input data for the SVM to categorize on the basis of word frequency information (Harrison and Luger 2002). SVMs are also used for image recognition, focusing on edge detection and shape description using gray scale or color intensity information (Cristianini and Shawe-Taylor 2000). In Figure 11.18, adapted from (Cristianini and Shawe-Taylor 2000), the SVM discriminates boundaries on a chess board. More details on SVMs and the full SVM learning algorithm may be found in (Burges 1998).

11.5 Hebbian Coincidence Learning

11.5.1 Introduction

Hebb's theory of learning is based on the observation that in biological systems when one neuron contributes to the firing of another neuron, the connection or pathway between the two neurons is strengthened. Hebb (1949) stated:

> When an axon of cell A is near enough to excite a cell B and repeatedly or persistently takes part in firing it, some growth process or metabolic change takes place in one or both cells such that A's efficiency, as one of the cells firing B, is increased.

Hebbian learning is appealing because it establishes behavior-based reward concepts on the neuronal level. Neural physiological research has confirmed that Hebb's idea that temporal proximity of the firing of connected neurons can modify synaptic strength, albeit in a much more complex fashion that Hebb's simple "increase in efficiency", is at least approximately correct. The particular learning law presented in this section is now referred to as Hebbian learning, even though his ideas were somewhat more abstract. This learning belongs to the *coincidence* category of learning laws which cause weight changes in response to localized events in neural processing. We describe the learning laws of this category by their local time and space properties.

Hebbian learning has been used in a number of network architectures. It is used in both supervised and unsupervised learning modes. The effect of strengthening the connection between two neurons, when one contributes to the firing of another, may be simulated mathematically by adjusting the weight on their connection by a constant times the sign of the product of their output values.

Let's see how this works. Suppose neurons i and j are connected so that the output of i is an input of j. We can define the weight adjustment on the connection between them, ΔW, as the sign of $c * (o_i * o_j)$, where c is a constant controlling the learning rate. In Table 11.4,

O_i is the sign of the output value of i and O_j of the output of j. From the first line of the table we see that when O_i and O_j are both positive, the weight adjustment, ΔW, is positive. This has the effect of strengthening the connection between i and j when i has contributed to j's "firing."

O_i	O_j	$O_i * O_j$
+	+	+
+	−	−
−	+	−
−	−	+

Table 11.4 The signs and product of signs of node output values.

In the second and third rows of Table 11.4, i and j have opposite signs. Since their signs differ, we want to inhibit i's contribution to j's output value. Therefore we adjust the weight of the connection by a negative increment. Finally, in the fourth row, i and j again have the same sign. This means that we increase the strength of their connection. This weight adjustment mechanism has the effect of reinforcing the path between neurons when they have similar signals and inhibiting them otherwise.

In the next sections we consider two types of Hebbian learning, unsupervised and supervised. We begin by examining an unsupervised form.

11.5.2   An Example of Unsupervised Hebbian Learning

Recall that in unsupervised learning a critic is not available to provide the "correct" output value; thus the weights are modified solely as a function of the input and output values of the neuron. The training of this network has the effect of strengthening the network's responses to patterns that it has already seen. In the next example, we show how Hebbian techniques can be used to model conditioned response learning, where an arbitrarily selected stimulus can be used as a condition for a desired response.

Weight can be adjusted, ΔW, for a node i in unsupervised Hebbian learning with:

$$\Delta W = c * f(X, W) * X$$

where c is the learning constant, a small positive number, $f(X, W)$ is i's output, and X is the input vector to i.

We now show how a network can use Hebbian learning to transfer its response from a primary or unconditioned stimulus to a conditioned stimulus. This allows us to model the type of learning studied in Pavlov's experiments, whereby simultaneously ringing a bell every time food was presented, a dog's salivation response to food was transferred to the bell. The network of Figure 11.19 has two layers, an input layer with six nodes and an output layer with one node. The output layer returns either +1, signifying that the output neuron has fired, or a −1, signifying that it is quiescent.

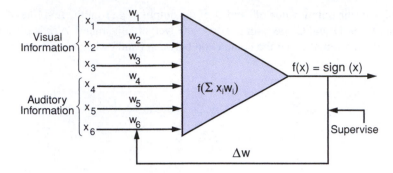

Figure 11.19 An example neuron for application of a hybrid Hebbian node where learning is supervised.

We let the learning constant be the small positive real number 0.2. In this example we train the network on the pattern $[1, -1, 1, -1, 1 -1]$ which is the concatenation of the two patterns, $[1, -1, 1]$ and $[-1, 1, -1]$. The pattern $[1, -1, 1]$ represents the unconditioned stimulus and $[-1, 1, -1]$ represents the new stimulus.

We assume that the network already responds positively to the unconditioned stimulus but is neutral with respect to the new stimulus. We simulate the positive response of the network to the unconditioned stimulus with the weight vector $[1, -1, 1]$, exactly matching the input pattern, while the neutral response of the network to the new stimulus is simulated by the weight vector $[0, 0, 0]$. The concatenation of these two weight vectors gives us the initial weight vector for the network, $[1, -1, 1, 0, 0, 0]$.

We now train the network on the input pattern, hoping to induce a configuration of weights which will produce a positive network response to the new stimulus. The first iteration of the network gives:

$$W * X = (1 * 1) + (-1 * -1) + (1 * 1) + (0 * -1) + (0 * 1) + (0 * -1)$$
$$= (1) + (1) + (1) = 3$$
$$f(3) = sign(3) = 1.$$

We now create the new weight W^2:

$$W^2 = [1, -1, 1, 0, 0, 0] + .2 * (1) * [1, -1, 1, -1, 1, -1]$$
$$= [1, -1, 1, 0, 0, 0] + [.2, -.2, .2, -.2, .2, -.2]$$
$$= [1.2, -1.2, 1.2, -.2, .2, -.2.]$$

We expose the adjusted network to the original input pattern:

$$W * X = (1.2 * 1) + (-1.2 * -1) + (1.2 * 1) + (-.2 * -1) + (.2 * 1) + (-.2 * -1)$$
$$= (1.2) + (1.2) + (1.2) + (+.2) + (.2) + (.2) = 4.2 \text{ and}$$
$$sign(4.2) = 1.$$

We now create the new weight W^3:

W^3 = [1.2, −1.2, 1.2, −.2, .2, −.2] + .2 * (1) * [1, −1, 1, −1, 1 −1]

    = [1.2, −1.2, 1.2, −.2, .2, −.2] + [.2, −.2, .2, −.2, .2, −.2]

    = [1.4, −1.4, 1.4, −.4, .4, −.4.]

It can now be seen that the vector product, W*X, will continue to grow in the positive direction, with the absolute value of each element of the weight vector increasing by .2 at each training cycle. After 10 more iterations of Hebbian training the weight vector will be:

W^{13} = [3.4, −3.4, 3.4, −2.4, 2.4, −2.4].

We now use this trained weight vector to test the network's response to the two partial patterns. We would like to see if the network continues to respond to the unconditioned stimulus positively and, more importantly, if the network has now acquired a positive response to the new, conditioned stimulus. We test the network first on the unconditioned stimulus [1, −1, 1]. We fill out the last three arguments of the input vector with random 1, and −1 assignments. For example, we test the network on the vector [1, −1, 1, 1, 1, −1]:

sign(W*X) = sign((3.4*1) + (−3.4*−1) + (3.4*1)

                + (−2.4*1) + (2.4*1) + (−2.4*−1))

        = sign(3.4 + 3.4 + 3.4 − 2.4 + 2.4 + 2.4)

        = sign(12.6) = +1.

The network thus still responds positively to the original unconditioned stimulus. We now do a second test using the original unconditioned stimulus and a different random vector in the last three positions [1, −1, 1, 1, −1, −1]:

sign(W*X) = sign((3.4*1) + (−3.4*−1) + (3.4*1)

                + (−2.4*1) + (2.4*−1) + (−2.4*−1))

        = sign(3.4 + 3.4 + 3.4 − 2.4 − 2.4 + 2.4)

        = sign(7.8) = +1.

The second vector also produces a positive network response. In fact we note in these two examples that the network's sensitivity to the original stimulus, as measured by its raw activation, has been strengthened, due to repeated exposure to that stimulus.

We now test the network's response to the new stimulus pattern, [−1, 1, −1], encoded in the last three positions of the input vector. We fill the first three vector positions with random assignments from the set {1, −1} and test the network on the vector [1, 1, 1, −1, 1, −1]:

sign(W*X) = sign((3.4*1) + (−3.4*−1) + (3.4*1)

                + (−2.4*1) + (2.4*1) + (−2.4*−1))

        = sign(3.4 − 3.4 + 3.4 + 2.4 + 2.4 + 2.4)

        = sign(10.6) = +1.

The pattern of the secondary stimulus is also recognized!

We do one final experiment, with the vector patterns slightly degraded. This could represent the stimulus situation where the input signals are slightly altered, perhaps because a new food and a different sounding bell are used. We test the network on the input vector [1, −1, −1, 1, 1, −1], where the first three parameters are one off the original unconditioned stimulus and the last three parameters are one off the conditioned stimulus:

$$\text{sign}(W*X) = \text{sign}((3.4*1) + (-3.4*-1) + (3.4*1)$$
$$+ (-2.4*1) + (2.4*1) + (-2.4*-1))$$
$$= \text{sign}(3.4 + 3.4 - 3.4 - 2.4 + 2.4 + 2.4)$$
$$= \text{sign}(5.8) = +1.$$

Even the partially degraded stimulus is recognized!

What has the Hebbian learning model produced? We created an association between a new stimulus and an old response by repeatedly presenting the old and new stimulus together. The network learns to transfer its response to the new stimulus without any supervision. This strengthened sensitivity also allows the network to respond in the same way to a slightly degraded version of the stimuli. This was achieved by using Hebbian coincidence learning to increase the strength of the network's response to the total pattern, an increase which has the effect of increasing the strength of the network's response to each individual component of the pattern.

11.5.3 Supervised Hebbian Learning

The Hebbian learning rule is based on the principle that the strength of the connection between neurons is increased whenever one neuron contributes to the firing of another. This principle can be adapted to a supervised learning situation by basing the connection weight adjustment on the desired output of the neuron rather than the actual output. For example, if the input of neuron A to neuron B is positive, and the *desired* response of neuron B is a positive output, then the weight on the connection from A to B is increased.

We examine an application of supervised Hebbian learning showing how a network can be trained to recognize a set of associations between patterns. The associations are given by a set of ordered pairs, $\{<X_1, Y_1>, <X_2, Y_2>, ..., <X_t, Y_t>\}$, where X_i and Y_i are the vector patterns to be associated. Suppose that the length of the X_i is n and the Y_i is m. We design the network to explicitly fit this situation. Therefore, it has two layers, an input layer of size n and an output layer of size m, as in Figure 11.20.

The learning formula for this network can be derived by starting with the Hebbian learning formula from the previous section:

$$\Delta W = c * f(X, W) * X$$

where $f(X, W)$ is the actual output of the network node. In supervised learning, we replace this actual output of a node with the desired output vector D, giving us the formula:

$$\Delta W = c * D * X$$

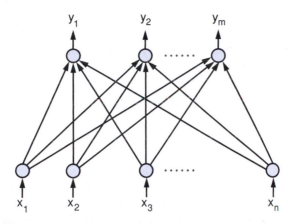

Figure 11.20 A supervised Hebbian network for learning pattern association.

Given a vector pair, $<X,Y>$ from the set of associated pairs, we apply this learning rule to the kth node in the output layer:

$$\Delta W_{ik} = c * d_k * x_i,$$

where ΔW_{ik} is the weight adjustment on the ith input to the kth node in the output layer, d_k is the desired output of the kth node, and x_i is the ith element of X. We apply this formula to adjust all the weights on all the nodes in the output layer. The vector $<x_1, x_2, ..., x_n>$ is just the input vector X and the vector $<d_1, d_2, ..., d_m>$ is the output vector Y. Applying the formula for individual weight adjustments across the entire output layer and collecting terms, we can write the formula for the weight adjustment on the output layer as:

$$\Delta W = c * Y * X,$$

where the vector product $Y*X$ is the *outer vector product*. The outer vector product YX is defined in general as the matrix:

$$YX = \begin{bmatrix} y_1 \bullet x_1 & y_1 \bullet x_2 & ... & y_1 \bullet x_m \\ y_2 \bullet x_1 & y_2 \bullet x_2 & ... & y_2 \bullet x_m \\ ... & ... & ... & ... \\ y_n \bullet x_1 & y_n \bullet x_2 & ... & y_n \bullet x_m \end{bmatrix}$$

To train the network on the entire set of associated pairs, we cycle through these pairs, adjusting the weight for each pair $<X_i, Y_i>$ according to the formula:

$$W^{t+1} = W^t + c*Y_i*X_i.$$

For the entire training set we get:

$$W^1 = W^0 + c (Y_1 * X_1 + Y_2 * X_2 + ... + Y_t * X_t),$$

where W^0 is the initial weight configuration. If we then initialize W^0 to the 0 vector, $<0, 0,$ ..., $0>$, and set the learning constant c to 1, we get the following formula for assigning network weights:

$$W = Y_1 * X_1 + Y_2 * X_2 + ... + Y_t * X_t.$$

A network which maps input vectors to output vectors using this formula for weight assignment is called a *linear associator*. We have shown that linear associator networks are based on the Hebbian learning rule. In practice this formula can be applied directly to initialize network weights without explicit training.

We next analyze the properties of the linear associator. This model, as we have just seen, stores multiple associations in a matrix of weight vectors. This raises the possibility of interactions between stored patterns. We analyze the problems created by these interactions in the next sections.

11.5.4 Associative Memory and the Linear Associator

The *linear associator* network was first proposed by Tuevo Kohonen (1972) and James Anderson et al. (1977). In this section we present the linear associator network as a method for storing and recovering patterns from memory. We examine different forms of memory retrieval, including the heteroassociative, autoassociative, and the interpolative models. We analyze the linear associator network as an implementation of interpolative memory based on Hebbian learning. We end this section by considering problems with interference or crosstalk which arise when encoding multiple patterns in memory.

We begin our examination of memory with some definitions. Patterns and memory values are represented as vectors. There is always an inductive bias in reducing the representation of a problem to a set of feature vectors. The associations which are to be stored in memory are represented as sets of vector pairs, $\{<X_1, Y_1>, <X_2, Y_2>, ..., <X_t, Y_t>\}$. For each vector pair $<X_i, Y_i>$, the X_i pattern is a key for retrieval of the Y_i pattern. There are three types of associative memories:

1. *Heteroassociative*: This is a mapping from X to Y such that if an arbitrary vector X is closer to the vector X_i than any other exemplar, then the associated vector Y_i is returned.

2. *Autoassociative*: This mapping is the same as the heteroassociative except that $X_i = Y_i$ for all exemplar pairs. Since every pattern X_i is related to itself, this form of memory is primarily used when a partial or degraded stimulus pattern serves to recall the full pattern.

3. *Interpolative*: This is a mapping Φ of X to Y such that when X differs from an exemplar, that is, $X = X_i + \Delta_i$, then the output of the $\Phi(X) = \Phi(X_i + \Delta_i) = Y_i + E$,

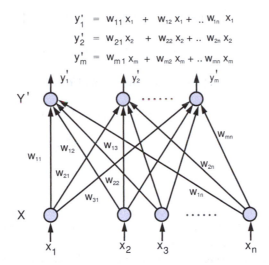

$$y'_1 = w_{11} x_1 + w_{12} x_1 + .. w_{1n} x_1$$
$$y'_2 = w_{21} x_2 + w_{22} x_2 + .. w_{2n} x_2$$
$$y'_m = w_{m1} x_m + w_{m2} x_m + .. w_{mn} x_m$$

Figure 11.21 The linear association network. The vector X_i is entered as input and the associated vector Y' is produced as output. y'_i is a linear combination of the x input. In training each y'_i is supplied with its correct output signals.

where $E = \Phi(\Delta_i)$. In an interpolative mapping, if the input vector is one of the exemplars X_i the associated Y_i is retrieved. If it differs from one of the exemplars by the vector Δ then the output vector also differs by the vector difference E, where $E = \Phi(\Delta)$.

The autoassociative and heteroassociative memories are used for retrieval of one of the original exemplars. They constitute memory in the true sense, in that the pattern that is retrieved is a literal copy of the stored pattern. We also may want to construct an output pattern that differs from the patterns stored in memory in some systematic way. This is the function of an interpolative memory.

The linear associator network in Figure 11.21 implements a form of interpolative memory. As shown in Section 11.5.3, it is based on the Hebbian learning model. The network weight initialization is described by the equation derived in Section 11.5.3:

$$W = Y_1 * X_1 + Y_2 * X_2 + ... + Y_t * X_t.$$

Given this weight assignment, the network will retrieve with an exact match one of the exemplars; otherwise it produces an interpolative mapping.

We next introduce some concepts and notation to help us analyze the behavior of this network. First we want to introduce a metric that allows us to define precisely distance between vectors. All our pattern vectors in the examples are *Hamming* vectors, that is vectors composed of +1 and −1 values only. We use *Hamming distance* to describe the distance between two Hamming vectors. Formally, we define a Hamming space:

$H^n = \{X = (x_1, x_2, ..., x_n)\}$, where each x_i is from the set $\{+1, -1\}$.

Hamming distance is defined for any two vectors from a Hamming space as:

$\|X, Y\|$ = the number of components by which X and Y differ.

For example, the Hamming distance, in four-dimensional Hamming space, between:

(1, −1, −1, 1) and (1, 1, −1, 1) is 1
(−1, −1, −1, 1) and (1, 1, 1, −1) is 4
(1, −1, 1, −1) and (1, −1, 1, −1) is 0.

We need two further definitions. First, the complement of a Hamming vector is that vector with each of its elements changed: +1 to −1 and −1 to +1. For example, the complement of (1, −1, −1, −1) is (−1, 1, 1, 1).

Second, we define the *orthonormality* of vectors. Vectors that are orthonormal are orthogonal, or perpendicular, and of unit length. Two orthonormal vectors, when multiplied together with the *dot product*, have all their cross-product terms go to zero. Thus, in an orthonormal set of vectors, when any two vectors, X_i and X_j, are multiplied the product is 0, unless they are the same vector:

$X_i X_j = \delta_{ij}$ where $\delta_{ij} = 1$ when $i = j$ and 0 otherwise.

We next demonstrate that the linear associator network defined above has the following two properties, with $\Phi(X)$ representing the mapping function of the network. First, for an input pattern X_i which exactly matches one of the exemplars, the network output, $\Phi(X_i)$, is Y_i, the associated exemplar. Second, for an input pattern X_k, which does not exactly match one of the exemplars, the network output, $\Phi(X_k)$, is Y_k, that is the linear interpolation of X_k. More precisely, if $X_k = X_i + \Delta_i$, where X_i is an exemplar, the network returns:

$Y_k = Y_i + E$, where $E = \Phi(\Delta_i)$.

We first show that, when the network input X_i is one of the exemplars, the network returns the associated exemplar.

$\Phi(X_i) = WX_i$, by the definition of the network activation function.

Since $W = Y_1 X_1 + Y_2 X_2 + ... + Y_i X_i + ... + Y_n X_n$, we get:

$$\Phi(X_i) = (Y_1 X_1 + Y_2 X_2 + ... + Y_i X_i + ... + Y_n X_n)X_i$$
$$= Y_1 X_1 X_i + Y_2 X_2 X_i + ... + Y_i X_i X_i + ... + Y_n X_n X_i, \text{ by distributivity.}$$

Since, as defined above, $X_i X_j = \delta_{ij}$:

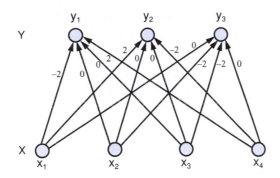

Figure 11.22 A linear associator network for the example in Section 11.5.4. The weight matrix is calculated using the formula presented in the previous section.

$$\Phi(X_i) = Y_1\delta_{1i} + Y_2\delta_{2i} + \dots + Y_i\delta_{ii} + \dots + Y_n\delta_{ni}.$$

By the orthonormality condition, $\delta_{ij} = 1$ when i = j and 0 otherwise. Thus we get:

$$\Phi(X_i) = Y_1{}^*0 + Y_2{}^*0 + \dots + Y_i{}^*1 + \dots + Y_n{}^*0 = Y_i.$$

It can also be shown that, for X_k not equal to any of the exemplars, the network performs an interpolative mapping. That is, for $X_k = X_i + \Delta_i$, where X_i is an exemplar,

$$\Phi(X_k) = \Phi(X_i + \Delta_i)$$
$$= Y_i + E,$$

where Y_i is the vector associated with X_i and

$$E = \Phi(\Delta_i) = (Y_1X_1 + Y_2X_2 + \dots + Y_nX_n)\, \Delta_i.$$

We omit the details of the proof.

We now give an example of linear associator processing. Figure 11.22 presents a simple linear associator network that maps a four-element vector X into a three-element vector Y. Since we are working in a Hamming space, the network activation function f is the *sign* function used earlier.

If we want to store the following two vector associations $<X_1, Y_1>$, $<X_2, Y_2>$ and:

$$X_1 = [1, -1, -1, -1] \leftrightarrow Y_1 = [-1, 1, 1],$$
$$X_2 = [-1, -1, -1, 1] \leftrightarrow Y_2 = [1, -1, 1].$$

Using the weight initialization formula for linear associators, with the outer vector product as defined in the previous section:

$$W = Y_1X_1 + Y_2X_2 + Y_3X_3 + \dots + Y_nX_n,$$

We can now calculate $Y_1X_1 + Y_2X_2$, the weight matrix for the network:

$$W = \begin{bmatrix} -1 & 1 & 1 & 1 \\ 1 & -1 & -1 & -1 \\ 1 & -1 & -1 & -1 \end{bmatrix} + \begin{bmatrix} -1 & -1 & -1 & 1 \\ 1 & 1 & 1 & -1 \\ -1 & -1 & -1 & 1 \end{bmatrix} = \begin{bmatrix} -2 & 0 & 0 & 2 \\ 2 & 0 & 0 & -2 \\ 0 & -2 & -2 & 0 \end{bmatrix}$$

We run the linear associator on one of the exemplars. We start with $X = [1, -1, -1, -1]$ from the first exemplar pair to get back the associated Y:

$y_1 = (-2*1) + (0*-1) + (0*-1) + (2*-1) = -4$, and sign$(-4) = -1$,
$y_2 = (2*1) + (0*-1) + (0*-1) + (-2*-1) = 4$, and sign$(4) = 1$, and
$y_3 = (0*1) + (-2*-1) + (-2*-1) + (0*-1) = 4$, and sign$(4) = 1$.

Thus $Y_1 = [-1, 1, 1]$, the other half of the exemplar pair, is returned.

We next show an example of linear interpolation of an exemplar. Consider the X vector $[1, -1, 1, -1]$:

$y_1 = (-2*1) + (0*-1) + (0*1) + (2*-1) = -4$, and sign$(-4) = -1$,
$y_2 = (2*1) + (0*-1) + (0*1) + (-2*-1) = 4$, and sign$(4) = 1$, and
$y_3 = (0*1) + (-2*-1) + (-2*1) + (0*-1) = 0$, and sign$(0) = 1$.

Notice that $Y = [-1, 1, 1]$ is not one of the original Y exemplars. Notice that the mapping preserves the values which the two Y exemplars have in common. In fact $[1, -1, 1, -1]$, the X vector, has a Hamming distance of 1 from each of the two X exemplars; the output vector $[-1, 1, 1]$ also has a Hamming distance of 1 from each of the other Y exemplars.

We summarize with a few observations regarding linear associators. The desirable properties of the linear associator depend on the requirement that the exemplar patterns comprise an orthonormal set. This restricts its practicality in two ways. First, there may be no obvious mapping from situations in the world to orthonormal vector patterns. Second, the number of patterns which can be stored is limited by the dimensionality of the vector space. When the orthonormality requirement is violated, interference between stored patterns occurs, causing a phenomenon called *crosstalk*.

Observe also that the linear associator retrieves an associated Y exemplar only when the input vector exactly matches an X exemplar. When there is not an exact match on the input pattern, the result is an interpolative mapping. It can be argued that interpolation is not memory in the true sense. We often want to implement a true memory retrieval function where an approximation to an exemplar retrieves the exact pattern that is associated with it. What is required is a *basin* of attraction to capture vectors in the surrounding region.

In the next section, we demonstrate an *attractor* version of the linear associator network.

11.6 Attractor Networks or "Memories"

11.6.1 Introduction

The networks discussed to this point are *feedforward*. In feedforward networks information is presented to a set of input nodes and the signal moves forward through the nodes or layers of nodes until some result emerges. Another important class of connectionist networks are *feedback* networks. The architecture of these nets is different in that the output signal of a node can be cycled back, directly or indirectly, as input to that node.

Feedback networks differ from feedforward networks in several important ways:

1. the presence of feedback connections between nodes,
2. a time delay, i.e., noninstantaneous signal propagation,
3. output of the network is the network's state upon convergence,
4. network usefulness depends on convergence properties.

When a feedback network reaches a time in which it no longer changes, it is said to be in a state of equilibrium. The state which a network reaches on equilibrium is considered to be the network output.

In the feedback networks of Section 11.6.2, the network state is initialized with an input pattern. The network processes this pattern, passing through a series of states until it reaches equilibrium. The network state on equilibrium is the pattern retrieved from memory. In Section 11.6.3, we consider networks that implement a heteroassociative memory, and in Section 11.6.4, an autoassociative memory.

The cognitive aspects of these memories are both interesting and important. They offer us a model for content addressable memory. This type of associator can describe the retrieval of a phone number, the feeling of sadness from an old memory, or even the recognition of a person from a partial facial view. Researchers have attempted to capture many of the associative aspects of this type of memory in symbol-based data structures, including semantic networks, frames, and object systems, as seen in Chapter 7.

An *attractor* is defined as a state toward which states in a neighboring region evolve across time. Each attractor in a network will have a region where any network state inside that region evolves toward that attractor. That region is called its *basin*. An attractor can consist in a single network state or a series of states through which the network cycles.

Attempts to understand attractors and their basins mathematically have given rise to the notion of a network energy function (Hopfield 1984). Feedback networks with an energy function that has the property that every network transition reduces total network energy are guaranteed to converge. We describe these networks in Section 11.6.3.

Attractor networks can be used to implement content addressable memories by installing the desired patterns as attractors in memory. They can also be used to solve optimization problems, such as the traveling salesperson problem, by creating a mapping between the cost function in the optimization problem and the network energy. The solution of the problem then comes through the reduction of total network energy. This type of problem solving is done with what is called a Hopfield network.

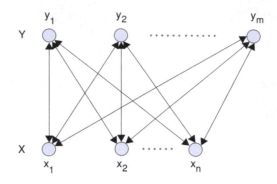

Figure 11.23 A BAM network for the examples of Section 11.6.2. Each node may also be connected to itself.

11.6.2 BAM, the Bi-directional Associative Memory

The BAM network, first described by Bart Kosko (1988), consists of two fully interconnected layers of processing elements. There can also be a feedback link connecting each node to itself. The BAM mapping of an n dimensional input vector X_n into the m dimensional output vector Y_m is presented in Figure 11.22. Since each link from X to Y is bi-directional, there will be weights associated with the information flow going in each direction.

Like the weights of the linear associator, the weights on the BAM network can be worked out in advance. In fact we use the same method for calculating network weights as that used in the linear associator. The vectors for the BAM architecture are taken from the set of Hamming vectors.

Given the N vector pairs that make up the set of exemplars we wish to store, we build the matrix as we did in Section 11.5.4:

$$W = Y_1 * X_1 + Y_2 * X_2 + ... + Y_t * X_t.$$

This equation gives the weights on the connections from the X layer to the Y layer, as can be seen in Figure 11.23. For example, w_{32} is the weight on the connection from the second unit on the X layer to the third unit on the Y layer. We assume that any two nodes only have one pathway between them. Therefore, the weights connecting nodes on the X and Y layers are identical in both directions. Thus, the weight matrix from Y to X is the transpose of the weight matrix W.

The BAM network can be transformed into an autoassociative network by using the same weight initialization formula on the set of associations $<X_1, X_1>$, $<X_2, X_2>$, ... Since the X and Y layers resulting from this procedure are identical we can eliminate the Y layer, resulting in a network which looks like Figure 11.24. We look at an example of an autoassociative network in Section 11.6.4.

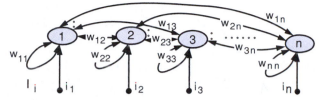

Figure 11.24 An autoassociative network with an input vector I_i. We assume single links between nodes with unique indices, thus $w_{ij} = w_{ji}$ and the weight matrix is symmetric.

The BAM network is used to retrieve patterns from memory by initializing the X layer with an input pattern. If the input pattern is a noisy or incomplete version of one of the exemplars, the BAM can often complete the pattern and retrieve the associated pattern.

To recall data with BAM, we do the following:

1. Apply an initial vector pair (X, Y) to the processing elements. X is the pattern for which we wish to retrieve an exemplar. Y is randomly initialized.

2. Propagate the information from the X layer to the Y layer and update the values at the Y layer.

3. Send the updated Y information back to the X layer, updating the X units.

4. Continue the preceding two steps until the vectors stabilize, that is until there is no further changes in the X and Y vector values.

The algorithm just presented gives BAM its feedback flow, its bidirectional movement toward equilibrium. The preceding set of instructions could have begun with a pattern at the Y level leading, upon convergence, to the selection of an X vector exemplar. It is fully bidirectional: we can take an X vector as input and can get a Y association on convergence or we can take a Y vector as input and get back a X association. We will see these issues worked through with an example in the next section.

Upon convergence, the final equilibrium state gives back one of the exemplars used to build the original weight matrix. If all goes as expected, we take a vector of known properties, either identical to or slightly different, from one of the exemplar vector pairs. We use this vector to retrieve the other vector in the exemplar pair. The distance is Hamming distance measured by component-wise comparison of the vectors, counting one for each element difference. Because of the orthonormality constraints, when BAM converges for a vector, it also converges for its complement. Thus we note that the complement of the vector also becomes an attractor. We give an example of this in the next section.

There are several things that can interfere with the BAM convergence. If too many exemplars are mapped into the weight matrix, the exemplars themselves can be too close together and produce pseudo-stabilities in the network. This phenomenon is called *crosstalk*, and occurs as local minima in the network energy space.

We next consider briefly the BAM processing. The multiplication of an input vector by the weight matrix computes the sums of the pairwise vector products of the vectors for

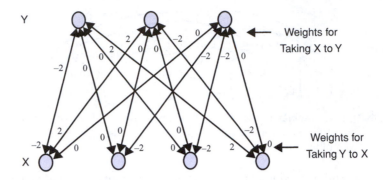

Figure 11.25 A BAM network for the examples of Section 11.6.3.

each element of the output vector. A simple thresholding function then translates the resultant vector back to a vector in the Hamming space. Thus:

net (Y) = WX, or for each Y_i component, net(Y_i) = $\Sigma w_{ij}{}^*x_j$,

with similar relationships for the X layer. The thresholding function f for net(Y) at the time t + 1 is also straightforward:

$$f(net^{t+1}) = \begin{cases} +1 & \text{if net} > 0 \\ f(net^t) & \text{if net} = 0 \\ -1 & \text{if net} < 0 \end{cases}$$

In the next section we illustrate this *bidirectional associative memory* processing with several examples.

11.6.3 Examples of BAM Processing

Figure 11.25 presents a small BAM network, a simple variation of the linear associator presented in Section 11.5.4. This network maps a four element vector X into a three element vector Y and vice versa. Suppose we want to create the two vector pair exemplars:

$x_1 = [1, -1, -1, -1] \leftrightarrow y_1 = [1, 1, 1]$, and
$x_2 = [-1, -1, -1, 1] \leftrightarrow y_2 = [1, -1, 1]$.

We now create the weight matrix according to the formula presented in the previous section:

$$W = Y_1X_1{}^t + Y_2X_2{}^t + Y_3X_3{}^t + \dots + Y_NX_N{}^t$$

$$W = \begin{bmatrix} 1 & -1 & -1 & -1 \\ 1 & -1 & -1 & -1 \\ 1 & -1 & -1 & -1 \end{bmatrix} + \begin{bmatrix} -1 & -1 & -1 & 1 \\ 1 & 1 & 1 & -1 \\ -1 & -1 & -1 & 1 \end{bmatrix} = \begin{bmatrix} 0 & -2 & -2 & 0 \\ 2 & 0 & 0 & -2 \\ 0 & -2 & -2 & 0 \end{bmatrix}$$

The weight vector for the mapping from Y to X is the transpose of W, or:

$$\begin{bmatrix} 0 & 2 & 0 \\ -2 & 0 & -2 \\ -2 & 0 & -2 \\ 0 & -2 & 0 \end{bmatrix}$$

We now select several vectors and test the BAM associator. Let's start with an exemplar pair, choosing the X component and seeing if we get the Y. Let X = [1, –1, –1, –1]:

Y_1 = (1*0) + (–1*–2) + (–1*–2) + (0*–1) = 4, and f(4) = 1,
Y_2 = (1*2) + (–1*0) + (–1*0) + (–1*–2) = 4, and f(4) = 1, and
Y_3 = (1*0) + (–1*–2) + (–1*–2) + (–1*0) = 4, and f(4) = 1.

Thus the other half of the exemplar pair is returned. The reader can make this Y vector an input vector and verify that the original X vector [1, –1, –1, –1] is returned.

For our next example, consider the X vector [1, 1, 1, –1], with Y randomly initialized. We map X with our BAM network:

Y_1 = (1*0) + (1*–2) + (1*–2) + (–1*0) = –4, and f(4) = –1,
Y_2 = (1*2) + (1*0) + (1*0) + (–1*–2) = 4, and f(4) = 1,
Y_3 = (1*0) + (1*–2) + (1*–2) + (–1*0) = –4, and f(4) = –1.

This result, with the thresholding function f applied to [–4, 4, –4], is [–1, 1, –1]. Mapping back to X gives:

X_1 = (–1*0) + (1*2) + (–1* 0) = 2,
X_2 = (–1*–2) + (1*0) + (–1*–2) = 4,
X_3 = (–1*–2) + (1*0) + (–1*–2) = 4,
X_4 = (–1*0) + (1*–2) + (–1*0) = –2.

The threshold function applied, again as above, gives the original vector [1, 1, 1, –1]. Since the starting vector produced a stable result with its first translation, we might think we have just discovered another prototype exemplar pair. In fact, the example we selected is the complement of the original <X_2, Y_2> vector exemplar! It turns out that in a BAM network, when a vector pair is established as an exemplar prototype, so is its complement. Therefore, our BAM network includes two more prototypes:

X_3 = [–1, 1, 1, 1] $\leftrightarrow$ Y_3 = [–1, –1, –1], and
X_4 = [1, 1, 1, –1] $\leftrightarrow$ Y_4 = [–1, 1, –1].

Let us next select a vector near an X exemplar, [1, –1, 1, –1]. Note that the Hamming distance from the closest of the four X exemplars is 1. We next randomly initialize the vector Y to [–1, –1, –1]:

$$Y_1^{t+1} = (1*0) + (-1*-2) + (1*-2) + (-1*0) = 0,$$
$$Y_2^{t+1} = (1*2) + (-1*0) + (1*0) + (-1*-2) = 4,$$
$$Y_3^{t+1} = (1*0) + (-1*-2) + (1*-2) + (-1*0) = 0.$$

The evaluation of the net function $f(Y_i^{t+1}) = f(Y_i^t)$ when $y_i^{t+1} = 0$, from the threshold equation at the end of Section 11.6.2. Thus, Y is $[-1, 1, -1]$ due to the random initialization of the first and third parameters of the Y^T to -1. We now take Y back to X:

$$X_1 = (-1*0) + (1*2) + (-1* 0) = 2,$$
$$X_2 = (-1*-2) + (1*0) + (-1*-2) = 4,$$
$$X_3 = (-1*-2) + (1*0) + (-1*-2) = 4,$$
$$X_4 = (-1*0) + (1*-2) + (-1*0) = -2.$$

The threshold function maps this result to the vector $X = [1, 1, 1, -1]$. We repeat the process taking this vector back to Y:

$$Y_1 = (1*0) + (1*-2) + (1*-2) + (-1*0) = -4,$$
$$Y_2 = (1*2) + (1*0) + (1*0) + (-1*-2) = 4,$$
$$Y_3 = (1*0) + (1*-2) + (1*-2) + (-1*0) = -4.$$

The threshold function applied to $[-4, 4, -4]$ again gives $Y = [-1, 1, -1]$. This vector is identical to the most recent version of Y, so the network is stable. This demonstrates that after two passes through the BAM net, a pattern that was close to X_4 converged to the stored exemplar. This would be similar to recognizing a face or other stored image with part of the information missing or obscured. The Hamming distance between the original X vector $[1, -1, 1, -1]$ and the X_4 prototype $[1, 1, 1, -1]$ was 1. The vector settled into the $<X_4, Y_4>$ exemplar pair.

In our BAM examples we started processing with the X element of the exemplar pair. Of course, we could have designed the examples from the Y vector, initializing X when necessary.

Hecht-Nielsen (1990, p. 82) presents an interesting analysis of the BAM network. He demonstrates that the orthonormal property for the linear associator network support for BAM is too restrictive. He gives an argument showing that the requirement for building the network is that the vectors be linearly independent, that is, that no vector can be created from a linear combination of other vectors in the space of exemplars.

11.6.4   Autoassociative Memory and Hopfield Nets

The research of John Hopfield, a physicist at California Institute of Technology, is a major reason connectionist architectures have their current credibility. He studied network convergence properties, using the concept of energy minimization. He also designed a family of networks based on these principles. As a physicist, Hopfield understood stabilities of physical phenomena as energy minimization points of the physical system. An example of this approach is the simulated annealing analysis of the cooling of metals.

Let us first review the basic characteristics of feedback associative networks. These networks begin with an initial state consisting of the input vector. The network then processes this signal through feedback pathways until it reaches a stable state. To use this architecture as an associative memory we would like the network to have two properties. First, starting from any initial state we would like a guarantee that the network will converge on some stable state. Second, we would like this stable state to be the one closest to the input state by some distance metric.

We look first at an autoassociative network built on the same principles as the BAM network. We noted in the previous section that BAM networks can be transformed into autoassociative networks by using identical vectors in the X and Y positions. The result of this transformation, as we see next, is a symmetric square weight matrix. Figure 11.23 of Section 11.6.2 offered an example.

The weight matrix for the autoassociative network that stores a set of vector exemplars $\{X_1, X_2, ..., X_n\}$ is created by:

$$W = \Sigma X_i X_i^t \qquad \text{for } i = 1, 2, ..., n.$$

When we create the autoassociative memory from the heteroassociative, the weight from node x_i to x_j will be identical to that from x_j to x_i and so the weight matrix will be symmetric. This assumption only requires that the two processing elements be connected by one path having a single weight. We may also have the special case, again with neural plausibility, that no network node is directly linked to itself, that is, there are no x_i to x_i links. In this situation the main diagonal of the weight matrix, w_{ij} where $i = j$, is all zeros.

As with BAM, we work out the weight matrix based on the patterns to be stored in memory. We clarify this with a simple example. Consider the three vector exemplar set:

$$X_1 = [1, -1, 1, -1, 1],$$
$$X_2 = [-1, 1, 1, -1, -1],$$
$$X_3 = [1, 1, -1, 1, 1].$$

We next calculate the weight matrix using $W = \Sigma X_i X_i^t$ for $i = 1, 2, 3$:

$$W = \begin{bmatrix} 1 & -1 & 1 & -1 & 1 \\ -1 & 1 & -1 & 1 & -1 \\ 1 & -1 & 1 & -1 & 1 \\ -1 & 1 & -1 & 1 & -1 \\ 1 & -1 & 1 & -1 & 1 \end{bmatrix} + \begin{bmatrix} 1 & -1 & -1 & 1 & 1 \\ -1 & 1 & 1 & -1 & -1 \\ -1 & 1 & 1 & -1 & -1 \\ 1 & -1 & -1 & 1 & 1 \\ 1 & -1 & -1 & 1 & 1 \end{bmatrix} + \begin{bmatrix} 1 & 1 & -1 & 1 & 1 \\ 1 & 1 & -1 & 1 & 1 \\ -1 & -1 & 1 & -1 & -1 \\ 1 & 1 & -1 & 1 & 1 \\ 1 & 1 & -1 & 1 & 1 \end{bmatrix}$$

$$W = \begin{bmatrix} 3 & -1 & -1 & 1 & 3 \\ -1 & 3 & -1 & 1 & -1 \\ -1 & -1 & 3 & -3 & -1 \\ 1 & 1 & -3 & 3 & 1 \\ 3 & -1 & -1 & 1 & 3 \end{bmatrix}$$

We use the thresholding function:

$$f(net^{t+1}) = \begin{cases} +1 & \text{if net} > 0 \\ f(net^t) & \text{if net} = 0 \\ -1 & \text{if net} < 0 \end{cases}$$

We first test the network with an exemplar, $X_3 = [1, 1, -1, 1, 1]$, and obtain:

$$X_3 * W = [7, 3, -9, 9, 7],$$

and with the threshold function, $[1, 1, -1, 1, 1]$. We see this vector stabilizes immediately on itself. This illustrates that the exemplars are themselves stable states or attractors.

We next test a vector which is Hamming distance 1 from the exemplar X_3. The network should return that exemplar. This is equivalent to retrieving a memory pattern from partially degraded data. We select $X = [1, 1, 1, 1, 1]$:

$$X * W = [5, 1, -3, 3, 5].$$

Using the threshold function gives the X_3 vector $[1, -1, -1, 1, 1]$.

We next take a third example, this time a vector whose Hamming distance is 2 away from its nearest prototype, let $X = [1, -1, -1, 1, -1]$. It can be checked that this vector is 2 away from X_3, 3 away from X_1, and 4 away from X_2. We begin:

$$X * W = [3, -1, -5, 5, 3], \text{ which with threshold yields } [1, -1, -1, 1, 1].$$

This doesn't seem to resemble anything, nor is it a stability point, since:

$$[1, -1, -1, 1, 1] * W = [9, -3, -7, 7, 9], \text{ which is } [1, -1, -1, 1, 1].$$

The net is now stable, but not with one of the original stored memories! Have we found another energy minimum? On closer inspection we note that this new vector is the complement of the original X_2 exemplar $[-1, 1, 1, -1, -1]$. Again, as in the case of the heteroassociative BAM network, our autoassociative network creates attractors for the original exemplars as well as for their complements, in this case we will have six attractors in all.

To this point in our presentation, we have looked at autoassociative networks based on a linear associator model of memory. One of John Hopfield's goals was to give a more general theory of autoassociative networks which would apply to any single-layer feedback network meeting a certain set of simple restrictions. For this class of single layer feedback networks Hopfield proved that there would always exist a network energy function guaranteeing convergence.

A further goal of Hopfield was to replace the discrete time updating model used previously with one that more closely resembles the continuous time processing of actual neurons. A common way to simulate continuous time asynchronous updating in Hopfield networks is to update nodes individually rather than as a layer. This is done using a random selection procedure for picking the next node to be updated, while also applying some method for ensuring that on average all the nodes in the network will be updated equally often.

The structure of a Hopfield network is identical to that of the autoassociative network above: a single layer of nodes completely connected (see Figure 11.23). The activation and thresholding also work as before. For node i,

$$x_i^{new} = \begin{cases} +1 & \text{if } \sum_j w_{ij}x_j^{old} > T_i, \\ x_i^{old} & \text{if } \sum_j w_{ij}x_j^{old} > T_i, \\ -1 & \text{if } \sum_j w_{ij}x_j^{old} < T_i, \end{cases}$$

Given this architecture, only one further restriction is required to characterize a Hopfield net. If w_{ij} is the weight on the connection into node i from node j, we define a Hopfield network as one which respects the weight restrictions:

$$w_{ii} = 0 \qquad \text{for all i,}$$
$$w_{ij} = w_{ji} \qquad \text{for all i, j.}$$

The Hopfield network does not typically have a learning method associated with it. Like the BAM, its weights are usually calculated in advance.

The behavior of Hopfield networks is now better understood than any other class of networks except perceptrons. This is because its behavior can be characterized in terms of a concise energy function discovered by Hopfield:

$$H(X) = -\sum_i \sum_j w_{ij}x_ix_j + 2\sum_i T_ix_i$$

We will now show that this energy function has the property that every network transition reduces the total network energy. Given the fact that H has a predetermined minimum and that each time H decreases it decreases by at least a fixed minimum amount, we can infer that from any state the network converges.

We first show that for an arbitrary processing element k which is the most recently updated, k changes state if and only if H decreases. The change in energy ΔH is:

$$\Delta H = H(X^{new}) - H(X^{old}).$$

Expanding this equation using the definition of H, we get:

$$\Delta H = -\sum_i \sum_j w_{ij}x_i^{new}x_j^{new} - 2\sum_i T_ix_i^{new} + \sum_i \sum_j w_{ij}x_i^{old}x_j^{old} + 2\sum_i T_ix_i^{old}$$

Since only x_k has changed, $x_i^{new} = x_i^{old}$ for i not equal to k. This means that the terms of the sum that do not contain x_k cancel each other out. Rearranging and collecting terms:

$$\Delta H = -2x_k^{new} \sum_j w_{kj} x_j^{new} + 2T_k x_k^{new} + 2x_k^{old} \sum_j w_{kj} x_j^{old} - 2T_k x_k^{old}.$$

Using the fact that $w_{ii} = 0$ and $w_{ij} = w_{ji}$ we can finally rewrite this as:

$$\Delta H = 2(x_k^{old} - x_k^{new}) \left[\sum_j w_{kj} x_j^{old} - T_k \right].$$

To show that ΔH is negative we consider two cases. First, suppose x_k has changed from −1 to +1. Then the term in square brackets must have been positive to make x_k^{new} be +1. Since $x_k^{old} - x_k^{new}$ is equal to −2, ΔH must be negative. Suppose that x_k has changed from 1 to −1. By the same line of reasoning, ΔH must again be negative. If x_k has not changed state, $x_k^{old} - x_k^{new} = 0$ and $\Delta H = 0$.

Given this result, from any starting state the network must converge. Furthermore, the state of the network on convergence must be a local energy minimum. If it were not then there would exist a transition that would further reduce the total network energy and the update selection algorithm would eventually choose that node for updating.

We have now shown that Hopfield networks have one of the two properties which we want in a network that implements associative memory. It can be shown, however, that Hopfield networks do not, in general, have the second desired property: they do not always converge on the stable state nearest to the initial state. There is no general known method for fixing this problem.

Hopfield networks can also be applied to the solution of optimization problems, such as the traveling salesperson problem. To do this the designer needs to find a way to map the cost function of the problem to the Hopfield energy function. By moving to an energy minimum the network will then also be minimizing the cost with respect to a given problem state. Although such a mapping has been found for some interesting problems, including the traveling salesperson problem, in general, this mapping from problem states to energy states is very difficult to discover.

In this section we introduced heteroassociative and autoassociative feedback networks. We analyzed the dynamical properties of these networks and presented very simple examples showing evolution of these systems toward their attractors. We showed how the linear associator network could be modified into an attractor network called the BAM. In our discussion of continuous time Hopfield networks, we saw how network behavior could be described in terms of an energy function. The class of Hopfield networks have guaranteed convergence because every network transition can be shown to reduce total network energy.

There still remain some problems with the energy-based approach to connectionist networks. First, the energy state reached need not be a global minimum of the system. Second, Hopfield networks need not converge to the attractor nearest to the input vector. This makes them unsuitable for implementing content addressable memories. Third, in using Hopfield nets for optimization, there is no general method for creating a mapping of constraints into the Hopfield energy function. Finally, there is a limit to the total number of energy minima that can be stored and retrieved from a network, and even more importantly, this number cannot be set precisely. Empirical testing of these networks shows that the number of attractors is a small fraction of the number of nodes in the net. These and other topics are ongoing issues for research (Hecht-Nielsen 1990, Zurada 1992, Freeman and Skapura 1991).

Biology-based approaches, such as genetic algorithms and cellular automata, attempt to mimic the learning implicit in the evolution of life forms. Processing in these models is also parallel and distributed. In the genetic algorithm model, for example, a population of patterns represents the candidate solutions to a problem. As the algorithm cycles, this population of patterns "evolves" through operations which mimic reproduction, mutation, and natural selection. We consider these approaches next, in Chapter 12.

11.7 Epilogue and References

We introduced connectionist learning in this chapter. We took an historical perspective in Section 11.1. For historical perspective see McCulloch and Pitts (1943), Oliver Selfridge (1959), Claude Shannon (1948), and Frank Rosenblatt (1958). Early psychological models are also important, especially those of Donald Hebb (1949). Cognitive science has continued to explore the relationship between cognition and brain architecture. Contemporary sources include *An Introduction to Natural Computation* (Ballard 1997), *Artificial Minds* (Franklin 1995), *The Cognitive Neuroscience of Action* (Jeannerod 1997), and *Rethinking Innateness: A Connectionist Perspective on Development* (Elman et al. 1996).

We have not addressed many important mathematical as well as computational aspects of connectionist architectures. For an overview, we recommend Robert Hecht-Nielsen (1990), James Freeman and David Skapura (1991), Jacek Zurada (1992), and Nello Cristianini and John Shawe-Taylor (2000). An excellent tutorial on Support Vector Machines is presented by Christopher Burges (1988). Neuro-dynammic programming is described by Bertsekas and Tsitsiklis (1996).

There are many issues, both representational and computational, that the learning research scientist must consider. These include architecture and connectivity selection for the network as well as determining what cognitive parameters of the environment are to be processed and what the results might "mean." There is also the issue of neural–symbol hybrid systems and how these might reflect different aspects of intelligence.

The backpropagation network is probably the most commonly used connectionist architecture, and thus we gave considerable space to its origins, use, and growth. The two volumes of *Parallel Distributed Processing* (Rumelhart et al.1986b) give an introduction to neural networks both as computational and cognitive tools. *Neural Networks and Natural Intelligence* (Grossberg 1988) is another thorough treatment of the subject.

There are also further questions for use of the backpropagation networks, including the number of hidden nodes and layers, selecting the training set, fine-tuning the learning constant, the use of bias nodes, and so on. Many of these issues come under the general heading of *inductive bias*: the role of the knowledge, expectations, and tools that the problem solver brings to problem solving. We address many of these issues in Chapter 17.

Many connectionist architecture designers have described their work. These include John Anderson et al. (1977), Stephan Grossberg (1976, 1988), Geoffrey Hinton and Terrance Sejnowski (1986), Robert Hecht-Nielsen (1982, 1989, 1990), John Hopfield (1982, 1984), Tuevo Kohonen (1972, 1984), Bart Kosko (1988), and Carver Mead (1989). More recent approaches, including graphical models, are presented by Michael Jordan (1999) and Brendan Frey (1998). A good modern textbook is written by Christopher Bishop (1995).

11.8 Exercises

1. Make a McCulloch–Pitts neuron that can calculate the logic function implies, $\Rightarrow$.

2. Build a perceptron net in LISP and run it on the classification example of Section 11.2.2.

   a. Generate another data set similar to that of Table 11.3 and run your classifier on it.
   b. Take the results of running the classifier and use the weights to determine the specification for the line separating the sets.

3. Build a backpropagation network in LISP or C++ and use it to solve the exclusive-or problem of Section 11.3.3. Solve the exclusive-or problem with a different backpropagation architecture, perhaps having two hidden nodes and no bias nodes. Compare the convergence speeds using the different architectures.

4. Write a Kohonen net in LISP or C++ and use it to classify the data of Table 11.3. Compare your results with those of Sections 11.2.2 and 11.4.2.

5. Write a counterpropagation net to solve the exclusive-or problem. Compare your results with those of the backpropagation net of Section 11.3.3. Use your counterpropagation net to discriminate between the classes of Table 11.3.

6. Use a backpropagation net to recognize the ten (hand drawn) digits. One approach would be to build a 4 x 6 array of points. When a digit is drawn on this grid it will cover some elements, giving them value 1, and miss others, value 0. This 24 element vector would be the input value for your net. You would build your own training vectors. Do the same task with a counterpropagation net; compare your results.

7. Select a different input pattern than that we used in Section 11.5.2. Use the unsupervised Hebbian learning algorithm to recognize that pattern.

8. Section 11.5.4 used the linear associator algorithm to make two vector pair associations. Select three (new) vector pair associations and solve the same task. Test whether your linear associator is interpolative; that is, can it associate near misses of the exemplars? Make your linear associator autoassociative.

9. Consider the bidirectional associative memory (BAM) of Section 11.6.3. Change the association pairs given in our example and create the weight matrix for the associations. Select new vectors and test your BAM associator.

10. Describe the differences between the BAM memory and the linear associator. What is *crosstalk* and how can it be prevented?

11. Write a Hopfield net to solve the traveling salesperson problem for ten cities.

MACHINE LEARNING: SOCIAL AND EMERGENT

12

What limit can we put to this power, acting during long ages and rigidly scrutinizing the whole constitution, structure and habits of each creature—favoring the good and rejecting the bad? I can see no limit to this power in slowly and beautifully adapting each form to the most complex relations of life.

—CHARLES DARWIN, *On the Origin of Species*

The First Law of Prophecy:
When a distinguished but elderly scientist states that something is possible, he is almost certainly right. When he states that something is impossible, he is very probably wrong.

The Second Law:
The only way of discovering the limits of the possible is to venture a little way past them into the impossible.

The Third Law:
Any sufficiently advanced technology is indistinguishable from magic.

—ARTHUR C. CLARKE, *Profiles of the Future*

12.0 Social and Emergent Models of Learning

Just as connectionist networks received much of their early support and inspiration from the goal of creating an artificial neural system, so also have a number of other biological analogies influenced the design of machine learning algorithms. This chapter considers learning algorithms patterned after the processes underlying evolution: shaping a population of individuals through the survival of its most fit members. The power of selection across a population of varying individuals has been demonstrated in the emergence of species in natural evolution, as well as through the social processes underlying cultural change. It has also been formalized through research in cellular automata, genetic algorithms, genetic programming, artificial life, and other forms of emergent computation.

Emergent models of learning simulate nature's most elegant and powerful form of adaptation: the evolution of plant and animal life forms. Charles Darwin saw "...no limit to this power of slowly and beautifully adapting each form to the most complex relations of life...". Through this simple process of introducing variations into successive generations and selectively eliminating less fit individuals, adaptations of increasing capability and diversity *emerge* in a population. Evolution and emergence occur in populations of *embodied* individuals, whose actions affect others and that, in turn, are affected by others. Thus, selective pressures come not only from the outside environment, but also from interactions between members of a population. An ecosystem has many members, each with roles and skills appropriate to their own survival, but more importantly, whose cumulative behavior shapes and is shaped by the rest of the population.

Because of their simplicity, the processes underlying evolution have proven remarkably general. Biological evolution produces species by selecting among changes in the genome. Similarly, cultural evolution produces knowledge by operating on socially transmitted and modified units of information. Genetic algorithms and other formal evolutionary analogs produce increasingly capable problem solutions by operating on populations of candidate problem solutions.

When the genetic algorithm is used for problem solving, it has three distinct stages: first, the individual potential solutions of the problem domain are encoded into representations that support the necessary variation and selection operations; often, these representations are as simple as bit strings. In the second stage, mating and mutation algorithms, analogous to the sexual activity of biological life forms, produce a new generation of individuals that recombine features of their parents. Finally, a *fitness* function judges which individuals are the "best" life forms, that is, most appropriate for the eventual solution of the problem. These individuals are favored in survival and reproduction, shaping the next generation of potential solutions. Eventually, a generation of individuals will be interpreted back to the original problem domain as solutions for the problem.

Genetic algorithms are also applied to more complex representations, including production rules, to evolve rule sets adapted to interacting with an environment. For example, genetic programming combines and mutates fragments of computer code in an attempt to evolve a program for solving problems such as capturing the invariants in sets of data.

An example of learning as social interaction leading to survival can be found in games such as *The Game of Life*, originally created by the mathematician John Horton Conway and introduced to the larger community by Martin Gardner in *Scientific American* (1970, 1971). In this game, the birth, survival, or death of individuals is a function of their own state and that of their near neighbors. Typically, a small number of rules, usually three or four, are sufficient to define the game. In spite of this simplicity, experiments with the game of life have shown it to be capable of evolving structures of extraordinary complexity and ability, including self replicating, multi-cellular "organisms" (Poundstone 1985).

An important approach for *artificial life*, or *a-life*, is to simulate the conditions of biological evolution through the interactions of finite state machines, complete with sets of states and transition rules. These automata are able to accept information from outside themselves, in particular, from their closest neighbors. Their transition rules include instructions for birth, continuing in life, and dying. When a population of such automata is set loose in a domain and allowed to act as parallel asynchronous cooperating agents, we sometimes witness the evolution of seemingly independent "life forms."

As another example, Rodney Brooks (1986, 1987) and his students have designed and built simple robots that interact as autonomous agents solving problems in a laboratory situation. There is no central control algorithm; rather cooperation emerges as an artifact of the distributed and autonomous interactions of individuals. The a-life community has regular conferences and journals reflecting their work (Langton 1995).

In Section 12.1 we introduce evolutionary or biology-based models with *genetic algorithms* (Holland 1975), an approach to learning that exploits parallelism, mutual interactions, and often a bit-level representation. In Section 12.2 we present *classifier systems* and *genetic programming*, relatively new research areas where techniques from genetic algorithms are applied to more complex representations, such as to build and refine sets of production rules (Holland et al. 1986) and to create and adapt computer programs (Koza 1992). In Section 12.3 we present *artificial life* (Langton 1995). We begin 12.3 with an introduction to "The Game of Life." We close with an example of emergent behavior from research at the Santa Fe Institute (Crutchfield and Mitchell 1995).

12.1 The Genetic Algorithm

Like neural networks, genetic algorithms are based on a biological metaphor: they view learning as a competition among a population of evolving candidate problem solutions. A "fitness" function evaluates each solution to decide whether it will contribute to the next generation of solutions. Then, through operations analogous to gene transfer in sexual reproduction, the algorithm creates a new population of candidate solutions.

Let P(t) define a population of candidate solutions, x_i^t, at time t:

$$P(t) = \{x_1^t, x_2^t, ..., x_n^t\}$$

We now present a general form of the genetic algorithm:

```
procedure genetic algorithm;

    begin
        set time t:= 0;
        initialize the population P(t);
        while the termination condition is not met do
            begin
                evaluate fitness of each member of the population P(t);
                select members from population P(t) based on fitness;
                produce the offspring of these pairs using genetic operators;
                replace, based on fitness, candidates of P(t), with these offspring;
                set time t := t +1
            end
    end.
```

This algorithm articulates the basic framework of genetic learning; specific implementations of the algorithm instantiate that framework in different ways. What percentage of the population is retained? What percentage mate and produce offspring? How often and to whom are the genetic operators applied? The procedure "replace the weakest candidates of P(t)" may be implemented in a simple fashion, by eliminating a fixed percentage of the weakest candidates. More sophisticated approaches may order a population by fitness and then associate a probability measure for elimination with each member, where the probability of elimination is an inverse function of its fitness. Then the replacement algorithm uses this measure as a factor in selecting candidates to eliminate. Although the probability of elimination would be very low for the fittest members of the society, there is a chance that even the best individuals could be removed. The advantage of this scheme is that it may save some individuals whose overall fitness is poor but that include some component that may contribute to a more powerful solution. This replacement algorithm has many names, including *Monte Carlo*, *fitness proportionate selection*, and *roulette wheel*.

Although the examples of Section 12.1.1 introduce more complex representations, we will introduce the representation issues related to genetic algorithms using simple bit strings to represent problem solutions. For example, suppose we want a genetic algorithm to learn to classify strings of 1s and 0s. We can represent a population of bit strings as a pattern of 1s, 0s, and #s, where # is a "don't care," that may match with either 0 or 1. Thus, the pattern 1##00##1 represents all strings of eight bits that begin and end with 1 and that have two 0s in the middle.

The genetic algorithm initializes P(0) to a population of candidate patterns. Typically, initial populations are selected randomly. Evaluation of candidate solutions assumes a fitness function, $f(x_i^t)$ that returns a measure of the candidate's fitness at time t. A common measure of a candidate's fitness tests it on a set of training instances and returns the percentage of correct classifications. Using such a fitness function, an evaluation assigns each candidate solution the value:

$$f(x_i^t)/m(P, t)$$

where m(P,t) is the average fitness over all members of the population. It is also common for the fitness measure to change across time periods, thus fitness could be a function of the stage of the overall problem solution, or $f(x_i^t)$.

After evaluating each candidate, the algorithm selects pairs for recombination. Recombination uses *genetic operators* to produce new solutions that combine components of their parents. As with natural evolution, the fitness of a candidate determines the extent to which it reproduces, with those candidates having the highest evaluations being given a greater probability of reproducing. As just noted, selection is often probabilistic, where weaker members are given a smaller likelihood of reproducing, but are not eliminated outright. That some less fit candidates survive is important since they can still contain some essential component of a solution, for instance part of a bit pattern, and reproduction may extract this component.

There are a number of genetic operators that produce offspring having features of their parents; the most common of these is *crossover*. Crossover takes two candidate solutions and divides them, swapping components to produce two new candidates. Figure 12.1 illustrates crossover on bit string patterns of length 8. The operator splits them in the

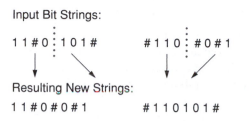

Input Bit Strings:

1 1 # 0 ⋮ 1 0 1 #   # 1 1 0 ⋮ # 0 # 1

Resulting New Strings:

1 1 # 0 # 0 # 1   # 1 1 0 1 0 1 #

Figure 12.1 Use of crossover on two bit strings of length eight. # is "don't care."

middle and forms two children whose initial segment comes from one parent and whose tail comes from the other. Note that splitting the candidate solution in the middle is an arbitrary choice. This split may be at any point in the representation, and indeed, this splitting point may be randomly adjusted or changed during the solution process.

For example, suppose the target class is the set of all strings beginning and ending with a 1. Both the parent strings in Figure 12.1 would have performed relatively well on this task. However, the first offspring would be much better than either parent: it would not have any false positives and would fail to recognize fewer strings that were actually in the solution class. Note also that its sibling is worse than either parent and will probably be eliminated over the next few generations.

Mutation is another important genetic operator. Mutation takes a single candidate and randomly changes some aspect of it. For example, mutation may randomly select a bit in the pattern and change it, switching a 1 to a 0 or #. Mutation is important in that the initial population may exclude an essential component of a solution. In our example, if no member of the initial population has a 1 in the first position, then crossover, because it preserves the first four bits of the parent to be the first four bits of the child, cannot produce an offspring that does. Mutation would be needed to change the values of these bits. Other genetic operators, e.g., *inversion*, could also accomplish this task, and are described in Section 12.1.1.

The genetic algorithm continues until some termination requirement is met, such as having one or more candidate solutions whose fitness exceeds some threshold. In the next section we give examples of genetic algorithm encodings, operators, and fitness evaluations for two situations: the CNF constraint satisfaction and the traveling salesperson problems.

12.1.1　Two Examples: CNF Satisfaction and the Traveling Salesperson

We next select two problems and discuss representation issues and fitness functions appropriate for their solutions. Three things should be noted: first, all problems are not easily or naturally encoded as bit level representations. Second, the genetic operators must preserve crucial relationships within the population, for example, the presence and uniqueness of all the cities in the traveling salesperson tour. Finally, we discuss an important relationship between the fitness function(s) for the states of a problem and the encoding of that problem.

The conjunctive normal form (CNF) satisfiability problem is straightforward: an expression of propositions is in conjunctive normal form when it is a sequence of clauses joined by an and ($\wedge$) relation. Each of these clauses is in the form of a disjunction, the or ($\vee$), of literals. For example, if the literals are a, b, c, d, e, and f, then the expression

$$(\neg a \vee c) \wedge (\neg a \vee c \vee \neg e) \wedge (\neg b \vee c \vee d \vee \neg e) \wedge (a \vee \neg b \vee c) \wedge (\neg e \vee f)$$

is in CNF. This expression is the conjunction of five clauses, each clause is the disjunction of two or more literals. We introduced propositions and their satisfaction in Chapter 2. We discussed the CNF form of propositional expressions, and offered a method of reducing expressions to CNF, when we presented resolution inferencing in Section 12.2.

CNF satisfiability means that we must find an assignment of true or false (1 or 0) to each of the six literals, so that the CNF expression evaluates to true. The reader should confirm that one solution for the CNF expression is to assign false to each of a, b, and e. Another solution has e false and c true.

A natural representation for the CNF satisfaction problem is a sequence of six bits, each bit, in order, representing true (1) or false (0) for each of the six literals, again in the order of a, b, c, d, e, and f. Thus:

1 0 1 0 1 0

indicates that a, c, and e are true and b, d, and f are false, and the example CNF expression is therefore false. The reader can explore the results of other truth assignments to the literals of the expression.

We require that the actions of each genetic operator produce offspring that are truth assignments for the CNF expression, thus each operator must produce a six-bit pattern of truth assignments. An important result of our choice of the bit pattern representation for the truth values of the literals of the CNF expression is that any of the genetic operators discussed to this point will leave the resulting bit pattern a legitimate possible solution. That is, crossover and mutation leave the resulting bit string a possible solution of the problem. Even other less frequently used genetic operators, such as *inversion* (reversing the order of the bits within the six-bit pattern) or *exchange* (interchanging two different bits in the pattern) leave the resulting bit pattern a legitimate possible solution of the CNF problem. In fact, from this viewpoint, it is hard to imagine a better suited representation than a bit pattern for the CNF satisfaction problem.

The choice of a fitness function for this population of bit strings is not quite as straightforward. From one viewpoint, either an assignment of truth values to literals will make the expression true or else the expression will be false. If a specific assignment makes the expression true, then the solution is found; otherwise it is not. At first glance it seems difficult to determine a fitness function that can judge the "quality" of bit strings as potential solutions.

There are a number of alternatives, however. One would be to note that the full CNF expression is made up of the conjunction of five clauses. Thus we can make up a rating system that will allow us to rank potential bit pattern solutions in a range of 0 to 5, depending on the number of clauses that pattern satisfies. Thus the pattern:

1 1 0 0 1 0 has fitness 1,
0 1 0 0 1 0 has fitness 2,
0 1 0 0 1 1 has fitness 3, and
1 0 1 0 1 1 has fitness 5, and is a solution.

This genetic algorithm offers a reasonable approach to the CNF satisfaction problem. One of its most important properties is the use of the implicit parallelism afforded by the population of solutions. The genetic operators have a natural fit to this representation. Finally, the solution search seems to fit naturally a parallel "divide and conquer" strategy, as fitness is judged by the number of problem components that are satisfied. In the chapter exercises the reader is encouraged to consider other aspects of this problem.

EXAMPLE 12.2.2: THE TRAVELING SALESPERSON PROBLEM

The traveling salesperson problem (TSP) is classic to AI and computer science. We introduced it with our discussion of graphs in Section 3.1. Its full state space requires the consideration of N! states where N is the number of cities to be visited. It has been shown to be NP-hard, with many researchers proposing heuristic approaches for its solution. The statement of the problem is simple:

> A salesperson is required to visit N cities as part of a sales route. There is a cost (e.g., mileage, air fare) associated with each pair of cities on the route. Find the least cost path for the salesperson to start at one city, visit all the other cities exactly once and return home.

The TSP has some very nice applications, including circuit board drilling, X-ray crystallography, and routing in VLSI fabrication. Some of these problems require visiting tens of thousands of points (cities) with a minimum cost path. One very interesting question in the analysis of the TSP class of problems is whether it is worth running an expensive workstation for many hours to get a near optimal solution or run a cheap PC for a few minutes to get "good enough" results for these applications. TSP is an interesting and difficult problem with many ramifications of search strategies.

How might we use a genetic algorithm to solve this problem? First, the choice of a representation for the path of cities visited, as well as the creation of a set of genetic operators for this path, is not trivial. The design of a fitness function, however, is very straightforward: all we need do is evaluate the path length. We could then order the paths by their length, the shorter the better.

Let's consider some obvious representations that turn out to have complex ramifications. Suppose we have nine cities to visit,1, 2, ..., 9, so we make the representation of a path the ordered listing of these nine integers. Suppose we simply make each city a four-bit pattern, 0001, 0010, ..., 1001. Thus, the pattern:

0001 0010 0011 0100 0101 0110 0111 1000 1001

represents a visit to each city in the order of its numbering. We have inserted blanks into the string only to make it easier to read. Now, what about the genetic operators? Crossover is definitely out, since the new string produced from two different parents would most probably not represent a path that visits each city exactly once. In fact, with crossover, some cities could be removed while others are visited more than once. What about mutation? Suppose the leftmost bit of the sixth city, 0110, is mutated to 1? 1110, or 14, is no longer a legitimate city. Inversion, and the swapping of cities (the four bits in the city pattern) within the path expression would be acceptable genetic operators, but would these be powerful enough to obtain a satisfactory solution? In fact, one way to look at the search for the minimum path would be to generate and evaluate all possible permutations of the N elements of the city list. The genetic operators must be able to produce all permutations.

Another approach to the TSP would be to ignore the bit pattern representation and give each city an alphabetic or numeric name, e.g., 1, 2, ..., 9; make the path through the cities an ordering of these nine digits, and then select appropriate genetic operators for producing new paths. Mutation, as long as it was a random exchange of two cities in the path, would be okay, but the crossover operator between two paths would be useless. The exchange of pieces of a path with other pieces of the same path, or any operator that shuffled the letters of the path (without removing, adding, or duplicating any cities) would work. These approaches, however, make it difficult to combine into offspring the "better" elements of patterns within the paths of cities of the two different parents.

A number of researchers (Davis 1985, Oliver et al. 1987) have created crossover operators that overcome these problems and let us work with the ordered list of cities visited. For example, Davis has defined an operator called *order crossover*. Suppose we have nine cities, 1, 2, ..., 9, and the order of the integers represents the order of visited cities.

Order crossover builds offspring by choosing a subsequence of cities within the path of one parent. It also preserves the relative ordering of cities from the other parent. First, select two cut points, indicated by a "|", which are randomly inserted into the same location of each parent. The locations of the cut points are random, but once selected, the same locations are used for both parents. For example, for two parents p1 and p2, with cut points after the third and seventh cities:

p1 = (1 9 2 | 4 6 5 7 | 8 3)
p2 = (4 5 9 | 1 8 7 6 | 2 3)

Two children c1 and c2 are produced in the following way. First, the segments between cut points are copied into the offspring:

c1 = (x x x | 4 6 5 7 | x x)
c2 = (x x x | 1 8 7 6 | x x)

Next, starting from the second cut point of one parent, the cities from the other parent are copied in the same order, omitting cities already present. When the end of the string is reached, continue on from the beginning. Thus, the sequence of cities from p2 is:

2 3 4 5 9 1 8 7 6

Once cities 4, 6, 5, and 7 are removed, since they are already part of the first child, we get the shortened list 2, 3, 9, 1, and 8, which then makes up, preserving the ordering found in p2, the remaining cities to be visited by c1:

c1 = (2 3 9 | 4 6 5 7 | 1 8)

In a similar manner we can create the second child c2:

c2 = (3 9 2 | 1 8 7 6 | 4 5)

To summarize, in order crossover, pieces of a path are passed on from one parent, p1, to a child, c1, while the ordering of the remaining cities of the child c1 is inherited from the other parent, p2. This supports the obvious intuition that the ordering of cities will be important in generating the least costly path, and it is therefore crucial that pieces of this ordering information be passed on from fit parents to children.

The order crossover algorithm also guarantees that the children would be legitimate tours, visiting all cities exactly once. If we wished to add a mutation operator to this result we would have to be careful, as noted earlier, to make it an exchange of cities within the path. The inversion operator, simply reversing the order of all the cities in the tour, would not work (there is no new path when all cities are inverted). However, if a piece within the path is cut out and inverted and then replaced, it would be an acceptable use of inversion. For example, using the cut | indicator as before, the path:

c1 = (2 3 9 | 4 6 5 7 | 1 8),

becomes under inversion of the middle section,

c1 = (2 3 9 | 7 5 6 4 | 1 8)

A new mutation operator could be defined that randomly selected a city and placed it in a new randomly selected location in the path. This mutation operator could also operate on a piece of the path, for example, to take a subpath of three cities and place them in the same order in a new location within the path. Other suggestions are in the exercises.

12.1.2 Evaluating the Genetic Algorithm

The preceding examples highlight the genetic algorithm's unique problems of knowledge representation, operator selection, and the design of a fitness function. The representation selected must support the genetic operators. Sometimes, as with the CNF satisfaction problem, the bit level representation is natural. In this situation, the traditional genetic operators of crossover and mutation could be used directly to produce potential solutions. The traveling salesperson problem was an entirely different matter. First, there did not seem to be any natural bit level representations for this problem. Secondly, new mutation and crossover operators had to be devised that preserved the property that the offspring had to be legal paths through all the cities, visiting each only once.

Finally, genetic operators must pass on "meaningful" pieces of potential solution information to the next generation. If this information, as in CNF satisfiability, is a truth value assignment, then the genetic operators must preserve it in the next generation. In the TSP problem, path organization was critical, so as we discussed, components of this path information must be passed on to descendants. This successful transfer rests both in the representation selected as well as in the genetic operators designed for each problem.

We leave representation with one final issue, the problem of the "naturalness" of a selected representation. Suppose, as a simple, if somewhat artificial, example, we want our genetic operators to differentiate between the numbers 6, 7, 8, and 9. An integer representation gives a very natural and evenly spaced ordering, because, within base ten integers, the next item is simply one more than the previous. With change to binary, however, this naturalness disappears. Consider the bit patterns for 6, 7, 8, and 9:

0110 0111 1000 1001

Observe that between 6 and 7 as well as between 8 and 9 there is a 1 bit change. Between 7 and 8, however, all four bits change! This representational anomaly can be huge in trying to generate a solution that requires any organizing of these four bit patterns. A number of techniques, usually under the general heading of *gray coding*, address this problem of non-uniform representation. For instance, a gray coded version of the first sixteen binary numbers may be found in Table 12.1. Note that each number is exactly one bit different from its neighbors. Using gray coding instead of standard binary numbers, the genetic operator's transitions between states of near neighbors is natural and smooth.

Binary	Gray
0000	0000
0001	0001
0010	0011
0011	0010
0100	0110
0101	0111
0110	0101
0111	0100
1000	1100
1001	1101
1010	1111
1011	1110
1100	1010
1101	1011
1110	1001
1111	1000

Table 12.1 The gray coded bit patterns for the binary numbers 0, 1, ..., 15.

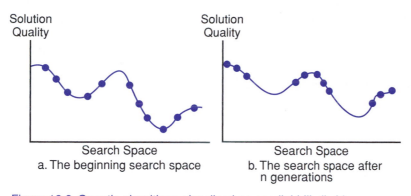

Figure 12.2 Genetic algorithms visualized as parallel hill climbing, adapted from Holland (1986).

An important strength of the genetic algorithm is in the parallel nature of its search. Genetic algorithms implement a powerful form of hill climbing that maintains multiple solutions, eliminates the unpromising, and improves good solutions. Figure 12.2, adapted from Holland (1986), shows multiple solutions converging toward optimal points in a search space. In this figure, the horizontal axis represents the possible points in a solution space, while the vertical axis reflects the quality of those solutions. The dots on the curve are members of the genetic algorithm's current population of candidate solutions. Initially, the solutions are scattered through the space of possible solutions. After several generations, they tend to cluster around areas of higher solution quality.

When we describe our genetic search as "hill climbing" we implicitly acknowledge moving across a "fitness landscape." This landscape will have its valleys, peaks, with local maxima and minima. In fact, some of the discontinuities in the space will be artifacts of the representation and genetic operators selected for the problem. This discontinuity, for example, could be caused by a lack of gray coding, as just discussed. Note also that genetic algorithms, unlike sequential forms of hill climbing, as in Section 4.1, do not immediately discard unpromising solutions. Through genetic operators, even weak solutions may continue to contribute to the makeup of future candidate solutions.

Another difference between genetic algorithms and the state space heuristics presented in Chapter 4 is the analysis of the present-state/goal-state difference. The information content supporting the A* algorithm, as in Section 4.3, required an estimate of "effort" to move between the present state and a goal state. No such measure is required with genetic algorithms, simply some measure of fitness of each of the current generation of potential solutions. There is also no strict ordering required of next states on an open list as we saw in state space search; rather, there is simply a population of fit solutions to a problem, each potentially available to help produce new possible solutions within a paradigm of parallel search.

An important source of the genetic algorithm's power is the *implicit parallelism* inherent in evolutionary operators. In comparison with state space search and an ordered open list, search moves in parallel, operating on entire families of potential solutions. By restricting the reproduction of weaker candidates, genetic algorithms may not only eliminate that solution, but all of its descendants. For example, the string, 101#0##1, if broken at its midpoint, can parent a whole family of strings of the form 101#____. If the parent is found to be unfit, its elimination also removes all of these potential offspring.

As genetic algorithms are more widely used in applied problem solving as well as in scientific modeling, there is increasing interest in attempts to understand their theoretical foundations. Several questions that naturally arise are:

1. Can we characterize types of problems for which GAs will perform well?

2. For what problem types do they perform poorly?

3. What does it even "mean" for a GA to perform well or poorly for a problem type?

4. Are there any laws that can describe the macrolevel of behavior of GAs? In particular, are there any predictions that can be made about the changes in fitness of subgroups of the population over time?

5. Is there any way to describe the differential effects of different genetic operators, crossover, mutation, inversion, etc., over time?

6. Under what circumstances (what problems and what genetic operators) will GAs perform better than traditional AI search methods?

Addressing many of these issues goes well beyond the scope of our book. In fact, as Mitchell (1996) points out, there are still more open questions at the foundations of genetic algorithms than there are generally accepted answers. Nonetheless, from the beginning of work in GAs, researchers, including Holland (1975), have attempted to understand how GAs work. Although they address issues on the macro level, such as the six questions just asked, their analysis begins with the micro or bit level representation.

Holland (1975) introduced the notion of a *schema* as a general pattern and a "building block" for solutions. A schema is a pattern of bit strings that is described by a template made up of 1, 0, and # (don't care). For example, the schema 1 0 # # 0 1 represents the family of six-bit strings beginning with a 1 0 and ending with a 0 1. Since the middle pattern # # describes four bit patterns, 0 0, 0 1, 1 0, 1 1, the entire schema represents four patterns of six 1s and 0s. Traditionally, each schema is said to describe a hyperplane (Goldberg 1989); in this example, the hyperplane cuts the set of all possible six-bit representations. A central tenet of traditional GA theory is that schemata are the building blocks of families of solutions. The genetic operators of crossover and mutation are said to manipulate these schemata towards potential solutions. The specification describing this manipulation is called the *schema theorem* (Holland 1975, Goldberg 1989). According to Holland, an adaptive system must identify, test, and incorporate structural properties hypothesized to give better performance in some environment. Schemata are meant to be a formalization of these structural properties.

Holland's schema analysis suggests that the fitness selection algorithm increasingly focuses the search on subsets of the search space with estimated best fitness; that is, the subsets are described by schemas of above average fitness. The genetic operator crossover puts high fitness building blocks together in the same string in an attempt to create ever more fit strings. Mutation helps guarantee that (genetic) diversity is never removed from the search; that is, that we continue to explore new parts of the fitness landscape. The genetic algorithm can thus be seen as a tension between opening up a general search process and capturing and preserving important (genetic) features in that search space. Although Holland's original analysis of GA search focused at the bit level, more recent work has extended this analysis to alternate representational schemes (Goldberg 1989). In the next section we apply GA techniques to more complex representations.

12.2 Classifier Systems and Genetic Programming

Early research in genetic algorithms focused almost exclusively on low-level representations, such as strings of {0, 1, #}. In addition to supporting straightforward instantiations of genetic operators, bit strings and similar representations give genetic algorithms much of the power of other subsymbolic approaches, such as connectionist networks. There are problems, however, such as the traveling salesperson, that have a more natural encoding at a more complex representational level. We can further ask whether genetic algorithms can be defined for still richer representations, such as *if... then...* rules or pieces of computer code. An important aspect of such representations is their ability to combine distinct, higher level knowledge sources through rule chaining or function calls to meet the requirements of a specific problem instance.

Unfortunately, it is difficult to define genetic operators that capture the syntactic and semantic structure of logical relationships while enabling effective application of operators such as crossover or mutation. One possible way to marry the reasoning power of rules with genetic learning is to translate logical sentences into bit strings and use the standard crossover operator. Unfortunately, under many translations most of the bit strings produced by crossover and mutation will fail to correspond to meaningful logical sentences. As an alternative to representing problem solutions as bit strings, we may define variations of crossover that can be applied directly to higher level representations such as *if... then...* rules or chunks of code in a higher level programming language. This section discusses examples of each approach to extending the power of genetic algorithms.

12.2.1 Classifier Systems

Holland (1986) developed a problem-solving architecture called *classifier systems* that applies genetic learning to rules in a production system. A classifier system (Figure 12.3) includes the familiar elements of a production system: production rules (here called classifiers), working memory, input sensors (or decoders), and outputs (or effectors). Unusual features of a classifier system include the use of competitive bidding for conflict resolution, genetic algorithms for learning, and the *bucket brigade algorithm* to assign credit and blame to rules during learning. Feedback from the outside environment provides

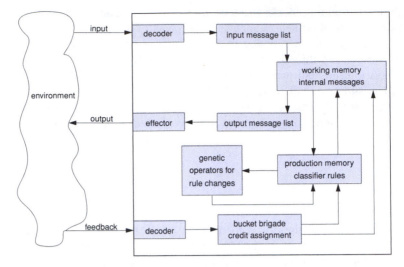

Figure 12.3 A classifier system interacting with the environment,
adapted from Holland (1986).

a means of evaluating the fitness of candidate classifiers, as required in genetic learning. The classifier system of Figure 12.3 has the following major components:

1. Detectors of input messages from the environment.

2. Detectors of feedback messages from the environment.

3. Effectors translating results of rule applications back to the environment.

4. A production rule set made up of a population of classifiers. Each classifier has an associated fitness measure.

5. A working memory for the classifier rules. This memory integrates the results of production rule firing with input information.

6. A set of genetic operators for production rule modification.

7. A system for giving credit to rules involved in producing successful actions.

In problem solving, the classifier performs as a traditional production system. The environment sends a message, perhaps a move in a game, to the classifier system's detectors. This event is decoded and placed as a pattern on the internal message list, the working memory for the production system. These messages, in the normal action of data-driven production system, match the condition patterns of the classifier rules. The selection of the "strongest activated classifiers" is determined by a bidding scheme, where a bid is a function of both the accumulated fitness of the classifier and the quality of the match between the input stimulus and its condition pattern. The classifiers with the closest match add messages (the action of the fired rules) to working memory. The revised message list may send messages to the effectors which act upon the environment or activate new classifier rules as the production system processing continues.

Classifier systems implement a form of reinforcement learning, Section 10.7. Based on feedback from a teacher or fitness evaluation function, the learner computes the fitness of a population of candidate rules and adapts this population using a variation of genetic learning. Classifier systems learn in two ways. First, there is a reward system that adjusts the fitness measures of the classifier rules, rewarding successful rule firings and penalizing errors. The credit assignment algorithm passes part of the reward or penalty back to any classifier rules that have contributed to the final rule firing. This distribution of differential rewards across interacting classifiers, as well as those that enabled their firing, is often implemented in a *bucket brigade* algorithm. The bucket brigade algorithm addresses the problem of assigning credit or blame in situations where the system's output may be the product of a sequence of rule firings. In the event of an error, how do we know which rule to blame? Is the responsibility that of the last rule to fire, or of some previous rule that provided it with faulty information? The bucket brigade algorithm allocates both credit and blame across a sequence of rule applications according to measures of each rule's contribution to the final conclusion. (An analogous assignment of blame for error was described with the backpropagation algorithm of Section 11.3; see Holland (1986) for more details.)

The second form of learning modifies the rules themselves using genetic operators such as mutation and crossover. This allows the most successful rules to survive and combine to make new classifiers, while unsuccessful rule classifiers disappear.

Each classifier rule consists of three components: the rule's condition matches data in the working memory in the typical production system sense. In learning, genetic operators can modify both the conditions and the actions of the production rules. The second component of the rule, the action, can have the effect of changing the internal message list (the production memory). Finally, each rule has a fitness measure. This parameter is changed, as just noted, both by successful as well as by unsuccessful activity. This measure is originally assigned to each rule on its creation by the genetic operators; for example, it may be set as the average fitness of its two parents.

A simple example illustrates the interactions of these components of a classifier system. Assume that a set of objects to be classified are defined by six attributes (conditions c_1, c_2, ..., c_6), and further suppose that each of these attributes can have five different values. Although the possible values of each attribute are of course different (for example, the value of c_3 might be color, while c_5 might describe the weather) we will, without loss of generality, give each attribute an integer value from $\{1, 2, ..., 5\}$. Suppose the conditions of these rules place their matching object in one of four classes: A1, A2, A3, A4.

Based on these constraints, each classifier will have the form:

$(c_1\ c_2\ c_3\ c_4\ c_5\ c_6) \rightarrow$ Ai, where i = 1, 2, 3, 4.

where each c_i in the condition pattern denotes the value $\{1, 2, ..., 5\}$ of the ith attribute of the condition. Usually, conditions can also assign a value of # or "don't care" to an attribute. Ai denotes the classification, A1, A2, A3, or A4. Table 12.2 presents a set of classifiers. Note that different condition patterns can have the same classification, as in rules 1 and 2, or the same patterns, as in rules 3 and 5, can lead to different classifications.

Condition (Attributes)		Action (Classification)	Rule Number
(1 # # # 1 #)	$\rightarrow$	A1	1
(2 # # 3 # #)	$\rightarrow$	A1	2
(# # 4 3 # #)	$\rightarrow$	A2	3
(1 # # # # #)	$\rightarrow$	A2	4
(# # 4 3 # #)	$\rightarrow$	A3	5
etc.			

Table 12.2 A set of condition $\rightarrow$ action classifiers to be "learned."

As described so far, a classifier system is simply another form of the ubiquitous production system. The only really novel feature of classifier rules in this example is their use of strings of digits and #s to represent condition patterns. It is this representation of conditions that constrains the application of genetic algorithms to the rules. The remainder of the discussion describes genetic learning in classifier systems.

In order to simplify the remainder of the example, we will only consider the classifier system's performance in learning the classification A1. That is, we will ignore the other classifications, and assign condition patterns a value of 1 or 0 depending on whether or not they support classification A1. Note that there is no loss of generality in this simplification; it may be extended to problems of learning more than one classification by using a vector to indicate the classifications that match a particular condition pattern. For example, the classifiers of Table 12.2 may be summarized by:

$$(1 \ \# \ \# \ \# \ 1 \ \#) \rightarrow (1 \ 0 \ 0 \ 0)$$
$$(2 \ \# \ \# \ 3 \ \# \ \#) \rightarrow (1 \ 0 \ 0 \ 0)$$
$$(1 \ \# \ \# \ \# \ \# \ \#) \rightarrow (0 \ 1 \ 0 \ 0)$$
$$(\# \ \# \ 4 \ 3 \ \# \ \#) \rightarrow (0 \ 1 \ 1 \ 0)$$

In this example, the last of these summaries indicates that the condition attributes support classification rules A2 and A3 and not A1 or A4. By replacing the 0 or 1 assignment with these vectors, the learning algorithm can evaluate the performance of a rule across multiple classifications.

In this example, we will use the rules in Table 12.2 to indicate the correct classifications; essentially, they will function as teachers or evaluators of the fitness of rules in the learning system. As with most genetic learners, we begin with a random population of rules. Each condition pattern is also assigned a *strength*, or *fitness*, parameter (a real number between 0.0, no strength, and 1.0, full strength. This strength parameter, s, is computed from the fitness of each rule's parents, and measures its historical fitness.

At each learning cycle, the rules attempt to classify the inputs and are then ranked by the teacher or fitness metric. For example, assume that at some cycle, the classifier has the following population of candidate classification rules, where the conclusion of 1 indicates that the pattern led to a correct classifcation and 0 that it did not:

$$(\# \# \# 2\ 1\ \#) \rightarrow 1 \qquad s = 0.6$$
$$(\# \# 3\ \# \# 5) \rightarrow 0 \qquad s = 0.5$$
$$(2\ 1\ \# \# \# \#) \rightarrow 1 \qquad s = 0.4$$
$$(\# 4\ \# \# \# 2) \rightarrow 0 \qquad s = 0.23$$

Suppose a new input message arrives from the environment: (1 4 3 2 1 5), and the teacher (using the first rule of Table 12.2) classifies this input vector as a positive example of A1. Let's consider what happens when working memory receives this pattern and the four candidate classifier rules try to match it. Rules 1 and 2 match. Conflict resolution is done through competitive bidding among matching rules. In our example, bidding is a function of the sum of the matches of the attribute values times the strength measure of the rule. "Don't care" matches have the value 0.5, while exact matches have value 1.0. To normalize we divide this result by the length of the input vector. Since the input vector matches the first classifier with two exact and four "don't cares," its bid is ((4 * 0.5 + 2 * 1) * 0.6) / 6, or 0.4. The second classifier also matches two attributes and has four "don't cares," so its bid is 0.33. In our example, only the classifier making the highest bid fires, but in more complex situations, it may be desirable for a percentage of the bids to be accepted.

The first rule wins and posts its action, a 1, indicating that this pattern is an example of A1. Since this action is correct, the fitness measure of rule 1 is increased to between its present value and 1.0. Had the action of this rule been incorrect, the fitness measure would have been lowered. If the system required multiple firings of the rule set to produce some result on the environment, all the rules responsible for this result would receive some proportion of the reward. The exact procedure by which the rule's fitness is calculated varies across systems and may be fairly complex, involving the use of the bucket brigade algorithm or some similar credit assignment technique. See Holland (1986) for details.

Once the fitness of the candidate rules has been computed, the learning algorithm applies genetic operators to create the next generation of rules. First, a selection algorithm will decide the most fit members of the rule set. This selection is based on the fitness measure, but may also include an additional random value. The random value gives rules with a poor fitness the opportunity to reproduce, helping to avoid a too hasty elimination of rules that, while performing poorly overall, may incorporate some element of the desired solution. Suppose the first two classifier rules of the example are selected to survive and reproduce. Randomly selecting a crossover position between the fourth and fifth elements,

$$(\# \# \# 2 \mid 1\ \#) \rightarrow 1 \qquad s = 0.6$$
$$(\# \# 3\ \# \mid \# 5) \rightarrow 0 \qquad s = 0.5$$

produces the offspring:

$$(\# \# 3\ \# \mid 1\ \#) \rightarrow 0 \qquad s = 0.53$$
$$(\# \# \# 2 \mid \# 5) \rightarrow 1 \qquad s = 0.57$$

The fitness measure of the children is a weighted function of the fitness of the parents. The weighting is a function of where the crossover point lies. The first offspring has 1/3 of the original 0.6 classifier and 2/3 of the original 0.5 classifier. Thus, the first offspring has strength of (1/3 * 0.6) + (2/3 * 0.5) = 0.53. With a similar calculation, the fitness of the second child is 0.57. The result of firing the classifier rule, always 0 or 1, goes with the majority of the attributes, thus preserving the intuition that these patterns are important in the outcomes of the rules. In a typical classifier system these two new rules, along with their parents, would make up the subset of classifiers for the operation of the system at the next time step.

A mutation operator may also be defined. A simple mutation rule would be to randomly change any attribute pattern to some other valid attribute pattern; for example, a 5 could be mutated to 1, 2, 3, 4 or #. Again, as noted in our discussion of GAs, mutation operators are seen as forcing diversity into the search for classifiers, while crossover attempts to preserve and build new children from successful pieces of parental patterns.

Our example was simple and intended primarily for illustrating the main components of the classifier system. In an actual system, more than one rule might fire and each pass their results along to the production memory. There is often a taxation scheme that keeps any classifier from becoming too prominent in the solution process by lowering its fitness each time it wins a bid. We also did not illustrate the bucket brigade algorithm, differentially rewarding rules supporting successful output messages to the environment. Also, the genetic operators do not usually rework the classifiers at every operation of the system. Rather, there is some general parameter for each application that decides, perhaps on analysis of feedback from the environment, when the classifiers should be evaluated and the genetic operators applied.

Finally, our example is taken from the classifier systems that Holland (1986) at the University of Michigan proposed. The Michigan approach can be viewed as a computational model of cognition, where the knowledge, (the classifiers), of a cognitive entity are exposed to a reacting environment and as a result undergo modification over time. We evaluate the success of the entire system over time, while the importance of the individual classifier is minimal. Alternative classifier systems have also been investigated, including work at the University of Pittsburgh (Michalski et al. 1983). The Pittsburgh classifier focuses on the roles of individual rules in producing new generations of classifiers. This approach implements a model of inductive learning proposed by Michalski.

In the next section we consider a different and particularly exciting application for GAs, the evolution of computer programs.

12.2.2 Programming with Genetic Operators

Through the last several subsections we have seen GAs applied to progressively larger representational structures. What began as genetic transformations on bit strings evolved to operations on *if... then...* rules. It can quite naturally be asked if genetic and evolutionary techniques might be applied to the production of other larger scale computational tools. There have been two major examples of this: the generation of computer programs and the evolution of systems of finite state machines.

Koza (1991, 1992) suggested that a successful computer program might evolve through successive applications of genetic operators. In genetic programming, the structures being adapted are hierarchically organized segments of computer programs. The learning algorithm maintains a population of candidate programs. The fitness of a program will be measured by its ability to solve a set of tasks, and programs are modified by applying crossover and mutation to program subtrees. Genetic programming searches a space of computer programs of varying size and complexity; in fact, the search space is the space of all possible computer programs composed of functions and terminal symbols appropriate to the problem domain. As with all genetic learners, this search is random, largely blind and yet surprisingly effective.

Genetic programming starts with an initial population of randomly generated programs made up of appropriate program pieces. These pieces, suitable for a problem domain, may consist of standard arithmetic operations, other related programming operations, and mathematical functions, as well as logical and domain-specific functions. Program components include data items of the usual types: boolean, integer, floating point, vector, symbolic, or multiple-valued.

After initialization, thousands of computer programs are genetically bred. The production of new programs comes with application of genetic operators. Crossover, mutation, and other breeding algorithms must be customized for the production of computer programs. We will see several examples shortly. The fitness of each new program is then determined by seeing how well it performs in a particular problem environment. The nature of the fitness measure will vary according to the problem domain. Any program that does well on this fitness task will survive to help produce the children of the next generation.

To summarize, *genetic programming* includes six components, many very similar to the requirements for GAs:

1. A set of structures that undergo transformation by genetic operators.

2. A set of initial structures suited to a problem domain.

3. A fitness measure, again domain dependent, to evaluate structures.

4. A set of genetic operators to transform structures.

5. Parameters and state descriptions that describe members of each generation.

6. A set of termination conditions.

In the following paragraphs we address each of these topics in more detail.

Genetic programming manipulates hierarchically organized program modules. LISP was (and still remains) the primary representation for the programming language components: Koza represents program segments as LISP symbol expressions, or *s-expressions*. (See Section 16.1 for a discussion of s-expressions, their natural representation as tree structures, and their evaluation as programs.)

Genetic operators manipulate s-expressions. In particular, operators map tree structures of s-expressions (LISP program segments) into new trees (new LISP program segments). Although this s-expression is the basis for Koza's early work, other researchers have more recently applied this approach to different programming paradigms.

Genetic programming will construct useful programs, given that the atomic pieces and evaluable predicates of the problem domain are available. When we set up a domain for the generation of a program sufficient to address a set of problems, we must first analyze what terminals are required for units in its solution as well as what functions are necessary to produce these terminals. As Koza notes (1992, p.86) "... the user of genetic programming should know ... that some composition of the functions and terminals he supplies can yield a solution of the problem."

To initialize the structures for adaptation by genetic operators, we must create two sets: F, the set of functions and T, the set of terminal values required for the domain. F can be as simple as {+, *, −, /} or may require more complex functions such as sin(X), cos(X), or functions for matrix operations. T may be the integers, reals, matrices, or more complex expressions. The symbols in T must be closed under the functions defined in F.

Next, a population of initial "programs" is generated by randomly selecting elements from the union of sets F and T. For example, if we begin by selecting an element of T, we have a degenerate tree of a single root node. More interestingly, when we start with an element from F, say +, we get a root node of a tree with two potential children. Suppose the initializer next selects * (with two potential children) from F, as the first child, and then terminal 6 from T as the second child. Another random selection might yield the terminal 8, and then the function + from F. Assume it concludes by selecting 5 and 7 from T.

The program we have randomly produced is represented in Figure 12.4. Figure 12.4a gives the tree after the first selection of +, 15.4b after selecting the terminal 6, and 15.4c the final program. A population of similar programs is created to initialize the genetic programming process. Sets of constraints, such as the maximum depth for programs to evolve, can help prune this population. Descriptions of these constraints, as well as different methods for generating initial populations, may be found in Koza (1992).

The discussion to this point addresses the issues of representation (s-expressions) and the set of tree structures necessary to initialize a situation for program evolution. Next, we require a fitness measure for populations of programs. The fitness measure is problem domain dependent and usually consists of a set of tasks the evolved programs must address. The fitness measure itself is a function of how well each program does on these tasks. A simple *raw fitness* score would add the differences between what the program produced and the results that the actual task from the problem domain required. Thus, raw fitness could be seen as the sum of errors across a set of tasks. Other fitness measures are possible, of course. Normalized fitness divides raw fitness by the total sum of possible errors and thus puts all fitness measures within the range of 0 to 1. Normalization can have an advantage when trying to select from a large population of programs. A fitness measure can also include an adjustment for the size of the program, for example, to reward smaller, more parsimonious programs.

Genetic operators on programs include both transformations on a tree itself as well as the exchange of structures between trees. Koza (1992) describes the primary transformations as *reproduction* and *crossover*. Reproduction simply selects programs from the

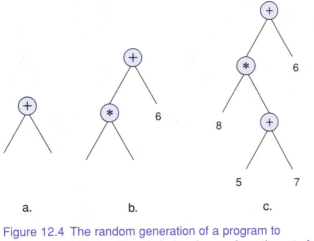

a.   b.   c.

Figure 12.4 The random generation of a program to
            initialize. The circled nodes are from the set of
            functions.

present generation and copies them (unchanged) into the next generation. Crossover exchanges subtrees between the trees representing two programs. For example, suppose we are working with the two parent programs of Figure 12.5, and that the random points indicated by | in parent a and parent b are selected for crossover. The resulting children are shown in Figure 12.6. Crossover can also be used to transform a single parent, by interchanging two subtrees from that parent. Two identical parents can create different children with randomly selected crossover points. The root of a program can also be selected as a crossover point.

There are a number of secondary, and much less used, genetic transforms of program trees. These include *mutation*, which simply introduces random changes in the structures of a program. For example, replacing a terminal value with another value or a function subtree. The *permutation* transform, similar to the inversion operator on strings, also works on single programs, exchanging terminal symbols, or subtrees, for example.

The state of the solution is reflected by the current generation of programs. There is no record keeping for backtrack or any other method for skipping around the fitness landscape. In this aspect genetic programming is much like the hill-climbing algorithm described in Section 4.1. The genetic programming paradigm parallels nature in that the evolution of new programs is a continuing process. Nonetheless, lacking infinite time and computation, termination conditions are set. These are usually a function both of program fitness and computational resources.

The fact that genetic programming is a technique for the computational generation of computer programs places it within the automatic programming research tradition. From the earliest days of AI, researchers have worked to automatically produce computer programs from fragmentary information (Shapiro 1992). Genetic programming can be seen as another tool for this important research domain. We conclude this section with a simple example of genetic programming taken from Mitchell (1996).

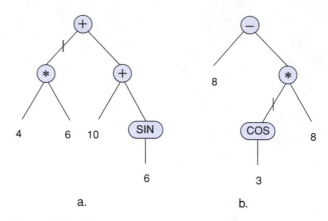

a. b.

Figure 12.5 Two programs, selected on fitness for crossover.
Points | from a and b are randomly selected for
crossover.

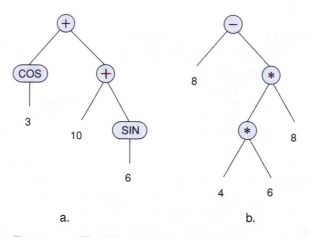

a. b.

Figure 12.6 The child programs produced by crossover of
the points in Figure 12.5.

EXAMPLE 3.2.1: EVOLVING A PROGRAM FOR KEPLER'S THIRD LAW OF PLANETARY
MOTION

Koza (1992) describes many applications of genetic programming to solve interesting
problems, but most of these examples are large and too complex for our present purposes.
Mitchell (1996), however, has created a simple example that illustrates many of the
concepts of genetic programming. Kepler's Third Law of Planetary Motion describes the
functional relationship between the orbital period, P, of a planet and its average distance,
A, from the sun.

The function for Kepler's Third Law, with c a constant is:

$$P^2 = cA^3$$

If we assume that P is expressed in units of earth years, and A is expressed in units of earth's average distance from the sun, then $c = 1$. The s-expression of this relationship is:

P = (sqrt (* A (* A A)))

Thus, the program we want to evolve is represented by the tree structure of Figure 12.7.

The selection of the set of terminal symbols in this example is simple; it is the single real value given by A. The set of functions could be equally simple, say {+, −, *, /, sq, sqrt}. Next we will create a beginning random population of programs. The initial population might include:

(* A (− (* A A) (sqrt A)))   fitness: 1
(/ A (/ (/ A A) (/ A A)))   fitness: 3
(+ A (* (sqrt A) A))   fitness: 0

(We explain the attached fitness measures shortly). As noted earlier in this section this initializing population often has a priori limits both of size and depth, given knowledge of the problem. These three examples are described by the programs trees of Figure 12.8.

Next we determine a suite of tests for the population of programs. Suppose we know some planetary data we want our evolved program to explain. For example, we have the planetary data in Table 12.3, taken from Urey (1952), which gives us a set of data points that our evolving programs must explain.

Planet	A (input)	P (output)
Venus	0.72	0.61
Earth	1.0	1.0
Mars	1.52	1.87
Jupiter	5.2	11.9
Saturn	9.53	29.4
Uranus	19.1	83.5

Table 12.3 A set of fitness cases, with planetary data taken from Urey (1952). A is Earth's semi-major axis of orbit and P is in units of earth-years.

Since the fitness measure is a function of the data points we want to explain, we define fitness as the number of outputs of the program that come within 20 per cent of the correct output values. We use this definition to create the fitness measures of the three programs of Figure 12.8. It remains for the reader to create more members of this initial population, to build crossover and mutation operators that can produce further generations of programs, and to determine termination conditions.

SQRT
*
A
*
A
A

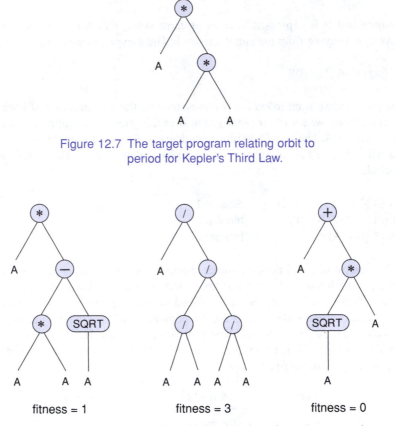

Figure 12.7 The target program relating orbit to period for Kepler's Third Law.

*
A
—
*
SQRT
A
A
A
fitness = 1
/
A
/
/
/
A
A
A
A
fitness = 3
+
A
*
SQRT
A
A
fitness = 0

Figure 12.8 Members from the initial population of programs to solve the orbital period problem.

12.3 Artificial Life and Society-Based Learning

Earlier in this chapter, we described a simplified version of "The Game of Life." This game, most effectively shown in computational visual simulations where succeeding generations rapidly change and evolve on a screen display, has a very simple specification. It was first proposed as a board game by the mathematician John Horton Conway, and made famous through Martin Gardner's discussion of it in *Scientific American* (1970, 1971). The Game of Life is a simple example of a model of computation called *cellular automata* (CA). Cellular automata are families of simple, finite-state machines that exhibit interesting, emergent behaviors through their interactions in a population.

The output of a Finite State Machine, as presented previously in Section 3.1, is a function of its present state and input values. The cellular automata makes the input to the present state a function of its "neighbor" states. Thus, the state at time (t + 1) is a function of its present state and *the state of its neighbors* at time t. It is through these interactions with neighbors that collections of cellular automata achieve much richer behaviors than simple finite state machines. Because the output of all states of a system is a function of their neighboring states, we can describe the evolution of a set of neighboring FSMs as society-based adaptation and learning.

For the societies described in this section, there is no explicit evaluation of the fitness of individual members. Fitness results from interactions in the population, interactions that may lead to the "death" of individual automata. Fitness is implicit in the survival of individuals from generation to generation. Learning among cellular automata is typically unsupervised; as occurs in natural evolution, adaptation is shaped by the actions of other, co-evolving members of the population.

A global, or society-oriented viewpoint also allows an important perspective on learning. We no longer need to focus exclusively on the individual, but can rather see invariances and regularities emerging within the society as a whole. This is an important aspect of the Crutchfield–Mitchell research presented in Section 12.3.2.

Finally, unlike supervised learning, evolution need not be "intentional". That is, the society of agents need not be seen as "going somewhere", say to some "omega" point. We did have a convergence bias when we used the explicit fitness measures in the earlier sections of this chapter. But as Stephen Jay Gould (1977, 1996) points out, evolution need not be viewed as making things "better", rather it just favors survival. The only success is continued existence, and the patterns that emerge are the patterns of a society.

12.3.1   The "Game of Life"

Consider the simple two-dimensional grid or game board of Figure 12.9. Here we have one square occupied, in black, with its eight nearest neighbors indicated by gray shading. The board is transformed over time periods, where the state of each square at time t + 1 is a function of its state and the state of these indicated nearest neighbors at time t. Three simple rules can drive evolution in the game: First, if any square, occupied or not, has

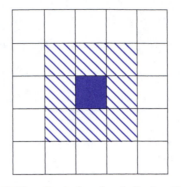

Figure 12.9 The shaded region indicates the set of neighbors for the "game of life."

exactly three of its nearest neighbors occupied, it will be occupied at the next time period. Second, if any occupied square has exactly two of its nearest neighbors occupied, it will be occupied in the next time period. Finally, for all other situations the square will not be occupied at the next time period.

One interpretation of these rules is that, for each generation or time period, life at any location, that is, whether or not the square is occupied and has state value 1, is a result of its own as well as its neighbors' life during the previous generation. Specifically, too dense a population of surrounding neighbors (more than three) or too sparse a neighboring population (less than two) at any time period will not allow life for the next generation.

Consider, for example, the state of life for Figure 12.10a. Here exactly two squares, indicated by an x, have exactly three occupied neighbors. At the next life cycle Figure 12.10b will be produced. Here again there are exactly two squares, indicated by y, with exactly three occupied neighbors. It can be seen that the state of the world will cycle back and forth between Figures 12.10a and 12.10b. The reader can determine what the next state will be for Figures 12.11a and 12.11b and examine other possible "world" configurations. Poundstone (1985) describes the extraordinary variety and richness of the structures that can emerge in the game of life, such as *gliders*, patterns of cells that move across the world through repeated cycles of shape changes.

Because of their ability to produce rich collective behaviors through the interactions of simple cells, cellular automata have proven a powerful tool for studying the mathematics of the emergence of life from simple, inanimate components. *Artificial life* is defined as *life made by human effort rather than by nature*. As can be seen in the previous example, artificial life has a strong "bottom up" flavor; that is, the atoms of a life-system are defined and assembled and their physical interactions "emerge." Regularities of this life form are captured by the rules of the finite state machine.

But how might a-life constructs be used? In biology, for example, the set of living entities provided by nature, as complex and diverse as they may be, are dominated by accident and historical contingency. We trust that there are logical regularities at work in the creation of this set, but there need not be, and it is unlikely that we will discover many of the total possible regularities when we restrict our view to the set of biological entities

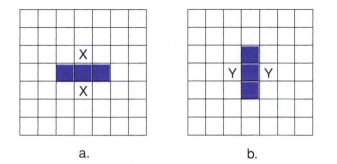

a.   b.

Figure 12.10 A set of neighbors generating the "blinking"
light phenomenon.

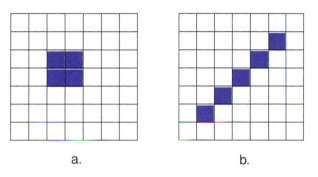

a.   b.

Figure 12.11 What happens to these patterns at the next
time cycle?

that nature actually provides. It is critical to explore the full set of possible biological regularities, some of which may have been eliminated by historical accident. We can always wonder what the present world would be like had not the dinosaurs' existence been peremptorily terminated. To have a theory of the actual, it is necessary to understand the limits of the possible.

Besides the determined effort of anthropologists and other scientists to fill in the gaps in knowledge of our actual evolution, there is continued speculation about rerunning the story of evolution itself. What might happen if evolution started off with different initial conditions? What if there were alternative intervening "accidents" within our physical and biological surroundings? What might emerge? What would remain constant? The evolutionary path that actually did occur on earth is but one of many possible trajectories. Some of these questions might be addressed if we could generate some of the many biologies that are possible.

A-life technology is not just an artifact of computational or biological domains. Research scientists from areas as diverse as chemistry and pharmacology have built synthetic artifacts, many related to the knowledge of actual entities existing in our world. For example, in the field of chemistry, research into the constitution of matter and the many

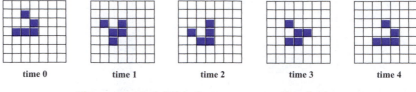

Figure 12.12 A "glider" moves across the display.

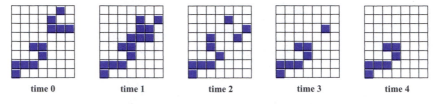

Figure 12.13 A "glider" is "consumed" by another "entity."

compounds that nature provides has led to analysis of these compounds, their constituent pieces, and their bonds. This analysis and recombination has led to the creation of numerous compounds that do not exist naturally. Our knowledge of the building blocks of nature has led us to our own synthetic versions, putting components of reality together in new and different patterns. It is through this careful analysis of natural chemical compounds that we come to some understanding of the set of possible compounds.

One tool for understanding possible worlds is to simulate and analyze society based movement and interaction effects. We have simple examples of this in the Game of Life. The sequence of time cycles demonstrated in Figure 12.12 implements the *glider* that was mentioned earlier. The glider sweeps across the game space by cycling among a small number of patterns. Its action is simple as it moves, in four time periods, to a new location one row further to the left and one row closer to the bottom of the grid.

An interesting aspect of the game of life is that entities such as the glider persist until interacting with other members of their society; what then happens can be difficult to understand and predict. For example, in Figure 12.13, we see the situation where two gliders emerge and engage. After four time periods, the glider moving down and to the left is "consumed" by the other entity. It is interesting to note that our ontological descriptions, that is, our use of terms such as "entity," "blinking light," "glider," "consumed," reflect our own anthropocentric biases on viewing life forms and interactions, whether artificial or not. It is very human of us to give names to regularities as they emerge within our social structures.

12.3.2 Evolutionary Programming

The "Game of Life" is an intuitive, highly descriptive example of cellular automata. We can generalize our discussion of cellular automata by characterizing them as finite state machines. We now discuss societies of linked FSMs and analyze them as emergent entities. This study is sometimes called *evolutionary programming*.

The history of evolutionary programming goes back to the beginning of computers themselves. John von Neumann, in a series of lectures in 1949, explored the question of what level of organizational complexity was required for self-replication to occur (Burks 1970). Burks cites von Neumann's goal as "... not trying to simulate the self-reproduction of a natural system at the level of genetics and biochemistry. He wished to abstract from the natural self-reproduction problem its logical form."

By removing chemical, biological, and mechanical details, von Neumann was able to represent the essential requirements for self-replication. von Neumann went on to design (it was never built) a self-reproducing automaton consisting of a two-dimensional cellular arrangement containing a large number of individual 29-state automata, where the next state for each automaton was a function of its current state and the states of its four immediate neighbors (Burks 1970, 1987).

Interestingly, von Neumann designed his self-replicating automaton, estimated to contain at least 40,000 cells, to have the functionality of a Universal Turing Machine. This universal computation device was also *construction universal*, in the sense that it was capable of reading an input tape, interpreting the data on the tape, and, through use of a construction arm, building the configuration described on the tape in an unoccupied part of the cellular space. By putting a description of the constructing automaton itself on the tape, von Neumann created a self-reproducing automaton (Arbib 1966).

Later Codd (1968) reduced the number of states required for a computationally universal, self-reproducing automaton from 29 to 8, but required an estimated 100,000,000 cells for the full design. Later Devore simplified Codd's machine to occupy only about 87,500 cells. In modern times, Langton created a self-replicating automaton, without computational universality, where each cell had only eight states and occupied just 100 cells (Langton 1986, Hightower 1992, Codd 1992). Current descriptions of these research efforts may be found in the proceedings of the a-life conferences (Langton 1989, Langton et al. 1992).

Thus, the formal analysis of self-replicating machines has deep roots in the theory of computation. Perhaps even more exciting results are implicit in empirical studies of a-life forms. The success of these programs is not indicated by some *a priori* fitness function, but rather by the simple fact that they can survive and replicate. Their mark of success is that they survive. On the darker side, we have experienced the legacy of computer viruses and worms that are able to work their way into foreign hosts, replicate themselves (usually destroying any information in the memory required for replication), and move on to infect yet other foreign hosts.

We conclude this section by discussing two research projects discussed earlier in our book, that of Rodney Brooks at MIT and Nils Nilsson and his students at Stanford. In the earlier presentations, Brooks' work came under the general heading of representation, Section 7.3, and Nilsson's under the topic of planning, Section 8.4.3. In the context of the present chapter, we recast these two earlier presentations in the context of artificial life and emergent phenomena.

Rodney Brooks (1991*a*, *b*) at MIT has built a research program based on the premise of a-life, namely that intelligence emerges through the interactions of a number of simple autonomous agents. Brook's approach, often described as "intelligence without representation" calls for a different approach to the creation of an artificial intelligence. Brooks argues:

> We must incrementally build up the capabilities of intelligent systems, having complete systems at each step of the way and thus automatically ensure that the pieces and their interfaces are valid.

> At each step we should build complete intelligent systems that we let loose in the real world with real sensing and real action. Anything less provides a candidate with which we can delude ourselves.

> We have been following this approach and have built a series of autonomous mobile robots. We have reached an unexpected conclusion:

> On examining very simple levels of intelligence we find that explicit representations and models of the world simply get in the way. It turns out to be better to use the world as its own model.

Brooks built a series of robots able to sense obstacles and move around the offices and hallways at MIT. They are able to wander, explore, and avoid other objects. Each of these entities is based on Brooks notion of a *subsumption architecture*, which "embodies the fundamental ideas of decomposition into layers of task achieving behaviors, and incremental composition through debugging in the real world." The intelligence of this system is an artifact of simple organization and embodied interactions with their environment. Brooks states "We wire finite state machines together into layers of control. Each layer is built on top of existing layers. Lower level layers never rely on the existence of higher level layers." Further references and alternative approaches to this problem include McGonigle (1990, 1998), Brooks (1987, 1991*a*); Lewis and Luger (2000).

Nils Nilsson and his students at Stanford, especially Scott Benson, designed a system for teleo-reactive agent control. In comparison with the efforts of Brooks, Nilsson's research offers a more global agent architecture along with component subsystems that can integrate the functions needed for robust, flexible performance in dynamic environments. These abilities include appropriate reaction to environmental situations based on agent's goals; selective attention to multiple competing goals; planning new action routines when innovation beyond designer-provided routines is necessary; and finally, learning the effects of actions so that the planner can use them to build ever more reliable plans.

Nilsson and his students (Nilsson 1994, Benson 1995, Benson and Nilsson 1995) designed a *teleo-reactive* (T-R) program for agent control, a program that directs an agent towards a goal in a manner that continuously takes into account changing environmental circumstances. This program operates very much with the flavor of a production system (Chapter 6) but also supports *durative action*, or action that takes place across arbitrary time periods, such as *go forward until....* Thus, unlike ordinary production systems, conditions must be continuously evaluated, and the action associated with the current highest true condition is always the one being executed. To summarize:

1. This research supports an architecture for planning that requires stereotypical programs of responses. The architecture also supports planning that allows agents to react appropriately and rapidly to commonly occurring situations (thus *reactive*). The agents' actions are also dynamic and goal-driven (thus *teleo*).

2. The agents must be able to maintain multiple time-varying goals and take actions that correspond to this organization of goals.

3. Since it is impossible to store all possible stereotypical situations, it is important for the agent to dynamically plan sequences of actions, and as environmental situations change, to re-plan as necessary.

4. In conjunction with continuously replanning according to environmental circumstances, it is important for the system to learn. This research, besides allowing the human to occasionally recode T-R programs, incorporates learning and adaptation methods that enable the agent to change its program automatically.

For further detail, the interested reader is directed to Nilsson (1994), Benson (1995), Benson and Nilsson (1995), Klein et al. (2000).

These two research efforts are samples from a very large population of agent-based research projects. These projects are fundamentally experimental. They ask questions of the natural world. The natural world responds with survival and growth for successful algorithms as well as the annihilation of a system incapable of adaptation. We will discuss this issue of artificial intelligence as empirical enquiry in more detail in the Epilogue, Chapter 17.

Finally, we consider research from the Santa Fe Institute: a case study in emergence.

12.3.3 A Case Study in Emergence (Crutchfield and Mitchell 1995)

Crutchfield and Mitchell explore the ability of evolution and interaction within simple systems to create higher-level collective information processing relationships. Their research offers an example of the (evolutionary or genetic algorithm supported) emergence of instances of global computation across a spatial system consisting of distributed and locally interacting cells or processors. The term *emergent computation* describes the appearance of global information processing structures in these systems. The goal of the Crutchfield and Mitchell research is to describe an architecture and mechanisms sufficient to evolve and support methods for emergent computation.

Specifically, a cellular automaton (CA) is made up of a number of individual cells; in fact, there are 149 cells in each automaton of the examples we present. These binary-state cells are distributed across a one-dimensional space with no global coordination. Each cell changes state as a function of its own state and the states of its two immediate neighbors. The CA forms a two-dimensional lattice as it evolves across time periods. The lattice starts out with an initial randomly generated set of N cells. In the example of Figure 12.14, there are 149 cells represented through the first 149 time steps of their evolution. (There is a zero time period and the cells are numbered from 0, 1, ..., 148). Two examples of these cellular automatas' behavior may be seen in the space-time diagrams of Figure 12.14. In these diagrams the ones are given as black cells and the zeros as white cells. Of course, different rules for the cell neighborhoods will produce different patterns in the space-time diagram of the CA.

Next we describe the rule set that determines the activity of the cells that make up each CA. Figure 12.15 presents a one-dimensional binary-state nearest neighbor CA, with $N = 11$ cells. Both the lattice and the rule table for updating the lattice are presented. The lattice is shown changing across one time step. The lattice is actually a cylinder, with the left end and the right end of the lattice at each time period being neighbors (this is important for applying the rule set). The rule table supports the local *majority vote* rule: if a local neighborhood of three cells has a majority of ones, then the center cell becomes a one at the next time step; otherwise, it becomes a zero at the next time step.

Crutchfield and Mitchell want to find a CA that performs the following collective computation, here called *majority wins*: if the initial lattice contains a majority of ones, the CA should evolve across time to all ones; otherwise, it should evolve to all zeros. They use CAs with neighborhoods containing seven cells, a center cell with three neighbors on each side. An interesting aspect of this research is that it is difficult to design a CA rule that performs the majority wins computation. In fact, in Mitchell et al. (1996), they show that the simple seven-neighbor "majority vote" rule does not perform the "majority wins" computation. The GA is used to search for a rule that will.

The genetic algorithm (GA), Section 12.1, is used to create the rule tables for different experiments with the CAs. Specifically, a GA is used to evolve the rules for the

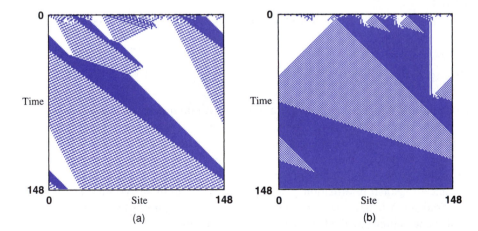

Figure 12.14 Space-time diagrams showing the behavior of two As, discovered by the genetic algorithm on different runs. They employ embedded particles for the nonlocal computation or general emerging patterns seen. Each space-time diagram iterates over a range of time steps, with 1s given as black cells, 0s as white cells; time increases down the page, from Crutchfield and Mitchell (1995).

one-dimensional binary-state cell population that makes up each CA. A fitness function is designed to reward those rules that support the majority wins result for the CA itself. Thus, over time, the GA built a rule set whose fitness was a function of its eventual success in enforcing global majority rules. The fittest rules in the population were selected to survive and randomly combined by crossover to produce offspring, with each offspring subject to a small probability of mutation. This process was iterated for 100 generations, with fitness estimated for a new set of initial cells at each generation. Full details may be found in Crutchfield and Mitchell (1995).

How can we quantify the emergent computation the more successful CAs are supporting? Like many spatially extended natural processes, the cell configurations often organize over time into spatial regions that are dynamically homogenous. Ideally, the analysis and determination of underlying regularities should be an automated process. In fact, Hanson and Crutchfield (1992) have created a language for minimal deterministic finite automaton and use it for describing the attractor-basins within each cellular automaton. This language can be used to describe our example.

Sometimes, as in Figure 12.14a, these regions are obvious to the human viewer as invariant domains, that is, regions in which the same pattern recurs. We will label these domains as Λ values, and then filter out the invariant elements, in order to better describe the interactions or computations effected by the intersections of these domains. Table 12.4 describes three Λ regions: Λ^0, the repeated 0s; Λ^1, the repeated 1s; and Λ^2, the repeated pattern 10001. There are other Λ domains in Figure 12.14a, but we now only discuss this subset.

With the filtering out of invariant elements of the Λ domains, we can see the interactions of these domains. In Table 12.4, we describe the interaction of six Λ areas, for example,

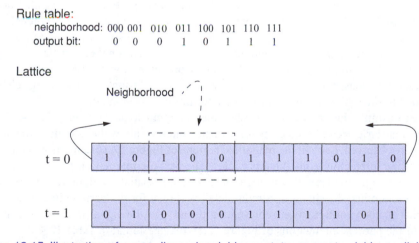

Figure 12.15 Illustration of a one-dimensional, binary-state, nearest-neighbor cellular automaton with N = 11. Both the lattice and the rule table for updating the lattice are illustrated. The lattice configuration is shown over one time step. The cellular automaton is circular in that the two end values are neighbors.

Regular Domains		
$\Lambda^0 = 0^*$	$\Lambda^1 = 1^*$	$\Lambda^2 = (10001)^*$
Particles (Velocities)		
$\alpha \sim \Lambda^1\Lambda^0 \,(1)$		$\beta \sim \Lambda^0\Lambda^1 \,(0)$
$\gamma \sim \Lambda^2\Lambda^0 \,(-2)$		$\delta \sim \Lambda^0\Lambda^2 \,(1/2)$
$\eta \sim \Lambda^2\Lambda^1 \,(4/3)$		$\mu \sim \Lambda^1\Lambda^2 \,(3)$
Interactions		
decay	$\alpha \rightarrow \gamma + \mu$	
react	$\alpha + \delta \rightarrow \mu, \; \eta + \alpha \rightarrow \gamma, \; \mu + \gamma \rightarrow \alpha$	
annihilate	$\eta + \mu \rightarrow \varnothing_1 \,, \gamma + \delta \rightarrow \varnothing_0$	

Table 12.4 Catalog of regular domains, particles (domain boundaries), particle velocities (in parentheses), and particle interactions of the space-time behavior of the CA of Figure 12.14a. The notation $p \sim \Lambda^x\Lambda^y$ means that p is the particle forming the boundary between regular domains Λ^x and Λ^y.

the particles at the frontiers of the Λ^1 and Λ^0 domains. The frontier, where the all 1 domain meets the all 0 domain, is called the *embedded particle* α. Crutchfield and Mitchell claim that the collection of embedded particles is a primary mechanism for carrying information (or signals) over long space-time continua. Logical operations on these particles or signals occur when they collide. Thus the collection of domains, domain walls, particles, and particle interactions for a CA represent the basic information-processing elements embedded in the CA's behavior, that is, the CA's intrinsic computation.

As an example, Figure 12.16 describes the emergent logic of Figure 12.14a. The Λ domain areas have been filtered of their invariant content to allow the domain wall particles to be easily observed. Each of the magnified regions of Figure 12.16 demonstrates the logic of two of the interacting embedded particles. The particle interaction $\alpha + \delta \rightarrow \mu$, shown in the upper right, implements the logic of mapping a spatial configuration representing signals α and δ into the signal μ. Similar detail is shown for the particle interaction $\mu + \gamma \rightarrow \alpha$, that maps a configuration representing μ and γ to the signal α. A more complete listing of the particle interactions of Figure 12.16 may be found in Table 12.4.

To summarize, an important result of the Crutchfield–Mitchell research is the discovery of methods for describing emergent computation within a spatially distributed system consisting of locally interacting cell processors. The locality of communication in the cells imposes a constraint of global communication. The role of the GAs is to discover local cell rules whose effect is to perform information processing over "large" space-time distances.

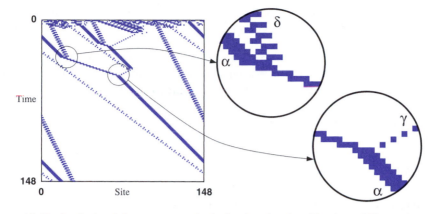

Figure 12.16 Analysis of the emergent logic for density classification of Figure 12.14a. This CA has three domains, six particles, and six particle iterations, as noted in Table 12.3. The domains have been filtered out using an 18-state nonlinear transducer; adapted from Crutchfield and Mitchell (1995).

Crutchfield and Mitchell have used ideas adopted from formal language theory to characterize these space-time patterns.

For Crutchfield and Mitchell, the result of the evolving automaton reflects an entirely new level of behavior that is distinct from the lower-level interactions of the distributed cells. Global particle-based interactions demonstrate how complex coordination can emerge within a collection of simple individual actions. The result of the GA operating on local cell rules showed how an evolutionary process, by taking advantage of certain non-linear pattern-forming actions of cells, produced a new level of behavior and the delicate balance necessary for effective emergent computation.

The results of the Crutchfield–Mitchell research are important in that they have, with GA support, demonstrated the emergence of higher-level invariances within a cellular automaton. Furthermore, they present computational tools, adapted from formal language theory, that can be used to describe these invariances. Continued research has the potential to elucidate the emergence of complexity: the defining characteristic of living things, and fundamental to understanding the origins of minds, species, and ecosystems.

12.4 Epilogue and References

Research on genetic algorithms and biology-based learning began with John Holland's design of genetic algorithms. His early research includes *Adaptation in Natural and Artificial Systems* (1975), a study on emergent phenomena in self-replicating systems (1976), and *Escaping Brittleness: The possibilities of general purpose learning algorithms applied to parallel rule-based systems* (1986), introducing *classifiers*. Some examples of work on the analysis of genetic systems can be found in Forrest and Mitchell (Forrest 1990,

Mitchell 1996, Forrest and Mitchell 1993*a*, 1993*b*). Other researchers, especially Goldberg (1989), Mitchell (1996), and Koza (1992, 1994) have continued the formal analysis of genetic algorithms and learning.

As noted above, Holland (1986) was also responsible for the original design of classifier systems. Classifiers create a macro or complete-system viewpoint of learning. Another similar view is represented by the SOAR project (Laird et al. 1986a, 1986b; Rosenbloom and Newell 1987; Rosenbloom et al. 1993).

John Koza is the primary designer of the genetic programming research area. His major contributions are described in: *Genetic Programming: On the programming of computers by means of natural selection* (1992) and *Genetic Programming II: Automatic discovery of reusable programs* (1994). The example of using genetic programs to learn Kepler's Third Law, Section 12.2.2, was suggested by Mitchell (1996).

The Game of Life was originally presented by the mathematician John Horton Conway, but made famous by Martin Gardner's discussion of it in *Scientific American* (1970, 1971). Research in the computational power of finite state machines goes back to the design of the first digital computers. John von Neumann was very active in this research, and in fact was the first to show that the FSM had the computational power of Turing's Universal Machine. Most of von Neumann's early research is presented in the writings of Arthur Burks (1966, 1970, 1987). Other researchers (Hightower 1992, Koza 1992) describe how a-life research evolved from this early work on FSMs. Other researchers in artificial life include Langton (1986) and Ackley and Littmann (1992). Proceedings of the early a-life conferences were edited by Langton (1989, 1990).

Dennett, *Darwin's Dangerous Ideas* (1995), and other philosophers have addressed the importance of evolutionary concepts in philosophical thinking. We also recommend *Full House: The Spread of Excellence from Plato to Darwin* (Gould 1996).

Besides the brief descriptions of agent research in Section 12.3 (Brooks 1986, 1987, 1991*a*, 1991*b*; Nilsson 1994; Benson and Nilsson 1995), there are many other projects in this domain, including Maes (1989, 1990) model of spreading activation in behavior networks, and the extension of the blackboard architecture by Hayes-Roth et al. (1993).The proceedings of the AAAI and IJCAI contain multiple articles from this important research domain. Crutchfield and Mitchell (1995) supported our presentation of Section 12.3.3.

12.5 Exercises

1. The genetic algorithm is intended to support the search for genetic diversity along with the survival of important skills (represented by genetic patterns) for a problem domain. Describe how different genetic operators can simultaneously support both these goals.

2. Discuss the problem of designing representations for genetic operators to search for solutions in different domains? What is the role of *inductive bias* here?

3. Consider the CNF-satisfaction problem of Section 12.1.1. How does the role of the number of disjuncts in the CNF expression bias the solution space? Consider other possible representations and genetic operators for the CNF-satisfaction problem. Can you design another fitness measure?

4. Build a genetic algorithm to solve the CNF-satisfaction problem.

5. Consider the traveling salesperson problem of Section 12.1.1. Discuss the problem of selecting an appropriate representation for this problem. Design other appropriate genetic operators and fitness measures for this problem.

6. Build a genetic algorithm to search for a solution for the traveling salesperson problem.

7. Discuss the role of representational techniques such as gray coding for shaping the search space for the genetic algorithm. Discuss two other problem domains where similar techniques will be important.

8. Read Holland's Schema Theorem (Mitchell 1996, Koza 1992). How does Holland's schema theory describe the evolution of the GA solution space? What does it have to say about problems not encoded as bit strings?

9. How does the Bucket Brigade Algorithm (Holland 1986) relate to the backpropagation algorithm (Section 14.3)?

10. Write a program to solve Kepler's Third Law of Motion Problem, described with a preliminary representation offered in Section 12.2.2.

11. Discuss the constraints (presented in Section 12.2.2) on using genetic programming techniques to solve problems. For example, what components of a solution cannot be evolved within the genetic programming paradigm?

12. Read the early discussion of the Game of Life in Gardner's column of *Scientific American* (1970, 1971). Discuss other a-life structures, similar to the *glider*, presented in Section 12.3.1.

13. Write an a-life program that implements the functionality of Figures 12.10–12.13.

14. The area of agent-based research was introduced in Section 12.3. We recommend further reading on any of the projects mentioned, but especially the Brooks, Nilsson and Benson, or Crutchfield and Mitchell research. Write a short paper on one of these topics.

15. Discuss the role of inductive bias in the representations, search strategies, and operators used in the models of learning presented in Chapter 12. Is this issue resolvable? That is, does the genetic model of learning work solely because of its representational assumptions or can it be translated into broader domains?

16. For further insights into evolution and the emergence of complexity, read and discuss *Darwin's Dangerous Idea* (Dennett 1995) or *Full House: The Spread of Excellence from Plato to Darwin* (Gould 1996).

ADVANCED TOPICS FOR AI PROBLEM SOLVING

Precision is not truth . . .

—HENRI MATISSE

Time present and time past
are both perhaps present in time future
and time future is contained in time past . . .

—T. S. ELIOT, "Burnt Norton"

. . . each larger pattern comes into being as the end product of a long sequence of tiny acts.

—CHRISTOPHER ALEXANDER

Automated Reasoning and Natural Language

Part V examines two important artificial intelligence applications: natural language understanding and automated reasoning. If we are ever to make claims of creating an artificial intelligence, we must address language, reasoning, and learning. Our solutions to these problems build on the tools and techniques introduced in the earlier sections of this book. Also, because of their importance, these problems have exerted a profound influence on the development of those tools and the overall direction of AI itself.

In the introduction to Part III we discussed the pluses and minuses of weak method problem solvers. The problems of using weak methods include the complexity of search spaces and the difficulties of representing specific knowledge of the world with general representations. In spite of the successes of expert systems and similar strong method solvers, many domains require general methods; in fact, the control strategies of expert systems themselves depend on good weak problem-solving methods. Much promising work on weak method problem solvers continues to be done by the *automated reasoning* or *theorem proving* community. These techniques have found application in a number of important areas including integrated circuit design and verification, proofs of program correctness, and indirectly, the creation of the PROLOG programming language. In Chapter 13 we address issues surrounding automated reasoning.

There are many reasons why *natural language understanding* has proven a difficult task for the AI community. Among the most important are the amounts of knowledge, ability, and experience required to support language use. Successful language comprehension requires an understanding of the natural world, human psychology, and social convention. It draws on skills as varied as logical reasoning and metaphor interpretation. Because of the complexity and ambiguity of human language, natural language understanding has motivated much of the research in knowledge representation. To date, these efforts have been only partly successful: using a knowledge-based approach, researchers have successfully developed programs that understand natural language in specific domains. Whether these techniques will eventually solve the language understanding problem itself continues to be a subject of debate.

The representational techniques presented in Chapter 7, such as semantic networks, scripts, and frames, have dominated work in natural language. More recently, the correlational analysis of language patterns has played a role in language understanding. Language utterances are not random creations of sounds or words, but happen in patterns. Bayesian techniques can model these language constructs. In Chapter 14 we examine syntactic, semantic, and stochastic techniques for natural language understanding.

With the advent of the World Wide Web and the extensive use of search engines by the general population, issues in natural language processing are even more important. *Text mining*, or the general search for useful information in unstructured text and *information summarization*, or the ability to "understand" text and extract its critical issues are important new technologies. The foundations for these software tools, symbol-based and stochastic pattern recognition, are presented in Chapter 14.

Finally, we build many of the data structures supporting natural language understanding in Part VI, including semantic net and frame systems in Sections 15.7 and 16.11 and a recursive descent semantic net parser in Section 15.9. We discuss some current limitations in understanding language, learning, and complex problem solving in Chapter 17.

13

AUTOMATED
REASONING

*For how is it possible, says that acute man, that when a concept is given me, I can go
beyond it and connect with it another which is not contained in it, in such a manner as if
the latter necessarily belonged to the former?*

—IMMANUEL KANT, "Prolegomena to a Future Metaphysics"

*Any rational decision may be viewed as a conclusion reached from certain premises. . . .
The behavior of a rational person can be controlled, therefore, if the value and factual
premises upon which he bases his decisions are specified for him.*

—SIMON, *Decision-Making and Administrative Organization*, 1944

Reasoning is an art and not a science. . . .

—WOS ET AL., *Automated Reasoning*, 1984

13.0 Introduction to Weak Methods
in Theorem Proving

Wos et al. (1984) describe an *automated reasoning* program as one that "employs an
unambiguous and exacting notation for representing information, precise inference rules
for drawing conclusions, and carefully delineated strategies to control those inference
rules." They add that applying strategies to inference rules to deduce new information is
an art: "A good choice for representation includes a notation that increases the chance for
solving a problem and includes information that, though not necessary, is helpful. A good
choice of inference rules is one that meshes well with the chosen representation. A good
choice for strategies is one that controls the inference rules in a manner that sharply
increases the effectiveness of the reasoning program."

Automated reasoning, as just described, uses weak problem-solving methods. It uses a uniform representation such as the first-order predicate calculus (Chapter 2), the Horn clause calculus (Section 13.3), or the clause form used for resolution (Section 13.2). Its inference rules are sound and, whenever possible, complete. It uses general strategies such as breadth-first, depth-first, or best-first search and, as we see in this chapter, heuristics such as *set of support* and *unit preference* to combat the combinatorics of exhaustive search. The design of search strategies, and especially heuristic search strategies, is very much an art; we cannot guarantee that they will find a useful solution to a problem using reasonable amounts of time and memory.

Weak method problem solving is an important tool in its own right as well as an essential basis for strong method problem solving. Production systems and rule-based expert system shells are both examples of weak method problem solvers. Even though the rules of the production system or rule-based expert system encode strong problem-solving heuristics, their application is supported by general (weak method) inference strategies.

Techniques for weak method problem solving have been the focus of AI research from its beginning. Often these techniques come under the heading of *theorem proving*, although we prefer the more generic title *automated reasoning*. We begin this chapter (Section 13.1) with an early example of automated reasoning, the *General Problem Solver*, and its use of *means–ends analysis* and *difference tables* to control search.

In Section 13.2 we present an important product of research in automated reasoning, the *resolution theorem prover*. We discuss the representation language, the resolution inference rule, the search strategies, and the answer extraction processes used in resolution theorem proving. As an example of Horn clause reasoning, in Section 13.3 we describe the inference engine for PROLOG, and show how that language contributes to a philosophy of declarative programming with an interpreter based on a resolution theorem prover. We conclude this chapter (Section 13.4) with some brief comments on *natural deduction*, equality handling, and more sophisticated inference rules.

13.1 The General Problem Solver and Difference Tables

The *General Problem Solver (GPS)* (Newell and Simon 1963b; Ernst and Newell 1969) came out of research by Allen Newell and Herbert Simon at Carnegie Mellon University, then Carnegie Institute of Technology. Its roots are in an earlier computer program called the *Logic Theorist (LT)* of Newell, Shaw, and Simon (Newell and Simon 1963a). The LT program proved many of the theorems in Russell and Whitehead's *Principia Mathematica* (Whitehead and Russell 1950).

As with all weak method problem solvers, the Logic Theorist employed a uniform representation medium and sound inference rules and adopted several strategies or heuristic methods to guide the solution process. The Logic Theorist used the propositional calculus (Section 2.1) as its representation medium. The inference rules were *substitution*, *replacement*, and *detachment*.

Substitution allows any expression to be substituted for every occurrence of a symbol in a proposition that is an axiom or theorem already known to be true. For instance, (B ∨ B) → B may have the expression ¬ A substituted for B to produce (¬ A ∨ ¬ A) → ¬ A.

Replacement allows a connective to be replaced by its definition or an equivalent form. For example, the logical equivalence of ¬ A ∨ B and A → B can lead to the replacement of (¬ A ∨ ¬ A) with (A → ¬ A).

Detachment is the inference rule we called modus ponens (Chapter 2).

The LT applies these inference rules in a breadth-first, goal-driven fashion to the theorem to be proved, attempting to find a series of operations that lead to axioms or theorems known to be true. The strategy of LT consists of four methods organized in an *executive routine*:

First, the substitution method is directly applied to the current goal, attempting to match it against all known axioms and theorems.

Second, if this fails to lead to a proof, all possible detachments and replacements are applied to the goal and each of these results is tested for success using substitution. If substitution fails to match any of these with the goal, then they are added to a *subproblem list*.

Third, the chaining method, employing the transitivity of implication, is used to find a new subproblem that, if solved, would provide a proof. Thus, if a → c is the problem and b → c is found, then a → b is set up as a new subproblem.

Fourth, if the first three methods fail on the original problem, go to the subproblem list and select the next untried subproblem.

The executive routine continues to apply these four methods until either the solution is found, no more problems remain on the subproblem list, or the memory and time allotted to finding the proof are exhausted. In this fashion, the logic theorist executes a goal-driven, breadth-first search of the problem space.

Part of the executive routine that enables the substitution, replacement, and detachment inference rules is the *matching process*. Suppose we wish to prove p → (q → p). The matching process first identifies one of the axioms, p → (q ∨ p), as more appropriate than the others—that is, more nearly matching in terms of a domain-defined difference—because the main connective, here →, is the same in both expressions. Second, the matching process confirms that the expressions to the left of the main connective are identical. Finally, matching identifies the difference between expressions to the right of the main connective. This final difference, between → and ∨, suggests the obvious replacement for proving the theorem. The matching process helps control the (exhaustive) search that would be necessary for applying all substitutions, replacements, and detachments. In fact, the matching eliminated enough of the trial and error to make the LT into a successful problem solver.

A sample LT proof shows the power of the matching process. Theorem 2.02 of *Principia Mathematica* is p → (q → p). Matching finds the axiom p → (q ∨ p) as appropriate for replacement. Substitution of ¬ q for q proves the theorem. Matching, controlling substitution, and replacement rules proved this theorem directly without any search through other axioms or theorems.

In another example, suppose we wish LT to prove:

$(p \rightarrow \neg p) \rightarrow \neg p$.

1.	$(A \vee A) \rightarrow A$	Matching identifies "best" axiom of five available.
2.	$(\neg A \vee \neg A) \rightarrow \neg A$	Substitution of $\neg A$ for A in order to apply
3.	$(A \rightarrow \neg A) \rightarrow \neg A$	replacement of $\rightarrow$ for $\vee$ and $\neg$,
4.	$(p \rightarrow \neg p) \rightarrow \neg p$	substitution of p for A.
QED		

The original LT proved this theorem in about 10 seconds using five axioms. The actual proof took two steps and required no search. Matching selected the appropriate axiom for the first step because its form was much like the conclusion it was trying to establish: (expression) $\rightarrow$ proposition. Then $\neg A$ was substituted for A. This allowed the replacement of the second and final step, which was itself motivated by the goal requiring a $\rightarrow$ rather than a $\vee$.

The Logic Theorist not only was the first example of an automated reasoning system but also demonstrated the importance of search strategies and heuristics in a reasoning program. In many instances LT found solutions in a few steps that exhaustive search might never find. Some theorems were not solvable by the LT, and Newell et al. pointed out improvements that might make their solution possible.

At about this time, researchers at Carnegie and others at Yale (Moore and Anderson 1954) began to examine think-aloud protocols of human subjects solving logic problems. Although their primary goal was to identify human processes that could solve this class of problem, researchers began to compare human problem solving with computer programs, such as the Logic Theorist. This was to become the first instance of what is now referred to as *information processing psychology*, where an explanation of the observed behavior of an organism is provided by a program of primitive information processes that generates that behavior (Newell et al. 1958). This research was also some of the first work that founded the modern discipline of *Cognitive Science* (see Section 16.2, Luger 1994).

Closer scrutiny of these first protocols showed many ways that LT's solutions differed from those of the human subjects. The human behavior showed strong evidence of a matching and difference reduction mechanism referred to as a *means–ends analysis*. In means–ends analysis the difference reduction methods (the *means*) were strongly linked to the specific differences to be reduced (the *ends*): the operators for difference reduction were indexed by the differences they could reduce.

In a very simple example, if the start statement was $p \rightarrow q$ and the goal was $\neg p \vee q$, the differences would include the $\rightarrow$ symbol in the start and $\vee$ in the goal (as well as the difference of p in the start and $\neg p$ in the goal). The difference table would contain the different ways that a $\rightarrow$ could be replaced by a $\vee$ and that $\neg$ could be removed. These transformations would be attempted one at a time until the differences were removed and the theorem was proven.

In most interesting problems the differences between start and goal could not be directly reduced. In this case an operator (from the table) was sought to partially reduce the difference. The entire procedure was applied recursively to these results until no differences existed. This might also require following different search paths, represented by different applications of reductions.

Figure 13.1a, from Newell and Simon (1963b), presents twelve transformation rules, the middle column, for solving logic problems. The right column gives directives as to when the transformations are to be used.

R 1.	$A \cdot B \to B \cdot A$ $A \lor B \to B \lor A$	Applies to main expression only.
R 2.	$A \supset B \to \sim B \supset \sim A$	Applies to main expression only.
R 3.	$A \cdot A \leftrightarrow A$ $A \lor A \leftrightarrow A$	A and B are two main expressions.
R 4.	$A \cdot (B \cdot C) \leftrightarrow (A \cdot B) \cdot C$ $A \lor (B \lor C) \leftrightarrow (A \lor B) \lor C$	A and $A \supset B$ are two main expressions.
R 5.	$A \lor B \leftrightarrow \sim(\sim A \cdot \sim B)$	$A \supset B$ and $B \supset C$ are two main expressions.
R 6.	$A \supset B \leftrightarrow \sim A \lor B$	
R 7.	$A \cdot (B \lor C) \leftrightarrow (A \cdot B) \lor (A \cdot C)$ $A \lor (B \cdot C) \leftrightarrow (A \lor B) \cdot (A \lor C)$	
R 8.	$A \cdot B \to A$ $A \cdot B \to B$	Applies to main expression only.
R 9.	$A \to A \lor X$	Applies to main expression only.
R 10.	$\left.\begin{array}{l}A \\ B\end{array}\right\} \to A \cdot B$	A and B are two main expressions.
R 11.	$\left.\begin{array}{l}A \\ A \supset B\end{array}\right\} \to B$	A and $A \supset B$ are two main expressions.
R 12.	$\left.\begin{array}{l}A \supset B \\ B \supset C\end{array}\right\} \to A \supset C$	$A \supset B$ and $B \supset C$ are two main expressions.

Figure 13.1a Transformation rules for logic problems, from Newell and Simon (1961).

1.	$(R \supset \sim P) \cdot (\sim R \supset Q)$	$\sim (\sim Q \cdot P)$
2.	$(\sim R \vee \sim P) \cdot (R \vee Q)$	Rule *6* applied to left and right of 1.
3.	$(\sim R \vee \sim P) \cdot (\sim R \supset Q)$	Rule *6* applied to left of 1.
4.	$R \supset \sim P$	Rule *8* applied to 1.
5.	$\sim R \vee \sim P$	Rule *6* applied to 4.
6.	$\sim R \supset Q$	Rule *8* applied to 1.
7.	$R \vee Q$	Rule *6* applied to 6.
8.	$(\sim R \vee \sim P) \cdot (R \vee Q)$	Rule *10* applied to 5. and 7.
9.	$P \supset \sim R$	Rule *2* applied to 4.
10.	$\sim Q \supset R$	Rule *2* applied to 6.
11.	$P \supset Q$	Rule *12* applied to 6. and 9.
12.	$\sim P \vee Q$	Rule *6* applied to 11.
13.	$\sim (P \cdot \sim Q)$	Rule *5* applied to 12.
14.	$\sim (\sim Q \cdot P)$	Rule *1* applied to 13. QED.

Figure 13.1b A proof of a theorem in propositional calculus, from Newell and Simon (1961).

Figure 13.1b presents a proof, from Newell and Simon (1963*b*), generated by a human subject. Before the proof, the transformation rules of Figure 13.1a are available to the subject, who, without experience in formal logic, is asked to change the expression $(R \supset \neg P) \bullet (\neg R \supset Q)$ to $\neg (\neg Q \bullet P)$. In the notation of Chapter 2 $\sim$ is $\neg$, $\bullet$ is $\wedge$, and $\supset$ is $\rightarrow$. The $\rightarrow$ or $\leftrightarrow$ in Figure 13.1a indicates a legal replacement. The rightmost column of Figure 13.1b indicates the rule of Figure 13.1a that is applied at each step of the proof.

Newell and Simon (1963*b*) called the problem-solving strategies of the human subject *difference reduction* and the general process of using transformations appropriate for reducing specific problem differences *means–ends analysis*. The algorithm for applying means–ends analysis using difference reductions is the *General Problem Solver (GPS)*.

Figure 13.2 presents the control diagram and the table of connections for GPS. The goal is to transform expression A into expression B. The first step is to locate a difference D between A and B. The subgoal, reduce D, is identified in the second box of the first line; the third box indicates that difference reduction is recursive. The "reduction" is the second line, where an operator Q is identified for the difference D. Actually, a list of operators is identified from the table of connections. This list provides ordered alternatives for difference reduction should the chosen operator not be acceptable, for example, by not

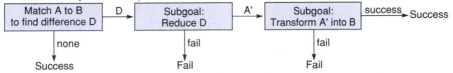

Goal: Transform object A into object B

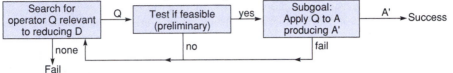

Goal: Reduce difference D between object A and object B

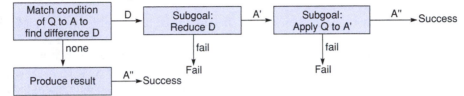

Goal: Apply operator Q to object A

For the logic task of the text:

Feasibility test (preliminary)
Is the mean connective the same (e.g., A•B → B fails against P∨Q)?
Is the operator too big (e.g., (A∨B)•(A∨C)→A∨(B•C) fails against P•Q)?
Is the operator too easy (e.g., A→A•A applies to anything)?
Are the side conditions satisfied (e.g., R8 applies only to main expressions)?

Table of connections

	R1	R2	R3	R4	R5	R6	R7	R8	R9	R10	R11	R12
Add terms			X				X		X	X	X	X
Delete terms			X				X	X		X	X	
Change connective					X	X	X					
Change sign					X							
Change lower sign		X			X	X						
Change grouping				X			X					
Change position	X	X										

X means some variant of the rule is relevant. GPS will pick the appropriate variant.

Figure 13.2 Flow chart and difference reduction table for the General Problem Solver, from Newell and Simon (1963b).

passing the *feasibility test*. In the third line of Figure 13.2 the operator is applied and D is reduced.

The GPS model of problem solving requires two components. The first is the general procedure just described for comparing two state descriptions and reducing their differences. The second component of GPS is the *table of connections*, giving the links between problem differences and the specific transformations that reduce them, appropriate to an application area. Figure 13.2, gives differences and their reductions (the twelve transformations from Figure 13.1a) for propositional calculus expressions. Other tables of connections could be for reducing differences in algebraic forms, or for tasks such as Towers of Hanoi, or for more complex games such as chess. A number of the different application areas of the GPS technique are described by Ernst and Newell (1969).

The structuring of the difference reductions of a problem domain helps organize the search for that domain. A heuristic or priority order for reduction of different difference classes is implicit in the order of the transformations within the difference reduction table. This priority order might put the more generally applicable transformations before the specialized ones or give whatever order some domain expert might deem most appropriate.

A number of research directions evolved from work in the General Problem Solver. One of these is the use of AI techniques to analyze human problem-solving behavior. In particular, the production system replaced the means–ends methods of GPS as the preferred form for modeling human information processing (Chapter 17). The production rules in modern rule-based expert systems replaced the specific entries in GPS's table of differences (Chapter 8).

In another interesting evolution of GPS, the difference table itself evolved in a further fashion, becoming the *operator table* for *planning* such as STRIPS and ABSTRIPS. Planning is important in robot problem solving. To accomplish a task, such as to go to the next room and bring back an object, the computer must develop a *plan*. This plan orchestrates the actions of the robot: put down anything it is now holding, go to the door of the present room, go through the door, find the required room, go through the door, go over to the object, and so on. Plan formation for STRIPS, the Stanford Research Institute Problem Solver (Fikes and Nilsson 1971, Fikes et al. 1972, Sacerdotti 1974) uses an operator table not unlike the GPS table of differences. Each operator (primitive act of the robot) in this table has an attached set of *preconditions* that are much like the feasibility tests of Figure 13.2. The operator table also contains *add* and *delete* lists, which update the model of the "world" once the operator is applied. We presented a STRIPS-like planner in Section 8.4. and then build it in PROLOG in Section 15.5.

To summarize, the first models of automated reasoning in AI are found in the Logic Theorist and General Problem Solver developed at Carnegie Institute. Already these programs offered the full prerequisites for weak method problem solving: a uniform representation medium, a set of sound inference rules, and a set of methods or strategies for applying these rules. The same components make up the *resolution proof procedures*, a modern and more powerful basis for automated reasoning.

13.2 Resolution Theorem Proving

13.2.1 Introduction

Resolution is a technique for proving theorems in the propositional or predicate calculus that has been a part of AI problem-solving research from the mid-1960s (Bledsoe 1977, Robinson 1965, Kowalski 1979b). Resolution is a sound inference rule that, when used to produce a *refutation* (Section 13.2.3), is also complete. In an important practical application, resolution theorem proving, particularly the resolution refutation system, has made the current generation of PROLOG interpreters possible (Section 13.3).

The resolution principle, introduced in an important paper by Robinson (1965), describes a way of finding contradictions in a database of clauses with minimum use of substitution. Resolution refutation proves a theorem by negating the statement to be proved and adding this negated goal to the set of axioms that are known (have been assumed) to be true. It then uses the resolution rule of inference to show that this leads to a contradiction. Once the theorem prover shows that the negated goal is inconsistent with the given set of axioms, it follows that the original goal must be consistent. This proves the theorem.

Resolution refutation proofs involve the following steps:

1. Put the premises or axioms into *clause form* (13.2.2).

2. Add the negation of what is to be proved, in clause form, to the set of axioms.

3. *Resolve* these clauses together, producing new clauses that logically follow from them (13.2.3).

4. Produce a contradiction by generating the empty clause.

5. The substitutions used to produce the empty clause are those under which the opposite of the negated goal is true (13.2.4).

Resolution is a sound inference rule in the sense of Chapter 2. However, it is not complete. Resolution is *refutation complete*; that is, the empty or null clause can always be generated whenever a contradiction in the set of clauses exists. More is said on this topic when we present strategies for refutation in Section 13.2.4.

Resolution refutation proofs require that the axioms and the negation of the goal be placed in a normal form called *clause form*. Clause form represents the logical database as a set of disjunctions of *literals*. A literal is an atomic expression or the negation of an atomic expression.

The most common form of resolution, called *binary resolution*, is applied to two clauses when one contains a literal and the other its negation. If these literals contain variables, the literals must be unified to make them equivalent. A new clause is then produced consisting of the disjuncts of all the predicates in the two clauses minus the literal and its negative instance, which are said to have been "resolved away." The resulting clause receives the unification substitution under which the predicate and its negation are found as "equivalent."

Before this is made more precise in the subsequent subsections, we take a simple example. Resolution produces a proof similar to one produced already with modus ponens. This is not intended to show that these inference rules are equivalent (resolution is actually more general than modus ponens) but to give the reader a feel for the process.

We wish to prove that "Fido will die" from the statements that "Fido is a dog" and "all dogs are animals" and "all animals will die." Changing these three premises to predicates and applying modus ponens gives:

1. All dogs are animals: $\forall(X)$ (dog (X) $\rightarrow$ animal (X)).

2. Fido is a dog: dog (fido).

3. Modus ponens and {fido/X} gives: animal (fido).

4. All animals will die: $\forall(Y)$ (animal (Y) $\rightarrow$ die (Y)).

5. Modus ponens and {fido/Y} gives: die (fido).

Equivalent reasoning by resolution converts these predicates to clause form:

PREDICATE FORM	CLAUSE FORM
1. $\forall(X)$ (dog) (X) $\rightarrow$ animal (X))	$\neg$ dog (X) $\vee$ animal (X)
2. dog (fido)	dog (fido)
3. $\forall(Y)$ (animal (Y) $\rightarrow$ die (Y))	$\neg$ animal (Y) $\vee$ die (Y)

Next, we negate the conclusion that Fido will die:

4. $\neg$ die (fido) $\neg$ die (fido)

Finally, we resolve clauses having opposite literals to produce new clauses by resolution as in Figure 13.3. This process is often called *clashing*.

The symbol □ in Figure 13.3 indicates that the empty clause is produced and the contradiction found. The □ symbolizes the clashing of a predicate and its negation: the situation where two mutually contradictory statements are present in the clause space. These are clashed to produce the empty clause. The sequence of substitutions (unifications) used to make predicates equivalent also gives us the value of variables under which a goal is true. For example, had we asked whether something would die, our negated goal would have been $\neg$ ($\exists$ (Z) die (Z)), rather than $\neg$ die(fido). The substitution {fido/Z} in Figure 13.3 would determine that fido is an instance of an animal that will die. The issues implicit in this example are made clear in the remainder of Section 13.2.

13.2.2   Producing the Clause Form for Resolution Refutations

The resolution proof procedure requires all statements in the database describing a situation to be converted to a standard form called *clause* form. This is motivated by the fact that resolution is an operator on pairs of disjuncts to produce new disjuncts. The form the database takes is referred to as a *conjunction of disjuncts*. It is a *conjunction* because all the clauses that make up the database are assumed to be true at the same time. It is a *disjunction* in that each of the individual clauses is expressed with disjunction (or $\vee$) as the connective. Thus the entire database of Figure 13.3 may be represented in clause form as:

($\neg$ dog (X) $\vee$ animal (X)) $\wedge$ ($\neg$ animal (Y) $\vee$ die (Y)) $\wedge$ (dog (fido)).

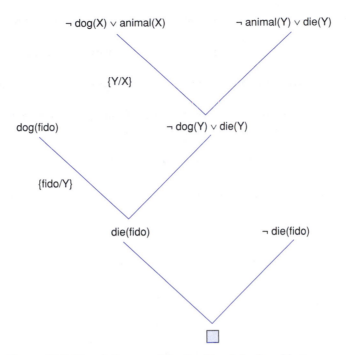

Figure 13.3 Resolution proof for the "dead dog" problem.

To this expression we add (by conjunction) the negation of what we wish to prove, in this case ¬ die(fido). Generally, the database is written as a set of disjunctions and the ∧ operators are omitted.

We now present an algorithm, consisting of a sequence of transformations, for reducing any set of predicate calculus statements to clause form. It has been shown (Chang and Lee 1973) that these transformations may be used to reduce any set of predicate calculus expressions to a set of clauses that are inconsistent if and only if the original set of expressions is inconsistent. The clause form will not be strictly equivalent to the original set of predicate calculus expressions in that certain interpretations may be lost. This occurs because skolemization restricts the possible substitutions for existentially quantified variables (Chang and Lee 1973). It will, however, preserve unsatisfiability. That is, if there was a contradiction (a refutation) within the original set of predicate calculus expressions, a contradiction exists in the clause form. The transformations do not sacrifice completeness for refutation proofs.

We demonstrate this process of conjunctive normal form reduction through an example and give a brief description rationalizing each step. These are not intended to be proofs of the equivalence of these transformations across all predicate calculus expressions.

In the following expression, according to the conventions of Chapter 2, uppercase letters indicate variables (W, X, Y, and Z); lowercase letters in the middle of the alphabet indicate constants or bound variables (l, m, and n); and early alphabetic lowercase letters indicate the predicate names (a, b, c, d, and e). To improve readability of the expressions, we use two types of brackets: ( ) and [ ], and remove redundant brackets. As an example, consider the following expression, where X, Y, and Z are variables and I a constant:

(i) $(\forall X)([a(X) \land b(X)] \rightarrow [c(X,I) \land (\exists Y)((\exists Z)[c(Y,Z)] \rightarrow d(X,Y))]) \lor (\forall X)(e(X))$

1. First we eliminate the $\rightarrow$ by using the equivalent form proved in Chapter 2: $a \rightarrow b \equiv \neg a \lor b$. This transformation reduces the expression in (i) above:

(ii) $(\forall X)(\neg [a(X) \land b(X)] \lor [c(X,I) \land (\exists Y)((\exists Z)[\neg c(Y,Z)] \lor d(X,Y))]) \lor (\forall X)(e(X))$

2. Next we reduce the scope of negation. This may be accomplished using a number of the transformations of Chapter 2. These include:

$\neg (\neg a) \equiv a$

$\neg (\exists X) a(X) \equiv (\forall X) \neg a(X)$

$\neg (\forall X) b(X) \equiv (\exists X) \neg b(X)$

$\neg (a \land b) \equiv \neg a \lor \neg b$

$\neg (a \lor b) \equiv \neg a \land \neg b$

Using the fourth equivalences (ii) becomes:

(iii) $(\forall X)([\neg a(X) \lor \neg b(X)] \lor [c(X,I) \land (\exists Y)((\exists Z)[\neg c(Y,Z)] \lor d(X,Y))]) \lor (\forall X)(e(X))$

3. Next we standardize by renaming all variables so that variables bound by different quantifiers have unique names. As indicated in Chapter 2, because variable names are "dummies" or "place holders," the particular name chosen for a variable does not affect either the truth value or the generality of the clause. Transformations used at this step are of the form:

$((\forall X)a(X) \lor (\forall X)b(X)) \equiv (\forall X)a(X) \lor (\forall Y)b(Y)$

Because (iii) has two instances of the variable X, we rename:

(iv) $(\forall X)([\neg a(X) \lor \neg b(X)] \lor [c(X,I) \land (\exists Y)((\exists Z) [\neg c(Y,Z)] \lor d(X,Y))]) \lor (\forall W)(e(W))$

4. Move all quantifiers to the left without changing their order. This is possible because step 3 has removed the possibility of any conflict between variable names. (iv) now becomes:

(v) $(\forall X)(\exists Y)(\exists Z)(\forall W)([\neg a(X) \lor \neg b(X)] \lor [c(X,I) \land (\neg c(Y,Z) \lor d(X,Y))] \lor e(W))$

After step 4 the clause is said to be in *prenex normal* form, because all the quantifiers are in front as a *prefix* and the expression or *matrix* follows after.

5. At this point all existential quantifiers are eliminated by a process called *skolemization*. Expression (v) has an existential quantifier for Y. When an expression contains an existentially quantified variable, for example, (∃Z)(foo(..., Z, ...)), it may be concluded that there is an assignment to Z under which foo is true. Skolemization identifies such a value. Skolemization does not necessarily show *how* to produce such a value; it is only a method for giving a name to an assignment that *must* exist. If k represents that assignment, then we have foo(..., k, ...). Thus:

(∃X)(dog(X)) may be replaced by dog(fido)

where the name fido is picked from the domain of definition of X to represent that individual X. fido is called a *skolem constant*. If the predicate has more than one argument and the existentially quantified variable is within the scope of universally quantified variables, the existential variable must be a function of those other variables. This is represented in the skolemization process:

(∀X) (∃Y) (mother(X,Y))

This expression indicates that every person has a mother. Every person is an X and the existing mother will be a function of the particular person X that is picked. Thus skolemization gives:

(∀X) mother(X, m(X))

which indicates that each X has a mother (the m of that X). In another example:

(∀X)(∀Y)(∃Z)(∀W)(foo(X,Y,Z,W))

is skolemized to:

(∀X)(∀Y)(∀W)(foo(X,Y,f(X,Y),W)).

The existentially quantified Y and Z are within the scope (to the right of) universally quantified X but not within the scope of W. Thus each will be replaced by a skolem function of X. Replacing Y with the skolem function f(X) and Z with g(X), (v) becomes:

(vi) (∀X)(∀W)([¬ a(X) ∨ ¬ b(X)] ∨ [c(X,l) ∧ (¬ c(f(X),g(X)) ∨ d(X,f(X)))]) ∨ e(W))

After skolemization, step 6 can take place, which simply drops the prefix.

6. Drop all universal quantification. By this point only universally quantified variables exist (step 5) with no variable conflicts (step 3). Thus all quantifiers can be dropped, and any proof procedure employed assumes all variables are universally quantified. Formula (vi) now becomes:

(vii) $[\neg a(X) \vee \neg b(X)] \vee [c(X,l) \wedge (\neg c(f(X),g(X)) \vee d(X,f(X)))] \vee e(W)$

7. Next we convert the expression to the conjunct of disjuncts form. This requires using the associative and distributive properties of $\wedge$ and $\vee$. Recall from Chapter 2 that

    $a \vee (b \vee c) = (a \vee b) \vee c$
    $a \wedge (b \wedge c) = (a \wedge b) \wedge c$

    which indicates that $\wedge$ or $\vee$ may be grouped in any desired fashion. The distributive property of Chapter 2 is also used, when necessary. Because

    $a \wedge (b \vee c)$

    is already in clause form, $\wedge$ is not distributed. However, $\vee$ must be distributed across $\wedge$ using:

    $a \vee (b \wedge c) = (a \vee b) \wedge (a \vee c)$

    The final form of (vii) is:

    (viii) $[\neg a(X) \vee \neg b(X) \vee c(X,l) \vee e(W)] \wedge$
    $[\neg a(X) \vee \neg b(X) \vee \neg c(f(X),g(X)) \vee d(X,f(X)) \vee e(W)]$

8. Now call each conjunct a separate clause. In the example (viii) above there are two clauses:

    (ixa) $\neg a(X) \vee \neg b(X) \vee c(X,l) \vee e(W)$
    (ixb) $\neg a(X) \vee \neg b(X) \vee \neg c(f(X),g(X)) \vee d(X,f(X)) \vee e(W)$

9. The final step is to *standardize the variables apart* again. This requires giving the variable in each clause generated by step 8 different names. This procedure arises from the equivalence established in Chapter 2 that

    $(\forall X)(a(X) \wedge b(X)) \equiv (\forall X) a(X) \wedge (\forall Y) b(Y)$

    which follows from the nature of variable names as place holders. (ixa) and (ixb) now become, using new variable names U and V:

    (xa) $\neg a(X) \vee \neg b(X) \vee c(X,l) \vee e(W)$
    (xb) $\neg a(U) \vee \neg b(U) \vee \neg c(f(U),g(U)) \vee d(U,f(U)) \vee e(V)$

The importance of this final standardization becomes apparent only as we present the unification steps of resolution. We find the most general unification to make two predicates within two clauses equivalent, and then this substitution is made across all the variables of the same name within each clause. Thus, if some variables (needlessly) share names with others, these may be renamed by the unification process with a subsequent (possible) loss of generality in the solution.

This nine-step process is used to change any set of predicate calculus expressions to clause form. The completeness property of resolution refutations is not lost. Next we demonstrate the resolution procedure for generating proofs from these clauses.

13.2.3　The Binary Resolution Proof Procedure

The *resolution refutation* proof procedure answers a query or deduces a new result by reducing the set of clauses to a contradiction, represented by the null clause ($\Box$). The contradiction is produced by resolving pairs of clauses from the database. If a resolution does not produce a contradiction directly, then the clause produced by the resolution, the *resolvent*, is added to the database of clauses and the process continues.

Before we show how the resolution process works in the predicate calculus, we give an example from the propositional or variable-free calculus. Consider two *parent* clauses p1 and p2 from the propositional calculus:

$$p1: a_1 \lor a_2 \lor \cdots \lor a_n$$
$$p2: b_1 \lor b_2 \lor \cdots \lor b_m$$

having two literals a_i and b_j , where $1 < i \le n$ and $1 \le j \le m$, such that $\neg a_i = b_j$. Binary resolution produces the clause:

$$a_1 \lor \cdots \lor a_{i-1} \lor a_{i+1} \lor \cdots \lor a_n \lor b_1 \lor \cdots \lor b_{j-1} \lor b_{j+1} \lor \cdots \lor b_m.$$

The notation above indicates that the resolvent is made up of the disjunction of all the literals of the two parent clauses except the literals a_i and b_j.

A simple argument can give the intuition behind the resolution principle. Suppose

$$a \lor \neg b \text{ and } b \lor c$$

are both true statements. Observe that one of b and $\neg b$ must always be true and one always false (b $\lor \neg$ b is a tautology). Therefore, one of

$$a \lor c$$

must always be true. a $\lor$ c is the resolvent of the two parent clauses a $\lor \neg$ b and b $\lor$ c.

Consider now an example from the propositional calculus, where we want to prove a from the following axioms (of course, I $\leftarrow$ m $\equiv$ m $\rightarrow$ I for all propositions I and m):

$$a \leftarrow b \land c$$
$$b$$
$$c \leftarrow d \land e$$

$e \vee f$

$d \wedge \neg f$

We reduce the first axiom to clause form:

$a \leftarrow b \wedge c$

$a \vee \neg (b \wedge c)$ by $l \rightarrow m \equiv \neg l \vee m$

$a \vee \neg b \vee \neg c$ by de Morgan's law

The remaining axioms are reduced, and we have the following clauses:

$a \vee \neg b \vee \neg c$

b

$c \vee \neg d \vee \neg e$

$e \vee f$

d

$\neg f$

The resolution proof is found in Figure 13.4. First, the goal to be proved, a, is negated and added to the clause set. The derivation of $\square$ indicates that the database of clauses is inconsistent.

To use binary resolution in the predicate calculus, where each literal may contain variables, there must be a process under which two literals with different variable names, or one with a constant value, can be seen as equivalent. Unification was defined in Section 2.3.2 as the process for determining consistent and most general substitutions for making two predicates equivalent.

The algorithm for resolution on the predicate calculus is very much like that on the propositional calculus except that:

1. A literal and its negation in parent clauses produce a resolvent only if they unify under some substitution σ. σ is then applied to the resolvent before adding it to the clause set. We require that σ be the most general unifier of the parent clauses.

2. The unification substitutions used to find the contradiction offer variable bindings under which the original query is true. We explain this process, called *answer extraction*, shortly.

Occasionally, two or more literals in one clause have a unifying substitution. When this occurs there may not exist a refutation for a set of clauses containing that clause, even though the set may be contradictory. For instance, consider the clauses:

$p(X) \vee p(f(Y))$

$\neg p(W) \vee \neg p(f(Z))$

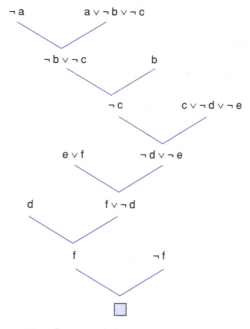

Figure 13.4 One resolution proof for an example
from the propositional calculus.

The reader should note that with simple resolution these clauses can be reduced only to equivalent or tautological forms but not to a contradiction, that is, no substitution can make them inconsistent.

This situation may be handled by *factoring* such clauses. If a subset of the literals in a clause has a most general unifier (Section 2.3.2), then the clause is replaced by a new clause, called a *factor* of that clause. The factor is the original clause with the most general unifier substitution applied and then redundant literals removed. For example, the two literals of the clause $p(X) \vee p(f(Y))$ will unify under the substitution $\{f(Y)/X\}$. We make the substitution in both literals to obtain the clause $p(f(Y)) \vee p(f(Y))$ and then replace this clause with its factor: $p(f(Y))$. Any resolution refutation system that includes factoring is refutation complete. Standardizing variables apart, Section 13.2.2 step 3 can be interpreted as a trivial application of factoring. Factoring may also be handled as part of the inference process in *hyperresolution* described in Section 13.4.2.

We now present an example of a resolution refutation for the predicate calculus. Consider the following story of the "happy student":

> Anyone passing his history exams and winning the lottery is happy. But anyone who studies or is lucky can pass all his exams. John did not study but he is lucky. Anyone who is lucky wins the lottery. Is John happy?

First change the sentences to predicate form:

Anyone passing his history exams and winning the lottery is happy.

$\forall$ X (pass (X,history) $\wedge$ win (X,lottery) $\rightarrow$ happy (X))

Anyone who studies or is lucky can pass all his exams.

$\forall$ X $\forall$ Y (study (X) $\vee$ lucky (X) $\rightarrow$ pass (X,Y))

John did not study but he is lucky.

$\neg$ study (john) $\wedge$ lucky (john)

Anyone who is lucky wins the lottery.

$\forall$ X (lucky (X) $\rightarrow$ win (X,lottery))

These four predicate statements are now changed to clause form (Section 13.2.2):

1. $\neg$ pass (X, history) $\vee$ $\neg$ win (X, lottery) $\vee$ happy (X)
2. $\neg$ study (Y) $\vee$ pass (Y, Z)
3. $\neg$ lucky (W) $\vee$ pass (W, V)
4. $\neg$ study (john)
5. lucky (john)
6. $\neg$ lucky (U) $\vee$ win (U, lottery)

Into these clauses is entered, in clause form, the negation of the conclusion:

7. $\neg$ happy (john)

The resolution refutation graph of Figure 13.5 shows a derivation of the contradiction and, consequently, proves that John is happy.

As a final example in this subsection we present the "exciting life" problem; suppose:

All people who are not poor and are smart are happy. Those people who read are not stupid. John can read and is wealthy. Happy people have exciting lives. Can anyone be found with an exciting life?

We assume $\forall$X (smart (X) $\equiv$ $\neg$ stupid (X)) and $\forall$Y (wealthy (Y) $\equiv$ $\neg$ poor (Y)), and get:

$\forall$X ($\neg$ poor (X) $\wedge$ smart (X) $\rightarrow$ happy (X))
$\forall$Y (read (Y) $\rightarrow$ smart (Y))
read (john) $\wedge$ $\neg$ poor (john)
$\forall$Z (happy (Z) $\rightarrow$ exciting (Z))

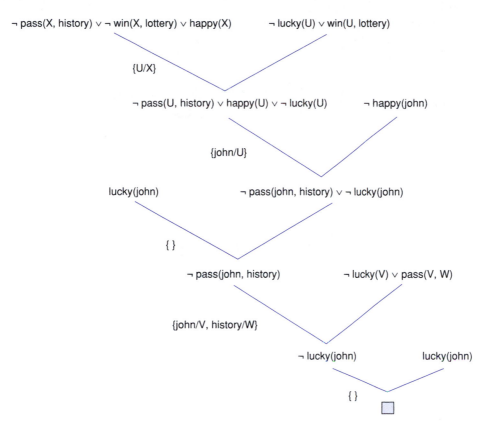

Figure 13.5 One resolution refutation for the "happy student" problem.

The negation of the conclusion is:

$\neg \exists W (\text{exciting} (W))$

These predicate calculus expressions for the "exciting life" problem are transformed into the following clauses:

poor (X) ∨ ¬ smart (X) ∨ happy (X)
¬ read (Y) ∨ smart (Y)
read (john)
¬ poor (john)
¬ happy (Z) ∨ exciting (Z)
¬ exciting (W)

The resolution refutation for this example is found in Figure 13.6.

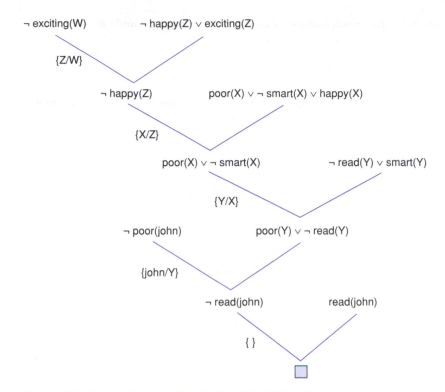

Figure 13.6 Resolution proof for the "exciting life" problem.

13.2.4 Strategies and Simplification Techniques for Resolution

A different proof tree within the search space for the problem of Figure 13.6 appears in Figure 13.7. There are some similarities in these proofs; for example, they both took five resolution steps. Also, the associative application of the unification substitutions found that john was the instance of the person with the "exciting life" in both proofs.

However, even these two similarities need not have occurred. When the resolution proof system was defined (Section 13.2.3) no order of clause combinations was implied. This is a critical issue: when there are N clauses in the clause space, there are N^2 ways of combining them or checking to see whether they can be combined at just the first level! The resulting set of clauses from this comparison is also large; if even 20% of them produce new clauses, the next round of possible resolutions will contain even more combinations than the first round. In a large problem this exponential growth will quickly get out of hand.

For this reason search heuristics are very important in resolution proof procedures, as they are in all weak method problem solving. As with the heuristics we considered in Chapter 4, there is no science that can determine the best strategy for any particular problem. Nonetheless, some general strategies can address the exponential combinatorics.

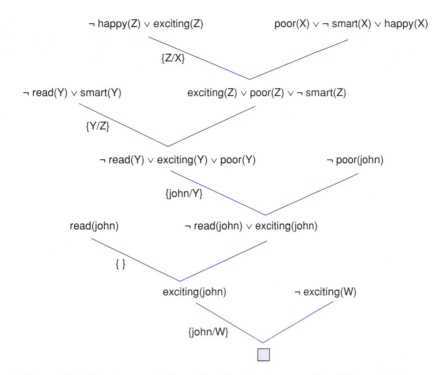

Figure 13.7 Another resolution refutation for the example of Figure 13.6.

Before we describe our strategies, we need to make several clarifications. First, based on the definition of unsatisfiability of an expression in Chapter 2, a *set of clauses is unsatisfiable* if no interpretation exists that establishes the set as satisfiable. Second, an inference rule is *refutation complete* if, given an unsatisfiable set of clauses, the unsatisfiability can be established by use of this inference rule alone. Resolution with factoring has this property (Chang and Lee 1973). Finally, a *strategy is complete* if by its use with a refutation-complete inference rule we can guarantee finding a refutation whenever a set of clauses is unsatisfiable. *Breadth-first* is an example of a complete strategy.

The *Breadth-First* Strategy. The complexity analysis of exhaustive clause comparison just described was based on breadth-first search. Each clause in the clause space is compared for resolution with every clause in the clause space on the first round. The clauses at the second level of the search space are generated by resolving the clauses produced at the first level with all the original clauses. We generate the clauses at the nth level by resolving all clauses at level $n - 1$ against the elements of the original clause set and all clauses previously produced.

This strategy can quickly get out of hand for large problems. It does have an interesting property, however. Like any breadth-first search, it guarantees finding the shortest solution path, because it generates every search state for each level before going any deeper. It also is a complete strategy in that, if it is continued long enough, it is guaranteed to find a refutation if one exists. Thus, when the problem is small, as are the ones we have presented as examples, the breadth-first strategy can be a good one. Figure 13.8 applies the breadth-first strategy to the "exciting life" problem.

The *Set of Support* Strategy.   An excellent strategy for large clause spaces is called the set of support (Wos and Robinson 1968). For a set of input clauses, S, we can specify a subset, T of S, called the set of support. The strategy requires that one of the resolvents in each resolution have an ancestor in the set of support. It can be proved that if S is unsatisfiable and S − T is satisfiable, then the set of support strategy is refutation complete (Wos et al. 1984).

If the original set of clauses is consistent, then any set of support that includes the negation of the original query meets these requirements. This strategy is based on the insight that the negation of what we want to prove true is going to be responsible for causing the clause space to be contradictory. The set of support forces resolutions between clauses of which at least one is either the negated goal clause or a clause produced by resolutions on the negated goal.

Figure 13.6 is an example of the set of support strategy applied to the exciting life problem. Because a set of support refutation exists whenever any refutation exists, the set of support can be made the basis of a complete strategy. One way to do this is to perform a breadth-first search for all possible sets of support refutations. This, of course, will be much more efficient than breadth-first search of all clauses. One need only be sure that all resolvents of the negated goal clause are examined, along with all their descendants.

The *Unit Preference* Strategy.   Observe that in the resolution examples seen so far, the derivation of the contradiction is indicated by the clause with no literals. Thus, every time

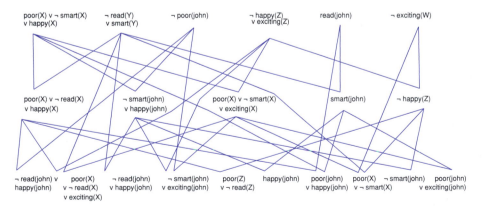

Figure 13.8 Complete state space for the "exciting life" problem generated
by breadth-first search (to two levels).

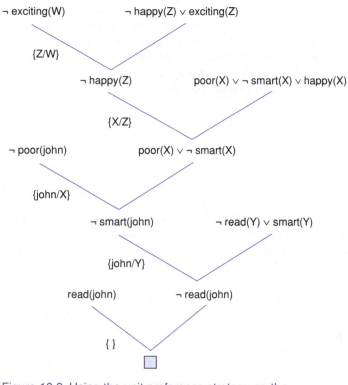

Figure 13.9 Using the unit preference strategy on the
"exciting life" problem.

we produce a resultant clause that has fewer literals than the clauses that are resolved to create it, we are closer to producing the clause of no literals. In particular, resolving with a clause of one literal, called a *unit* clause, will guarantee that the resolvent is smaller than the largest parent clause. The unit preference strategy uses units for resolving whenever they are available. Figure 13.9 uses the unit preference strategy on the exciting life problem. The unit preference strategy along with the set of support can produce a more efficient complete strategy.

Unit resolution is a related strategy that requires that one of the resolvents always be a unit clause. This is a stronger requirement than the unit preference strategy. We can show that unit resolution is not complete using the same example that shows the incompleteness of linear input form.

The *Linear Input Form* Strategy. The linear input form strategy is a direct use of the negated goal and the original axioms: take the negated goal and resolve it with one of the axioms to get a new clause. This result is then resolved with one of the axioms to get another new clause, which is again resolved with one of the axioms. This process continues until the empty clause is produced.

At each stage we resolve the clause most recently obtained with an axiom derived from the original problem statement. We never use a previously derived clause, nor do we resolve two of the axioms together. The linear input form is not a complete strategy, as can be seen by applying it to the following set of four clauses (which are obviously unsatisfiable). Regardless of which clause is taken as the negation of the goal, the linear input strategy cannot produce a contradiction:

$\neg\, a \vee \neg\, b$

$a \vee \neg\, b$

$\neg\, a \vee b$

$a \vee b$

Other Strategies and Simplification Techniques.   We have not attempted to present an exhaustive set of strategies or even the most sophisticated techniques for proving theorems using resolution inference. These are available in the literature, such as Wos et al. (1984) and Wos (1988). Our goal is rather to introduce the basic tools for this research area and to describe how these tools may be used in problem solving. The resolution proof procedure is but another weak method problem-solving technique.

In this sense, resolution may serve as an inference engine for the predicate calculus, but an engine that requires much analysis and careful application of strategies before success. In a problem large enough to be interesting, randomly clashing expressions together with resolution is as hopeless as striking random terminal keys and hoping a quality paper will result. The number of combinations is that large!

The examples used in this chapter are trivially small and have all the clauses necessary (and only those necessary) for their solution. This is seldom true of interesting problems. We have given several simple strategies for combating these combinatorial complexities, and we will conclude this subsection by describing a few more important considerations in designing a resolution-based problem solver. Later we show (in Section 13.3) how a resolution refutation system, with an interesting combination of search strategies, provides a "semantics" for *logic programming*, especially for the design of PROLOG interpreters.

A combination of strategies can be quite effective in controlling search—for instance, the use of set of support plus unit preference. Search heuristics may also be built into the design of rules (by creating a left-to-right ordering of literals for resolving). This order can be most effective for pruning the search space. This implicit use of strategy is important in PROLOG programming (Section 13.3).

The generality of conclusions can be a criterion for designing a solution strategy. On one side it might be important to keep intermediate solutions as general as possible, as this allows them to be used more freely in resolution. Thus the introduction of any resolution with clauses that require specialization by binding variables, such as {john/X}, should be put off as long as possible. If, on the other side, a solution requires specific variable bindings, such as in the analysis of whether John has a staph infection, the {john/Person} and {staph/Infection} substitutions may restrict the search space and increase the probability and speed of finding a solution.

An important issue in selecting a strategy is the notion of completeness. It might be very important in some applications to know that a solution will be found (if one exists). This can be guaranteed by using only complete strategies.

We can also increase efficiency by speeding up the matching process. We can eliminate needless (and costly) unifications between clauses that cannot possibly produce new resolvents by indexing each clause with the literals it contains and whether they are positive or negative. This allows us directly to find potential resolvents for any clause. Also, we should eliminate certain clauses as soon as they are produced. First, any tautological clause need never be considered; these can never be falsified and so are of no use in a solution attempt.

Another type of clause that gives no new information is one that can be *subsumed*, that is, when a new clause has a more general instance already in the clause space. For example, if p(john) is deduced for a space that already contains $\forall$ X(p(X)), then p(john) may be dropped with no loss; in fact, there is a saving because there are fewer clauses in the clause space. Similarly, p(X) subsumes the clause p(X) $\vee$ q(X). Less general information does not add anything to more general information when both are in the clause space.

Finally, *procedural attachment* evaluates or otherwise processes without further search any clause that can yield new information. It does arithmetic, makes comparisons between atoms or clauses, or "runs" any other deterministic procedure that can add concrete information to the problem solving or in any manner constrain the solution process. For example, we may use a procedure to compute a binding for a variable when enough information is present to do so. This variable binding then restricts possible resolutions and prunes the search space.

Next we show how answers may be extracted from the resolution refutation process.

13.2.5 Answer Extraction from Resolution Refutations

The instances under which an hypothesis is true are exactly the substitutions with which the refutation is found. Therefore, retaining information on the unification substitutions made in the resolution refutation gives information for the correct answer. In this subsection we give three examples of this and introduce a bookkeeping method for extracting answers from a resolution refutation.

The answer recording method is simple: retain the original conclusion that was to be proved and, into that conclusion, introduce each unification that is made in the resolution process. Thus the original conclusion is the "bookkeeper" of all unifications that are made as part of the refutation. In the computational search for resolution refutations, this might require extra pointers, such as when more than one possible choice exists in the search for a refutation. A control mechanism such as backtracking may be necessary to produce alternative solution paths. But still, with a bit of care, this added information may be retained.

Let us see some examples of this process. In Figure 13.6, where a proof was found for the existence of a person with an exciting life, the unifications of Figure 13.10 were made. If we retain the original goal and apply all the substitutions of the refutation to this clause, we find the answer of which person it is who has an exciting life.

Figure 13.10 shows how a resolution refutation not only can show that "no one leads an exciting life" is false but also, in the process of that demonstration, can produce a happy person, John. This is a general result, where the unifications that produce a refutation are the same ones that produce the instances under which the original query is true.

A second example is the simple story:

Fido the dog goes wherever John, his master, goes. John is at the library. Where is Fido?

First we represent this story in predicate calculus expressions and then reduce these expressions to clause form. The predicates:

at (john,X) → at (fido,X)

at (john,library)

The clauses:

¬ at (john,Y) ∨ at (fido,Y)

at (john,library)

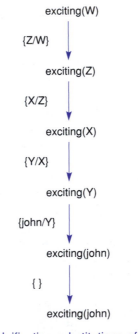

Figure 13.10 Unification substitutions of Figure 13.6
applied to the original query.

The conclusion negated:

¬ at (fido,Z), Fido is nowhere!

Figure 13.11 gives the answer extraction process. The literal keeping track of unifications is the original question (where is Fido?):

at (fido,Z)

Once again, the unifications under which the contradiction is found tell how the original query is true: Fido is at the library.

The final example shows how the skolemization process can give the instance under which the answer may be extracted. Consider the following situation:

Everyone has a parent. The parent of a parent is a grandparent. Given the person John, prove that John has a grandparent.

The following sentences represent the facts and relationships in the situation above. First, Everyone has a parent:

$(\forall X)(\exists Y) p(X,Y)$

A parent of a parent is a grandparent.

$(\forall X)(\forall Y)(\forall Z) p(X,Y) \wedge p(Y,Z) \rightarrow gp(X,Z)$

The goal is to find a W such that gp(john,W) or $\exists$ (W)(gp(john,W)). The negation of the goal is ¬ $\exists$ (W)(gp(john,W)) or:

¬ gp(john,W)

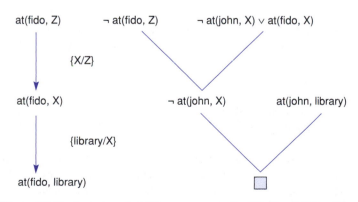

Figure 13.11 Answer extraction process on the "finding fido" problem.

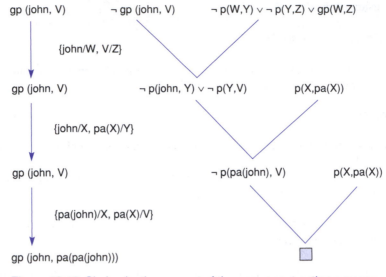

Figure 13.12 Skolemization as part of the answer extraction process.

In the process of putting the predicates above in clause form for the resolution refutation, the existential quantifier in the first predicate (everyone has a parent) requires a skolem function. This skolem function would be the obvious function: take the given X and find the parent of X. Let's call this the pa(X) for "find a parental ancestor for X ." For John this would be either his father or his mother. The clause form for the predicates of this problem is:

p(X,pa(X))
¬ p(W,Y) ∨ ¬ p(Y,Z) ∨ gp(W,Z)
¬ gp(john,V)

The resolution refutation and answer extraction process for this problem are presented in Figure 13.12. Note that the unification substitutions in the answer are

gp(john,pa(pa(john)))

The answer to the question of whether John has a grandparent is to "find the parental ancestor of John's parental ancestor." The skolemized function allows us to compute this result.

The general process for answer extraction just described may be used in all resolution refutations, whether they be with the general unifications as in Figures 13.10 and 13.11 or from evaluating the skolem function as in Figure 13.12. The process yields an answer. The method is really quite simple: the instances (unifications) under which the contradiction is found are exactly those under which the opposite of the negated conclusion (the original query) is true. Although this subsection has not demonstrated how this is true in every instance, it has shown several examples of how the process works; further discussion can be found in the literature (Nilsson 1980, Wos et al. 1984).

13.3 PROLOG and Automated Reasoning

13.3.1 Introduction

Only by understanding the implementation of a computer language can we properly guide its use, control its side effects, and have confidence in its results. In this section we describe the semantics of PROLOG, and relate it to the issues in automated reasoning presented in the previous section.

A serious criticism of the resolution proof procedure, Section 13.2, is that it requires a totally homogeneous database to represent the problem. When predicate calculus descriptors are reduced or transformed to clause form, important problem-solving information is left out. The omitted information is not the truth or fallacy of any part of the problem but rather the control hints or procedural descriptions on how to *use* the information. For example, a negated goal clause in a resolution format might be of the form:

$$a \lor \neg b \lor c \lor \neg d$$

where a, b, c, and d are literals. The resolution inference mechanism applies a search strategy to deduce the empty clause. All literals are open to the strategy and the one used depends on the particular strategy selected. The strategies used to guide resolution theorem proving are weak heuristics; they do not incorporate deep knowledge of a specific problem domain.

For example, the negated goal clause in the resolution example above might be a transformation of the predicate calculus statement:

$$a \leftarrow b \land \neg c \land d$$

This can be understood as "to see whether a is true go out and see whether b is true and c is false and d is true." The rule was intended as a procedure for solving a and implements heuristic information specific to this use. Indeed, the subgoal b might offer the easiest way to falsify the entire predicate, so the order "try b then see whether c is false then test d" could save much problem-solving time. The implicit heuristic says "test the easiest way to falsify the problem first, then if this is passed go ahead and generate the remaining (perhaps much more difficult) part of the solution." Human experts design procedures and relationships that not only are true but also contain information critical for *using* this truth. In most interesting problem-solving situations we cannot afford to ignore these heuristics (Kowalski 1979*b*).

In the next section we introduce Horn clauses and use their procedural interpretation as an explicit strategy that preserves this heuristic information.

13.3.2 Logic Programming and PROLOG

To understand the mathematical foundations of PROLOG, we first define *logic programming*. Once we have made this definition, we will add an explicit search strategy to logic programming to approximate the search strategy, sometimes referred to as the *procedural semantics*, of PROLOG. To get full PROLOG, we also discuss the use of *not* and the *closed world assumption*.

Consider the database of clauses prepared for resolution refutation, as in Section 13.2. If we restrict this set to clauses that have at most one positive literal (zero or more negative literals), we have a clause space with some interesting properties. First, problems describable with this set of clauses preserve unsatisfiability for resolution refutations, or are refutation complete, Section 13.2. Second, an important benefit of restricting our representation to this subclass of all clauses is a very efficient search strategy for refutations: a linear input form, unit preference based, left-to-right and depth-first goal reduction. With well-founded recursion (recursive calls that eventually terminate) and occurs checking, this strategy guarantees finding refutations if the clause space is unsatisfiable (van Emden and Kowalski 1976). A Horn clause contains at most one positive literal, which means it is of the form

$$a \lor \neg b_1 \lor \neg b_2 \lor \cdots \lor \neg b_n$$

where a and all the b_is are positive literals. To emphasize the key role of the one positive literal in resolutions, we generally write Horn clauses as implications with the positive literal as the conclusion:

$$a \leftarrow b_1 \land b_2 \land \cdots \land b_n$$

Before we discuss further the search strategy, we formally define this subset of clauses, called *Horn clauses*. These, together with a *nondeterministic* goal reduction strategy, are said to constitute a *logic program*.

DEFINITION

LOGIC PROGRAM

A *logic program* is a set of universally quantified expressions in first-order predicate calculus of the form:

$$a \leftarrow b_1 \land b_2 \land b_3 \land \cdots \land b_n$$

The a and b_i are all positive literals, sometimes referred to as atomic goals. The a is the clause *head*, the conjunction of b_i, the *body*.

These expressions are the *Horn clauses* of the first-order predicate calculus. They come in three forms: first, when the original clause has no positive literals; second, when it has no negative literals; and third, when it has one positive and one or more negative literals. These cases are 1, 2, and 3, respectively:

1. $\leftarrow b_1 \wedge b_2 \wedge \cdots \wedge b_n$
    called a *headless* clause or *goals* to be tried: b_1 and b_2 and . . . and b_n.

2. $a_1 \leftarrow$
    $a_2 \leftarrow$
    .
    .
    .
    $a_n \leftarrow$
    called the *facts*.

3. $a \leftarrow b_1 \wedge \cdots \wedge b_n$
    called a *rule* relation.

Horn clause calculus allows only the forms just presented; there may be only one literal to the left of $\leftarrow$ and this literal must be positive. All literals to the right of $\leftarrow$ are also positive.

The reduction of clauses that have at most one positive literal into Horn form requires three steps. First, select the positive literal in the clause, if there is a positive literal, and move this literal to the very left (using the commutative property of $\vee$). This single positive literal becomes the *head* of the Horn clause, as just defined. Second, change the entire clause to Horn form by the rule:

$$a \vee \neg b_1 \vee \neg b_2 \vee \cdots \vee \neg b_n \equiv a \leftarrow \neg (\neg b_1 \vee \neg b_2 \vee \cdots \vee \neg b_n)$$

Finally, use de Morgan's law to change this specification to:

$$a \leftarrow b_1 \wedge b_2 \cdots \wedge b_n$$

where the commutative property of $\wedge$ can be used to order the b_i subgoals.

It should be noted that it may not be possible to transform clauses from an arbitrary clause space to Horn form. Some clauses, such as $p \vee q$, have no Horn form. To create a Horn clause, there can be at most one positive literal in the original clause. If this criterion is not met it may be necessary to rethink the original predicate calculus specification for the problem. The payoff for Horn form representation is an efficient refutation strategy, as we see shortly.

The computation algorithm for logic programs proceeds by nondeterministic goal reduction. At each step of the computation where there is a goal of the form:

$$\leftarrow a_1 \wedge a_2 \wedge \cdots \wedge a_n$$

the interpreter *arbitrarily* chooses some a_i for $1 \leq i \leq n$. It then *nondeterministically* chooses a clause:

$$a^1 \leftarrow b_1 \wedge b_2 \wedge \cdots \wedge b_n$$

such that the a^1 unifies with a_i with substitution ς and uses this clause to reduce the goal. The new goal then becomes:

$$\leftarrow (a_1 \wedge \cdots \wedge a_{i-1} \wedge b_1 \wedge b_2 \wedge \cdots \wedge b_n \wedge a_{i+1} \wedge \cdots \wedge a_n)\varsigma$$

This process of nondeterministic goal reduction continues until the computation terminates with the goal set empty.

If we eliminate the nondeterminism by imposing an order on the reduction of subgoals, we do not change the result of the computation. All results that can be found nondeterministically can be found through an exhaustive ordered search. However, by reducing the amount of nondeterminism, we can define strategies that prune unnecessary branches from the space. Thus, a major concern of practical logic programming languages is to provide the programmer with facilities to control and, when possible, reduce the amount of nondeterminism. These facilities allow the programmer to influence both the order in which the goals are reduced and the set of clauses that are used to reduce each goal. (As in any graph search, precautions must be taken to prevent infinite cycles in the proof.)

The abstract specification of a logic program has a clean semantics, that of the resolution refutation system. van Emden and Kowalski (1976) show that the smallest interpretation on which a logic program is true is *the* interpretation of the program. The price paid by practical programming languages, such as PROLOG, is that executing programs by these may compute only a subset of their associated interpretations (Shapiro 1987).

Sequential PROLOG is an approximation to an interpreter for the logic programming model, designed for efficient execution on von Neumann computers. This is the interpreter that we have used so far in this text. Sequential PROLOG uses both the order of goals in a clause and the order of clauses in the program to control the search for a proof. When a number of goals are available, PROLOG always pursues them left to right. In the search for a unifiable clause on a goal, the possible clauses are checked in the order they are presented by the programmer. When each selection is made, a backtracking pointer is placed with the recorded unification that allows other clauses to be used (again, in the programmer's order) should the original selection of a unifiable clause fail. If this attempt fails across all possible clauses in the clause space, then the computation fails. With *cut*, an attempt to use efficiently the depth-first backtracking search, Section 15.1.5, the interpreter may not, in fact, visit all clause combinations (interpretations) in the search space.

More formally, given a goal:

$$\leftarrow a_1 \wedge a_2 \wedge a_3 \wedge \cdots \wedge a_n$$

and a program P, the PROLOG interpreter sequentially searches for the first clause in P whose head unifies with a_1. This clause is then used to reduce the goals. If:

$$a^1 \leftarrow b_1 \wedge b_2 \wedge \ldots \wedge b_n$$

is the reducing clause with ξ the unification, the goal clause then becomes:

$$\leftarrow (b_1 \wedge b_2 \wedge \cdots \wedge b_n \wedge a_2 \wedge a_3 \wedge \cdots \wedge a_n)\xi$$

The PROLOG interpreter then continues by trying to reduce the leftmost goal, b_1 in this example, using the first clause in the program P that unifies with b_1. Suppose it is:

$$b^1 \leftarrow c_1 \wedge c_2 \wedge \cdots \wedge c_p$$

under unification ϕ. The goal then becomes:

$$\leftarrow (c_1 \wedge c_2 \wedge \cdots \wedge c_p \wedge b_2 \wedge \cdots \wedge b_n \wedge a_2 \wedge a_3 \wedge \cdots \wedge a_n)\xi \, \phi$$

Note that the goal list is treated as a stack enforcing depth-first search. If the PROLOG interpreter ever fails to find a unification that solves a goal it then backtracks to its most recent unification choice point, restores all bindings made since that choice point, and chooses the next clause that will unify (by the order in P). In this way, PROLOG implements its left-to-right, depth-first search of the clause space.

If the goal is reduced to the null clause ($\square$) then the composition of unifications that made the reductions:

$$\leftarrow (\square)\xi \, \phi \cdots \omega$$

(here $\xi \, \phi \cdots \omega$), provides an interpretation under which the original goal clause was true.

Besides backtracking on the order of clauses in a program, sequential PROLOG allows the *cut* or "!". As described in Section 15.1.5, a cut may be placed in a clause as a goal itself. The interpreter, when encountering the cut, is committed to the current execution path and in particular to that subset of unifications made since the choice of the clause containing the cut. It also commits the interpreter to the choice of that clause itself as the only method for reducing the goal. Should failure be encountered within the clause after the cut, the entire clause fails.

Procedurally, the cut makes it unnecessary to retain backtrack pointers for the reducing clause and all its components *before* the cut. Thus, cut can mean that only some of the possible interpretations of the model are ever computed.

We summarize our discussion of sequential PROLOG by comparing it to the resolution refutation model of Section 13.2.

1. The resolution clause space is a superset of Horn clause expressions in logic programming. Each clause must have at most one positive literal to be in Horn form.

2. The following structures represent the problem in Horn form:
   a. The goals,

   $$\leftarrow b_1 \wedge b_2 \wedge \cdots \wedge b_n$$

   are a list of clause statements that make up the goals to be tested by resolution refutation. Each a_i is in turn negated, unified with, and reduced until the empty clause is found (if this is possible).

b. The facts,

$$a_1 \leftarrow$$
$$a_2 \leftarrow$$
.
.
.
$$a_n \leftarrow$$

are each separate clauses for resolution. Finally,

c. The Horn clause rules or axioms,

$$a \leftarrow b_1 \wedge b_2 \wedge \cdots \wedge b_n$$

allow us to reduce matching subgoals.

3. With a unit preference, *linear input form* strategy (always preferring fact clauses and using the negated goal and its descendant resolvents; see Section 13.2.4) and applying a left-to-right, depth-first (with backtracking) order for selecting clauses for resolutions, the resolution theorem prover is acting as a PROLOG interpreter. Because this strategy is refutation complete, its use guarantees that the solution will be found (provided that part of the set of interpretations is not pruned away by using cut).

4. Finally, the composition of unifications in the proof provides the answer (interpretation) for which the goal is true. This is exactly equivalent to the answer extraction process of Section 13.2.5. Recording the composition of unifications in the goal literal produces each answer interpretation.

An important issue with current PROLOG interpreters is the *closed world* assumption implicit in their implementation. In predicate calculus, the proof of $\neg\, p(X)$ is exactly the proof that $p(X)$ is logically false. That is, $p(X)$ is false under every interpretation that makes the axiom set true. The PROLOG interpreter, based on the unification algorithm of Chapter 2, offers a more restricted result than the general resolution refutation of Section 13.2. Rather than trying all interpretations, it examines only those explicit in the database. We now axiomatize these constraints to see exactly the restrictions implicit in PROLOG.

For every predicate p, and every variable X belonging to p, suppose $a_1, a_2, \ldots, a_n$ make up the domain of X. The PROLOG interpreter, using unification, enforces:

1. The *unique name* axiom. For all atoms of the domain $a_i \not\equiv a_j$ unless they are identical. This implies that atoms with distinct names are distinct.

2. The *closed world* axiom.

$$p(X) \rightarrow p(a_1) \vee p(a_2) \vee \cdots \vee p(a_n).$$

This means the only possible instances of a relation are those implied by the clauses present in the problem specification.

3. The *domain closure* axiom.

$$(X = a_1) \lor (X = a_2) \lor \cdots \lor (X = a_n).$$

This guarantees that the atoms occurring in the problem specification constitute all and the only atoms.

These three axioms are implicit in the action of the PROLOG interpreter. They may be seen as added to the set of Horn clauses making up a problem description and thus as constraining the set of possible interpretations to a PROLOG query.

Intuitively, this means that PROLOG assumes as false all goals that it cannot prove to be true. This can introduce anomalies: if a goal's truth value is actually unknown to the current database, PROLOG will assume it to be false.

Other limitations are implicit in PROLOG, as they seem to be in all computing languages. The most important of these, besides the problem of negation as failure, represent violations of the semantic model for logic programming. In particular, there are the lack of an occurs check (see Section 2.3; this allows a clause to unify with a subset of itself) and the use of cut. The current generation of PROLOG interpreters should be looked at pragmatically. Some problems arise because "no efficient way is currently known" to get around the issue (the occurs check); others arise from attempts to optimize use of the depth-first with backtrack search (the cut). Many of the anomalies of PROLOG are a result of trying to implement the nondeterministic semantics of pure logic programming on a sequential computer. This includes the problems introduced by the cut.

In the final section of Chapter 13 we introduce alternative inferencing schemes for automated reasoning.

13.4 Further Issues in Automated Reasoning

We described weak method problem solvers as using (a) a *uniform representation medium* for (b) *sound inference rules* that focus on syntactic features of the representation and are guided by (c) *methods or strategies* for combating the combinatorics of exhaustive search. We conclude this chapter with further comments on each of these aspects of the weak method solution process.

13.4.1 Uniform Representations for Weak Method Solutions

The resolution proof procedure requires us to place all our axioms in clause form. This uniform representation then allows us to resolve clauses and simplifies the design of problem-solving heuristics. One major disadvantage of this approach is that much valuable heuristic information can be lost in this uniform encoding.

The if . . . then format of a rule often conveys more information for use of modus ponens or production system search than one of its syntactic variants. It also offers us an efficient way to use the rule. For instance, suppose we want to represent the abductive inference, Section 9.0, If the engine does not turn over and the lights do not come on then the battery may be dead. This rule suggests how to check the battery.

The disjunctive form of the same rule obscures this heuristic information about how the rule should be applied. If we express this rule in predicate calculus $\neg$ turns_over $\wedge \neg$ lights $\rightarrow$ battery, the clause form of this rule is this: turns_over $\vee$ lights $\vee$ battery. This clause can have a number of equivalent forms, and each of these represents a different implication.

$$(\neg \text{ turns\_over} \wedge \neg \text{ lights}) \rightarrow \text{battery}$$
$$(\neg \text{ turns\_over} \rightarrow (\text{battery} \vee \text{lights}))$$
$$(\neg \text{ battery} \wedge \neg \text{ lights}) \rightarrow \text{turns\_over}$$
$$(\neg \text{ battery} \rightarrow (\text{turns\_over} \vee \text{lights}))$$

and so on.

To retain heuristic information in the automated reasoning process several researchers, including Nilsson (1980) and Bundy (1988), advocate reasoning methods that encode heuristics by forming rules according to the way in which the human expert might design the rule relationships. We have proposed this approach already in our and/or graph reasoning in Section 3.3 and the PROLOG form of automated reasoning of Section 13.3. Rule-based expert systems also allow the programmer to control search through the structure of rules. We develop the idea further with the next two examples, one data-driven and the second goal-driven. Both of these retain the form of implications and use this information to guide search through an and/or graph.

Consider, for use in data-driven reasoning, the following facts, rules (axioms), and goal:

Fact:

$$(a \vee (b \wedge c))$$

Rules (or axioms):

$$(a \rightarrow (d \wedge e))$$
$$(b \rightarrow f)$$
$$(c \rightarrow (g \vee h))$$

Goal:

$$\leftarrow e \vee f$$

The proof of $e \vee f$ is found in the and/or graph of Figure 13.13. Note the use of and connectors on $\vee$ relations and the or connectors on $\wedge$ relations in the data-driven search space. If we are given that either a or b $\wedge$ c is true, then we must reason with both disjuncts to guarantee that our argument is truth preserving; hence these two paths are conjoined. When b and c are true, on the other hand, we can continue to explore either of these conjuncts. Rule matching takes any intermediate state, such as c, and replaces it with the conclusion of a rule, such as (g ∨ h), whose premise matches that state. The discovery of both states e and f in Figure 13.13 indicates that the goal (e ∨ f) is established.

In a similar fashion we can use matching of rules on and/or graphs for goal-driven reasoning. When a goal description includes a ∨, as in the example of Figure 13.14, then either alternative can be explored independently to establish the goal. If the goal is a conjunction, then, of course, both conjuncts must be established.

Goal:

    (a ∨ (b ∧ c))

Rules (or axioms):

    (f ∧ d) → a

    (e → (b ∧ c))

    (g → d)

Fact:

    f ∧ g

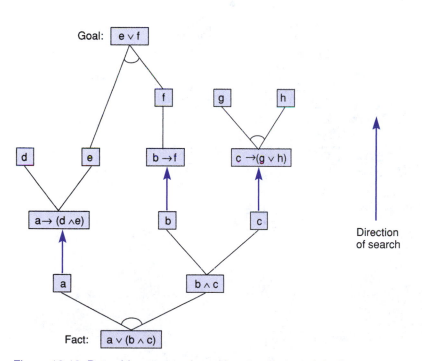

Figure 13.13 Data-driven reasoning with an and/or graph in the propositional calculus.

Although these examples are taken from the propositional calculus, a similar search is generated using predicate calculus facts and rules. Unification makes literals compatible for applying inference rules across different branches of the search space. Of course, unifications must be consistent (that is, unifiable) across different and branches of the search space.

This subsection has suggested solution methods to help preserve heuristic information within the representational medium for weak method problem solving. This is essentially the way the inference engines of expert systems allow the programmer to specify control and heuristic information in a rule. Expert systems rely on the rule form, such as the ordering of rules or the ordering of the premises within a rule, for control of search rather than depending totally on general weak problem-solving methods. What is lost in this approach is the ability to apply uniform proof procedures, such as resolution, across the full set of rules. As can be noted in the examples of Figures 13.13 and 13.14, modus ponens may still be used, however. Production system control using either depth-first, breadth-first, or best-first search offers one weak method reasoning architecture for implementing rule systems (see examples in Chapters 4, 6, 8, 15, and 16).

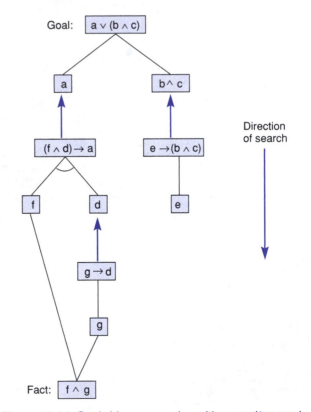

Figure 13.14 Goal-driven reasoning with an and/or graph in the propositional calculus.

13.4.2 Alternative Inference Rules

Resolution is the most general sound inference rule we have presented so far. Several more sophisticated inference rules have been created in an attempt to make resolution more efficient. We briefly consider two of these: *hyperresolution* and *paramodulation*.

Resolution, as we have presented it, is actually a special variant called *binary resolution*: exactly two parent clauses are clashed. A successful application of hyperresolution replaces a sequence of binary resolutions to produce one clause. Hyperresolution clashes, in a single step, a clause with some negative literals, referred to as the *nucleus*, and a number of clauses with all positive literals, called the *satellites*. These satellites must have one positive literal that will match with a negative literal of the nucleus. There must also be one satellite for each negative literal of the nucleus. Thus the result of an application of hyperresolution is a clause with all positive literals.

An advantage of hyperresolution is that a clause of all positive literals is produced from each hyperresolution inference, and the clause space itself is kept smaller because no intermediate results are produced. Unifications across all clauses in the inference step must be consistent.

As an example of hyperresolution, consider the following clause set:

$\neg$ married(X,Y) $\lor$ $\neg$ mother(X,Z) $\lor$ father(Y,Z)

married(kate,george) $\lor$ likes(george,kate)

mother(kate,sarah)

We draw a conclusion in one step using hyperresolution:

father(george,sarah) $\lor$ likes(george,kate)

The first clause in the example is the nucleus; the second two are satellites. The satellites are all positive, and there is one for each negative literal in the nucleus. Note how the nucleus is just the clause form for the implication:

married(X,Y) $\land$ mother(X,Z) $\rightarrow$ father(Y,Z)

The conclusion of this rule is part of the final result. Note that there are no intermediate results, such as:

$\neg$ mother(kate,Z) $\lor$ father(george,Z) $\lor$ likes(george,kate)

which we would find in any binary resolution proof applied to the same clause space.

Hyperresolution is sound and complete when used by itself. When combined with other strategies, such as set of support, completeness may be compromised (Wos et al. 1984). It does require special search strategies to organize the satellite and nucleus clauses, although in most environments where hyperresolution is used, the clauses are often indexed by the name and positive or negative property of each literal. This makes it efficient to prepare the nucleus and satellite clauses for the hyperresolution inference.

An important and difficult issue in the design of theorem-proving mechanisms is the control of equality. Especially complex are application areas, such as mathematics, where most facts and relationships have multiple representations, such as can be obtained by applying the associative and commutative properties to expressions. To convince yourself of this with a very simple example, consider the multiple ways the arithmetic expression 3 + (4 + 5) can be represented, including 3 + ((4 + 0) + 5). This is a complex issue in that expressions need to be substituted for, unified with, and checked for equality with other expressions within automated mathematical problem solving.

Demodulation is the process of rephrasing or rewriting expressions so they automatically take on a chosen canonical form. The unit clauses used to produce this canonical form are *demodulators*. Demodulators specify the equality of different expressions, allowing us to replace an expression with its canonical form. With proper use of demodulators all newly produced information is reduced to a specified form before it is placed in the clause space. For example, we might have a demodulator:

    equal(father(father(X)),grandfather(X))

and the new clause:

    age(father(father(sarah)),86).

Before adding this new clause to the clause space, we apply the demodulator and add instead:

    age(grandfather(sarah),86).

The equality problem here is one of naming. Do we wish to classify a person as father(father(X)) or grandfather(X)? Similarly, we can pick out canonical names for all family relations: a brother(father(Y)) is uncle(Y), etc. Once we pick the canonical names to store information under, we then design demodulators such as the equal clause to reduce all new information to this determined form. Note that demodulators are always unit clauses.

Paramodulation is a generalization of equality substitution at the term level. For example, given the expression:

    older(mother(Y),Y)

and the equality relationship:

    equal(mother(sarah),kate)

we can conclude with paramodulation:

    older(kate,sarah)

Note the term-level matching and replacement of {sarah/Y} and mother(sarah) for kate. A vital difference between demodulation and paramodulation is that the latter allows a nontrivial replacement of variables in both the arguments of the equality predicate and the predicate into which the substitution is made. Demodulation does replacement based on the demodulator. Multiple demodulators may be used to get an expression into its final form; paramodulation is usually used only once in any situation.

We have given simple examples of these powerful inference mechanisms. They should be seen as more general techniques for use in a resolution clause space. Like all the other inference rules we have seen, these are tightly linked to the chosen representation and must be controlled by appropriate strategies.

13.4.3 Search Strategies and Their Use

Sometimes the domain of application puts special demands on the inference rules and heuristics for guiding their use. We have already seen the use of demodulators for assistance in equality substitution. Bledsoe, in his *natural deduction system*, identifies two important strategies for preparing theorems for resolution proof. He calls these strategies s*plit* and *reduce* (Bledsoe 1971).

Bledsoe designed his strategies for use in mathematics and, in particular, for application to *set theory*. The effect of these strategies is to break a theorem into parts to make it easier to prove by conventional methods such as resolution. Split takes various mathematical forms and splits them to appropriate pieces. The proof of $A \wedge B$ is equivalent to the proof of A and the proof of B. Similarly, the proof of $A \leftrightarrow B$ is the proof of $A \rightarrow B$ and the proof of $A \leftarrow B$.

The heuristic reduce also attempts to break down large proofs to their components. For example, the proof of $s \in A \cap B$ may be decomposed into the proofs of $s \in A$ and $s \in B$. Another example might be to prove some property true of $\neg (A \cup B)$ by proving the property for $\neg A$ and for $\neg B$. By breaking up larger proofs into smaller pieces, Bledsoe hopes to contain the search space. His heuristics also include a limited use of equality substitution.

As mentioned throughout this book, the appropriate use of heuristics is very much an art that takes into account the application area as well as the representation and inference rules used. We close this chapter by citing some general proverbs, all of which are sometimes false but which can, with careful use, be very effective. These proverbs sum up thoughts taken from researchers in the area (Bledsoe 1971, Nilsson 1980, Wos et al. 1984, Dallier 1986, Wos 1988) as well as our own reflections on weak method problem solvers. We state them without further comment.

Use, whenever possible, clauses with fewer literals.

Break the task into subtasks before employing general inferencing.

Use equality predicates whenever this is appropriate.

Use demodulators to create canonical forms.

Use paramodulation when inferencing with equality predicates.

Use strategies that preserve "completeness."

Use set of support strategies, for these contain the potential contradiction.

Use units within resolution, as these shorten the resulting clause.

Perform subsumption checks with new clauses.

Use an ordering mechanism on clauses and literals within the clauses that reflect your intuitions and problem-solving expertise.

13.5 Epilogue and References

Automated reasoning programs and other weak method problem solvers are very important in artificial intelligence. They are used both to design general search strategies in game playing and theorem proving and to support much of our knowledge-based reasoning. Thus we see them in the design of "shells" for expert systems and inference mechanisms for network representations.

Weak method solvers require choosing a representational medium, inference mechanisms, and search strategies. These three choices are intricately interwoven and cannot be made in isolation from each other. The application domain also affects the choice of representation, inference rules, and strategies. The "proverbs" at the end of the previous section should be considered in making these choices.

Resolution is the process of constraining possible interpretations until it is seen that the clause space with the inclusion of the negated goal is inconsistent. This text does not go into the soundness of resolution or the completeness of resolution refutations. The arguments for these important issues are based on Herbrand's theorem (Chang and Lee 1973) and the notion of possible interpretations of the clause set. The interested reader is encouraged to go to the references for these proofs.

A number of other references are appropriate: Chang and Lee (1973) is a very readable introductory text. *Automated Theorem Proving: A Logical Basis* offers a formal approach (Loveland 1978). A number of classic early papers in the field are collected in a series *The Automation of Reasoning: Collected Papers, 1957 to 1970* (Siekmann and Wrightson 1983*a*, *b*). Nilsson (1980), Weyhrauch (1980), Genesereth and Nilsson (1987), Kowalski (1979*b*), Lloyd (1984), Wos et al. (1984), and Wos (1988) offer valuable summaries of important concepts in automated reasoning. Robinson (1965) and Bledsoe (1977) have made fundamental contributions to the field. An important theorem-proving research contribution is made by Boyer and Moore (1979). The early theorem-proving work by Newell and Simon and their colleagues at Carnegie Institute of Technology is reported in *Computers and Thought* (Feigenbaum and Feldman 1963) and *Human Problem Solving* (Newell and Simon 1972).

For the past 25 years CADE, the Conference on Automated DEduction, has been the major forum for the presentation of new results in automated reasoning. Model checking, verification systems, and scalable knowledge representation systems, are current research issues (McAllester 1999, Ganzinger et al. 1999). Important research continues by Larry Wos and his colleagues at Argonne National Laboratory. Veroff (1997) has published a set of essays in automated reasoning in honor of Wos. Bundy's work (1983, 1988) in automated reasoning at the University of Edinburgh is important. Research also continues on extending the Boyer-Moore theorem prover at the University of Texas, Austin, see *Computer-Aided Reasoning: ACL2 Case Studies*, Kaufmann et al. (2000).

13.6 Exercises

1. Take the logic-based financial advisor of Section 2.4, put the predicates describing the problem into clause form, and use resolution refutations to answer queries such as whether a particular investor should make an investment(combination).

2. Use resolution to prove Wirth's statement in Exercise 12, Chapter 2.

3. Use resolution to answer the query in Example 3.3.4.

4. In Chapter 6 we presented a simplified form of the knight's tour. Take the path3 rule, put it in clause form, and use resolution to answer queries such as path3(3,6). Next, use the recursive path call, in clause form, to answer queries.

5. How might you use resolution to implement a "production system" search?

6. How would you do data-driven reasoning with resolution? Use this to address the search space of Exercise 1. What problems might arise in a large problem space?

7. Use resolution for queries in the farmer, wolf, goat, and cabbage problem of Section 15.3.

8. Use resolution to solve the following puzzle problem from Wos et al. (1984). There are four people: Roberta, Thelma, Steve, and Pete. The four hold eight different jobs. Each person has exactly two jobs. The jobs are, without sex bias, chef, guard, nurse, telephonist, police officer, teacher, actor, and boxer. The nurse is a male. The husband of the chef is the telephonist. Roberta is not a boxer. Pete has no education past the ninth grade. Roberta, the chef, and the police officer went golfing together. Who holds which jobs? Show how the addition of a sex bias changes the problem.

9. Work out two examples for hyperresolution where the nucleus has at least four literals.

10. Write a demodulator for sum that would cause clauses of the form equal(ans, sum(5, sum(6, minus(6)))) to be reduced to equal(ans, sum(5, 0)). Write a further demodulator to reduce this last result to equal(ans, 5).

11. Pick a "canonical set" of six family relations. Write demodulators to reduce alternative forms of relations to the set. For example, your "mother's brother" is "uncle."

12. Take the happy student problem of Figure 13.5 and apply three of the refutation strategies of Section 13.2.4 to its solution.

13. Put the following predicate calculus expression in clause form:

$$\forall (X)(p(X) \rightarrow \{\forall (Y)[p(Y) \rightarrow p(f(X,Y))] \wedge \neg \forall (Y)[q(X,Y) \rightarrow p(Y)]\})$$

14. Create the **and/or** graph for the following data-driven predicate calculus deduction.

    Fact: $\neg d(f) \vee [b(f) \wedge c(f)]$.
    Rules: $\neg d(X) \rightarrow \neg a(X)$ and $b(Y) \rightarrow e(Y)$ and $g(W) \leftarrow c(W)$.
    Prove: $\neg a(Z) \vee e(Z)$.

15. Prove the linear input form strategy is not refutation complete.

16. Create the **and/or** graph for the following problem. Why is it impossible to conclude the goal:

    $r(Z) \vee s(Z)$?
    Fact: $p(X) \vee q(X)$.
    Rules: $p(a) \rightarrow r(a)$ and $q(b) \rightarrow s(b)$.

17. Use factoring and resolution to produce a refutation for the following clauses: $p(X) \vee p(f(Y))$ and $\neg p(W) \vee \neg p(f(Z))$. Try to produce a refutation without factoring.

18. Derive a resolution proof of the theorem of Figure 13.1.

19. An alternative semantic model for logic programming is that of *Flat Concurrent PROLOG*. Compare the semantics of PROLOG seen in Section 13.3 with that of Flat Concurrent PROLOG (Shapiro 1987).

UNDERSTANDING NATURAL LANGUAGE

14

Quid opus est verbis? (What need is there for words?)

—TERENCE

I understand a fury in your words,
But not the words.

—WILLIAM SHAKESPEARE, *Othello*

They have been at a great feast of languages,
and stolen the scraps.

—WILLIAM SHAKESPEARE, *Love's Labour's Lost*

I wish someone would tell me what "Ditty wah ditty" means.

—ARTHUR BLAKE

14.0 The Natural Language Understanding Problem

Communicating with natural language, whether as text or as speech acts, depends heavily on our knowledge and expectations within the domain of discourse. Understanding language is not merely the transmission of words: it also requires inferences about the speaker's goals, knowledge, and assumptions, as well as about the context of the interaction. Implementing a natural language understanding program requires that we represent knowledge and expectations of the domain and reason effectively about them. We must consider such issues as nonmonotonicity, belief revision, metaphor, planning, learning, and the practical complexities of human interaction. But these are the central problems of artificial intelligence itself!

Consider, for example, the following lines from Shakespeare's *Sonnet XVIII*:

Shall I compare thee to a summer's day?
Thou art more lovely and more temperate:
Rough winds do shake the darling buds of May,
And summer's lease hath all too short a date:

We cannot understand these lines through a simplistic, literal treatment of meaning. Instead, we must address such issues as:

1. What were Shakespeare's intentions in writing? We must know a great deal about human love and its social conventions to begin to understand these lines. Or was he just trying to get something to his publisher so he could be paid?

2. Why did Shakespeare compare his beloved to a summer's day? Does he mean that she is 24 hours long and can cause sunburn or that she makes him feel the warmth and beauty of summer?

3. What inferences does the passage require? Shakespeare's intended meaning does not reside explicitly in the text; it must be inferred using metaphors, analogies, and background knowledge. For instance, how do we come to interpret the references to rough winds and the brevity of summer as lamenting the shortness of human life and love?

4. How does metaphor shape our understanding? The words are not mere references to explicit objects such as blocks on a table: the heart of the poem's meaning is in the selective attribution of properties of a summer's day to the beloved. Which properties are attributed, and which are not, and above all, why are some properties important while others are ignored?

5. Must a computer-based text-to-speech system know something about the iambic pentameter? How could a computer summarize what this poem is "about," or retrieve it intelligently from a corpus of poetry?

We cannot merely chain together the dictionary meanings of Shakespeare's words and call the result understanding. Instead, we must employ a complex process of understanding the words, parsing the sentence, constructing a representation of the semantic meaning, and interpreting this meaning in light of our knowledge of the problem domain.

Our second example is part of a web ad for a faculty position in computer science.

The Department of Computer Science of the University of New Mexico . . . is conducting a search to fill two tenure-track positions. We are interested in hiring people with interests in:
    Software, including analysis, design, and development tools . . .
    Systems, including architecture, compilers, networks . . .
    ...
Candidates must have completed a doctorate in . . .
The department has internationally recognized research programs in adaptive computation, artificial intelligence, . . . and enjoys strong research collaborations with the Santa Fe Institute and several national laboratories . . .

Several questions arise in understanding this job ad:

1. How does the reader know that this ad is for a faculty position, when only tenure-track is explicitly stated? For how long are people hired as tenure-track?

2. What software and software tools are required for working in a university environment, when none were explicitly mentioned? Cobol, PROLOG, UML? A person would need a lot of knowledge about university teaching and research to understand these expectations.

3. What do internationally recognized programs and collaborations with interesting institutions have to do with a university job ad?

4. How could a computer summarize what this ad is about? What must it know to intelligently retrieve this ad from the web for a job-hunting PhD candidate?

There are (at least!) three major issues involved in understanding language. First, a large amount of human knowledge is assumed. Language acts describe relationships in an often complex world. Knowledge of these relationships must be part of any understanding system. Second, language is pattern based: phonemes are components of words and words make phrases and sentences. Phoneme, word, and sentence orders are not random. Communication is impossible without a rather constrained use of these components. Finally, language acts are the product of agents, either human or computer. Agents are embedded in complex environments with both individual and sociological dimensions. Language acts are purposive.

This chapter provides an introduction to the problems of natural language understanding and the computational techniques developed for their solution. Although in this chapter we focus primarily on the understanding of text, speech-understanding and generation systems must also solve these problems, as well as the additional difficulties associated with the recognition and disambiguation of words grounded in a particular context.

Early AI programs, because of the knowledge required to understand unconstrained language, made progress by restricting their focus to *microworlds*, limited applications that required minimal domain knowledge. One of the earliest programs to take this approach was Terry Winograd's SHRDLU (Winograd 1972), which could converse about a *blocks world* consisting of differently shaped and colored blocks and a hand for moving them about, as in Figure 14.1.

SHRDLU could respond to English-language queries such as "What is sitting on the red block?" "What shape is the blue block on the table?" or "Place the green pyramid on the red brick." It could handle pronoun references such as "Is there a red block? Pick it up." It could even understand ellipses, such as "What color is the block on the blue brick? Shape?" Because of the simplicity of the blocks world, it was possible to provide the system with complete knowledge of the world. Because the blocks world did not involve the more difficult problems of commonsense reasoning such as understanding time, causality, possibilities, or beliefs, the techniques for representing this knowledge were relatively straightforward. In spite of its limited domain, SHRDLU did provide a model for the integration of syntax and semantics and demonstrated that a program with sufficient knowledge of a domain of discourse could communicate meaningfully in natural language.

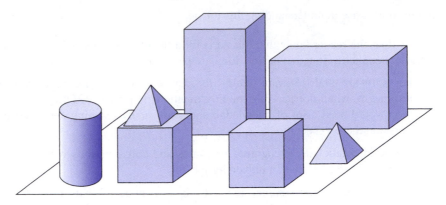

Figure 14.1 A blocks world, adapted from Winograd (1972).

Complementary to the knowledge-intensive component of language understanding just described is to model the patterns and expectations in the language expressions themselves. *Markov Chains* offer us a powerful tool for capturing these regularities. In language use, for example, articles and adjectives generally precede nouns rather than follow them and certain nouns and verbs tend to occur together. Markov models can also capture the relationships between language patterns and the worlds they describe.

In Section 14.1 we present a symbolic approach to understanding language. Section 14.2 presents a syntactic analysis; Section 14.3 combines syntax and semantics using augmented transition network parsing. Section 14.4 presents the stochastic approach to capturing regularities in language expressions. Finally, in Section 14.5 we consider several applications where natural language understanding programs are useful: question answering, accessing information in databases, and web queries and text summarization.

14.1 Deconstructing Language: A Symbolic Analysis

14.1.1 Introduction

Language is a complicated phenomenon, involving processes as varied as the recognition of sounds or printed letters, syntactic parsing, high-level semantic inferences, and even the communication of emotional content through rhythm and inflection. To manage this complexity, linguists have defined different levels of analysis for natural language:

1. *Prosody* deals with the rhythm and intonation of language. This level of analysis is difficult to formalize and often neglected; however, its importance is evident in the powerful effect of poetry or religious chants, as well as the role played by rhythm in children's wordplay and the babbling of infants.

2. *Phonology* examines the sounds that are combined to form language. This branch of linguistics is important for computerized speech recognition and generation.

3. *Morphology* is concerned with the components (morphemes) that make up words. These include the rules governing the formation of words, such as the effect of prefixes (un-, non-, anti-, etc.) and suffixes (-ing, -ly, etc.) that modify the meaning of root words. Morphological analysis is important in determining the role of a word in a sentence, including its tense, number, and part of speech.

4. *Syntax* studies the rules for combining words into legal phrases and sentences, and the use of those rules to parse and generate sentences. This is the best formalized and thus the most successfully automated component of linguistic analysis.

5. *Semantics* considers the meaning of words, phrases, and sentences and the ways in which meaning is conveyed in natural language expressions.

6. *Pragmatics* is the study of the ways in which language is used and its effects on the listener. For example, pragmatics would address the reason why "Yes" is *usually* an inappropriate answer to the question "Do you know what time it is?"

7. *World knowledge* includes knowledge of the physical world, the world of human social interaction, and the role of goals and intentions in communication. This general background knowledge is essential to understand the full meaning of a text or conversation.

Although these levels of analysis seem natural and are supported by psychological evidence, they are, to some extent, artificial divisions that have been imposed on language. All of these interact extensively, with even low-level intonations and rhythmic variations having an effect on the meaning of an utterance, for example, the use of sarcasm. This interaction is evident in the relationship between syntax and semantics, and although some division along these lines seems essential, the exact boundary is difficult to characterize. For example, sentences such as "They are eating apples" have multiple parsings, resolved only by attention to meaning in context. Syntax also affects semantics, as is seen by the role of phrase structure in interpreting the meaning of a sentence.

Although the exact nature of the distinction between syntax and semantics is often debated, both the psychological evidence and its utility in managing the complexity of the problem argue for its retention. We address these deeper issues of language understanding and interpretation again in Chapter 17.

14.1.2 Stages of Language Analysis

Although the specific organization of natural language understanding programs varies with different philosophies and applications—e.g., a front end for a database, an automatic translation system, a story understanding program—all of them must translate the original sentence into an internal representation of its meaning. Generally, natural language understanding follows the stages of Figure 14.2.

The first stage is *parsing*, which analyzes the syntactic structure of sentences. Parsing both verifies that sentences are syntactically well formed and also determines a linguistic structure. By identifying the major linguistic relations such as subject–verb, verb–object,

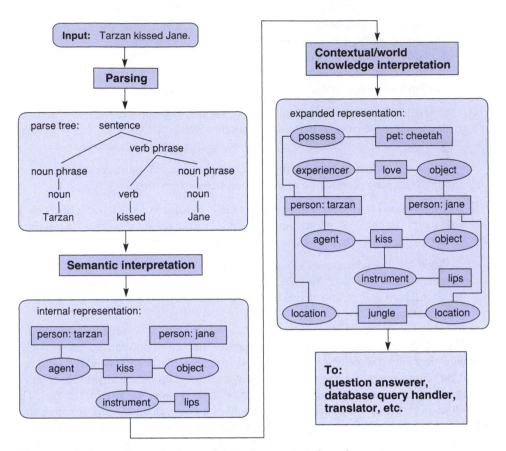

Figure 14.2 Stages in producing an internal representation of a sentence.

and noun–modifier, the parser provides a framework for semantic interpretation. This is often represented as a *parse* tree. The parser employs knowledge of language syntax, morphology, and some semantics.

The second stage is *semantic interpretation*, which produces a representation of the meaning of the text. In Figure 14.2 this is shown as a conceptual graph. Other representations commonly used include conceptual dependencies, frames, and logic-based representations. Semantic interpretation uses knowledge about the meaning of words and linguistic structure, such as case roles of nouns or the transitivity of verbs. In Figure 14.2, the program used knowledge of the meaning of kiss to add the default value of lips for the instrument of kissing. This stage also performs semantic consistency checks. For example, the definition of the verb kiss may include constraints that the object be a person if the agent is a person, that is, Tarzan kisses Jane and does not (normally) kiss Cheetah.

In the third stage, structures from the knowledge base are added to the internal representation of the sentence to produce an expanded representation of the sentence's meaning. This adds the necessary world knowledge required for complete understanding, such as the facts that Tarzan loves Jane, that Jane and Tarzan live in the jungle, and that

Cheetah is Tarzan's pet. This resulting structure represents the meaning of the natural language text and is used by the system for further processing.

In a database front end, for example, the extended structure would combine the representation of the query's meaning with knowledge about the organization of the database. This could then be translated into an appropriate query in the database language (see Section 14.5.2). In a story understanding program, this extended structure would represent the meaning of the story and be used to answer questions about it (see the discussion of scripts in Chapter 7 and of text summarization in Section 14.5.3).

These stages exist in all systems, although they may or may not correspond to distinct software modules. For example, many programs do not produce an explicit parse tree but generate the internal semantic representation directly. Nevertheless, the tree is implicit in the parse of the sentence. *Incremental parsing* (Allen 1987) is a commonly used technique in which a fragment of the internal representation is produced as soon as a significant part of the sentence is parsed. These fragments are combined into a complete structure as the parse proceeds. They are also used to resolve ambiguities and guide the parser.

14.2 Syntax

14.2.1 Specification and Parsing Using Context-Free Grammars

Chapters 3 and 15 introduce the use of *rewrite rules* to specify a grammar. The rules listed below define a grammar for simple transitive sentences such as "The man likes the dog." The rules are numbered for reference.

1. sentence ↔ noun_phrase verb_phrase
2. noun_phrase ↔ noun
3. noun_phrase ↔ article noun
4. verb_phrase ↔ verb
5. verb_phrase ↔ verb noun_phrase
6. article ↔ a
7. article ↔ the
8. noun ↔ man
9. noun ↔ dog
10. verb ↔ likes
11. verb ↔ bites

Rules 6 through 11 have English words on the right-hand side; these rules form a dictionary of words that may appear in sentences. These words are the *terminals* of the grammar and define a *lexicon* of the language. Terms that describe higher-level linguistic concepts (sentence, noun_phrase, etc.) are called *nonterminals*. Nonterminals appear in this typeface. Note that terminals do not appear in the left-hand side of any rule.

A legal sentence is any string of terminals that can be *derived* using these rules. A derivation begins with the nonterminal symbol sentence and produces a string of terminals through a series of substitutions defined by the rules of the grammar. A legal substitution replaces a symbol that matches the left-hand side of a rule with the symbols on the right-hand side of that rule. At intermediate stages of the derivation, the string may contain both terminals and nonterminals and is called a *sentential form*. A derivation of the sentence "The man bites the dog" is given by:

STRING	APPLY RULE #
sentence	1
noun_phrase verb_phrase	3
article noun verb_phrase	7
The noun verb_phrase	8
The man verb_phrase	5
The man verb noun_phrase	11
The man bites noun_phrase	3
The man bites article noun	7
The man bites the noun	9
The man bites the dog	

This is an example of a *top-down* derivation: it begins with the sentence symbol and works down to a string of terminals. A bottom-up derivation starts with a string of terminals and replaces right-hand-side patterns with those from the left-hand side, terminating when all that remains is the sentence symbol.

A derivation can be represented as a tree structure, known as a *parse tree*, in which each node is a symbol from the set of rules of the grammar. The tree's interior nodes are nonterminals; each node and its children correspond, respectively, to the left- and right-hand side of a rule in the grammar. The leaf nodes are terminals and the sentence symbol is the root of the tree. The parse tree for "The man bites the dog" appears in Figure 14.3.

Not only does the existence of a derivation or parse tree prove that a sentence is legal in the grammar, but it also determines the structure of the sentence. The *phrase structure* of the grammar defines the deeper linguistic organization of the language. For example, the breakdown of a sentence into a noun_phrase and a verb_phrase specifies the relation between an action and its agent. This phrase structure plays an essential role in semantic interpretation by defining intermediate stages in a derivation at which semantic processing may take place.

Parsing is the problem of constructing a derivation or a *parse tree* for an input string from a formal definition of a grammar. Parsing algorithms fall into two classes: *top-down parsers*, which begin with the top-level sentence symbol and attempt to build a tree whose leaves match the target sentence, and *bottom-up parsers*, which start with the words in the sentence (the terminals) and attempt to find a series of reductions that yield the sentence symbol.

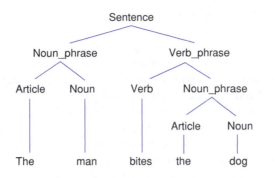

Figure 14.3 Parse tree for the sentence "The man bites the dog."

One difficulty, that can add huge complexity to the parsing problem, is in determining which of several potentially applicable rules should be used at any step of the derivation. If the wrong choice is made, the parser may fail to recognize a legal sentence. For example, in attempting to parse the sentence "The dog bites" in a bottom-up fashion, rules 7, 9, and 11 produce the string article noun verb. At this point, an erroneous application of rule 2 would produce article noun_phrase verb; this could not be reduced to the sentence symbol. The parser should have used rule 3 instead. Similar problems can occur in a top-down parse.

The problem of selecting the correct rule at any stage of the parse is handled either by allowing the parser to set backtrack pointers and return to the problem situation if an incorrect choice was made (as in *recursive descent parsers,* see Section 15.9) or by using look-ahead to check the input string for features that will help determine the proper rule to apply. With either approach, we must take care to control the complexity of execution while guaranteeing a correct parse.

The inverse problem is that of *generation*, or producing legal sentences from an internal semantic representation. Generation starts with a representation of some meaningful content (such as a semantic network or conceptual dependency graph) and constructs a grammatically correct sentence that communicates this meaning. However, generation is not merely the reverse of understanding; it encounters unique difficulties and requires separate methodologies.

Because parsing is particularly important in the processing of programming languages as well as natural language, researchers have developed a number of different parsing algorithms. These include both top-down and bottom-up strategies. Though a complete survey of parsing algorithms is beyond the scope of this chapter, we do consider *transition network* parsers in some detail. Although transition network parsers themselves are not sufficiently powerful for the analysis of natural language, they form the basis for *augmented transition networks*, which have proved to be a useful and powerful tool for natural language work.

14.2.2 Transition Network Parsers

A transition network parser represents a grammar as a set of finite-state machines or *transition networks*. Each network corresponds to a single nonterminal in the grammar. Arcs in the networks are labeled with either terminal or nonterminal symbols. Each path through the network, from the start state to the final state, corresponds to some rule for that nonterminal; the sequence of arc labels on the path is the sequence of symbols on the right-hand side of the rule. The grammar of Section 14.2.1 is represented by the transition networks of Figure 14.4. When there is more than one rule for a nonterminal, the corresponding network has multiple paths from the start to the goal. For example, the rules noun_phrase ↔ noun and noun_phrase ↔ article noun are captured by alternative paths through the noun_phrase network of Figure 14.4.

Finding a successful transition through the network for a nonterminal corresponds to the replacement of that nonterminal by the right-hand side of a grammar rule. For example, to parse a sentence, a transition network parser must find a transition through the sentence network. It begins in the start state (S$_{initial}$) and takes the noun_phrase transition and then the verb_phrase transition to reach the final state (S$_{final}$). This is equivalent to replacing the original sentence symbol with the pair of symbols noun_phrase verb_phrase.

In order to cross an arc, the parser examines its label. If the label is a terminal symbol, the parser checks the input stream to see whether the next word matches the arc label. If it does not match, the transition cannot be taken. If the arc is labeled with a nonterminal symbol, the parser retrieves the network for that nonterminal and recursively attempts to find a path through it. If the parser fails to find a path through this network, the top-level arc cannot be traversed. This causes the parser to backtrack and attempt another path through the network. Thus, the parser tries to find a path through the sentence network; if it succeeds, the input string is a legal sentence in the grammar.

Consider the simple sentence "Dog bites." The first steps in parsing this sentence are illustrated in Figure 14.5:

1. The parser begins with the sentence network and tries to move along the arc labeled noun_phrase. To do so, it retrieves the network for noun_phrase.

2. In the noun_phrase network, the parser first tries the transition marked article. This causes it to branch to the network for article.

3. It fails to find a path to the finish node of the article network because the first word of the sentence, "Dog," matches neither of the arc labels. The parser fails and backtracks to the noun_phrase network.

4. The parser attempts to follow the arc labeled noun in the noun_phrase network and branches to the network for noun.

5. The parser successfully crosses the arc labeled "dog," because this corresponds to the first word of the input stream.

6. The noun network returns success. This allows the arc labeled noun in the noun_phrase network to be crossed to the final state.

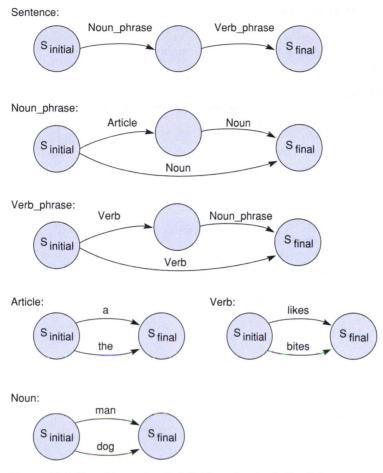

Figure 14.4 Transition network definition of a simple English grammar.

7. The noun_phrase network returns success to the top-level network, allowing the transition of the arc labeled noun_phrase.

8. A sequence of similar steps is followed to parse the verb_phrase portion of the sentence.

Pseudo-code for a transition network parser appears below. It is defined using two mutually recursive functions, parse and transition. Parse takes a grammar symbol as argument: if the symbol is a terminal, parse checks it against the next word in the input stream. If it is a nonterminal, parse retrieves the transition network associated with the symbol and calls transition to find a path through the network. Transition takes a state in a transition network as argument and tries to find a path through that network in a depth-first fashion. To parse a sentence, call parse(sentence).

```
function parse(grammar_symbol);

begin
  save pointer to current location in input stream;
  case

    grammar_symbol is a terminal:
      if grammar_symbol matches the next word in the input stream
        then return (success)
        else begin
          reset input stream;
          return (failure)
        end;
    grammar_symbol is a nonterminal:
      begin
        retrieve the transition network labeled by grammar symbol;
        state := start state of network;
        if transition(state) returns success
        then return (success)
        else begin
          reset input stream;
          return (failure)
        end
      end

  end
end.


function transition (current_state);

begin
  case

    current_state is a final state:
      return (success)
    current_state is not a final state:
      while there are unexamined transitions out of current_state
        do begin
          grammar_symbol := the label on the next unexamined transition;
          if parse(grammar_symbol) returns (success)
            then begin
              next_state := state at end of the transition;
              if transition(next_state) returns success;
                   then return (success)
            end
        end
      return (failure)

  end
end.
```

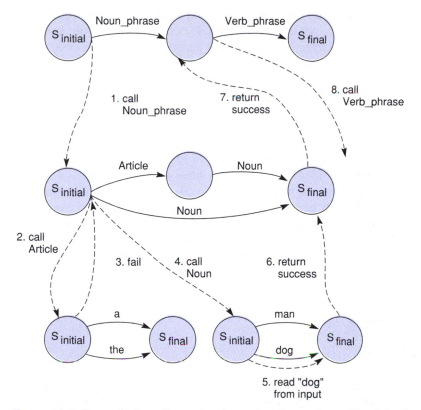

Figure 14.5 Trace of a transition network parse of the sentence "Dog bites."

Because the parser may make a mistake and have to backtrack, parse retains a pointer to the current location in the input stream. This allows the input stream to be reset to this location in the event the parser backtracks.

This transition network parser determines whether a sentence is grammatically correct, but it does not construct a parse tree. This may be accomplished by having the functions return a subtree of the parse tree instead of the symbol success. Modifications that would accomplish this are:

1. Each time the function parse is called with a terminal symbol as argument and that terminal matches the next symbol of input, it returns a tree consisting of a single leaf node labeled with that symbol.

2. When parse is called with a nonterminal, grammar_symbol, it calls transition. If transition succeeds, it returns an ordered set of subtrees (described below). Parse combines these into a tree whose root is grammar_symbol and whose children are the subtrees returned by transition.

3. In searching for a path through a network, transition calls parse on the label of each arc. On success, parse returns a tree representing a parse of that symbol. Transition saves these subtrees in an ordered set and, on finding a path through the network, returns the ordered set of parse trees corresponding to the sequence of arc labels on the path.

14.2.3 The Chomsky Hierarchy and Context-Sensitive Grammars

In Section 14.2.1, we defined a small subset of English using a *context-free grammar*. A context-free grammar allows rules to have only a single nonterminal on their left-hand side. Consequently, the rule may be applied to any occurrence of that symbol, regardless of its context. Though context-free grammars have proved to be a powerful tool for defining programming languages and other formalisms in computer science, there is reason to believe that they are not powerful enough, by themselves, to represent the rules of natural language syntax. For example, consider what happens if we add both singular and plural nouns and verbs to the grammar of Section 14.2.1:

noun ↔ men
noun ↔ dogs
verb ↔ bites
verb ↔ like

The resulting grammar will parse sentences like "The dogs like the men", but it also accepts "A men bites a dogs." The parser accepts these sentences because the rules don't use context to determine when singular and plural forms need be coordinated. The rule defining a sentence as a noun_phrase followed by a verb_phrase does not require that the noun and verb agree on number, or that articles agree with nouns.

Context-free languages can be extended to handle these situations, but a more natural approach is for the grammer to be context sensitive, where the components of the parse tree are designed to constrain each other. Chomsky (1965) first proposed a world of hierarchical and ever more powerful grammers (Hopcroft and Ullman 1979). At the bottom of this hierarchy is the class of *regular languages*, whose grammar may be defined using a finite-state machine, Section 3.1. Regular languages have many uses in computer science, but they are not powerful enough to represent the syntax of most programming languages.

The *context-free languages* are above the regular languages in the Chomsky hierarchy. Context-free languages are defined using rewrite rules such as in Section 14.2.1; context-free rules may only have one nonterminal symbol on their left-hand side. Transition network parsers are able to parse the class of context-free languages. It is interesting to note that if we *do not* allow recursion in a transition network parser i.e., arcs may be labeled only with terminal symbols and transitions may not "call" another network, then the class of languages that may be so defined corresponds to regular expressions. Thus, regular languages are a proper subset of the context-free languages.

The *context-sensitive* languages form a proper superset of the context-free languages. These are defined using *context-sensitive grammars* which allow more than one symbol on the left-hand side of a rule and make it possible to define a context in which that rule can be applied. This ensures satisfaction of global constraints such as number agreement and other semantic checks. The only restriction on context-sensitive grammar rules is that the right-hand side be at least as long as the left-hand side (Hopcroft and Ullman 1979).

A fourth class, forming a superset of the context-sensitive languages, is the class of *recursively enumerable* languages. Recursively enumerable languages may be defined using unconstrained production rules; because these rules are less constrained than context-sensitive rules, the recursively enumerable languages are a proper superset of the context-sensitive languages. This class is not of interest in defining the syntax of natural language, although it is important in the theory of computer science. The remainder of this section focuses on English as a context-sensitive language.

A simple context-free grammar for sentences of the form article noun verb that enforces number agreement between article and noun and subject and verb is given by:

sentence ↔ noun_phrase verb_phrase
noun_phrase ↔ article number noun
noun_phrase ↔ number noun
number ↔ singular
number ↔ plural
article singular ↔ a singular
article singular ↔ the singular
article plural ↔ some plural
article plural ↔ the plural
singular noun ↔ dog singular
singular noun ↔ man singular
plural noun ↔ men plural
plural noun ↔ dogs plural
singular verb_phrase ↔ singular verb
plural verb_phrase ↔ plural verb
singular verb ↔ bites
singular verb ↔ likes
plural verb ↔ bite
plural verb ↔ like

In this grammar, the nonterminals singular and plural offer constraints to determine when different article, noun, and verb_phrase rules can be applied, ensuring number agreement. A derivation of the sentence "The dogs bite" using this grammar is given by:

sentence.
noun_phrase verb_phrase.
article plural noun verb_phrase.
The plural noun verb_phrase.
The dogs plural verb_phrase.
The dogs plural verb.
The dogs bite.

Similarly, we can use context-sensitive grammars to perform checks for semantic agreement. For example, we could disallow sentences such as "Man bites dog" by adding a nonterminal, act_of_biting, to the grammar. This nonterminal could be checked in the rules to prevent any sentence involving "bites" from having "man" as its subject.

Though context-sensitive grammars can define language structures that cannot be captured using context-free grammars, they have a number of disadvantages for the design of practical parsers:

1. Context-sensitive grammars increase drastically the number of rules and non-terminals in the grammar. Imagine the complexity of a context-sensitive grammar that would include number, person, and all the other forms of agreement required by English.

2. They obscure the phrase structure of the language that is so clearly represented in the context-free rules.

3. By attempting to handle more complicated checks for agreement and semantic consistency in the grammar itself, they lose many of the benefits of separating the syntactic and semantic components of language.

4. Context-sensitive grammars do not address the problem of building a semantic representation of the meaning of the text. A parser that simply accepts or rejects sentences is not sufficient; it must return a useful representation of the sentence's semantic meaning.

In the next section we examine *augmented transition networks* (ATNs), an extension of transition networks that can define context-sensitive languages but has several advantages over context-sensitive grammars in the design of parsers.

14.3 Syntax and Knowledge with ATN Parsers

An alternative to context-sensitive grammars is to retain the simpler structure of context-free grammar rules but augment these rules with attached procedures that perform the necessary contextual tests. These procedures are executed when a rule is invoked in parsing. Rather than using the grammar to describe such notions as number, tense, and person, we represent these as *features* attached to terminals and nonterminals of the grammar. The procedures attached to the rules of the grammar access these features to assign values and perform the necessary tests. Grammars that use augmentations of context-free grammars to implement context sensitivity include *augmented phrase structure grammars* (Heidorn 1975, Sowa 1984), *augmentations of logic grammars* (Allen 1987), and the *augmented transition network* (ATN).

In this section we present ATN parsing and outline the design of a simple ATN parser for sentences about the "dogs world" introduced in Section 14.2.1. We address the first two steps of Figure 14.2: creation of a parse tree and its use to construct a representation of the sentence's meaning. We use conceptual graphs in this example, although ATN parsers can also be used with script, frame, or logic representations.

14.3.1   Augmented Transition Network Parsers

Augmented transition networks extend transition networks by allowing procedures to be attached to the arcs of the networks. An ATN parser executes these attached procedures when it traverses the arcs. The procedures may assign values to grammatical features and perform tests, causing a transition to fail if certain conditions (such as number agreement) are not met. These procedures also construct a parse tree, which is used to generate an internal semantic representation of the sentence's meaning.

We represent both terminals and nonterminals as identifiers (e.g., verb, noun_phrase) with attached features. For example, a word is described using its morphological root, along with features for its part of speech, number, person, etc. Nonterminals in the grammar are similarly described. A noun phrase is described by its article, noun, number, and person. Both terminals and nonterminals can be represented using framelike structures with named slots and values. The values of these slots specify grammatical features or pointers to other structures. For example, the first slot of a sentence frame contains a pointer to a noun phrase definition. Figure 14.6 shows the frames for the sentence, noun_phrase, and verb_phrase nonterminals in our simple grammar.

Individual words are represented using similar structures. Each word in the dictionary is defined by a frame that specifies its part of speech (article, noun, etc.), its morphological root, and its significant grammatical features. In our example, we are only checking for number agreement and only record this feature. More sophisticated grammars indicate person and other features. These dictionary entries may also indicate the conceptual graph definition of the word's meaning for use in semantic interpretation. The complete dictionary for our grammar appears in Figure 14.7.

Figure 14.8 presents an ATN for our grammar, with pseudo-code descriptions of the tests performed at each arc. Arcs are labeled with both nonterminals of the grammar (as in Figure 14.4) and numbers; these numbers are used to indicate the function attached to each arc. These functions must run successfully in order to traverse the arc.

When the parser calls a network for a nonterminal, it creates a new frame for that non-terminal. For example, on entering the noun_phrase network it creates a new noun_phrase frame. The slots of the frame are filled by the functions for that network. These slots may be assigned values of grammatical features or pointers to components of

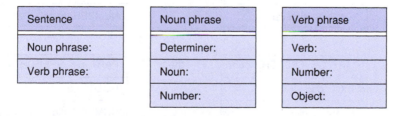

Figure 14.6 Structures representing the sentence, noun phrase, and verb phrase nonterminals of the grammar.

the syntactic structure (e.g., a verb_phrase can consist of a verb and a noun_phrase). When the final state is reached, the network returns this structure.

When the network traverses arcs labeled noun, article, and verb, it reads the next word from the input stream and retrieves that word's definition from the dictionary. If the word is not the expected part of speech, the rule fails; otherwise the definition frame is returned.

In Figure 14.8 frames and slots are indicated using a Frame.Slot notation; e.g., the number slot of the verb frame is indicated by VERB.NUMBER. As the parse proceeds, each function builds and returns a frame describing the associated syntactic structure. This structure includes pointers to structures returned by lower-level networks. The top-level

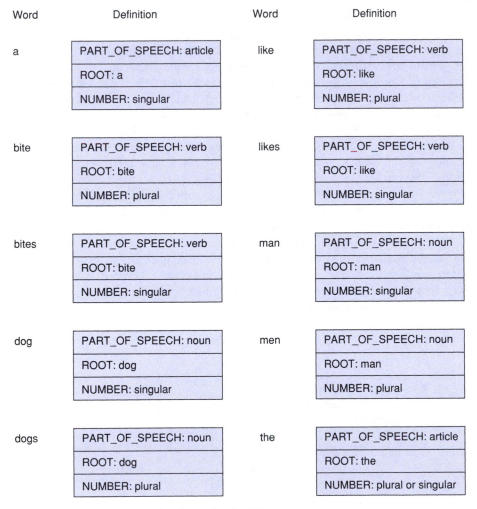

Figure 14.7 Dictionary entries for a simple ATN.

sentence function returns a **sentence** structure representing the parse tree for the input. This structure is passed to the semantic interpreter. Figure 14.9 shows the parse tree that is returned for the sentence "The dog likes a man."

The next phase of natural language processing takes the parse tree, such as that of Figure 14.9, and constructs a semantic representation of the domain knowledge and meaning content of the sentence.

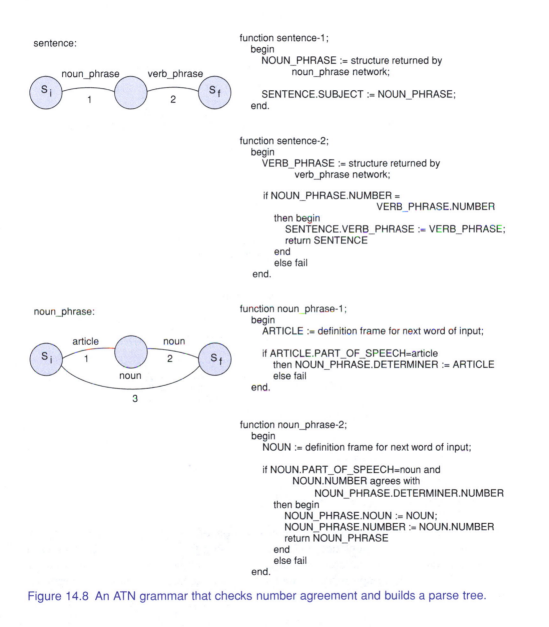

```
function sentence-1;
    begin
        NOUN_PHRASE := structure returned by
            noun_phrase network;

        SENTENCE.SUBJECT := NOUN_PHRASE;
    end.


function sentence-2;
    begin
        VERB_PHRASE := structure returned by
            verb_phrase network;

        if NOUN_PHRASE.NUMBER =
                            VERB_PHRASE.NUMBER
            then begin
                SENTENCE.VERB_PHRASE := VERB_PHRASE;
                return SENTENCE
            end
            else fail
    end.


function noun_phrase-1;
    begin
        ARTICLE := definition frame for next word of input;

        if ARTICLE.PART_OF_SPEECH=article
            then NOUN_PHRASE.DETERMINER := ARTICLE
            else fail
    end.


function noun_phrase-2;
    begin
        NOUN := definition frame for next word of input;

        if NOUN.PART_OF_SPEECH=noun and
                NOUN.NUMBER agrees with
                    NOUN_PHRASE.DETERMINER.NUMBER
            then begin
                NOUN_PHRASE.NOUN := NOUN;
                NOUN_PHRASE.NUMBER := NOUN.NUMBER
                return NOUN_PHRASE
            end
            else fail
    end.
```

Figure 14.8 An ATN grammar that checks number agreement and builds a parse tree.

```
function noun_phrase-3
    begin
        NOUN := definition frame for next word of input;

        if NOUN.PART_OF_SPEECH=noun
            then begin
                NOUN_PHRASE.DETERMINER := unspecified;
                NOUN_PHRASE.NOUN := NOUN
                NOUN_PHRASE.NUMBER := NOUN.NUMBER
            end
            else fail
    end.
```

verb_phrase:

```
function verb_phrase-1
    begin
        VERB := definition frame for next word of input;

        if VERB.PART_OF_SPEECH=verb
            then begin
                VERB_PHRASE.VERB := VERB;
                VERB_PHRASE.NUMBER := VERB.NUMBER;
            end;
    end.
```

```
function verb_phrase-2
    begin
        NOUN_PHRASE := structure returned by
                              noun_phrase network;

        VERB_PHRASE.OBJECT := NOUN_PHRASE;
        return VERB_PHRASE
    end.
```

```
function verb_phrase-3
    begin
        VERB := definition frame for next word of input;

        if VERB.PART_OF_SPEECH=verb
            then begin
                VERB_PHRASE.VERB := VERB;
                VERB_PHRASE.NUMBER := VERB.NUMBER;
                VERB_PHRASE.OBJECT := unspecified;
                return VERB_PHRASE;
            end;
    end.
```

Figure 14.8 (cont'd) An ATN grammar that checks number agreement and builds a parse tree.

14.3.2 Combining Syntax and Semantic Knowledge

The semantic interpreter constructs a representation of the input string's meaning by beginning at the root, or sentence node, and traversing the parse tree. At each node, it recursively interprets the children of that node and combines the results into a single conceptual graph; this graph is passed up the tree. For example, the semantic interpreter builds a representation of the verb_phrase by recursively building representations of the

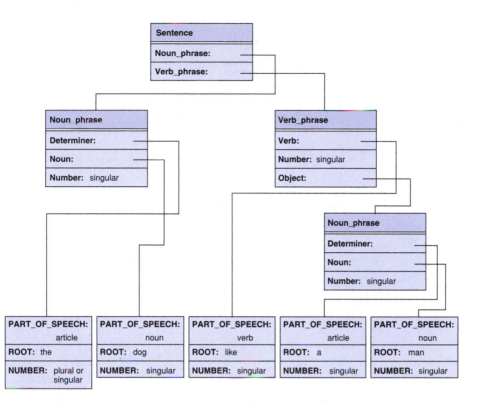

Figure 14.9 Parse tree for the sentence "The dog likes a man" returned by an ATN parser.

node's children, verb and noun_phrase, and joining these to form an interpretation of the verb phrase. This is passed to the sentence node and combined with the representation of the subject.

Recursion stops at the terminals of the parse tree. Some of these, such as nouns, verbs, and adjectives, cause concepts to be retrieved from the knowledge base. Others, such as articles, do not directly correspond to concepts in the knowledge base but qualify other concepts in the graph.

The semantic interpreter in our example uses a knowledge base for the "dogs world." Concepts in the knowledge base include the objects dog and man and the actions like and bite. These concepts are described by the type hierarchy of Figure 14.10.

In addition to concepts, we must define the relations that will be used in our conceptual graphs. For this example, we use the following concepts:

agent links an act with a concept of type animate. agent defines the relation between an action and the animate object causing the action.

experiencer links a state with a concept of type animate. It defines the relation between a mental state and its experiencer.

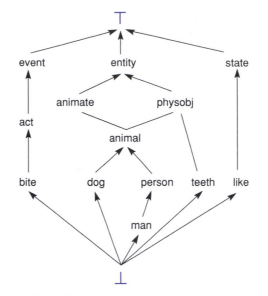

Figure 14.10 Type hierarchy used in "dogs world" example.

instrument links an act with an entity and defines the instrument used in an action.

object links an event or state with an entity and represents the verb–object relation.

part links concepts of type physobj and defines the relation between whole and part.

The verb plays a particularly important role in building an interpretation, as it defines the relationships between the subject, object, and other components of the sentence. We represent each verb using a *case frame* that specifies:

1. The linguistic relationships (agent, object, instrument, and so on) appropriate to that particular verb. Transitive verbs, for example, have an object; intransitive verbs do not.

2. Constraints on the values that may be assigned to any component of the case frame. For example, in the case frame for the verb "bites," we have asserted that the agent must be of the type dog. This causes "Man bites dog" to be rejected as semantically incorrect.

3. Default values on components of the case frame. In the "bites" frame, we have a default value of teeth for the concept linked to the instrument relation.

The case frames for the verbs like and bite appear in Figure 14.11.

We define the actions that build a semantic representation with rules or procedures for each potential node in the parse tree. Rules for our example are described as pseudo-code

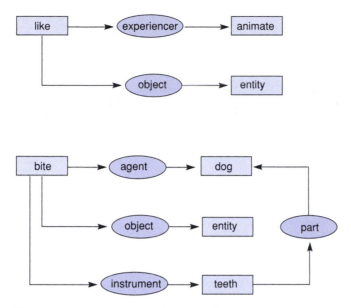

Figure 14.11 Case frames for the verbs "like" and "bite."

procedures. In each procedure, if a specified join or other test fails, that interpretation is rejected as semantically incorrect:

procedure sentence;

begin
    call noun_phrase to get a representation of the subject;
    call verb_phrase to get a representation of the verb_phrase;
    using join and restrict, bind the noun concept returned for the subject to
        the agent of the graph for the verb_phrase
end.

procedure noun_phrase;

begin
    call noun to get a representation of the noun;
    case
        the article is indefinite and number singular: the noun concept is generic;
        the article is definite and number singular: bind marker to noun concept;
        number is plural: indicate that the noun concept is plural
    end case
end.

```
procedure verb_phrase;

    begin
        call verb to get a representation of the verb;
        if the verb has an object
            then begin
                call noun_phrase to get a representation of the object;
                using join and restrict, bind concept for object to object of the verb
            end
    end.

procedure verb;

    begin
        retrieve the case frame for the verb
    end.

procedure noun;

    begin
        retrieve the concept for the noun
    end.
```

Articles do not correspond to concepts in the knowledge base but determine whether their noun concept is generic or specific. We have not discussed the representation of plural concepts; refer to Sowa (1984) for their treatment as conceptual graphs.

Using these procedures, along with the concept hierarchy of Figure 14.10 and the case frames of Figure 14.11, we trace the actions of the semantic interpreter in building a semantic representation of the sentence "The dog likes a man" from the parse tree of Figure 14.9. This trace appears in Figure 14.12.

The actions taken in the trace are (numbers in parentheses refer to Figure 14.12):

1. Beginning at the sentence node, call sentence.

2. sentence calls noun_phrase.

3. noun_phrase calls noun.

4. noun returns a concept for the noun dog (1 in Figure 14.12).

5. Because the article is definite, noun_phrase binds an individual marker to the concept (2) and returns this concept to sentence.

6. sentence calls verb_phrase.

7. verb_phrase calls verb, which retrieves the case frame for like (3).

8. verb_phrase calls noun_phrase, which then calls noun to retrieve the concept for man (4).

9. Because the article is indefinite, noun_phrase leaves this concept generic (5).

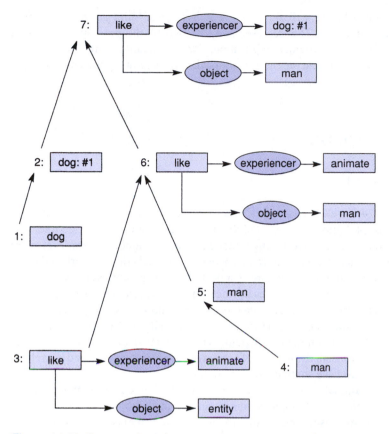

Figure 14.12 Construction of a semantic representation from the parse tree of Figure 14.9.

10. The verb_phrase procedure restricts the entity concept in the case frame and joins it with the concept for man (6). This structure is returned to sentence.

11. sentence joins concept dog: #1 to the experiencer node of the case frame (7).

This conceptual graph represents the meaning of the sentence.

Language generation is a related problem addressed by natural language understanding programs. The generation of English sentences requires the construction of a semantically correct output from an internal representation of meaning. For example, the agent relation indicates a subject–verb relationship between two concepts. Simple approaches allow the appropriate words to be plugged into stored sentence *templates*. These templates are patterns for sentences and fragments, such as noun phrases and prepositional phrases. The output is constructed by walking the conceptual graph and combining these fragments. More sophisticated approaches to language generation use transformational grammars to map meaning into a range of possible sentences (Winograd 1972, Allen 1987).

In Section 14.5 we will show how a program can build an internal representation of natural language text. This representation is used by the program in a number of ways, depending on the particular application. Two applications are presented. But first, in Section 14.4, we present stochastic approaches for capturing the patterns and regularities of language.

14.4 Stochastic Tools for Language Analysis

14.4.1 Introduction

In Section 14.1 we discussed the "pattern-based" component of language understanding. In Sections 14.2 and 14.3 we noted that the semantic and knowledge intensive aspects of language could be enabled through phonemic, verbal, and sentence-level representational structures. In this section we introduce stochastic models that support, at these same levels, pattern based analysis of structures supporting language comprehension.

Statistical language techniques are methods which arise when we view natural language as a random process. In everyday parlance, randomness suggests lack of structure, definition, or understanding. However, viewing natural language as a random process *generalizes* the deterministic viewpoint. That is, statistical (or stochastic) techniques can accurately model both those parts of language which are well defined as well as those parts which indeed do have some degree of randomness.

Viewing language as a random process allows us to redefine many of the basic problems within natural language understanding in a rigorous, mathematical manner. It is an interesting exercise, for example, to take several sentences, say the previous paragraph including periods and parentheses, and to print out these same words ordered by a random number generator. The result will make very little sense. It is interesting to note (Jurafsky and Martin 2000) that these same pattern-based constraints operate on many levels of linguistic analysis, including acoustic patterns, phonemic combinations, the analysis of grammatical structure, and so on. As an example of the use of stochastic tools, we consider the problem of part-of-speech tagging.

Most people are familiar with this problem from grammar class. We want to label each word in a sentence as a noun, verb, preposition, adjective, and so on. In addition, if the word is a verb, we may want to know if it is active, passive, transitive, or intransitive. If the word is a noun, whether it is singular or plural and so on. Difficulty arises with words like "swing." If we say, "front porch swing," swing is a noun but if we say "swing at the ball" then swing is a verb. We present next a quote from Picasso with its correct part of speech labels:

Art	is	a	lie	that	lets	us	see	the	truth.
Noun	Verb	Article	Noun	Pronoun	Verb	Pronoun	Verb	Article	Noun

To begin our analysis, we first define the problem formally. We have a set of words in our language $S_w = \{w_1, ..., w_n\}$, for example {a, aardvark, ..., zygote}, and a set of parts of speech or tags $S_t = \{t_1, ..., t_m\}$. A sentence with n words is a sequence of n random variables $W_1, W_2, ..., W_n$. These are called *random* variables because they can take on any of the values in S_w with some probability. The tags, $T_1, T_2, ..., T_n$, are also a sequence of random variables. The value that T_i takes on will be denoted t_i and the value of W_i is w_i. We want to find the sequence of values for these tags which is most likely, given the words in the sentence. Formally, we want to pick $t_1, ..., t_n$ to maximize:

$$P(T_1 = t_1, ..., T_n = t_n \mid W_1 = w_1, ..., W_n = w_n)$$

Recall from Section 9.3 that $P(X \mid Y)$ stands for *the probability of* X *given that* Y *has occurred*. It is customary to drop reference to the random variables and just write:

$$P(t_1, ..., t_n \mid w_1, ..., w_n) \qquad\qquad \text{equation 1}$$

Note that if we knew this probability distribution exactly and if we had enough time to maximize over all possible tag sets, we would always get the best possible set of tags for the words considered. In addition, if there really were only one correct sequence of tags for each sentence, an idea your grammar teacher may have espoused, this probabilistic technique would always find that correct sequence! Thus the probability for the correct sequence would be 1 and that for all other sequences 0. This is what we meant when we said that the statistical viewpoint can generalize the deterministic one.

In reality, because of limited storage space, data, and time, we cannot use this technique and must come up with some type of approximation. The rest of this section deals with better and better ways to approximate equation 1.

First note that we can rewrite equation 1 in a more useful manner:

$$P(t_1, ..., t_n \mid w_1, ..., w_n) = P(t_1, ..., t_n, w_1, ..., w_n) / P(w_1, ..., w_n)$$

and since we maximize this by choosing $t_1, ..., t_n$, we can simplify equation 1 to:

$$P(t_1, ..., t_n, w_1, ..., w_n) =$$

$$P(t_1)P(w_1 \mid t_1)P(t_2 \mid t_1, w_1) ... P(t_n \mid w_1, ..., w_n, t_1, ..., t_{n-1}) =$$

$$\prod_{i=1}^{n} P(t_i \mid t_1, ..., t_{i-1}, w_1, ..., w_{i-1}) P(w_i \mid t_1, ..., t_{i-1}, w_1, ..., w_{i-1}) \qquad \text{equation 2}$$

Notice that equation 2 is equivalent to equation 1.

14.4.2   A Markov Model Approach

In practice, and as seen earlier in our discussion of Section 9.3, it is usually a complex task to maximize equations with probabilities conditioned on many other random variables, such as we find in equation 2. There are three reasons for this: first, it is difficult to store the probability of a random variable conditioned on many other random variables because the number of possible probabilities increases exponentially with the number of conditioning variables. Secondly, even if we could store all of the probability values, it is often difficult to estimate their values. Estimation is usually done empirically by counting the number of occurrences of an event in a hand-tagged training set and thus, if an event occurs only a few times in the training set, we will not get a good estimate of its probability. That is, it is easier to estimate P(cat | the) than P(cat | The dog chased the) since there will be fewer occurrences of the latter in the training set. Finally, finding the chain of tags that maximizes structures like equation 2 would take too long, as will be shown next.

First, we need to make some useful approximations of equation 2. The first rough attempt is:

$$P(t_i \mid t_1, ..., t_{i-1}, w_1, ..., w_{i-1}) \text{ approaches } P(t_i \mid t_{i-1})$$

and

$$P(w_i \mid t_1, ..., t_{i-1}, w_1, ..., w_{i-1}) \text{ approaches } P(w_i \mid t_i).$$

These are called *Markov assumptions* because they assume that the present thing under consideration is independent of things in the far past.

Plugging these approximations back into equation 2, we get

$$\prod_{i=1}^{n} P(t_i \mid t_{i-1}) \, P(w_i \mid t_i) \qquad\qquad\qquad \text{equation 3}$$

Equation 3 is straightforward to work with because its probabilities can be easily estimated and stored. Recall that equation 3 is just an estimate of $P(t_1, ..., t_n \mid w_1, ..., w_n)$ and we still need to maximize it by choosing the tags, i.e., $t_1, ..., t_n$. Fortunately, there is a dynamic programming algorithm called the Viterbi algorithm (Viterbi 1967, Forney 1973) which will allow us to do this. The Viterbi algorithm calculates the probability of t^2 tag sequences for each word in the sentence where t is the number of possible tags. For a particular step, the tag sequences under consideration are of the following form:

article article	{best tail}
article verb	{best tail}
...	
article noun	{best tail}
...	
...	
noun article	{best tail}
...	
noun noun	{best tail}

where {best tail} is the most likely sequence of tags found dynamically for the last n − 2 words for the given n − 1 tag.

There is an entry in the table for every possible value for tag number $n - 1$ and tag number n (hence we have the t^2 tag sequences). At each step, the algorithm finds the maximal probabilities and adds one tag to each best tail sequence. This algorithm is guaranteed to find the tag sequence which maximizes equation 3 and it runs in $O(t^2 s)$, where t is the number of tags and s is the number of words in the sentence. If $P(t_i)$ is conditioned on the last n tags rather than the last two, the Viterbi algorithm will take $O(t^n s)$. Thus we see why conditioning on too many past variables increases the time taken to find a maximizing value.

Fortunately, the approximations used in equation 3 work well. With about 200 possible tags and a large training set to estimate probabilities, a tagger using these methods is about 97% accurate, which approaches human accuracy. The surprising accuracy of the Markov approximation along with its simplicity makes it useful in many applications. For example, most speech recognition systems use what is called the *trigram* model to provide some "grammatical knowledge" to the system for predicting words the user has spoken. The trigram model is a simple Markov model which estimates the probability of the current word conditioned on the previous two words. It uses the Viterbi algorithm and other techniques just described. For more detail on this and related techniques see Jurafsky and Martin (2000).

14.4.3 A Decision Tree Approach

An obvious problem with the Markov approach is that it considers only local context. If instead of tagging words with simple parts of speech, we wish to do things like identify an agent, identify an object, or decide whether verbs are active or passive, then a richer context is required. The following sentence illustrates this problem:

The policy announced in December by the President guarantees lower taxes.

In fact, the *President* is the agent but a program using a Markov model would likely identify the *policy* as agent and *announced* as an active verb. We can imagine that a program would get better at probabilistically choosing the agent of this type of sentence if it could ask questions like, "Is the current noun inanimate?" or "Does the word *by* appear a few words before the noun under consideration?"

Recall that the tagging problem is equivalent to maximizing equation 2, i.e.,

$$\prod_{i=1}^{n} P(t_i \mid t_1, ..., t_{i-1}, w_1, ..., w_{i-1}) \, P(w_i \mid t_1, ..., t_{i-1}, w_1, ..., w_{i-1}).$$

Theoretically, considering a larger context involves simply finding better estimates for these probabilities. This suggests that we might want to use answers to the grammatical questions above to refine the probabilities.

There are several ways we can address this issue. First, we can combine the Markov approach with the parsing techniques presented in the first three sections of this chapter. A second method allows us to find probabilities conditioned on *yes* or *no* questions with the

ID3 algorithm (presented in detail in Section 10.3 and built in LISP in Section 16.13) or some equivalent algorithm. ID3 trees have the added bonus that out of a very large set of possible questions, they will choose only those which are good at refining probability estimates. For more complicated natural language processing tasks such as parsing, ID3-based trees are often preferred over Markov models. We next describe how to use ID3 to construct a decision tree for use in parsing.

Recall that in the above section we asked the question "Is the current noun inanimate?". We can ask questions like this only if we know which words are animate and which words are inanimate. In fact there is an automated technique which can assign words to these types of classes for us. The technique is called *mutual information clustering*. The mutual information shared between two random variables X and Y is defined as follows:

$$I(X;Y) = \sum_{x \in X} \sum_{y \in Y} P(x, y) \log_2 \frac{P(x, y)}{P(x)P(y)}$$

To do mutual information clustering over a vocabulary of words, we start by putting each word in the vocabulary into a distinct set. At each step, we compute the average mutual information between sets using a bigram, that is a next word model, and a merge of two word sets is chosen which minimizes the loss in average mutual information for all classes.

For example, if initially we have the words cat, kitten, run, and green, at the first step of the algorithm, we have the sets:

{cat} {kitten} {run} {green}.

It is likely that the probability of the next word, given that the previous word was cat, is about equal to the probability of the next word, given that the previous word was kitten. In other words:

P(eats | cat) is about the same as P(eats | kitten)
P(meows | cat) is about the same as P(meows | kitten)

Thus, if we let X1, X2, Y1, and Y2 be random variables such that:

X1 = {{cat}, {kitten}, {run}, {green}}
Y1 = word following X1
X2 = {{cat, kitten}, {run}, {green}}
Y2 = word following X2,

then the mutual information between X2 and Y2 is not much less than the mutual information between X1 and Y1, thus cat and kitten will likely be combined. If we continue this procedure until we have combined all possible classes, we get a binary tree.

Then, *bit codes* can be assigned to words based on the branches taken within the tree that reaches the leaf node that has that word in it. This reflects the semantic meaning of the word. For example:

```
cat   = 01100011
kitten = 01100010
```

Furthermore, we might find that "noun-like" words will be all those words that have a 1 in the leftmost bit and that words which most likely represent inanimate objects may be those whose 3rd bit is a 1.

This new encoding of dictionary words allows the parser to ask questions more effectively. Note that the clustering does not take context into account so that, even though "book" may be clustered as a "noun-like" word, we will want our model to tag it as a verb when it is found in the phrase "book a flight."

14.4.4 Parsing and Other Language Applications for Stochastic Techniques

Stochastic techniques have already been used in many domains of computational linguistics and there is still a great deal of opportunity to apply them to areas which have resisted traditional, symbolic approaches.

The use of statistical methods in parsing was first motivated by the problem of ambiguity. Ambiguity arises from the fact that there are often several possible parses for a given sentence and we need to choose which parse might be the best one. For example, the sentence Print the file on the printer can be parsed using either of the two trees presented in Figure 14.13.

In situations such as this, grammar rules alone are not sufficient for choosing the correct parse. In the Print the file on the printer case we need to consider some information about context and semantics. In fact, the primary use of stochastic techniques in the parsing domain is to help resolve ambiguities. In the current example, we can use the same tool used in part of speech tagging, the ID3 algorithm. ID3 assists us in predicting the probability that a parse is correct based on semantic questions about the sentence. In the case when there is some syntactic ambiguity in the sentence, we can then choose that parse which has the highest probability of being correct. As usual, this technique requires a large *training corpus* of sentences with their correct parses.

Recently, people in the statistical natural language modeling community have become more ambitious and have tried to use statistical techniques without a grammar to do parsing. Although the details of grammarless parsing are beyond the scope of this book, suffice it to say that it is related more to pattern recognition than to the traditional parsing techniques covered earlier in this chapter.

Grammarless parsing has been quite successful. In experiments comparing a traditional grammar-based parser with a grammarless one on the task of parsing the same set of sentences, the grammar-based parser achieved a score, using a popular metric, the *crossing-brackets* measure, of 69% and the grammarless parser 78% (Magerman 1994).

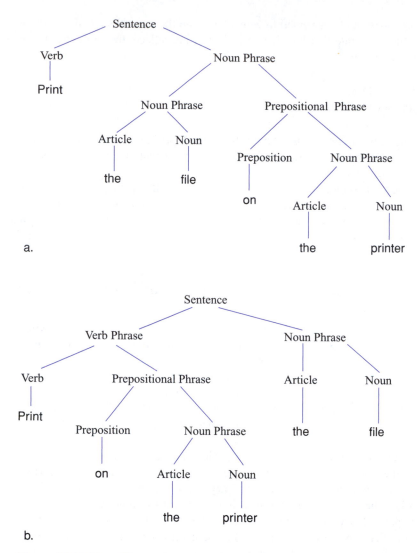

Figure 14.13 Two different parses of "Print the file on the printer."

These results are good, although not outstanding. More importantly, the grammar in the traditional parser was developed meticulously by a trained linguist over the course of about ten years, while the grammarless parser used essentially no hard-coded linguistic information, only sophisticated mathematical models which could infer the needed information from the training data. For more on grammarless parsing and related issues see Manning and Schutze (1999).

Speech understanding, converting speech to text, and handwriting recognition are three further areas which have a long history of using stochastic methods for modeling language. The most commonly used statistical method in these areas is the trigram model for next word prediction. The strength of this model is in its simplicity: it predicts the next word based on the last two words. Recently, there has been work in the statistical language community to maintain the simplicity and ease of use of this model while incorporating grammatical constraints and longer distance dependencies. This new approach uses what are called *grammatical trigrams*. The grammatical trigrams are informed by basic associations between pairs of words (i.e., subject–verb, article–noun, and verb–object). Collectively, these associations are called a *link grammar*. The link grammar is much simpler and easier to construct than the traditional grammars used by linguists and works well with probabilistic methods.

Berger et al. (1994) describe a statistical program, Candide, which translates French text to English text. Candide uses both statistics and information theory to develop a probability model of the translation process. It trains only on a large corpus of French and English sentence pairs and gets results comparable to and in some cases better than Systran (Berger et al. 1994), a commercial translation program. Of particular interest is the fact that the Candide system does no traditional parsing in the translation process. Instead it uses the grammatical trigrams and link grammars just mentioned.

There are several other areas where rigorous stochastic language modeling techniques have not yet been tried but where they may yield useful results. Information extraction, or the problem of obtaining a certain amount of concrete information from a written text, along with WWW searching are two of these potential areas. Further details on stochastic approaches to natural language processing can be found in Jurafsky and Martin (2000) and Manning and Schutze (1999).

14.5 Natural Language Applications

14.5.1 Story Understanding and Question Answering

An interesting test for natural language understanding technology is to write a program that can read a story or other piece of natural language text and answer questions about it. In Chapter 7 we discussed some of the representational issues involved in story understanding, including the importance of combining background knowledge with the explicit content of the text. As illustrated in Figure 14.2, a program can accomplish this by performing network joins between the semantic interpretation of the input and conceptual graph structures in a knowledge base. More sophisticated representations, such as scripts, Section 7.1.4, can model more complex situations involving events occurring over time.

Once the program has built an expanded representation of the text, it can intelligently answer questions about what it has read. The program parses the question into an internal representation and matches that query against the expanded representation of the story. Consider the example of Figure 14.2. The program has read the sentence "Tarzan kissed Jane" and built an expanded representation.

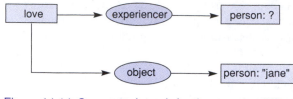

Figure 14.14 Conceptual graph for the question "Who loves Jane?"

Assume that we ask the program "Who loves Jane?" In parsing the question, the interrogative, who, what, why, etc., indicates the intention of the question. *Who* questions ask for the agent of the action; *what* questions ask for the object of the action; *how* questions ask for the means by which the action was performed, and so on. The question "Who loves Jane?" produces the graph of Figure 14.14. The agent node of the graph is marked with a ? to indicate that it is the goal of the question. This structure is then joined with the expanded representation of the original text. The concept that becomes bound to the person: ? concept in the query graph is the answer to the question: "Tarzan loves Jane." As an example of this approach, we build a recursive descent semantic net parser in PROLOG in Section 15.9.

14.5.2   A Database Front End

The major bottleneck in designing natural language understanding programs is the acquisition of sufficient knowledge about the domain of discourse. Current technology is limited to narrow domains with well-defined semantics. An application area that meets these criteria is the development of natural language front ends for databases. Although databases store enormous amounts of information, that information is highly regular and narrow in scope; furthermore, database semantics are well defined. These features, along with the utility of a database that can accept natural language queries, make database front ends an important application of natural language understanding technology.

The task of a database front end is to translate a question in natural language into a well-formed query in the database language. For example, using the SQL database language as a target (Ullman 1982), the natural language front end would translate the question "Who hired John Smith?" into the query:

```
SELECT MANAGER
FROM MANAGER_OF_HIRE
WHERE EMPLOYEE = 'John Smith'
```

In performing this translation, the program must do more than translate the original query; it must also decide where to look in the database (the MANAGER_OF_HIRE relation), the name of the field to access (MANAGER), and the constraints on the query (EMPLOYEE = 'John Smith'). None of this information was in the original question; it

employee	manager	employee	salary
John Smith	Jane Martinez	John Smith	$35,000.00
Alex Barrero	Ed Angel	Alex Barrero	$42,000.00
Don Morrison	Jane Martinez	Don Morrison	$50,000.00
Jan Claus	Ed Angel	Jan Claus	$40,000.00
Anne Cable	Bob Veroff	Anne Cable	$45,000.00

manager_of_hire: employee_salary:

Figure 14.15 Two relations in an employee database.

was found in a knowledge base that knew about the organization of the database and the meaning of potential questions.

A *relational database* organizes data in relations across domains of entities. For example, suppose we are constructing a database of employees and would like to access the salary of each employee and the manager who hired her. This database would consist of three *domains*, or sets of entities: the set of managers, the set of employees, and the set of salaries. We could organize these data into two relations, employee_salary, which relates an employee and her salary, and manager_of_hire, which relates an employee and her manager. In a relational database, relations are usually displayed as tables that enumerate the instances of the relation. The columns of the tables are often named; these names are called *attributes* of the relation. Figure 14.15 shows the tables for the employee_salary and the manager_of_hire relations. Manager_of_hire has two attributes, the employee and the manager. The values of the relation are the pairs of employees and managers.

If we assume that employees have a unique name, manager, and salary, then the employee name can be used as a *key* for both the salary and the manager attributes. An attribute is a key for another attribute if it uniquely determines the value of elements for the other attribute. A valid query indicates a target attribute and specifies a value or set of constraints; the database returns the specified values of the target attribute. We can indicate the relationship between keys and other attributes graphically in a number of ways, including *entity-relationship diagrams* (Ullman 1982) and *data flow diagrams* (Sowa 1984). Both of these approaches display the mapping of keys onto attributes using directed graphs.

We can extend conceptual graphs to include diagrams of these relationships (Sowa 1984). The database relation that defines the mapping is indicated by a rhombus, which is labeled with the name of the relation. The attributes of the relation are expressed as concepts in a conceptual graph and the direction of the arrows indicates the mapping of keys onto other attributes. The entity-relation graphs for the employee_salary and manager_of_hire relations may be seen in Figure 14.16.

In translating from English to a formal query, we must determine the record that contains the answer, the field of that record that is to be returned, and the values of the keys that determine that field. Rather than translating directly from English into the database

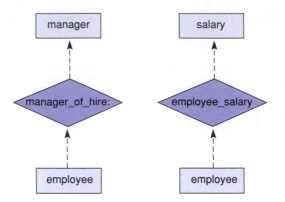

Figure 14.16 Entity-relationship diagrams of the manager_of_hire and employee_salary relations.

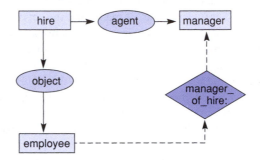

Figure 14.17 Knowledge base entry for "hire" queries.

language, we first translate into a more expressive language such as conceptual graphs. This is necessary because many English queries are ambiguous or require additional interpretation to produce a well-formed database query. The use of a more expressive representation language helps this process.

The natural language front end parses and interprets the query into a conceptual graph, as described earlier in this chapter. It then combines this graph with information in the knowledge base using join and restrict operations. In this example, we want to handle queries such as "Who hired John Smith?" or "How much does John Smith earn?" For each potential query, we store a graph that defines its verb, the case roles for that verb, and any relevant entity-relationship diagrams for the question. Figure 14.17 shows the knowledge base entry for the verb "hire."

The semantic interpreter produces a graph of the user's query and joins this graph with the appropriate knowledge base entry. If there is an attached entity relation graph that maps keys into the goal of the question, the program can use this entity relation graph to form a

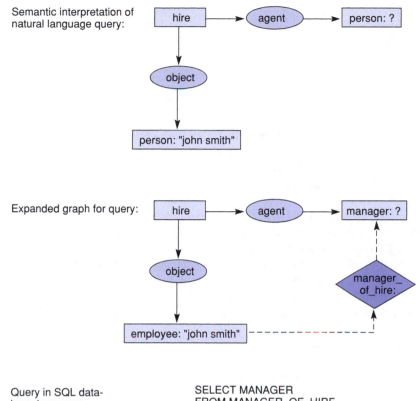

Semantic interpretation of natural language query:

Expanded graph for query:

Query in SQL data-base language:

```
SELECT MANAGER
FROM MANAGER_OF_HIRE
WHERE EMPLOYEE = "john smith"
```

Figure 14.18 Development of a database query from the graph of a natural language input.

database query. Figure 14.18 shows the query graph for the question "Who hired John Smith?" and the result of joining this with the knowledge base entry from Figure 14.17. It also shows the SQL query that is formed from this graph. Note that the name of the appropriate record, the target field, and the key for the query were not specified in the natural language query. These were inferred by the knowledge base.

In Figure 14.18 the agent and object of the original query were known only to be of type person. To join these with the knowledge base entry for hire, they were first restricted to types manager and employee, respectively. The type hierarchy could thus be used to perform type checking on the original query. If john smith were not of type employee, the question would be invalid and the program could detect this.

Once the expanded query graph is built, the program examines the target concept, flagged with a ?, and determines that the manager_of_hire relation mapped a key onto this concept. Because the key is bound to a value of john smith, the question was valid and the program would form the proper database query. Translation of the entity relationship graph into SQL or some other language is straightforward.

Although this example is simplified, it illustrates the use of a knowledge-based approach to building a natural language database front end. The ideas in our example are expressed in conceptual graphs but could be mapped into other representations such as frames or predicate logic-based languages.

14.5.3 An Information Extraction and Summarization System for the Web

The World Wide Web offers many exciting challenges as well as opportunities for artificial intelligence and natural language understanding software. One of the biggest is the need for intelligent software to summarize "interesting" web-based materials.

After locating information, perhaps by key-word match or use of a more sophisticated search-engine, an *information extraction system* takes as input this unrestricted text and then summarizes it with respect to a prespecified domain or topic of interest. It finds useful information about the domain and encodes this information in a form suitable for report to the user or for populating a structured database.

In contrast to an in-depth natural language understanding system, information extraction systems skim a text to find relevant sections and then focus only on processing these sections. The information extraction system of Figure 14.19, for example, summarizes information from Computer Science job advertisements. For the example of Section 14.0:

Sample Computer Science Job Ad (an excerpt):

> The Department of Computer Science of the University of New Mexico. . . is conducting a search to fill two tenure-track positions. We are interested in hiring people with research interests in:
> Software, including analysis, design, and development tools. . .
> Systems, including architecture, compilers, networks. . .
>   ...
> Candidates must have completed a doctorate in. . .
> The department has internationally recognized research programs in adaptive computation, artificial intelligence, . . . and enjoys strong research collaborations with the Santa Fe Institute and several national laboratories. ...

Sample Partially Filled Template:

> Employer: Department of Computer Science, University of New Mexico
> Location City: Albuquerque
> Location State: NM 87131
> Job Description: Tenure track faculty
> Job Qualifications: PhD in . . .
> Skills Required: software, systems, . . .
> Platform Experience: . . .
> About the Employer: (text attached)

Figure 14.19 Sample text, template summary, and information extraction for computer science advertisement.

1. Text:	The Department of Computer Science of the University of New Mexico is conducting a search to fill two track track positions. We are interested in hiring . . .
2. Tokenization and Tagging:	The/det Department/noun of/prep ...
3. Sentence Analysis:	Department/subj is conducting/verb search/obj ...
4. Extraction:	**Employer**: Department of Computer Science **Job Description**: Tenure track position ...
5. Merging:	tenure track position = faculty New Mexico = NM ...
6. Template Generation:	As in Figure 14.19

Figure 14.20 An architecture for information extraction, from Cardie (1997).

In early attempts at information extraction, natural language systems varied in their approaches. On one extreme, systems processed text using traditional tools: a full syntactic breakdown of each sentence which was accompanied by a detailed semantic analysis. Discourse level processing often followed. At the other extreme, systems used keyword matching techniques with little or no knowledge or linguistic level analysis. As more systems were built and evaluated, however, the limitations of these extreme approaches became obvious. A more modern architecture for information extraction, adapted from Cardie (1997), is presented in Figure 14.20. Although the details of this architecture may differ across applications, the figure indicates the main functions performed in extraction.

First, each sentence of the "interesting" web site is tokenized and tagged. The stochastic tagger presented in Section 14.4 could be used for this. The sentence analysis stage that follows performs parsing that produces noun groups, verbs, prepositional phrases and other grammatical constructs. Next the extraction phase finds and labels semantic entities relevant to the extraction topic. In our example, this will identify employer name, location, job requirements, etc.

The extraction phase is the first entirely domain-specific stage of the process. During extraction, the system identifies specific relations among relevant components of the text. In our example, the Department of Computer Science is seen as the employer and the location is seen as University of New Mexico. The merging phase must address issues such as synonym reference and anaphora resolution. Example of synonyms are *tenure-track* position and *faculty* position as well as *New Mexico* and *NM*. Anaphora resolution links *Department of Computer Science* in the first sentence with *we* in sentence two.

The discourse-level inferences made during merging assist the template generation phase, which determines the number of distinct relationships in the text, maps these extracted pieces of information onto each field of the template, and produces the final output template.

In spite of recent progress, current information extraction systems still have problems. First, the accuracy and robustness of these systems can be improved greatly, as errors in extraction seem to follow from a rather shallow understanding of the input text. Second, building an information extraction system in a new domain can be difficult and time consuming (Cardie 1997). Both of these problems are related to the domain-specific nature of the extraction task. The information extraction process improves if its linguistic knowledge sources are tuned to the particular domain, but manually modifying domain-specific linguistic knowledge is both difficult and error prone.

Nonetheless, a number of interesting applications now exist. Glasgow et al. (1997) built a system to support underwriters in analysis of life insurance applications. Soderland et al. (1995) have a system to extract symptoms, physical findings, test results, and diagnoses from medical patient records for insurance processing. There are programs to analyze newspaper articles to find and summarize joint business ventures (MUC-5 1994), systems that automatically classify legal documents (Holowczak and Adam 1997), and programs that extract information from computer job listings (Nahm and Mooney 2000).

14.5.4 Using Learning Algorithms to Generalize Extracted Information

A final application brings together many of the ideas presented in this chapter as well as algorithms from machine learning (Sections 10.3 and 16.13). Cardie and Mooney (1999) and Nahm and Mooney (2000) have suggested that information extracted from text may be generalized by machine learning algorithms and the result reused in the information extraction task.

The approach is straightforward. Completed, or even partially filled text summarization templates as seen, for example, in Figure 14.19 are collected from appropriate web sites. The resulting template information is then stored in a relational database where learning algorithms, such as ID3 or C4.5 are used to extract decision trees, which, as seen in Section 10.3, can reflect rule relationships implicit in the data sets. (This technique we referred to as *data mining*.) Mooney and his colleagues propose that these newly discovered relationships then be used for refining the original templates and knowledge structures used in the information extraction. Examples of this type of information that might be discovered from the computer science job application analysis of Section 14.5.3 might include: if the position is computer science faculty then experience on a particular computing platform is not required; if universities are hiring faculty members then research experience is required, etc. Further details may be found in Nahm and Mooney (2000).

14.6 Epilogue and References

As this chapter suggests, there are a number of approaches to defining grammars and parsing sentences in natural language. We have presented ATN parsers and Markov models as typical examples of these approaches. The serious student should be aware of other possibilities. These include *transformational grammars*, *semantic grammars*, *case grammars*, and *feature and function grammars* (Winograd 1983, Allen 1995). Transformational grammars use context-free rules to represent the *deep structure*, or meaning, of the sentence. This deep structure may be represented as a parse tree that not only consists of terminals and nonterminals but also includes a set of symbols called *grammatical markers*. These grammatical markers represent such features as number, tense, and other context-sensitive aspects of linguistic structure. Next, a higher-level set of rules called transformational rules transform between this deep structure and a *surface structure*, which is closer to the actual form the sentence will have. For example, "Tom likes Jane" and "Jane is liked by Tom" have the same deep structure but different surface structures.

Transformational rules act on parse trees themselves, performing the checks that require global context and produce a suitable surface structure. For example, a transformational rule may check that the number feature of the node representing the subject of a sentence is the same as the number feature of the verb node. Transformational rules may also map a single deep structure into alternative surface structures, such as changing active to passive voice or forming an assertion into a question. Although transformational grammars are not discussed in this text, they are an important alternative to augmented phrase structure grammars.

Terry Winograd offers a comprehensive treatment of grammars and parsing in *Language as a Cognitive Process* (1983). This book offers a thorough treatment of transformational grammars. *Natural Language Understanding* by James Allen (1987, 1995) provides an overview of the design and implementation of natural language understanding programs. *Introduction to Natural Language Processing* by Mary Dee Harris (1985) is another general text on natural language expanding the issues raised in this chapter. We also recommend Gerald Gazdar and Chris Mellish (1989), *Natural Language Processing in PROLOG*. Charniak (1993) and Charniak et al. (1993) address issues in stochastic approaches to language and part-of-speech tagging.

The semantic analysis of natural language involves a number of difficult issues that are addressed in knowledge representation (Chapter 7). In *Computational Semantics*, Charniak and Wilks (1976) have articles addressing these issues. Because of the difficulty in modeling the knowledge and social context required for natural language interaction, many authors have questioned the possibility of moving this technology beyond constrained domains. Early research in discourse analysis may be found in Linde (1974), Grosz (1977) and Grosz and Sidner (1990) *Understanding Computers and Cognition* by Winograd and Flores (1986), *Minds, Brains, and Programs* by John Searle (1980) and *On the Origin of Objects* (Smith 1996) address these issues.

Inside Computer Understanding by Schank and Riesbeck (1981) discusses natural language understanding using conceptual dependency technology. *Scripts, Plans, Goals and Understanding* by Schank and Abelson (1977) discusses the role of higher-level knowledge organization structures in natural language programs.

Speech Acts by John Searle (1969) discusses the role of pragmatics and contextual knowledge in modeling discourse. Fass and Wilks (1983) have proposed *semantic preference theory* as a vehicle for modeling natural language semantics. Semantic preference is a generalization of case grammars that allows transformations on case frames. This provides greater flexibility in representing semantics and allows the representation of such concepts as metaphor and analogy. For a full discussion of the Chomsky hierarchy see Hopcroft and Ullman (1979). We are indebted to John Sowa (1984) for our treatment of conceptual graphs.

Recent presentations of language processing techniques can be found in *Speech and Language Processing* by Jurafsky and Martin (2000), *Foundations of Statistical Natural Language Processing* by Manning and Schutze (1999), and *Survey of the State of the Art in Human Language Technology*, Cole (1997), and the Winter 1997 edition of the *AI Magazine*.

Excellent references for keeping up with the research trends in natural language understanding, both from the traditional as well as from the stochastic viewpoints, are the annual proceedings of the AI conferences: AAAI and IJCAI, published by AAAI Press through MIT Press and the *Journal of the Association for Computational Linguistics*.

14.7 Exercises

1. Classify each of the following sentences as either syntactically incorrect, syntactically correct but meaningless, meaningful but untrue, or true. Where in the understanding process is each of these problems detected?

   Colorless green ideas sleep furiously.
   Fruit flies like a banana.
   Dogs the bite man a.
   George Washington was the fifth president of the USA.
   This exercise is easy.
   I want to be under the sea in an octopus's garden in the shade.

2. Discuss the representational structures and knowledge necessary to understand the following sentences.

   The brown dog ate the bone.
   Attach the large wheel to the axle with the hex nut.
   Mary watered the plants.
   The spirit is willing but the flesh is weak.
   My kingdom for a horse!

3. Parse each of these sentences using the "dogs world" grammar of Section 14.2.1. Which of these are illegal sentences? Why?

   The dog bites the dog.
   The big dog bites the man.
   Emma likes the boy.
   The man likes.
   Bite the man.

4. Extend the dogs world grammar so it will include the illegal sentences in Exercise 3.

5. Parse each of these sentences using the context-sensitive grammar of Section 14.2.3.

   The men like the dog.
   The dog bites the man.

6. Produce a parse tree for each of the following sentences. You will have to extend our simple grammars with more complex linguistic constructs such as adverbs, adjectives, and

prepositional phrases. If a sentence has more than one parsing, diagram all of them and explain the semantic information that would be used to choose a parsing.

> Time flies like an arrow but fruit flies like a banana.
> Tom gave the big, red book to Mary on Tuesday.
> Reasoning is an art and not a science.
> To err is human, to forgive divine.

7. Extend the dogs world grammar to include adjectives in noun phrases. Be sure to allow an indeterminate number of adjectives. Hint: use a recursive rule, adjective_list, that either is empty or contains an adjective followed by an adjective list. Map this grammar into transition networks.

8. Add the following context-free grammar rules to the dogs world grammar of Section 14.2.1. Map the resulting grammar into transition networks.

> sentence ↔ noun_phrase verb_phrase prepositional_phrase
> prepositional_phrase ↔ preposition noun_phrase
> preposition ↔ with
> preposition ↔ to
> preposition ↔ on

9. Define an ATN parser for the dogs world grammar with adjectives (Exercise 7) and prepositional phrases (Exercise 8).

10. Define concepts and relations in conceptual graphs needed to represent the meaning of the grammar of Exercise 9. Define the procedures for building a semantic representation from the parse tree.

11. Extend the context-sensitive grammar of Section 14.2.3 to test for semantic agreement between the subject and verb. Specifically, men should not bite dogs, although dogs can either like or bite men. Perform a similar modification to the ATN grammar.

12. Expand the ATN grammar of Section 14.2.4 to include *who* and *what* questions.

13. Describe how the Markov models of Section 14.4 might be combined with the more symbolic approach to understanding language of Sections 14.1–14.3.

14. Extend the database front end example of Section 14.5.2 so that it will answer questions of the form "How much does Don Morrison earn?" You will need to extend the grammar, the representation language, and the knowledge base.

15. Take the previous problem and put its words, including punctuation, in random order.

16. Assume that managers are listed in the employee_salary relation with other employees in the example of Section 14.5.2. Extend the example so that it will handle queries such as "Find any employee that earns more than his or her manager."

17. How might the stochastic approaches of Section 14.4 be combined with the techniques for database analysis found in Section 14.5.

18. Use of the stochastic approach for discovering patterns in a relational database is an important area of current research, sometime referred to as *data mining* (see Section 14.3). How might this work be used to answer queries, such as those posed in Section 14.5 about relational databases?

19. As a project, build an information extraction system for some knowledge domain to be used on the WWW. See Section 14.5 for suggestions.

PART VI

LANGUAGES AND PROGRAMMING TECHNIQUES FOR ARTIFICIAL INTELLIGENCE

for now we see as through a glass darkly . . .

—PAUL TO THE CORINTHIANS

The map is not the territory; the name is not the thing named.

—ALFRED KORZYBSKI

What have I learned but the proper use of several tools?

—GARY SNYDER, "What Have I Learned"

Languages, Understanding, and Levels of Abstraction

In Part VI we first discuss the issues involved in selecting a language for artificial intelligence programming. Then, in the chapters dedicated to LISP and PROLOG, we introduce a number of programming techniques for use in building intelligent systems. The primary function of AI programming is to construct the representation and control structures needed for intelligent problem solving. The requirements of these structures to a great extent determine the features that an AI implementation language should provide. In the Introduction to Part VI, we first enumerate the language features desired for AI programming and then introduce the LISP and PROLOG programming languages. Not only are these two of the most frequently used languages in artificial intelligence: their syntactic and semantic features also encourage powerful ways of thinking about problems and their solutions. The remarkable influence these languages have had on the historical development of AI is as much a product of their ability to function as "tools for thinking" as it is a reflection of their strengths as programming languages.

The ability to form higher-level abstractions from the particulars of experience is one of the most powerful and fundamental abilities of the human mind. Abstraction allows us to consolidate the details of a complicated domain into a general characterization of its organization and behavior; these abstractions allow us to understand the full range of particulars found in that domain. If we enter a strange house, for example, we will be able to find our way around: the organization of the living room, bedrooms, kitchen, and bathrooms generally conforms to a standard model of a house. The abstraction lets us make sense of the variations found in different houses. A picture may be worth a thousand words, but an abstraction can concisely represent the important features of an entire class of pictures.

When we form theories to describe classes of phenomena, the significant qualitative and quantitative features of the class are abstracted out from the details that characterize its individual members. This loss of detail is compensated for by the descriptive and predictive power of a valid theory. Abstraction is an essential tool for understanding and managing the complexity of the world around us, as well as that of our own mental structures. Indeed, this process of abstraction occurs continuously and recursively in the act of knowing: knowledge is built in layers of abstraction, from the mechanisms that extract structure from the chaos of raw sensory stimuli all the way up to the most subtle of scientific theories. Ultimately, most of our ideas are about other ideas.

Hierarchical abstraction, the organization of experience into increasingly abstract classes and descriptions, is an essential tool for understanding the behavior and organization of complex systems, including computer programs. Just as the behavior of an animal may be studied without concern for the underlying physiology of its nervous system, an algorithm has a characterization of its own, quite separate from the program that implements it.

Consider, for example, two different implementations of binary search, one written in FORTRAN using arrays and calculations on array indices and the other written in C++ using pointers to implement binary search trees. In a deep sense, these programs are the same, even though the particulars of their implementations differ. This separation of an algorithm from the code used to implement it is only one example of hierarchical abstraction in computer science.

Allen Newell has distinguished between the *knowledge level* and the *symbol level* of describing an intelligent system (Newell 1982). The symbol level is concerned with the particular formalisms used to represent problem-solving knowledge; the discussion of predicate logic as a representation language in Chapter 2 is an example of such a symbol-level consideration. Above the symbol level is the knowledge level, concerned with the knowledge content of the program and the way in which that knowledge is used.

This distinction is reflected in the architecture of knowledge-based systems and the development style it supports. Because users understand programs in terms of their knowledge and capabilities, it is important that AI programs have a clear knowledge-level characterization. The separation of the knowledge base from the underlying control structure makes this point of view explicit and simplifies the development of coherent, knowledge-level behavior. Similarly, the symbol level defines a representation language, such as logic or production rules, for the knowledge base. Its separation from the knowledge level allows the programmer to address issues of expressiveness, efficiency

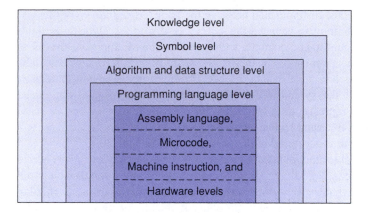

Figure VI.1 Levels of a knowledge-based system, adapted from Newell (1982).

and ease of programming that are not relevant to the program's higher-level behavior. The implementation of the symbol-level representation constitutes a still lower level of program organization and defines an additional set of design considerations, as in Figure VI.1.

The importance of the multi-level approach to system design cannot be overemphasized: it allows a programmer to ignore the complexity hidden at lower levels and focus on issues appropriate to the current level of abstraction. It allows the theoretical foundations of artificial intelligence to be kept free of the nuances of a particular implementation or programming language. It allows us to modify an implementation, improving its efficiency or porting it to another machine, without affecting its specification and behavior at higher levels.

The knowledge level defines the capabilities of an intelligent system. The knowledge content is independent of the formalisms used to represent it, as long as the representation language is sufficiently expressive. Knowledge-level concerns include such questions as: What queries will be made of the system? What objects and relations are important in the domain? How is new knowledge added to the system? Will facts change over time? How will the system need to reason about its knowledge? Does the domain of discourse have a well-understood taxonomy? Does the domain involve uncertain or missing information? Careful analysis at this level is an important step in designing the architecture of the program and in choosing the particular method of representation used at the symbol level.

At the symbol level, decisions are made about the structures used to represent and organize knowledge. The selection of a representation language is a primary symbol-level concern. As we have seen in Chapters 7, 8, and 9, logic is only one of many formalisms currently available for knowledge representation. Not only must a representation language be able to express the knowledge required for an application, but it also must be concise, modifiable, computationally efficient and must assist the programmer in acquiring and organizing the knowledge base. These goals often conflict and necessitate trade-offs in the design of representation languages.

Just as we have distinguished between the knowledge and symbol levels of a program, we can also distinguish between the symbol level and the algorithms and data structures used to implement it. For example, with the exception of efficiency, the behavior of a logic-based problem solver should be unaffected by the choice between a hash table and a binary tree to implement a table of its symbols. These are implementation decisions and should be invisible at the symbol level. Many of the algorithms and data structures used in implementing representation languages for AI are common computer science techniques such as binary trees and tables; others are more specific to AI and are presented in pseudo-code throughout the text and in the chapters on LISP and PROLOG.

Below the algorithm/data structure level is the language level. It is here that the implementation language for the program becomes significant. Even though good programming style requires that we build barriers of abstraction between the particular features of a programming language and the layers above it, the unique needs of symbol-level programming exert a profound influence on the design and use of AI programming languages. In addition, language design must accommodate the constraints it inherits from still lower levels of computer architecture, including the operating system, the underlying hardware architecture and the limitations physical computers must place on resources such as memory and processor speed. The techniques LISP and PROLOG use to mediate the needs of the symbol level and the requirements of the underlying architecture are both a source of their utility and also an intellectual achievement of great importance and elegance.

We next introduce the major AI programming languages, PROLOG and LISP.

An Overview of PROLOG and LISP

PROLOG

PROLOG is the best-known example of a *logic programming language*. A logic program is a set of specifications in formal logic; PROLOG uses the first-order predicate calculus. Indeed, the name itself comes from PROgramming in LOGic. An interpreter executes the program by systematically making inferences from logic specifications. The idea of using the representational power of the first-order predicate calculus to express specifications for problem solving is one of the central contributions PROLOG has made to computer science in general and to artificial intelligence in particular. The benefits of using first-order predicate calculus for a programming language include a clean and elegant syntax and well-defined semantics.

The implementation of PROLOG has its roots in research on theorem proving by J.A. Robinson (1965), especially the creation of algorithms for resolution refutation. Robinson designed a proof procedure called *resolution*, which is the primary method for computing with PROLOG. The chapter on automated theorem proving demonstrates *resolution refutation systems*; see Sections 13.2 and 13.3.

Because of these features, PROLOG has proved to be a useful vehicle for investigating such experimental programming issues as automatic code generation, program verification, and design of high-level specification languages. PROLOG and other logic-based languages support a declarative programming style—that is, constructing a program in terms of high-level descriptions of a problem's constraints—rather than a procedural programming style—writing programs as a sequence of instructions for performing an algorithm. This mode of programming essentially tells the computer "what is true" and "what needs to be done" rather than "how to do it." This allows programmers to focus on problem solving as sets of specifications for a domain rather than the details of writing low-level algorithmic instructions for "what to do next."

The first PROLOG program was written in Marseille, France, in the early 1970s as part of a project in natural language understanding (Colmerauer et al. 1973, Roussel 1975, Kowalski 1979*a*). The theoretical background for the language is discussed in the work of Kowalski, Hayes, and others (Kowalski 1979*a*, 1979*b*; Hayes 1977, Lloyd 1984). The major development of the PROLOG language was carried out from 1975 to 1979 at the department of artificial intelligence of the University of Edinburgh. The group in Edinburgh responsible for the implementation of PROLOG were David H.D. Warren and Fernando Pereira. They produced the first PROLOG interpreter robust enough for delivery to the general computing community. This product was built on the DEC-system 10 and could operate in both interpretive and compiled modes (Warren et al. 1979). Further descriptions of this early code and comparisons of PROLOG with LISP may be found in Warren et al. (1977). This "Warren and Pereira" PROLOG became the early standard, and the book *Programming in PROLOG* (Clocksin and Mellish 1984) was the chief vehicle for delivering PROLOG to the computing community. Our text uses this standard, which has come to be known as the Edinburgh syntax.

The advantages of the language have been demonstrated by research projects designed to evaluate and extend the expressive power of logic programming. Discussion of many such applications can be found in the Proceedings of the International Joint Conference on Artificial Intelligence and the Symposium on Logic Programming. See also the references at the end of Chapter 15.

LISP

LISP was first proposed by John McCarthy in the late 1950s. The language was originally intended as an alternative model of computation based on the theory of recursive functions. In an early paper, McCarthy (1960) outlined his goals: to create a language for symbolic rather than numeric computation, to implement a model of computation based on the theory of recursive functions (Church 1941), to provide a clear definition of the language's syntax and semantics, and to demonstrate formally the completeness of this computational model. Although LISP is one of the oldest computing languages still in existence (along with FORTRAN and COBOL), the careful thought given to its original design and the extensions made to the language through its history have kept it in the vanguard of programming languages. In fact, this programming model has proved so effective that a number of other languages have been based on functional programming, e.g., SCHEME, ML, and FP.

The list is the basis of both programs and data structures in LISP: LISP is an acronym for LISt Processing. LISP provides a powerful set of list-handling functions implemented internally as linked pointer structures. LISP gives programmers the full power and generality of linked data structures while freeing them from the responsibility for explicitly managing pointers and pointer operations.

Originally, LISP was a compact language, consisting of functions for constructing and accessing lists, defining new functions, detecting equality, and evaluating expressions. The only means of program control were recursion and a single conditional. More complicated functions, when needed, were defined in terms of these primitives. Through time, the best of these new functions became part of the language itself. This process of extending the language by adding new functions led to the development of numerous dialects of LISP, often including hundreds of specialized functions for data structuring, program control, real and integer arithmetic, input/output (I/O), editing LISP functions, and tracing program execution. These dialects are the vehicle by which LISP has evolved from a simple and elegant theoretical model of computing into a rich, powerful, and practical environment for building large software systems. Because of the proliferation of early LISP dialects, the Defense Advanced Research Projects Agency in 1983 proposed a standard dialect of the language, known as Common LISP.

Although Common LISP has emerged as the lingua franca of LISP dialects, a number of other dialects continue to be widely used. One of these is SCHEME, an elegant rethinking of LISP that has been used both for AI development and for teaching the fundamental concepts of computing. The dialect we use throughout our text is Common LISP.

Selecting an Implementation Language

As artificial intelligence has matured and demonstrated its applicability to a range of practical problems, its almost exclusive reliance on LISP and PROLOG has diminished. The circumstances of software development, such as the need to easily interface with legacy code, the use of AI as modules of large, conventional programs, and the need to conform to development standards imposed by corporate or government customers has led to the development of AI systems in a variety of languages, including Smalltalk, C, C++, and Java. Nonetheless, LISP and PROLOG continue to be important for prototyping and development and an important part of any AI programmer's skill set.

In addition, these languages have served as proving grounds for many of the features that continue to be incorporated into modern programming languages. Perhaps the best example of this is the Java language, which profits from its use of dynamic binding, automatic memory management, and other features that were pioneered in AI languages. It seems as though the rest of the programming world is still trying to catch up to the standards set by AI languages. As this evolution continues, knowledge of LISP, PROLOG, or Smalltalk and the programming techniques they enable will only increase in value. We are confident that this will be true, whether you continue to use one of these classic AI languages, or find yourself programming in C++, Objective C, Java or one of their other competitors, descendants, or distant cousins.

AN INTRODUCTION TO PROLOG

All the objects of human reason or inquiry may naturally be divided into two kinds, to wit, "Relations of Ideas" and "Matters of Fact."

—DAVID HUME, *An Inquiry Concerning Human Understanding*

The only way to rectify our reasonings is to make them as tangible as those of the mathematicians, so that we can find our error at a glance, and when there are disputes among persons we can simply say, "Let us calculate... to see who is right."

—LEIBNIZ, *The Art of Discovery*

15.0 Introduction

As an implementation of logic programming, PROLOG makes many interesting contributions to AI problem solving. These include its *declarative semantics*, a means of directly expressing problem relationships in AI, as well as with built-in unification, some high-powered techniques for pattern matching and search. We address many of the important issues of PROLOG and logic programming in this chapter.

In Section 15.1 we present the basic PROLOG syntax and several simple programs. These programs demonstrate the use of the predicate calculus as a representation language. We show how to monitor the PROLOG environment and demonstrate the use of the *cut* with PROLOG's built in depth-first search.

In Section 15.2 we create *abstract data types* (ADTs) in PROLOG. These ADTs include *stacks*, *queues*, and *priority queues*, which are then used to build a production system in Section 15.3 and to design control structures for the search algorithms of Chapters 3, 4, and 7 in Section 15.4. In Section 15.5 we create a *planner*, after the material presented in Section 8.4. In Section 15.6 we introduce *meta-predicates*, predicates whose domains of interpretation are PROLOG expressions themselves. For example, atom(X) succeeds if X is bound to an atom. Meta-predicates may be used for imposing type constraints on

PROLOG interpretations. In Section 15.7 meta-predicates are used for building *meta-interpreters* in PROLOG. Meta-interpreters are used to build a PROLOG interpreter in PROLOG, as well as to build interpreters for rule chaining and inheritance searches.

In Section 15.8 we demonstrate PROLOG as a language for machine learning, with examples of version space search and explanation-based learning from Chapter 10. In Section 15.9 we build a recursive descent semantic net parser, based on ideas developed in Chapter 14. The chapter ends with the discussion of the general issues of programming in logic and procedural versus declarative problem solving.

15.1 Syntax for Predicate Calculus Programming

15.1.1 Representing Facts and Rules

Although there are numerous dialects of PROLOG, the syntax used throughout this text is the original Warren and Pereira C-PROLOG (Clocksin and Mellish 2003). To simplify our presentation of PROLOG, our version of predicate calculus syntax in Chapter 2 used many PROLOG conventions. There are, however, a number of differences between PROLOG and predicate calculus syntax. In C-PROLOG, for example, the symbol :- replaces the $\leftarrow$ of first-order predicate calculus. Other symbols differ from those used in Chapter 2:

ENGLISH	PREDICATE CALCULUS	PROLOG
and	$\wedge$	,
or	$\vee$	;
only if	$\leftarrow$	:-
not	$\neg$	not

As in Chapter 2, predicate names and bound variables are expressed as a sequence of alphanumeric characters beginning with an alphabetic. Variables are represented as a string of alphanumeric characters beginning (at least) with an uppercase alphabetic. Thus:

likes(X, susie).

or, better,

likes(Everyone, susie).

could represent the fact that "everyone likes Susie." Or,

likes(george, Y), likes(susie, Y).

could represent the set of things (or people) that are liked by both George and Susie.

Similarly, suppose it was desired to represent in PROLOG the following relationships: "George likes Kate and George likes Susie." This could be stated as:

```
likes(george, kate), likes(george, susie).
```

Likewise, "George likes Kate or George likes Susie":

```
likes(george, kate); likes(george, susie).
```

Finally, "George likes Susie if George does not like Kate":

```
likes(george, susie) :- not(likes(george, kate)).
```

These examples show how the predicate calculus connectives ∧, ∨, ¬, and ← are expressed in PROLOG. The predicate names (likes), the number or order of parameters, and even whether a given predicate always has the same number of parameters are determined by the design requirements (the implicit "semantics") of the problem. There are no expressive limitations, other than the syntax of well-formed formulae, in the language.

A PROLOG program is a set of specifications in the first-order predicate calculus describing the objects and relations in a problem domain. The set of specifications is referred to as the *database* for that problem. The PROLOG interpreter responds to questions about this set of specifications. Queries to the database are patterns in the same logical syntax as the database entries. The PROLOG interpreter uses pattern-directed search to find whether these queries logically follow from the contents of the database.

The interpreter processes queries, searching the database in left to right depth-first order to find out whether the query is a logical consequence of the database of specifications. PROLOG is primarily an interpreted language. Some versions of PROLOG run in interpretive mode only, while others allow compilation of part or all of the set of specifications for faster execution. PROLOG is an interactive language; the user enters queries in response to the PROLOG prompt: ?-.

Suppose that we wish to describe a "world" consisting of George's, Kate's, and Susie's likes and dislikes. The database might contain the following set of predicates:

```
likes(george, kate).
likes(george, susie).
likes(george, wine).
likes(susie, wine).
likes(kate, gin).
likes(kate, susie).
```

This set of specifications has the obvious interpretation, or mapping, into the world of George and his friends. This world is a model for the database (Section 2.3). The interpreter may then be asked questions:

```
?- likes(george, kate).
yes
```

```
?- likes(kate, susie).
yes
?- likes(george, X).
X = kate
;
X = susie
;
X = wine
;
no
?- likes(george, beer).
no
```

Note several things in these examples. First, in the request likes(george, X), successive user prompts (;) cause the interpreter to return all the terms in the database specification that may be substituted for the X in the query. They are returned in the order in which they are found in the database: kate before susie before wine. Although it goes against the philosophy of nonprocedural specifications, a determined order of evaluation is a property of most interpreters implemented on sequential machines. The PROLOG programmer must be aware of the order in which PROLOG searches entries in the database.

Also note that further responses to queries are produced when the user prompts with the ; (or). This forces a backtrack on the most recent result. Continued prompts force PROLOG to find all possible solutions to the query. When no further solutions exist, the interpreter responds no.

The above example also illustrates the *closed world assumption* or *negation as failure*. PROLOG assumes that "anything is false whose opposite is not provably true." In the query likes(george, beer), the interpreter looks for the predicate likes(george, beer) or some rule that could establish likes(george, beer). Failing this, the request is false. Thus, PROLOG assumes that all knowledge of the world is present in the database.

The closed world assumption introduces a number of practical and philosophical difficulties in the language. For example, failure to include a fact in the database often means that its truth is unknown; the closed world assumption treats it as false. If a predicate were omitted or there were a misspelling, such as likes(george, beeer), the response remains no. The negation-as-failure issue is a very important topic in AI research. Though negation as failure is a simple way to deal with the problem of unspecified knowledge, more sophisticated approaches, such as multivalued logics (true, false, unknown) and nonmonotonic reasoning (see Section 9.1), provide a richer interpretive context.

The PROLOG expressions used in the database above are examples of *fact* specifications. PROLOG also lets us define *rules* to describe relationships between facts using the logical implication, :- . In creating a PROLOG rule, only one predicate is permitted on the left-hand side of the if symbol, :-; this predicate must be a *positive literal*, which means it cannot be negated (Section 13.3). All predicate calculus expressions that contain implication or equivalence relationships ($\leftarrow$, $\rightarrow$, and $\leftrightarrow$) must be reduced to this form, referred to as *Horn clause logic*. In Horn clause form, the left-hand side (conclusion) of an implication must be a single positive literal. The *Horn clause calculus* is equivalent to the full first-order predicate calculus for proofs by refutation, see details in Chapter 13.

Suppose we add to the specifications of the previous database a rule for determining whether two people are friends. This may be defined:

friends(X, Y) :- likes(X, Z), likes(Y, Z).

This expression might be interpreted as "X and Y are friends if there exists a Z such that X likes Z and Y likes Z ." Two issues are important here. First, because neither the predicate calculus nor PROLOG has global variables, the scope (extent of definition) of X, Y, and Z is limited to the friends rule. Second, values bound to, or unified with, X, Y, and Z are consistent across the entire expression. The treatment of the friends rule by the PROLOG interpreter is seen in the following example.

With the friends rule added to the set of specifications of the preceding example, we can query the interpreter:

?- friends(george, susie).
yes

To solve the query, PROLOG searches the database using the backtrack algorithm presented in Chapters 3 and 6. The query friends(george, susie) is matched or unified with the conclusion of the rule friends(X, Y) :- likes(X, Z), likes(Y, Z), with X as george and Y as susie. The interpreter looks for a Z such that likes(george, Z) is true. This is first attempted using the first fact in the database, with Z as kate.

The interpreter then tries to determine whether likes(susie, kate) is true. When it is found to be false, using the closed world assumption, this value for Z (kate) is rejected. The interpreter then backtracks to find a second value for Z in likes(george, Z).

likes(george, Z) then matches the second clause in the database, with Z bound to susie. The interpreter then tries to match likes(susie, susie). When this also fails, the interpreter goes back to the database (backtracks) for yet another value for Z. This time wine is found in the third predicate, and the interpreter goes on to show that likes(susie, wine) is true. In this case wine is the binding that ties george and susie. PROLOG tries to match goals with patterns in the order in which the patterns are entered in the database.

It is important to state the relationship between universal and existential quantification in the predicate calculus and the treatment of variables in a PROLOG program. When a variable is placed in the specifications of a PROLOG database, the variable is assumed to be universally quantified. For example, likes(susie, Y) means, according to the semantics of the previous examples, "Susie likes everyone." In the course of interpreting some query, any term, or list or predicate, may be bound to Y. Similarly, in the rule friends(X, Y) :- likes(X, Z), likes(Y, Z), any X, Y, and Z that meet the specifications of the expression are acceptable variable bindings.

To represent an existentially quantified variable in PROLOG, we may take two approaches. First, if the existential value of a variable is known, that value may be entered directly into the database. Thus, likes(george, wine) is an instance of likes(george, Z) and may be thus entered into the database, as it was in the previous examples.

Second, to find an instance of a variable that makes an expression true, we query the interpreter. For example, to find whether a Z exists such that likes(george, Z) is true, we put this query directly to the interpreter. It will find whether a value of Z exists under which the expression is true. Some PROLOG interpreters find all existentially quantified values; C-PROLOG requires repeated user prompts (;) to get all values.

15.1.2 Creating, Changing, and Monitoring the PROLOG Environment

In creating a PROLOG program the database of specifications is created first. In an interactive environment the predicate assert adds new predicates to specifications. Thus:

    ?- assert(likes(david, sarah)).

adds this predicate to the computing specifications. Now, with the query:

    ?- likes(david, X).
    X = sarah.

is returned. assert allows further control in adding new specifications to the database: asserta(P) asserts the predicate P at the beginning of all the predicates P, and assertz(P) adds P at the end of all the predicates named P. This is important for search priorities and building heuristics. To remove a predicate P from the database retract(P) is used. (It should be noted that in many PROLOGs assert can be unpredictable in that the exact entry time of the new predicate into the environment can vary depending on what other things are going on, affecting both the indexing of asserted clauses and backtracking.)

It soon becomes tedious to create a set of specifications using the predicates assert and retract. Instead, the programmer takes her favorite editor and creates a file containing all the PROLOG specifications. Once this file is created (let's call it myfile) and PROLOG is called, then the file is placed in the database by the PROLOG command consult. Thus:

    ?- consult(myfile).
    yes

adds the predicates in myfile to the database. A short form of the consult predicate, and better for adding multiple files to the database, uses the list notation, to be seen shortly:

    ?- [myfile].
    yes

The predicates read and write are important for user communication. read(X) takes the next term from the current input stream and binds it to X. Input expressions are terminated with a ".". write(X) puts X in the output stream. If X is unbound then an integer preceded by an underline is printed (_69). This integer represents the internal bookkeeping on variables necessary in a theorem-proving environment (see how variables are *standardized apart* in Section 13.2.2).

The PROLOG predicates see and tell are used to read information from and place information into files. see(X) opens the file X and defines the current input stream as originating in X. If X is not bound to an available file see(X) fails. Similarly, tell(X) opens a file for the output stream. If no file X exists, tell(X) creates a file named by the bound value of X. seen(X) and told(X) close the respective files.

A number of PROLOG predicates are important in helping us keep track of the state of the PROLOG database as well as the state of computing about the database; the most important of these are listing, trace, and spy. If we use listing(predicate_name) where predicate_name is the name of a predicate, such as member (Section 15.1.3), all the clauses with that predicate name in the database are returned by the interpreter. Note that the number of arguments of the predicate is not indicated; in fact, all uses of the predicate, regardless of the number of arguments, are returned.

trace allows the user to monitor the progress of the PROLOG interpreter. This monitoring is accomplished by printing to the output file every goal that PROLOG attempts, which is often more information than the user wants to have. The tracing facilities in many PROLOG environments are rather cryptic and take some study and experience to understand. The information available in a trace of a running PROLOG program usually includes the following:

1. The depth level of recursive calls (marked left to right on line).
2. When a goal is tried for the first time (sometimes call is used).
3. When a goal is successfully satisfied (with an exit).
4. When a goal has further matches possible (a retry).
5. When a goal fails because all attempts to satisfy it have failed (fail is often used).
6. The goal notrace stops the exhaustive tracing.

When a more selective trace is required the goal spy is useful. This predicate usually takes a predicate name as argument but sometimes is defined as a prefix operator where the predicate to be monitored is listed after the operator. Thus, spy member causes the interpreter to print to output all uses of the predicate member. spy can also take a list of predicates followed by their arities: spy[member/2, append/3] sets monitoring of the interpreter on all uses of the goals member with two arguments and append with three. nospy removes these spy points.

15.1.3 Lists and Recursion in PROLOG

The previous subsections presented PROLOG syntax in several simple examples. These examples introduced PROLOG as an engine for computing with predicate calculus expressions (in Horn clause form). This is consistent with all the principles of predicate calculus inference presented in Chapter 2. PROLOG uses unification for pattern matching and returns the bindings that make an expression true. These values are unified with the variables in a particular expression and are not bound in the global environment.

Recursion is the primary control mechanism for PROLOG programming. We will demonstrate this with several examples. But first we consider some simple list-processing examples. The list is a data structure consisting of ordered sets of elements (or, indeed, lists). Recursion is the natural way to process the list structure. Unification and recursion come together in list processing in PROLOG. The list elements themselves are enclosed by brackets [ ] and are separated by commas. Examples of PROLOG lists are:

```
[1, 2, 3, 4]
[[george, kate], [allen, amy], [don, pat]]
[tom, dick, harry, fred]
[ ]
```

The first elements of a list may be separated from the tail of the list by the bar operator, |. The tail of a list is the list with its first element removed. For instance, when the list is [tom,dick,harry,fred], the first element is tom and the tail is the list [dick, harry, fred]. Using the vertical bar operator and unification, we can break a list into its components:

If [tom, dick, harry, fred] is matched to [X | Y], then X = tom and Y = [dick, harry, fred].

If [tom,dick,harry,fred] is matched to pattern [X, Y | Z], then X = tom , Y = dick , and Z = [harry, fred].

If [tom, dick, harry, fred] is matched to [X, Y, Z | W], then X = tom, Y = dick, Z = harry, and W = [fred].

If [tom, dick, harry, fred] is matched to [W, X, Y, Z | V], then W = tom, X = dick, Y = harry, Z = fred, and V = [ ] .

[tom, dick, harry, fred] will not match [V, W, X, Y, Z | U] .

[tom, dick, harry, fred] will match [tom, X | [harry, fred]], to give X = dick.

Besides "tearing lists apart" to get at particular elements, unification can be used to "build" the list structure. For example, if X = tom, Y = [dick], and L unifies with [X | Y], then L will be bound to [tom, dick]. Thus terms separated by commas before the | are all elements of the list, and the structure after the | is always a list, the tail of the list.

Let's take a simple example of recursive processing of lists: the member check. We define a predicate to determine whether an item, represented by X, is in a list. This predicate member takes two arguments, an element and a list, and is true if the element is a member of the list. For example:

```
?- member(a, [a, b, c, d, e]).
yes
?- member(a, [1, 2, 3, 4]).
no
?- member(X, [a, b, c]).
X = a
;
X = b
;
X = c
;
no
```

To define member recursively, we first test if X is the first item in the list:

member(X, [X | T]).

This tests whether X and the first element of the list are identical. If they are not, then it is natural to check whether X is an element of the rest (T) of the list. This is defined by:

member(X, [Y | T]) :- member(X, T).

The two lines of PROLOG for checking list membership are then:

member(X, [X | T]).
member(X, [Y | T]) :- member(X, T).

This example illustrates the importance of PROLOG's built-in order of search with the terminating condition placed before the recursive call, to be tested before the algorithm recurs. If the order of the predicates is reversed, the terminating condition may never be checked. We now trace member(c,[a,b,c]), with numbering:

1: member(X, [X | T]).
2: member(X, [Y | T]) :- member(X, T).

?- member(c, [a, b, c]).
        call 1. fail, since c ≠ a
        call 2. X = c, Y = a, T = [b, c], member(c, [b,c])?
                call 1. fail, since c ≠ b
                call 2. X = c, Y = b, T = [c], member(c, [c])?
                        call 1. success, c = c
                yes (to second call 2.)
        yes (to first call 2.)
yes

Good PROLOG style suggests the use of *anonymous variables*. These serve as an indication to the programmer and interpreter that certain variables are used solely for pattern-matching purposes, with the variable binding itself not part of the computation process. Thus, when we test whether the element X is the same as the first item in the list we usually say: member(X, [X|_]). The use of the _ indicates that even though the tail of the list plays a crucial part in the unification of a query, the content of the tail of the list is unimportant. In the member check the anonymous variable should be used in the recursive statement as well, where the value of the head of the list is unimportant:

member(X, [X | _]).
member(X, [_ | T]) :- member(X, T).

Writing out a list one element to a line is a nice exercise for understanding both lists and recursive control. Suppose we wish to write out the list [a,b,c,d]. We could define the recursive command:

```
writelist([ ]).
writelist([H | T]) :- write(H), nl, writelist(T).
```

This predicate writes one element of the list on each line, as nl requires the output stream controller to begin a new line. If we wish to write out a list in reversed order the recursive predicate must come before the write command. This guarantees that the list is traversed to the end before any element is written. At that time the last element of the list is written followed by each preceding element as the recursive control comes back up to the top. A reverse write of a list would be:

```
reverse_writelist([ ]).
reverse_writelist([H | T]) :- reverse_writelist(T), write(H), nl.
```

The reader should run writelist and reverse_writelist with trace to observe the behavior of these predicates.

15.1.4 Recursive Search in PROLOG

In Section 6.2 we introduced the 3×3 knight's tour problem for the predicate calculus. We represented the board squares for the knight moves like this:

1	2	3
4	5	6
7	8	9

The legal moves are represented in PROLOG using a move predicate. The path predicate defines an algorithm for finding a path of zero or more moves between its arguments. Note that path is defined recursively:

```
move(1, 6).     move(3, 4).     move(6, 7).     move(8, 3).
move(1, 8).     move(3, 8).     move(6, 1).     move(8, 1).
move(2, 7).     move(4, 3).     move(7, 6).     move(9, 4).
move(2, 9).     move(4, 9).     move(7, 2).     move(9, 2).

path(Z, Z).
path(X, Y) :- move(X, W), not(been(W)), assert(been(W)), path(W, Y).
```

This definition of path is a PROLOG implementation of the algorithm defined in Chapter 6. As noted above, assert is a built-in PROLOG predicate that always succeeds and has the side effect of placing its argument in the database of specifications. The been predicate is used to record previously visited states and avoid loops.

This use of the been predicate violates the program designer's goal of creating predicate calculus specifications that do not use global variables. Thus been(3), when asserted into the database, is indeed a fact available to any other procedure in the database and, as such, has global extension. Even more important, creating global structures to alter program control violates the basic tenet of the production system model, where the logic (of problem specifications) is kept separate from the control of the program. Here been structures were created as global specifications to modify the execution of the program itself.

As we proposed in Chapter 3, a list may be used to keep track of visited states and thus keep the path call from looping. The member predicate is used to detect duplicate states (loops). This approach remedies the problems of using global been(W) assertions. The PROLOG-based specification of the following clauses exactly implements the depth-first graph search with the backtracking algorithm of Chapters 3 and 6:

```
path(Z, Z, L).
path(X, Y, L) :- move(X, Z), not(member(Z, L)), path(Z, Y, [Z | L]).
```

using the member predicate as defined previously.

The third parameter of path is the local variable representing the list of states that have already been visited. When a new state is generated (using the move predicate) and this state is not already on the list of visited states, not(member(Z, L)), it is placed on the front of the state list [Z | L] for the next path call.

It should be noted that all the parameters of path are local and their current values depend on where they are called in the graph search. Each recursive call adds a state to this list. If all continuations from a certain state fail, then that particular path call fails. When the interpreter backs up to the parent call, the third parameter, representing the list of states visited, has its previous value. Thus, states are added to and deleted from this list as the backtracking search moves through the graph.

When the path call finally succeeds, the first two parameters are identical. The third parameter is the list of states visited on the solution path, in reverse order. Thus we can print out the steps of the solution. The PROLOG specification for the knight's tour problem using lists and a depth-first search employing backtrack may be obtained by using this definition of path with the move specifications and member predicates just presented.

The call to the PROLOG interpreter path(X,Y,[X]), where X and Y are replaced by numbers between 1 and 9, finds a path from state X to state Y, if the path exists. The third parameter initializes the path list with the starting state X. Note that there is no typing distinction in PROLOG: the first two parameters are any representation of states in the problem space and the third is a list of states. Unification makes this generalization of pattern matching across data types possible. Thus, path is a general depth-first search algorithm that may be used with any graph. In Section 15.3 we use this to implement a production system solution to the farmer, wolf, goat, and cabbage problem, with state specifications replacing square numbers in the call to path.

We now present the solution for the 3×3 knight's tour. It is left as an exercise to solve the full 8×8 knight's tour problem in PROLOG. (See exercises in Chapters 15 and 16.) For this trace we refer to the two parts of the path algorithm by number:

```
1. is path(Z, Z, L).
2. is path(X, Y, L) :- move(X, Z), not(member(Z, L)), path(Z, Y, [Z | L]).
?- path(1, 3, [1]).
```

path(1, 3, [1]) attempts to match 1. fail 1 ≠ 3.
path(1, 3, [1]) matches 2. X is 1, Y is 3, L is [1]
   move(1, Z) matches Z as 6, not(member(6, [1])) is true, call path(6, 3, [6,1])
    path(6, 3, [6, 1]) attempts to match 1. fail 6 ≠ 3.
    path(6, 3, [6, 1]) matches 2. X is 6, Y is 3, L is [6, 1].
      move(6, Z) matches Z as 7, not(member(7, [6, 1])) is true, path(7, 3, [7, 6, 1])
      path(7, 3, [7, 6, 1]) attempts to match 1. fail 7 ≠ 3.
      path(7, 3, [7, 6, 1]) matches 2. X is 7, Y is 3, L is [7, 6, 1].
        move(7, Z) is Z = 6, not(member(6, [7, 6, 1])) fails, backtrack!
        move(7, Z) is Z = 2, not(member(2, [7, 6, 1])) true, path(2, 3, [2, 7, 6, 1])
        path call attempts 1, fail, 2 ≠ 3.
        path matches 2, X is 2, Y is 3, L is [2, 7, 6, 1]
          move matches Z as 7, not(member(...)) fails, backtrack!
          move matches Z as 9, not(member(...)) true, path(9, 3, [9, 2, 7, 6, 1])
          path fails 1, 9 ≠ 3.
          path matches 2, X is 9, Y is 3, L is [9, 2, 7, 6, 1]
            move is Z = 4, not(member(...)) true, path(4, 3, [4, 9, 2, 7, 6, 1])
            path fails 1, 4 ≠ 3.
            path matches 2, X is 4, Y is 3, L is [4, 9, 2, 7, 6, 1]
              move Z = 3, not(member(...)) true, path(3, 3, [3, 4, 9, 2, 7, 6, 1])
                path attempts 1, true, 3 = 3, yes
      yes
     yes
    yes
   yes
  yes
 yes

In summary, the recursive path call is a *shell* or general control structure for search in a graph: in path(X, Y, L), X is the present state; Y is the goal state. When X and Y are identical, the recursion terminates. L is the list of states on the current path to state Y, and as each new state Z is found with the call move(X, Z) it is placed on the list: [Z | L]. The state list is checked, using not(member(Z, L)), to be sure the path does not loop.

The difference between the state list L in the path call above and the closed set in Chapter 3 is that closed records all states visited, while the state list L keeps track of only the present path. It is straightforward to expand the record keeping in the path call to record all visited states and we do this in Section 15.4.

15.1.5 The Use of Cut to Control Search in PROLOG

The *cut* is represented by an exclamation point, !. The syntax for cut is that of a goal with no arguments, that has several side effects: first, when originally encountered it always succeeds, and second, if it is "failed back to" in backtracking, it causes the entire goal in which it is contained to fail. For a simple example of the effect of the cut, recall the two-move path call from the knight's tour example. The predicate path2 could be created:

path2(X, Y) :- move(X, Z), move(Z, Y).

(There is a two-move path between X and Y if there exists an intermediate stop Z between them.) For this example, assume part of the knight's database:

```
move(1, 6).
move(1, 8).
move(6, 7).
move(6, 1).
move(8, 3).
move(8, 1).
```

The interpreter is asked to find all the two-move paths from 1; there are four answers:

```
?- path2(1, W).
W = 7
;
W = 1
;
W = 3
;
W = 1
;
no
```

When path2 is altered with cut, only two answers result:

path2(X, Y) :- move(X, Z), !, move(Z, Y).

```
?- path2(1, W).
W = 7
;
W = 1
;
no
```

This happens because variable Z takes on only one value (the first value it is bound to), namely 6. Once the first subgoal succeeds, Z is bound to 6 and the cut is encountered. This prohibits further backtracking to the first subgoal and any further bindings for Z.

There are several uses for the cut in programming. First, as this example demonstrated, it allows the programmer to control explicitly the shape of the search tree. When further (exhaustive) search is not required, the tree can be explicitly pruned at that point. This allows PROLOG code to have the flavor of function calling: when one set of values (bindings) is "returned" by a PROLOG predicate (or set of predicates) and the cut is encountered, the interpreter does not search for other unifications. If that set of values does not lead on to a solution then no further values are attempted.

A second use of cut controls recursion. For example in the path call:

```
path(Z, Z, L).
path(X, Z, L) :- move(X, Y), not(member(Y, L)), path(Y, Z, [Y|L]), !.
```

the addition of cut means that (at most) one solution to the graph search is produced. Only one solution is produced because further solutions occur after the clause path(Z, Z, L) is satisfied. If the user asks for more solutions, path(Z, Z, L) fails, and the second path call is reinvoked to continue the (exhaustive) search of the graph. When the cut is placed after the recursive path call, the call cannot be reentered (backed into) for further search.

Important side effects of the cut are to make the program run faster and to conserve memory locations. When cut is used within a predicate, the pointers in memory needed for backtracking to predicates to the left of the cut are not created. This is, of course, because they will never be needed. Thus, cut produces the desired solution, and only the desired solution, with more efficient use of memory.

The cut can also be used with recursion to reinitialize the path call for further search within the graph. This will be demonstrated with the general search algorithms presented in Section 15.3. For this purpose we also need to develop several abstract data types.

15.2 Abstract Data Types (ADTs) in PROLOG

Programming in any environment is enhanced by procedural abstractions and information hiding. Because the set, stack, queue, and priority queue data structures were the support constructs for the graph search algorithms of Chapters 3, 4, and 6, we build them in PROLOG in the present section and then use them in the design of the PROLOG search algorithms presented later in this chapter.

Recursion, lists, and pattern matching, as emphasized throughout this book, are the primary tools for building and searching graph structures. These are the pieces with which we build our ADTs. All list handling and recursive processing that define the ADT are "hidden" within the ADT abstraction, quite different than the normal static data structure.

15.2.1 The ADT Stack

A *stack* is a linear structure with access at one end only. Thus all elements must be added to, pushed, and removed, popped, from the structure at that end of access. The stack is sometimes referred to as a last-in-first-out (LIFO) data structure. We saw its use with depth-first search in Section 3.2.3. The operators that we will define for a stack are:

1. Test whether the stack is empty.

2. Push an element onto the stack.

3. Pop, or remove, the top element from the stack.

4. Peek (often called Top) to see the top element on the stack without popping it.

5. Member_stack, which checks whether an element is in the stack.

6. Add_list, which adds a list of elements to the stack.

Operators 5 and 6 may be built from 1–4.

We now build these operators in PROLOG. As just noted, we use the list primitives:

1. empty_stack([ ]). This predicate can be used either to test a stack to see whether it is empty or to generate a new empty stack.

2–4. stack(Top, Stack, [Top | Stack]). This predicate performs the push, pop, and peek predicates depending on the variable bindings of its arguments. For instance, push produces a new stack as the third argument when the first two arguments are bound. Likewise, pop produces the top element of the stack when the third argument is bound to the stack. The second argument will then be bound to the new stack, once the top element is popped. Finally, if we keep the stack as the third argument, the first argument lets us peek at its top element.

5. member_stack(Element, Stack) :- member(Element, Stack). This allows us to determine whether an element is a member of the stack. Of course, the same result could be produced by creating a recursive call that peeked at the next element of the stack and then, if this element did not match Element, popped the stack. This would continue until the empty stack predicate was true.

6. add_list_to_stack(List, Stack, Result) :- append(List, Stack, Result). List is added to Stack to produce Result, a new stack. Of course, the same result could be obtained by popping List and pushing each element onto a temporary stack until empty stack is true of List. We then pop the temporary stack and push each element onto the Stack until empty stack is true of the temporary stack. append is described in detail in Section 15.10.

A final predicate for printing a stack in reverse order is reverse_print_stack. This is very useful when a stack has, in reversed order, the current path from the start state to the present state of the graph search. We will see several examples of this in the following subsections.

```
reverse_print_stack(S) :- empty_stack(S).
reverse_print_stack(S) :-
    stack(E, Rest, S),
    reverse_print_stack(Rest),
    write(E), nl.
```

15.2.2 The ADT Queue

A *queue* is a first-in-first-out (FIFO) data structure. It is often characterized as a list where elements are taken off (dequeued) from one end and added to (enqueued) at the other end. The queue was used for defining breadth-first search in Chapters 3 and 4. The queue operators are:

1. empty_queue([ ]). This predicate either tests whether a queue is empty or initializes a new empty queue.

2. enqueue(E, [ ], [E]).
   enqueue(E, [H | T], [H | Tnew]) :- enqueue(E, T, Tnew). This recursive predicate adds the element E to a queue, the second argument. The new augmented queue is the third argument.

3. dequeue(E, [E | T], T). This predicate produces a new queue, the third argument, that is the result of taking the next element, the first argument, off the original queue, the second argument.

4. dequeue(E, [E | T], _). This predicate lets us peek at the next element, E, of the queue.

5. member_queue(Element, Queue) :- member(Element, Queue). This tests whether Element is a member of Queue.

6. add_list_to_queue(List, Queue, Newqueue) :- append(Queue, List, Newqueue). This enqueues an entire list of elements.

Of course, 5 and 6 can be created using 1–4; append is presented in Section 15.10.

15.2.3   The ADT Priority Queue

A *priority queue* orders the elements of a regular queue so that each new entrant to the priority queue is placed in its sorted order. The dequeue operator removes the "best" sorted element from the priority queue. We used the priority queue in the design of best-first search in Chapter 4.

Because the priority queue is a sorted queue, many of its operators are the same as the queue operators, in particular, empty_queue, member_queue, dequeue (the "best" of the sorted elements will be next for the dequeue), and peek. enqueue in a priority queue is the insert_pq operator, as each new item is placed in its proper sorted order.

```
insert_pq(State, [ ], [State]) :- !.
insert_pq(State, [H | Tail], [State, H | Tail]) :-
     precedes(State, H).
insert_pq(State, [H | T], [H | Tnew]) :-
     insert_pq(State, T, Tnew).
precedes(X, Y) :- X < Y.                        %order operator depends on types compared
```

The first argument of this predicate is the new element that is to be inserted. The second argument is the previous priority queue, and the third argument is the augmented priority queue. The precedes predicate checks that the order of elements is preserved.

Another priority queue operator is insert_list_pq. This predicate is used to merge an unsorted list or set of elements into the priority queue, as is necessary when adding the children of a state to the priority queue for best-first search (Chapter 4 and Section 15.4.3). insert_list_pq uses insert_pq to put each individual new item into the priority queue:

```
insert_list_pq([ ], L, L).
insert_list_pq([State | Tail], L, New_L) :-
    insert_pq(State, L, L2),
    insert_list_pq(Tail, L2, New_L).
```

15.2.4   The ADT Set

Finally, we describe the ADT set. A *set* is a collection of elements with no element repeated. Sets can be used for collecting all the children of a state or for maintaining closed in a search algorithm, as in Chapters 3 and 4. A set of elements, e.g., {a,b}, is represented as a list, [a,b], with order not important. The set operators include empty_set, member_set, delete_if_in, and add_if_not_in. We have operators for combining and comparing sets, including union, intersection, set_difference, subset, and equal_set.

```
empty_set([ ]).
member_set(E, S) :-
    member(E, S).
delete_if_in_set(E, [ ], [ ]).
delete_if_in_set(E, [E | T], T) :- !.
delete_if_in_set(E, [H | T], [H | T_new]) :-
    delete_if_in_set(E, T, T_new), !.
add_if_not_in_set(X, S, S) :-
    member(X, S), !.
add_if_not_in_set(X, S, [X | S]).
union([ ], S, S).
union([H | T], S, S_new) :-
    union(T, S, S2),
    add_if_not_in_set(H, S2, S_new),!.
subset([ ], _).
subset([H | T], S) :-
    member_set(H, S),
    subset(T, S).
intersection([ ], _, [ ]).
intersection([H | T], S, [H | S_new]) :-
    member_set(H, S),
    intersection(T, S, S_new), !.
intersection([_ | T], S, S_new) :-
    intersection(T, S, S_new), !.
set_difference([ ], _, [ ]).
set_difference([H | T], S, T_new) :-
    member_set(H, S),
    set_difference(T, S, T_new), !.
set_difference([H | T], S, [H | T_new]) :-
    set_difference(T, S, T_new), !.
equal_set(S1, S2) :-
    subset(S1, S2),
    subset(S2, S1).
```

15.3 A Production System Example in PROLOG

In this section we write a production system solution to the farmer, wolf, goat, and cabbage problem. The problem is stated as follows:

> A farmer with his wolf, goat, and cabbage come to the edge of a river they wish to cross. There is a boat at the river's edge, but, of course, only the farmer can row. The boat also can carry only two things (including the rower) at a time. If the wolf is ever left alone with the goat, the wolf will eat the goat; similarly, if the goat is left alone with the cabbage, the goat will eat the cabbage. Devise a sequence of crossings of the river so that all four characters arrive safely on the other side of the river.

In the next paragraphs we present a production system solution to this problem. First, we observe that the problem may be represented as a search through a graph. To do this we consider the possible moves that might be available at any time in the solution process. Some of these moves are eventually ruled out because they produce states that are unsafe (something will be eaten).

For the moment, suppose that all states are safe, and simply consider the graph of possible states. The boat can be used in four ways: to carry the farmer and wolf, the farmer and goat, the farmer and cabbage, and the farmer alone. A state of the world is some combination of the characters on the two banks. Several states of the search are represented in Figure 15.1. States of the world may be represented using the predicate, state(F, W, G, C), with the location of the farmer as first parameter, location of the wolf as second parameter, the goat as third, and the cabbage as fourth. We assume that the river runs "north to south" and that the characters are on either the east, e, or west, w, bank. Thus, state(w, w, w, w) has all characters on the west bank to start the problem.

It must be pointed out that these choices are conventions that have been arbitrarily chosen by the authors. Indeed, as researchers in AI continually point out, the selection of an appropriate representation is often the most critical aspect of problem solving. These conventions are selected to fit the predicate calculus representation in PROLOG. Different states of the world are created by different crossings of the river, represented by changes in the values of the parameters of the state predicate as in Figure 15.1. Other representations are certainly possible.

We now describe a general graph for this river-crossing problem. For the time being, we ignore the fact that some states are unsafe. In Figure 15.2 we see the beginning of the graph of possible moves back and forth across the river. Since the farmer always rows, it is not necessary to have a separate representation for the location of the boat. Figure 15.2 represents part of the graph that is to be searched for a solution path.

The recursive path call previously described provides the control mechanism for the production system search. The production rules are the rules for changing state in the search. We define these as move rules in PROLOG form.

Because PROLOG uses Horn clauses, a production system designed in PROLOG must either represent production rules directly in Horn clause form or translate rules to this format. We take the former option here (and show how *if... then...* rules are changed to Horn clauses in Section 13.2). Horn clauses require that the pattern for the present state

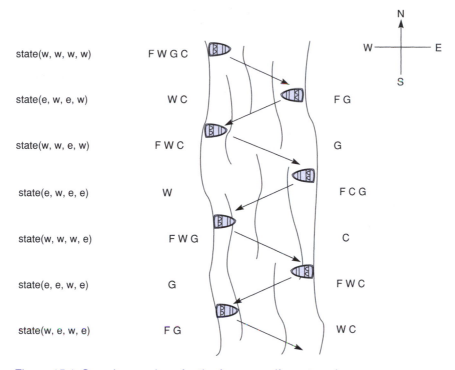

state(w, w, w, w)   F W G C

state(e, w, e, w)   W C   F G

state(w, w, e, w)   F W C   G

state(e, w, e, e)   W   F C G

state(w, w, w, e)   F W G   C

state(e, e, w, e)   G   F W C

state(w, e, w, e)   F G   W C

N
W———|———E
S

Figure 15.1 Sample crossings for the farmer, wolf, goat, and
cabbage problem.

and the pattern for the next state both be placed in the head of the Horn clause, or to the left of :-. These are the arguments to the move predicate. The conditions that the production rule requires to fire and return the next state are placed to the right of :-. As shown in the following example, these conditions can also be expressed as unification constraints.

The first rule we define is for the farmer to take the wolf across the river. This rule must account for both the transfer from east to west and the transfer from west to east, and it must not be applicable when the farmer and wolf are on opposite sides of the river. Thus, it must transform state(e, e, G, C) to state(w, w, G, C) and state(w, w, G, C) to state(e, e, G, C). It must also fail for state(e, w, G, C) and state(w, e, G, C). The variables G and C represent the fact that the third and fourth parameters can be bound to either e or w. Whatever their values, they remain the same after the move of the farmer and wolf. Some of the states produced may indeed be "unsafe."

The following move rule operates only when the farmer and wolf are in the same location and takes them to the opposite side of the river. Note that the goat and cabbage do not change their present location (whatever it might be).

```
move(state(X, X, G, C), state(Y, Y, G, C)) :- opp(X, Y).
opp(e, w).
opp(w, e).
```

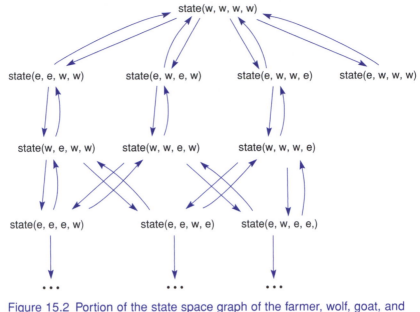

Figure 15.2 Portion of the state space graph of the farmer, wolf, goat, and cabbage problem, including unsafe states.

This rule fires when a state (the present location in the graph) is presented to the first parameter of move in which the farmer and wolf are at the same location. When the rule fires, a new state, the second parameter of move, is produced with the value of X opposite, opp, the value of Y. Two conditions are satisfied to produce the new state: first, that the values of the first two parameters are the same and, second, that both of their new locations are opposite their old.

The first condition was checked implicitly in the unification process, in that move is not even called unless the first two parameters are the same. This test may be done explicitly by using the following rule:

move(state(F, W, G, C), state(Z, Z, G, C)) :- F = W, opp(F, Z).

This equivalent move rule first tests whether F and W are the same and, only if they are (on the same side of the river), assigns the opposite value of F to Z. Note that PROLOG can do "assignment" by the binding of variable values in unification. Bindings are shared by all occurrences of a variable in a clause, and the scope of a variable is limited to the clause in which it occurs.

Pattern matching, a powerful tool in AI programming, is especially important in pruning search. States that do not fit the patterns in the rule are automatically pruned. In this sense, the first version of the move rule offers a more efficient representation because unification does not even consider the state predicate unless its first two parameters are identical.

Next, we create a predicate to test whether each new state is safe, so that nothing is eaten in the process of crossing the river. Again, unification plays an important role in this definition. Any state where the second and third parameters are the same and opposite the first parameter is unsafe; the wolf eats the goat. Alternatively, if the third and fourth parameters are the same and opposite the first parameter, the state is unsafe: the goat eats the cabbage. These unsafe situations may be represented with the following rules.

```
unsafe(state(X, Y, Y, C)) :- opp(X, Y).
unsafe(state(X, W, Y, Y)) :- opp(X, Y).
```

Several points should be mentioned here. First, if a state is to be not unsafe (i.e., safe), according to the definition of not in PROLOG, neither of these unsafe predicates can be true. Thus, neither of these predicates can unify with the current state or, if they do unify, their conditions must not be satisfied. Second, not in PROLOG is not exactly equivalent to the logical ¬ of the first-order predicate calculus; not is rather "negation by failure of its opposite." The reader should test a number of states to verify that unsafe does what it is intended to do. Now, not unsafe is added to the previous production rule:

```
move(state(X, X, G, C), state(Y, Y, G, C)) :-
    opp(X, Y), not(unsafe(state(Y, Y, G, C))).
```

The not unsafe test calls unsafe, as mentioned above, to see whether the generated state is an acceptable new state in the search. When all criteria are met, including the check in the path algorithm that the new state is not a member of the visited-state list, path is (recursively) called on this state to go deeper into the graph. When path is called, the new state is added to the visited-state list.

In a similar fashion, we can create the three other production rules to represent the farmer taking the goat, cabbage, and himself across the river. We have added a writelist command to each production rule to print a trace of the current rule.

The reverse_print_stack command is used in the terminating condition of path to print out the final solution path. Finally, we add a fifth "pseudorule" that always fires, because no conditions are placed on it, when all previous rules have failed; it indicates that the path call is backtracking from the current state, and then it itself fails. This pseudorule is added to assist the user in seeing what is going on as the production system is running.

We now present the full production system program in PROLOG to solve the farmer, wolf, goat, and cabbage problem. The PROLOG predicates unsafe, writelist, and the ADT stack predicates of Section 15.2.1, must also be included:

```
move(state(X, X, G, C), state(Y, Y, G, C)) :-
    opp(X, Y), not(unsafe(state(Y, Y, G, C))),
    writelist(['try farmer takes wolf', Y, Y, G, C]).
move(state(X, W, X, C), state(Y, W, Y, C)) :-
    opp(X, Y), not(unsafe(state(Y, W, Y, C))),
    writelist(['try farmer takes goat', Y, W, Y, C]).
move(state(X, W, G, X), state(Y, W, G, Y)) :-
    opp(X, Y), not(unsafe(state(Y, W, G, Y))),
    writelist(['try farmer takes cabbage', Y, W, G, Y]).
```

```
move(state(X, W, G, C), state(Y, W, G, C)) :-
    opp(X, Y), not(unsafe(state(Y, W, G, C))),
    writelist(['try farmer takes self', Y, W, G, C]).
move(state(F, W, G, C), state(F, W, G, C)) :-
    writelist(['   BACKTRACK from:', F, W, G, C]), fail.
path(Goal, Goal, Been_stack) :-
    write('Solution Path Is: '), nl,
    reverse_print_stack(Been_stack).
path(State, Goal, Been_stack) :-
    move(State, Next_state),
    not(member_stack(Next_state, Been_stack)),
    stack(Next_state, Been_stack, New_been_stack),
        path(Next_state, Goal, New_been_stack), !.
opp(e, w).
opp(w, e).
```

The code is called by requesting go, which initializes the recursive path call. To make running the program easier, we can create a predicate, called test, that simplifies the input:

```
go(Start, Goal) :-
    empty_stack(Empty_been_stack),
    stack(Start, Empty_been_stack, Been_stack),
    path(Start, Goal, Been_stack).

test :- go(state(w,w,w,w), state(e,e,e,e)).
```

The algorithm backtracks from states that allow no further progress. You may also use trace to monitor the various variable bindings local to each call of path. It may also be noted that this program is a general program for moving the four creatures from any (legal) position on the banks to any other (legal) position, including asking for a path from the goal back to the start state. Other interesting features of production systems, including the fact that different orderings of the rules can produce different searches through the graph, are presented in the exercises. A partial trace of the execution of the program, showing only rules actually used to generate new states, is presented next:

```
?- test.
try farmer takes goat e w e w
try farmer takes self w w e w
try farmer takes wolf e e e w
try farmer takes goat w e w w
try farmer takes cabbage e e w e
try farmer takes wolf w w w e
try farmer takes goat e w e e
   BACKTRACK from e,w,e,e
   BACKTRACK from w,w,w,e
try farmer takes self w e w e
try farmer takes goat e e e e
```

Solution Path Is:
state(w,w,w,w)
state(e,w,e,w)
state(w,w,e,w)
state(e,e,e,w)
state(w,e,w,w)
state(e,e,w,e)
state(w,e,w,e)
state(e,e,e,e)

In summary, this PROLOG program implements a production system solution to the farmer, wolf, goat, and cabbage problem. The move rules make up the content of the production memory. The working memory is represented by the arguments of the path call. The production system control mechanism is defined by the recursive path call. Finally, the ordering of rules for generation of children from each state (conflict resolution) is determined by the order in which the rules are placed in the production memory.

15.4 Designing Alternative Search Strategies

As the previous subsection demonstrated, and as is made more precise in Section 15.7, PROLOG itself uses depth-first search with backtracking. We now show how the alternative search strategies of Chapters 3, 4, and 6 can be implemented in PROLOG. Our implementations of depth-first, breadth-first, and best-first search use open and closed lists to record states in the search. When search fails at any point we do not go back to the preceding values of open and closed. Instead, open and closed are updated within the path call and the search continues with these new values. The cut is used to keep PROLOG from storing the old versions of open and closed.

15.4.1 Depth-First Search Using the Closed List

Because the values of variables are restored when recursion backtracks, the list of visited states in the depth-first path algorithm of Section 15.3 records states only if they are on the current path to the goal. Although the testing each "new" state for membership in this list prevents loops, it still allows branches of the space to be reexamined if they are reached along paths generated earlier but abandoned at that time as unfruitful. A more efficient implementation keeps track of all the states that have ever been encountered. This more complete collection of states made up the list called closed in Chapter 3, and Closed_set in the following algorithm.

Closed_set holds all states on the current path plus the states that were rejected when the algorithm backtracked out of them; thus, it no longer represents the path from the start to the current state. To capture this path information, we create the ordered pair [State, Parent] to keep track of each state and its parent; the Start state is represented by [Start, nil]. These state–parent pairs will be used to re-create the solution path from the Closed_set.

We now present a shell structure for depth-first search in PROLOG, keeping track of both open and closed and checking each new state to be sure it was not previously visited. path has three arguments, the Open_stack, Closed_set, maintained as a set, and the Goal state. The current state, State, is the next state on the Open_stack. The stack and set operators are found in Section 15.2.

Search starts by a go predicate that initializes the path call. Note that go places the Start state with the nil parent, [Start, nil], alone on Open_stack; Closed_set is empty:

```
go(Start, Goal) :-
    empty_stack(Empty_open),
    stack([Start, nil], Empty_open, Open_stack),
    empty_set(Closed_set),
    path(Open_stack, Closed_set, Goal).
```

The three-argument path call is:

```
path(Open_stack, _, _) :-
    empty_stack(Open_stack),
    write('No solution found with these rules').
path(Open_stack, Closed_set, Goal) :-
    stack([State, Parent], _, Open_stack), State = Goal,
    write('A Solution is Found!'), nl,
    printsolution([State, Parent], Closed_set).
path(Open_stack, Closed_set, Goal) :-
    stack([State, Parent], Rest_open_stack, Open_stack),
    get_children(State, Rest_open_stack, Closed_set, Children),
    add_list_to_stack(Children, Rest_open_stack, New_open_stack),
    union([[State, Parent]], Closed_set, New_closed_set),
    path(New_open_stack, New_closed_set, Goal), !.
get_children(State, Rest_open_stack, Closed_set, Children) :-
    bagof(Child, moves(State, Rest_open_stack,
        Closed_set, Child), Children).
moves(State, Rest_open_stack, Closed_set, [Next, State]) :-
    move(State, Next),
    not(unsafe(Next)),                          % test depends on problem
    not(member_stack([Next,_], Rest_open_stack)),
    not(member_set([Next,_], Closed_set)).
```

We assume a set of move rules, and, if necessary, an unsafe predicate:

```
move(Present_state, Next_state) :- ...           % test first rule.
move(Present_state, Next_state) :- ...           % test second rule.
....
```

The first path call terminates search when the Open_stack is empty, which means there are no more states on the open list to continue the search. This usually indicates that the graph has been exhaustively searched. The second path call terminates and prints out the solution path when the solution is found. Since the states of the graph search are maintained as [State, Parent] pairs, printsolution will go to the Closed_set and recursively rebuild the solution path. Note that the solution is printed from start to goal.

```
printsolution([State, nil], _) :-
    write(State), nl.
printsolution([State, Parent], Closed_set) :-
    member_set([Parent, Grandparent], Closed_set),
    printsolution([Parent, Grandparent], Closed_set),
    write(State), nl.
```

The third path call uses bagof, a PROLOG predicate standard to most interpreters. bagof lets us gather all the unifications of a pattern into a single list. The second parameter to bagof is the pattern predicate to be matched in the database. The first parameter specifies the components of the second parameter that we wish to collect. For example, we may be interested in the values bound to a single variable of a predicate. All bindings of the first parameter resulting from these matches are collected in a list and bound to the third parameter.

In this program, bagof collects the states reached by firing *all* of the enabled production rules. Of course, this is necessary to gather all descendants of a particular state so that we can add them, in proper order, to open. The second argument of bagof, a new predicate named moves, calls the move predicates to generate all the states that may be reached using the production rules. The arguments to moves are the present state, the open list, the closed set, and a variable that is the state reached by a good move. Before returning this state, moves checks that the new state, Next, is not a member of either rest_open_stack, open once the present state is removed, or closed_set. bagof calls moves and collects all the states that meet these conditions. The third argument of bagof thus represents the new states that are to be placed on the Open_stack.

In some implementations, bagof fails when no matches exist for the second argument and thus the third argument is empty. This can be remedied by substituting (bagof(X, moves(S, T, C, X), List); List = [ ]) for the current calls to bagof in the code.

Finally, because the states of the search are represented as state–parent pairs, the member check predicates, e.g., member_set, must be revised to reflect the structure of the pattern matching. We need to test to see if a state–parent pair is identical to the first element of a list of state–parent pairs and then recur if it isn't:

```
member_set([State, Parent], [[State, Parent]| _]).
member_set(X, [_|T]) :- member_set(X, T).
```

15.4.2 Breadth-First Search in PROLOG

We now present the *shell* of an algorithm for breadth-first search using explicit open and closed lists. The shell can be used with the move rules and unsafe predicates for any search problem. This algorithm is called by:

```
go(Start, Goal) :-
    empty_queue(Empty_open_queue),
    enqueue([Start, nil], Empty_open_queue, Open_queue),
    empty_set(Closed_set),
    path(Open_queue, Closed_set, Goal).
```

Start and Goal have their obvious values. Again we create the ordered pair [State, Parent], as we did with depth and breadth search, to keep track of each state and its parent; the Start state is represented by [Start, nil]. This will be used by printsolution to re-create the solution path from the Closed_set. The first parameter of path is the Open_queue, the second is the Closed_set, and the third is the Goal. *Don't care* variables, those whose values are not used in a clause, are written as _.

```
path(Open_queue, _, _) :-
    empty_queue(Open_queue),
    write('Graph searched, no solution found.').
path(Open_queue, Closed_set, Goal) :-
    dequeue([State, Parent], Open_queue,_), State = Goal,
    write('Solution path is: '), nl,
    printsolution([State, Parent], Closed_set).
path(Open_queue, Closed_set, Goal) :-
    dequeue([State, Parent], Open_queue, Rest_open_queue),
    get_children(State, Rest_open_queue, Closed_set, Children),
    add_list_to_queue(Children, Rest_open_queue, New_open_queue),
    union([[State, Parent]], Closed_set, New_closed_set),
    path(New_open_queue, New_closed_set, Goal), !.
get_children(State, Rest_open_queue, Closed_set, Children) :-
    bagof(Child, moves(State, Rest_open_queue,
        Closed_set, Child), Children).
moves(State, Rest_open_queue, Closed_set, [Next, State]) :-
    move(State, Next),
    not(unsafe(Next)),                              % test depends on problem
    not(member_queue([Next,_], Rest_open_queue)),
    not(member_set([Next,_], Closed_set)).
```

This algorithm is a shell in that no move rules are given. These must be supplied to fit the specific problem domain. The queue and set operators are found in Section 15.2.

The first path termination condition is defined for the case that path is called with its first argument, Open_queue, empty. This happens only when no more states in the graph remain to be searched and the solution has not been found. A solution is found in the second path predicate when the head of the open_queue and the Goal state are identical.

When path does not terminate, the bagof and moves predicates gather all the children of the current state and maintain the queue. The actions of these predicates were described in the previous section. In order to recreate the solution path, we saved each state as a state–parent pair, [State, Parent]. The start state has the parent nil. As noted in Section 15.4.1, the state–parent pair representation makes necessary a slightly more complex pattern matching in the member, moves, and print_solution predicates.

15.4.3 Best-First Search in PROLOG

Our shell for best-first search is a modification of the breadth-first algorithm in which the open queue is replaced by a priority queue, ordered by heuristic merit, for each new call to path. In our algorithm, we attach a heuristic measure permanently to each new state on open and use this measure for ordering states on open. We also retain the parent of each state. This information is used by printsolution, as in breadth-first search, to build the solution path once the goal is found.

To keep track of all required search information, each state is represented as a list of five elements: the state description, the parent of the state, an integer giving the depth in the graph of its discovery, an integer giving the heuristic measure of the state, and the integer sum of the third and fourth elements. The first and second elements are found in the usual way; the third is determined by adding one to the depth of its parent; the fourth is determined by the heuristic measure of the particular problem. The fifth element, used for ordering the states on the open_pq, is $f(n) = g(n) + h(n)$, as presented in Chapter 4.

As before, the move rules are not specified; they are defined to fit the specific problem. The ADT operators for set and priority queue are presented in Section 15.2. heuristic, also specific to each problem, is a measure applied to each state to determine its heuristic weight, the value of the fourth parameter in its descriptive list.

This algorithm has two termination conditions and is called by:

```
go(Start, Goal) :-
    empty_set(Closed_set),
    empty_pq(Open),
    heuristic(Start, Goal, H),
    insert_pq([Start, nil, 0, H, H], Open, Open_pq),
    path(Open_pq, Closed_set, Goal).
```

nil is the parent of Start and H its heuristic evaluation. The code for best-first search is:

```
path(Open_pq, _,_) :-
    empty_pq(Open_pq),
    write('Graph searched, no solution found.').
path(Open_pq, Closed_set, Goal) :-
    dequeue_pq([State, Parent, _, _, _], Open_pq,_),
    State = Goal,
    write('The solution path is: '), nl,
    printsolution([State, Parent, _, _, _], Closed_set).
path(Open_pq, Closed_set, Goal) :-
    dequeue_pq([State, Parent, D, H, S], Open_pq, Rest_open_pq),
    get_children([State, Parent, D, H, S], Rest_open_pq, Closed_set, Children, Goal),
    insert_list_pq(Children, Rest_open_pq, New_open_pq),
    union([[State, Parent, D, H, S]], Closed_set, New_closed_set),
    path(New_open_pq, New_closed_set, Goal), !.
```

get_children is a predicate that generates all the children of State. It uses bagof and moves predicates as in the previous searches. Details are found in Section 15.4.1. Move rules, a safe check for legal moves, and a heuristic must be specifically defined for each application. The member check must be specifically designed for five element lists.

```
get_children([State, _, D, _, _], Rest_open_pq, Closed_set, Children, Goal) :-
    bagof(Child, moves([State, _, D, _, _], Rest_open_pq,
    Closed_set, Child, Goal), Children).
moves([State, _, Depth, _, _], Rest_open_pq, Closed_set,
        [Next, State, New_D, H, S], Goal) :-
    move(State, Next),
    not(unsafe(Next)),% determined by application
    not(member_pq([Next, _, _, _, _], Rest_open_pq)),
    not(member_set([Next, _, _, _, _], Closed_set)),
    New_D is Depth + 1,
    heuristic(Next, Goal, H),% determined by application
    S is New_D + H.
```

Finally, printsolution prints the solution path. It recursively finds State–Parent pairs by matching the first two elements in the state description with the first two elements of the five element lists that make up the Closed_set. The start state has nil as its parent.

```
printsolution([State, nil, _, _, _], _) :-
    write(State), nl.
printsolution([State, Parent, _, _, _], Closed_set) :-
    member_set([Parent, Grandparent, _, _, _], Closed_set),
        printsolution([Parent, Grandparent, _, _, _], Closed_set),
    write(State), nl.
```

15.5 A PROLOG Planner

In Section 6.3 we described a predicate calculus-based planning algorithm. It was predicate calculus (PC) based in that the PC representation was chosen for both the state of the planning world descriptions as well as the change of state rules. In this section we create a PROLOG version of that algorithm.

We represent the states of the world, including the begin and goal states, as lists of predicates. Two states, the start and goal states for our example, are described:

```
start = [handempty, ontable(b), ontable(c), on(a,b), clear(c), clear(a)]
goal = [handempty, ontable(a), ontable(b), on(c,b), clear(a), clear(c)]
```

These states are seen, along with a portion of the search space, in Figures 15.3 and 15.4.

The moves in this blocks world are described using *add* and *delete* lists, as in Section 8.4. The move predicates have three arguments. First is the move predicate name with its arguments. The second argument is the list of preconditions: the predicates that must be true in the description of the state of the world for the move rule to be applied to that state. The third argument is the add and delete list: the predicates that are added to and deleted from the state of the world to create the new state of the world that results from applying the move rule. Notice how useful the ADT set operators of union, intersection, set difference, etc., are in manipulating the preconditions and the *add* and *delete* lists.

Four of the moves within this world may be described:

```
move(pickup(X), [handempty, clear(X), on(X,Y)],
     [del(handempty), del(clear(X)), del(on(X,Y)),
     add(clear(Y)), add(holding(X))]).
```

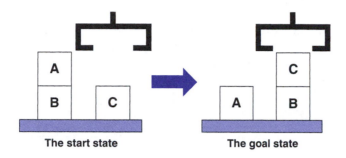

The start state   The goal state

Figure 15.3 The start and goal states for the blocks world problem.

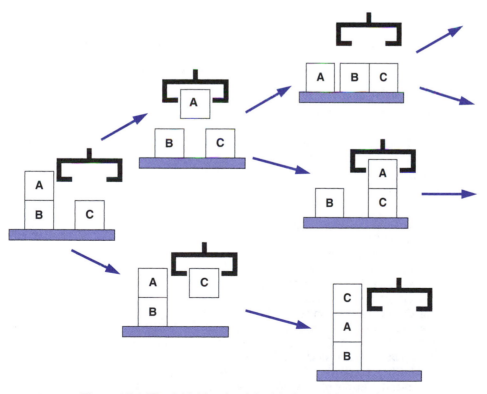

Figure 15.4 The initial levels of the blocks world state space.

```
move(pickup(X), [handempty, clear(X), ontable(X)],
    [del(handempty), del(clear(X)), del(ontable(X)),
    add(holding(X))]).
move(putdown(X), [holding(X)],
    [del(holding(X)), add(ontable(X)),
    add(clear(X)), add(handempty)]).
move(stack(X,Y), [holding(X), clear(Y)],
    [del(holding(X)), del(clear(Y)), add(handempty),
    add(on(X,Y)), add(clear(X))]).
```

Finally, we have the recursive controller for the plan generation. The first plan predicate gives the successful termination conditions for the plan, namely, when the goal is produced. The final plan predicate states that after exhaustive search, no plan is possible. The recursive plan generator:

1. Searches for a move relationship.

2. Checks, using the subset operator, whether the state's Preconditions are met.

3. The change_state predicate produces a new Child_state using the add and delete list.

4. member_stack makes sure the new state has not been visited before.

5. The stack operator pushes the new Child_state onto the New_moves_stack.

6. The stack operator pushes the original Name state onto the New_been_stack.

7. The recursive plan call searches for the next state using the Child_state and an updated New_move_stack and Been_stack.

A number of supporting utilities, built on the stack and set ADTs of Sections 15.2.1 and 15.2.4 are included. Of course, the search being stack-based, is depth-first with backtracking and terminates with the first path found to a goal. It is left as an exercise to build breadth-first and best-first planners.

```
plan(State, Goal, _, Move_stack) :-
    equal_set(State, Goal),
    write('moves are'), nl,
    reverse_print_stack(Move_stack).
plan(State, Goal, Been_stack, Move_stack) :-
    move(Name, Preconditions, Actions),
    conditions_met(Preconditions, State),
    change_state(State, Actions, Child_state),
    not(member_stack(Child_state, Been_stack)),
    stack(Name, Been_stack, New_been_stack),
    stack(Child_state, Move_stack, New_move_stack),
        plan(Child_state, Goal, New_been_stack, New_move_stack), !.
plan(_, _, _) :- write('No plan possible with these moves!').
```

```
conditions_met(P, S) :-
    subset(P, S).
    change_state(S, [ ], S).
change_state(S, [add(P) | T], S_new) :-
    change_state(S, T, S2),
    add_if_not_in_set(P, S2, S_new), !.
change_state(S, [del(P) | T], S_new) :-
    change_state(S, T, S2),
    delete_if_in_set(P, S2, S_new), !.
reverse_print_stack(S) :-
    empty_stack(S).
reverse_print_stack(S) :-
    stack(E, Rest, S),
        reverse_print_stack(Rest),
    write(E), nl.
```

Finally, we create a go predicate to initialize the arguments for plan, as well as a test predicate to demonstrate an easy method to save repeated creation of the same input string.

```
go(Start, Goal) :-
    empty_stack(Move_stack),
    empty_stack(Been_stack),
    stack(Start, Been_stack, New_been_stack),
    plan(Start, Goal, New_been_stack, Move_stack).
test :-
    go([handempty, ontable(b), ontable(c), on(a,b), clear(c), clear(a)],
        [handempty, ontable(a), ontable(b), on(c,b), clear(a), clear(c)]).
```

15.6 PROLOG: Meta-Predicates, Types and Unification

15.6.1 Meta-Logical Predicates

Meta-logical constructs extend the expressive power of any programming environment. We refer to these predicates as *meta* because they are designed to match, query, and manipulate other predicates that make up the specifications of the problem domain. That is, they can be used to reason about PROLOG predicates rather than the terms or objects these other predicates denote. We need meta-predicates in PROLOG for (at least) five reasons:

1. To determine the "type" of an expression.

2. To add "type" constraints to logic programming applications.

3. To build, take apart, and evaluate PROLOG structures.

4. To compare values of expressions.

5. To convert predicates passed as data to executable code.

We have already described how global structures, which are those that can be accessed by the entire clause set, are entered into a PROLOG program. The command assert(C) adds the clause C to the current set of clauses.

There are dangers associated with programming with assert and retract. Because they create and remove global structures, these commands introduce side effects and may cause other problems associated with poorly structured programs. Yet, it is sometimes necessary to use global structures. We do this when creating *semantic nets* and *frames* in a PROLOG environment. We may also use global structures to describe new results as they are found with our rule-based shell. We want this information to be global so that other predicates (rules) may access it when appropriate.

Other meta-predicates that are useful for manipulating representations include:

var(X) succeeds only when X is an unbound variable.

nonvar(X) succeeds only when X is bound to a nonvariable term.

=.. creates a list from a predicate term.

For example, foo(a, b, c) =.. Y unifies Y with [foo, a, b, c]. The head of the list Y is the function name, and its tail is the function's arguments. =.. also can be used "backward," of course. Thus, if X =.. [foo, a, b, c] succeeds, then X has the value foo(a, b, c).

functor(A, B, C) succeeds with A a term whose principal functor has name B and arity C.

For example, functor(foo(a, b), X, Y) will succeed with variables X = foo and Y = 2. functor(A, B, C) can also be used with any of its arguments bound in order to produce the others, such as all the terms with a certain name and/or arity.

clause(A, B) unifies B with the body of a clause whose head unifies with A.

If p(X) :- q(X) exists in the database, then clause(p(a), Y) will succeed with Y = q(a). This is useful for controlling rule chaining in an interpreter.

any_predicate(..., X, ...) :- X executes predicate X, the argument of any predicate.

Thus a predicate, here X, may be passed as a parameter and executed at any desired time. call(X), where X is a clause, also succeeds with the execution of predicate X. This short list of meta-logical predicates will be very important in building and interpreting the AI data structures of the preceding chapters. Because PROLOG can manipulate its own structures in a straightforward fashion, it is easy to implement interpreters that modify the PROLOG semantics, as we see next.

15.6.2 Types in PROLOG

For a number of problem-solving applications, the unconstrained use of unification can introduce unintended error. PROLOG is an untyped language; unification simply matches patterns, without restricting them according to type. For example, append(nil, 6, 6) is deducible from the definition of **append**. Strongly typed languages such as Pascal have shown how type checking can help the programmer avoid these problems. A number of researchers have proposed the introduction of *types* to PROLOG (Neves et al. 1986, Mycroft and O'Keefe 1984).

Typed data are particularly appropriate in a relational database (Neves et al. 1986, Malpas 1987). The rules of logic can be used as constraints on the data and the data can be typed to enforce consistent and meaningful interpretation of the queries. Suppose that a department store database has inventory, suppliers, supplier_inventory, and other appropriate relations. We define a database as relations with named fields that can be thought of as sets of tuples. For example, inventory might consist of 4-tuples, where:

< Pname, Pnumber, Supplier, Weight > ∈ inventory

only when Supplier is the supplier name of an inventory item numbered Pnumber that is called Pname and has weight Weight. Suppose also

< Supplier, Snumber, Status, Location > ∈ suppliers

only when Supplier is the name of a supplier numbered Snumber who has status Status and lives in city Location, and

< Supplier, Pnumber, Cost, Department > ∈ supplier_inventory

only if Supplier is the name of a supplier of part number Pnumber in the amount of Cost to department Department.

We may define PROLOG rules that implement various queries and perform type checking in these relations. For instance, the query "are there suppliers of part number 1 that live in London?" is given in PROLOG as:

```
?- getsuppliers(Supplier,1, london).
```

The rule:

```
getsuppliers(Supplier, Pnumber, City) :-
    cktype(City, suppliers, city),
    suppliers(Supplier, _, _,City),
    cktype(Pnumber, inventory, number),
    supplier_inventory(Supplier, Pnumber, _, _),
    cktype(Supplier, inventory, name).
```

implements this query and also enforces the appropriate constraints across the tuples of the database. First the variables Pnumber and City are bound when the query unifies with the head of the rule; our predicate cktype tests that Supplier is an element of the set of suppliers, that 1 is a legitimate inventory number, and that london is a suppliers city.

We define cktype to take three arguments: a value, a relation name, and a field name, and to check that each value is of the appropriate type for that relation. For example, we may define lists of legal values for Supplier, Pnumber, and City and enforce data typing by requiring member checks of candidate values across these lists. Alternatively, we may define logical constraints on possible values of a type; for example, we may require that inventory numbers be less than 1000.

We should note the differences in type checking between standard languages such as Pascal and PROLOG. We might define a Pascal data type for suppliers as:

```
type supplier = record
      sname: string;
      snumber: integer;
      status: boolean;
      location: string
      end
```

The Pascal programmer defines new types, here supplier, in terms of already defined types, such as boolean or integer. When the programmer uses variables of this type, the compiler automatically enforces type constraints on their values.

In PROLOG, we could represent the supplier relation as instances of the form:

```
supplier(sname(Supplier),
      snumber(Snumber),
      status(Status),
      location(Location)).
```

We implement type checking by using rules such as getsuppliers and cktype.

The distinction between Pascal and PROLOG type checking is clear and important: the Pascal type declaration tells the compiler the form for both the entire structure (record) and the individual components (boolean, integer, string) of the data type. In Pascal we declare variables to be of a particular type (record) and then create procedures to access these typed structures.

```
procedure changestatus (X: supplier);
      begin
            if X.status then. . . .
```

Because it is nonprocedural, PROLOG does not separate the declaration from the use of data types, and type checking is done as the program is executing. Consider the rule:

```
supplier_name(supplier(sname(Supplier), snumber(Snumber),
      status(true), location (london))) :-
integer(Snumber), write(Supplier).
```

supplier_name takes as argument an instance of the supplier predicate and writes the name of the supplier. However, this rule will succeed only if the supplier's number is an integer, the status is active (true), and the supplier lives in London. An important part of the type check is handled by the unification algorithm (true, london) and the rest is the built-in system predicate integer. Further constraints could restrict values to be from a particular list; for example, Snumber could be constrained to be from a list of supplier numbers. We define constraints on database queries using rules such as cktype and supplier_name to implement type checking when the program is executed.

So far, we have seen three ways that data may be typed in PROLOG. First, and most powerful, is the use of unification to constrain variable assignment. Second, PROLOG itself provides predicates to do limited type checking. We saw this with meta-predicates such as var(X), clause(X,Y), and integer(X). The third limited use of typing occurred in the inventory example where rules checked lists of legitimate suppliers, pnumbers, and cities to enforce type constraints.

A fourth, and more radical, approach is the complete predicate and data type check proposed by Mycroft and O'Keefe (1984). Here all predicate names are typed and given a fixed arity. Furthermore, all variable names are themselves typed. A strength of this approach is that the constraints on the constituent predicates and variables of the PROLOG program are themselves enforced by a (meta) PROLOG program. Even though the result may be slower program execution, the security gained through total type enforcement may justify this cost.

Rather than providing built-in type checking as a default, PROLOG allows run-time type checking under complete programmer control. This approach offers a number of benefits for AI programmers, including the following:

1. The programmer is not forced to adhere to strong type checking at all times. This allows us to write predicates that work across any type of object. For example, the member predicate performs general member checking, regardless of the type of elements in the list.

2. Flexibility in typing helps exploratory programming. Programmers can relax type checking in the early stages of program development and introduce it to detect errors as they come to better understand the problem.

3. AI representations seldom conform to the built-in data types of languages such as Pascal, C++, or Java. PROLOG allows types to be defined using the full power of predicate calculus. The database example showed this flexibility.

4. Because type checking is done at run time rather than compile time, the programmer determines when the program should perform a check. This allows programmers to delay type checking until it is necessary or until certain variables have become bound.

5. Programmer control of type checking at run time also lets us write programs that create and enforce new types during execution. This could be of use in a learning program, for example.

15.6.3 Unification, the Engine for Predicate Matching and Evaluation

An important feature of PROLOG programming is the interpreter's behavior as a resolution-based theorem prover, presented in Section 13.3. As a theorem prover PROLOG performs a series of resolutions on database entries, rather than sequentially evaluating statements and expressions like a traditional language. This has an important result: variables are bound (assigned values, instantiated, ...) by unification and *not* by evaluation unless, of course, an evaluation is explicitly requested. This programming paradigm has several implications.

The first and perhaps most important result is the relaxation of the requirement to specify variables as input or output. We have already seen some of the power of this in the append predicate, which could either join lists together, test whether two lists are correctly appended, or break a list into parts consistent with the definition of append. We also see unification as a matcher and constraint handler for parsing and generating sentences in Section 15.9.

Unification is a powerful technique for rule-based and frame-based expert systems. All production systems require a form of this matching, and it is often necessary to write a unification algorithm in languages that don't provide it (see, for example, Section 16.6 for a LISP implementation of unification).

An important difference between unification-based computing and the use of more traditional languages is that unification performs syntactic matches (with appropriate parameter substitutions) on structures. It does *not* evaluate expressions. Suppose, for example, we wished to create a successor predicate that succeeds if its second argument is the arithmetic successor of its first. Not understanding unification, one might be tempted to define successor:

successor (X, Y) :- Y = X + 1.

This will fail because the = operator does not evaluate its arguments but only attempts to unify the expressions on either side. This predicate succeeds if Y unifies with the structure X + 1. Because 4 does not unify with 3 + 1, the call successor(3, 4) fails! On the other hand, = can test for equivalence, as defined by unification, of *any* two expressions.

To correctly define successor and other arithmetic predicates, we need to evaluate arithmetic expressions. PROLOG provides an operator, is, for this evaluation. is evaluates the expression on its right-hand side and attempts to unify the result with the object on its left. Thus,

X is Y + Z

unifies X with the value of Y added to Z. Because it performs arithmetic evaluation:

1. If Y and Z do not have values (are not bound at execution time) evaluation of the is causes a run-time error. Thus

2. X is Y + Z cannot (as one might think with a declarative programming language) give a value to Y when X and Z are bound.

3. Programs must use is to evaluate expressions containing arithmetic operators, +, −, *, /, and mod.

Finally, as in the predicate calculus, variables in PROLOG may have one and only one binding. Once given a value, through local assignment or unification, they can never take on a new value, except through a backtrack in the and/or search space of the current interpretation. Thus, is does not function like a traditional assignment operator; an expression such as X is X + 1 will always fail.

Using is, we can now properly define successor(X, Y) as:

successor (X, Y) :- Y is X + 1.

This will have the correct behavior as long as X is bound to a numeric value. It can be used either to compute Y, given X, or to test values of X and Y:

```
?- successor (3, X).
X = 4
yes
?- successor (3, 4).
yes
?- successor (4, 2).
no
?- successor (Y, 4).
failure, error in arithmetic expression
```

As this discussion illustrates, PROLOG does not evaluate expressions as a default as in traditional languages. The programmer must explicitly indicate evaluation using is. Explicit control of evaluation, as also found in LISP, makes it easy to treat expressions as data, passed as parameters, and creating or modifying them as needed within the program.

This feature, like the ability to manipulate predicate calculus expressions as data and execute them using call, greatly simplifies the development of different interpreters, such as the expert system shell of the next section.

We close this discussion of the power of unification-based computing with an example that does string catenation through the use of *difference lists*. As an alternative to the standard PROLOG list notation, we can represent a list as the difference of two lists. For example, [a, b] is equivalent to [a, b | [ ]] – [ ] or [a, b, c] – [c]. This representation has certain expressive advantages over the traditional list syntax. When the list [a, b] is represented as the difference [a, b | Y] – Y, it actually describes the potentially infinite class of all lists that have a and b as their first two elements. Now this representation has an interesting property, namely addition:

$$X - Z = X - Y + Y - Z$$

We can use this property to define the following single-clause logic program where X – Y is the first list, Y – Z is the second list, and X – Z is the result of catenating them:

catenate(X – Y, Y – Z, X – Z).

This operation joins two lists of any length in constant time by unification on the list structures, rather than by repeated assignment based on the length of the lists (as with append). Thus the catenate call gives:

Addition of difference lists:

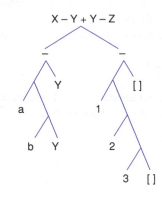

After binding Y to [1, 2, 3], binding Z to [ ], and performing the addition:

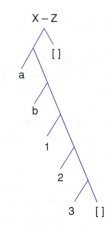

Figure 15.5 Tree diagrams of catenation using difference lists.

```
?- catenate ([a, b | Y] – Y, [1, 2, 3] – [ ], W).
Y = [1, 2, 3]
W = [a, b, 1, 2, 3] – [ ]
```

As noted in Figure 15.5, the (subtree) value of Y in the second parameter is unified with both occurrences of Y in the first parameter of catenate. This demonstrates the power of unification, not simply for substituting values for variables but also for matching general structures: all occurrences of Y take the value of the entire subtree. The example also illustrates the advantages of an appropriate representation. Thus difference lists represent a whole class of lists, including the desired catenation.

In this section we have discussed a number of idiosyncrasies and advantages of PROLOG's unification-based approach to computing. Unification is at the heart of PROLOG's declarative semantics.

15.7 Meta-Interpreters in PROLOG

15.7.1 An Introduction to Meta-Interpreters: PROLOG in PROLOG

In both LISP and PROLOG, it is easy to write programs that manipulate expressions written in the language syntax. We call such programs *meta-interpreters*. For example, an expert system shell interprets a set of rules and facts that describe a particular problem. Although the rules of a problem situation are written in the syntax of the underlying language, the meta-interpreter redefines their semantics.

As an example of a meta-interpreter, we define the semantics of pure PROLOG using PROLOG itself. solve takes as its argument a PROLOG goal and processes it according to the semantics of PROLOG:

```
solve(true) :-!.
solve(not A) :- not(solve(A)).
solve((A, B)) :-!, solve(A), solve(B).
solve(A) :- clause(A, B), solve(B).
```

If we assume the following simple set of assertions,

```
p(X, Y) :- q(X), r(Y).
q(X) :- s(X).
r(X) :- t(X).
s(a).
t(b).
t(c).
```

solve has the behavior we expect of PROLOG:

```
?- solve(p(a, b)).
yes
?- solve(p(X, Y)).
X = a, Y = b;
X = a, Y = c;
no
?- solve(p(f, g)).
no
```

solve implements the same left-to-right, depth-first, goal-directed search as the built-in PROLOG interpreter.

The ability to easily write meta-interpreters for a language has certain theoretical advantages. For example, McCarthy wrote a simple LISP meta-interpreter as part of a proof that the language is Turing complete (McCarthy 1960). From a more practical standpoint, we can use meta-interpreters to extend or modify the semantics of the underlying language to better fit our application. This is the programming methodology of *meta-linguistic abstraction*, the creation of a high-level language that is designed to help solve a specific problem.

For example, we may wish to modify the standard PROLOG semantics so as to ask the user about the truth value of any goal that does not succeed in the knowledge base. We can do so by adding the following clauses to the end of the previous definitions of solve:

```
solve(A) :- askuser(A).
askuser(A) :- write(A),
       write('? Enter true if the goal is true, false otherwise'),nl,
       read(true).
```

Because we add this definition to the end of the other solve rules, it is called only if all of these fail. solve invokes askuser to query the user for the truth value of the goal A. askuser prints the goal and instructions for answering. read(true) attempts to unify the user's input with the term true, failing if the user enters false (or anything that will not unify with true). In this way we have changed the semantics of solve and extended the behavior of PROLOG. An example, using the simple knowledge base defined above, illustrates the behavior of the augmented solve predicate:

```
?- solve(p(f, g)).
s(f)? Enter true if the goal is true, false otherwise
true.
t(g)? Enter true if the goal is true, false otherwise
true.
yes
```

Another extension to the meta-interpreter allows it to respond to "why" queries. When the interpreter asks the user a question, the user can respond with why; the appropriate response to this query is the current rule that the program is trying to solve. We implement this by storing the stack of rules in the current line of reasoning as the second parameter to solve. Whenever solve calls clause to backward chain on a goal, it places the selected rule on the stack. Thus, the rule stack records the chain of rules from the top-level goal to the current subgoal.

Because the user may now enter two valid responses to a query, askuser calls respond, which either succeeds if the user enters true (as before) or prints the top rule on the stack if the user enters why. respond and askuser are mutually recursive, so that after printing the answer to a why query, respond calls askuser to query the user about the goal again. Note, however, that it calls askuser with the tail of the rule stack. Thus, a series of why queries will simply chain back up the rule stack until the stack is exhausted, letting the user trace the entire line of reasoning.

```
solve(true, _) :-!.
solve(not(A), Rules) :- not(solve(A, Rules)).
solve((A, B), Rules) :- !, solve(A, Rules), solve(B, Rules).
solve(A, Rules) :- clause(A, B), solve(B, [(A :- B) | Rules]).
solve(A, Rules) :- askuser(A, Rules).
askuser(A, Rules) :- write(A),
    write('? Enter true if goal is true, false otherwise'),nl,
    read(Answer), respond(Answer, A, Rules).
respond(true, _, _).
respond(why, A, [Rule | Rules]) :- write(Rule), nl,
    askuser(A, Rules).
respond(why, A, [ ]) :- askuser(A, [ ]).
```

For example, we may run solve on the simple database introduced earlier in the section. Note how successive why queries trace back up the line of reasoning.

```
?- solve(p(f, g), [ ]).
s(f)? Enter true if goal is true, false otherwise
why.
q(f) :- s(f)
s(f)? Enter true if goal is true, false otherwise
why.
p(f,g) :- (q(f), r(g))
s(f)? Enter true if goal is true, false otherwise
true.
t(g)? Enter true if goal is true, false otherwise
true.
yes
```

A useful extension to the solve predicate constructs a proof tree for any successful goal. The ability to build proof trees provides expert system shells with the means of responding to "how" queries; it is also important to any algorithm, such as explanation-based learning (Section 10.5), that reasons about the results of a problem solver.

We may modify the pure PROLOG interpreter to recursively build a proof tree for a goal as it solves that goal. In the definition that follows, the proof is returned as the second parameter of the solve predicate. The proof of the atom true is that atom; this halts the recursion. In solving a goal A using a rule A :- B, we construct the proof of B and return the structure (A :- ProofB). In solving a conjunction of goals, A and B, we simply conjoin the proof trees for each goal: (ProofA,ProofB).

The definition of a meta-interpreter that constructs proof trees is:

```
solve(true, true) :-!.
solve(not(A), not ProofA) :- not(solve(A, ProofA)).
solve((A, B),(ProofA, ProofB)) :- solve(A, ProofA), solve(B, ProofB).
solve(A, (A :- ProofB)) :- clause(A, B), solve(B, ProofB).
solve(A, (A :- given)) :- askuser(A).
askuser(A, Proof) :- write(A),
    write('enter true if goal is true, false otherwise'), read(true).
```

Running this on our simple database gives the results:

```
?- solve(p(a, b), Proof).
Proof = p(a, b) :-
    ((q(a) :-
         (s(a) :-
              true)),
      (r(b) :-
         (t(b) :-
              true)))
```

In the next section, we use these techniques to implement an expert system shell. exshell uses a knowledge base in the form of rules to solve problems. It asks the user for needed information, keeps a record of case-specific data, responds to how and why queries, and implements the certainty factor algebra of Chapter 9. Although this program, exshell, is much more complex than the PROLOG meta-interpreters discussed above, it is just an extension of this methodology. Its heart is a solve predicate that implements a back-chaining search of rules and facts.

15.7.2   Shell for a Rule-Based Expert System

In this section we present the key predicates used in the design of an interpreter for a goal-driven, rule-based expert system. At the end of this section, we demonstrate the performance of exshell using an automotive diagnostic knowledge base. If the reader would prefer to read through this trace before examining exshell's key predicates, we encourage looking ahead.

An exshell knowledge base consists of rules and specifications of queries that can be made to the user. Rules are represented using a two-parameter rule predicate of the form rule(R, CF). The first parameter is an assertion to the knowledge base, written using standard PROLOG syntax. Assertions may be PROLOG rules, of the form (G :- P), where G is the head of the rule and P is the conjunctive pattern under which G is true. The first argument to the rule predicate may also be a PROLOG fact. CF is the confidence the designer has in the rule's conclusions. exshell implements the certainty algebra of MYCIN, presented in Chapter 9. CFs range from 100, a fact that is true, to –100, something that is known to be false. If the CF is around 0, the truth value is unknown. Typical rules from a knowledge base for diagnosing automotive failures are:

```
rule((bad_component(starter) :- (bad_system(starter_system),
    lights(come_on))), 50).
rule(fix(starter, 'replace starter'),100).
```

The first rule states that if the bad system is shown to be the starter system and the lights come on, then conclude that the bad component is the starter, with a certainty of 50. The second asserts the fact that we may fix a broken starter by replacing it, with a certainty of 100. exshell uses the rule predicate to retrieve those rules that conclude about a given goal, just as the simpler versions of solve used the built-in clause predicate to retrieve rules from the global PROLOG database.

exshell supports user queries for unknown data; however, because we do not want the interpreter to ask for every unsolved goal, we allow the programmer to specify exactly what information may be so obtained. We do this with the askable predicate:

    askable(car_starts).

specifies that the interpreter may ask the user for the truth of the car_starts goal when nothing is known or can be concluded about that goal.

In addition to the programmer-defined knowledge base of rules and askables, exshell maintains its own record of case-specific data. Because the shell asks the user for information, it needs to remember what it has been told; this prevents the program from asking the same question twice during a consultation (decidedly non-expert behavior!).

The heart of the exshell meta-interpreter is a predicate of four arguments called, surprisingly, solve. The first of these arguments is the goal to be solved. On successfully solving the goal, exshell binds the second argument to the confidence in the goal as computed from the knowledge base. The third argument is the rule stack, used in responding to why queries, and the fourth is the cutoff threshold for the certainty factor algebra. This allows pruning of the search space if the confidence falls below the threshold.

In attempting to satisfy a goal, G, solve first tries to match G with any facts that it already has obtained from the user. We represent known facts using the two-parameter known(A, CF) predicate. For example, known(car_starts, 85) indicates that the user has already told us that the car starts, with a confidence of 85. If the goal is unknown, solve attempts to solve the goal using its knowledge base. It handles the negation of a goal by solving the goal and multiplying the confidence in that goal by -1. It solves conjunctive goals in left-to-right order. If G is a positive literal, solve tries any rule whose head matches G. If this fails, solve queries the user. On obtaining the user's confidence in a goal, solve asserts this information to the database using a known predicate.

```
% Case 1: truth value of goal is already known
solve(Goal, CF, _, Threshold) :-
    known(Goal, CF), !,
    above_threshold(CF, Threshold).            % Test confidence threshold
% Case 2: negated goal
solve(not(Goal), CF, Rules, Threshold) :-!,
    invert_threshold(Threshold, New_threshold),
    solve(Goal, CF_goal, Rules, New_threshold),
    negate_cf(CF_goal, CF).
% Case 3: conjunctive goals
solve((Goal_1,Goal_2), CF, Rules, Threshold) :- !,
    solve(Goal_1, CF_1, Rules, Threshold),
    above_threshold(CF_1, Threshold),
    solve(Goal_2, CF_2, Rules, Threshold),
    above_threshold(CF_2, Threshold),
    and_cf(CF_1, CF_2, CF).                     % Compute CF for and
```

```
% Case 4: back chain on a rule in knowledge base
solve(Goal, CF, Rules, Threshold) :-
    rule((Goal :- (Premise)), CF_rule),
    solve(Premise, CF_premise, [rule((Goal :- Premise), CF_rule)|Rules], Threshold),
    rule_cf(CF_rule, CF_premise, CF),
    above_threshold(CF, Threshold).
% Case 5: fact assertion in knowledge base
solve(Goal, CF, _, Threshold) :-
    rule(Goal, CF),
    above_threshold(CF, Threshold).
% Case 6: ask user
solve(Goal, CF, Rules, Threshold) :-
    askable(Goal),
    askuser(Goal, CF, Rules), !,
    assert(known(Goal, CF)),
    above_threshold(CF, Threshold).
```

We start a consultation using a two-argument version of solve. The first argument is the top-level goal in the knowledge base, and the second is a variable that will be bound to the confidence in the goal's truth as inferred from the knowledge base. solve/2 prints a set of instructions to the user, calls retractall(known(_,_)) to clean up any residual information from previous uses of exshell, and calls solve/4 with appropriate values.

```
solve(Goal, CF) :-
    print_instructions,
    retractall(known(_, _)),
    solve(Goal, CF, [ ], 20).                                    % A threshold of 20
```

print_instructions tells the user the allowable responses to an exshell query:

```
print_instructions :-
    nl, write('Response must be either:'),
    nl, write(' A confidence in the truth of the query.'),
    nl, write(' This is a number between −100 and 100.'),
    nl, write(' why.'),
    nl, write(' how(X), where X is a goal'), nl.
```

The next set of predicates computes certainty factors. (exshell uses a form of the Stanford certainty factor algebra presented in Section 9.2.1.) The certainty factor of the and of two goals is the minimum of the certainty factors of the individual goals; the certainty factor of the negation of a fact is −1 times the certainty of that fact. Confidence in a fact concluded using a rule equals the certainty of the premise times the certainty factor in the rule. above_threshold determines whether the value of a certainty factor is too low given a particular threshold. exshell uses the threshold value to prune a goal if its certainty gets too low. Note that we define above_threshold separately for negative and positive values of the threshold. A positive threshold enables us to prune if the goal's confidence is less than the threshold. However, a negative threshold indicates that we are trying to prove a goal false. Thus for negative goals we prune search if the value of the goal's confidence is greater than the threshold. invert_threshold is called to multiply the threshold by −1.

```
and_cf(A, B, A) :-
    A = < B.
and_cf(A, B, B) :-
    B < A.
negate_cf(CF, Negated_CF) :-
    Negated_CF is - 1 * CF.
rule_cf(CF_rule, CF_premise,CF) :-
    CF is (CF_rule * CF_premise/100).
above_threshold(CF, T) :-
    T >= 0, CF >= T.
above_threshold(CF, T) :-
    T < 0, CF =< T.
invert_threshold(Threshold, New_threshold) :-
    New_threshold is -1 * Threshold.
```

askuser writes out a query and reads the user's answer; the respond predicates take the appropriate action for each user input.

```
askuser(Goal, CF, Rules) :-                          % Ask user for answer to goal
    nl, write('User query:'),
    write(Goal), nl, write('?'),
    read(Answer),
    respond(Answer, Goal, CF, Rules).                % Processes answer
```

The user can respond to the query with a CF between 100 and −100, indicating his confidence in the goal's truth, why to ask why the question was asked, or how(X) to inquire how result X was established.

The response to a why query is the rule currently on top of the rule stack. As with our previous implementation, successive why queries will chain back up the rule stack, enabling the user to reconstruct the entire line of reasoning. If the user answer matches how(X), respond calls build_proof to build a proof tree for X and write_proof to print that proof in a readable form. There is a "catchall" respond for unknown input values.

```
% Case 1: user enters a valid confidence factor
respond(CF, _, CF, _) :-
    number(CF),
    CF =< 100, CF >= −100.
% Case 2: user enters a why query
respond(why, Goal, CF, [Rule | Rules]) :-
    write_rule(Rule),
    askuser(Goal, CF, Rules).
respond(why, Goal, CF, [ ]) :-
    write('Back to top of rule stack.'),
    askuser(Goal, CF, [ ]).
```

```
% Case 3: user enters a how query. Build and print a proof
respond(how(X), Goal, CF, Rules) :-
    build_proof(X, CF_X, Proof), !,
    write(X), write(' was concluded with certainty '), write(CF_X), nl, nl,
    write('The proof is '), nl, nl,
    write_proof(Proof, 0), nl, nl,
    askuser(Goal, CF, Rules).
% User enters how query, could not build proof
respond(how(X), Goal, CF, Rules) :-
    write('The truth of '), write(X), nl,
    write('is not yet known.'), nl,
    askuser(Goal, CF, Rules).
% Case 4: unrecognized input
respond(_, Goal, CF, Rules) :-
    write('Unrecognized response.'), nl,
    askuser(Goal, CF, Rules).
```

The definition of build_proof is almost completely parallel to that of solve/4. However, build_proof does not ask the user for unknown facts, as these have already been saved as part of the case-specific data. build_proof constructs a proof tree as it proves the goal.

```
build_proof(Goal, CF, (Goal, CF :- given)) :-
    known(Goal, CF), !.
build_proof(not Goal, CF, not Proof) :-
    !, build_proof(Goal, CF_goal, Proof), negate_cf(CF_goal, CF).
build_proof((Goal_1, Goal_2), CF, (Proof_1, Proof_2)) :-
    !, build_proof(Goal_1, CF_1, Proof_1),
    build_proof(Goal_2, CF_2, Proof_2), and_cf(CF_1, CF_2, CF).
build_proof(Goal, CF, (Goal, CF :- Proof)) :-
    rule((Goal :- Premise), CF_rule),
    build_proof(Premise, CF_premise, Proof),
    rule_cf(CF_rule, CF_premise, CF),
build_proof(Goal, CF, (Goal, CF :- fact)) :-
    rule(Goal, CF).
```

The final predicates create a simple user interface. As is so often true, the interface requires the bulk of the code! First, we define a predicate to write out a rule in a readable format:

```
write_rule(rule((Goal :- (Premise)), CF)) :-
    write(Goal), write(':-'), nl,
    write_premise(Premise), nl,
    write('CF = '), write(CF), nl.
write_rule(rule(Goal, CF)) :-
    write(Goal), nl,
    write('CF = '), write(CF), nl.
```

write_premise writes the conjuncts of a rule premise:

```prolog
write_premise((Premise_1, Premise_2)) :-
    !, write_premise(Premise_1),
    write_premise(Premise_2).
write_premise(not Premise) :-
    !, write('   '), write(not), write(' '), write(Premise), nl.
write_premise(Premise) :-
    write('   '), write(Premise), nl.
```

write_proof prints out a proof, using indentation to show the structure of the tree:

```prolog
write_proof((Goal, CF :- given), Level) :-          % Prints proof tree, with
    indent(Level), write(Goal),                     % indentation for levels of tree
write(' CF= '), write(CF),
    write(' was given by the user'), nl, !.
write_proof((Goal, CF :- fact), Level) :-
    indent(Level), write(Goal), write(' CF = '), write(CF),
    write(' was a fact in the knowledge base'), nl, !.
write_proof((Goal, CF :- Proof), Level) :-
    indent(Level), write(Goal), write(' CF = '), write(CF), write(' :-'),
    nl, New_level is Level + 1, write_proof(Proof, New_level), !.
write_proof(not Proof, Level) :-
    indent(Level), write((not)), nl,
    New_level is Level + 1, write_proof(Proof, New_level), !.
write_proof((Proof_1, Proof_2),Level) :-
    write_proof(Proof_1, Level), write_proof(Proof_2, Level), !.
indent(0).
indent(I) :-
    write('   '), I_new is I - 1, indent(I_new).
```

As an illustration of the behavior of exshell, consider the following sample knowledge base for diagnosing car problems. The top-level goal is fix/1. The knowledge base decomposes the problem solution into finding the bad system, finding the bad component within that system, and finally linking the diagnosis to advice for its solution. Note that the knowledge base is incomplete; there are sets of symptoms that it cannot diagnose. In this case, exshell simply fails. Extending the knowledge base to some of these cases and adding a rule that succeeds if all others fail are interesting challenges and left as exercises.

```prolog
rule((fix(Advice) :-                                % Top-level query
    (bad_component(X), fix(X,Advice))), 100).
rule((bad_component(starter) :-
    (bad_system(starter_system), lights(come_on))), 50).
rule((bad_component(battery) :-
    (bad_system(starter_system), not lights(come_on))), 90).
rule((bad_component(timing) :-
    (bad_system(ignition_system), not tuned_recently)), 80).
rule((bad_component(plugs) :-
    (bad_system(ignition_system), plugs(dirty))), 90).
```

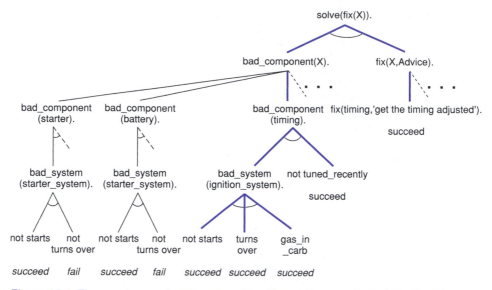

Figure 15.6 The graph searched in automotive diagnostic consultation. Dashed lines indicate branches not examined and the bold lines indicate the final solution.

```
rule((bad_component(ignition_wires) :-
    (bad_system(ignition_system), not plugs(dirty), tuned_recently)), 80).
rule((bad_system(starter_system) :-
    (not car_starts, not turns_over)), 90).
rule((bad_system(ignition_system) :-
    (not car_starts, turns_over, gas_in_carb)), 80).
rule((bad_system(ignition_system) :-
    (runs(rough), gas_in_carb)), 80).
rule((bad_system(ignition_system) :-
    (car_starts, runs(dies), gas_in_carb)), 60).
rule(fix(starter, 'replace starter'), 100).              %Advice for problems
rule(fix(battery, 'replace or recharge battery'), 100).
rule(fix(timing, 'get the timing adjusted'), 100).
rule(fix(plugs, 'replace spark plugs'), 100).
rule(fix(ignition_wires, 'check ignition wires'), 100).
askable(car_starts).                                     % May ask user about goal
askable(turns_over).
askable(lights(_)).
askable(runs(_)).
askable(gas_in_carb).
askable(tuned_recently).
askable(plugs(_)).
```

Next, exshell uses this knowledge base. Figure 15.6 illustrates the search space: solid lines are searched, dotted lines are not searched, and bold lines indicate the solution.

```
?- solve(fix(X), CF).
Response must be either:
      A confidence in the truth of the query.
            This is a number between −100 and 100.
      why.
      how(X), where X is a goal
User query:car_starts
? −100.
User query:turns_over
? 85.
User query:gas_in_carb
? 75.
User query:tuned_recently
? −90.
      X = 'get the timing adjusted' CF = 48.0
```

We now run the same problem situation with how and why queries. Compare the responses with the corresponding subtrees and paths in Figure 15.6:

```
?- solve(fix(X), CF).
Response must be either:
      A confidence in the truth of the query.
            This is a number between −100 and 100.
      why.
      how(X), where X is a goal
User query:car_starts
? −100.
User query:turns_over
? why.
bad_system(starter_system):-
      not car_starts
      not turns_over
CF = 90
User query:turns_over
? why.
bad_component(starter):-
      bad_system(starter_system)
      lights(come_on)
CF = 50
User query:turns_over
? why.
fix(_0):-
      bad_component(starter)
      fix(starter,_0)
CF = 100
User query:turns_over
? why.
Back to top of rule stack.
User query:turns_over
```

```
? 85.
User query:gas_in_carb
? 75.
User query:tuned_recently
? why.
bad_component(timing):-
    bad_system(ignition_system)
    not tuned_recently
CF = 80
User query:tuned_recently
? how(bad_system(ignition_system)).
bad_system(ignition_system) was concluded with certainty 60.0
The proof is
bad_system(ignition_system) CF= 60.0 :-
    not  car_starts CF = -100 was given by the user
    turns_over CF =  85 was given by the user
    gas_in_carb CF = 75 was given by the user
User query:tuned_recently
? -90.
    X = 'get the timing adjusted' CF = 48.0
```

15.7.3   Semantic Nets in PROLOG

We next implement inheritance for a simple semantic network (Section 7.1). Our language ignores the important distinction between classes and instances. This restricted language simplifies the implementation of inheritance.

In the semantic net of Figure 15.7, nodes represent individuals such as the canary tweety and classes such as ostrich, crow, robin, bird, and vertebrate. isa links represent the class hierarchy relationship. We adopt canonical forms for the data relationships within the net. We use an isa(Type, Parent) predicate to indicate that Type is a member of Parent and a hasprop(Object, Property, Value) predicate to represent property relations. hasprop indicates that Object has Property with Value. Object and Value are nodes in the network, and Property is the name of the link that joins them.

A partial list of predicates describing the bird hierarchy of Figure 15.7 is:

```
isa(canary, bird).                   isa(robin, bird).
isa(ostrich, bird).                  isa(penguin, bird).
isa(bird, animal).                   isa(fish, animal).
isa(opus, penguin).                  isa(tweety, canary).
hasprop(tweety, color, white).       hasprop(robin, color, red).
hasprop(canary, color, yellow).      hasprop(penguin, color, brown).
hasprop(bird, travel, fly).          hasprop(fish, travel, swim).
hasprop(ostrich, travel, walk).      hasprop(penguin, travel, walk).
hasprop(robin, sound, sing).         hasprop(canary, sound, sing).
hasprop(bird, cover, feathers).      hasprop(animal, cover, skin).
```

We create a recursive search algorithm to find whether an object in our semantic net has a particular property. Properties are stored in the net at the most general level at which they are true. Through inheritance, an individual or subclass acquires the properties of its superclasses. Thus the property fly holds for bird and all its subclasses. Exceptions are located at the specific level of the exception. Thus, ostrich and penguin travel by walking instead of flying. The hasproperty predicate begins search at a particular object. If the information is not directly attached to that object, hasproperty follows isa links to superclasses. If no more superclasses exist and hasproperty has not located the property, it fails.

```
hasproperty(Object, Property, Value) :-
        hasprop(Object, Property, Value).
```

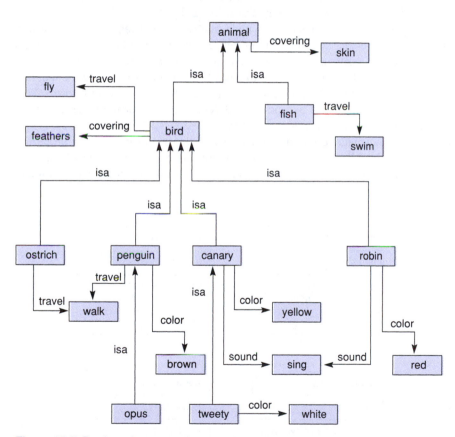

Figure 15.7 Portion of a semantic network describing birds and other animals.

```
hasproperty(Object, Property, Value) :-
    isa(Object, Parent),
    hasproperty(Parent, Property, Value).
```

hasproperty searches the inheritance hierarchy in a depth-first fashion. In the next section, we show how inheritance can be applied to a frame-based representation and implement both tree and multiple-inheritance relations.

15.7.4   Frames and Schemata in PROLOG

Semantic nets can be partitioned, with additional information added to node descriptions, to give them a frame structure. We redefine the bird example of the previous subsection using frames, where each frame represents a collection of relationships of the semantic net and the isa slots of the frame define the frame hierarchy (Figure 15.8).

The first slot of each frame names the node, such as name(tweety) or name(vertebrate). The second slot gives the inheritance links between the node and its parents. Because our example has a tree structure, each node has only one link, the isa predicate with one argument. The third slot in the node's frame is a list of features that describe that node. In this list we use any PROLOG predicate such as flies, feathers, or color(brown). The final slot in the frame is the list of exceptions and default values for the node, again either a single word or predicate indicating a property.

In our frame language, each frame organizes its slot names into lists of properties and default values. This allows us to distinguish these different types of knowledge and give them different behaviors in the inheritance hierarchy. Although our implementation allows

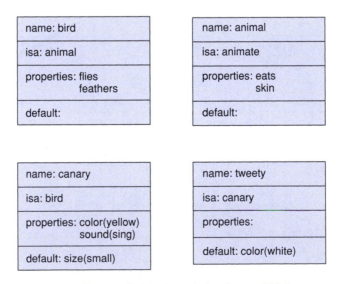

Figure 15.8 Frames from a knowledge base of birds.

subclasses to inherit properties from both lists, other representations are possible and may be useful in certain applications. We may wish to specify that only default values are inherited. Or we may wish to build a third list containing the properties of the class itself rather than the members, sometimes called *class values*. For example, we may wish to state that the class canary names a species of songbird. This should not be inherited by subclasses or instances: tweety does not name a species of songbird. Further extensions to this example are suggested in the exercises at the end of the chapter.

We now represent the relationships in Figure 15.8 with the PROLOG fact predicate frame with four arguments. We may use the methods suggested in Section 15.6.2 to check the parameters of the frame predicate for appropriate type, for instance, to ensure that the third frame slot is a list that contains only values from a fixed list of properties.

```
frame(name(bird),
    isa(animal),
    [travel(flies), feathers],
    [ ]).
frame(name(penguin),
    isa(bird),
    [color(brown)],
    [travel(walks)]).
frame(name(canary),
    isa(bird),
    [color(yellow), call(sing)],
    [size(small)]).
frame(name(tweety),
    isa(canary),
    [ ],
    [color(white)]).
```

Once the full set of descriptions and inheritance relationships are defined for the frame of Figure 15.8, we create procedures to infer properties from this representation:

```
get(Prop, Object) :-
    frame(name(Object), _, List_of_properties,_),
    member(Prop, List_of_properties).
get(Prop, Object) :-
    frame(name(Object), _, _ List_of_defaults),
    member(Prop, List_of_defaults).
get(Prop, Object) :-
    frame(name(Object), isa(Parent),_,_),
    get(Prop, Parent).
```

If the frame structure allows multiple inheritance of properties (see also Section 16.12), we make this change both in our representation and in our search strategy. First, in the frame representation we make the argument of the isa predicate the list of superclasses of the Object. Thus, each superclass in the list is a parent of the entity named in the first argument of frame. If opus is a penguin and a cartoon_char we represent this:

```
frame(name(opus),
    isa([penguin, cartoon_char]),
    [color(black)],
    [ ]).
```

Now, we test for properties of opus by recurring up the isa hierarchy for both penguin and cartoon_char. We add the additional solve definition between the third and fourth get predicates of the previous example.

```
get(Prop, Object) :-
    frame(name(Object), isa(List), _, _),
    get_multiple(Prop, List).
```

We define get_multiple by:

```
get_multiple(Prop, [Parent | _]) :-
    get(Prop, Parent).
get_multiple(Prop, [_ | Rest]) :-
    get_multiple(Prop, Rest).
```

With this inheritance preference, properties of penguin and its superclasses will be examined before those of cartoon_char.

Finally, any PROLOG procedure may be attached to a frame slot. As we have built the frame representation in our examples, this would entail adding a PROLOG rule, or list of PROLOG rules, as a parameter of frame. This is accomplished by enclosing the entire rule in parentheses, as we did for rules in exshell, and making this structure an argument of the frame predicate. For example, we could design a list of response rules for opus, giving him different responses for different questions.

This list of rules, each rule in parentheses, would then become a parameter of the frame and, depending on the value of X passed to the opus frame, would define the appropriate response. More complex examples could be rules describing the control of a thermostat or creating a graphic image appropriate to a set of values. These examples are presented in Section 16.12, where attached procedures, often called methods, play an important role in object-oriented representations.

15.8 Learning Algorithms in PROLOG

15.8.1 Version Space Search in PROLOG

In Chapter 10, we presented a number of symbol-based machine learning algorithms. In this section and the next, we implement two of them: *version space search* and *explanation-based learning*. The algorithms themselves are presented in Chapter 10; here we implement them in PROLOG. PROLOG is used for machine learning because, as these implementations illustrate, besides its built-in pattern matching, its meta-level reasoning capabilities simplify the construction and manipulation of new representations.

We first implement the specific to general search and then the full bi-directional candidate elimination algorithm. We also give hints on how to construct the general to specific version space search. These search algorithms are independent of the representation used for concepts, as long as that representation supports appropriate generalization and specialization operations. We use a representation of objects as lists of features. For example, we describe a small, red, ball with the list:

[small, red, ball]

We represent the concept of all small, red things by including a variable in the list:

[small, red, X]

This representation is called a *feature vector,*. It is less expressive than full logic, e.g., it cannot represent the class "all red or green balls." However, it simplifies generalization, and provides a strong inductive bias (Section 10.4). We generalize a feature vector by substituting a variable for a constant, for example, the most specific common generalization of [small, red, ball] and [small, green, ball] is [small, X, ball]. This vector will cover both of the specializations and is the most specific vector to do so.

We define a feature vector as covering another if the first is either identical to or more general than the second. Note that unlike unification, covers is asymmetrical: values exist for which X covers Y, but Y does not cover X. For example, [X, red, ball] covers [large, red, ball] but the reverse is not true. We define covers for feature vectors as:

```
covers([ ], [ ]).
covers([H1|T1], [H2|T2]) :-              % variables cover each other
     var(H1), var(H2), covers(T1, T2).
covers([H1|T1], [H2|T2]) :-              % a variable covers a constant
     var(H1), atom(H2), covers(T1, T2).
covers([H1|T1], [H2|T2]) :-              % matching constants
     atom(H1), atom(H2), H1 = H2,
     covers(T1, T2).
```

We next need to determine whether one feature vector is strictly more general than another; i.e., the vectors are not identical. We define the more_general/2 predicate as:

```
more_general(X, Y) :- not(covers(Y, X)), covers(X, Y).
```

We implement generalization of feature vectors as a predicate, generalize with three arguments, where the first argument is a feature vector representing an hypothesis (this vector may contain variables), the second argument is an instance, containing no variables. generalize binds its third argument to the most specific generalization of the hypothesis that covers the instance. generalize recursively scans the feature vectors, comparing corresponding elements. If two elements match, the result contains the value of the hypotheses vector in that position; if two elements do not match, it places a variable in the corresponding position of the generalized feature vector. Note the use of the expression not(Feature \= Inst_prop), in the second definition of generalize; this double negative enables us to test if two atoms will unify without actually performing the unification and forming any unwanted variable bindings. We define generalize:

```
generalize([ ], [ ], [ ]).
generalize([Feature|Rest], [Inst_prop|Rest_inst], [Feature|Rest_gen]) :-
    not(Feature \= Inst_prop), generalize(Rest, Rest_inst, Rest_gen).
generalize([Feature|Rest], [Inst_prop|Rest_inst], [_|Rest_gen]) :-
    Feature \= Inst_prop, generalize(Rest, Rest_inst, Rest_gen).
```

These predicates define the essential operations on feature vector representations. The remainder of the implementations that follow are independent of any specific representation, and may be adapted to a variety of representations and generalization operators.

As discussed in Section 10.2, we may search a concept space in a specific to general direction by maintaining a list H of candidate hypotheses. The hypotheses in H are the most specific concepts that cover all the positive examples and none of the negative examples seen so far. The heart of the algorithm is process with five arguments. The first argument to process is a training instance, positive(X) or negative(X), indicating that X is a positive or negative example. The second and third arguments are the current list of hypotheses and the list of negative instances. On completion, process binds its fourth and fifth arguments to the updated lists of hypotheses and negative examples, respectively.

The first clause in the definition initializes an empty hypothesis set to the first positive instance. The second handles positive training instances by generalizing candidate hypotheses to cover the instance. It then deletes all over-generalizations by removing those that are more general than some other hypothesis and eliminating any hypothesis that covers some negative instance. The third clause in the definition handles negative examples by deleting any hypothesis that covers those instances.

```
process(positive(Instance), [ ], N, [Instance], N).
process(positive(Instance), H, N, Updated_H, N) :-
    generalize_set(H, Gen_H, Instance),
    delete(X, Gen_H, (member(Y, Gen_H),
        more_general(X, Y)), Pruned_H),
    delete(X, Pruned_H, (member(Y, N),
    covers(X, Y)), Updated_H).
process(negative(Instance), H, N, Updated_H, [Instance|N]) :-
    delete(X, H, covers(X, Instance), Updated_H).
process(Input, H, N, H, N):-                        %Catches mistyped input
    Input \= positive(_),
    Input \= negative(_),
    write('Enter either positive(Instance) or negative(Instance) '), nl.
```

An interesting aspect of this implementation is the delete predicate, a generalization of the usual process of deleting all matches of an element from a list. One of the arguments to delete is a test that determines which elements to remove from the list. Using bagof, delete matches its first argument (usually a variable) with each element of its second argument (this must be a list). For each such binding, it then executes the test specified in argument three; this test is any sequence of callable PROLOG goals. If a list element causes this test to fail, delete includes that element in the resulting list. It returns the result in its final argument. The delete predicate is an excellent example of the power of meta reasoning in PROLOG: by letting us pass in a specification of the elements we want to delete from a list, delete gives us a general tool for implementing a range of list operations. Thus, delete lets us define the various filters used in process/5 in an extremely compact fashion. We define delete:

```
delete(X, L, Goal, New_L) :-
    (bagof(X, (member(X, L), not(Goal)), New_L); New_L = [ ]).
```

Generalize_set is a straightforward predicate that recursively scans a list of hypotheses and generalizes each one against a training instance. Note that this assumes that we may have multiple candidate generalizations at one time. In fact, the feature vector representation of Section 10.2 only allows a single most specific generalization. However, this is not true in general and we have defined the algorithm for the general case.

```
generalize_set([ ], [ ], _).
generalize_set([Hypothesis|Rest], Updated_H, Instance):-
    not(covers(Hypothesis, Instance)),
    (bagof(X, generalize(Hypothesis, Instance, X), Updated_head);
        Updated_head = [ ]),
    generalize_set(Rest, Updated_rest, Instance),
    append(Updated_head, Updated_rest, Updated_H).
generalize_set([Hypothesis|Rest], [Hypothesis|Updated_rest], Instance) :-
    covers(Hypothesis, Instance),
    generalize_set(Rest, Updated_rest, Instance).
```

specific_to_general implements a loop that reads and processes training instances.

```
specific_to_general(H, N) :-
    write('H = '), write(H), nl, write('N = '), write(N), nl, write('Enter Instance: '),
    read(Instance), process(Instance, H, N, Updated_H, Updated_N),
        specific_to_general(Updated_H, Updated_N).
```

The following transcript illustrates the execution of the algorithm.

```
?- specific_to_general([], []).
H = [ ]
N = [ ]
Enter Instance: positive([small, red, ball]).
H = [[small, red, ball]]
N = [ ]
Enter Instance: negative([large, green, cube]).
H = [[small, red, ball]]
N = [[large, green, cube]]
Enter Instance: negative([small, blue, brick]).
```

```
H = [[small, red, ball]]
N = [[small, blue, brick], [large, green, cube]]
Enter Instance: positive([small, green, ball]).
H = [[small, _66, ball]]
N = [[small, blue, brick], [large, green, cube]]
Enter Instance: positive([large, blue, ball]).
H = [[_116, _66, ball]]
N = [[small, blue, brick], [large, green, cube]]
```

The second version of the algorithm searches in a general to specific direction, as presented in Section 10.2.2. In this version, the set of candidate hypotheses are initialized to the most general possible concept. In the case of the feature vector representation, this is a list of variables. It then specializes candidate concepts to prevent them from covering negative instances. In the feature vector representation, this involves replacing variables with constants. When given a new positive instance, it eliminates any candidate hypothesis that fails to cover that instance.

We implement this algorithm in a way that closely parallels the specific to general search just described, including the use of the general delete predicate to define the various filters of the list of candidate concepts.

In defining a general to specific search, process will have six arguments. The first five reflect the specific to general version: the first a training instance of the form positive(Instance) or negative(Instance); the second is a list of candidate hypotheses; these are the most general hypotheses that cover no negative instances. The third argument is the list of positive examples, used to delete any overly specialized candidate hypothesis. The fourth and fifth arguments are the updated lists of hypotheses and positive examples, respectively. The sixth argument is a list of allowable variable substitutions for specializing concepts. Specialization by substituting a constant for a variable requires the algorithm to know the allowable constant values for each field of the feature vector. These values will have to be passed in as the sixth argument of process. In our example of [Size, Color, Shape] vectors, a sample list of types might be: [[small, medium, large], [red, white, blue], [ball, brick, cube]]. Note that the position of each sublist determines the position in a feature vector where those values are used; for example, the first sublist defines allowable values for the first position of a feature vector.

We leave construction of this algorithm as an exercise (28). For guidance we include a run of our implementation:

```
?- general_to_specific([[_, _, _]], [ ], [[small, medium, large], [red, blue, green],
    [ball, brick, cube]]).
H = [[_0, _1, _2]]
P = [ ]
Enter Instance: positive([small, red, ball]).
H = [[_0, _1, _2]]
P = [[small, red, ball]]
Enter Instance; negative([large, green, cube]).
H = [[small, _89, _90], [_79, red, _80], [_69, _70, ball]]
P = [[small, red, ball]]
```

Enter Instance: negative([small, blue, brick]).
H = [[_79, red, _80],[_69, _70, ball]]
P = [[small, red, ball]]
Enter Instance: positive([small, green, ball]).
H = [[_69,_70,ball]]
P = [[small, green, ball], [small, red, ball]]

15.8.2   The Candidate Elimination Algorithm

The full candidate elimination algorithm, as defined in Section 10.2.2, is a combination of the two single direction searches. As before, the heart of the algorithm is the definition of process, with six arguments. The first argument to process is a training instance. Arguments two and three are G and S, the sets of maximally general and maximally specific hypotheses respectively. The fourth and fifth arguments are bound to the updated versions of these sets. The sixth argument of process lists allowable variable substitutions for specializing feature vectors.

On positive instances, process generalizes S, the set of most specific generalizations, to cover the training instance. It then eliminates any elements of S that have been over generalized. It also eliminates any elements of G that fail to cover the training instance. It is interesting to note that an element of S is overly general if there is no element of G that covers it; this is true because G contains those candidate hypotheses that are both maximally general and cover no negative instances. process uses delete to eliminate these hypotheses.

On a negative training instance, process specializes all hypotheses in G to exclude that instance. It also eliminates any candidates in S that cover the negative instance. As discussed above, specialization of feature vectors requires replacing variables with constants. This requires that we pass a list of allowable substitutions as the sixth argument to process. We define process:

```
process(negative(Instance), G, S, Updated_G, Updated_S, Types) :-
    delete(X, S, covers(X, Instance), Updated_S),
    specialize_set(G, Spec_G, Instance, Types),
    delete(X, Spec_G, (member(Y, Spec_G), more_general(Y, X)), Pruned_G),
    delete(X, Pruned_G, (member(Y, Updated_S), not(covers(X, Y))), Updated_G).
process(positive(Instance), G, [ ], Updated_G, [Instance],_) :-         % Initialize S
    delete(X, G, not(covers(X, Instance)), Updated_G).
process(positive(Instance), G, S, Updated_G, Updated_S,_) :-
    delete(X, G, not(covers(X, Instance)), Updated_G),
    generalize_set(S, Gen_S, Instance),
    delete(X, Gen_S, (member(Y, Gen_S), more_general(X, Y)), Pruned_S),
    delete(X, Pruned_S, not((member(Y, Updated_G), covers(Y, X))), Updated_S).
process(Input, G, P, G, P,_) :-
    Input \= positive(_), Input \= negative(_),
    write('Enter either positive(Instance) or negative(Instance): '), nl.
```

generalize_set generalizes all members of a set of candidate hypotheses to cover a training instance. It is identical to the version defined for the specific to general search. specialize_set takes a set of candidate hypotheses and computes all maximally general specializations of those hypotheses that exclude (do not cover) a training instance. Note the use of bagof to get all specializations.

```
specialize_set([ ], [ ], _, _).
specialize_set([Hypothesis|Rest], Updated_H, Instance, Types) :-
    covers(Hypothesis, Instance),
    (bagof(Hypothesis, specialize(Hypothesis, Instance,Types), Updated_head);
        Updated_head = [ ]),
specialize_set(Rest, Updated_rest, Instance, Types),
    append(Updated_head, Updated_rest, Updated_H).
    specialize_set([Hypothesis|Rest], [Hypothesis|Updated_rest], Instance, Types) :-
    not (covers(Hypothesis, Instance)),
        specialize_set(Rest, Updated_rest, Instance, Types).
```

specialize finds an element of a feature vector that is a variable. It binds that variable to a constant value that it selects from the list of allowable values, and which does not match the training instance. Recall that specialize_set called specialize with bagof to get all specializations. If we call specialize once, it will only substitute a constant into the first variable; the use of bagof causes it to produce all specializations.

```
specialize([Prop|_], [Inst_prop|_], [Instance_values|_]) :-
    var(Prop),
    member(Prop, Instance_values), Prop \= Inst_prop.
specialize([_|Tail], [_|Inst_tail], [_|Types]) :-
    specialize(Tail, Inst_tail, Types).
```

The definitions of generalize, more_general, covers, and delete are the same as in the specific to general algorithm defined above. candidate_elim implements a top-level read-process loop, printing out the current G set, the S set, and calls process on the input.

```
candidate_elim([G],[S],_) :-
    covers(G,S),covers(S,G),
    write('target concept is: '), write(G),nl.
candidate_elim(G, S, Types) :-
    write('G= '), write(G), nl, write('S= '), write(S), nl, write('Enter Instance: '),
    read(Instance),
    process(Instance, G, S, Updated_G, Updated_S, Types),
        candidate_elim(Updated_G, Updated_S, Types).
```

To conclude this section we present a trace of the candidate elimination algorithm. Note initializations of G, S, and the list of allowable substitutions:

```
?- candidate_elim([[_, _, _]], [ ], [[small, medium, large], [red, blue, green],
    [ball, brick, cube]]).
```

```
G= [[_0, _1, _2]]
S= [ ]
Enter Instance: positive([small, red, ball]).
G= [[_0, _1, _2]]
S= [[small, red, ball]]
Enter Instance: negative([large, green, cube]).
G= [[small, _96, _97], [_86, red, _87], [_76, _77, ball]]
S= [[small, red, ball]]
Enter Instance: negative([small, blue, brick]).
G= [[_86, red, _87], [_76, _77, ball]]
S= [[small, red, ball]]
Enter Instance: positive([small, green, ball]).
G= [[_76, _77, ball]]
S= [[small, _351, ball]]
Enter Instance: positive([large, red, ball]).
target concept is: [_76, _77, ball]
yes
```

15.8.3 Explanation-Based Learning in PROLOG

In this section, we present a PROLOG implementation of the explanation-based learning algorithm of Section 10.4.2. Our implementation is based upon Kedar-Cabelli and McCarty's formulation (Kedar-Cabelli and McCarty 1987), called prolog_ebg, and illustrates the power of unification in PROLOG. Even though it is quite difficult to implement explanation based learning in many languages, the PROLOG version is fairly simple.

Instead of building an explanation structure and maintaining separate sets of specific and general substitutions as done in Section 10.4, this algorithm builds both the proof of the training instance and the generalized proof tree concurrently.

In this example, we represent proof trees as we did in exshell (Section 15.7.2). When prolog_ebg discovers a fact, it returns this fact as the leaf of a proof tree. The proof of conjunctive goals is the conjunction of the proof of the conjuncts. The proof of a goal that requires rule chaining is represented as (Goal :- Proof), where Proof becomes bound to the proof tree for the rule premise.

The heart of the algorithm is prolog_ebg. This predicate takes four arguments: the first is the goal being proved in the training example, the second is the generalization of that goal. If the domain theory enables a proof of the specific goal, it binds the third and fourth arguments to a proof tree for the goal and the generalization of that proof. For instance, implementing the cup example from Section 10.5.2, we would call prolog_ebg with the arguments:

    prolog_ebg(cup(obj1), cup(X), Proof, Gen_proof).

We assume that PROLOG has the domain theory and training instance of Section 10.4.2. prolog_ebg succeeds; Proof and Gen_proof are the proof trees of Figure 10.17.

Prolog_ebg is a straightforward variation of the meta-interpreter of Section 15.7.2. The primary difference is in solving the goal and the generalized goal in parallel. A further interesting aspect of the algorithm is the use of the predicate duplicate to create two versions of each rule: the first version is the rule as it appears in the domain theory, the second binds variables in the rule to the values in the training instance. Define prolog_ebg:

```
prolog_ebg(A, GenA,  A, GenA) :- clause(A, true).
prolog_ebg((A, B), (GenA, GenB), (AProof, BProof), (GenAProof, GenBProof)) :- !,
    prolog_ebg(A, GenA, AProof, GenAProof),
        prolog_ebg(B, GenB, BProof, GenBProof).
prolog_ebg(A, GenA, (A :- Proof), (GenA :- GenProof)) :-
    clause(GenA, GenB),
    duplicate((GenA :- GenB), (A :- B)),
        prolog_ebg(B, GenB, Proof, GenProof).
```

Duplicate relies upon the behavior of assert and retract to create a copy of a PROLOG expression with all new variables.

```
duplicate(Old, New) :- assert('$marker'(Old)), retract('$marker'(New)).
```

Extract_support returns the sequence of the highest level operational nodes, as defined by the predicate operational. The predicate implements a recursive tree walk, terminating the recursion when it finds nodes in the proof tree that qualifies as operational.

```
extract_support(Proof, Proof) :- operational(Proof).
extract_support((A :- _), A) :- operational(A).
extract_support((AProof, BProof), (A, B)) :-
    extract_support(AProof, A),
    extract_support(BProof, B).
extract_support((_ :- Proof), B) :- extract_support(Proof, B).
```

The final component of the algorithm constructs the learned rule, using prolog_ebg and extract_support:

```
ebg(Goal, Gen_goal, (Gen_goal :- Premise)) :-
    prolog_ebg(Goal, Gen_goal, _, Gen_proof),
    extract_support(Gen_proof, Premise).
```

We illustrate the execution of these predicates with the example of learning structural definitions of cups from Section 10.5.2 (Mitchell et al. 1986). We begin with a domain theory for cups and other physical objects. The theory includes the rules:

```
cup(X) :- liftable(X), holds_liquid(X).
holds_liquid(Z) :- part(Z, W), concave(W), points_up(W).
liftable(Y) :- light(Y), part(Y, handle).
light(A):- small(A).
light(A):- made_of(A, feathers).
```

The learner is also given the following example, in which obj1 is known to be a cup:

```
small(obj1).
part(obj1, handle).
owns(bob, obj1).
part(obj1, bottom).
part(obj1, bowl).
points_up(bowl).
concave(bowl).
color(obj1, red).
```

The operationality criteria define those predicates that may be used in a rule:

```
operational(small(_)).
operational(part(_, _)).
operational(owns(_, _)).
operational(points_up(_)).
operational(concave(_)).
```

A run of the algorithm on the cup example illustrates the behavior of these predicates:

```
?- prolog_ebg(cup(obj1), cup(X), Proof, Gen_proof).
X = _0,
Proof = cup(obj1) :-
    ( (liftable(obj1) :-
            ( (light(obj1) :-
                    small(obj1)), part(obj1, handle))),
        (holds_liquid(obj1) :-
            (part(obj1, bowl),
                concave(bowl), points_up(bowl))))
Gen_prooof = cup(_0) :-
    ( (liftable(_0) :-
            ( (light(_0) :-
                    small(_0)),
                part(_0, handle))),
        (holds_liquid(_0) :-
            (part(_0, _106),
                concave(_106),
                points_up(_106))))
```

When we give extract_support the generalized proof from the previous execution of prolog_ebg, it returns the operational nodes of the proof, in left to right order:

```
?- extract_support((cup(_0) :-
    ( (liftable(_0) :-
            ( (light(_0) :-
                    small(_0)),
                part(_0, handle))),
        (holds_liquid(_0) :-
            (part(_0,_106), concave(_106),
                points_up(_106))))), Premise),
```

```
_0 = _0, _106 = _1,
Premise =  (small(_0), part(_0,handle)), part(_0,_1),  concave(_1), points_up(_1)
```

Finally, ebg uses these predicates to construct a new rule from the example.

```
?- ebg(cup(obj1), cup(X), Rule).
X = _0,
Rule = cup(_0) :-
      ( (small(_0), part(_0, handle)), part(_0,_110), concave(_110), points_up(_110))
```

15.9 Natural Language Processing in PROLOG

15.9.1 Semantic Representations for Natural Language Processing

Because of its built-in search and pattern matching, PROLOG easily accommodates natural language processing. We can write natural language grammars directly in PROLOG, as we see for the context-free and context-sensitive grammars of Section 15.9.2. Semantic representations are also easy to create in PROLOG, as we see for case frames in this section. Semantic relationships may be captured either using the first-order predicate calculus or by a meta-interpreter for another representation, as suggested by the frame system of Section 15.7.4. Finally, semantic inference, such as join, restrict, and inheritance in conceptual graphs, can be done directly in PROLOG as we see in Section 15.9.3.

As presented in Section 7.2, conceptual graphs can be translated directly into predicate calculus and hence into PROLOG. The conceptual relation nodes become the predicate name, and the arity of the relation indicates the number of arguments of the predicate. Each PROLOG predicate, as with each conceptual graph, represents a single proposition.

The conceptual graphs of Figure 7.14 may be rendered in PROLOG as:

```
bird(X), flies(X).
dog(X), color (X, Y), brown(Y).
child(X), parents(X, Y, Z), father(Y), mother(Z).
```

where X, Y, and Z are bound to the appropriate individuals. Type information can be added to parameters as indicated in Section 15.6. We can also define the type hierarchy through a variation of isa predicates.

Case frames, Section 14.3.2, are also easily built in PROLOG. Each verb is paired with a list of the semantic relations assumed to be part of the verb. These may include agents, instruments, and objects. We next offer examples of the verbs give and bite. For example, the verb give requires a subject, object, and indirect object. In the English sentence "John gives Mary the book," this structure takes on the obvious assignments. We can define defaults in a case frame by binding the appropriate variable values. For example, we could give bite a default instrument of teeth, and, indeed indicate that the instrument for biting, teeth, belong to the agent! Case frames for these two verbs might be:

```
verb(give,
    [human (Subject),
      agent (Subject, give),
      act_of_giving (give),
      object (Object, give),
      inanimate (Object),
      recipient (Ind_obj, give),
      human (Ind_obj) ] ).

verb(bite,
    [animate (Subject),
      agent (Subject, Action),
      act_of_biting (Action),
      object (Object, Action),
      animate (Object),
      instrument (teeth, Action),
      part_of (teeth, Subject) ] ).
```

Logic programming offers a powerful medium for building grammars as well as representations for semantic meanings. We next build recursive descent parsers in PROLOG, and then add syntactic and semantic constraints to these parsers.

15.9.2   A Recursive Descent Context-Free Parser in PROLOG

Consider the subset of English grammar rules below. These rules are "declarative" in the sense that they simply define relationships among parts of speech. With this subset of rules a large number of simple sentences can be judged as well formed or not.

Sentence ↔ NounPhrase VerbPhrase
NounPhrase ↔ Noun
NounPhrase ↔ Article Noun
VerbPhrase ↔ Verb
VerbPhrase ↔ Verb NounPhrase

Adding some vocabulary to the grammar rules:

Article(a)
Article(the)
Noun(man)
Noun(dog)
Verb(likes)
Verb(bites)

Figure 15.9 is the parse tree of "the man bites the dog," with and constraints in the grammar reflected by and links in the tree. The grammar rules have a natural fit to PROLOG, for example, a sentence is a nounphrase followed by a verbphrase:

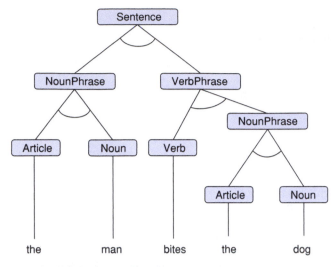

Figure 15.9 The and/or parse tree for "The man bites the dog".

sentence(Start, End) :- nounphrase(Start, Rest), verbphrase(Rest, End).

Each PROLOG rule takes two parameters, the first a sequence of words in list form. The rule attempts to determine whether some initial part of the list is a legal part of speech. Any remaining tail of the list will match the second parameter, as we are parsing the sentence left-to-right. If the sentence rule succeeds, the second parameter of sentence will be what remains after the nounphrase and verbphrase parse. If the list is a sentence, this is [ ]. Two alternative forms of noun phrases and verb phrases are defined.

The sentence itself, for simplicity, is described as a list: [the,man,likes,the,dog]. The list is broken up and passed to the various grammar rules to be examined for syntactic correctness. Note how the "pattern matching" works on the list in question: pulling off the head, or the head and second element; passing on what is left over; and so on. The utterance predicate takes the list to be parsed as its argument and calls the sentence rule, initializing the second parameter of sentence to [ ]. The complete grammar is defined:

```
utterance(X) :- sentence(X, [ ]).
sentence(Start,End) :- nounphrase(Start, Rest), verbphrase(Rest, End).
nounphrase([Noun | End], End) :- noun(Noun).
nounphrase([Article, Noun | End], End) :- article(Article), noun(Noun).
verbphrase([Verb | End], End) :- verb(Verb).
verbphrase([Verb | Rest], End) :- verb(Verb), nounphrase(Rest, End).
article(a).
article(the).
noun(man).
noun(dog).
verb(likes).
verb(bites).
```

Example sentences may be tested for well-formedness:

```
?- utterance([the, man, bites, the, dog]).
yes
?- utterance([the, man, bites, the]).
no
```

The interpreter can also fill in possible legitimate words to incomplete sentences:

```
?- utterance([the, man, likes, X]).
X = man
;
X = dog
;
no
```

Finally, the same code may be used to generate the set of all well-formed sentences using this limited dictionary and set of grammar rules:

```
?- utterance(X).
[man, likes]
;
[man, bites]
;
[man, likes, man]
;
[man, likes, dog]
etc.
```

If the user continues asking for more solutions, eventually all possible well-formed sentences that can be generated from the grammar rules and our vocabulary are returned as values for X. Note that the PROLOG search is left to right and depth-first.

The grammar rules specify a subset of legitimate sentences of English. The PROLOG grammar code represents these specifications. The interpreter is asked questions about them and the answer is a function of the specifications and the question asked. Since there are no constraints enforced across the subtrees that make up the full parse of a sentence, see Figure 15.9, the parser/generator for this grammar is said to be *context free*.

In the following sections we extend the context-free grammar of Section 15.9.2 to include further syntactic and semantic constraints. For example, we may want some grammatical structures to be less likely than others, such as a noun by itself being less likely than an article followed by a noun. Further, we may want the sentence "The man bites the dog" to be less likely than the sentence "The dog bites the man". Finally, if our vocabulary includes the verb like (as well as likes), we want "The man likes the dog" to be acceptable, but "The man like the dog" to fail. In the next sections we address these issues. The parsers for Sections 15.9.3 and 15.9.4 were suggested by Professor Mark Steedman of the University of Edinburgh and transformed to the syntax of this book by Ms. Monique Morin of the University of New Mexico.

15.9.3   A Probabilistic Context-Free Parser (Steedman and Morin)

Our first extension is to build a *probabilistic context-free parser*. To do this, we add a probabilistic parameter, Prob, to each grammar rule. Note that the probability that a sentence will be a noun phrase followed by a verb phrase is 1.0, while the probability that a noun phrase is simply a noun is less than the probability of it being an article followed by a noun. These probabilities are reflected in pr facts for each grammar rule, r1, r2, ..., r5.

The full probability of a particular sentence, Prob, however, is calculated by combining a number of probabilities: that of the rule itself together with the probabilities of each of its constituents. Thus the full probability Prob of r1 is a product of the probabilities that a particular noun phrase is combined with a particular verb phrase. Further, the probability for the third rule, r3, will be the product of that type noun phrase occurring (r3) times the probabilities of the particular article and noun that make up the noun phrase. These noun/article probabilities are given in the two argument dictionary "fact" predicates.

```
utterance(Prob, X) :- sentence(Prob, X, [ ]).
sentence(Prob, Start, End) :- nounphrase(P1, Start, Rest), verbphrase(P2, Rest, End),
    pr(r1, P), Prob is P*P1*P2.
nounphrase(Prob, [Noun|End], End) :- noun(P1, Noun),
    pr(r2, P), Prob is P*P1.
nounphrase(Prob, [Article, Noun|End], End) :- article(P1, Article), noun(P2, Noun),
    pr(r3, P), Prob is P*P1*P2.
verbphrase(Prob, [Verb|End], End) :- verb(P1, Verb),
    pr(r4, P), Prob is P*P1.
verbphrase(Prob, [Verb|Rest], End) :- verb(P1, Verb), nounphrase(P2, Rest, End),
    pr(r5, P), Prob is P*P1*P2.


pr(r1, 1.0).
pr(r2, 0.3).
pr(r3, 0.7).
pr(r4, 0.2).
pr(r5, 0.8).


article(0.25, a).
article(0.75, the).
noun(0.65, man).
noun(0.35, dog).
verb(0.9, likes).
verb(0.1, bites).
```

We now run several example sentences as well as offer general patterns of sentences, i.e., sentences beginning with specific patterns of words such as "The dog bites...". Finally, we ask for all possible sentences that can be generated under these constraints.

```
?- utterance(Prob, [the, man, likes, the, dog]).
Prob = 0.0451474
Yes
```

```
?- utterance(Prob, [bites, dog])
No
?- utterance(Prob, [the, man, dog]).
No

?- utterance(Prob, [the, dog, bites, X]).
Prob = 0.0028665
X = man
;
Prob = 0.0015435
X = dog
;
No

?- utterance(Prob, [the, dog, bites, X|Y]).
Prob = 0.0028665
X = man
Y = [ ]
;
Prob = 0.0015435
X = dog
Y = [ ]
;
Prob = 0.00167212
X = a
Y = [man] ;
etc.

?- utterance(Prob, X).
Prob = 0.0351
X = [man, likes]
;
Prob = 0.0039
X = [man, bites]
;
Prob = 0.027378
X = [man, likes, man]
;
Prob = 0.014742
X = [man, likes, dog]
etc.
```

15.9.4 A Probabilistic Lexicalized C-F Parser (Steedman and Morin)

We next demonstrate a *probabilistic lexicalized context-free parser*. This is a much more constrained system in which the probabilities, besides giving measures for the various grammatical structures and individual words as in the previous section, also describe the possible combinations of words (thus, it is a *lexicalized* parser). For example, we now measure the likelihood of both noun-verb and verb-object word combinations. Constraining noun-verb combinations gives us much of the power of context-sensitive parsing, Section 15.9.5, where noun-verb agreement is enforced, as well as the ability to assign low confidences to noun-verb combinations that do not make semantic sense.

There are a number of goals here, including prioritizing the "quality" of utterances in the language by using the probabilistic measure of them occurring. Thus, we can determine that a possible sentence fails for syntactic or semantic reasons by seeing that it produces a very low or zero probability measure, rather than by the interpreter simply saying "no".

In the following grammar we have hard coded the probabilities of various structure and word combinations. In a real system, lexical information could be better obtained by sampling appropriate corpora with noun-verb or verb-object bigrams. We discussed the n-gram approach to language analysis in Section 14.4 where the probability of word combinations were described (two words—*bigrams*, three words—*trigrams*, etc.). These probabilities are usually determined by sampling over a large collection of sentences, called a *corpus*. The result was the ability to assess the likelihood of these word combinations, e.g., to determine the probability of the verb "bite" following the noun "dogs".

In the following examples the Prob value is made up of the probabilities of the particular sentence structure, the probabilities of the verb-noun and verb-object combinations, and the probabilities of individual words.

```
utterance(Prob, X) :- sentence(Prob, Verb, Noun, X, [ ]).
sentence(Prob, Verb, Noun, Start, End) :-
    nounphrase(P1, Noun, Start, Rest), verbphrase(P2, Verb, Rest, End),
    pr(r1, P),                          % Probability of this sentence structure
    pr([r1, Verb, Noun], PrDep),        % Probability this noun and verb go together
    pr(shead, Verb, Pshead),            % Probability this verb heads the sentence
    Prob is Pshead*P*PrDep*P1*P2.
nounphrase(Prob, Noun, [Noun|End], End) :- noun(P1, Noun),
    pr(r2, P), Prob is P*P1.
nounphrase(Prob, Noun, [Article, Noun|End], End) :-
    article(P1, Article), noun(P2, Noun), pr(r3, P),
    pr([r3, Noun, Article], PrDep),     % Probability this article and noun go together
    Prob is P*PrDep*P1*P2.
verbphrase(Prob, Verb, [Verb|End], End) :- verb(P1, Verb),
    pr(r4, P), Prob is P*P1.
verbphrase(Prob, Verb, [Verb|Rest], End) :-
    verb(P1, Verb), nounphrase(P2, Object, Rest, End),
    pr([r5, Verb, Object], PrDep),      % Probability this verb and object go together
    pr(r5, P), Prob is P*PrDep*P1*P2.

pr(r1, 1.0).
pr(r2, 0.3).
pr(r3, 0.7).
pr(r4, 0.2).
pr(r5, 0.8).
```

```
article(1.0, a).
article(1.0, the).
article(1.0, these).
noun(1.0, man).
noun(1.0, dogs).
verb(1.0, likes).
verb(1.0, bite).

pr(shead, likes, 0.5).
pr(shead, bite, 0.5).

pr([r1, likes, man], 1.0).
pr([r1, likes, dogs], 0.0).
pr([r1, bite, man], 0.0).
pr([r1, bite, dogs], 1.0).
pr([r3, man, a], 0.5).
pr([r3, man, the], 0.5).
pr([r3, man, these], 0.0).
pr([r3, dogs, a], 0.0).
pr([r3, dogs, the], 0.6).
pr([r3, dogs,  these], 0.4).
pr([r5, likes, man], 0.2).
pr([r5, likes, dogs], 0.8).
pr([r5, bite, man], 0.8).
pr([r5, bite, dogs], 0.2).
```

The **Prob** measure gives the likelihood of the utterance; words that aren't sentences return No.

```
?- utterance(Prob, [a, man, likes, these, dogs]).
Prob = 0.03136
?- utterance(Prob, [a, man, likes, a, man]).
 Prob = 0.0098
?- utterance(Prob, [a, man, likes, a, man]).
Prob = 0.0098
?- utterance(Prob, [the, dogs, likes, these, man]).
Prob = 0
?- utterance(Prob, [the, dogs]).
No
?- utterance(Prob, [the, dogs, X|Y])
Prob = 0
X = likes  Y = []
;
Prob = 0.042
X = bite  Y = []
;
Prob = 0
X = likes  Y = [man]
;
....
```

```
Prob = 0.04032
X = bite  Y = [man]
;
Prob = 0.01008
X = bite  Y = [dogs]
;
Prob = 0.04704
X = bite  Y = [a, man]
etc
?- utterance(Prob, X).
Prob = 0.03
X = [man, likes]
;
Prob = 0
 X = [man, bite]
;
Prob = 0.0072
X = [man, likes, man]
;
Prob = 0.0288
X = [man, likes, dogs]
;
Prob = 0.0084
X = [man, likes, a, man]
etc
```

15.9.5 A Context-Sensitive Parser in PROLOG

A *context-sensitive* parser addresses the issues of the previous section in a different manner. Suppose we desire to have proper noun–verb agreement enforced by the grammar rules themselves. In the dictionary entry for each word its singular or plural form can be noted as such. Then in the grammar specifications for nounphrase and verbphrase a further parameter is used to signify the number of each phrase. This enforces the constraint that a singular noun has to be associated with a singular verb. Similar constraints for article–noun combinations can also be enforced. The technique we are using is constraining sentence components by enforcing variable bindings across the subtrees of the parse of the sentence (note the and links in the parse tree of Figure 15.9).

Context sensitivity increases the power of a context-free grammar considerably. These additions are made by extending the PROLOG code of Section 15.9.2:

```
utterance(X) :- sentence(X, [ ]).
sentence(Start, End) :- nounphrase(Start, Rest, Number),
    verbphrase(Rest, End, Number).
nounphrase([Noun | End], End, Number) :- noun(Noun, Number).
nounphrase([Article, Noun | End], End, Number) :- noun(Noun, Number),
    article(Article, Number).
```

```
verbphrase([Verb | End], End, Number) :- verb(Verb, Number).
verbphrase([Verb | Rest], End, Number) :- verb(Verb, Number),
    nounphrase(Rest, End,_).

article(a, singular).
article(these, plural).
article(the, singular).
article(the, plural).
noun(man, singular).
noun(men, plural).
noun(dog, singular).
noun(dogs, plural).
verb(likes, singular).
verb(like, plural).
verb(bites, singular).
verb(bite, plural).
```

Sentences may now be tested. The answer to the second query is no, because the subject (men) and the verb (likes) do not agree in number.

```
?- utterance([the, men, like, the, dog]).
yes
?- utterance([the, men, likes, the, dog]).
no
```

If we enter the following goal, X returns all verb phrases that complete the plural "the men ..." with all verb phrases with noun–verb number agreement. The final query returns all sentences with article–noun as well as noun–verb agreement.

```
?- utterance([the, men | X]).
?- utterance(X).
```

In the context-sensitive example we use the parameters of dictionary entries to introduce more information on the meanings of each of the words that make up the sentence. This approach may be generalized to a powerful parser for natural language. More and more information may be included in the dictionary of the word components used in the sentences, implementing a knowledge base of the meaning of English words. For example, men are animate and human. Similarly, dogs may be described as animate and nonhuman. With these descriptions new rules may be added for parsing, such as "humans do not bite animate nonhumans" to eliminate sentences such as [the, man, bites, the, dog]. We add these constraints in the following section.

15.9.5   A Recursive Descent Semantic Net Parser in PROLOG

We next extend the set of context-sensitive grammar rules to include some possibilities of semantic consistency. We do this by matching case frames for the verbs of sentences to semantic descriptions of subjects and objects. After each match, we constrain these semantic net subgraphs to be consistent with each other. We do this by performing graph operations, such as join and restrict, to each piece of the graph as it is returned up the parse tree.

We first present the grammar rules. Notice that the top-level predicate utterance, returns not just a sentence but also a Sentence_graph. Each component of the grammar relationships, such as nounphrase and verbphrase, call join to merge together the constraints of their respective graphs.

```
utterance(X, Sentence_graph) :-
    sentence(X, [ ], Sentence_graph).
sentence(Start, End, Sentence_graph) :-
    nounphrase(Start, Rest, Subject_graph),
    verbphrase(Rest, End, Predicate_graph),
    join([agent(Subject_graph)], Predicate_graph, Sentence_graph).
nounphrase([Noun | End], End, Noun_phrase_graph) :-
    noun(Noun, Noun_phrase_graph).
nounphrase([Article, Noun | End], End, Noun_phrase_graph) :-
    article(Article),
    noun(Noun, Noun_phrase_graph).
verbphrase([Verb | End], End, Verb_phrase_graph) :-
    verb(Verb, Verb_phrase_graph).
verbphrase([Verb | Rest], End, Verb_phrase_graph) :-
    verb(Verb, Verb_graph),
    nounphrase(Rest, End, Noun_phrase_graph),
    join([object(Noun_phrase_graph)], Verb_graph, Verb_phrase_graph).
```

We next present predicates for the graph join and restriction operations. These are meta-predicates because their domain is other PROLOG structures. These operators are seen as utilities that propagate constraints across the pieces of semantic nets they merge.

```
join(X, X, X).
join(A, B, C) :-
    isframe(A), isframe(B), !,
    join_frames(A, B, C, not_joined).
join(A, B, C) :-
    isframe(A), is_slot((B), !,
    join_slot_to_frame(B, A, C).
join(A, B, C) :-
    isframe(B), is_slot(A), !,
    join_slot_to_frame(A, B, C).
join(A, B, C) :-
    is_slot(A), is_slot(B), !,
    join_slots(A, B, C).
```

join_frames recursively matches each slot (property) of the first frame to matching slots of the second. join_slot_to_frame takes a slot and a frame and searches the frame for matching slots. join_slots matches two slots, taking the type hierarchy into account:

```
join_frames([A | B], C, D, OK) :-
    join_slot_to_frame(A, C, E) , !,
    join_frames(B, E, D, ok).
join_frames([ A | B], C, [A | D], OK) :-
    join_frames(B, C, D, OK), !.
join_frames([], A, A, ok).
join_slot_to_frame(A, [B | C], [D | C]) :-
    join_slots(A, B, D).
join_slot_to_frame(A, [B | C], [B | D]) :-
    join_slot_to_frame(A, C, D).
join_slots(A, B, D) :-
    functor(A, FA, _), functor(B, FB, _),
    match_with_inheritance(FA, FB, FN),
    arg(1, A, Value_a), arg(1, B, Value_b),
    join(Value_a, Value_b, New_value),
    D =.. [FN | [New_value]].
isframe([_ | _]).
isframe([ ]).
is_slot(A) :- functor(A, _, 1).
```

Finally, we create the dictionary entries, the inheritance hierarchy, and the case frames for the verbs. In this example, we use a simple hierarchy that lists all valid specializations; the third argument to match_with_inheritance is the common specialization of the first two. A more realistic implementation would maintain a graph of the hierarchies and search it for common specializations. Implementation of this is left as an exercise.

```
match_with_inheritance(X, X, X).
match_with_inheritance(dog, animate, dog).
match_with_inheritance(animate,dog, dog).
match_with_inheritance(man, animate, man).
match_with_inheritance(animate, man, man).
article(a).
article(the).
noun(fido, [dog(fido)]).
noun(man, [man(X)]).
noun(dog, [dog(X)]).
verb(likes, [action([liking(X)]), agent([animate(X)]), object([animate(Y)])]).
verb(bites, [action([biting(Y)]), agent([dog(X)]), object([animate(Z)])]).
```

We now parse several sentences and print out the Sentence_graph:

```
?- utterance([the, man, likes, the, dog], X).
X = [action([liking(_54)]), agent([man(_23)]), object([dog(_52)])].
?- utterance([fido, likes, the, man], X).
X = [action([liking(_62)]), agent([dog(fido)]), object([man(_70)])].
?- utterance([the, man, bites, fido], Z).
no
```

The first sentence states that some man, with name unknown, likes an unnamed dog. The last sentence, although it was syntactically correct, did not meet the semantic constraints, where a dog had to be the agent of the verb bites. In the second sentence, a particular dog, Fido, likes an unnamed man. In the following example we ask whether Fido can bite an unnamed man:

```
?- utterance([fido, bites, the, man], X).
X = [action([biting(_12)]), agent([dog(fido)]), object([man(_17)])].
```

This parser may be extended in many interesting directions, for instance, by adding adjectives, adverbs, and prepositional phrases, or by allowing compound sentences. These additions must be both matched and constrained as they are merged into the sentence graph for the full sentence. Each dictionary item may also have multiple meanings that are only accepted as they meet the general requirements of the sentence. See the exercises for further examples.

15.10 Epilogue and References

In traditional computing languages such as FORTRAN and C, the logic for the problem's specification and the control for executing the solution algorithm are inextricably mixed together. A program in these languages is simply a sequence of things to be done to get an answer. This is the accepted notion of *applicative* or *procedural* languages. PROLOG, however, separates the logic or specification for a problem application from the execution or control of the use of that specification. In artificial intelligence programs, there are many reasons for this separation, as pointed out in Chapters 6, 7, and 8.

Needless to say, PROLOG has not yet achieved a state of computing nirvana! It is still possible, however, to show how logic programming, as represented by the PROLOG language, exhibits many of the benefits of a nonprocedural semantics.

We next present an example of the *declarative/nonprocedural* nature of PROLOG. Consider the predicate append:

```
append([ ], L, L).
append([X|T], L, [X|NL]) :- append(T, L, NL).
```

append is nonprocedural in that it defines a relationship between lists rather than a series of operations for joining two lists. Consequently, different queries will cause it to compute different aspects of this relationship. We can understand append by tracing its execution in joining two lists together. If the following call is made, the response is:

```
?- append([a, b, c], [d, e], Y).
Y = [a, b, c, d, e]
```

The execution of append is not tail recursive, in that the local variable values are accessed after the recursive call has succeeded. In this case, X is placed on the head of the list ([X | NL]) after the recursive call has finished. This requires that a record of each call be kept on the PROLOG stack. For purposes of reference in the following trace:

```
1. is append([ ], L, L).
2. is append([X|T], L, [X|NL]) :- append(T, L, NL).
```

```
?- append([a, b, c], [d, e], Y).
    try match 1, fail [a, b, c] ≠ [ ]
    match 2, X is a, T is [b, c], L is [d, e], call append([b, c], [d, e], NL)
      try match 1, fail [b, c] ≠ [ ]
      match 2, X is b, T is [c], L is [d, e], call append([c], [d, e], NL)
        try match 1, fail [c] ≠ [ ]
        match 2, X is c, T is [ ], L is [d, e], call append([ ], [d, e], NL)
          match 1, L is [d, e] (for BOTH parameters), yes
        yes, N is [d, e], [X|NL] is [c, d, e]
      yes, NL is [c, d, e], [X|NL] is [b, c, d, e]
    yes, NL is [b, c, d, e], [X|NL] is [a, b, c, d, e]
  Y = [a, b, c, d, e], yes
```

In most PROLOG algorithms, the parameters of the predicates seem to be intended as either "input" or "output"; most definitions assume that certain parameters would be bound in the call and others would be unbound. This need not be so. In fact, there is no commitment at all to parameters being input or output! PROLOG code is intended to be simply a set of specifications of what is true, a statement of the logic of the situation. Thus, append specifies the relationship between three lists, such that the third list is the catenation of the first onto the front of the second.

To demonstrate this fact we can give append a different set of goals:

```
?- append([a, b], [c], [a, b, c]).
yes
?- append([a], [c], [a, b, c]).
no
?- append(X, [b, c], [a, b, c]).
X = [a]
?- append(X, Y, [a, b, c]).
X = [ ]
Y = [a, b, c]
;
X = [a]
Y = [b, c]
;
X = [a, b]
Y = [c]
;
X = [a, b, c]
Y = [ ]
;
no
```

In the last query, PROLOG returns all the lists X and Y that, when appended together, give [a,b,c], four pairs of lists in all. As mentioned above, append gives a statement of the logic of a relationship that exists among three lists. What the interpreter produces depends on the query.

The notion of solving a problem based on a set of specifications for correct relationships in a domain area, coupled with the action of a theorem prover, is exciting and important. As seen in this chapter, it is an important tool in areas as diverse as natural language understanding, databases, compiler writing, and machine learning. How the PROLOG interpreter works cannot be properly understood without the concepts of resolution theorem proving, especially the Horn clause refutation process, which is presented in Section 13.2, resolution-based theorem proving, and Section 13.3, PROLOG as an instance of a resolution refutation system.

PROLOG is a general-purpose language, and we have ignored a great number of its important concepts and control mechanisms because of the space limitations of this book. We recommend that the interested reader pursue some of the many excellent texts available, such as *Programming in Prolog* (Clocksin and Mellish 2003), *Computing with Logic* (Maier and Warren 1988), *The Art of PROLOG* (Sterling and Shapiro 1986), *The Craft of PROLOG* (O'Keefe 1990), *Techniques of PROLOG Programming* (VanLe 1993), *Mastering PROLOG* (Lucas 1996), or *Advanced PROLOG: Techniques and Examples* (Ross 1989). *Knowledge Systems through PROLOG* (King 1991) and *Natural Language Processing in PROLOG* (Gazdar and Mellish 1989) examine the use of PROLOG in a number of important artificial intelligence applications.

We introduced PROLOG meta-predicates in Section 15.6 and demonstrated through the rest of the chapter how these predicates offered a powerful tool for reasoning about the problem-solving environment itself. For further research in the use of meta-predicates we recommend Bundy et al. (1979) and Bundy and Welham (1981). A more complete discussion of PROLOG types, as well as suggestions for building a type checker, is presented in *A Polymorphic Type System for Prolog* by Alan Mycroft and Richard O'Keefe (1984). The use of rule stacks and proof trees in the design of rule-based expert systems was suggested by Leon Sterling and Ehud Shapiro (1986).

Building AI representations such as semantic nets, frames, and objects is discussed in a number of books, especially *Knowledge Systems and Prolog* by Adrian Walker, Michael McCord, John Sowa, and Walter Wilson (1987) and *PROLOG: A Relational Language and Its Applications* by John Malpas (1987).

The PROLOG representation medium is so applicable for natural language understanding that many projects use PROLOG to model language. In fact, the first PROLOG interpreter was designed to analyze French using *metamorphosis grammars* (Colmerauer 1975). Fernando Pereira and David Warren (1980) created *definite clause grammars*. Veronica Dahl (1977), Dahl and McCord (1983), Michael McCord (1982, 1986), and John Sowa (Sowa 1984, Walker et al. 1987) have all contributed to this research. The two stochastic interpreters for sentence parsing presented in Section 15.9 were adopted from the work of Professor Mark Steedman of the University of Edinburgh. These parsers were implemented in the PROLOG syntax of this book by Monique Morin of the University of

New Mexico. The code for these parsers and the other examples in this and the following chapter may be obtained from the author's website http://www.cs.unm.edu/~luger/.

The intellectual roots of PROLOG reside in the theoretical concepts of using logic for problem specification. Expecially recommended are *Logic for Problem Solving* (Kowalski 1979*b*) and *Algorithm = logic + control* (Kowalski 1979*a*).

There is ongoing interest in logic programming environments other than PROLOG. These include parallel logic programming languages, Shapiro (1987). Nadathur and Tong (1999), in *Realizing Modularity in Lambda Prolog*, describe Lambda PROLOG, a higher-order logic programming language. *The Goedel Programming Language*, by Hill and Lloyd (1994), presents the Goedel language. Finally, Somogyi, Henderson, and Conway (1995) describe Mercury. Goedel and Mercury are two relatively new declarative logic programming environments.

15.11 Exercises

1. Create a relational database in PROLOG. Represent the data tuples as facts and the constraints on the data tuples as rules. Suitable examples might be from stock in a department store or records in a personnel office.

2. Write a PROLOG program to answer Wirth's "I am my own grandfather" problem (Chapter 2, Exercise 12).

3. Write the "member check" program in PROLOG. What happens when an item is not in the list? Query to the "member" specification to break a list into its component elements.

4. Design a PROLOG program unique(Bag, Set) that takes a Bag (a list that may contain duplicate elements) and returns a Set (no elements are repeated).

5. Write a PROLOG program to count the elements in a list (a list within the list counts as one element). Write a program to count the atoms in a list (count the elements within any sublist). Hint: several meta-predicates such as atom() can be helpful.

6. Write the PROLOG code for the farmer, wolf, goat, and cabbage problem, Section 15.3.
   a. Execute this code and draw a graph of the search space.
   b. Alter the rule ordering to produce alternative solution paths.
   c. Use the shell in the text to produce a breadth-first problem.
   d. Describe a heuristic that might be appropriate for this problem.
   e. Build the heuristic search solution.

7. Do a to e as in Exercise 6 for the missionary and cannibal problem:
   Three missionaries and three cannibals come to the bank of a river they wish to cross. There is a boat that will hold only two, and any of the group is able to row. If there are ever more missionaries than cannibals on any side of the river the cannibals will get converted. Devise a series of moves to get all the people across the river with no conversions.

8. Use your code to check alternative forms of the missionary and cannibal problem—for example, when there are four missionaries and four cannibals and the boat holds only two.

What if the boat can hold three? Try to generalize solutions for the whole class of missionary and cannibal problems.

9. Write PROLOG code to solve the full 8×8 knight's tour problem. Use the production system architecture proposed in this chapter and Chapter 6. Do tasks a to e in Exercise 6.

10. Do a to e as in Exercise 6 for the water jugs problem:
    There are two jugs, one holding 3 and the other 5 gallons of water. A number of things can be done with the jugs: they can be filled, emptied, and dumped one into the other either until the poured-into jug is full or until the poured-out-of jug is empty. Devise a sequence of actions that will produce 4 gallons of water in the larger jug. (Hint: use only integers.)

11. Take the **path** algorithm presented for the knight's tour problem in the text. Rewrite the path call in the recursive code to the following form:

    path(X, Y) :- path(X, W), move(W, Y).

    Examine the trace of this execution and describe what is happening.

12. Write a program to pass values up to the top level of a game tree or graph:

    a. Using MIN-MAX.
    b. Using alpha-beta pruning of the tree.
    c. Using both of these on the game of tic-tac-toe.

13. Write a PROLOG program to build the search process for the financial advisor program that was used in Chapters 2–5. Use the production system architecture. Add several more advisory rules to make the program more interesting.

14. Finish the code for the planner of Section 15.5. Add code for a situation that requires a new set of moves, such as adding a pyramid or sphere that could not be stacked on.

15. Design a breadth-first search planner for the planner of Section 15.5. Add heuristics to the search of your planning algorithm. Can you specify a heuristic that is admissible?

16. Create a triangle table-like structure to use with your planner. Use it to save, and generalize, where possible, successful move sequences.

17. Create the full set of ADT predicates for the **priority queue** in Section 15.2.

18. Create a type check that prevents the **append(nil, 6, 6)** anomaly.

19. Is the difference list catenate really a linear time append (Section 15.6)? Explain.

20. Create the "inventory supply" database of Section 15.6.2. Build type checks for a set of six useful queries on these data tuples.

21. Extend the definition of PROLOG in PROLOG (Section 15.7) to include **or, and**, and cut.

22. Fill out the rules used with the **exshell** cars example in the text. You might add new subsystems for the transmission or brakes.

23. Create a knowledge base in a new domain for **exshell**.

24. Currently, if **exshell** cannot solve a goal using the rule base, it fails. Extend **exshell** so if it cannot prove a goal using the rules, and if it is not askable, it will call that goal as a PROLOG query. Adding this option requires changes to both **solve** and **build_proof**.

25. **exshell** allows the user to respond to queries by entering a confidence in the query's truth, a why query, or a how query. Extend **respond** to allow the user to answer with **y** if the query is true, **n** if it is false. This corresponds to certainty factors of 100 and −100.

26. Take the conceptual graphs used to describe the "dogs world" of Section 7.2. Translate each of the graphs used into PROLOG notation. Design PROLOG rules for the **restrict, join,** and **simplify** operations. Hint: create a list of the propositions whose conjunction make up a graph; then the operations on the graphs are accomplished by manipulations of these lists.

27. Implement a frame system with inheritance that supports the definition of three kinds of slots: properties of a class that may be inherited by subclasses, properties that are inherited by instances of the class but not by subclasses, and properties of the class and its subclasses that are not inherited by instances (class properties). Discuss the benefits, uses, and problems with this distinction.

28. Implement a general to specific search of the version space using the feature vector representation of Section 10.4.1. We specialize feature vectors by replacing variables with constants; since this requires telling the algorithm of allowable values for each field of the feature vector, we must pass this in as an extra argument. The following definition of **run_general**, the top-level goal, illustrates the necessary initializations for the example used in the text: objects may be **small, medium** or **large**, their color may be **red, blue** or **green**, and their shape may be **ball, brick** or **cube**.

    ```
    run_general :-
    general_to_specific([[_, _, _]], [ ],
    [[small, medium, large], [red, blue, green], [ball, brick, cube]]).
    ```

29. Implement the domain theory for the float example in Chapter 10; run it with **prolog_ebg**.

30. Extend the definition of **ebg** so that after it constructs a new rule, it asserts it to the logic database where it may be used in future queries. Test the performance of the resulting system using a theory for a suitably rich domain. You might do this by constructing a theory for a domain of your choice, or extending the theory from the cup example to allow it to explain different types of cups such as Styrofoam cups, cups without handles, etc.

31. Chapter 16 presents a LISP implementation of the ID3 algorithm from Chapter 13. Using this implementation as a reference, implement ID3 in PROLOG. Do not think of this as simply translating the LISP code to PROLOG. The languages are different and, like different natural languages, require different idioms to say the same thing. Make your PROLOG follow what you feel is a lucid and pleasing PROLOG style.

32. Build in PROLOG the ATN parser of Section 14.2.4. Add **who** and **what** questions.

33. Write the PROLOG code for a subset of English grammar rules, as in the context-free and context-sensitive parsers found in Sections 15.9.2 and 15.9.5. Add:

    a. Adjectives and adverbs that can modify verbs and nouns, respectively.
    b. Prepositional phrases. (Can you do this with a recursive call?)
    c. Compound sentences (two sentences joined by a conjunction).

34. Extend the stochastic context-free parser of Section 15.9.3 to include appropriate probabilities for the new sentence structures built in Exercise 33. Explore the possibility of obtaining probabilities for these sentence structures from a treebank for natural language processing. Examples may be found on the www.

35. Add probabilities for more word pair relationships as demonstrated in the lexicalized context-free parser of Section 15.9.4.

36. Explore the possibility of obtaining the probabilistic bigram values for the noun–verb, verb–object, and other word pairs of Section 15.9.3 from an actual corpus linguistics. Several of these may be found on the www.

37. The simple natural language parsers presented in Section 15.9 will accept grammatically correct sentences that may not have a commonsense meaning, such as "the man bites the dog." These sentences may be eliminated from the grammar by augmenting the parser to include some notion of what is semantically plausible. Design a small "semantic network" in PROLOG (see comments in text) to allow you to reason about some aspect of the possible interpretations of the English grammar rules, such as when it is reasonable for the man to bite the dog.

35. Rework the semantic net parser of Section 14.3.2 to allow a richer representation of class hierarchies. Specifically, rewrite the definition of match_with_inheritance so that instead of enumerating the common specializations of two items, it computes this by searching a type hierarchy.

AN INTRODUCTION TO LISP

"The name of the song is called 'Haddocks' Eyes.'"

"Oh, that's the name of the song, is it?" Alice said, trying to feel interested.

"No, you don't understand," the Knight said, looking a little vexed. "That's what the name is called. The name really is 'The Aged Aged Man.'"

"Then I ought to have said 'That's what the song is called'?" Alice corrected herself.

"No, you oughtn't: that's quite another thing! The song is called 'Ways and Means': but that's only what it's called you know!"

"Well, what is the song, then?" said Alice, who was by this time completely bewildered.

"I was coming to that," the Knight said.

—LEWIS CARROLL, *Through the Looking Glass*

See simplicity in the complicated.

—LAO TZU

16.0 Introduction

For the 40-plus years of its existence, LISP has been an important language for artificial intelligence programming. Originally designed for symbolic computing, LISP has been extended and refined over its lifetime in direct response to the needs of AI applications. LISP is an *imperative* language: LISP programs describe *how* to perform an algorithm. This contrasts with *declarative* languages such as PROLOG, whose programs are assertions that define relationships and constraints in a problem domain. However, unlike traditional imperative languages, such as FORTRAN or C++, LISP is *functional*: its syntax and semantics are derived from the mathematical theory of recursive functions. The power of functional programming, combined with a rich set of high-level tools for building symbolic data structures such as predicates, frames, networks, and objects, is responsible for LISP's popularity in the AI community. LISP is widely used as a language for implementing AI tools and models, particularly in the research community, where its high-level functionality and rich development environment make it an ideal language for building and testing prototype systems.

In this chapter we introduce the syntax and semantics of Common LISP, with particular emphasis on the features of the language that make it useful for AI programming: the use of lists to create symbolic data structures, and the implementation of interpreters and search algorithms to manipulate these structures. Examples of LISP programs that we develop in this chapter include search engines, pattern matchers, theorem provers, rule-based expert system shells, semantic networks, algorithms for learning, and object-oriented simulations. It is not our goal to provide a complete introduction to LISP; a number of excellent texts (see the epilogue to this chapter) do this in far greater detail than our space allows. Instead, we focus on using LISP to implement the representation languages and algorithms of artificial intelligence programming.

16.1 LISP: A Brief Overview

16.1.1 Symbolic Expressions, the Syntactic Basis of LISP

The syntactic elements of the LISP programming language are *symbolic expressions*, also known as *s-expressions*. Both programs and data are represented as s-expressions: an s-expression may be either an *atom* or a *list*. LISP atoms are the basic syntactic units of the language and include both numbers and symbols. Symbolic atoms are composed of letters, numbers, and the following non-alphanumeric characters:

$$* - + / @ \$ \% \^{} \& \_ < > \sim .$$

Examples of LISP atoms include:

```
3.1416
100
×
hyphenated-name
*some-global*
nil
```

A list is a sequence of either atoms or other lists separated by blanks and enclosed in parentheses. Examples of lists include:

```
(1 2 3 4)
(tom mary john joyce)
(a (b c) (d (e f)))
( )
```

Note that lists may be elements of lists. This nesting may be arbitrarily deep and allows us to create symbol structures of any desired form and complexity. The empty list, "( )", plays a special role in the construction and manipulation of LISP data structures and is given the special name nil. nil is the only s-expression that is considered to be both an atom and a list. Lists are extremely flexible tools for constructing representational structures. For example, we can use lists to represent expressions in the predicate calculus:

```
(on block-1 table)
(likes bill X)
(and (likes george kate) (likes bill merry))
```

We use this syntax to represent predicate calculus expressions in the unification algorithm of this chapter. The next two examples suggest ways in which lists may be used to implement the data structures needed in a database application. Section 16.1.5 describes the implementation of a simple data retrieval system using these representations.

```
((2467 (lovelace ada) programmer) (3592 (babbage charles) computer-designer))
((key-1 value-1) (key-2 value-2) (key-3 value-3))
```

An important feature of LISP is its use of LISP syntax to represent programs as well as data. For example, the lists,

```
(* 7 9)
(− (+ 3 4) 7)
```

may be interpreted as arithmetic expressions in a prefix notation. This is exactly how LISP treats these expressions, with (* 7 9) representing the product of 7 and 9. When LISP is invoked on the computer, the user enters an interactive dialogue with the LISP interpreter. The interpreter prints a prompt (in the examples in this text: >), reads the user input, attempts to evaluate that input, and, if successful, prints the result. For example:

```
> (* 7 9)
63
>
```

Here, the user enters (* 7 9) and the LISP interpreter responds with 63, i.e., the *value* associated with that expression. LISP then prints another prompt and waits for more user input. This cycle is known as the *read-eval-print loop* and is the heart of the LISP interpreter.

When given a list, the LISP evaluator attempts to interpret the first element of the list as the name of a function and the remaining elements as its arguments. Thus, the s-expression (f x y) is equivalent to the more traditional mathematical function notation f(x,y). The value printed by LISP is the result of *applying* the function to its arguments. LISP expressions that may be meaningfully evaluated are called *forms*. If the user enters an expression that may not be correctly evaluated, LISP prints an error message and allows the user to trace and correct the problem. A sample LISP session appears below:

```
> (+ 14 5)
19
> (+ 1 2 3 4)
10
> (− (+ 3 4) 7)
0
> (* (+ 2 5) (− 7 (/ 21 7)))
28
> (= (+ 2 3) 5)
t
> (> (* 5 6) (+ 4 5))
t
> (a b c)
Error: invalid function: a
```

Several of the examples above have arguments that are themselves lists, for example (− (+ 3 4) 7). This indicates the composition of functions, in this case "subtract 7 from the *result* of adding 3 to 4". The word "result" is emphasized here to indicate that the function—is not passed the s-expression "(+ 3 4)" as an argument but rather the result of *evaluating* that expression.

In evaluating a function, LISP first evaluates its arguments and then applies the function indicated by the first element of the expression to the results of these evaluations. If the arguments are themselves function expressions, LISP applies this rule recursively to their evaluation. Thus, LISP allows nested function calls of arbitrary depth. It is important to remember that, by default, LISP evaluates everything. LISP uses the convention that numbers always evaluate to themselves. If, for example, 5 is typed into the LISP interpreter, LISP will respond with 5. Symbols, such as x, may have a value *bound* to them. If a symbol is bound, the binding is returned when the symbol is evaluated (one way in which symbols become bound is in a function call; see Section 16.1.2). If a symbol is unbound, it is an error to evaluate that symbol.

For example, in evaluating the expression (+ (* 2 3) (* 3 5)), LISP first evaluates the arguments, (* 2 3) and (* 3 5). In evaluating (* 2 3), LISP evaluates the arguments 2 and 3, which return their respective arithmetic values; these values are multiplied to yield 6. Similarly, (* 3 5) evaluates to 15. These results are then passed to the top-level addition, which is evaluated, returning 21. A diagram of this evaluation appears in Figure 16.1.

In addition to arithmetic operations, LISP includes a large number of functions that operate on lists. These include functions to construct and combine lists, to access elements of lists, and to test various properties. For example, list takes any number of arguments and constructs a list of those elements. nth takes a number and a list as arguments and returns the indicated element of the list. By convention, nth begins counting with 0. Examples of these and other list manipulation functions include:

```
> (list 1 2 3 4 5)
(1 2 3 4 5)
> (nth 0 '(a b c d))
a
```

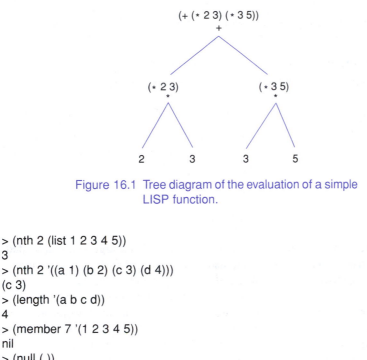

Figure 16.1 Tree diagram of the evaluation of a simple
LISP function.

```
> (nth 2 (list 1 2 3 4 5))
3
> (nth 2 '((a 1) (b 2) (c 3) (d 4)))
(c 3)
> (length '(a b c d))
4
> (member 7 '(1 2 3 4 5))
nil
> (null ( ))
t
```

We discuss list-handling functions in greater detail in Section 16.1.5. The concepts of this section are summarized in the following definition.

DEFINITION

S-EXPRESSION

An s-expression is defined recursively:

1. An atom is an s-expression.
2. If $s_1, s_2, ..., s_n$ are s-expressions,
    then so is the list $(s_1 \, s_2 \, ... \, s_n)$.

A list is a nonatomic s-expression.
A form is an s-expression that is intended to be evaluated. If it is a list, the first element is treated as the function name and the subsequent elements are evaluated to obtain the function arguments.

In evaluating an s-expression:

If the s-expression is a number, return the value of the number.

> If the s-expression is an atomic symbol, return the value bound to that symbol; if it is not bound it is an error.

> If the s-expression is a list, evaluate the second through the last arguments and apply the function indicated by the first argument to the results.

LISP represents both programs and data as s-expressions. Not only does this simplify the syntax of the language but also, when combined with the ability to control the evaluation of s-expressions, it makes it easy to write programs that treat other LISP programs as data. This simplifies the implementation of interpreters in LISP.

16.1.2 Control of LISP Evaluation: quote and eval

In the previous section, several of the examples included list arguments preceded by a single quotation mark: '. The ', which can also be represented by the function quote, is a special function which does not evaluate its argument but prevents evaluation, often because its argument is to be treated as data rather than an evaluable form.

When evaluating an s-expression, LISP will first try to evaluate all of its arguments. If the interpreter is given the expression (nth 0 (a b c d)), it will first try to evaluate the argument (a b c d). This attempted evaluation will result in an error, because a, the first element of this s-expression, does not represent any known LISP function. To prevent this, LISP provides the user with the built-in function quote. quote takes one argument and returns that argument without evaluating it. For example:

```
> (quote (a b c))
(a b c)
> (quote (+ 1 3))
(+ 1 3)
```

Because quote is used so often, LISP allows it to be abbreviated by a single quotation mark. Thus, the preceding examples could be written:

```
> '(a b c)
(a b c)
> '(+ 1 3)
(+ 1 3)
```

In general, quote is used to prevent the evaluation of arguments to a function when these arguments are intended to be treated as data rather than evaluable forms. In the earlier examples of simple arithmetic, quote was not needed, because numbers always evaluate to themselves. Consider the effect of quote in the following calls to the list function:

```
> (list (+ 1 2) (+ 3 4))
(3 7)
```

```
> (list '(+ 1 2) '(+ 3 4))
((+ 1 2) (+ 3 4))
```

In the first example, the arguments are not quoted; they are therefore evaluated and passed to list according to the default evaluation scheme. In the second example, quote prevents this evaluation, with the s-expressions themselves being passed as arguments to list. Even though (+ 1 2) is a meaningful LISP form, quote prevents its evaluation. The ability to prevent evaluation of programs and manipulate them as data is an important feature of LISP.

As a complement to quote, LISP also provides a function, eval, that allows the programmer to evaluate an s-expression at will. eval takes one s-expression as an argument: this argument is evaluated as is usual for arguments to functions; however, the result is then evaluated *again* and this final result is returned as the value of the eval expression. Examples of the behavior of eval and quote include:

```
> (quote (+ 2 3))
(+ 2 3)
> (eval (quote (+ 2 3)))                    ; eval undoes the effect of quote
5
> (list '* 2 5)                             ; this constructs an evaluable s-expression
(* 2 5)
> (eval (list '* 2 5))                      ; this constructs and evaluates it
10
```

The eval function is precisely what is used in the ordinary evaluation of s-expressions. By making quote and eval available to the programmer, LISP greatly simplifies the development of *meta-interpreters*: variations on the standard LISP interpreter that define alternative or extended behaviors for the LISP language. This important programming methodology is illustrated in the "infix-interpreter" of Section 16.7 and the design of an expert system shell in Section 16.10.

16.1.3 Programming in LISP: Creating New Functions

Common LISP includes a large number of built-in functions, including:

A full range of arithmetic functions, supporting integer, rational, real and complex arithmetic.

A variety of looping and program control functions.

List manipulation and other data structuring functions.

Input/output functions.

Forms for the control of function evaluation.

Functions for the control of the environment and operating system.

LISP includes too many functions to list in this chapter; for a more detailed discussion, consult a specialized LISP text or the manual for your particular implementation.

In LISP, we program by defining new functions, constructing programs from this already rich repertoire of built-in functions. These new functions are defined using defun, which is short for define function. Once a function is defined it may be used in the same fashion as functions that are built into the language.

Suppose, for example, the user would like to define a function called square that takes a single argument and returns the square of that argument. square may be created by having LISP evaluate the following expression:

```
(defun square (x)
    (* x x))
```

The first argument to defun is the name of the function being defined; the second is a list of the formal parameters for that function, which must all be symbolic atoms; the remaining arguments are zero or more s-expressions, which constitute the body of the new function, the LISP code that actually defines its behavior. Unlike most LISP functions, defun does not evaluate its arguments; instead, it uses them as specifications to create a new function. As with all LISP functions, however, defun returns a value, although the value returned is simply the name of the new function.

The important result of evaluating a defun is the side effect of creating a new function and adding it to the LISP environment. In the above example, square is defined as a function that takes one argument and returns the result of multiplying that argument by itself. Once a function is defined, it must be called with the same number of arguments, or "actual parameters," as there are formal parameters specified in the defun. When a function is called, the actual parameters are bound to the formal parameters. The body of the function is then evaluated with these bindings. For example, the call (square 5) causes 5 to be bound to the formal parameter x in the body of the definition. When the body (* x x) is evaluated, LISP first evaluates the arguments to the function. Because x is bound to 5 by the call, this leads to the evaluation of (* 5 5).

More concisely, the syntax of a defun expression is:

```
(defun <function name> (<formal parameters>) <function body>)
```

In this definition, descriptions of the elements of a form are enclosed in angle brackets: < >. We use this notational convention throughout this text to define LISP forms. Note that the formal parameters in a defun are enclosed in a list.

A newly defined function may be used just like any built-in function. Suppose, for example, that we need a function to compute the length of the hypotenuse of a right triangle given the lengths of the other two sides. This function may be defined according to the Pythagorean theorem, using the previously defined square function along with the built-in function sqrt. We have added a number of comments to this sample code. LISP supports "end of line comments": it ignores all text from the first ";" to the end of the same line.

```
(defun hypotenuse (x y)                    ; the length of the hypotenuse is
    (sqrt (+ (square x)                    ; the square root of the sum of
            (square y))))                  ; the squares of the other sides.
```

This example is typical in that most LISP programs are built up of relatively small functions, each performing a single well-defined task. Once defined, these functions are used to implement higher-level functions until the desired "top-level" behavior has been defined.

16.1.4 Program Control in LISP: Conditionals and Predicates

LISP branching is also based on function evaluation: control functions perform tests and, depending on the results, selectively evaluate alternative forms. Consider, for example, the following definition of the absolute value function (note that LISP has a built-in function, abs, that computes absolute value):

```
(defun absolute-value (x)
    (cond ((< x 0) (− x))                  ; if x is less than 0, return −x
          ((>= x 0) x)))                   ; otherwise, return x unchanged
```

This example uses the function, cond, to implement a conditional branch. cond takes as arguments a number of *condition–action pairs*:

```
(cond (< condition1 >  < action1 >)
      (< condition2 > < action2 >)
        . . .
      (< conditionn > < actionn >))
```

Conditions and actions may be arbitrary s-expressions, and each pair is enclosed in parentheses. Like defun, cond does not evaluate all of its arguments. Instead, it evaluates the conditions in order until one of them returns a non-nil value. When this occurs, it evaluates the associated action and returns this result as the value of the cond expression. None of the other actions and none of the subsequent conditions are evaluated. If all of the conditions evaluate to nil, cond returns nil.

An alternative definition of absolute-value is:

```
(defun absolute-value (x)
    (cond  ((< x 0)  (− x))                ; if x is less than 0, return −x
           (t   x)))                       ; otherwise, return x unchanged
```

This version notes that the second condition, (>= x 0), is always true if the first is false. The "t" atom in the final condition of the cond statement is a LISP atom that roughly corresponds to "true." By convention, t always evaluates to itself; this causes the last action to be evaluated if all preceding conditions return nil. This construct is extremely useful, as it provides a way of giving a cond statement a default action that is evaluated if and only if all preceding conditions fail.

Although any evaluable s-expressions may be used as the conditions of a cond, generally these are a particular kind of LISP function called a *predicate*. A predicate is simply a function that returns a value of either true or false depending on whether or not its arguments possess some property. The most obvious examples of predicates are the relational operators typically used in arithmetic such as =, >, and >=. Here are some examples of arithmetic predicates in LISP:

```
> (= 9 (+ 4 5))
t
> (>= 17 4)
t
> (< 8 (+ 4 2))
nil
> (oddp 3)                          ; oddp tests whether its argument is odd or not
t
> (minusp 6)                        ; minusp tests whether its argument is less than 0
nil
> (numberp 17)                      ; numberp tests whether its argument is numeric
t
> (numberp nil)
nil
> (zerop 0)                         ; zerop is true if its argument is 0, nil otherwise
t
> (plusp 10)                        ; plusp is true if its argument is strictly greater than 0
t
> (plusp -2)
nil
```

Note that the predicates in the above examples do not return "true" or "false" but rather t or nil. LISP is defined so that a predicate may return nil to indicate "false" and anything other than nil (not necessarily t) to indicate "true." An example of a function that uses this feature is the member predicate. member takes two arguments, the second of which must be a list. If the first argument is a member of the second, member returns the suffix of the second argument, which contains the first argument as its initial element; if it is not, member returns nil. For example:

```
> (member 3 '(1 2 3 4 5))
(3 4 5)
```

One rationale for this convention is that it allows a predicate to return a value that, in the "true" case, may be of use in further processing. It also allows any LISP function to be used as a condition in a cond form.

As an alternative to cond, the if form takes three arguments. The first is a test. If evaluates the test; if it returns a non-nil value, the if form evaluates its second argument and returns the result, otherwise it returns the result of evaluating the third argument. In cases involving a two-way branch, the if construct generally provides cleaner, more readable code than cond. For example, absolute-value could be defined using the if form:

```
(defun absolute-value (x)
  (if (< x 0) (- x)  x))
```

In addition to if and cond, LISP offers a wide selection of alternative control constructs, including iterative constructs such as do and while loops. Although these functions provide LISP programmers with a wide range of control structures that fit almost any situation and programming style, we will not discuss them in this section; the reader is referred to a more specialized LISP text for this information.

One of the more interesting program control techniques in LISP involves the use of the logical connectives and, or, and not. not takes one argument and returns t if its argument is nil and nil otherwise. Both and and or may take any number of arguments and behave as you would expect from the definitions of the corresponding logical operators. It is important to note, however, that and and or are based on *conditional evaluation*.

In evaluating an and form, LISP evaluates its arguments in left-to-right order, stopping when any one of the arguments evaluates to nil or the last argument has been evaluated. Upon completion, the and form returns the value of the last argument evaluated. It therefore returns non-nil only if all its arguments return non-nil. Similarly, the or form evaluates its arguments only until a non-nil value is encountered, returning this value as a result. Both functions may leave some of their arguments unevaluated, as may be seen by the behavior of the print statements in the following example. In addition to printing its argument, in some LISP environments print returns a value of nil on completion.

```
> (and (oddp 2) (print "second statement was evaluated"))
nil
> (and (oddp 3) (print "second statement was evaluated"))
second statement was evaluated
> (or (oddp 3) (print "second statement was evaluated"))
t
> (or (oddp 2) (print "second statement was evaluated"))
second statement was evaluated
```

Because (oddp 2) evaluates to nil in the first expressions, the and simply returns nil without evaluating the print form. In the second expression, however, (oddp 3) evaluates to t and the and form then evaluates the print. A similar analysis may be applied to the or examples. It is important to be aware of this behavior, particularly if some of the arguments are forms whose evaluations have side effects, such as the print function. The conditional evaluation of logical connectives makes them useful in controlling the flow of execution of LISP programs. For example, an or form may be used to try alternative solutions to a problem, evaluating them in order until one of them returns a non-nil result.

16.1.5   Functions, Lists, and Symbolic Computing

Although the preceding sections introduced LISP syntax and demonstrated a few useful LISP functions, they did so in the context of simple arithmetic examples. The real power of LISP is in symbolic computing and is based on the use of lists to construct arbitrarily complex data structures of symbolic and numeric atoms, along with the forms needed for manipulating them. We illustrate the ease with which LISP handles symbolic data structures, as well as the naturalness of data abstraction techniques in LISP, with a simple database example. Our database application requires the manipulation of employee records containing name, salary, and employee number fields.

These records are represented as lists, with the name, salary, and number fields as the first, second, and third elements of a list. Using nth, it is possible to define access functions for the various fields of a data record. For example:

```
(defun name-field (record)
    (nth 0 record))
```

will have the behavior:

```
> (name-field '((Ada Lovelace) 45000.00 38519))
(Ada Lovelace)
```

Similarly, the functions salary-field and number-field may be defined to access the appropriate fields of a data record. Because a name is itself a list containing two elements, a first name and a last name, it is useful to define functions that take a name as argument and return either the first or last name as a result.

```
(defun first-name (name)
    (nth 0 name))
```

will have the behavior:

```
> (first-name (name-field '((Ada Lovelace) 45000.00 338519)))
Ada
```

In addition to accessing individual fields of a data record, it is also necessary to implement functions to create and modify data records. These are defined using the built-in LISP function: list. list takes any number of arguments, evaluates them, and returns a list containing those values as its elements. For example:

```
> (list 1 2 3 4)
(1 2 3 4)
> (list '(Ada Lovelace) 45000.00 338519)
((Ada Lovelace) 45000.00 338519)
```

As the second of these examples suggests, list may be used to define a constructor for records in the database:

```
(defun build-record (name salary emp-number)
    (list name salary emp-number))
```

will have the behavior:

```
> (build-record '(Alan Turing) 50000.00 135772)
((Alan Turing) 50000.00 135772)
```

Now, using build-record and the access functions, we may construct functions that return a modified copy of a record. For example replace-salary will behave:

```
(defun replace-salary-field (record new-salary)
(build-record (name-field record)
    new-salary
    (number-field record)))
> (replace-salary-field '((Ada Lovelace) 45000.00 338519) 50000.00)
((Ada Lovelace) 50000.00 338519)
```

Note that this function does not actually update the record itself but produces a modified copy of the record. This updated version may be saved by binding it to a global variable using setf (Section 16.1.8). Although LISP provides forms that allow a particular element in a list to be modified in the original structure (i.e. without making a copy), good LISP programming style generally avoids their use, and they are not covered in this text. For LISP applications involving all but extremely large structures, modifications are generally done by creating a new copy of the structure.

In the above examples, we created an abstract data type for employee records. The various access and update functions defined in this section implement a specialized language appropriate to the meaning of the records, freeing the programmer from concerns about the actual list structures being used to implement the records. This simplifies the development of higher-level code, as well as making that code much easier to maintain and understand.

Generally, AI programs manipulate large amounts of varied knowledge about problem domains. The data structures used to represent this knowledge, such as objects and semantic networks, are complex, and humans generally find it easier to relate to this knowledge in terms of its meaning rather than the particular syntax of its internal representation. Therefore, data abstraction techniques, always good computer science, are essential tools for the AI programmer. Because of the ease with which LISP supports the definition of new functions, it is an ideal language for data abstraction.

16.1.6 Lists as Recursive Structures

In the previous section, we used nth and list to implement access functions for records in a simple "employee" database. Because all employee records were of a determinate length (three elements), these two functions were sufficient to access the fields of records. However, these functions are not adequate for performing operations on lists of unknown length, such as searching through an unspecified number of employee records. To do this, we must be able to scan a list iteratively or recursively, terminating when certain conditions are met (e.g., the desired record is found) or the list is exhausted. In this section we introduce list operations, along with the use of recursion to create list-processing functions.

The basic functions for accessing the components of lists are car and cdr. car takes a single argument, which must be a list, and returns the first element of that list. cdr also takes a single argument, which must be a list, and returns that list with its first argument removed. For example:

```
> (car '(a b c))                                    ; note that the list is quoted
a
> (cdr '(a b c))
(b c)
> (car '((a b) (c d))); the first element of a list may be a list
(a b)
> (cdr '((a b) (c d)))
((c d))
> (car (cdr '(a b c d)))
b
```

The way in which car and cdr operate suggests a recursive approach to manipulating list structures. To perform an operation on each of the elements of a list:

1. If the list is empty, quit.

2. Otherwise, operate on the element and recurse on the remainder of the list.

Using this scheme, we can define a number of useful list-handling functions. For example, Common LISP includes the predicates member, which determines whether one s-expression is a member of a list, and length, which determines the length of a list. We define our own versions of these functions: my-member takes two arguments, an arbitrary s-expression and a list, my-list. It returns nil if the s-expression is not a member of the my-list; otherwise it returns the list containing the s-expression as its first element:

```
(defun my-member (element my-list)
     (cond ((null my-list) nil)                      ; element not in list
           ((equal element (car my-list)) my-list)    ; element found
           (t (my-member element (cdr my-list)))))    ; recursive step
```

my-member has the behavior:

```
> (my-member 4 '(1 2 3 4 5 6))
(4 5 6)
> (my-member 5 '(a b c d))
nil
```

Similarly, we may define our own versions of length and nth:

```
(defun my-length (my-list)
     (cond ((null my-list) 0)
           (t (+ (my-length (cdr my-list)) 1))))
```

```
(defun my-nth (n my-list)
    (cond ((zerop n) (car my-list))              ; zerop tests if its argument is zero
        (t (my-nth (− n 1) (cdr my-list)))))
```

It is interesting to note that these examples, though presented here to illustrate the use of car and cdr, reflect the historical development of LISP. Early versions of the language did not include as many built-in functions as Common LISP does; programmers defined their own functions for checking list membership, length, etc. Over time, the most generally useful of these functions have been incorporated into the language standard. As an easily extensible language, Common LISP makes it easy for programmers to create and use their own library of reusable functions.

In addition to the functions car and cdr, LISP provides a number of functions for constructing lists. One of these, list, which takes as arguments any number of s-expressions, evaluates them, and returns a list of the results, was introduced in Section 16.1.1. A more primitive list constructor is the function cons, that takes two s-expressions as arguments, evaluates them, and returns a list whose car is the value of the first argument and whose cdr is the value of the second:

```
> (cons 1 '(2 3 4))
(1 2 3 4)
> (cons '(a b) '(c d e))
((a b) c d e)
```

cons bears an inverse relationship to car and cdr in that the car of the value returned by a cons form is always the first argument to the cons, and the cdr of the value returned by a cons form is always the second argument to that form:

```
> (car (cons 1 '(2 3 4)))
1
> (cdr (cons 1 '(2 3 4)))
(2 3 4)
```

An example of the use of cons is seen in the definition of the function filter-negatives, which takes a list of numbers as an argument and returns that list with any negative numbers removed. filter-negatives recursively examines each element of the list; if the first element is negative, it is discarded and the function returns the result of filtering the negative numbers from the cdr of the list. If the first element of the list is positive, it is "consed" onto the result of filtering negatives from the rest of the list:

```
(defun filter-negatives (number-list)
    (cond ((null number-list) nil)                          ; termination condition
        ((plusp (car number-list)) (cons (car number-list)
                                    (filter-negatives (cdr number-list))))
        (t (filter-negatives (cdr number-list)))))
```

This function behaves:

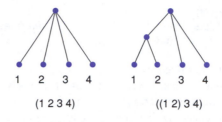

Figure 16.2 Mapping lists onto trees, showing structural differences.

```
> (filter-negatives '(1 −1 2 −2 3 −4))
(1 2 3)
```

This example is typical of the way cons is often used in recursive functions on lists. car and cdr tear lists apart and "drive" the recursion; cons selectively constructs the result as the recursion "unwinds." Another example of this use of cons is in redefining the built-in function append:

```
(defun my-append (list1 list2)
     (cond ((null list1) list2)
            (t (cons (car list1) (my-append (cdr list1) list2)))))
```

which yields the behavior:

```
> (my-append '(1 2 3) '(4 5 6))
(1 2 3 4 5 6)
```

Note that the same recursive scheme is used in the definitions of my-append, my-length, and my-member. Each definition uses the car function to remove an element from the list, allowing a recursive call on the shortened list; the recursion "bottoms out" on the empty list. As the recursion unwinds, the cons function reassembles the solution. This particular scheme is known as *cdr recursion*, because it uses the cdr function to linearly scan the elements of a list.

16.1.7 Nested Lists, Structure, and car/cdr Recursion

Although both cons and append may be used to combine smaller lists into a single list, it is important to note the difference between these two functions. If cons is called with two lists as arguments, it makes the first of these a new first element of the second list, whereas append returns a list whose elements are the elements of the two arguments:

```
> (cons '(1 2) '(3 4))
((1 2) 3 4)
> (append '(1 2) '(3 4))
(1 2 3 4)
```

The lists (1 2 3 4) and ((1 2) 3 4) have fundamentally different structures. This difference may be noted graphically by exploiting the isomorphism between lists and trees. The simplest way to map lists onto trees is to create an unlabeled node for each list, with descendants equal to the elements of that list. This rule is applied recursively to the elements of the list that are themselves lists; elements that are atoms are mapped onto leaf nodes of the tree. Thus, the two lists mentioned above generate the different tree structures illustrated in Figure 16.2.

This example illustrates the representational power of lists, particularly as a means of representing any tree structure such as a search tree or a parse tree (Figure 16.1). In addition, nested lists provide a way of hierarchically structuring complex data. In the employee records example of Section 16.1.4, the name field was itself a list consisting of a first name and a last name. This list could be treated as a single entity or its individual components could be accessed.

The simple cdr-recursive scheme discussed in the previous section is not sufficient to implement all manipulations on nested lists, because it does not distinguish between items that are lists and those that are simple atoms. Suppose, for example, that the length function defined in Section 16.1.6 is applied to a nested list structure:

```
> (length '((1 2) 3 (1 (4 (5)))))
3
```

In the above example, length returns 3 because the list has 3 elements, (1 2), 3, and (1 (4 (5))). This is, of course, the correct and desired behavior for a length function.

On the other hand, if we want the function to count the number of *atoms* in the list, we need a different recursive scheme, one that, in addition to scanning along the elements of the list, "opens up" non-atomic list elements and recursively applies itself to the task of counting their atoms. We define this function, called count-atoms, which behaves:

```
(defun count-atoms (my-list)
    (cond ((null my-list) 0)
          ((atom my-list) 1)
          (t (+ (count-atoms (car my-list))          ; open up an element
                (count-atoms (cdr my-list))))))       ; scan down the list
> (count-atoms '((1 2) 3 (((4 5 (6)))))
6
```

The above definition is an example of car-cdr recursion. Instead of just recurring on the cdr of the list, count-atoms also recurs on the car of its argument, with the + function combining the two components into an answer. Recursion halts when it encounters an atom or empty list. One way of thinking of this scheme is that it adds a second dimension to simple cdr recursion, that of "going down into" each of the list elements. Compare the diagrams of calls to length and count-atoms in Figure 16.3. Note the similarity of car-cdr recursion and the recursive definition of s-expressions given in Section 16.1.1.

Another example of the use of car-cdr recursion is in the definition of the function flatten. flatten takes as argument a list of arbitrary structure and returns a list that consists of the same atoms in the same order but with all the atoms at the same level. Note the

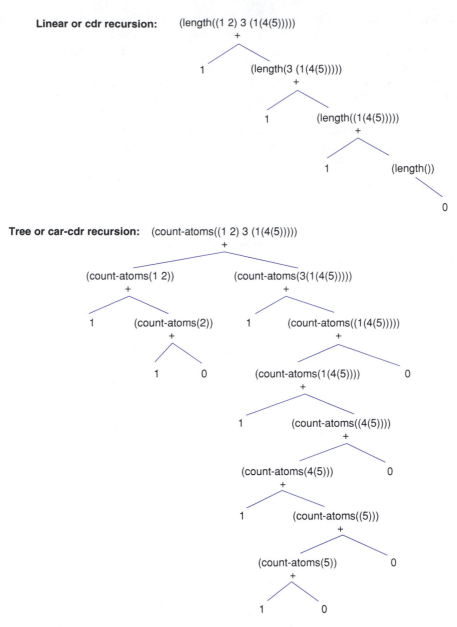

Figure 16.3 Diagrams of linear and tree recursive executions.

similarity between the definition of flatten and that of count-atoms: both use car-cdr recursion to tear apart lists and drive the recursion, both terminate when the argument is either null or atomic, and both use a second function (append or +) to construct an answer from the results of the recursive calls.

```
(defun flatten (lst)
    (cond ((null lst) nil)
          ((atom lst) (list lst))
          (t (append (flatten (car lst))(flatten (cdr lst))))))
```

Examples of the behavior of flatten include:

```
> (flatten '(a (b c) (((d) e f))))
(a b c d e f)
> (flatten '(a b c))                                    ; this list is already flattened
(a b c)
> (flatten '(1 (2 3) (4 (5 6) 7)))
(1 2 3 4 5 6 7)
```

car-cdr recursion is the basis of our implementation of unification in Section 16.6.

16.1.8 Binding Variables Using set

LISP is based on the theory of recursive functions; early LISP was the first example of a functional or *applicative* programming language. An important aspect of purely functional languages is the lack of any side effects as a result of function execution. This means that the value returned by a function call depends only on the function definition and the value of the parameters in the call. Although LISP is based on mathematical functions, it is possible to define LISP forms that violate this property. Consider the following LISP interaction:

```
> (f 4)
5
> (f 4)
6
> (f 4)
7
```

Note that f does not behave as a true function in that its output is not determined solely by its actual parameter: each time it is called with 4, it returns a different value. Execution of the function creates a side effect that influences the behavior of future calls. f is implemented using a LISP built-in function called set:

```
(defun f (x)
    (set 'inc (+ inc 1))
    (+ x inc))
```

set takes two arguments. The first must evaluate to a symbol; the second may be an arbitrary s-expression. set evaluates the second argument and assigns this value to the symbol defined by the first argument. In the above example, if inc is first set to 0 by the call (set 'inc 0), each subsequent evaluation will increment its parameter by one.

set requires that its first argument evaluate to a symbol. In many cases, the first argument is simply a quoted symbol. Because this is done so often, LISP provides an alternative form, setq, that does not evaluate its first argument. Instead, setq requires that the first argument be a symbol. For example, the following forms are equivalent:

```
> (set 'x 0)
0
> (setq x 0)
0
```

Although this use of set makes it possible to create LISP objects that are not pure functions in the mathematical sense, the ability to bind a value to a variable in the global environment is a useful feature. Many programming tasks are most naturally implemented using this ability to define objects whose state persists across function calls. The classic example of this is the "seed" in a random number generator: each call to the function changes and saves the value of the seed. Similarly, it would be natural for a database program (such as was described in Section 16.1.3) to store the database by binding it to a variable in the global environment.

So far, we have seen two ways of giving a value to a symbol: explicitly, by assignment using set or setq, or implicitly, when a function call binds the calling parameters to the formal parameters in the definition. In the examples seen so far, all variables in a function body were either *bound* or *free*. A bound variable is one that appears as a formal parameter in the definition of the function, while a free variable is one that appears in the body of the function but is not a formal parameter. When a function is called, any bindings that a bound variable may have in the global environment are saved and the variable is rebound to the calling parameter. After the function has completed execution, the original bindings are restored. Thus, setting the value of a bound variable inside a function body has no effect on the global bindings of that variable, as seen in the LISP interaction:

```
> (defun foo (x)
    (setq x (+ x 1))                    ; increment bound variable x
    x)                                  ; return its value
foo
> (setq y 1)
1
> (foo y)
2
> y                                     ; note that value of y is unchanged
1
```

In the example that began this section, x was bound in the function f, whereas inc was free in that function. As we demonstrated in the example, free variables in a function definition are the primary source of side effects in functions.

An interesting alternative to set and setq is the generalized assignment function, setf. Instead of assigning a value to a symbol, setf evaluates its first argument to obtain a memory location and places the value of the second argument in that location. When binding a value to a symbol, setf behaves like setq:

```
> (setq x 0)
0
> (setf x 0)
0
```

However, because we may call setf with any form that corresponds to a memory location, it allows a more general semantics. For example, if we make the first argument to setf a call to the car function, setf will replace the first element of that list. If the first argument to setf is a call to the cdr function, setf will replace the tail of that list. For example:

```
> (setf x '(a b c))                          ; x is bound to a list
(a b c)
> x                                          ; the value of x is a list
(a b c)
> (setf (car x) 1)              ; the car of x corresponds to a location in memory
1
> x                            ; note that setf changed the value of the car of x
(1 b c)
> (setf (cdr x) '(2 3))
(2 3)
> x                                          ; note that x now has a new tail
(1 2 3)
```

We may call setf with most LISP forms that correspond to a memory location; these include symbols and functions such as car, cdr, and nth. Thus, setf allows the program designer great flexibility in creating, manipulating, and even replacing components of LISP data structures.

16.1.9 Defining Local Variables Using let

let is another useful function for explicitly controlling the binding of variables. let allows the creation of local variables. As an example of the use of let, consider a function to compute the roots of a quadratic equation. The function quad-roots will take as arguments the three parameters a, b, and c of the equation $ax^2 + bx + c = 0$ and return a list of the two roots of the equation. These roots will be calculated from the formula

$$x = \frac{-b \pm \sqrt{b^2 - 4ac}}{2a}$$

For example:

```
> (quad-roots 1 2 1)
(−1.0 −1.0)
> (quad-roots 1 6 8)
(−2.0 −4.0)
```

In computing quad-roots, the value of

$$\sqrt{b^2 - 4ac}$$

is used twice. For reasons of efficiency, as well as elegance, we should compute this value only once, saving it in a variable for use in computing the two roots. Based on this idea, an initial implementation of quad-roots might be:

```
(defun quad-roots-1 (a b c)
    (setq temp (sqrt (− (* b b) (* 4 a c))))
        (list (/ (+ (− b) temp) (* 2 a))
            (/ (− (− b) temp) (* 2 a))))
```

Note that the above implementation assumes that the equation does not have imaginary roots, as attempting to take the square root of a negative number would cause the sqrt function to halt with an error condition. Modifying the code to handle this case is straightforward and not relevant to this discussion.

Although, with this exception, the code is correct, evaluation of the function body will have the side effect of setting the value of temp in the global environment:

```
> (quad-roots-1 1 2 1)
(−1.0 −1.0)
> temp
0.0
```

It is much more desirable to make temp local to the function quad-roots, thereby eliminating this side effect. This can be done through the use of a let block. A let expression has the syntax:

```
(let (<local-variables>) <expressions>)
```

where the elements of (<local-variables>) are either symbolic atoms or pairs of the form:

```
(<symbol> <expression>)
```

When a let form (or block as it is usually called) is evaluated, it establishes a local environment consisting of all of the symbols in (<local-variables>). If a symbol is the first element of a pair, the second element is evaluated and the symbol is bound to this result; symbols that are not included in pairs are bound to nil. If any of these symbols are already bound in the global environment, these global bindings are saved and restored when the let block terminates.

After these local bindings are established, the <expressions> are evaluated in order within this environment. When the let statement terminates, it returns the value of the last expression evaluated within the block.

The behavior of the let block is illustrated by the following example:

```
> (setq a 0)
0
> (let ((a 3) b)
      (setq b 4)
      (+ a b))
7
> a
0
> b
ERROR – b is not bound at top level.
```

In this example, before the let block is executed, a is bound to 0 and b is unbound at the top-level environment. When the let is evaluated, a is bound to 3 and b is bound to nil. The setq assigns b to 4, and the sum of a and b is returned by the let statement. Upon termination of the let, a and b are restored to their previous values, including the unbound status of b.

Using the let statement, quad-roots can be implemented with no global side effects:

```
(defun quad-roots-2 (a b c)
(let (temp)
      (setq temp (sqrt (− (* b b) (* 4 a c))))
      (list (/ (+ (− b) temp) (* 2 a))
            (/ (− (− b) temp) (* 2 a)))))
```

Alternatively, temp may be bound when it is declared in the let statement, giving a somewhat more concise implementation of quad-roots. In this final version, the denominator of the formula, 2a, is also computed once and saved in a local variable, denom:

```
(defun quad-roots-3 (a b c)
(let ((temp (sqrt (− (* b b) (* 4 a c))))
      (denom (* 2 a)))
      (list (/ (+ (− b) temp) denom)
            (/ (− (− b) temp) denom))))
```

In addition to avoiding side effects, quad-roots-3 is the most efficient of the three versions, because it does not recompute values unnecessarily.

16.1.10 Data Types in Common LISP

LISP provides the user with a number of built-in data types. These include integers, floating-point numbers, strings, and characters. LISP also includes such structured types as arrays, hash tables, sets, and structures. All of these types include the appropriate operations on the type and predicates for testing whether an object is an instance of the type. For example, lists are supported by such functions as listp, which identifies an object as a list; null, which identifies the empty list, and constructors and accessors such as list, nth, car, and cdr.

However, unlike such strongly typed languages as C or Pascal, where all expressions can be checked for type consistency before run time, in LISP it is the data objects that are typed, rather than variables. Any LISP symbol may bind to any object. This provides the programmer with the power of typing but also with a great deal of flexibility in manipulating objects of different or even unknown types. For example, we may bind any object to any variable at run time. This means that we may define data structures such as frames, without fully specifying the types of the values stored in them. To support this flexibility, LISP implements run-time type checking. So if we bind a value to a symbol, and try to use this value in an erroneous fashion at run time, the LISP interpreter will detect an error:

```
> (setq x 'a)
a
> (+ x 2)
> > Error: a is not a valid argument to +.
> > While executing: +
```

Users may implement their own type checking using either built-in or user-defined type predicates. This allows the detection and management of type errors as needed.

The preceding pages are not a complete description of LISP. Instead, they are intended to call the reader's attention to interesting features of the language that will be of use in implementing AI data structures and algorithms. These features include:

1. The naturalness with which LISP supports a data abstraction approach to programming.

2. The use of lists to create symbolic data structures.

3. The use of cond and recursion to control program flow.

4. The recursive nature of list structures and the recursive schemes involved in their manipulation.

5. The use of quote and eval to control function evaluation.

6. The use of set and let to control variable bindings and side effects.

The remainder of this chapter builds on these ideas to demonstrate the use of LISP for typical AI programming tasks such as pattern matchers and search algorithms.

16.2 Search in LISP: A Functional Approach to the Farmer, Wolf, Goat, and Cabbage Problem

To introduce AI programming in LISP, we next represent and solve the farmer, wolf, goat, and cabbage problem:

A farmer with his wolf, goat, and cabbage come to the edge of a river they wish to cross. There is a boat at the river's edge, but, of course, only the farmer can row it. The boat also can carry only two things (including the rower) at a time. If the wolf is ever left alone with the goat, the wolf will eat the goat; similarly, if the goat is left alone with the cabbage, the goat will eat the cabbage. Devise a sequence of crossings of the river so that all four characters arrive safely on the other side of the river.

This problem was first presented in PROLOG in Section 15.3. The LISP version searches the same space and has structural similarities to the PROLOG solution; however, it differs in ways that reflect LISP's imperative/functional orientation. The LISP solution searches the state space in a depth-first fashion using a list of visited states to avoid loops.

The heart of the program is a set of functions that define states of the world as an abstract data type. These functions hide the internals of state representation from higher-level components of the program. States are represented as lists of four elements, where each element denotes the location of the farmer, wolf, goat, or cabbage, respectively. Thus, (e w e w) represents the state in which the farmer (the first element) and the goat (the third element) are on the east bank and the wolf and cabbage are on the west. The basic functions defining the state data type will be a constructor, make-state, which takes as arguments the locations of the farmer, wolf, goat, and cabbage and returns a state, and four access functions, farmer-side, wolf-side, goat-side, and cabbage-side, which take a state and return the location of an individual. These functions are defined:

```
(defun make-state (f w g c) (list f w g c))
(defun farmer-side (state)
    (nth 0 state))
(defun wolf-side (state)
    (nth 1 state))
(defun goat-side (state)
    (nth 2 state))
(defun cabbage-side (state)
    (nth 3 state))
```

The rest of the program is built on these state access and construction functions. In particular, they are used to implement the four possible actions the farmer may take: rowing across the river alone or with either the wolf, goat, or cabbage.

Each move uses the access functions to tear a state apart into its components. A function called opposite (to be defined shortly) determines the new location of the individuals that cross the river, and make-state reassembles these into the new state. For example, the function farmer-takes-self may be defined:

```
(defun farmer-takes-self (state)
   (make-state (opposite (farmer-side state))
               (wolf-side state)
               (goat-side state)
               (cabbage-side state)))
```

Note that this function returns the new state, regardless of whether it is safe or not. A state is unsafe if the farmer has left the goat alone with the cabbage or left the wolf alone with the goat. The program must find a solution path that does not contain any unsafe states. Although this "safe" check may be done at a number of different stages of the program, our approach is to perform it in the move functions. This is implemented by using a function called safe, which we also define shortly. safe has the following behavior:

```
> (safe '(w w w w))                      ; safe state, return unchanged.
(w w w w)
> (safe '(e w w e))                      ; wolf eats goat, return nil.
nil
> (safe '(w w e e))                      ; goat eats cabbage, return nil.
nil
```

safe is used in each move function to filter out the unsafe states. Thus, any move that moves to an unsafe state will return nil instead of that state. The recursive path algorithm can check for this nil and use it to prune that state. In a sense, we are using safe to implement a production system style condition-check prior to determining if a move rule can be applied. Using safe, a final definition of the four move functions is next:

```
(defun farmer-takes-self (state)
    (safe (make-state (opposite (farmer-side state))
                      (wolf-side state)
                      (goat-side state)
                      (cabbage-side state))))
(defun farmer-takes-wolf (state)
    (cond ((equal (farmer-side state) (wolf-side state))
           (safe (make-state (opposite (farmer-side state))
                             (opposite (wolf-side state))
                             (goat-side state)
                             (cabbage-side state))))
          (t nil)))
(defun farmer-takes-goat (state)
    (cond ((equal (farmer-side state) (goat-side state))
           (safe (make-state (opposite (farmer-side state))
                             (wolf-side state)
                             (opposite (goat-side state))
                             (cabbage-side state))))
          (t nil)))
(defun farmer-takes-cabbage (state)
    (cond ((equal (farmer-side state) (cabbage-side state))
           (safe (make-state (opposite (farmer-side state))
                             (wolf-side state)
                             (goat-side state)
                             (opposite (cabbage-side state)))))
          (t nil)))
```

Note that the last three move functions include a conditional test to determine whether the farmer and the prospective passenger are on the same side of the river. If they are not, the functions return nil. The move definitions use the state manipulation functions already presented and a function opposite, which returns the opposite of a given side:

```
(defun opposite (side)
    (cond ((equal side 'e) 'w)
          ((equal side 'w) 'e)))
```

LISP provides a number of different predicates for equality. The most stringent, eq, is true only if its arguments evaluate to the same object, i.e., point to the same memory location. equal is less strict: it requires that its arguments be syntactically identical, as in:

```
> (setq l1 '(1 2 3))
(1 2 3)
> (setq l2 '(1 2 3))
(1 2 3)
> (equal l1 l2)
t
> (eq l1 l2)
nil
> (setq l3 l1)
(1 2 3)
> (eq l1 l3)
t
```

We define safe using a cond to check for the two unsafe conditions: (1) the farmer on the opposite bank from the wolf and the goat and (2) the farmer on the opposite bank from the goat and the cabbage. If the state is safe, it is returned unchanged; otherwise, safe returns nil:

```
(defun safe (state)
    (cond ((and (equal (goat-side state) (wolf-side state))        ; wolf eats goat
                (not (equal (farmer-side state) (wolf-side state)))) nil)
          ((and (equal (goat-side state) (cabbage-side state))     ; goat eats cabbage
                (not (equal (farmer-side state) (goat-side state)))) nil)
          (t state)))
```

path implements the backtracking search of the state space. It takes as arguments a state and a goal and first checks to see whether they are equal, indicating a successful termination of the search. If they are not equal, path generates all four of the neighboring states in the state space graph, calling itself recursively on each of these neighboring states in turn to try to find a path from them to a goal. Translating this simple definition directly into LISP yields:

```
(defun path (state goal)
    (cond ((equal state goal) 'success)
          (t (or (path (farmer-takes-self state) goal)
                 (path (farmer-takes-wolf state) goal)
                 (path (farmer-takes-goat state) goal)
                 (path (farmer-takes-cabbage state) goal)))))
```

This version of the path function is a simple translation of the recursive path algorithm from English into LISP and has several "bugs" that need to be corrected. It does, however, capture the essential structure of the algorithm and should be examined before continuing to correct the bugs. The first test in the cond statement is necessary for a successful completion of the search algorithm. When the equal state goal pattern matches, the recursion stops and the atom success is returned. Otherwise, path generates the four descendant nodes of the search graph and then calls itself on each of the nodes in turn.

In particular, note the use of the or form to control evaluation of its arguments. Recall that an or evaluates its arguments in turn until one of them returns a non-nil value. When this occurs, the or terminates without evaluating the other arguments and returns this non-nil value as a result. Thus, the or not only is used as a logical operator but also provides a way of controlling branching within the space to be searched. The or form is used here instead of a cond because the value that is being tested and the value that should be returned if the test is non-nil are the same.

One problem with this definition is that a move function may return a value of nil if the move may not be made or if it leads to an unsafe state. To prevent path from attempting to generate the children of a nil state, it must first check whether the current state is nil. If it is, path should return nil.

The other issue that needs to be addressed in the implementation of path is that of detecting potential loops in the search space. If the above implementation of path is run, the farmer will soon find himself going back and forth alone between the two banks of the river; that is, the algorithm will be stuck in an infinite loop between identical states, both of which it has already visited. To prevent this from happening, path is given a third parameter, been-list, a list of all the states that have already been visited. Each time that path is called recursively on a new state of the world, the parent state will be added to been-list. path uses the member predicate to make sure the current state is not a member of been-list, i.e., that it has not already been visited. This is done by checking the current state for membership in been-list before generating its descendants. path is now defined:

```
(defun path (state goal been-list)
    (cond ((null state) nil)
          ((equal state goal) (reverse (cons state been-list)))
          ((not (member state been-list :test #'equal))
              (or (path (farmer-takes-self state) goal (cons state been-list))
                  (path (farmer-takes-wolf state) goal (cons state been-list))
                  (path (farmer-takes-goat state) goal (cons state been-list))
                  (path (farmer-takes-cabbage state) goal (cons state been-list))))))
```

In the above implementation, member is a Common LISP built-in function that behaves in essentially the same way as the my-member function defined in this chapter. The only difference is the inclusion of :test #'equal in the argument list. Unlike our "home-grown" member function, the Common LISP built-in form allows the programmer to specify the function that is used in testing for membership. This wrinkle increases the flexibility of the function and should not cause too much concern in this discussion.

Rather than having the function return just the atom success, it is better to have it return the actual solution path. Because the series of states on the solution path is already contained in the been-list, this list is returned instead. Because the goal is not already on been-list, it is consed onto the list. Also, because the list is constructed in reverse order (with the start state as the last element), the list is reversed (constructed in reverse order using another LISP built-in function, reverse) prior to being returned.

Finally, because the been-list parameter should be kept "hidden" from the user, a top-level calling function may be written that takes as arguments a start and a goal state and calls path with a nil value of been-list:

```
(defun solve-fwgc (state goal) (path state goal nil))
```

Let us compare the LISP version of the farmer, wolf, goat, and cabbage problem with the PROLOG solution presented in Section 15.3. Not only does the LISP program solve the same problem, but it also searches exactly the same state space as the PROLOG version. This underscores the point that the state space conceptualization of a problem is independent of the implementation of a program for searching that space. Because both programs search the same space, the two implementations have strong similarities; the differences tend to be subtle but provide an interesting contrast between declarative and procedural programming styles.

States in the PROLOG version are represented using a predicate, state(e,e,e,e), and the LISP implementation uses a list. These two representations are more than syntactic variations on one another. The LISP representation of state is defined not only by its list syntax but also by the access and move functions that constitute the abstract data type "state." In the PROLOG version, states are patterns; their meaning is determined by the way in which they match other patterns in PROLOG rules which could also be lists.

The LISP version of path is slightly longer than the PROLOG version. One reason for this is that the LISP version must implement a search strategy, whereas the PROLOG version takes advantage of PROLOG's built-in search algorithm. The control algorithm is explicit in the LISP version but is implicit in the PROLOG version. Because PROLOG is built on declarative representation and theorem-proving techniques, the PROLOG program is more concise and has a flavor of describing the problem domain, without directly implementing the search algorithm. The price paid for this conciseness is that much of the program's behavior is hidden, determined by PROLOG's built-in inference strategies. Programmers may also feel more pressure to make the problem solution conform to PROLOG's representational formalism and search strategies. LISP, on the other hand, allows greater flexibility for the programmer. The price paid here is that the programmer cannot draw on a built-in representation or search strategy and must implement it explicitly.

16.3 Higher-Order Functions and Abstraction

One of the most powerful techniques that LISP and other functional programming languages provide is the ability to define functions that take other functions as parameters or return them as results. These are called *higher-order functions* and constitute an important tool for procedural abstraction.

16.3.1 Maps and Filters

A *filter* is a function that applies a test to the elements of a list, eliminating those that fail the test. filter-negatives, presented earlier in this chapter, was an example of a filter. *Maps* take a list of data objects and apply a function to each one, returning a list of the results. This idea may be further generalized through the development of general maps and filters that take as arguments both lists and the functions or tests that are to be applied to their elements.

To begin with an example, recall the function filter-negatives from Section 16.1.6. This function took as its argument a list of numbers and returned that list with all negative values deleted. Similarly, a function to filter out all the even numbers in a list may be defined:

```
(defun filter-evens (number-list)                        ; termination condition
    (cond ((null number-list) nil)
          ((oddp (car number-list))
              (cons (car number-list) (filter-evens (cdr number-list))))
          (t (filter-evens (cdr number-list)))))
```

Because these two functions differ *only* in the name of the predicate used to filter elements from the list, it is natural to think of generalizing them into a single function that takes the filtering predicate as a second parameter.

This may be defined using a LISP form called funcall, which takes as arguments a function and a series of arguments and applies that function to those arguments:

```
(defun filter (list-of-elements test)
    (cond ((null list-of-elements) nil)
          ((funcall test (car list-of-elements))
              (cons (car list-of-elements) (filter (cdr list-of-elements) test)))
          (t (filter (cdr list-of-elements) test))))
```

The function, filter, applies the test to the first element of the list. If the test returns non-nil, it conses the element onto the result of filtering the cdr of the list; otherwise, it just returns the filtered cdr. This function may be used with different predicates passed in as parameters to perform a variety of filtering tasks:

```
> (filter '(1 3 -9 5 -2 -7 6) #'plusp)                   ; Filter out all negative numbers
(1 3 5 6)
> (filter '(1 2 3 4 5 6 7 8 9) #'evenp)                  ; Filter out all odd numbers
(2 4 6 8)
> (filter '(1 a b 3 c 4 7 d) #'numberp)                  ; Filter out all non-numbers
(1 3 4 7)
```

When a function is passed as a parameter, as in the above examples, it should be preceded by a #' instead of just '. The purpose of this convention is to flag arguments that are functions so that they may be given appropriate treatment by the LISP interpreter. In particular, when a function is passed as an argument in Common LISP, the bindings of its free variables (if any) must be retained. This combination of function definition and bindings of free variables is called a *lexical closure*; the #' informs LISP that the lexical closure must be constructed and passed with the function. More formally, funcall is defined:

```
(funcall <function> <arg₁> <arg₂> ... <arg_n>)
```

In this definition, <function> is a LISP function and $<arg_1>$ ... $<arg_n>$ are zero or more arguments to the function. The result of evaluating a funcall is the same as the result of evaluating <function> with the specified arguments as actual parameters.

apply is a similar function that performs the same task as funcall but requires that its arguments be in a list. Except for this syntactic difference, apply and funcall behave the same; the programmer can choose the function that seems more convenient for a given application. These two functions are similar to eval in that all three of them allow the user to specify that function evaluation should take place. The difference is that eval requires its argument to be an s-expression that is evaluated; funcall and apply take a function and its arguments as separate parameters. Examples of the behavior of these functions are:

```
> (funcall #'plus 2 3)
5
> (apply #'plus '(2 3))
5
> (eval '(plus 2 3))
5
> (funcall #'car '(a b c))
a
> (apply #'car '((a b c)))
a
```

Another important class of higher-order functions consists of mapping functions, functions that will apply a given function to all the elements of a list. Using funcall, we define the simple mapping function map-simple, which returns a list of the results of applying a functional to all the elements of a list. It has the behavior:

```
(defun map-simple (func list)
    (cond ((null list) nil)
          (t (cons  (funcall func (car list))
                    (map-simple func (cdr list))))))
> (map-simple #'1+ '(1 2 3 4 5 6))
(2 3 4 5 6 7)
> (map-simple #'listp '(1 2 (3 4) 5 (6 7 8)))
(nil nil t nil t)
```

map-simple is a simplified version of a LISP built-in function mapcar, that allows more than one argument list, so that functions of more than one argument can be applied to corresponding elements of several lists:

```
> (mapcar #'1+ '(1 2 3 4 5 6))               ; this is the same as map-simple
(2 3 4 5 6 7)
```

```
> (mapcar #'+ '(1 2 3 4) '(5 6 7 8))
(6 8 10 12)
> (mapcar #'max '(3 9 1 7) '(2 5 6 8))
(3 9 6 8)
```

mapcar is only one of many mapping functions provided by LISP, as well as only one of many higher-order functions built into the language.

16.3.2   Functional Arguments and Lambda Expressions

In the preceding examples, function arguments were passed by their name and applied to a series of arguments. This requires that the functions be previously defined in the global environment. Frequently, however, it is desirable to pass a function definition directly, without first defining the function globally. This is made possible through the lambda expression.

Essentially, the lambda expression allows us to separate a function definition from the function name. The origin of lambda expressions is in the *lambda calculus*, a mathematical model of computation that provides (among other things) a particularly thoughtful treatment of this distinction between an object and its name. The syntax of a lambda expression is similar to the function definition in a defun, except that the function name is replaced by the term lambda. That is:

```
(lambda (<formal-parameters>) <body>)
```

Lambda expressions may be used in place of a function name in a funcall or apply. The funcall will execute the body of the lambda expression with the arguments bound to the parameters of the funcall. As with named functions, the number of formal parameters and the number of actual parameters must be the same. For example:

```
> (funcall #'(lambda (x) (* x x)) 4)
16
```

Here, x is bound to 4 and the body of the lambda expression is then evaluated. The result, the square of 4, is returned by funcall. Other examples of the use of lambda expressions with funcall and apply are:

```
> (apply #'(lambda (x y) (+ (* x x) y)) '(2 3))
7
> (funcall #'(lambda (x) (append x x)) '(a b c))
(a b c a b c)
> (funcall #'(lambda (x1 x2) (append (reverse x1) x2)) '(a b c) '(d e f))
(c b a d e f)
```

Lambda expressions may be used in a higher-order function such as mapcar in place of the names of globally defined functions. For example:

```
> (mapcar #'(lambda (x) (* x x)) '(1 2 3 4 5))
(1 4 9 16 25)
> (mapcar #'(lambda (x) (* x 2)) '(1 2 3 4 5))
(2 4 6 8 10)
> (mapcar #'(lambda (x) (and (> x 0) (< x 10))) '(1 24 5 −9 8 23))
(t nil t nil t nil)
```

Without lambda expressions the programmer must define every function in the global environment using a defun, even though that function may be used only once. Lambda expressions free the programmer from this necessity: if it is desired to square each element in a list, the lambda form is passed to mapcar as the first of the above examples illustrates. It is not necessary to define a squaring function first.

16.4 Search Strategies in LISP

The use of higher-order functions provides LISP with a powerful tool for procedural abstraction. In this section, we use this abstraction technique to implement general algorithms for breadth-first, depth-first, and best-first search. These algorithms implement the search algorithms from Chapters 3 and 4, using open and closed lists to manage search through the state space.

16.4.1 Breadth-First and Depth-First Search

The LISP implementation of breadth-first search maintains the open list as a first-in-first-out (FIFO) structure. We will define open and closed as global variables. This is done for several reasons: first to demonstrate the use of global structures in LISP; second, to contrast the LISP solution with that in PROLOG; and third, it can be argued that since the primary task of this program is to solve a search problem, the state of the search may be represented globally. Finally, since open and closed may be large, their use as global variables seems justified. General arguments of efficiency for the local vs global approach often depend on the implementation details of a particular language. Global variables in Common LISP are written to begin and end with *. Breadth-first search is defined:

```
(defun breadth-first ( )
    (cond ((null *open*) nil)
            (t (let ((state (car *open*)))
                (cond ((equal state *goal*) 'success)
                        (t (setq *closed* (cons state *closed*))
                        (setq *open* (append (cdr *open*)
                        (generate-descendants state *moves*)))
                            (breadth-first)))))))
(defun run-breadth (start goal)
    (setq *open* (list start))
    (setq *closed* nil)
    (setq *goal* goal)
    (breadth-first))
```

In this implementation, the *open* list is tested: if it is nil, the algorithm returns nil, indicating failure; otherwise it examines the first element of *open*. If this is equal to the goal, the algorithm halts and returns success; otherwise, it calls generate-descendants to produce the children of the current state, adds them to the *open* list, and recurs. run-breadth is an initialization function that sets the initial values of *open*, *closed*, and *goal*. generate-descendants is passed both the state and *moves* as parameters. *moves* is a list of the functions that generate moves. In the farmer, wolf, goat, and cabbage problem, assuming the move definitions of Section 16.2, *moves* would be:

```
(setq *moves*
    '(farmer-takes-self farmer-takes-wolf farmer-takes-goat farmer-takes-cabbage))
```

generate-descendants takes a state and returns a list of its children. In addition to generating child states, it disallows duplicates in the list of children and eliminates any children that are already in the open or closed list. In addition to the state, generate-descendants is given a list of moves; these may be the names of defined functions, or they may be lambda definitions. generate-descendants uses a let block to save the result of a move in the local variable child. We define generate-descendants:

```
(defun generate-descendants (state moves)
    (cond ((null moves) nil)
          (t (let ((child (funcall (car moves) state))
                   (rest (generate-descendants state (cdr moves))))
               (cond ((null child) rest)
                     ((member child rest :test #'equal) rest)
                     ((member child *open* :test #'equal) rest)
                     ((member child *closed* :test #'equal) rest)
                     (t (cons child rest)))))))
```

As first noted in Section 16.2, the calls to the member function use an additional parameter, :test #'equal. The member function allows the user to specify any test for membership. This allows us to use predicates of arbitrary complexity and semantics to test membership. Though LISP does not require that we specify the test, the default comparison is the predicate eq. eq requires that two objects be identical, which means they have the same location in memory; we are using a weaker comparison, equal, that only requires that the objects have the same value. By binding the global variable *moves* to an appropriate set of move functions, the search algorithm just presented may be used to search any state space graph in a breadth-first fashion.

One difficulty that remains with this implementation is its inability to print the list of states along the path from a start to a goal. Although all the states that lead to the goal are present in the closed list when the algorithm halts, these are mixed with all other states from earlier levels of the search space. We can solve this problem by recording both the state and its parent, and reconstructing the solution path from this information. For example, if the state (e e e e) generates the state (w e w e), a record of both states, ((w e w e) (e e e e)), is placed on *open*. Later, after the children of the state have been generated, the same (<state> <parent>) pair is placed on *closed*.

When the current state equals the goal, the ancestor information is used to build the path from the goal to the start state by going back to successive parents. This augmented version of breadth-first search begins by defining state records as an abstract data type:

```
(defun build-record (state parent) (list state parent))
(defun get-state (state-tuple) (nth 0 state-tuple))
(defun get-parent (state-tuple) (nth 1 state-tuple))
(defun retrieve-by-state (state list)
    (cond ((null list) nil)
            ((equal state (get-state (car list))) (car list))
            (t (retrieve-by-state state (cdr list)))))
```

build-record constructs a (<state> <parent>) pair. get-state and get-parent access the appropriate fields of a record. retrieve-by-state takes a state and a list of state records and returns the record whose state field matches that state.

build-solution uses retrieve-by-state to chain back from state to parent, constructing a list of successive states that led to a goal. When initializing *open*, we will give the starting state a parent of nil; build-solution stops when passed a null state.

```
(defun build-solution (state)
    (cond ((null state) nil)
            (t (cons state (build-solution (get-parent (retrieve-by-state state *closed*)))))))
```

The remainder of the algorithm is similar to the breadth-first search of Section 3.2:

```
(defun run-breadth (start goal)
    (setq *open* (list (build-record start nil)))
    (setq *closed* nil)
    (setq *goal* goal)
    (breadth-first))
(defun breadth-first ( )
  (cond ((null *open*) nil)
          (t (let ((state (car *open*)))
              (setq *closed* (cons state *closed*))
                  (cond ((equal (get-state state) *goal*) (build-solution *goal*))
                        (t (setq *open* (append (cdr *open*)
                          (generate-descendants (get-state state) *moves*)))
                              (breadth-first)))))))
(defun generate-descendants (state moves)
    (cond ((null moves) nil)
            (t (let ((child (funcall (car moves) state))
                    (rest (generate-descendants state (cdr moves))))
                (cond ((null child) rest)
                      ((retrieve-by-state child rest) rest)
                      ((retrieve-by-state child *open*) rest)
                      ((retrieve-by-state child *closed*) rest)
                      (t (cons (build-record child state) rest)))))))
```

Depth-first search may be implemented by modifying breadth-first search to maintain open as a stack. This simply involves reversing the order of the arguments to append.

16.4.2 Best-First Search

Best-first search may be implemented through straightforward modifications to the breadth-first search algorithm. Specifically, the heuristic evaluation is saved along with each state. The tuples on *open* are then sorted according to this evaluation. The data type definitions for state records are an extension of those used in breadth-first search:

```
(defun build-record (state parent depth weight)
    (list state parent depth weight))
(defun get-state (state-tuple) (nth 0 state-tuple))
(defun get-parent (state-tuple) (nth 1 state-tuple))
(defun get-depth (state-tuple) (nth 2 state-tuple))
(defun get-weight (state-tuple) (nth 3 state-tuple))
(defun retrieve-by-state (state list)
    (cond ((null list) nil)
            ((equal state (get-state (car list))) (car list))
            (t (retrieve-by-state state (cdr list)))))
```

best-first and generate-descendants are defined:

```
(defun best-first ( )
    (cond ((null *open*) nil)
            (t (let ((state (car *open*)))
                (setq *closed* (cons state *closed*))
                (cond ((equal (get-state state) *goal*) (build-solution *goal*))
                        (t (setq *open*
                            (insert-by-weight
                                (generate-descendants (get-state state)
                                        (+ 1 (get-depth state)) *moves*) (cdr *open*)))
                        (best-first)))))))
(defun generate-descendants (state depth moves)
    (cond ((null moves) nil)
            (t (let ((child (funcall (car moves) state))
                    (rest (generate-descendants state depth (cdr moves))))
                (cond ((null child) rest)
                        ((retrieve-by-state child rest) rest)
                        ((retrieve-by-state child *open*) rest)
                        ((retrieve-by-state child *closed*) rest)
                        (t (cons (build-record child state depth
                                        (+ depth (heuristic child))) rest)))))))
```

The only differences between best-first and breadth-first search are the use of insert-by-weight to sort the records on *open* by heuristic weights and the computation of search depth and heuristic weights in generate-descendants.

Completion of best-first requires a definition of insert-by-weight. This function takes an unsorted list of state records and inserts them, one at a time, into their appropriate positions in *open*. It also requires a problem-specific definition of heuristic. This function takes a state and, using the global *goal*, computes a heuristic weight for that state. We leave the definition of these functions as an exercise for the reader.

16.5 Pattern Matching in LISP

Pattern matching is an important AI methodology that has already been discussed in the PROLOG chapters and the discussion of production systems. In this section we implement a recursive pattern matcher and use it to build a pattern-directed retrieval function for a simple database.

The heart of this retrieval system is a function called match, which takes as arguments two s-expressions and returns t if the expressions match. Matching requires that both expressions have the same *structure*, as well as having identical atoms in corresponding positions. In addition, match allows the inclusion of variables, denoted by ?, in an s-expression. Variables are allowed to match with any s-expression, either a list or an atom, but do not save bindings, as with full unification. Examples of the desired behavior for match appear below. If the examples seem reminiscent of the PROLOG examples in Chapter 15, this is because match is actually a simplified version of the unification algorithm that forms the heart of PROLOG, as well as many other pattern-directed AI systems. In Section 16.6 we expand match into the full unification algorithm by allowing named variables and returning a list of bindings required for a match.

```
> (match '(likes bill wine) '(likes bill wine))
t
> (match '(likes bill wine) '(likes bill milk))
nil
> (match '(likes bill ?) '(likes bill wine))          ; example with a variable
t
> (match '(likes ? wine) '(likes bill ?))             ; note variables in both expressions
t
> (match '(likes bill ?) '(likes bill (prolog lisp smalltalk)))
t
> (match '(likes ?) '(likes bill wine))
nil
```

match is used to define a function called get-matches, which takes as arguments two s-expressions. The first argument is a pattern to be matched against elements of the second s-expression, which must be a list. get-matches returns a list of the elements of the list that match the first argument. In the example below, get-matches is used to retrieve records from an employee database as described earlier in this chapter.

Because the database is a large and relatively complex s-expression, we have bound it to the global variable *database* and use that variable as an argument to get-matches. This was done to improve readability of the examples.

```
> (setq *database* '(((lovelace ada) 50000.00 1234)
                      ((turing alan) 45000.00 3927)
                      ((shelley mary) 35000.00 2850)
                      ((vonNeumann john) 40000.00 7955)
                      ((simon herbert) 50000.00 1374)
                      ((mccarthy john) 48000.00 2864)
                      ((russell bertrand) 35000.00 2950))
*database*
> (get-matches '((turing alan) 45000.00 3927) *database*)
((turing alan) 45000.00 3927)
> (get-matches '(? 50000.00 ?) *database*)                ; all people who make 50000
(((lovelace ada) 50000.00 1234) ((simon herbert) 50000.00 1374))
> (get-matches '((? john) ? ?) *database*)                ; all people named john
(((vonNeumann john) 40000.00 7955) ((mccarthy john) 48000.00 2864))
```

We implement get-matches with cdr recursion to look for elements that match with the first argument (the pattern). All elements of the database that match the pattern are consed together to form the answer for the pattern. get-matches is defined:

```
(defun get-matches (pattern database)
    (cond ((null database) ( ))
          ((match pattern (car database))                ; match found, add to result
              (cons (car database) (get-matches pattern (cdr database))))
          (t (get-matches pattern (cdr database)))))
```

The heart of the system is the match function, a predicate that determines whether or not two s-expressions containing variables actually match. match is based on the idea that two lists match if and only if their respective cars and cdrs match, suggesting a car-cdr recursive scheme for the algorithm. The recursion terminates when either of the arguments is atomic (this includes the empty list, nil, which is both an atom and a list). If both patterns are the same atom or if one of the patterns is a variable atom, ?, which can match with anything, then termination is with a successful match; otherwise, the match will fail. Notice that if either of the patterns is a variable, the other pattern need not be atomic; variables may match with s-expressions of arbitrary complexity.

Because the handling of the terminating conditions is complex, the implementation of match uses a function called match-atom that takes two arguments, one or both of which is an atom, and checks to see whether the patterns match. By hiding this complexity in match-atom the car-cdr recursive structure of match is more apparent:

```
(defun match (pattern1 pattern2)
    (cond (or (atom pattern1) (atom pattern2))          ; one of the patterns is atomic
              (match-atom pattern1 pattern2))           ; call match-atom, otherwise
          (t (and (match (car pattern1) (car pattern2)) ; match both car and cdr
              (match (cdr pattern1) (cdr pattern2))))))
```

The implementation of match-atom makes use of the fact that when it is called, at least one of the arguments is an atom. Because of this assumption, a simple test for equality of patterns is all that is needed to test that both patterns are the same atom (including both being a variable); it will fail either if the two patterns are different atoms or if one of them is nonatomic. If the first test fails, the only way a match can succeed is if one of the patterns is a variable. This check constitutes the remainder of the function definition. Finally, a function variable-p is defined to test whether or not a pattern is a variable. Treating variables as an abstract data type now will simplify later extensions to the function (for example, the extension of the function to named variables as in PROLOG).

```
(defun match-atom (pattern1 pattern2)
    (or (equal pattern1 pattern2)          ; both patterns are the same, or
        (variable-p pattern1)              ; one of them is a variable.
        (variable-p pattern2)))
(defun variable-p (x)  (equal x '?))
```

16.6 A Recursive Unification Function

In Section 16.5 we implemented a recursive pattern-matching algorithm that allowed the inclusion of unnamed variables in patterns. Now we extend this simple pattern matcher into the full unification algorithm presented in Chapter 2. The function, unify, allows named variables in both of the patterns to be matched, and returns a list of the variable bindings required for the match. This unification function is the basis of the inference systems developed later in this chapter.

As in Section 16.5, patterns are either constants, variables, or list structures. In a full unification algorithm, variables may be distinguished from one another by their names. Named variables are going to be represented as lists of the form (var <name>), where <name> is usually an atomic symbol. (var x), (var y), and (var newstate) are all examples of legal variables.

The function unify takes as arguments two patterns to be matched and a set of variable substitutions (bindings) to be employed in the match. Generally, this set will be empty (nil) when the function is first called. On a successful match, unify returns a (possibly empty) set of substitutions required for a successful match. If no match was possible, unify returns the symbol failed; nil is used to indicate an empty substitution set, i.e., a match in which no substitutions were required. An example of the behavior of unify, with comments, appears below.

```
> (unify '(p a (var x)) '(p a b) ( ))        ; returns substitution of b for (var x)
(((var x) . b))
> (unify '(p (var y) b) '(p a (var x)) ( ))  ; variables appear in both patterns
(((var x) . b) ((var y) . a))
> (unify '(p (var x)) '(p (q a (var y))) ( )) ; variable bound to more complex pattern
(((var x) q a (var y)))
> (unify '(p a) '(p a) ( ))                   ; nil indicates no substitution required
nil
> (unify '(p a) '(q a) ( ))                   ; returns the atom failed to indicate failure
failed
```

We explain the "." notation, as in ((var x) .b), after we present the function unify. unify, like the pattern matcher of Section 16.5, uses a car-cdr recursive scheme and is defined by:

```
(defun unify (pattern1 pattern2 substitution-list)
    (cond ((equal substitution-list 'failed) 'failed)
            ((varp pattern1) (match-var pattern1 pattern2 substitution-list))  ; varp tests
            ((varp pattern2) (match-var pattern2 pattern1 substitution-list))  ; if variable
            ((is-constant-p pattern1)
                (cond ((equal pattern1 pattern2) substitution-list)
                        (t 'failed)))
            ((is-constant-p pattern2) 'failed)
            (t (unify (cdr pattern1) (cdr pattern2)
                        (unify (car pattern1) (car pattern2) substitution-list)))))
```

On entering unify, the algorithm first checks whether the substitution list is equal to failed. This could occur if a prior attempt to unify the cars of two patterns had failed. If this condition is met, the function returns failed.

Next, if either pattern is a variable, the function match-var is called to perform further checking and possibly add a new binding to the substitution list. If neither pattern is a variable, unify tests whether either is a constant, returning the unchanged substitution list if they are the same constant, failed otherwise.

The last item in the cond statement implements the tree-recursive decomposition of the problem: first, the cars of the patterns are unified using the bindings in substitution-list. The result is passed as the third argument to the call of unify on the cdrs of both patterns. This allows the variable substitutions made in matching the cars to be applied to other occurrences of those variables in the cdrs of both patterns.

match-var, for the case of matching a variable and a pattern, is defined by:

```
(defun match-var (var pattern substitution-list)
    (cond ((equal var pattern) substitution-list)
            (t (let ((binding (get-binding var substitution-list)))
                (cond (binding (unify (get-binding-value binding) pattern substitution-list))
                        ((occursp var pattern) 'failed)
                        (t (add-substitution var pattern substitution-list)))))))
```

match-var first checks whether the variable and the pattern are the same; unifying a variable with itself requires no added substitutions, so substitution-list is returned unchanged.

If var and pattern are not the same, match-var checks whether the variable is already bound. If a binding exists, unify is called recursively to match the *value* of the binding with pattern. Note that this binding value may be a constant, a variable, or a pattern of arbitrary complexity; requiring a call to the full unification algorithm to complete the match.

If no binding currently exists for var, the function calls occursp to test whether var appears in pattern. The *occurs check* is needed to prevent attempts to unify a variable with a pattern containing that variable, leading to a circular structure. For example, if (var x) was bound to (p (var x)), any attempt to apply those substitutions to a pattern would result in an infinite loop. If var appears in pattern, match-var returns failed; otherwise, it adds the new substitution pair to substitution-list using add-substitution.

unify and match-var are the heart of the unification algorithm. occursp (which performs a tree walk on a pattern to find any occurrences of the variable in that pattern), varp, and is-constant-p (which test whether their argument is a variable or a constant, respectively) appear below. Functions for handling substitution sets are discussed below.

```
(defun occursp (var pattern)
    (cond ((equal var pattern) t)
             ((or (varp pattern) (is-constant-p pattern)) nil)
             (t (or (occursp var (car pattern))
                     (occursp var (cdr pattern))))))
(defun is-constant-p (item)
    (atom item))
(defun varp (item)
    (and (listp item)
             (equal (length item) 2)
             (equal (car item) 'var)))
```

Sets of substitutions are represented using a built-in LISP data type called the *association list* or *a-list*. This is the basis for the functions add-substitutions, get-binding, and binding-value. An association list is a list of data records, or *key/data* pairs. The car of each record is a *key* for its retrieval; the cdr of each record is called the *datum*. The datum may be a list of values or a single atom. Retrieval is implemented by the function assoc, which takes as arguments a key and an association list and returns the first member of the association list that has the key as its car. An optional third argument to assoc specifies the test to be used in comparing keys. The default test is the Common LISP function eql, a form of equality test requiring two arguments be the same object (i.e., either the same memory location or the same numeric value). In implementing substitution sets, we will specify a less strict test, equal, which requires only that the arguments match syntactically (i.e., are designated by identical names). An example of assoc's behavior appears below:

```
> (assoc 3 '((1 a) (2 b) (3 c) (4 d)))
(3 c)
> (assoc 'd '((a b c) (b c d e) (d e f) (c d e)) :test #'equal)
(d e f)
> (assoc 'c '((a . 1) (b . 2) (c . 3) (d . 4)) :test #'equal)
(c . 3)
```

Note that assoc returns the entire record matched on the key; the datum may be retrieved from this list by the cdr function. Also, notice that in the last call the members of the a-list are not lists but a structure called *dotted pairs*, e.g., (a . 1).

The dotted pair, or cons pair, is actually the fundamental constructor in LISP. It is the result of consing one s-expression onto another; the list notation that we have used throughout the chapter is just a notational variant of dotted pairs. For example, the value returned by (cons 1 nil) is actually (1 . nil); this is equivalent to (1). Similarly, the list (1 2 3) may be written in dotted pair notation as (1 . (2 . (3 . nil))). Although the actual effect of a cons is to create a dotted pair, the list notation is cleaner and is generally preferred.

If two atoms are consed together, the result is always written using dotted pair notation. The cdr of a dotted pair is the second element in the pair, rather than a list containing the second atom. For example:

```
> (cons 'a 'b)
(a . b)
> (car '(a . b))
a
> (cdr '(a . b))
b
```

Dotted pairs occur naturally in association lists when one atom is used as a key for retrieving another atom, as well as in other applications that require the formation and manipulation of pairs of atomic symbols. Because unifications often substitute a single atom for a variable, dotted pairs appear often in the association list returned by the unification function.

Along with assoc, Common LISP defines the function acons, which takes as arguments a key, a datum and an association list and returns a new association list whose first element is the result of consing the key onto the datum. For example:

```
> (acons 'a 1 nil)
((a . 1))
```

Note that when acons is given two atoms, it adds their cons to the association list:

```
> (acons 'pets '(emma jack clyde)
    '((name . bill) (hobbies music skiing movies) (job . programmer)))
((pets emma jack clyde) (name . bill) (hobbies music skiing movies)
    (job . programmer))
```

Members on an association list may be either dotted pairs or lists.

Association lists provide a convenient way to implement a variety of tables and other simple data retrieval schemes. In implementing the unification algorithm, we use association lists to represent sets of substitutions: the keys are the variables, and the data are the values of their bindings. The datum may be a simple variable or constant or a more complicated structure.

Using association lists, the substitution set functions are defined:

```
(defun get-binding (var substitution-list)
    (assoc var substitution-list :test #'equal))
(defun get-binding-value (binding) (cdr binding))
(defun add-substitution (var pattern substitution-list)
    (acons var pattern substitution-list))
```

This completes the implementation of the unification algorithm. We will use it in Section 16.8 to implement a simple PROLOG interpreter, and in Section 16.10 to build an expert system shell.

16.7 Interpreters and Embedded Languages

The top level of the LISP interpreter is known as the *read-eval-print* loop. This describes the interpreter's behavior in reading, evaluating, and printing the value of s-expressions entered by the user. The eval function, defined in Section 16.1.4, is the heart of the LISP interpreter; using eval, it is possible to write LISP's top-level read-eval-print loop in LISP itself. In the next example, we develop a simplified version of this loop. This version is simplified chiefly in that it does not have the error-handling abilities of the built-in loop, although LISP does provide the functionality needed to implement such capabilities.

To write the read-eval-print loop, we use two more LISP functions, read and print. read is a function that takes no parameters; when it is evaluated, it returns the next s-expression entered at the keyboard. print is a function that takes a single argument, evaluates it, and then prints that result to standard output. Another function that will prove useful is terpri, a function of no arguments that causes a newline character to standard output. terpri also returns a value of nil on completion. Using these functions, the read-eval-print loop is based on a nested s-expression:

```
(print (eval (read)))
```

When this is evaluated, the innermost s-expression, (read), is evaluated first. The value returned by the read, the next s-expression entered by the user, is passed to eval, where it is evaluated. The result of this evaluation is passed to print, where it is sent to the display screen. To complete the loop we add a print expression to output the prompt, a terpri to output a newline after the result has been printed, and a recursive call to repeat the cycle. Thus, the final read-eval-print loop is defined:

```
(defun my-read-eval-print ( )          ; this function takes no arguments
  (print ':)                           ; output a prompt, ours is a ":"
  (print (eval (read)))                ; read-eval-print
  (terpri)                             ; output a newline
  (my-read-eval-print))                ; do it all again
```

This may be used "on top of" the built-in interpreter:

```
> (my-read-eval-print)
:(+ 1 2)                                               ; note the new prompt
3
:                                                      ; etc.
```

As this example illustrates, by making functions such as quote and eval available to the user, LISP gives the programmer a high degree of control over the handling of functions. Because LISP programs and data are both represented as s-expressions, we may write programs that perform any desired manipulations of LISP expressions prior to evaluating them. This underlies much of LISP's power as an imperative representation language because it allows arbitrary LISP code to be stored, modified, and evaluated when needed. It also makes it simple to write specialized interpreters that may extend or modify the behavior of the built-in LISP interpreter in some desired fashion. This capability is at the heart of many LISP-based expert systems, that read user queries and respond to them according to the expertise contained in their knowledge base.

As an example of the way in which such a specialized interpreter may be implemented in LISP, we may modify my-read-eval-print so that it evaluates arithmetic expressions in an infix rather than a prefix notation, as in the following example (note the modified prompt, infix->):

```
infix-> (1 + 2)
3
infix-> (7 − 2)
5
infix-> ((5 + 2) * (3 − 1))          ; the loop should allow nesting of expressions
14
```

To simplify the example, the infix interpreter handles only arithmetic expressions. A further simplification restricts the interpreter to binary operations and requires that all expressions be fully parenthesized, eliminating the need for more sophisticated parsing techniques or worries about operator precedence. However, it does allow expressions to be nested to arbitrary depth and handles LISP's binary arithmetic operators.

We modify the previously developed read-eval-print loop by adding a function that translates infix expressions into prefix expressions prior to passing them on to eval. A first attempt at writing this function might look like:

```
(defun simple-in-to-pre (exp)
      (list (nth 1 exp)          ; middle element (operator) becomes first element.
            (nth 0 exp)                                        ; first operand
            (nth 2 exp)                                       ; second operand
```

simple-in-to-pre is effective in translating simple expressions; however, it is not able to correctly translate nested expressions, that is, expressions in which the operands are themselves infix expressions. To handle this situation properly, the operands must also be translated into prefix notation. Recursion is halted by testing the argument to determine whether it is a number, returning it unchanged if it is. The completed version of the infix-to-prefix translator is:

```
(defun in-to-pre (exp)
      (cond ((numberp exp) exp)
            (t (list (nth 1 exp)
                     (in-to-pre (nth 0 exp))
                     (in-to-pre (nth 2 exp))))))
```

Using this translator, the read-eval-print loop may be modified to interpret infix expressions, as defined below:

```
(defun in-eval ( )
    (print 'infix->)
    (print (eval (in-to-pre (read))))
    (terpri)
    (in-eval))
```

This allows the interpretation of binary expressions in infix form:

```
> (in-eval)
infix->(2 + 2)
4
infix->((3 * 4) − 5)
7
```

In the above example, we have implemented a new language, the language of infix arithmetic, in LISP. Because of the facilities LISP provides for symbolic computing (lists and functions for their manipulation) along with the ability to control evaluation, this was much easier to do than in many other programming languages. This example illustrates an important AI programming methodology, that of *meta-linguistic abstraction*. Very often in AI programming, a problem is not completely understood, or the program required to solve a problem is extremely complex. *Meta-linguistic abstraction* uses the underlying programming language, in this case, LISP, to implement a specialized, high-level language that may be more effective for solving a particular class of problems. The term "meta-linguistic abstraction" refers to our use of the base language to implement this other programming language, rather than to directly solve the problem. As we saw in Section 15.6, PROLOG also gives the programmer the power to create meta-level interpreters. The power of meta-interpreters to support programming in complex domains was also discussed in the introduction to Part VI.

16.8 Logic Programming in LISP

As an example of meta-linguistic abstraction, we develop a LISP-based logic programming interpreter, using the unification algorithm from Section 16.6. Like PROLOG, our logic programs consist of a database of facts and rules in the predicate calculus. The interpreter processes queries (or goals) by unifying them against entries in the logic database. If a goal unifies with a simple fact, it succeeds; the solution is the set of bindings generated in the match. If it matches the head of a rule, the interpreter recursively attempts to satisfy the rule premise in a depth-first fashion, using the bindings generated in matching the head. On success, the interpreter prints the original goal, with variables replaced by the solution bindings.

For simplicity's sake, this interpreter supports conjunctive goals and implications: or and not are not defined, nor are features such as arithmetic, I/O, or the usual PROLOG built-in predicates. Although we do not implement full PROLOG, and the exhaustive nature of the search and absence of the *cut* prevent the proper treatment of recursive predicates, the shell captures the basic behavior of the logic programming languages. The addition to the interpreter of the other features just mentioned is an interesting exercise.

16.8.1 A Simple Logic Programming Language

Our logic programming interpreter supports Horn clauses, a subset of full predicate calculus. Well-formed formulas consist of terms, conjunctive expressions, and rules written in a LISP-oriented syntax. A compound term is a list in which the first element is a predicate name and the remaining elements are the arguments. Arguments may be either constants, variables, or other compound terms. As in the discussion of unify, we represent variables as lists of two elements, the word var followed by the name of the variable. Examples of terms include:

```
(likes bill music)
(on block (var x))
(friend bill (father robert))
```

A conjunctive expression is a list whose first element is and and whose subsequent arguments are either simple terms or conjunctive expressions:

```
(and (smaller david sarah) (smaller peter david))
(and (likes (var x) (var y)) (likes (var z) (var y)))
(and (hand-empty) (and (on block-1 block-2) (on block-2 table)))
```

Implications are expressed in a syntactically sweetened form that simplifies both their writing and recognition:

```
(rule if <premise> then <conclusion>)
```

where <premise> is either a simple or conjunctive proposition and <conclusion> is always a simple proposition. Examples of rules include:

```
(rule if (and (likes (var x) (var z))
              (likes (var y) (var z)))
    then (friend (var x) (var y)))
(rule if (and (size (var x) small)
              (color (var x) red)
              (smell (var x) fragrant))
    then (kind (var x) rose))
```

The logical database is a list of facts and rules bound to a global variable, *assertions*. We can define an example knowledge base of likes relationships by a call to setq (we could also have used the LISP function defvar):

```
(setq *assertions*
    '((likes george beer)
      (likes george kate)
      (likes george kids)
      (likes bill kids)
      (likes bill music)
      (likes bill pizza)
      (likes bill wine)
      (rule
        if (and (likes (var x) (var z))
                (likes (var y) (var z)))
        then (friend (var x) (var y)))))
```

The top level of the interpreter is a function, logic-shell, that reads goals and attempts to satisfy them against the logic database bound to *assertions*. Given the above database, logic-shell will have the following behavior (comments follow the ;):

```
> (logic-shell)                              ; logic-shell prompts with a ?
?(likes bill (var x))        ; successful queries are printed with substitutions
(likes bill kids)
(likes bill music)
(likes bill pizza)
(likes bill wine)
?(likes george kate)
(likes george kate)
?(likes george taxes)                        ; failed query returns nothing
?(friend bill george)
(friend bill george)             ; from (and(likes bill kids)(likes george kids))
?(friend bill roy)           ; roy does not exist in knowledge base, query fails
?(friend bill (var x))
(friend bill george)             ; from (and(likes bill kids)(likes george kids))
(friend bill bill)                 ; from (and(likes bill kids)(likes bill kids))
(friend bill bill)               ; from (and(likes bill music)(likes bill music))
(friend bill bill)               ; from (and(likes bill pizza)(likes bill pizza))
(friend bill bill)                 ; from (and(likes bill wine)(likes bill wine))
?quit
bye
>
```

Before discussing the implementation of the logic programming interpreter, we introduce the *stream* data type.

16.8.2   Streams and Stream Processing

As the preceding example suggests, even a small knowledge base can produce complex behaviors. It is necessary not only to determine the truth or falsity of a goal but also to determine the variable substitutions that make that goal to be true in the knowledge base.

A single goal can match with different facts, producing different substitution sets; conjunctions of goals require that all conjuncts succeed and also that the variable bindings be consistent throughout. Similarly, rules require that the substitutions formed in matching a goal with a rule conclusion be made in the rule premise when it is solved. The management of these multiple substitution sets is the major source of complexity in the interpreter. Streams help address this complexity by focusing on the movement of a sequence of candidate variable substitutions through the constraints defined by the logic database.

A *stream* is a sequence of data objects. Perhaps the most common example of stream processing is a typical interactive program. The data from the keyboard are viewed as an endless sequence of characters, and the program is organized around reading and processing the *current* character from the input stream. Stream processing is a generalization of this idea: streams need not be produced by the user; they may also be generated and modified by functions. A *generator* is a function that produces a continuing stream of data objects. A *map function* applies some function to each of the elements of a stream. A *filter* eliminates selected elements of a stream according to the constraints of some predicate.

The solutions returned by an inference engine may be represented as a stream of different variable substitutions under which a goal follows from a knowledge base. The constraints defined by the knowledge base are used to modify and filter a stream of candidate substitutions, producing the result. Consider, for example, the conjunctive goal:

```
(and (likes bill (var z))
     (likes george (var z)))
```

using the logic database from the preceding section. The stream-oriented view regards each of the conjuncts in the expression as a *filter* for a stream of substitution sets. Each set of variable substitutions in the stream is applied to the conjunct and the result is matched against the knowledge base. If the match fails, that set of substitutions is eliminated from the stream; if it succeeds, the match may create new sets of substitutions by adding new bindings to the original substitution set.

Figure 16.4 illustrates the stream of substitutions passing through this conjunctive goal. It begins with a stream of candidate substitutions containing only the empty substitution set and grows after the first proposition matches against multiple entries in the database. It then shrinks to a single substitution set as the second conjunct eliminates substitutions that do not allow (likes george (var z)) to succeed. The resulting stream, ((((var z) . kids))), contains the only variable substitution that allows both subgoals in the conjunction to succeed in the knowledge base.

As this example illustrates, a goal and a single set of substitutions may generate several new substitution sets, one for each match in the knowledge base. Alternatively, a goal will eliminate a substitution set from the stream if no match is found. The stream of substitution sets may grow and shrink as it passes through a series of conjuncts.

The basis of stream processing is a set of functions to create, augment, and access the elements of a stream. We can define a simple set of stream functions using lists and the standard list manipulators. The functions that constitute a list-based implementation of the stream data type are:

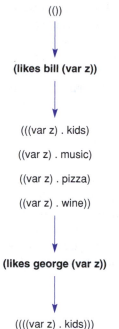

(())

(likes bill (var z))

(((var z) . kids)
((var z) . music)
((var z) . pizza)
((var z) . wine))

(likes george (var z))

((((var z) . kids)))

Figure 16.4 Stream of variable substitutions filtered
through conjunctive subgoals.

```
; Cons-stream adds a new first element to a stream
(defun cons-stream (element stream) (cons element stream))
; head-stream returns the first element of the stream
(defun head-stream (stream) (car stream))
; tail-stream returns the stream with its first element deleted.
(defun tail-stream (stream) (cdr stream))
; empty-stream-p is true if the stream is empty
(defun empty-stream-p (stream) (null stream))
; make-empty-stream creates an empty stream
(defun make-empty-stream ( ) nil)
; combine-stream appends two streams.
(defun combine-streams (stream1 stream2)
    (cond ((empty-stream-p stream1) stream2)
          (t (cons-stream (head-stream stream1)
                (combine-streams
                        (tail-stream stream 1)
                        stream2)))))
```

Although the implementation of streams as lists does not allow the full power of stream-based abstraction, the definition of a stream data type helps us to view the program from a data flow point of view. For many problems, such as the logic programming interpreter of Section 16.8.3, this provides the programmer with a powerful tool for organizing and simplifying the code. In Section 16.9 we discuss some limitations of this list-based implementation of streams and present an alternative approach using streams with delayed evaluation.

16.8.3   A Stream-Based Logic Programming Interpreter

We invoke the interpreter through a function called logic-shell, a straightforward variation of the read-eval-print loop discussed in Section 16.7. After printing a prompt, "?," it reads the next s-expression entered by the user and binds it to the symbol goal. If goal is equal to quit, the function halts; otherwise, it calls solve to generate a stream of substitution sets that satisfy the goal. This stream is passed to print-solutions, which prints the goal with each of these different substitutions. The function then recurs. logic-shell is defined by:

```
(defun logic-shell ( )
    (print '? )
    (let ((goal (read)))
        (cond ((equal goal 'quit) 'bye)
                (t (print-solutions goal (solve goal nil))
                    (terpri)
                    (logic-shell)))))
```

solve is the heart of the interpreter. solve takes a goal and a set of substitutions and finds all solutions that are consistent with the knowledge base. These solutions are returned as a stream of substitution sets; if there are no matches, solve returns the empty stream. From the stream processing point of view, solve is a *source*, or *generator*, for a stream of solutions. solve is defined by:

```
(defun solve (goal substitutions)
    (declare (special *assertions*))
    (if (conjunctive-goal-p goal)
        (filter-through-conj-goals (body goal)
            (cons-stream substitutions (make-empty-stream)))
        (infer goal substitutions *assertions*)))
```

The declaration special tells the LISP compiler that *assertions* is a *special*, or global, variable and should be bound dynamically in the environment in which solve is called. (This special declaration is not required in many modern versions of LISP.)

solve first tests whether the goal is a conjunction; if it is, solve calls filter-through-conj-goals to perform the filtering described in Section 16.8.2. If goal is not a conjunction, solve assumes it is a simple goal and calls infer, defined below, to solve it against the knowledge base.

solve calls filter-through-conj-goals with the body of the conjunction (i.e., the sequence of conjuncts with the and operator removed) and a stream that contains only the initial substitution set. The result is a stream of substitutions representing all of the solutions for this goal. We define filter-through-conj-goals by:

```
(defun filter-through-conj-goals (goals substitution-stream)
    (if (null goals)
            substitution-stream
            (filter-through-conj-goals (cdr goals)
                    (filter-through-goal (car goals) substitution-stream))))
```

If the list of goals is empty, the function halts, returning substitution stream unchanged. Otherwise, it calls filter-through-goal to filter substitution-stream through the first goal on the list. It passes this result on to a recursive call to filter-through-conj-goals with the remainder of the goal list. Thus, the stream is passed through the goals in left-to-right order, growing or shrinking as it passes through each goal.

filter-through-goal takes a single goal and uses it as a filter to the stream of substitutions. This filtering is done by calling solve with the goal and the first set of substitutions in the substitution stream. The result of this call to solve is a stream of substitutions resulting from matches of the goal against the knowledge base. This stream will be empty if the goal does not succeed under any of the substitutions contained in the stream, or it may contain multiple substitution sets representing alternative bindings. This stream is combined with the result of filtering the tail of the input stream through the same goal:

```
(defun filter-through-goal (goal substitution-stream)
    (if (empty-stream-p substitution-stream)
            (make-empty-stream)
            (combine-streams
                    (solve goal (head-stream substitution-stream))
                    (filter-through-goal goal (tail-stream substitution-stream)))))
```

To summarize, filter-through-conj-goals passes a stream of substitution sets through a sequence of goals, and filter-through-goal filters the substitution stream through a single goal. A recursive call to solve solves the goal under each substitution set.

Whereas solve handles conjunctive goals by calling filter-through-conj-goals, simple goals are handled by the function infer, defined next, which takes a goal and a substitution set and finds all solutions in the knowledge base. infer's third parameter, kb, is a database of logical expressions. When solve first calls infer, it passes the knowledge base contained in the global variable *assertions*. infer searches kb sequentially, trying the goal against each fact or rule conclusion.

The recursive implementation of infer builds the backward-chaining search typical of PROLOG and most expert system shells. It first checks whether kb is empty, returning an empty stream if it is. Otherwise, it binds the first item in kb to the symbol assertion using a let* block. let* is like let except it is guaranteed to evaluate the initializations of its local variables in sequentially nested scopes, i.e., it provides an order to the binding and visibility of preceding variables. It also defines the variable match: if assertion is a rule, let initializes match to the substitutions required to unify the goal with the conclusion of the rule; if assertion is a fact, let binds match to those substitutions required to unify assertion with the goal. After attempting to unify the goal with the first element of the knowledge base, infer tests whether the unification succeeded. If it failed to match, infer recurs, attempting to solve the goal using the remainder of the knowledge base. If the unification succeeded and assertion is a rule, infer calls solve on the premise of the rule using the augmented set of substitutions bound to match. combine-stream joins the resulting stream of solutions to that constructed by calling infer on the rest of the knowledge base. If assertion is not a rule, it is a fact; infer adds the solution bound to match to those provided by the rest of the knowledge base. Note that once the goal unifies with a fact, it is solved; this terminates the search. We define infer:

```
(defun infer (goal substitutions kb)
    (if (null kb)
        (make-empty-stream)
        (let* ((assertion (rename-variables (car kb)))
                (match (if (rulep assertion)
                        (unify goal (conclusion assertion) substitutions)
                        (unify goal assertion substitutions))))
            (if (equal match 'failed)
                (infer goal substitutions (cdr kb))
                (if (rulep assertion)
                    (combine-streams
                        (solve (premise assertion) match)
                        (infer goal substitutions (cdr kb)))
                    (cons-stream match (infer goal substitutions (cdr kb)))))))))
```

Before the first element of kb is bound to assertion, it is passed to rename-variables to give each variable a unique name. This prevents name conflicts between the variables in the goal and those in the knowledge base entry; e.g., if (var x) appears in a goal, it must be treated as a different variable than a (var x) that appears in the rule or fact. The simplest way to handle this is by renaming all variables in the assertion with unique names. We define rename-variables at the end of this section.

This completes the implementation of the core of the logic programming interpreter. To summarize, solve is the top-level function and generates a stream of substitution sets that represent solutions to the goal using the knowledge base. filter-through-conj-goals solves conjunctive goals in a left-to-right order, using each goal as a filter on a stream of candidate solutions: if a goal cannot be proven true against the knowledge base using a substitution set in the stream, filter-through-conj-goals eliminates those substitutions from the stream. If the goal is a simple literal, solve calls infer to generate a stream of all substitutions that make the goal succeed against the knowledge base. Like PROLOG, our logic programming interpreter takes a goal and finds all variable bindings that make it true against a given knowledge base.

All that remain are functions for accessing components of knowledge base entries, managing variable substitutions, and printing solutions. print-solutions takes as arguments a goal and a stream of substitutions. For each set of substitutions in the stream, it prints the goal with variables replaced by their bindings in the substitution set.

```
(defun print-solutions (goal substitution-stream)
     (cond ((empty-stream-p substitution-stream) nil)
           (t (print (apply-substitutions goal (head-stream substitution-stream)))
              (terpri)
              (print-solutions goal (tail-stream substitution-stream)))))
```

The replacement of variables with their values under a substitution set is done by apply-substitutions, which does a car-cdr recursive tree walk on a pattern. If the pattern is a constant, it is returned unchanged. If it is a variable, apply-substitutions tests if it is bound. If it is unbound, the variable is returned; if it is bound, apply-substitutions calls itself recursively on the value of this binding. Note that the binding value may be either a constant, another variable, or a pattern of arbitrary complexity.

```
(defun apply-substitutions (pattern substitution-list)
     (cond ((is-constant-p pattern) pattern)
           ((varp pattern)
            (let ((binding (get-binding pattern substitution-list)))
                 (cond (binding (apply-substitutions (get-binding-value binding)
                                                     substitution-list))
                       (t pattern))))
           (t (cons (apply-substitutions (car pattern) substitution-list)
                    (apply-substitutions (cdr pattern) substitution-list)))))
```

infer renamed the variables in each knowledge base entry before matching it with a goal. This is necessary to prevent undesired name collisions in matches. For example, the goal (p a (var x)) should match with the knowledge base entry (p (var x) b), because the scope of each (var x) is restricted to a single expression. As unification is defined, however, this match will not occur. Name collisions are prevented by giving each variable in an expression a unique name. The basis of our renaming scheme is a Common LISP built-in function called gensym that takes no arguments; each time it is called, it returns a unique symbol consisting of a number preceded by #:G. For example:

```
> (gensym)
#:G4
> (gensym)
#:G5
> (gensym)
#:G6
>
```

Our renaming scheme replaces each variable name in an expression with the result of a call to gensym. rename-variables performs certain initializations (described below) and calls rename-rec to make substitutions recursively in the pattern. When a variable is encountered, the function rename is called to return a new name. To allow multiple occurrences of a variable in a pattern to be given consistent names, each time a variable is renamed, the new name is placed in an association list bound to the *special* variable *name-list*. The special declaration makes all references to the variable dynamic and shared among these functions. Thus, each access of *name-list* in rename will access the instance of *name-list* declared in rename-variables. rename-variables initializes *name-list* to nil when it is first called on an expression. These functions are defined:

```
(defun rename-variables (assertion)
     (declare (special *name-list*))
     (setq *name-list* nil)
     (rename-rec assertion))
(defun rename-rec (exp)
     (declare (special *name-list*))
     (cond ((is-constant-p exp) exp)
           ((varp exp) (rename exp))
           (t (cons (rename-rec (car exp))(rename-rec (cdr exp))))))
(defun rename (var)
     (declare (special *name-list*))
     (list 'var (or (cdr (assoc var *name-list* :test #'equal))
               (let ((name (gensym)))
                    (setq *name-list* (acons var name *name-list*))name))))
```

The final functions access components of rules and goals and are self-explanatory:

```
(defun premise (rule) (nth 2 rule))
(defun conclusion (rule) (nth 4 rule))
(defun rulep (pattern)
     (and (listp pattern)
          (equal (nth 0 pattern) 'rule)))
(defun conjunctive-goal-p (goal)
     (and (listp goal)
          (equal (car goal) 'and)))
(defun body (goal) (cdr goal))
```

16.9 Streams and Delayed Evaluation

As we demonstrated in the implementation of logic-shell, a stream-oriented view can help with the organization of a complex program. However, our implementation of streams as lists did not provide the full benefit of stream processing. In particular, this implementation suffers from inefficiency and an inability to handle infinitely long data streams.

In the list implementation of streams, all of the elements must be computed before that stream (list) can be passed on to the next function. In logic-shell this leads to an exhaustive search of the knowledge base for each intermediate goal in the solution process. In order to produce the first solution to the top-level goal, the program must produce a list of all solutions. Even if we want only the first solution on this list, the program must still search the entire solution space. What we would really prefer is for the program to produce just the first solution by searching only that portion of the space needed to produce that solution and then to delay finding the rest of the goals until they are needed.

A second problem is the inability to process infinitely long streams. Although this problem does not arise in logic-shell, it occurs naturally in the stream-based solution to many problems. Assume, for example, that we would like to write a function that returns a stream of the first n odd Fibonacci numbers. A straightforward implementation would use a generator to produce a stream of Fibonacci numbers, a filter to eliminate even-valued numbers from the stream, and an accumulator to gather these into a solution list of n elements; see Figure 16.5. Unfortunately, the stream of Fibonacci numbers is infinite in length and we cannot decide in advance how long a list will be needed to produce the first n odd numbers.

Instead, we would like the generator to produce the stream of Fibonacci numbers one at a time and pass each number through the filter until the accumulator has gathered the n values required. This behavior more closely fits our intuitive notion of evaluating a stream than does the list-based implementation. We will accomplish this through the use of *delayed evaluation*.

Instead of letting the generator run to completion to produce the entire stream of results, we let the function produce the first element of the stream and then freeze or delay its execution until the next element is needed. When the program needs the next element of the stream, it causes the function to resume execution and produce only that element and again delay evaluation of the rest of the stream. Thus, instead of containing the entire list of numbers, the stream consists of just two components, its first element and the frozen computation of the rest of the stream; see Figure 16.6.

We use *function closures* to create the delayed portion of the stream illustrated in Figure 16.4. A closure consists of a function, along with all its variable bindings in the current environment; we may bind a closure to a variable, or pass it as a parameter, and evaluate it using funcall. Essentially, a closure "freezes" a function application until a later time. We can create closures using the LISP form function. For example, consider the following LISP transcript:

```
> (setq v 10)
10
> (let ((v 20)) (setq f_closure (function (lambda ( ) v))))
#<COMPILED-LEXICAL-CLOSURE #x28641E>
> (funcall f_closure)
20
> v
10
```

The initial setq binds v to 10 in the global environment. In the let block, we create a local binding of v to 20 and create a closure of a function that returns this value of v. It is interesting to note that this binding of v does not disappear when we exit the let block, because it is retained in the function closure that is bound to f_closure. It is a lexical binding, however, so it doesn't shadow the global binding of v. If we subsequently evaluate this closure, it returns 20, the value of the local binding of v, even though the global v is still bound to 10.

The heart of this implementation of streams is a pair of functions, delay and force. delay takes an expression as argument and does not evaluate it; instead it takes the unevaluated argument and returns a closure. force takes a function closure as argument and uses funcall to force its application. These functions are defined:

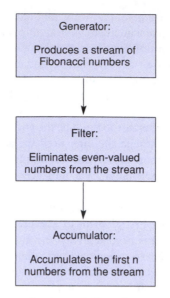

Figure 16.5 Stream implementation of a program to find the first n odd Fibonacci numbers.

A list-based stream containing an indeterminate number of elements:

$(e_1 \quad e_2 \quad e_3 \quad e_4 \ldots)$

A stream with delayed evaluation of its tail containing only two elements but capable of producing any number of elements:

$(e_1 \quad . <\text{delayed evaluation of remainder of stream}>)$

Figure 16.6 List-based versus delayed evaluation implementations of streams.

```
(defmacro delay (exp) '(function (lambda ( ) ,exp)))
(defun force (function-closure)
    (funcall function-closure))
```

delay is an example of a LISP form called a *macro*. We cannot define delay using defun because all functions so defined evaluate their arguments before executing the body. Macros give us complete control over the evaluation of their arguments. We define macros using the defmacro form. When a macro is executed, it does not evaluate its arguments. Instead, it binds the unevaluated s-expressions in the call to the formal parameters and evaluates its body *twice*. The first evaluation is called a *macro-expansion*; the second evaluates the resulting form.

To define the delay macro, we introduce another LISP form, the *backquote* or '. Backquote prevents evaluation just like a quote, except that it allows us to evaluate selectively elements of the backquoted expression. Any element of a backquoted s-expression preceded by a comma is evaluated and its value inserted into the resulting expression.

For example, assume the call (delay (+ 2 3)). The expression (+ 2 3) is not evaluated; instead it is bound to the formal parameter, exp. When the body of the macro is evaluated the first time, it returns the backquoted expression with the formal parameter, exp, replaced by its value, the unevaluated s-expression (+ 2 3). This produces the expression (function (lambda () (+ 2 3))). This is evaluated again, returning a function closure.

If we later pass this closure to force, it will evaluate the expression (lambda () (+ 2 3)). This is a function that takes no arguments and whose body evaluates to 5. Using force and delay, we can implement streams with delayed evaluation. We rewrite cons-stream as a macro that takes two arguments and conses the value of the first onto the delayed evaluation of the second. Thus, the second argument may be a function that will return a stream of any length; it is not evaluated. We define tail-stream so that it forces the evaluation of the tail of a stream. These are defined:

```
(defmacro cons-stream (exp stream) '(cons ,exp (delay ,stream)))
(defun tail-stream (stream) (force (cdr stream)))
```

We also redefine combine-streams as a macro that takes two streams but does not evaluate them. Instead, it uses delay to create a closure for the second stream and passes this and the first stream to the function comb-f. comb-f is similar to our earlier definition of combine-streams, except that in the event that the first stream is empty, it forces evaluation of the second stream. If the first stream is not empty, the recursive call to comb-f is done using our delayed version of cons-stream. This freezes the recursive call in a closure for later evaluation.

```
(defmacro combine-streams (stream1 stream2)
   '(comb-f ,stream1 (delay ,stream2)))
(defun comb-f (stream1 stream2)
   (if (empty-stream-p stream1)
      (force stream2)
      (cons-stream (head-stream stream1)
            (comb-f (tail-stream stream1) stream2))))
```

If we add these definitions to the versions of head-stream, make-empty-stream, and empty-stream-p from Section 16.8.2, we have a complete stream implementation with delayed evaluation.

We can use these functions to solve our problem of producing the first n odd Fibonacci numbers. fibonacci-stream returns a stream of all the Fibonacci numbers; note that fibonacci-stream is a nonterminating recursive function. Delayed evaluation prevents it from looping forever; it produces the next element only when needed. filter-odds takes a stream of integers and eliminates the even elements of the stream. accumulate takes a stream and a number n and returns a *list* of the first n elements of the stream.

```
(defun fibonacci-stream (fibonacci-1 fibonacci-2)
    (cons-stream (+ fibonacci-1 fibonacci-2)
                    (fibonacci-stream fibonacci-2 (+ fibonacci-1 fibonacci-2))))
(defun filter-odds (stream)
    (cond ((evenp (head-stream stream)) (filter-odds (tail-stream stream)))
          (t (cons-stream (head-stream stream) (filter-odds (tail-stream stream))))))
(defun accumulate-into-list (n stream)
    (cond ((zerop n) nil)
          (t (cons (head-stream stream) (accumulate-into-list
             (– n 1)(tail-stream stream))))))
```

To obtain a list of the first 25 odd Fibonacci numbers, we call accumulate-into-list:

```
(accumulate-into-list 25 (filter-odds (fibonacci-stream 0 1)))
```

We may use these stream functions in the definition of the logic programming interpreter of Section 16.8 to improve its efficiency under certain circumstances. Assume that we would like to modify print-solutions so that instead of printing all solutions to a goal, it prints the first and waits for the user to ask for the additional solutions. Using our implementation of lists as streams, the algorithm would still search for all solutions before it could print out the first. Using delayed evaluation, the first solution will be the head of a stream, and the function evaluations necessary to find the additional solutions will be frozen in the tail of the stream.

In the next section we modify this logic programming interpreter to implement a LISP-based expert system shell. Before presenting the expert system shell, however, we mention two additional stream functions that are used in its implementation. In Section 16.3, we presented a general mapping function and a general filter for lists. These functions, map-simple and filter, can be modified to function on streams. We use filter-stream and map-stream in the next section; their implementation is an exercise.

16.10   An Expert System Shell in LISP

The expert system shell developed in this section is an extension of the backward-chaining engine of Section 16.8. The major modifications include the use of certainty factors to manage uncertain reasoning, the ability to ask the user for unknown facts, and the use of a working memory to save user responses. This expert system shell is called lisp-shell.

16.10.1 Implementing Certainty Factors

The logic programming interpreter returned a stream of the substitution sets under which a goal logically followed from a database of logical assertions. Bindings that did not allow the goal to be satisfied using the knowledge base were either filtered from the stream or not generated in the first place. In implementing reasoning with certainty factors, however, simple truth values are replaced by a numeric value between −1 and 1.

This requires that the stream of solutions to a goal not only contain the variable bindings that allow the goal to be satisfied; they must also include measures of the confidence under which each solution follows from the knowledge base. Consequently, instead of processing streams of substitution sets, lisp-shell processes streams of pairs: a set of substitutions and a number representing the confidence in the truth of the goal under those variable substitutions.

We implement stream elements as an abstract data type: the functions for manipulating the substitution and certainty factor pairs are subst-record, which constructs a pair from a set of substitutions and a certainty factor; subst-list, which returns the set of bindings from a pair; and subst-cf, which returns the certainty factor. Internally, records are represented as dotted pairs, of the form (<substitution list>. <cf>). The functions that handle these pairs are:

```
; Returns the list of variable bindings from a substitution/certainty factor pair.
(defun subst-list (substitutions)
    (car substitutions))
; Returns the certainty factor from a substitution/certainty factor pair.
(defun subst-cf (substitutions)
    (cdr substitutions))
; Forms a substitution set/certainty factor pair.
(defun subst-record (substitutions cf)
    (cons substitutions cf))
```

Similarly, rules and facts are stored in the knowledge base with an attached certainty factor. Facts are represented as dotted pairs, (<assertion>. <cf>), where <assertion> is a positive literal and <cf> is its certainty measure. Rules are in the format (rule if <premise> then <conclusion> <cf>), where <cf> is the certainty factor. A sample rule for the domain of recognizing flowers is:

```
(rule
    if (and (rose (var x)) (color (var x) red))
    then (kind (var x) american-beauty) 1)
```

The functions for handling rules and facts are:

```
; Returns the premise of a rule.
(defun premise (rule)
    (nth 2 rule))
; Returns the conclusion of a rule.
(defun conclusion (rule)
    (nth 4 rule))
; Returns the cf of a rule.
(defun rule-cf (rule)
    (nth 5 rule))
```

```
; Tests whether a given pattern is a rule.
(defun rulep (pattern)
    (and (listp pattern)
        (equal (nth 0 pattern) 'rule)))
; Returns the pattern part of a fact.
(defun fact-pattern (fact)
    (car fact))
; Returns the cf of a fact.
(defun fact-cf (fact)
    (cdr fact))
```

Using these functions, we implement the balance of the rule interpreter through a series
of modifications to the logic programming interpreter (Section 16.8).

16.10.2 Architecture of lisp-shell

solve is the heart of lisp-shell. solve does not return a solution stream directly but first
passes it through a filter that eliminates any substitutions whose certainty factor is less than
0.2. This prunes results that lack sufficient confidence.

```
(defun solve (goal substitutions)
    (filter-stream
        (if (conjunctive-goal-p goal)
            (filter-through-conj-goals
                (cdr (body goal))
                (solve (car (body goal)) substitutions))
            (solve-simple-goal goal substitutions))
        # '(lambda (x) (< 0.2 (subst-cf x))))))
```

This has changed only slightly from the definition of solve in logic-shell. It is still a
conditional statement that distinguishes between conjunctive goals and simple goals. One
difference is the use of the general filter filter-stream to prune any solution whose certainty
factor falls below a certain value. This test is passed as a lambda expression that checks
whether or not the certainty factor of a substitution set/cf pair is less than 0.2. The other
difference is to use solve-simple-goal in place of infer. Handling simple goals is
complicated by the ability to ask for user information. We define solve-simple-goal as:

```
(defun solve-simple-goal (goal substitutions)
    (declare (special *assertions*))
    (declare (special *case-specific-data*))
    (or (told goal substitutions *case-specific-data*)
        (infer goal substitutions *assertions*)
        (ask-for goal substitutions)))
```

solve-simple-goal uses an or form to try three different solution strategies in order. First
it calls told to check whether the goal has already been solved by the user in response to a

previous query. User responses are bound to the global variable *case-specific-data*; told searches this list to try to find a match for the goal. This keeps lisp-shell from asking for the same piece of information twice. If this fails, solve-simple-goal attempts to infer the goal using the rules in *assertions*. Finally, if these fail, it calls ask-for to query the user for the information. These functions are defined below.

The top-level read-solve-print loop has changed little, except for the inclusion of a statement initializing *case-specific-data* to nil before solving a new goal. Note that when solve is called initially, it is not just passed the empty substitution set, but a pair consisting of the empty substitution set and a cf of 0. This certainty value has no real meaning: it is included for syntactic reasons until a meaningful substitution set and certainty factor pair is generated by user input or a fact in the knowledge base.

```
(defun lisp-shell ()
    (declare (special *case-specific-data*))
    (setq *case-specific-data* ( ))
    (prin1 'lisp-shell> )                              ; prin1 does not output a new line
    (let ((goal (read)))
    (terpri)
    (cond ((equal goal 'quit) 'bye)
            (t (print-solutions goal (solve goal (subst-record nil 0)))
                (terpri)
                (lisp-shell)))))
```

filter-through-conj-goals is not changed, but filter-through-goal must compute the certainty factor for a conjunctive expression as the minimum of the certainties of the conjuncts. To do so, it binds the first element of substitution-stream to the symbol subs in a let block. It then calls solve on the goal and this substitution set; the result is passed through the general mapping function, map-stream, which takes the stream of substitution pairs returned by solve and recomputes their certainty factors as the minimum of the certainty factor of the result and the certainty factor of the initial substitution set, subs. These functions are defined:

```
(defun filter-through conj-goals (goals substitution-stream)
    (if (null goals)
            substitution-stream
            (filter-through-conj-goals (cdr goals)
            (filter-through-goal (car goals) substitution-stream))))
(defun filter-through-goal (goal substitution-stream)
    (if (empty-stream-p substitution-stream)
            (make-empty-stream)
            (let ((subs (head-stream substitution-stream)))
                (combine-streams
                (map-stream (solve goal subs)
                # '(lambda (x) (subst-record (subst-list x)(min (subst-cf x)
                    (subst-cf subs)))))
                (filter-through-goal goal (tail-stream substitution-stream))))))
```

The definition of infer has been changed to take certainty factors into account. Although its overall structure reflects the version of infer written for the logic programming interpreter, we must now compute the certainty factor for solutions to the goal from the certainty factors of the rule and the certainties of solutions to the rule premise. solve-rule calls solve to find all solutions to the premise and uses map-stream to compute the resulting certainties for the rule conclusion.

```
(defun infer (goal substitutions kb)
    (if (null kb)
        (make-empty-stream)
        (let* ((assertion (rename-variables (car kb)))
               (match (if (rulep assertion)
                          (unify goal conclusion assertion) (subst-list substitutions))
                          (unify goal assertion (subst-list substitutions)))))
            (if (equal match 'failed)
                (infer goal substitutions (cdr kb))
                (if (rulep assertion)
                    (combine-streams
                      (solve-rule assertion (subst-record match (subst-cf substitutions)))
                      (infer goal substitutions (cdr kb)))
                    (cons-stream (subst-record match (fact-cf assertion))
                      (infer goal substitutions (cdr kb)))))))))
((defun solve-rule (rule substitutions)
    (map-stream (solve (premise rule) substitutions)
        # '(lambda (x) (subst-record
            (subst-list x)
            (* (subst-cf x) (rule-cf rule))))))
```

Finally, print-solutions is modified to take certainty factors into account:

```
(defun print-solutions (goal substitution-stream)
    (cond ((empty-stream-p substitution-stream) nil)
        (t (print (apply-substitutions goal (subst-list (head-stream substitution-stream))))
            (write-string "cf =")
            (prin1 (subst-cf (head-stream substitution-stream)))
            (terpri)
            (print-solutions goal (tail-stream substitution-stream)))))
```

The remaining functions, such as apply-substitutions and functions for accessing components of rules and goals, are unchanged from their definition in Section 16.8.

The remainder of lisp-shell consists of the functions ask-for and told, which handle user interactions. These are straightforward, although the reader should note that we have made some simplifying assumptions. In particular, the only response allowed to queries is either "y" or "n." This causes the binding set passed to ask-for to be returned with a cf of either 1 or −1, respectively; the user may not give an uncertain response directly to a query. ask-rec prints a query and reads the answer, repeating until the answer is either y or n. The reader may expand ask-rec to take on any value within the −1 to 1 range. (−1 and 1, of course, offers an arbitrary range; particular applications may use other ranges.)

askable verifies whether the user may be asked for a particular goal. Any asked goal must exist as a pattern in the global list *askables*; the architect of an expert system may in this way determine which goals may be asked and which may only be inferred from the knowledge base. told searches through the entries in the global *case-specific-data* to find whether the user has already answered a query. It is similar to infer except it assumes that everything in *case-specific-data* is stored as a fact. We define these functions:

```
(defun ask-for (goal substitutions)
    (declare (special *askables*))
    (declare (special *case-specific-data*))
    (if (askable goal *askables*)
        (let* ((query (apply-substitutions goal (subst-list substitutions)))
               (result (ask-rec query)))
            ((setq *case-specific-data* (cons (subst-record query result)
                    *case-specific-data*))
            (cons-stream (subst-record (subst-list substitutions) result)
                (make-empty-stream))))))
(defun ask-rec (query)
    (prin1 query)
    (write-string ">")
        (let ((answer (read)))
        (cond ((equal answer 'y) 1)
                ((equal answer 'n) – 1)
                (t (print "answer must be y or n")
                    (terpri)
                    (ask-rec query)))))
(defun askable (goal askables)
    (cond ((null askables) nil)
            ((not (equal (unify goal (car askables) ( )) 'failed)) t)
            (t (askable goal (cdr askables)))))
(defun told (goal substitutions case-specific-data)
    (cond ((null case-specific-data) (make-empty-stream))
            (t (combine-streams
                    (use-fact goal (car case-specific-data) substitutions)
                    (told goal substitutions (cdr case-specific-data))))))
```

This completes the implementation of our LISP-based expert system shell. In the next section we use lisp-shell to build a simple classification expert system.

16.10.3 Classification Using lisp-shell

We now present a small expert system for classifying trees and bushes. Although it is far from botanically complete, it illustrates the use and behavior of the tool. The knowledge base resides in two global variables: *assertions*, which contains the rules and facts of the knowledge base, and *askables*, which lists the goals that may be asked of the user. The knowledge base used in this example is constructed by two calls to setq:

```
(setq *assertions* '(
    (rule
        if (and (size (var x) tall) (woody (var x)))
        then (tree (var x)) .9)
    (rule
        if (and (size (var x) small) (woody (var x)))
        then (bush (var x)) .9)
    (rule
        if (and (tree (var x)) (evergreen (var x))(color (var x) blue))
        then (kind (var x) spruce) .8)
    (rule
        if (and (tree (var x)) (evergreen (var x))(color (var x) green))
        then (kind (var x) pine) .9)
    (rule
        if (and (tree (var x)) (deciduous (var x)) (bears (var x) fruit))
        then (fruit-tree (var x)) 1)
    (rule
        if (and (fruit-tree (var x)) (color fruit red) (taste fruit sweet))
        then (kind (var x) apple-tree) .9)
    (rule
        if (and (fruit-tree (var x)) (color fruit yellow) (taste fruit sour))
        then (kind (var x) lemon-tree) .8)
    (rule
        if (and (bush (var x)) (flowering (var x)) (thorny (var x)))
        then (rose (var x)) 1)
    (rule
        if (and (rose (var x)) (color (var x) red))
        then (kind (var x) american-beauty) 1)))
(setq *askables* '(
    (size (var x) (var y))
    (woody (var x))
    (soft (var x))
    (color (var x) (var y))
    (evergreen (var x))
    (thorny (var x))
    (deciduous (var x))
    (bears (var x) (var y))
    (taste (var x) (var y))
    (flowering (var x))))
```

A sample run of the trees knowledge base appears below. The reader is encouraged to
trace through the rule base to observe the order in which rules are tried, the propagation of
certainty factors, and the way in which possibilities are pruned when found to be false:

```
> (lisp-shell)
lisp-shell>(kind tree-1 (var x))
(size tree-1 tall) >y
(woody tree-1) >y
(evergreen tree-1) >y
```

```
(color tree-1 blue) >n
color tree-1 green) >y
(kind tree-1 pine) cf 0.81
(deciduous tree-1) >n
(size tree-1 small) >n

lisp-shell>(kind bush-2 (var x))
(size bush-2 tall) >n
(size bush-2 small) >y
(woody bush-2) >y
(flowering bush-2) >y
(thorny bush-2) >y
(color bush-2 red) >y
(kind bush-2 american-beauty) cf 0.9

lisp-shell>(kind tree-3 (var x))
(size tree-3 tall) >y
(woody tree-3) >y
(evergreen tree-3) > n
(deciduous tree-3) >y
(bears tree-3 fruit) >y
(color fruit red) >n
(color fruit yellow) >y
(taste fruit sour) >y
(kind tree-3 lemon-tree) cf 0.72
(size tree-3 small) >n
lisp-shell>quit
bye
?
```

In this example, several anomalies may be noted. For example, the shell occasionally asks whether a tree is small even though it was told the tree is tall, or it asks whether the tree is deciduous even though the tree is an evergreen. This is typical of the behavior of expert systems. The knowledge base does not know anything about the relationship between tall and small or evergreen and deciduous: they are just patterns to be matched. Because the search is exhaustive, all rules are tried. If a system is to exhibit deeper knowledge than this, the relationships must be coded in the knowledge base. For example, a rule may be written that states that small implies not tall. In this example, lisp-shell is not capable of representing these relationships because we have not implemented the not operator. This extension is left as an exercise.

16.11   Semantic Networks and Inheritance in LISP

This section introduces the implementation of semantic networks in LISP. As a family of representations, semantic networks provide a basis for a large variety of inferences; we do not discuss all of these, but focus on a basic approach to constructing network representations using *property lists*. After these are discussed and used to define a simple semantic network, we define a function for class inheritance. The ideas illustrated in this section are important precursors of the object-oriented programming techniques of Section 16.12.

LISP is a convenient language for representing any graph structure, including semantic nets. Lists provide the ability to create computational objects of arbitrary complexity and these objects may be bound to names, allowing for easy reference and the definition of relationships between them. Indeed, all LISP data structures are based on an internal implementation as chains of pointers, a natural isomorph to graph structures.

For example, labeled graphs may be represented using association lists: each node is an entry in an association list with all the arcs out of that node stored in the datum of the node as a second association list. Arcs are described by an association list entry that has the arc name as its key and the arc destination as its datum. Using this representation, the built-in association list functions are used to find the destination of a particular arc from a given node. For example, the labeled, directed graph of Figure 16.7 is represented by the association list:

```
((a (1 . b))
   (b (2 . c))
   (c (2 . b) (3 . a)))
```

This approach is the basis of many network implementations. Another way to implement semantic networks is through the use of *property lists*.

Essentially, property lists are a built-in feature of LISP that allow named relationships to be attached to symbols. Rather than using setq to bind an association list to a symbol, with property lists we can program the direct attachment of named attributes to objects in the global environment. These are bound to the symbol not as a value but as an additional component called the property list.

Functions for managing property lists are get, setf, remprop, and symbol-plist. get, which has the syntax

```
(get <symbol> <property-name>)
```

retrieves a property from <symbol> by its <property-name>. For example, if the symbol rose has a color property of red and a smell property of sweet, then get would have the behavior:

```
(get 'rose 'color)

red
(get 'rose 'smell)
sweet
(get 'rose 'party-affiliation)
nil
```

As the last of these calls to get illustrates, if an attempt is made to retrieve a nonexistent property, one that is not on the property list, get returns a value of nil.

Properties are attached to objects using the setf function, which has the syntax:

Figure 16.7 A simple labeled directed graph.

(setf *<form>* *<value>*)

setf is a generalization of setq. The first argument to setf is taken from a large but specific list of forms. setf does not use the value of the form but the location where the value is stored. The list of forms includes car and cdr. setf places the value of its second argument in that location. For example, we may use setf along with list functions to modify lists in the global environment, as the following transcript shows:

```
? (setq x '(a b c d e))

(a b c d e)
? (setf (nth 2 x) 3)
3
? x
(a b 3 d e)
```

We use setf, along with get, to change the value of properties. For instance, we may define the properties of a rose by:

```
> (setf (get 'rose 'color) 'red)
red
> (setf (get 'rose 'smell) 'sweet)
sweet
```

remprop takes as arguments a symbol and a property name and causes a named property to be deleted. For example:

```
> (get 'rose 'color)
red
> (remprop 'rose 'color)
color
> (get 'rose 'color)
nil
```

symbol-plist takes as argument a symbol and returns its property list. For example:

```
> (setf (get 'rose 'color) 'red)
red
> (setf (get 'rose 'smell) 'sweet)
sweet
> (symbol-plist 'rose)
(smell sweet color red)
```

Using property lists, it is straightforward to implement a semantic network. For example, the following calls to setf implement the semantic network description of species of birds from Figure 15.7. The isa relations define inheritance links.

```
(setf (get 'animal 'covering) 'skin)
(setf (get 'bird 'covering) 'feathers)
(setf (get 'bird 'travel) 'flies)
(setf (get 'bird 'isa) animal)
(setf (get 'fish 'isa) animal)
(setf (get 'fish 'travel) 'swim)
(setf (get 'ostrich 'isa) 'bird)
(setf (get 'ostrich 'travel) 'walk)
(setf (get 'penguin 'isa) 'bird)
(setf (get 'penguin 'travel) 'walk)
(setf (get 'penguin 'color) 'brown)
(setf (get 'opus 'isa) 'penguin)
(setf (get 'canary 'isa) 'bird)
(setf (get 'canary 'color) 'yellow)
(setf (get 'canary 'sound) 'sing)
(setf (get 'tweety 'isa) 'canary)
(setf (get 'tweety 'color) 'white)
(setf (get 'robin 'isa) 'bird)
(setf (get 'robin 'sound) 'sings)
(setf (get 'robin 'color) 'red)
```

Using this representation of semantic nets, we now define hierarchical inheritance. This is simply a search along isa links until a parent is found with the desired property. The parents are searched in a depth-first fashion, and search stops when an instance of the property is found. This is typical of the inheritance algorithms provided by many commercial systems. Variations on this approach include the use of breadth-first search as a search strategy.

inherit-get is a variation of get that first tries to retrieve a property from a symbol; if this fails, inherit-get calls get-from-parents to implement the search. get-from-parents takes as its first argument either a single parent or a list of parents; the second argument is a property name. If the parameter parents is nil, the search halts with failure. If parents is an atom, it calls inherit-get on the parent to either retrieve the property from the parent itself or continue the search. If parents is a list, get-from-parents calls itself recursively on the car and cdr of the list of parents. The tree walk based function inherit-get is defined by:

```
(defun inherit-get (object property)
    (or (get object property)
        (get-from-parents (get object 'isa) property)))
(defun get-from-parents (parents property)
    (cond ((null parents) nil)
          ((atom parents) (inherit-get parents property))
          (t (or (get-from-parents (car parents) property)
                 (get-from-parents (cdr parents) property)))))
```

16.12   Object-Oriented Programming Using CLOS

In spite of the many advantages of functional programming, some problems are best conceptualized in terms of objects that have a state that changes over time. Simulation programs are typical of this. Imagine trying to build a program that will predict the ability of a steam heating system to heat a large building: we can simplify the problem by thinking of it as a system of objects (rooms, thermostats, boilers, steam pipes, etc.) that interact to change the temperature and behavior of each other over time. Object-oriented languages support an approach to problem solving that lets us decompose a problem into interacting objects. These objects have a state that can change over time, and a set of functions or methods that define the object's behaviors. Essentially, object-oriented programming lets us solve problems by constructing a model of the problem domain as we understand it. This model-based approach to problem solving is a natural fit for artificial intelligence, an effective programming methodology in its own right, and a powerful tool for thinking about complex problem domains.

There are a number of languages that support object-oriented programming. Some of the most important are Smalltalk, C++, Java and the Common LISP Object System (CLOS). At first glance, LISP, with its roots in functional programming, and object orientation, with its emphasis on creating objects that retain their state over time, may seem worlds apart. However, many features of the language, such as dynamic type checking and the ability to create and destroy objects dynamically, make it an ideal foundation for constructing an object-oriented language. Indeed, LISP was the basis for many of the early object-oriented languages, such as Flavors, KEE, and ART. As the Common LISP standard was developed, the LISP community has accepted CLOS as the preferred way to do object-oriented programming in LISP.

In order to fully support the needs of object-oriented programming, a programming language must provide three capabilities: 1) *encapsulation*, 2) *polymorphism*, and 3) *inheritance*. The remainder of this introduction defines these capabilities and gives an introduction to the way in which CLOS supports them.

1. **Encapsulation.** All modern programming languages allow us to create complex data structures that combine atomic data items into a single entity. Object-oriented encapsulation is unique in that it combines both data items and the procedures used for their manipulation into a single structure, called a *class*. For example, the abstract data types seen previously (e.g., Section 15.2) may quite properly be seen

as classes. In some object-oriented languages, such as Smalltalk, the encapsulation of procedures (or methods as they are called in the object-oriented community) in the object definition is explicit. CLOS takes a different approach, using LISP's type-checking to provide this same ability. CLOS implements methods as *generic functions*. These functions check the type of their parameters to guarantee that they can only be applied to instances of a certain object class. This gives us a logical binding of methods to their objects.

2. **Polymorphism.** The word polymorphic comes from the roots "poly," meaning *many*, and "morph," meaning *form*. A function is polymorphic if it has many different behaviors, depending on the types of its arguments. Perhaps the most intuitive example of polymorphic functions and their importance is a simple drawing program. Assume that we define objects for each of the shapes (square, circle, line) that we would like to draw. A natural way to implement this is to define a method named draw for each object class. Although each individual method has a different definition, depending on the shape it is to draw, all of them have the same name. Every shape in our system has a draw behavior. This is much simpler and more natural than to define a differently named function (draw-square, draw-circle, etc.) for every shape. CLOS supports polymorphism through generic functions. A generic function is one whose behavior is determined by the types of its arguments. In our drawing example, CLOS enables us to define a generic function, draw, that includes code for drawing each of the shapes defined in the program. On evaluation, it checks the type of its argument and automatically executes the appropriate code.

3. **Inheritance.** Inheritance is a mechanism for supporting class abstraction in a programming language. It lets us define general classes that specify the structure and behavior of their specializations, just as the class "tree" defines the essential attributes of pine trees, poplars, oaks, and other different species. In Section 16.11, we built an inheritance algorithm for semantic networks; this demonstrated the ease of implementing inheritance using LISP's built-in data structuring techniques. CLOS provides us with a more robust, expressive, built-in inheritance algorithm.

16.12.1 Defining Classes and Instances in CLOS

The basic data structure in CLOS is the class. A class is a specification for a set of like object instances. We define classes using the defclass macro. defclass has the syntax:

```
(defclass <class-name> (<superclass-name>*)
    (<slot-specifier>*))
```

<class-name> is a symbol. Following the class name is a list of direct superclasses; these are the class's immediate parents in the inheritance hierarchy. This list may be empty. Following the list of parent classes is a list of zero or more slot specifiers. A slot specifier is either the name of a slot or a list consisting of a slot name and zero or more slot options:

```
slot-specifier ::= slotname | (slot-name [slot-option])
```

For instance, we may define a class, rectangle, which has slots for length and width:

```
> (defclass rectangle()
     (length width))
#<standard-class rectangle>
```

make-instance allows us to create instances of a class, taking as its argument a class name and returning an instance of that class. It is the instances of a class that actually store data values. We may bind a symbol, rect, to an instance of rectangle using make-instance and setq:

```
> (setq rect (make-instance 'rectangle))
#<rectangle #x286AC1>
```

The slot options in a defclass define optional properties of slots. Slot options have the syntax (where " | " indicates alternative options):

```
slot-option ::= :reader <reader-function-name> |
                :writer <writer-function-name> |
                :accessor <reader-function-name> |
                :allocation <allocation-type> |
                :initarg <initarg-name> |
                :initform <form>
```

We declare slot options using keyword arguments. Keyword arguments are a form of optional parameter in a LISP function. The keyword, which always begins with a ":", precedes the value for that argument. Available slot options include those that provide accessors to a slot. The :reader option defines a function called reader-function-name that returns the value of a slot for an instance. The :writer option defines a function named writer-function-name that will write to the slot. :accessor defines a function that may read a slot value or may be used with setf to change its value. In the following transcript, we define rectangle to have slots for length and width, with slot accessors get-length and get-width, respectively. After binding rect to an instance of rectangle using make- instance, we use the accessor, get-length, with setf to bind the length slot to a value of 10. Finally, we use the accessor to read this value.

```
> (defclass rectangle ()
      ((length :accessor get-length)
       (width :accessor get-width)))
#<standard-class rectangle>
> (setq rect (make-instance 'rectangle))
#<rectangle #x289159>
> (setf (get-length rect) 10)
10
> (get-length rect)
10
```

In addition to defining accessors, we can access a slot using the primitive function slot-value. slot-value is defined for all slots; it takes as arguments an instance and a slot name and returns the value of that slot. We can use it with setf to change the slot value. For example, we could use slot-value to access the width slot of rect:

```
> (setf (slot-value rect 'width) 5)
5
> (slot-value rect 'width)
5
```

:allocation lets us specify the memory allocation for a slot. allocation-type may be either :instance or :class. If allocation type is :instance, then CLOS allocates a local slot for each instance of the type. If allocation type is :class, then all instances share a single location for this slot. In class allocation, all instances will share the same value of the slot; changes made to the slot by any instance will affect all other instances. If we omit the :allocation specifier, allocation defaults to :instance.

:initarg allows us to specify an argument that we can use with make-instance to specify an initial value for a slot. For example, we can modify our definition of rectangle to allow us to initialize the length and width slots of instances:

```
> (defclass rectangle ()
    ((length :accessor get-length :initarg init-length)
     (width :accessor get-width :initarg init-width)))
#<standard-class rectangle>
>(setq rect (make-instance 'rectangle 'init-length 100 'init-width 50))
#<rectangle #x28D081>
> (get-length rect)
100
> (get-width rect)
50
```

:initform lets us specify a form that CLOS evaluates on each call to make-instance to compute an initial value of the slot. For example, if we would like our program to ask the user for the values of each new instance of rectangle, we may define a function to do so and include it in an initform:

```
> (defun read-value (query) (print query)(read))
read-value
> (defclass rectangle ()
    ((length :accessor get-length :initform (read-value "enter length"))
     (width :accessor get-width :initform (read-value "enter width"))))
#<standard-class rectangle>
> (setq rect (make-instance 'rectangle))
"enter length" 100
"enter width" 50
#<rectangle #x290461>
> (get-length rect)
100
> (get-width rect)
50
```

16.12.2 Defining Generic Functions and Methods

A generic function is a function whose behavior depends upon the type of its arguments. In CLOS, generic functions contain a set of *methods*, indexed by the type of their arguments. We call generic functions with a syntax like that of regular functions; the generic function retrieves and executes the method associated with the type of its parameters.

CLOS uses the structure of the class hierarchy in selecting a method in a generic function; if there is no method defined directly for an argument of a given class, it uses the method associated with the "closest" ancestor in the hierarchy. Generic functions provide most of the advantages of "purer" approaches of methods and message passing, including inheritance and overloading. However, they are much closer in spirit to the functional programming paradigm that forms the basis of LISP. For instance, we can use generic functions with mapcar, funcall, and other higher-order constructs in the LISP language.

We define generic functions using either defgeneric or defmethod. defgeneric lets us define a generic function and several methods using one form. defmethod enables us to define each method separately, although CLOS combines all of them into a single generic function. defgeneric has the (simplified) syntax:

```
(defgeneric f-name lambda-list <method-description>*)
<method-description> ::= (:method specialized-lambda-list form)
```

defgeneric takes a name of the function, a lambda list of its arguments, and a series of zero or more method descriptions. In a method description, specialized-lambda-list is just like an ordinary lambda list in a function definition, except that a formal parameter may be replaced with a (symbol parameter-specializer) pair: symbol is the name of the parameter, and parameter-specializer is the class of the argument. If an argument in a method has no parameter specializer, its type defaults to t, which is the most general class in a CLOS hierarchy. Parameters of type t can bind to any object. The specialized lambda list of each method specifier must have the same number of arguments as the lambda list in the defgeneric. A defgeneric creates a generic function with the specified methods, replacing any existing generic functions.

As an example of a generic function, we may define classes for rectangles and circles and implement the appropriate methods for finding areas:

```
(defclass rectangle ()
    ((length :accessor get-length :initarg init-length)
     (width :accessor get-width :initarg init-width)))
(defclass circle ()
    ((radius :accessor get-radius :initarg init-radius)))
(defgeneric area (shape)
    (:method ((shape rectangle))
        (* (get-length shape)
           (get-width shape)))
    (:method ((shape circle))
        (* (get-radius shape) (get-radius shape) pi)))
```

```
(setq rect (make-instance 'rectangle 'init-length 10 'init-width 5))
(setq circ (make-instance 'circle 'init-radius 7))
```

We can use the area function to compute the area of either shape:

```
> (area rect)
50
> (area circ)
153.93804002589985
```

We can also define methods using defmethod. Syntactically, defmethod is similar to defun, except it uses a specialized lambda list to declare the class to which its arguments belong. When we define a method using defmethod, if there is no generic function with that name, defmethod creates one; if a generic function of that name already exists, defmethod adds a new method to it. For example, we could add the class square to the above definitions by:

```
(defclass square ()
  ((side :accessor get-side :initarg init-side)))
(defmethod area ((shape square))
  (* (get-side shape)
     (get-side shape)))
(setq sqr (make-instance 'square 'init-side 6))
```

defmethod does not change the previous definitions of the area function; it simply adds a new method to the generic function:

```
> (area sqr)
36
> (area rect)
50
> (area circ)
153.93804002589985
```

16.12.3 Inheritance in CLOS

CLOS is a multiple-inheritance language. Along with offering the program designer a very flexible representational scheme, multiple inheritance introduces the potential for creating anomalies when inheriting slots and methods. If two or more ancestors have defined the same method, it is crucial to know which method any instance of those ancestors will inherit. CLOS resolves potential ambiguities by defining a *class precedence* list, which is a total ordering of all classes within a class hierarchy.

Each defclass lists the direct parents of a class in left-to-right order. Using the order of direct parents for each class, CLOS computes a partial ordering of all the ancestors in the inheritance hierarchy. From this partial ordering, it derives the total ordering of the class precedence list through a topological sort. The precedence list follows two rules:

1. Any direct parent class precedes any more distant ancestor.

2. In the list of immediate parents of defclass, each class precedes those to its right.

CLOS computes the class precedence list for an object by topologically sorting its ancestor classes according to the following algorithm. Let C be the class for which we are defining the precedence list:

1. Let S_c be the set of C and all its superclasses.

2. For each class, c, in S_c, define the set of ordered pairs:

    $$R_c = \{(c, c_1), (c_1, c_2), (c_2, c_3) \ldots (c_{n-1}, c_n)\}$$

    where c_1 through c_n are the direct parents of c in the order they are listed in defclass. Note that each R_c defines a total order.

3. Let R be the union of the R_cs for all elements of S_c. R may or may not define a partial ordering. If it does not define a partial ordering, then the hierarchy is inconsistent and the algorithm will detect this.

4. Topologically sort the elements of R by:

    4.1 Begin with an empty precedence list, P.

    4.2 Find a class in R having no predecessors. Add it to the end of P and remove the class from S_c and all pairs containing it from R. If there are several classes in S_c with no predecessor, select the one that has a direct subclass nearest the end in the current version of P.

    4.3 Repeat steps 4.1 and 4.2 until no element can be found that has no predecessor in R.

5. If S_c is not empty, then the hierarchy is inconsistent; it may contain ambiguities that cannot be resolved using this technique.

Because the resulting precedence list is a total ordering, it resolves any ambiguous orderings that may have existed in the class hierarchy. CLOS uses the class precedence list in the inheritance of slots and the selection of methods.

In selecting a method to apply to a given call of a generic function, CLOS first selects all applicable methods. A method is applicable to a generic function call if each parameter specializer in the method is consistent with the corresponding argument in the generic function call. A parameter specializer is consistent with an argument if the specializer either matches the class of the argument or the class of one of its ancestors.

CLOS then sorts all applicable methods using the precedence lists of the arguments. CLOS determines which of two methods should come first in this ordering by comparing their parameter specializers in a left-to-right fashion. If the first pair of corresponding parameter specializers are equal, CLOS compares the second, continuing in this fashion until it finds corresponding parameter specializers that are different. Of these two, it designates as more specific the method whose parameter specializer appears leftmost in the precedence list of the corresponding argument. After ordering all applicable methods, the default method selection applies the most specific method to the arguments. For more details, see Steele (1990).

16.12.4 Example: A Thermostat Simulation

The properties of object-oriented programming that make it a natural way to organize large and complex software implementations are equally applicable in the design of knowledge bases. In addition to the benefits of class inheritance for representing taxonomic knowledge, the message-passing aspect of object-oriented systems simplifies the representation of interacting components.

As a simple example, consider the task of modeling the behavior of a steam heater for a small office building. We may naturally view this problem in terms of interacting components. For example:

> Each office has a thermostat that turns the heat in that office on and off; this functions independently of the thermostats in other offices.
>
> The boiler for the heating plant turns itself on and off in response to the heat demands made by the offices.
>
> When the demand on the boiler increases, there may be a time lag while more steam is generated.
>
> Different offices place different demands on the system; for example, corner offices with large windows lose heat faster than inner offices. Inner offices may even gain heat from their neighbors.
>
> The amount of steam that the system may route to a single office is affected by the total demand on the system.

These points are only a few of those that must be taken into account in modeling the behavior of such a system; the possible interactions are extremely complex. An object-oriented representation allows the programmer to focus on describing one class of objects at a time. We would represent thermostats, for example, by the temperature at which they call for heat, along with the speed with which they respond to changes in temperature.

The steam plant could be characterized in terms of the maximum amount of heat it can produce, the amount of fuel used as a function of heat produced, the amount of time it takes to respond to increased heat demand, and the rate at which it consumes water.

A room could be described in terms of its volume, the heat loss through its walls and windows, the heat gain from neighboring rooms, and the rate at which the radiator adds heat to the room.

The knowledge base is built up of classes such as room and thermostat, which define the properties of the class, and instances such as room-322 and thermostat-211, which model individuals.

The interactions between components are described by messages between instances. For example, a change in room temperature would cause a message to be sent to an instance of the class thermostat. If this new temperature is low enough, the thermostat would switch after an appropriate delay. This would cause a message to be sent to the steam plant requesting more heat. This would cause the steam plant to consume more oil, or, if the plant is already operating at maximum capacity, to route some heat away from other rooms to respond to the new demand. This would cause other thermostats to trip, and so on.

Using this simulation, we can test the ability of the system to respond to external changes in temperature, measure the effect of heat loss, or determine whether the projected heating is adequate. We could use this simulation in a diagnostic program to verify that a hypothesized fault could indeed produce a particular set of symptoms. For example, if we have reason to believe that a heating problem is caused by a blocked steam pipe, we could introduce such a fault into the simulation and see whether it produces the observed symptoms.

The significant thing about this example is the way in which an object-oriented approach allows knowledge engineers to deal with the complexity of the simulation. It enables them to build the model a piece at a time, focusing only on the behaviors of simple classes of objects. The full complexity of the system behavior emerges when we execute the model.

The basis of our CLOS implementation of this model is a set of object definitions. Thermostats have a single slot called setting. The setting of each instance is initialized to 65 using initform. heater-thermostat are a subclass of thermostat for controlling heaters (as opposed to air conditioners); they have a single slot that will be bound to an instance of the heater class. Note that the heater slot has a class allocation; this captures the constraint that the thermostats in different rooms of a building control the single building heater.

```
(defclass thermostat ()
    ((setting :initform 65
            :accessor therm-setting)))
(defclass heater-thermostat (thermostat)
    ((heater :allocation :class
            :initarg heater-obj)))
```

A heater has a state (on or off) which is initialized to off, and a location. It also has a slot, rooms-heated, that will be bound to a list of objects of type room. Note that instances, like any other structure in LISP, may be elements of a list.

```
(defclass heater ()
    ((state :initform 'off
            :accessor heater-state)
    (location :initarg loc)
    (rooms-heated)))
```

room has slots for temperature, initialized to 65 degrees; thermostat, which will be bound to an instance of thermostat; and name, the name of the room.

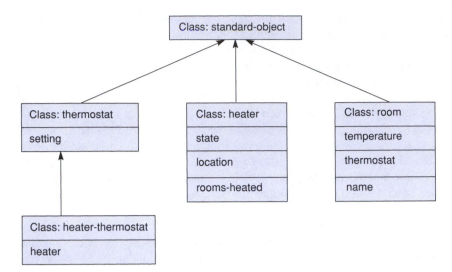

Figure 16.8 Class hierarchy for thermostat simulation.

```
(defclass room ()
        ((temperature :initform 65
                :accessor room-temp)
        (thermostat :initarg therm
                :accessor room-thermostat)
        (name :initarg name
                :accessor room-name)))
```

These class definitions define the hierarchy of Figure 16.8.

We represent our particular simulation as a set of instances of these classes. We will implement a simple system of one room, one heater, and one thermostat:

```
(setf office-heater (make-instance 'heater 'loc 'office))
(setf room-325 (make-instance 'room
                'therm (make-instance 'heater-thermostat
                                'heater-obj office-heater)
                'name 'room-325))
(setf (slot-value office-heater 'rooms-heated) (list room-325))
```

Figure 16.9 shows the definition of instances, the allocation of slots, and the bindings of slots to values.

We define the behavior of rooms through the methods change-temp, check-temp, and change-setting. change-temp sets the temperature of a room to a new value, prints a message to the user, and calls check-temp to determine whether the heater should come on. Similarly, change-setting changes the thermostat setting and calls check-temp, which simulates the thermostat. If the temperature of the room is less than the thermostat setting, it sends the heater a message to turn on; otherwise it sends an off message.

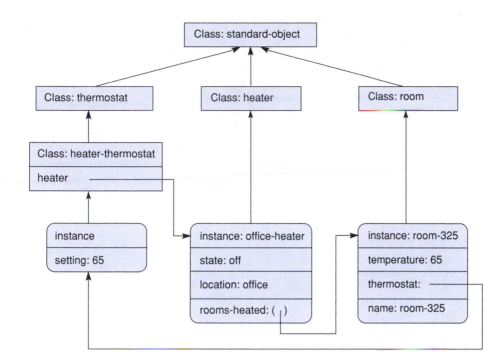

Figure 16.9 Thermostat simulation showing instances, initial values, and
slot allocation.

```
(defmethod change-temp ((place room) temp-change)
    (let ((new-temp (+ (room-temp place) temp-change)))
            (setf (room-temp place) new-temp)
            (terpri)
            (prin1 "the temperature in")
            (prin1 (room-name place))
            (prin1 " is now ")
            (prin1 new-temp)
            (terpri)
            (check-temp place)))

(defmethod change-setting ((room room) new-setting)
    (let ((therm (room-thermostat room)))
            (setf (therm-setting therm) new-setting)
            (prin1 "changing setting of thermostat in")
            (prin1 (room-name room))
            (prin1 " to ")
            (prin1 new-setting)
            (terpri)
            (check-temp room)))
```

```
(defmethod check-temp ((room room))
    (let* ((therm (room-thermostat room))
           (heater (slot-value therm 'heater)))
        (cond ((> (therm-setting therm) (room-temp room))
                  (send-heater heater 'on))
              (t (send-heater heater 'off)))))
```

The heater methods control the state of the heater and change the temperature of the rooms. send-heater takes as arguments an instance of heater and a message, new-state. If new-state is on it calls the turn-on method to start the heater; if new-state is off it shuts the heater down. After turning the heater on, send-heater calls heat-rooms to increase the temperature of each room by one degree.

```
(defmethod send-heater ((heater heater) new-state)
    (case new-state
        (on (if (equal (heater-state heater) 'off)
               (turn-on heater))
               (heat-rooms (slot-value heater 'rooms-heated) 1))
        (off (if (equal (heater-state heater) 'on)
               (turn-off heater)))))
(defmethod turn-on ((heater heater))
    (setf (heater-state heater) 'on)
    (prin1 "turning on heater in")
    (prin1 (slot-value heater 'location))
    (terpri))
(defmethod turn-off ((heater heater))
    (setf (heater-state heater) 'off)
    (prin1 "turning off heater in")
    (prin1 (slot-value heater 'location))
    (terpri))
(defun heat-rooms (rooms amount)
        (cond ((null rooms) nil)
              (t (change-temp (car rooms) amount)
                 (heat-rooms (cdr rooms) amount))))
```

The following transcript illustrates the behavior of the simulation.

```
> (change-temp room-325 5)
"the temperature in "room-325" is now "60
"turning on heater in "office
"the temperature in "room-325" is now "61
"the temperature in "room-325" is now "62
"the temperature in "room-325" is now "63
"the temperature in "room-325" is now "64
"the temperature in "room-325" is now "65
"turning off heater in "office
nil
```

```
> (change-setting room-325 70)
"changing setting of thermostat in "room-325" to "70
"turning on heater in "office
"the temperature in "room-325" is now "66
"the temperature in "room-325" is now "67
"the temperature in "room-325" is now "68
"the temperature in "room-325" is now "69
"the temperature in "room-325" is now "70
"turning off heater in "office
nil
```

16.13   Learning in LISP: The ID3 Algorithm

In this section, we implement the ID3 induction algorithm described in Section 10.3. ID3 infers decision trees from a set of training examples, which enables classification of an object on the basis of its properties. Each internal node of the decision tree tests one of the properties of a candidate object, and uses the resulting value to select a branch of the tree. It continues through the nodes of the tree, testing various properties, until it reaches a leaf, where each leaf node denotes a classification. ID3 uses an information theoretic test selection function to order tests so as to construct a (nearly) optimal decision tree.

The ID3 algorithm requires that we manage a number of complex data structures, including objects, properties, sets, and decision trees. The heart of our implementation is a set of structure definitions, aggregate data types similar to records in Pascal or structures in C. Using defstruct, Common LISP allows us to define types as collections of named slots; defstruct constructs functions needed to create and manipulate objects of that type.

Along with the use of structures to define data types, we exploit higher order functions such as mapcar. As the stream-based approach to our expert system shell demonstrated, the use of maps and filters to apply functions to lists of objects can often capture the intuition behind an algorithm with greater clarity than less expressive programming styles. The ability to treat functions as data, to bind function closures to symbols and process them using other functions, is a cornerstone of LISP programming style.

16.13.1 Defining Structures Using defstruct

Using defstruct, we can define a new *data type*, employee, by evaluating the form:

```
(defstruct employee
        name
        address
        serial-number
        department
        salary)
```

Here, employee is the name of the defined type; name, address, serial number, department and salary are the names of its slots. Evaluation of this defstruct does not create any instances of an employee record; instead, it defines the type, and the functions needed to create and manipulate objects of this type. defstruct takes as its arguments a symbol, which will become the name of a new type, and a number of slot specifiers. Here, we have defined five slots by name; slot specifiers also allow us to define different properties of slots, including type and initialization information, see Steele (1990).

Evaluating the defstruct form has a number of effects, for example:

```
(defstruct <type name>
      <slot name 1>
      <slot name 2>
      ...
      <slot name n>)
```

defstruct defines a function, named according to the scheme: make-<type name>, that lets us create instances of this type. For example, after defining the structure, employee, we may bind new-employee to an object of this type by evaluating:

```
(setq new-employee (make-employee))
```

We can also use slot names as keyword arguments to the make function, giving the instance initial values. For example:

```
(setq new-employee
      (make-employee
            :name '(Doe Jane)
            :address "1234 Main, Randolph, Vt"
            :serial-number 98765
            :department 'Sales
            :salary 4500.00))
```

defstruct makes <type name> the name of a data type. We may use this name with typep to test if an object is of that type, for example:

```
> (typep new-employee 'employee)
t
```

Furthermore, defstruct defines a function, <type-name>-p, that we may also use to test if an object is of the defined type. For instance:

```
> (employee-p new-employee)
t
> (employee-p '(Doe Jane))
nil
```

Finally, defstruct defines an accessor for each slot of the structure. These accessors are named according to the scheme:

```
<type name>-<slot name>
```

In our example, we may access the values of various slots of new-employee using these accessors:

```
> (employee-name new-employee)
(Doe Jane)
> (employee-address new-employee)
 "1234 Main, Randolph, Vt"
> (employee-department new-employee)
Sales
```

We may also use these accessors in conjunction with setf to change the slot values of an instance. For example:

```
> (employee-salary new-employee)
4500.0
> (setf (employee-salary new-employee) 5000.00)
5000.0
> (employee-salary new-employee)
5000.0
```

So we see that using structures, we can define predicates and accessors of a data type in a single LISP form. These definitions are central to our implementation of the ID3 algorithm.

When given a set of examples of known classification, ID3 induces a tree that will correctly classify all the training instances, and has a high probability of correctly classifying unseen objects. In the discussion of ID3 in Section 10.3, we described training instances in a tabular form, explicitly listing the properties and their values for each instance. For example, Table 10.1 lists a set of instances for learning to predict an individual's credit risk. Throughout this section, we will continue to refer to this problem.

Tables are only one way of representing examples; it is more general to think of them as objects that may be tested for various properties. Our implementation makes few assumptions about the representation of objects. For each property, it requires a function of one argument that may be applied to an object to return a value of that property. For example, if credit-profile-1 is bound to the first example in Table 10.1, and history is a function that returns the value of an object's credit history, then:

```
> (history credit-profile-1)
bad
```

Similarly, we require functions for the other properties of a credit profile:

```
> (debt credit-profile-1)
high
> (collateral credit-profile-1)
none
> (income credit-profile-1)
0-to-15k
> (risk credit-profile-1)
high
```

Next we select a representation for the credit assignment example, making objects as association lists in which the keys are property names and their data are property values. Thus, the first example of Table 10.1 is represented by the association list:

```
((risk . high) (history . bad) (debt . high) (collateral . none) (income . 0-15k))
```

We now use defstruct to define instances as structures. We represent the full set of training instances as a list of association lists and bind this list to examples:

```
(setq examples
 '(((risk . high) (history . bad) (debt . high) (collateral . none) (income . 0-15k))
  ((risk . high) (history . unknown) (debt . high) (collateral . none) (income . 15k-35k))
  ((risk . moderate) (history . unknown)(debt . low)(collateral . none)(income . 15k-35k))
  ((risk . high) (history . unknown) (debt . low) (collateral . none) (income . 0-15k))
  ((risk . low) (history . unknown) (debt . low) (collateral . none) (income . over-35k))
  ((risk . low) (history . unknown) (debt . low) (collateral . adequate) (income . over-35k))
  ((risk . high) (history . bad) (debt . low) (collateral . none) (income . 0-15k))
  ((risk . moderate) (history . bad) (debt . low) (collateral . adequate) (income . over-35k))
  ((risk . low) (history . good) (debt . low) (collateral . none) (income . over-35k))
  ((risk . low) (history . good) (debt . high) (collateral . adequate) (income . over-35k))
  ((risk . high) (history . good) (debt . high) (collateral . none) (income . 0-15k))
  ((risk . moderate) (history . good) (debt . high) (collateral . none) (income . 15k-35k))
  ((risk . low) (history . good) (debt . high) (collateral . none) (income . over-35k))
  ((risk . high) (history . bad) (debt . high) (collateral . none) (income . 15k-35k))))
```

Since the purpose of a decision tree is the determination of risk for a new individual, test instances will include all properties except risk:

```
(setq test-instance
     '((history . good) (debt . low) (collateral . none) (income . 15k-35k)))
```

Given this representation of objects, we next define properties:

```
(defun history (object)
    (cdr (assoc 'history object :test #'equal)))
(defun debt (object)
    (cdr (assoc 'debt object :test #'equal)))
(defun collateral (object)
    (cdr (assoc 'collateral object :test #'equal)))
(defun income (object)
    (cdr (assoc 'income object :test #'equal)))
(defun risk (object)
    (cdr (assoc 'risk object :test #'equal)))
```

A property is a function on objects; we represent these functions as a slot in a structure that includes other useful information:

```
(defstruct property
    name
    test
    values)
```

The test slot of an instance of property is bound to a function that returns a property value. name is the name of the property, and is included solely to help the user inspect definitions. values is a list of all the values that may be returned by test. Requiring that the values of each property be known in advance simplifies the implementation greatly, and is not unreasonable.

We now define decision trees using the following structures:

```
(defstruct decision-tree
    test-name
    test
    branches)
(defstruct leaf
    value)
```

Thus a decision tree is either an instance of decision-tree or an instance of leaf. leaf has one slot, a value corresponding to a classification. Instances of type decision-tree represent internal nodes of the tree, and consist of a test, a test-name and a set of branches. test is a function of one argument that takes an object and returns the value of a property. In classifying an object, we apply test to it using funcall and use the returned value to select a branch of the tree. test-name is the name of the property. We include it to make it easier for the user to inspect decision trees; it plays no real role in the program's execution. branches is an association list of subtrees: the keys are the possible values returned by test; the data are subtrees.

For example, the tree of Figure 10.13 would correspond to the following set of nested structures. The #S is a convention of Common LISP I/O; it indicates that an s-expression represents a structure.

```
#S(decision-tree
    :test-name income
    :test #<Compiled-function income #x3525CE>
    :branches
        ((0-15k . #S(leaf :value high))
         (15k-35k .
            #S(decision-tree
                :test-name history
                :test #<Compiled-function history #x3514D6>
                :branches
                    ((good . #S(leaf :value moderate))
                     (bad . #S(leaf :value high))
                     (unknown .
                        #S(decision-tree
                            :test-name debt
                            :test  #<Compiled-function debt #x351A7E>
                            :branches
                                ((high . #S(leaf :value high))
                                 (low . #S(leaf :value  moderate))))))))
         (over-35k .
            #S(decision-tree :test-name history
                :test #<Co...d-fun.. history #x3514D6>
                :branches
                    ((good . #S(leaf :value low))
                     (bad . #S(leaf :value moderate))
                     (unknown . #S(leaf :value low))))))))
```

Although a set of training examples is, conceptually, just a collection of objects, we will make it part of a structure that includes slots for other information used by the algorithm. We define example-frame as:

```
(defstruct example-frame
    instances
    properties
    classifier
    size
    information)
```

instances is a list of objects of known classification; this is the training set used to construct a decision tree. properties is a list of objects of type property; these are the properties that may be used in the nodes of that tree. classifier is also an instance of property; it represents the classification that ID3 is attempting to learn. Since the examples are of known classification, we include it as another property. size is the number of examples in the instances slot; information is the information content of that set of examples. We compute size and information content from the examples. Since these values take time to compute and will be used several times, we save them in these slots.

As you recall from Section 10.3, ID3 constructs trees recursively. Given a set of examples, each an instance of example-frame, it selects a property and uses it to partition the set of training instances into non-intersecting subsets. Each subset contains all the instances that have the same value for that property. The property selected becomes the test at the current node of the tree. For each subset in the partition, ID3 recursively constructs a subtree using the remaining properties. The algorithm halts when a set of examples all belong to the same class, at which point it creates a leaf.

Our final structure definition is partition, a division of an example set into subproblems using a particular property. We define the type partition:

```
(defstruct partition
    test-name
    test
    components
    info-gain)
```

In an instance of partition, the test slot is bound to the property used to create the partition. test-name is the name of the test, included for readability. components will be bound to the subproblems of the partition. In our implementation, components is an association list: the keys are the different values of the selected test; each datum is an instance of example-frame. info-gain is the information gain that results from using test as the node of the tree. As with size and information in the example-frame structure, this slot caches a value that is costly to compute and is used several times in the algorithm. By organizing our program around these data types, we make our implementation more clearly reflect the structure of the algorithm.

16.13.2 The ID3 Algorithm

The heart of our implementation is the function build-tree, which takes an instance of example-frame, and recursively constructs a decision tree.

```
(defun build-tree (training-frame)
    (cond
        ; Case 1: empty example set
            ((null (example-frame-instances training-frame))
             (make-leaf :value "unable to classify: no examples"))
        ; Case 2: all tests have been used
            ((null (example-frame-properties training-frame))
             (make-leaf :value (list-classes training-frame)))
```

```
; Case 3: all examples in same class
    ((zerop (example-frame-information training-frame))
     (make-leaf :value (funcall
         (property-test (example-frame-classifier training-frame))
         (car (example-frame-instances training-frame)))))
; Case 4: select test and recur
    (t (let ((part (choose-partition (gen-partitions training-frame))))
        (make-decision-tree
            :test-name (partition-test-name part)
            :test (partition-test part)
            :branches (mapcar #'(lambda (x)
                            (cons (car x) (build-tree (cdr x))))
                        (partition-components part)))))))
```

Using cond, build-tree analyzes four possible cases. In case 1, the example frame does not contain any training instances. This might occur if ID3 is given an incomplete set of training examples, with no instances for a given value of a property. In this case it creates a leaf consisting of the message: "unable to classify: no examples."

The second case occurs if the properties slot of training-frame is empty. In recursively building the decision tree, once the algorithm selects a property, it deletes it from the properties slot in the example frames for all subproblems. If the example set is inconsistent, the algorithm may exhaust all properties before arriving at an unambiguous classification of training instances. In this case, it creates a leaf whose value is a list of all classes remaining in the set of training instances.

The third case represents a successful termination of a branch of the tree. If training-frame has an information content of zero, then all of the examples belong to the same class (this follows from Shannon's definition of information, see Section 13.3). The algorithm halts, returning a leaf node in which the value is equal to this remaining class.

The first three cases terminate tree construction; the fourth case recursively calls build-tree to construct the subtrees of the current node. gen-partitions produces a list of all possible partitions of the example set, using each test in the properties slot of training-frame. choose-partition selects the test that gives the greatest information gain. After binding the resulting partition to the variable part in a let block, build-tree constructs a node of a decision tree in which the test is that used in the chosen partition, and the branches slot is bound to an association list of subtrees. Each key in branches is a value of the test and each datum is a decision tree constructed by a recursive call to build-tree. Since the components slot of part is already an association list in which the keys are property values and the data are instances of example-frame, we implement the construction of subtrees using mapcar to apply build-tree to each datum in this association list.

gen-partitions takes one argument, training-frame, an object of type example-frame-properties, and generates all partitions of its instances. Each partition is created using a different property from the properties slot. gen-partitions employs a function, partition, that takes an instance of an example frame and an instance of a property; it partitions the examples using that property. Note the use of mapcar to generate a partition for each element of the example-frame-properties slot of training-frame.

```
(defun gen-partitions (training-frame)
    (mapcar #'(lambda (x) (partition training-frame x))
        (example-frame-properties training-frame)))
```

choose-partition searches a list of candidate partitions and chooses the one with the highest information gain:

```
(defun choose-partition (candidates)
    (cond ((null candidates) nil)
          ((= (list-length candidates) 1)(car candidates))
          (t (let ((best (choose-partition (cdr candidates))))
       (if (> (partition-info-gain (car candidates)) (partition-info-gain best))
           (car candidates)
           best)))))
```

Partition is the most complex function in the implementation. It takes as arguments an example frame and a property, and returns an instance of a partition structure:

```
(defun partition (root-frame property)
    (let ((parts (mapcar #'(lambda (x) (cons x (make-example-frame)))
                    (property-values property))))
        (dolist (instance (example-frame-instances root-frame))
            (push instance (example-frame-instances
                (cdr (assoc (funcall (property-test property) instance) parts)))))
        (mapcar #'(lambda (x)
            (let ((frame (cdr x)))
                (setf (example-frame-properties frame)
                    (remove property (example-frame-properties root-frame)))
                (setf (example-frame-classifier frame)
                    (example-frame-classifier root-frame))
                (setf (example-frame-size frame)
                    (list-length (example-frame-instances frame)))
                (setf (example-frame-information frame)
                    (compute-information
                        (example-frame-instances frame)
                        (example-frame-classifier root-frame)))))
        parts)
    (make-partition
        :test-name (property-name property)
        :test (property-test property)
        :components parts
        :info-gain (compute-info-gain root-frame parts))))
```

partition begins by defining a local variable, parts, using a let block. It initializes parts to an association list whose keys are the possible values of the test in property, and whose data will be the subproblems of the partition. partition implements this using the dolist macro. dolist binds local variables to each element of a list and evaluates its body for each binding At this point, they are empty instances of example-frame: the instance slots of each subproblem are bound to nil. Using a dolist form, partition pushes each element of the instances slot of root-frame onto the instances slot of the appropriate subproblem in parts. push is a LISP macro that modifies a list by adding a new first element; unlike cons, push permanently adds a new element to the list.

This section of the code accomplishes the actual partitioning of root-frame. After the dolist terminates, parts is bound to an association list in which each key is a value of property and each datum is an example frame whose instances share that value. Using mapcar, the algorithm then completes the information required of each example frame in parts, assigning appropriate values to the properties, classifier, size and information slots. It then constructs an instance of partition, binding the components slot to parts.

list-classes is used in case 2 of build-tree to create a leaf node for an ambiguous classification. It employs a do loop to enumerate the classes in a list of examples. The do loop initializes classes to all the values of the classifier in training-frame. For each element of classes, it adds it to classes-present if it can find an element of the instances slot of training-frame that belongs to that class.

```lisp
(defun list-classes (training-frame)
    (do
        ((classes (property-values (example-frame-classifier training-frame))
                    (cdr classes))
         (classifier (property-test (example-frame-classifier training-frame)))
         classes-present)                                    ; local var accumulates result
        ((null classes) classes-present)                     ; exit clause
        (if (member (car classes) (example-frame-instances training-frame)
                        :test #'(lambda (x y) (equal x (funcall classifier y))))
            (push (car classes) classes-present))))
```

The remaining functions compute the information content of examples. compute-information determines the information content of a list of examples. It counts the number of instances in each class, and computes the proportion of the total training set belonging to each class. Assuming this proportion equals the probability that an object belongs to a class, it computes the information content of examples using Shannon's definition:

```lisp
(defun compute-information (examples classifier)
    (let ((class-count
            (mapcar #'(lambda (x) (cons x 0)) (property-values classifier)))
          (size 0))
        ; count number of instances in each class
        (dolist (instance examples)
            (incf size)
            (incf (cdr (assoc (funcall (property-test classifier) instance)
                    class-count))))
        ; compute information content of examples
```

```
(sum #'(lambda (x) (if (= (cdr x) 0) 0
            (* -1
            (/ (cdr x) size)
            (log (/ (cdr x) size) 2))))
    class-count)))
```

compute-info-gain gets the information gain of a partition by subtracting the weighted average of the information in its components from that of its parent examples.

```
(defun compute-info-gain (root parts)
    (- (example-frame-information root)
        (sum #'(lambda (x) (* (example-frame-information (cdr x))
                (/ (example-frame-size (cdr x))
                    (example-frame-size root))))
            parts)))
```

sum computes the values returned by applying f to all elements of list-of-numbers:

```
(defun sum (f list-of-numbers)
    (apply '+ (mapcar f list-of-numbers)))
```

This completes the implementation of build-tree. The remaining component of the algorithm is a function, classify, that takes as arguments a decision tree as constructed by build-tree, and an object to be classified; it determines the classification of the object by recursively walking the tree. The definition of classify is straightforward: classify halts when it encounters a leaf, otherwise it applies the test from the current node to the instance, and uses the result as the key to select a branch in a call to assoc.

```
(defun classify (instance tree)
    (if (leaf-p tree)
        (leaf-value tree)
        (classify instance
            (cdr (assoc (funcall (decision-tree-test tree) instance)
                (decision-tree-branches tree))))))
```

Using the object definitions just defined, we now call build-tree on the credit example of Table 10.1. We bind tests to a list of property definitions for history, debt, collateral and income. classifier tests the risk of an instance. Using these definitions we bind the credit examples to an instance of example-frame.

```
(setq tests
    (list (make-property
                :name 'history
                :test #'history
```

```
                  :values '(good bad unknown))
            (make-property
                  :name 'debt
                  :test #'debt
                  :values '(high low))
            (make-property
                  :name 'collateral
                  :test #'collateral
                  :values '(none adequate))
            (make-property
                  :name 'income
                  :test #'income
                  :values '(0-to-15k 15k-to-35k over-35k))))


(setq classifier
      (make-property
            :name 'risk
            :test #'risk
            :values '(high moderate low)))


(setq credit-examples
      (make-example-frame
            :instances examples
            :properties tests
            :classifier classifier
            :size (list-length examples)
            :information (compute-information examples class)))
```

Using these definitions, we may now induce decision trees, and use them to classify instances according to their credit risk:

```
> (setq credit-tree (build-tree credit-examples))
#S(decision-tree
      :test-name income
      :test #<Compiled-function income #x3525CE>
      :branches
            ((0-to-15k . #S(leaf :value high))
            (15k-to-35k .
                  #S(decision-tree
                        :test-name history
                        :test #<Compiled-function history #x3514D6>
                        :branches
                              ((good . #S(leaf :value moderate))
                              (bad . #S(leaf :value high))
                              (unknown .
                                    #S(decision-tree
                                          :test-name debt
```

```
            :test  #<Compiled-function debt #x351A7E>
            :branches
                    ((high . #S(leaf :value high))
                     (low . #S(leaf :value  moderate)))))))))
                   (over-35k .
                        #S(decision-tree :test-name history
                                :test #<Compiled-function history #x...6>
                                :branches
                                    ((good . #S(leaf :value low))
                                     (bad . #S(leaf :value moderate))
                                     (unknown . #S(leaf :value low)))))))))


>(classify '((history . good) (debt . low (collateral . none) (income . 15k-to-35k))
        credit-tree)
moderate
```

16.14   Epilogue and References

Both PROLOG and LISP are based on formal mathematical models of computation: PROLOG on logic and theorem proving, LISP on the theory of recursive functions. This sets these languages apart from more traditional languages whose architecture is just a refinement of the architecture of the underlying computing hardware. By deriving their syntax and semantics from mathematical notations, LISP and PROLOG inherit both expressive power and clarity.

Although PROLOG, the newer of the two languages, has remained close to its theoretical roots, LISP has been extended until it is no longer a purely functional programming language. LISP is, above all, a practical programming language that has grown to support the full range of modern techniques. These techniques include functional and applicative programming, data abstraction, stream processing, delayed evaluation, and object-oriented programming.

The strength of LISP is that it has built up a range of modern programming techniques as extensions of its core model of functional programming. This set of techniques, combined with the power of lists to create a variety of symbolic data structures, forms the basis of modern LISP programming. This chapter is intended to illustrate that style.

In designing the algorithms of this chapter, we have been influenced by Abelson and Sussman's book *The Structure and Interpretation of Computer Programs* (1985). Steele (1990) offers an essential guide to using Common LISP. Valuable tutorials and textbooks on LISP programming include *LISP* (Winston and Horn 1984), *Common LISPCraft* (Wilensky 1986), *Artificial Intelligence Programming*, Charniak et al. (1987), *Common LISP Programming for Artificial Intelligence* (Hasemer and Domingue 1989), *Common LISP: A Gentle Introduction to Symbolic Computation* (Touretzky 1990), *On LISP: Advanced Techniques for Common LISP* (Graham 1993), and *ANSI Common Lisp* (Graham 1995).

A number of books explore the use of LISP in the design of AI problem solvers. *Building Problem Solvers* (Forbus and deKleer 1993) is an encyclopedic treatment of AI algorithms in LISP and an invaluable reference for AI practitioners. Also, see any of a number of general AI texts that take a more LISP-centered approach to the basic material, including *Artificial Intelligence with Common LISP* (Noyes 1992) and *The Elements of Artificial Intelligence Using Common LISP* by Steven Tanimoto (1990).

16.14 Exercises

1. Newton's method for solving roots takes an estimate of the value of the root and tests it for accuracy. If the guess does not meet the required tolerance, it computes a new estimate and repeats. Pseudo-code for using Newton's method to get the square root of a number is:
   function root-by-newtons-method (x, tolerance)

   > guess := 1;
   > repeat
   >   guess := 1/2(guess + x/guess)
   > until absolute-value(x − guess · guess) < tolerance

   Write a recursive LISP function to compute square roots by Newton's method.

2. a. Write a recursive LISP function that will reverse the elements of a list. (Do not use the built-in reverse function.) What is the complexity of your implementation? It is possible to reverse a list in linear time; can you do so?

   b. Write a LISP function that will take a list nested to any depth and print the mirror image of that list. For instance, the function should have the behavior:
   > (mirror '((a b) (c (d e))))
   (((e d) c) (b a))

3. Write a random number generator in LISP. This function must maintain a global variable, seed, and return a different random number each time the function is called. For a description of a reasonable random number algorithm, consult any basic algorithms text.

4. Write the functions initialize, push, top, pop, and list-stack to maintain a global stack. These functions should behave:

   > (initialize)
   nil
   > (push 'foo)
   foo
   > (push 'bar)
   bar
   > (top)
   bar
   > (list-stack)
   (bar foo)
   > (pop)
   bar
   > (list-stack)
   (foo)

5. Sets may be represented using lists. Note that these lists should not contain any duplicate elements. Write your own LISP implementations of the set operations of union, intersection, and set difference. (Do not use Common LISP's built-in versions of these functions.)

6. The towers of Hanoi problem is based on the following legend:

   In a Far Eastern monastery, there is a puzzle consisting of three diamond needles and 64 gold disks. The disks are of graduated sizes. Initially, the disks are all stacked on a single needle in decreasing order of size. The monks are attempting to move all the disks to another needle under the following rules:

   a. Only one disk may be moved at a time.
   b. No disk can ever rest on a smaller disk.

   Legend has it that when the task has been completed, the universe will end.

   Write a LISP program to solve this problem. For safety's sake (and to write a program that will finish in your lifetime) do not attempt the full 64-disk problem. Three or four disks is more reasonable.

7. Write a compiler for arithmetic expressions of the form:

   (op operand1 operand2)

   where op is either +, −, *, or / and the operands are either numbers or nested expressions. An example is (* (+ 3 6) (− 7 9)). Assume that the target machine has instructions:

   (move value register)
   (add register-1 register-2)
   (subtract register-1 register-2)
   (times register-1 register-2)
   (divide register-1 register-2)

   All the arithmetic operations will leave the result in the first register argument. To simplify, assume an unlimited number of registers. Your compiler should take an arithmetic expression and return a list of these machine operations.

8. Implement a depth-first backtracking solution (such as was used to solve the farmer, wolf, goat, and cabbage problem in Section 16.2) to the missionary and cannibal problem:

   Three missionaries and three cannibals come to the bank of a river they wish to cross. There is a boat that will hold only two people, and any of the group can row it. If there are ever more missionaries than cannibals on any side of the river the cannibals will get converted. Devise a series of moves to get everyone across the river with no conversions.

9. Implement a depth-first solution to the water jugs problem:

   There are two jugs, one holding 3 gallons and the other 5 gallons of water. A number of things that can be done with the jugs: they can be filled, emptied, and dumped one into the other either until the poured-into jug is full or until the poured-out-of jug is empty. Devise a sequence of actions that will produce 4 gallons of water in the larger jug. (Hint: only integer values of water are used.)

10. Implement build-solution and eliminate-duplicates for the breadth-first search algorithm of Section 16.3.

11. Use the breadth-first search algorithm of Exercise 10 to solve:

    a.   The farmer, wolf, goat, and cabbage problem (see Section 16.2).
    b.   The missionary and cannibal problem (see Exercise 8).
    c.   The water jugs problem (see Exercise 9).

Compare the breadth-first results to the depth-first results. The differences will probably be the most telling for the water jugs problem. Why?

12. Finish implementing best-first search using the general path algorithm described in Section 16.3.3. Use this along with appropriate heuristics to solve each of the three problems mentioned in Exercise 11.

13. Write a LISP program to solve the 8-queens problem. (This problem is to find a way to place eight queens on a chessboard so that no queen may capture any other through a single move, i.e., no two queens are on the same row, column, or diagonal.)

14. Write a LISP program to solve the full 8×8 version of the knight's tour problem.

15. The implementations of breadth-first, depth-first, and best-first search using open and closed lists are all very similar; they differ only in the way in which open is maintained. Write a general search function that can implement any of these three searches by defining the function for maintaining open as a parameter.

16. Rewrite print-solutions in the logic programming interpreter so that it prints the first solution and waits for a user response (such as a carriage return) before printing the second solution.

17. Modify the logic programming interpreter to handle or and not. Disjunctive expressions should succeed if at least one of the disjuncts succeeds; in processing a disjunctive expression, the interpreter should return the union of all the solutions returned by the disjuncts. Negation is a bit more difficult, since a negated goal can succeed only if the goal itself fails. Thus, it is not possible to return any variable bindings for a negated goal. This is a result of the closed world assumption and negation as failure described in Section 13.3.

18. Implement the general map and filter functions, map-stream and filter-stream, described in Section 16.8.

19. Rewrite the solution to the first n odd Fibonacci numbers problem so that it uses the general stream filter, filter-stream, instead of filter-odds. Modify this to return the first n even Fibonacci numbers and then modify it again to return the squares of the first n Fibonacci numbers.

20. Expand the logic programming interpreter to include LISP write statements. This will allow rules to print messages directly to the user. Hint: modify solve first to examine if a goal is a write statement. If it is, evaluate the write and return a stream containing the initial substitution set.

21. Expand the logic programming language to include arithmetic comparisons, =, <, and >.

Hint: as in Exercise 20, modify solve to detect these comparisons before calling infer. If an expression is a comparison, replace any variables with their values and evaluate it. If it returns nil, solve should return the empty stream; if it returns non-nil, solve should return a stream containing the initial substitution set. Assume that the expressions do not contain unbound variables. For a more challenging exercise, define = so that it will function like the PROLOG is operator and assign a value to an unbound variable and simply do an equality test if all elements are bound.

22. Use the logic programming interpreter with arithmetic (Exercise 21) to solve the financial advisor problem of Chapter 2.

23. Select a problem such as automotive diagnosis or classifying different species of animals and solve it using lisp-shell.

24. Expand the expert system shell of Section 16.10 to allow the user responses other than y or n. For example, we may want the user to be able to provide bindings for a goal. This may be done by changing ask-for and the related functions to let the user also enter a pattern, which is matched against the goal. If the match succeeds, ask for a certainty factor.

25. Extend lisp-shell to include not. For an example of how to treat negation using uncertain reasoning, refer to Chapter 8 and the PROLOG-based expert system shell in Chapter 15.

26. Write an ATN parser (Section 12.3) for a subset of English.

27. Add to the CLOS simulation of Section 16.12 a cooling system so that if any room's temperature gets above a certain temperature it starts to cool. Also add a "thermal" factor to each room so that it heats and cools as a function of its volume and insulation value.

28. Create a CLOS simulation in another domain, e.g., an ecological scenario.

29. Run the ID3 algorithm in another problem domain and set of examples of your choice.

PART VII

EPILOGUE

The potential of computer science, if fully explored and developed, will take us to a higher plane of knowledge about the world. Computer science will assist us in gaining a greater understanding of intellectual processes. It will enhance our knowledge of the learning process, the thinking process, and the reasoning process. Computer science will provide models and conceptual tools for the cognitive sciences. Just as the physical sciences have dominated humanity's intellectual endeavors during this century as researchers explored the nature of matter and the beginning of the universe, today we are beginning the exploration of the intellectual universe of ideas, knowledge structures, and language. I foresee significant advances continuing to be made that will greatly alter our lives. . . . I can foresee an understanding of how to organize and manipulate knowledge . . .

—J. HOPCROFT, ACM Turing Award Lecture, 1987

What is mind? No matter.
What is matter? Never mind . . .

—HOMER SIMPSON

It's what we learn after we know it all that is important.

—EARL WEAVER, Baltimore Orioles

Reflections on the Nature of Intelligence

Although this book has flirted with the larger philosophical implications of artificial intelligence, we have chiefly emphasized the engineering techniques used to build intelligent computer-based artifacts. In these final pages, we would like to return to those deeper issues, to consider the philosophical foundations of artificial intelligence, to re-evaluate the possibility of a science of intelligence using AI techniques, and to speculate on the future progress of the discipline.

As we have noted throughout our book, research on human cognition and problem solving has made important contributions to the theory of artificial intelligence and the design of AI programs. And conversely, work in AI has led to many insights for both model construction and empirical testing in many disciplines, including biology, linguistics, and cognitive psychology. In concluding our presentation, we would like to revive this eclectic spirit and consider such issues as the limits of representations, the importance of physical embodiment to mental processes, and the role of culture in the growth and interpretation of knowledge. These questions lead us to further scientific and philosophical questions, such as those surrounding the falsifiability of models and the nature and capabilities of the scientific method itself. Our observations lead us to argue for an interdisciplinary approach that couples work in AI with the findings of psychology, linguistics, biology, anthropology, epistemology, and the other fields that explore the full range of human thought and its products. We believe that by exploring both the intersections of these disciplines, as well as the tensions between them, we can better understand the processes that underlie intelligence, whether biologically or mechanically based.

Traditionally, work in artificial intelligence was based on the physical symbol system hypothesis (Newell and Simon 1976). Research from that perspective produced increasingly sophisticated data structures and search strategies that, in turn, led to many important successes both in creating tools that can achieve elements of intelligent behavior, as well as in illuminating the many components that make up human intelligence. It is important to note, however, that much of the practice of AI that emerged from this early approach rested on assumptions which derive from philosophical rationalism. As defined by the rationalist tradition, intelligence itself is largely seen as a process of logical reasoning, scientific problem solving, and a straightforward, empirical approach to understanding the universe. We feel that philosophical rationalism has overly constrained both the current methods of artificial intelligence as well as the scope of its inquiry.

Throughout this book, we have presented many more recent developments, including alternative models of learning, agent-based and distributed problem solving, approaches to embodied and situated intelligence, as well as the insights of evolutionary computation and artificial life. These approaches to understanding intelligence offer much needed alternatives to a rationalist reductionism. Biological and social models of intelligence have shown that human intelligence is very much a product of our bodies and senses, of our cultural and social institutions, of the art we create and have enjoyed, of the stories we have been told and pass on. By establishing methods for building computer simulations of many of these complex processes, such as evolution or the adaptation of neural patterns in the human brain, these recent approaches have given AI a new and powerful set of tools to complement its more traditional techniques.

Artificial intelligence, like most of computer science, is a young field. Where physics and biology can measure their progress in centuries, modern computing still reckons its age in decades. In Chapter 17 we attempt to integrate the findings of AI's different approaches into a unified science of intelligent systems. We propose that science and engineering, philosophy, and our own aesthetic judgments must lead us in our continuing creation of new artifacts and experiments, which when used appropriately, can offer insight into the more general science of intelligent systems. This chapter continues the long tradition introduced in Chapter 1 of establishing an epistemological grounding for AI, not so much to answer its critics (in fact, many of their challenges still await answers) but in the positive sense, of attempting to explore and illuminate the path ahead.

ARTIFICIAL INTELLIGENCE AS EMPIRICAL ENQUIRY

Computer science is an empirical discipline. We would have called it an experimental science, but like astronomy, economics, and geology, some of its unique forms of observation and experience do not fit a narrow stereotype of the experimental method. Nonetheless, they are experiments. Each new machine that is built is an experiment. Actually constructing the machine poses a question to nature; and we listen for the answer by observing the machine in operation and analyzing it by all analytical and measurement means available. Each new program that is built is an experiment. It poses a question to nature, and its behavior offers clues to an answer. Neither machines nor programs are black boxes; they are artifacts that have been designed, both hardware and software, and we can open them up and look inside. We can relate their structure to their behavior and draw many lessons from a single experiment.

—A. NEWELL AND H. A. SIMON, *ACM Turing Award Lecture, 1976*

The study of thinking machines teaches us more about the brain than we can learn by introspective methods. Western man is externalizing himself in the form of gadgets.

—WILLIAM S. BURROUGHS, *Naked Lunch*

Where is the knowledge we have lost in information?

—T. S. ELIOT, *Choruses from the Rock*

17.0 Introduction

For many people, one of the most surprising aspects of work in artificial intelligence is the extent to which AI, and indeed much of computer science, turns out to be an empirical discipline. This is surprising because most people initially think of these fields in terms of their mathematical, or alternatively, their engineering foundations. From the mathematical viewpoint, sometimes termed the "neat" perspective, there is the rationalist desire to bring standards of proof and analysis to the design of intelligent computational devices. From the engineering, or "scruffy" perspective, the task is often viewed as simply making successful artifacts that society wants to call "intelligent". Unfortunately, or fortunately, depending upon your philosophy, the complexity of intelligent software and the ambiguities inherent in its interactions with the worlds of human activity frustrate analysis from either the purely mathematical or purely engineering perspectives.

Furthermore, if artificial intelligence is to achieve the level of a science and become a critical component of the *science of intelligent systems*, a mixture of analytic and empirical methods must be included in the design, execution, and analysis of its artifacts. On this viewpoint each AI program can be seen as an experiment: it proposes a question to the natural world and the results are nature's response. Nature's response to our design and programmatic commitments shapes our understanding of formalism, mechanism, and finally, of the nature of intelligence itself (Newell and Simon 1976).

Unlike many of the more traditional studies of human cognition, we as designers of intelligent computer artifacts can inspect the internal workings of our "subjects". We can stop program execution, examine internal state, and modify structure at will. As Newell and Simon (1976) note, the structure of computers and their programs indicate their potential behavior: they may be examined, and their representations and search algorithms understood. The power of computers as tools for understanding intelligence is a product of this duality. Appropriately programmed computers are capable of both achieving levels of semantic and behavioral complexity that beg to be characterized in psychological terms as well as offer an opportunity for an inspection of their internal states that is largely denied scientists studying most other intellectual life forms.

Fortunately for continuing work in AI, as well as for establishing a science of intelligent systems, more modern psychological techniques, especially those related to neural physiology, have also shed new light on the many modes of human intelligence. We know now, for example, that human intelligent function is not monolithic and uniform. Rather it is modular and distributed. Its power is seen in the sense organs, such as the human retina, that can screen and preprocess visual information. Similarly, human learning is not a uniform and homogenous faculty. Rather learning is a function of multiple environments and differing systems, each adapted to achieve specialized goals. MRI analysis, along with PET scans and allied neural physical imaging procedures, all support a diverse and cooperative picture of the internal workings of actual intelligent systems.

If work in AI is going to reach the level of a science, we must also address important philosophical issues, especially those related to epistemology, or the question of how an intelligent system "knows" its world. These issues range from the question of what is the object of study of artificial intelligence to deeper issues, such as questioning the validity and utility of the physical symbol system hypothesis. Further questions include what a "symbol" is in the symbol system approach to AI and how symbols might relate to sets of weighted nodes in a connectionist model. We also question the role of rationalism expressed in the inductive bias seen in most learning programs and how this compares to the unfettered lack of structure often seen in unsupervised, reinforcement, and emergent approaches to learning. Finally, we must question the role of embodiment, situatedness, and sociological bias in problem solving. We conclude our discussion of philosophical issues by proposing a *constructivist epistemology* that fits comfortably with both our commitment to AI as a science as well as to AI as empirical enquiry.

And so in this final chapter we return again to the questions asked in Chapter 1: What is intelligence? Can it be formalized? How can we build mechanisms that exhibit it? How can artificial and human intelligence fit into a larger context of a science of intelligent systems? In Section 17.1 we begin with a revised definition of artificial intelligence which shows how current work in AI, although rooted in the physical symbol system hypothesis of Newell and Simon, has extended both its tools, techniques, and inquiries into a much broader context. We explore these alternative approaches to the question of intelligence, and consider their powers for the design of intelligent machines and for being a component in the science of intelligence systems. In Section 17.2, we point out how many of the techniques of modern cognitive psychology, neuroscience, as well as epistemology may be used to better understand the artificial intelligence enterprise.

Finally, in Section 17.3, we discuss some of the challenges that remain both for modern AI practitioners as well as for epistemologists. For even though the traditional approaches to AI have often been guilty of a rationalist reductionism, new interdisciplinary insights and tools also have related shortcomings. For example, the creators of the genetic algorithm and the designers of a-life research define the world of intelligence from a Darwinian viewpoint: "What is, is what survives". Knowledge is also seen as "knowing how" rather than "knowing what" in a complex situated world. For the scientist, answers require explanations, and "success" or "survival" are not of themselves sufficient.

In this final chapter, we will discuss the future of AI by exploring the philosophical questions that must be addressed to create a computational science of intelligence. We conclude that AI's empirical methodology is an important tool, and perhaps one of the best available, for exploring the nature of intelligence.

17.1 Artificial Intelligence: A Revised Definition

17.1.1 Intelligence and the Physical Symbol System Hypothesis

Based on our experience of the last 16 chapters, we offer a revised definition of artificial intelligence:

> AI is the study of the mechanisms underlying intelligent behavior through the construction and evaluation of artifacts designed to enact those mechanisms.

On this definition, artificial intelligence is less a theory about the mechanisms underlying intelligence and more an empirical methodology for constructing and testing possible models for supporting such a theory. It is a commitment to the scientific method of designing, running, and evaluating experiments with the goal of model refinement and further experiment. Most importantly however, this definition, like the field of AI itself, directly attacks centuries of philosophical obscurantism about the nature of mind. It gives people who would understand what is perhaps our defining characteristic as humans an alternative to religion, superstition, Cartesian dualism, new-age placebos, or the search for intelligence in some as yet undiscovered quirk of quantum mechanics (Penrose 1989). If the science supporting artificial intelligence has made any contribution to human knowledge, it is in confirming that intelligence is not some mystic vapor permeating men and angels, but rather the effect of a set of principles and mechanisms that can be understood and applied in the design of intelligent machines. It must be noted that our revised definition of AI does *not* define intelligence; rather it proposes a coherent role for *artificial* intelligence in exploring the nature and expression of intelligent phenomena.

From an historical perspective, the dominant approach to artificial intelligence involved the construction of representational formalisms and their associated search-based reasoning mechanisms. The guiding principle of early AI methodology was the *physical symbol system* hypothesis, first articulated by Newell and Simon (1976). This hypothesis states:

> The necessary and sufficient condition for a physical system to exhibit general intelligent action is that it be a physical symbol system.
>
> *Sufficient* means that intelligence can be achieved by any appropriately organized physical symbol system.
>
> *Necessary* means that any agent that exhibits general intelligence must be an instance of a physical symbol system. The necessity of the physical symbol system hypothesis requires that any intelligent agent, whether human, space alien, or computer, achieve intelligence through the physical implementation of operations on symbol structures.
>
> *General intelligent action* means the same scope of action seen in human action. Within physical limits, the system exhibits behavior appropriate to its ends and adaptive to the demands of its environment.

Newell and Simon have summarized the arguments for the *necessity* as well as the *sufficiency* of this hypothesis (Newell and Simon 1976, Newell 1981, Simon 1981). In subsequent years both AI and cognitive science explored the territory delineated by this hypothesis.

The physical symbol system hypothesis has led to four significant methodological commitments: (a) the use of symbols and systems of symbols as a medium to describe the world; (b) the design of search mechanisms, especially heuristic search, to explore the space of potential inferences those symbol systems could support; and (c) the disembodiment of cognitive architecture, by which we mean it was assumed that an appropriately designed symbol system could provide a full causal account of intelligence, regardless of its medium of implementation. Finally (d), on this viewpoint, AI became empirical and constructivist: it attempted to understand intelligence by building working models of it.

On the symbol system view, tokens in a language, referred to as *symbols*, were used to denote or reference something other than themselves. Like verbal tokens in a natural language, symbols stood for or referred to things in an intelligent agent's world. Tarski (1956, Section 2.3) could offer the possibility of a *science of meaning* in these object–referent relationships.

Furthermore, AI's use of symbols goes beyond the questions addressed in a Tarskian semantics, extending symbols to represent all forms of knowledge, skill, intention, and causality. Such constructive efforts rely on the fact that symbols, together with their semantics, can be embedded in formal systems. These define a *representation language*. The ability to formalize symbolic models is essential to modeling intelligence as a running

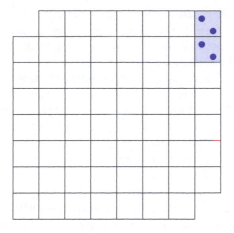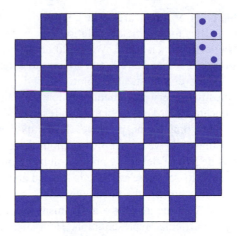

Figure 17.1 Truncated chessboard with two squares covered by a domino.

computer program. In previous chapters we studied several representations in detail: the predicate calculus, semantic networks, scripts, conceptual graphs, frames, and objects. The mathematics of formal systems allows us to argue such issues as soundness, completeness, and complexity, as well as discuss the organization of knowledge structures. The evolution of representational formalisms has allowed us to establish more complex (richer) semantic relationships. For example, inheritance systems constitute a semantic theory of taxonomic knowledge. By formally defining a class inheritance, such languages simplify the construction of intelligent programs and provide testable models of the organization of possible categories of intelligence itself.

Closely bound to representational schemata and their use in reasoning is the notion of search. Search became the step-by-step examination of problem states within a state space framework (an a priori semantic commitment) looking for solutions, subproblem goals, problem symmetries, or whatever aspect of the problem might be under consideration. Representation and search are linked because a commitment to a particular representation determines a space to be searched. Indeed, some problems can be made more difficult, or even impossible, through a poor choice of a representation language. The discussion of inductive bias later in this chapter illustrates this point.

A dramatic and often cited example of this interplay between search and representation as well as the difficulty of choosing an appropriate representation (can this process of optimizing the selection of representations be automated?) is the problem of placing dominos on a truncated chessboard. Assume that we have a chessboard and a set of dominos such that each domino will cover exactly two squares of the board. Also, assume that the board has some missing squares; in Figure 17.1 the upper left-hand corner and the lower right-hand corner have been removed.

The truncated chessboard problem asks whether there is a way of placing dominos on the board so that each square of the chessboard is covered and each domino covers exactly two squares. We might try to solve the problem by trying all placements of dominos on the board; this is the obvious search-based approach and is a natural consequence of representing the board as a simple matrix, ignoring such seemingly irrelevant features as the color of the squares. The complexity of such a search is enormous, and would require heuristics for an efficient solution. For example, we might prune partial solutions that leave single squares isolated. We could also start by solving the problem for a smaller board, such as 2×2 and 3×3, and attempt to extend the solution to the 8×8 situation.

A more sophisticated solution, relying on a more complex representational scheme, notes that every placement of a domino must cover both a black and a white square. This truncated board has 32 black squares but only 30 white squares; thus the desired placement is not going to be possible. This raises a serious question for purely symbol-based reasoners: do we have representations that allow problem solvers to access knowledge with this degree of flexibility and creativity? How can a particular representation automatically change its structure as more is learned about a problem domain?

Heuristics are the third component, along with representation and search, of symbol-based AI. A heuristic is a mechanism for organizing search across the alternatives offered by a particular representation. Heuristics are designed to overcome the complexity of exhaustive search, the barrier to useful solutions for many classes of interesting problems. In computing, just as for humans, intelligence requires the informed choice of "what to do next". Throughout the history of AI research, heuristics have taken many forms.

The earliest problem-solving techniques, such as *hill climbing* in Samuel's checker-playing program (Section 4.1) or *means–ends analysis* in Newell, Shaw, and Simon's General Problem Solver (Section 13.1), came into AI from other disciplines, such as *operations research*, and have gradually matured into general techniques for AI problem solving. Search properties, including *admissibility, monotonicity,* and *informedness,* are important results from these early studies. These techniques are often referred to as *weak methods.* Weak methods were general search strategies intended to be applicable across entire classes of problem domains (Newell and Simon 1972, Ernst and Newell 1969). We saw these methods and their properties in Chapters 2, 3, 4, 6, and 13.

We introduced *strong methods* for AI problem solving with the rule-based expert system, model-based and case-based reasoning, and symbol-based learning of Chapters 8, 9, and 10. In contrast to weak problem solvers, strong methods focus on the information specific to each problem area, such as internal medicine or integral calculus, rather than on designing heuristic methods that generalize across problem areas. Strong methods underlie expert systems and other knowledge-intensive approaches to problem solving. Strong methods emphasize such issues as the amount of knowledge needed for problem solving, learning, and knowledge acquisition, the syntactic representation of knowledge, the management of uncertainty, and issues related to the quality of knowledge.

Why have we not built many truly intelligent symbol-based systems?

There are many criticisms that can be leveled at the *physical symbol system* characterization of intelligence. Most of these are captured by considering the issues of semantic meaning and the *grounding* of the symbols of an intelligent agent. The nature of "meaning", of course, also impacts the idea of intelligence as search through pre-interpreted symbol structures and the "utility" implicit in the use of heuristics. The notion of meaning in traditional AI is very weak, at best. Furthermore, the temptation of moving towards a more mathematics-based semantics, such as the Tarskian possible worlds approach, seems wrong-headed. It reinforces the rationalist project of replacing the flexible and evolving intelligence of an embodied agent with a world where clear and distinct ideas are directly accessible.

The *grounding* of meaning is an issue that has forever frustrated both the proponents and critics of the AI and cognitive science enterprises. The grounding issue asks how symbols can have meaning. Searle (1980) makes just this point in his discussion of the so-called *Chinese Room*. Searle places himself in a room intended for translating Chinese sentences into English; there he receives a set of Chinese symbols, looks the symbols up in a large Chinese symbol cataloging system, and then outputs the appropriately linked sets of English symbols. Searle claims that although he himself knows absolutely no Chinese, his "system" can be seen as a Chinese-to-English translation machine.

There *is* a problem here. Although anyone who has worked in the research areas of machine translation or natural language understanding (Chapter 14), might argue that the Searle "translation machine", blindly linking one set of symbols to another set of symbols, would produce results of minimal quality, the fact remains that many current intelligent systems have a very limited ability to interpret sets of symbols in a "meaningful" fashion. This problem of too weak a supporting semantics also pervades many computationally based sensory modalities, whether they be visual, kinesthetic, or verbal.

In the areas of human language understanding, Lakoff and Johnson (1999) argue that the ability to create, use, exchange, and interpret meaning-symbols comes from a human's embodiment within an evolving social context. This context is physical, social, and right-now; it supports and enables the human ability to survive, evolve, and reproduce. It makes possible a world of analogical reasoning, the use and appreciation of humor, and the experiences of music and art. Our current generation of AI tools and techniques are very far away indeed from being able to encode and utilize any equivalent "meaning" system.

As a direct result of this weak semantic encoding, the traditional AI search/heuristic methodology explores states and contexts of states that are pre-interpreted. This means that an AI program's creator "imputes" or "lays on" to the symbols of the program various contexts of semantic meaning. A direct result of this pre-interpreted encoding is that intelligence-rich tasks, including learning and language, can only produce some computed function of that interpretation. Thus, many AI systems have very limited abilities to evolve new meaning associations as they explore their environments (Luger et al. 2002).

Finally, as a direct result of our current limited semantic modeling abilities, those applications where we are able to abstract away from a rich embodied and social context and at the same time capture the essential components of problem solving with pre-interpreted symbol systems are our most successful endeavors. Many of these were addressed throughout this book. However, even these areas remain brittle, without multiple interpretations, and with only limited ability to automatically recover from failures.

Across its brief history, the artificial intelligence research community has explored the ramifications of the physical symbol system hypothesis, and has developed its own challenges to that previously dominant view. As illustrated in the later chapters of this book, the explicit symbol system and search are not the only possible representational media for capturing intelligence. Models of computing based on the architecture of the animal brain as well as on the processes of biological evolution also provide useful frameworks for understanding intelligence in terms of scientifically knowable and empirically reproducible processes. In the following sections of this final chapter we explore the ramifications of these approaches.

17.1.2 Connectionist or "Neural" Computing

A significant alternative to the physical symbol system hypothesis is the research into neural networks and other biologically inspired models of computing. Neural networks, for example, are computational and physically instantiated models of cognition not totally reliant on explicitly referenced and pre-interpreted symbols that characterize a world. Because the "knowledge" in a neural network is distributed across the structures of that network, it is often difficult, if not impossible, to isolate individual concepts to specific nodes and weights of the network. In fact, any portion of the network may be instrumental in the representation of different concepts. Consequently, neural networks offer a counterexample, at least to the *necessary* clause of the physical symbol system hypothesis.

Neural networks and genetic architectures shift the emphasis of AI away from the problems of symbolic representation and sound inference strategies to issues of learning and adaptation. Neural networks, like human beings and other animals, are mechanisms for adapting to the world: the structure of a trained neural network is shaped by learning, as much as by design. The intelligence of a neural network does not require that the world be recast as an explicit symbolic model. Rather, the network is shaped by its interactions with the world, reflected through the implicit traces of experience. This approach has made a number of contributions to our understanding of intelligence, giving us a plausible model of the mechanisms underlying the physical embodiment of mental processes, a more viable account of learning and development, a demonstration of the ability of simple, and local adaptations to shape a complex system in response to actual phenomena. Finally, they offer a powerful research tool for cognitive neuroscience.

Precisely because they are so different, neural nets can answer a number of questions that may be outside the expressive abilities of symbol-based AI. An important class of such questions concerns perception. Nature is not so generous as to deliver our perceptions to a processing system as neat bundles of predicate calculus expressions. Neural networks offer a model of how we might recognize "meaningful" patterns in the chaos of sensory stimuli.

Because of their distributed representation, neural networks are often more robust than their explicitly symbolic counterparts. A properly trained neural network can effectively categorize novel instances, exhibiting a human-like perception of similarity rather than strict logical necessity. Similarly, the loss of a few neurons need not seriously compromise the performance of a large neural network. This results from the often extensive redundancy inherent in network models.

Perhaps the most appealing aspect of connectionist networks is their ability to learn. Rather than attempting to construct a detailed symbolic model of the world, neural networks rely on the plasticity of their own structure to adapt directly to external experiences. They do not construct a model of the world so much as they are shaped by their experience within the world. Learning is one of the most important aspects of intelligence. It is also the problem of learning that raises some of the hardest questions for work in neural computing.

Why have we not built a brain?

In fact, the current generation of engineered connectionist systems bear very little resemblance to the human neuronal system! Because the topic of *neural plausibility* is a critical research issue, we begin with that question and then consider development and learning. Recent research in cognitive neuroscience (Squire and Kosslyn 1998, Gazzaniga 2000, Hugdahl and Davidson 2003) brings new insight to the understanding of human cognitive architecture. We describe briefly some findings and comment on how they relate to the AI enterprise. We consider issues from three levels: first, the neuron, second, the level of neural architecture, and finally we discuss cognitive representation or the *encoding* problem.

First, at the level of the individual neuron, Shephard (1998) and Carlson (1994) identify many different types of neuronal architectures for cells, each of which is specialized as to its function and role within the larger neuronal system. These types include *sensory receptor cells* typically found in the skin and passing input information to other cell structures, *interneurons* whose primary task is to communicate within cell clusters, *principle neurons* whose task is to communicate between cell clusters, and *motor neurons* whose task is system output.

Neural activity is electrical. Patterns of ion flows into and out of the neuron determine whether a neuron is active or resting. The typical neuron has a resting charge of -70mV. When a cell is active, certain chemicals are released from the axon terminal. These chemicals, called *neurotransmitters*, influence the postsynaptic membrane, typically by fitting into specific receptor sites, like a key into a lock, initiating further ion flows. Ion flows, when they achieve a critical level, about -50mV, produce an *action potential*, an all-or-none triggering mechanism indicating that the cell has fired. Thus neurons communicate through sequences of binary codes.

Postsynaptic changes from the action potential are of two sorts, *inhibitory*, found mainly in interneuron cell structures, or *excitatory*. These positive and negative potentials are constantly being generated throughout the synapses in the dendritic system. Whenever the net effect of all these events is to alter the membrane potentials of related neurons from -70mV to about -50mV, the threshold is crossed and massive ion flows are again initiated into those cells' axons.

Secondly, on the level of neural architecture, there are approximately 10^{10} total neurons in the cerebral cortex, a thin convoluted sheet covering the entire cerebral hemisphere. Much of the cortex is folded in on itself, increasing the total surface area. From the computational perspective we need to know not only the total number of synapses, but also the fan-in and fan-out parameters. Shephard (1998) estimates both these numbers to be about 10^5.

Finally, aside from the differences in the cells and architectures of neural and computer systems, there is a deep problem of cognitive representation. We are ignorant, for example, of how even simple memories are encoded in cortex. Of how, for example, a face is recognized, and how recognition of a face can link an agent to feelings of joy or sadness. We know a huge amount about the physical/chemical aspects of the brain, but relatively little about how the neural system encodes and uses "patterns" within its context.

One of the more difficult questions facing researchers, in both the neural and computing communities, is the role of innate knowledge in learning: can effective learning ever occur on a *tabula rasa*, or *blank slate*, starting with no initial knowledge and learning entirely from experience? Or must learning start out with some prior inductive bias? Experience in the design of machine learning programs suggests that some sort of prior knowledge, usually expressed as an inductive bias, is necessary for learning in complex environments.

The ability of connectionist networks to converge on a meaningful generalization from a set of training data has proven sensitive to the number of artificial neurons, the network topology, and the specific learning algorithms used. Together, these factors constitute as strong an inductive bias as can be found in any symbolic representation. Research into human development supports this conclusion. There is increasing evidence, for example, that human infants inherit a range of "hard-wired" cognitive biases that enable learning of concept domains such as language and commonsense physics. Characterizing innate biases in neural networks is an active area of research (Elman et al. 1996).

The issue of innate biases becomes even more confounding when we consider more complex learning problems. For example, suppose we are developing a computational model of scientific discovery and want to model Copernicus' shift from a geocentric to heliocentric view of the universe. This requires that we represent both the Copernican and Ptolemaic views in a computer program. Although we could represent these views as patterns of activations in a neural network, our networks would tell us nothing about their behavior *as theories*. Instead, we prefer explanations such as "Copernicus was troubled by the complexity of the Ptolemaic system and preferred the simpler model of letting the planets revolve around the sun." Explanations such as this require symbols. Clearly, connectionist networks must be capable of supporting symbolic reasoning; after all, human beings are neural networks, and they seem to manipulate symbols tolerably well. Still, the neural foundation of symbolic reasoning is an important and open research problem.

Another problem is the role of development in learning. Human children cannot simply learn on the basis of available data. Their ability to learn in specific domains appears in well-defined developmental stages (Karmiloff-Smith 1992). An interesting question is whether this developmental progression is solely a result of human biology and embodiment, or whether it reflects some logically necessary limits on the ability of an intelligence to learn invariances in its world. Could developmental stages function as a mechanism for decomposing the problem of learning about the world into more manageable subproblems? Might a series of artificially imposed developmental restrictions provide artificial networks with a necessary framework for learning about a complex world?

The application of neural networks to practical problems raises a number of additional research issues. The very properties of neural networks that make them so appealing, such as adaptability and robustness in light of missing or ambiguous data, also create problems for their practical application. Because networks are trained, rather than programmed, behavior is difficult to predict. There are few guidelines for designing networks that will converge properly in a given problem domain. Finally, explanations of *why* a network arrived at a particular conclusion are often difficult to construct and may take the form of a statistical argument. These are all areas of current research.

One can ask then, whether connectionist networks and more symbolic AI are that different as models of intelligence. They both share a number of important commonalities, especially that intelligence is ultimately encoded as computation and has fundamental and formal limits, such as the Church/Turing hypothesis (Luger 1994, Chapter 2). Both approaches also offer models of mind shaped by application to practical problems. Most importantly, however, both approaches deny philosophical dualism and place the foundations of intelligence in the structure and function of physically realized devices.

We believe that a full reconciliation of these two very different approaches to capturing intelligence is inevitable. When it is accomplished, a theory of how symbols may reduce to patterns in a network and, in turn, influence future adaptation of that network, will be an extraordinary contribution. This will support a number of developments, such as integrating network-based perceptual and knowledge-intensive reasoning facilities into a single intelligence. In the meantime, however, both research communities have considerable work to do, and we see no reason why they should not continue to coexist. For those who feel uncomfortable with two seemingly incommensurable models of intelligence, even physics functions well with the intuitively contradictory notion that light is sometimes best understood as a wave and sometimes as a particle, although both viewpoints may well be subsumed by string theory (Greene 1999).

17.1.3 Agents, Emergence, and Intelligence

Agent-based computation and modular theories of cognition raise another set of interesting issues for researchers building artificial intelligences. One important school of thought in cognitive science holds that the mind is organized into sets of specialized functional units (Minsky 1985, Fodor 1983). These modules are specialists and employ a range of innate structures and functions, from "hard-wired" problem solving to inductive biases, that account for the diversity of problems they, as practical agents, must address. This makes sense: how can a single neural network or other system be trained to handle functions as diverse as perception, motor control, memory, and higher-level reasoning? Modular theories of intelligence provide both a framework for answering these questions and a direction for continued research into issues such as the nature of innate biases in individual modules as well as mechanisms of module interaction.

Genetic and emergent models of computation offer one of the newest and most exciting approaches to understanding both human and artificial intelligence. By demonstrating that globally intelligent behavior can arise from the cooperation of large numbers of restricted, independent, and individual agents, genetic and emergent theories view complex results through the interrelationships of relatively simple structures.

In an example from Holland (1995), the mechanisms that keep a large city such as New York supplied with bread demonstrate the fundamental processes underlying the emergence of intelligence in an agent-based system. It is unlikely that we could write a centralized planner that would successfully supply New Yorkers with the rich variety of daily breads to which they are accustomed. Indeed, the Communist world's unfortunate experiment with central planning revealed the limitations of such approaches! However, in spite of the practical difficulties of writing a centralized planning algorithm that will keep New York supplied with bread, the loosely coordinated efforts of the city's many bakers, truckers, suppliers of raw materials, as well as its retailers, solve the problem quite nicely. As in all agent-based emergent systems, there is no central plan. No one baker has more than a very limited knowledge of the city's bread requirements; each baker simply tries to optimize his or her own business opportunities. The solution to the global problem emerges from the collective activities of these independent and local agents.

By demonstrating how highly goal-directed, robust, nearly optimal behaviors can arise from the interactions of local individual agents, these models provide yet another answer to old philosophical questions of the origins of mind. The central lesson of emergent approaches to intelligence is that full intelligence can and does arise from the interactions of many simple, individual, local, and embodied agent intelligences.

The second major feature of emergent models is their reliance on Darwinian selection as the basic mechanism that shapes the behavior of the individual agents. In the bakery example, it seems that each individual baker does not behave in a manner that is, in some sense, globally optimal. Rather, the source of their optimality is not of a central design; it is the simple fact that bakers who do a poor job of satisfying the needs of their local customers generally fail. It is through the tireless, persistent operations of these selective pressures that individual bakers arrive at the behaviors that lead to their individual survival as well as to a useful emergent collective behavior.

The combination of a distributed, agent-based architecture and the adaptive pressures of natural selection are a powerful model of the origins and operations of mind. Evolutionary psychologists (Cosmides and Tooby 1992, 1994; Barkow et al. 1992) have provided a model of the way in which natural selection has shaped the development of the innate structure and biases in the human mind. The basis of evolutionary psychology is a view of the mind as highly modular, as a system of interacting, highly specialized agents. Indeed, discussions of evolutionary psychology often compare the mind to a Swiss army knife, a collection of specialized tools that can be applied to solving different problems.

There is increasing evidence that human minds are, indeed, highly modular. Fodor (1983) offers a philosophical argument for the modular structure of mind. Minsky (1985) explores the ramifications of modular theories for artificial intelligence. This architecture is important to theories of the evolution of mind. It would be difficult to imagine how evolution could shape a single system as complex as a mind. It is, however, plausible that evolution, working over millions of years, could successively shape individual, specialized cognitive skills. As evolution of the brain continued, it could also work on combinations of modules, forming the mechanisms that enable the modules to interact, to share information, and to cooperate to perform increasingly complex cognitive tasks (Mithen 1996).

Theories of neuronal selection (Edelman 1992) show how these same processes can account for the adaptation of the individual neural system. Neural Darwinism models the adaptation of neural systems in Darwinian terms: the strengthening of particular circuits in the brain and the weakening of others is a process of selection in response to the world. In contrast to symbolic learning methods, which attempt to extract information from training data and use that information to build models of the world, theories of neuronal selection examine the effect of selective pressures on populations of neurons and their interactions. Edelman (1992, page 81) states:

> In considering brain science as a science of recognition I am implying that recognition is not an instructive process. No direct information transfer occurs, just as none occurs in evolutionary or immune processes. Instead, recognition is selective.

Agent technologies offer models of social cooperation as well. Using agent-based approaches, economists have constructed informative (if not completely predictive) models of economic markets. Agent technologies have exerted an increasing influence on the design of distributed computing systems, the construction of internet search tools and implementation of cooperative work environments.

Finally, agent-based models have exerted an influence on theories of consciousness. For example, Daniel Dennett (1991) has based an account of the function and structure of consciousness on an agent architecture of mind. He begins by arguing that it is incorrect to ask where consciousness is located in the mind/brain. Instead, his *multiple draft theory of consciousness* focuses on the role of consciousness in the interactions of agents in a distributed mental architecture. In the course of perception, motor control, problem solving, learning, and other mental activities, we form coalitions of interacting agents. These coalitions are highly dynamic, changing in response to the needs of different situations. Consciousness, for Dennett, serves as a binding mechanism for these coalitions, supporting agent interaction and raising critical coalitions of interacting agents to the foreground of cognitive processing.

What issues limit an agent-based approximation of intelligence?

Agent-based and "emergent" approaches have opened up a number of problems that must be solved if their promise is to be realized. For example, we have yet to fill in all the steps that have enabled the evolution of higher-level cognitive abilities such as language. Like paleontologists' efforts to reconstruct the evolution of species, tracing the development of these higher-level problems will take a great deal of additional detailed work. We must both enumerate the agents that underlie the architecture of mind and trace their evolution across time.

Another important problem for agent-based theories is in explaining the interactions between modules. Although the "Swiss army knife" model of mind is a useful intuition builder, the modules that compose mind are not as independent as the blades of a pocket knife. Minds exhibit extensive, highly fluid interactions between cognitive domains: we can talk about things we see, indicating an interaction between visual and linguistic modules. We can construct buildings that enable a specific social purpose, indicating an interaction between technical and social intelligence. Poets can construct tactile metaphors for visual scenes, indicating a fluid interaction between visual and tactile modules. Defining the representations and processes that enable these inter-module interactions is an active area of research (Karmiloff-Smith 1992, Mithen 1996, Lakoff and Johnson 1999).

Practical applications of agent-based technologies are also becoming increasingly important. Using agent-based computer simulations, it is possible to model complex systems that have no closed-form mathematical description, and were heretofore impossible to study in this detail. Simulation-based techniques have been applied to a range of phenomena, such as the adaptation of the human immune system and the control of complex processes, including particle accelerators, the behavior of global currency markets, and the study of weather systems. The representational and computational issues that must be solved to implement such simulations continue to drive research in knowledge representations, algorithms, and even the design of computer hardware.

Further practical problems that agent architectures must deal with include protocols for inter-agent communication, especially when local agents often have limited knowledge of the problem at large or indeed of what knowledge other agents might already possess. Furthermore, few algorithms exist for the decomposition of larger problems into coherent agent-oriented subproblems, or indeed how limited resources might be distributed among agents. These and other agent-related issues were presented in Section 7.4.2.

Perhaps the most exciting aspect of emergent theories of mind is their potential for placing mental activities within a unified model of the emergence of order from chaos. Even the brief overview provided in this section has cited work using emergent theories to model a range of processes, from the evolution of the brain over time, to the forces that enable learning in individuals, to the construction of economic and social models of behavior. There is something extraordinarily appealing in the notion that the same processes of emergent order as shaped by Darwinian processes can explain intelligent behavior at a variety of resolutions, from the interactions of individual neurons, to the shaping of the modular structure of the brain, to the functioning of economic markets and social systems. It may be that intelligence has a fractal geometry, where the same emerging processes appear at whatever level of resolution we view the system at large.

17.1.4 Probabilistic Models and the Stochastic Technology

As early as the 1950s, stochastic techniques were used to address the understanding and generation of natural language expressions. Claude Shannon (1948) applied probabilistic models, including discrete Markov chains, to the task of language processing. Shannon (1951) also borrowed the notion of entropy from thermodynamics as a way of measuring the information capacity of a message. Also about this time Bell Labs created the first statistical system able to recognize the ten digits, 0, ..., 9, as spoken by an individual speaker. It functioned at 97-99% accuracy (Davis et al. 1952, Jurafsky and Martin 2000).

Through the 1960s and 1970s Bayesian approaches to reasoning continued very much in the background of AI research activity. Natural language technology explored many of the symbol-based approaches described in Section 7.1. Although many expert systems, for example MYCIN, created their own "certainty factor algebras" as seen in Section 9.2.1, several, including PROSPECTOR, took the Bayesian approach (Duda et al. 1979*a*). The complexity of such systems quickly become intractable, however. As we pointed out in Section 8.3.1, the full use of Bayes' rule for a realistic sized medical diagnosis program of 200 diseases and 2000 symptoms would require the collection and integration of eight hundred million pieces of information.

In the late 1980s Judea Pearl (1988) offered a computationally tractable model for diagnostic reasoning in the context of causal relationships within a problem domain: Bayesian belief networks. BBNs relax two constraints of the full Bayesian model. First, an implicit "causality" is assumed in stochastic inference; that is, reasoning goes from cause to effect and is not circular, i.e., an effect cannot circle back to cause itself. This supports representing BBNs as a directed acyclic graph (Section 3.1). Second, BBNs assume the direct parent of a node supports full causal influence on that node. All other nodes are assumed to be conditionally independent or have influence small enough to be ignored.

Pearl's research (1988, 2000) renewed interest in stochastic approaches for modeling the world. As we saw in Section 9.3, BBNs offered a very powerful representational tool for diagnostic (abductive) inference. This is true especially with the dynamic nature of both human and stochastic systems: as the world changes across time, our understanding is enriched: some causes turn out to explain more of what we see while other potential causes are "explained away". Research in the design of stochastic systems as well as their supporting inference schemes is really only in its infancy.

The late 1980s also saw new research energy applied to issues of natural language processing. As noted in Section 14.4, these stochastic approaches included new parsing, tagging, and many other techniques for disambiguating language expressions. A full range of these approaches may be found in books on speech recognition and tasks in language processing (Manning and Schutz 1999, Jurafsky and Martin 2000).

With the renewed interest and successes in the stochastic approaches to characterizing intelligent behavior, a person can quite naturally wonder what its limitations might be.

Is intelligence fundamentally stochastic?

There is a tremendous attraction towards a stochastic viewpoint for agent interactions in a changing world. Many might argue that a human's "representational system" is fundamentally stochastic, i.e., conditioned by the world of perceptions and causes in which it is immersed. Certainly the behaviorist/empiricist viewpoint would find this conjecture attractive. Situated and embedded action theorists might go even further and hypothesize that the conditioned relationships an agent has with its physical and social environment offer a sufficient explanation of the successful agent's accommodation with that world.

These conjectures are altogether too simple, however. Let's look at language. One of the strengths of oral and written expression, as Chomsky and others have pointed out, is its *generative* nature. This means that, within the set of vocabulary and language forms available, new and previously unexperienced expressions naturally occur. This happens both on the level of creating novel sentences as well as with individual words, verbizing, for instance: "Google that topic". How can a stochastic account of language ever generalize to new expressions? Furthermore, the limitations of collected language information, whether corpora, treebanks, or other data sets, can radically restrict use of the stochastic technology. This is because the collected information must offer an appropriate setting (or prior) for interpreting the current novel situation.

Stochastic models of application domains, for an aircraft engine or transmission system say, have similar limitations. There, of necessity, will always be *closed world* or *minimal model* assumptions, Section 9.1, for models of any realistically complex system. This means both an a priori limitation of the phenomena that any model can account for, as well as an inability to predict novel situations.

On a higher explanatory level, it may be difficult, if not impossible, for a model to account for a shift out of its own explanatory system, or paradigm. In what sense, as noted in Section 17.1.2, can a model possibly explain theories or higher-level rearrangements of conceptual views, that is, re-evaluate issues related to the adequacy of the model itself with, perhaps, the need to shift to different viewpoints? These topics remain important research issues and constraints on the stochastic approaches to understanding uncertainty.

But, the fact remains that, often without explicit instruction, agents "make" quite successful models. As we see from a constructivist viewpoint, Section 17.2, some model is a sine qua non for an agent to understand its world, i.e., if there is no a priori commitment to what the world is "about", phenomena are neither perceived nor understood!

Besides the philosophical arguments just presented, there are a number of practical limitations to the use of stochastic systems. The current generation of BBNs are propositional in nature. It is not possible to articulate general laws or relationships such as "for all X, p(X) implies ...", see Chapter 2. It is important to add the further expressive power of a variable-based calculus to such systems. Furthermore, it is also impossible in current BBNs to have recursive relationships, where a rule is defined in terms of itself. Research to develop first-order stochastic representational systems, addressing these issues of general, variable based, and recursive relationships, is an important domain for continuing research (Pfeffer et al. 1999, Pfeffer 2001, Pless and Luger 2001, 2003). It is also important to explore the application of stochastic models in neuro/psychological applications, where they have, currently, very little use.

We next discuss those psychological and philosophical aspects of human intelligence that impact the creation, deployment, and evaluation of an artificial intelligence.

17.2 The Science of Intelligent Systems

It is not a coincidence that a major subgroup of the artificial intelligence community has focused its research on understanding *human* intelligence. Humans provide the prototypical examples of intelligent activity, and AI engineers, even though they are usually *not* committed to "making programs that act like humans", seldom ignore human solutions. Some applications such as diagnostic reasoning are often deliberately modeled on the problem solving processes of human experts working in that area. Even more importantly, understanding human intelligence is a fascinating and open scientific challenge in itself.

Modern *cognitive science*, or *the science of intelligent systems* (Luger 1994), began with the advent of the digital computer, even though, as we saw in Chapter 1, there were many intellectual forebears of this discipline, from Aristotle through Descartes and Boole, to more modern theorists such as Turing, McCulloch and Pitts, the founders of the *neural net* model, and John von Neumann, an early proponent of a-life. The study became a science, however, with the ability to design and run experiments based on these theoretical notions, and to an important extent, this came about with the arrival of the computer. Finally, we must ask, "Is there an all inclusive science of intelligence?" We can further ask, "Can a science of intelligent systems support construction of artificial intelligences?"

In the following sections we discuss briefly how the psychological, epistemological, and sociological sciences support research and development in AI.

17.2.1 Psychological Constraints

Early research in cognitive science examined human solutions to logic problems, simple games, planning, and concept learning (Feigenbaum and Feldman 1963, Newell and Simon

1972, Simon 1981). Coincident with their work on the Logic Theorist, Section 13.1, Newell and Simon began to compare their computational approaches with the search strategies used by human subjects. Their data consisted of *think-aloud protocols*, descriptions by human subjects of their thoughts during the process of devising a problem solution, such as a logic proof. Newell and Simon then compared these protocols with the behavior of the computer program solving the same problem. The researchers found remarkable similarities and interesting differences across both problems and subjects.

These early projects established the methodology that the discipline of *cognitive science* would employ during the following decades:

1. Based on data from humans solving particular classes of problems, design a representational scheme and related search strategy for solving the problem.

2. Run the computer-based model to produce a trace of its solution behavior.

3. Observe human subjects working on these same problems and keep track of measurable parameters of their solution process, such as those found in think-aloud protocols, eye movements, and written partial results.

4. Analyze and compare the human and computer solutions.

5. Revise the computer model for the next round of tests and comparisons with the human subjects.

This empirical methodology is described in Newell and Simon's Turing award lecture, quoted at the beginning of this chapter. An important aspect of cognitive science is the use of experiments to validate a problem-solving architecture, whether it be a production system, connectionist, emergent, or an architecture based on the interaction of distributed agents.

In recent years, an entirely new dimension has been added to this paradigm. Now, not just programs can be deconstructed and observed in the act of problem solving, but humans and other life forms can be as well. A number of new imaging techniques have been included in the tools available for observing cortical activity. These include *magnetoencephalography* (MEG), which detects the magnetic fields generated by populations of neurons. Unlike the electrical potentials generated by these populations, the magnetic field is not smeared by the skull and scalp, and thus a much greater resolution is possible.

A second imaging technology is *positron emission tomography*, or PET. A radioactive substance, typically 0^{15} is injected into the bloodstream. When a particular region of the brain is active, more of this agent passes by sensitive detectors than when the region is at rest. Comparison of resting and active images can potentially reveal functional localization at a resolution of about 1cm (see Stytz and Frieder 1990).

Another technique for neural analysis is *functional magnetic resonance imaging*, or fMRI. This approach has emerged from more standard structured imaging based on nuclear magnetic resonance (NMR). Like PET, this approach compares resting with active neuronal states to reveal functional localization.

A further contribution to the localization of brain function, with an important link to the imaging techniques just mentioned, is software algorithms developed by Barak Pearlmutter and his colleagues (Pearlmutter and Parra 1997, Tang et al. 1999, 2000*a*, 2000*b*). These researchers are able to take the complex noise patterns often seen as the output of various neural imaging techniques and break them into their separate components. This is an essential step in analysis, as the patterns of normal steady state existence, such as eye movements, breathing, and heartbeats, are interwoven with the other neuron firing patterns we want to understand.

The result of recent research in cognitive neuroscience (Squire and Kosslyn 1998, Shephard 1998, Gazzaniga 2000) has added greatly to our understanding of the neural components involved in intelligent activity. Even though an analysis and critique of these results is beyond the scope of this book, we list and reference several important issues:

In the area of perception and attention there is the *binding problem*. Researchers such as Anne Triesman (1993, 1998) note that perceptual representations depend on distributed neural codes for relating the parts and properties of objects to each other, and ask what mechanism is needed to "bind" the information relating to each object and to distinguish that object from others.

In the area of visual search, what neural mechanisms support the perception of objects embedded in large complex scenes? Some experiments show that the suppression of information from irrelevant objects plays an important role in the selection of search targets (Luck 1998). Furthermore how do we "learn" to see (Sagi and Tanne 1998)?

In the area of plasticity in perception, Gilbert (1992, 1998) contends that what we see is not strictly a reflection of the physical characteristics of a scene, but rather is highly dependent on the processes by which our brain attempts to interpret that scene.

How does the cortical system represent and index temporally related information, including interpretation of perceptions and production of motor activity (Ivry 1998)?

In memory studies, stress hormones released during emotionally arousing situations modulate memory processes (Cahill and McGaugh 1998). This relates to the *grounding* problem: how are thoughts, words, perceptions meaningful to an agent? In what sense can there possibly be a "sadness (or tears) in things," the *lacremae rerum* of Virgil?

The acoustic–phonetic aspects of speech provide important organizing principles for linking neuroscience research to cognitive and linguistic theories (Miller et al. 1998). How are syntactic and semantic components of cortex integrated (Gazzaniga 2000)?

How does an individual acquire a specific language and what neurophysiological stages support this development (Kuhl 1993, 1998)?

How is development understood, what is *critical period plasticity*, and the adult reorganizations seen in mammalian somatosensory systems (O'Leary et al. 1999)? Are developmental stages critical for "building" intelligence? See Karmiloff-Smith (1992) and Gazzaniga (2000) for further discussion.

The practice of artificial intelligence certainly does not require extensive knowledge of these and related neuro/psychological domains. However, this type of knowledge can support the engineering of intelligent artifacts as well as help locate research and development in AI within the context of the larger science of intelligence systems. Finally, the creation of a psychological, neurophysiological, and computational synthesis is truly exciting. But this requires a mature epistemology, which we discuss next.

17.2.2 Epistemological Issues

If you don't know where you are going, you will wind up somewhere else. . .

—YOGI BERRA (attributed)

The development of artificial intelligence has been shaped by a number of important challenges and questions. Natural language understanding, planning, reasoning in uncertain situations, and machine learning are all typical of those types of problems that capture some essential aspect of intelligent behavior. More importantly, intelligent systems operating in each of these domains require knowledge of purpose, practice, and performance in situated and socially embedded contexts. To better understand these issues, we examine the *epistemological commitment* of a program that is intended to be "intelligent".

The epistemological commitment reflects both the semantics supporting symbol use as well as the structures of symbols employed. The task in these situations is to discover and exploit the *invariances* existing in a problem domain. "Invariant" is a term used to describe the regularities or significant manipulable aspects of complex environments. In the present discussion, the terms *symbols* and *symbol systems* are used generically, from the explicit symbols of the Newell and Simon (1976) tradition, to the nodes and network architecture of a connectionist system, to the emergent tokens of genetic and artificial life. Although the points we make next are general across most of AI, we will focus our discussion on issues in machine learning, as we have created multiple examples and algorithms for learning throughout this book.

In spite of progress in machine learning, it remains one of the most difficult problems facing artificial intelligence. There are three issues limiting our current understanding and research progress: first, the problem of *generalization and overlearning*, second, the role of *inductive bias* in learning, and third, the *empiricist's dilemma* or addressing the idea of constraint-free learning. The last two problems are related: the implicit inductive bias of many learning algorithms is an expression of the rationalists' problem of being biased by expectations, that is, what we learn often seems to be a direct function of what we expect to learn. From the opposite viewpoint, as we saw in a-life research, where there are very few *a priori* expectations of what is to be learned, is it really sufficient to say, "Build it and it will happen"? According the attribution to Yogi Berra at the beginning of this section, it probably won't! The next sections briefly address these issues.

The generalization problem

The examples we used to introduce the various learning models—symbol-based, connectionist, and emergent—were usually very constrained. For example, connectionist architectures often contained only a few nodes or one partial hidden layer. This is appropriate in

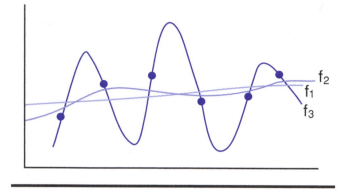

Figure 17.2 A set of data points and three
function approximations.

that the main learning laws can be adequately explained in the context of a few neurons
and partial layers. It can be very misleading in that neural net applications are usually
considerably larger and that the problem of scale IS important. For instance, for
backpropagation learning, a large number of training examples and larger networks are
generally required to solve problems of any significant practical interest. Many researchers
comment extensively on the matter of selecting appropriate numbers of input values, the
ratio between input parameters and hidden nodes, and the training trials necessary before
convergence can be expected (Hecht-Nielsen 1990, Zurada 1992, Freeman and Skapura
1991). In fact, the quality and quantity of training data are important issues for any
learning algorithm. Without an appropriate bias or extensive built-in knowledge, a learning
algorithm can be totally misled attempting to find patterns in noisy, sparse, or even bad
data. Other than acknowledging that these are difficult, important, and open issues, this
"engineering" aspect of learning is not addressed in our book.

A related problem is the issue of "sufficiency" in learning. When can we say our
algorithms are sufficient for capturing the important constraints or invariants of a problem
domain? Do we reserve a portion of our original data to test our learning algorithms? Does
the amount of data we have relate to the quality of learning? Perhaps the sufficiency
judgement is heuristic or aesthetic: we humans often see our algorithms as "good enough".

Let us illustrate this generalization problem with an example, using a form of
backpropagation to induce a general function from a set of data points. Figure 17.2 might
represent data points we are asking our algorithm to generalize. The lines across this set of
points represent functions induced by a learning algorithm. Remember that once the
algorithm is trained we will want to offer it new data points and have the algorithm produce
a good generalization for these data also.

The induced function f_1 might represent a fairly accurate least mean squares fit. With
further training the system might produce f_2, which seems a fairly "good" fit to the set of
data points; but still, f_2 does not exactly capture the data points. Further training can
produce functions that exactly fit the data but may offer terrible generalizations for further
input data. This phenomenon is referred to as *overtraining* a network. One of the strengths

of backpropagation learning is that in many application domains it is known to produce effective generalizations, that is, functional approximations which fit the training data well *and also* handle new data correctly. However, identifying the point where a network passes from an undertrained to an overtrained state is nontrivial. It is naive to think that one can present a neural network, or for that matter any other learning tool, with raw data and then simply step aside and watch while it produces the most effective and useful generalizations for addressing new similar problems.

We conclude by placing this generalization issue back into its epistemological context. When problem solvers make and utilize representations (whether symbols, nodes of networks, or whatever) for the solution process, they are creating invariants, and most probably systems of invariants, for exploring the problem/solution domain and producing related generalizations. This very viewpoint brought to the problem solving process biases the eventual success of the endeavour. In the next subsection, we address this issue further.

Inductive bias, the rationalist's a priori

The automated learning of Chapters 10 to 12, and for that matter most AI techniques, reflected the a priori biases of their creators. The problem of inductive bias is that the resulting representations and search strategies offer a medium for encoding an already interpreted world. They rarely offer mechanisms for questioning our interpretations, generating new viewpoints, or for backtracking and changing perspectives when they are unproductive. This implicit bias leads to the rationalist epistemological trap of seeing in the world exactly and only what we expect or are trained to see.

The role of inductive bias must be made explicit in each learning paradigm. Furthermore, just because no inductive bias is acknowledged, doesn't mean it does not exist and critically affect the parameters of learning. In symbol-based learning the inductive bias is usually obvious, for example, using a semantic net for concept learning. In Winston's (1975a) learning algorithms, biases include the conjunctive relationship representation and the importance of using "near misses" for constraint refinement. We see similar biases in the use of particular predicates for version space search, Section 10.1, decision trees in ID3, Section 10.3, or even rules for Meta-DENDRAL, Section 10.5.

As we have intimated throughout Chapters 10 and 11, however, many aspects of connectionist and genetic learning also assume an inductive bias. For instance, the limitations of perceptron networks led to the introduction of hidden nodes. We may well ask what contribution the hidden nodes make in solution generation. One way of understanding the role of hidden nodes is that they add dimensions to the representation space. As a simple example, we saw in Section 11.3.3 that the data points for the *exclusive-or* problem were not linearly separable in two dimensions. The learned weight on the hidden node, however, provides another dimension to the representation. In three dimensions, the points are separable using a two-dimensional plane. Given the two dimensions of the input space and the hidden node, the output layer of this network can then be seen as an ordinary perceptron, which is finding a plane that separates the points in a three-dimensional space.

A complementary perspective is that many of the "different" learning paradigms shared (sometimes not obvious) common inductive biases. We pointed out many of these: the relationship between clustering with CLUSTER/2 in Section 10.5, the perceptron in

Section 11.2, and prototype networks in Section 11.3. We noted that counterpropagation, the coupled network that uses unsupervised competitive learning on the Kohonen layer together with supervised Hebbian learning on the Grossberg layer, is in many ways similar to backpropagation learning. In counterpropagation, clustered data on the Kohonen layer plays a role similar to the generalizations learned by the hidden nodes that use backpropagation.

In many important ways, the tools we presented are similar. In fact, even the discovery of prototypes representing clusters of data offers the complementary case to function approximation. In the first situation, we are attempting to classify sets of data; in the second, we are generating functions that explicitly divide data clusters from each other. We saw this when the minimum distance classification algorithm used by the perceptron also gave the parameters defining the linear separation.

Even the generalizations that produce functions can be seen from many different viewpoints. Statistical techniques, for example, have for a long time been able to discover data correlations. Iterative expansion of Taylor series can be used to approximate most functions. Polynomial approximation algorithms have been used for over a century to approximate functions for fitting data points.

To summarize, the commitments made within a learning scheme, whether symbol-based, connectionist, or emergent, to a very large extent mediate the results we can expect from the problem-solving effort. When we appreciate this synergistic effect throughout the process of the design of computational problem solvers we can often improve our chances of success as well as interpret our results more insightfully.

The empiricist's dilemma

If current approaches to machine learning, especially supervised learning, possess a dominant inductive bias, unsupervised learning, including many of the genetic and evolutionary approaches, has to grapple with the opposite problem, sometimes called *the empiricist's dilemma*. Themes of these research areas include: solutions will emerge, alternatives are evolved, populations reflect the survival of the fittest. This is powerful stuff, especially situated in the context of parallel and distributed search power. But there is a problem: How can we know we are someplace when we are not sure where we are going?

Plato, more than 2000 years ago, posed this problem in the words of the slave Meno:

> And how can you enquire, Socrates, into that which you do not already know? What will you put forth as the subject of the enquiry? And if you find out what you want, how will you ever know that this is what you did not know (Plato 1961)?

Several researchers have demonstrated that Meno was correct, see Mitchell (1997) and the *No Free Lunch* theorems of Wolpert and Macready (1995). The empiricist, in fact, does require the remnants of a rationalist's a priori to save the science!

Nonetheless, there remains great excitement about unsupervised and evolutionary models of learning; for example, in creating networks based on exemplars or energy minimization, which can be seen as fixed-point attractors or basins for complex relational invariances. We watch as data points "settle" toward attractors and are tempted to see these new architectures as tools for modeling dynamic phenomena. What, we might ask, are the limits of computation in these paradigms?

In fact, researchers have shown (Siegelman and Sontag 1991) that recurrent networks are computationally complete, that is, equivalent to the class of Turing Machines. This Turing equivalence extends earlier results: Kolmogorov (1957) showed that for any continuous function there exists a neural network that computes that function. It has also been shown that a one hidden-layer backpropagation network can approximate any of a more restricted class of continuous functions (Hecht-Nielsen 1989). Similarly, we saw in Section 12.3 that von Neumann created finite state automata that were Turing complete. Thus connectionist networks and finite state automata appear to be but two more classes of algorithms capable of computing virtually any computable function. Furthermore, inductive biases DO apply to unsupervised as well as genetic and emergent models of learning; representational biases apply to the design of nodes, networks, and genomes, and algorithmic biases apply to the search, reward, and selection operators.

What is it then, that unsupervised learners, whether connectionist, genetic, or evolving finite state machines in their various forms, can offer?

1. One of the most attractive features of connectionist learning is that most models are data or example driven. That is, even though their architectures are explicitly designed, they learn by example, generalizing from data in a particular problem domain. But the question still arises as to whether the data is sufficient or clean enough not to perturb the solution process. And how can the designer know?

2. Genetic algorithms also support a powerful and flexible search of a problem space. Genetic search is driven both by the diversity enforced by mutation as well as by operators such as crossover and inversion that preserve important aspects of parental information for succeeding generations. How can the program designer preserve and nurture this diversity/preservation trade-off?

3. Genetic algorithms and connectionist architectures may be viewed as instances of parallel and asynchronous processing. Do they indeed provide results through parallel asynchronous effort not possible with explicit sequential programming?

4. Even though the neural and sociological inspiration is not important for many modern practitioners of connectionist and genetic learning, these techniques do reflect many important aspects of natural evolution and selection. We saw models for error reduction learning with perceptron, backpropagation, and Hebbian models. We also saw the autoassociative Hopfield nets in Section 11.3.4. Various models of evolution were reflected in the paradigms of Chapter 12.

5. Finally, all learning paradigms are tools for empirical enquiry. As we capture the invariants of our world, are our tools sufficiently powerful and expressive to ask further questions related to the nature of perception, learning, and understanding?

In the next section we propose that a constructivist epistemology, coupled with the experimental methods of modern artificial intelligence, offer the tools and techniques for continuing the exploration of a science of intelligent systems.

The constructivist's rapprochement

Theories are like nets: he who casts, captures. . .

—L. WITTGENSTEIN

Constructivists hypothesize that all understanding is the result of an interaction between energy patterns in the world and mental categories imposed on the world by the intelligent agent (Piaget 1954, 1970; von Glasersfeld 1978). Using Piaget's descriptions, we *assimilate* external phenomena according to our current understanding and *accommodate* our understanding to the "demands" of the phenomena.

Constructivists often use the term *schemata* to describe the *a priori* structure used to organize experience of the external world. This term is taken from the British psychologist Bartlett (1932) and its philosophical roots go back to Kant (1781/1964). On this viewpoint, observation is not passive and neutral but active and interpretive.

Perceived information, Kant's *a posteriori* knowledge, never fits precisely into our preconceived, and *a priori*, schemata. From this tension, the schema-based biases the subject uses to organize experience are either modified or replaced. The need for accommodation in the face of unsuccessful interactions with the environment drives a process of cognitive equilibration. Thus, the constructivist epistemology is fundamentally one of cognitive evolution and refinement. An important consequence of constructivism is that the interpretation of any situation involves the imposition of the observer's concepts and categories on reality (an inductive bias).

When Piaget (1954, 1970) proposed a constructivist approach to understanding, he called it *genetic epistemology*. The lack of a comfortable fit of current schemata to the world "as it is" creates a cognitive tension. This tension drives a process of schema revision. Schema revision, Piaget's *accommodation*, is the continued evolution of an agent's understanding towards *equilibration*.

Schema revision and continued movement toward equilibrium is a genetic predisposition of an agent for an accommodation to the structures of society and the world. It combines both these forces and represents an embodied predisposition for survival. Schema modification is both an *a priori* result of our genetics as well as an *a posteriori* function of society and the world. It reflects the embodiment of a survival-driven agent, of a being in space and time.

There is a blending here of the empiricist and rationalist traditions, mediated by the goals of agent survival. As embodied, agents can comprehend nothing except that which first passes through their senses. As accommodating, agents survive through learning the general patterns of an external world. What is perceived is mediated by what is expected; what is expected is influenced by what is perceived: that is, these two functions can only be understood in terms of each other.

Finally, we, as agents, are seldom consciously aware of the schemata that support our interactions with the world. As the sources of bias and prejudice both in science and society, we are more often than not unaware of a priori schemata. These are constitutive of our equilibration with the world and not (usually) a perceptible element of a conscious mental life.

Finally, why is a constructivist epistemology particularly useful in addressing the problems of understanding intelligence? How can an agent within an environment understand its own understanding of that situation? We believe constructivism also addresses the *epistemological access* problem in both philosophy and psychology. For more than a century there has been a struggle in both these disciplines between two factions, the positivist, which proposes to infer mental phenomena from observable physical behavior, and a more phenomenological approach which allows the use of first person reporting to access cognitive phenomena. This factionalism exists because both modes of access to psychological phenomena require some form of model construction and inference.

In comparison to physical objects like chairs and doors, which often, naively, seem to be directly accessible, the mental states and dispositions of an agent seem to be particularly difficult to characterize. In fact, we contend that this dichotomy between the direct access to physical phenomena and the indirect access to the mental is illusory. The constructivist analysis suggests that no experience of things is possible without the use of some model or schema for organizing that experience. In scientific inquiry, as well as in our normal human experiences, this implies that *all* access to phenomena is through exploration, approximation, and continued model refinement.

So what is the project of the AI practitioner?

As AI practitioners, we are constructivists. We build, test, and refine models. But what is it that we are approximating in our model-building activity? We discuss this issue in the following paragraphs but first we make a simple epistemological observation: Rather than trying to capture the essence of "things outside" us, the AI problem-solver is best served by attempting to emulate the model building, refining, and equilibration heuristics of the intelligent agent itself (Luger et al. 2002).

Only the extreme solipsist (or the mentally challenged) would deny the "reality" of an extra-subject world. But what is this so called "real world"? Besides being a complex combination of "hard things" and "soft things", it is also a system of atoms, molecules, quarks, gravity, relativity, cells, DNA, and (perhaps even) superstrings. For all these concepts are but exploratory models driven by the explanatory requirements of equilibration-driven agents. Again, these exploratory models are not about an external world. Rather, they capture the dynamic equilibrating tensions of the intelligent and social agent, of a material intelligence evolving and continually calibrating itself within space and time.

But access to and creation of "the real" is also achieved through agent commitment. An embodied agent *creates the real* through an existential affirmation that a perceived model of its expectations is good-enough for addressing some of its practical needs and purposes. This act of commitment grounds the symbols and systems of symbols the agent uses in its material and social contexts. These constructs are grounded because they are affirmed as good-enough for achieving aspects of its purpose. This grounding is also seen in agent language use. Searle (1969) is correct in his notion of speech phenomena as *acts*. This *grounding* issue is part of why computers have fundamental problems with expressions of intelligence, including their demonstrations of language and learning. What disposition might a computer be given that affords it appropriate purposes and goals? Although Dennett (1987) would impute grounding to a computer solving problems requiring and using "intelligence", the lack of *sufficient* grounding is easily seen in the computer's simplifications, brittleness, and often limited appreciation of context.

The use and grounding of symbols by animate agents implies even more. The particulars of the human agent's embodiment and social contexts mediate its interactions with its world. Auditory and visual systems sensitive to a particular bandwidth; viewing the world as an erect biped, having arms, legs, hands; being in a world with weather, seasons, sun, and darkness; part of a society with evolving goals and purposes; an individual that is born, reproduces, and dies: these are critical components that support metaphors of understanding, learning, and language; these mediate the expressions of art, life, and love.

> Shall I compare thee to a summer's day?
> Thou art more lovely and more temperate:
> Rough winds do shake the darling buds of May,
> And summer's lease hath all too short a date...
> *Shakespeare Sonnet XVIII*

We conclude with a summary of critical issues that both support and delimit current efforts at creating a science of intelligent systems.

17.3 AI: Current Challenges and Future Directions

like the geometer who strives
  to square the circle and cannot find
  by thinking the principle needed,

was I at that new sight. . .

—DANTE, *Paradiso*

Although the use of AI techniques to solve practical problems has demonstrated its utility, the use of these techniques to found a general science of intelligence is a difficult and continuing problem. In this final section we return to the questions that led us to enter the field of artificial intelligence and to write this book: is it possible to give a formal, computational account of the processes that enable intelligence?

The computational characterization of intelligence begins with the abstract specification of computational devices. Research through the 1930s, 40s, and 50s began this task, with Turing, Post, Markov, and Church all contributing formalisms that describe computation. The goal of this research was not just to specify what it meant to compute, but rather to specify limits on what could be computed. The Universal Turing Machine (Turing 1950) is the most commonly studied specification, although Post's rewrite rules, the basis for production system computing (Post 1943), is also an important contribution. Church's model (1941), based on partially recursive functions, offers support for modern high-level functional languages, such as Scheme and Standard ML.

Theoreticians have proven that all of these formalisms have equivalent computational power in that any function computable by one is computable by the others. In fact, it is possible to show that the universal Turing machine is equivalent to any modern computational device. Based on these results, the Church–Turing hypothesis makes the even stronger argument: that no model of computation can be defined which is more powerful than these known models. Once we establish equivalence of computational specifications, we have freed ourselves from the medium of mechanizing these specifications: we can implement our algorithms with vacuum tubes, silicon, protoplasm, or tinker toys. The automated design in one medium can be seen as equivalent to mechanisms in another. This makes the empirical enquiry method even more critical, as we experiment in one medium to test our understanding of mechanisms implemented in another.

One of the possibilities is that the universal machine of Turing and Post may be too general. Paradoxically, intelligence may require a less powerful computational mechanism with more focused control. Levesque and Brachman (1985) have suggested that human intelligence may require more computationally efficient (although less expressive) representations, such as Horn clauses for reasoning, the restriction of factual knowledge to ground literals, and the use of computationally tractable truth maintenance systems. Agent-based and emergent models of intelligence also seem to espouse this philosophy.

Another point addressed by the formal equivalence of our models of mechanism is the duality issue and the mind–body problem. At least since the days of Descartes (Section 1.1), philosophers have asked the question of the interaction and integration of mind, consciousness, and a physical body. Philosophers have offered every possible response, from total materialism to the denial of material existence, even to the supporting intervention of a benign god! AI and cognitive science research reject Cartesian dualism in favor of a material model of mind based on the physical implementation or instantiation of symbols, the formal specification of computational mechanisms for manipulating those symbols, the equivalence of representational paradigms, and the mechanization of knowledge and skill in embodied models. The success of this research is an indication of the validity of this model (Johnson-Laird 1988, Dennett 1987, Luger et al. 2002).

Many consequential questions remain, however, within the epistemological foundations for intelligence in a physical system. We summarize again several of these critical issues.

1. **The representation problem.** Newell and Simon hypothesized that the physical symbol system and search are necessary and sufficient characterizations of intelligence (see Section 17.1). Are the successes of the neural or sub-symbolic models and of the genetic and emergent approaches to intelligence refutations of the physical symbol hypothesis, or are they simply other instances of it?

   Even a weak interpretation of this hypothesis—that the physical symbol system is a *sufficient* model for intelligence—has produced many powerful and useful results in the modern field of cognitive science. What this argues is that we can implement physical symbol systems that will demonstrate intelligent behavior. Sufficiency allows creation and testing of symbol-based models for many aspects of human performance (Pylyshyn 1984, Posner 1989). But the strong interpretation—that the physical symbol system and search are *necessary* for intelligent activity—remains open to question (Searle 1980, Weizenbaum 1976, Winograd and Flores 1986, Dreyfus and Dreyfus 1985, Penrose 1989).

2. **The role of embodiment in cognition.** One of the main assumptions of the physical symbol system hypothesis is that the particular instantiation of a physical symbol system is irrelevant to its performance; all that matters is its formal structure. This has been challenged by a number of thinkers (Searle 1980, Johnson 1987, Agre and Chapman 1987, Brooks 1989, Varela et al. 1993) who essentially argue that the requirements of intelligent action in the world require a physical embodiment that allows the agent to be fully integrated into that world. The architecture of modern computers does not support this degree of situatedness, requiring that an artificial intelligence interact with its world through the extremely limited window of contemporary input/output devices. If this challenge is correct, then, although some form of machine intelligence may be possible, it will require a very different interface than that afforded by contemporary computers. (For further comments on this topic see Section 14.0, issues in natural language understanding, and Section 17.2.2, on epistemological constraints.)

3. **Culture and intelligence.** Traditionally, artificial intelligence has focused on the individual mind as the sole source of intelligence; we have acted as if an explanation of the way the brain encodes and manipulates knowledge would be a complete explanation of the origins of intelligence. However, we could also argue that knowledge is best regarded as a social, rather than as an individual construct. In a *meme-based* theory of intelligence (Edelman 1992), society itself carries essential components of intelligence. It is possible that an understanding of the social context of knowledge and human behavior is just as important to a theory of intelligence as an understanding of the dynamics of the individual mind/brain.

4. **Characterizing the nature of interpretation.** Most computational models in the representational tradition work with an already interpreted domain: that is, there is an implicit and *a priori* commitment of the system's designers to an interpretive context. Under this commitment there is little ability to shift contexts, goals, or representations as the problem solving evolves. Currently, there is little effort at illuminating the process by which humans construct interpretations.

   The Tarskian view of semantics as a mapping between symbols and objects in a domain of discourse is certainly too weak and doesn't explain, for example, the fact that one domain may have different interpretations in the light of different practical goals. Linguists have tried to remedy the limitations of Tarskian semantics by adding a theory of pragmatics (Austin 1962). Discourse analysis, with its fundamental dependence on symbol use in context, has dealt with these issues in recent years. The problem, however, is broader in that it deals with the failure of referential tools in general (Lave 1988, Grosz and Sidner 1990).

   The semiotic tradition started by C. S. Peirce (1958) and continued by Eco, Seboek, and others (Eco 1976, Grice 1975, Sebeok 1985) takes a more radical approach to language. It places symbolic expressions within the wider context of signs and sign interpretation. This suggests that the meaning of a symbol can only be understood in the context of its role as interpretant, that is, in the context of an interpretation and interaction with the environment (see Section 17.2.2).

5. **Representational indeterminacy.** Anderson's representational indeterminacy conjecture (Anderson 1978) suggests that it may in principle be impossible to determine what representational scheme best approximates the human problem solver in the context of a particular act of skilled performance. This conjecture is founded on the fact that every representational scheme is inextricably linked to a larger computational architecture, as well as search strategies. In the detailed analysis of human skill, it may be impossible to control the process sufficiently so that we can determine the representation; or establish a representation to the point where a process might be uniquely determined. As with the uncertainty principle of physics, where phenomena can be altered by the very process of measuring them, this is an important concern for constructing models of intelligence but need not limit their utility.

But more importantly, the same criticisms can be leveled at the computational model itself where the inductive biases of symbol and search in the context of the Church–Turing hypothesis still under constrain a system. The perceived need of some optimal representational scheme may well be the remnant of a rationalist's dream, while the scientist simply requires models sufficiently robust to constrain empirical questions. The proof of the quality of a model is in its ability to offer an interpretation, to predict, and to be revised.

6. **The necessity of designing computational models that are falsifiable.** Popper (1959) and others have argued that scientific theories must be falsifiable. This means that there must exist circumstances under which the model is *not* a successful approximation of the phenomenon. The obvious reason for this is that *any* number of confirming experimental instances are not sufficient for confirmation of a model. Furthermore, much new research is done in direct response to the failure of existing theories.

The general nature of the physical symbol system hypothesis as well as situated and emergent models of intelligence may make them impossible to falsify and therefore of limited use as models. The same criticism can be made of the conjectures of the phenomenological tradition (see point 7). Some AI data structures, such as the semantic network, are so general that they can model almost anything describable, or as with the universal Turing machine, any computable function. Thus, when an AI researcher or cognitive scientist is asked under what conditions his or her model for intelligence will *not* work, the answer can be difficult.

7. **The limitations of the scientific method.** A number of researchers (Winograd and Flores 1986, Weizenbaum 1976) claim that the most important aspects of intelligence are not and, in principle, cannot be modeled, and in particular not with any symbolic representation. These areas include learning, understanding natural language, and the production of speech acts. These issues have deep roots in our philosophical tradition. Winograd and Flores's criticisms, for example, are based on issues raised in phenomenology (Husserl 1970, Heidegger 1962).

Most of the assumptions of modern AI can trace their roots back from Carnap, Frege, and Leibniz through Hobbes, Locke, and Hume to Aristotle. This tradition argues that intelligent processes conform to universal laws and are, in principle, understandable.

Heidegger and his followers represent an alternative approach to understanding intelligence. For Heidegger, reflective awareness is founded in a world of embodied experience (a life-world). This position, shared by Winograd and Flores, Dreyfus, and others, argues that a person's understanding of things is rooted in the practical activity of "using" them in coping with the everyday world. This world is essentially a context of socially organized roles and purposes. This context, and human functioning within it, is not something explained by propositions and understood by theorems. It is rather a flow that shapes and is itself continuously created. In a fundamental sense, human expertise is not knowing *that*, but rather, within a world of evolving social norms and implicit purposes, knowing *how*. We are inherently unable to place our knowledge and most of our intelligent behavior into language, either formal or natural.

Let us consider this point of view. First, as a criticism of the *pure* rationalist tradition, it is correct. Rationalism asserts that all human activity, intelligence, and responsibility can, in principle at least, be represented, formalized, and understood. Most reflective people do not believe this to be the case, reserving important roles for emotion, self-affirmation and responsible commitment (at least!). Aristotle himself said, in his *Essay on Rational Action*, "Why is it that I don't feel compelled to perform that which is entailed?" There are many human activities outside the realms of science that play an essential role in responsible human interaction; these cannot be reproduced by or abrogated to machines.

This being said, however, the scientific tradition of examining data, constructing models, running experiments, and examining results with model refinement for further experiments has brought an important level of understanding, explanation, and ability to predict to the human community. The scientific method is a powerful tool for increasing human understanding. Nonetheless, there remain a number of caveats to this approach that scientists must understand.

First, scientists must not confuse the model with the phenomenon being modeled. The model allows us to progressively approximate the phenomenon: there will, of necessity, always be a "residue" that is not empirically explained. In this sense also representational indeterminacy is *not* an issue. A model is used to explore, explain, and predict; and if it allows scientists to accomplish this, it is successful (Kuhn 1962). Indeed, different models may successfully explain different aspects of a phenomenon, such as the wave and particle theories of light.

Furthermore, when researchers claim that aspects of intelligent phenomena are outside the scope and methods of the scientific tradition, this statement itself can only be verified by using that very tradition. The scientific method is the only tool we have for explaining in what sense issues may still be outside our current understanding. Every viewpoint, even that from the phenomenological tradition, if it is to have any meaning, must relate to our current notions of explanation—even to be coherent about the extent to which phenomena cannot be explained.

The most exciting aspect of work in artificial intelligence is that to be coherent and contribute to the endeavor we must address these issues. To understand problem solving, learning, and language we must comprehend the philosophical level of representations and knowledge. In a humbling way we are asked to resolve Aristotle's tension between *theoria* and *praxis*, to fashion a union of understanding and practice, of the theoretical and practical, to live between science and art.

AI practicioners are tool makers. Our representations, algorithms, and languages are tools for designing and building mechanisms that exhibit intelligent behavior. Through experiment we test both their computational adequacy for solving problems as well as our own understanding of intelligent phenomena.

Indeed, we have a tradition of this: Descartes, Leibniz, Bacon, Pascal, Hobbes, Babbage, Turing, and others whose contributions were presented in Chapter 1. Engineering, science, and philosophy; the nature of ideas, knowledge, and skill; the power and limitations of formalism and mechanism; these are the limitations and tensions with which we must live and from which we continue our explorations.

17.4 Epilogue and References

We refer the reader to the references at the end of Chapter 1 and add *Computation and Cognition* (Pylyshyn 1984) and *Understanding Computers and Cognition* (Winograd and Flores 1986). For issues in cognitive science see Newell and Simon (1972), Pylyshyn (1973, 1980), Norman (1981), Churchland (1986), Posner (1989), Luger (1994), Franklin (1995), Ballard (1997), Elman et al. (1996), and Jeannerod (1997).

Haugeland (1981, 1997), Dennett (1978) and Smith (1996) describe the philosophical foundations of a science of intelligent systems. Anderson's (1990) book on cognitive psychology offers valuable examples of information processing models. Pylyshyn (1984) and Anderson (1978, 1982, 1983a) give detailed descriptions of many critical issues in cognitive science, including a discussion of representational indeterminacy. Dennett (1991) applies the methodology of cognitive science to an exploration of the structure of consciousness itself. We also recommend books on the philosophy of science (Popper 1959, Kuhn 1962, Bechtel 1988, Hempel 1965, Lakatos 1976, Quine 1963).

Finally, *Philosophy in the Flesh* (Lakoff and Johnson 1999), suggests possible answers to the grounding problem. *The Embodied Mind* (Varela et al.1993), Suchman (1987), and *Being There* (Clark 1997) describe aspects of embodiment that support intelligence.

We leave the reader with address information for two important groups:

The American Association for Artificial Intelligence
445 Burgess Drive
Menlo Park, CA 94025

Computer Professionals for Social Responsibility
P.O. Box 717
Palo Alto, CA 94301

BIBLIOGRAPHY

Abelson, H., and Sussman, G.J. 1985. *Structure and Interpretation of Computer Programs*. Cambridge, MA: MIT Press.

Ackley, D.H. and Littman, M. 1992. Interactions between learning and evolution. In Langton et al., eds (1992).

Ackley, D.H., Hinton, G.E., and Sejnowski, T.J. 1985. A learning algorithm for Boltzmann machines. *Cognitive Science* 9.

Adler, M.R., Davis, A.B., Weihmayer, R., and Worrest, R.W. 1989. Conflict resolution strategies for nonhierarchical distributed agents. *Distributed Artificial Intelligence,* Vol. 112. San Francisco: Morgan Kaufmann.

Agre, P. and Chapman, D. 1987. Pengi: an implementation of a theory of activity. *Proceedings of the Sixth National Conference on Artificial Intelligence,* pp. 268–272. CA: Morgan Kaufmann.

Aho, A.V. and Ullman, J.D. 1977. *Principles of Compiler Design*. Reading, MA: Addison-Wesley.

Allen, J. 1987. *Natural Language Understanding*. Menlo Park, CA: Benjamin/Cummings.

Allen, J. 1995. *Natural Language Understanding*, 2nd ed. Menlo Park, CA: Benjamin/Cummings.

Allen, J., Hendler, J., and Tate, A. 1990. *Readings in Planning*. Los Altos, CA: Morgan Kaufmann.

Alty, J.L. and Coombs, M.J. 1984. *Expert Systems: Concepts and Examples*. Manchester: NCC Publications.

Anderson, J.A., Silverstein, J.W., Ritz, S.A., and Jones, R.S. 1977. Distinctive features, categorical perception and probability learning: Some applications of a neural model. *Psychological Review*, 84:413–451.

Anderson, J.R. 1978. Arguments concerning representations for mental imagery. *Psychological Review*, 85:249–277.

Anderson, J.R. 1982. Acquisition of cognitive skill. *Psychological Review*, 89:369–406.

Anderson, J.R. 1983*a*. Acquisition of proof skills in geometry. In Michalski et al. (1983).

Anderson, J.R. 1983*b*. *The Architecture of Cognition*. Cambridge, MA: Harvard University Press.

Anderson, J.R. 1990. *Cognitive Psychology and its Implications*. New York: W.H. Freeman.

Anderson, J.R. and Bower, G.H. 1973. *Human Associative Memory*. Hillsdale, NJ: Erlbaum.

Andrews, P. 1986. *An Introduction to Mathematical Logic and Type Theory: To Truth Through Proof*. New York: Academic Press.

Appelt, D. 1985. *Planning English Sentences*. London: Cambridge University Press.

Arbib, M. 1966. Simple self-reproducing universal automata. *Information and Control* 9:177–189.

Aspray, W. and Burks, A.W., ed. 1987. *Papers of John Von Neumann on Computing and Computer Theory*. Cambridge, MA: MIT Press.

Auer, P., Holte, R.C., and Maass, W. 1995. Theory and application of agnostic pac-learning with small decision trees. *Proceedings of the Twelfth International Conference on Machine Learning,* pp. 21–29. San Francisco: Morgan Kaufmann.

Austin, J.L. 1962. *How to Do Things with Words.* Cambridge, MA: Harvard University Press.

Bach, E. and Harms, R., eds 1968. *Universals of Linguistic Theory.* New York: Holt, Rinehart and Winston.

Bacon, F. 1620. *Novum Organum.* Londini: Apud (Bonham Norton and) Joannem Billium.

Ballard, D. 1997. *An Introduction to Natural Computation.* Cambridge, MA: MIT Press.

Balzer, R., Erman, L.D., London, P.E., and Williams, C. 1980. HEARSAY III: A domain independent framework for expert systems. *Proceedings of the First Annual National Conference on Artificial Intelligence.* Cambridge, MA: MIT Press.

Bareiss, E.R., Porter, B.W., and Weir, C.C. 1988. Protos: An exemplar-based learning apprentice. *International Journal of Man–Machine Studies,* 29:549–561.

Barker, V.E. and O'Connor, D.E. 1989. Expert Systems for configuration at DIGITAL: XCON and Beyond. *Communications of the ACM,* 32(3):298–318.

Barkow, J.H., Cosmides, L., and Tooby, J. 1992. *The Adapted Mind.* New York: Oxford Univ. Press.

Barr, A. and Feigenbaum, E., eds 1989. *Handbook of Artificial Intelligence.* Los Altos, CA: William Kaufman.

Bartlett, F. 1932. *Remembering.* London: Cambridge University Press.

Bateson, G. 1979. *Mind and Nature: A Necessary Unity.* New York: Dutton.

Bayes, T. 1763. Essay towards solving a problem in the doctrine of chances. *Philosophical Transactions of the Royal Society of London.* London: The Royal Society, pp. 370–418.

Bechtel, W. 1988. *Philosophy of Mind.* Hillsdale, NJ: Erlbaum.

Bellman, R.E. 1957. *Dynamic Programming.* Princeton, NJ: Princeton University Press.

Benson, S. 1995. Action Model Learning and Action Execution in a Reactive Agent. *Proceedings of the International Joint Conference on Artificial Intelligence (IJCAI-95).* Morgan Kaufmann.

Benson, S. and Nilsson, N. 1995. Reacting, Planning and Learning in an Autonomous Agent. *Machine Intelligence 14.* Edited by K. Furukawa, D. Michie, and S. Muggleton. Oxford: Clarendon Press.

Berger, A., Brown, P., Della Pietra, S., Della Pietra, V., Gillett, J., Lafferty, J., Mercer, R., Printz, H., and Ures, L. 1994. The Candide System for Machine Translation. *Human Language Technology: Proceedings of the ARPA Workshop on Speech and Natural Language.* San Mateo, CA: Morgan Kaufmann.

Bernard, D.E., Dorais, G.A., Fry, C., Gamble, E.B., Kanefsky, B., Kurien, J., Millar, W., Muscettola, N., Nayak, P.P., Pell, B., Rajan, K., Rouquette, N., Smith, B., and Williams, B.C. 1998. Design of the remote agent experiment for spacecraft autonomy. *Proceedings of the IEEE Aerospace Conference,* Snomass, CO.

Bertsekas, D.P. and Tsitsiklis, J.N. 1996. *Neuro-Dynamic Programming.* Belmont, MA: Athena.

Bishop, C.H. 1995. *Neural Networks for Pattern Recognition.* Oxford: Oxford University Press.

Bledsoe, W.W. 1971. Splitting and reduction heuristics in automatic theorem proving. *Artificial Intelligence,* 2:55–77.

Bledsoe, W.W. 1977. Non-resolution theorem proving. *Artificial Intelligence,* 9(1):1–35.

Bobrow, D.G. 1975. Dimensions of representation. In Bobrow and Collins (1975).

Bobrow, D.G. and Collins A., eds 1975. *Representation and Understanding.* New York, Academic Press.

Bobrow, D.G. and Winograd, T. 1977. An overview of KRL, a knowledge representation language. *Cognitive Science* 1(1):3–46.

Bond, A.H. and Gasser, L., eds 1988. *Readings in Distributed Artificial Intelligence.* San Francisco: Morgan Kaufmann.

Boole, G. 1847. *The Mathematical Analysis of Logic.* Cambridge: MacMillan, Barclay & MacMillan.

Boole, G. 1854. *An Investigation of the Laws of Thought*. London: Walton & Maberly.

Boyer, R.S. and Moore, J.S. 1979. *A Computational Logic*. New York: Academic Press.

Brachman, R.J. 1979. On the epistemological status of semantic networks. In Brachman and Levesque (1985).

Brachman, R.J. 1985. I lied about the trees. *AI Magazine* 6(3).

Brachman, R.J. and Levesque, H.J. 1985. *Readings in Knowledge Representation*. Los Altos, CA: Morgan Kaufmann.

Brachman, R.J., Fikes, R.E., and Levesque, H.J. 1985. KRYPTON: A functional approach to knowledge representation. In Brachman and Levesque (1985).

Brachman, R.J., Levesque, H.J., and Reiter, R., eds 1990. *Proceedings of the First International Conference on Principles of Knowledge Representation and Reasoning*, Los Altos, CA: Morgan Kaufmann.

Brodie, M.L., Mylopoulos, J. and Schmidt, J.W. 1984. *On Conceptual Modelling*. New York: Springer-Verlag.

Brooks, R.A. 1986. A robust layered control system for a mobile robot. *IEEE Journal of Robotics and Automation*. 4:14–23.

Brooks, R.A. 1987. A hardware retargetable distributed layered architecture for mobile robot control. *Proceedings IEEE Robotics and Automation*, pp. 106–110. Raleigh, NC.

Brooks R.A. 1989. A robot that walks: Emergent behaviors from a carefully evolved network. *Neural Computation* 1(2):253–262.

Brooks, R.A. 1991*a*. Intelligence without representation, *Artif. Intell.* 47(3):139–159.

Brooks, R.A. 1991*b*. Challenges for complete creature architectures. In Meyer and Wilson 1991.

Brooks, R.A., 1997. The cog project, *Journal of the Robotics Society of Japan, Special Issue (Mini) on Humanoid*, Vol. 15(7) T. Matsui, (ed.).

Brooks, R. and Stein, L. 1994. Building brains for bodies. *Autonomous Robots*, 1:7–25.

Brown, J.S. and Burton, R.R. 1978. Diagnostic models for procedural bugs in basic mathematical skills. *Cognitive Science*, 2:155–192.

Brown, J.S. and VanLehn, K. 1980. Repair theory: A generative theory of bugs in procedural skills. *Cognitive Science*, 4:379–426.

Brown, J.S., Burton, R.R., and deKleer, J. 1982. Pedagogical, natural language and knowledge engineering techniques in SOPHIE. In Sleeman and Brown (1982).

Brownston, L., Farrell, R., Kant E., and Martin, N. 1985. *Programming Expert Systems in OPS5: An Introduction to Rule-Based Programming*. Reading, MA: Addison-Wesley.

Buchanan, B.G. and Mitchell, T.M. 1978. Model-directed learning of production rules. In Waterman and Hayes-Roth (1978).

Buchanan, B.G. and Shortliffe, E.H., eds 1984. *Rule-Based Expert Systems: The MYCIN Experiments of the Stanford Heuristic Programming Project*. Reading, MA: Addison-Wesley.

Bundy, A. 1983. *Computer Modelling of Mathematical Reasoning*. New York: Academic Press.

Bundy, A. 1988. The use of explicit plans to guide inductive proofs. Lusk, R. and Overbeek, R. eds *Proceedings of CADE 9*, pp. 111–120, New York: Springer Verlag.

Bundy, A. and Welham, R. 1981. Using meta-level inference for selective application of multiple rewrite rules in algebraic manipulation, *Artificial Intelligence*, 16:189–212.

Bundy, A., Byrd, L., Luger, G., Mellish, C., Milne, R., and Palmer, M. 1979. Solving mechanics problems using meta-level inference. *Proceedings of IJCAI-1979*, pp. 1017–1027. Morgan Kaufmann.

Burges, C.J.C. 1998. A tutorial on support vector machines for pattern recognition. *Data Mining and Knowledge Discovery*, 2(2):161–167.

Burks, A.W. 1966. *Theory of Self Reproducing Automata*. University of Illinois Press.

Burks, A.W. 1970. *Essays on Cellular Automata*. University of Illinois Press.

Burks, A.W. 1987. Von Neumann's self-reproducing automata. In Aspray and Burks (1987).

Burmeister, B., Haddadi, A., and Matylis, G. 1997. Applications of multi-agent systems in traffic and transportation. *IEEE Transactions in Software Engineering*, 144(1):51–60.

Burstall, R.M. and Darlington, J.A. 1977. A transformational system for developing recursive programs. *JACM*, 24 (January).

Busuoic, M. and Griffiths, D., 1994. Cooperating intelligent agents for service management in communications networks. *Proceedings of 1993 Workshop on Cooperating Knowledge Based Systems*, University of Keele, UK, 213–226.

Butler, M., ed. 1998. *Frankenstein, or The Modern Prometheus: the 1818 text by Mary Shelly*. New York: Oxford University Press.

Cahill, L. and McGaugh, J.L. 1998. Modulation of memory storage. In Squire and Kosslyn (1998).

Carbonell, J.G. 1983. Learning by analogy: Formulating and generalizing plans from past experience. In Michalski et al. (1983).

Carbonell, J.G. 1986. Derivational analogy: A theory of reconstructive problem solving and expertise acquisition. In Michalski et al. (1986).

Carbonell, J.G., Michalski, R.S., and Mitchell, T.M. 1983. An overview of machine learning. In Michalski et al. (1983).

Cardie, C. 1997. Empirical methods in information extraction. *AI Magazine*, Winter, 65–79.

Cardie, C. and Mooney, R.J. 1999. Machine learning and natural language. *Machine Learning*, 34:5–9.

Carlson, N.R. 1994, *Physiology of Behavior, 5th ed*. Needham Heights MA: Allyn Bacon.

Carnap, R. 1948, On the application of inductive logic. *Philosophy and Phenomenological Research*, 8:133–148.

Ceccato, S. 1961. *Linguistic Analysis and Programming for Mechanical Translation*. New York: Gordon & Breach.

Chang, C.L. and Lee, R.C.T. 1973. *Symbolic Logic and Mechanical Theorem Proving*. New York: Academic Press.

Charniak, E. 1972. Toward a model of children's story comprehension. Report No. TR-266, AI Laboratory, MIT.

Charniak, E. 1993. *Statistical Language Learning*. Cambridge, MA: MIT Press.

Charniak, E. and McDermott, D. 1985. *Introduction to Artificial Intelligence*. Reading, MA: Addison-Wesley.

Charniak, E. and Shimony, S. 1990. Probabilistic semantics for cost based abduction. *Proceedings of the Eighth National Conference on Artificial Intelligence*, pp. 106–111. Menlo Park, CA: AAAI Press/ MIT Press.

Charniak, E. and Wilks, Y. 1976. *Computational Semantics*. Amsterdam: North-Holland.

Charniak, E., Riesbeck, C.K., McDermott, D.V., and Meehan, J.R. 1987. *Artificial Intelligence Programming*, 2nd ed. Hillsdale, NJ: Erlbaum.

Charniak, E., Hendrickson, C., Jacobson, N., and Perkowitz, M. 1993. Equations for part-of-speech tagging. *Proceedings of the Eleventh National Conference on Artificial Intelligence*. Menlo Park, CA: AAAI/MIT Press.

Chen, L. and Sycara, K. 1998. Webmate: a personal agent for browsing and searching. *Proceedings of Second International Conference on Autonomous Agents (Agents 98)*, pp. 132–139, New York: ACM Press.

Chomsky, N. 1965. *Aspects of the Theory of Syntax*. Cambridge, MA: MIT Press.

Chorafas, D.N. 1990. *Knowledge Engineering*. New York: Van Nostrand Reinhold.

Chung, K.T. and Wu, C.H. 1997. Dynamic scheduling with intelligent agents. *Metra Application Note 105*. Palo Alto: Metra.

Church, A. 1941. The calculi of lambda-conversion. *Annals of Mathematical Studies*. Vol. 6, Princeton: Princeton University Press.

Churchland, P. S., 1986, *Neurophilosophy: Toward a Unified Science of the Mind/Brain*, Cambridge, MA: MIT Press.

Clancy, W.J. 1983. The advantages of abstract control knowledge in expert system design. *AAAI-3*. AAAI Press.

Clancy, W.J. 1985. Heuristic Classification. *Artificial Intelligence*, 27:289–350.

Clancy, W.J. and Shortliffe, E.H. 1984a. Introduction: Medical artificial intelligence programs. In Clancy and Shortliffe (1984b).

Clancy, W.J. and Shortliffe, E.H., eds 1984b. *Readings in Medical Artificial Intelligence: the First Decade*. Reading, MA: Addison-Wesley.

Clark, A. 1997. *Being There: Putting Brain, Body, and World Together Again*. Cambridge, MA: MIT Press.

Clocksin, W.F. and Mellish, C.S. 2003. *Programming in PROLOG*, 5th ed. New York: Springer-Verlag.

Codd, E.F. 1968. *Cellular Automata*. New York: Academic Press.

Codd, E.F. 1992. Private communication to J.R. Koza. In Koza (1992).

Cohen, P.R. and Feigenbaum, E.A. 1982. *The Handbook of Artificial Intelligence*. Vol. 3. Los Altos, CA: William Kaufmann.

Cole, R.A., ed. 1997. *Survey of the State of the Art in Human Language Technology*. New York: Cambridge University Press.

Cole, P. and Morgan, J.L., ed. 1975. *Studies in Syntax*. Vol. 3. New York: Academic Press.

Collins A. and Quillian, M.R. 1969. Retrieval time from semantic memory. *Journal of Verbal Learning & Verbal Behavior*, 8:240–247.

Colmerauer, A. 1975. Les Grammaires de Metamorphose, Groupe Intelligence Artificielle, Université Aix-Marseille II.

Colmerauer, A., Kanoui, H., Pasero, R., and Roussel, P. 1973. *Un Système de Communication Homme-machine en Francais*. Research Report, Groupe Intelligence Artificielle, Université Aix-Marseille II, France.

Coombs, M.J., ed. 1984. *Developments in Expert Systems*. New York: Academic Press.

Corera, J.M., Laresgoiti, I. and Jennings, N.R. 1996. Using arcon, part 2: Electricity transportation management. *IEEE Expert*, 11(6):71–79.

Cormen, T.H., Leiserson, C.E., and Rivest, R.J. 1990. *Introduction to Algorithms*. Cambridge, MA: MIT Press.

Cosmides, L. and Tooby, J. 1992. Cognitive adaptations for social exchange. In Barkow et al. (1992)

Cosmides, L. and Tooby, J. 1994. Origins of domain specificity: the evolution of functional organization. In Hirschfeld and Gelman (1994).

Cotton, S., Bundy, A. and Walsh, T. 2000. Automatic invention of integer sequences. *Proceedings of the AAAI-2000*, Cambridge, MA: MIT Press.

Crick, F.H. and Asanuma, C. 1986. Certain aspects of the anatomy and physiology of the cerebral cortex. In McClelland et al. (1986).

Cristianini, N. and Shawe-Taylor, J. 2000. *An Introduction to Support Vector Machines and other Kernel-Based Learning Methods*. Cambridge UK: Cambridge University Press.

Crutchfield, J.P. and Mitchell, M. 1995. The Evolution of Emergent Computation. *Working Paper 94-03-012*. Santa Fe Institute.

Cussens, J. 2001. Parameter estimation in stochastic logic programs. *Machine Learning*, 44:245–271.

Cutosky, M.R., Fikes, R.E., Engelmore, R.S., Genesereth, M.R., Mark, W.S., Gruber, T., Tenenbaum, J.M., and Weber, C.J. 1993. PACT: An experiment in integrating concurrent engineering systems. *IEEE Transactions on Computers*, 26(1):28–37.

Dahl, V. 1977. Un Système Deductif d'Interrogation de Banques de Donnes en Espagnol, PhD thesis, Université Aix-Marseille.

Dahl, V. and McCord, M.C. 1983. Treating Coordination in Logic Grammars. *American Journal of Computational Linguistics*, 9:69–91.

Dallier, J.H. 1986. *Logic for Computer Science: Foundations of Automatic Theorem Proving*. New York: Harper & Row.

Darr, T.P. and Birmingham, W.P. 1996. An attribute-space representation and algorithm for concurrent engineering. *AIEDAM* 10(1):21–35.

Davis, E. 1990. *Representations of Commonsense Knowledge*. Los Altos, CA: Morgan Kaufmann.

Davis, K.H., Biddulph, R., and Balashek, S. 1952. Automatic recognition of spoken digits. *Journal of the Acoustical Society of America,* 24(6):637–642.

Davis, L. 1985. Applying Adaptive Algorithms to Epistatic Domains. *Proceedings of the International Joint Conference on Artificial Intelligence*, pp. 162–164. Morgan Kaufmann.

Davis, M., Matijasevic, Y., and Robinson, J. 1976. Hilbert's tenth problem: Diophantine equations; Positive aspects of a negative solution. *Proceedings of Symposia in Pure Mathematics*, 28:323–378.

Davis, R. 1982. Applications of meta level knowledge to the construction, maintenance, and use of large knowledge bases. In Davis and Lenat (1982).

Davis, R. and Hamscher, W. 1992. Model-based reasoning: Trouble shooting. In H.E. Shrobe (ed) *Exploring Artificial Intelligence: Survey Talks from the National Conferences on Artificial Intelligence*. San Francisco: Morgan Kaufmann. Reprinted in Hamscher et al., (eds). 1992. *Readings in Model Based Diagnosis* San Francisco: Morgan Kaufmann.

Davis, R. and Lenat, D.B. 1982. *Knowledge-based Systems in Artificial Intelligence*. New York: McGraw-Hill.

Davis, R., Shrobe, H., Hamscher, W., Wieckert, K., Shirley, M., and Polit, S. 1982. Diagnosis Based on Description of Structure and Function. *Proceedings of the National Conference on Artificial Intelligence*. Menlo Park, CA: AAAI Press.

Dechter, R. 1996. Bucket elimination: A unifying framework for probabilistic inference. *Proceedings of Conference on Uncertainty in AI (UAI-96)*.

deDombal, F.T., Staniland, J.R., and Clamp, S.E. 1974. Human and computer-aided diagnosis of abdominal pain: Further report with emphasis on performance of clinicians. *British Medical Journal*, 1:376–380.

DeGroot, M.H. 1989. *Probability and Statisics*, 2nd ed. Reading, MA: Addison-Wesley.

DeJong, G. and Mooney, R. 1986. Explanation-based learning: An alternative view. *Machine Learning*, 1(2):145–176.

deKleer, J. 1975. Qualitative and quantitative knowledge of classical mechanics. *Technical Report AI-TR-352*, AI Laboratory, MIT.

deKleer, J. 1976. *Local methods for localizing faults in electronic circuits* (MIT AI Memo 394). Cambridge, MA: MIT.

deKleer, J. 1984. Choices without backtracking. *Proceedings of the Fourth National Conference on Artificial Intelligence*, Austin, TX, pp. 79–84. Menlo Park, CA: AAAI Press.

deKleer, J. 1986. An assumption based truth maintenance system, *Artificial Intelligence*, 28:127–162.

deKleer, J. and Williams, B.C. 1987. Diagnosing multiple faults. *Artificial Intelligence* 32(1):92–130.

deKleer, J. and Williams, B.C. 1989. Diagnosis with behavioral modes. *Proceedings of the International Joint Conference on Artificial Intelligence*, pp. 1324–1330. Cambridge MA: MIT Press.

Dempster, A.P. 1968. A generalization of Bayesian inference. *Journal of the Royal Statistical Society*, 30 (Series B):1–38.

Dennett, D.C. 1978. *Brainstorms: Philosophical Essays on Mind and Psychology*. Montgomery, AL: Bradford.

Dennett, D.C. 1984. *Elbow Room: The Varieties of Free Will Worth Wanting*. London: Cambridge University Press.

Dennett, D.C. 1987. *The Intentional Stance*. Cambridge MA: MIT Press.

Dennett, D.C. 1991. *Consciousness Explained*. Boston: Little, Brown.

Dennett, D.C. 1995. *Darwin's Dangerous Idea: Evolution and the Meanings of Life*. New York: Simon & Schuster.

Descartes, R. 1680. *Six Metaphysical Meditations, Wherein it is Proved That there is a God and that Man's Mind is really Distinct from his Body*. W. Moltneux, translator. London: Printed for B. Tooke.

Dietterich, T.G. 1986. Learning at the knowledge level. *Machine Learning*, 1(3):287–316.

Dietterich, T.G. and Michalski, R.S. 1981. Inductive learning of structural descriptions: Evaluation criteria and comparative review of selected methods. *Proceedings IJCAI 6*. William Kaufmann.

Dietterich, T.G. and Michalski, R.S. 1986. Learning to predict sequences. In Michalski et al. (1986).

Domingos, P. and and Pazzani, M. 1997. On the optimality of the simple Bayesian classifier under zero-one loss. *Machine learning*, 29:103–130.

Doorenbos, R., Etzioni. O., and Weld, D. 1997. A scalable comparison shopping agent for the World Wide Web. *Proceedings of the First International Conference on Autonomous Agents (Agents 97)*, pp. 39–48.

Doyle, J. 1979. A truth maintenance system. *Artificial Intelligence*, 12:231–272.

Doyle, J. 1983. Some theories of reasoned assumptions: An essay in rational psychology. *Tech. Report CS-83-125*. Pittsburgh: Carnegie Mellon University.

Dressler, O. 1988. An extended basic ATMS. *Proceedings of the Second International Workshop on Non-Monotonic Reasoning*, pp. 143–163. Edited by Reinfrank, deKleer, Ginsberg and Sandewall. Lecture Notes in Artificial Intelligence 346. Heidelberg: Springer-Verlag.

Dreyfus, H.L. and Dreyfus, S.E. 1985. *Mind Over Machine*. New York: Macmillan/The Free Press.

Druzdel, M.J. 1996. Qualitative Verbal Explanations in Bayesian Belief Networks. *AISB Quar.*, 94:43–54.

Druzdel, M.J. and Henrion, M. 1993. Efficient reasoning in qualitative probabilistic networks. *Proceedings of the 11th National Conference on Artificial Intelligence (AAAI-93)*, pp. 548–553. The AAAI Press/MIT Press.

Duda, R.O., and Hart, P.E. 1973. *Pattern Classification and Scene Analysis*. New York: John Wiley.

Duda, R.O., Gaschnig, J., and Hart, P.E. 1979*a*. Model design in the PROSPECTOR consultant system for mineral exploration. In Michie (1979).

Duda, R.O., Hart, P.E., Konolige, K., and Reboh, R. 1979*b*. *A computer-based consultant for mineral exploration*. SRI International.

Durfee, E.H. and Lesser, V. 1989. Negotiating task decomposition and allocation using partial global planning. *Distributed Artificial Intelligence: Vol II*, Gasser, L and Huhns, M., eds San Francisco: Morgan Kaufmann, 229–244.

Durkin, J. 1994. Expert *Systems: Design and Development*. New York: Macmillan.

Eco, U. 1976. *A Theory of Semiotics*. Bloomington, Indiana: University of Indiana Press.

Edelman, G.M. 1992. *Bright Air, Brilliant Fire: On the Matter of the Mind*. New York: Basic Books.

Elman, J.L., Bates, E.A., Johnson, M.A., Karmiloff-Smith, A., Parisi, D., and Plunkett, K. 1996. *Rethinking Innateness: A Connectionist Perspective on Development*. Cambridge, MA: MIT Press.

Engelmore, R. and Morgan, T., ed. 1988. *Blackboard Systems*, London: Addison-Wesley.

Erman, L.D., Hayes-Roth, F., Lesser, V., and Reddy, D. 1980. The HEARSAY II speech understanding system: Integrating knowledge to resolve uncertainty. *Computing Surveys*, 12(2):213–253.

Erman, L.D., London, P.E., and Fickas, S.F. 1981. The design and an example use of HEARSAY III. In *Proceedings IJCAI 7*. William Kaufmann.

Ernst, G.W. and Newell, A. 1969. *GPS: A Case Study in Generality and Problem Solving*. New York: Academic Press.

Euler, L. 1735. The seven bridges of Konigsberg. In Newman (1956).

Evans, T.G. 1968. A heuristic program to solve geometric analogy problems. In Minsky (1968).

Falkenhainer, B. 1990. Explanation and theory formation. In Shrager and Langley (1990).

Falkenhainer, B., Forbus, K.D., and Gentner, D. 1989. The structure mapping engine: Algorithm and examples. *Artificial Intelligence*, 41(1):1–64.

Fass, D. and Wilks, Y. 1983. Preference semantics with ill-formedness and metaphor. *American Journal of Computational Linguistics IX*, pp. 178–187.

Feigenbaum, E.A., and Feldman, J., eds 1963. *Computers and Thought*. New York: McGraw-Hill.

Feigenbaum, E.A. and McCorduck, P. 1983. *The Fifth Generation: Artificial Intelligence and Japan's Computer Challenge to the World*. Reading, MA: Addison-Wesley.

Fikes, R.E. and Nilsson, N.J. 1971. STRIPS: A new approach to the application of theorem proving to artificial intelligence. *Artificial Intelligence*, 1(2):189–208.

Fikes, R.E., Hart, P.E., and Nilsson, N.J. 1972. Learning and executing generalized robot plans. *Artificial Intelligence*, 3(4):251–88.

Fillmore, C.J. 1968. The case for case. In Bach and Harms (1968).

Fischer, K., Muller, J.P., and Pischel, M. 1996. Cooperative transportation scheduling: An application domain for DAI. *Applied Artificial Intelligence*, 10(1):1–34.

Fisher, D.H. 1987. Knowledge acquisition via incremental conceptual clustering. *Machine Learning*, 2:139–172.

Fisher, D. H., Pazzani, M.J., and Langley, P. 1991. *Concept Formation: Knowledge and Experience in Unsupervised Learning*. San Mateo, CA: Morgan Kaufmann Publishing.

Fisher, R.A. 1922. On the mathematical foundation of theoretical statistics. *Philosophical Transactions of the Royal Society of London*, Series A 222:309–368.

Fodor, J.A. 1983. *The Modularity of Mind*. Cambridge, MA: MIT Press.

Forbus, K.D. and deKleer, J. 1988. Focusing the ATMS. *Proceedings of the Seventh National Conference on Artificial Intelligence*, pp. 193–198. AAAI Press/ MIT Press.

Forbus, K.D. and deKleer, J. 1993. *Building Problem Solvers*. Cambridge, MA: MIT Press.

Ford. K.M. and Hayes, P.J. 1995. Turing Test Considered Harmful. *Proceedings of International Joint Conference on Artificial Intelligence*, Montreal. Morgan Kaufmann.

Ford. K.M., Glymour, C. and Hayes, P.J. 1995. *Android Epistemology*. Cambridge: MIT Press.

Forgy, C.L. 1982. RETE: a fast algorithm for the many pattern/many object pattern match problem. *Artificial Intelligence*, 19(1):17–37.

Forney, G.D., Jr. 1973. The Viterbi Algorithm. *Proceedings of the IEEE (*March), pp. 268–278.

Forrest, S. 1990. Emergent Computation: Self-organizing, collective, and cooperative phenomena in natural and artificial computing networks. *Physica D*, 42:1–11.

Forrest, S. and Mitchell, M. 1993*a*. What makes a problem hard for a genetic algorithm? Some anomalous results and their explanation. *Machine Learning*, 13:285–319.

Forrest, S. and Mitchell, M. 1993*b*. Relative building block fitness and the building block hypothesis. In Whitley (1993).

Francis, W.N. 1979. A taged corpus – problems and prospects. In Greenbaum, S., Leech, G., and Svartvik, J. (eds), *Studies in English Linguistics for Randolph Quirk*, pp. 192–209. New York: Longman.

Franklin, S. 1995. *Artificial Minds*. Cambridge, MA: MIT Press.

Freeman, J.A. and Skapura, D.M. 1991. *Neural Networks: Algorithms, Applications and Programming Techniques*. New York: Addison-Wesley.

Frege, G. 1879. *Begriffsschrift, eine der arithmetischen nachgebildete Formelsprache des reinen Denkens*. Halle: L. Niebert.

Frege, G. 1884. *Die Grundlagen der Arithmetic*. Breslau: W. Koeber.

Frey, B.J. 1998. *Graphical Models for Machine Learning and Digital Communication*. Cambridge: MIT Press.

Friedman, N. 1998. The Bayesian structural EM algorithm, *Proceedings of the Fourteenth Conference of Uncertainty in Artificial Intelligence*, pp. 252–262. San Francisco: Morgan Kaufmann.

Gadamer, H.G. 1976. *Philosophical Hermeneutics.* Translated by D.E. Linge. Berkeley: University of California Press.

Galileo Galilei 1638. *Discorsi E Dimonstrazioni Matematiche Introno a Due Nuove Scienze.* Leiden.

Gallier, J.H. 1986. *Logic for Computer Science: Foundations of Automatic Theorem Proving.* New York: Harper and Row.

Ganzinger, H., Meyer, C., and Veanes, M. 1999. The two-variable guarded fragment with transitive relations. *Proceedings of the Annual Symposium on Logic in Computer Science*, pp. 24–34.

Gardner, M. 1970. Mathematical Games. *Scientific American* (October 1970).

Gardner, M. 1971. Mathematical Games. *Scientific American* (February 1971).

Garey, M. and Johnson, D. 1979. *Computers and Intractability: A Guide to the Theory of NP-Completeness.* San Francisco: Freeman.

Gazdar, G. and Mellish, C. 1989. *Natural Language Processing in PROLOG: An Introduction to Computational Linguistics.* Reading, MA: Addison-Wesley.

Gazzaniga, M.S. ed. 2000. *The New Cognitive Neurosciences*, 2nd ed. Cambridge: MIT Press.

Genesereth, M. and Nilsson, N. 1987. *Logical Foundations of Artificial Intelligence.* Los Altos, CA: Morgan Kaufmann.

Genesereth, M.R. 1982. The role of plans in intelligent teaching systems. In Sleeman and Brown (1982).

Gennari, J.H., Langley, P., and Fisher, D. 1989. Models of incremental concept formation. *Artificial Intelligence*, 40(1–3):11–62.

Gentner, D. 1983. Structure-mapping: A theoretical framework for analogy. *Cognitive Science*, 7:155–170.

Ghahramani, Z. and Jordan, M.I. 1997. Factorial hidden Markov models. *Machine Learning*, 29:245–274.

Giarratano, J. and Riley, G. 1989. *Expert Systems: Principles and Programming.* PWS-Kent Publishing Co.

Gilbert, C.D. 1992. Horizontal integration and cortical dynamics. *Neuron*, 9:1–13.

Gilbert, C.D. 1998. Plasticity in visula perception and physiology. In Squire and Kosslyn (1998).

Ginsburg, M., ed. 1987. *Readings in Non-monotonic Reasoning.* San Francisco: Morgan Kaufmann.

Glasgow, B., Mandell, A., Binney, D., Ghemri, L., and Fisher, D. 1997. MITA: An information extraction approach to analysis of free-form text in life insurance applications. *Proceedings of the Ninth Conference of Innovative Applications of Artificial Intelligence*, pp. 992–999.

Gluck, M. and Corter, J. 1985. Information, uncertainty and the utility of categories. *Seventh Annual Conference of the Cognitive Science Society, Irvine, Calif.*

Glymour, C. and Cooper, G.F., eds 1999. *Computation, Causation and Discovery.* Cambridge: MIT Press.

Glymour, C., Ford, K., and Hayes, P. 1995*a*. The Prehistory of Android Epistemology. In Glymour et al. (1995*b*).

Glymour, C., Ford, K., and Hayes, P. 1995*b*. *Android Epistemology.* Menlo Park, CA: AAAI Press.

Goldberg, D.E. 1989. *Genetic Algorithms in Search, Optimization and Machine Learning.* Reading, MA: Addison-Wesley.

Goodwin, J. 1982. An Improved Algorithm for Non-Monotonic Dependency Net Update. *Technical Report LITH-MAT-R-82-23.* Department of Computer Science and Information Science, Linköping University, Linköping, Sweden.

Gould, S.J. 1977. Ontogeny and Phylogeny. Cambridge MA: Belknap Press.

Gould, S.J. 1996. *Full House: The Spread of Excellence from Plato to Darwin.* NY: Harmony Books.

Graham, P. 1993. *On LISP: Advanced Techniques for Common LISP.* Englewood Cliffs, NJ: Prentice Hall.

Graham, P. 1995. *ANSI Common Lisp.* Englewood Cliffs, NJ: Prentice Hall.

Greene, B. 1999. *The Elegent Universe: Superstrings, Hidden Dimensions, and the Quest for the Ultimate Theory.* New York: Norton.

Grice, H.P. 1975. Logic and conversation. In Cole and Morgan (1975).

Grossberg, S. 1976. Adaptive pattern classification and universal recoding. I. Parallel development and coding of neural feature detectors. *Biological Cybernetics*, 23:121–134.

Grossberg, S. 1982. *Studies of Mind and Brain: Neural Principles of Learning, Perception, Development, Cognition and Motor Control.* Boston: Reidel Press.

Grossberg, S., ed. 1988. *Neural Networks and Natural Intelligence.* Cambridge, MA: MIT Press.

Grosz, B. 1977. The representation and use of focus in dialogue understanding. PhD thesis, University of California, Berkeley.

Grosz, B. and Sidner, C.L. 1990. Plans for discourse. *Intentions in Communications*, Cohen, P.R. and Pollack, M.E., eds, pp. 417–444. Cambridge, MA: MIT Press.

Hall, R.P. 1989. Computational approaches to analogical reasoning: A comparative analysis, 39(1):39–120.

Hammond, K., ed. 1989. *Case Based Reasoning Workshop.* San Mateo, CA: Morgan Kaufmann.

Hamscher, W., Console, L., and deKleer, J. 1992. *Readings in Model-based Diagnosis.* San Mateo, CA: Morgan Kaufmann.

Hanson, J.E. and Crutchfield, J.P. 1992. The Attractor-basin portrait of a cellular automaton. *Journal of Statistical Physics*, 66(5/6):1415–1462.

Harmon, P. and King, D. 1985. *Expert Systems: Artificial Intelligence in Business.* New York: Wiley.

Harmon, P., Maus, R., and Morrissey, W. 1988. *Expert Systems: Tools and Applications.* New York: Wiley.

Harris, M.D. 1985. *Introduction to Natural Language Processing.* Englewood Cliffs NJ: Prentice Hall.

Harrison, C.D. and Luger, G.F. 2002. Data mining using web spiders (submitted). *UNM Computer Science Technical Report TR-CS-2001-34.*

Hasemer, T. and Domingue, J. 1989. *Common LISP Programming for Artificial Intelligence.* Reading, MA: Addison-Wesley.

Haugeland, J., ed. 1981. *Mind Design: Philosophy, Psychology, Artificial Intelligence.* Cambridge, MA: MIT Press.

Haugeland, J. 1985. *Artificial Intelligence: the Very Idea.* Cambridge/Bradford, MA: MIT Press.

Haugeland, J., ed. 1997. *Mind Design: Philosophy, Psychology, Artificial Intelligence*, 2nd ed. Cambridge, MA: MIT Press.

Haussler, D. 1988. Quantifying inductive bias: AI learning algorithms and Valiant's learning framework. *Artificial Intelligence*, 36:177–222.

Hayes, P.J. 1977. In defense of logic. *Proceedings IJCAI-77*, pp. 559–564, Cambridge, MA. William Kaufmann.

Hayes, P.J. 1979. The logic of frames. In Metzing (1979).

Hayes-Roth, B. 1995. Agents on stage: Advancing the state of the art in AI. *Proceedings of the Fourteenth IJCAI.* Cambridge, MA: MIT Press, 967–971.

Hayes-Roth, B., Pfleger, K., Morignot, P., and Lalanda, P. 1993. Plans and Behavior in Intelligent Agents. *Technical Report, Knowledge Systems Laboratory (KSL-95-35).*

Hayes-Roth, F., Waterman, D., and Lenat, D. 1984. *Building Expert Systems.* Reading, MA: Addison-Wesley.

Hebb, D.O. 1949. *The Organization of Behavior.* New York: Wiley.

Hecht-Nielsen, R. 1982. Neural analog processing. *Proc. SPIE*, 360, pp. 180–189. Bellingham, WA.

Hecht-Nielsen, R. 1987. Counterpropagation networks. *Applied Optics*, 26:4979–4984 (Dec 1987).

Hecht-Nielsen, R. 1989. Theory of the backpropagation neural network. *Proceedings of the International Joint Conference on Neural Networks, I*, pp. 593–611. New York: IEEE Press.

Hecht-Nielsen, R. 1990. *Neurocomputing*. New York: Addison-Wesley.

Heidegger, M. 1962. *Being and Time*. Translated by J. Masquarrie and E. Robinson. New York: Harper & Row.

Heidorn, G.E. 1975. Augmented phrase structure grammar. In Schank and Nash-Webber (1975).

Helman, D.H., ed. 1988. *Analogical Reasoning*. London: Kluwer Academic.

Helman, P. and Veroff, R. 1986. *Intermediate Problem Solving and Data Structures: Walls and Mirrors*, Menlo Park, CA: Benjamin/Cummings.

Hempel, C.G. 1965. *Aspects of Scientific Explanation*. New York: The Free Press.

Hightower, R. 1992. *The Devore universal computer constructor*. Presentation at the Third Workshop on Artificial Life, Santa Fe, NM.

Hill, P.A. and Lloyd, J.W. 1994. *The Goedel Programming Language*. Cambridge, MA: MIT Press.

Hillis, D.W. 1985. *The Connection Machine*. Cambridge, MA: MIT Press.

Hinton, G.E. and Sejnowski, T.J. 1986. Learning and relearning in Boltzmann machines. In McClelland et al. (1986).

Hinton, G.E. and Sejnowski, T.J. 1987. Neural network architectures for AI. Tutorial, AAAI Conference.

Hobbes, T. 1651. *Leviathan*. London: Printed for A. Crooke.

Hobbs, J.R. and Moore, R.C. 1985. *Formal Theories of the Commonsense World*. Norwood, NJ: Ablex.

Hodges, A. 1983. *Alan Turing: The Enigma*. New York: Simon and Schuster.

Hofstadter, D. 1995. *Fluid Concepts and Creative Analogies*, New York: Basic Books.

Holland, J.H. 1975. *Adaptation in Natural and Artificial Systems*. University of Michigan Press.

Holland, J.H. 1976. Studies of the spontaneous emergence of self-replicating systems using cellular automata and formal grammars. In Lindenmayer and Rozenberg (1976).

Holland, J.H. 1986. Escaping brittleness: The possibilities of general purpose learning algorithms applied to parallel rule-based systems. In Michalski et al. (1986).

Holland, J.H. 1995. *Hidden Order: How Adaptation Builds Complexity*. Reading, MA: Addison-Wesley.

Holland, J.H., Holyoak, K.J, Nisbett, R.E., and Thagard, P.R. 1986. *Induction: Processes of Inference, Learning and Discovery*. Cambridge, MA: MIT Press.

Holowczak, R.D. and Adam, N.R. 1997. Information extraction-based multiple-category document classification for the global legal information network. *Proceedings of the Ninth Conference on Innovative Applications of Artificial Intelligence*, pp. 1013–1018.

Holyoak, K.J. 1985. The pragmatics of analogical transfer. *The Psychology of Learning and Motivation*, 19:59–87.

Hopcroft, J.E. and Ullman, J.D. 1979. *Introduction to Automata Theory, Languages and Computation*. Reading, MA: Addison-Wesley.

Hopfield, J.J. 1982. Neural networks and physical systems with emergent collective computational abilities. *Proceedings of the National Academy of Sciences*, 79:2554–2558.

Hopfield, J.J. 1984. Neurons with graded response have collective computational properties like those of two state neurons. *Proceedings of the National Academy of Sciences*, 81:3088–3099.

Horowitz, E. and Sahni, S. 1978. *Fundamentals of Computer Algorithms*. Rockville, MD: computer Science Press.

Huang, C. and Darwiche, A. 1996. Inference in belief networks: A procedural guide, *International Journal of Approximate Reasoning*, 15(3), pp. 225–263.

Hugdahl, K. and Davidson, R.J., eds 2003. *The Asymmetrical Brain*. Cambridge: MIT Press.

Hume, D. 1748. *An Inquiry Concerning Human Understanding*. New York: Bobbs-Merrill.

Husserl, E. 1970. *The Crisis of European Sciences and Transcendental Phenomenology*. Translated by D. Carr. Evanston, IL: Northwestern University Press.

Husserl, E. 1972. *Ideas: General Introduction to Pure Phenomenology*. New York: Collier.

Huygens, C. 1657. Ratiociniis in ludo aleae. In van Schoot, F. (ed.), *Exercitionum Mathematicorum*. Amseterdam: Elsevier.

Ignizio, J.P. 1991. *Introduction to Expert Systems: The Development and Implementation of Rule-Based Expert Systems*. New York: McGraw-Hill.

Ivry, I.B. 1998. The representation of temporal information in perception and motor control. In Squire and Kosslyn (1998).

Jackson, P. 1986. *Introduction to Expert Systems*. Reading, MA: Addison-Wesley.

Jeannerod, M. 1997. *The Cognitive Neuroscience of Action*. Oxford: Blackwell.

Jennings, N.R. 1995. Controlling cooperative problem solving in industrial multi-agent systems using joint intentions. *Artificial Intelligence*, 75:195–240.

Jennings, N.R. and Wooldridge, M. 1998. Applying agent technology. *Agent Technology: Foundations, Applications, and Markets*, Jennings, N.R. and Wooldridge, M., eds Berlin: Springer-Verlag.

Jennings, N.R., Sycara, K.P., and Wooldridge, M. 1998. A roadmap for agent research and development. *Journal of Autonomous Agents and MultiAgent Systems*, 1(1):7–36.

Johnson, L. and Keravnou, E.T. 1985. *Expert Systems Technology: A Guide*. Cambridge, MA: Abacus Press.

Johnson, M. 1987. *The Body in the Mind: The Bodily Basis of Meaning, Imagination and Reason*. Chicago: University of Chicago Press.

Johnson-Laird, P.N. 1983. *Mental Models*. Cambridge, MA: Harvard University Press.

Johnson-Laird, P.N. 1988. *The Computer and the Mind*. Cambridge, MA: Harvard University Press.

Jordan, M., ed. 1999. *Learning in Graphical Models*. Boston: Kluwer Academic.

Josephson, J.R. and Josephson, S.G., ed. 1994. *Abductive Inference: Computation, Philosophy and Technology*. New York: Cambridge University Press.

Jurafsky, D. and Martin, J.H. 2000, *Speech and Language Processing*, Upper Saddle River, NJ: Prentice Hall.

Kant, I. 1781/1964. *Immanuel Kant's Critique of Pure Reason*, Smith, N.K. translator. New York: St Martin's Press.

Karmiloff-Smith, A., 1992. *Beyond Modularity: A Developmental Perspective on Cognitive Science*. Cambridge, MA: MIT Press.

Kaufmann, M., Manolios, P., and Moore. J.S., eds 2000. *Computer-Aided Reasoning: ACL2 Case Studies*. Boston: Kluwer Academic.

Kautz, H., Selman, B., and Shah, M. 1997. The hidden web. *AI Magazine* 18(2):27–35.

Kedar-Cabelli, S.T. 1988. Analogy – From a unified perspective. In Helman (1988).

Kedar-Cabelli, S.T. and McCarty, L.T. 1987. Explanation-based generalization as resolution theorem proving. *Proceedings of the Fourth International Workshop on Machine Learning*.

Keravnou, E.T. and Johnson, L. 1986. *Competent Expert Systems: A Case Study in Fault Diagnosis*. London: Kegan Paul.

King, S.H. 1991. *Knowledge Systems Through PROLOG*. Oxford: Oxford University Press.

Klahr, D. and Waterman, D.A. 1986. *Expert Systems: Techniques, Tools and Applications*. Reading, MA: Addison-Wesley.

Klahr, D., Langley, P., and Neches, R., ed. 1987. *Production System Models of Learning and Development*. Cambridge, MA: MIT Press.

Klein, W.B., Westervelt, R.T., and Luger, G.F. 1999. A general purpose intelligent control system for particle accelerators. *Journal of Intelligent & Fuzzy Systems*. New York: John Wiley.

Klein, W.B., Stern, C.R., Luger, G.F., and Pless, D. 2000. Teleo-reactive control for accelerator beamline tuning. *Artificial Intelligence and Soft Computing: Proceedings of the IASTED International Conference*. Anaheim: IASTED/ACTA Press.

Kodratoff, Y. and Michalski, R.S., ed. 1990. *Machine Learning: An Artificial Intelligence Approach.* Vol. 3. Los Altos, CA: Morgan Kaufmann.

Kohonen, T. 1972. Correlation matrix memories, *IEEE Transactions Computers*, 4:353–359.

Kohonen, T. 1984. *Self-Organization and Associative Memory.* Berlin: Springer-Verlag.

Koller, D. and Pfeffer, A. 1997. Object-oriented Bayesian networks. *Proceedings of the Thirteenth Annual Conference on Uncertainty in Artificial Intelligence.* San Francisco: Morgan Kaufmann.

Koller, D. and Pfeffer, A. 1998. Probabalistic frame-based systems. *Proceedings of the Fifteenth Annual Conference on Uncertainty in Artificial Intelligence.* San Francisco: Morgan Kaufmann.

Kolmogorov, A.N. 1950. *Foundations of the Theory of Probability.* New York: Chelsea.

Kolmogorov, A.N. 1957. On the representation of continuous functions of many variables by superposition of continuous functions of one variable and addition (in Russian). *Dokl. Akad Nauk USSR*, 114:953–956.

Kolmogorov, A.N. 1965. Three approaches to the quantative definition of information. *Problems in Information Transmission*, 1(1):1–7.

Kolodner, J.L. 1987. Extending problem solver capabilities through case based inference. *Proceedings of the Fourth International Workshop on Machine Learning.* CA: Morgan Kaufmann.

Kolodner, J.L. 1988*a*. Retrieving events from a case memory: A parallel implementation. *Proceedings of the Case Based Reasoning Workshop.* Los Altos, CA: Morgan Kaufmann.

Kolodner, J.L., ed. 1988*b*. *Case Based Reasoning Workshop.* San Mateo, CA: Morgan Kaufmann.

Kolodner, J.L. 1991. Improving human decision making through case-based decision aiding. *AI Magazine*, 12(2):52–68.

Kolodner, J.L. 1993. *Case-based Reasoning.* San Mateo, CA: Morgan Kaufmann.

Korf, R.E. 1987. Search. In Shapiro (1987).

Korf, R.E. 1998. Artificial intelligence search algorithms. In *CRC Handbook of Algorithms and Theory of Computation*, M.J. Atallah, ed. Boca Raton, FL: CRC Press.

Korf, R.E. 1999. Sliding-tile puzzles and Rubic's Cube in AI research. *IEEE Intelligent Systems*, Nov, 8–12.

Kosko, B. 1988. Bidirectional associative memories. *IEEE Transactions Systems, Man & Cybernetics,* 18:49–60.

Kosoresow, A.P. 1993. A fast-first cut protocol for agent coordination. *Proceedings of the Eleventh National Conference on Artificial Intelligence*, pp. 237–242. Cambridge, MA: MIT Press.

Koton, P. 1988*a*. Reasoning about evidence in causal explanation. *Proceedings of AAAI-88.* Cambridge, MA: AAAI Press/MIT Press.

Koton, P. 1988*b*. Integrating case-based and causal reasoning. *Proceedings of the Tenth Annual Conference of the Cognitive Science Society.* Northdale, NJ: Erlbaum.

Kowalski, R. 1979*a*. Algorithm = Logic + Control. *Communications of the ACM*, 22:424–436.

Kowalski, R. 1979*b*. *Logic for Problem Solving.* Amsterdam: North-Holland.

Koza, J.R. 1991. Genetic evolution and co-evolution of computer programs. In Langton et al. (1992).

Koza, J.R. 1992. *Genetic Programming: On the Programming of Computers by Means of Natural Selection.* Cambridge, MA: MIT Press.

Koza, J.R. 1994. *Genetic Programming II: Automatic Discovery of Reusable Programs.* Cambridge, MA: MIT Press.

Krulwich, B. 1996. The BarginFinder agent: Comparison price shopping on the internet. *Bots, and other Internet Beasties,* Williams, J., ed. 257–263, Indianapolis: Macmillan.

Kucera, H. and Francis, W.N. 1967. *Computational Analysis of Present-Day American English.* Providence, RI: Brown University Press.

Kuhl, P.K. 1993. Innate predispositions and the effects of experience in speech perception: The native language magnet theory. *Developmental Neurocognition: Speech and Face Processing in the*

First Year of Life, Boysson-Bardies, B., de Schonen, S., Jusczyk, P., McNeilage, P. and Morton, J. eds, pp. 259–274. Netherlands: Kluwer Academic.

Kuhl, P.K. 1998. Learning and representation in speech and language. In Squire and Kosslyn (1998).

Kuhn, T.S. 1962. *The Structure of Scientific Revolutions*. Chicago: University of Chicago Press.

Laird, J., Rosenbloom, P., and Newell, A. 1986*a*. Chunking in SOAR: The Anatomy of a General Learning Mechanism. *Machine Learning* 1(1):11–46.

Laird, J., Rosenbloom, P., and Newell, A. 1986*b*. *Universal Subgoaling and Chunking: The automatic Generation and Learning of Goal Hierarchies*. Dordrecht: Kluwer.

Lakatos, I. 1976. *Proofs and Refutations: The Logic of Mathematical Discovery*. Cambridge: Cambridge University Press.

Lakoff, G. 1987. *Women, Fire and Dangerous Things*. Chicago: University of Chicago Press.

Lakoff, G, and Johnson, M., 1999. *Philosophy in the Flesh*, New York: Basic Books.

Langley, P. 1995. *Elements of Machine Learning*. San Francisco: Morgan Kaufmann.

Langley, P., Bradshaw, G.L., and Simon, H.A. 1981. Bacon 5: The discovery of conservation laws. *Proceedings of the Seventh International Joint Conference on Artificial Intelligence*. William Kaufmann.

Langley, P., Zytkow, J., Simon, H.A., and Bradshaw, G.L. 1986. The search for regularity: Four aspects of scientific discovery. In Michalski et al. (1986).

Langley, P., Simon, H.A., Bradshaw, G.L., and Zytkow, J.M. 1987. *Scientific Discovery: Computational Explorations of the Creative Processes*. Cambridge, MA: MIT Press.

Langton, C.G. 1986. Studying artificial life with cellular automata. *Physica D*, 22:120–149.

Langton, C.G. 1989. *Artificial Life: Santa Fe Institute Studies in the Sciences of Complexity, VI*. Reading, MA: Addison-Wesley.

Langton, C.G. 1990. Computation at the edge of chaos: Phase transitions and emergent computation. *Physica D.*, 42:12–37.

Langton, C.G. 1995. *Artificial Life: An Overview*. Cambridge, MA: MIT Press.

Langton, C.G., Taylor, C., Farmer, J.D., and Rasmussen, S. 1992. *Artificial Life II, SFI Studies in the Sciences of Complexity*. Vol. 10. Reading, MA: Addison-Wesley.

Laplace, P. 1816. *Essai Philosophique sur la Probabilitates, 3rd ed*. Paris: Courcier Imprimeur.

Larkin, J.H., McDermott, J., Simon, D.P., and Simon, H.A. 1980. Models of competence in solving physics problems. *Cognitive Science*, 4:317–345.

Laskey, K. and Mahoney, S. 1997. Network fragments: Representing knowledge for constructing probabalistic models. *Proceedings of the Thirteenth Annual Conference on Uncertainty in Artificial Intelligence*. San Francisco: Morgan Kaufmann.

Lauritzen, S.L. and Spiegelhalter, D.J. 1988. Local computations with probabilities on graphical structures and their application to expert systems. *Journal of the Royal Statistical Society*, B 50(2):157–224.

Lave, J. 1988. *Cognition in Practice*. Cambridge: Cambridge University Press.

Leake, D.B. 1992. *Constructing Explanations: A Content Theory*. Northdale, NJ: Erlbaum.

Leake, D.B., ed. 1996. *Case-based Reasoning: Experiences, Lessons and Future Directions*. Menlo Park: AAAI Press.

Leibniz, G.W. 1887. *Philosophische Schriften*. Berlin.

Lenat, D.B. 1977. On automated scientific theory formation: a case study using the AM program. *Machine Intelligence*, 9:251–256.

Lenat, D.B. 1982. AM: an artificial intelligence approach to discovery in mathematics as heuristic search. In Davis and Lenat (1982).

Lenat, D.B. 1983. EURISKO: A program that learns new heuristics. *Artificial Intelligence*, 21(1, 2):61–98.

Lenat, D.B. and Brown, J.S. 1984. Why AM and Eurisko appear to work. *Artificial Intelligence*, 23(3):269–294.

Lennon, J. and McCartney, P. 1968. Rocky Raccoon. *The White Album*. Apple Records.

Lesser, V.R. and Corkill, D.D. 1983. The distributed vehicle monitoring testbed. *AI Magazine*, 4(3):15–33.

Levesque, H. 1984. Foundations of a functional approach to knowledge representation. *Artificial Intelligence*, 23(2):155–212.

Levesque, H.J. 1989. A knowledge level account of abduction. *Proceedings of the Eleventh International Joint Conference on Artificial Intelligence*, pp. 1051–1067. San Mateo, CA: Morgan Kaufmann.

Levesque, H.J. and Brachman, R.J. 1985. A fundamental tradeoff in knowledge representation and reasoning (revised version). In Brachman and Levesque (1985).

Lewis, J.A. and Luger, G.F., 2000. A constructivist model of robot perception and performance. In *Proceedings of the Twenty Second Annual Conference of the Cognitive Science Society*. Hillsdale, NJ: Erlbaum.

Lieberman, H. 1995. Letizia: An agent that assists web browsing. *Proceedings of the Fourteenth International Joint Conference on Artificial Intelligence*, 924–929. Cambridge, MA: MIT Press.

Lifschitz, V. 1984. Some Results on Circumscription. *AAAI 1984*. AAAI Press.

Lifschitz, V. 1986. Pointwise Circumscription: Preliminary Report. *Proceedings of the Fifth National Conference on Artificial Intelligence*, pp. 406–410. Menlo Park, CA: AAAI Press.

Linde, C. 1974. Information structures in discourse. *PhD thesis*, Columbia University.

Lindenmayer, A. and Rosenberg, G., ed. 1976. *Automata, Languages, Development*. New York: North-Holland.

Lindsay, R.K. Buchanan, B.G. Feigenbaum, E.A., and Lederberg, J. 1980. *Applications of artificial intelligence for organic chemistry: the DENDRAL project*. New York: McGraw-Hill.

Ljunberg, M. and Lucas, A. 1992. The OASIS air traffic management system. *Proceedings of the Second Pacific Rim International Conference on AI (PRICAI-92)*, Korea Information Science Society Center for Artificial Intelligence Research (KAIST). Seoul, Korea.

Lloyd, J.W. 1984. *Foundations of Logic Programming*. New York: Springer-Verlag.

Lovelace, A. 1961. Notes upon L.F. Menabrea's sketch of the Analytical Engine invented by Charles Babbage. In Morrison and Morrison (1961).

Loveland, D.W. 1978. *Automated Theorem Proving: a Logical Basis*. New York: North-Holland.

Lucas, R. 1996. *Mastering PROLOG*. London: UCL Press.

Luck, S.J. 1998. Cognitive and neural mechanisms in visual search. In Squire and Kosslyn (1998).

Luger, G.F. 1978. Formal analysis of problem solving behavior. In *Cognitive Psychology: Learning and Problem Solving*, Milton Keynes: Open University Press.

Luger, G.F. 1994. *Cognitive Science: The Science of Intelligent Systems*. San Diego and New York: Academic Press.

Luger, G.F. 1995. *Computation & Intelligence: Collected Readings*. CA: AAAI Press/MIT Press.

Luger, G.F., Lewis, J.A., and Stern, C. 2002. Problem-solving as model refinement: Towards a constructivist epistemology. *Brain, Behavior, and Evolution*, Basil: Karger; 59:87–100.

Maes, P. 1989. The dynamics of action selection. *Proceedings of the 11th International Joint Conference on Artificial Intelligence*, pp. 991–997. Los Altos, CA: Morgan Kaufmann.

Maes, P. 1990. *Designing Autonomous Agents*. Cambridge, MA: MIT Press.

Maes, P. 1994. Agents that reduce work and information overload. *Communications of the ACM*, 37(7):31–40.

Magerman, D. 1994. Natural Language as Statistical Pattern Recognition, PhD dissertation, Stanford University, Department of Computer Science.

Maier, D. and Warren, D.S. 1988. *Computing with Logic*. Menlo Park, CA: Benjamin/Cummings.

Malpas, J. 1987. *PROLOG: A Relational Language and its Applications*. Englewood Cliffs, NJ: Prentice Hall.

Manna, Z. and Pnueli, A. 1992. *The Temporal Logic of Reactive and Concurrent Systems: Specification*. Berlin: Springer-Verlag.

Manna, Z. and Waldinger, R. 1985. *The Logical Basis for Computer Programming*. Reading, MA: Addison-Wesley.

Manning, C.D. and Schutze, H. 1999. *Foundations of Statistical Natural Language Processing*. Cambridge, MA: MIT Press.

Marcus, M. 1980. *A Theory of Syntactic Recognition for Natural Language*. Cambridge, MA: MIT Press.

Markov, A., 1954. A theory of algorithms, *National Academy of Sciences*, USSR.

Marshall, J.B. 1999. *Metacat: A Self-Watching Cognitive Architecture for Analogy-Making and High-Level Perception*. PhD dissertation, Department of Computer Science, Indiana University.

Martin, A. 1997. *Computational Learning Theory: An Introduction*. Cambridge: Cambridge University Press.

Martins, J. 1990. The truth, the whole truth, and nothing but the truth: an indexed bibliography to the literature on truth maintenance systems. *AI Magazine*, 11(5):7–25.

Martins, J. 1991. A structure for epistemic states. *New Directions for Intelligent Tutoring Systems*. Costa, ed. NATO ASI Series F. Heidelberg: Springer-Verlag.

Martins, J. and Shapiro, S.C. 1983. Reasoning in multiple belief spaces. *Proceedings of the Eighth IJCAI*. San Mateo, CA: Morgan Kaufmann.

Martins, J. and Shapiro, S.C. 1988. A Model for Belief Revision. *Artificial Intelligence*. 35(1):25–79.

Masterman, M. 1961. Semantic message detection for machine translation, using Interlingua. *Proceedings of the 1961 International Conference on Machine Translation*.

McAllester, D.A. 1978. *A three-valued truth maintenance system*. MIT AI Lab., Memo 473.

McAllester, D.A. 1999. PAC-Bayesian model averaging, *Proceedings of the Twelfth ACM Annual Conference on Computational Learning Theory COLT-99*. New York: ACM Press.

McCarthy, J. 1960. Recursive functions of symbolic expressions and their computation by machine. *Communications of the ACM*, 3(4):184–195.

McCarthy, J. 1968. Programs with common sense. In Minsky (1968), pp. 403–418.

McCarthy, J. 1977. Epistemological problems in artificial intelligence. *Proceedings IJCAI-77*, pp. 1038–1044. William Kaufmann.

McCarthy, J. 1980. Circumscription—A form of non-monotonic reasoning. *Artificial Intelligence*, 13:27–39.

McCarthy, J. 1986. Applications of Circumscription to Formalizing Common Sense Knowledge. *Artificial Intelligence*, 28:89–116.

McCarthy, J. and Hayes, P.J. 1969. Some philosophical problems from the standpoint of artificial intelligence. In Meltzer and Michie (1969).

McClelland, J.L., Rumelhart, D.E., and The PDP Research Group. 1986. *Parallel Distributed Processing*. 2 vols. Cambridge, MA: MIT Press.

McCord, M.C. 1982. Using slots and modifiers in logic grammars for natural language. *Artificial Intelligence*, 18:327–367.

McCord, M.C. 1986. Design of a PROLOG based machine translation system. *Proceedings of the Third International Logic Programming Conference*, London.

McCulloch, W.S. and Pitts, W. 1943. A logical calculus of the ideas immanent in nervous activity. *Bulletin of Mathematical Biophysics*, 5:115–133.

McDermott, D. 1978. Planning and acting. *Cognitive Science* 2:71–109.

McDermott, D. and Doyle, J. 1980. Non-monotonic logic I. *Artificial Intelligence*, 13:14–72.

McDermott, J. 1981. R1, The formative years. *AI Magazine* (summer 1981).

McDermott, J. 1982. R1: A rule based configurer of computer systems. *Artificial Intelligence*, 19:39–88.

McGonigle, B. 1990. Incrementing intelligent systems by design. *Proceedings of the First International Conference on Simulation of Adaptive Behavior (SAB-90)*.

McGonigle, B. 1998. Autonomy in the making: Getting robots to control themselves. *International Symposium on Autonomous Agents*. Oxford: Oxford University Press.

McGraw, K.L. and Harbison-Briggs, K. 1989. *Knowledge Acquisition: Principles and Guidelines*, Englewood Cliffs, NJ: Prentice-Hall.

Mead, C. 1989. *Analog VLSI and Neural Systems*. Reading, MA: Addison-Wesley.

Meltzer, B. and Michie, D. 1969. *Machine Intelligence 4*. Edinburgh: Edinburgh University Press.

Merleau-Ponty, M. 1962. *Phenomenology of Perception*. London: Routledge & Kegan Paul.

Metzing, D., ed. 1979. *Frame Conceptions and Text Understanding*. Berlin: Walter de Gruyter and Co.

Meyer, J.A. and Wilson, S.W., eds 1991. *From animals to animats. Proceedings of the First International Conference on Simulation of Adaptive Behavior*. Cambridge, MA: MIT Press/Bradford Books.

Michalski, R.S. and Stepp, R.E. 1983. Learning from observation: conceptual clustering. In Michalski et al. (1983).

Michalski, R.S., Carbonell, J.G., and Mitchell, T.M., eds 1983. *Machine Learning: An Artificial Intelligence Approach*. Vol. 1. Palo Alto, CA: Tioga.

Michalski, R.S., Carbonell, J.G., and Mitchell, T.M., eds 1986. *Machine Learning: An Artificial Intelligence Approach*. Vol. 2. Los Altos, CA: Morgan Kaufmann.

Michie, D. 1961. Trial and error. *Science Survey, Part 2*, Barnett, S.A. and McClaren, A., eds, 129–145. Harmondsworth UK: Penguin.

Michie, D., ed. 1979. *Expert Systems in the Micro-electronic Age*. Edinburgh: Edinburgh Univ. Press.

Miller, S.L., Delaney, T.V., and Tallal, P. 1998. Speech and other central auditory processes: Insights from cognitive neuroscience. In Squire and Kosslyn (1998).

Minsky, M., ed. 1968. *Semantic Information Processing*. Cambridge, MA: MIT Press.

Minsky, M. 1975. A framework for representing knowledge. In Brachman and Levesque (1985).

Minsky, M. 1985. *The Society of Mind,* New York: Simon and Schuster.

Minsky, M. and Papert, S. 1969. *Perceptrons: An Introduction to Computational Geometry*. Cambridge, MA: MIT Press.

Minton, S. 1988. *Learning Search Control Knowledge*. Dordrecht: Kluwer Academic Publishers.

Mitchell, M. 1993. *Analogy-Making as Perception*. Cambridge, MA: MIT Press.

Mitchell, M. 1996. *An Introduction to Genetic Algorithms*. Cambridge, MA: The MIT Press.

Mitchell, M., Crutchfield, J., and Das, R. 1996. Evolving cellular automata with genetic algorithms: A review of recent work. *Proceedings of the First International Conference on Evolutionary Computation and Its Applications*. Moscow, Russia: Russian Academy of Sciences.

Mitchell, T.M. 1978. Version spaces: an approach to concept learning. *Report No. STAN-CS-78-711*, Computer Science Dept., Stanford University.

Mitchell, T M. 1979. An analysis of generalization as a search problem. *Proceedings IJCAI, 6*.

Mitchell, T.M. 1980. The need for biases in learning generalizations. *Technical Report CBM-TR-177*. Department of Computer Science, Rutgers University, New Brunswick, NJ.

Mitchell, T.M. 1982. Generalization as search. *Artificial Intelligence*, 18(2):203–226.

Mitchell, T.M. 1997. *Machine Learning*. New York: McGraw Hill.

Mitchell, T.M., Utgoff, P.E., and Banarji, R. 1983. Learning by experimentation: Acquiring and refining problem solving heuristics. In Michalski, Carbonell, and Mitchell (1983).

Mitchell, T.M., Keller, R.M., and Kedar-Cabelli, S.T. 1986. Explanation-based generalization: A unifying view. *Machine Learning*, 1(1):47–80.

Mithen, S. 1996. *The Prehistory of the Mind*. London: Thames & Hudson.

Mockler, R.J. and Dologite, D.G. 1992. *An Introduction to Expert Systems*, New York: Macmillan.

Mooney, R.J. 1996. Comparative experiments on disambiguating word senses: An illustration of the role of bias in machine learning. In *Proceedings of the Conference on Empirical Methods in Natural Language Processing (EMNLP-96)*. Philadelphia PA. pp. 82–91.

Moore, O.K. and Anderson, S.B. 1954. Modern logic and tasks for experiments on problem solving behavior. *Journal of Psychology*, 38:151–160.

Moore, R.C. 1982. The role of logic in knowledge representation and commonsense reasoning. *Proceedings AAAI-82*. The AAAI Press.

Moore, R.C. 1985. Semantical considerations on nonmonotonic logic. *Artificial Intelligence*, 25(1):75–94.

Moret, B.M.E. and Shapiro, H.D. 1991. *Algorithms from P to NP*, vol 1. Redwood City, CA: Benjamin/Cummings.

Morrison, P. and Morrison, E., eds 1961. *Charles Babbage and His Calculating Machines*. NY: Dover.

MUC-5, 1994. *Proceedings of the Fifth Message Understanding Conference*, San Francisco: Morgan Kaufmann.

Mycroft, A. and O'Keefe, R.A. 1984. A polymorphic type system for PROLOG. *Artificial Intelligence*, 23: 295–307.

Mylopoulos, J. and Levesque, H.J. 1984. An overview of knowledge representation. In Brodie et al. (1984).

Nadathur, G. and Tong, G. 1999. Realizing modularity in lambda Prolog. *Journal of Functional and Logic Programming*, 9, Cambridge, MA: MIT Press.

Nagel, E. and Newman, J.R. 1958. *Godel's Proof*. New York: New York University Press.

Nahm, U.Y. and Mooney R.J. 2000. A mutually beneficial integration of data mining and information extraction. *Proceedings of the American Assoc. for Artificial Intelligence Conf.*, The AAAI Press/The MIT Press. pp. 627–632.

Neches, R., Langley, P. and Klahr, D. 1987. Learning, development and production systems. In Klahr et al. (1987).

Negoita, C. 1985. *Expert Systems and Fuzzy Systems*. Menlo Park, CA: Benjamin/Cummings.

Neves, J.C. F. M, Luger, G.F., and Carvalho, J.M. 1986. A formalism for views in a logic data base. In *Proceedings of the ACM Computer Science Conference*, Cincinnati, OH.

Newell, A. 1981. Physical symbol systems. In Norman (1981).

Newell, A. 1982. The knowledge level. *Artificial Intelligence*, 18(1):87–127.

Newell, A. 1990. *Unified Theories of Cognition*. Cambridge, MA: Harvard University Press.

Newell, A. and Simon, H.A. 1956. The logic theory machine. *IRE Transactions of Information Theory*, 2:61–79.

Newell, A. and Simon, H.A. 1961. GPS: a program that simulates human thought. *Lernende Automaten*, H. Billing ed. pp. 109–124. Munich: R. Oldenbourg KG.

Newell, A. and Simon, H.A. 1963*a*. Empirical explorations with the Logic Theory Machine: a case study in heuristics. In Feigenbaum and Feldman (1963).

Newell, A. and Simon, H.A. 1963*b*. GPS: a program that simulates human thought. In Feigenbaum and Feldman (1963).

Newell, A. and Simon, H.A. 1972. *Human Problem Solving*. Engelwood Cliffs, NJ: Prentice Hall.

Newell, A. and Simon, H.A. 1976. Computer science as empirical inquiry: symbols and search. *Communications of the ACM*, 19(3):113–126.

Newell, A., Shaw, J.C., and Simon, H.A. 1958. Elements of a theory of human problem solving. *Psychological Review*, 65:151–166.

Newell, A., Rosenbloom, P.S., and Laird, J.E. 1989. Symbolic architectures for cognition. In Posner (1989).

Newman, J.R. 1956. *The World of Mathematics*. New York: Simon and Schuster.

Ng, H.T. and Mooney, R.J. 1990. On the Role of Coherence in Abductive Explanation. *Proceedings of the Eighth National Conference on Artificial Intelligence*, pp. 347–342. Menlo Park, CA: AAAI Press/ MIT Press.

Nii, H.P. 1986*a*. Blackboard systems: The blackboard model of problem solving and the evolution of blackboard architectures. *AI Magazine*, 7(2):38–53.

Nii, H.P. 1986*b*. Blackboard systems: Blackboard application systems from a knowledge based perspective. *AI Magazine*, 7(3):82–106.

Nii, H.P. and Aiello, N. 1979. AGE: A knowledge based program for building knowledge based programs. *Proceedings IJCAI 6*.

Nilsson, N.J. 1965. *Learning Machines*. New York: McGraw-Hill.

Nilsson, N.J. 1971. *Problem-Solving Methods in Artificial Intelligence*. New York: McGraw-Hill.

Nilsson, N.J. 1980. *Principles of Artificial Intelligence*. Palo Alto, CA: Tioga.

Nilsson, N.J. 1994. Teleo-Reactive Programs for Agent Control. *Journal of Artificial Intelligence Research*, 1:139–158.

Nilsson, N.J., 1998. *Artificial Intelligence: A New Synthesis*. San Francisco: Morgan Kaufmann.

Nishibe, Y., Kuwabara, K., Suda, T., and Ishida, T. 1993. Distributed channel allocation in atm networks. *Proceedings of the IEEE Globecom Conference*, 12.2.1–12.2.7.

Nordhausen, B. and Langley, P. 1990. An integrated approach to empirical discovery. In Shrager and Langley (1990).

Norman, D.A. 1972. Memory, knowledge and the answering of questions. *CHIP Technical Report 25*, Center for Human Information Processing, University of California, San Diego.

Norman, D.A. 1981. *Perspectives on Cognitive Science*. Hillsdale, NJ: Erlbaum.

Norman, D.A., Rumelhart, D.E., and the LNR Research Group. 1975. *Explorations in Cognition*. San Francisco: Freeman.

Noyes, J.L. 1992. *Artificial Intelligence with Common LISP: Fundamentals of Symbolic and Numeric Computing*. Lexington, MA: D. C. Heath and Co.

O'Keefe, R. 1990. *The Craft of PROLOG*. Cambridge, MA: MIT Press.

O'Leary, D.D.M., Yates, P., and McLaughlin, T. 1999. Mapping sights and smells in the brain: distinct chanisms to achieve a common goal. *Cell* 96:255–269.

Oliver, I.M., Smith, D.J., and Holland, J.R.C. 1987. A Study of Permutation Crossover Operators on the Traveling Salesman Problem. *Proceedings of the Second International Conference on Genetic Algorithms*, pp. 224–230. Hillsdale, NJ: Erlbaum & Assoc.

Oliveira, E., Fonseca, J.M., and Steiger-Garcao, A. 1997. MACIV: A DAI based resource management system. *Applied Artificial Intelligence*, 11(6):525–550.

Papert, S. 1980. *Mindstorms*. New York: Basic Books.

Pascal, B. 1670. *Pensées de M. Pascal sur la Religion et sur quelques autre Sujets*. Paris: Chez Guillaume Desprez.

Patil, R., Szolovits, P., and Schwartz, W. 1981. Causal understanding of patient illness in medical diagnosis. *Proceedings of the International Joint Conference on Artificial Intelligence*. Palo Alto, CA: Morgan Kaufmann.

Pearl, J. 1984. *Heuristics: Intelligent Strategies for Computer Problem Solving*. Reading, MA: Addison-Wesley.

Pearl, J. 1988. *Probabilistic Reasoning in Intelligent Systems: Networks of Plausible Inference*. Los Altos, CA: Morgan Kaufmann.

Pearl, J. 2000. *Causality*. New York: Cambridge University Press.

Pearlmutter, B.A. and Parra, L.C. 1997. Maximum likelihood blind source separation: A context-sensitive generalization of ICA. *Advances in Neural Information Processing Systems*, 9, Cambridge, MA: MIT Press.

Peirce, C.S. 1958. *Collected Papers 1931–1958*. Cambridge MA:Harvard University Press.

Penrose, R. 1989. *The Emperor's New Mind*. Oxford: Oxford University Press.

Pereira, F. and Warren, D.H.D. 1980. Definite clause grammars for language analysis—A survey of the formalism and a comparison with augmented transition networks. *Artificial Intelligence,* 13:231–278.

Perlis, D. 1988. Autocircumscription. *Artificial Intelligence*, 36:223–236.

Perriolat, F., Sakaret, P., Varga, L.Z., and Jennings, N.J. 1996. Using archon: Particle accelerator Control, 11(6): 80–86.

Pfeffer, A. 2001. IBAL: A probabilistic rational programming language. In *Proceedings of International Joint Conference on Artificial Intelligence*, 733–740. Cambridge MA: MIT Press.

Pfeffer, A., Koller, D., Milch, B., and Takusagawa, K. 1999. SPOOK: A system for probabilistic object-oriented knowledge representation. *Proceedings of the Fifteenth Annual Conference on Uncertainty in Artificial Intelligence*. San Francisco: Morgan Kaufmann.

Piaget, J. 1954. *The Construction of Reality in The Child*. New York: Basic Books.

Piaget, J. 1970. *Structuralism*. New York: Basic Books.

Pinker, S. 1994. *The Language Instinct*. New York: William Morrow and Company.

Plato 1961. *The Collected Dialogues of Plato*, Hamilton, E. and Cairns, H., eds Princeton: Princeton University Press.

Pless, D. and Luger, G.F. 2001. Towards general analysis of recursive probability models. In *Proceedings of Uncertainty in Artificial Intelligence Conference—2001*. San Francisco: Morgan Kaufmann.

Pless, D. and Luger, G.F. 2003. EM learning of product distributions in a first-order stochastic logic language. *Artificial Intelligence and Soft Computing: Proceedings of the IASTED International Conference*. Anaheim: IASTED/ACTA Press. Also available as *University of New Mexico Computer Science Technical Report TR-CS-2003-01*.

Pless, D., Luger, G.F., and Stern, C. 2000. A new object-oriented stochastic modeling language. *Artificial Intelligence and Soft Computing: Proceedings of the IASTED International Conference*. Anaheim: IASTED/ACTA Press.

Polya, G. 1945. *How to Solve It*. Princeton, NJ: Princeton University Press.

Popper, K.R. 1959. *The Logic of Scientific Discovery*. London: Hutchinson.

Porphyry 1887. Isagoge et in Aristotelis categorias commentarium. In A. Busse, ed. *Commentaria in Aristotelem Graeca*, 4(1).

Posner, M.I. 1989. *Foundations of Cognitive Science*. Cambridge, MA: MIT Press.

Post, E. 1943. Formal reductions of the general combinatorial problem. *American Journal of Mathematics*, 65:197–268.

Poundstone, W. 1985. *The Recursive Universe: Cosmic Complexity and the Limits of Scientific Knowledge*. New York: William Morrow and Company.

Prerau, D.S. 1990. *Developing and Managing Expert Systems: Proven Techniques for Business and Industry*. Reading, MA: Addison-Wesley.

Pylyshyn, Z.W. 1973. What the mind's eye tells the mind's brain: a critique of mental imagery. *Psychological Bulletin*, 80:1–24.

Pylyshyn, Z.W. 1980. The causal power of machines. *Behavioral and Brain Sciences* 3:442–444.

Pylyshyn, Z.W. 1984. *Computation and Cognition: Toward a Foundation for Cognitive Science*. Cambridge, MA: MIT Press.

Quillian, M.R. 1967. Word concepts: A theory and simulation of some basic semantic capabilities. In Brachman and Levesque (1985).

Quine, W.V.O. 1963. *From a Logical Point of View*, 2nd ed. New York: Harper Torchbooks.

Quinlan, J.R. 1983. Learning efficient classification procedures and their application to chess endgames. In Michalski et al. (1983).

Quinlan, J.R. 1986a. Induction of decision trees. *Machine Learning*, 1(1):81–106.

Quinlan, J.R. 1986b. The effect of noise on concept learning. In Michalski et al. (1986).

Quinlan, J.R. 1993. *C4.5: Programs for Machine Learning*. San Francisco: Morgan Kaufmann.

Quinlan, J R. 1996. Bagging, Boosting and C4.5. *Proceedings AAAI 96*. Menlo Park, CA: AAAI Press.

Quinlan, P. 1991. *Connectionism and Psychology*. Chicago: University of Chicago Press.

Rabiner, L.R. 1989. A tutorial on hidden Markov models and selected applications in speech recognition. *Proc. IEEE*, 77 (2), 257-286.

Raphael, B. 1968. SIR: A computer program for semantic information retrieval. In Minsky (1968).

Reddy, D.R. 1976. Speech recognition by machine: A review. *Proceedings of the IEEE 64* (May 1976).

Reggia, J., Nau, D.S., and Wang, P.Y. 1983. Diagnostic expert systems based on a set covering model. *International Journal of Man–Machine Studies*, 19(5):437–460.

Reinfrank, M. 1989. Fundamental and Logical Foundations of Truth Maintenance. Linköping Studies in Science and Technology, Dissertation 221, Department of Computer and Information Science, Linköping University, Linköping, Sweden.

Reiter, R. 1978. On closed world databases. In Webber and Nilsson (1981).

Reiter, R. 1980. A logic for default reasoning. *Artificial Intelligence*, 13:81–132.

Reiter, R. 1985. On reasoning by default. In Brachman and Levesque (1985).

Reiter, R. and Criscuolo, G. 1981. On interacting defaults. *Proceedings of the International Joint Conference on Artificial Intelligence*. William Kaufmann.

Reitman, W.R. 1965. *Cognition and Thought*. New York: Wiley.

Rich, E. and Knight, K. 1991. *Artificial Intelligence*, 2nd ed. New York: McGraw-Hill.

Rissland, E.L. 1983. Examples in legal reasoning: Legal hypotheticals. *Proceedings of IJCAI-83*. San Mateo, CA: Morgan Kaufman.

Rissland, E.L. and Ashley, K. 1987. HYPO: A case-based system for trade secrets law. *Proceedings, First International Conference on Artificial Intelligence and Law*.

Roberts, D.D. 1973. *The Existential Graphs of Charles S. Pierce*. The Hague: Mouton.

Robinson, J.A. 1965. A machine-oriented logic based on the resolution principle. *Journal of the ACM*, 12:23–41.

Rochester, N., Holland, J.H., Haibit, L.H., and Duda, W.L. 1988. Test on a cell assembly theory of the actuation of the brain, using a large digital computer. In J.A. Anderson and E. Rosenfeld, eds 1988. *Neurocomputing: Foundations of Research*. Cambridge, MA: MIT Press.

Rosch, E. 1978. Principles of categorization. In Rosch and Lloyd (1978).

Rosch, E. and Lloyd, B.B., ed. 1978. *Cognition and Categorization*, Hillsdale, NJ: Erlbaum.

Rosenblatt, F. 1958. The perceptron: A probabilistic model for information storage and organization in the brain. *Psychological Review*, 65:386–408.

Rosenblatt, F. 1962. *Principles of Neurodynamics*. New York: Spartan.

Rosenbloom, P.S. and Newell, A. 1987. Learning by chunking, a production system model of practice. In Klahr et al. (1987).

Rosenbloom, P.S., Lehman, J.F., and Laird, J.E. 1993. Overview of Soar as a unified theory of cognition: Spring 1993. *Proceedings of the Fifteenth Annual Conference of the Cognitive Science Society*. Hillsdale, NJ: Erlbaum.

Ross, T. 1989. *Advanced PROLOG*. Reading, MA: Addison-Wesley.

Ross, S.M. 1988. *A First Course in Probability, 3rd ed*. London: Macmillan.

Ross, T. 1995. *Fuzzy Logic with Engineering Applications*. New York: McGraw-Hill.

Roussel, P. 1975. PROLOG: *Manuel de Reference et d'Utilisation*. Groupe d'Intelligence Artificielle, Université d'Aix-Marseille, Luminy, France.

Rumelhart, D.E. and Norman, D.A. 1973. Active semantic networks as a model of human memory. *Proceedings IJCAI-3*. William Kaufmann.

Rumelhart, D.E., Lindsay, P.H., and Norman, D.A. 1972. A process model for long-term memory. In Tulving and Donaldson (1972).

Rumelhart, D.E., Hinton, G.E., and Williams, R J. 1986*a*. Learning internal representations by error propagation. In McClelland et al. (1986).

Rumelhart, D.E., McClelland, J.L., and The PDP Research Group. 1986*b*. *Parallel Distributed Processing.* Vol. 1. Cambridge, MA: MIT Press.

Russell, S.J. 1989. *The Use of Knowledge in Analogy and Induction.* San Mateo, CA: Morgan Kaufmann.

Russell, S.J. and Norvig, P. 1995, 2003. *Artificial Intelligence: A Modern Approach.* Englewood Cliffs, NJ: Prentice-Hall.

Russell, S.J. and Norvig, P. 2003. *Artificial Intelligence: A Modern Approach*, 2nd ed. Englewood Cliffs, NJ: Prentice-Hall.

Sacerdotti, E.D. 1974. Planning in a hierarchy of abstraction spaces. *Artificial Intelligence*, 5:115–135.

Sacerdotti, E.D. 1975. The non linear nature of plans. *Proceedings IJCAI 4.*

Sacerdotti, E.D. 1977. *A Structure of Plans and Behavior.* New York: Elsevier.

Sacks, O. 1987. *The Man who Mistook his Wife for a Hat.* New York: Simon & Schuster.

Sagi, D. and Tanne, D. 1998. Perceptual learning: Learning to see. In Squire and Kosslyn (1998).

Samuel, A.L. 1959. Some studies in machine learning using the game of checkers, *IBM Journal of R & D*, 3:211–229.

Schank, R.C. 1982. *Dynamic Memory: A Theory of Reminding and Learning in Computers and People.* London: Cambridge University Press.

Schank, R.C. and Abelson, R. 1977. *Scripts, Plans, Goals and Understanding.* Hillsdale, NJ: Erlbaum.

Schank, R.C. and Colby, K.M., ed. 1973. *Computer Models of Thought and Language.* San Francisco: Freeman.

Schank, R.C. and Nash-Webber, B.L., ed. 1975. *Theoretical Issues in Natural Language Processing.* Association for Computational Linguistics.

Schank, R.C. and Rieger, C.J. 1974. Inference and the computer understanding of natural language. *Artificial Intelligence* 5(4):373–412.

Schank, R.C. and Riesbeck, C.K., ed. 1981. *Inside Computer Understanding: Five Programs Plus Miniatures.* Hillsdale, NJ: Erlbaum.

Scholkopf, B., Smola, A., Williamson, R., and Bartlett, P. 1998. New support vector algorithms. *Technical Report NC-TR-98-031*, NeuroCOLT Working Group.

Schoonderwoerd, R., Holland, O., and Bruten, J. 1997. Ant-like agents for load balancing in telecommunications networks. *Proceedings of the First International Conference on Autonomous Agents (Agents-97)* pp. 209–216.

Schrooten, R. and van de Velde, W. 1997. Software agent foundation for dynamic interactive electronic catalogues. *Applied Artificial Intelligence*, 11(5):459–482.

Schwuttke, U.M. and Quan, A.G. 1993. Enhancing performance of cooperating agents in real-time diagnostic systems. *Proceedings of the Thirteenth International Joint Conference on Artificial Intelligence*, pp. 332–337. Morgan Kaufmann.

Searle, J. 1969. *Speech Acts.* London: Cambridge University Press.

Searle, J.R. 1980. Minds, brains and programs. *The Behavioral and Brain Sciences*, 3:417–424.

Sebeok, T.A. 1985. *Contributions to the Doctrine of Signs.* Lanham, MD: Univ, Press of America.

Sedgewick, R. 1983. *Algorithms.* Reading, MA: Addison-Wesley.

Sejnowski, T.J. and Rosenberg, C.R. 1987. Parallel networks that learn to pronounce English text. *Complex Systems*, 1:145–168.

Selfridge, O. 1959. Pandemonium: A paradigm for learning. *Symposium on the Mechanization of Thought.* London: HMSO.

Selman, B. and Levesque, H.J. 1990. Abductive and Default Reasoning: A Computational Core. *Proceedings of the Eighth National Conference on Artificial Intelligence*, pp. 343–348. Menlo Park, CA: AAAI Press/MIT Press.

Selz, O. 1913. *Uber die Gesetze des Geordneten Denkverlaufs*. Stuttgart: Spemann.

Selz, O. 1922. *Zur Psychologie des Produktiven Denkens und des Irrtums*. Bonn: Friedrich Cohen.

Shafer, G., and Pearl, J., eds 1990. *Readings in Uncertain Reasoning*, Los Altos, CA: Morgan Kaufmann.

Shannon, C. 1948. A mathematical theory of communication. *Bell System Technical Journal*, 27:379–423.

Shannon, C. 1951. Prediction and entropy of printed English. *Bell System Technical Journal*, 30:54–60.

Shapiro, E. 1987. *Concurrent Prolog: Collected Papers*, 2 vols. Cambridge, MA: MIT Press.

Shapiro, S.C., 1971. A net structure for semantic information storage, deduction, and retrieval. *Proceedings of the Second International Joint Conference of Artificial Intelligence*, pp. 512–523. William Kaufmann.

Shapiro, S.C., 1979. The SNePS semantic network processing system. In N.V. Findler, ed. *Associative Networks: Representation and Use of Knowledge by Computers*. New York: Academic Press, pp. 179–203.

Shapiro, S.C., ed. 1987. *Encyclopedia of Artificial Intelligence*. New York: Wiley-Interscience.

Shapiro, S.C., ed. 1992. *Encyclopedia of Artificial Intelligence*. New York: Wiley.

Shavlik, J.W. and Dietterich, T.G., ed. 1990. *Readings in Machine Learning*. San Mateo, CA: Morgan Kaufmann.

Shavlik, J.W., Mooney, R.J., and Towell, G.G. 1991. Symbolic and neural learning algorithms: An experimental comparison. *Machine Learning*, 6(1):111–143.

Shephard, G.M. 1998. *The Synaptic Organization of the Brain*. New York: Oxford University Press.

Shrager, J. and Langley, P., eds 1990. *Computational Models of Scientific Discovery and Theory Formation*. San Mateo, CA: Morgan Kaufmann.

Siegelman, H. and Sontag, E.D. 1991. Neural networks are universal computing devices. *Technical Report SYCON 91-08*. New Jersey: Rutgers Center for Systems and Control.

Siegler, R.S., ed. 1978. *Children's Thinking: What develops*. Hillsdale, NJ: Erlbaum.

Siekmann, J.H. and Wrightson, G., ed. 1983*a*. *The Automation of Reasoning: Collected Papers from 1957 to 1970*. Vol I. New York: Springer-Verlag.

Siekmann, J.H. and Wrightson, G., ed. 1983*b*. *The Automation of Reasoning: Collected Papers from 1957 to 1970*. Vol II. New York: Springer-Verlag.

Simmons, R.F. 1966. Storage and retrieval of aspects of meaning in directed graph structures. *Communications of the ACM*, 9:211–216.

Simmons, R.F. 1973. Semantic networks: Their computation and use for understanding English sentences. In Schank (1972).

Simon, D.P. and Simon, H.A. 1978. Individual differences in solving physics problems. In Siegler (1978).

Simon, H.A. 1981. *The Sciences of the Artificial*, 2nd ed. Cambridge, MA: MIT Press.

Simon, H.A. 1983. Why should machines learn? In Michalski et al. (1983).

Sims, M.H. 1987. Empirical and analytic discovery in IL. *Proceedings of the Fourth International Workshop on Machine Learning*. Los Altos, CA: Morgan Kaufmann.

Skinner, J.M. and Luger, G.F. 1991. A synergistic approach to reasoning for autonomous satellites. *Proceedings for NATO Conference of the Advisory Group for Aerospace Research and Development*.

Skinner, J.M. and Luger, G.F. 1992. An architecture for integrating reasoning paradigms. *Principles of Knowledge Representation and Reasoning*. B. Nobel, C. Rich and W. Swartout, eds. San Mateo, CA: Morgan Kaufmann.

Skinner, J.M. and Luger, G.F. 1995. Contributions of a case-based reasoner to an integrated reasoning system. *Journal of Intelligent Systems*. London: Freund.

Sleeman, D. and Brown, J S. 1982. *Intelligent Tutoring Systems*. New York: Academic Press.

Smart, G. and Langeland-Knudsen, J. 1986. *The CRI Directory of Expert Systems*. Oxford: Learned Information (Europe) Ltd.

Smith, B.C. 1985. Prologue to reflection and semantics in a procedural language. In Brachman and Levesque (1985).

Smith, B.C. 1996. *On the Origin of Objects*. Cambridge, MA: MIT Press.

Smith, R.G. and Baker, J.D. 1983. The dipmeter advisor system: a case study in commercial expert system development. *Proc. 8th IJCAI*, pp. 122–129. William Kaufmann.

Smoliar, S.W. 1985. A View of Goal-oriented Programming, Schlumberger-Doll Research Note.

Soderland, S., Fisher, D., Aseltine, J., and Lehnert, W. 1995. CRYSTAL: Inducing a conceptual dictionary. *Proceedings of the Fourteenth International Joint Conference on Artificial Intelligence*, pp. 1314–1319. Morgan Kaufmann.

Soloway, E., Bachant, J., and Jensen, K. 1987. Assessing the maintainability of XCON-in-RIME: Coping with the problems of a very large rule base. *Proceedings AAAI-87*. Los Altos, CA: Morgan Kaufmann.

Somogyi, Z., Henderson, F., and Conway, C. 1995. Mercury: An efficient purely declarative logic programming language. *Proceedings of the Australian Computer Science Conference*, pp. 499–512.

Sowa, J.F. 1984. *Conceptual Structures: Information Processing in Mind and Machine*. Reading, MA: Addison-Wesley.

Squire, L.R. and Kosslyn, S.M., eds 1998. *Findings and Current Opinion in Cognitive Neuroscience*, Cambridge: MIT Press.

Steele, G.L., 1990, *Common LISP: The Language*, 2nd ed. Bedford, MA: Digital Press.

Sterling, L. and Shapiro, E. 1986. *The Art of Prolog: Advanced Programming Techniques*. Cambridge, MA: MIT Press.

Stern, C.R. 1996. *An Architecture for Diagnosis Employing Schema-based Abduction*, PhD dissertation, Department of Computer Science, University of New Mexico.

Stern, C.R. and Luger, G.F. 1992. A model for abductive problem solving based on explanation templates and lazy evaluation. *International Journal of Expert Systems*, 5(3):249–265.

Stern, C.R. and Luger, G.F. 1997. Abduction and abstraction in diagnosis: a schema-based account. *Situated Cognition: Expertise in Context.* Ford et al. eds. Cambridge, MA: MIT Press.

Stubblefield, W.A. 1995. *Source Retrieval in Analogical Reasoning: An Interactionist Approach. PhD dissertation*, Department of Computer Science, University of New Mexico.

Stubblefield, W.A. and Luger, G.F. 1996. Source Selection for Analogical Reasoning: An Empirical Approach. *Proceedings: Thirteenth National Conference on Artificial Intelligence*. AAAI Press/ The MIT Press.

Stytz, M.P. and Frieder, O. 1990.Three dimensional medical imagery modalities: An overview. *Critical Review of Biomedical Engineering*, 18:11–25.

Suchman, L. 1987. *Plans and Situated Actions: The Problem of Human Machine Communication*. Cambridge: Cambridge University Press.

Sussman, G.J. 1975. *A Computer Model of Skill Acquisition*. Cambridge, MA: MIT Press.

Sutton, R.S. 1988. Learning to predict by the method of temporal differences. *Machine Learning*, 3:9–44.

Sutton, R.S. 1990. Integrated architectures for learning, planning, and reacting based on approximating dynamic programming. *Proceedings of the Seventh International Conference on Machine Learning*, pp. 216–224. San Francisco: Morgan Kaufmann.

Sutton, R.S. 1991. Dyna: An integrated architecture for learning, planning, and reacting. *SIGART Bulletin*, 2:160–164, ACM Press.

Sutton, R.S. and Barto, A.G. 1998. *Reinforcement Learning*. Cambridge: MIT Press.

Sycara, K., Decker, K., Pannu, A., Williamson, M., and Zeng, D. 1996. Distributed intelligent agents. *IEEE Expert*, 11(6):36–46.

Tang, A.C., Pearlmutter, B.A., and Zibulevsky, M. 1999. Blind source separation of neuromagnetic responses. *Computational Neuroscience 1999*, Proceedings published in *Neurocomputing*.

Tang, A.C., Pearlmutter, B.A., and Zibulevsky, M., Hely, T.A., and Weisend, M. 2000a. A MEG study of response latency and variability in the human visual system during a visual-motor integration task. *Advances in Neural Info. Proc. Sys*: San Francisco: Morgan Kaufmann.

Tang, A.C., Phung, D., and Pearlmutter, B.A. 2000b. Direct measurement of interhemispherical transfer time (IHTT) for natural somatasensory stimulation during voluntary movement using MEG and blind source separation. *Society of Neuroscience Abstracts*.

Takahashi, K., Nishibe, Y., Morihara, I., and Hattori, F. 1997. Intelligent pp.: Collecting shop and service information with software agents. *Applied Artificial Intelligence*, 11(6):489–500.

Tanimoto, S.L. 1990. *The Elements of Artificial Intelligence using Common LISP*. New York: W.H. Freeman.

Tarski, A. 1944. The semantic conception of truth and the foundations of semantics. *Philos. and Phenom. Res.*, 4:341–376.

Tarski, A. 1956. *Logic, Semantics, Metamathematics*. London: Oxford University Press.

Tesauro, G.J. 1994. TD-Gammon, a self-teaching backgammon program achieves master-level play. *Neural Computation*, 6(2):215–219.

Tesauro, G.J. 1995. Temporal difference learning and TD-Gammon. *Communications of the ACM*, 38:58–68.

Thagard, P. 1988. Dimensions of analogy. In Helman (1988).

Touretzky, D.S. 1986. *The Mathematics of Inheritance Systems*. Los Altos, CA: Morgan Kaufmann.

Touretzky, D.S. 1990. *Common LISP: A Gentle Introduction to Symbolic Computation*. Redwood City, CA: Benjamin/Cummings.

Trappl, R. and Petta, P. 1997. *Creating Personalities for Synthetic Actors*. Berlin: Springer-Verlag.

Treisman, A. 1993. The perception of features and objects. *Attention: Selection, Awareness, and Control: A Tribute to Donald Broadbent*. Badderly, A. and Weiskrantz, L. eds, pp. 5–35. Oxford: Clarendon Press.

Treisman, A. 1998. The binding problem. In Squire and Kosslyn (1998).

Tulving, E. and Donaldson, W. 1972. *Organization of Memory*. New York: Academic Press.

Turing, A.A. 1950. Computing machinery and intelligence. *Mind*, 59:433–460.

Turner, R. 1984. *Logics for Artificial Intelligence*. Chichester: Ellis Horwood.

Ullman, J.D. 1982. *Principles of Database Systems*. Rockville, MD: Computer Science Press.

Urey, H.C. 1952. *The Planets: Their Origin and Development*. Yale University Press.

Utgoff, P.E. 1986. Shift of bias in inductive concept learning. In Michalski et al. (1986).

Valiant, L.G. 1984. A theory of the learnable. *CACM*, 27:1134–1142.

van der Gaag, L.C., ed. 1996. Special issue on Bayesian Belief Networks. *AISB Quarterly*. 94.

van Emden, M. and Kowalski, R. 1976. The semantics of predicate logic and a programming language. *Journal of the ACM*, 23:733–742.

VanLe, T. 1993. *Techniques of PROLOG Programming with Implementation of Logical Negation and Quantified Goals*. New York: Wiley.

Varela, F.J., Thompson, E., and Rosch, E. 1993. *The Embodied Mind: Cognitive Science and Human Experience*. Cambridge, MA: MIT Press.

Veloso, M., Bowling, M., Achim, S., Han, K. and Stone, P. 2000. CNITED-98 RoboCup-98 small robot world champion team. *AI Magazine*, 21(1):29–36.

Vere, S.A. 1975. Induction of concepts in the predicate calculus. *Proceedings IJCAI 4*.

Vere, S.A. 1978. Inductive learning of relational productions. In Waterman and Hayes-Roth (1978).

Veroff, R., ed. 1997. *Automated Reasoning and its Applications.* Cambridge, MA: MIT Press.

Viterbi, A.J. 1967. Error bounds for convolutional codes and an asymtotically optimum decoding algorithm. *IEEE Transactions on Information Theory*, IT-13(2):260–269.

von Glaserfeld, E. 1978. An introduction to radical constructivism. *The Invented Reality*, Watzlawick, ed., pp. 17–40, New York: Norton.

Walker, A., McCord, M., Sowa, J.F., and Wilson, W.G. 1987. *Knowledge Systems and PROLOG: A Logical Approach to Expert Systems and Natural Language Processing.* Reading, MA: Addison-Wesley.

Warren, D.H.D. 1976. Generating conditional plans and programs. *Proc. AISB Summer Conference,* Edinburgh, pp. 334–354.

Warren, D.H.D., Pereira, L.M., and Pereira, F. 1977. PROLOG–the language and its implementation compared with LISP. *Proceedings, Symposium on AI and Programming Languages, SIGPLAN Notices*, 12:8.

Warren, D.H.D., Pereira, F., and Pereira, L.M. 1979. *User's Guide to DEC-System 10 PROLOG.* Occasional Paper 15, Department of Artificial Intelligence, University of Edinburgh.

Waterman, D. and Hayes-Roth, F. 1978. *Pattern Directed Inference Systems.* New York: Academic Press.

Waterman, D.A. 1968. Machine Learning of Heuristics. *Report No. STAN-CS-68-118*, Computer Science Dept, Stanford University.

Waterman, D.A. 1986. *A Guide to Expert Systems.* Reading, MA: Addison-Wesley.

Watkins, C.J.C.H. 1989. *Learning from Delayed Rewards.* PhD Thesis, Cambridge University.

Wavish, P. and Graham, M. 1996. A situated action approach to implementing characters in computer games. *Applied Artificial Intelligence*, 10(1): 53–74.

Webber, B.L. and Nilsson, N.J. 1981. *Readings in Artificial Intelligence.* Los Altos, CA: Tioga Press.

Weiss, S.M. and Kulikowski, C.A. 1991. *Computer Systems that Learn.* San Mateo, CA: Morgan Kaufmann.

Weiss, S.M., Kulikowski, C.A., Amarel, S., and Safir, A. 1977. A model-based method for computer-aided medical decision-making. *Artificial Intelligence*, 11(1–2):145–172.

Weizenbaum, J. 1976. *Computer Power and Human Reason.* San Francisco: W. H. Freeman.

Weld, D.S. 1994. An introduction to least committment planning. *AI Magazine* 15(4):16–35.

Weld, D.S. and deKleer, J., eds 1990. *Readings in Qualitative Reasoning about Physical Systems.* Los Altos, CA: Morgan Kaufmann.

Wellman, M.P. 1990. Fundamental concepts of qualitative probabilistic networks. *Artificial Intelligence*, 44(3):257–303.

Weyhrauch, R.W. 1980. Prolegomena to a theory of mechanized formal reasoning. *Artificial Intelligence*, 13(1,2):133–170.

Whitehead, A.N. and Russell, B. 1950. *Principia Mathematica*, 2nd ed. London: Cambridge University Press.

Whitley, L.D., ed. 1993. *Foundations of Genetic Algorithms 2.* Los Altos, CA: Morgan Kaufmann.

Widrow, B. and Hoff, M.E. 1960. Adaptive switching circuits. *1960 IRE WESTCON Convention Record*, pp. 96–104. New York.

Wilensky, R. 1986. *Common LISPCraft*, New York: Norton Press.

Wilks, Y.A. 1972. *Grammar, Meaning and the Machine Analysis of Language.* London: Routledge & Kegan Paul.

Williams, B.C. and Nayak, P.P. 1996a. Immobile robots: AI in the new millennium. *AI Magazine* 17(3): 17–34.

Williams, B.C. and Nayak, P.P. 1996b. A model-based approach to reactive self-configuring systems. *Proceedings of the AAAI-96*, pp. 971–978. Cambridge, MA: MIT Press.

Williams, B.C. and Nayak, P.P. 1997. A reactive planner for a model-based executive. *Proceedings of the International Joint Conference on Artificial Intelligence*, Cambridge, MA: MIT Press.

Winograd, T. 1972. *Understanding Natural Language*. New York: Academic Press.

Winograd, T. 1973. A procedural model of language understanding. In Schank and Colby (1973).

Winograd, T. 1983. *Language as a Cognitive Process: Syntax*. Reading, MA: Addison-Wesley.

Winograd, T. and Flores, F. 1986. *Understanding Computers and Cognition*. Norwood, NJ: Ablex.

Winston, P.H. 1975*a*. Learning structural descriptions from examples. In Winston (1975*b*).

Winston, P.H., ed. 1975*b*. *The Psychology of Computer Vision*. New York: McGraw-Hill.

Winston, P.H. 1992. *Artificial Intelligence*, 3rd ed. Reading, MA: Addison-Wesley.

Winston, P.H. and Horn, B.K.P. 1984. *LISP*. Reading, MA: Addison-Wesley.

Winston, P.H., Binford, T.O., Katz, B., and Lowry, M. 1983. Learning physical descriptions from functional definitions, examples and precedents. *National Conference on Artificial Intelligence in Washington, D. C.*, Morgan Kaufmann, pp. 433–439.

Wirth, N. 1976. *Algorithms + Data Structures = Programs*. Engelwood Cliffs, NJ: Prentice-Hall.

Wittgenstein, L. 1953. *Philosophical Investigations*. New York: Macmillan.

Wolpert, D.H. and Macready, W.G. 1995. *The No Free Lunch Theorems for Search*, Technical Report SFI-TR-95-02-010. Santa Fe, NM: The Santa Fe Institute.

Wolstencroft, J. 1989. Restructuring, reminding and repair: What's missing from models of analogy. *AICOM*, 2(2):58–71.

Woods, W. 1985. What's in a Link: Foundations for Semantic Networks. In Brachman and Levesque (1985).

Wooldridge, M. 1998. Agent-based computing. *Interoperable Communication Networks*. 1(1):71–97.

Wooldridge, M. 2000. *Reasoning about Rational Agents*, Cambridge, MA: MIT Press.

Wos, L. and Robinson, G.A. 1968, Paramodulation and set of support, *Proceedings of the IRIA Symposium on Automatic Demonstration, Versailles*. New York: Springer-Verlag, pp. 367–410.

Wos, L. 1988. *Automated Reasoning, 33 Basic Research Problems*. Englewood Cliffs, NJ: Prentice Hall.

Wos, L. 1995. The field of automated reasoning. In *Computers and Mathematics with Applications*, 29(2):xi–xiv.

Wos, L., Overbeek, R., Lusk, E., and Boyle, J. 1984. *Automated Reasoning: Introduction and Applications*. Englewood Cliffs, NJ: Prentice-Hall.

Xiang, Y., Poole, D., and Beddoes, M. 1993. Multiply sectioned Bayesian networks and junction forests for large knowledge based systems. *Computational Intelligence* 9(2):171–220.

Xiang, Y., Olesen, K.G., and Jensen, F.V. 2000. Practical issues in modeling large diagnostic systems with multiply sectioned Bayesian networks. *International Journal of Pattern Recognition and Artificial Intelligence*, 14(1):59–71.

Yager, R.R. and Zadeh, L.A. 1994. *Fuzzy Sets, Neural Networks and Soft Computing*. New York: Van Nostrand Reinhold.

Zadeh, L. 1983. Commonsense knowledge representation based on fuzzy logic. *Computer*, 16:61–65.

Zurada, J.M. 1992. *Introduction to Artificial Neural Systems*. New York: West Publishing.

Url listings:
IIa: http://www-formal.stanford.edu/jmc/history/dartmouth/dartmouth.html, 28 Jan 2004

AUTHOR INDEX

Chang, C. L. 77, 557, 567, 588
Chapman, D. 27, 225, 228, 850
Charniak, E. 121, 244, 349, 631, 816
Chen, L. 268
Chomsky, N. 604, 837
Chorafas, D. N. 330
Chung , K. T. 268
Church, A. 639, 848
Churchland, P. S. 853
Clancy, W. J. 329
Clark, A. 223, 226, 228, 272, 273, 853
Clarke, A. C. 20, 507
Clocksin, W. F. 639, 642, 718
Codd, E. F. 535
Cohen, P. R. 330
Colby, K. M. 32, 236, 238
Cole, R. A. 632
Collins, A. 230, 272
Colmerauer, A. 639, 718
Conway, J. H. 508, 530, 542
Conway, T. 718
Coombs, M. J. 329, 330
Cooper, G. F. 363
Corera, J. M. 268
Corkill, D. D. 217, 220
Cormen, T. 121
Corter, J. 440
Cosmides, L. 834
Cotton, S. 28, 434
Crick, F. 29
Crisculo, G. 339, 380
Cristianini, N. 483, 484, 505
Crutchfield, J. P. 509, 531, 537–541, 542
Cussens, J. 382
Cutosky, M. R. 268

Dahl, V. 718
Dallier, J. H. 587
Dante 4, 848
Darlington, J. A. 12
Darr, T. P. 268
Darwiche, A. 382
Darwin, C. 4, 507, 508
Davidson, R. J. 831
Davis, E. 380
Davis, K. H. 836
Davis, L. 514
Davis, M. 6
Davis, R. 28, 433
Davis, W. 242, 268, 269
Dechter, R. 371, 847
deDombal, F. T. 190
DeGroot, M. H. 191
DeJong, G. 28, 424, 427

deKleer, J. 272, 298,327,330, 342, 343, 348, 380, 816
deMorgan 539
Dempster, A. P. 350, 359
Dennett, D. C. 32, 79, 226, 272, 542, 543, 835, 849, 853
Descartes, R. 7–8, 16, 849, 853
Dietterich, T. G. 429, 449
Dologite, D. G. 329, 330
Domingos, P. 191
Domingue, J. 816
Doorenbos, R. 269
Doyle, J. 337, 338, 340, 342, 380
Dressler, O. 342
Dreyfus, H. L. 17, 850, 852
Dreyfus, S. E. 17, 850, 852
Druzdel, M. J. 371, 381
Duda, R. O. 23, 186, 190, 191, 836
Durfee, E. H. 267
Durkin, J. 23, 329, 330

Eco, U. 850
Edelman, G. M. 834, 850
Einstein, A. 165, 333
Eliot, T. S. 193, 453, 545, 823
Elman, J. L. 505, 832, 853
Engelmore, R. 228
Erman, L. D. 217, 219, 220
Ernst, G. W. 548, 553, 828
Euler, L. 8, 80–82
Evans, T. G. 262, 275

Falkenhainer, B. 431
Fass, D. 631
Feigenbaum. E. A. 32, 223, 277, 330, 450, 588, 838
Feldman, J. 450, 588, 838
Fermat, 45
Fikes, R. E. 8, 319–9–320, 323, 424, 554
Fillmore, C. J. 235
Fischer, K. 268
Fisher, D. H. 190, 307, 363, 438, 450
Flores, F. 8, 16–17, 32, 36, 631, 850, 851, 852, 853
Fodor, J. A. 833, 834
Forbus, K. D. 816
Ford, K. 15, 32, 190
Forgy, C. L. 297, 307
Forrest, S. 541
Francis, W. N. 183
Franklin, S. 505, 853
Freeman, J. A. 505, 842
Frege, G. 10, 12, 32, 231, 852
Frey, B. J. 506

Rosenberg, C. R. 121, 471
Rosenblatt, F. 458, 505
Rosenbloom, P. S. 542
Ross, T. 191, 354, 357, 381, 381, 718
Roussel, P. 639
Rumelhart, D. E. 231, 236, 465, 505
Russell, B. 11–12, 21, 32, 49, 224, 333, 453, 548
Russell, S. 191, 322, 330

Sacerdotti, E. 330, 332, 554
Sacks, O. 227
Sagi, D. 840
Sahni, S. 92, 121
Samuel, A. L. 127–128, 161, 306, 308, 450, 828
Schank, R. 32, 236–238, 240, 241–242, 244, 330, 631
Schickard, W. 6
Schrooten, R. 269
Schutze, H. 25, 191, 622, 632, 837
Schwutkke, U. M. 268
Scott, D. 12
Searle, J. 8, 17, 631, 847, 850
Seboek, T. A. 850
Sedgewick, R. 121
Sejnowski, T. 459, 471, 506
Selfridge, O. 32, 505
Selman, B. 348
Selz, O. 231, 272
Shafer, G. 335, 350, 359, 380
Shakespeare, W. 591, 592, 848
Shannon, C. 35, 412, 505, 810, 836
Shapiro, E. 578, 590, 718, 719
Shapiro, H. 161
Shapiro, S. C. 32, 232, 235, 330, 342, 344, 347, 380, 381, 527
Shavlik, J. W. 449, 472
Shaw, J. C. 49, 224, 828
Shawe-Taylor, J. 483, 484, 505
Shelley, M. 1, 4
Shephard, G. M. 831, 840
Shimony, S. 349
Shortliffe, E. H. 23, 329, 350
Shrager, J. 434, 450
Sidner, C. L. 631, 850
Siegelman, H. 845
Siekmann, J. H. 588
Simmons, R. F. 232, 235
Simon, D. P. 203
Simon, H. A. 8, 15, 20–21, 30, 32, 35, 49, 121, 123, 155, 193, 201–202, 203, 216, 219, 223, 224, 287, 388, 547, 548, 551–552, 588, 822, 823, 824, 826, 828, 839, 841, 853
Simpson, H. 821
Sims, M. H. 434

Skapura, D. M. 505, 842
Skinner, J. M. 219, 306, 307, 309, 330
Smart, G. 330
Smith, B. C. 225, 631, 853
Smith, R. G. 23
Smoliar, S. W. 330
Snyder, G. 635
Soderland, S. 630
Soloway, E. 203
Somogyi, Z. 718
Sontag, S. 845
Sowa, J. 226, 227, 231, 248, 272, 604, 614, 625, 631, 718
Spiegelhalter, D. J. 369, 371, 381, 382
Spock 385
Squire, L. R. 831, 840
Steedman, M. 707–810, 718
Steele, G. 798, 804, 816
Stein, L. 261
Stepp, R. E. 436
Sterling, L. 718
Stern, C. 226, 227, 231, 248, 272, 604, 614, 625, 631, 718
Stoller, M. 123
Strachey, C. 12
Stubblefield, W. A. 307, 308, 434, 450
Stytz, M. P. 839
Suchman, L. 853
Sussman, G. J. 28, 816
Sutton, R. S. 443, 444, 447, 448, 449, 450
Sycara, K. 266, 267, 268, 269, 270

Takahashi, K. 269
Tang, A. C. 839
Tanne, D. 840
Tanimoto, S. L. 816
Tarski, A. 5, 12, 826
Tesauro, G. J. 447, 49
Terence, 591
Thagard, P. 449
Tong, G. 718
Tooby, J. 834
Touretzky, D. S. 339, 380, 816
Trappl, R. 269
Treisman, A. 840
Tsitsiklis, J. N. 450, 505
Tsu, L. 723
Turing, A. 5, 6–11, 13–16, 30, 32, 838, 848, 853
Turner, R. 256, 380
Twain, M. 453

Ullman, J. D. 120, 196, 604, 605, 624, 625, 631
Urey, H. C. 529
Utgoff, P. E. 419

Valiant, L. G. 422
van de Velde, W. 269
van der Gaag, L. C. 381
van Emden, M. 576, 578
VanLe, T. 718
VanLehn, K. 330, 331
Varela, F. J. 850, 853
Veloso, M. 226, 266
Veroff, R. 22, 77, 121, 589
Vere, S. A. 449
von Glaserfeld, E. 846
von Neumann, J. 12, 455, 535, 542, 838, 845

Waldinger, R. 51, 77
Walker, A. 718
Warren, D. H. D. 339, 630
Warren, D. S. 718
Waterman, D. 23, 220, 278, 329, 330
Watkins, C. J. 448, 449, 450
Wavish, P. 269
Weaver, E. 821
Weiss, S. M. 330, 449
Weizenbaum, J. 32, 850, 851
Weld, D. S. 272, 324, 327
Wellman, M. P. 382, 718
Weyhrauch, R. W. 380, 588

Whitehead, A. N. 11–12, 21, 32, 49, 224, 548
Widrow, B. 465
Wilensky, R. 816
Wilks, Y. 32, 232, 236, 631
Williams, B. C. 302, 304, 326–329, 330
Wilson, W. 718
Winograd, T. 8, 16–17, 25, 32, 36, 272, 593, 594, 615, 630, 631, 850, 851, 853
Winston, P. H. 28, 121, 392, 425, 816, 843, 852
Wirth, N. 78
Wittgenstein, L. 16–17, 438, 476, 846
Wolpert, D. H. 844
Wolstencroft, J. 430
Woods, W. 239
Wooldridge, M. 225, 228, 266, 267, 270
Wos, L. 77, 547, 568, 575, 585, 587, 588, 589
Wrightson 588
Wu, C. H. 268

Xiang, Y. 378, 379, 382

Yager, R. R. 346

Zadeh, L. A. 240, 353, 357, 381
Zurada, J. M. 467, 476, 478, 505, 842

SUBJECT INDEX

LISP (continued)
    read-eval-print loop 725, 765–767
    recursion 725–741
    s-expression 724–727
    semantic networks 787–791
    simulation 791, 798
    slot options 792–793
    slot-specifiers 792–793
    special declaration 775–776
    state space search 746–751
    streams 769–780
    streams and delayed evaluation 776–780
    thermostat simulation 798–803
    tree-recursion 738–741
    unification 761–765
LISP functions
    * 725
    + 725
    − 725
    < 732
    = 726, 732
    > 726, 732
    >= 732
    ' 726–729
    acons 764
    and 725, 733
    append 738
    apply 753
    assoc 763
    car 736
    case 802
    cdr 736
    cond 731–733
    cons 737
    declare 776
    defclass 792
    defgeneric 795
    defmacro 778–779
    defmethod 795–796
    defun 730
    eq 749
    equal 749
    eval 729, 765
    funcall 752–753
    gensym 775
    get 788–789
    if 732–733
    length 727
    let 743–745
    let* 773
    list 726, 729, 737
    listp 745
    mapcar 753–754
    max 754

member 727, 732, 736
minusp 732
not 749
nth 726–727
null 727, 745
numberp 732
oddp 732
or 733
plusp 732
print 765
quote 728
read 765
remprop 788–789
set 741–743
setf 741–743, 788–789
setq 741–743
sqrt 731
symbol-plist 790
terpri 765
zerop 732
/ 724–726
Livingstone 302–305, 326–328
logic programming 575–581, 638–639
Logic Theorist 21, 49, 223–224
logic-based truth maintenance system 343–344, 350
logical inference 62–65
logically follows 64
LOGO 282
Loopy Logic 379
LT (see Logic Theorist)

machine learning 28, 385–543, 694–704
    and heuristic search 392
    and knowledge representation 391
    agglomerative clustering 399
    AM 28, 433–434
    analogical reasoning 430–433
    autoassociative memory (see associative memory,
        Hopfield networks)
    associative memory 455, 490–505 (see also
        semantic networks, conceptual graphs)
    BACON 434
    bagging 416–417
    boosting 416–417
    BAM, bi-directional associative memory 496–500
    C4.5 417, 630
    candidate elimination 397–408, 699–701
    category formation (see conceptual clustering)
    CLUSTER/2 389, 419, 436–437, 476
    COBWEB 389, 437–441, 476
    coincidence learning 484
    competitive learning 454–455, 474–484
    concept learning 389
    concept space 392, 396–397

transition network parser 600–616
traveling salesperson 91–93, 455, 513–515
triangle tables 319–323
truncated chessboard problem 827–828
truth maintenance system 337–344
   assumption-based truth maintenance 342–344, 348
   chronological backtracking 339
   dependency-directed backtracking 340
   justification-based truth maintenance 340–342
   logic-based truth maintenance 343–344, 350
   multiple belief reasoner 344
Turing machine 848
Turing test 13

unification 66–72, 562, 671–679, 761–765
uniform representations for weak method solutions 581
unit preference strategy 548, 569

universal instantiation 64–65
unsatisfiability 567
unsupervised learning 389, 433–441, 454, 476–478, 484–488

validity 63
Vapnik Chervonenkis dimension 482–483
version space search 396–408, 694–699
Viterbi 376–379, 618
   (see also dynamic programming)

weak method problem solving 223–224
well-formed formula 46–47
winner-take-all learning 454–455, 474–476
working memory 200
world knowledge 595

XCON 23, 203